Futargh O'Donnell

CIVIL PROCEDURE IN THE SUPERIOR COURTS

AUSTRALIA

LBC Information Services
Sydney

CANADA AND THE USA

Carswell

NEW ZEALAND

Brooker's
Wellington

SINGAPORE AND MALAYSIA

Thomson Information (S.E. Asia)
Singapore

Civil Procedure in the Superior Courts

HILARY DELANY

B.A.(Mod.), M.Litt., Ph.D., Barrister-at-Law
Fellow of Trinity College, Dublin
Senior Lecturer in Law, Trinity College, Dublin

and

DECLAN MCGRATH

LL.B., LL.M., Barrister-at-Law, Attorney-at-Law
Lecturer in Law, Trinity College, Dublin and
The Honorable Society of King's Inns

DUBLIN
ROUND HALL SWEET & MAXWELL
2001

Published in 2001 by
Round Hall Ltd
43 Fitzwilliam Place
Dublin 2

Typeset by
Gough Typesetting Services
Dublin

Printed by
MPG Books, Cornwall

ISBN 1-85800-241-9

In memory of my Mother

(D.McG.)

To R.G.K, S.N.W and D.J.O'M.

(H.D.)

FOREWORD

It has been both a privilege and pleasure for me to read the proofs of this book prior to its publication.

In deciding to write this text the authors undertook an enormous task. They have succeeded in producing a comprehensive text book which is full of concentrated legal pemmican but in a most digestible form.

Each chapter deals with a particular area of the courts' jurisdiction and sets forth in a way that will be of use to both practitioner and academic the relevant legal principles applicable and the up to date case law on the topic. As the authors combine both academia and practice, they are ideally suited to produce this work.

In my view this book will be of inestimable value to any practitioner when called upon to consider any aspect of civil procedure of the Superior Courts.

I hope that the book has the success which it richly deserves and will be found on the shelves of any lawyer who has to consider any aspect of the area covered by the book.

Peter Kelly
October 2001

PREFACE

The aim of this book is to provide a comprehensive treatment and analysis of some of the main areas of civil practice and procedure in the Superior Courts. There are a number of topics, for example, taxation of costs, which is already the subject of an excellent text, which we have not attempted to cover, and admittedly pressure of time (and in particular publishers' deadlines!) has meant that we were unable to address specific areas in this book which we hope to remedy in future editions. To this end we would welcome comments and suggestions on improvements which might be made to the format and content of the text.

While we envisage that the book will prove particularly useful to practitioners, it also provides detailed commentary which, it is hoped, may be of assistance to those who are interested in a more academic treatment of civil procedure. It must be acknowledged that the existing texts of O'Floinn *Practice and Procedure in the Superior Courts*, Wylie's *Judicature Acts* and the various editions of the White Book already provide an invaluable resource to the practitioner and indeed were the first port of call of the authors in writing this book. However, we had both been struck by the sheer volume of case law, often unreported, dealing with aspects of civil procedure, and felt that a more detailed exposition was merited and would be of benefit.

In researching this book, the authors were struck by the dynamism of this area. There appears to be an increasing emphasis on procedural issues in recent times and there are a large number of important decisions which have been handed down by the courts in the last number of years. In addition, the Rules of the Superior Courts have been the subject of a large number of amendments with the authors counting 45 Statutory Instruments which have brought into effect new provisions since the promulgation of the current Rules in 1986. The number and importance of some of these changes creates its own problems and the time may be opportune for a set of consolidating Rules.

Indeed, the pace of change in this area is likely to accelerate. In England, the Woolf reforms have introduced sweeping changes to the civil procedure rules in that jurisdiction and it would seems almost inevitable that at least some of those reforms will be implemented here also. The authors understand that a number of matters including case management and the impact of technology are been actively considered at the moment. It may be that when we return to this project in a second edition, the canvas against which it will be written will have changed significantly.

If a new set of consolidated Rules is to be introduced, then the opportunity should be taken to simplify, rationalise and modernise them. The lineage of the current Rules to those first introduced as a Schedule to the Supreme Court of Judicature (Ireland) Act 1877 is clear and the continued relevance of authorities decided in the aftermath of the introduction of those Rules and collated in Wylie's *Judicature Acts* is striking. However, the amendment and expansion of the Rules over the following century has resulted in a set of Rules which are complex and unwieldy, contradictory and overlapping in parts and virtually impenetrable in places.

Like many books, this one has been in gestation for a number of years, with one of the authors harbouring ambitions to write in the area since his interest in the subject was awakened by the lectures of Brian Spierin SC in the King's Inns. The authors also wish to acknowledge the invaluable contributions of a considerable number of individuals to the book which, more than most, reflects the combined knowledge and experience of many persons. In that regard, we would particularly like to thank the Honourable Mr Justice Peter Kelly who kindly wrote the foreword, and Garrett Simons, James O'Reilly SC and Gerard Hogan SC who read a number of chapters and made numerous useful suggestions. In addition, we wish to thank the following individuals, David Barniville, Rory Brady SC, Rachel Casey, Cathryn Costello, Tríona Daly, James Doherty, Jarlath Fitzsimons, Louise Hartigan, Ruth Heard, Brian Kennedy, Finbarr McElligott, Betty McGuigan and Alex Schuster.

We would like to record our special thanks to Trevor Redmond who did Trojan work as our research assistant and in copyediting the text and compiling the tables. We would also like to express our appreciation to Gilbert Gough for the excellent job which he did in typesetting the text, to Patricia Baker who compiled the index and to the staff at Round Hall Ltd, particularly Catherine Dolan, for their practical assistance in preparing this book for publication.

We have endeavoured to state the law as of 1 October 2001.

Hilary Delany
Declan McGrath

5 October 2001

CONTENTS

TABLE OF CONTENTS

TABLE OF CASES

TABLE OF STATUTES

TABLE OF ORDERS

OTHER TABLES

ARTICLES OF THE CONSTITUTION

CHAPTER ONE

THE STRUCTURE AND JURISDICTION OF THE COURTS

THE STRUCTURE AND COMPOSITION OF THE COURTS

Introduction

1.001 Article 34.1 of the Constitution of Ireland 1937 provides that "justice shall be administered in courts established by law by judges appointed in the manner prescribed by the Constitution....". Article 34.2 goes on to provide that these courts shall comprise courts of first instance and a court of final appeal and Article 34.3.1° states that:

> The Courts of First Instance shall include a High Court invested with full original jurisdiction in and power to determine all matters and questions whether of law or fact, civil or criminal.

Pursuant to similar provisions in the Constitution of Saorstát Éireann 1922,[1] the Courts of Justice Act 1924 had provided for the establishment of the Supreme Court, the Court of Criminal Appeal, the High Court, the Circuit Court and the District Court. While the 1937 Constitution envisaged the establishment of a 'new' court system, this did not take place until the enactment of the Courts (Establishment and Constitution) Act 1961 which effectively re-established the courts listed above. The Superior Courts as established by the Courts (Establishment and Constitution) Act 1961 with which this book is concerned are a court of final appeal, the Supreme Court,[2] and a court of first instance invested with full original jurisdiction, the High Court.[3]

Composition of the Supreme Court

1.002 S.7(1) of the Courts (Supplemental Provisions) Act 1961 provides that the Supreme Court shall be a superior court of record with such appellate and other jurisdiction as is prescribed by the Constitution. Since 1995, by virtue of s.7(3) of the 1961 Act, inserted by s.7 of the Courts and Court Officers Act 1995, the Supreme Court may sit in two or more divisions simultaneously. An

---

[1] Articles 64-72.
[2] S.1 of the Courts (Establishment and Constitution) Act 1961.
[3] S.2 of the Courts (Establishment and Constitution) Act 1961.

appeal to or other matter cognisable under Article 12[4] or Article 26[5] of the Constitution or a question of the validity of any law having regard to the provisions of the Constitution shall be heard and determined by not less than five judges.[6] In practice cases raising constitutional issues are heard by five judges even where the validity of a law is not impugned. The Chief Justice or in his absence the senior ordinary judge of the Supreme Court for the time being available, may determine that an appeal or other matter cognisable by the Supreme Court may be heard and determined by a division of five or three judges.[7]

S.1(2) of the Courts (Establishment and Constitution) Act 1961, as amended by s.6(1) of the Courts and Court Officers Act 1995, now provides that the Supreme Court shall be constituted of a president, known as "The Chief Justice" and not more than seven ordinary judges[8] and s.1(3) further provides that the President of the High Court shall be *ex officio* an additional judge of the Supreme Court. S.1(4) allows the Chief Justice to request any ordinary judge, where a sufficient number of judges of the Supreme Court are not available for the transaction of the business of the court, to sit on the hearing of a matter before the Supreme Court.

Composition of the High Court

1.003 S.8(1) of the Courts (Supplemental Provisions) Act 1961 establishes the High Court as a superior court of record with such original and other jurisdiction as is prescribed by the Constitution. S.2(2) of the Courts (Establishment and Constitution) Act 1961 provides that the High Court shall be comprised of a president, known as "The President of the High Court" and such number of ordinary judges as may from time to time be fixed by legislation. S.2 of the Courts (No. 2) Act 1997 currently fixes that number at not more than 24, although where the President of the Law Reform Commission is a judge of the High Court, that number may be exceeded by one.[9]

---

[4] Article 12.3.1° provides that the question of whether the President has become permanently incapacitated shall be established to the satisfaction of the Supreme Court consisting of not less than five judges.

[5] Article 26.2.1° provides that the Supreme Court consisting of not less than five judges shall consider every question referred to it by the President for a decision under that article which provides a mechanism for challenging the constitutionality of a Bill.

[6] S.7(5) of the Courts (Supplemental Provisions) Act 1961 as inserted by s.7 of the Courts and Court Officers Act 1995. No upper limit is set on the number of judges and in *Sinnott v Minister for Education* Supreme Court, 12 July 2001 a court consisting of seven judges heard the case.

[7] S.7(4) of the Courts (Supplemental Provisions) Act 1961 as inserted by s.7 of the Courts and Court Officers Act 1995.

[8] Where a Supreme Court judge is appointed President of the Law Reform Commission, this number may be exceeded by one, see s.3 of the Courts (No. 2) Act 1997, amending s.14 of the Law Reform Commission Act 1975.

[9] S.3 of the Courts (No. 2) Act 1997 which amends s.14 of the Law Reform Commission Act 1975.

S.4 of the Courts (No. 2) Act 1997 provides that a person who, after the commencement of the Act, is appointed as the presiding judge of the Supreme Court or the High Court shall be so appointed for a period of seven years – in which case he shall not be eligible for re-appointment – or until he reaches retirement age, whichever occurs first. However, where a judge completes a seven year term as a presiding judge, he may continue as a judge of that court until retirement.

Qualification as a Judge of the Superior Courts

1.004 A person who is for the time being a practising barrister of not less than 12 years standing shall be qualified for appointment as a judge of the Supreme Court or the High Court and for this purpose service as a judge of the Circuit Court,[10] of the Court of Justice or Court of First Instance of the European Union, or as Advocate General of the Court of Justice shall be deemed to be practice at the Bar.[11] In addition, s.5(2)(e) of the Courts (Supplemental Provisions) Act 1961[12] provides that a judge of the Circuit Court of four years standing shall also be qualified for appointment as a judge of the Supreme Court or the High Court and a practising solicitor of not less than ten years standing may now qualify for appointment as a judge of the Circuit Court.[13] In *State (Walshe) v Murphy*[14] Finlay P rejected the argument that the effect of Article 36.ii of the Constitution was to confine the legislature to regulating the terms of appointment and number of judges of the District Court. In his view "the provisions of Article 36 of the Constitution are not only consistent with the right of the legislature to provide the qualifications for the appointment of judges to the courts established under the Constitution but may be properly interpreted as expressly authorising the determination of such qualifications".[15]

THE JURISDICTION OF THE HIGH COURT

Original Jurisdiction

The Meaning of "Full Original Jurisdiction"

1.005 Article 34.3.1° states that the High Court shall be invested with "full original jurisdiction in and power to determine all matters and questions whether

---

[10] S.5(2)(b) of the Courts (Supplemental Provisions) Act 1961.
[11] S.5(2)(c) of the Courts (Supplemental Provisions) Act 1961 inserted by s.28 of the Courts and Court Officers Act 1995.
[12] Inserted by s.28 of the Courts and Court Officers Act 1995.
[13] S.30 of the Courts and Court Officers Act 1995 which amends s.17 of the Courts (Supplemental Provisions) Act 1961.
[14] [1981] IR 275.
[15] *Ibid.* at 286.

of law or fact, civil or criminal". However, as the Supreme Court pointed out in *Tormey v Ireland*[16] there are some matters and questions which are not amenable to determination by any court and the provision should be read as being confined to "all justiciable matters and questions". The object of Article 34.3.1° was described by Gannon J in *R. v R.*[17] as being to ensure that a court existed to which recourse may be had "in any event or upon any occasion and in any circumstances where there may exist a wrong for which in justice a remedy may be required". However, Article 34.3.1° must not be interpreted as requiring the High Court to hear and determine all justiciable matters as the judgment of McMahon J in *Ward v Kinahan Electrical Ltd*[18] makes clear. The plaintiff, resisting an application by the defendant to have the action remitted, contended that the section was invalid on the grounds that Article 34.3.1° of the Constitution gives every citizen the right to have his case, however trivial, determined in the High Court. McMahon J rejected his argument stating that in his opinion Article 34.3.1° could "not be construed as conferring a universal right of recourse to the High Court for the determination of all justiciable disputes"[19] and he concluded that business which falls within the full original jurisdiction of the High Court may be assigned within the express and implied limits laid down in the Constitution to some other court. A similar view was taken by Gannon J in *R. v R.*[20] in which the plaintiff sought to bring family law proceedings in the High Court which according to the relevant legislation were within the jurisdiction of the lower courts. Gannon J held that while by virtue of Article 34.3.1° the High Court retained jurisdiction in relation to such matters, it was open to that court to decline to entertain proceedings on the grounds that the relief sought was available in the lower courts.[21]

One problematic aspect of his judgment was his assertion that it was incorrect to contend that the Oireachtas might confer jurisdiction in the matters under consideration on other courts to the exclusion of the High Court. This point of view cannot be reconciled with the conclusion reached by the Supreme Court in *Tormey v Ireland*[22] which merits consideration in some detail.

---

[16] [1985] IR 289, [1985] ILRM 375.

[17] [1984] IR 296, 307-308. In Kelly *The Irish Constitution* eds. Hogan and Whyte (3rd ed., 1995) at 410 it is asserted that while the Supreme Court in *Tormey v Ireland* [1985] IR 289, [1985] ILRM 375 subsequently appeared to take a different view on whether Article 34.3.1° allowed exclusive jurisdiction to be vested in the lower courts, it did not take issue with the analysis of Gannon J as to the object of the article.

[18] [1984] IR 292.

[19] *Ibid.* at 295.

[20] [1984] IR 296.

[21] See also *O'R. v O'R.* [1985] IR 367 and *Deighan v Hearne* [1986] IR 603.

[22] [1985] IR 289, [1985] ILRM 375. Henchy J stated at 296, 380 that: "if in exercise of its powers under Article 34.3.4°, parliament commits certain matters or questions to the jurisdiction of the District Court or of the Circuit Court, the functions of hearing and determining those matters and questions may, expressly or by necessary implication, be given exclusively to those courts".

The plaintiff had been sent forward for trial on indictment to the Dublin Circuit Court and sought a transfer of his trial to the Central Criminal Court, or alternatively to a circuit outside Dublin. He contended, *inter alia*, that s.32(1) of the Courts Act 1981, which repealed s.6 of the Courts Act 1964 – which had made provision for the transfer of trials to the Central Criminal Court – was unconstitutional on the grounds that it was inconsistent with Article 34.3.1° of the Constitution. The Supreme Court expressed the view that despite its unqualified and unambiguous terms Article 34.3.1° could not be read entirely literally. Henchy J said that the jurisdiction to hear and determine matters vested by the Constitution in courts or bodies other than the High Court must be taken to be capable of being exercised in certain instances to the exclusion of the High Court, otherwise the allocation of jurisdiction would be overlapping and unworkable. As he stated: "Article 34.3.4° amounts to a recognition of the fact that the High Court is not expected to be a suitable forum for hearing and determining at first instance all justiciable matters".[23] Henchy J added that while the jurisdiction of the High Court must be deemed to be "full" in the sense that all justiciable matters, except those removed by the Constitution itself from the original jurisdiction of the High Court, shall be within the original jurisdiction of that court, the Oireachtas may still commit certain matters to the District or Circuit Courts. However, this did not mean that such matters are put beyond the original jurisdiction of the High Court and while legislation may give sole jurisdiction to the lower courts, the full original jurisdiction of the High Court can be invoked in judicial review proceedings to ensure that justice is done.

The net effect of these decisions would seem to be that "full original jurisdiction" must be broadly interpreted. As the decisions in *Ward* and *R. v R.* illustrate, the High Court may decline to hear matters which properly fall within the jurisdiction of the lower courts and yet as *Tormey* shows, where these lower courts are given jurisdiction, the full original jurisdiction of the High Court can be invoked in review proceedings.

1.006 This supervisory jurisdiction exercised by the High Court over decisions made by lower courts and administrative tribunals in judicial review proceedings is an important one which cannot be completely ousted[24] by legislation. As Gavan Duffy J commented in *Murren v Brennan*[25] statutory provisions purporting to make the decision of administrative authorities final "cannot exclude the constitutional jurisdiction of the High Court in a case deemed by the High Court to call for interference". This view is borne out by the approach

---

[23] *Ibid.* at 295, 378-379.
[24] Although limitations put on the availability of judicial review *e.g.* by imposing strict time limits on the bringing of proceedings have been upheld as constitutional, see *Brady v Donegal County Council* [1989] ILRM 282.
[25] [1942] IR 466, 476.

of Henchy J in *Tormey v Ireland*[26] where he stated that the full jurisdiction of the High Court is there to be invoked in review proceedings and to this extent "no justiciable matter or question may be excluded from the range of the original jurisdiction of the High Court".

1.007 In monetary terms the cases which the High Court hears are those where the claim for damages exceeds £30,000[27] which will be extended to €100,000 from 1 January 2002.[28] In addition, it has specific jurisdiction in matters relating to the winding up of companies and the appointment of an examiner and in relation to bankruptcy cases. The High Court also exercises wardship jurisdiction in "lunacy and minor matters".[29]

The Constitutionality of Legislation

1.008 Article 34.3.2° provides that the High Court shall have jurisdiction to determine the constitutional validity of any law and states that no such question shall be raised in any court other than the High Court or the Supreme Court.[30] This provision has been interpreted as only applying to statutes passed after the coming into force of the 1937 Constitution.[31] However, the effect of Article 50, which continues in force all pre-existing legislation to the extent that it is not inconsistent with the Constitution, and Article 34.3.1°, gives the High Court jurisdiction to pronounce on the constitutionality of such legislation. By virtue of Article 34.3.2° courts other than the High Court and the Supreme Court may not consider the constitutionality of post-1937 legislation "whether by pleading, argument or otherwise".

1.009 The constitutional validity of legislation may be challenged in any case in which the issue is relevant. While the question will usually be raised in plenary proceedings seeking declaratory relief, such an issue may equally be raised in judicial review proceedings, where an injunction is sought or as part of a defence in a civil or criminal action. Order 60 of the Rules of the Superior Courts 1986 makes provision for the service of notice on the Attorney General in any matter where the constitutional validity of legislation is challenged where he is not already a party. Where any question as to the interpretation of the Constitution arises, the Attorney General should be joined if the High Court so directs. His joinder in such "interpretation" litigation is not automatic. Order

---

[26] [1985] IR 289, 297, [1985] ILRM 375, 380.
[27] See s.2(3)(a) of the Courts Act 1991.
[28] S.12 of the Courts and Court Officers Act 2001.
[29] S.9(1) of the Courts (Supplemental Provisions) Act 1961.
[30] This issue is dealt with in detail in Collins and O'Reilly *Civil Proceedings and the State in Ireland: A Practitioner's Guide* (1990) Chapter 5. See also Kelly *The Irish Constitution* eds. Hogan and Whyte (3rd ed., 1994).
[31] *State (Sheerin) v Kennedy* [1966] IR 379, 388.

60, rule 3 provides that such notice shall state concisely the nature of the proceedings and the contentions of the parties to the proceedings, and rule 4 provides that the Attorney General shall be entitled to appear in the matter and become a party to it as regards the question which arises.[32]

Appellate Jurisdiction

1.010 The High Court exercises appellate jurisdiction both in the form of appeals from decisions of the Circuit Court and by way of case stated from decisions of the District Court. Ss. 37 and 38 of the Courts of Justice Act 1936 govern appeals from decisions of the Circuit Court.[33] S.37 makes provision for an appeal to the High Court sitting in Dublin from a decision in a civil action at the hearing of which no oral evidence was given and s.38 provides for appeals to the High Court sitting in Dublin or on Circuit in other cases. Both sections provide for a "rehearing"[34] but it should be noted that s.37 states that "no evidence which was not given and received in the Circuit Court shall be given or received on the hearing of such appeal without the special leave of the judge hearing such appeal". S.39 of the Act of 1936 provided that the decision of the High Court on an appeal under Part IV of that Act shall be "final and conclusive and not appealable".

S.51 of the Courts (Supplemental Provisions) Act 1961 extends the provisions of s.2 of the Summary Jurisdiction Act 1857 to allow any party to summary proceedings before the District Court to request a district judge, after he has heard and determined a matter, to state a case to the High Court on a point of law.[35] In addition, s.52 of the Courts (Supplemental Provisions) Act 1961 provides a mechanism for a consultative case stated which allows for the stating of a case for the opinion of the High Court in the course of proceedings before the District Court.[36]

---

[32] See further paragraphs 6.026–6.027.

[33] See Delany, *The Courts Acts 1924–1997* (2nd ed., 2000) at 132-139.

[34] See *Powerscourt v Doran* [1941] Ir Jur Rep 83 in relation to s.38.

[35] See *infra* Chapter 22. See also Delany, *The Courts Acts 1924–1997* (2nd ed., 2000) at 265-268 and Collins and O'Reilly, *Civil Proceedings and the State in Ireland: A Practitioner's Guide* (1990) at 1-16.

[36] See *infra* Chapter 22. See also Delany, *The Courts Acts 1924–1997* (2nd ed., 2000) at 269-273 and Collins and O'Reilly, *Civil Proceedings and the State in Ireland: A Practitioner's Guide* (1990) at 17-22.

8 *Civil Procedure*

THE JURISDICTION OF THE SUPREME COURT

Original Jurisdiction

Cases Expressly Provided for by the Constitution

1.011 Article 34.4.1° provides that the court of final appeal shall be called the Supreme Court. However, as Walsh J made clear in the course of his judgment in *State (Browne) v Feran*[37] this does not mean that the Supreme Court shall be only a court of final appeal and it does possess limited original jurisdiction. Two constitutional provisions confer express jurisdiction in this regard. First, Article 12.3.1° provides that the question of whether the President has become permanently incapacitated must be established to the satisfaction of the Supreme Court consisting of not less than five judges. Secondly, Article 26.2.1° provides that the Supreme Court consisting of not less than five judges shall consider every question referred to it by the President for a decision under that article which provides a mechanism for challenging the constitutionality of a Bill. Article 26 applies to any Bill passed by both Houses of the Oireachtas other than a money Bill, a Bill containing a proposal to amend the Constitution, or a Bill the time for the consideration of which has been abridged under Article 24. Having heard arguments by or on behalf of the Attorney General and by counsel assigned by the court to argue against the Bill, the Supreme Court is required to pronounce its decision in open court as soon as may be and in any case not later than 60 days after the date of the reference. Article 26.2.2° provides that the decision of the majority shall be the decision of the court and that no other opinion shall be disclosed. Where the Supreme Court decides that any provision of a Bill is repugnant to the Constitution, the President shall decline to sign it and in every other case, the President shall sign the Bill as soon as may be after the decision of the Supreme Court has been pronounced.[38]

Cases not Expressly Provided for by the Constitution

1.012 The question of the extent to which the Supreme Court may exercise original jurisdiction in other cases is not free from doubt. In *State (Browne) v Feran*[39] Walsh J commented that so far as the Supreme Court and the High Court are concerned, the provisions of Article 36 appear to allow jurisdiction to be added to that already derived from the Constitution. He suggested that an original jurisdiction might therefore be conferred upon the Supreme Court although in such a case it would be "a court of first and final instance".[40] This

---

[37] [1967] IR 147, 157.
[38] Article 26.3.1° and 26.3.3°.
[39] [1967] IR 147.
[40] *Ibid.* at 157.

issue was considered in some detail by the Supreme Court in *AG (SPUC (Ireland) Ltd) v Open Door Counselling Ltd (No. 2)*.[41] Here, the second named defendant sought an order from the Supreme Court discharging an injunction restraining the defendant from assisting pregnant women to travel abroad for the purpose of obtaining an abortion, following the amendment of Article 40.3.3°. These amendments made it clear that the subsection should not limit freedom to travel or to obtain or make available in the State, information relating to services lawfully available in another state. The majority of the Supreme Court refused the relief sought, Finlay CJ stating that the court had no originating jurisdiction apart from that expressly granted to it by the Constitution or by statute to hear a case stated. The Chief Justice added that the court has consistently declined, "otherwise than in the most exceptional circumstances, dictated by the necessity of justice"[42] to consider an issue of constitutional law which has not yet been fully argued and decided in the High Court. Given the tenor of the remarks made by Walsh J in *State (Browne) v Feran* this seems a rather restrictive approach. Also relevant in this context is the dissenting judgment of Denham J. She stated that while the Supreme Court is fundamentally an appellate court it is not exclusively so. Although she accepted that the Supreme Court should not in general hear and determine an issue which has not been tried by another court, Denham J expressed the view that in addition to the exceptions explicitly set out in the Constitution, there are rare implied exceptions to this principle which arise when a constitutional right or justice requires to be protected and where the Supreme Court determines it has a duty to intervene.

1.013 Recent *dicta* on this issue illustrate that there is still some difference of opinion amongst the members of the Supreme Court about the correct approach in such cases. In *Dunnes Stores Ireland Co. v Ryan*[43] Keane CJ stated quite clearly that it was not open to the Supreme Court to determine an issue of constitutional law which had not been the subject of adjudication in the High Court. However, in *Blehein v Murphy*[44] Denham J, while stressing that apart from a few exceptions the Supreme Court is a court of appeal, acknowledged that in exceptional circumstances a non-appellate jurisdiction might be invoked. She concluded that "in exceptional circumstances the Supreme Court will consider issues of constitutional law which have not been argued in the High Court"[45] and relied on the *dicta* of Finlay CJ in *AG (SPUC) v. Open Door Counselling Ltd (No. 2)* to support such a proposition.[46]

---

[41] [1994] 2 IR 333.

[42] *Ibid.* at 341.

[43] Supreme Court, 8 February 2000.

[44] [2000] 2 IR 231, [2000] 2 ILRM 481.

[45] *Ibid.* at 489. Although in the circumstances, Denham J was satisfied that there were no exceptional circumstances to justify invoking the exception to the rule.

[46] This reasoning was also applied by analogy by Denham J in *Re Greendale Developments (No. 3)* [2000] 2 IR 514, [2001] 1 ILRM 161 in relation to the circumstances in

Appellate Jurisdiction

Introduction

1.014 Article 34.4.3° provides that the Supreme Court shall, with such exceptions and subject to such regulations as may be proscribed by law, have appellate jurisdiction from all decisions of the High Court. Neither the scope of nor the manner in which the Supreme Court's appellate jurisdiction should be exercised is set out in the Constitution. The procedure governing the bringing of such appeals is set out in Order 58 of the Rules of the Superior Courts.[47] Order 58, rule 1 requires that all appeals to the Supreme Court shall be "by way of rehearing", although this phrase has been quite restrictively interpreted. As Henchy J stated in *Northern Bank Finance Ltd v Charlton*[48] the court will normally be precluded from hearing witnesses whose oral evidence was the core of the hearing before the High Court and the appeal will be "by way of rehearing" only to the extent that this will be possible by examining documentary evidence, save for exceptional cases.[49] In addition, he observed that while the Supreme Court may exercise appellate jurisdiction on questions of both law and fact, the court should be slow to interfere with findings of fact arrived at by the High Court unless the evidence which was acted on could not reasonably have been correct. In effect, the Supreme Court has, as McCarthy J commented in *Hay v O'Grady*,[50] limited its jurisdiction by its own decisions.

1.015 As noted above, Article 34.4.3° provides that the Supreme Court shall, subject to certain exceptions have appellate jurisdiction from "all decisions" of the High Court. The finding of the Supreme Court in *Campus Oil Ltd v Minister for Industry and Energy*[51] that a determination that certain questions of interpretation of the EC Treaty should be referred to the European Court of Justice was not a "decision" within the meaning of Article 34.4.3° was a restrictive one and more recent cases illustrate a more flexible attitude towards this issue. In *SPUC (Ireland) Ltd v Grogan*[52] the plaintiff sought to appeal a determination by the High Court to postpone consideration of whether it was entitled to an injunction pending the reference of certain questions to the European Court of Justice. The Supreme Court distinguished the *Campus Oil*

---

which the Supreme Court might intervene where a final order had been made. In her view a very heavy onus lies on a person seeking to have such a jurisdiction exercised and it will only be in the most exceptional circumstances where a constitutional right or justice requires to be protected that the Supreme Court would consider whether a final judgment or order should be rescinded or varied.

[47] See further Chapter 20.
[48] [1979] IR 149.
[49] *Ibid.* at 188.
[50] [1992] 1 IR 210, 217, [1992] ILRM 689, 694.
[51] [1983] IR 82.
[52] [1989] IR 753, [1990] ILRM 350.

decision and held that such a determination constituted a decision which might be appealed to the Supreme Court. As Finlay CJ observed: "no mere absence of formal words from a High Court order could be permitted to remove from the appellate jurisdiction of this Court a determination of a High Court judge which affects one of the parties involved and has all the characteristics of a decision".[53] A similarly broad interpretation of what constitutes a decision for this purpose is evident in the case of *Dublin Wellwoman Centre Ltd v Ireland*.[54] The third named defendants sought to appeal a determination made by a High Court judge, Carroll J, that she did not need to disqualify herself from hearing a case and the plaintiffs argued that this was not a "decision" which might be appealed to the Supreme Court. Denham J allowed the appeal stating that there had been a determination of an issue and that it affected the interests of one of the parties. In addition, the determination had all the characteristics of a decision and the fact that it was an issue preliminary to a trial did not divest it of such status. The Supreme Court concluded that it was satisfied that both in substance and in form the judgment and order of the High Court was a "decision" within the meaning of Article 34.4.3° and that consequently an appeal lay to the Supreme Court.

Exceptions to and Regulation of the Supreme Court's Appellate Jurisdiction

1.016 Article 34.4.3° contemplates that exceptions to and regulation of the Supreme Court's appellate jurisdiction may be prescribed by law. However, it should be noted that Article 34.4.4° provides that no law shall be enacted excepting from the appellate jurisdiction of the Supreme Court cases which involve questions as to the validity of any law having regard to the provisions of the Constitution. In addition, Article 34.4.5° provides that there shall be only one judgment of the Supreme Court on a question as to the validity of a law having regard to the Constitution and the existence of any other opinion shall not be disclosed.

One of the most commonly encountered exceptions to the Supreme Court's jurisdiction is found in s.39 of the Courts of Justice Act 1936, as re-enacted by s.48 of the Courts (Supplemental Provisions) Act 1961. This provides that a decision of the High Court on appeal from the Circuit Court "shall be final and conclusive and not appealable." This provision was considered by the Supreme Court in *Eamonn Andrews Productions Ltd v Gaiety Theatre Enterprises Ltd*[55] where it was held that it constituted a valid exception to the appellate jurisdiction of that court pursuant to Article 34.4.3°.

---

[53] *Ibid.* at 763, 354-355. Quoted with approval by Denham J in *Dublin Wellwoman Centre Ltd v Ireland* [1995] 1 ILRM 408, 417.

[54] [1995] 1 ILRM 408.

[55] [1973] IR 295, 360.

1.017 In addition to creating exceptions to the Supreme Court's appellate jurisdiction, it has also been regulated by legislation requiring that the leave of the
High Court be obtained before an appeal can be brought. An example of this is
s.52 of the Courts (Supplemental Provisions) Act 1961 which provides that an
appeal shall only lie from a determination of the High Court on a consultative
case stated with the leave of that court. This aspect of s.52 was considered by
the Supreme Court in *Minister for Justice v Wang Zhu Jie*.[56] Counsel for the
appellant submitted, *inter alia*, that the decision of the High Court judge to
refuse leave to appeal was a "decision of the High Court" within the meaning of
Article 34.4.3° of the Constitution and that therefore there was a constitutional
right of appeal to the Supreme Court from such a decision. It was further contended that even if the provisions of s.52(2) were to be construed as a form of
regulation or exception applicable to the decision of the High Court in such a
case, they did not unambiguously except the decision of the High Court on a
case stated from the provisions of Article 34.4.3° and that, accordingly, a right
of appeal existed. In refusing to entertain the appeal, Finlay CJ stated that the
provisions of Article 34.4.3° clearly envisaged and provided for exceptions to
and regulation of the general right of appeal from decisions of the High Court to
the Supreme Court to be prescribed by law, namely by Act of the Oireachtas.
The Chief Justice concluded that the provisions of s.52 should be construed as
effecting an exception from the absolute right of appeal, provided for in Article
34.4.3° of the Constitution, from decisions of the High Court to the Supreme
Court and substituting therefor a regulated right of appeal, which is subject to
the final discretion of the judge of the High Court answering the consultative
case stated.

1.018 It was clearly stated by Walsh J in *People (AG) v Conmey*[57] that any
statutory provision which has as its object the excepting of some decisions of
the High Court from the appellate jurisdiction of the Supreme Court or a provision seeking to confine the scope of such appeals must be "clear and unambiguous". Similarly, as O'Higgins CJ commented in the same case, since the
appellate jurisdiction of the Supreme Court is written into the Constitution it
"can only be restricted or regulated by legislation clearly intended to have this
effect". These principles were accepted by Finlay CJ in the Supreme Court
decision in *Holohan v Donohoe*[58] in which the court rejected the argument that
by virtue of s.96 of the Courts of Justice Act 1924, as re-enacted by s.48 of the
Courts (Supplemental Provisions) Act 1961, the Supreme Court did not have
jurisdiction to substitute its own assessment of damages in an appropriate case

---

[56] [1993] 1 IR 426, [1991] ILRM 823.
[57] [1975] IR 341, 360. This *dicta* has been approved in numerous subsequent cases. See
   e.g. *Irish Asphalt Ltd v An Bord Pleanála* [1996] 2 IR 179, [1997] 1 ILRM 81 and *Irish
   Hardware Association v South Dublin County Council* [2001] 2 ILRM 291.
[58] [1986] IR 45, [1986] ILRM 250.

for that made by the High Court. Henchy J stated that an exception or regulation of the Supreme Court's appellate jurisdiction cannot have the limiting effect contended for unless it clearly and unambiguously carries that meaning. In his opinion, s.96 could not be said to be so clear and unambiguous in its scope as to deprive the court of jurisdiction to make such order as it deemed necessary for the purpose of doing justice, and in particular to assess damages rather than order a new trial on the issue of damages.

1.019 The *Conmey* principles were also applied by the Supreme Court in *Hanafin v Minister for the Environment*[59] in holding that the Referendum Act 1994 could not be construed as excepting from the appellate jurisdiction of the Supreme Court an appeal from a decision of the High Court on a referendum petition. In the view of Hamilton CJ the "fundamental position" is as follows:

> ... [I]f it is the intention of the legislature to oust, except from or regulate the appellate jurisdiction of this Court to hear and determine appeals from the decisions of the High Court, such intention must be expressed in clear and unambiguous terms and it is a matter for interpretation by the court as to whether or not any provision of any law which purports to except from or regulate the appellate jurisdiction of this Court is effective so to do.[60]

Hamilton CJ added that he agreed with the submission of counsel for the Attorney General that the Oireachtas in enacting legislation designed to except or regulate the jurisdiction of the Supreme Court in this regard should not be restricted to the use of any particular formula or combination of words to give effect to its intention. Provided the intention is clearly and unambiguously expressed, the failure to use words contained in other Acts is of no significance and what is important is the intention expressed in the use of such words.

1.020 Article 34.4.3° also provides that the Supreme Court shall have such appellate jurisdiction from such decisions of other courts as may be prescribed by law. S.16 of the Courts of Justice Act 1947 confers jurisdiction on a Circuit Court judge to state a case to the Supreme Court.[61]

---

[59] [1996] 2 IR 321.

[60] *Ibid.* at 389.

[61] See *infra* Chapter 22. See also Delany, *The Courts Acts 1924–1997* (2nd ed., 2000) at 181-187 and Collins and O'Reilly, *Civil Proceedings and the State in Ireland: A Practitioner's Guide* (1990) at 23-26. Note that s.38(3) of the Courts of Justice Act 1936 confers a similar jurisdiction on a High Court judge hearing an appeal under that section. See *infra* Chapter 22. See also Delany, *The Courts Acts 1924–1997* (2nd ed., 2000) at 136-139 and Collins and O'Reilly, *Civil Proceedings and the State in Ireland: A Practitioner's Guide* (1990) at 26-31.

Decisions of the Supreme Court shall be Final and Conclusive

1.021 It should be noted that Article 34.4.6° provides that the decision of Supreme Court shall be final and conclusive. This must now be read in the light of Article 234 EC[62] which provides that if a question is raised as to the interpretation of the EC Treaties, the validity and interpretation of acts of the Community institutions or the interpretation of the statutes of bodies established by act of the Council, the Supreme Court must, if it considers it necessary to enable it to give judgment, request the European Court of Justice to give a preliminary ruling.

The effect of this article has been examined recently by the Supreme Court in some detail in *Re Greendale Developments Ltd (No. 3)*,[63] in which the applicants sought to have a judgment and orders of the Supreme Court set aside. In refusing the application, Hamilton CJ stated as follows:

> The common law and public policy recognized the desire for finality in proceedings *inter partes* and Article 34.4.6° of the Constitution incorporated into the Constitution this desire and expressed it in clear and unambiguous terms. It provided that the decision of the Supreme Court shall in all cases be final and conclusive. The said provision is expressed to apply in all cases and there is nothing in the circumstances of this appeal which would justify disregarding the said provision.[64]

Denham J agreed that the application should be dismissed although she expressed the view that the Supreme Court's jurisdiction to protect constitutional rights and justice extends to an inherent duty to protect constitutional justice even where there has been what appears to be a final judgment and order. However, in her view a very heavy onus rests on a person seeking to have such jurisdiction exercised and it would only be in the most exceptional circumstances that the Supreme Court would consider whether a final judgment or order should be rescinded or varied. Barron J adopted a similar approach and stated that the provision of the Constitution requiring decisions of the Supreme Court to be final and conclusive must prevail unless there has been a clear breach of the principles of natural justice in which the applicant has not acquiesced and it is such that a failure to remedy it would damage the authority of the Supreme Court.

---

[62] Formerly Article 177 of the Treaty of Rome.
[63] [2000] 2 IR 514, [2001] 1 ILRM 161.
[64] *Ibid.* at 536, 183.

CHAPTER TWO

COMMENCEMENT OF PROCEEDINGS

INTRODUCTION

2.001 Proceedings may be commenced in the High Court by either (i) an originating summons; (ii) a petition; or (iii) an originating motion. The use of an originating summons is, by far, the most common because Order 1, rule 1 stipulates that save as otherwise provided in the Rules, civil proceedings in the High Court must be instituted by an originating summons.

ORIGINATING SUMMONS PROCEDURE

2.002 An originating summons is a document which informs a defendant of the existence of legal proceedings and the plaintiff's claim and instructs him to take the steps specified therein if the claim is disputed. Order 1 provides for three types of originating summons: (i) a plenary summons which is used for the commencement of plenary proceedings with pleadings and a hearing on oral evidence,[1] (ii) a summary summons which is used for the commencement of summary proceedings without pleadings to be heard on affidavit (with or without oral evidence),[2] and (iii) a special summons which is used for the commencement of certain specified proceedings and is grounded on an affidavit describing the claim in detail.[3] Before going on to examine each of these in detail, some common features should be noted.

2.003 The solicitor for the plaintiff is required to state in the summons the address and occupation or description of the plaintiff and the name of his firm and its registered place of business where proceedings may be served[4] or, if the plaintiff sues in person, he must indorse upon the summons his occupation or description and an address for service within the jurisdiction.[5] The summons must also contain the name and registered place of business of the solicitor to be served or, in the case of a party who does not act by a solicitor, the name and address for service of that party.[6]

---

[1] Order 1, rule 2. This is required to conform to Form No. 1 in Appendix A, Part I.
[2] Order 1, rule 3. This is required to conform to Form No. 2 in Appendix A, Part I.
[3] Order 1, rule 4. This is required to conform to Form No. 3 in Appendix A, Part I except where a form is otherwise prescribed.
[4] Order 4, rule 14.
[5] Order 4, rule 15.
[6] Order 121, rule 4.

A summons must also include an indorsement of claim[7] which is the part of the summons that sets out the relief sought. As will be seen below, the degree of particularity required in this regard varies according to the type of summons. A plenary summons is merely required to contain a general indorsement of claim which sets out the relief sought in general terms.[8] In contrast, a summary or special summons must contain a special indorsement of claim which sets out with particularity the relief sought and the grounds on which it is sought.[9]

There are also a number of other indorsements which may be required on a summons depending on the type of claim and the parties. For example, where the indorsement of claim concerns a claim which, by virtue of the Jurisdiction of Courts and Enforcement of Judgments Act 1998, the court has power to hear and determine, it must be indorsed before issue with: (i) a statement that the court has power under the 1998 Act to hear and determine the claim specifying the particular provision or provisions of the Brussels Convention under which the court should assume jurisdiction; and (ii) a statement that no proceedings between the parties concerning the same cause of action is pending between the parties in another contracting state.[10] Particular indorsements are also required on summonses in proceedings for the recovery of land,[11] where a party sues or is sued in a representative capacity,[12] probate actions,[13] a claim that an account be taken,[14] actions by moneylenders,[15] and actions under hire-purchase agreements.[16]

Plenary Summons

2.004 A plenary summons is to be used for the commencement of plenary proceedings with pleadings and a hearing on oral evidence.[17] The summons derives its name from the type of hearing which obtains at trial *i.e.* a plenary hearing with oral evidence. It is the default summons because Order 1, rule 6 provides that in all proceedings (other than to take a minor into wardship) commenced by originating summons, procedure by plenary summons is mandatory except where procedure by summary or special summons is required or authorised by the Rules. Therefore, whenever relief is sought and no other specific

---

[7] Order 4, rule 1.
[8] Order 4, rule 2.
[9] Order 4, rule 4.
[10] Order 4, rule 1A (inserted by the Rules of the Superior Courts (No. 1) 1989 (SI No. 14 of 1989).
[11] Order 4, rules 6–8.
[12] Order 4, rule 9.
[13] Order 4, rule 10.
[14] Order 4, rule 11.
[15] Order 4, rule 12.
[16] Order 4, rule 13. *Cf. McMullan Bros Ltd v Ryan* [1958] IR 94.
[17] Order 1, rule 2.

procedure is specified, then a plenary summons should be used. In addition, if relief is sought which is not appropriate to a summary or special summons in addition to relief that would be appropriate, then proceedings should be commenced by way of plenary summons.[18]

Indorsement of Claim

2.005 The indorsement of claim on a plenary summons, entitled "General Indorsement of Claim", is merely designed to give the defendant notice of the general nature of the plaintiff's claim. This is clear from Order 4, rule 3 which stipulates that it not necessary to set forth the precise ground of complaint or the precise remedy or relief to which the plaintiff considers himself entitled. This level of generality is justified on the basis that the plenary summons is simply used as a means of instituting proceedings and is followed by a statement of claim which will set out with particularity the precise nature of the plaintiff's claim and relief sought and the grounds on which it is sought.

The indorsement of claim is required to set out the relief claimed and the grounds thereof expressed in general terms in such one of the forms in Appendix B, Part II, as shall be applicable to the case.[19]

2.006 It should be noted that the indorsement of claim must seek substantive as opposed to interlocutory relief.[20] In *Murphy v GM PB PC Ltd*,[21] the respondents contended that a plenary summons seeking an interlocutory order pursuant to s.3(1) of the Proceeds of Crime Act 1996 was defective because it did not contain any claim for substantive relief under s.4 of that Act. Reliance was placed on the decision of the Supreme Court in *Caudron v Air Zaire*,[22] where leave to serve proceedings out of the jurisdiction under Order 11, rule 1(g) was refused on the basis that the relief sought, namely an injunction, was merely interlocutory in nature and no substantive relief was claimed in the indorsement of claim. Finlay CJ considered the sample indorsements set out in Appendix B,

---

[18] See, for example, *Barden v Downes* [1940] IR 131. It was held that there is no jurisdiction on a special summons issued by a mortgagee for an order for sale of mortgaged premises to make an order for payment on the personal covenant contained in the mortgage deed but that the two claims could be combined on a plenary summons.

[19] Order 4, rule 2. Part II includes a long list of sample indorsements which share a common characteristic of brevity as can be seen from the following examples: "The plaintiff's claim is for damages for injury to the plaintiff by the negligence of the defendant, his servants or agents." and "The plaintiff's claim is for damages for breach of contract to accept and pay for goods." If none of the enumerated examples are applicable, then the indorsement must be set out in such other similarly concise form as the nature of the case may require.

[20] *Caudron v Air Zaire* [1985] IR 716, [1986] ILRM 10; *Murphy v GM PB PC Ltd* High Court (O'Higgins J) 4 June 1999.

[21] High Court (O'Higgins J) 4 June 1999.

[22] [1985] IR 716, [1986] ILRM 10.

Part II and said that they universally bore the characteristic that they were the ultimate relief being sought by the plaintiff in the action. Although O'Higgins J acknowledged that there were very significant differences between the type of injunction contemplated by the Proceeds of Crime Act and that sought in the *Caudron* case, he stated that the pleading point was a valid one because s.3 merely provides for interlocutory as opposed to final relief which is provided for in s.4.

Summary Summons

2.007 As the name suggests, a summary summons is used where proceedings are suitable for summary disposition without pleadings[23] and on affidavit. It is designed to enable a plaintiff to recover judgment against a defendant expeditiously in circumstances where the plaintiff's claim is easily quantifiable and the defendant does not have any valid defence.

Proceedings which may be Commenced by Summary Summons

2.008 Proceedings can only be commenced by summary summons where required or authorised by the Rules[24] and Order 2, rule 1 *permits* a summary summons to be used for three classes of claim:

(1) In all actions where the plaintiff seeks only to recover a debt or liquidated demand in money payable by the defendant, with or without interest, arising –

    (a) upon a contract, express or implied (as, for instance, on a bill of exchange, promissory note, or cheque, or other simple contract debt); or

    (b) on a bond or contract under seal for payment of a liquidated amount of money; or

    (c) on a statute when the sum ought to be recovered is a fixed sum of money or in the nature of a debt other than a penalty;[25] or

---

[23] Order 20, rule 1 provides that when summary summons procedure is used, no statement of claim or other pleading can be delivered except by order of the court.

[24] Order 1, rule 6.

[25] But note Order 68, rule 3 which provides that proceedings for the recovery of any tax or duty under the care and management of the Revenue Commissioners, or for any fine, penalty or forfeiture in connection with any such tax or duty or incurred under or imposed by the Acts relating to customs or excise, or for the delivery of an affidavit or an account, whether on oath or not, or for the furnishing or explanations or documents in connection with any such tax or duty, or for the condemnation of goods under the Customs Acts, may be brought by summary summons (or if the circumstances so require, by plenary summons). See *Bedford v Butler* [1972] IR 434.

(d) on a guarantee, whether under seal or not, where the claim against the principal is in respect of a debt or liquidated demand only; or
(e) on a trust.

(2) In actions where a landlord seeks to recover possession of land, with or without a claim for rent or mesne profits –

(a) against a tenant whose term has expired or has been duly determined by a notice to quit; or
(b) for non-payment of rent.

(3) Claims in which the plaintiff in the first instance desires to have an account taken.

In addition, procedure by summary summons may be adopted in the case of a claim not coming within one of these classes where all the parties to the case consent.[26]

(i) Actions to Recover a Debt or Liquidated Demand in Money
2.009 The essence of this class of claim is that it is for a liquidated sum of money *i.e.* a sum which has been ascertained or is capable of being ascertained by calculation. It is, thus, to be distinguished from a claim for unascertained damages, for example, in an action for personal injuries. It is usually a straightforward matter to determine whether a claim is liquidated or not, but the following points should be noted. First, in accordance with a long line of authority distinguishing between liquidated damages and penalties,[27] a sum stipulated as payable under a contract in the event of default will only be recoverable as a liquidated demand if it constitutes a genuine pre-estimate of the damages incurred as opposed to a penalty.[28] Second, an action on a *quantum meruit i.e.* where the sum claimed is not fixed by contract but is, rather, grounded on a promise, expressed or implied, to pay the plaintiff the reasonable value of work

---

[26] Order 2, rule 2.
[27] See *Irish Telephone Rentals v ICS Building Society* [1992] 2 IR 525, [1991] ILRM 880; *Robophone Facilities Ltd v Blank* [1966] 1 WLR 1428, [1966] 3 All ER 128 and *Dunlop Pneumatic Tyre Co. Ltd v New Garage and Motor Co. Ltd* [1915] AC 79, [1914-15] All ER 739. In *Dunlop*, Lord Dunedin explained that the "essence of a penalty is a payment of money stipulated as *in terrorem* of the offending party; the essence of liquidated damages is a genuine covenanted pre-estimate of damage" and a sum stipulated in a contract will be held to be a penalty if it is "extravagant and unconscionable in amount in comparison with the greatest loss that could conceivably be proved to have followed from the breach" (at 86-87).
[28] *United Dominion Trust Ltd v Patterson* [1973] NI 142. *Cf. Toomey v Murphy* [1897] 2 IR 601.

and labour done is a liquidated demand.[29] Third, although reference is made to
a debt or liquidated *demand* in money, it is not necessary that a prior demand
for payment be made, provided that the debt or sum of money is payable at the
time of issue of the summons, unless the parties have agreed in the contract or
instrument sued upon that an actual demand will be a condition precedent to the
existence of an enforceable debt.[30] Fourth, interest can only be claimed where
it is provided for and ascertainable under the terms of the contract or instrument
sued upon or fixed by statute as otherwise it is not a liquidated claim.[31]

(ii) Actions to Recover Possession of Land
2.010 It can be seen that sub-rule (2) permits a landlord to use a summary
summons to commence ejectment proceedings against a tenant[32] in three distinct situations: (i) where the tenancy[33] has expired by the efflux of time; (ii)
where the tenancy has been determined by a notice to quit;[34] or (iii) where a
year's rent is in arrears and the tenancy is of a type to which s.52 of Deasy's

---

[29] In *Stephenson v Weir* (1879) 4 LR Ir 369, 372, Palles CB said that "demands for work
and labour on a *quantum meruit*, or for goods sold, although the price was not fixed by
contract, are clearly 'liquidated demands'; that when the value of the work or the
goods, as the case may be, is ascertained, that value determines, and therefore liqui-
dates the claim". See also *Kilgariff v McGrane* (1881) 8 LR Ir 354 (doctor's fees);
Whelan v Kelly (1884) 14 LR Ir 387. But see, *contra*, *Shortal v Farrell* (1869) IR 3 CL
506 and *Spratt v Lonergan* (1880) 14 ILTR 86.

[30] *Joachimson v Swiss Bank Corporation* [1921] 3 KB 110, 117, *per* Bankes LJ. See, for
example, *Bank of Ireland v Connell* [1942] IR 1 where the terms of the guarantee being
sued on stipulated that the guarantors were obliged to pay two days after demand made
by the bank and it was held that until a demand was made, no cause of action accrued.
It was further held that the summary summons in that case was flawed because it was
not based on the first effective demand that gave rise to the cause of action.

[31] *Stokes v Kerwick* (1921) 56 ILTR 24; *Gold Ores Reduction Co. Ltd v Parr* [1892] 2 QB
14.

[32] In *Bray UDC v Skelton* [1947] Ir Jur Rep 33, it was held by Dixon J that, it is essential,
if the proceedings are to be properly constituted, that either the tenant, or some person
who is shown to be the assignee or the legal personal representative of the tenant or the
successor, in some other way, to the tenant's interest should be defendant.

[33] All tenancies come within the scope of the sub-rule including weekly tenancies
(*McGillicuddy v Cassidy* [1911] 2 IR 632) and tenancies at will (*Delany (Blanchardstown
Mills Ltd) v Jones* [1938] IR 826).

[34] In *Keating v Mulcahy* [1926] IR 214, the Supreme Court rejected the contention that a
summary summons could only be used where there had been a determination by a notice
to quit prescribed by statute or common law and not a determination by a notice to quit
in accordance with a provision in the contract of tenancy. In *Meares v Connolly* [1930]
IR 333, it was held by O'Byrne J, following *Keating*, that procedure by summary summons is not available in actions for the recovery of land founded on a notice to quit
where the right to serve the notice depends on a contingency. However, it is submitted
that the better view is that of Fitzgibbon J in *Keating* who opined that, provided a
tenancy is determined by a notice to quit, it is immaterial that it is based on a forfeiture
or the happening of a contingency.

Act applies.[35] It is important to note that the availability of the summary summons procedure is strictly limited to these three categories[36] and cannot be used, for example, if the tenancy has been determined by forfeiture.[37] If ejectment proceedings are improperly commenced by summary summons, the court has no power to amend the summary summons and allow the action to proceed as if commenced by plenary summons.[38]

(iii) Claims to Have an Account Taken

2.011 The taking of accounts, which may be ordered by the court to be taken at any stage of proceedings,[39] is normally ancillary to the prosecution, by a plaintiff, of a substantive cause of action.[40] However, sub-rule (3) provides that the summary summons procedure may be used where the plaintiff, *in the first instance*, desires to have an account taken.[41] The italicised words seem to indicate that this relief is sufficient, in and of itself, to ground a summary summons and no other cause of action is necessary.

(iv) Agreement of the Parties

2.012 It is possible for the parties to agree that procedure by summary summons be adopted in the case of a claim not falling within the classes specified in Order 2, rule 1.[42] This course of action may be adopted where no real conflict of evidence arises and the parties are desirous of an expeditious disposition of the proceedings. If there is a serious conflict of evidence or the proceedings are otherwise unsuitable for summary disposition, then procedure by way of summary summons is inappropriate because the proceedings are likely to be adjourned to plenary hearing.[43]

---

[35] In *Bank of Ireland v Lady Lisa Ireland Ltd* [1992] 1 IR 404, [1993] ILRM 235 and *Keating v Mulcahy* [1926] IR 214, it was held that the reference to "non-payment of rent" in sub-rule (2) had to be taken as referring to the special procedure arising under s.52 of Deasy's Act (Landlord and Tenant (Amendment) (Ireland) Act 1860) permitting ejectment proceedings to be brought without further notice whenever a year's rent is in arrears in respect of land held under the form of tenure referred to therein.

[36] *Bray UDC v Skelton* [1947] Ir Jur Rep 33.

[37] *Bank of Ireland v Lady Lisa Ireland Ltd* [1992] 1 IR 404, [1993] ILRM 235; *Keating v Mulcahy* [1926] IR 214.

[38] *Keating v Mulcahy* [1926] IR 214; *Meares v Connolly* [1930] IR 333; *Bank of Ireland v Lady Lisa Ireland Ltd* [1992] 1 IR 404, [1993] ILRM 235.

[39] Order 33, rule 2.

[40] Though see Order 36, rule 8 which makes special provision as to trial where the matter in dispute consists wholly or in part of matters of account which cannot be tried conveniently in the ordinary way.

[41] *Cf.* Order 4, rule 11 which provides that, in all cases in which the plaintiff, in the first instance, desires to have an account taken, the summons must be indorsed with the claim that such account be taken.

[42] Order 2, rule 2.

[43] See, further, chapter 16.

Indorsement of Claim

2.013 Order 4, rule 4 provides that the indorsement of claim on a summary summons is entitled a "Special Indorsement of Claim" and must state specifically and with all necessary particulars the relief claimed and the grounds thereof.[44] It is required to be in such one of the forms in Appendix B, Part III as is applicable to the case, or, if none is applicable, then such other similarly concise form as the nature of the case may require.[45]

The basic principle as to what is required for a valid indorsement was identified by Kingsmill Moore J in *Bond v Holton*[46] who stated that "[u]nless an indorsement on a summary summons states the cause of action or states facts which, if true, unequivocally constitute a cause of action which may be brought by summary summons, it is a bad indorsement."[47] What is required in that regard was elaborated upon by Hanna J in *Caulfield v Bolger*.[48] He considered the phrase "necessary particulars" used in rule 4 and said:

> In my judgment it connotes such particulars as are essential to make the indorsement a good statement of claim both in particularity of fact and in law. It is the analogue of the statement of claim in plenary proceedings. While it contemplates an abbreviated and concise form, this is no bar to its containing all essentials of a correct pleading.[49]

2.014 Applying this principle to a claim for a debt or liquidated demand, sufficient particulars to establish the cause of action must be given. For example, if the claim is based on a contract then the existence of the contract[50] and any

---

[44] Order 4, rule 4.

[45] Order 4, rule 4.

[46] [1959] IR 302, 310-311.

[47] He went on to say that if a summons fails to specify a cause of action, the defendant is entitled to have the action dismissed or struck out. He rejected the contention that any defect in this regard could be cured by adjourning the proceedings to plenary hearing saying that a defendant should not be forced to a plenary hearing without knowing the cause of action which is alleged against him and the facts which are relied on as proving the cause of action.

[48] [1927] IR 117, 124.

[49] This approach was endorsed by Maguire P in *Keogh v O'Connor* [1943] Ir Jur Rep 11, 12, who agreed that an indorsement of claim "must set out, even if in an abbreviated form, all the particulars of correct pleading". That case concerned a claim for recovery of alleged over-payments of rent and the indorsement was held to be defective in that it did not contain any statement as to the circumstances of any letting at any particular time, what the standard rent was, or how the over-payments alleged to be due were made up.

[50] In *Bond v Holton* [1959] IR 302, it was held that the plaintiff's summary summons disclosed no cause of action where he pleaded an offer but not an acceptance and, therefore, failed to plead the existence of a contract.

conditions precedent to bringing an action such as the service of a demand[51] or the satisfaction of a statutory requirement[52] must be pleaded. If the proceedings are based on the dishonour of a cheque, it is necessary to aver notice of dishonour of the cheque.[53] If a claim is made for interest, the terms of the agreement or the provisions of the statute pursuant to which it is claimed that the interest is payable must be pleaded.[54]

If the relief sought is ejectment, the existence of a tenancy must be pleaded[55] and full particulars of the tenancy agreement and its determination given. However, it may not be necessary to actually set out all of these particulars in the indorsement of claim if they are given in a notice to quit which is incorporated by reference into the summons.[56]

2.015 In addition to properly pleading the cause of action, it is also necessary to include in the indorsement sufficient particulars of the claim that the defendant can decide whether he should pay or resist the claim.[57] This test was adopted by Murnaghan J in *Stacey and Harding Ltd v O'Callaghan*,[58] who stated:

> It is not easy, nor do I propose, to lay down any hard and fast rule as to what is and what is not a sufficient indorsement.... Each case must be considered in the light of the particular claim made, and must depend on the particular circumstances. I will say, however, that such particulars must be given in every case as may reasonably be necessary to enable the defendant to know whether he ought to pay or resist...

---

[51] If a demand is a necessary agreement of the cause of action, then the special indorsement must contain an averment that a demand was made and give particulars: *Bank of Ireland v Connell* [1942] IR 1, 13-14.

[52] See *Caulfield v Bolger* [1927] IR 117 where the claim was for costs incurred by a solicitor on behalf of a client. Under s.2 of the Attorneys and Solicitors (Ireland) Act 1849, no solicitor could maintain an action for the recovery of costs until the expiration of one month after the delivery to the party to be charged, of a bill of such costs, signed by the solicitor. Hanna J regarded it as well settled that compliance with this condition had to be averred with the necessary particulars in a statement of claim and, therefore, he held that the special indorsement of claim was defective because this had not been done. However, it is not necessary to plead compliance with statutory requirements if they do not constitute conditions precedent to bringing a claim: *McMullan Bros Ltd v Ryan* [1958] IR 94.

[53] *Cf. Royal Bank of Ireland v O'Rourke* [1962] IR 159 and *Northern Bank v Bailey* [1894] 2 IR 18.

[54] *Gold Ores Reduction Co. Ltd v Parr* [1892] 2 QB 14.

[55] See *Burke v Hardiman* (1894) 28 ILTR 129 where it was held that a special indorsement of claim ought to allege a contract of tenancy and state the parties thereto. But *cf. Ormathwaite v Riordan* (1894) 28 ILTR 147 and *Dunne v Farr* (1900) 34 ILTR 174.

[56] *Keating v Mulcahy* [1926] IR 214; *M'Donnell v Kavanagh* (1903) 4 NIJR 189.

[57] *Jackson v Kelly* (1878) 12 ILTR 136; *Stacey and Harding Ltd v O'Callaghan* [1958] IR 320.

[58] [1958] IR 320, 322.

In that case, the plaintiff had issued a summary summons for the price of goods sold and delivered by them to the defendant. The sum claimed was stated in the indorsement of claim to be "for goods sold and delivered by the plaintiffs to the defendant at the defendant's request within the last six years, detailed particulars of which said goods have already been furnished by the plaintiffs to the defendant". The indorsement set out neither the nature and dates of the transactions giving rise to the claim nor the method by which and date on which the amount claimed was arrived at. It was held by Murnaghan J that the indorsement was too vague. He was of the opinion that, as a general rule it is insufficient merely to set out in the indorsement of claim words to the effect that "particulars have already been furnished to the defendant" without more. However, he did acknowledge that, in a particular case, especially where the particulars are very lengthy, it may be sufficient after giving some general particulars, to refer to the fact that detailed particulars were on a certain date furnished to the defendant.[59]   In practice, it is common to particularise the claim by providing the dates between which the goods or services were supplied.[60]

Indorsement as to Costs

2.016 If the claim is one for a liquidated sum only,[61] the indorsement of claim, besides stating the amount claimed, must state the amount claimed for costs, and state that, on payment of the amount of the demand plus costs within six days after service,[62] or in the case of a summons for service out of the jurisdiction, within the time limited for appearance, further proceedings will be stayed.[63] A summons endorsed with an excessive sum for costs, will, on the application of the defendant before appearance, be set aside as irregular with costs.[64]

---

[59] See also *Beaufort v Ledwith* [1894] 2 IR 16 (indorsement held to be defective because it failed to set out the dates on which the items mentioned in the particulars became payable); *Phelan v Shanks* (1884) 18 ILTR 13 (held that special indorsement must state the dates and particulars of sums admitted to have been paid on account). *Cf. Hibernian Joint Stock Co v M'Donnell* (1878) 12 ILTR 106 (held that an indorsement, claiming only a portion of a sum stated to be due, but without giving any particulars of any credit given, was a good special indorsement).

[60] *Cf. Kilgariff v M'Grane* (1881) 8 LR Ir 354 in which it was held that a claim by a doctor on a *quantum meruit* had not been pleaded with sufficient particularity where no dates were given for when the attendances began or ended or when the work was done.

[61] An indorsement as to costs is not required where the claim is for recovery of possession of land: *Doyle v Patterson* [1934] IR 116, 123.

[62] The six day period is not extended by the service of an amended summons: *O'Connell v Hanlon* (1898) 32 ILTR 95.

[63] Order 4, rule 5(1). The amount of costs which can be claimed is detailed in Order 4, rule 5(2). If this indorsement is omitted, then it is open to the defendant to bring a motion to dismiss the proceedings on the basis of this irregularity prior to entering an appearance: *Allen v Quigley* (1878) 12 ILTR 46.

[64] *Roberts v Casey* (1888) 22 ILTR 8.

It should be noted that liability to pay the amount claimed for costs arises once the summons is issued.[65] A defendant will, therefore, be liable to pay these costs even if he or she pays the amount of the demand before service but after issue of the summons[66] and if the defendant refuses to pay the costs, then the plaintiff can enter final judgment for the amount of the costs alone.[67]

Special Summons

2.017 Like a summary summons, a special summons is utilised for proceedings which are generally capable of summary disposition without pleadings[68] or the necessity for oral evidence. However, it is used for cases which involve pure issues of law or discrete issues of fact. This is evident from a perusal of the matters listed in Order 3 that may be disposed of by special summons.

Proceedings which may be Commenced by Special Summons

2.018 Order 3 lists 21[69] classes of claim that *may* be commenced by special summons:

(1) The administration of the real or personal estate of a deceased person,[70] or the administration of the trust of any deed or instrument save where there is a charge of wilful default or breach of trust.[71]

---

[65] The plaintiff cannot, however, recover costs incurred prior to the issue of the summons: *Allen v O'Callaghan* (1876) 10 ILTR 131.

[66] *O'Malley v Guardians of the Poor of the Kilmallock Union* (1888) 22 LR Ir 326; *Simonds, Hunt & Montgomery v Cronin* (1910) 44 ILTR 47; *Murphy v Kearns* (1924) 58 ILTR 29. But *cf. Joseph Morton (Banbridge) Ltd v Boyle* [1959] NI 141.

[67] *Simonds, Hunt & Montgomery v Cronin* (1910) 44 ILTR 47; *Murphy v Kearns* (1924) 58 ILTR 29.

[68] Order 20, rule 1 provides that when procedure by special summons is used, no statement of claim or other pleading can be delivered except by order of the court.

[69] There were originally 22 classes of claim as is evident from the numbering but class 13 was deleted by the Rules of Superior Courts (No. 1) 1990 (SI No. 97 of 1990). Class 21 was amended and subdivided into two sub-classes by the Rules of the Superior Courts (No.2) (Amendment to Order 3) 2001 (SI No. 269 of 2001).

[70] Or persons: in *O'Kelly v Kelly* (1900) 34 ILTR 140, an order for the administration of the estates of two deceased was obtained on foot of one summons.

[71] See, further, Order 54, rules 1 and 2. Apart from cases involving charges of wilful default or breach of trust, there may be other issues arising out of the administration of an estate or trust which are not suitable for trial by special summons and in *Neilan v Farrell* (1892) 29 LR Ir 12 and *Buckley v Hartnett* [1943] IR 191, it was held that procedure by special summons is inappropriate where a question arises outside the ordinary course of administration. In *Meegan v Harvey* (1939) 73 ILTR 167, it was held by the Northern Ireland Court of Appeal that the court did not have any jurisdiction, on an administration summons, to determine questions of fact as against persons claiming dehors the estate.

(2)   The determination of any question affecting the rights or interests of any person claiming to be creditor, devisee, legatee, next-of-kin or heir-at-law of a deceased person, or *cestui que trust* under the trust of any deed or instrument, or claiming by assignment or otherwise under any such person.[72]

(3)   The payment into court of any money in the hands of[73] executors, administrators or trustees.[74]

(4)   A direction to any executors, or administrators or trustees to do or abstain from doing any particular act in their character as such executors or administrators or trustees (including the furnishing and vouching of accounts).[75]

(5)   The approval of any sale, purchase, compromise, or other transaction in connection with the administration of any estate or trust.[76]

(6)   The determination[77] of any question arising in the administration of any

---

[72] See, further, Order 54, rules 1 and 2.

[73] In *Nutter v Holland* [1894] 3 Ch 408, a literal interpretation of the phrase "in the hands of" was taken such that proceedings may only be commenced by special summons where the money is actually in the hands of the executor, administrator or trustee and not in circumstances where the money is not actually in his or her hands even though he or she is responsible for it.

[74] See, further, Order 54, rules 1 and 2.

[75] See, further, Order 54, rules 1 and 2. The court may refuse to give directions to do or abstain from doing an act which is outside the scope of the relevant trust, instrument or will: *Suffolk v Lawrence* 32 WR 899. In *Manning v Manning* (1894) 28 ILTR 33, the applicant sought an order directing the defendants, the executors of the deceased, to sell certain lands and divide the proceeds among the parties entitled, pursuant to the trust for sale contained in the will of the deceased. Porter MR stated that this class was framed to deal with the situation where executors sought the advice of the court and, perhaps, where difficulties had arisen in the discharge of their duties but not for the purpose of enabling parties to come to court to ask the court to direct the executors to do what they had already been directed to do by the testator.

[76] See, further, Order 54, rules 1 and 2. In *Pickard v Wheater* (1886) 31 Ch D 247, 249, Pearson J pointed out that pursuant to this class, the court is given the power only to approve a sale not to order a sale. Construing this class by reference to the preceding classes, he said that it: "refers to the approval of any sale which could be made by the executors or trustees of a will or deed, and which, but for this order, the executors or trustees might have been obliged to make at their own discretion, or for which they could have obtained the direction of the court only in a proper administration action. I do not think that the rule gives the court any power to direct a sale in a case in which it had no power to do so previously."

[77] Order 54, rule 5 stipulates that: "It shall not be obligatory on the court to pronounce or make a judgment or order for the administration of any trust or of the estate of any deceased persons if the questions between the parties can be properly determined without such judgment or order."

estate or trust or the ascertainment of any class of creditors, legatees, devisees, next-of-kin, or others.[78]

(7) The determination[79] of any question of construction arising under any deed, will, or other written instrument, and a declaration of the rights of the persons interested.[80]

(8) The determination, under s.14(2) of the Finance Act 1894, of a dispute as to the proportion of estate duty to be borne by any property or person.[81]

(9) Any relief under the Settled Land Acts 1882 to 1890,[82] or the Conveyancing Acts 1881 to 1911.

(10) Where no proceeding is pending by reason whereof the infant is a ward of court, an application as to the following: ss. 12, 16 and 17 of the Infants Property Act 1830 as extended to Ireland by the Infants Property (Ireland) Act 1835;[83] s.4 of the Leasing Powers Act for Religious Worship in Ireland 1855, as extended by the Glebe Lands (Ireland) Act 1875, and the Leases for Schools (Ireland) Act 1881.[84]

(11) The appointment of a trustee or a new trustee with or without a vesting or other consequential order; or a vesting order or other order consequential on the appointment of a new trustee, where the appointment is made by the court or out of court; or a vesting or other consequential order in any case where a judgment or order has been given or made for the sale, conveyance or transfer of any land or stock; or a vesting order under s.39 of the Trustee Act 1893; or an order directing a person to convey.

(12) The determination of any question under s.9 of the Vendor and Purchaser Act 1874.[85]

---

[78] See, further, Order 54, rules 1 and 2. In *Meegan v Harvey* (1939) 73 ILTR 167, Andrews LCJ took the view that this class is confined to questions arising *in* the administration of an estate and, therefore, did not extend to the determination of a claim which was against the estate and, thus, arose *outside* of the administration of the estate.

[79] See Order 54, rule 5, *supra*.

[80] See, further, Order 54, rules 1 and 2.

[81] The heading of a summons under this class is proscribed by Order 54, rule 4.

[82] See, further, Order 72.

[83] S.16 was repealed, so far as it refers to married women, by s.19 of the Married Women's Status Act 1957.

[84] As originally drafted, class 10 contained three subclasses of which the applications listed form subclass (a). Subclass (b) dealt with the settlement of the property of an infant on marriage under the Infants Settlements Act 1855 but this statute was repealed by s.8 of the Age of Majority Act 1985. Subclass (c) which dealt with the guardianship, care and maintenance or advancement of any infant was deleted by the Rules of the Superior Courts (No.1) 1990 (SI No. 97 of 1990).

[85] In *Martin v Irish Permanent Building Society* High Court (McWilliam J) 30 July 1980, McWilliam J explained that s.9 of the Vendor and Purchaser Act 1874 is designed to provide a comparatively simple procedure for resolving disputes between vendors and

(14) Any relief under ss. 42 or 44 of the Trustee Act 1893.

(15) Sale, delivery of possession by a mortgagor, or redemption; reconveyance, or delivery of possession by a mortgagee.[86]

(16) Any relief in respect of funds lodged in court pursuant to s.69 of the Land Clauses Consolidation Act 1845.[87]

(17) An interpleader order.[88]

(18) Applications in connection with the lodgment in court of any funds, the investment of any funds lodged in court, or the payment out of any funds lodged in court, whether pursuant to the provisions of any statute or otherwise, where there is no pending proceedings in respect thereof and no other procedure prescribed or required by the Rules.[89]

(19) Applications for the taxation and delivery of bills of costs[90] and for the delivery by any solicitor of deeds, documents and papers where there is no pending proceeding in which the application may be made.

(20) Any other proceeding in which procedure by special summons is required[91] or authorised[92] by the Rules.

---

purchasers and it is not suited to deciding complex issues of law and fact. Thus, a vendor and purchaser summons cannot be used as a procedure for investigation of title by the court (*Martin v. Irish Permanent Building Society* High Court (McWilliam J) 30 July 1980; *Mulligan v Dillon* High Court (McWilliam J) 7 November 1980) or where a question of fraud arises (*Re Delany's and Deegan's Contract* [1905] 1 IR 602).

[86] Order 54, rule 3 provides that any mortgagee or mortgagor, whether legal or equitable, or any person entitled to or having property subject to a legal or equitable charge, or any person having the right to foreclose or redeem any mortgage, whether legal or equitable, may take out a special summons for relief of the kind specified in class 15. In *Barden v Downes* [1940] IR 131, it was held that there is no jurisdiction, on a special summons issued by a mortgagee for an order for sale of the mortgaged premises, to make an order for payment on the personal covenant contained in the mortgage deed and, therefore, if both of these reliefs are sought, the mortgagee will either have to issue separate special and summary summonses or combine both reliefs on a plenary summons.

[87] See, further, Order 77.

[88] See, further, Order 57. Rule 4 provides that, where the applicant is a defendant, application for relief may be made by motion on notice at any time after the commencement of the proceedings. In any other case, the application must be by special summons.

[89] See, further, Order 77.

[90] See, further, Order 99, Part IV.

[91] The categories of proceedings which must be commenced by special summons under the Rules include: (a) an application under the Solicitors Acts 1954 and 1960 (as amended) relating to the control of a solicitor's property (Order 53, rules 19 & 20); (b) all family law proceedings under Order 70A other than an application under rule 27 (Order 70A, rule 2, as substituted by Rules of the Superior Courts (No. 3) 1997 (SI No. 343 of 1997)); (c) an application under the Settled Land Acts 1882 to 1890 (Order 72, rule 2(1); (d) an application by an assurance company for an order for the payment and

(21) (a) Any other proceeding which is required or authorised by law to be brought in a summary manner[93] and for which no other procedure is prescribed by the Rules;[94]

---

transfer of a deposit out of court (Order 88, rule 2); (e) an application pursuant to s.16 of the Auctioneers and Houses Agents Act 1947 (Order 89, rule 1); (f) an appeal under ss. 299, 300 or 301 of the Social Welfare (Consolidation) Act 1981 (as amended) or the referral of a question by the minister under s.299 of the Act (Order 90, rules 1 & 5); (g) an application under s.78(2) of the Housing Act 1966 (Order 92, rule 1); (h) an appeal under s.11(1)(d) of the Fisheries (Consolidation) Act 1959 (Order 93, rule 1); (i) appeals from various professional disciplinary bodies (Order 95, rule 1); (j) an application under s.62(7) of the Registration of Title Act 1964 by an owner of a charge for possession of registered land (Order 96, rule 14); (k) an application for release under s.50 of the Extradition Act 1965 (Order 98, rule 1); (l) an application under s.2 of the Attorneys and Solicitors (Ireland) Act 1849 if no proceedings are pending (Order 99, rule 15); (m) an application under s.5(3) of the Registration of Business Names Act 1963 (Order 100, rule 2); (n) an appeal under the Housing (Miscellaneous Provisions) Act 1979 (Order 101, rule 1); (o) an appeal under s.9 of the Transport (Tour Operators and Travel Agents) Act 1982 (Order 102, rule 1); (p) an appeal under the Redundancy Payments Acts 1967 and 1971 or the Minimum Notice and Terms of Employment Act 1973 and any question referred by the minister under these Acts (Order 105, rules 1 & 5); (q) an application under s.3 of the Trade Union Act 1971 (Order 107, rule 1); (r) an application under ss. 16 or 26 of the Industrial and Provident Societies (Amendment) Act 1978 (Order 109, rule 1); (s) an appeal or referral under s.13 of the Housing (Private Rented Dwellings) (Amendment) Act 1983 (Order 112, rules 1 & 5) and (t) an application by a party pursuant to Article 28.4.3° seeking the disclosure of discussions at meetings of the Government (Order 132, rule 2 (as inserted by the Rules of the Superior Courts (No. 2) (Applications Pursuant to Article 28.4.3° of the Constitution) 1998) (SI No. 281 of 1998); (u) applications pursuant to the Child Abduction and Enforcement of Custody Orders Act 1991 (Order 133, rule 2(1) (as inserted by the Rules of the Superior Courts (No. 1) (Child Abduction and Enforcement of Custody Orders Act 1991) 2001 (SI No. 94 of 2001) and (v) applications pursuant to the Investor Compensation Act 1998 (Order 75C, rule 2) (as inserted by the Rules of the Superior Courts (No. 3) (Investor Compensation Act 1998) 2001 (SI No. 270 of 2001).

[92] The following categories of proceedings may be commenced by special summons: (a) an application by a client for the delivery of a cash account, or the payment of moneys or the delivery of securities by his or her solicitor (Order 53, rule 22); (b) certain applications specified in Order 56, rule 4 by any party to a reference under an arbitration; (c) certain admiralty actions specified in Order 64, rule 3 or where all the parties to admiralty proceedings consent (order 64, rule 4); (d) an application in a winding up by the court for leave to disclaim any part of the property of a company pursuant to s.290(1) of the Companies Act 1963 (Order 74, rule 84(1)); (e) an application by any person claiming to be interested under a deed for the determination of any question of construction arising under the instrument and for a declaration of the rights of the persons interested (Order 83, rule 1).

[93] Examples of proceedings which are required to be brought in a summary manner and hence by special summons include applications pursuant to: s.58 of the Waste Management Act 1996; s.25 of the Animal Remedies Act 1993; s.28A of the Air Pollution Act 1987 (as amended); ss. 5 & 6 of the Foreshore (Amendment) Act 1992; and s.10 of the Local Government (Water Pollution) Act 1977 (as substituted by s.7 of the Local Government (Water Pollution) (Amendment) Act 1990. Examples of proceedings which may be brought in a summary manner and hence by special summons include applications

(b) Any other proceeding which is required or authorised by law and for
     which no other procedure is prescribed by the Rules.[95]

(22) Such other matters as the court may think fit to dispose of by special sum-
     mons.

2.019 A number of observations can be made about the foregoing classes of
claim. First, it should be noted that where procedure by special summons is
required or permitted, whether under the Rules and/or statute, the reliefs which
may be claimed and/or obtained are limited to those contemplated by the relevant rule or statutory provision. In the case of a statutory provision, it is a
matter of statutory construction to determine what issues may be determined
and reliefs sought under the relevant provision. For example, in *Archer v
Fleming*,[96] the plaintiff brought an application by way of special summons pursuant to s.50 of the Extradition Act 1965 seeking a number of reliefs including
a declaration that the information on oath on which the warrant for his arrest
was based was false and did not justify the issue of the warrant. Finlay P commented that:

> A special summons under the Extradition Act 1965, seeking relief pursu-
> ant to s.50 is, I am quite satisfied, quite clear confined to achieving an
> order under that section and a consideration of section 50 makes it quite
> clear that it does not include giving to the High Court any jurisdiction to
> make any general declaration with regard to the truth or falsity of any
> document leading to the making of an extradition order.[97]

Similarly, in *Martin v Irish Permanent Building Society*,[98] the plaintiff brought
an application by way of special summons pursuant to s.9 of the Vendor and
Purchaser Act 1874 at the instance of the defendant which refused to advance
money to the plaintiff on the security of a home proposed to be purchased by

---

pursuant to: s.6 of the Arbitration (International Commercial) Act 1998; ss. 26 & 28 of
the Investor Compensation Act 1998; s.3 of the Comptroller and Auditor General and
Committees of the Houses of the Oireachtas (Special Provisions) Act 1998; ss. 12, 13
& 84 of the Central Bank Act 1997 (as amended); s.4 of the Tribunals of Inquiry
(Evidence) (Amendment) Act 1997; and ss. 14, 24, 29 & 65 of the Stock Exchange Act
1995 (as amended).

[94] See, for example, the Powers of Attorney Act 1996. S.4(2) specifies that applications
under Part II of that Act are to be made in a summary manner but rather than proceeding by way of special summons, Order 129 (inserted by the Rules Of the Superior
Courts (No. 1) (Powers of Attorney Act 1996) 2000 (SI No. 66 of 2000)) provides for
the various applications to be made by way of *ex parte* motions and motions on notice.

[95] A revamped class 21 was inserted in Order 3 by the Rules of the Superior Courts (No.
2) (Amendment to Order 3) 2001.

[96] High Court (Finlay P) 21 January 1980.

[97] *Ibid*. at 6.

[98] High Court (McWilliam J) 30 July 1980.

him unless he obtained a declaration from the court with regard to the Family Home Protection Act 1976. McWilliam J commented that:

> Both parties to this transaction are under a complete misapprehension as to the function and jurisdiction of the court. The Vendor and Purchaser Act 1874, provides a comparatively simple procedure for resolving disputes between vendors and purchasers. It is not intended to provide a procedure for investigation of title by the court where no dispute has arisen between the parties.[99]

2.020 Second, the mere fact that a claim falls within the literal wording of one of the classes does not mean that a special summons should be used. As noted above, the special summons procedure is designed to dispose of matters summarily on affidavit and if complex legal and, especially, factual issues are raised, these are better dealt with by the plenary summons procedure which provides for pleadings and oral evidence.

Third, it will not necessarily be fatal if proceedings are instituted by special summons and all or part of the relief does not fall within one of the permitted categories because class 22 permits the court to dispose of such matters by way of special summons as it thinks appropriate.[100] In addition, there may be circumstances where the court might exercise its discretion pursuant to class 22 to direct that particular proceedings be commenced by special summons.

Fourth, the range of circumstances where a special summons may be used to commence proceedings has been greatly expanded by the amendment of class 21 by the Rules of the Superior Courts (No. 2) (Amendment to Order 3) 2001.[101] Previously, proceedings could only be brought under class 21 where the proceedings were required or authorised by *statute* to be brought in a *summary manner*. If the proceedings were required or authorised by statutory instrument or the phrase "in a summary manner" was not used, then it seemed as if a plenary summons had to be used, notwithstanding that the proceedings might be suitable for disposition by the special summons procedure unless reliance could be placed on class 22. Now, proceedings may be brought whenever the proceeding is required or authorised to be brought by *law* (which includes applications pursuant to a statutory instrument) and it is not necessary that the phrase "in a summary manner" be used by the draftsman.

---

[99] *Ibid.* at 3-4.
[100] The inclusion of class 22 would seem to reverse the effect of the decision of Haugh J in *Buckley v Hartnett* [1943] IR 191, that where a claim had been incorrectly commenced by way of special summons, the court had no power to amend the summons to convert it into a plenary summons or to adjourn it to plenary hearing.
[101] SI No. 269 of 2001.

Indorsement of Claim

2.021 A special summons is designed to be the sole pleading in the action and, therefore, it is required to contain a full indorsement of claim entitled "Special Indorsement of Claim" which must state specifically and with all necessary particulars the relief claimed and the grounds thereof.[102] Sample indorsements are set out in Appendix B, Part III and the indorsement must be in such one of these forms as shall be applicable to the case, or, if none is applicable, then such other similarly concise form as the nature of the case may require.

The same principles apply to drafting a special indorsement for a special summons as to one for a summary summons. Thus, as outlined above, it must plead all the particulars of law and fact necessary to ground the plaintiff's claim for relief with sufficient detail that the defendant can make an informed decision as to whether to appear and resist the plaintiff's claim or not.

Grounding Affidavit

2.022 After the special summons has issued, an affidavit verifying the claim indorsed thereon must be filed in the Central Office.[103] Notice of the filing of this affidavit must be given to the parties concerned. Although it is not necessary to do so, it is common to serve the affidavit and summons together.

Issue of Summonses

2.023 A summons cannot be served until it is issued.[104] This is done by bringing the draft summons and a number of copies to the Central Office[105] where an officer will insert the date of issue on the summons,[106] seal it with the seal of the High Court, mark it with a record number[107] and return it to the solicitor or the plaintiff where he sues in person.[108] The form of the record number will vary

---

[102] Order 4, rule 4.

[103] Order 38, rule 1.

[104] Order 5, rule 9. The issue of a summons in probate proceedings must be preceded by the filing of an affidavit made by the plaintiff or one of the plaintiffs in verification of the indorsement on the summons and, once the summons is issued, the plaintiff must, if he has not already done so, lodge a caveat in the Probate Office entitled in the estate of the deceased person.

[105] Order 5, rule 1 requires that, save as otherwise provided by the Rules, every originating summons must be issued out of the Central Office. Order 65, rule 1 stipulates that proceedings to make a minor a ward of court are issued out of the Office of Wards of Court.

[106] Order 5, rule 8 requires a summons to bear the date of issue.

[107] Order 5, rule 9.

[108] It should be noted that a limited liability company cannot represent itself and must, therefore, be represented by a solicitor: *Battle v Irish Art Promotion Centre Ltd* [1968] IR 252. See further, Chapter 6, paragraph 6.021.

according to the type of summons, a plenary summons will be given a record number in the form "2000 No.100P", a summary summons in the form "2000 No.100S" and a special summons in the form "2000 No.100Sp". Once a summons has been sealed and marked with a record number, it is deemed to have been issued[109] and time for the purposes of the Statute of Limitations will stop running.

The solicitor or plaintiff is obliged to leave a signed copy of the summons with the officer who will mark, stamp and file it and cause an entry of the particulars thereof to be made in the appropriate Cause Book.[110] Such other copies as are required for service will also be marked and stamped.

Issue of Summons for Service out of the Jurisdiction

2.024 Order 5, rule 14(1) provides that, save as is otherwise provided for in the Rules, no summons for service out of the jurisdiction, or of which notice is to be given out of the jurisdiction, can be issued without leave of the court. However, an originating summons to which Order 11A, rule 2 applies and which is to be served out of the jurisdiction, or of which notice is to be given out of the jurisdiction, may be issued without leave of the court, if, but only if, it complies with the following conditions:[111]

(a) each claim made by the summons is one which, by virtue of the 1998 Act, the court has power to hear and determine; and

(b) the summons is indorsed before it is issued with a statement that the court has power under the 1998 Act to hear and determine the claim and specifying the particular provision or provisions of the 1968 Convention under which the court should assume jurisdiction; and

(c) the summons is indorsed with a statement that no proceedings concerning the said cause of action are pending between the parties in another contracting state.

Assignment of Summonses

2.025 The general rule is that a summons should not be assigned to any particular judge[112] but Order 5, rule 4 lists a number of matters which must be assigned to such judge or judges as the President of the High Court may from

---

[109] Order 5, rule 9.
[110] Order 5, rules 10–12. The requirement for and format of the Cause Books is dealt with in Order 5, rule 7. A separate Cause Book is kept for proceedings in revenue cases (Order 68, rule 18).
[111] Rule 14(2) (inserted by the Rules of the Superior Courts (No. 1) 1989 (SI No. 14 of 1989)).
[112] Order 5, rule 3.

time to time assign. These matters include every special summons relating to any particular class of claim. Where a claim falls within one of these categories the officer of the Central Office is obliged to mark and assign the summons to the judge or judges assigned.[113] In addition, if the summons relates to a matter which is required pursuant to Order 5, rule 4, to be assigned to a particular judge, the officer issuing the summons must mark and assign the summons for the judge assigned.

Where a summons has been assigned to a particular judge or has (whether assigned or not) been heard by a particular judge, every subsequent summons, notice of motion or petition, relating to the same matter, or so connected therewith as to be conveniently dealt with by the same judge must, whenever practicable be marked by the proper officer with the name of such judge, and the party or solicitor presenting such summons, notice of motion, or petition must, if there is to his knowledge such relation or connection, so certify.[114]

Concurrent Summonses

2.026 Order 6, rule 1 provides that the plaintiff in any proceedings may, at the time of, or at any time during the twelve months after the issuing of the originating summons,[115] issue one or more concurrent summonses.[116] Each concurrent summons will bear the same date of issue as the original summons and will be marked with a seal bearing the word concurrent and its date of issue. The original and concurrent summons will, thus, correspond except that, if the plaintiff wishes, each can be directed solely to the defendant to be served therewith.[117]

Concurrent summonses are commonly used where there are multiple defendants, some of whom are within the jurisdiction and some of whom are outside.[118] This is because the time limited for appearance will be different for the two categories of defendant.[119] In this situation, the plaintiff should bring an *ex*

---

[113] Order 5, rule 5. Any case of doubt or difficulty is to be determined by the Master and the assignment or non-assignment of any summons at the time of issue is without prejudice to the power of the Master to vary or alter such assignment or non-assignment.

[114] Order 5, rule 6. The certificate is required to be in the form set out in Appendix A, Part I, Form No. 5 and must be countersigned by the registrar of the judge to whom such summons had been assigned or by whom such summons had been heard as the case may be.

[115] It is possible to issue a concurrent summons after the expiration of this 12 month period if the court enlarges time pursuant to Order 122, rule 7: see *Smalpage v Tonge* (1886) 17 QBD 644.

[116] However, such concurrent summons will only remain in force for the period during which the original summons in such proceedings is in force.

[117] *Harte v Mulligan* (1907) 41 ILTR 213; *Traill v Porter* (1878) 1 LR Ir 60, 62.

[118] Express provision is made for this situation in Order 6, rule 2.

[119] In *Traill v Porter* (1878) 1 LR Ir 60, the Vice-Chancellor took the view that whenever different times for appearance are allowed to different defendants, a concurrent summons must be used.

parte application for liberty to serve the summons or notice on the defendants resident outside the jurisdiction unless the defendants are resident in a Convention country in which case an order for liberty to serve is not necessary. Then, the plaintiff should issue a concurrent summons in accordance with Order 6 which is served on the defendants resident within the jurisdiction.[120] However, there is nothing in Order 6 which restricts the issue of concurrent summonses to the foregoing situation and in the English decision of *Smalpage v Tonge*,[121] it was held that a concurrent summons could be issued for service out of the jurisdiction even though the original summons had been issued for service within the jurisdiction and although there was only one defendant to the action.

Renewal of Summonses

2.027 Order 8, rule 1 of the Rules of the Superior Courts stipulates that an originating summons remains in force for the purpose of service for a period of 12 months from the date of issue.[122] After the expiration of that period, service of the summons cannot be validly effected unless it is renewed in accordance with the provisions of Order 8, rule 1.[123] It provides that an order renewing the summons may be made where the court is satisfied that reasonable efforts have been made to serve the defendant or where other good reason exists. Given that a plaintiff who fails to serve a summons within the 12 month period limited for service has the option of issuing a fresh summons, the real significance of the renewal of proceedings lies in the fact that a summons which is renewed is considered to have remained in force from the date of issue and will be effective to prevent the proceedings becoming statute barred.[124]

Application for Leave to Renew Summons

2.028 An application for leave to renew a summons is generally made *ex parte* but may also be made by way of motion on notice to the defendant. However, it if is made *ex parte*, then (as will be seen below) it is open to the defendant to bring a motion to set aside the order renewing the summons.[125] The application

---

[120] The original summons should be directed only to the defendant outside the jurisdiction and the concurrent summons only to the defendant within the jurisdiction.

[121] (1886) 17 QBD 644.

[122] The 12 month period is inclusive of the date of issue: Order 8, rule 1.

[123] In *Baulk v Irish National Insurance Co. Ltd* [1969] IR 66, 71, Walsh J rejected the contention that a summons became a nullity after the expiration of the 12 month period and expressed the view that, if the summons is served outside of this period, the defect in service would be cured by the entry of an unconditional appearance to the summons. See, to the same effect, *Sheldon v Brown Bayley's Steelworks Ltd* [1953] 2 QB 393, [1953] 2 All ER 894.

[124] Order 8, rule 1.

[125] Order 8, rule 2.

is grounded on the affidavit of the solicitor for the plaintiff setting out the reason(s) why service was not effected and why renewal is sought. If the 12 month period has not expired, the application is made to the Master for leave to renew the summons. However, if the period has expired, then an application must be made to the court to extend time for leave to renew the summons.[126] The Master or the court, as the case may be, if satisfied that reasonable efforts have been made to serve the defendant or that other good reason exists, may order that the summons be renewed for six months.[127] Each of these grounds for renewal will be examined below.

(i) Reasonable Efforts to Effect Service

2.029 The first category is relatively straightforward though questions may arise as to the reasonableness of the efforts made to effect service. The Master and the court will be astute to ensure that alleged difficulties in service are not used to conceal dilatoriness on the part of the plaintiff. In particular, the plaintiff will have to explain why one of the alternatives to personal service such as obtaining an order for substituted service was not availed of.

(ii) Other Good Reason

2.030 The starting point in considering the meaning of the phrase "other good reason" is the decision of the Supreme Court in *Baulk v Irish National Insurance Co. Ltd.*[128] The plaintiff's claim for damages arose out of personal injuries he suffered in a car accident which occurred in August 1962. The defendants were aware from October 1962 of the plaintiff's intention to sue but proceedings were not actually issued until 6 June 1964. No attempt was made to serve the summons and in October 1966 an application for leave to renew the summons was made by which time, the claim, if made by a fresh summons, would have been statute barred. The High Court refused to grant leave and the plaintiff appealed to the Supreme Court.

Walsh J (with whom Ó Dálaigh CJ concurred) took the view that the phrase "other good reason" was not "exclusively referrable to the question of service but refers also to any other reason which might move the court, in the interests of doing justice between the parties, to grant the renewal."[129] He said that it

---

[126] It would appear from the wording of Order 8, rule 1, that where an application is made to the court outside the 12 month period, two orders should be sought: (i) an order extending time for making the application for leave to renew the summons; and (ii) an order granting leave to renew the summons.

[127] Order 8, rule 1. It is stipulated that the six month period runs from the date of renewal inclusive and that the summons may be renewed from time to time during the currency of the renewed summons. The summons is renewed by being stamped with the date of renewal in the Central Office upon delivery to the appropriate officer by the plaintiff or his or her solicitor of a Memorandum of Renewal of Summons in the Form No. 4 in Appendix A, Part I.

[128] [1969] IR 66.

[129] *Ibid.* at 71-72.

was erroneous to equate the position where proceedings have been commenced by the issue of a summons that has not been served with the position where proceedings have not been issued at all and he took the view that "the fact that the Statute of Limitations would defeat any new proceedings, which might be necessitated by the failure to grant the renewal sought, could itself be a good cause to move the court to grant the renewal."[130] Turning to the circumstances of the case, he pointed out that the defendants had been aware from an early point of the plaintiff's intention to sue them and he concluded that no injustice would be done, in the wide sense of the term, by granting leave for renewal of the summons:

> [I]f the plaintiff can establish negligence against the deceased driver but does not have his summons renewed because the period of limitation for the institution of a new action has already expired, the plaintiff will suf-fer an injustice by a refusal to renew this summons through being de-prived of such damages as he would be entitled to. In my view, in the circumstances of this case, it would be an injustice to the plaintiff to employ the rules of court for the purpose of preventing him from pro-ceeding with the action which he commenced within time when there is no other course open to him which will enable him to have his claim against the defendants determined.[131]

2.031 The decision in *Baulk* was subsequently followed by a majority of the Supreme Court in *McCooey v Minister for Finance*,[132] where Ó'Dálaigh CJ identified its *ratio* as being that the fact that new proceedings would be statute barred if renewal was refused constituted a good reason for granting a renewal.[133]

The interpretation placed on *Baulk* in *McCooey* was open to criticism on the basis that it undermined the policy basis of the Statute of Limitations that "persons with good causes of action should pursue them with reasonable dili-gence and that defendants should not be put in a position in which, through the expiration of time, they have lost the evidence to resist a stale claim by reason of death or defective recollection of witnesses or by the destruction of relevant documents."[134] It would seem to defeat the purpose of having strict time limits within which proceedings must be commenced if a plaintiff can be dilatory in serving proceedings and then rely on the expiration of the limita-tion period in order to obtain a renewal of the summons. Of course, as Walsh

---

[130] *Ibid.* at 72.
[131] *Ibid.* at 72.
[132] [1971] IR 159.
[133] See also *Walshe v CIE* [1985] ILRM 180 where O'Hanlon J applied *Baulk* and *McCooey* and granted leave to renew a summons in circumstances where the plaintiff had, at an early stage, made known to the defendant his intention to bring proceedings and where fresh proceedings would be statute barred.
[134] *Per* FitzGerald J in *McCooey v Minister for Finance* [1971] IR 159, 167.

J pointed out in *Baulk*, if renewal is not permitted, a plaintiff may suffer an injustice in being unable to pursue what may be a well-founded claim. However, this is caused by the plaintiff's own failure to respect the limitation period and may be matched by the injustice to the defendant in having to meet a stale claim that would otherwise be statute barred. It is not surprising, therefore, that the courts in recent times have resiled to some extent from the broad interpretation of *Baulk* adopted in *McCooey*.

2.032 The first signs of dissatisfaction with this approach came in *Prior v Independent Television News*.[135] The plaintiff had sued the defendant for libel arising out of a "News at Ten" programme in 1983 which claimed that he and another man were kidnappers. A plenary summons was issued in November 1988 but never served. In February 1992, the plaintiff sought to renew the summons and argued that unless the summons was renewed, he would be unable to maintain his claim against the defendant which would be statute barred. The defendant maintained that it had no knowledge of the claim until January 1992, by which stage none of its staff had any recollection of or knowledge in relation to the programme or events in question.

Barron J examined the decisions in *Baulk* and *McCooey* and identified the cardinal principle as being that "where proceedings have not been heard on the merits it may be unjust that they should be barred by procedural difficulties". However, he went on to stress that:

> The question of prejudice to the defendant is equally important as prejudice to the plaintiff. I must balance the hardship which the plaintiff will suffer by reason of being deprived of a hearing of his cause of action against that which the defendant may suffer by reason of being required to defend the proceedings after a lapse of time...[136]

In the instant case, the plaintiff had recovered substantial damages against defendants in other libel cases. Barron J took the view that, while this fact did not go to the merits of the action or the ability of the defendants to defend the proceedings, it did largely counterbalance the element which would normally weigh in the plaintiff's favour if a summons was not renewed, *viz.* that he would be deprived of damages. In addition, there had been considerable delay in the case (by this stage it was nine years since the programme had been broadcast) and this delay had not been caused by any fault on the part of the defendant. This delay had prejudiced the defendant in that its ability to defend the claim had been seriously impaired. The learned judge concluded that there was nothing in the plaintiff's claim to justify making the defendant meet the claim notwith-

---

[135] [1993] 1 IR 399, [1993] ILRM 638.
[136] *Ibid.* at 403, 641.

standing this impairment and, in the circumstances, justice required that leave to renew the summons should be refused.

2.033 The principles laid down in *Prior* were subsequently applied in *Sullivan v Church of Ireland*.[137] The plaintiff applied in March 1995 to renew a plenary summons dated 6 March 1987 claiming damages for negligence arising out of events on 12 March 1984. No attempt had been made to serve the summons and the defendant first became aware that it had been issued on 3 September 1993. In her judgment, Laffoy J identified the central issue as being whether the interests of justice would be served by renewing the summons or by refusing to renew it. The first question to ask was whether the plaintiff would suffer an injustice if the summons was not renewed and the second was whether the defendant would suffer an injustice if the summons was renewed. Turning to the facts of the case, she accepted that the defendant was not in a position, at this remove, to adduce reliable credible evidence to meet the plaintiff's claim and that its ability to defend the plaintiff's claim had been seriously impaired. In particular, an important witness had died. Thus, the defendant would be severely prejudiced if it was put into a position of having to defend the plaintiff's claim at this remove. Also of significance was that at the time the summons was issued (just within the limitation period), there was no clear unequivocal notification by the plaintiff to the defendant that he was pursuing a claim against the defendant. A further six and a half years elapsed before the plaintiff apprised the defendant that the summons had been issued. In the circumstances, she was satisfied that the delay in the case had been so gross and excessive that the interests of justice could only be served by refusing to renew the summons.

2.034 A similar approach was adopted by the Supreme Court in *O'Brien v Fahy*.[138] The plaintiff had been injured in an accident at the defendant's riding stables on 24 July 1988 and the plenary summons was issued on 23 July 1991. On 5 June 1992, the plaintiff's solicitor wrote to the defendants giving them their first intimation that proceedings were contemplated against them. The summons was finally served on 29 July 1992 at a point when it was no longer in force and the plaintiff applied for a renewal of the summons. Barrington J, delivering the judgment of the Supreme Court, emphasised that the fact that a plaintiff's cause of action would be statute barred if renewal was not granted was not the only matter to which the court had to pay attention. He laid emphasis on the fact that, in the instant case, the defendant had only been informed of the intention to bring proceedings four years after the cause of action accrued and as a result of this delay was greatly prejudiced in making his defence. He continued:

---

[137] High Court (Laffoy J) 7 May 1996.
[138] Supreme Court, *ex tempore*, 21 March 1997.

It appears to me that the lapse of such a time without knowing that a claim was going to be made is something which itself implies prejudice and when the defendant and her solicitor are prepared to swear affidavits that in fact it is not a theoretical prejudice but an actual prejudice which the defendant would suffer; one must set that against the loss to the plaintiff, if as a result of a refusal to renew the summons which is out of time, her claim becomes statute-barred.[139]

He concluded that, in the circumstances, the balance of justice was in favour of refusing the application for an order extending time for leave to renew the summons.

2.035 *O'Brien v Fahy* was subsequently followed in *Roche v Clayton*.[140] O'Flaherty J, delivering the judgment of the Supreme Court, stressed that while a judge has a wide discretion whether to renew a summons:

[The court] must make an order that renders justice between the two immediate parties to the litigation.... It is not a good reason ... to renew a summons simply to prevent the defendant availing of the Statute of Limitations. The Statute of Limitations must be available on a reciprocal basis to both sides of any litigation.[141]

The net effect of the case law would seem to be that the phrase "other good reason" is treated by the courts as being synonymous with the interests of justice.[142] Thus, an order granting leave to renew a summons will only be made where it is in the interests of justice to do so *i.e.* where the injustice to the plaintiff in not being able to pursue his or her claim outweighs any injustice which would be caused to the defendant by renewing the summons.[143]

2.036 In deciding where the balance of justice lies, it is necessary to assess, first, whether the plaintiff would suffer an injustice if the summons is not renewed. Where the effect of not renewing the summons is that the plaintiff's claim will be statute barred, then obviously the plaintiff will be prejudiced but whether this amounts to an injustice to the plaintiff depends on the reason for the delay in service. If the court concludes that the plaintiff or his or her solici-

---

[139] *Ibid.* at 4.

[140] [1998] 1 IR 596.

[141] *Ibid.* at 600. See also *O'Reilly v Northern Telecom (Ireland) Ltd* [1999] 1 IR 214, [1999] 1 ILRM 371.

[142] *Cf. per* Walsh J in *Baulk v Irish National Insurance Co. Ltd* [1969] IR 66, 71-72.

[143] *Baulk v Irish National Insurance Co. Ltd* [1969] IR 66, 72; *Prior v Independent Television News* [1993] 1 IR 399, 403, [1993] ILRM 638, 641; *Sullivan v Church of Ireland* High Court (Laffoy J) 7 May 1996; *Foran v O'Connell* High Court (Morris J) 6 May 1997; *Roche v Clayton* [1998] 1 IR 596.

tor is culpable for this delay, then no injustice will result from the statute barring of the plaintiff's proceedings which is attributable to his or her own default. Thus, explanations by the defendant for the delay in service which have been rejected by the courts as good reasons include: that the firm of solicitors handling the case had broken up;[144] that the plaintiff was let down by a solicitor;[145] or that the plaintiff employee did not wish to jeopardise his position with the defendant employer.[146] However, if the failure to effect service can be explained or excused in some way as where it was not caused or contributed to by the plaintiff or his solicitor or was due to a genuine mistake, then a good reason may be found to exist. In *Martin v Moy Contractors Ltd*,[147] Lynch J, delivering the judgment of the Supreme Court, cautioned that "it would be wrong to say that mere oversight or inadvertence or carelessness can never be excused as amounting to 'other good reason'" and he instanced as an example, a case in which the plenary summons had expired in the recent past. In that case, the Supreme Court dismissed an appeal from a decision of Morris P in the High Court who refused to set aside an order renewing a plenary summons five years after the time limited for service had expired so that it could be served on one of eight defendants in circumstances where it had been served on the other seven defendants and the failure to serve it on that defendant was due to an oversight.

If the plaintiff succeeds in satisfying the court that a good reason for renewal may exist, then the court must proceed to assess the prejudice, if any, which would be caused to the defendant.[148] In assessing prejudice to the defendant two related factors are very important: (i) the date on which the defendant first became aware of the plaintiff's intention to sue;[149] and (ii) the lapse of time between the accrual of the cause of action and/or the expiration of the period limited for service and the application for a renewal. The importance of these factors lies in their value as indicators of prejudice.[150] If a long period of

---

144 *Kerrigan v Massey Bros (Funerals) Ltd* High Court (Geoghegan J) 15 March 1994.
145 *Roche v Clayton* [1998] 1 IR 596.
146 *O'Reilly v Northern Telecom (Ireland) Ltd* [1999] 1 IR 214, [1999] 1 ILRM 371.
147 Supreme Court 11 February 1999.
148 *Prior v Independent Television News* [1993] 1 IR 399, [1993] ILRM 638; *Sullivan v Church of Ireland* High Court (Laffoy J) 7 May 1996. *Cf. Kerrigan v Massey Bros (Funerals) Ltd* High Court (Geoghegan J) 15 March 1994 where Geoghegan J held that if the plaintiff fails to establish a good reason, there is no need to proceed to consider the question of whether the defendant would be prejudiced.
149 See the emphasis placed on this factor in *Kerrigan v Massey Bros (Funerals) Ltd* High Court (Geoghegan J) 15 March 1994, *Sullivan v Church of Ireland* High Court (Laffoy J) 7 May 1996 and *O'Brien v Fahy* Supreme Court, *ex tempore,* 21 March 1997 and *O'Reilly v Northern Telecom (Ireland) Ltd* [1999] 1 IR 214, [1999] 1 ILRM 371.
150 See *Prior v Independent Television News* [1993] 1 IR 399, [1993] ILRM 638; *Sullivan v Church of Ireland* High Court (Laffoy J) 7 May 1996 and *O'Brien v Fahy* Supreme Court, *ex tempore,* 21 March 1997. *Cf. Foran v O'Connell* High Court (Morris J) 6 May 1997, and *Martin v Moy Contractors Ltd* Supreme Court, 11 February 1999, where the lack of any prejudice to the defendant was a very important factor in the decision to renew the summons.

time has elapsed before the defendant became aware of the plaintiff's intention to sue and/or since the cause of action accrued, then prejudice to the defendant in terms of his ability to defend the claim will be presumed.[151] If, in addition, the defendant can demonstrate that this presumed prejudice has crystallised into actual prejudice such that his or her ability to defend the claim has been impaired, this factor will weigh very heavily against renewal.[152]

Motion to Set Aside Renewal of Summons

2.037 As noted above, if an application to renew a summons is made *ex parte*, then it is open to a defendant, before entering an appearance, to bring a motion on notice to the plaintiff to set aside the order renewing the summons.[153] In *Behan v Bank of Ireland*,[154] Morris J emphasised that this application is not in the nature of an appeal from the order renewing the summons but rather:

> [I]t is incumbent upon the moving party to demonstrate that facts exist which significantly alter the nature of the plaintiff's application to the extent of satisfying the court that, had these facts been known at the original hearing, the order would not have been made.[155]

Those facts may either be facts which were withheld from the court in breach of the plaintiff's obligation of *uberrimae fides* or facts such as those relating to prejudice on the part of the defendant which were not within the plaintiff's knowledge but which change the assessment of where the balance of justice lies.

PETITION PROCEDURE

2.038 Petitions are generally used to commence proceedings where there is no identifiable defendant[156] and where the proceedings may require to be brought to the notice of a potentially large number of people. It is a form of process used

---

[151] See *O'Brien v Fahy* Supreme Court, *ex tempore*, 21 March 1997 and *Martin v Moy Contractors Ltd* Supreme Court, 11 February 1999.

[152] See *Sullivan v Church of Ireland* High Court (Laffoy J) 7 May 1996 and *O'Brien v Fahy* Supreme Court, *ex tempore*, 21 March 1997.

[153] Order 8, rule 2.

[154] High Court (Morris J) 14 December 1995.

[155] *Ibid.* at 3. *Cf. Kerrigan v Massey Bros (Funerals) Ltd* High Court (Geoghegan J) 15 March 1994, where Geoghegan J set aside the order of Carroll J renewing the summons in circumstances where he was satisfied that if all the facts had been before her, he was satisfied that she would not have made the order.

[156] *Cf.* Order 125, rule 1 which defines the term 'petitioner' as including any person making an application to the court, either by petition or motion, otherwise than as against a defendant".

in particular to commence proceedings in company law and other matters which require advertisement to the general public.

Proceedings which may be Commenced by Petition

2.039 A petition can only be used to initiate proceedings where the Rules specifically provide[157] and provision is made for a miscellany of proceedings to be commenced by petition as follows:

(1) All originating applications to the President of the High Court for the exercise by him of all or any of the powers conferred by the Lunacy Regulation (Ireland) Act 1871 or otherwise conferred upon or possessed by him in respect of the persons or property of persons of weak or unsound mind.[158]

(2) Appeals under s.10 of the Finance Act 1894 (as amended).[159]

(3) Appeals under the Succession Duty Act 1853.[160]

(4) Matrimonial Causes and Matters pursuant to Order 70.

(5) Proceedings under the Legitimacy Declaration Act (Ireland) 1868.[161]

(6) Petitions to wind up a company pursuant to Order 74.

(7) Miscellaneous other applications under the Companies Acts specified in Order 75, rule 4.

(8) Applications for the appointment of an Examiner under the Companies (Amendment) Act 1990.[162]

(9) Bankruptcy petitions under Order 76.

(10) Parliamentary election petitions under Order 97.

(11) Appeals under s.14(1) of the Business Names Act 1963.[163]

Contents of Petition

2.040 There is no standard form for a petition and its contents will vary depending on the type of application or appeal being made. However, it is stipulated that every petition must be indorsed by the solicitor for the petitioner with

---

[157] Order 1, rule 1.
[158] Order 67, rule 3(1).
[159] Order 68, rule 9.
[160] Order 68, rule 16.
[161] Order 71, rule 2.
[162] Order 75A, rule 3 (as inserted by the Rules of the Superior Courts (No. 3) 1991 (SI No. 147 of 1991).
[163] Order 100, rule 3.

the address and occupation or description of the petitioner and the name of the solicitor's firm and its registered place of business where proceedings may be served or, if the petitioner brings the petition in person, he must indorse upon it his occupation or description and an address for service within the jurisdiction.[164] In addition, Order 5, rule 16 provides that, at the foot of every petition presented to the court, and of every copy thereof, a statement must be made of the persons, if any, intended to be served therewith, and if no person is intended to be served a statement to that effect must be made at the foot of the petition and of every copy thereof.

Presentation of Petition

2.041 Order 5, rule 15 provides that, save as otherwise provided by the Rules, every petition to the court must be presented by leaving it with the proper officer at the Central Office. Subject thereto, the other provisions of Order 5 apply to a petition in the same manner as they apply to an originating summons. Order 5, rule 17 provides that unless the court gives leave to the contrary, there must be at least two clear days between the service and the date for the hearing of the petition.

ORIGINATING MOTION PROCEDURE

2.042 The originating motion procedure is another, and increasingly utilised means, for initiating proceedings which are suitable for disposal without pleadings and, often, on affidavit.[165] The distinguishing feature and utility of the procedure lies in the fact that the motion is returned before a judge a set period of time after it is issued and will, thereafter, appear at periodic intervals before a judge until such time as it is listed for trial or disposed of. Proceedings commenced by originating motion, therefore, tend to be disposed of in a relatively expeditious manner.

Proceedings which may be Commenced by Originating Motion

2.043 Procedure by originating motion can only be used where provision is made for it in the Rules[166] and provision is made for a miscellany of proceed-

---

[164] Order 4, rule 16. In addition, Order 121, rule 4 requires it to contain the name and registered place of business of any solicitor to be served or, in the case of a party who does not act by a solicitor, the name and address for service of such person.

[165] It should be noted that, in the absence of pleadings, the issues to be decided by the court will be identified in the affidavits filed by the parties and a party will not be permitted to raise a point at the hearing which is not raised on affidavit: *South Dublin County Council v Balfe* High Court (Costello J) 3 November 1995 at 4-5.

[166] Order 1, rule 1.

ings to be commenced in this manner including the following:

(1) Appeals and applications to the President of the High Court under Parts IV, V and VI of the Solicitors Act 1954.[167]

(2) Appeals to the High Court under s.7 of the Solicitors (Amendment) Act 1960 (as substituted by s.17 of the Solicitors (Amendment) Act 1994) and applications under s.11 of the 1994 Act.[168]

(3) Applications under the Companies Act 1990.[169]

(4) Applications for judicial review unless the court directs that it made by way of plenary summons.[170]

(5) Applications for the review of a decision to award a public contract within the scope of certain public procurement Directives.[171]

(6) Applications or appeals under the Registration of Title Act 1964.[172]

(7) Applications for an injunction under s.160 of the Planning and Development Act 2000.[173]

(8) Applications for an order under s.28 of the Air Pollution Act 1987.[174]

(9) Appeals under s.5 of the Hepatitis C Compensation Tribunal Act 1997.[175]

(10) Applications under ss. 14 & 23 of the Industrial and Provident Societies (Amendment) Act 1978.[176]

(11) Appeals against the decisions of designated authorities under the European Communities (General System for Recognition of Higher Education Diplomas) Regulations 1991 or under the European Communities (Second General System for the Recognition of Professional Education and Training) Regulations 1996.[177]

---

[167] Order 53, rule 12.

[168] Order 53, rule 26 (as inserted by the Rules of the Superior Courts (No.1) (Solicitors (Amendment) Act 1994) 1998 (SI No. 14 of 1998)).

[169] Order 75B, rule 3 (as inserted by the Rules of the Superior Courts (No. 4) 1991 (SI No. 278 of 1991)).

[170] Order 84, rule 22(1).

[171] Order 84A, rule 2 (as inserted by the Rules of the Superior Courts (No. 4) (Review of the Award of Public Contracts) 1998 (SI No. 374 of 1998)).

[172] Order 96, rule 2.

[173] Order 103 (as amendd by the Rules of the Superior Courts (No. 1) 1996).

[174] Order 103A, rule 2 (as inserted by the Rules of the Superior Courts (No. 2) 1996 (SI No. 377 of 1996)).

[175] Order 105A, rule 1 (as inserted by the Rules of the Superior Courts (No. 7) (Appeals from the Hepatitis C Compensation Tribunal) 1998 (SI No. 392 of 1998)).

[176] Order 109, rule 6.

[177] Order 113A (as inserted by the Rules of the Superior Courts (No. 5) 1997 (SI No. 346 of 1997)).

(12) Appeals pursuant to ss. 42(1), 42(2) or 42(3) of the Freedom of Information Act 1997.[178]

(13) Applications or appeals pursuant to the Committees of the House of the Oireachtas (Compellability, Privileges and Immunities of Witnesses) Act 1997.[179]

Contents of Motion

2.044 There is no standard format for an originating notice of motion and its contents will vary depending on the type of application or appeal being made. However, it is stipulated that every originating notice of motion must be indorsed by the solicitor for the applicant with the address and occupation or description of the applicant and the name of the solicitor's firm and its registered place of business where proceedings may be served or, if the applicant brings the application or appeal in person, he must indorse upon it his occupation or description and an address for service within the jurisdiction.[180]

DEFECT IN THE ORIGINATING PROCEDURE

2.045 If the wrong originating procedure is used as, for example, if a summary summons is used in circumstances where procedure by summary summons is not available, then the defendant may bring an application pursuant to Order 124, rule 1 to strike out the proceedings.[181] However, an application to set aside any proceedings for irregularity will not be entertained unless it is made within a reasonable time or if the party applying has taken any fresh step after knowledge of the irregularity.[182] At the hearing of the motion, the court is given a broad jurisdiction and the "proceedings may be set aside either wholly or in part as irregular, or amended, or otherwise dealt with in such manner and upon such terms as the court shall think fit".[183]

---

[178] Order 130, rule 2 (as inserted by the Rules of the Superior Courts (No. 3) (Freedom of Information Act 1997) 1998 (SI No. 325 of 1998)).

[179] Order 131, rule 2 (as inserted by the Rules of the Superior Courts (No. 5) (Committees of the Houses of the Oireachtas (Compellability, Privileges and Immunities of Witnesses) Act 1997) 1998 (SI No. 381 of 1998)).

[180] Order 4, rule 16. In addition, Order 121, rule 4 requires it to contain the name and registered place of business of any solicitor to be served or, in the case of a party who does not act by a solicitor, the name and address for service of such person.

[181] The application must be made by way of notice of motion which states the grounds on which it is sought to strike out the proceedings (Order 124, rule 3) and failure to make the application in the required form may disentitle the defendant to relief (*Murphy v GM PB PC Ltd* High Court (O'Higgins J) 4 June 1999).

[182] Order 124, rule 2.

[183] Order 124, rule 1.

Whether the court will exercise its discretion to strike out the proceedings depends on the nature of the error. If the wrong originating procedure has been used as, for example, when a summary summons is used in circumstances where it is not available, then the court is likely to take the view that the proceedings are fundamentally flawed and dismiss them.[184] However, if there is merely a defect in the indorsement of claim which can be rectified by an amendment, then the court is more likely to grant leave to amend the pleadings rather than strike out the proceedings. This was the course of action adopted in *Murphy v GM PB PC Ltd*,[185] where the respondents contended that the plenary summons was defective because the indorsement of claim merely sought interlocutory relief and did not include any claim for substantive relief. O'Higgins J agreed that the summons was defective for this reason but exercised his discretion not to strike out the proceedings because the application had not been made promptly and in the correct manner and the defect in pleading was of a technical nature which could not conceivably have caused prejudice to the respondents. He took the view that it would, therefore, be unfair to allow the respondents to avail of the defect of pleading at that point and he permitted the applicants to make the appropriate amendments to the plenary summons.

---

[184] See, for example, *Meares v Connolly* [1930] IR 333; *Bray UDC v Skelton* [1947] Ir Jur Rep 33 and *Bank of Ireland v Lady Lisa (Ireland) Ltd* [1992] 1 IR 404, [1993] ILRM 235.
[185] High Court (O'Higgins J) 4 June 1999.

Chapter Three

SERVICE

SERVICE OF SUMMONSES

Introduction

3.001 In *Fox v Taher*,[1] Costello P identified the object of service as being "to bring home to defendants the nature of the proceedings and the documents relating to the claim being made against them". For this reason, it is vital that proper service be effected and the Rules of the Superior Courts contain detailed requirements in this regard.

Personal Service

3.002 The default rule with regard to service is laid down by Order 9, rule 2 which provides that service of any summons[2] must, except where otherwise specified by the Rules, be effected by personal service where this is reasonably practicable. Rule 3 specifies that personal service is effected "by delivering a copy of the summons to the defendant in person and showing him the original or duplicate original".[3] This provision was considered by Costello P in *Petronelli v Collins*.[4] A private investigator acting for the plaintiff averred that she had handed the defendant a copy of the summons with a sticker attached to it on which he signed his autograph. On being handed back these items, she removed the sticker, handed the copy summons to the defendant, showed him the original summons and said "Mr Collins you are served". Costello P was satisfied that if this evidence was correct, the service was valid and in accordance with rule 3. The defendant averred that a woman had attempted to hand him an envelope which he had not accepted and that he had not been shown any document. However, Costello P expressed the view that "serious inconsistencies" between the version of events given by the defendant and other witnesses weakened the credibility of this testimony and he concluded that the defendant had been properly served with the summons in the circumstances.

---

[1] High Court (Costello P) 24 January 1996.
[2] Order 9, rule 16 provides that Order 9 shall apply as far as practicable to the originating document in proceedings not commenced by summons.
[3] Order 9, rule 3.
[4] High Court (Costello P) 19 July 1996.

Service on a Solicitor

3.003 Order 9, rule 1 stipulates that service of a summons on a defendant will not be required if "the defendant, by his solicitor, accepts service, and undertakes in writing to enter an appearance".[5] It is, therefore, clear that service may be effected on a solicitor but only where he or she accepts service on behalf of his or her client and is authorised to do so.[6] In order to establish this authority, it is common practice, where the institution of proceedings is preceded by an exchange of correspondence, for the solicitors for the prospective plaintiff to ask the solicitors for the defendant whether they are authorised to accept service and service on the solicitors will only be effected if an affirmative response is received. If the solicitor for the defendant refuses to accept service of proceedings, then Order 9, rule 1 will not apply and service in the normal way will have to be effected.[7]

Service on Particular Defendants

3.004 Order 9, rules 4-7 make provision in relation to service on particular defendants. Where a husband and wife are both defendants in proceedings, they should both be served unless the court orders otherwise.[8] Where an infant is a defendant, service on his father, mother or guardian or on the person with whom he resides or under whose care he is shall, unless the court orders otherwise, be deemed good service. In addition, the court may order that service made or to be made on an infant himself shall be deemed good service.[9] Where a lunatic or person of unsound mind is a defendant, service on the committee of the lunatic or on the individual with whom the person of unsound mind resides or under whose care he is, shall be deemed good service unless the court orders otherwise.

Order 9, rule 7 makes specific provision in relation to service on a corporation aggregate, the inhabitants of a county district, county, city or town and provides that where any statute makes provision for service on a corporation or body of persons, corporate or incorporate, a summons may be served in the manner so provided. The most important example of such a statutory provision is s.379(1) of the Companies Act 1963 which provides that a document

---

[5] Note that Order 12, rule 12 provides that "A solicitor not entering an appearance in pursuance of his written undertaking to do so shall be liable to an attachment."

[6] Although note the decision in *Thompson v Sherrard* (1903) 37 ILTR 64 in which a solicitor accepted service of a summons on behalf of two brothers. Subsequently, another solicitor acting for one of the brothers informed the plaintiff that the service of the writ was bad in relation to his client. Boyd J made an order declaring the service already effected on this brother good service and directed that a copy of the order be served on the solicitor acting for him.

[7] See *Fox v Taher* High Court (Costello P) 24 January 1996.

[8] Order 9, rule 4.

[9] Order 9, rule 5.

may be served on a company by leaving it at or sending it by post to the registered office of the company or, if the company has not given notice to the Registrar of Companies of the situation of its registered office, by registering it at the office for the registration of companies. Section 379(2) further provides that any document left at or sent by post to the place for the time being recorded by the Registrar as the situation of the registered office of a company shall be deemed to have been left at or sent by post to the registered office of the company notwithstanding that the situation of its registered office may have been changed. Although s.379 does not require service by registered post, it is prudent to use registered post as this makes it easier to prove the posting.

Service in Particular Actions

3.005 Order 9, rules 8-11 make provision in relation to service in particular actions, specifically those for the recovery of land. Rule 10 provides that in such actions service may be effected either by personal service on the person to be served at any place within the jurisdiction or by delivering a copy of the summons to the wife, husband, child, father, mother, brother or sister of such person at his house, office or place of business and by showing such person the original or duplicate original of the summons. This differs from the provisions of rule 2 which deals with other types of action, in that service may not be effected on a defendant's "servant or clerk" and it may also be effected in this manner whether the person to be served is within the jurisdiction or not.

Service on Connected Persons

3.006 As stated above, personal service is required only if it is "reasonably practicable" and, sometimes, it will not be possible to effect personal service as where the defendant deliberately evades service or threatens the process server. For this reason, Order 9, rule 2 provides that where it appears that the defendant is personally within the jurisdiction[10] and due and reasonable diligence[11] has been exercised in endeavouring to effect personal service, service may be effected by delivering a copy of the summons at his house or place of business, to his wife, husband, child, father, mother, brother, sister or to any servant of the defendant and by showing such person the original or duplicate original of the summons.

If service is effected in this manner, then it will be necessary, if an issue subsequently arises as to service, to obtain an order pursuant to Order 9, rule 15 deeming service to be sufficient. This application is grounded upon an affi-

---

[10] Service in such a manner may be set aside if the defendant is not personally within the jurisdiction.

[11] "Due and reasonable diligence" is usually interpreted as meaning that three attempts have been made at reasonable hours to effect service.

davit of the process server[12] which should: (i) aver that the defendant is within the jurisdiction or was within the jurisdiction at the appropriate time; (ii) detail the attempts made to effect personal service and aver that due and reasonable diligence has been exercised in endeavouring to effect personal service; (iii) describe the manner in which service was effected, and (iv) state the belief of the deponent that the defendant has notice of the proceedings.

3.007 The requirements of rule 2 were considered in *Uwaydah v Nolan*[13] where the plaintiff sought an order pursuant to Order 9, rule 15, deeming service on the wife of the first named defendant to be sufficient service on him. The summons server had spoken to the first named defendant's wife on two occasions by telephone before calling to the house and was told by her that she did not know what time her husband would be home. It was submitted on behalf of the first named defendant that his wife could not have been validly served since he was permanently resident and domiciled out of the jurisdiction and had not been within the jurisdiction on the date of the alleged service. While Barron J accepted the Australian decision of *Laurie v Carroll*[14] as authority for the proposition that service within the jurisdiction cannot in general be effected when the defendant is not within the jurisdiction, except where he has left to avoid service, he was satisfied that there was *prima facie* evidence of the first named defendant's presence within the jurisdiction at the relevant time. The onus of disproving this lay on the first named defendant and in his view, this onus had not been discharged. Accordingly, Barron J made an order deeming good the service actually effected.

Deeming Service Sufficient

3.008 Where an issue arises or is likely to arise as to the sufficiency of service effected, an application may be made pursuant to Order 9, rule 15 to have the service actually effected declared sufficient. Although applications pursuant to rule 15 are most commonly brought where service has been effected on a person connected to the defendant, the court is given a broad discretion to cure a deficiency in service where "just grounds" exist for doing so. Although no further elaboration of what constitutes just grounds is given, the exercise of the court's power is informed by what Morris J identified in *Lancefort Ltd v An Bord Pleanála*[15] as the purpose and object of proper service, namely "to ensure that the party concerned is adequately informed of the matters contained in the notice so as to suffer no prejudice". Thus, failure to effect service in strict compliance with the requirements laid down in the Rules will not be

---

[12] Order 9, rule 2.
[13] High Court (Barron J) 21 February 1997.
[14] (1958) 98 CLR 310.
[15] High Court (Morris J) 13 May 1997.

fatal where the proceedings have actually been brought to the attention of the defendant and he has not suffered any prejudice thereby.

3.009 A good example of the application of rule 15 can be seen in *Fox v Taher*[16] where Costello P refused an application to set aside an order previously made by Kinlen J deeming service in the proceedings good. The defendant's solicitors had written to the plaintiff stating that they would accept service in this country of any proceedings which the plaintiff might institute against him arising out of a dispute in relation to litigation in which the plaintiff had acted for the defendant. However, when the plaintiff's solicitor brought a copy of the summons to a meeting with the member of the firm of solicitors acting for the defendant, he refused to accept service of the proceedings and to enter an appearance. Costello P expressed the view that "the whole object of the power of the court to deem service good is to deal with a situation such as arose in this case". In his view it was clear that the defendant's solicitors were in "daily if not hourly contact" with him and that notice of the proceedings would have been made available almost immediately to him. Costello P therefore held that he was quite satisfied that Kinlen J had properly exercised his jurisdiction in making the order deeming service good.

It should be noted that the power granted under rule 15 is discretionary in nature and will not be exercised where the Rules have been deliberately flouted.

Application to Set Aside Service

3.010 Order 12, rule 26 allows a defendant on whom notice of proceedings have been served to apply before entering an appearance to set aside the service of such proceedings or to discharge the order authorising such service. So, in *O'Toole v Ireland*,[17] Costello J granted the application of the fourth named defendant to set aside the order of the court authorising service out of the jurisdiction on the basis that it did not fall within the terms of Order 11, rule 1(h)[18] and was not a "necessary or proper party to the proceedings". Similarly in *Rye Valley Foods Ltd v Fisher Frozen Foods Ltd*[19] O'Sullivan J granted the defendant's application to have service of a plenary summons set aside. He held that the court did not have jurisdiction to hear the plaintiff's claim on the basis that any alleged defects in goods which became apparent in the plaintiff's premises within the jurisdiction did not constitute of itself a breach of contract on the defendant's part occurring in Ireland for the purposes of Order 11, rule 1(e).[20]

---

[16] High Court (Costello P) 24 January 1996.
[17] [1992] ILRM 218.
[18] Considered *infra*.
[19] High Court (O'Sullivan J) 10 May 2000.
[20] Considered *infra*. See also *Analog Devices BV v Zurich Insurance Co.* High Court (Lavan J) 18 May 2001.

It is clear from the wording of Order 12, rule 26 that an application to set aside service must be made before an appearance is entered. Therefore if the defendant enters an unconditional appearance this would seem to cure any defect in the service effected.[21]

Substituted Service

3.011 Order 10, rule 1 provides that if it appears to the court that a plaintiff is "from any cause unable to effect prompt personal service", the court may make an order for substituted service or for the substitution for service of notice by advertisement or otherwise. This procedure is in some respects more satisfactory than that permitted by Order 9 which does not involve obtaining a court order as it may be difficult to prove that the person actually served was one of those specified in the rule.

Application for Substituted Service

3.012 An application for substituted service is made *ex parte* grounded on an affidavit setting out the grounds on which the application is made.[22] The affidavit must be sworn by the person who has attempted to effect service and should set out:

(i) Where the defendant is believed to reside and/or carry on business.

(ii) The attempts which have been made to effect personal service (usually three) and the reason why they were unsuccessful. It must be established that reasonable attempts were made in this regard *i.e.* that service was attempted at a time and place where the defendant would reasonably be expected to be.

(iii) An averment that the defendant is still to be found at those addresses and, if it is the case, an averment as to the belief of the deponent that the defendant is evading service.

(iv) The suggested means of substituted service. It is important to satisfy the court that the suggested method will be effective to inform the defendant of the existence of the proceedings. For example, if service is to be effected on a person connected with the defendant, the plaintiff will have to satisfy the court that the person is in close contact with the defendant and can reasonably be expected to bring the summons to his notice.

(v) A prayer for an order directing service in the suggested way.

---

[21] *Murphy v GM PB PC Ltd* High Court (O'Higgins J) 4 June 1999 at 9.
[22] Order 10, rule 2.

If the court decides to make an order for substituted service, it will usually fix an extended time within which an appearance is to be entered. A copy of the order must be served with the summons or notice.[23]

The Form of Substituted Service

3.013 The form of substituted service which is ordered by the court will depend on the circumstances. The most common form is service of the summons by registered post[24] but other examples include putting it through the letterbox at the defendant's residence or pinning it to the door of his residence or business premises. Alternatively, an order may be made for the substitution for service of notice by advertisement or otherwise.[25]

In certain circumstances, leave may be given to serve a solicitor who has been acting for the defendant in the matter out of which the claim arose.[26] This may even be done where the solicitor's retainer has been withdrawn provided he has been in communication with his former client shortly before the application for substituted service was made as the decision of the Supreme Court in *Shelswell-White v O'Connor*[27] illustrates. Budd J had refused the application saying that "justice demands that actions involving serious allegations and grave consequences should not be litigated without the knowledge of a defendant and without his being aware of what is happening".[28] However, the Supreme Court granted the application on the basis that in all reasonable probability the summons would come to the notice of the defendant. Lavery J quoted with approval from *Halsbury* that, where an application is made for substituted service or service out of the jurisdiction, "it must be shown that there is a practical impossibility of actual service and that the method of substituted service asked for will in all reasonable probability be effective to bring knowledge of the writ to the defendant."[29] In *Smyth v Dolan*[30] the court refused to set aside an order giving leave to substitute service by serving the defendant's solicitor personally where it was established that the defendant was within the jurisdiction at the date of the issue of the writ even if he was outside it on the date the order was made.

---

[23] Order 10, rule 3.

[24] See, for example, *Irish Agricultural Wholesale Society v Saint Enda's Co-operative* [1924] 2 IR 41 where leave was given to effect service through the post on the grounds that it would be unsafe for the process server to effect personal service without military protection.

[25] Order 10, rule 1. In *Mahon v Skeehan* (1953) 88 ILTR 36, Davitt P held that publication of a condensed form of the contents of a summons in the press complied with this requirement in the circumstances.

[26] *Walsh v Kennedy* (1934) 68 ILTR 238. See also *Re Slattery* [1941] Ir Jur Rep 13.

[27] (1961) 95 ILTR 113.

[28] *Ibid.* at 114.

[29] *Ibid.* at 115. See *Halsburys Laws of England* (Hailsham Edition) Vol 26 at 30.

[30] (1913) 47 ILTR 287.

Challenging an Order for Substituted Service

3.014 If an order for substituted service was made but the defendant was not put on notice of the proceedings, he can later challenge any order made in his absence on that ground. So, in *Grimes v Wallace*[31] where Barron J was satisfied that the applicant was resident out of the jurisdiction at all material times and that this fact had been communicated to the relevant party, he held that an order for substituted service should not have been made.

Proof of Service

3.015 The person serving the summons is required, within three days after service, to indorse on it the day and date of service and an affidavit of service of such summons must specify the date on which the endorsement was made.[32] If it is necessary to prove service and the person who effected service is unable to swear an affidavit of service, it may be possible to prove service in some other way. For example, in *Nicholson v McDonald*[33] the process server had become seriously ill and the court permitted an assistant in the plaintiff's solicitor's office who was acquainted with the former's handwriting to make an affidavit verifying the endorsement of service.

SERVICE OUT OF THE JURISDICTION

Introduction

3.016 Order 11 rule 1 provides that service out of the jurisdiction of an originating summons or notice of an originating summons[34] may be allowed in a number of circumstances listed in the rule. It also provides that it does not apply to a summons to which Order 11A applies, namely proceedings governed by the Brussels Convention and the Jurisdiction of Courts and Enforcement of Judgments (European Communities) Act 1998.[35] Order 11 applies to "situations in which the defendant is not present within the jurisdiction but in which the case is so closely connected with Ireland or with Irish law that there is a justification for it being tried within the jurisdiction".[36] As Walsh J made

---

[31] High Court (Barron J) 4 March 1994.
[32] Order 9, rule 12. It would appear that the affidavit must specify the precise mode in which service was effected, see *O'Sullivan v Murphy* (1884) 18 ILTR 102.
[33] (1903) 38 ILTR 36.
[34] Order 11, rule 8 provides that where the defendant is not, or is not known or believed to be, a citizen of Ireland, notice of the summons, and not the summons itself, shall be served upon him.
[35] See the *dicta* of Geoghegan J in *Schmidt v Home Secretary* [1995] 1 ILRM 301, 305.
[36] *Per* Walsh J in *Grehan v Medical Incorporated* [1986] IR 528, 532, [1986] ILRM 627, 629.

it clear in *Grehan v Medical Incorporated*[37] the jurisdiction to allow service out of the jurisdiction is discretionary and not mandatory in nature. He stated as follows:

> There is of course a heavy burden on the court to examine the circumstances of each case before exercising its discretion to make an order for service out of the jurisdiction. It would be clearly wrong to refuse it on the application of any technical rule which insists on one element occurring in the jurisdiction as it would be equally inappropriate if the court were to permit service out of the jurisdiction where the case only had a tenuous connection with the country on its facts and in terms of the law likely to govern questions of liability and related matters.[38]

It is necessary when bringing an application under Order 11 that an applicant should bring himself within one of the situations enumerated in rules 1(a)-(q)[39] and that the court, when giving leave for service out of the jurisdiction should specifically mention in the order the particular class of action within which the intended claim falls.[40]

Circumstances in which Order 11 applies

3.017 Although rule 1 contains 16 subparagraphs, only the four most frequently invoked are considered here:

> (e) the action is one brought to enforce, rescind, dissolve, annul, or otherwise affect a contract, or to recover damages or other relief for or in respect of the breach of a contract:
>
> (i) made within the jurisdiction; or
>
> (ii) made by or through an agent trading or residing within the juris-

---

[37] [1986] IR 528, 532. See also *M'Crea v Knight* [1896] 2 IR 619, 625 *per* Fitzgibbon LJ; *Joynt v M'Crum* [1899] 1 IR 217, 224 *per* Chatterton VC; *Bennett v Cook* (1901) 35 ILTR 153, 154 *per* Fitzgibbon LJ; *Kutchera v Buckingham International Holdings Ltd* [1988] IR 61, 73, [1988] ILRM 501, 509.

[38] *Ibid.* at 542.

[39] *Brennan v Lockyer* [1932] IR 100, 107 *per* Kennedy CJ. See also *Shipsey v British and South American Steam Navigation Co.* [1936] IR 65, 88 *per* Fitzgibbon J; *International Commercial Bank plc v Insurance Corporation of Ireland plc* [1989] IR 453, 459, [1989] ILRM 788, 791-792 *per* Costello J. However, the *dicta* of Porter MR in *Russell v Le Bert* [1896] 1 IR 334, 339 (referred to by Walsh J in *Grehan v Medical Incorporated* [1986] IR 528, 532, [1986] ILRM 627, 630) should also be noted, namely that "it is desirable that the rules in reference to service out of the jurisdiction should be construed widely" and should apply to cases clearly within the spirit of the rules.

[40] *Shipsey v British and South American Steam Navigation Co.* [1936] IR 65, 83 *per* Kennedy CJ; *Short v Ireland* [1996] 2 IR 188, 198-199 *per* O'Hanlon J.

diction on behalf of a principal trading or residing out of the jurisdiction; or

(iii) by its terms or by implication to be governed by Irish law, or is one brought in respect of a breach committed within the jurisdiction of a contract wherever made, even though such breach was preceded or accompanied by a breach out of the jurisdiction which rendered impossible the performance of the part of the contract which ought to have been performed within the jurisdiction;

3.018 The most common basis for making an order pursuant to Order 11, rule 1(e) is that the contract has been made within the jurisdiction[41] or that the breach has been committed within the jurisdiction regardless of where the contract was made.[42] The substantive principles relating to these requirements have been considered in detail elsewhere[43] but a number of procedural points should be noted. First, it was made clear by Kennedy CJ in *Brennan v Lockyer*[44] that it is not sufficient to aver in the affidavit grounding the application that the contract upon which the intending plaintiff relies was made in the jurisdiction. It was necessary, in his opinion, "that the affidavit should set out the facts which will enable the court to determine for itself where the contract was made and not to accept what is merely the deponent's opinion or conclusion upon undisclosed facts, without regard to the material upon which the interested party's conclusion is based".

3.019 It is also important that the cause of action fits within the terms of the relevant paragraph of rule 1 pursuant to which the application is made. In *Campbell v Holland Dredging Co. (Ireland) Ltd*[45] the defendants applied to vacate an order allowing service out of the jurisdiction on the grounds that the action by the plaintiff for damages in respect of the death of her husband was one brought in tort and consequently was not one falling within the provisions of rule 1(e). Counsel for the plaintiff submitted that the cause of action also arose out of the deceased's contract with the defendants and that it was an appropriate case for the court to exercise its jurisdiction under paragraph (e). However, Keane J pointed out that if the order being challenged and the service effected thereunder were allowed to stand, there would be nothing to prevent the plaintiff from confining her proceedings to a claim for damages in respect of a tort committed outside the jurisdiction and in his opinion, "this

---

[41] *E.g. M'Crea v Knight* [1896] 2 IR 619; *Tedcastle McCormick & Co. v Robertson* [1929] IR 597; *Kelly v Cruise Catering Ltd* [1994] 2 ILRM 394.

[42] *E.g. O'Mara v Dodd* [1912] 2 IR 55; *Taher Meats (Ireland) Ltd v State Company for Foodstuff Trading* [1991] 1 IR 443.

[43] See Binchy *Irish Conflicts of Law* (1988) at 139-147.

[44] [1932] IR 100, 107.

[45] High Court (Keane J) 3 March 1989.

would not be consistent with the care which the courts must exercise in assuming a jurisdiction which normally belongs to other states". Accordingly Keane J concluded that he should vacate the order previously made. However, it would appear from the decision of the Supreme Court in *United Meat Packers (Ballaghaderreen) Ltd v Nordstern Allgemeine Versicherungs AG*[46] that provided an order is simply made under rule 1(e), it may not be fatal if the application is made pursuant to the incorrect subparagraph (i), (ii) or (iii). Order 11, rule 1(e)(ii) confers jurisdiction where there is a breach of a contract made by an agent within the jurisdiction on behalf of a principal outside the jurisdiction and (iii) confers jurisdiction where a breach of a contract occurs within the jurisdiction, irrespective of where the contract was made. In the High Court the plaintiff applied under rule (e)(iii) and was granted leave to serve a summons outside the jurisdiction. Some of the defendants applied to set aside service of the notice on the grounds that the contract was not made within the jurisdiction by their agent. Carroll J granted the relief sought and said it could not be assumed that another judge would grant service outside the jurisdiction pursuant to subparagraph (iii) on the evidence which had been before the court, although she pointed out that the plaintiff was free to make another application under Order 11, rule 1(e)(iii). However, on appeal the Supreme Court reversed her decision and held that the relief sought by the defendants must be refused. O'Flaherty J stated that while in the course of the affidavit which was sworn on behalf of the plaintiff subparagraph 1(e)(ii) had been mistakenly relied upon, the order when it was drawn up did not refer to subparagraphs and simply stated that it had been made under rule 1(e). In his view the correct enquiry was whether there was evidence before the court which established that the court had jurisdiction under Order 11, rule 1(e) which was the order on foot of which leave was granted.

(f) the action is founded on a tort committed within the jurisdiction;

3.020 An extensive treatment of the substantive questions involved in deciding whether a tort can be said to have been committed within the jurisdiction is contained elsewhere[47] but many of the important principles relating to the exercise of jurisdiction pursuant to rule 1(f) are summarised by Walsh J in the course of his judgment in *Grehan v Medical Incorporated*.[48] He stated that the issue of whether a tort has been committed within the jurisdiction within the meaning of the rule is not merely a mechanical one because this would lead to arbitrary results. He continued as follows:

The court must have regard to the implications for the plaintiff or the

---

[46] [1996] 2 ILRM 260 (HC); [1997] 2 ILRM 553 (SC).
[47] See Binchy *Irish Conflicts of Law* (1988) at 147-153.
[48] [1986] IR 528, [1986] ILRM 627.

defendant if the trial is to take place within the State. The task of the court is to interpret and to apply the rule in a way designed to ensure that justice and practical common sense prevail. The court therefore should interpret the rule in the light of a broad policy and in the light of its choice of law implications. If more than one possible interpretation of the rule is available, the one which serves to encourage the operation of sensible choice of law rules should be followed rather than the one which would tend to frustrate them.[49]

Walsh J concluded that the test for the application of rule 1(f) should be whether any significant element in the commission of the tort had occurred within the jurisdiction.[50]

(g) any injunction is sought as to anything to be done within the jurisdiction, or any nuisance within the jurisdiction is sought to be prevented or removed, whether damages are or are not also sought in respect thereof;

3.021 It is clear that in order to come within the terms of rule 1(g) the injunction must be one sought in the originating summons and must not be relief of an ancillary nature. This issue was given detailed consideration by both the High Court and the Supreme Court in *Caudron v Air Zaire*.[51] Barr J held that where the court is satisfied that "in justice or convenience" an injunction ought to be granted in relation to property of the proposed defendant within its jurisdiction, then whether the injunction amounts to substantive relief or not, service out should be granted. However, this decision was reversed by the Supreme Court which held that the injunction must be one "necessarily and properly sought in the originating summons" and cannot be one which is sought "not as part of the endorsement of claim on the summons but rather by means of a motion *ex parte* or on notice".[52] This approach seems to have been implicitly approved of by Costello J in *Taher Meats (Ireland) Ltd v State Company for Foodstuff Trading*[53] in which he held that in addition to jurisdiction under rule 1(e), the court had jurisdiction to make the order giving leave to serve out of the jurisdiction under rule 1(g) as the plaintiff's claim to an injunction was of a substantive nature and not merely ancillary to other relief.

[49] *Ibid.* at 541, 637.
[50] See also *An Bord Trachtala v Waterford Foods plc* High Court (Keane J) 25 November 1992.
[51] [1986] ILRM 10.
[52] *Ibid.* at 21.
[53] [1991] 1 IR 443.

Civil Procedure

(h) any person out of the jurisdiction is a necessary or proper party to an action properly brought against some other person duly served within the jurisdiction;

3.022 As Barrington J stated in *Short v Ireland*[54] "the standard test to be applied in exercising this jurisdiction is whether the person out of the jurisdiction would, if he were within the jurisdiction, be a proper person to be joined as a defendant in the action against the other defendants".

It has also been clearly established that the party served within the jurisdiction must legitimately be a defendant and the court will not permit rule 1(h) to be used in order to serve a defendant outside the jurisdiction where the defendant within the jurisdiction was sued solely for the purpose of seeking to ensure that service might be effected pursuant to the rule.[55] The test suggested by the English Court of Appeal in *Witted v Galbraith*[56] which has been applied in this jurisdiction is "Supposing that both the defendant[s] ... were resident within the jurisdiction, would they both have been joined in the action?" However, where there is a "real substantial cause of action against both defendants" rule 1(h) may properly be invoked.[57]

3.023 The effect of Order 11, rule 1(h) was considered by Costello J in *International Commercial Bank plc v Insurance Corporation of Ireland*[58] where he stated as follows:

> Order 11, rule 1(h) ... means that the Irish courts will assume jurisdiction over a claim against a foreign domiciliary, even though the cause of action may have arisen outside the jurisdiction, once the foreign domiciliary can be regarded as a proper party to an action brought by a plaintiff in this country against an Irish domiciliary. It is also to be borne in mind that the claim against the foreign domiciliary need not be the same as that against the Irish domiciliary, once he can be regarded as a 'proper' party in the action against the Irish domiciliary.... The effect of Order 11, rule 1(h) is, therefore, to allow the court to assume jurisdiction in respect of a claim which may not be within any of the other subparagraphs of Order 11, rule 1 once there is a co-defendant in the action who can be served within the jurisdiction.

Costello J concluded that he could see no reason why rule 1(h) could not be applied to a third party notice and held that such a notice may be issued against

---

[54] [1996] 2 IR 188, 216. Applied by Lavan J in *Analog Devices BV v Zurich Insurance Co.* High Court (Lavan J) 18 May 2001.
[55] *Sharples v Eason & Son* [1911] 2 IR 436; *Ross v Eason & Son* [1911] 2 IR 459.
[56] [1893] 1 QB 577, 579.
[57] *Cooney v Wilson* [1913] 2 IR 402, 407. See also *Joynt v M'Crum* [1899] 2 IR 217.
[58] [1989] IR 452, 460, [1989] ILRM 788, 793. See also *Analog Devices BV v Zurich Insurance Co.* High Court (Lavan J) 18 May 2001.

a person out of the jurisdiction when the person out of the jurisdiction is a necessary or proper party to an action brought against some person duly served within the jurisdiction. The Supreme Court dismissed the third party's appeal. Finlay CJ stated that a claim for indemnity against a third party is clearly a proceeding instituted in a manner other than by originating summons and as such, by virtue of Order 11, rule 11 the provisions of rule 1(h) must be applied to it "so far as practicable and applicable". He concluded that there was nothing in the terms of rule 1(h) which would justify restricting its application to service on persons who were necessary or proper parties to the plaintiff's claim.

3.024 The circumstances in which Order 11, rule 1(h) will apply were also considered in *Short v Ireland*[59] in the context of proceedings brought by the plaintiffs in an attempt to prevent the further development of the Thorp nuclear reprocessing plant in Cumbria. In the High Court, Costello J held that the link between the proceedings brought against the State and the claim made against the third named defendant, British Nuclear Fuels Ltd, was sufficiently close to enable rule 1(h) to be invoked. He distinguished the facts of the case before him from those in *O'Toole v Ireland*[60] in which he said there had been no obvious connection between the types of relief sought against the defendants or even in relation to the causes of action put forward against them. The Supreme Court dismissed the third named defendant's appeal from the order refusing to set aside leave to serve notice of the plenary summons outside the jurisdiction. Barrington J stated that no one could have doubted that if the third named defendant were resident within the jurisdiction it would be a proper defendant in the case and he concluded that O'Hanlon J had been correct in allowing service out of the jurisdiction under this head.

Factors for the Consideration of the Court

3.025 Order 11, rule 2 provides that when a court is considering an application for service out of the jurisdiction, "it shall have regard to the amount or value of the claim or property affected and to the comparative cost and convenience of proceedings in Ireland or in the place of the defendant's residence". So, where an assessment of the issues of the comparative cost and convenience shows that a trial should not take place in the jurisdiction, no order allowing service out will be made[61] or it may subsequently be set aside.[62] The court should take into account the comparative cost and convenience to the parties generally and not

---

[59] [1996] 2 IR 188, [1997] ILRM 161.
[60] [1992] ILRM 218.
[61] *M'Crea v Knight* [1896] 2 IR 619, 626 where Fitzgibbon LJ stated that in this context "'convenience' . . . means fitness, propriety and suitableness – each and all three in the most general sense". See also *Bennett v Cook* (1901) 35 ILTR 153.
[62] *Murray v Finkle* (1914) 48 ILTR 178.

merely to one party[63] and the court must be provided with sufficient information to enable it to exercise its discretion properly as to the comparative cost and convenience of taking proceedings within the jurisdiction or elsewhere.[64]

Making an Application for Leave

3.026 Order 11, rule 6 stipulates that an application for leave to serve a summons or notice of a summons on a defendant out of the jurisdiction must be made before the issue of the summons. However, in *Traynor v Fagan*,[65] Barrington J stated that it would be wrong to deduce from rule 6 that the Central Office should refuse to issue proceedings when a proposed defendant is resident out of the jurisdiction unless the plaintiff has obtained an order of the court or can produce a letter from a solicitor within the jurisdiction agreeing to accept service.

The application is made *ex parte* grounded on an affidavit containing sufficient information to enable the court to exercise its discretion under Order 11 in the applicant's favour.[66] The affidavit should be sworn by the plaintiff[67] and:

(i)   state which of the provisions of rule 1(a)-(q) applies and set out the facts which bring the alleged cause of action within the rule.[68]

(ii)   exhibit the plenary summons or notice which is intended to be served.

(iii)   state the belief of the deponent that the plaintiff has a good cause of action.[69]

(iv)   state the place or country in which the defendant is or is likely to be found.[70]

---

[63] *Tedcastle McCormick & Co. v Robertson* [1929] IR 597, 602 *per* Kennedy CJ. See also *Kelly v Cruise Catering Ltd* [1994] 2 ILRM 394.

[64] *Brennan v Lockyer* [1932] IR 100, 109 *per* Kennedy CJ.

[65] [1985] IR 586.

[66] Order 11, rule 5. Rule 6 specifies that this affidavit, when no proceeding is pending, is to be entitled as between the parties to the intended proceedings *i.e.* "intended plaintiff" and "intended defendant" and "In the Matter of the Courts of Justice Acts 1924 to 1961 and the Courts (Supplemental Provisions) Acts 1961 to 1981".

[67] *Cf. M'Evers v O'Neill* (1879) 4 LR Ir 517 where the affidavit had been sworn by the guardian and uncle of the plaintiff in proceedings for breach of promise of marriage. Fitzgerald B stated that it would have been more satisfactory if the affidavit had been sworn by the plaintiff herself but the facts contained therein must be assumed to be the facts within the deponent's knowledge and were sufficient to sustain the order made.

[68] *Brennan v Lockyer* [1932] IR 100, 107.

[69] Order 11, rule 5. In *Short v Ireland* [1996] 2 IR 188 O'Hanlon J in the High Court adverted to the fact that there was no formal statement in the affidavits that in the belief of the deponent the plaintiff had a good cause of action but stated that he proposed to overlook this breach of procedural requirements in the exercise of his discretion. The Supreme Court did not go into this question but upheld the decision of the High Court that the case for service out of the jurisdiction under Order 11 had been made out.

[70] Order 11, rule 5.

(v)   state whether the defendant is an Irish citizen or not.

(vi) specify why Ireland is a convenient forum to hear and determine the matter.[71]

(vii) contain a prayer for relief.

As with all *ex parte* applications, an application for leave must be made *uberrimae fides* and an order for service out of the jurisdiction may be discharged if the party obtaining does not comply with his duty to disclose all material facts.[72] In *Brennan v Lockyer*[73] Kennedy CJ stated that an affidavit which does not fully recite the relevant facts but avers as a fact what is really a conclusion of fact "is not such an honest disclosure of facts as the court should act upon".

Order Giving Leave for Service

3.027 Any order giving leave to effect service or give notice out of the jurisdiction shall limit a time after service within which the person to be served is to enter an appearance.[74] The time limited for entering an appearance will depend on the place or country where or within which the summons is to be served or the notice given. In addition, Order 11, rule 8 provides that where the defendant is not, or is not known or believed to be an Irish citizen, notice of the summons and not the summons itself shall be served on him. This is because service of proceedings in another jurisdiction on a citizen of another state was seen, historically, as an infringement of the sovereignty of the state of citizenship of the individual. So, in *O'Connor v Commercial General and Marine Ltd*[75] it was held that service of a summons, rather than notice of the summons on a company incorporated in Belgium at its place of business in Brussels, was not service effected in accordance with the rules and should be set aside. Similarly, in *Short v Ireland*[76] O'Hanlon J found that notice of the summons and not the summons itself should have been served on the third named defendant. He suggested that this was a requirement "which should be observed meticulously"[77] and concluded that this slip up in the manner of service was a matter of some significance. He therefore decided to set aside the service already effected and made an order renewing the plenary summons so that notice of the summons might be served on the third named defendant in the manner prescribed by the

---

[71] Order 11, rule 2.
[72] *Attorney General (Johnston) v Irish Society* (1892) 26 ILTR 56.
[73] [1932] IR 100, 107.
[74] Order 11, rule 7.
[75] [1996] 2 ILRM 291.
[76] [1996] 2 IR 188.
[77] *Ibid.* at 199.

Rules.[78] However, in some circumstances it would appear that non-compliance with the provisions of Order 11, rule 8 may be overlooked where an alternative method of service is effected. In *Murphy v GM PB PC Ltd*[79] O'Higgins J pointed out that service of a plenary summons rather than notice of the summons on the third named defendant out of the jurisdiction was not in compliance with the rules. However, he expressed the view that the unconditional appearance to the summons entered by this defendant cured any defect it. O'Higgins also made reference to the fact that there had been good service on this defendant as a result of service accepted by his solicitor on his behalf within the jurisdiction. He therefore concluded that in all the circumstances of the case, he would overlook any defect in service.

Order 11 makes no provision in relation to the mode of service and personal service shall be effected unless the court orders otherwise. Order 11, rule 10 provides that where an order is made giving leave to serve a summons or notice thereof out of the jurisdiction, a copy of the order must be served with the summons or notice. In addition, Order 11, rule 11 provides that the order shall apply "so far as practicable and applicable" to proceedings instituted by originating summons or in some other manner and to any order or notice in such proceedings.

Service out of the Jurisdiction under the Jurisdiction of Courts and Enforcement of Judgments Act 1998

3.028 The provisions of Order 11A[80] apply to proceedings which are governed by the terms of the Brussels Convention 1968 and subsequent Accession Convention and the Jurisdiction of Courts and Enforcement of Judgments Act 1998.[81] Order 11A provides that service of an originating summons or notice of an originating summons out of the jurisdiction is permissible without the leave of the court if the following conditions are complied with. The claim made by the summons must be one which by virtue of the 1998 Act the court has power to hear and determine and no proceedings between the parties concerning the same cause of action can be pending between the parties in another contracting state. In addition, the defendant must be domiciled in a contracting state, or the proceedings commenced by the originating summons must be ones to which the provisions of Article 16 of the 1968 Convention concerning exclusive jurisdiction apply, or the defendant must be party to an agreement conferring jurisdic-

---

[78] Note that the Supreme Court dismissed the cross-appeal brought by the plaintiff seeking to overturn the order of O'Hanlon J in so far as it ordered re-service of notice of the proceedings.

[79] High Court (O'Higgins J) 4 June 1999.

[80] Inserted by the Rules of the Superior Courts (No. 1) 1989 (SI No. 14 of 1989).

[81] This Act was brought into force on 1 December 1999 by the Jurisdiction of Courts and Enforcement of Judgments Act 1998 (Commencement) Order 1999 (SI No. 353 of 1999).

tion to which the provisions of Article 17 of the Convention concerning prorogation of, or submission to jurisdiction apply.

3.029 Order 5, rule 14 provides that an originating summons to which Order
11A, rule 2 applies which is to be served out of the jurisdiction may be issued
without the leave of the court provided the summons is indorsed before it is
issued with a statement that the court has power under the 1998 Act to hear
and determine the claim and specifying the particular provision(s) of the 1968
Convention under which the court should assume jurisdiction, and also with a
statement that no proceedings concerning the said cause of action are pending
between the parties in another contracting state. If the indorsements required
by Order 5, rule 14 are omitted altogether or not included correctly, applications to amend the summons may be dealt with in accordance with the principles applied to purely domestic proceedings.[82]

3.030 A number of the conditions contained in Order 11A, rule 2 merit further
consideration. In order for the claim made by the summons to be one which by
virtue of the 1998 Act the court has power to hear and determine, it must fall
within the scope of the Brussels Convention 1968 and subsequent Accession
Conventions. Article 1 of the convention provides that it shall apply in civil and
commercial matters[83] whatever the nature of the court or tribunal[84] but states
that it shall not extend in particular to revenue, customs or administrative matters and shall not apply to the status or legal capacity of natural persons, rights
in property arising out of a matrimonial relationship, wills and succession; bankruptcy, proceedings relating to the winding up of insolvent companies or other
legal persons, judicial arrangements, compositions and analogous proceedings;
social security or arbitration.[85] Order 11A, rule 2(2) gives effect to the *lis alibi
pendens* rule set out in Article 21 of the Brussels Convention which provides
that where proceedings involving the same cause of action[86] and between the
same parties are brought in the courts of different contracting states, any court
other than the court first seised of the action shall, of its own motion, decline
jurisdiction. The concept of domicile referred to in Order 11A, rule 2(3) is according to Order 11A, rule 8 to be determined in accordance with the provisions
of Articles 52 and 53 of the Convention and s.15 of the 1998 Act. As Costello J
stated in *Deutsche Bank AG v Murtagh*[87] "this means that the traditional com-

---

[82] See Newman (1996) DULJ (ns) 79, at 95-101.
[83] In *Gourdian v Nadler* (Case 133/78) [1979] ECR 733, [1979] 3 CMLR 180 the Court
of Justice stated that the concept of "civil and commercial matters" must be interpreted
according to the general legal principles common to the law of the contracting states.
[84] See *Lufttransportunternehmen GmbH & Co. KG v Eurocontrol* (Case 29/76) [1976]
ECR 1541, 1551, [1977] 1 CMLR 88, 100.
[85] On the scope of the convention, see Byrne *The European Union and Lugano Conventions* (2nd ed., 1994) at 14-35.
[86] See *The Nordglimt* [1988] QB 183, [1988] 2 WLR 338, [1988] 2 All ER 531.
[87] [1995] 2 IR 122, 128, [1995] 1 ILRM 381, 385.

mon law principles relating to the concept of domicile are not to be applied, instead the court will consider whether the defendant is 'ordinarily resident' in the State." Article 16 of the convention sets out the circumstances in which the court referred to shall have exclusive jurisdiction regardless of domicile and Article 17, which deals with prorogation of jurisdiction, effectively allows parties where one or more of them are domiciled in a contracting state, to agree that a court or courts of a contracting state shall have exclusive jurisdiction.[88]

3.031 Order 11A, rule 3 provides time limits for entering an appearance, including an appearance entered solely to contest jurisdiction. Such an appearance must be entered five weeks after the service of the summons exclusive of the day of service where an originating summons or notice of an originating summons is to be served in the European territory of another contracting state, or within a period of six weeks in the case of any non-European territory of a contracting state.

Order 11A, rule 4 deals with cases where there are two or more defendants, not all of whom are domiciled in a contracting state, and requires that where a co-defendant is not domiciled in a contracting state, the provisions of Order 11 requiring leave to serve proceedings out of the jurisdiction shall apply. Rule 4(2) provides that in the case of proceedings to which the provisions of Order 16 or Order 17 concerning exclusive jurisdiction and prorogation of jurisdiction respectively apply, service on all co-defendants, even if not every co-defendant is domiciled in a contracting state, shall be governed by the provisions of Order 11A which do not require leave.

3.032 Rule 5(1) deals with cases where the parties to a contract have agreed, without conferring jurisdiction for the purposes of Article 17 of the convention, that service of a summons may be effected at any place within or without the jurisdiction in any manner specified in such contract and deems service in accordance with such agreement good wherever the parties are resident. If no place or mode of service is specified in the contract, service shall be effected in accordance with the Rules. Rule 5(2) relates to cases where a contract contains an agreement conferring jurisdiction for the purposes of Article 17 and provides that in such cases where an originating summons is issued for service out of the jurisdiction without leave and is served in accordance with the Rules of the Superior Courts, it shall be deemed to have been duly served. Order 11A, rules 6 and 7 correspond to the provisions in Order 11, rules 8 and 9. Rule 6 provides that where a defendant is not, or is not known or believed to be a citizen of Ireland, notice of the summons itself shall be served upon him and rule 7 provides that notice in lieu of summons shall be given in the same manner in which summonses are served.

---

[88] See e.g. *Holfeld Plastics Ltd v ISAP OMV Group SpA* High Court (Geoghegan J) 19 March 1999.

Finally, it should be noted that an order granting liberty to serve out of the jurisdiction will be set aside where the matter should have been dealt with by the convention procedure set out in Order 11A.[89]

3.033 Council Regulation EC No. 1348/2000 on the service in member states of judicial and extrajudicial documents in civil and commercial matters came into force in Ireland on 31 May 2001. The regulation requires the member states to designate transmitting and receiving agencies and makes provision in relation to the transmission and service of documents. It applies to all member states of the European Union with the exception of Denmark, to which the Hague Convention of the Service Abroad of Judicial and Extrajudicial Documents 1965 continues to apply.

Concurrent Summonses

3.034 Order 6 provides that the plaintiff in any proceedings may, at the time of, or at any time during the twelve months after the issuing of the originating summons, issue one or more concurrent summons or summonses. Each concurrent summons will bear the same date of issue as the original summons and will be marked with a seal bearing the word concurrent and its date of issue.

Concurrent summonses are commonly used by a plaintiff if some of the defendants are resident within the jurisdiction and some of them outside. In this situation, the plaintiff will bring an *ex parte* application for liberty to serve the summons or notice on the defendants resident outside the jurisdiction and then issue a concurrent summons in accordance with Order 6 which is served on the defendants resident within the jurisdiction.

SERVICE OF OTHER DOCUMENTS

Service of Documents Within the Jurisdiction

3.035 Order 121 makes provision in relation to the service of non-originating documents and "document" in the context of this order includes a pleading, notice, affidavit or order.[90] The delivery or service of such documents, for which personal service is not required, shall be effected by leaving the document or a copy thereof at, or sending it or a copy thereof by registered pre-paid post to, the residence or place of business in the State of the person to be served or the place of business in the State of the solicitor acting for him in the proceedings to which the document relates.[91] Order 121, rule 2A makes similar provision in

---

[89] *Schmidt v Home Secretary of the Government of the UK* [1995] 1 ILRM 301.
[90] Order 121, rule 1.
[91] Order 121, rule 2.

relation to the delivery or service of any document under the Jurisdiction of Courts and Enforcement of Judgments (European Communities) Act 1998 for which personal service is not required. Order 121, rule 3 provides that the delivery or service by post of any document, which is authorised to be delivered or served by post, shall be deemed to have been served at the time it would have been delivered in the ordinary course of post. However, this presumption will be rebutted by evidence that the document was not delivered.[92]

Any document to be served or delivered shall contain the name and registered place of business of the solicitor for the party serving it and the name and registered place of business of the solicitor to be served, or if a party does not act through a solicitor, his name and address for service.[93]

Service of Documents out of the Jurisdiction Pursuant to Order 11B

3.036 Order 11B[94] makes provision for the service of documents outside the jurisdiction in accordance with the Hague Convention for the Service Abroad of Judicial and Extra Judicial Documents 1965.[95] Order 11B, rule 2 states that it applies to the service of any summons or other document where such service is required to be effected out of the jurisdiction and in a convention country and where leave has been granted or is unnecessary and where a request for service has been made to the Central Authority, which in this jurisdiction means the Master of the High Court. Order 11B, rule 3 provides that any party to proceedings of a civil or commercial nature and any competent authority or judicial officer[96] who wishes to have a document served pursuant to the Hague Convention may lodge the following with the Central Authority:

(a)   a request for service of the document, the format of which is specified in the Annex to the convention.[97]

(b)   two copies of the document to be served with an additional copy for each person to be served.

(c)   a translation of each document into the official language or one of the official languages of the State addressed.

(d)   an undertaking to pay the costs of service.

---

[92] *Re J. Bird Moyer & Co. (Ireland) Ltd* (1964) 98 ILTR 202.

[93] Order 121, rule 4.

[94] Inserted by the Rules of the Superior Courts (No. 3) 1994 (SI No. 101 of 1994).

[95] See the Law Reform Commission Report on the Service of Documents Abroad in Civil Proceedings – the Hague Convention LRC 22–1987.

[96] Order 11B, rule 2(3) provides that the Central Authority, a practising solicitor, a county registrar or a District Court clerk are declared to be competent authorities or competent judicial officers for the purposes of this article.

[97] See Appendix AA Form 1 in the Rules of the Superior Courts.

As noted above, Council Regulation EC No. 1348/2000 on the service in member states of judicial and extrajudicial documents in civil and commercial matters, which came into force on 31 May 2001, now applies in all member states of the European Union with the exception of Denmark, to which the Hague Convention continues to apply.

Service of Foreign Process

3.037 Order 121A[98] regulates the service of foreign proceedings within the jurisdiction pursuant to the Hague Convention for the Service Abroad of Judicial and Extra Judicial Documents 1965. It makes provision for the service of "foreign process" which is defined to mean "any document initiating or relating to proceedings in a convention country or in a foreign country which has been forwarded to the Central Authority[99] for service in the State". Rule 2 provides that the order applies to the service of any foreign process on any person in the State where the Master has received a request for service on that person by the Central Authority of another convention country or from an authority or judicial officer competent under the law of the state in which the documents originate or has received from the Department of Foreign Affairs a letter of request for service of process from a court or tribunal of a foreign state on a person in the State with a recommendation from the Minister for Foreign Affairs that it is desirable that effect should be given to such request. Rule 3 then sets out the procedure which should be followed when the Master receives a request for service in accordance with the order.

---

[98] Inserted by the Rules of the Superior Courts (No. 3) 1994 (SI No. 101 of 1994).
[99] The Master of the High Court, see Order 121A, rule 1.

CHAPTER FOUR

APPEARANCE

ENTRY AND EFFECT OF APPEARANCE

4.001 The entry of an appearance, which is dealt with in Order 12 of the Rules of the Superior Courts 1986, is a very important step in proceedings because it constitutes an acknowledgement by the defendant of their existence and generally indicates an intention to defend.

Time for Entry

4.002 An appearance by a defendant to a plenary summons or summary summons must be entered within eight days after the service of the summons, exclusive of the day of service, unless the court otherwise orders.[1] An appearance to a special summons can be entered at any time and a defendant to proceedings commenced by special summons is not entitled, without leave of the court, to be heard in such proceedings unless he has entered an appearance. Special provision is made for the entry of an appearance to an originating summons in respect of proceedings issued for service out of the jurisdiction under Order 11A, rule 2.[2] This must be entered: (a) within five weeks after service of the summons exclusive of the day of service where an originating summons or notice of an originating summons is to be served in the European territory of another contracting state, or (b) within six weeks after the service of the summons exclusive of the day of service where an originating summons or notice of an originating summons is served in any non-European territory of a contracting state or on any co-defendant who is not domiciled in a contracting state.

The significance of the time limit for entry of an appearance is that an application for judgment in default of appearance cannot be made before the time so limited has expired. However, the expiration of the time limit does not prevent the defendant from entering an appearance subject to the exceptions provided for in the Rules. Order 12, rule 13 provides that a defendant, save in actions for the recovery of land, may appear at any time before judgment.[3] However, if he

---

[1] Order 12, rule 2(1).

[2] Order 12, rule 2(3) (as inserted by the Rules of the Superior Courts (No.1) 1989 (SI No. 14 of 1989)).

[3] In the case of actions for the recovery of land, rule 15 provides that a person served with the proceedings will not be permitted to appear after the time limited for appearance without leave of the court which should be made by way of motion on notice to the plaintiff (*Cuttiford v Ellis* (1879) 13 ILT 89). Rule 17 provides that an appearance en-

appears at any time after the time limited for appearance, he shall not, unless the Court shall otherwise order, be entitled to any further time for delivering his defence or for any other purpose than if he had appeared within the time limited for appearance.

Special provision is made in Order 12 in relation to appearances in probate actions[4] and proceedings for the recovery of land.[5]

Entering an Appearance

4.003 An appearance is entered by the defendant delivering to the proper officer[6] a memorandum in writing in the form set out at Appendix A, Part II, Form No. 1,[7] dated on the day of its delivery and containing the name of the defendant's solicitor,[8] or stating that the defendant defends in person.[9] If the appearance is entered by a solicitor, the memorandum must state his registered place of business[10] and, if the defendant is defending in person, the memorandum must state an address for service within the jurisdiction where summonses and other forms of process may be left for him.[11] If the memorandum does not contain such address, it cannot be received and if any such address is illusory or fictitious, the appearance may be set aside by the court or the Master on the application of the plaintiff.[12] If the memorandum of appearance is in the proper

---

tered without leave after the time limited for appearance has expired is void and it may be set aside on the application of the plaintiff (see *Stanley v Hart* (1933) 67 ILTR 33).

[4] Rules 14 and 27-29.

[5] Rules 15-25.

[6] Appearances are entered in the Central Office of the High Court except in the case of lunacy and minor matters which are entered in the Office of Wards of Court (Order 12, rule 1).

[7] Order 12, rule 9.

[8] If two or more defendants in the same action appear by the same solicitor and at the same time, the names of all the defendants so appearing must be entered in one memorandum: Order 12, rule 11.

[9] Order 12, rule 3. Alternatively, Order 12, rule 4 provides that, in the case of a defendant desiring to enter an appearance in person, he or she may, in lieu of delivering to the proper officer the memorandum of appearance and the duplicate thereof, enter the appearance through the post by sending to the proper officer by pre-paid registered letter: (a) a memorandum of appearance and two duplicates thereof both duly filled up; (b) a postal order for the prescribed fee payable on entering an appearance; (c) two envelopes sufficiently stamped, one addressed to the plaintiff's solicitor (or to the plaintiff it he or she sues in person) at the address for service, and the other addressed to the defendant entering the appearance. On receipt of the foregoing, the proper officer must forthwith enter the appearance as of the date when he received the memorandum, and mark the duplicates with the official stamp showing the date on which the appearance is entered, and must post one duplicate to the plaintiff or his solicitor and the other duplicate to the defendant.

[10] Order 12, rule 6.

[11] Order 12, rule 7.

[12] Order 12, rule 8. *Cf. City and County Building Society v Hayes* (1882) 16 ILTR 105,

form and complies with the Rules, the officer will enter the appearance in the appropriate Cause Book.[13] The officer will also stamp a number of duplicates of the memorandum with the date of entry of the appearance and return them to the defendant or his solicitor as the case may be.[14]

On the same day as the appearance is entered, the defendant must give notice of his appearance to the plaintiff's solicitor or, if the plaintiff sues in person, to the plaintiff himself by serving the stamped duplicate memorandum.[15] This may be served in the ordinary way at the address for service, or by prepaid letter directed to that address and posted on the day of entering appearance in due course of post. In the case of a plenary summons, the memorandum must include a notice stating whether the defendant requires a statement of claim or not.[16]

It should be noted that a limited liability company cannot enter an appearance in person which must, therefore, be entered by a solicitor on its behalf.[17] Special provision in the Rules is also made in respect of an infant, who cannot enter an appearance except by his or her guardian *ad litem*,[18] and a person of unsound mind who may defend by his or her committee or guardian appointed for that purpose.[19]

Withdrawal of Appearance

4.004 Unlike the position under the English Rules,[20] there is no express provision made in the Rules for the withdrawal of an appearance once entered. However, in *Taher Meats (Ireland) Ltd v State Company for Foodstuff Trading*,[21] it was held by Costello J that, despite the lack of an express provision in the Rules, the court has an inherent jurisdiction to rectify an error and he discharged the appearance made by the second defendant which he was satis-

---

where the defendant gave the address of an unoccupied house and, as an alternative to setting aside the appearance, leave was given for substituted service of the statement of claim by affixing a copy on the unoccupied house and serving the wife of the defendant.

[13] Order 12, rule 10.

[14] Order 12, rule 3 provides that the duplicate memorandum so stamped is a certificate that the appearance was entered on the day indicated by the stamp.

[15] Order 12, rule 5(1).

[16] Order 12, rule 5(1).

[17] *Battle v Irish Art Promotion Centre Ltd* [1968] IR 252.

[18] Order 15, rule 18. No order for the appointment of such guardian is necessary but the solicitor applying to enter such appearance must make and file an affidavit in the Form No.4 in Appendix A, Part II. See further paragraph 6.024.

[19] Order 15, rule 17. See further paragraph 6.025.

[20] Order 21, rule 1 of the English Rules of the Supreme Court provides that a party who has entered an appearance may withdraw it with the leave of the court. Order 21, rule 1 of the Rules of the Supreme Court in Northern Ireland is to similar effect.

[21] [1991] 1 IR 443.

fied had been entered by mistake.[22] The nature of the mistake required before a court will exercise this inherent jurisdiction is not discussed in *Taher*, but the effect of the English and Northern Irish authorities is that, where a party or his solicitor enters an appearance under a misapprehension of fact, he may be allowed to withdraw it, at least where no prejudice has occurred as a result; but where he has taken that step ill-advisedly or through an incorrect appreciation of the law or his rights under it, he will not generally be permitted to withdraw the appearance.[23]

Effect of Appearance

4.005 The entry of an unconditional appearance is an acknowledgement that the defendant is on notice of the proceedings and, therefore, constitutes a waiver of the right to object to any defect in service such as the service of an expired summons.[24] It will also preclude the defendant from relying on any irregularity in the form of the summons.[25] However, it will not affect any substantive defences that may be raised by the defendant as where a defendant argues that the court has no jurisdiction to hear the matter because the wrong originating procedure was used or where the defendant relies on a deficiency in the indorsement of claim.

Conditional Appearance

4.006 Apart from Order 12, rule 2(3) which makes provision for appearances to be entered solely to contest jurisdiction under the Brussels Convention, the Rules do not contain any recognition of the concept of a conditional appearance. Indeed, Order 12, rule 26 dealing with applications to set aside the service of proceedings specifies that such an application should be brought *prior* to entering an appearance which clearly militates against the idea. However, it is accepted that a defendant can enter a conditional appearance and that this

---

[22] See also *Campbell International Trading House Ltd v Peter van Aart* [1992] 2 IR 305, 317, [1992] ILRM 663, 666, where Finlay CJ also seemed to accept that an appearance could be set aside on the basis of a mistake.

[23] *Bradford v Department of the Environment* [1986] NI 41, 43 (*per* Carswell J). *Cf. Volkes v Eastern Health and Social Services Board* [1990] NI 388; *Firth v John Mowlem Ltd* [1978] 1 WLR 1184, [1978] 3 All ER 331; *Somportex Ltd v Philadelphia Chewing Gum Corporation* [1968] 3 All ER 26.

[24] *Baulk v Irish National Insurance Co. Ltd* [1969] IR 66, 71 (*per* Walsh J); *Volkes v Eastern Health and Social Services Board* [1990] NI 388; *Sheldon v Brown Bayley's Steelworks Ltd* [1953] 2 QB 393, [1953] 3 WLR 542, [1953] 2 All ER 894.

[25] See, for example, *Doyle v Patterson* [1934] IR 116, where it was held that the defendant who had entered an unconditional appearance could not rely on an irregularity in the indorsement as to costs to have the summons declared a nullity. See also *Allen v Quigley* (1878) 12 ILTR 46 and *O'Connell v Golden* (1928) 63 ILTR 49.

will preserve his right to subsequently bring a motion challenging the jurisdiction of the court or the service of the proceedings.[26] An appearance entered in such circumstances should state clearly on its face that it is made for the purpose of contesting jurisdiction.

Appearance to Contest Jurisdiction under the Brussels Convention

4.007 Article 18 of the Brussels Convention[27] provides that, apart from jurisdiction derived under the other provisions of the convention, a court of a contracting state before whom a defendant enters an appearance will have jurisdiction unless that appearance is entered solely to contest jurisdiction. Provision in that regard is made in Order 12, rule 2(3) which permits an appearance to an originating summons in respect of proceedings issued for service out of the jurisdiction under Order 11A, rule 2 to be entered solely to contest jurisdiction.

These provisions were examined by the Supreme Court in *Campbell International Trading House Ltd v Peter van Aart*.[28] The defendant had entered an unconditional appearance to proceedings instituted by the plaintiff but subsequently brought a motion seeking to have the proceedings struck out on the ground, *inter alia*, that the court had no jurisdiction to entertain the action. Finlay CJ explained that:

> Having regard to the terms of Article 18, it is quite clear that if a person wishes or intends to contest the jurisdiction of the court in proceedings brought pursuant to the Act and the convention, it is necessary in entering an appearance that they should so indicate. It may not be necessary to do it in any particular form; conceivably it is not necessary to do it exactly contemporaneously with the entry of appearance, but it is certainly necessary to do it by some method, informing the plaintiff of the fact that the purpose of the entry of an appearance is to contest jurisdiction. That could be done, conceivably, by a letter accompanying the appearance, by a letter immediately following the appearance, or by a notice of motion accompanying or following the appearance and contesting the jurisdiction.[29]

In the instant case, the defendant had entered an unconditional appearance and had not given an indication of an intention to contest jurisdiction. Given the

---

[26] See *Fox v Taher* High Court (Costello P) 24 January 1996 and *Minister for Agriculture v Alte Leipziger Versicherung Aktiengesellschaft* [2000] 4 IR 32, [2001] 1 ILRM 519 where the concept of a conditional appearance received a measure of curial endorsement. *Cf.* the reporter's note to *Kutchera v Buckingham International Holdings Ltd* [1988] IR 61.

[27] European Convention on Jurisdiction and Enforcement of Judgments in Civil and Commercial Matters 1968.

[28] [1992] 2 IR 305, [1992] ILRM 663.

[29] *Ibid.* at 317, 666.

absence of any factor such as mistake and the lapse of time since the appearance had been entered, the court was satisfied that the jurisdiction pursuant to Article 18 had been acquired.

4.008 Article 18 was considered further by Finlay CJ in *Devrajan v Ballagh*[30] where he stated that its "obvious purpose as a matter of justice is that a plaintiff seeking and invoking the jurisdiction of the courts of one particular contracting state should be on the earliest possible notice of the fact that the jurisdiction is being contested." In that case, the applicant had instituted proceedings in the District Court against the notice party, a company domiciled in the Netherlands. A notice of intention to defend was filed within the requisite period but six months later, the notice party wrote to the applicant informing him that the notice had been filed for the purposes of contesting jurisdiction. The court concluded that, having regard to the applicant's contention as to the effects of limitation periods under Dutch law on his claim and the absence of any justification for the notice party's delay in informing him of the intention to contest jurisdiction, it would be unfair to permit the notice party to contest jurisdiction after such a delay.

It should be noted that if a defendant enters an appearance solely for the purpose of contesting jurisdiction, he will not be precluded from defending the case on the merits if he subsequently abandons or fails in the challenge to jurisdiction.[31]

DEFAULT OF APPEARANCE

4.009 If the defendant fails to enter an appearance within the time limited for doing so, the plaintiff can proceed to seek judgment in default of appearance. The procedures for doing so are laid down in Orders 13 and 13A and vary depending on the type of summons and claim at issue. However, one requirement which is common to each default procedure should be highlighted at the outset, namely that, in all cases, a plaintiff who wishes to seek judgment in default of appearance must file an affidavit of service of the summons or notice

---

[30] [1993] 3 IR 377, 380.
[31] *Campbell International Trading House Ltd v Peter van Aart* [1992] 2 IR 305, 317, [1992] ILRM 663, 666. The standard form of appearance entered to contest jurisdiction expressly provides for that possibility; see, for example, *Minister for Agriculture v Alte Leipziger Versicherung Aktiengesellschaft* [2000] 4 IR 32, [2001] 1 ILRM 519 where the "memorandum of appearance to contest the jurisdiction of the court" stipulated that: "such appearance is limited to an appearance for contesting the jurisdiction of the court to hear and determine the plaintiff's claim pursuant to the Jurisdiction of Courts and Enforcement of Judgments Acts 1988 to 1993 and without prejudice to such appearance the defendant reserves the right in the alternative to defend these proceedings".

in lieu of summons, as the case may be, *before*[32] taking any proceedings in default.[33] This requirement is strictly enforced as can be seen from the decision of *Crane & Sons v Wallis*,[34] where O'Brien LC emphasised that the question was one of jurisdiction and not one of merely dispensing with a formality.[35] That decision is illustrative of the general attitude of the courts towards default judgments. The courts are understandably reluctant to grant final judgment against a defendant who has not been heard and, therefore, strict compliance with the default procedures set out below is required. In *Crane & Sons v Wallis*[36] Ronan LJ approved the statement of Buckley LJ in *Hamp-Adams v Hall*,[37] that "[w]here a plaintiff proceeds by default, every step in the proceeding must strictly comply with the rules; that is a matter *strictissimi juris*."

The provisions of Order 13 are complex with different rules prescribed for different classes of claim. For ease of exposition, it is proposed to examine the default procedures under the heading of liquidated and unliquidated claims.

Liquidated Claims

4.010 Order 13 sets out a summary procedure which can, in the generality of cases, be used to enter judgment in the Central Office without recourse to court where the claim is for a liquidated sum only and no appearance has been entered. This procedure can be used where there has been default of appearance either to a plenary summons or a summary summons indorsed with a claim for a liquidated demand.

If the defendant or all the defendants (if more than one) fail to appear, then the plaintiff, after filing an affidavit of service of the summons or notice in lieu of the summons,[38] may enter final judgment in the Central Office for the sum specified in an affidavit of debt as the sum then actually due[39] (which cannot exceed the sum indorsed on the summons) together with interest (if any) to the date of the judgment and costs.[40] It would appear that interest pursuant to s.22 of the Courts Act 1981[41] can also be awarded by the Regis-

---

[32] In *Fitzpatrick v Daly* (1935) 69 ILTR 179, the court dismissed a motion for judgment in default of appearance where the affidavit of service of the summons was defective, notwithstanding that a sufficient supplemental affidavit was subsequently filed.
[33] Order 13, rule 2.
[34] [1915] 2 IR 411.
[35] *Ibid.* at 415.
[36] [1915] 2 IR 411, 418.
[37] [1911] 2 KB 942, 944.
[38] Order 13, rule 2. The affidavit must establish that service was properly effected and if an order for substituted service was obtained that the terms of the order were strictly complied with.
[39] This is required by Order 13, rule 18 and is sometimes referred to as an affidavit of debt.
[40] Order 13, rule 3.
[41] S.22 provides that: "Where in any proceedings a court orders the payment by any person of a sum of money (which expression includes in this section, damages) the judge

trar of the Central Office in an appropriate case although the practice is not to do this.[42]

If there are several defendants, of whom one or more appear, to the summons and another or others of them fail to appear, the plaintiff may enter final judgment against those that have not appeared (and issue execution upon such judgment), without prejudice to his right to proceed against such of the defendants as have appeared.[43] Indeed, it is not a necessary prerequisite to proceeding against a defendant for judgment in default that the plaintiff has even served the other defendants.

4.011 In *Parker v Hamilton*,[44] the plaintiff issued proceedings against two defendants for a liquidated sum on foot of a promissory note under which they were jointly and severally liable. Only one of the defendants had been served with the summons and the plaintiff sought judgment in default of appearance against the defendant who had been served. Andrews J could not see any reason why the plaintiff could not do this and ordered that final judgment be marked against the defendant who had not appeared notwithstanding the non-service of the other defendant, and without requiring the plaintiff to discontinue or abandon his action against the defendant who had not been served. An example of where a plaintiff subsequently decided to proceed against other defendants who had not been served initially can be seen in *M'Carroll v Green*.[45] The plaintiff issued proceedings against four defendants on foot of a joint and several promissory note. Three of the defendants were duly served and judgment marked against them, but execution was never levied. Subsequently, the fourth defendant was served and a motion was issued seeking judgment in default of appearance. It was held that the plaintiff was entitled to

---

concerned may, if he thinks fit, also order the payment by the person of interest at the rate *per annum* standing specified for the time being in s.26 of the Debtors (Ireland) Act 1840, on the whole or any part of the sum in respect of the whole or any part of the period between the date when the cause of action accrued and the date of judgment." This is subject to qualification in relation to compound interest, interest payable pursuant to contract, bills of exchange and personal injuries contained in subs (2) and (3).

[42] S.50(2) of the Courts and Court Officers Act 1995 provides that: "Where, in the case of a claim in the High Court for a debt or a liquidated sum, an application is made for judgment in default of appearance, the Registrar of the Central Office may exercise the discretion to award interest conferred by s.22 of the Courts Act 1981." The interaction between this section and Order 13, rule 19 which provides that a plaintiff who is entitled to enter final judgment in the Central Office may apply to the court *ex parte* for an order for judgment inclusive of interest pursuant to s.22 is unclear. *Cf. Mellowhide Products Ltd v Barry Agencies Ltd* [1983] ILRM 152.

[43] Order 13, rule 8. See *Montgomerie v Ferris* (1887) 20 LR Ir 282, *Rice v Dillon* (1890) 28 LR Ir 376 and *Pim Bros Ltd v Coyle* [1903] 2 IR 457.

[44] (1892) 30 LR Ir 156.

[45] (1908) 42 ILTR 116.

enter such judgment, notwithstanding that judgment had already entered against the other defendants but that the plaintiff should levy only one set of costs.

Leave of the Master or the Court

4.012 Order 13 singles out two classes of case where, because of the inequality of bargaining power between the parties and the potential vulnerability of at least some of the defendants, judgment cannot be entered in the Central Office without the leave of the Master or the Court having first been obtained: (i) proceedings by moneylenders; and (ii) proceedings on foot of a hire-purchase agreement. The application for leave is made, in the first instance, to the Master but he may, in lieu of giving or refusing leave to enter judgment, place the summons in the court list for hearing.[46]

(i) Proceedings by Moneylenders[47]

4.013 Rule 3 provides that, in the case of proceedings by a moneylender, or the personal representative of a moneylender, or an assignee, for the recovery of money lent by the moneylender, or the enforcement of any agreement or security relating to any such money, judgment cannot be entered in default of appearance unless the leave of the Master or the court, as the case may be, has been obtained in accordance with the provisions of rule 14.[48] Rule 14 requires the application for leave to be made by notice returnable before the Master not less than four clear days after service of the notice and stipulates that such notice cannot be issued until the time limited for entering an appearance has expired and a proper affidavit of service of the summons has been filed.[49] At the hearing of the application, the Master or the court, as the case may be, if satisfied by affidavit or otherwise that the notice has been duly served, and whether the defendant appears or not, may give leave to enter final judgment for the whole or part of the claim, and as regards any part of the claim as to which leave to enter final judgment is refused, may give any such directions or make any such order as might have been given or made upon the hearing of the summons or of a motion for judgment, as the case might be, if the defendant had entered an appearance, upon such terms as to notice to the defendant and otherwise as may be thought just.[50]

---

[46] Order 13, rule 16.

[47] The term 'moneylender' is defined in s.2 of the Consumer Credit Act 1995.

[48] Order 13, rule 3.

[49] Order 13, rule 14(1) & (2). The notice may be served personally or by registered post, addressed to the defendant at his last known place of address.

[50] Order 13, rule 14(3) also provides that the Master or the court may exercise the powers of the court under s.1(1) of the Moneylenders Act 1900 (as amended by s.17 of the Moneylenders Act 1933) but these provisions were repealed by s.19 of the Consumer Credit Act 1995.

(ii) Proceedings on foot of Hire-Purchase Agreements

4.014 Similarly, in actions to recover a debt or liquidated demand arising under a hire-purchase agreement or credit-sale agreement[51] or any contract of guarantee relating to such an agreement, judgment cannot be entered in default of appearance unless the leave of the Master or the court, as the case may be, has been obtained in accordance with the provisions of rule 15.[52] The procedure for applying for leave is the same as that under rule 14 but the role of the Master or the court seems to be more limited and may involve ensuring that the requirements of the Consumer Credit Act 1995 have been complied with.[53]

Joinder of Liquidated Claim and other Claims

4.015 In the case of a plenary summons indorsed with a claim for a liquidated demand together with a claim or other claims, the plaintiff may enter final judgment for the liquidated demand, together with interest (if any) and costs against the defendant or defendants failing to appear and may proceed, in accordance with the appropriate procedure, in respect of the other claim or claims.

Unliquidated Claims

Motion for Judgment in Default of Appearance

4.016 If a defendant fails to enter an appearance to a plenary summons within the time limited for an appearance, the procedure which is adopted in most cases is for the plaintiff to bring a motion for judgment in default of appearance against the defendant or, where there is more than one defendant, against such of those defendants as have not appeared.[54]

(i) Notice of Motion

4.017 If the plaintiff's claim is for unliquidated damages, then the notice of motion should seek the following reliefs: (a) an order pursuant to Order 13 granting such judgment against the defendant upon the statement of claim as the court shall consider the plaintiff to be entitled to and (b) an order that damages be assessed at a date to be fixed by the court by a judge and jury or

---

[51] These terms were originally defined in the Hire Purchase Act 1946 but their definition is now to be found in s.2 of the Consumer Credit Act 1995.

[52] Order 13, rule 3.

[53] Order 13, rule 15 stipulates that "judgment shall not be entered until an affidavit shall have been filed stating that the requirements specified in s.3 or s.4 (as the case may be) of the Hire Purchase Act 1946, as amended by ss. 21 and 22 of the Hire Purchase Act 1960, have been complied with." However, these provisions were repealed by s.19 of the Consumer Credit Act 1995, Part VI of which deals with hire-purchase agreements.

[54] Order 13, rules 6 & 9.

judge sitting alone as appropriate.[55] If the claim is for equitable relief, then the notice of motion should specify the relief sought and must be grounded upon an affidavit setting out sufficient grounds to enable the court to exercise its discretion in favour of the plaintiff.

(ii) Preliminary Steps
4.018 Before the notice of motion is issued or served, the plaintiff must file two documents in the Central Office: (i) an affidavit of service of the plenary summons or notice in lieu of the summons; and (ii) a statement of claim endorsed with a certificate signed and dated by the solicitors for the plaintiff certifying that no appearance has been entered.[56]

(iii) Service of the Motion
4.019 The motion is brought on notice to the defendant(s) in default[57] and should be served personally.[58] If the institution of proceedings has been preceded by an exchange of correspondence with a solicitor acting on behalf of the defendant, then it is common practice to write to the solicitor informing him or her that the motion has issued but service on that solicitor is not required or, indeed, will not suffice because he or she has not come on record until such time as an appearance is entered.

(iv) Proofs
4.020 The proofs required for the motion are as follows:

(i)   The notice of motion

(ii)   The grounding affidavit (if any).

(iii) The original plenary summons endorsed with the particulars of service within three days thereof as required by Order 9, rule 12.

(iv)   An affidavit of service of the summons showing that it was properly served.

(v)   An affidavit of service of the notice of motion on the defendant.

---

[55] *Cf.* Order 13, rule 6.
[56] Order 13, rule 6. It should be noted that in general, under Order 20, it is not necessary to file a statement of claim and delivery *inter partes* suffices.
[57] See *Casey v Hickey* (1928) 62 ILTR 163.
[58] Order 121, rule 5 provides that, where no appearance has been entered for a party, any document which is not required to be served personally and for which no other mode of service is directed, may be served by filing it in the Central Office. However, in *Taylor v Huband-Smith* (1920) 55 ILTR 120, it was held that this rule was not applicable and that personal service of a notice of motion for judgment in default of appearance is required. *Cf. Provincial Bank of Ireland v Phelan* [1909] 2 IR 698. If personal service, cannot be effected, an order for substituted service can be obtained (see, for example, *Philip Harrington Daly & Co. v JVC (UK) Ltd* High Court (O'Hanlon J) 16 March 1995).

(vi) A copy of the filed statement of claim with a certificate endorsed on it by the plaintiff's solicitor to the effect that no appearance has been entered.

(v) Hearing of the Motion

4.021 Given that the motion is for judgment in default of appearance there will not, by definition, be a solicitor on record and it will, therefore, be categorised as a motion for the sitting of the court and should be called over as such at the beginning of the list. It is common for an appearance to be entered before the motion comes on for hearing and if this is the case, then the only issue will be as to costs which will generally be awarded to the plaintiff but may be reserved if the court considers that the motion was issued precipitately. Alternatively, the defendant (or a solicitor or barrister instructed on his behalf) may appear and indicate an intention to enter an appearance. In this situation, the court will grant, as a matter of course, an extension of time within which to file an appearance (usually one or two weeks) and, again, the only real issue will be as to costs.

It is rare for a defendant not to appear but if this happens, then the court will grant judgment if it is satisfied as to service of the summons and the notice of motion.[59] However, the order will not be drawn up until the solicitor for the plaintiff lodges a certificate of no appearance (which is bespoken at the Central Office) with the Registrar.[60]

If the plaintiff is seeking unliquidated damages, the court will not assess the damages at that point but will, instead, direct that they be assessed at a later date by a judge sitting alone or a judge and jury as appropriate.[61] Where there are multiple defendants and one or more of them have not appeared but one or more of them have appeared, then the damages (if any) to be awarded against the defendants in default will be ascertained at the trial of the proceedings against the other defendant(s) unless the court otherwise directs.[62] If equitable relief is sought, this will be granted if the court is satisfied, on the basis of the grounding affidavit, that the plaintiff has established grounds for relief.

---

[59] But *cf. Rattigan v Waldron* Supreme Court, 3 November 1970 where the Supreme Court upheld the order of Murnaghan J refusing to grant judgment on foot of the plaintiff's motion for judgment in default of appearance and dismissed her action on the basis that the statement of claim filed by her did not disclose any stateable cause of action against the defendant.

[60] Practice Direction of 16 February 2001.

[61] Order 13, rule 6 provides that the plaintiff may apply for the "ascertainment of any damages to which the plaintiff may be entitled, with a jury in case any party is entitled to a jury and requires such, but otherwise without a jury, and in the latter case the court may fix the amount of such damages itself on evidence by affidavit or otherwise, or may refer the matter to the Master to determine."

[62] Order 13, rule 9.

Judgment as to Costs

4.022 Order 13, rule 13 provides that in any case in which the defendant is not entitled to enter final judgment in the Central Office and in which the defendant fails, or all the defendants if more than one, fail to appear, but in which, by reason of payment, satisfaction, abatement of nuisance, or for any other reason, it is unnecessary for the plaintiff to proceed, he may by leave of the Master, to be obtained by motion on notice, enter judgment for costs. The motion must be filed and then served in the manner in which service of the summons was effected or in such other manner as the Master may direct.[63] The Master may, in lieu of giving or refusing leave to enter judgment, place the summons in the court list for hearing.[64]

Miscellaneous

4.023 Special provision is made in Order 13 in relation to default of appearance by a defendant to proceedings for the recovery of land,[65] summonses indorsed with a claim for the delivery of specific goods,[66] summonses indorsed with a claim on any bond, covenant or agreement within the meaning of s.145 of the Common Law Procedure Amendment Act (Ireland) 1853,[67] proceedings brought by moneylenders,[68] or actions to recover a debt or liquidated demand arising under a hire-purchase agreement or credit-sale agreement.[69] In addition, Order 13, rule 1 lays down the procedure to be adopted where no appearance is entered to a summons for a defendant who is an infant or a person of unsound mind not so found by inquisition.

Rule 17 contains a default provision that in all proceedings not otherwise specifically provided for in Order 13, if the party served with the summons does not appear within the time limited for appearance, upon the filing by the plaintiff of a proper affidavit of service and, where appropriate, of a statement of claim, the proceedings may proceed as if such party had appeared, subject, as to actions where an account is claimed, to the provisions of Order 37.[70]

---

[63] Rule 13.
[64] Order 13, rule 16.
[65] Rules 4 and 5.
[66] Rule 7.
[67] Rule 12.
[68] Rule 14.
[69] Rule 15.
[70] Order 37, rule 13 provides that, where a summary summons has been indorsed with a claim for an account under Order 2, or where the indorsement on a summons involves taking an account, and the defendant fails to appear, the Master shall forthwith make an order for the proper accounts, with all necessary inquires and directions.

SETTING ASIDE A JUDGMENT OBTAINED IN DEFAULT OF APPEARANCE

4.024 Order 13, rule 11 provides that where final judgment is entered pursuant to any of the rules of this order, the court may set aside or vary such judgment upon such terms as may be just. The rule does not give any indication of the grounds upon which this discretion may be exercised but the case law has identified two distinct categories of case: (i) where there was some irregularity in the proceedings or the procedure by which the judgment which it is sought to set aside or vary was obtained; and (ii) where the judgment was obtained in a regular manner but the defendant may have a good defence to the claim and the interests of justice require that he should be given the opportunity to defend the proceedings. The main difference between the two categories is that in the case of an irregular judgment, an affidavit of merits is not required[71] but in the case of a regular judgment, it is essential.[72] In addition, the court is unlikely to impose terms for the setting aside of an irregular judgment[73] but may well do so, depending on the circumstances, where it sets aside a regular judgment.

Irregular Judgment

4.025 As noted above, the courts require strict compliance with the default procedures. In *Crane & Sons v Wallis*,[74] Molony LJ stated that he regarded it "as a matter of the greatest importance that in the case of a judgment by default the rules should be strictly complied with." In that case, the standard of strict compliance was found not to have been met in circumstances where the plaintiff had failed to file an affidavit of service before applying for judgment in default.[75] One case which seems to demand an inordinate degree of exactitude is *Martin v Pilkington*[76] where judgment was set aside on the basis of the mis-description of one of the defendants, who was widowed, as a spinster. However, this case may well turn on its own particular facts.

In a number of cases, applications to set aside have been successful on the basis of a defect in service as in *Poole v Stewart*,[77] where the defendant was out of the jurisdiction at the time of attempted service and *Irwin & Co. v Austin &*

---

[71] *Irwin & Co. v Austin & Sons* (1907) 41 ILTR 190; *Martin v Williams* (1868) IR 3 CL 5.
[72] *Petronelli v Collins* High Court (Costello P) 19 July 1996; *Maher v Dixon* [1995] 1 ILRM 218.
[73] See, for example, *Crane & Sons v Wallis* [1915] 2 IR 411; *Martin v Pilkington* [1942] Ir Jur Rep 51; *Poole v Stewart* (1903) 37 ILTR 74.
[74] [1915] 2 IR 411, 421.
[75] See also *Martin v Pilkington* [1942] Ir Jur Rep 51 where a default judgment was set aside on the basis of the mis-description of one of the defendants. However, this case may turn on its own particular facts.
[76] [1942] Ir Jur Rep 51.
[77] (1903) 37 ILTR 74.

Sons,[78] where reasonable attempts had not been made to effect personal service. It appeared from these decisions that it was sufficient merely to rely on the defect in service and that it was not necessary to show that the defendant had not actually been on notice of the proceedings. However, in *Royal Bank of Ireland v Nolan*,[79] Dixon J pointed out that the fundamental purpose of service was to give the defendant notice of proceedings and held that where an application to set aside a judgment is brought on the basis of an irregularity in service, it is a prerequisite to relief that the defendant swear an affidavit establishing that he did not have notice of the proceedings.

The court will require that a plaintiff who seeks to invoke the default procedures under the Rules should, himself, comply with those Rules. Thus, in *O'Foghludha v McLean*,[80] it was held that the plaintiff was not entitled to obtain judgment in default of appearance on foot of a summary summons in circumstances where he refused to serve an English translation of the summons, which was in Irish, as required by the then equivalent to Order 120, rule 3.

Regular Judgment

4.026 The discretion of the court to set aside a regular judgment obtained in default of appearance is based on the principle identified by Lord Atkins in *Evans v Bartlam*[81] that "unless and until the court has pronounced a judgment upon the merits or by consent, it is to have the power to revoke the expression of its coercive power where that has been obtained only by a failure to follow any of the rules of procedure". This jurisdiction, thus, seeks to avoid the injustice that might otherwise result if a defendant, with a good defence on the merits was precluded from contesting a claim made against him. It follows logically from this rationale, that the court can only exercise its discretion in favour of setting aside the default judgment where it is satisfied that the defendant may have a good defence and, for this reason, an affidavit of merits establishing this is essential.[82] In *Maher v Dixon*,[83] Budd J stated that rule 11 gives the court "an untrammelled discretion" but only if a satisfactory affidavit of merits has been sworn.

4.027 One case where this prerequisite was not satisfied is *O'Callaghan Ltd v*

---

[78] (1907) 41 ILTR 190. See also *Kirwin v Geoghegan* (1878) 2 LR Ir 57.
[79] (1958) 92 ILTR 60.
[80] [1934] IR 469.
[81] [1937] AC 473, 480, [1937] 2 All ER 646, 650.
[82] *Petronelli v Collins* High Court (Costello P) 19 July 1996; *Maher v Dixon* [1995] 1 ILRM 218; *Clarke v. City of Dublin Steampacket Co.* (1891) 25 ILTR 21. In *Clarke*, it was held that the affidavit need not be made in any particular form or by any particular person if the court is satisfied as to its efficiency.
[83] [1995] 1 ILRM 218, 221.

O'Donovan.[84] The plaintiff issued plenary proceedings against the defendants for a balance due for work done by the plaintiff. The plaintiff issued two motions for judgment in default of appearance. The first was comprised by a consent order extending the time for entering an appearance which was, nonetheless, not entered. Judgment was obtained on foot of the second motion. The first named defendant then brought a motion to set aside the judgment. He did not dispute that the plaintiff was owed the sum claimed but sought to set aside the judgment on the basis that he had been acting merely as an agent for the second named defendant and the money was owed by the second named defendant and not by him. In the High Court, Morris J refused the application stating that:

> The court must be satisfied that there is a valid and *bona fide* defence on the part of the defendant.... The affidavits presented by the first named defendant fall far short of establishing an absolute or even a good defence.... I am satisfied that the defendant was aware of what the consequences would be, there was no question of misadventure here in the obtaining of judgment. I do not believe the case now being made by the defendant and I refuse the application.

Lynch J for the Supreme Court said that Morris J had applied the proper test and he approved of the formulation of the test in *The Saudi Eagle,*[85] that: "a defendant who is asking the court to exercise its discretion in its favour should show that he has a defence which has a real prospect of success". He was not satisfied that the affidavits filed and the exhibits thereto supported the defence put forward by the first named defendant and dismissed the appeal.

Grounds on Which the Court May Exercise its Discretion

4.028 The most common ground for seeking to set aside a regular judgment is on the basis that there was some element of surprise. A good example can be seen in *Maher v Dixon*[86] where the third defendant, a limited liability company, sought to set aside a judgment granted against it in 1987. The application was based on the affidavit of the principal of the third defendant who averred that he had purchased the company "off the shelf" in 1993, had no knowledge of the plaintiff or the defendant and only became aware of the judgment in 1994. Budd J was satisfied that a stateable case had been made out that the third defendant, a "shelf" company, had not been trading at the time of the plaintiff's accident and, therefore, he could not have been employed by it. He, therefore, set aside the judgment with directions as to pleadings and discovery and awarded the costs of the motion to the plaintiff.

---

[84] Supreme Court 13 May 1997.
[85] [1986] 2 Lloyd's Rep 221, 223.
[86] [1995] 1 ILRM 218.

4.029 In *Fox v Taher*,[87] an application was also made on the basis of surprise. The plaintiff had acted as solicitor for the defendants in certain proceedings and a dispute subsequently arose between the plaintiff and the first named defendant in relation to the quantum of the plaintiff's costs. Proceedings were instituted and judgment in default of appearance was entered against the defendants. A motion was brought to set aside this judgment on the ground of surprise. The solicitors for the defendants claimed that they were taken by surprise by the judgment and did not consider that a judgment in default of appearance could be obtained in the Central Office on foot of the statement of claim because it was in such terms that a liquidated sum had not been properly claimed in it and that only by leave of the court could judgment be obtained. Costello J said it was more accurate to say that judgment was obtained by virtue of a mistake on their part but said:

> I do not think it matters very much whether I come to the view that the judgment was obtained by mistake or by surprise because the court has to do justice in this situation. The court has a very wide discretion in setting aside judgments and I think that an injustice would be done to the defendants by allowing the judgment to stand.[88]

He was satisfied that, at all times, the defendants wished to contest the jurisdiction of the Irish courts to hear the plaintiff's claim and they were waiting for the matter to be brought before the court. In those circumstances, he took the view that justice required that the defendants should be given an opportunity to make their case.

As can be seen, Costello J in *Fox v Taher* emphasised the very wide discretion enjoyed by the court. Therefore, while surprise and mistake[89] are the most common grounds for seeking to set aside a judgment, the court enjoys "an untrammelled discretion"[90] which can be exercised in any case where the interests of justice require that a defendant be allowed to defend proceedings. This is clear from *Maher v Dixon*,[91] where Budd J approved of the following passage from the judgment of Lord Atkin in *Evans v Bartlam*:[92]

> The discretion is in terms unconditional.... It was suggested in argument that ... the applicant must satisfy the court that there is a reasonable

---

[87] High Court (Costello J) 24 January 1996.
[88] *Ibid.* at 7.
[89] See, for example, *M'Master v M'Assey* (1859) 9 ICLR App xii, where a judgment obtained in default of appearance was set aside where the defendant had allowed judgment to go by default because he was not aware at the time that his infancy would have been a good defence.
[90] *Per* Budd J in *Maher v Dixon* [1995] 1 ILRM 218, 221.
[91] [1995] 1 ILRM 218.
[92] [1937] AC 473, 480, [1937] 2 All ER 646, 650.

explanation why judgment was allowed to go by default, such as mistake, accident, fraud or the like. I do not think that any such rule exists, though obviously the reason, if any, for allowing the judgment, and thereafter applying to set it aside is one of the matters to which the court will have regard in exercising its discretion. If there were a rigid rule that no one could have a default judgment set aside who knew at the time and intended that there should be a judgment signed, the … rules would be deprived of most of their efficacy.

4.030 An example of a case where there was no reasonable explanation for allowing judgment to go by default is *Petronelli v Collins*.[93] The plaintiff issued proceedings to enforce a judgment obtained in earlier US proceedings and obtained judgment in default of appearance. The defendant subsequently sought to set aside this judgment on the ground that service had not been effected properly and that he had no notice of the proceedings. Costello P considered the evidence put forward by the parties on the issue of service and concluded that there were serious inconsistencies in the evidence given by the defendant. He, therefore accepted the evidence adduced by the plaintiff and concluded that the defendant had been properly served and had notice of the proceedings. He also rejected the defendant's contention that the judgment had been obtained by surprise. He was satisfied that the defendant must have been aware that proceedings of some sort were being taken against him and that he had chosen to deliberately ignore the proceedings. Nevertheless, he set aside the judgment on terms because the defendant had sworn a satisfactory affidavit of merits which raised issues of substance as to whether an Irish court should decline to exercise its jurisdiction to enforce the US judgment.

Imposition of Terms

4.031 It is, of course, necessary for the court to do justice between the parties[94] and the court will be conscious that an injustice should not be caused to the plaintiff who has obtained the benefit of a regular judgment. Therefore, rule 11 provides that the court may set aside or vary a default judgment "upon such terms as may be just". For example, in *Fox v Taher*,[95] where it was accepted by the defendants that some money was owing to the plaintiff, Costello J considered that a serious injustice to the plaintiff would be done if some provision was not made for their payment and the plaintiff had to wait years for the case to come to trial. He therefore set aside the judgment obtained in default of appearance on terms that the defendants pay the plaintiff £100,000 (which he consid-

[93] High Court (Costello P) 19 July 1996.
[94] *Fox v Taher* High Court (Costello J) 24 January 1996.
[95] High Court 24 January 1996.

ered a reasonable figure in part-payment of the fees owed) plus the costs of obtaining the default judgment and the costs of the motion.

A court is particularly likely to impose terms if it concludes that the defendant was culpable in allowing judgment to go by default. Thus, in *Petronelli v Collins*,[96] Costello P imposed terms that the defendant pay the amount of the judgment into court until further order. He took the view that this was a proper case for the imposition of such a condition as the defendant had deliberately decided to ignore the proceedings and the affidavit evidence filed in support of the application was unsatisfactory (he had rejected a number of the factual contentions made therein).

Application by Persons other than the Defendant

4.032 Although an application to set aside or vary a judgment obtained in default will most commonly be brought by a defendant, it may also be brought by the plaintiff[97] and, in exceptional circumstances, by a non-party who is adversely affected. An example can be seen in *Mehaffey v Mehaffey*,[98] where judgment was allowed to be marked by collusion between the plaintiff and the defendant in an action against an administrator of a deceased intestate for money. The applicant was a next-of-kin who was not a party to the record but his interest in the assets of the deceased was prejudicially affected by the judgment. It was held that, in the exceptional circumstances of the case, the applicant had such a specific interest in the assets of the deceased as to entitle him to an order in the action, setting aside the judgment, and giving him leave to intervene.

DEFAULT OF APPEARANCE UNDER THE JURISDICTION OF COURTS AND ENFORCEMENT OF JUDGMENTS ACT 1998

4.033 Special provision is made in Order 13A[99] in relation to claims governed by the Brussels Convention and the Jurisdiction of Courts and Enforcement of Judgments Act 1998.

Claims which the Court has Power to Hear and Determine

4.034 In the case of default of appearance by any defendant to an originating summons concerning a claim which by virtue of the 1998 Act, the court has

---

[96] High Court (Costello P) 19 July 1996.
[97] See, for example, *The Wise Finance Co. Ltd v O'Regan* High Court (Laffoy J) 26 June 1998.
[98] [1905] 2 IR 292.
[99] Inserted by the Rules of the Superior Courts (No.1) 1989 (SI No. 14 of 1989).

power to hear and determine, the plaintiff must: (1) in the case of a plenary summons, deliver a statement of claim by filing the same in the Central Office; (2) in the case of a special summons, file a grounding affidavit in the Central Office; or, (3) in the case of a summary summons, file an affidavit in the Central Office verifying the facts relied upon, prior to applying for judgment in default of appearance.[100]

Summons Issued for Service out of the Jurisdiction

4.035 Where an originating summons has been issued for service out of the jurisdiction under Order 11A, rule 2, the plaintiff is not entitled to enter judgment in default of appearance except with the leave of the court.[101] Order 13A, rule 2 stipulates that the application for leave must be made on notice to the defendant in default and must be supported by an affidavit stating that in the deponent's belief: (1) each claim made by the summons is one which by virtue of the 1998 Act the court has power to hear and determine;[102] (2) no other court has exclusive jurisdiction within the meaning of the Brussels Convention to hear and determine such claim; and (3) where the summons or notice of the summons is served out of the jurisdiction under Order 11A, rule 2, that such service satisfies the requirement of the Brussels Convention;[103] and giving in each case the source of grounds of such belief. Otherwise, the provisions of Order 13 are stated to apply, in so far as practicable.[104]

Summons Served out of the Jurisdiction under the Hague Convention

4.036 Order 11B, rule 4[105] provides that where proceedings have been issued for service out of jurisdiction under Order 11A, rule 2 and transmitted abroad for service in accordance with Order 11B, judgment in default of appearance can only be entered with leave of the court and cannot be entered unless and until it is established that:

(a)   the document was served by a method prescribed by the internal law of the State addressed for the service of documents in domestic actions upon persons who are within its territory; or

---

[100]   Order 13A, rule 3.
[101]   Order 13A, rule 1.
[102]   Under Article 20 of the convention, the court may, of its own motion, refuse jurisdiction unless the proceedings fall within the provisions of the convention.
[103]   Under Article 27(2) of the convention, judgment in default of appearance may be refused recognition unless the defendant is shown to have been duly served in sufficient time to arrange his defence.
[104]   Order 13A, rule 4.
[105]   Inserted by the Rules of the Superior Courts (No.3) 1994 (SI No. 101 of 1994).

(b)   the document was actually delivered to the defendant or to his residence by
      another method provided for by the Hague Convention;

and in either case, that service or delivery was effected in sufficient time to
enable the defendant to defend.

Compliance with these requirements is usually proved by means of a certificate of service issued by the Central Authority of the State addressed. Article 6 of the convention requires the Central Authority of the State addressed, or
any authority which he may have designated, to complete a certificate of service
stating that the document has been served and specifying the method, the place
and the date of service and the person to whom the document was delivered.
Under Order 11B, rule 3(6), a certificate of service received under Article 6
from the Central Authority of the State addressed must be transmitted forthwith
to the party who lodged the request and it is provided that any such certificate
purporting to have been issued by such Central Authority in the form prescribed
is *prima facie* evidence of the facts stated therein. However, the court may give
leave to enter judgment even if no certificate of service or delivery has been
received from the Central Authority of the State addressed, provided that:

(a)   the document was transmitted by one of the methods provided for in the
      convention;

(b)   a period of time (of not less than six months) considered adequate by the
      court has elapsed since the transmission of the document;

(c)   no certificate of any kind has been received and that every reasonable
      effort has been made to obtain it through the competent authorities of the
      State addressed.[106]

An application for judgment in default of appearance must be made by motion
on notice supported by an affidavit verifying the plaintiff's claim for relief and
the steps taken in the proceedings, supported by adequate proof thereof.[107] The
affidavit must also contain the statements of belief required by Order 13A, rule
2.[108]

Setting Aside Default Judgment

4.037   Order 11B, rule 4(6) deals with applications to set aside default judgments. It provides that an application to set aside any judgment obtained in
default must be made by motion on notice and grounded on the affidavit of the
moving party and the court may, if satisfied that:

---

[106]   Order 11B, rule 4(5).
[107]   Order 11B, rule 4(4).
[108]   Order 11B, rule 4(1).

(a) the application was made within a reasonable time after the defendant had knowledge of the judgment and

(b) the defendant, without any fault on his part, did not have knowledge of the document in sufficient time to defend or knowledge of the judgment in sufficient time to appeal, as the case may be and

(c) the defendant has disclosed a *prima facie* defence to the action on the merits,

set aside the judgment or extend the time for appealing same, as the case may be, on such terms and conditions as appear just. There is no indication in rule 4(6) as to whether it applies just to cases where a summons has been transmitted for service out of the jurisdiction in accordance with Order 11B or whether it applies to all cases where a summons has been issued for service out of the jurisdiction under Order 11A, rule 2. It is submitted that the latter is the preferable interpretation.

CHAPTER FIVE

PLEADINGS

INTRODUCTION

5.001 The term "pleading" is a generic one applied to a variety of documents[1] which set out the contents of the claim or defence of a party to proceedings and, thus, identify the issues between the parties. It is important that a claim or defence be pleaded properly because if an allegation of fact is not pleaded, no evidence can be adduced in relation to it[2] and no finding in relation to it can be made by the court of trial.[3]

PLEADINGS

Purpose of Pleadings

5.002 The purpose of a pleading has been "conveniently and compendiously"[4] stated by Fitzgerald J in *Mahon v Celbridge Spinning Co Ltd*:[5]

> The whole purpose of a pleading, be it a statement of claim, defence or reply, is to define the issues between the parties, to confine the evidence at the trial to the matters relevant to those issues, and to ensure that the trial may proceed to judgment without either party being taken at a disadvantage by the introduction of matters not fairly to be ascertained from the pleadings. In other words a party should know in advance, in broad outline, the case he will have to meet at the trial.[6]

In accordance with these purposes, a pleading should, therefore, set out the

---

[1] Order 125, rule 1 provides that the term includes an originating summons, statement of claim, defence, counterclaim, reply, petition and answer. There is some doubt as to whether a notice for particulars and the replies thereto are pleadings but Macken J in *Leinster Leader Ltd v Williams Group Tullamore Ltd* High Court (Macken J) 9 July 1999 favoured the view that they are not.
[2] See *Callan v Marum* (1870) IR 5 CL 315.
[3] See *Wrenn v Bus Átha Cliath* Supreme Court, 31 March 1995 (trial judge not entitled to make finding of contributory negligence because it had not been pleaded).
[4] *Per* Keane J in *McGee v O'Reilly* [1996] 2 IR 229, 233.
[5] [1967] IR 1.
[6] *Ibid.* at 3. This passage was approved in *Wildgust v Bank of Ireland* [2001] 1 ILRM 24, *McGee v O'Reilly* [1996] 2 IR 229 and *Behan v Medical Council* [1993] 3 IR 523; [1993] ILRM 240.

claim or defence of a party concisely[7] and "in language and terms easily understood by the reasonably intelligent layman".[8] If this is done, then the issues between the parties will be evident which will not only facilitate trial of those issues and preparation for trial but also, thereby, save costs. It can be seen that the aim of many of the rules and principles of pleadings examined below is to ensure that these objectives are achieved by ensuring that all relevant matters are pleaded whilst avoiding either prolixity or undue terseness.

Form of Pleadings

5.003 The form of pleadings is dictated by the Rules and each pleading should contain a heading in accordance with Appendix B, Part IV,[9] the record number of the action, the court (if any) to which the action is assigned, the title of the action and the description of the pleading.[10] In addition, it must contain the name and registered place of business of the solicitor for the party serving the same and also the name and registered place of business of the solicitor to be served or, in the case of a party who does not act by a solicitor, the name and address for service of such person.[11]

The main body of the pleading should set out the claim or defence of the party clearly and legibly[12] and to that end, it must be divided into paragraphs numbered consecutively[13] with each cause of action or defence relied upon set out in a separate paragraph.[14]

It is not necessary for a pleading to be signed by counsel but, where pleadings have been drafted or settled by counsel, they should be signed by him (or them).[15] If they have not been settled by counsel, then they should be signed by the solicitor who drafted them or by the party if he sues or defends in person.[16]

Although adherence to the foregoing rules is important and any departure may well be the subject of judicial criticism, Order 19, rule 26 stipulates that no

---

[7] Order 19, rule 1 specifies that pleadings should be as brief as the nature of the case will admit.

[8] *Per* Walsh J in *P.W. v CIE* [1967] IR 137, 140.

[9] Part IV contains headings for a statement of claim, a defence and a reply and Order 19, rule 4 provides that these headings, where applicable, must be used for all pleadings.

[10] Order 19, rule 11.

[11] Order 121, rule 4.

[12] Order 19, rule 9 provides that every pleading which contains less than fifteen folios (every figure being counted as one word) may be either printed or written, or partly printed and partly written and every other pleading, not being a petition, shall be printed unless otherwise ordered by the court.

[13] Order 19, rule 3. It is also provided that dates, sums and numbers should be expressed in figures and not in words.

[14] *Dunne v Clancy* (1880) 6 LR Ir 395. *Cf. Hoban v McPherson* (1904) 39 ILTR 153.

[15] Order 19, rule 3.

[16] Order 19, rule 3.

technical objection can be raised to any pleading on the ground of any alleged want of form.

Principles of Pleading

Material Facts and not Evidence Should be Pleaded

5.004 Order 19, rule 3 lays down what has been described as the "golden rule of pleading",[17] namely that:

> Every pleading shall contain, and contain only, a statement in summary form of the material facts on which the party pleading relies for his claim or defence, as the case may be, but not the evidence by which they are to be proved …

There are two aspects to this rule which require to be considered: (i) that a party must plead the material facts on which he relies; and (ii) that a party must not plead the evidence by which those material facts are to be proved.

5.005 The concept of "material facts" was considered by Palles CB in *Rattray v Cork and Macroom Railway Co.*,[18] who stated that these are "the facts constituting the cause of action, or the matter of defence, as the case may be"[19] *i.e.* the facts which must be proved by a party in order to succeed in the claim being made or the defence being raised. An example of what is required in that regard can be seen in *Wildgust v Bank of Ireland*.[20] At the trial, the plaintiffs sought to make a case based on negligent misstatement but objection was taken by the second named defendant on the basis that this cause of action had not been properly pleaded and that it had been prejudiced in its defence as a result. Having considered the elements of the tort of negligent misstatement as laid down in *Hedley Byrne & Co. Ltd v Heller & Partners Ltd*[21] and examining the statement of claim and particulars, the Supreme Court concluded that a claim of negligent misstatement had not been properly pleaded. McGuinness J stated that the statement of claim failed to plead the material facts required to establish such a claim in that it: (i) did not state that a duty of care was owed by the second named defendant to the plaintiffs; (ii) it did not state that the communication in question was made to the plaintiffs or their agents; (iii) it did not state that the plaintiffs relied on the communication or that the second named defendant knew that they would rely on it; and (iv) it did not clearly set out that the

---

[17] *Per* Lord MacDermott LCJ in *Atkinson v Stewart and Partners Ltd* [1967] NI 146, 147.
[18] (1879) 4 LR Ir 386.
[19] *Ibid.* at 388. See also *Lacey v Kendall* (1883) 17 ILTR 112.
[20] [2001] 1 ILRM 24.
[21] [1964] AC 465, [1964] 3 WLR 101, [1963] 2 All ER 575.

plaintiffs acted to their detriment in reliance on the communication. In addition, it did not set out that the communication was untrue. In the circumstances, she took the view that the second named defendant had been justified in considering that the parts of the statement of claim relied on as grounding the claim of negligent misstatement related to a separate allegation of *mala fides* made by the plaintiffs.

5.006 The other aspect of rule 3 is that it seeks to avoid prolixity and the inclusion of unnecessary and extraneous matters in pleadings by confining them to material facts and excluding the evidence by which those material facts are to be proved. The line between those facts which are material and should be pleaded and those which are merely evidence of the existence or non-existence of material facts and which, therefore, should not be pleaded is not precise but accords in general terms with the distinction drawn in the law of evidence between facts in issue (*factum probandum*) and facts relevant to an issue (*factum probans*). As will be seen below, portions of pleadings which are unduly prolix and set out the evidence by which the material facts are to be proved can be struck out as embarrassing.[22]

5.007 The general principle laid down in rule 3 is reinforced by a number of other specific rules laid down in Order 19. Of these, one of the most important is rule 21 which provides that if the contents of any document are material, it is sufficient to state the effect thereof as briefly as possible in a pleading without setting out the whole of the document or any part thereof unless the precise words of the document are material, *e.g.* the document containing the alleged libel in a libel action. Also of note is rule 14 which deals with conditions precedent,[23] rule 22 which deals with establishing intention or knowledge,[24] rule 23 which deals with allegations of notice,[25] and rule 24 which deals with allegations of contractual and other relations.[26]

---

[22] Order 19, rule 27. See *Crawford v British Medical Association* (1881) 15 ILTR 86; *Doyle v Hort* (1878) 12 ILTR 172.

[23] Rule 14 provides that any condition precedent, the performance or occurrence of which is intended to be contested must be distinctly specified in his pleading by the plaintiff or defendant (as the case may be) and subject thereto, an averment of the performance or occurrence of all conditions precedent necessary for the case of the plaintiff or defendant shall be implied in his pleading. See *Jones v Quinn* (1878) 2 LR Ir 516, 13 ILTR 16 and *Newry and Armagh Railway Co. v Ulster Railway Co.* (1869) IR 4 CL 62.

[24] Rule 22 provides that, if it is material to allege malice, fraudulent intention, knowledge or any other condition of the mind of any person, it is sufficient to allege same as a fact without setting out the circumstances from which same is to be inferred.

[25] Rule 23 provides that, if it is material to allege notice to any person of any fact, matter, or thing, it is sufficient to allege such notice as a fact, unless the form or the precise terms of such notice, or the circumstances from which such notice is to be inferred is material.

[26] Rule 24 provides that, if any contract or any relation between any persons is to be

5.008 As stated above, the material facts which are required to be pleaded are those which are necessary to establish the claim or defence of a party. It follows that any fact which does not have to be proved by a party in order to succeed is not material and does not have to be pleaded. This is the rationale behind rule 25 which provides that a party is not required to allege any matter in a pleading which the law presumes in his favour or as to which the burden of proof lies upon the other side unless it has first been specifically denied. Although rule 25 is not mentioned, the principle encapsulated therein appears to be the basis of the decision of Griffin J in *Mullen v Quinnsworth Ltd*,[27] that it is not necessary to expressly plead *res ipsa loquitur* and that a plaintiff can rely on it if the facts pleaded and proved show that the doctrine is applicable.[28] That holding is justifiable on the basis that, although there has been considerable debate as to the precise nature of the presumption created by the doctrine of *res ipsa loquitur*,[29] it is clearly something that the law presumes in favour of the plaintiff and, thus, is not required to be pleaded. That said, the issue is not settled[30] and, hence, the safer course of action would be to expressly plead it as is generally done.

Denials Should Deal Specifically with the Substance of Each Allegation of Fact

5.009 Order 19, rule 17 seeks to prevent parties from making pregnant or blanket denials and thereby failing to consider and make any attempt to identify the matters which are actually at issue between the parties.[31] It provides that it is not sufficient for a defendant in his defence, to deny generally the grounds alleged by the statement of claim, or for a plaintiff in his reply to deny generally the grounds alleged in a defence by way of counterclaim, but each party must deal specifically with each allegation of fact of which he does not admit the truth, except damages.[32] Thus, it is not sufficient for a defendant (or a plaintiff

---

implied from a series of letters or conversations, or otherwise from a number of circumstances, it is sufficient to allege such contract or relation as a fact, and to refer generally to such letters, conversations, or circumstances without setting them out in detail. It is further provided that, if in such case the person so pleading desires to rely in the alternative upon more contracts or relations than one as to be implied from such circumstances, he may state the same in the alternative.

[27] [1990] 1 IR 59.

[28] Following on this point by Johnson J in *O'Reilly v Lavelle* [1990] 2 IR 372.

[29] See McMahon and Binchy, *Law of Torts* (3rd ed., 2000), § 9.41.

[30] McCarthy J in *Mullen v Quinnsworth* [1990] 1 IR 59, 67 left the question open.

[31] See *Lee Conservancy Board v Button* (1879) 12 Ch D 383, 397 where Malins VC was critical of the practice of denying everything in the defence. It should be noted that Order 21, rule 8 makes provision for a costs penalty in the event of unreasonable denials. It provides that, where the court is of opinion that any allegations of fact denied or not admitted by the defendant ought to have been admitted, it may make such order as shall be just with respect to any extra costs occasioned by their having been denied or not admitted.

[32] *Cf.* Order 19, rule 19 which provides that, if an allegation is made with divers circumstances, it will not be sufficient to deny it along with those circumstances.

as the case may be) to make a general denial or traverse of a pleading but he must, instead, traverse each material allegation[33] made in the pleading.[34] In *Dunne v Clancy*,[35] a counterclaim in its first paragraph set out a contract and an alleged breach and in the second paragraph a contract and several specific breaches. The plaintiff in his reply stated that he did not admit the statements in the first paragraph and denied the statements in the second paragraph. Both paragraphs of the reply were set aside as embarrassing on the ground that each conflated the issue of the making of the alleged contract and the breach of it.

5.010 The general principle laid down in rule 17 is reinforced by a number of more specific rules contained in Order 21. Rule 3 provides that, in actions for a debt or a liquidated demand in money, a mere denial of the debt is inadmissible. This rule is complemented by rule 4 which provides that, in actions upon bills of exchange, promissory notes, or cheques, a defence in denial must deny some matter of fact such as the drawing, making, endorsing, accepting, presenting or notice of dishonour of the bill or note. It is further provided in rule 5 that, in actions for a debt or liquidated demand arising upon a contract including a bill of exchange, promissory note, cheque or other simple contract debt or on a bond or contract under seal for payment of a liquidated amount of money, a defence in denial must deny such matters of fact, from which the liability of the defendant is alleged to arise, as are disputed. Thus, in an action for goods sold and delivered, the defence must deny the order or contract, the delivery or the amount claimed.

5.011 Order 19, rule 19 deals with a different problem, that of overly specific denials in pleadings. It stipulates that, when a party in any pleading denies an allegation of fact in the previous pleading of the opposite party, he must not do so evasively, but must answer the point of substance. Thus, if for example, it is alleged that a party received a certain sum of money, it is not sufficient to deny that he received that particular amount, the party must deny that he received that sum or any part thereof or else set out how much he received.[36] The application of this principle can be seen in *Rowley v Laffan*[37] where, in an action for ejectment for non-payment of rent, the denial of the defendant that he was a

---

[33] See *Quirk v Fitzgerald* (1879) 13 ILTR 64 where it was held that where a proposition is the gist of an action a general traverse is not allowable and a specific denial must be made but where it is not the gist of the action, a general denial is sufficient.

[34] *Jones v Quinn* (1878) 2 LR Ir 516, 13 ILTR 16; *Barclay v McHugh* (1878) 12 ILTR 176; *Harris v Great Britain Mutual Life Assurance Society* (1878) 2 LR Ir 512, 13 ILTR 65n. But *cf. Peclar v Johnstone* (1919) 53 ILTR 31 where it was held that a denial by the defendant of "each of the several acts in the statement of claim alleged" was held to be a sufficient compliance with the equivalent of rule 17.

[35] (1880) 6 LR Ir 395.

[36] Order 19, rule 19.

[37] (1882) 10 LR Ir 9.

tenant of the plaintiffs was held to be embarrassing and defective in not answering the substance of the plaintiff's claim by denying that there was a subsisting tenancy in any person under the plaintiffs.

All Defences Should be Expressly Pleaded

5.012 Order 19, rule 15 lays down the important principle that a defendant in his defence and a plaintiff in his reply (if any) must raise all matters which show that the action or counterclaim is not maintainable, or that the transaction is either void or voidable in point of law or such other grounds of defence or reply as, which if not raised, would be likely to take the other party by surprise or would raise issues of fact not arising out of the preceding pleadings.[38] The examples given in the rule of such grounds are fraud, Statute of Limitations, release, payment, performance, facts showing illegality either by statute or common law, or Statute of Frauds.[39] This rule is further reinforced by rule 20 which provides that when a contract, promise, or agreement is alleged in any pleading, a bare denial of the same by the opposite party shall be construed only as a denial in fact of the express contract, promise, or agreement alleged, or of the matters of fact from which the same may be implied by law, and not as a denial of the legality or sufficiency in law of such contract, promise, or agreement, whether with reference to the Statute of Frauds or otherwise.

5.013 An application of this principle can be seen in *Callan v Marum*,[40] where, to a claim for "work done and materials provided by the plaintiff for the defendant at his request", the defendant pleaded "that no work was done or materials provided by the plaintiff for the defendant as alleged". It was held that it was not competent for the defendant under such a plea to show that, although work and materials were actually done and provided, they were done and provided under a special contract, the terms of which the plaintiff had not complied with. Such a defence should have been made the subject of a special plea not denying that the work and materials were done and provided but stating that they were done and provided under a special contract and showing that, under the terms

---

[38] *Cf. Murphy v Times Newspapers Ltd* [2000] 1 IR 522. In that case, the Supreme Court rejected the submission of the plaintiff that the defendants could not rely on s. 22 of the Defamation Act 1961 in a libel action because it was not expressly pleaded in the defence. Although Keane J relied on Order 19, rule 3 in reaching that conclusion, the decision is, perhaps, best explained by reference to Order 19, rule 15, because it was clear that the plaintiff would not be surprised by the invocation of s. 22 in the circumstances of the case.

[39] See also Order 21, rule 7 which stipulates that, if either party wishes to deny the right of any other party to claim as executor, or as trustee, whether in bankruptcy or otherwise, or as assignee in bankruptcy, or in any representative or other alleged capacity, or the alleged constitution of any partnership firm, he shall deny the same specifically.

[40] (1870) IR 5 CL 315.

and conditions of that contract, the plaintiff was not entitled to recover for such work and materials.[41]

5.014 A case where this principle was found not to have been violated in the circumstances is *McKnight v McLaughlin*.[42] The plaintiff claimed damages for personal injuries sustained in a collision between his motorcycle and a car driven by the defendant. At the trial, the defendant sought to lead evidence of the defect in the braking system of the car and it was objected to on behalf of the plaintiff who submitted that this matter ought to have been specifically raised on the pleadings. However, it was held by Black LJ that, as a matter of pleading, the defendant in an action based upon negligence was entitled, on a defence containing a bare denial of negligence, to show that the accident was due to the fault of some third person not a party to the proceedings. In the circumstances of this case, the plaintiff ought to have been able to anticipate that the defendant might seek to rely, by way of defence to the action, upon the defect in the mechanical condition of his car which had been mentioned in correspondence and accordingly could not complain that he had been taken by surprise.[43]

Any Fact Not Denied is Taken as Admitted

5.015 The basic rule as laid down by Order 19, rule 13 is that any allegation of fact in any pleading (except a petition), if not denied specifically or by necessary implication, or stated to be not admitted in the pleading of the opposite party, will be taken to be admitted, except as against an infant, or person of unsound mind. The general principle laid down in that rule is tempered to some degree by Order 21, rule 6, which provides that no denial or defence is necessary as to damages claimed or their amount and these are deemed to be put in issue in all cases unless expressly admitted.

   As can be seen from the terms of rule 13, its application can be avoided not only by an express denial but also if a party states that he does not admit the allegation of fact made. The difference between the two pleas is that one is a positive denial of the state of affairs while the other merely seeks to put the other party on proof of their case. The latter plea in often used in respect of procedural, jurisdictional or technical matters.

5.016 It suffices to avoid the application of rule 13 if a party denies a matter by necessary implication though in determining whether this has been done, the terms of rules 7, 15, 20 discussed above should be considered. In general, the courts will afford some degree of latitude to the party pleading the denial but

---

[41] But *cf. Beattie v McCracken* (1856) 6 ICLR 259 and *Mosely v McMullen* (1856) 6 ICLR 69.
[42] [1963] NI 34.
[43] See also *Rumbold v London County Council* (1909) 25 TLR 541 and *Southport Corp. v Esso Petroleum Co. Ltd* [1953] 3 WLR 773, 781, [1953] 2 All ER 1204, 1212.

one case where a very strict approach was taken is *Commissioners of Church Temporalities in Ireland v McAuley*.[44] The plaintiffs brought an action for recovery of land for non-payment of rent. The statement of claim alleged that the defendant held the land from the plaintiff for a certain period of time. The defence stated that the defendant "does not hold" the land as alleged. The court accepted that the plaintiffs were entitled to mark judgment on the basis that the defendant had not denied the plaintiffs' claim by using the present tense and, not having denied the allegations, he was taken to have admitted it.

If a party fails to deny a matter in either his defence or reply as the case may be and thereby makes formal admissions of material facts, it is open to the opposing party to move for such judgment as he may be entitled. Order 32, rule 6 provides that any party may at any stage of a cause or matter, where admissions of fact have been made, either on the pleadings or otherwise apply to the court for such judgment or order as upon such admissions he may be entitled to, without waiting for the determination of any other question between the parties, and the court may upon such application make such order, or give such judgment, as the court may think just.[45]

Delivery of Pleadings

5.017 All pleadings are required to be delivered between the parties[46] but (with the exception of originating summonses) service by post suffices.[47] The periods of time afforded to parties to deliver a statement of claim, defence and reply respectively are dealt with in Orders 21–23 and are discussed below but a number of general points should be noted. First, the time for delivering and filing any pleading can be extended by consent in writing without the necessary for an application to court.[48] Second, the long vacation is not to be reckoned in the

---

[44] (1879) 13 ILTR 123.

[45] See *Massy v Donovan* (1879) 3 LR Ir 85 and *MacMahon v Thompson* (1878) 13 ILTR 93.

[46] Order 19, rule 11. Rule 10 specifies that every pleading or other document required to be delivered to a party, or between parties, shall be delivered to the solicitor of every party who appears by a solicitor, or to the party if he does not appear by a solicitor, but if no appearance has been entered for any party, then such pleading or document shall be delivered by being filed with the proper officer of the Central Office.

[47] Order 121, rule 2 provides that the delivery or service of any document under the Rules for which personal service is not required, shall be effected by leaving the document or a copy thereof (as may be appropriate) at, or sending the document or a copy thereof (as may be appropriate) by registered prepaid post to the residence or place of business in the State of the person to be served or the place of business in the State of the solicitor (if any) acting for him in the proceedings to which the document relates. Order 121, rule 3 further provides that the service by post of any document, which is authorised to be delivered or served by post, shall be deemed to have been served at the time at which it would be delivered in the ordinary course of post.

[48] Order 122, rule 8.

computation of the time allowed for delivery of pleadings[49] and, unless directed by the court or on consent, a pleading cannot be delivered during the long vacation.[50]

Costs of Pleadings

5.018 Order 19, rule 1 provides that pleadings must be as brief as the nature of the case will admit, and the Taxing Master in adjusting the costs of the action must, at the instance of any party, or may without any request, inquire into any unnecessary prolixity, and order the costs occasioned by such prolixity to be borne by the party chargeable with same.[51]

PARTICULARS OF PLEADING

Introduction

5.019 In *Cooney v Browne*,[52] Hamilton J explained that the ordinary use and purpose of particulars is "to define the issues between parties to any action or proceeding and thereby to prevent either party being taken by surprise and incidentally to limit as much as possible the length and expense of trials."[53] They thus serve the general purposes of pleadings by further narrowing and clarifying the issues between the parties.[54] It follows that a party providing particulars will be bound thereby and will not be permitted to introduce evidence relating to any matter falling outside the scope of the particulars[55] unless the opposing party is otherwise aware of the matter and would not be taken by surprise.[56]

---

[49] Order 122, rule 5.

[50] Order 122, rule 4.

[51] *Cf.* Order 1, rule 5 which provides that any costs occasioned by the use of any forms of summonses or of indorsements thereon, other or more prolix than the forms prescribed in the Rules shall be borne by the party using same unless the court otherwise directs.

[52] [1985] IR 185.

[53] *Ibid.* at 188. See, to the same effect *Behan v Medical Council* [1993] 3 IR 523, [1993] ILRM 240; *Shepperton Investment Co. Ltd v Concast (1975) Ltd* High Court (Barron J) 21 December 1992; *P.W. v CIE* [1967] IR 137, 140; *Caulfield v George Bell & Co. Ltd* (1957) 93 ILTR 108, 111; *Jevens v Marine Transport Services Ltd* Supreme Court, 5 December 1972; *Spedding v Fitzpatrick* (1888) 38 Ch D 410, 413. *Cf. Fahy v Pullen* (1968) 102 ILTR 81 where Ó Dálaigh CJ adopted the words of MacDermott LCJ in *Patterson v Donnell* [1954] NI 96, 98, that "[t]he object of further and better particulars is to promote a satisfactory process of adjudication and to guard against a party being taken by surprise."

[54] See *Behan v Medical Council* [1993] 3 IR 523 where Morris J stated the object of particulars by reference to the purposes of pleading identified by Fitzgerald J in *Mahon v Celbridge Spinning Co. Ltd* [1967] IR 1, 3, and *McGee v O'Reilly* [1996] 2 IR 229, 233 where Keane J stated that, in considering whether particulars should be ordered in any case, those purposes must be borne in mind.

[55] *P.W. v CIE* [1967] IR 137, 141. Cf. *Hogan v Jones* Supreme Court, 31 July 1990.

[56] *Fahy v Pullen* (1968) 102 ILTR 81.

Particulars may be required in two situations: (i) under the Rules, particulars of certain pleas are required; and (ii) in any case, a party may request further and better particulars of a claim or defence and if he is dissatisfied with the replies may apply to the court to compel that party to furnish replies.

Particulars of Pleading

5.020 In certain instances, the Rules require a party to expand upon the bare material facts on which his claim or defence is based and provide particulars which clarify the nature of the case which he is making. Most important in this regard is Order 19, rule 5 which requires a party to provide particulars in his pleading[57] in respect of three categories of plea: (i) civil wrongs, (ii) allegations of fraud and misrepresentation, and (iii) debts.[58]

Civil Wrongs

5.021 If a civil wrong *i.e.* a tort, breach of contract or breach of trust is alleged, particulars of such wrong, any personal injuries suffered and any items of special damage must be set out in the statement of claim or counterclaim and particulars of any contributory negligence must be set out in the defence.[59]

(i) Particulars of Civil Wrong

5.022 A bald plea of negligence, breach of contract *etc.* would, in many instances, provide little information to the opposing party as to how he was alleged to have breached his duty of care or the contract at issue prejudicing the ability of that party to prepare for trial and leading to him being unfairly surprised at the trial. Hence, the necessity for particulars of negligence, breach of contract *etc.* which identify precisely how that party is alleged to have breached his duty of care or the contract between the parties.

An example of a case where sufficient particulars of negligence were not provided is *Mitchell v Arthurs*.[60] The plaintiff workman sued for damages arising out of the fall of bricks from scaffolding and pleaded that the defendant "so

---

[57] The required particulars must be stated in the pleading and it is not sufficient to incorporate them by reference: *Kingston v Corker* (1892) 29 LR Ir 364, 367.

[58] See also Order 19, rule 6 which requires certain specified particulars in probate actions.

[59] Order 19, rule 5(1) provides that in all cases alleging a wrong within the meaning of the Civil Liability Acts 1961 to 1964, particulars of such wrong, any personal injuries suffered and any items of special damage must be set out in the statement of claim or counterclaim and particulars of any contributory negligence must be set out in the defence. S.2 of the 1961 Act defines a "wrong" as meaning "a tort, breach of contract or breach of trust, whether the act is committed by the person to whom the wrong is attributed or by one for whose acts he is responsible, and whether or not the act is also a crime, and whether or not the wrong is intentional".

[60] (1883) 17 ILTR 102.

carelessly, negligently, and unskilfully erected the scaffolding, that a large number of bricks fell on the plaintiff". The statement of claim was struck out as embarrassing on the basis that it merely made a general plea of negligence and failed to specify the particular defects in the scaffolding complained of.

5.023 Serious question marks have, however, been raised as to whether particulars of negligence as commonly pleaded actually succeed in identifying the issues in the case and preventing unfairness or surprise. This is because of the increasing tendency in recent years for lawyers, particularly counsel, to engage in "defensive pleading" and provide copious and generic particulars of negligence which bear little relation to the facts of the case. This tendency is particularly notable in personal injury cases and has been the subject of trenchant judicial criticism. In *Caulfield v George Bell & Co. Ltd*,[61] Murnaghan J referred with disapproval to the practice of slavishly copying particulars of negligence from precedents and stated that it was his experience that:

> [W]hat nowadays in the vast majority of cases passes for "particulars of negligence" is a type of dragnet often in the guise of a supplementary pleading, not intended to give any information to the defendant but on the contrary designed to cover all possible cases which the plaintiff might by some lucky chance find himself at the last moment able to make against the defendant.[62]

In a similar vein, Black LJ in *Atkinson v Stewart and Partners Ltd*,[63] referred to the phenomenon of particulars "containing in the guise of particulars long and assorted lists of allegations of negligence the majority of which are not even attempted to be substantiated at the trial and are indeed shown by the evidence to be wholly devoid of foundation."[64] He pointed out that pleadings framed in this way "so far from serving the objects of particulars, are calculated to embarrass the fair conduct of the action" and took the view that judges should not to be slow to deal with such pleadings by making special orders as to costs and in a specially bad case they may be forced to treat a pleading of this type as an abuse of the process of the court.[65]

(ii) Particulars of Damage
5.024 Rule 5(1) also requires particulars of any personal injuries suffered and special damages. Apart from enabling the opposing party to prepare for trial, an

---

[61] (1957) 93 ILR 108.
[62] *Ibid.* at 110. See, to the same effect, *per* Lord MacDermott LCJ in *Atkinson v Stewart and Partners Ltd* [1954] NI 146, 153.
[63] [1954] NI 146.
[64] *Ibid.* at 165.
[65] *Ibid.* at 165.

additional reason for requiring such particulars is that the great majority of personal injury cases settle before trial and those particulars greatly assist that process. However, it must be said that, quite often, these particulars set out a considerable amount of evidence in the statement of claim contrary to Order 19, rule 3.

Allegations of Fraud

5.025 The long established practice of the courts has been to require allegations of fraud to be specially pleaded.[66] Rule 5(2) now provides that, in all cases alleging misrepresentation, fraud, breach of trust, wilful or undue influence[67] and in all other cases in which particulars may be necessary, particulars (with dates and items if necessary) must be set out in the pleadings. The rationale of this requirement was explained by Barrington J in *Hanly v Finnerty*[68] in relation to a plea of undue influence as follows:

> Undue influence is a plea similar to fraud and it appears to me that it would be quite unfair to require a party against whom a plea of undue influence is made to go into court without any inkling of the allegations of fact on which the plea of undue influence rests. Because of the seriousness of the plea counsel will not lightly put his name to a pleading containing a plea of undue influence so that his solicitor will usually have in his possession some allegations of fact which justify the raising of the plea or at least excuse the plea from being irresponsible.[69]

Thus, a party is not only required to expressly plead fraud or misrepresentation *etc.*,[70] but he must also give full particulars of its nature and how it is alleged to have occurred.[71] However, it should be noted that, given the difficulty of proving fraudulent intention, malice or any other condition of the mind (which is often a matter of inference to be drawn from the proven facts), it suffices to allege this as a fact without setting out the circumstances from which the same is to be inferred.[72]

---

[66] *Barclay v McHugh* (1878) 12 ILTR 176.
[67] See *Hanly v Finnerty* [1981] ILRM 198, where it was held by Barrington J that the necessity to provide particulars of undue influence extended to probate cases.
[68] [1981] ILRM 198.
[69] *Ibid.* at 202.
[70] *Doyle v Hort* (1878) 12 ILTR 172; *Roper v Cox* (1882) 10 LR Ir 200, 203. *Cf. Byrne v Muzio* (1881) 8 LR Ir 396.
[71] *Barclay v McHugh* (1878) 12 ILTR 176; *Bastow v Bradshaw* (1881) 8 LR Ir 30. *Cf. Moore v McGlynn* [1894] 1 IR 74. *Cf. Kingston v Corker* (1892) 29 LR Ir 364.
[72] Order 19, rule 22.

Debt

5.026 Order 19, rule 5(3) provides that, in any case where the particulars, being of debt, expenses or damages, exceed three folios that fact must be stated with a reference to full particulars already delivered or to be delivered with the pleadings.[73]

Seeking Further and Better Particulars

5.027 In any case where a party is unsure of the case that he has to meet or is concerned that he may be surprised at the trial, he can seek further and better particulars of the relevant pleading by serving a notice for particulars. If the opposing party fails to furnish replies thereto, then the party may apply, pursuant to Order 19, rule 7, to compel him to furnish replies.[74] Rule 7 provides that a further and better statement of the nature of a claim or defence, or further and better particulars of any matter stated in any pleading, notice or written proceeding requiring particulars, may in all cases be ordered, upon such terms, as to costs or otherwise, as may be just.

In recent years, there has been an increasing reliance on notices for particulars as a means of ascertaining information about an opponent's case with the service of elaborate and standardised notices now commonplace. This trend has been the subject of judicial criticism with Keane J in *McGee v O'Reilly*[75] cautioning against the use of particulars for purposes other than the elucidation of pleadings:

> In our system of civil litigation, the case is ultimately decided having regard to the oral evidence adduced at the trial. The machinery of pleadings and particulars, while of critical importance in ensuring that the parties know the case that is being advanced against them and that matters extraneous to the issues as thus defined will not be introduced at the trial, is not a substitute for the oral evidence of witnesses and their cross-examination before the trial judge.[76]

Similarly, in *Coyle v Hannan*,[77] the Northern Ireland Court of Appeal emphasised that a defendant cannot obtain particulars of matters which are not alleged

---

[73] *Cf. James v Hunter* (1879) 13 ILT 375.

[74] If a party is not satisfied that sufficient particulars of his opponent's claim has been made, the proper course of action is to bring a motion to compel replies rather than a motion to strike out the pleading on the ground that it fails to disclose a reasonable change of action pursuant to Order 19, rule 28: *Tromso Sparebank v Beirne* High Court (Costello J) 14 March 1988.

[75] [1996] 2 IR 229.

[76] *Ibid.* at 234.

[77] [1974] NI 160.

in the statement of claim and took the view that the notice for particulars in that case was an attempt to serve interrogatories under the guise of seeking particulars which was something that the court would not sanction.[78]

Particulars Which May be Ordered

5.028 In considering whether particulars should be ordered, a court will have regard to the purpose of pleadings as identified by Fitzgerald J in *Mahon v Celbridge Spinning Co. Ltd*.[79] Thus, the general principle is that particulars will be ordered if they are necessary to clarify the issues so that the party requesting them can know the case he has to meet or if there is a danger that he may be taken by surprise at the trial of the action.[80] The courts enjoy a broad discretion in that regard and, as acknowledged by Murnaghan J in *Caulfield v George Bell & Co. Ltd*,[81] the exercise of that discretion will often depend "on a view of fairness or convenience which is essentially a matter of degree".[82]

5.029 The leading case is *McGee v O'Reilly*.[83] The plaintiff was a minor and sought damages against the defendants for alleged negligence arising out of the failure to diagnose meningitis. The first defendant was a medical doctor who had attended the plaintiff at his home on a number of occasions. In relation to one of these occasions, it was alleged that he did not examine the plaintiff and that he advised his parents to continue the medication which the plaintiff was on at the time. In his defence, the defendant denied that no examination had taken place on this occasion and stated that he had advised the plaintiff's parents to bring the plaintiff back to hospital immediately. Arising out of that plea, the first defendant was requested to provide particulars of (i) any symptoms found or observations made by the first named defendant upon examination of the plaintiff on that occasion; (ii) the history allegedly given by the parents of the plaintiff; (iii) any diagnosis made and (iv) the advice allegedly given to the parents of the plaintiff to bring him back to hospital. Not being satisfied with the particulars provided, the plaintiff brought a motion for further and better particulars.

Applying the tests laid down in *Mahon*, Keane J held that the plaintiff was not entitled to the particulars sought. The defendant had specifically pleaded that he visited the plaintiff on the particular occasion and advised his parents to

---

[78] See also *Lister v Thompson* (1890) 7 TLR 107.

[79] [1967] IR 1, 3.

[80] *McGee v O'Reilly* [1996] 2 IR 229, 233; *Behan v Medical Council* [1993] 3 IR 523, [1993] ILRM 240. *Cf. Jevens v Marine Transport Services Ltd* Supreme Court, 5 December 1972; *Atkinson v Stewart and Partners Ltd* [1954] NI 146; *Savage v Kirk* (1906) 40 ILTR 82; *Lynch v Dublin, Wicklow and Wexford Railway* (1901) 40 ILTR 83n, 1 NIJR 233.

[81] (1957) 93 ILTR 108.

[82] *Ibid.* at 111.

[83] [1996] 2 IR 229.

bring him to hospital immediately. So far as this part of the case was concerned, the issues were defined between the parties and would be confined at the trial to matters relevant to those issues. There was no ground on which it could be suggested that the trial of the action could conclude with the plaintiff having been taken at a disadvantage by the introduction of matters which could not fairly be ascertained from the defence. At the very least, the plaintiff knew in broad outline what was going to be said at the trial in relation to the visit.

5.030 A similar approach was taken in *Behan v Medical Council*.[84] The plaintiff, a consultant psychiatrist, was the subject of an inquiry by the first defendant following a complaint made by one of the plaintiff's patients. The plaintiff obtained leave to seek an order of prohibition by way of judicial review to prevent the inquiry and pursuant to the order granting leave, he delivered a statement of claim. The first defendant then delivered a defence which constituted a direct traverse of the plaintiff's claim. The plaintiff served a notice for particulars in relation to the defence and, being dissatisfied with the replies thereto, he brought a motion seeking to compel the first defendant to provide further and better particulars. In the High Court, Morris J, having referred to the decision in *Mahon* and having considered the notice for particulars and the replies thereto, held that the plaintiff was fully informed of all matters arising from the first defendant's defence and that an order for further and better particulars was unnecessary.[85] His conclusion was upheld on appeal by the Supreme Court[86] with Finlay CJ going so far as to describe the notices for particulars as an abuse of the processes of the court.

5.031 In *Cooney v Browne*,[87] Henchy J distinguished between the situation where particulars are sought in order to plead and that where they are sought for the purpose of the hearing. In the latter case, he said that "they should not be ordered unless they are necessary or desirable for the purpose of a fair hearing".[88] This would be the case where the pleading in question was so general or imprecise that the other side did not know the case he would have to meet at the trial. In those circumstances, he would be entitled to such particulars as would inform him of the range of evidence (as distinct from any particular items of

---

[84] [1993] 3 IR 523, [1993] ILRM 240.
[85] In reaching that conclusion, he appears to have acceded to the submission of counsel for the first named defendant that, *per* Astbury J in *Weinberger v Inglis* [1918] 1 Ch 133, 137: "As a general rule the court never orders a defendant to give particulars of facts and matters which the plaintiff has to prove in order to succeed and this is especially the case where the defendant has confined himself to putting the plaintiff to the proof of allegations in the statement of claim, the onus of establishing which lies upon him."
[86] Supreme Court, 27 January 1993.
[87] [1985] IR 185.
[88] *Ibid.* at 191.

evidence) that he would have to deal with at the trial. In the instant case, the defendant was ordered to provide particulars of a rolled-up plea in its defence to a libel action on the basis that:

> In this case, the factual elements of the article complained of are so numerous and so unspecific that it would be unfair to expect the plaintiff to come to court and present his case properly without knowing in advance the true range of the factual case that will be presented in support of the rolled-up plea. It would, of course, be unfair to require the defendants to make a detailed disclosure of their evidence in advance, but all they are asked to do is to identify the matters in the article which they claim to be matters of fact and to state the facts which they intend to prove at the trial for the purpose of supporting those factual statements in the article.[89]

The learned judge concluded that such disclosure was not unfair and indeed was highly desirable, if not necessary, in the interests of a fair trial.

The extent to which a party can refuse to furnish replies to a notice for particulars on the basis that the matter is within the knowledge of the party making the request is unclear. In *Fanin & Co. Ltd v Surgical Distributors Ltd*[90] the Supreme Court held that a plaintiff in a libel action could not be compelled to furnish particulars of the names and addresses of the person to whom publication was made except in special circumstances. Walsh J, delivering the judgment of the court, stated that the principle underlying this conclusion was that the defendant was usually in a better position than anybody to know to whom he had published the alleged libel. However, in *Shepperton Investment Co. Ltd v Concast (1975) Ltd*[91] Barron J took the view that, even where a matter is within his knowledge, a party is entitled to tie his opponent to a particular case to ensure that he will not be taken by surprise at the trial of the action.

Time at Which Particulars May be Sought

5.032 Particulars may be sought at any stage in the proceedings either before or after the pleadings have closed. However, an order compelling replies to particulars may be refused if a party has delayed unduly in bringing the application.[92] Particulars will not be ordered to be delivered before the defence or reply, as appropriate, unless the court is of the opinion that they are necessary or desirable to enable the defendant or plaintiff, as the case may be, to plead or ought for any other special reason to be so delivered.[93]

---

[89] *Ibid.* at 191-2.
[90] Supreme Court, 27 February 1975.
[91] High Court (Barron J) 21 December 1992
[92] *Tromso Sparebank v Beirne* High Court (Costello J) 14 March 1988.
[93] Order 19, rule 7(3).

Particulars Which May be Furnished

5.033 Any particulars furnished must fall within the four corners of the relevant pleading and, while they can clarify and elaborate upon the pleading, they cannot amplify or alter any claim made therein.[94] If a party wishes to do this, then he will have to amend the underlying pleading.

Continuing Obligation to Provide Particulars

5.034 A party is required to furnish particulars on the basis of the facts as they are known at the time of pleadings[95] and is not under a general continuing obligation to provide updated or supplementary particulars. However, if new information comes to light in relation to matters of which particulars have been provided and which could cause surprise if relied upon, then the party should furnish supplemental particulars or otherwise put the opposing party on notice.[96]

Failure to Provide Particulars

5.035 If a party, having been ordered to do so, fails to provide particulars, then an order may be made striking out the relevant pleading or the proceedings. The inherent jurisdiction of the court to do this was confirmed in *Church & General Insurance plc v Moore*.[97] The respondent claimed a sum by way of summary summons and, the matter having been adjourned to plenary hearing, the respondent sought particulars of the defence delivered on behalf of the appellant. These were not forthcoming and the respondent obtained an order in the High Court compelling the appellant to deliver certain particulars. This order was not complied with and, by consent, it was subsequently ordered that the particulars be delivered by a certain date and in default of doing so, the defence of the appellant would be struck out. The replies to particulars were not delivered and the High Court ordered that the defence be struck out. However, a stay was placed on the order for two weeks and it was provided that in the event of the appellant complying with the previous orders within that period and paying into court to the credit of the action a sum of £50,000, execution would be further stayed pending the trial of the action. The appellant provided the particulars required and appealed to the Supreme Court against the requirement to pay money into court.

As to the question of whether the trial judge had been entitled to make an order striking out the defence of the appellant to the proceedings, Hamilton CJ, delivering the judgment of the court, took the view that:

---

[94] *Cf. Fahy v Pullen* (1968) 102 ILTR 81.
[95] *Fahy v Pullen* (1968) 102 ILTR 81.
[96] *Fahy v Pullen* (1968) 102 ILTR 81; *O'Driscoll v Irish Shell and BP Ltd* [1968] IR 215.
[97] [1996] 1 ILRM 202. *Cf. Fagan v Burgess* High Court (Barron J) 29 January 1997.

> While the Rules of the Superior Courts do not specifically provide for the striking out of a defence in the event of failure to comply with an order made by the court to provide "further and better particulars", as is provided in the event of failure to answer interrogatories or make discovery of documents, I am satisfied that a court has an inherent jurisdiction to enforce orders made by it and if there is failure to comply with an order, then in certain circumstances an order can be made dismissing a claim for want of prosecution or striking out a defence.[98]

In order for this to occur, there had to be: (i) an order that further and better particulars be provided; (ii) the imposition of terms; (iii) the provision that if the order is not complied with within a certain time, the action shall be dismissed or the defence struck out. These conditions were satisfied here and therefore the trial judge had been entitled to make an order striking out the defence. However, he concluded that the trial judge had no jurisdiction to impose a stay requiring the payment of monies into court because the court was thereby imposing a penalty on the appellant for failure to comply with the orders of the court and the inherent jurisdiction of the court and the power given by Order 19, rule 7 is for the purpose of ensuring compliance with orders made by the court. The requirement to pay into court the sum of £50,000 was not necessary to secure compliance with the orders of the court.

Failure to Seek Particulars

5.036 If a party does not seek particulars, it follows that he is satisfied that he knows the case that he has to meet and he cannot, thereafter, be heard to complain at the trial that he has been taken by surprise by the introduction of evidence relating to any matter which fairly arises from the pleadings.[99] As O'Daly J stated in *MacNaughton v Murphy*,[100] "a defendant who does not choose to seek any further particulars of a broad allegation … must not complain if something capable of being brought within it but which he did not expect confronts him at the trial".[101] In *P.W. v CIE*,[102] objection was taken by the defendant to the admission of evidence as to the certain adverse *sequelae* of personal injuries suffered by the plaintiff. It was held by the Supreme Court that if the defendants desired to have the information necessary to enable them to meet the plaintiff's case, they should have sought particulars of the *sequelae* of the injuries alleged in addition to seeking particulars of those injuries. Walsh J observed that:

---

[98] *Ibid.* at 208. See also *Davey v Bentinck* [1893] 1 QB 185.
[99] *Hewson v Cleeve* [1904] 2 IR 536.
[100] [1961] Ir Jur Rep 41.
[101] *Ibid.* at 44.
[102] [1967] IR 137.

> Any particular injury may provide several *sequelae*…. It therefore be-
> hoves every defendant, who looks for the necessary information to enable
> him to meet the plaintiff's case, to seek not only particulars of the injuries
> alleged, but also to seek information as to the *sequelae*…. If the defend-
> ant does not ask for particulars of *sequelae*, he can scarcely be heard to
> complain that he was not furnished with any.[103]

Similarly, if a party seeks further and better particulars, he cannot complain of
inadequate replies[104] or the late delivery[105] or non-delivery of replies thereto if
he fails to issue a motion to compel replies. However, a party who refuses to
provide particulars when requested may be held strictly to what he has pleaded
with any ambiguity construed against him.[106]

Procedure

5.037 Where a party desires particulars, the first step is to apply to the other
party for the particulars by means of a Notice for Particulars.[107] If the party is
dissatisfied with the replies furnished, he should then write to the other party
identifying the inadequacies in the replies and requesting further and better particulars.[108] If the other party still fails or refuses to provide the requested particulars, then a motion may be brought seeking an order compelling replies.
This application is brought in the High Court by way of motion on notice to the
party from whom the replies are sought.[109]

An order for particulars does not operate as a stay of the proceedings but if
the court makes an order compelling a party to provide replies, the applicant
has, unless the order otherwise provides, the same length of time for pleading
after the delivery of the particulars that he had at the date of the service of the
notice of the application.[110]

---

[103] *Ibid.* at 141.

[104] *P.W. v CIE* [1967] IR 137, *cf. Shepperton Investment Co. Ltd v Concast (1975) Ltd*
High Court (Barron J) 21 December 1992 where it was held that, where a partial reply
is given that limits the issue, then the other party by not following up the matter must
accept any amplification of the answer at the trial which does not go beyond the limit
set by the answer.

[105] *Houlihan v O'Sullivan* (1930) 64 ILTR 178.

[106] *Shepperton Investment Co. Ltd v Concast (1975) Ltd* High Court (Barron J) 21 December 1992.

[107] Order 19, rule 7(2).

[108] In *Tromso Sparebank v Beirne* High Court (Costello J) 14 March 1988, Costello J
stated that a party applying to compel replies would be in danger of losing the costs of
the motion if he did not write a letter indicating in what respects the reply is inadequate.

[109] Order 52, rule 2 and *cf.* Order 63, rule 1.

[110] Order 19, rule 8.

PLEADING IN PLENARY PROCEEDINGS

Introduction

5.038 The pleadings in a High Court plenary action are:

(i)   plenary summons

(ii) appearance

(iii) statement of claim

(iv) defence

(v)   reply.

The first two pleadings have been discussed in Chapter Two and Four respectively and, therefore, only the last three are examined below.

Statement of Claim

5.039 The statement of claim is the document which sets out the plaintiff's claim and the relief sought. In the words of O'Byrne J in *Irish People's Assurance Society v City of Dublin Assurance Co.*,[111] the object of a statement of claim "is to show the defendant the case which is being made against him, and which he has to meet at the trial of the action".[112]

Requirement for a Statement of Claim

5.040 A statement of claim is not required to be delivered unless the defendant when entering his appearance, or within 8 days thereafter, gives notice in writing to the plaintiff or his solicitor that he requires a statement of claim to be delivered.[113] Thus, no statement of claim need be delivered if the defendant fails to enter an appearance unless the plaintiff wishes to proceed to judgment in default of appearance.[114] If the plaintiff delivers a statement of claim without being required to do so, or the defendant unnecessarily requires it, the court may make such order as to the costs occasioned thereby as shall be just.[115]

---

[111] [1928] IR 204, 207.

[112] This statement was approved by Murnaghan J in *Caulfield v George Bell & Co. Ltd* (1957) 93 ILTR 108, 110, who opined that insufficient emphasis was placed on the latter part of the quotation.

[113] Order 20, rules 2 & 3. *Cf.* rule 5 dealing with probate actions.

[114] Order 20, rule 4.

[115] Order 20, rule 4.

Delivery of the Statement of Claim

5.041 The plaintiff may, if he wishes, deliver the statement of claim with the plenary summons or notice in lieu thereof[116] and this is frequently done. Otherwise, it must be delivered within 21 days from the receipt of notice from the defendant that he requires a statement of claim.[117]

Contents of Statement of Claim

5.042 The statement of claim must set out the plaintiff's claim and the relief sought with clarity and particularity in accordance with the principles of pleading set out above. Thus, it should state specifically the relief which the plaintiff claims, either simply or in the alternative.[118] If the plaintiff seeks relief in respect of several distinct claims or causes of action founded upon separate and distinct grounds, they should be stated, so far as possible, separately and distinctly.[119] It should be noted that there is nothing to prevent the plaintiff setting up two or more separate claims and claiming relief in respect thereto in the alternative.[120]

Amplification of the Plaintiff's Case

5.043 Order 20, rule 6 provides that whenever a statement of claim is delivered the plaintiff may therein alter, modify or extend his claim without any amendment of the indorsement on the summons. However, it was held in *Moore v Alwill*[121] that it is not possible to add, under the guise of amplification, a new and distinct cause of action not covered by the indorsement of the summons and such an amendment was liable to be set aside. So, in *Teevan v Cavan Creameries Ltd*,[122] it was held that it was not possible for the plaintiff to add in to his statement of claim, a claim for damages for libel which had not been made in his plenary summons. Where it becomes necessary to make an amendment of this nature, the plaintiff should first obtain leave to amend the plenary summons.

Brussels Convention

5.044 Special provision is made in Order 19 with regard to claims falling within

---

[116] Order 20, rule 2.

[117] Order 20, rule 2.

[118] Order 20, rule 7. Although it is common practice to do so, it is not necessary to ask for general or other relief which may always be given, as the court may think just, to the same extent as if it had been asked for.

[119] See *Hoban v McPherson* (1878) 1 LR Ir 564; *Doyle v Hort* (1878) 12 ILTR 172.

[120] *Cf. Phonographic Performance (Ireland) Ltd v Cody* [1998] 4 IR 504, [1994] 2 ILRM 241 (HC).

[121] (1881) 8 LR Ir 245.

[122] (1903) 3 NIJR 306.

the scope of the Brussels Convention. Rule 3A[123] provides that where a statement of claim concerns a claim which, by virtue of the Jurisdiction of Courts and Enforcement of Judgments Act 1998, the court has power to hear and determine, it must be endorsed with: (i) a statement that the court has power under the 1998 Act to hear and determine the claim specifying the particular provision or provisions of the Brussels Convention in respect of which the court should assume jurisdiction; and (ii) a statement that no proceedings between the parties concerning the same cause of action is pending between the parties in another contracting state.

Defence and Counterclaim

5.045 The function of the defence is to put the plaintiff on proof of those matters which the defendant requires him to prove and also to set out the defence of the defendant to the proceedings including any set-off or counterclaim he may have.

Delivery of the Defence

5.046 If a defendant enters an appearance to a plenary summons, then he is required to deliver his defence and counterclaim (if any): (a) if he does not require a statement of claim, within 28 days from the entry of appearance; or (b) in any other case within 28 days from the date of delivery of the statement of claim or from the time limited for appearance, whichever is later.[124] Delivery of the defence after the expiration of the relevant time is permissible without the leave of the court[125] unless the late delivery causes prejudice to the plaintiff as where the case has been fixed for trial.[126]

Contents of Defence

5.047 The defence must state clearly and intelligibly set forth the defendant's defence to the proceedings including any set-off or counterclaim which it is sought to assert. If the defendant seeks to assert several distinct defences and/or counterclaims founded on separate and distinct grounds, they should be stated, so far as possible, separately and distinctly.[127] If the defendant so wishes, he may set up mutually inconsistent defences.[128] It is not necessary to deny damages claimed or their amount because these are deemed to be put in issue in all cases unless expressly admitted.[129]

---

[123] Inserted by the Rules of the Superior Courts (No. 1) 1989 (SI No. 14 of 1989).
[124] Order 21, rule 1.
[125] *Schofield v Skehan* (1880) 14 ILTR 26; *Kennane v Mackey* (1889) 24 LR Ir 495.
[126] *Wilson v Noble* (1884) 11 LR Ir 546.
[127] *Cf. Hoban v McPherson* (1878) 1 LR Ir 564; *Doyle v Hort* (1878) 12 ILTR 172.
[128] *Phonographic Performance (Ireland) Ltd v Cody* [1998] 4 IR 504, [1994] 2 ILRM 241 (HC).
[129] Order 21, rule 6.

Set-off and Counterclaim[130]

5.048 Order 19, rule 2 provides that a defendant in any action may set-off, or set up by way of counterclaim against the claims of the plaintiff, any right or claim, whether such set-off or counterclaim sounds in damages or not subject to the discretion of the court to refuse the defendant to avail of it if, in the opinion of the court, such set-off or counterclaim cannot be conveniently disposed of in the pending action. The application of this rule is considered in conjunction with Order 21, rule 14 below.[131]

Such set-off or counterclaim has the same effect as a cross action, enabling the court to pronounce a final judgment in the same action, both on the original and on the cross claim. In addition, if the set-off or counterclaim is established as a defence against the plaintiff's claim, the court may, if the balance is in favour of the defendant, give judgment for the defendant for such balance, or may otherwise adjudge to the defendant such relief as he may be entitled to upon the merits of the case.[132]

Drafting of a Counterclaim

5.049 Order 21, rule 9 requires a defendant, who seeks to rely upon any grounds as supporting a right of counterclaim, to state specifically that he does so by way of counterclaim. This requirement is usually satisfied by distinguishing the counterclaim from the main body of the defence by means of a separate heading.[133] However, it is not necessary to repeat in the counterclaim, facts which are set out in the defence provided that they are adopted for the purpose of the counterclaim.[134]

Independence of Counterclaim

5.050 As stated, the counterclaim sets up a cross-action which is independent of the plaintiff's claim. Therefore, if the action of the plaintiff is stayed, discontinued, or dismissed, the counterclaim may nevertheless be proceeded with.[135] For example, in *Seddon's Pneumatic Tyre Co. v Sweeny*,[136] a defendant applied to dismiss an action for want of prosecution and for judgment on a counterclaim to which a reply had been delivered. The court granted the application for a dismissal but went on to rule on the counterclaim holding that it was an independent action.

---

[130] *Cf. Ryan v Fraser* (1884) 16 LR Ir 253 as to the difference between a set-off and a counterclaim.

[131] See paragrahs 5.052–5.054.

[132] Order 21, rule 16. *Cf. Hannan v Laffan* (1881) 15 ILTR 32; *Ryan v Fraser* (1884) 16 LR Ir 253.

[133] *Cf. Robins v McDonnell* (1879) 13 ILTR 91.

[134] *Morony v Guest* (1878) 1 LR Ir 564.

[135] Order 21, rule 15.

[136] (1895) 29 ILTR 96.

Counterclaims Against Third Persons

5.051 Order 21, rule 10[137] permits a defendant to set out a counterclaim against third persons who are not parties to the proceedings in addition to a counter-claim against the plaintiff.[138] However, this can only be done where there is a connection between the third person made a defendant to the proceedings and the original cause of action[139] and between the relief sought against the third person and that sought against the plaintiff.[140] Where that third person is not already a party to the action, he must be made a party to the action by being served with the defence.[141] Thereafter, that party may deliver a reply to the counterclaim.[142] It is important to note that, regardless of the fact that the third person may not be made a party to the proceedings until some considerable period of time after they have commenced, for the purposes of the Statute of Limitations, the proceedings against that person are considered to have been commenced on the same date as the original action.[143]

Separate Trial of a Counterclaim

5.052 It is not necessary that a counterclaim relate to the claim(s) made by the plaintiff in his statement of claim. In *Quinn v Hession*,[144] Palles CB expressed the view that:

> [U]pon the true construction of the Judicature Act, and the Rules for carrying it into effect, any claim of a defendant against a plaintiff, whether connected or disconnected with the original subject-matter of the action, can be made the subject of a counter-claim.... the power of counter-claim-

---

[137] Rule 10 provides that: "Where a defendant by his defence sets up any counterclaim which raises questions between himself and the plaintiff along with any other persons, he shall add to the title of his defence a further title similar to the title in a statement of claim setting forth the names of all the persons who, if such counterclaim were to be enforced by the cross-action, would be defendants to such cross-action, and shall deliver his defence to such of them as are parties to the action within the period within which he is required to deliver it to the plaintiff."

[138] *Cf. Arthur v Arthur* (1879) 3 LR Ir 1 (relief in the counterclaim must be sought against the plaintiff as well as against third parties).

[139] *O'Connor v Anderson* (1880) 14 ILTR 14.

[140] *Barclay v McHugh* (1878) 12 ILTR 176. *Cf. Quinn v Hession* (1878) 4 LR Ir 35.

[141] Order 21, rule 11. Service is regulated in accordance with the rules applied to the service of a summons and every defence so served must be indorsed in the Form No. 3 in Appendix C. Rule 12 provides that the third person served with the defence and counterclaim must appear thereto as if he had been served with a summons to appear in an action.

[142] Order 21, rule 14. This must be done within the time limited for delivery of a defence to a statement of claim.

[143] *Strick v Treacy* High Court (O'Hanlon J) 10 June 1993.

[144] (1878) 4 LR Ir 35.

ing by the defendant against the plaintiff [i]s to be limited by convenience, and by convenience alone.[145]

It is, therefore, possible that a counterclaim could raise matters which are entirely unrelated to the plaintiff's claim and which cannot be conveniently dealt with in conjunction therewith. For this reason, Order 21, rule 14 provides that the plaintiff or other party to a counterclaim may, at any time before delivering his reply, apply to the court for an order that such counterclaim ought to be excluded and the claim raised thereby disposed of in an independent action. On the hearing of such an application, the court is empowered to make such order as shall be just.

5.053 The construction of rule 14 was considered in *Scofish International Ltd v Owners of MV "Anton Lopatin"*[146] where Barr J said that:

> This rule makes it clear that it lies within the discretion of the court to decide whether a defendant should be permitted to include a counterclaim with his defence and that in deciding whether it is proper to allow such a claim to be brought in this action, the court must review the situation and endeavour to do justice between the parties having regard to all of the circumstances.[147]

That case involved a dispute arising out of the provisioning of a fishing vessel. After the institution of proceedings, the parties entered into an agreement to prorogate the exclusive jurisdiction of the High Court in Ireland to try the dispute. Subsequently, the defendant delivered a defence and counterclaim in which it counterclaimed for an alleged breach of contract on the part of the plaintiffs, wrongful arrest of its shipping vessel and libel.

The plaintiffs submitted that, having regard to the terms of the prorogation agreement, it was not open to the defendant to bring the counterclaims because their consent to the jurisdiction of the Irish High Court was specifically limited to the determination of their claims in the action and did not include any counterclaim that the defendant might bring. It was also submitted that, in all the circumstances, the court should exercise its discretion against the defendant and direct that its counterclaim for libel should be tried as a separate cause of action. The defendant, however, submitted that it was clear at all times to the plaintiffs that it intended to counterclaim.

Barr J rejected, as not well-founded, the submission of the plaintiffs that the defendant had no authority to counterclaim in the action having regard to the terms of the prorogation agreement. He stated that the defendant's counterclaim

---

[145] *Ibid.* at 41.
[146] High Court (Barr J) 18 October 1994.
[147] *Ibid.* at 6.

for damages for alleged breach concerned the same agreement which was the basis for the plaintiffs' claim and were all intimately connected. Furthermore, he found that the defendant's intention to counterclaim was known to the plaintiffs when the jurisdiction agreement was entered into by the parties. Although it did not specifically refer to any counterclaim arising out of the contract between the parties, he took the view that in making the prorogation agreement as to jurisdiction, the likelihood was that the parties had in mind that the Irish court was being clothed with jurisdiction to deal with all aspects of the contract in question. Furthermore, the parties specifically agreed that their dispute would be tried according to Irish law which includes a defendant's right to counterclaim arising out of the same transaction which was the subject matter of the plaintiffs' claim, subject to the discretion of the court to disallow it pursuant to rule 14. He, therefore, concluded that the defendant's counterclaim for damages for inducing breach of contract and damages for the alleged wrongful arrest of the vessel all arose out of the same business relationship which was the subject-matter of the plaintiffs' claim and was, therefore, properly within the ambit of the counterclaim in the action.

He then went on to consider the defendant's counterclaim for libel which he said raised two issues for consideration. The first was whether it was so closely related to the issues raised in the plaintiffs' claim that for convenience it should be dealt with in the action by way of counterclaim. The second was whether the court should authorise the proposed counterclaim in the instant action even though the plaintiffs were entitled to have that particular issue tried by jury. The learned judge said that the crucial factor was that the plaintiffs had a *prima facie* right to have the issue of defamation tried by jury. The other issues raised in the action were not justiciable by jury. He was, therefore, satisfied that if the defendants wished to persist in bringing an action for libel against the plaintiffs, then they should await the outcome of the instant action. He therefore acceded to the plaintiffs' application that the defendant's claim for defamation should not proceed in the instant action by way of counterclaim but, if brought, should be the subject-matter of a separate action.

5.054 The convenience of trying a counterclaim together with the action of the plaintiff was also considered in *McCarthy v McNulty*,[148] in the context of an application by the defendants for leave to amend the defence in order to include a counterclaim. The plaintiff claimed damages for personal injuries arising out of an accident involving a car owned by him but driven by another uninsured driver. A number of other actions arising out of the accident had been settled by the second named defendant, the Motor Insurers' Bureau of Ireland, and it sought to amend the defence to include a counterclaim for the monies paid to settle those actions. The plaintiff resisted this application on the basis that the issues

---

[148] Supreme Court, 22 October 1999.

raised were complex and difficult and that it would not be convenient or just to permit the counterclaim to proceed. Leave to amend was granted in the High Court and the plaintiff appealed.

Denham J, delivering the judgment of the Supreme Court, stated that the inherent jurisdiction of the courts together with the jurisdiction conferred by Order 19, rule 2 and Order 21, rule 14 enable the court to exercise its discretion. In the instant case, this had been exercised in favour of allowing the counterclaim and there was no evidence that it would be inconvenient, embarrassing or unjust to the plaintiff to allow the counterclaim to be tried. She went on to say that:

> In considering the issues of convenience and justice the criteria proposed by [counsel for the defendants] are relevant. It is desirable to have finality in litigation, multiplicity of suits should be avoided and it is very important to take steps to reduce the costs of litigation.[149]

She acknowledged that the counterclaim raised serious and complex issues but concluded that, in all the circumstances of the case, they could be conveniently disposed of in the pending action and the justice of the situation favoured that course.

Reply and Subsequent Pleadings

Delivery of a Reply

5.055 It is not necessary to deliver a reply where its purpose would merely be to deny and put in issue all material statements of fact in the defence.[150] Therefore, a reply will, generally, only be delivered if the plaintiff wishes to plead a defence to the set-off or counterclaim of the defendant. In those circumstances, the reply will function as a defence in the cross-action created by the counterclaim and is subject to the same rules.[151] If the plaintiff decides to deliver a reply, then this must be done within 14 days from the delivery of the defence or the last of the defences unless that period is extended by the court[152] or by consent in writing.[153]

---

[149] *Ibid.* at 7.

[150] Order 23, rule 1 and Order 27, rule 11. *Cf.* Order 19, rule 18 which provides that, the plaintiff by his reply may join issue upon the defence and such joinder of issue will operate as a denial of every material allegation of fact in the pleading upon which the issue is joined, but it may except any facts which the party may be willing to admit, and shall then operate as a denial of the facts not so admitted.

[151] Order 23, rule 5.

[152] Order 23, rule 2.

[153] Order 122, rule 8.

Contents of a Reply

5.056 The rules applicable to the contents of a defence discussed above apply equally to a reply.[154] Thus, it is not sufficient for the plaintiff in his reply to deny generally the grounds alleged in a defence by way of counterclaim and he is required to deal specifically with each allegation of fact in the defence of which he does not admit the truth except damages.[155] It should be noted that the reply is a separate pleading to the statement of claim and, if the plaintiff wishes to rely on any facts in the statement of claim for the purpose of the reply, then express reference to the statement of claim should be made.[156]

A cardinal rule is that a reply can only deal with matters raised in the defence and cannot raise any new ground or claim or contain any allegation of fact inconsistent with the statement of claim.[157] For example, in *Taggart v Hunter*,[158] the plaintiff sued for a liquidated sum and the defendant in his defence pleaded a debt allegedly due to him by the plaintiff by way of set-off to the plaintiff's claim. It was held that the plaintiff in his reply could not set-off another debt due by the defendant to him but not included in his original claim. Similarly, in *O'Farrell v Stephenson*,[159] the plaintiff in an action for the recovery of land, alleged in his statement of claim a title to the premises sought to be recovered under a particular demise. The defence alleged that this demise had been surrendered and, in his reply, the plaintiff admitted that he did not hold under that demise but alleged a title in himself as representing the lessor under another lease. It was held that the plaintiff's reply should be set aside as having made a case wholly different from that made by the statement of claim.

If a plaintiff wishes to put forward a new or inconsistent claim, then he can only do so by amending his statement of claim.[160]

Rejoinder

5.057 In some cases, a defendant may wish to deliver a rejoinder to the reply of the plaintiff but it is clearly undesirable that the process of exchanging pleadings should go on *ad infinitum*. For this reason, Order 23, rule 3 provides that no pleading subsequent to reply other than a joinder of issue[161] shall be pleaded

---

[154] Order 23, rule 5 which provides that, where a counterclaim is pleaded, a reply thereto shall be subject to the rules applicable to a defence.
[155] Order 19, rule 17.
[156] *O'Grady v Warren* (1878) 12 ILTR 150.
[157] Order 19, rule 16. See *Taggart v Hunter* (1893) 27 ILTR 95; *O'Farrell v Stephenson* (1878) 12 ILTR 81; *Duckworth v McClelland* (1878) 12 ILTR 169. *Cf. Kidd v Kidd* (1884) 18 ILTR 5; *O'Sullivan v Hamilton* (1881) 15 ILTR 96; *Kingston v Corker* (1892) 29 LR Ir 365; *Byrne v Figatner* (1903) 37 ILTR 153.
[158] (1893) 27 ILTR 95.
[159] (1878) 12 ILTR 81.
[160] *Keane v Ryan* (1942) 76 ILTR 69; *Duckworth v McClelland* (1878) 12 ILTR 169.
[161] It should be noted that Order 27, rule 11 stipulates that when the pleadings close, all material statements of fact in the pleading last delivered shall be deemed to have been

without leave of the court, and then only upon such terms as the court shall think fit.[162] Such will be granted very sparingly because, as explained by Johnson J in *Great Horseless Carriage Co. v Flanagan*,[163] "[s]ince the Judicature Act every court has set itself against unnecessary length of pleadings, and now if the matter can be disposed of on the ordinary pleadings leave will not be given to file special pleadings."

In *Johnson, Mahony & Co. v Kelly*,[164] an application was made *ex parte* for leave to deliver a rejoinder. The action was brought for a balance on a stock-broker's account. The defence pleaded a special settlement and the reply alleged a special term. The defendant then sought to rejoin, pleading a waiver of the special term. However, Murphy J took the view that "it was against the spirit of the Judicature Act and modern pleading to allow pleading after reply, where by any possibility it could be avoided." In the instant case, the plea of waiver could have been pleaded in the defence (though in anticipation) and he refused to give liberty to deliver a rejoinder, giving liberty instead to amend the defence. A similar course of action was taken by Johnson J in *Great Horseless Carriage Co. v Flanagan*.[165]

If leave to deliver a rejoinder is given, then this must be delivered within four days of the delivery of the reply unless time is extended by the court.[166]

Closure of Pleadings

5.058 If the plaintiff does not deliver a reply, or the defendant does not deliver a rejoinder within the period allowed for that purpose, the pleadings are deemed to be closed at the expiration of that period.[167] In *Webb v Kerr*,[168] it was held that a reply delivered outside the time limited for reply was irregular and that pleadings had closed and could not be re-opened without the leave of the court. However, the provisions of Order 122, rule 8 should be noted which provides that the time for delivering any pleading may be enlarged by consent in writing without application to the court.

---

denied and put in issue. Therefore, it is not necessary to deliver a rejoinder to join issue on the reply.

[162] The application for leave should be made on notice: *Monck v Smythe* [1895] 1 IR 200.

[163] (1898) 32 ILTR 152.

[164] (1895) 29 ILTR 128.

[165] (1898) 32 ILTR 152.

[166] Order 23, rule 4.

[167] Order 27, rule 11. See also, Order 23, rule 6 which provides that: "As soon as any party has joined issue upon the preceding pleading of the opposite party simply without adding any further or other pleading thereto, or has made default as mentioned in Order 27, rule 11, the pleadings as between such parties shall be deemed to be closed."

[168] (1884) 14 LR Ir 294.

DEFAULT OF PLEADING

Introduction

5.059 If a party fails to deliver a pleading within the time limited for doing so, then it is open to an opposing party to seek judgment in default of pleading. The procedures for seeking such judgment, which vary according to the pleading which has not been delivered and the type of claim involved, are laid down in Order 27. For ease of exposition, it is proposed to examine the default provisions under the following three headings: (i) default in delivery of a statement of claim; (ii) default in delivery of a defence; and (ii) default in the delivery of other pleadings.

Default in Delivery of Statement of Claim

5.060 Order 27, rule 1 provides that if the plaintiff, being required to do so, does not deliver a statement of claim within the time allowed for that purpose, the defendant may apply to the court to dismiss the action with costs for want of prosecution. On the hearing of such an application, the court may order the action to be dismissed or may make such other order on such terms as the court shall think just.[169] Dismissal of proceedings for want of prosecution is dealt with in Chapter 11 and rule 1 will not be dealt with further here.

Default in Delivery of Defence

Liquidated Claims and other Summary Actions

5.061 If the plaintiff's claim is for a debt or liquidated demand only, or for the recovery of land, or for the delivery of specific goods, and the defendant does not, within the time allowed for that purpose, deliver a defence, the plaintiff may enter final judgment in the Central Office with costs.[170] The form of judgment granted will depend on the nature of the claim. In the case of a claim for a debt or liquidated demand, judgment will be entered for the amount claimed.[171] Alternatively, if the plaintiff's claim is for recovery of land, or for the delivery of specific goods, judgment will be granted, as the case may be, that the person whose title is asserted in the statement of claim recover possession of the land or that the specific goods be delivered without giving the defendant the option of retaining such goods without paying the value thereof.[172] If the plaintiff's claim includes a claim for other relief such as damages, then he may enter final

---

[169] Order 27, rule 1.

[170] Order 27, rule 2.

[171] Order 27, rule 2. This rule must be read subject to rule 15 (dealing with actions by moneylenders) and rule 16 (actions to recover a debt or liquidated demand arising under a hire-purchase agreement or credit-sale agreement).

[172] Order 27, rule 2.

judgment as outlined for the summary portion of his claim and then apply in accordance with the rules governing judgment in default of defence in the case of unliquidated claims.[173] If there are multiple defendants, and one of them defaults, then the plaintiff may enter final judgement against the defendant in default and issue execution without prejudice to his right to proceed with his action against the other defendants.[174]

Where the claim is for a debt or liquidated demand, judgment by default cannot be entered until an affidavit of debt specifying the sum then actually due has been filed.[175]

Unliquidated Claims

5.062 Default in the delivery of a defence in respect of claims other than those dealt with above is governed by rules 8, 9 and 10 of Order 27.

21 Day Warning Letter

5.063 If a defendant fails to deliver a defence within the time limited for doing so, the first step is for the plaintiff to write to the defendant giving him notice of his intention to serve a notice of motion for judgment and consenting to the late delivery of the defence within 21 days of the date of the letter. This is an essential precondition to the issue of a motion for judgment in default of defence[176] unless the plaintiff applies *ex parte* and obtains an order for short service from the Master.[177] In order to succeed, the plaintiff will have to establish special reasons making it necessary to serve the motion with greater urgency.[178]

Issue of the Motion

5.064 If no defence is delivered within the 21 day period specified in the warning letter, the plaintiff can serve a notice of motion for judgment in default of defence which is returnable to a date not less than 14 clear days from the date of the service of the notice.[179] If, not later than seven days after the service of notice of the motion for judgment, the defendant delivers a defence to the plaintiff, and not later than six days before the return date lodges a copy thereof in the Central Office with a certified copy of the said notice of motion attached

---

[173] Order 27, rule 3.

[174] Order 27, rule 4.

[175] Order 27, rule 13.

[176] Although Order 27, rule 9(1) only requires a 21 day warning letter in contract and tort cases, the practice is to require it in all cases.

[177] Even if an order is obtained, not less than four clear days notice of the motion must be given to the defendant.

[178] Order 27, rule 9.

[179] Order 27, rule 9(2). The notice of motion must be filed not later than six days before the return date.

thereto, the said motion for judgment will not be put in the judge's list but will be struck out.[180] In that event, the defendant is required to pay to the plaintiff the sum of £100 as costs of the motion.

Notice of Motion

5.065 If the plaintiff's claim is for unliquidated damages, then the notice of motion should seek the following reliefs: (a) an order pursuant to Order 27, rule 8 granting such judgment against the defendant upon the statement of claim as the court shall consider the plaintiff to be entitled to and (b) an order setting the action down for trial by a judge and jury or judge sitting alone as appropriate.[181] If the claim is for equitable relief, then the notice of motion should specify the relief sought and must be grounded upon an affidavit setting out sufficient grounds to enable the court to exercise its discretion in favour of the plaintiff.

Proofs

5.066 The proofs required for the motion are as follows:

(i) The notice of motion.

(ii) The grounding affidavit (if any).

(iii) An affidavit of service of the motion on the defendant.

(iv) A copy of the appearance entered by the defendant.

(v) A copy of the filed statement of claim with a certificate endorsed on it by the plaintiff's solicitor to the effect that no defence has been delivered.

(vi) 21-day warning letter.

Hearing of the Motion

5.067 If the defendant has not delivered the defence before the hearing of the motion, then it is common for him (or his legal advisers) to appear and seek an extension of time within which to file a defence. It is the "virtually invariable practice of the court"[182] to grant an extension of time (usually two to three

---

[180] Order 27, rule 9(3).

[181] Order 27, rule 8 provides that: "Any damages to which the plaintiff may be entitled shall be ascertained by the Judge with a jury in case any party requires and is entitled to one, but otherwise without a jury, and, if without a jury, either by the Judge or by the Master or by the Examiner, as the Judge may direct on evidence by affidavit or otherwise." Rule 10 provides that, if there are several defendants, one of whom defaults in the delivery of his defence, then the plaintiff may (if the cause of action is severable) set down the action at once on motion for judgment against the defendant so making default, or may set it down against him at the time when it is entered for trial or set down on motion for judgment against the other defendants.

[182] *Ewing v Kelly* High Court (O'Sullivan J) 16 May 2000 at 9.

weeks) and, if the plaintiff has sent the required 21 day warning letter, he will generally be awarded the costs of the motion.

If the defendant does not appear, then the court will grant judgment if satisfied as to the service of the notice of motion. However, if the plaintiff is seeking unliquidated damages, the court will not proceed to assess the damages but will, instead, direct that they be assessed at a later date by a judge sitting alone or a judge and jury as appropriate. If equitable relief is sought, this will be granted if the court is satisfied, on the basis of the grounding affidavit, that the plaintiff has established grounds for relief.[183]

It should be noted that where judgment in default of defence is granted, the order will not be drawn unless and until the plaintiff's solicitor lodges with the Registrar (if not already produced to the court) a certificate of no defence, that is a copy of the statement of claim with an indorsement thereon signed by the plaintiff's solicitor dated as of the date of the order that no defence has been delivered to the statement of claim.[184]

Miscellaneous Claims

5.068 Special provision is made in Order 27 in relation to default in delivery of defence by a defendant in proceedings brought for the recovery of land,[185] probate actions,[186] by moneylenders[187] and actions to recover a debt or liquidated demand arising under a hire-purchase agreement or credit-sale agreement.[188]

Default in Delivery of Other Pleadings

5.069 An application for judgment in default will not lie where a plaintiff fails to deliver a reply or a defendant fails to deliver a rejoinder within the time limited for that purpose because of the operation of rule 11 which provides that in that event, the pleadings shall be deemed to be closed at the expiration of that period and all material statements of fact in the pleading last delivered shall be deemed to have been denied and put in issue. However, rule 12 provides that, in any case in which issues arise in an action other than between the plaintiff and defendant (as in a third party action of where a counterclaim is made against a third party who is made defendant to the counterclaim), if any party to any such issue makes default in delivering any pleading, the opposite party may apply to the court for such judgment, if any, as upon the pleadings he may appear to be

---

[183] *Cf. Doherty v Kelly* (1879) 13 ILTR 59 where specific performance of an agreement in writing was sought and no defence was entered by the defendant, it was held that, before granting judgment in default and ordering specific performance, the agreement would have to be produced and proved.

[184] Practice Direction of 26 February 2001.

[185] Rules 5 and 6.

[186] Rule 7.

[187] Rule 15.

[188] Rule 16.

entitled to. On such application, the court may order judgment to be entered accordingly, or make such order as may be necessary to do complete justice between the parties.

Setting Aside Default Judgment

5.070 Order 27, rule 14 provides that any judgment by default, whether under that order or under any other of the Rules, may be set aside by the court upon such terms as to costs or otherwise as the court may think fit. Where an action has been set down under rule 8, such setting down may be dealt with by the court in the same way as if a judgment in default had been signed when the case was set down.

STRIKING OUT PLEADINGS

Introduction

5.071 Order 19 contains two rules which make provision for the striking out of pleadings. Rule 27 deals with the problem of unnecessary or scandalous pleadings and rule 28 with pleadings which do not disclose a reasonable cause of action or defence. Rule 28 is considered in chapter 12 so it is only necessary to deal with the application of rule 27 here.

Unnecessary or Scandalous Pleadings

5.072 Rule 27 confers a broad discretion upon the court to strike out pleadings, providing that:

> The court may at any stage of the proceedings order to be struck out or amended any matter in any indorsement or pleading which may be unnecessary or scandalous, or which may tend to prejudice, embarrass, or delay the fair trial of the action; and may in any such case, if it shall think fit, order the costs of the application to be paid as between solicitor and client.

Speaking of the contemporary equivalent of rule 27, Chatterton VC in *Morony v Guest*,[189] referred to its antecedence and stated that:

> This beneficial rule affords a ready and simple remedy for what was formerly the subject of formal objection, and extends it to matters not the subject of objection. But the rule is not to be abused, nor are pleadings to

---

[189] (1878) 1 LR Ir 564.

be scanned too finely, with regard to the power of amendment conferred, nor can a party dictate to his opponent how he ought to plead. The court must in each case consider whether the pleading substantially comes within the terms of the rule. A party is not to be called upon to answer statements which are irrelevant to the case, or which are pleaded in an unfair, ambiguous, or prolix manner; but the court should confine the rule to cases which come within the terms of it.[190]

5.073 More recently, Smyth J in *Riordan v Hamilton*,[191] stressed that:

The purpose of pleadings is to convey what the nature of the action is. Pleadings should not be used as an opportunity of placing unnecessary or scandalous matters on the record of the court, or as an opportunity of disseminating such matters when they have nothing to do with any dispute between the parties.

Although the rule is broadly drafted, it can be seen to be directed towards three main problems: (i) where a party pleads unnecessary matters; (ii) scandalous pleadings *i.e.* where a party pleads matters which are untrue and/or calculated to cause embarrassment to or otherwise scandalise the opposing party; and (iii) prejudicial pleadings *i.e.* pleadings which may delay, embarrass or otherwise prejudice the fair trial of the action as, for example, where a party fails to plead his case with sufficient clarity and particularity such that the opposing party does not know the case that he has to meet.

Unnecessary Pleadings

5.074 Parts of pleadings which include matters which are irrelevant to the issues in dispute between the parties will be struck out as unnecessary.[192] For example, in *Robins v McDonnell*,[193] a paragraph was struck out of the defence which contained neither a defence to the claim nor a counterclaim but was pleaded in order to preserve the possibility of a future claim. Pleadings which are prolix can also be struck out on this basis. As outlined above, Order 19, rule 3 seeks to avoid prolixity in pleading by stipulating that only the material facts and not the evidence by which they are to be proved should be pleaded. If a party contravenes this rule and pleads matters of evidence or otherwise in a prolix manner, then an application may be brought to strike out the unnecessary parts of the pleading.[194] It should be noted that it is not necessary to show, in order to suc-

---

[190] *Ibid.* at 570-1.
[191] High Court (Smyth J) 26 June 2000 at 5.
[192] *Cf. Laloutte v Robson* (1878) 12 ILTR 171.
[193] (1879) 13 ILTR 91.
[194] See *Crawford v British Medical Association* (1881) 15 ILTR 86; *Williamson v McClintock* (1892) 30 LR Ir 436; *Provincial Bank of Ireland v Brocklebank* (1890) 26

ceed in such an application, that the opposing party is actually embarrassed or prejudiced by the prolixity.[195]

Scandalous Pleadings

5.075 Pleadings will be regarded as scandalous where they seek to introduce extraneous matters for purposes and motives unconnected with the subject matter of the dispute between the parties. This will particularly be the case where that material is calculated to or has the effect of embarrassing or causing distress or offence to the opposing party.

In *Riordan v Hamilton*,[196] the plaintiff sought certain reliefs against the defendants who were all members of the Supreme Court. In his pleadings, he had made a number of serious and intemperate allegations against the defendants and Smyth J, having considered the pleadings, concluded they should be struck out as scandalous. The learned judge held that allegations are not to be considered scandalous where they would be admissible in evidence to show the truth of any allegation in the pleadings which is material to the relief claimed.[197] However, unnecessary imputations can be struck out as scandalous.[198] Applying those principles to the pleadings before him, he commented:

> In the pleadings here there are allegations which are totally unnecessary to any reasonably balanced or strongly held views of a plaintiff as against a defendant. . . . I need not go through them but merely highlight further what I would regard as contemptuous language and scandalous allegations. It is perfectly in order for a litigant to say that a defendant has acted in a particular way. However, what has been imputed here is not only over the top but is being deliberately used for the purpose of trying to advance some view which does not accord with fairness, common sense, justice, constitutional right or with any modicum of decency.[199]

Prejudicial Pleadings

5.076 Pleadings may prejudice or embarrass the opposing party and the fair trial of an action for a number of reasons. Most commonly, the complaint of embarrassment or prejudice is put on the basis that a pleading is so vague or imprecise that the opposing party does not know the case which it has to meet. The courts will require a party to plead his case properly and set out his cause of

---

LR Ir 572; *Barclay v McHugh* (1878) 12 ILTR 176; *Lacey v Kendall* (1883) 17 ILTR 112; *Doyle v Hort* (1878) 12 ILTR 172.
[195] *Williamson v McClintock* (1892) 30 LR Ir 436; *Lacey v Kendall* (1883) 17 ILTR 112
[196] High Court (Smyth J) 26 June 2000.
[197] *Christie v Christie* (1873) LR 8 Ch App 499.
[198] *Murray v Epsom Local Board* [1897] 1 Ch 35.
[199] High Court (Smyth J) 26 June 2000 at 6.

action with precision and if he fails to do so, then the relevant pleading may be struck out.[200] For example, a statement of claim may be embarrassing if it is capable of covering and intended to cover two different causes of action and does not state them clearly and intelligibly.[201]

A pleading may also be embarrassing where it introduces wholly immaterial matters which would lead to the introduction of irrelevant evidence at the trial of the action[202] or where it includes a speculative plea in the hope that evidence at the trial might substantiate it.[203]

A pleading will not be held to be embarrassing simply because it sets up inconsistent claims or defences. In *Phonographic Performance (Ireland) Ltd v Cody*,[204] the plaintiff was a limited company, the members of which were record companies and which carried on the business of administering the copyright in sound recordings. By virtue of s.17(4) of the Copyright Act 1963, the plaintiff was entitled to receive "equitable remuneration" from anyone who broadcast sound recordings in which it held copyright. The plaintiff issued proceedings against the defendants, the manager and owner of a hotel in which there was a disco, claiming injunctive relief restraining the defendants from causing certain specified sound recordings to be played in their premises without the payment of equitable remuneration. In their defence, the defendants put in issue the plaintiff's averments that copyright subsisted in the recordings specified in the statement of claim and that the plaintiff was the owner or exclusive licensee of those copyrights. In the alternative, they pleaded that they were willing to pay the plaintiff such equitable remuneration as it might be entitled to pursuant to the 1963 Act. The plaintiff brought a motion seeking, *inter alia*, an order striking out so much of the defence as put in issue the plaintiff's ownership of the copyright. It was submitted by the plaintiff that the defendants should not be permitted to plead two wholly inconsistent grounds of defence. Keane J in the High Court was satisfied that there was nothing to prevent a defendant from relying on a number of alternative defences. This was a well accepted method of pleading which should not, of itself, be the cause of any prejudice, embarrassment or delay to the plaintiff within the meaning of rule 27.

---

[200] *Cf. Lacey v Kendall* (1883) 17 ILTR 112; *Molloy v Lewers* (1882) 12 LR Ir 39.

[201] *Hoban v McPherson* (1904) 39 ILTR 153; *Doyle v Hort* (1878) 12 ILTR 172.

[202] *Quinn v Hession* (1878) 4 LR Ir 35.

[203] *Kennedy v Midland Oil Co. Ltd* (1976) 110 ILTR 26 (held that the defendant's plea of contributory negligence should be struck out in circumstances where it admitted that it was not in possession of evidence to support the plea but desired to be in a position to rely on such evidence as might be adduced in the course of the hearing of the action).

[204] [1998] 4 IR 504, [1994] 2 ILRM 241 (HC).

AMENDMENT OF PLEADINGS

Introduction

5.077 Amendment of pleadings[205] is dealt with in Order 28 which embodies the principle that the interests of justice are best served if the real issues in controversy between the parties are before the court. Thus, a party will generally be entitled to amend his pleadings so as to achieve this objective provided that irreparable prejudice is not thereby suffered by the opposing party.

Order 28 distinguishes between amendment at two stages of the proceedings: (1) a party may seek to amend a pleading shortly after its delivery without any necessity for leave; or (2) a party may apply to the court at any time for leave to amend his pleadings and such amendment may be allowed upon such terms as may be just.

Amendment Without Leave

5.078 Order 28 makes provision for parties to amend their pleadings without leave within certain limited time periods. Rule 2 provides that a plaintiff may amend his statement of claim once at any time before the expiration of the time limited for a reply and before replying or, where no defence has been delivered, at any time before the expiration of four weeks from the date of the last appearance entered by a defendant.[206] Rule 3 affords a similar facility to a defendant who has set up a counterclaim or set-off and he may amend such counterclaim or set-off at any time within six days from the delivery of the reply or the expiration of the time allowed for delivery thereof, whichever is shorter.[207] The costs of and occasioned by any such amendments are borne by the party making same unless the court otherwise orders.[208]

---

[205] It was held in *Ahern v Minister for Industry and Commerce* [1990] 1 IR 55 that Order 28 could not be relied upon in order to amend a statement grounding an application for judicial review. However, Order 28 will apply in circumstances where judicial review proceedings are commenced by plenary summons or are adjourned to plenary hearing with an order that points of claim/points of defence or a statement of claim/defence be exchanged: *O'Leary v Minister for Transport, Energy and Communications* [2001] 1 ILRM 132.

[206] It should be noted that rule 2 can only be relied upon by a plaintiff to amend his statement of claim without leave if an appearance has been entered and not in a case where no appearance has been entered: *Mercantile Credit Co. of Ireland v Moynagh* [1958] IR 265.

[207] Order 28, rule 5 provides that, where any party has amended his pleadings under rule 2 or rule 3, the opposing party must plead to the amended pleading, or amend his pleading within the time he then has to plead or within eight days from the delivery of the amendment, whichever is longer. If the opposing party has pleaded before the delivery of the amendment, and does not plead again or amend within these times, he is deemed to rely on his original pleading in answer to such amendment.

[208] Order 28, rule 13.

This right of amendment is, however, subject to the entitlement of the opposing party, within eight days after the delivery to him of the amended pleading, to apply pursuant to rule 4 to the court to disallow the amendment, or any part thereof.[209] On the hearing of such application, the court may, if satisfied that the justice of the case requires it, disallow the amendment, or allow it subject to such terms as to costs or otherwise as may be just.

Amendment with Leave

Introduction

5.079 The starting point in dealing with applications for leave to amend pleadings is Order 28, rule 1 which provides that:

> The court may, at any stage of the proceedings, allow either party to alter or amend his indorsement or pleadings in such manner and on such terms as may be just, and all such amendments shall be made as may be necessary for the purpose of determining the real questions in controversy between the parties.

Rule 1 is based on the proposition that the interests of justice are best served if the real issues in controversy between the parties are before and can be determined by the court. Thus, the traditional approach of the courts was that a party should not be punished for any error in pleading and should be permitted and indeed was entitled to make such amendments to the pleadings as were necessary to ensure that the real questions in controversy between the parties were before the court unless that amendment would prejudice the opposing party.[210] Perhaps the best known exposition of this view is to be found in the following passage from the judgment of Bowen LJ in *Cropper v Smith*:[211]

> It is a well established principle that the object of the court is to decide the rights of the parties not to punish them for mistakes they made in the conduct of their case, by deciding otherwise than in accordance with their rights.... I know of no kind of error or mistake which if not fraudulent or intended to overreach, the court ought not to correct if it can be done without prejudice to the other party. Courts do not exist for the sake of discipline but for the sake of deciding matters in controversy, and I do not regard such amendment as a matter of grace or favour.... it seems to me that as soon as it appears that the way in which the party has framed his case will not lead to a decision on the real matters in controversy, it is as

---

[209] Order 28, rule 4.

[210] See *Cropper v Smith* (1884) 26 Ch D 700, 710-11; *Ketteman v Hansel Properties Ltd* [1987] AC 189, 202, [1988] 1 All ER 38, 48.

[211] (1884) 26 Ch D 700.

much a matter of right on his part to have it corrected if it can be done without injustice as anything else in the case is a matter of right.[212]

5.080 A more recent statement of principle along the same lines, which has been approved in a number of decisions,[213] is to be found in the judgment of Lynch J in *Director of Public Prosecutions v Corbett*:[214]

> The day is long past when justice could be defeated by mere technicalities which did not materially prejudice the other party. While courts have a discretion as to amendment that discretion must be exercised judicially and where an amendment can be made without prejudice to the other party and thus enable the real issues to be tried the amendments should be made.[215]

More recent cases have emphasised that the court enjoys a wide discretion under Order 28[216] which may be exercised to refuse to grant leave to amend not only because of prejudice but also on the basis of the conduct of the applicant as where he has delayed in bringing the application and/or has failed to provide a satisfactory explanation for the failure to plead the matter in the first instance.

Real Questions in Controversy

5.081 It is a fundamental prerequisite to any successful application under rule 1 that the amendment sought is necessary in order for the purpose of determining the real questions in controversy between the parties. This simply means that the amendment must raise or relate to an issue between the parties arising from the subject matter of the proceedings. This is evident from the decision of the Supreme Court in *O'Leary v Minister for Transport, Energy and Communications*.[217] The applicant was a former chairman of CIE who instituted judicial review proceedings seeking an order of *certiorari* to quash the decision of the first named respondent to dismiss him. Leave to amend his points of claim to introduce a claim of conspiracy was refused by Kelly J in the High Court[218] on

---

[212] *Ibid.* at 710-11. This passage has been quoted with approval in a number of cases including *Aer Rianta v Walsh Western International Ltd* [1997] 2 ILRM 45, 51; *Cornhill v Minister for Agriculture* High Court (O'Sullivan J) 13 March 1998; *Palomos Properties Ltd v Brooks* [1996] 3 IR 597, 603.

[213] *Bell v Pederson* [1995] 3 IR 511, 518, [1996] 1 ILRM 290, 296; *O'Leary v Minister for Transport, Energy and Communications* [2001] 1 ILRM 132, 143.

[214] [1992] ILRM 674.

[215] *Ibid.* at 678. This statement of principle was approved by Kinlen J in *Bell v Pederson* [1995] 3 IR 511, 518, [1996] 1 ILRM 290, 296 and the Supreme Court in *O'Leary v Minister for Transport, Energy and Communications* [2001] 1 ILRM 132, 143.

[216] *Bell v Pederson* [1996] 1 ILRM 290, 297 (*per* Kinlen J).

[217] [2001] 1 ILRM 132.

[218] [2000] 1 ILRM 391.

the basis that the addition of the conspiracy claim was not necessary for the purposes of determining the real question in controversy between the parties which was whether the applicant had resigned or had been dismissed. However, it was held by the Supreme Court that, although the claim of conspiracy was not, in itself, necessary for determining the question of whether the applicant had been dismissed or resigned, it would, if established, be relevant to the claim that the minister was bound to comply with the provisions of natural and/or constitutional justice and to the issue of damages. The court, therefore, decided to grant leave.

5.082 Provided that a proposed amendment raises an issue relevant to the proceedings, it is not a bar to granting leave that it fundamentally alters the nature of the proceedings by introducing a new cause of action or ground for relief. In *Wolfe v Wolfe*,[219] Herbert J following the earlier decision of Morris J in *Rubotham v M. & B. Bakeries Ltd*,[220] held that, in the absence of special circumstances, the mere novelty of a proposed amendment does not represent a barrier to its being permitted by the courts.

5.083 Similarly, it is immaterial that the proposed amendment seeks to make a case which is significantly different from that originally made by the applicant for leave. In *Aer Rianta v Walsh Western International Ltd*,[221] the plaintiff instituted proceedings claiming damages for breach of a contract allegedly entered into between the parties pursuant to which the defendant agreed to transport goods for the plaintiff. In its defence, the defendant admitted that, by a series of consignment notes, the defendant as carrier agreed to transport a consignment of goods for the plaintiff to Moscow but, following a change of solicitors, an application was subsequently brought by the defendant seeking liberty to amend its defence by substituting for the admission of a contractual relationship between the parties, an express denial of same with a plea that any arrangement made by the plaintiff in relation to the said consignment was made with a Dutch company, Walsh Western BV, and not with the defendant. Delivering the judgment of a majority of the Supreme Court, Murphy J took the view that the real and virtually only controversy between the parties was whether or not the contracting party was the defendant or the Dutch company and that the defendant should be permitted to raise that defence.

5.084 In deciding whether an amendment is necessary for the determination of the real issues between the parties, it is not the function of the court to make any adjudication on the merits of the proposed amendment or its likelihood of success. This is clear from the decision of O'Sullivan J in *Cornhill v Minister for*

---

[219] [2001] 1 ILRM 389.
[220] [1993] ILRM 219.
[221] [1997] 2 ILRM 45.

Agriculture.[222] The proceedings arose out of the destruction of intervention beef in a fire. The defendant claimed to be indemnified by the plaintiff insurance companies who instituted proceedings seeking declaratory relief that the defendant was not entitled to an indemnity on the grounds, *inter alia*, of non-disclosure. They subsequently sought to make a number of amendments to the statement of claim which were resisted by the defendant on the basis, *inter alia*, that the onus was on the plaintiff to establish by credible evidence that the proposed amendments raised a real issue between the parties and the plaintiff had failed to discharge this onus. For their part, the plaintiffs submitted that the appropriate test was simply the threshold one of whether the plea would have been a proper plea in the original statement of claim and would have survived an attack under Order 19, rule 28 on the basis that it disclosed no reasonable cause of action.

O'Sullivan J preferred the submission of the plaintiffs, taking the view that "an amendment of the pleadings should be allowed if it would have been appropriate in the original pleadings, would have withstood an attack under Order 19 Rule 28" subject to the provision that no injustice was thereby done to the opposing party.[223] His conclusion in this regard was bolstered by a consideration of the judgment of Murphy J in *Aer Rianta* who opined that any difficulties faced by the defendant in establishing the new defence which it sought to raise were matters to be explored at the trial and not upon the application for leave. A similar approach was taken in *O'Leary v Minister for Transport, Energy and Communications*.[224] Emphasis was placed by the defendant on the fact that the claim of conspiracy which the applicant wished to make by means of the proposed amendment was based completely on hearsay. However, it was held that, notwithstanding the great difficulties which the applicant would face in establishing a claim of conspiracy, the allegations were, nevertheless, of a very serious nature and could not be dismissed as being frivolous or vexatious. It was, therefore, concluded by the Supreme Court that, on balance, to refuse to permit the applicant to pursue this claim would be to do him an injustice.

Prejudice to the Other Party

5.085 Leave to amend will not be granted where to do so would prejudice the other party to the proceedings. Prejudice in this context does not refer to the effect of the amendment sought on the party's chances of success in the proceedings. In *Aer Rianta v Walsh Western International Ltd*,[225] Murphy J explained that it is "inescapable that every amendment to a defence is intended to raise, and presumably will raise, further obstacles for a plaintiff".[226] He ap-

---

[222] High Court (O'Sullivan J) 13 March 1998.
[223] *Ibid.* at 9.
[224] [2001] 1 ILRM 132.
[225] [1997] 2 ILRM 45, 51.
[226] [1997] 2 ILRM 45, 51.

proved of a passage from the judgment of Lord Keith in *Ketteman v Hansel Properties Ltd*,[227] where his Lordship explained that:

> The sort of injury which is here in contemplation is something which places the other party in a worse position from the point of view of presentation of his case than he would have been in if his opponent had pleaded the subject-matter of the proposed amendment at the proper time.... It is not a relevant type of prejudice that allowance of the amendment will or may deprive him of a success which he would achieve if the amendment were not to be allowed.[228]

Examples of such prejudice include the death of a witness,[229] the loss of an early hearing date[230] or the delaying of the trial.[231] In *Shepperton Investment Co. Ltd v Concast (1975) Ltd*,[232] Barron J took the view that it would be unjust to the defendant to permit the plaintiff to add a new claim in circumstances where it had taken eight years for the proceedings to come to trial and a long delay would be likely before the matter would be ready for trial again.

5.086 It will generally be insufficient for a party resisting an application for leave to make general allegations of prejudice and it will be necessary to point to some specific prejudice. In *O'Neill v Canada Life Assurance (Ireland) Ltd*,[233] the Supreme Court rejected the defendant's argument of prejudice on this basis arising from the plaintiff's application to broaden his claim. While the court accepted that the nature of the case being made by the amendment would create difficulties for the first defendant because of fading memories, it had not been suggested that there were any particular witnesses who were no longer available. Furthermore, much of the case which the plaintiff sought to make would be based on documentation in the possession of the employer which should still be available to the defendant's witnesses to refresh their memory. In the circumstances, Murphy J concluded that a case had not been made out that an amendment at that stage would be so embarrassing or so unfair as to be unjust to the defendants and he was satisfied that allowing the amendment would not cause any real injustice to the defendants.

---

[227] [1987] AC 189, [1988] 1 All ER 38.

[228] *Ibid.* at 203, 49. This definition of prejudice was also approved in *Cornhill v Minister for Agriculture* High Court (O'Sullivan J) 13 March 1998 at 8 and *Palomos Properties Ltd v Brooks* [1996] 3 IR 597, 603-604.

[229] *Cf. O'Leary v Minister for Transport* [2001] 1 ILRM 132.

[230] *Cf. Aer Rianta v Walsh Western International Ltd* [1997] 2 ILRM 45.

[231] *Shepperton Investment Co. Ltd v Concast (1975) Ltd* High Court (Barron J) 21 December 1992; *McFadden v Dundalk & Dowdallshill Coursing Club Ltd* Supreme Court, 22 April 1994.

[232] High Court (Barron J) 21 December 1992.

[233] Supreme Court (*ex tempore*) 27 January 1999.

5.087 Leave to amend will not be refused if the prejudice which is relied on by the other side is capable of being ameliorated in some other way, for example by an adjournment or an order as to costs. In *Director of Public Prosecutions v Corbett,*[234] Lynch J stated that:

> If there might be prejudice which could be overcome by an adjournment then the amendments should be made and an adjournment granted to over-come the possible prejudice and if the amendment might put the other party to extra expense that can be regulated by a suitable order as to costs or by the imposition of a condition that the amending party shall indem-nify the other party against such expenses.[235]

One very specific type of prejudice deserving of separate consideration is where the effect of a proposed amendment would be to deprive the affected party of the benefit of the Statute of Limitations.

Statute of Limitations

5.088 The traditional common law approach can be seen in *Weldon v Neal*[236] where Lord Esher in the Court of Appeal stated that:

> We must act on the settled rule of practice, which is that amendments are not admissible when they prejudice the rights of the opposite party as existing at the date of such amendments. If an amendment were allowed setting up a cause of action which, if the writ were issued in respect thereof at the date of the amendment, would be barred by the Statute of Limita-tions, it would be allowing the plaintiff to take advantage of her former writ to defeat the statute and taking away an existing right from the de-fendant, a proceeding which, as a general rule, would be, in my opinion, improper and unjust. Under very peculiar circumstances, the court might perhaps have power to allow such an amendment, but certainly as a gen-eral rule it will not do so.[237]

A similar approach was adopted by the Supreme Court in *Bank of Ireland v Connell,*[238] with Murnaghan J commenting that:

> Where the amendment sought is one that affects the operation of the Stat-ute of Limitations the rule has consistently been followed since the Judi-

---

[234] [1992] ILRM 674.
[235] *Ibid.* at 678.
[236] (1887) 19 QBD 394.
[237] *Ibid.* at 395.
[238] [1942] IR 1.

cature Act that an amendment will not be allowed if it prejudices the rights of the opposite party as existing at the date of the amendment.[239]

5.089 However, a different approach is evident in the decision of Keane J in *Krops v Irish Forestry Board Ltd.*[240] The plaintiff had commenced proceedings on 17 October 1990 claiming damages from the defendants arising out of the death of his wife when the car in which she was travelling was struck by a falling tree. The statement of claim pleaded negligence, breach of duty and breach of statutory duty on the part of the defendants and on 28 November 1994, an application was made to amend the statement of claim to add a plea of nuisance. The first defendant claimed that if the amendment was allowed, it would be deprived of a defence to that claim under the Statute of Limitations. The plaintiff argued that as no new facts were being alleged, the first defendant could not be prejudiced.

Keane J allowed the plaintiff to amend his statement of claim. He pointed out that although the rule in *Weldon v Neal*[241] "was stated in reasonably wide terms in that decision, it was abundantly clear that the plaintiff was seeking, not merely to add new causes of action to that already pleaded, but to make fresh allegations of fact which had never been pleaded, in circumstances where the Statute of Limitations had already run".[242] He went on to note that the rule, as stated in such general terms, came to be seen as unduly restrictive of the general power of the court to amend pleadings where it seemed just to do so and, in particular, where it was necessary to determine the real question in issue between the parties and that the English courts had sought to confine it. In the absence of authority, he approached the question as a matter of principle:

> the pleadings which initiate an action in this court carry with them from the time they are issued or delivered the potentiality of being amended by the court in the exercise of its general jurisdiction to allow a party to amend his indorsement or pleadings "in such manner and on such terms as may be just". Where, as here, an amendment, if allowed, will not in any way prejudice or embarrass the defendant by new allegations of fact, no injustice is done to him by permitting the amendment. In that sense, it is true to say that the amendment does not in truth deprive him of a defence under the Statute of Limitations 1957: since the proceedings were always capable of amendment in such manner as might be just and in order to allow the real question in controversy between the parties to be determined, it cannot be said that the defendant was at any stage in a position to rely on the Statute of Limitations 1957.[243]

---

[239] *Ibid.* at 11.
[240] [1995] 2 IR 113, [1995] 2 ILRM 290.
[241] (1887) 19 QBD 394, 395.
[242] [1995] 2 IR 113, 118.
[243] *Ibid.* at 121.

He went on to express the view that:

> Where, as here, the plaintiff seeks to add a new cause of action arising out of – to borrow the words of the English rule – "the same facts or substantially the same facts", there seems no reason why this court, even in the absence of a corresponding rule in this jurisdiction, should be precluded from permitting such an amendment.[244]

Although Keane J does not overrule *Weldon v Neal*, his judgment indicates that it will, at a minimum, be narrowly construed.

Conduct of the Applicant

5.090 The courts enjoy a wide discretion which they will exercise against an applicant who attempts to gain an unfair advantage or to surprise his opponent in making an application for leave to amend.[245] Such cases are, however, rare and more generally the issue for the court under this heading is whether the applicant has delayed unduly in making his application.

The first question is whether the applicant is actually guilty of delay. In this regard, it is important to note that even if an application for leave is made at a relatively late stage of the proceedings, it may still be made at the first reasonable opportunity. For example, in *O'Neill v Canada Life Assurance (Ireland) Ltd*,[246] the plaintiff brought an action against the first defendant for wrongful dismissal and the second defendant for slander. Five years after the commencement of proceedings, he brought an application seeking leave to amend the statement of claim so as to include an allegation that under the terms of his contract with the first defendant, his employers had an implied obligation to conduct their business in a proper fashion and in particular not to conduct it in such a way as would unfairly or improperly damage his reputation. This amendment was based on evolving English jurisprudence in the area, in particular, the decision of the House of Lords in *Malik v Bank of Credit and Commerce International*.[247] The first defendant contended that there had been inordinate delay and that it was embarrassed by the late amendment. However, the Supreme Court accepted that the evolution in the law explained, at least in part, the delay in making this case.

5.091 Even if an applicant has delayed unduly, that will only deprive him of his entitlement to amend his pleadings if that delay is culpable in some manner. An example of such culpability can be seen in *Doyle v C. & D. Providers (Wex-*

---

[244] *Ibid.*
[245] *Cf. Shepperton Investment Co. Ltd v Concast (1975) Ltd* High Court (Barron J) 21 December 1992.
[246] Supreme Court (*ex tempore*) 27 January 1999.
[247] [1998] AC 20, [1997] 3 WLR 95, [1997] 3 All ER 1.

ford) Ltd.[248] The case involved a breach of contract action in the Circuit Court. At the trial, the defendants made a preliminary objection that the claim was statute barred and this was upheld by the trial judge. The plaintiff appealed this decision and at the start of the appeal applied to amend the civil bill so as to include a further allegation of fraud against the defendant. As an explanation for his failure to make this allegation earlier, the plaintiff claimed that he had at all times been anxious to raise the allegation but that his legal advisers had told him he did not have sufficient grounds to put forward such a serious allegation. O'Hanlon J took the view that, in fact, the only basis on which the plaintiff sought to amend the civil bill at such a late stage, when an appeal to the High Court was about to commence, was in reliance on evidence given on behalf of the defendant in the original Circuit Court action. However, he pointed out that this evidence could have been obtained earlier by the delivery of interrogatories if the plaintiffs had really been as anxious to introduce the plea of fraud as he claimed. He, therefore, refused to allow an amendment in circumstances where the Circuit Court proceedings had been allowed to continue to a conclusion and a decision given.[249]

In order to assess whether the delay has been culpable or not, the courts will examine the reasons offered to explain or excuse it. In *Palomos Properties Ltd v Brooks*,[250] Flood J explained that:

> [W]ithin the facts underlying the claim before the court there must be such evidence from which an inference can reasonably be drawn as to why the plea which is sought to be introduced by way of amendment was not put in the original defence or express evidence given to explain the failure in a manner which renders the omission broadly excusable if not actually justifiable.[251]

5.092 If an applicant fails to offer an explanation, the court will infer that none exists and this will weigh heavily against the applicant.[252] In *McFadden v Dundalk & Dowdallshill Coursing Club Ltd*,[253] the plaintiff brought proceedings claiming damages for personal injuries against the defendants arising out

---

[248] [1994] 3 IR 57.

[249] *Cf. Carroll v Sheridan* High Court (O'Hanlon J) 28 October 1982 (leave to make fundamental amendment of pleadings in the course of the hearing of a Circuit Court appeal was refused as it would have effectively introduced a new course of action which the defendant was unprepared to meet).

[250] [1996] 3 IR 597.

[251] *Ibid* at 605. This passage was endorsed by Kinlen J in *Bell v Pederson* [1995] 3 IR 511, 518, [1996] 1 ILRM 290, 296.

[252] See *Shepperton Investment Co. Ltd v Concast (1975) Ltd* High Court (Barron J) 21 December 1992. Cf. *James McMahon Ltd v Michael Lynch Ltd* High Court (Flood J) 20 November 1996.

[253] Supreme Court, 22 April 1994.

of an accident which occurred in 1987. Three days before the hearing was due to take place in December 1993, an application was made by the defendant to amend their defence to raise the plea that the plaintiff was a member of the club and that, therefore, he could not sue as a member of an unincorporated body. The Supreme Court refused to allow the amendment, taking the view that this was a "purely technical point" which was "quite clearly without any merits though it may be a good legal point".[254] The court took the view that it was too late to make such a technical point and pointed out that no explanation was given on affidavit as to why the matter was not adverted to or why it was not in the original defence or why there was not any application made earlier.

5.093 *McFadden* was subsequently distinguished in *Aer Rianta v Walsh West-ern International Ltd*.[255] The plaintiff instituted proceedings on 2 December 1994 for damages for breach of a contract allegedly entered into between the parties. It was claimed that under the terms of this contract, the defendant agreed to transport goods to Moscow for the plaintiff. In a defence delivered on 14 July 1995, the defendant admitted that, by a series of consignment notes, the defend-ant as carrier agreed to transport a consignment of goods for the plaintiff to Moscow. In July 1996, a notice of change of solicitor was filed. The defendant subsequently brought an application seeking liberty to amend its defence by substituting for the admission of a contractual relationship between the parties, an express denial of same with a plea that any arrangement made by the plain-tiff in relation to the said consignment was made with Walsh Western BV and not with the defendant.

The defendant's application was refused in the High Court by Johnson J who placed reliance on the fact that there had been absolutely no explanation from the defendant's former solicitors as to why the admission that the defend-ant was the carrier had been made. However, Murphy J in the Supreme Court pointed out it had been stated on affidavit that the defendant did not instruct its former legal advisers to make the admission which had been made by reason of error or inadvertence on the part of the defendant's former legal advisers. If this was the case, then it was understandable that the former solicitors would be unwilling or at least reluctant to make the admission which would be implicit in the explanation as to how the error occurred. In the circumstances, he con-cluded that justice required that the amendment be allowed.

Bona Fide Errors

5.094 As stated by Bowen LJ in *Cropper v Smith*,[256] "the object of the course is to decide the rights of the parties not to punish them for mistakes they made in

---

[254] *Ibid.* at 3.
[255] [1997] 2 ILRM 45.
[256] (1883) 26 Ch D 700, 710.

the conduct of their case". Therefore, as can be seen from the decision of the Supreme Court in *Glennon v McMorrow*,[257] leave to amend will be granted if the court is satisfied that the failure to plead a particular matter was due to a *bona fide* mistake unless irremediable prejudice would be caused to the other side.

Glennon involved a family dispute in which serious allegations of sexual abuse were made against the plaintiff by two brothers resulting in a defamation action. By reason of an error at the time of drafting, neither of the defendants pleaded qualified privilege in their defence and this error was only spotted when counsel advised on proofs. The defendants then applied for leave to amend their defences to make a plea of qualified privilege. The Supreme Court granted leave on the basis that it was quite satisfied that the drafting error was the result of "an unfortunate mistake" and it was "proper that the mistake should be put right". The court distinguished other cases where leave to amend had been re-fused on the basis that they concerned attempts to raise technical defences at the last moment which had no particular merits in the circumstances of those cases having regard to the lateness at which the application was made or having re-gard to some other circumstances that there was no proper explanation as to why those defences were not pleaded earlier. The court was concerned to ensure that no injustice was caused to the plaintiff by reason of the amendment and in addition to awarding him the costs of any consequential amendments necessi-tated by the amendment, special provision for costs was made in the event of the plaintiff deciding to abandon the actions as a result of the amendment.

Terms on Which Leave may be Granted

5.095 In dealing with an application for leave to amend, the court must try and do justice between all the parties to the proceedings[258] and, to that end, it may and frequently will grant leave on terms. Generally, the opposing party will be entitled to any costs arising out of the application to amend including the costs of the motion and the costs or expenses arising out of the amendment.[259] De-pending on the circumstances, the court may order that the party seeking the amendment provide an indemnity for any extra expense incurred by the other side in dealing with the amendment,[260] lodge monies in court towards security for the further costs of the action,[261] or pay all costs up to a certain point.[262]

If the adjournment of a trial is necessitated by reason of an application for

---

[257] Supreme Court (*ex tempore*) 14 December 1998.
[258] *Bell v Pederson* [1996] 1 ILRM 290, 297; *Cornhill v Minister for Agriculture* High Court (O'Sullivan J) 13 March 1998; *Shepperton Investment Co. Ltd v Concast (1975) Ltd* High Court (Barron J) 21 December 1992.
[259] *Aer Rianta v Walsh Western International Ltd* [1997] 2 ILRM 45.
[260] *Bell v Pederson* [1996] 1 ILRM 290; *Wolfe v Wolfe* [2001] 1 ILRM 389.
[261] *Fallon v Naughton* [1953-54] Ir Jur Rep 12.
[262] See *Stanley v Aer Lingus Teo* (1972) 114 ILTR 26.

an amendment, then the party applying for it will have to pay the costs wasted thereby. In *Wolfe v Wolfe*,[263] an issue arose as to the costs which should be awarded in such circumstances. Herbert J granted the petitioners liberty to re-amend their petition but pointed out that, as a result of the amendment, the respondents would have to prepare for and meet a substantially new case raising new issues of fact and very complex issues of law. He took the view, therefore, that an order for "costs of the day" in favour of the respondents as defined by Order 99, rule 37(33),[264] would not be sufficient for the attainment of justice or for enforcing or defending the rights of the respondents. Such an order would fail to recognise the fundamental importance of the re-amendment, the time and circumstances at and under which the re-amendment came to be sought, and the probable impact of the re-amendment on the future course and conduct of the proceedings. He was of the opinion that what would do justice between the parties was an order for costs in favour of the respondents on a party and party basis but confined to counsel's fees, witness allowances and expenses, their solicitor's proper charges for attending in court and such other fees and disbursements and charges as related solely to the preparation of the adjourned trial and which would required to be repeated or would be of no value at the next hearing.

Time at Which Leave may be Obtained

5.096 Although applications for leave to amend are generally brought in advance of a trial, Order 28, rule 1 provides that the court may grant leave for the amendment of pleadings "at any stage of the proceedings". Therefore, an application for leave may be brought during the course of a trial and even after judgment has been handed down.

(i) Amendment in the Course of a Trial

5.097 In *Wildgust v Bank of Ireland*[265] it was stressed by McGuinness J, delivering the judgment of the Supreme Court, that the amendment of pleadings in the course of a trial was not a desirable practice and should not frequently be permitted. However, she went on to hold that on the facts of that case, such an exceptional course was warranted. This was because, although the plaintiffs had failed to properly plead a claim of negligent misstatement which they wished to make, the second named defendant had been made aware in general terms of

---

[263] [2001] 1 ILRM 389.
[264] Order 99, rule 37(33) provides that: "When a cause, being in the list for hearing is ordered to be adjourned upon payment of costs of the day, the party to pay the same shall pay to each party to whom costs are awarded if entitled to appear by three counsel £180.00, if by two counsel £110.00, and if by one counsel £70.00 unless the court shall otherwise direct. The foregoing sums do not include witnesses expenses."
[265] [2001] 1 ILRM 24, 39.

the plaintiffs' claim from the course of the proceedings as a whole. In those circumstances, the court concluded that the trial judge should have permitted an amendment of the pleadings mid-trial rather than putting the matter back for a new trial. The latter course was one which would place an undue burden on the plaintiffs which was not necessitated by the level of possible prejudice against the defendant arising out of the continuation of the trial.

Another case where the circumstances justified an amendment of the pleadings during the course of the trial is *W.(F.) v BBC*.[266] The plaintiff claimed damages for personal injury arising out of a broadcast by the defendant in which the identity of the plaintiff as a victim of sexual abuse was disclosed. During the course of the trial, it emerged that a consultant psychologist retained by the defendant had been guilty of misconduct and gross negligence in his examination of the plaintiff and Barr J acceded to an application by the plaintiff to amend the statement of claim by including a claim for aggravated damages. He proceeded to award aggravated damages to the plaintiff.

(ii) Amendment After the Conclusion of a Trial

5.098 Although it is possible for pleadings to be amended at the end of proceedings before judgment is given and even after judgment is given,[267] the trial judge must ensure that fair procedures are observed and that the opposing party is given an adequate opportunity to meet the case against him. In *Balkanbank v Taher*,[268] the plaintiff had failed to plead that its claim was a derivative action brought on behalf of the shareholders of a company and this contention was first made in the closing submissions of counsel for the plaintiff. However, the trial judge took the view that this matter had been dealt with in the submissions of both parties and he made an order that the plaintiff's claim was to be treated as a derivative action in accordance with the relevant exception to the rule in *Foss v Harbottle*[269] and granted liberty to the plaintiff to deliver an amended statement of claim. Six days later, the statement of claim was amended and further orders were made. On appeal, the defendants argued that the post-judgment amendment had radically changed the nature of the proceedings and that they had been seriously prejudiced in that they did not have sufficient time and opportunity to deal with the issue and raise any defences that might be open in a derivative action.

The Supreme Court allowed the appeal on this ground. Fair procedures required that a party to an action should be given notice of the nature of the claim and an adequate opportunity of defending all aspects of it but this had not been afforded to the defendants. It was not in accordance with such procedures for

[266] High Court (Barr J) 25 March 1999.
[267] See *Cox v ESB (No. 2)* [1943] IR 231.
[268] Supreme Court, 19 January 1995.
[269] (1843) 2 Hare 461.

the statement of claim to be amended in a manner which radically altered the nature of the plaintiff's claim after judgment had been given thereon.

In *Flynn v Director of Public Prosecutions*,[270] an application by the plaintiff for leave to amend at the hearing of the action was refused by the trial judge even though it was not opposed by the defendant. Finlay CJ, delivering the judgment of the Supreme Court, stated that:

> In general, amendments of a pleading which are not opposed by the other party and are not, on the face of them, vexatious or frivolous should be allowed by the court, even at a late stage.[271]

However, he was satisfied, on the facts, that no injustice to the plaintiff had resulted from the refusal to grant leave to amend.

Miscellaneous

Amending a Pleading

5.099 Although it is permissible to identify the amendments to a pleading which a party wishes to make by making hand written alterations on the copy which has been previously delivered,[272] the universal practice is to re-type the pleading with the amendments clearly underlined. The amended pleading must also be marked with the date of the order, if any, under which it was amended and the day on which such amendment was made *e.g.* "Amended the [   ] day of [   ] 2001 pursuant to the order of Mr. Justice [   ] dated the [   ] of [   ] 2001".[273]

Failure to Amend Pleadings Within Time

5.100 Rule 7 provides that, if a party who has obtained an order for leave to amend does not amend accordingly within the time limited for that purpose by the order, or if no time is thereby limited, then within 14 days from the date of the order, such order to amend shall, on the expiration of such limited time as aforesaid become *ipso facto* void, unless the time is extended by the court.

---

[270] [1986] ILRM 290.

[271] *Ibid.* at 293.

[272] Order 28, rule 8 provides that an indorsement or pleading may be amended by written alterations in the copy which has been delivered, and by additions on paper to be interleaved therewith if necessary, unless the amendments require the insertion of more than 144 words in any one place, or are so numerous, or of such a nature that the making of them in writing would render the document difficult or inconvenient to read, in either of which cases the amendment must be made by delivering the document as amended, which must be printed when printing is required under Order 19, rule 9.

[273] Order 28, rule 9.

Delivery of Amended Pleading

5.101 Rule 10 provides that whenever any indorsement or pleading is amended, such amended document must be delivered to the opposite party within the time allowed for amending same.[274]

---

[274] See *Mercantile Credit Co. of Ireland v Moynagh* [1958] IR 265 where it was held that the plaintiff was not entitled to judgment in default of appearance on foot of an amended statement of claim in circumstances where it had not delivered it to the defendant by filing or otherwise.

CHAPTER SIX

PARTIES

JOINDER OR REMOVAL OF PARTIES

Introduction

6.001 Order 15 of the Rules of the Superior Courts 1986 provides for the addition or substitution of parties in an action and allows an order to be made discharging a person from proceedings in circumstances where he is not a necessary party. It allows for the addition, substitution or removal either "upon or without the application of either party"[1] and gives the court extensive powers to dispose of proceedings in a more expeditious and cost efficient manner where the circumstances of the case justify it. The aim and object of Order 15 of the Rules of the Superior Courts, as suggested by Budd J in *O'Reilly v Granville,*[2] is "to ensure that all the proper parties are before the court so as to enable full justice to be done between the parties who are really interested in the matters at issue having regard to the nature of the proceedings and the granting of appropriate relief in the circumstances of the case".

Joinder of Plaintiffs

6.002 Order 15, rule 1 provides for the joining of persons in an action as plaintiffs[3] where their alleged right to relief arises out of the same transaction or series of transactions or where, if such persons brought separate actions, any common question of law or fact would arise. However, where it appears to the court that such joinder might embarrass or delay the trial of proceedings, it may order separate trials. As the wording of rule 1 makes clear, it is a prerequisite to a successful application pursuant to this rule, that the rights claimed by the plaintiffs arise out of the "same transaction or series of transactions". In *Reddy v Dublin Corporation*[4] an action was brought against the corporation by a number of their employees and a preliminary point as to the right of the plaintiffs to be joined in one action was raised by Gavan Duffy J. His finding that he had no jurisdiction to try the case in view of the provisions of Order 15, rule 1 was upheld by the Supreme Court. O'Byrne J stated that the question for consideration might be restricted to one point, namely whether the rights claimed

---

[1] Order 15, rule 13.
[2] [1971] IR 90.
[3] See *e.g. O'Cearbhaill v An Bord Telecom* High Court (Lardner J) 1 April 1993.
[4] [1941] IR 255.

by the plaintiffs arose out of the same transaction or series of transactions. He concluded that it was difficult to see how their respective rights could be said to arise out of the same transaction or series of transactions as each was separately employed with his own special duties and terms of employment. In each case the rights of the particular plaintiff had to be determined by reference to the work on which he was engaged and this depended upon his own employment and was peculiar to him.

Where Action Commenced in the Name of Wrong Person as Plaintiff

6.003 Order 15, rule 2 provides that where an action has been commenced in the name of the wrong person as a plaintiff, the court may order any other person to be substituted or added as plaintiff if it is satisfied that there has been a *bona fide* mistake and that "it is necessary for the determination of the real matter in dispute so to do". However, an order pursuant to the rule will not be made where to do so would constitute a new action.[5] The application of this rule was considered in *Southern Mineral Oil Ltd v Cooney (No. 2)*[6] in which the applicant companies' application to have the liquidator substituted as the applicant in the proceedings was dismissed by Shanley J. He stated that there was no evidence of a *bona fide* mistake such as would be necessary to establish before the jurisdiction conferred by rule 2 could be exercised. The liquidator had clearly intended to institute proceedings in the name of the companies, and his mistake, it if was a mistake, was to sue in the companies' names in the belief that the companies were possessed of the cause of action as opposed to the liquidator himself. In his view, this was not a category of mistake to which rule 2 applied. Shanley J also adopted a requirement set out by Millett J in *Re Probe Data Systems*[7] to the effect that the mistake must not be misleading or such as to cause any reasonable doubt as to the identity of the intended plaintiff. He stated that applying that principle, it seemed clear that to allow an amendment would be to suggest that the respondents were at all material times in no real doubt but that the intended applicant was in fact the liquidator, which was patently not the case. For these reasons, Shanley J concluded that he would refuse liberty to substitute the liquidator for the companies.

6.004 A useful example of a *bona fide* mistake which would allow an order for the substitution of a plaintiff to be made is provided by the decision of Geoghegan J in *BV Kennemerland Groep v Montgomery*.[8] Geoghegan J stated that it was not seriously disputed that the proceedings had been brought in the name of the wrong plaintiff and that the circumstances in which this error had occurred were

---

[5] *Kirby v Arthur* (1878) 12 ILTSJ 75 and *Crawford v Donnelly* (1889) 23 LR Ir 511.
[6] [1999] 1 IR 237.
[7] [1989] BCLC 561, 563.
[8] [2000] 1 ILRM 370.

fully explained in affidavits. He expressed the view that it was perfectly clear that the defendants would have at all material times known that the wrong company was named as plaintiff and said that subject to a question in relation to whether the action was statute barred, justice required that he make the substitution sought. Geoghegan J stated that under Order 15, rule 2 the court has a discretion to refuse to make such an order on the grounds that it would be futile in practice if the action would be statute barred beyond any doubt, but this was far from being the situation in the case before him and he made the order sought.[9]

Where a person has been improperly or unnecessarily joined as a co-plaintiff and a defendant has set up a counterclaim or set-off, he may obtain the benefit of this by establishing his counterclaim or set-off as against the parties other than the co-plaintiff despite the mis-joinder.[10]

Joinder of Defendants

6.005 Order 15 also deals with the joinder of defendants and rule 4 provides that all persons may be joined as defendants against whom the right to any relief is alleged to exist whether jointly, severally or in the alternative.[11] Rule 5 goes on to provide that it is not necessary that each defendant shall be interested in all the relief sought or every cause of action[12] included in the proceedings but the court may make any order necessary to prevent any defendant from being embarrassed or put to expense by being required to attend any proceedings in which he has no interest. The causes of action do not have to be the same against every defendant,[13] and where leave is sought to join another party as co-defendant, "it is not necessary that each defendant should be interested in the entire relief sought".[14] Lord O'Brien LCJ considered the meaning of rule 5 in *O'Keeffe v Walsh*[15] and stated that it did not mean that wholly separate and distinct causes of action might be combined in one action against different defendants. In his opinion it meant that causes of action, the proofs of which were interlaced and which are connected with and derive from one subject of complaint may be included in one action.[16]

Where the plaintiff is in doubt as to the person from whom he is entitled to redress, he may join two or more defendants and the question of whether, and if

---

[9] See further *infra* in relation to Order 15, rule 13.
[10] Order 15, rule 3.
[11] See generally, Kerr, *The Civil Liability Acts* (2nd ed., 1999).
[12] As Gibson J stated in *O'Keeffe v Walsh* [1903] 2 IR 681, 715 "cause of action" has more than one sense and may mean in the wide sense, the subject matter of the complaint, the grievance founding the action or it may signify technical cause of action.
[13] *Blake v Moore* (1881) 8 LR Ir 95 and *Creaton v Midland and Great Western Railway Co.* (1882) 10 LR Ir 74.
[14] *Per* Palles CB in *Creaton v Midland and Great Western Railway Co.* (1882) 10 LR Ir 74, 77.
[15] [1903] 2 IR 681.
[16] *Ibid.* at 705.

so, to what extent any of the defendants is liable may be determined as between all the parties.[17] However, as the decision of the Supreme Court in *Higgins v Patterson*[18] makes clear, while a plaintiff is free to take proceedings against additional defendants, the trial judge may enter judgment for one of these defendants at the conclusion of the plaintiff's evidence where the evidence has not established any facts which would have justified a finding of liability on this defendant's part. As FitzGerald J stated while "the provisions of Order 15, rule 7 may well be of assistance to a plaintiff on the question of costs where he finds himself in a position that evidence is not available to him to establish negligence against any particular defendant or defendants ... [i]t does not ... appear to justify a departure from the principle that he who affirms must prove".[19]

Joinder or Removal of Parties Pursuant to Order 15, rules 13 and 14

Introduction

6.006 The principal object of these rules is to prevent the defeating of any cause or matter by reason of the mis-joinder or non-joinder of parties.[20] As Murphy J pointed out in *Allied Irish Coal Supplies Ltd v Powell Duffryn International Fuels Ltd,*[21] as the first sentence of rule 13 indicates, the provision was originally made to alleviate the hardship which was caused by the rigid application of "legal technicalities". It provides that no cause or matter shall be defeated by reason of the mis-joinder or non-joinder of parties and that the court may in every case deal with the matter in controversy so far as regards the rights and interests of the parties actually before it. The court may at any stage in the proceedings[22] and either upon or without the application of either party, on such terms as may appear to the court to be just, order that the names of any parties improperly joined may be struck out or that additional parties be joined.

Improperly Joined Parties May be Struck Out

6.007 A party named in an action as a plaintiff without his consent may apply to have his name struck out[23] and the court has no authority to permit a party's name to be used as a plaintiff without his sanction.[24] Similarly, a defendant may

---

[17] Order 15, rule 7.
[18] [1971] IR 111.
[19] *Ibid.* at 122.
[20] *Per* Andrews LCJ in *Kelly v Rafferty* [1948] NI 187, 188 in relation to the then equivalent rules in Northern Ireland.
[21] [1998] 2 IR 519, 532, [1998] 2 ILRM 61, 68.
[22] Note that as McGuinness J stated in *McG. v W. (No. 2)* [2000] 1 ILRM 121, 125-126 "this rule deals solely with the joinder of parties before the conclusion of an action and before the making of final orders".
[23] *Montgomery v Montgomery* (1856) 6 ICLR 522.
[24] *Sullivan v Sullivan* (1856) 6 ICLR 523.

apply to the court to be discharged from proceedings on the ground that he is not a necessary party. So, in *Fuller v Dublin County Council*[25] the Supreme Court allowed the application of the second named defendant to be discharged from an action, the test being, in the opinion of Henchy J, whether the presence in the proceedings of this defendant was justifiable by the plaintiffs as necessary for the proper prosecution of the claim.[26]

Addition of Parties

6.008 Rule 13 provides that the names of any parties may be added, whether plaintiffs or defendants, who ought to have been joined, or "whose presence before the court may be necessary in order to enable the court effectually and completely to adjudicate upon and settle all the questions involved in the cause or matter". As Murphy J stated in *Allied Irish Coal Supplies Ltd v Powell Duffryn International Fuels Ltd*,[27] the words "cause or matter" in this context mean the action as it stands between the existing parties[28] and the court has jurisdiction to refuse to add parties for the purpose of introducing a new cause of action.[29] Similarly in *Kelly v Rafferty*[30] Andrews LCJ stated that this wording suggested that "the framers of the rule had only in contemplation ... such amendment of parties as would enable the court finally and completely to determine the rights and interests of all parties in the action actually before the courts." The provisions of the equivalent rule applicable in Northern Ireland were considered in some detail by Andrews LCJ in *Kelly* in which he dismissed an application by a non-party for an order that he might be made a defendant in an existing action. Andrews LCJ stated that he could find no words in the rule which enabled the court, either at the instance of a third person who the plaintiff had deliberately refrained from suing, or of its own motion, to direct the joinder of a person as a defendant who was admittedly not a necessary party to the maintenance of the action which the plaintiff had chosen to take and which he believed be could bring to a successful conclusion. Nor was there anything in the rule which would justify the conclusion that the court would compel the plaintiff to make a new claim inconsistent with, and effectively in substitution for, the one he has made.[31] Andrews LCJ stated that if the court were to make the order sought, the plaintiff would be forced to plead a cause of action which

---

[25] [1976] IR 20.

[26] *Ibid.* at 28.

[27] [1998] 2 IR 519, 532, [1998] 2 ILRM 61, 68.

[28] See *Amon v Raphael Tuck and Sons Ltd* [1956] 1 QB 357, 369, [1956] 2 WLR 372, 382, [1956] 1 All ER 273, 279.

[29] [1998] 2 IR 519, 532-533, [1998] 2 ILRM 61, 68. See also *Raleigh v Goschen* [1898] 1 Ch 73.

[30] [1948] NI 187, 189.

[31] *Ibid.* at 189.

would be inconsistent with the case which he had already made. He concluded as follows:

> No case has been cited, and in my opinion no case is to be found, except in a representative action, in which a person, not a party, and against whom no relief is claimed by the plaintiff, was joined as a defendant at his own request, and solely on his own application, against the will of the plaintiff who had deliberately refrained from making any claim or seeking any relief against him.[32]

6.009 A slighty less restrictive view was expressed by Lynch J in *Fincoriz SAS di Bruno Tassan Din v Ansbacher & Co. Ltd,*[33] which also concerned an application by a third party seeking to be joined as a defendant in an action. Lynch J stated that *prima facie* a plaintiff is entitled to sue whoever he wishes and not to have to sue a person he does not wish to sue. As a general principle Lynch J said that in order for a defendant to be joined without the consent and, *a fortiori*, against the wishes of a plaintiff, exceptional circumstances must exist. It must be established that the proposed defendants are parties who ought to have been joined initially, or it must be shown at the time of the application to the court that their presence will as a matter of probability be necessary in order to enable the court effectually and completely to adjudicate upon and settle all questions involved in the cause or matter. On the facts before him, Lynch J was satisfied that the court could not effectually and completely adjudicate upon and settle all questions involved in the proceedings without the presence of the applicant and another company, and he made an order joining them as defendants.

Application by a Plaintiff to Join an Additional Defendant

6.010 The particular considerations which may be relevant where a plaintiff seeks to join an additional defendant were examined by both the High Court and the Supreme Court in *Allied Irish Coal Supplies Ltd v Powell Duffryn International Fuels Ltd*[34] in which the plaintiff's application to join a parent company as a co-defendant in existing proceedings was dismissed. Laffoy J stated that the onus on the plaintiff was no greater than to demonstrate that it had a stateable case against the proposed defendant. In addition, she expressed the view that it was not appropriate to attempt to resolve conflicts of evidence, such as those which arose on the affidavits filed, and that the proper approach was to determine whether there was a stateable case on the basis that the plaintiff's version of the disputed facts was the true one. She concluded that even if the plaintiff had a stateable case for the joinder of the parent company as a co-

---

[32] *Ibid.* at 194.
[33] High Court (Lynch J) 20 March 1987.
[34] [1998] 2 IR 519, [1997] ILRM 306 (HC), [1998] 2 ILRM 61 (SC).

defendant, the court would not order its joinder because as the claim against the company was statute barred, it would serve no useful purpose to do so. Her decision was upheld by the Supreme Court and Murphy J considered the issue of the *locus standi* of the existing defendant to resist the application for the addition of a new defendant. He stated that in general a plaintiff may institute proceedings against any defendant without seeking the permission of another but it must be borne in mind that the joinder of a defendant in an existing action may well cause delay or add unnecessarily to the cost of proceedings. In his view the court had a discretion as to whether to order the addition of a new defendant and the submissions of an existing defendant might well be of assistance to the court in determining how such discretion should be exercised so the requisite *locus standi* did exist.

Murphy J also stated that it is a well established rule of practice that a court will not permit a person to be made a defendant in an existing action at a time when he could rely on the Statute of Limitations as barring the plaintiff from bringing a fresh action against him.[35] This is relevant in view of the fact that the Supreme Court had previously in *O'Reilly v Granville*[36] allowed a plaintiff's application to add an additional defendant although the limitation period had expired as against that defendant, the court's attitude being that the statute was a matter of defence and did not arise until pleaded.[37] The issue subsequently arose in *Southern Mineral Oil Ltd v Cooney (No. 2)*[38] which concerned an application to substitute a liquidator for companies as the applicant in proceedings. Shanley J quoted the *dicta* of Murphy J in *Allied Coal* referred to above[39] and said that he felt bound to follow this decision. He concluded that there was nothing in the affidavits before the court which suggested that the limitation period had not expired and that the decision of the Supreme Court in *Allied Coal* required that he did not allow the substitution of a plaintiff in circumstances where his cause of action was clearly statute barred.

6.011 An attempt was made by Geoghegan J in *BV Kennemerland Groep v Montgomery*[40] to clarify these principles although as noted above the case concerned an application to substitute a plaintiff on the grounds of a *bona fide* mistake and the order sought was made pursuant to rule 2 rather than rule 13.

---

[35] *Ibid.* at 533, 69. See also *Liff v Peasley* [1980] 1 WLR 781, [1980] 1 All ER 623 and *Ketteman v Hansel Properties Ltd* [1987] AC 189, [1987] 2 WLR 312, [1988] 1 All ER 38.

[36] [1971] IR 90.

[37] Although note that Budd J stated that "[I]f it were apparent beyond doubt that the statute applied to the case, an application to add the proposed defendant as a party might very well be refused as a futile operation …" (at 106).

[38] [1999] 1 IR 237.

[39] *Supra* footnote 35

[40] [2000] 1 ILRM 370.

Geoghegan J referred to the earlier decisions and said that he thought it highly unlikely that the Supreme Court in *Allied Irish Coal* would have intended to overrule *O'Reilly* without actually saying so.[41] On that basis, he characterised the former decision as "simply a restatement of a long established principle that a court will not add a defendant under Order 15, rule 13 if the action is quite clearly statute barred". Geoghegan J stated that he did not think that it could be taken as authority for the proposition that if there is doubt as to whether a plea based on the Statute of Limitations would be successful or not, the court making the decision as to whether to join the additional party has to there and then decide the limitation issue and accede to or refuse the application accordingly. On the facts, Geoghegan J said that it was far from being the case that the action was clearly statute barred and he made the order sought, although he stressed that he was doing so under rule 2 and that the principles which apply in relation to a rule 13 application do not necessarily apply equally to the former type of case.

6.012 Where an application is made to join an additional defendant, as the wording of rule 13 illustrates, it must be shown to be necessary "in order to enable the court effectually and completely to adjudicate upon and settle all the questions involved in the cause or matter". This issue was considered by Lynch J in the High Court in *Fusco v O'Dea*[42] in which the plaintiff, who was seeking his release pursuant to s.50 of the Extradition Act 1965, sought to join the government of the United Kingdom as a defendant and to serve a motion for discovery upon it. It was held by Lynch J that the proper defendant in such proceedings was the garda who had backed the warrant in the State and that this party was a sufficient defendant to enable the court effectually and completely to adjudicate upon and settle all the questions involved in the matter. He was satisfied that it was neither appropriate nor necessary to join the government of the United Kingdom[43] and in addition held that it was not necessary that an order for third party discovery be made against the government.[44]

---

[41] Geoghegan J stated that it seemed somewhat doubtful whether the decision in *O'Reilly* was ever cited to the Supreme Court in *Allied Irish Coal* as it was surprising that there was no reference to the decision in the judgments.

[42] [1994] 2 IR 93.

[43] Counsel for the plaintiff had indicated that the only reason for seeking to join the government was in order to obtain discovery against it and made it clear that as an alternative, he would be content with an order for third party discovery pursuant to Order 31, rule 29. It should be noted that it had been held by Kenny J in *International Trading Ltd v Dublin Corporation* [1974] IR 373, prior to the introduction of the procedure for third party procedure in Order 31, rule 29, that the court would not make an order adding a party as a defendant merely for the purpose of obtaining discovery of documents against the proposed defendant.

[44] The sole issue for the determination by the Supreme Court on appeal was whether an

Substitution of Parties

6.013 An application may also be made to substitute a party for an existing one as the decision in *Southern Mineral Oil Ltd v Cooney (No. 2)*[45] considered above illustrates. However, where relevant the provisions of Order 15, rule 2 which have already been examined must be borne in mind in this context and it must be shown that there has been a *bona fide* mistake and that it is necessary for the determination of the real matter in dispute that the substitution be made. In addition, where the facts of the case require it, the court may make an order substituting a notice party as plaintiff instead of the existing one.[46]

Procedure for Adding, Substituting or Striking out a Party

6.014 Order 15, rule 13 provides that the court may "at any stage in the proceedings" order that the names of any parties may be struck out or added. In addition, rule 14 provides that an application "to add or strike out or substitute" may be made at any time before trial by way of motion or at the trial of the action in a summary manner. Where the application is made before the trial, it should be made by motion on notice to the Master of the High Court[47] and not less than two clear days notice of such motion shall be given.[48] Such an application may be made *ex parte* to the Master where it is necessitated by the death of a party, an event causing a change or transmission of interest or liability, or the coming into existence of a person interested in the matter.[49] While such motions are on notice to the parties already involved, the usual rule of practice is that it is not necessary for the proposed defendant to be present in court for the hearing of the motion but that he may come to court at a later date seeking to have an order joining him set aside.

Where the trial of the action has commenced, the application to add, strike out or substitute a party may be made in a summary manner. As the *dicta* of Fitzgibbon LJ in *Keys v Hore*[50] makes clear, where a further party's interests are involved, the statement of claim may be amended and served on the additional defendant.

---

order for third party discovery could be made against a foreign government and it was held that such an order could not be made save in circumstances where that government had submitted to the jurisdiction of the courts.
[45] [1999] 1 IR 237.
[46] *Ulster Bank Ltd v Crawford* High Court (Laffoy J) 20 December 1999.
[47] Order 63, rule 1(12).
[48] Order 63, rule 4.
[49] Order 17, rule 4.
[50] 13 ILTR 58.

Miscellaneous Provisions

6.015 Order 15, rule 15 provides that where the additional or substituted party is a defendant, the plaintiff must, unless ordered otherwise by the court, file an amended copy of the summons and serve the new defendant with the amended summons or notice in the same manner as the original defendants were served. If a statement of claim had been previously delivered, it must be amended in such manner as is necessary or desirable, unless the court orders otherwise. A copy of this amended statement of claim shall be delivered to the new defendant either at the time he is served with the summons or notice or within four day of the entry of an appearance by him. Finally, it should be noted that rule 13 provides that the proceeding as against the new party "shall be deemed to have begun only on the making of the order adding such party".[51]

Applications to Join Parties at the Appellate Stage

6.016 Additional parties may be joined in proceedings before the Supreme Court where it is "in the interests of justice"[52] to do so. In *O'Keeffe v An Bord Pleanála*[53] in which the plaintiff had obtained judicial review before the High Court of a decision of the respondent quashing a decision to grant planning permission to a third party, this party sought liberty to be joined as a respondent in the subsequent appeal before the Supreme Court. The Supreme Court joined the third party that had successfully obtained planning permission, having concluded that in the interests of justice it was necessary that this party, which would be clearly affected by the result of the appeal, be added. However, it did so on the terms that it would not be allowed to introduce fresh evidence or to raise any issue not raised in the High Court. Recently in *TDI Metro Ltd v Delap (No. 1)*,[54] considered in more detail below, the Supreme Court made an order joining the Attorney General as a notice party to proceedings for the purposes of an appeal, but on the basis that additional grounds could not be added to the appeal.

An application by a non-party to be added as an appellant in an action in which it was not a party in the High Court was rejected by the Supreme Court in *O'Cearbhaill v An Bord Telecom Éireann*[55] in circumstances where the purpose of the application was to raise grounds of appeal relating to issues not considered and determined in the High Court. Finlay CJ stated that apart from what he was satisfied would be the very substantial injustice which an order permitting this party to enter into the appeal would cause, it was clear that it

---

[51] This may have implications for the computation of the relevant limitation period, see *McGuinness v Amrstrong Patents Ltd* [1980] IR 289.
[52] *Per* Finlay CJ in *O'Keeffe v An Bord Pleanála* [1993] 1 IR 39, [1992] ILRM 237.
[53] [1993] 1 IR 39, [1992] ILRM 237.
[54] [2000] 4 IR 337, [2001] 1 ILRM 321. See further *infra* at paragraph 6.032.
[55] Supreme Court 16 July 1993.

was quite inconsistent with the appellate jurisdiction of the Supreme Court that there should be any consideration and determination of an issue which had not been tried before the High Court.[56]

Finally, it should be noted that as the decision in *McG. v W. (No. 2)*[57] considered below makes clear, an order will not be made joining a notice party to proceedings for the sole purpose of appealing a decision in circumstances where judgment has been given and final orders perfected by the High Court.

JOINDER AND CONSOLIDATION OF CAUSES OF ACTION

6.017 Order 18, rule 1 provides that a plaintiff may unite several causes of action in the same proceedings. However, it goes on to provide that where such causes of action cannot be conveniently tried together, the court may order separate trials or make such other order as may be necessary or expedient to dispose of the matters.

Where a defendant alleges that a plaintiff has united several causes of action which cannot conveniently be disposed of together, he may apply at any time to the court for an order confining the proceedings to such of the causes of action as may be conveniently disposed of together.[58] In *Byrne v Triumph Engineering Ltd*[59] the plaintiff brought claims against different defendants in respect of personal injuries sustained in separate incidents at work. The defendants in the first claim brought a motion pursuant to rule 8 seeking separate trials in respect of the two causes of action which was supported by the defendant in the other claim. Hamilton J refused the relief sought concluding that the two causes of action could be conveniently disposed of together and the defendants' appeal was dismissed. In the view of the majority of the Supreme Court[60] the defendants had not discharged the onus of establishing that a joint trial could not conveniently take place. O'Higgins CJ stated that it did not appear to him that any difficulty could be caused by a separate consideration of the evidence as to liability and damages in respect of each accident.

---

[56] Finlay CJ pointed out that in *O'Keeffe v An Bord Pleanála* [1993] 1 IR 39, [1992] ILRM 237 it had been made a specific condition that the party intervening was confined to making submissions on the grounds which had been filed by the existing appellants, all of which had been determined in the High Court.

[57] [2000] 1 ILRM 121; [2000] 4 IR 1, [2000] 2 ILRM 451. See *infra* at paragraph 6.033.

[58] Order 18, rule 8.

[59] [1982] IR 220, [1982] ILRM 317

[60] Note that Kenny J delivered a dissenting judgment in which he expressed the view that it would be inconvenient and might lead to injustice to try the two causes of action together.

6.018 Order 18, rule 9 provides that where it appears to the court that causes of action are such that they cannot all be conveniently disposed of together, the court may order any of such causes of action to be excluded and consequential amendments to be made and may make such order as to costs as may be just. In *Baillie Stewart v Sefton*[61] the plaintiff sued a number of defendants in respect of alleged defamatory material in a book and two further defendants in respect of alleged defamatory matter in a television interview concerning its contents. These two defendants brought a motion seeking to have the statement of claim struck out as against them as being vexatious or embarrassing. It was held by Murnaghan J that any cause of action as against these defendants was distinct and separate from any that might exist on the basis of the words used in the book and he accepted the submission of counsel that these two defendants were embarrassed by the causes of action being joined in the same proceedings. Since the plaintiff's claim against these defendants would be statute barred if the statement of claim were struck out as against them, he ordered that an amended statement of claim be delivered and that the cause of action against the two defendants be tried separately.

Where a plaintiff does not take steps to unite several causes of action in the same proceedings, matters pending in the High Court may be consolidated by order of the court on the application of any party and whether or not all the parties consent to the order.[62] The principles to be applied in considering an application to consolidate were set out by McCarthy J in *Duffy v News Group Newspapers Ltd*[63] as follows:

(1) Is there a common question of law or fact of sufficient importance?

(2) Is there a substantial saving of expense or inconvenience?

(3) Is there a likelihood of confusion or miscarriage of justice?

McCarthy J stated that while the wording of Order 49, rule 6 is very wide, that does not mean that a heavy burden does not lie on those who seek to join or consolidate actions. In the circumstances he concluded that he would not order the consolidation of the actions, nor the joint trial of them in the case before him, but he did direct that the actions be tried in succession and that the trials should be presided over by the same judge.

As an alternative to consolidation, the court has an inherent jurisdiction to order that cases be heard simultaneously, as in *O'Neill v Ryanair Ltd*.[64]

---

[61] [1964] IR 36.
[62] Order 49, rule 6.
[63] [1992] 2 IR 369, 376, [1992] ILRM 835, 838.
[64] [1992] 1 IR 160.

SUING IN A REPRESENTATIVE CAPACITY

6.019 Parties may also bring or defend an action in a representative capacity and Order 15, rule 9 provides that where numerous persons have the same interest in a cause or matter, one or more persons may sue or be sued or may be authorised by the court to defend a matter on behalf or for the benefit of all interested persons. A motion should be brought seeking a representative order authorising the party or parties to sue on behalf of persons whose names and addresses are exhibited in the affidavit grounding the application.

The court will not make a representative order where there is no evidence to suggest that a plaintiff has been authorised to sue on behalf of other persons.[65] In addition, the court will not make such an order where the proposed representative defendant is unwilling to act.[66] Order 4, rule 9 provides that where a plaintiff sues or a defendant is sued in a representative capacity, the indorsement of claim shall show in what capacity the party sues or is sued.[67]

Where a representative action is properly taken, the decision of the court will bind every interested party who cannot make out a special case for exempting himself from the decision provided there is no fraud or collusion in the conduct of the proceedings.[68] Conversely, as a general principle only parties to the proceedings may benefit directly from any order made by the court.[69]

An issue relating to the taking of a case by numerous plaintiffs having the same interest in a matter was discussed by Murphy J in *Greene v Minister for Agriculture*,[70] although it was not material in the case having regard to the decision which he reached. The action was brought by six plaintiffs named in the title to the proceedings and in their statement of claim, they stated that the action was being taken on behalf of all the farmers listed in a schedule thereto, although no such schedule was in fact annexed. A list of 1,390 plaintiffs was transmitted to the defendants in lieu of the schedule and Murphy J concluded that these listed plaintiffs had authorised the proceedings to be taken on their behalf and in their name.

REPRESENTATION OF PARTIES

Representation by a Barrister or Solicitor

6.020 As a general principle a litigant may be represented before the courts by a barrister instructed by a solicitor,[71] by a solicitor who is on record for that

---

[65] *Madigan v Attorney General* [1986] ILRM 136, 148.
[66] *Firth Finance and General Ltd v McNarry* [1987] NI 125.
[67] In such of the forms in Appendix B, Part I as shall be applicable to the case.
[68] *Moore v Attorney General* [1930] IR 471, 489 *per* Kennedy CJ.
[69] *Murphy v Attorney General* [1982] IR 241.
[70] [1990] 2 IR 17, [1990] ILRM 364.
[71] Note that Rule 4.1 of the Code of Conduct for the Bar of Ireland provides that subject

party,[72] or by himself. The extent to which there are exceptions to this general principle is subject to some doubt, although the assistance of a so called "McKenzie friend"[73] has been accepted as valid in this jurisdiction in relation to matters other than of a matrimonial nature or which must be heard *in camera*.[74]

Whether Right to Representation by a Lay Person

6.021 While it is well established that a litigant may appear on his own behalf,[75] the question of whether a lay person may appear on behalf of others is more problematic. The issue was considered by the Supreme Court in *Battle v Irish Art Promotion Centre Ltd*[76] in which the applicant, who was the managing director and a major shareholder of the defendant company, applied *ex parte* for liberty to conduct the company's defence at the hearing of the plaintiff's action. The application was dismissed by the Supreme Court, Ó Dálaigh CJ stating that "in the absence of statutory exception, a limited company cannot be represented in court proceedings by its managing director or other officer or servant". While Ó Dálaigh CJ expressed sympathy with the purpose which the applicant had in mind, *viz.* to safeguard his business reputation, he stated that as the law stood, he could not substitute his *persona* for that of the company.

This decision and a number of authorities from other jurisdictions were considered by Budd J in his judgment in *P.M.L.B. v P.H.J.*[77] in which a preliminary issue was raised as to whether the plaintiff litigant was entitled to represent her husband and her son, who had reached the age of majority. In reply to a submission by counsel for the defendant that only three categories of persons have a right of audience in court, namely a litigant in person, a solicitor and counsel briefed by a solicitor, Budd J stated that he thought that there might be certain rare exceptions to that general rule. He quoted at some length from the decision of the New Zealand Court of Appeal in *Re G.J. Mannix Ltd*[78] in which the

---

to such exceptions as may be authorised by the Bar Council a barrister may not act in a professional capacity except upon the instructions of a solicitor or, in appropriate cases, a patent agent or a trade mark agent.

[72] S.17 of the Courts Act 1971 extended the right of audience of solicitors to all courts. As Budd J stated in *P.M.L.B. v P.H.J.* High Court (Budd J) 5 May 1992, s.17 provided that a qualified solicitor should have a right of audience in any court where he is appearing for a party in an action. As he commented "this would appear to be a statutory exception to the general rule of common law that only counsel on behalf of a litigant has the right of audience in court".

[73] See further *infra*.

[74] *R.D. v McGuinness* [1999] 2 IR 411, [1999] 1 ILRM 549.

[75] Recent examples include *Riordan v An Taoiseach (No. 1)* [1999] 4 IR 32, *Riordan v An Taoiseach (No. 2)* [1999] 4 IR 343 and *Murphy v Minister for Justice* [2001] 2 ILRM 144.

[76] [1968] IR 252.

[77] High Court (Budd J) 5 May 1992.

[78] [1984] 1 NZLR 309.

court accepted that there is a residual discretion to allow unqualified advocates to appear before them. However, as Cooke J stated it should be regarded as a "reserve or occasional expedient"[79] and in the words of Somers J, such cases are "likely to be rare".[80] Budd J stated that the discretionary approach adopted by the New Zealand Court of Appeal was preferable but expressed the view that he did not think that the plaintiff's case came anywhere near the rare and exceptional cases envisaged by that court. He then went on to say that the Supreme Court decision in *Battle* appeared to indicate that on principle a non-lawyer litigant does not have a right of audience for another litigant and that even if this is not a correct construction of the principle and the law as set out in *Mannix* is correct, he did not think that the plaintiff's case was an exceptional one in that sense.[81]

Circumstances in Which Litigant Entitled to Assistance of "McKenzie Friend"

6.022 A related issue is the question of whether a lay litigant who has chosen to conduct his case without solicitor or counsel is entitled to the help of another individual to give advice and otherwise assist during the hearing. The term used to describe such an individual is "McKenzie friend" which derives from a decision of the English Court of Appeal in *McKenzie v McKenzie*[82] in which Davies LJ cited with approval the following *obiter* comment from the judgment of Lord Tenterden in *Collier v Hicks*:[83]

> Any person, whether he be a professional man or not, may attend as a friend of either party, may take notes, may quietly make suggestions, and give advice; but no one can demand to take part in the proceedings as an advocate, contrary to the regulations of the court as settled by the discretion of the justices.

Some confusion arose about the extent of this so called right in the wake of *McKenzie* in the decision of the Divisional Court in *R v Leicester City Justices, ex p. Barrow*.[84] Watkins LJ, in concluding that the applicants in the case before the court had not been prejudiced by the justices' refusal to allow the assistance

---

[79] *Ibid.* at 314.
[80] *Ibid.* at 317.
[81] High Court, 5 May 1992 at 44. Budd J stated that there was a further compelling reason why the court should not exercise its discretion in favour of permitting the plaintiff to represent her husband and son, assuming the court had such a discretion, namely conflict of interest on the basis that there had been ongoing litigation between the husband and wife for more than ten years.
[82] [1971] P 33, [1970] 3 WLR 472, [1970] 3 All ER 1034.
[83] (1831) 2 B & Ad 663, 669.
[84] [1991] 2 QB 260, [1991] 3 WLR 368, [1991] 3 All ER 935.

which they had sought, stressed that while a court has a discretion to allow an unrepresented litigant to receive the assistance of a friend in the course of representing himself, there is no actual right to have such assistance. The Court of Appeal allowed the applicants' appeal, Lord Donaldson MR stating that a party has a right to present his own case and in doing so to arm himself with such assistance as he thinks appropriate, subject to the right of the court to intervene. He continued as follows:

> [I]f a party arms himself with assistance in order the better *himself* to present his case, it is not a question of seeking the leave of the court. It is a question of the court objecting and restricting him in the use of this assistance, if it is clearly unreasonable in nature or degree or if it becomes apparent that the 'assistance' is not being provided *bona fide*, but for an improper purpose or is being provided in a way which is inimical to the proper and efficient administration of justice by, for example, causing the party to waste time, advising the introduction of irrelevant issues or the asking of irrelevant or repetitious questions.[85]

However, it should be noted that Lord Donaldson stressed that the only "right" is that of the litigant to reasonable assistance which can take many forms. So as the Court of Appeal made clear in *R v Bow County Court, ex p. Pelling*[86] a McKenzie friend personally has no rights with regard to litigation.[87]

6.023 The issue of the circumstances in which a litigant may be entitled to the assistance of a "McKenzie friend" have recently been considered in this jurisdiction by Macken J in *R.D. v McGuinness*.[88] The applicant lay litigant appeared before the respondent in the District Court in relation to an application for a barring order which was being sought by his wife, proceedings which were of an *in camera* nature. He sought liberty to be assisted by another person

---

[85] *Ibid.* at 289, 379, 946. This is in line with the approach adopted by Lord Woolf MR in *R. v Bow County Court, ex p. Pelling* [1999] 1 WLR 1807, 1824-1825, [1999] 4 All ER 751, 757-758. He summarised his position as follows (at 1827, 760): "In relation to proceedings in public, a litigant in person should be allowed to have the assistance of a *McKenzie* friend unless the judge is satisfied that fairness and the interests of justice do not require a litigant in person to have the assistance of a *McKenzie* friend."

[86] [1999] 1 WLR 1807, [1999] 4 All ER 751. See also the decision of Neuberger J in *Izzo v Phillip Ross & Co.* Chancery Division, 31 July 2001 where he made it clear that any application of this nature must be considered with great care on a case-by-case basis and stressed that litigants should be aware that the court might not be prepared to let them be represented by a friend.

[87] In the decision of the Divisional Court Otton LJ stressed (at 1813) that such a person is not like a professional advocate who has rights of audience which exist independently of any particular client and who could legitimately complain if he were excluded from appearing in court.

[88] [1999] 2 IR 411, [1999] 1 ILRM 549.

who might take notes on his behalf and assist him generally during the hearing but the respondent concluded that he would not allow this person to remain in court during what was an *in camera* hearing. The applicant then instituted proceedings seeking a declaration that when acting in person he was entitled to be accompanied by a friend who might take notes on his behalf, quietly make suggestions and assist him generally during the hearing, relying on an order made by the Supreme Court in *Quinn v Bank of Ireland*.[89] On the general issue of a party's entitlement to the assistance of a "McKenzie friend", Macken J stated as follows:

> I am satisfied that in so far as this jurisdiction is concerned, all other things being equal and in relation to matters other than the matters of a matrimonial nature or of a nature which the law prescribes should be heard *in camera*, the Supreme Court is satisfied and has decreed that a party who prosecutes proceedings in person is entitled to be accompanied in court by a friend who may take notes on his behalf, quietly make suggestions and assist him generally during the hearing, but who may not act as advocate.[90]

However, Macken J said that she would be reluctant to find that the long standing view of the legislature that all matters of a matrimonial nature were to be heard otherwise than in public ought to be set aside or modified in favour of attendance in court of a member of the public as a "McKenzie friend" unless there was overwhelming evidence that a fair hearing could not be secured by the applicant.[91] In the circumstances, having regard to the fact that the applicant was in the view of the respondent a very articulate person and that the court itself had experience of protecting persons who appeared before it in family law matters without legal representation, Macken J concluded that there was no evidence to suggest that by appearing in person without a "McKenzie friend", the applicant would be deprived of a fair hearing.

---

[89] Supreme Court, 13 October 1995.

[90] *Ibid.* at 421, 558.

[91] This is similar to the approach adopted by Lord Woolf MR in *R. v Bow County Court, ex p. Pelling* [1999] 1 WLR 1807, [1999] 4 All ER 751 where he stated that where proceedings are in private, then the nature of the proceedings may make it undesirable in the interests of justice for a *McKenzie* friend to assist.

REPRESENTATION OF PERSONS UNDER A DISABILITY

Representation of Infants

6.024 Order 15, rule 16 provides that an infant may sue as plaintiff by his next friend and may defend proceedings by his guardian appointed for that purpose.[92] Where the plaintiff is an infant the consent of his next friend should be filed in the Central Office at the same time as the summons is issued[93] and rule 20 provides that that before the name of any person shall be used as next friend of an infant or other party, or as relator, such person shall sign a written authority to the solicitor for that purpose and the authority shall be filed in the Central Office. Any party acting in such a manner necessarily acts for the next friend and not for the infant.[94] Where the next friend of an infant plaintiff dies during the action, a new next friend may be appointed on an *ex parte* application to the court.[95] Where the infant attains full age, the next friend or guardian may apply on affidavit to the Registrar in the Central Office for a certificate that the plaintiff or defendant may proceed to defend in his name.[96] So, in *Almack v Moore*[97] Palles CB made it clear that until the court has actually determined that an infant is of age, the next friend is *dominus litus*.

An infant may not enter an appearance except by his guardian *ad litem*.[98] Rule 18 goes on to provide that no order for the appointment of such guardian shall be necessary but the solicitor applying to enter such appearance shall make and file an affidavit in Form No. 4 in Appendix A Part II of the Rules. Where a solicitor enters an appearance *bona fide* and without knowledge of the fact that his client is an infant, he may be personally liable for the costs incurred by the defendant in seeking to have the summons set aside on the ground of irregularity as the plaintiff had not sued by his next friend.[99] In addition, it should be noted that the court has jurisdiction to discharge a guardian of infants on his own application.[100]

Representation of Persons of Unsound Mind

6.025 A person of unsound mind may sue as plaintiff by his committee[101] or next friend and may defend proceedings by his committee or guardian appointed

---

[92] The guardian *ad litem* must be properly appointed, see *Smith v Smith* (1868) IR 3 Eq 19.

[93] *Erwin v Blythe* (1883) 17 ILTR 24.

[94] *Almack v Moore* (1878) 2 LR Ir 90.

[95] *Daly v Daly* (1882) 9 LR Ir 383.

[96] Order 15, rule 16.

[97] (1878) 2 LR Ir 90.

[98] Order 15, rule 18.

[99] *Lindsay v McCord* (1897) 33 ILTR 71.

[100] *Re Grays, Minors* (1891) 27 LR Ir 609.

[101] The committee must be appointed by the court pursuant to Order 67, rule 57.

for that purpose.[102] As noted above, rule 20 requires that before the name of the next friend is used in any action, such person must sign a written authority to the solicitor for that purpose and the authority shall be filed in the appropriate court office. An application for the appointment of a guardian *ad litem* should be made by way of motion to the Master of the High Court on an *ex parte* basis.[103] It must be supported by an affidavit containing sufficient detail about the defendant's state of mind[104] and showing that the proposed guardian is a fit and proper person to act[105] and that there is no conflict of interest between him and the person he is to act for.[106] Where a person becomes of unsound mind during the course of proceedings such an application may be made at that point.[107]

ROLE OF THE ATTORNEY GENERAL IN PROCEEDINGS

Right of the Attorney General to Notice of Constitutional Issues

6.026 Order 60, rule 1 provides that where any question as to the validity of any law having regard to the Constitution arises in any action, notice must be served on the Attorney General by the party having carriage of the proceedings if the former is not already a party. It was held by Carroll J in *State (D. & D.) v Groarke*[108] that Order 60, rule 1 required that the Attorney General be notified if a question as to the validity of any law was to be considered, including statutes enacted prior to the coming into force of the Constitution of Ireland 1937. She stated that she could not accept that Order 60 should be interpreted so that it would be possible for a pre-Constitution statute to be declared unconstitutional in an action between two private parties without the knowledge of the Attorney General. Carroll J therefore declined to consider any of the issues directed to the constitutionality of the Children Act 1908 on the basis that no notice had been served on the Attorney General as required by Order 60, rule 1.

Order 60, rule 2 provides that if any question as to the interpretation of the Constitution, other than a question referred to in rule 1, arises in an action or matter, the party having carriage of the proceedings shall, if the court so directs, serve notice upon the Attorney General. Questions referred to in rules 1 and 2 as arising in any action or matter have been interpreted as meaning an action actually in being. In *R . v R.*[109] the plaintiff served notice under Order 60 and

---

[102] Order 15, rule 17.
[103] Order 63, rule 1(3).
[104] *Watson v Knilans* (1874) 8 ILTR 157.
[105] *Gaffney v Gaffney* (1896) 31 ILTR 11.
[106] *Dobbin v Belling* (1872) IR 6 Eq 623.
[107] *Wolfe v Wolfe* (1875) IR 9 Eq 392.
[108] [1988] IR 187. Carroll J did not follow the earlier decision of *State (D.C.) v Midland Health Board* High Court (Keane J) 31 July 1986.
[109] [1984] IR 296.

stated that an issue concerning the validity of specified statutory provisions "may arise in this action". Gannon J stated that Order 60, rules 1 and 2 seem to require that before proceeding under this order, a question must have arisen involving an adverse contention and in the case before him, none had been made. As the defendant had not been called upon to argue against the validity of the impugned statutory provisions, the plaintiff and the Attorney General had difficulty in presenting arguments on the issue.

6.027 Order 60, rule 3 provides that the notice shall state concisely the nature of the proceedings in which the question or dispute arises and the contentions of the party or parties to the proceedings. Upon service of the notice, the Attorney General shall be entitled to appear in the action or matter and become a party as regards the question which arises. Once involved in an action as a notice party, the Attorney General may take an active part in the proceedings where he considers it appropriate. So, in *Murphy v Roche*,[110] the Attorney General who had been served with notice of the proceedings, brought an appeal against an order made by the High Court directing that a preliminary point of law be determined. He argued that because the issue of negligence had been raised in the defence and was to be determined in the action, the trial of any question involving a constitutional issue as a preliminary point was inappropriate and might prove to be the determination by the court of an issue of constitutional law in the form of a moot. The Supreme Court allowed the Attorney General's appeal and varied the order of the High Court, holding that where the issues between the parties can be finally disposed of by the resolution of an issue of law other than a constitutional one, the court should consider that issue first and if it determines the case, should decline to express any view on the constitutional issue. Similarly, in *Brady v Donegal County Council*[111] in which legislation had been declared unconstitutional in the High Court, the Attorney General as notice party appealed to the Supreme Court raising issues which had not previously been considered. The Supreme Court allowed the appeal and remitted the entire action for re-trial by the High Court.[112]

The Role of the Attorney General in Enforcing Public Rights[113]

Introduction

6.028 It has been stated that the Attorney General is the legal representative of the public in all litigation in which the public may be involved as an interested

---

[110] [1987] IR 106.

[111] [1989] ILRM 282.

[112] The action was subsequently compromised between the applicant and the respondents.

[113] See generally Casey, *The Irish Law Officers* (1996).

party, whether as plaintiff, defendant or otherwise.[114] So, the Attorney General
has traditionally been recognised as the appropriate person to assert and defend
the public interest[115] and may institute proceedings as the guardian of public
rights.[116] While his role as the representative of the public interest is no longer
an exclusive one,[117] he is still regarded as having a power and in some senses a
duty to enforce public rights and uphold constitutional guarantees.[118]

Relator Actions

6.029 The Attorney General may institute proceedings at the relation of a private individual or body in respect of a public matter.[119] Where the Attorney
General sues with a relator, the latter need have no personal interest in the
subject matter except his interest as a member of the public.[120] In such cases the
Attorney General alone is the plaintiff[121] and remains *dominus litus* throughout
the proceedings.[122] So, the Attorney's consent must be obtained where it is
sought to amend pleadings and he must be kept informed of the manner in which
the litigation is proceeding and of any steps which it is proposed to take. The
relator's solicitors will have carriage of the case and must agree to pay the costs
of the proceedings which will include any undertaking in damages which may
be required.[123] Order 15, rule 20 provides that before the name of any person is
used as a relator, a written authority must be given to his solicitor for that purpose and filed in the appropriate court office.

Proceedings instituted by individuals may be converted into a relator action
where the litigant lacks the necessary *locus standi*, so in *Attorney General
(Society for the Protection of Unborn Children (Ireland) Ltd) v Open Door*

---

[114] *Moore v Attorney General* [1930] IR 471, 495 *per* Kennedy CJ.
[115] *Campus Oil Ltd v Minister for Industry and Energy (No. 2)* [1983] IR 88, [1984]
ILRM 45.
[116] See *e.g. Attorney General v Paperlink Ltd* [1984] ILRM 373 where relief was granted
against the defendants in order to protect the state postal monopoly. See also *Incorporated Law Society of Ireland v Carroll* [1995] 3 IR 145.
[117] *Society for the Protection of Unborn Children (Ireland) Ltd v Coogan* [1989] IR 734,
[1990] ILRM 70. See further *infra.*
[118] *Attorney General v X.* [1992] 1 IR 1, [1992] ILRM 401 and *Attorney General v Hamilton* [1993] 2 IR 250, [1993] ILRM 81, [1993] ILRM 821.
[119] See Collins and O'Reilly, *Civil Proceedings and the State in Ireland: A Practitioner's
Guide* (1990) Chapter 7.
[120] *Attorney General (Society for the Protection of Unborn Children (Ireland) Ltd) v Open
Door Counselling Ltd* [1987] ILRM 477, 486 *per* Hamilton P.
[121] Although the relator may be named as a co-plaintiff where a separate issue arises in
respect of which he would have been entitled to issue proceedings.
[122] *Attorney General (Humphreys) v Governors of Erasmus Smith Schools* [1910] 1 IR
325, 331 *per* Holmes LJ. See also *Attorney General (Martin) v Dublin Corporation*
[1983] ILRM 254, 257.
[123] *Attorney General (Martin) v Dublin Corporation* [1983] ILRM 254.

Counselling Ltd[124] when the defendants challenged the plaintiff's standing in their defences, the plaintiff sought and obtained leave to amend the proceedings which were converted into an action in the name of the Attorney General at the relation of the original plaintiff.

Recent Developments

6.030 In general terms the courts have tended to adopt a fairly flexible approach in more recent cases towards the question of the *locus standi*[125] of a person seeking to assert public rights and towards the role of private individuals in matters involving enforcement of the government's legal obligations[126] and compliance with the Constitution.[127]

The most important decision in this area is that of the Supreme Court in *Society for the Protection of Unborn Children (Ireland) Ltd v Coogan*[128] where the majority of the court held that the Attorney General did not have an exclusive right to take proceedings seeking to enforce compliance with the provisions of the Constitution and that any citizen with a *bona fide* concern and interest for the protection of a constitutionally guaranteed right may initiate such an action. Finlay CJ stated as follows:

> If it were to be accepted as is contended on behalf of the defendants that only the Attorney General could sue to protect such a constitutional right as that involved in this case, that would, I am satisfied, be a major curtailment of the duty and power of the courts to defend and uphold the Constitution.[129]

In addition, as Walsh J pointed out, there may well be occasions on which the defendant could legitimately be named as a defendant in proceedings brought to defend or vindicate constitutional rights, and in his view "it would be an intolerable situation if the defence or vindication of constitutional rights was to be

---

[124] [1988] IR 593, [1987] ILRM 477, [1989] ILRM 19. See also *Martin v Dublin Corporation* High Court (Costello J) 14 November 1978 and *Attorney General (Martin) v Dublin Corporation* [1983] ILRM 254.

[125] See *Irish Permanent Building Society Ltd v Caldwell (No. 2)* [1981] ILRM 242, although note the more cautious approach of Keane J in *Irish Permanent Building Society Ltd v Caldwell (No. 1)* [1979] ILRM 273.

[126] In *State (Sheehan) v Ireland* [1987] IR 550, [1988] ILRM 437 both Costello J in the High Court and McCarthy J in his dissenting judgment in the Supreme Court took a broad approach to this question. However, the approach of the majority of the Supreme Court (see the judgment of Henchy J) suggested a more restrictive approach.

[127] *Crotty v Ireland* [1987] IR 713, [1987] ILRM 400 and *McGimpsey v Ireland* [1990] 1 IR 110, [1990] ILRM 441.

[128] [1989] IR 734, [1990] ILRM 70.

[129] *Ibid.* at 742, 73.

confined to the very officer of State who had been entrusted with the task of defending such impugned activities".[130]

However, the approach adopted by the High Court and Supreme Court in *Incorporated Law Society of Ireland v Carroll*[131] in which both courts tended to re-emphasise the importance of relator proceedings should also be noted. The plaintiffs sought declarations that the defendants had contravened certain provisions of the Solicitors Act 1954 and injunctive relief restraining further purported contraventions. In refusing the relief sought by the plaintiffs, Blayney J concluded that "as what is in issue is the enforcement of a public right, the only party who can bring civil proceedings to enforce it is the Attorney General".[132]

Applications by the Attorney General to be joined in proceedings

6.031 The Attorney General may bring an application seeking to intervene in proceedings, although he has no entitlement to intervene and the issue is one for the discretion of the court. In addition, it is clear that the Attorney General may be joined at the appeal stage of proceedings. In *Brady v Cavan County Council*[133] the Attorney General was permitted to intervene and was heard by the Supreme Court in an *amicus curiae* role because, it was submitted on his behalf, issues of general public concern were raised.

6.032 In *TDI Metro Ltd v Delap (No. 1)*[134] the Attorney General brought an application seeking to intervene for the first time in an appeal taken by the notice party against a decision of the High Court quashing the applicant's conviction of an offence relating to the unauthorised erection of an advertising hoarding on the basis that the notice party did not have the power to prosecute summarily. It was argued on behalf of the Attorney General that there was a general public interest in the prosecution of indictable offences in a summary manner and that the Attorney General was an appropriate person to be heard having regard to his role in representing the public interest. Denham J stated that while the Attorney General does not have a right entitling him to intervene in or be joined to proceedings, he does have a right to apply to the court and it is a matter for the determination of the court whether to grant the application. She expressed the view that the Attorney General might be joined to proceedings either in the High Court or the Supreme Court and that there is no bar to the joinder of a party at the appeal stage[135] although she stated that the addition of

---

[130] *Ibid.* at 744, 75.
[131] [1995] 3 IR 145.
[132] *Ibid.* at 174.
[133] [1999] 4 IR 99, [2000] 1 ILRM 81.
[134] [2000] 4 IR 337, [2001] 1 ILRM 321.
[135] See *O'Keeffe v An Bord Pleanála* [1993] 1 IR 39, [1992] ILRM 237. See further *supra.*

the Attorney General does not permit further grounds to be added.[136] She concluded that there was a clear public interest in the case before the court relating to the prosecution of offences and that the Attorney General was an appropriate constitutional officer to be heard having regard to his role in representing the public interest. Hardiman J agreed and said that while the Attorney General had no entitlement to intervene in any proceedings he wishes, the court has a discretion to allow a party to be joined in the proceedings even at the appeal stage where this is considered to be necessary in the interests of justice and where there is no specific rule of law excluding the additional parties at that stage of the proceedings. Hardiman J concluded that the Attorney General should be joined as a party to the proceedings for the purposes of the appeal although he stated that in most circumstances the Attorney General should confine himself to the issues raised by the facts and pleadings. In relation to the issue of costs, he stated as follows:

> In my view it is appropriate, when the Attorney General seeks to intervene in this way that he should, at least as a general rule, abide his own costs and, in the court's discretion, some or all of the costs of other parties. It is quite possible that the proceedings will be prolonged or become more elaborate by reason of the Attorney's presence than if the matter had simply been argued between the original parties. If the Attorney General's legitimate interest is the basis of his intervention, it may be proper that some or all of the costs be paid out of the public purse rather than by the private parties. This may be appropriate whether or not the contentions advanced by the Attorney find favour with the court.[137]

6.033 It is clear from the decision in *McG. v W. (No. 2)*[138] that an order will not be made joining the Attorney General as a notice party to proceedings for the sole purpose of appealing a decision in circumstances where judgment has been given and final orders perfected by the High Court. McGuinness J had made an order pursuant to s.29(1) of the Family Law Act 1995 recognising the decree of dissolution of the marriage between the petitioner and the notice party granted outside the jurisdiction. At that point, the parties believed that the proceedings were concluded but the Attorney General on becoming aware of the decision, sought to be joined as a notice party so that he could appeal against it. McGuinness J refused the order sought and stated that while in hindsight it might have been an advantage had the Attorney General been joined in the proceedings, the absence of the Attorney as a party did not disable the court from making a declaration under the section. The Attorney General's appeal to

---

[136] Referring to *O'Cearbhaill v. An Bord Telecom* Supreme Court, 16 July 1993.
[137] [2000] 1 ILRM 321, 337.
[138] [2000] 1 ILRM 121 (HC); [2000] 4 IR 1, [2000] 2 ILRM 451 (SC).

the Supreme Court was dismissed, Denham J stating that whilst the Family Law Act 1995 allows for the joining of the Attorney General as a party to the proceedings, it is not mandatory. The parties are given a choice as to whether to give notice to the Attorney General and the latter is given a choice as to whether to join the proceedings or not. In her view while the Attorney General may be joined to "proceedings", in the case before her, the proceedings had concluded, the order and judgment had been given and there were no extant proceedings to which he could be joined.

CHAPTER SEVEN

DISCOVERY

INTRODUCTION

The Nature and Purpose of Discovery

7.001 Discovery describes the procedure whereby a litigant in civil proceedings obtains prior to the trial disclosure of documents in the possession or control of another party, or occasionally from a non-party, which are relevant to the litigation. As Matthews and Malek point out: "although much information can be obtained voluntarily, some cannot, and often the most relevant information is in the hands of the opposing party, who will certainly not disclose it willingly if it hurts his own case".[1] Accordingly, it was accepted that some form of compulsory disclosure procedure would be necessary to ensure that justice is done and it was in order to meet this requirement that the discovery process was developed. It has long been recognised that discovery of documents is an "extremely valuable legal procedure".[2] However, there is also growing judicial awareness of the fact that it imposes a considerable burden on litigants and that there is "a danger that this valuable legal procedure may be invoked unnecessarily or applied oppressively".[3] As McCracken J recently commented in *Hannon v Commissioners of Public Works*[4] "the court is entitled to take into account the extent to which discovery of documents might become oppressive, and should be astute to ensure that the procedure of discovery is not used as a tactic in the war between the parties". Clearly the courts are increasingly aware of the possible misuse of the discovery process and it is interesting that in a number of recent cases dealing with different aspects of the procedure, the underlying rationale behind the judgments has been similar, namely that orders for discovery should only be made where they are necessary.

As Finlay CJ stated in *AIB Banks plc v Ernst & Whinney*[5] "the basic purpose and reason for the procedure of discovery ... is to ensure as far as possible that the full facts concerning any matter in dispute before the court are capable of being presented to the court by the parties concerned, so that justice on full information, rather than on a limited or partial revelation of the facts arising in

---

[1] *Disclosure* (2nd ed., 2000) at 4.
[2] *Per* Murphy J in *Irish Nationwide Building Society v Charlton* Supreme Court, 5 March 1997 at 13.
[3] *Ibid.* at 13.
[4] High Court (McCracken J) 4 April 2001 at 4.
[5] [1993] 1 IR 375, 390.

a particular action, may be done." While the aim of discovery could be said to be "to aid a party in the progress of litigation"[6] and to prevent "unfair evidential advantage being taken at the trial",[7] it should also be availed of "to remove some issues from the debate thus saving time and costs".[8] Therefore one of the purposes of discovery could also be described as being "to help to define the issues as sharply as possible in advance so that the actual hearing is allowed to take its course as smoothly as possible".[9] A useful summary of the aims of the discovery process is provided by Henchy J in the course of his judgment in *McCarthy v O'Flynn*[10] in the following terms:

> The aim of the relevant rules is to enable a party to learn, in advance of the trial, of the existence of the documents on which his opponent might rely at the trial; to give the party who has obtained an order for discovery an opportunity of seeking production for inspection of any of those documents; and to debar the party who has made discovery from introducing in evidence at the trial documents which he ought to have, but has not, discovered.

Limitations on the Use of Discovery

7.002 Discovery has been described as "an instrument to advance the cause of justice"[11] and it has been clearly stated that the purpose of discovery is to aid a party in the process of litigation and that it is not to be invoked so as to enable a person to plead a cause of action which he is not otherwise in a position to do.[12] Similarly the court will not make an order adding a party as a defendant to proceedings in circumstances where the plaintiff seeks the order merely for the purpose of obtaining discovery of documents from the proposed defendant.[13]

---

[6] *Galvin v Graham Twomey* [1994] 2 ILRM 315, 318 *per* O'Flaherty J.

[7] *McCarthy v O'Flynn* [1979] IR 127, 129 *per* Henchy J.

[8] *Ibid. per* O'Flaherty J.

[9] *AIB Banks plc v Ernst & Whinney* [1993] 1 IR 375, 396 *per* O'Flaherty J. See also *Spring Grove Services (Ireland) Ltd v O'Callaghan* High Court (Herbert J) 31 July 2000 at 9.

[10] [1979] IR 127, 129.

[11] *AIB Banks plc v Ernst & Whinney* [1993] 1 IR 375, 396 *per* O'Flaherty J.

[12] *Galvin v Graham Twomey* [1994] 2 ILRM 315, 318 *per* O'Flaherty J. So, in the context of defamation proceedings, it was essential for the plaintiff to be able to prove publication of a defamatory matter; he could not be permitted to institute proceedings and then hope to be able to amend his pleadings by obtaining discovery and thereby make his case.

[13] *International Trading Group Ltd v Dublin Corporation* [1974] IR 373. Kenny J quoted with approval from the judgment of Lord Denning in *Norwich Pharmacal Co. v Commissioners of Customs and Excise* [1972] 3 WLR 870, 876, [1972] 3 All ER 813, 817 to the effect that "it would be intolerable if an innocent person without any interest in a case were to be subjected to an action simply to get papers or information out of

It is generally accepted that documents, having been disclosed on foot of a discovery order, are subject to an implied undertaking that they will not be used for any purpose other than the proper conduct of the action, or as Murphy J commented in *Countyglen plc v Carway*[14] "discovery is made solely for the purposes of the particular litigation in which the order is made". This point was explained in the following terms by Finlay CJ in *Ambiorix Ltd v Minister for the Environment (No. 1)*:[15]

> As a matter of general principle, of course, a party obtaining the production of documents by discovery in an action is prohibited by law from making any use of any description of such documents or the information contained in them otherwise than for the purpose of the action. To go outside that prohibition is to commit contempt of court.

The rationale behind this principle was explained by Keane J in *Greencore Group plc v Murphy*[16] as being that an order requiring the production of documents is an invasion of the right of the person against whom the order is made to keep his own documents to himself and it is for this reason that the courts will require that such documents are only used for the purpose of the particular legal proceedings in which they are produced. However, it would appear from the judgment of Kelly J in *Roussel v Farchepro Ltd*[17] that the principle set out by Finlay CJ in *Ambiorix* may be modified in limited circumstances. The plaintiff applied for leave to use documents discovered by the seventh named defendant in a claim for infringement of patents in proceedings pending before courts outside the jurisdiction in Spain and Switzerland. Kelly J referred to both the *dicta* of Finlay CJ in *Ambiorix* and to that of O'Flaherty J in *Megaleasing Ltd v Barrett*[18] but he said that in his view these statements were made *obiter* and that neither of them constituted a binding authority on him. He also made reference to the speech of Lord Oliver in *Crest Homes plc v Marks*[19] which he said made it "abundantly clear" that it is permissible to modify or vary an undertaking not to use discovered documents for any collateral purpose. To adopt an inflexible view in relation to the issue would in his opinion result in the court's hands being unduly and unnecessarily tied and be likely to give rise to injustice and to frustrate the constitutional obligation which is imposed upon the court to

---

him". Note that Order 31, rule 29 of the Rules of the Superior Courts 1986 introduced the concept of non-party discovery which will be considered in detail *infra*.

[14] [1995] 1 IR 208, 218, [1995] 1 ILRM 481, 490. See also the *dicta* of Keane J in *Fields v Woodland Products Ltd* High Court (Keane J) 16 July 1999.

[15] [1992] 1 IR 277, 286, [1992] ILRM 209, 215. Quoted with approval by Kelly J in *Cooper Flynn v RTE* [2000] 3 IR 344, [2001] 1 ILRM 208.

[16] [1995] 3 IR 520, [1996] 1 ILRM 210.

[17] [1999] 3 IR 567, [2000] 1 ILRM 321.

[18] [1993] ILRM 497, 507

[19] [1987] 1 AC 829, [1987] 3 WLR 293, [1987] 2 All ER 1074.

administer justice. Kelly J then proceeded to consider the circumstances in which an undertaking not to use discovered documents for another purpose should be modified or released and stated that these circumstances would of course vary from case to case. The appropriate approach was for the court to look at all the circumstances, including if necessary, the circumstances of the original disclosure, the nature and strength of the evidence, the type of wrongdoing which is alleged to be involved and the interests of both parties and any public interest at stake. In the case before him, Kelly J was satisfied that there were special circumstances in relation to the Spanish proceedings[20] as there was an element of urgency and there was no danger of a loss of confidentiality by reason of the way in which the documents would be dealt with by the Spanish court. Kelly J concluded that he was satisfied that there would be a risk of injustice to the plaintiff if these documents were not disclosed and no risk of injustice to the seventh named defendant and he therefore made an order permitting the use of the documents for the Spanish courts.

7.003 It has been stressed on a number of occasions that discovery, like other procedures of an interlocutory nature, is "a means to an end and should never be allowed to take on a life of [its] own"[21] and criticisms have been made to the effect that such interlocutory matters may be used "to hold up the business of the courts".[22] Clearly the courts must ensure that what may be a valuable and often very necessary legal procedure is used in order to further the aim of achieving justice between the parties to an action and not to unnecessarily delay or increase the costs of proceedings. These concerns have been aptly summed up by Murphy J in the course of his judgment in *Irish Nationwide Building Society v Charlton*:[23]

> Discovery of documents is an extremely valuable legal procedure. On the other hand it can be a very burdensome one. Perhaps this burden has been accentuated by the proliferation of documentary records and the improvement in recent years of photocopying equipment. There is a danger that this valuable legal procedure may be invoked unnecessarily or applied oppressively. It will always involve delay and expense. In virtually every commercial case it is the greatest single cause of delay in obtaining a judicial determination on the real issues between the parties. It may be

---

[20] Although not in relation to the Swiss proceedings. He concluded that in the case of the Swiss litigation he ought to refuse the relief sought by the plaintiff on the basis that he was not satisfied that injustice would be caused to the plaintiff by taking this course and he felt that there was a danger of such injustice being caused to the party disclosing the information by reason of confidentiality being lost. In addition, he pointed to the fact that there was no urgency involved in obtaining these documents.
[21] *AIB Banks plc v Ernst & Whinney* [1993] 1 IR 375, 398 *per* O'Flaherty J.
[22] *Stafford v Revenue Commissioners* Supreme Court, 27 March 1996 *per* O'Flaherty J.
[23] Supreme Court, 5 March 1997 at 13.

that litigants should consider more carefully whether in particular cases discovery is required.

These comments illustrate a growing judicial awareness of the pitfalls of over-reliance on the discovery process and of the need to avoid its use in situations where it is clearly not warranted.[24] As O'Flaherty J commented in *Murphy v Minister for Defence*[25] "[w]hile there will be many cases where, of course, discovery is an essential requirement to make sure that justice is done there will be many simple, straightforward cases where a motion for discovery would be needless". However, it must be said that discovery will be deemed necessary in order to achieve the aims referred to above in a large number of cases and these comments could be said to reflect a degree of exasperation at the use of the discovery process as a delaying tactic.

A further potential abuse which has been referred to is the practice of swamping the opposing party with a huge volume of material with a view to overburdening him or in the hope that it will lead to a significant document being overlooked. While it will be difficult to establish that a party engaged in such deliberate conduct, the comment has been made that "to engage in such a tactic is as much an abuse as to withhold relevant information".[26]

TIME OF DISCOVERY

7.004 Discovery will generally not be granted until after the statement of claim and defence have been delivered as prior to this the issues in dispute between the parties are unlikely to be clear.[27] Order 31, rule 12(4)(4) provides that an application for discovery, whether pursuant to rule 12(1) or (4) shall be made not later than 28 days after the action has been set down, or in matters which are not set down, 28 days after it has been listed for trial. The subrule goes on to provide that the time limit may be extended by agreement between the parties or by order of the court where "it appears just and reasonable so to do".

Traditionally a plaintiff would not be entitled to an order for discovery before delivery of the statement of claim unless the court was satisfied by reason of material contained in an affidavit that a special case had been made out.[28] It has long been accepted that such an order is "an exceptional one" at this stage in the proceedings although it will be made in a proper case where the circum-

---

[24] See also *Brooks Thomas Ltd v Impac* [1999] 1 ILRM 171.

[25] [1991] 2 IR 161, 167.

[26] *AIB Banks plc v Ernst & Whinney* [1993] 1 IR 375, 397 *per* O'Flaherty J.

[27] As Lawton LJ commented in *R.H.M. Foods Ltd v Bovril Ltd* [1982] 1 WLR 661, 665, [1982] 1 All ER 673, 677: "Until at least a statement of claim has been delivered the court can seldom know what are the matters in question in the action".

[28] *Hunter v Nelson* (1881) 15 ILTR 16.

stances demand it.[29] Similarly, discovery has been granted to defendants before a defence has been delivered in circumstances where the defendants sought to ascertain the damage which the plaintiff had suffered with a view to paying money into court with the defence.[30]

7.005 More recently it has been reiterated that while the courts do have jurisdiction to order that discovery be made before delivery of a statement of claim, such an order will only be made "in the most exceptional circumstances",[31] *e.g.* in order to avoid substantial unnecessary amendments being made to the pleadings.[32] This issue was considered by Morris J, as he then was, in *Law Society of Ireland v Rawlinson and Hunter*,[33] which concerned a claim of negligence brought by the plaintiff against the defendant, a firm of accountants which had acted for a solicitor whose clients had made claims against the plaintiff's compensation fund. The plaintiff claimed to be entitled to discovery even though no statement of claim had been delivered as it had been advised that until it had access to the defendant's files, it would not be possible to prepare a properly particularised and comprehensive statement of claim. The defendant contended that the normal practice is that discovery is only made after a statement of claim has been delivered and is never given in order to allow a plaintiff to trawl through a defendant's papers in the hope of discovering a basis for a claim. Morris J stated that it was in his view well settled that while the court does have the power to make an order for discovery under Order 31 rule 12 prior to delivery of the statement of claim, such an order should only be made in the most exceptional circumstances. Morris J also quoted the following passage from the headnote to the judgment of Rogers J in the Australian decision of *Gollin Holdings Ltd v Adcock*:[34]

> The rule that discovery cannot be had before pleading should give way to the demands of justice in particular instances and in particular where the application is not a 'fishing expedition' and the nature of the claim has been made clear.

Morris J concluded that applying these principles to the matter before him, there were facts and circumstances in the case which would render it an exceptional

---

[29] *Stewart v Ratner Safe Company* (1907) 41 ILTR 74; *Kinsella v Flanagan* (1901) 35 ILTR 98. See also *Walshe v Gallagher* [1955-56] Ir Jur Rep 51 in which Murnaghan J commented that such an order would only be made "in very special circumstances".
[30] *Megaw v M'Diarmid* (1882) 10 LR Ir 376.
[31] *Gale v Denman Picture Houses Ltd* [1930] 1 KB 588, 590 *per* Scrutton LJ. *Law Society of Ireland v Rawlinson and Hunter* [1997] 3 IR 592.
[32] *Speyside Estate and Trust Co. Ltd v Wraymond Freeman (Blenders) Ltd* [1950] 1 Ch 96, [1949] 2 All ER 796.
[33] [1997] 3 IR 592.
[34] [1981] NSWLR 691.

one. In this regard Morris J referred to the complexity of the case, the nature of the plaintiff's statutory obligations to make good the solicitor's default from the compensation fund, the fact that there existed a stateable case capable of being pleaded in general terms and the desirability of having a concise and clear statement of claim which would enable the defendant to know the case it had to meet. In his view it appeared beyond doubt that the plaintiff was already in possession of information which would enable it "to prepare and deliver a statement of claim reflecting the basic ingredients of the case which [it] wish[es] to make against the defendant" and it was not a "trawling exercise".

The importance of this point was emphasised by Laffoy J in *AMEC plc v Bord Gais Éireann*[35] in which a number of defendants challenged the plaintiffs' entitlement to obtain discovery against them. While the statement of claim and defence had been delivered, these defendants contended that they were entitled to proper particulars of the plaintiffs' claim before they should be called upon to make discovery. It was submitted on their behalf that where, as in the case before the court, the allegations were vague and the plaintiff was unable to particularise them, the court should not order discovery to assist the plaintiff to make his case. Laffoy J referred to the principles set out in the *Law Society* case and in particular to the point made by Morris J that the plaintiff in that case was in possession of such information as would enable it to prepare and deliver a statement of claim reflecting the basic ingredients of the case it wished to make and that there existed a stateable case capable of being pleaded in general terms. In her view, when the motion in the case before her was issued, the plaintiffs had pleaded their claims against the defendants with sufficient clarity to ensure that these defendants knew the claims being made against them and the issues between the parties had been established. While Laffoy J expressed no view as to whether the plaintiffs had adequately particularised their claims in response to the defendants' requests for further particulars, she stated that she had no doubt that on the present state of the pleadings, the plaintiffs were entitled to an order for discovery against these defendants.

7.006 Where a preliminary issue of law arises, it will be appropriate to dispose of it before ordering discovery.[36] So in *McCabe v Ireland*[37] the Supreme Court upheld the decision of the High Court directing the trial of preliminary issues of law and postponing the making of an order of discovery.

Finally, it should be noted that in certain circumstances, discovery has been ordered after judgment. In *Henessey v Lavery*[38] the plaintiffs had obtained judgment for an injunction and an account of profits against a defendant and discov-

---

[35] High Court (Laffoy J) 4 July 1997.
[36] See Order 31, rule 19.
[37] [2000] 1 ILRM 410.
[38] [1903] 1 IR 87.

ery was granted to enable the plaintiff to test the accuracy of the account which
the defendant had lodged.

INTER PARTES DISCOVERY

Introduction

7.007 Order 31, rule 12(1) as initially set out in the Rules of the Superior
Courts 1986[39] provided that a party might apply to the court for an order directing discovery without filing an affidavit and that the court might refuse or adjourn such an application if satisfied that it was not necessary, or not necessary
at that stage of the proceedings.[40] Rule 12(3) went on to provide that an order
should not be made "if and so far as the court shall be of opinion that it is not
necessary either for disposing fairly of the cause or matter or for saving costs".[41]
Commenting on these original provisions, Finlay CJ stated as follows in the
course of his judgment in *AIB Banks plc v Ernst & Whinney*:[42]

> It would appear that the court should only adjourn or refuse such an appli-
> cation if it is satisfied that it is not necessary, either at all or at the time at
> which it is made, either for disposing fairly of the cause or matter or for
> saving costs. The onus of establishing that would appear, *prima facie* to
> lie upon the party against whom discovery is sought and who resists it....
> [T]he proper construction of rule 12 dealing with discovery by a party, is
> that the court's discretion to refuse it is confined to its being satisfied that
> either in the form of the application itself or in respect of the time at which
> it is made, it is not necessary either for disposing fairly of the cause or
> matter, or for saving costs.

The meaning of the requirement that discovery shall not be ordered if it is not
"necessary either for disposing fairly of the cause or matter or for saving costs"
was considered by Kelly LJ in his judgment in *Lanigan v Chief Constable*[43]
and he brought together a number of statements which in his view contained

---

[39] Rules of the Superior Courts (No. 2) 1999 (Discovery) (SI No. 233 of 1999) substituted
a new rule 12 which will be considered *infra*.
[40] Geoghegan J commented in *Bailey v Flood* High Court (Geoghegan J) 15 May 1998 at
5 that this rule was interpreted to mean that the court could only refuse to make an
order for discovery if satisfied that it was not necessary or not necessary at that stage of
the proceedings. See also *AIB Banks plc v Ernst and Whinney* [1993] 1 IR 375, 389,
referred to *infra*.
[41] This subrule remained unaltered when a new rule 12 was substituted by Rules of the
Superior Courts (No. 2) 1999 (Discovery) (SI No. 233 of 1999).
[42] [1993] 1 IR 375, 388-389.
[43] [1991] NI 42, 52.

useful indications of what 'necessity' meant in this context. These were as follows:

> 1. [Are the statements sought] "very likely to contain material which would give substantial support to [the plaintiffs'] contentions? Would he be deprived of the means of proper presentation of his case?" (Lord Fraser in *Air Canada v Secretary of State for Trade* [1983] 2 AC 394).

> 2. [Can it be said] "there [is] a likelihood that the documents would support the case of the party seeking discovery?" [Is there] "something beyond speculation, some concrete ground for belief which takes the case beyond a mere 'fishing' expedition?" (Lord Wilberforce in *Air Canada*).

The meaning of the phrase "necessary for disposing fairly of the cause or matter" has recently been considered by Kelly J in *Cooper Flynn v Radio Telefís Éireann*[44] in the context of Order 31, rule 18 which provides for inspection of documents. Kelly J said that he derived considerable assistance from the English authorities to which he had been referred and there is no reason to suggest that the relevant ones should not also apply in the context of discovery.[45]

7.008 Order 31, rule 12(4) was added in 1993[46] and provided that an order directing discovery should generally not be made unless the applicant had previously applied for voluntary discovery and the person to whom such a request was made had failed to make such discovery within a reasonable time. Rule 12(4)(1) goes on to provide that where the parties agree or because of the urgency of the matter, the nature of the case or any other circumstances which seem appropriate to the court, the court may make an order for discovery without the necessity for prior application in writing. Rule 12(4)(2) provides that an agreement to make discovery on such a voluntary basis shall "be made in like manner and form and have such effect as if directed by order of the court". Accordingly, a party may apply to the court for an order of discovery pursuant to rule 12(1) where the other party has refused to make voluntary discovery, or has failed to do so within a reasonable time or where because of the special circumstances of the case the court deems the voluntary discovery process unnecessary.

Signs of a more rigorous attitude being displayed by the judiciary towards the interpretation of rule 12 had been growing more obvious. It is particularly evident in the judgment of the Supreme Court in *Brooks Thomas Ltd v Impac Ltd*[47] where Lynch J refused to order discovery of documents in which he could

---

[44] [2000] 3 IR 344, [2001] 1 ILRM 208.
[45] See *infra* Inspection.
[46] Inserted by Rules of the Superior Courts (No. 2) 1993 (SI No. 265 of 1993). See Brady (1999) 4 BR 58.
[47] [1999] 1 ILRM 171.

only see a "tenuous relevance" on the grounds that they were not necessary either for disposing fairly of the action or for saving costs. He added that the delay in bringing the case to trial stemmed from the parties seeking discovery which seemed to him quite unnecessary "instead of getting on with the case and achieving finality".[48]

Changes to the Discovery Process

7.009 The increasing dissatisfaction with the manner in which rule 12 was being utilized culminated in the substitution of a new rule with effect from 3 August 1999 which substantially altered the discovery process in a number of material ways.[49] First, the written application seeking voluntary discovery is now required to specify the precise categories of documents in respect of which discovery is sought and must also set out reasons why each category of documents is required. However, as pointed out above, it should be noted that a proviso sets out that where, by reason of the urgency of the matter, the consent of the parties, the nature of the case or any other circumstances which to the court seem appropriate, the court may make an order as appears proper, without the necessity for such prior application in writing.[50] Secondly, the notice of motion is required to specify the precise categories of documents in respect of which discovery is sought. Thirdly, motions for discovery must now be grounded on an affidavit[51] which shall verify that the discovery sought is necessary for disposing fairly of the matter or for saving costs and shall furnish the reasons why each category of documents is required to be discovered. These new requirements have resulted in a number of important changes both in relation to the type of order of discovery being sought and to the manner in which the court's discretion will be exercised.[52] It will no longer suffice to seek a general order for discovery seeking all relevant documents in the other party's posses-

---

[48] *Ibid.* at 177. This decision was distinguished by Herbert J in *Spring Grove Services (Ireland) Ltd v O'Callaghan* High Court (Herbert J) 31 July 2000 where he stated that it was impossible to suggest that the trial would be unnecessarily and unreasonably delayed by the motion for further discovery or that it had been so delayed by previous applications for discovery.

[49] Rules of the Superior Courts (No.2) (Discovery) 1999 (SI No. 233 of 1999).

[50] Rule 12(4)(1). See *Brian Greene & Co. Ltd v Instruelec Services Ltd* High Court (McKechnie J) 19 February 2001.

[51] It is interesting to note that at the conclusion of his judgment in *Brooks Thomas Ltd v Impac Ltd* [1999] 1 ILRM 171, 178 Lynch J made the following comment: "In view of the trend in modern times to seek discovery in almost every case the Superior Court Rules Committee might consider changing rule 12(1) so as to require an affidavit before discovery is ordered".

[52] Brady has commented (1999) 4 BR 58, 59 that the new provisions are an indication of a shift in attitude by the judiciary towards the process of discovery and that: "[a] more rigourous and analytical approach to the grant of discovery will, in future, be a feature of this procedure".

sion or power and precise categories of documents will have to be specified. In addition, while under the original rule 12(1) the onus of establishing that an order for discovery was not necessary appeared to lie on the party against whom discovery is sought, the substituted rule clearly requires the party seeking the order to verify that the discovery is necessary and to furnish reasons why each category of documents is required to be discovered.

7.010 The manner in which these new provisions should be interpreted was considered by Morris P in his judgment in *Swords v Western Proteins Ltd*[53] which concerned an appeal from an order of the Master that the defendants should make discovery. The Master had ordered the defendants to make discovery of, *inter alia*, an accident report form and all documents relating to the reporting and investigation of an accident in which the plaintiff was involved up to the date when the defendant was made aware of the plaintiff's intention to bring legal proceedings in relation to the accident. Counsel for the defendant submitted that the Master had misdirected himself in allowing discovery of these documents. Counsel submitted that in contravention of Order 31, rule 12(4) the letters written by the plaintiff's solicitor made no attempt to specify the precise category of documents in respect of which discovery was sought, that no reason had been furnished setting out why each category of documents was required to be discovered and that no reasonable period of time for discovery had been allowed. In addition, counsel contended that when the matter first came before the Master, the grounding affidavit failed to verify that the discovery of the documents sought was necessary and that it did not give reasons indicating why each category was required to be discovered. He submitted that while a supplemental affidavit filed by the plaintiff may have done this, the Master had been wrong in law in adjourning the matter to enable such an affidavit to be filed.

Morris P stated that he was satisfied that the amendment to Order 31, rule 12 had been made for the purpose of addressing a problem which had given rise to delay and potential injustice over a number of years. He continued as follows:

> Accordingly I believe that SI No. 233 of 1999 imposed a clearly defined obligation upon a party seeking discovery to pinpoint the documents or category of documents required and required that party to give the reasons why they were required. Blanket discovery became a thing of the past. The new rule was brought into being to ensure in the first instance that the party against whom discovery was being sought would, upon receipt of the preliminary letter, be in a position to know the document or category of documents referred to and be able to exercise a judgment on whether the reasons given for requiring those documents to be discovered was valid. He would then be in a position to know if he was required to

---

[53] [2001]1 ILRM 481. See Delany (2001) 19 ILT 57 and Kavanagh (2001) 6 BR 273.

comply with the request. If he disputed his obligation to make discovery the court would know by reference to this letter precisely why the moving party sought the documents in question and the grounds upon which the moving party believed that the documents sought to be discovered might help to dispose fairly of the cause or save costs.[54]

Morris P held that if the letter of application did not comply with the rules then the Master had no power to make a determination even where an elaborate affidavit is filed in support of the application. In his opinion the Master derived his jurisdiction to determine the questions which arise between the parties from the identification of the issues in the applicant's originating letter or letters. This is an important point and illustrates that considerable thought must be put into the contents of the letter seeking voluntary discovery and that the specific requirements of the rules must be complied with at this stage and not just when the grounding affidavit is being drawn up.

Applying these principles to the case before him, Morris P stated that, in as much as the plaintiff's solicitor's letter had identified the documents as "accident report book/record details", no effort had been made to specify the precise categories of documents sought. In addition, Morris P was satisfied that there had been a failure on the part of the plaintiff's solicitors to furnish reasons why each of the categories of documents was required to be discovered.

Turning to the submissions made in relation to the requirements of rule 12 as to the contents of the affidavit, Morris P pointed out that when the matter came before the Master the only affidavit was that of the plaintiff's solicitors which neither verified that discovery was necessary for the purpose of disposing fairly of the cause or matter or to save costs nor did it furnish reasons why each category of documents was required. However, the solicitor had obtained leave from the Master to file a supplemental affidavit which in the view of Morris P complied with the requirements of the rule. He added that he had no doubt that it was within the Master's jurisdiction to give the plaintiff an opportunity to file a supplemental affidavit to enable him to comply with the rules of court. In response to a further argument put by counsel for the defendant that the limits of the Master's jurisdiction in this regard are as set out in Order 31, rule 12(2), Morris P stressed that in his view the Master had an overall jurisdiction to adjourn a case if the interests of justice required it and that his authority was not derived solely from the provisions of rule 12(2).

Despite the considerable importance which Morris P appeared to place in his judgment in *Swords* on the requirements relating to the content of the application in writing seeking voluntary discovery, in practice some latitude is being permitted in this regard. So, where precise categories of documents have not

---

[54] *Ibid.* at 487. Note that in *Burke v Director of Public Prosecutions* Supreme Court, 21 June 2001 Keane CJ expressed his agrement with the view adopted by Morris P in relation to the object of SI No. 233 of 1999 and its importance.

been specified in the original application, the High Court may subsequently allow some elaboration thereof.

This is borne out by the approach adopted by McKechnie J in *Brian Greene & Co. Ltd v Instruelec Services Ltd*[55] in which he made an order for discovery notwithstanding the Master's refusal to do so on the grounds that the letter seeking voluntary discovery was insufficiently precise. However, it should be pointed out that this case came within the terms of the proviso in rule 12(4)(1), on the basis that the parties consented to an order for discovery being made, and in such circumstances there had been compliance with the rules and the court clearly had jurisdiction to make the order sought.

What is a Document?

7.011 There is no definition of the word "document" set out in Order 31, although over the years a process of judicial interpretation has built up a fairly accurate picture of how the word may be defined in this context. An early definition contained in the judgment of Darling J in *R v Daye*[56] is "any written thing capable of being evidence is properly described as a document and it is immaterial on what the writing may be inscribed".

Originally a rather narrow interpretation was also given to the word in this jurisdiction and in *Lynch v Fleming*[57] McLoughlin J stated that a document did not appear to be capable of being interpreted as the thoughts or ideas of any person and concluded that X-ray plates or photographs did not come within the definition for the purposes of discovery. However, the decision in *Lynch* was overruled by the Supreme Court in *McCarthy v O'Flynn*[58] and both the judgments of Henchy and Kenny JJ contain useful *dicta* on this issue. Henchy J stated that the word "document" should be construed so that it would "comprehend the full range of things which could become part of the court file at the end of the hearing of the proceedings" and in that sense would clearly include X-ray films. He stated as follows:

> I think that where the word occurs in the discovery rules it should be construed in terms of the scheme and purpose of those rules. Thus read, I consider that the word includes any thing which, if adduced in evidence at the hearing of the proceedings, would be put in, or become annexed to, the court file of the proceedings. All such things are part of the documentation of the case and qualify for preservation as part of the court archives.[59]

Kenny J expressed the view that the statement of Darling J in *R v Daye* was

---

[55] High Court (McKechnie J) 19 February 2001.
[56] [1908] 2 KB 333, 340.
[57] [1953-54] Ir Jur Rep 45.
[58] [1979] IR 127.
[59] *Ibid.* at 129.

defective as it did not refer to the main characteristic of a document, namely that it is something which gives information.[60] In his opinion an X-ray plate or photograph gives information and so it is a document and the defendant was entitled to discovery of it.

A number of English authorities were referred to by Kenny J in the course of his judgment in *McCarthy* and it is useful to consider them briefly as they refer to different types of "documents". In *Lyell v Kennedy (No. 3)*,[61] the Court of Appeal accepted that photographs were documents for the purposes of discovery. Subsequently in *Grant v Southwestern & County Properties Ltd*[62] Walton J held that tape recordings of evidence or information can also be regarded as documents in the context of the discovery process[63] and rejected the argument that they could not be classed as documents because they could not be inspected visually. As he stated: "the mere interposition of necessity of an instrument for deciphering the information cannot make any difference in principle".[64]

7.012 More recently the question has arisen whether computer records can be regarded as documents and this was considered by Vinelott J in *Derby and Co. Ltd v Weldon (No. 9)*.[65] He concluded that a computer database or information stored in back up files are documents for the purposes of discovery. He added:

> Similarly, there can be no distinction in principle between the tape used to record a telephone conversation in *Grant v Southwestern & County Properties Ltd* which was an ordinary analogue tape.... and a compact disc or digital tape on which sound, speech as well as music, is mapped by co-ordinates and recorded in the form of groups of binary numbers. And no clear dividing line can be drawn between digital tape recording messages and the database of a computer on which information which has been fed into the computer is analysed and recorded in a variety of media in binary language.

Recently in *Irish Nationwide Building Society v Charlton*[66] Murphy J commented that "what is included in [the word 'documents'] may be open to some

---

[60] This echoes the view put forward by Humphreys J in *Hill v R* [1945] KB 329, 332-333 that "a document must be something which teaches you and from which you can learn something *i.e.* it must be something which affords information".

[61] (1884) 27 Ch D 1. See *Grant v Southwestern & County Properties Ltd* [1975] Ch 185, 191, [1974] 3 WLR 221, 226, [1974] 2 All ER 465, 469-470 *per* Walton J.

[62] [1975] Ch 185, [1974] 3 WLR 221, [1974] 2 All ER 465.

[63] Matthews and Malek in *Disclosure* (2nd ed., 2000) at 93 suggest that "[g]iven the position regarding audio tapes, there is no reason to doubt that video and audio discs are also documents for the purposes of [discovery]".

[64] [1975] Ch 185, 197, [1974] 3 WLR 221, 231, [1974] 2 All ER 465, 474.

[65] [1991] 1 WLR 652, [1991] 2 All ER 901.

[66] Supreme Court, 5 March 1997.

debate". However, the broad interpretation placed on the word in *McCarthy v O'Flynn* would suggest that a flexible attitude will be adopted by the judiciary in this jurisdiction and there is nothing to suggest that the *dicta* of Vinelott J in *Derby* will not be followed,[67] or indeed developed if and when this is deemed necessary.

"Relating to any Matter in Question"

7.013 O'Flaherty J stressed in *Stafford v Revenue Commissioners*[68] that "the most singular thing about discovery is that the documents sought to be discovered have to be relevant to the matter in issue".[69] Order 31, rule 12(1) requires a party to make discovery of documents which are or have been in his possession or power "relating to any matter in question therein". The question of what documents will be relevant in this context was considered by Brett LJ in *Compagnie Financiere et Commerciale du Pacifique v Peruvian Guano Company*[70] and his *dicta* have been referred to in numerous cases since and merit being set out in full.

> It seems to me that every document relates to the matters in question in the action, which not only would be evidence upon any issue, but also which, it is reasonable to suppose, contains information which *may* – not which *must* – either directly or indirectly enable the party requiring the affidavit either to advance his own case or to damage the case of his adversary. I have put in the words 'either directly or indirectly' because, as it seems to me, a document can properly be said to contain information which may enable the party requiring the affidavit either to advance his own case or damage the case of his adversary, if it is a document which may fairly lead him to a train of inquiry, which may have either of these two consequences.

This statement was quoted with approval by Kenny J in *Sterling-Winthrop v*

---

[67] This *dicta* was referred to by Denham J in her judgment in *Keane v An Bord Pleanála* [1997] 1 IR 184 in considering principles of statutory interpretation.

[68] Supreme Court, 27 March 1996. A dispute arose about the importation of a bronze statute and the Revenue Commissioners sought and obtained an order for discovery in wide terms relating to previous importations. On the issue of relevance, O'Flaherty J concluded that the documents dealing with previous importations were not relevant to the matter that would have to be resolved in the litigation before him and he amended the order made by the Master on this basis.

[69] Clearly there will be limits to the scope of the term "relevance", see *e.g. Blascaod Mór Teo v Commissioners of Public Works* [1994] 2 IR 372.

[70] (1882) 11 QBD 55, 63. Although as Murray J stated in *Aquatechnologie Ltd v National Standards Authority of Ireland* Supreme Court, 10 July 2000 at 11 there is nothing in this statement which is intended to qualify the principle that documents sought on discovery must be relevant, directly or indirectly, to the matters in issue between the parties.

Farbenfabriken Bayer AG[71] in which he refused an application by the plaintiffs for further discovery on the grounds, *inter alia*, that the plaintiffs had failed to show that further documents relevant to the issues in the action were in the possession of the defendants. These principles were also approved by Costello J in *Irish Shell Ltd v Dan Ryan Ltd*[72] in which he formulated the test of relevance in the following terms: "a discovery affidavit must not merely comprise those documents which would support or defeat any issue in the case but which could reasonably be said to contain information which might either directly or indirectly enable a plaintiff who has sought discovery to advance his own case or damage the case of a defendant". However, as Murray J made it clear in *Aquatechnologie Ltd v National Standards Authority of Ireland*[73] an applicant for discovery must show that it is reasonable for the court to suppose that the documents contain information which may enable the applicant to advance his own case or to damage the case of his adversary. As he stated "an applicant is not entitled to discovery based on mere speculation or on the basis of what has been traditionally characterized as a fishing expedition".[74] Similarly, as McCracken J stated in *Hannon v Commissioners of Public Works*,[75] "a party may not seek discovery of a document in order to find out whether the document may be relevant. A general trawl through the other parties' documentation is not permitted under the rules."

The *Compagnie Financiere* principles were also followed and applied by Flood J in *Woodfab Ltd v Coillte Teoranta*[76] in which the plaintiff claimed declarations in relation to the defendant's alleged abuse of a dominant position in the raw timber market in Ireland and sought an order seeking further and better discovery or, an order striking out the defence in default of such discovery. The High Court was required to consider which documents related to any matter in question and were discoverable. Flood J said that the documents to be produced were not confined to those which would be evidence to prove or disprove any matter in question but should include those which it was reasonable to suppose contained information which might enable the party requiring the affidavit either to advance his own case or damage that of his adversary. In the case before him, Flood J concluded that documents which went to show the manner in which the defendant conducted its business with customers were relevant.

---

[71] [1967] IR 97, 102. See also *Golden Vale Co-operative Creameries Ltd v Barrett* High Court (Hamilton P) 6 June 1986; *Irish Nationwide Building Society Ltd v Charlton* Supreme Court, 5 March 1997; *Kennedy v Law Society* Supreme Court, 28 November 1997; *Hughes v Garda Commissioner* High Court (Laffoy J) 20 January 1998 at 2; *Brooks Thomas Ltd v Impac Ltd* [1999] 1 ILRM 171, 176.
[72] High Court (Costello J) 22 April 1986 at 3.
[73] Supreme Court, 10 July 2000.
[74] *Ibid.* at 11.
[75] High Court (McCracken J) 4 April 2001 at 4.
[76] High Court (Flood J) 11 August 1995.

7.014 Morris J, as he then was, made it clear in *McKenna v Best Travel Ltd*[77] that it is only documents which would support or defeat an issue which arises in an existing action which are relevant and required to be discovered. The plaintiff sought damages for personal injuries sustained while on holiday in the Holy Land. The first named defendant went into voluntary liquidation and the plaintiff sought details of the insurance company which indemnified this defendant. The Master of the High Court made an order directing the first named defendant to disclose the identity of the insurance company and the defendant successfully appealed against the order. As Morris J stated, unless documents enable the plaintiff to advance his case or damage his opponent's, they will not be discoverable. He went on to say that none of the issues identified in the pleadings related to the first named defendant's indemnifiers and he concluded that documents which went outside these issues should not be required to be discovered. The fact that "relevance must be tested by the pleadings and particulars"[78] is also borne out by the conclusion reached by Blayney J in *Irish Intercontinental Bank Ltd v Brady.*[79] Blayney J was of the opinion that the pleadings in the case did not disclose any issue to which documents in the possession of auctioneers appointed by the plaintiff could be relevant and that therefore the defendant was not entitled to discovery of them. A similar point was made by McCracken J in his judgment in *Hannon v Commissioners of Public Works*[80] where he stressed that relevance must be determined in relation to the pleadings in the specific case and not by submissions as to alleged facts put forward in affidavits unless such submissions relate back to the pleadings, or in the case of an application for further and better discovery, to previously discovered documents.

7.015 It should be pointed out that it has been recognised, both in England and in this jurisdiction, that applying the *Compagnie Financiere* test to the facts of a case is often by no means straightforward and that "there is ample room for error"[81] in its application. This was made clear by Blayney J in the course of his judgment in *Irish Nationwide Building Society v Charlton*[82] when he referred to the fact that there may be "very real difficulty" in applying the test to the circumstances of a particular action. He continued as follows:

> Frequently the deponent will be familiar with the documents in his possession, power or procurement but [will] have little understanding of the manner in which the contents of any such document might advance the case of either party. It is this problem which imposes on the solicitor to the

---

[77] [1995] 1 IR 577, [1995] 2 ILRM 471.
[78] Halsbury 4th ed., volume 13 paragraph 38. Quoted with approval by Johnson J in *Murphy v Donohoe Ltd* [1996] 1 IR 123, 129, [1995] 2 ILRM 509, 512.
[79] Supreme Court, 1 June 1995.
[80] High Court (McCracken J) 4 April 2001.
[81] *The Consul Corfitson* [1917] AC 550, 553.
[82] Supreme Court, 5 March 1997.

party making discovery the duty to take positive steps to ensure that his client appreciates the extent of the obligation imposed by an order for discovery. The solicitor owes a duty to the court carefully to go through the documents disclosed by the client to make sure, as far as possible, that no relevant document has been withheld from disclosure.

This raises the question of who should decide upon the issue of relevance in a given case. In *Yates v Ciba Geigy Agro Ltd*[83] Barron J stated that whether or not documents are relevant is primarily a matter for the deponent of the affidavit of discovery but that where it can be shown that the deponent has misunderstood the issues or that his view that the documents are not relevant is wrong, discovery of these documents can be ordered. This issue was also considered by both Murphy J in the High Court[84] and Finlay CJ in the Supreme Court in *Bula Ltd v Crowley*.[85] Murphy J commented that "discovery is a procedure which is left to the integrity of the parties themselves ... [and] ... the deponent who swears the affidavit has the final word on what is relevant and it is difficult, if not impossible, for the court to go behind that". However, Finlay CJ stated that he was not satisfied that such an absolute protection of the decision by a deponent with regard to the question of discovery was warranted on principle and this approach would be supported by the subsequent comments of Murphy J in *Irish Nationwide Building Society v Charlton*[86] in relation to the difficulties which a deponent may have in identifying what is relevant for the purposes of discovery.

Possession or Power

7.016 Rule 12 envisages discovery of documents "which are or have been in [the] possession or power" of the deponent of the affidavit of discovery. The wording makes clear that documents are discoverable if they either "are or have been" in that party's possession or power; as Lord Diplock stated in *Lonrho Ltd v Shell Petroleum Co. Ltd*:[87] "The phrase ... looks to the present and the past, not to the future". So, as Lord Diplock went on to say, in the absence of a presently enforceable right to the documents, there is nothing to compel a party to take steps which will enable him to acquire one in the future.

In addition, Appendix C Form No. 10 at paragraph 7 sets out the appropriate form of averment for a party swearing an affidavit as to documents and requires that party to swear, *inter alia*, that according to the best of his knowledge, information and belief, there is not now and never was in his possession, custody or power, or that of his solicitors or agents, any documents other than

---

[83] High Court (Barron J) 29 April 1986.

[84] High Court (Murphy J) 19 December 1989 (*ex tempore*).

[85] [1991] 1 IR 220, 223, [1990] ILRM 756, 758.

[86] Supreme Court, 5 March 1997 at 15.

[87] [1980] 1 WLR 627, 635.

those set out. As O'Flaherty J commented in *Bula Ltd v Tara Mines Ltd*[88] three concepts come into play, namely possession, custody and power, and they are to be considered disjunctively.

It has been suggested by Dunn J in the English decision of *B. v B.*[89] that "possession" means the right to the possession of a document and does not require actual physical possession and there is no reason to suggest that the courts in this jurisdiction would disagree with such an approach. A fairly flexible interpretation was also placed on the words "possession or power" by Barron J in *Yates v Ciba Geigy Agro Ltd*[90] in which the plaintiff sought, *inter alia*, discovery of a report which the defendant averred was in the possession of its parent company. Barron J stated that "possession alone is not the test" and that documents may be in the power or procurement of a party even though they are not in his possession. In his view there was no reason to suppose that a request for the documents in question by the defendant would be refused and he said that *prima facie* they must be regarded as being available to the defendant if requested.[91] Barron J referred to the decision of Finlay P in *Northern Bank Finance Corporation v Charlton*[92] to support the argument that "documents not being in the power of a party may still be within his procurement".[93] In that case it was held that documents in the possession of a company were in the procurement of the plaintiff on the basis that if they were sought by it from the directors, having regard to the fact that they were nominees of the plaintiff, there was no reason to believe that they would refuse such a request.

7.017 However, more recent Supreme Court decisions would suggest that the interpretation placed on "possession or power" in *Yates* and *Northern Bank* was too broad and as Kinlen J pointed out in *Quinlivan v Conroy*[94] "interestingly enough, the order makes no use of the word 'procurement'". The plaintiff sought discovery of a number of official reports into the events surrounding his escape from prison. Kinlen J stated that the defendants were senior police officers who had sworn that they had never had the documents sought in their pos-

---

[88] [1994] 1 ILRM 111, 113.

[89] [1978] Fam 181, 186, [1978] 3 WLR 624, 628.

[90] High Court (Barron J) 29 April 1986.

[91] This finding can be contrasted with that the converse situation in *Lonrho Ltd v Shell Petroleum Co. Ltd* [1980] 1 WLR 627 in which the House of Lords held that since documents in the possession of subsidiary companies could not be obtained from them without their consent, they were not within the power of the parent company. However, it would appear that the real test is whether the company seeking the documents, whether it be the parent or subsidiary, has the right to obtain the documents without the other party's consent, and in practice it would seem to make no difference whether it is the parent or the subsidiary company which is seeking access to the documents.

[92] High Court (Finlay P) 26 May 1977.

[93] However it should be noted that the Rules speak of "possession or power" and not procurement and for this reason, this *dicta* should be treated with a degree of caution.

[94] [1999] 1 IR 271.

session or power and dismissed the application. The Supreme Court dismissed the plaintiff's appeal holding that the documents sought were not relevant to any live issue in the litigation, nor would any of them advance the case of the plaintiff. In addition, in the view of O'Flaherty J the defendants did not have any enforceable legal right to obtain the documents in question, which as had been held by the Supreme Court in *Bula Ltd v Tara Mines Ltd*,[95] it was necessary to show in order to establish that documents are within the "power" of a party for the purposes of Order 31, rule 12. The most widely accepted definition of when a document is in the power of a person is certainly the one laid down by O'Flaherty J in *Bula Ltd v Tara Mines Ltd* in the following terms:

> A document is within the power of a party if he has an enforceable legal right to obtain from whoever actually holds the document inspection of it without the need to obtain the consent of anyone else.[96]

In that case, the plaintiffs issued a motion seeking discovery of certain documents in the possession of advisers retained in the past by one of the defendants, the Minister for Energy. The order was refused by Murphy J on the grounds that the matter should be more appropriately dealt with under Order 31, rule 29 and the plaintiffs appealed to the Supreme Court. O'Flaherty J stated that final documents, approved by the professional adviser for the sight of the minister were documents within the "power" of the minister and were discoverable under rule 12. He drew a distinction between documents which can be required to be handed over to the client and those which the adviser is entitled to retain as being his property.[97] O'Flaherty J concluded that the order for discovery made in the High Court should be extended to include documents within the power of the minister (*i.e.* the final documents not the other preparatory documents which were personal to the adviser and therefore not discoverable) and that an order under rule 29 would not be the appropriate procedure in this case.

---

[95] [1994] 1 ILRM 111, 113.

[96] *Ibid*. at 113. See also the definition set out by Dunn J in *B. v B.* [1978] Fam 181, 186, [1978] 3 WLR 624, 628 that "'power' means an enforceable right to inspect the document or to obtain possession or control of the document from the person who ordinarily has it in fact". See also *Lonrho Ltd v Shell Petroleum Co. Ltd* [1980] 1 WLR 627, 635 *per* Lord Diplock.

[97] O'Flaherty J referred to the *dicta* of McKinnon LJ in *Leicestershire County Council v Faraday and Partners Ltd* [1941] 2 KB 205, 216 in which he distinguished the following types of situations. First, if an agent brings into existence certain documents while in the employment of his principal, they are the principal's documents and the principal can claim that the agent should hand them over. However, where an agent has prepared documents for his own assistance in carrying out his work which are not documents brought into existence by the agent on behalf of his principal, they cannot be said to be the property of the principal.

7.018 The approach in *Bula* has also been followed recently by the Supreme Court in *Johnson v Church of Scientology*[98] in which the defendant appealed against an order of the High Court that certain documents must be procured and discovered. Counsel for the defendants contended that a rule which limits discovery to documents which are or have been the property of a party, or are or have been in his physical custody or are under his absolute dominion sets clear limits to the duty to disclose. He further submitted that a rule that requires a party to "procure" documents which are not within these categories is potentially boundless and requires searches to be undertaken by people who are not under the control of the party for documents which the party has never seen and has no right to obtain. Denham J in allowing the defendants' appeal held that documents which are in the possession, custody or power of a party must be discovered and that a document is in the power of party when that party has an enforceable legal right to obtain the document. She concluded that the documents at issue in the case before her were not in the possession, custody or power of the defendants and that, as the defendants had no enforceable legal right to obtain them, the plaintiff was not entitled to the discovery sought.

7.019 The distinction between documents which are within the power of a client as opposed to his adviser, explored by O'Flaherty J in *Bula Ltd v Tara Mines Ltd*, was also considered by Hamilton CJ in *Quigley v Burke*,[99] when the Supreme Court had to consider whether a nominal ledger prepared by an accountant for the appellant taxpayer was "within the possession and power" of the appellant for the purposes of the Income Tax Act 1967 or whether it was part of the accountant's working papers and outside the scope of that definition. The accountant had not been engaged by the appellant for the purpose of preparing an audit of his business but rather as a tax agent in order to prepare the necessary accounts and documentation to be used on the appellant's behalf in his appeal against an income tax assessment, and in the course of fulfilling this obligation, the accountant had prepared the nominal ledger. Hamilton CJ concluded that it was quite clear that the accountant had been employed to prepare and submit the accounts necessary to enable a proper assessment of his income tax liability to be made and that while in the appellant's employment, the accountant had prepared the nominal ledger. In his opinion the appellant was entitled to obtain the ledger from his agent and consequently he was satisfied that the ledger was in his possession or power.

The definition of when a document is within the power of a party set out above by O'Flaherty J was applied by Blayney J in *Irish Intercontinental Bank Ltd v Brady*[100] in which the court had to consider whether the defendant was entitled to an order directing the plaintiff to make discovery of documents in the

---

[98] [2001] 2 ILRM 110.
[99] Supreme Court, 7 November 1995.
[100] Supreme Court, 1 June 1995.

possession of the receiver of a company which the defendant had owned. The essential question was whether the bank had an enforceable legal right to obtain inspection of the documents in the possession of the receiver without his consent. Blayney J pointed out that the receiver, although appointed by the bank, was not the agent of the bank but rather of the company. Because he was not the bank's agent, it could not without his consent inspect documents in his possession relating to the receivership, and it followed that the bank could not be required to discover these documents.

Further and Better Discovery

7.020 While Order 31, rule 20(3) of the Rules of the Superior Courts 1986 provides that a party to an action may be required to state by affidavit whether specified documents are or have been in his possession or power, "whether an affidavit ... shall or shall not already have been ordered or made", there is no specific provision in the rules providing for the making of an order for further and better discovery. However, it is well established that the courts have an inherent jurisdiction to order further discovery although it has been stressed that the court should not permit a party "to indulge in an exploratory or fishing expedition"[101] in this regard. A fishing or exploratory operation was described by O'Sullivan J in *McDonnell v Sunday Business Post Ltd*[102] in this context as being "one where there was no stated objective or delimitation by reference to the pleadings" and he said that the fact that discovery may be comprehensive and wide ranging does not mean that it is *ipso facto* an exploratory or fishing operation.

In *Components Tube Co. Ltd v Naylor*[103] a decision of the Queen's Bench Division, Kenny J stated that a court will order a further and better affidavit of documents to be filed where there are reasonable grounds for suspecting that there are additional documents in existence which are relevant to the action and in the possession, power or procurement of the person against whom a further affidavit of discovery is sought.[104] However, in *Lysaght v Mullen*,[105] decided the same year, Porter MR stressed that a court will not order further and better discovery on the basis of a "mere suspicion" that there are other relevant documents within the possession, power or procurement of the deponent. A similar point was made by Kenny J in *Sterling-Winthrop Group Ltd v Farbenfabriken Bayer Aktiengesellschaft*[106] where he stated that such an order will not be made when the application is based solely on an affidavit alleging that the other party

---

[101] *Per* Finlay CJ in *Bula Ltd v Crowley* [1991] 1 IR 220, 223, [1990] ILRM 756, 758.
[102] High Court (O'Sullivan J) 2 February 2000.
[103] (1898) 32 ILTR 37.
[104] This principle was laid down in *Lyell v Kennedy* (1884) 27 Ch D 1.
[105] (1898) 32 ILTR 65.
[106] [1967] IR 97.

has documents in his possession relevant to the action which have not been disclosed.

7.021 The circumstances in which a court may reach the conclusion that there are further documents in existence which are relevant to the action and in the possession of the deponent were set out by Brett LJ in *Compagnie Financiere et Commerciale du Pacifique v Peruvian Guano Co.*[107] in the following terms. He stated that the question must be whether from the description either in the first affidavit itself or in the list of documents referred to in that affidavit or in the pleadings, there are still documents in the possession of the party making the original affidavit which contain information which may, either directly or indirectly enable the party requiring the further affidavit either to advance his own case or to damage the case of his adversary. Similar language was employed by Kenny J in *Sterling-Winthrop Group Ltd v Farbenfabriken Bayer Aktiengesellschaft*[108] where he stated that the court will order a further affidavit where it is satisfied from the pleadings, from the affidavit already filed, from the documents referred to in the affidavit of discovery or from an admission by the party who has made the affidavit that there are documents in the deponent's possession relating to issues in the action which have not been disclosed in the original affidavit. He continued as follows:

> The court will also order a further affidavit when there are grounds, derived from the documents discovered, for suspecting that there are other relevant documents in the possession of the party who has made the affidavit or where there are reasonable grounds for believing that that person making the affidavit of discovery has misunderstood the issues in the case and has, in consequence, omitted documents from it.[109]

It should also be noted that Kenny J referred to the decision in *British Association of Glass Bottle Manufacturers Ltd v Nettlefold*[110] in which Viscount Haldane VC commented that while as a general rule it is not possible to go behind the original affidavit in the absence of admissions in that or some other document, this rule is qualified where the basis on which the affidavit has been made turns out to have been wrong. If the party making the affidavit has misconceived his case then the court can refuse to recognise an affidavit as conclusive.[111]

---

[107] (1882) 11 QBD 55. See also *Spring Grove Services (Ireland) Ltd v O'Callaghan* High Court (Herbert J) 31 July 2000 at 9 and *Hannon v Commissioners of Public Works* High Court (McCracken J) 4 April 2001 at 2.

[108] [1967] IR 97.

[109] *Ibid.* at 100.

[110] [1912] AC 709.

[111] These principles were applied by the Supreme Court in *Kreglinger and Fernau v Irish National Insurance Co.* Supreme Court, 2 July 1954 (see [2000] 2 ILRM 386).

Reference should also be made to the views expressed by Finlay CJ in *Bula Ltd v Crowley*[112] where he stated that "a court should be satisfied, as a matter of probability, that an error has occurred in an omission from an affidavit of discovery of documents on the basis of irrelevancy before making any order for further discovery". These principles were recently applied by the Supreme Court in *Phelan v Goodman*[113] where the court concluded that the evidence was insufficient to satisfy it that relevant documents were or had been in the possession of the defendant which should have been but had not been discovered by him.

7.022 An application for further and better discovery will not be granted where it is believed that additional documents have come into existence since the date on which the original affidavit was sworn. This was established in *Bula Ltd v Tara Mines Ltd (No. 5)*[114] in which the plaintiffs' application for further and better discovery relating to documents which had not been in existence at the time of the swearing of the original affidavit was refused. The Supreme Court held that Murphy J had been correct in concluding that there was no authority for the proposition that an order of discovery imposed a general obligation upon the party against whom it was directed to make discovery of documents subsequently coming into existence and Finlay CJ stated that "there is no question of any principle of continuing automatic obligation for discovery of documents created and brought into existence after the filing of an affidavit of discovery".[115] However, he went on to comment that it would not be correct to say that there may not be cases where the court would in the interests of justice direct the discovery and production of a specified document which had come into existence after the filing of an affidavit of discovery, but he added that this jurisdiction should only be used very sparingly and in accordance with certain "very limited and restricted" conditions which he laid down in the following terms.

> I am, first, satisfied that in any instance where a party seeks such a discovery he must specify documents, and not merely indicate the possibility of a type or range of document. Secondly, I am satisfied that in any instance where the documents specified are created out of proceedings and would therefore *prima facie* be exempt from production as privileged documents that the court should not make an order unless it is satisfied on proof that for some special reason that exemption must be lifted. Thirdly, I am satisfied that the court should not make such an order where it has not been established to its satisfaction that the party seeking it is unable to

---

[112] [1991] 1 IR 220, 223, [1990] ILRM 756, 758. See also *Hannon v Commissioners of Public Works* High Court (McCracken J) 4 April 2001 at 3.
[113] [2000] 2 IR 577, [2000] 2 ILRM 378.
[114] [1994] 1 IR 487.
[115] *Ibid.* at 496.

obtain the document or a copy of it by any other means, or has not already obtained a copy of it from other sources or by other means. Lastly, I am satisfied that if such an application were to succeed in the rare circumstances in which it would be appropriate, it would be necessary for the party seeking it to prove not only a general probability of relevance but a significant importance of a specified or identifiable kind.[116]

7.023 This situation where documents come into existence after the filing of an original affidavit of discovery can be contrasted with that where documents which existed prior to this only come to the notice of a deponent after he has sworn the affidavit. In such cases, while it is not necessary to bring an application for further and better discovery, a continuing obligation to disclose such documents exists as a result of the original order for discovery made. This was made clear by Morris P in his judgment in *Murphy v Times Newspapers Ltd.*[117] The plaintiff brought an application for further and better discovery and his counsel informed the court that the purpose of this application was to require the defendants to bring their discovery up to date on the basis that as so much time had passed since they had made discovery in August 1989, it was probable that additional documentation had come into their hands which was material to the issues to be tried by the court. Morris P stated that he was satisfied that the application fell to be dealt with in accordance with the principles laid down by Kenny J in *Sterling-Winthrop Group Ltd v Farbenfabriken Bayer Atkiengesellschaft* and said that on the basis of this authority he was satisfied that it was not appropriate that the court should make an order for further and better discovery to bring the discovery up to date. He continued as follows:

> To make such an order the court must be satisfied that documents which should have been discovered were not, for one of the reasons enumerated by Kenny J, in fact discovered and that in reality this type of order should only be made for the purpose of clarifying an ambiguity or remedying a problem which might exist in the interpretation of the original order.[118]

Morris P concluded that if documents, which should be discovered, had, since the date of the swearing of the original affidavit, come into the hands of the defendants, then, without any need for an additional order, they were governed by the terms of the original order for discovery made by the Master in 1989.

The court has the power to order that an additional affidavit be sworn or may, as it did in *Irish Nationwide Building Society v Charlton*,[119] require a plaintiff to review the totality of their discovery and deliver one affidavit in

---

[116] *Ibid.* at 498.
[117] High Court (Morris P) 23 March 1998.
[118] *Ibid.* at 4.
[119] Supreme Court, 5 March 1997.

substitution for earlier attempts "so that the total discovery on behalf of the plaintiffs will be clear and unambiguous".[120]

FAILURE TO COMPLY WITH DISCOVERY

7.024 Order 31, rule 21 provides that if any party fails to comply with an order for discovery, or for inspection of documents or to answer interrogatories, he shall be liable to a number of consequences. He shall be liable to attachment,[121] and also if a plaintiff, to have his action dismissed for want of prosecution,[122] or if a defendant, to have his defence, if any, struck out.[123] The case law which has built up in this area concerns the latter power which will place the defendant in the same position as if he had not defended the claim and it has been described as a "drastic remedy".[124] However, as O'Flaherty J stated in *Decospan NV v Benhouse Ltd*[125] "the rule is quite clear that the court may order that the defence be struck out if discovery has not been made within a given time".

Detailed consideration was given by the Supreme Court in *Mercantile Credit Co. of Ireland v Heelan*[126] to the nature of the power to strike out a defence for failure to comply with discovery and to the circumstances in which it should be exercised. Hamilton CJ stressed that the striking out of a defence is "a serious matter" and that the court's power in this regard should not be exercised so as to punish a party for failure to comply with a discovery order within the time limited by the order.[127] He stated as follows:

> The power given by the said rule to the court to strike out the defence of a defendant who has failed to comply with an order of discovery is discretionary and not obligatory, and should not be exercised unless the court is satisfied that the plaintiff is endeavouring to avoid giving discovery, and not where the omission or neglect to comply with the order is not a culpa-

---

[120] *Ibid.* at 16.

[121] Order 44 of the RSC.

[122] Order 63, rule 1(8).

[123] Order 63, rule 1(9). Equally, an application may be brought by a defendant seeking an order striking out a plaintiff's defence to a counterclaim, as in *Northern Bank Finance Corporation Ltd v Charlton* High Court (Finlay P) 26 May 1977. Finlay P held that the plaintiff's failure to discover certain documents was not the type of failure "consisting of an attempt to evade true discovery or to conceal from the other party or from the court documents relevant to the hearing of the action" which would justify the court striking out their defence to the counterclaim.

[124] *Phonographic Performance (Ireland) Ltd v Cody* [1998] 4 IR 504, 510, [1994] 2 ILRM 241, 246.

[125] [1995] 2 ILRM 620, 623.

[126] [1998] 1 IR 81.

[127] This echoes what was stated by Stamp LJ in *Husband's of Marchwood Ltd v Drummond Walker Developments Ltd* [1975] 1 WLR 603, 606, [1975] 2 All ER 30, 32.

ble one, for instance, if it is due to loss of memory or illness. It should only be made where there is wilful default or negligence on the part of a defendant and then only upon application to the court for an order to that effect.[128]

Hamilton CJ concluded that while the second named defendant had undoubtedly delayed in complying with various orders for discovery and had prolonged the proceedings, the interests of justice appeared to require that he be afforded an opportunity of controverting the plaintiff's claim. In the circumstances, the court was satisfied that the order striking out the second named defendant's defence should not have been made.

7.025 Further consideration was given to these principles by both the High Court and the Supreme Court in *Murphy v J. Donohoe Ltd* (the *Fiat* case).[129] The plaintiffs brought proceedings in respect of personal injuries sustained by them when a car belonging to their father, the fourth named defendant, caught fire. This defendant brought a motion against the second and fifth named defendants pursuant to Order 31, rule 21 seeking to have their defences struck out on the grounds that they had failed to comply with an order for discovery. It appeared that these defendants had failed to disclose the fact that similar fires had affected the model of car in question. It was argued on behalf of these defendants that the failure to make discovery was not due to any deliberate act on their part but was attributable to "a combination of inefficiency, stupidity, confusion or incompetence". Johnson J did not accept this and concluded that he could not rely on them to honestly fulfil the requirements imposed upon them by the orders of the court and made an order striking out the defences of these defendants. However, the Supreme Court reversed this decision and allowed their appeal. Barrington J stated that "Order 31, rule 21 exists to ensure that parties to litigation comply with orders for discovery. It does not exist to punish a defaulter but to facilitate the administration of justice by ensuring compliance with the orders of the court."[130] He said that undoubtedly cases exist in which one party may not be able to get a fair trial because of the other party's wilful refusal to comply with an order for discovery and in such cases it may be necessary to dismiss the plaintiff's claim or to strike out the defendant's defence, but that such cases will be extreme ones. While he accepted that Johnson J had reached the conclusion that the case before him was an extreme one, there were in his view matters to which the learned trial judge did not appear to have attached sufficient weight. Barrington J concluded that having regard to these factors, including the fact that these defendants' legal advisers had placed a

---

[128] [1998] 1 IR 81, 85.
[129] [1996] 1 IR 123, [1995] 2 ILRM 509 (HC), [1996] 1 ILRM 481 (SC).
[130] *Ibid.* at 142, 488.

restrictive interpretation on the order and that they had declared they would make further and better discovery, he would allow the appeal.

Undoubtedly the essential question which the court must answer in such cases is whether there has been wilful default or negligence on the part of a litigant and where documents have been deliberately concealed, the appropriate remedy will clearly be to strike out a defence. This latter point was made by Barron J in his judgment in *Radiac Abrasives Inc v Prendergast*,[131] although as his judgment in that decision makes clear, it may be difficult to satisfy a court that such deliberate conduct has in fact occurred.

NON PARTY DISCOVERY

Introduction

7.026 Prior to the coming into force of the Rules of the Superior Courts 1986 an order for discovery of documents could not be made against a person who was not a party to the action before the court. In addition, as the judgment of Kenny J in *International Trading Group Ltd v Dublin Corporation*[132] made clear, the courts would not make an order adding a party as a defendant to an action where the plaintiff sought the order merely for the purpose of obtaining discovery of documents from the proposed defendant.

Now Order 31, rule 29 provides that where it appears to the court that any person not a party to the action is likely to have or have had in his possession, custody or power any documents which are relevant to an issue arising or likely to arise in the cause or matter, discovery of such documents may be directed by the court.[133] Commenting on the provisions of rule 29 in *Allied Irish Banks plc v Ernst & Whinney*[134] McCarthy J stated that the rule is there "to advance the course of justice" by seeking to ensure that the parties to an action may be fully informed about all relevant documents prior to the trial and that it "extend[ed] the scope of discovery in a very material and helpful way". The terms of rule 29 make it clear that the provisions of Order 31 shall apply *mutatis mutandis* as if the order had been directed to a party to the action.[135] This means that for example the requirement to seek voluntary discovery set out in rule 12(4) will apply and as Barron J pointed out in *Holloway v Belenos Publications Ltd (No.*

[131] High Court (Barron J) 13 March 1996.
[132] [1974] IR 373.
[133] As Barron J stated in *Holloway v Belenos Publications Ltd (No. 2)* [1988] IR 494, 495, [1988] ILRM 685, 686 the rule "breaks new ground" by allowing for discovery to be directed against a person who is not a party to the action. In his view the power to order discovery is part of the inherent jurisdiction of the court and rule 29 is one "giving altered effect to that inherent jurisdiction".
[134] [1993] 1 IR 375, 393.
[135] *Allied Irish Banks plc v Ernst and Whinney* [1993] 1 IR 375, 393; *Holloway v Belenos Publications Ltd (No. 1)* [1987] IR 405, 408, [1987] ILRM 790, 793.

2)[136] an order for discovery under rule 29 will have the same attributes and consequences as an order under rule 12. However, as Keane J commented in the course of his judgment in *Kennedy v Law Society*[137] "an order for third party discovery should not be lightly made" and it is clear from the wording of the rule and the case law which has evolved in relation to it that "much stricter requirements"[138] have to be observed before a litigant can obtain an order for non-party discovery than obtain in relation to obtaining an order against another party. These requirements have been given consideration in a number of decisions which it is useful to examine in some detail.

7.027 In *Holloway v Belenos Publications Ltd (No. 1)*[139] Costello J stated that before a court can make an order under rule 29, "it must be satisfied that 'it is likely' that the notice party has or had in its possession, power or procurement documents which are relevant to an issue that is likely to arise in the action" and he stressed that the court has a discretion as to whether to make an order or not. He continued that the court has no power to make an order merely for the purposes of permitting a party to inspect the files of a non-party to ascertain whether they contain any relevant documents and that the court must have evidence that relevant documents exist and that it is likely that the notice party has relevant documents in his possession power or procurement.[140] In addition, he stated that the costs of the discovery by the notice party are to be borne by the moving party[141] but if the moving party is successful in the action they may be recoverable from the unsuccessful party. Finally Costello J commented that unless it is clear that a party does not wish to be heard, a motion under rule 29 should be served on all the parties to the action.

7.028 The most comprehensive examination of the provisions of rule 29 carried out to date has been by the Supreme Court in *Allied Irish Banks plc v Ernst & Whinney*.[142] Finlay CJ stated that where discovery is sought pursuant to rule 29, the onus lies on the applicant to establish, first, that the party named is likely to have or have had documents in his possession, custody or power and secondly, that they are documents which are relevant to an issue arising or likely to arise in the cause or matter.[143] The Chief Justice continued by saying that

---

[136] [1988] IR 494, 496, [1988] ILRM 685, 687.

[137] Supreme Court, 28 November 1997.

[138] *Bailey v Flood* High Court (Geoghegan J) 15 May 1998 at 5.

[139] [1987] IR 405, [1987] ILRM 790.

[140] See also *O'Connell v Radio Telefís Éireann* High Court (Blayney J) 2 November 1988 at 4.

[141] See also *Allied Irish Banks plc v Ernst and Whinney* [1993] 1 IR 375, 395 *per* McCarthy J and *Bula Ltd v Tara Mines Ltd* [1994] 1 ILRM 111, 112 *per* O'Flaherty J.

[142] [1993] 1 IR 375.

[143] See also the judgment of McCarthy J at 397 and *Lewis v Minister for Enterprise and Employment* High Court (Costello P) 9 October 1996.

even after it has been established to the satisfaction of the court that a person not a party has, or is likely to have, in his possession documents which are relevant to an issue arising, the court still has a further discretion which relates in particular to the oppression or prejudice which may be caused to the person called upon to discover documents not capable of being adequately compensated by the payment of the costs of making discovery. In relation to the form of an order which a court should make pursuant to rule 29 Finlay CJ commented that they should "either by the annexing of pleadings or by a schedule to the order, identify the issues, by reference to the pleadings, to which an alleged relevance occurs". In addition, O'Flaherty J stated that he would encourage parties applying for discovery against strangers to seek to define the categories of documents as definitely as possible, in advance of the application to the court.

7.029 The statements made about the nature of the discretion conferred upon the court by rule 29 were reiterated by O'Donovan J in *Ulster Bank Ltd v Byrne*.[144] He stated that the onus lies on the applicant for discovery to show that the party named is likely to have relevant documents in his possession, custody or power and stated that even if this is established, "the court still has a further discretion to refuse the application if it considers that particular oppression or prejudice will be caused to the person called upon to make discovery which is not capable of being adequately compensated by the payment by the party seeking discovery of the costs of the making thereof."[145] The plaintiff referred to the decision of the Supreme Court in *Murphy v Kirwan*[146] and suggested that when in an application for third party discovery a party to the cause or matter has been guilty of fraud or other malpractice then the application for discovery should be granted irrespective of the relevance of the documents sought to be discovered or of any oppression or prejudice which may be caused to the person called on to make the discovery. O'Donovan J rejected that suggestion and said that in his opinion, *Murphy* did not in any way alter the principles laid down in *Allied Irish Banks plc v Ernst & Whinney* that documents were to be relevant to the issue in respect of which those documents are sought to be discovered, notwithstanding that one of the parties may be alleging fraud.

7.030 It should be noted that the power of the Superior Court Rules Committee to make rule 29 was called into question on two occasions. In *Holloway v Belenos Publications Ltd (No. 2)*[147] the notice parties resisted an application for discovery on the grounds that the Rules Committee had no power to make the rule,

---

[144] High Court (O'Donovan J) 10 July 1997.
[145] *Ibid.* at 5. See also the *dicta* of Egan J in *Fusco v O'Dea* [1994] 2 IR 93, 102, [1994] 2 ILRM 389, 392 to the effect that an order made pursuant to rule 29 is in the court's discretion and is not available as of right.
[146] [1993] 3 IR 501, [1994] 1 ILRM 293.
[147] [1988] IR 494, [1988] ILRM 685.

contending that it related to a matter of substantive law and went beyond the limitation of practice and procedure. Barron J rejected this argument and concluded that in his view the rule was one of practice and procedure. He stated that the right to discovery against a non-party does not create an independent enforceable right against such a person and that it has no existence independent of the proceedings in which it is sought. A similar challenge was made in *Fitzpatrick v Independent Newspapers Ltd*[148] in which the notice parties opposed the motion brought under rule 29 on the grounds that the rule was invalid as being *ultra vires* the rule making committee. Costello J rejected this contention and held that any order made pursuant to rule 29 could properly be regarded as a procedural one and that the rules committee is clearly empowered to enable the courts to make such orders.

Interpretation of Order 31, Rule 29

7.031 While the utility of a provision such as rule 29 is obvious, it is important to note that the courts have tended to interpret it in a rather restrictive fashion. A clear example of the inflexible interpretation placed on rule 29 is the judgment of the Supreme Court in *Fusco v O'Dea*[149] in which the court was required to consider whether to order third party discovery against a foreign sovereign government, namely the government of Great Britain and Northern Ireland. Egan J commented that the wording of rule 29 is silent as to the issue of its possible application to third parties outside the jurisdiction but continued that "although the rule is drafted widely ... it is arguable that it should be construed narrowly."[150] In his view parties outside the jurisdiction should only be made amenable to the jurisdiction of the Irish courts in specified circumstances and to grant an order for discovery against a third party outside the jurisdiction would subject such a party to the jurisdiction of our courts in circumstances other than those provided for in Order 11 of the RSC. In addition, Egan J stated that the situation as regards discovery against a foreign sovereign government is complicated by the principle of state immunity. In his view where a foreign state has submitted to the jurisdiction of the courts by for example initiating proceedings, it must be prepared to make discovery, but he was of the opinion that discovery would not otherwise lie as it would undermine the principle of immunity. Egan J concluded by saying that rule 29 was an unusual provision as it required a stranger to an action to make discovery and that it should be interpreted strictly and should not be read as conferring an extra-territorial jurisdiction on the Irish courts in this regard. This reasoning applied *a fortiori* to the position of a sovereign government and Egan J upheld the decision refusing the relief sought.

---

[148] [1988] IR 132, [1988] ILRM 707.
[149] [1994] 2 IR 93, [1994] 2 ILRM 389.
[150] *Ibid.* at 102, 392.

7.032 This decision illustrates the rather narrow construction placed on the scope of rule 29 and this is further borne out by the decision in *Chambers v Times Newspapers Ltd*,[151] which indicates the reluctance of the courts to order third party discovery if it can be avoided and there is a real alternative. The defendants sought an order pursuant to Order 31, rule 29 directing the Registrars of the Special Criminal Court and Court of Criminal Appeal to make discovery of the book of evidence and the transcripts of a criminal prosecution in which the plaintiff had been tried and convicted of a number of offences. The defendants, who were the publisher and editor of a newspaper, submitted that they sought this information in order to properly defend a claim for defamation brought against them by the plaintiff. The issue which arose during the course of the hearing was that given that the documents were *prima facie* available and in the possession of the plaintiff, was it desirable to involve a non party in the proceedings by making an order for discovery of these documents against it. It was submitted on behalf of the notice party that as a general principle an order for discovery against a non party should only be made where the documents sought to be discovered are not available as a consequence of an order for discovery made against a party to the action.[152] Morris P referred to the *dicta* of McCarthy J in *Allied Irish Banks plc v Ernst & Whinney*[153] to the effect that although certain documents were available to the defendants, that did not preclude them from pursuing the same documents in the possession of a third party and stated that while this statement was not part of the *ratio* of the case, he accepted it as a clear indication that in an appropriate case the court should make an order for non party discovery even though the documents might be discovered by a party to the action. However, Morris P stated that the court should be slow to put someone who is not a party to an action to the trouble of making discovery if it can be avoided and he was satisfied that an order should only be made against a non party in circumstances where the documents in question are not readily available to be discovered by a party to the action or where in the particular circumstances of the case, the interests of justice require that it should be done. The defendants submitted that it was not known whether the plaintiff still had the documents which they sought in his possession and that it was unreasonable to require them to depend upon the plaintiff producing these documents by way of discovery when they were essential to the defence of the action. Morris P did not accept that argument and said that while it would appear *prima facie* that the plaintiff had been convicted of serious offences in the Special Criminal Court it did not follow that he would not make full and proper

---

[151] [1999] 2 IR 424, [1999] 1 ILRM 504.
[152] This contention was in line with a statement made by Costello J in *Fitzpatrick v Independent Newspapers* [1988] IR 132, [1988] ILRM 707 to the effect that he agreed with the submission of counsel for the notice parties that as a general rule the court should not make an order under rule 29 against non-parties if the documents which are sought are otherwise available to the party seeking the order.
[153] [1993] 1 IR 375, 394.

discovery, and more importantly, there was no reason to think that his solicitors would not ensure that proper discovery was made. Given that there was no satisfactory evidence that the documents were not available to be discovered by the plaintiff or that proper discovery would not be made, Morris P concluded that the court should not order non party discovery. He stated as follows:

> I believe that as a general principle third party discovery, with all the inconvenience which it involves, should only be ordered when there is no realistic alternative available.[154]

However, he added that he realised the importance of the documents sought to the defendants and stated that if these documents were not available to be produced on discovery by the plaintiff, he would be prepared to make the order sought. Accordingly he decided to adjourn the application generally with liberty to re-enter and stated that if requested by the defendants he would make an order of discovery against the plaintiff.

7.033 Finally the High Court has recently considered in *Dunne v Fox*[155] what should be the proper basis for taxation of costs payable by a litigant who has obtained an order under Order 31, rule 29 to the person against whom the order has been obtained. Laffoy J stated that it is of particular importance to have regard to Order 99 of the Rules of the Superior Courts in construing Order 31, rule 29, and that the provision in relation to costs embodied in rule 29 is mandatory both as to the right to costs and the amount of costs. She set out the following principles:

> First, all expenditure reasonably incurred is within the range allowable on taxation. Thus the range of expenditure allowable is broader than is allowable on taxation on a party and party basis. However, in my view the requirement that expenditure be reasonably incurred necessitates that it should be of a reasonable amount; expenditure which is gross or extravagant in amount could hardly be regarded as having been reasonably incurred. Thus, the range of expenditure allowable corresponds to the range allowable on taxation as between solicitor and client. Secondly, the onus

---

[154] [1999] 2 IR 424, 430, [1999] 1 ILRM 504, 509. This approach would also appear to underlie the conclusion reached by the Supreme Court in *Bula Ltd v Tara Mines Ltd* [1994] 1 ILRM 111 in which the court held that documents prepared by a non party for the defendant minister were within the "power" of the defendant and as such discoverable in an application brought pursuant to rule 12. This can be contrasted with the conclusion reached by Murphy J in the High Court who refused the application for discovery under rule 12 and suggested that the matter should be more appropriately dealt with under rule 29.

[155] High Court (Laffoy J) 3 April 1998.

is on the person who incurred the expenditure and is seeking indemnity in respect of it to show that the expenditure was reasonably incurred.[156]

Laffoy J held that the taxing master had correctly identified the range of expenditure on the part of the non party allowable on taxation, namely the costs reasonably incurred, but that he had been mistaken as to where the burden of proof lay in relation to this question and that he had erred in law in ruling that the non party should be given the benefit of the doubt on this point. Laffoy J concluded that the non party had established that the amounts charged were reasonable in the circumstances.

MISCELLANEOUS ISSUES RELATING TO DISCOVERY

Discovery Orders Made by a Tribunal

7.034 An interesting question which arose recently in relation to proceedings before tribunals of inquiry established pursuant to the Tribunals of Inquiry Act 1921 is whether as a matter of law High Court practice and procedure relating to non party discovery ought to be applied in relation to discovery orders made by a tribunal. This question was considered in some detail and ultimately rejected by Geoghegan J in the course of his judgment in *Bailey v Flood*[157] which concerned an application for judicial review of orders for discovery and production made by the respondent against the applicants' bank. The applicants submitted that in the case of a tribunal everybody against whom an order for discovery is made and who is affected by an order is a non party by definition because there are no "parties" to a tribunal. The applicants placed reliance on this contention because if it were accepted, they would go on to argue that the tribunal would have to give reasons justifying an order for discovery or production before it was issued. Geoghegan J commented that if a tribunal was confined in its power to make discovery orders to the parameters of rule 29, it would in his opinion considerably curb the tribunal's powers of investigation and he concluded that the rules relating to discovery by non parties did not have any application to tribunals of inquiry. He stated that the concept of non party discovery was not known to parliament at the time the Tribunals of Inquiry Act 1921 was enacted and in his view the Act permitted ordinary discovery on the assumption that the person against whom the order is made is a party rather than a non party. Geoghegan J therefore concluded that the sole member of the tribunal of inquiry had power to make an order for discovery against a person as though that person was a party.

---

[156] At 13-14.
[157] High Court (Geoghegan J) 15 May 1998.

Discovery in Judicial Review Proceedings

7.035 Order 84, rule 25 of the 1986 Rules provides that "any interlocutory application may be made to the court in proceedings on an application for judicial review" and goes on to provide that "interlocutory application" includes an order under Order 31. Such applications are rarely brought in practice because as Lord Diplock noted in the course of his speech in *O'Reilly v Mackman*[158] "the facts ... can seldom be a matter of relevant dispute upon an application for judicial review".[159] As Glidwell LJ commented in his judgment in *R v Secretary of State for the Home Department ex p. Harrison*:[160]

> [I]nevitably, because of the nature of the jurisdiction, discovery in judicial review will be appropriate in far fewer cases and will frequently, even when it is ordered, be more circumscribed in its extent than it commonly is in relation to an action begun by writ.

Similarly Carswell J concluded in *Re Glor na Gael's Application*[161] that "there is a definite distinction to be made between discovery in judicial review and discovery in plenary actions". In his view there was a consistent trend in judicial review proceedings against ordering discovery of documents relating to the issue of unreasonableness unless material existed upon which the applicant could make a case that the evidence put before the court by the respondent was inaccurate or false.

7.036 Finally, O'Hanlon J made it clear in *McDaid v Minister for the Marine*[162] that judicial review proceedings should not be used to obtain discovery of documents with a view to instituting plenary proceedings. The court was satisfied that the applicant, who was the daughter of an individual who had drowned when a fishing vessel was lost at sea, was contemplating instituting proceedings for damages but that she had not done so because the full circumstances of the accident were not known. Judicial review proceedings were brought seeking to require the respondent to make available a preliminary report into the tragedy but O'Hanlon J stated that it seemed to him that the real relief being sought by the applicant was an order for discovery. In these circumstances he concluded that an action by way of judicial review was "not an appropriate method of dealing with a problem of the kind which faces the applicant in the present proceedings".

---

[158] [1983] 2 AC 237, 282, [1982] 3 WLR 1096, 1107, [1982] 3 All ER 1124, 1132.
[159] However, there have been a number of decisions dealing with discovery in judicial review proceedings *e.g. Ahern v Minister for Industry and Commerce* High Court (Lardner J) 11 March 1988.
[160] English Court of Appeal 1987. (Referred to in *Re Glor na Gael's Application* [1991] NI 117, 130-131.)
[161] [1991] NI 117, 129.
[162] High Court (O'Hanlon J) 7 September 1994.

Discovery in Other Types of Proceedings

7.037 While discovery in proceedings before the Superior Courts is provided for in the Rules of Court, there are many other forms of proceedings, usually quasi-judicial or administrative in character, where no provision is made for discovery of documents prior to a hearing. The constitutional implications of this position were considered by the Supreme Court in *Nolan v Irish Land Commission*[163] which concerned a hearing before the defendants' lay commissioners of the plaintiff's objections to a decision that his land was "required" pursuant to the Land Act 1931. Prior to the hearing and at its commencement the plaintiff applied unsuccessfully for discovery and inspection of documents and he sought a declaration that he was entitled to such procedural entitlements despite the fact that no provision had been made for them in the statutory rules governing such proceedings. The question which the court had to consider was whether it could be said that if discovery and inspection were not granted, the plaintiff would be deprived of an adequate opportunity to answer the case for acquisition brought against him by the defendants. O'Higgins CJ agreed that in the absence of discovery and inspection of the appropriate documents which had been considered by the lay commissioners prior to certification, the requirements of natural justice would not be observed. Griffin J stressed the importance of ensuring that both parties can approach any hearing "with all the cards faced upwards on the table". He stated that the absence of appropriate procedures would not be a bar to granting an order for discovery if the interests of justice required it and pointed out that Article 40.3 of the Constitution provides a guarantee to the citizen of basic fairness of procedures. Griffin J was of the view that in the absence of discovery the plaintiff would not have an effective opportunity of meeting the case against him and concluded that discovery was essential in the interests of justice.

7.038 While the *Nolan* decision would suggest that the courts have an inherent power to order discovery in proceedings in order to safeguard the interests of justice, it should be pointed out that Carroll J took a much more restrictive approach towards this question in *Phillips v Medical Council*.[164] She pointed out that the Medical Practitioners Act 1978 gave the respondent's Fitness to Practice Committee power to order production of documents but did not make provision for ordering discovery against a third party. She stated that it would have been a simple matter to provide for discovery in the legislation if it had been intended and she was not satisfied that any inherent power to order discovery existed. Carroll J concluded that it should have been possible to implement fair procedures in relation to documents using the powers given in the legislation and held that the order for discovery made was *ultra vires*. It would appear

[163] [1981] IR 23.
[164] [1992] ILRM 469.

that the essential question which the court must ask in such cases is whether the absence of discovery would infringe an individual's right to basic fairness of procedures and that no hard and fast rule can be laid down in relation to the specific types of proceedings in relation to which discovery may be necessary in the interests of justice.

Jurisdiction to Make Discovery where it is the Sole Object of the Proceedings

7.039 As Finlay CJ stated in *Megaleasing UK Ltd v Barrett*[165] the granting of an order for discovery in an action solely instituted for this purpose prior to taking proceedings against a defendant is "a power which for good reasons must be sparingly used", although he acknowledged that where it is appropriate to make such an order "it may be of very considerable value towards the attainment of justice".[166]

The issue was considered in some detail by the House of Lords in *Norwich Pharmacal Co. v Customs and Excise Commissioners*[167] in which the plaintiff obtained an order for discovery to compel the defendants to reveal the identity of importers who, as statistics published by the defendants revealed, were importing a chemical compound in alleged infringement of the plaintiff's patent. However, as Lord Morris stated "the plaintiffs are in a position to assert that the persons who have imported, whoever they are, must have been infringers, and, therefore, wrongdoers"[168] or as Viscount Dilhorne expressed it, discovery can be granted where wrongdoing has been established to determine who was responsible for it. The importance of confining actions for sole discovery to those where clear proof of wrongdoing exists was confirmed by the Supreme Court in *Megaleasing UK Ltd v Barrett*.[169] Invoices raised by the defendants against the first named plaintiff were paid although the plaintiff claimed that on investigation, no satisfactory explanation could be found of any value for goods or services provided by the defendants to whom the payments were made. The plaintiffs alleged that the defendants had either wittingly or unwittingly become involved in the tortious acts of others so as to facilitate wrongdoing and that they were under a duty to give the plaintiffs full information in relation to this wrongdoing so as they could take action against the alleged wrongdoers. In the course of a judgment in which he granted the order of discovery sought by the plaintiffs, Costello J stated that "persons come under a duty to assist one injured if they have information or documents available" and that "once a *prima facie*

---

[165] [1993] ILRM 497.
[166] *Ibid.* at 503.
[167] [1974] AC 133, [1973] 3 WLR 164, [1973] 2 All ER 943. See further O'Brien (2001) 6 Bar Rev 241.
[168] *Ibid.* at 178, 171, 951.
[169] [1993] ILRM 497.

case of wrongdoing exists the duty arises". However, the Supreme Court allowed the defendants' appeal and followed the approach adopted by the House of Lords in *Norwich Pharmacal*. Finlay CJ stated as follows:

> I am, accordingly, driven to the conclusion that the existing authorities upon which the judgment of the High Court are largely based, which are the authorities of the English courts, do in fact confine the remedy to cases where a very clear proof of a wrongdoing exists, and possibly, so far as applies to an action for discovery alone prior to the institution of any other proceedings, to cases where what is really sought are the names and identity of the wrongdoers, rather than factual information concerning the commission of the wrong.[170]

Similarly, McCarthy J stressed that the jurisdiction in question must be sparingly exercised and stated that "a procedure of the kind is plainly open to abuse which the courts must be alert to prevent".[171] O'Flaherty J also said that he would confine the requirement in cases of this nature to the disclosure of names where wrongdoing is established and stated that if the scope of this type of action was ever to be widened, it would require the fullest disclosure on the part of the applicants so that all information is laid before the court at the earliest possible moment.

7.040 A recent decision which shows a definite disinclination on the part of the courts to extend the circumstances in which an action for sole discovery may be permitted is that of the Supreme Court in *Doyle v Garda Commissioner*.[172] The plaintiff made a complaint to the European Commission on Human Rights alleging that the United Kingdom was in breach of its obligations under Article 2 of the European Convention on Human Rights by reason of the alleged failure of the RUC to investigate properly the car bomb explosions which had occurred in Dublin and Monaghan in 1974. In aid of this complaint, the plaintiff issued a plenary summons seeking discovery of all documentation in the possession of the Garda Síochána concerning their investigations into the bombings. The plaintiff's application was dismissed by the High Court[173] and on appeal, by the Supreme Court. Barrington J stated that there is no doubt that the High Court has jurisdiction at common law to entertain an action for sole discovery but added that the authorities have established that this is a jurisdiction which should be exercised sparingly and he said it has been exercised only where the plaintiff has been in a position to prove that he has suffered a wrong but he was not, and the defendant was, in a position to establish the identity of the wrongdoer.

---

[170] *Ibid.* at 504.
[171] *Ibid.* at 505.
[172] [1999] 1 IR 249, [1998] 2 ILRM 523.
[173] [1999] 1 IR 249, [1998] 1 ILRM 229.

Barrington J quoted from the decision of the Supreme Court in *Megaleasing UK Ltd v Barrett* but pointed out that the case before him was very different to the type of case at issue in that decision or in the other relevant English authorities[174] which contemplated a situation where the plaintiff had established a wrong but could not establish the identity of the wrongdoer and was not therefore in a position to institute proceedings. In addition, Barrington J pointed out that an action for sole discovery is a plenary action and must proceed on the basis of evidence or agreed facts. No evidence had been produced to show that the United Kingdom had been guilty of any wrongdoing or to support the allegations of the plaintiff and in the view of Barrington J this was therefore not an appropriate case for sole discovery.

Whether an Order for Discovery can be Made on the Basis that only Lawyers can Inspect the Documents

7.041 The question of whether an order for discovery could be made on the basis that only the lawyers involved in the case could inspect the documents was considered by the Supreme Court in *Burke v Central Independent Television plc*.[175] The plaintiffs instituted proceedings claiming damages for libel allegedly published in a TV programme broadcast on the fund-raising activities of the IRA. The Master ordered that both parties should make discovery and the defendant objected to the production of certain documents on grounds of privilege, *inter alia*, because it might put lives at risk and because they had been supplied in confidence on the understanding that they would not be disclosed to a third party. Murphy J rejected the claim of privilege but ordered the production of the documents subject to the qualification that only the lawyers involved in the case would be entitled to examine them. On appeal by the defendant, the Supreme Court held that the making of an order of discovery on those terms was not a procedure which could be adopted by the court. If the plaintiffs' lawyers had access to the documents, they might be significant in relation to cross-examination of witnesses but they would be unable to use the documents or to explain their failure to do so to their clients and this would constitute an undesirable breach of the proper trust which should exist between a lawyer and a client. Therefore Finlay CJ was satisfied that an order should be made protecting the documents from being delivered or discovered or from being produced in evidence. He said that he reached that conclusion on the basis that in respect of the protection of a life where the competing constitutional right involved is not another life, the court must act if it is satisfied that there is a plausible risk to that life.

[174] *Norwich Pharamcal Co. v Customs and Excise Commissioners* [1974] AC 133, [1973] 3 WLR 164, [1973] 2 All ER 943 and *Orr v Diaper* (1876) 4 Ch D 92.
[175] [1994] 2 IR 61, [1994] 2 ILRM 161.

7.042 This can be contrasted with the approach taken by the Supreme Court in the earlier decision of *Ambiorix Ltd v Minister for the Environment (No. 1)*,[176] in which the plaintiff property development companies sought a declaration that a decision to declare a site as a 'designated area' under s.6 of the Urban Renewal Act 1986 was *ultra vires*. Lardner J ordered discovery of documents which had come into existence for the purpose of arriving at the challenged decision including those containing representations made by third parties to government departments. Before the Supreme Court, it was accepted that these submissions would contain details, financial and otherwise, which would be of no relevance to the issue relating to executive privilege which the court was required to decide. Finlay CJ made the point that a party obtaining discovery is prohibited from making use of such documents otherwise than for the purpose of the action and stated that the court has an inherent jurisdiction to take any necessary steps to prohibit any infringement of this restriction. He concluded that by restricting inspection of the documents in question to lawyers on behalf of the plaintiffs, who would give an undertaking that they would not reveal their contents to their clients except with the leave of the court, the commercial and financial interests of the parties who had made the representations would be protected and the order drawn up by the court reflected this conclusion. The different conclusions reached in the *Burke* and *Ambiorix* decisions on this point have recently been considered by the Supreme Court in *Ward v Special Criminal Court*.[177] O'Flaherty J quoted from *Burke* and the following statement from the decision of the Court of Appeal in *R v Davis*[178] namely that "it would wholly undermine counsel's relationship with his client if he were privy to issues in court but could reveal neither the discussions nor even the issues to his client". He expressed the view that *Ambiorix* was "a very special case" for the purposes of this principle and pointed out that if the court were to follow the approach adopted there it would lead to arbitrary distinctions being drawn between situations in which a litigant is represented by lawyers and those in which he conducts his own case. This view would appear to be the correct one and it is unlikely that the courts will depart from the principles laid down in *Burke* apart from in an exceptional case.

The Role of Legal Advisers in Discovery

7.043 The respective roles of the deponent of an affidavit of discovery and his solicitor were considered by Murphy J in *Irish Nationwide Building Society v Charlton*[179] in the context of determining what is "relevant" for the purposes of discovery. As Murphy J stated, often the deponent will be familiar with the

---

[176] [1992] 1 IR 277, [1992] ILRM 209.
[177] [1998] 2 ILRM 493.
[178] [1993] 1 WLR 613, 616-617, [1993] 2 All ER 643, 647.
[179] Supreme Court, 5 March 1997.

documents in his possession or power but will have little understanding of the manner in which they may advance his own case or damage his opponents. He continued as follows:

> It is this problem which imposes on the solicitor to the party making discovery the duty to take positive steps to ensure that his client appreciates the extent of the obligation imposed by an order for discovery. The solicitor owes a duty to the court carefully to go through the documents disclosed by the client to make sure, as far as possible, that no relevant document has been withheld from disclosure (see *Woods v Martins Bank Ltd* [1959] 1 QB 55). However, the deponent cannot abdicate his duty in relation to disclosure to his legal advisers nor could the lawyer accept the responsibility of inspecting all of the documents in the possession of his clients. Careful consultation between the solicitor and the client should enable the deponent to extract all documents in his possession or procurement which are relevant – in the wide sense to which that word in used in relation to discovery – to matters in issue in the proceedings and to obtain the advice of his lawyers, if necessary, in relation to any particular document the discoverability of which might be in doubt.

Clearly the court will attach some importance to the advice given by legal advisers in relation to the question of which documents are "relevant" and ought to be disclosed. This was made clear by Barrington J delivering the judgment of the Supreme Court in *Murphy v J. Donohoe Ltd*[180] which concerned an application to have the defences of some of the defendants struck out for failure to comply with discovery. One of the factors which he said the trial judge had attached insufficient weight to in making a decision to accede to the application was that the legal advisers of the relevant defendants had placed a restrictive interpretation on the original discovery order. In the view of Barrington J if these defendants were acting on advice from independent legal advisers who were prepared to stand over this advice in court, this was a factor which mitigated the default of the defendants, even in the event of the trial judge holding that this advice was wrong. For this and other reasons, the Supreme Court decided to allow the appeal against the striking out of the defences.[181]

Cross-examination on an Affidavit of Discovery

7.044 The circumstances in which cross-examination of an affidavit of discovery may be permitted are rare. They were considered in *Duncan v Governor of Portlaoise Prison*.[182] The applicant had been detained on foot of an order of the

---

[180] [1996] 1 IR 123, [1996] 1 ILRM 481.
[181] See further paragraph 7.025.
[182] [1997] 1 IR 558.

Special Criminal Court which it subsequently transpired was invalid. He was released and re-arrested and remanded in custody in Portlaoise Prison. An application was made for an inquiry pursuant to Article 40.4.2° of the Constitution into the lawfulness of his detention and in the course of these proceedings the applicant sought discovery against the respondent and a number of notice parties. The notice parties made affidavits of discovery which contained claims of legal professional and executive privilege. The applicant sought *inter alia* an order directing an oral hearing of the claims of privilege and served a notice of intention to cross-examine in respect of the notice parties' affidavits of discovery, claiming that he was entitled to test the claim of privilege and the issue of whether the notice parties had further documents which ought to have been discovered by way of cross-examination. Kelly J refused the relief sought, although he stated that he did not accept that "in Irish law an affidavit of discovery must be considered as conclusive and can never be the subject of cross-examination." He said that the courts should have the ability to adjudicate fully on the adequacy and accuracy of an affidavit of discovery, which in exceptional cases may involve cross-examination of the deponent of an affidavit. However, Kelly J stated that the circumstances in which it might be permissible to cross-examine on an affidavit of discovery were extremely rare because of the variety of other remedies which are available with a view to testing matters contained in an affidavit of discovery including orders for further and better discovery, the delivery of interrogatories and the inspection by the court itself of documents referred to in an affidavit. He said that the rare circumstances which merit cross-examination need not be specified, but it should only arise where it was both necessary and where other remedies proved inadequate. He concluded that cross-examination on the affidavits which had been made was neither necessary nor appropriate in the circumstances of the case before him.

Discovery of Privileged Documents

7.045 As a general principle, issues relating to discovery and privilege are entirely distinct and the fact that a claim of privilege may subsequently successfully be made is not a ground for refusing discovery of a document. However, sometimes in the interests of expediency, normal procedures may not be followed as the decision of Geoghegan J in *Haughey v Moriarty*[183] illustrates. The decision deals with the issue of public interest immunity in the context of a motion of discovery brought by the plaintiffs against the Moriarty Tribunal and the State in the course of their wide-ranging challenge to the tribunal. With regard to the discovery sought from the tribunal, Geoghegan J was satisfied that only one of the documents sought was relevant, namely a copy of the confidential letter sent by the tribunal to the Government Chief Whip. Ordinarily this

---

[183] High Court (Geoghegan J) 20 January 1998.

finding would have been sufficient to dispose of the motion for discovery leaving for another day, the question of whether the document was immune from production. However, in the circumstances of the case, the judge decided to telescope the normal discovery procedure and adjudicate upon the claim of public interest immunity. He stated as follows:

> Normally, an alleged public interest in the confidentiality of a particular document is not itself a ground for refusing discovery. If an order for discovery is made, such a document has to be listed in the ordinary way but privilege can be pleaded in respect of it. But given the urgency of this action in that, in the absence of an early hearing the proceedings of the tribunal may be delayed, it was agreed that the confidentiality issue would be dealt with on the hearing of the application for discovery itself the rationale being that if such a plea would in the event be upheld the making of the order for discovery would be pointless. Accordingly, what would normally be two stages in the discovery process have in this instance, in the interest of speedy and fair procedures been merged into one.[184]

Material Which Would be Used Solely for Cross-Examination of a Witness as to Credit

7.046 A submission was made by counsel for the appellant in *Stafford v Revenue Commissioners*,[185] which concerned a challenge to decisions made by the respondents in relation to the importation of a bronze statute, that if the application for discovery had really been sought to attack the credit of her client, it should not be granted. In relation to this submission, O'Flaherty J stated that he was prepared to adopt the following statement from Matthews and Malek on *Discovery*[186] as representing the current position in Irish law:

> Discovery will not be ordered of material which would be used solely for cross-examination of a witness as to credit, since it would be oppressive if a party was obliged to disclose any document which might provide material for cross-examination as to his credibility as a witness.

O'Flaherty J concluded that discovery of documents relating to the importation of goods on previous occasions would not be relevant to the proceedings before the court and should not be granted.

---

[184] *Ibid.* at 10.
[185] Supreme Court, 27 March 1996.
[186] (1992). Now see *Disclosure* 2nd edition, 2000.

Conclusions

7.047 It is clear that the judiciary are becoming increasingly wary of what might be described as excessive use of the discovery process. At the conclusion of his judgment in *Brooks Thomas Ltd v Impac Ltd*[187] Lynch J made reference to "the trend in modern times to seek discovery in almost every case". O'Flaherty J has also commented on the growing frequency with which interlocutory applications are being brought and he stated in *Stafford v Revenue Commissioners*[188] "not for the first time", that "these interlocutory matters are used to hold up the business of the courts". It will be interesting to observe the extent to which the new rule 12 will alter the practice which has developed over recent years.

PROCEDURE FOR BRINGING DISCOVERY APPLICATION

Inter Partes Discovery

Voluntary Discovery

7.048 When a party has identified the documents of which he or she wishes to have discovery, the first step is to write to the other side seeking voluntary discovery. The former practice of the High Court that this was an essential prerequisite to obtaining an order for discovery is now enshrined in Order 31, rule 12 which provides that an order for discovery cannot be made unless the party has previously requested voluntary discovery. This requirement may only be dispensed with in limited circumstances where by reason of urgency, the consent of the parties, the nature of the case or other circumstances, the court deems it appropriate to deal with the matter.[189]

The request for voluntary discovery must specify the precise categories of documents in respect of which discovery is sought and the reasons why each category is sought. These reasons will usually be closely tied to the issues raised by the pleadings and the particularity required will be dictated by the degree of connection between the documents sought and the issues in the case *i.e.* the more obvious the relevance of the documents sought, the less elaborate will be the reason required. It may be further necessary in some instances to give reasons why a party believes that documents within a specified category may exist. A reasonable period to make discovery must be allowed and what is a reasonable period will depend on the circumstances.

---

[187] [1999] 1 ILRM 171, 178. Lynch J suggested that for this reason the Superior Courts Rules Committee might consider changing the provisions of rule 12(1) so as to require an affidavit before discovery is ordered.

[188] Supreme Court, 27 March 1996 at 7.

[189] Order 31, rule 12(4).

An agreement by a party to make voluntary discovery in terms agreed with the other side has, from a practical perspective, the same effect as if a court order in those terms had been made because Order 31, rule 12(4)(2) provides that such discovery must be made in the same manner and form as if it had been ordered by the High Court and will have the same effect. Thus, an affidavit of discovery in the proper form must be sworn. In addition, the same remedies for default in making discovery within the time agreed are available provided that the party requested to make voluntary discovery was informed that: (a) voluntary discovery was being sought pursuant to Order 31, rule 12(4); (b) agreement to make discovery would require it to be made in like manner and form and would have such effect as if directed by order; and (c) failure to make discovery might result in an application to penalise the default.[190] It follows that for an agreement for voluntary discovery to have binding effect, these matters should be specified as a matter of course in any request for voluntary discovery.

Motion for Discovery

7.049 If the other party fails or refuses to make discovery, then an application to the Master[191] by way of motion on notice to the party from whom discovery is sought may be made. The notice of motion must specify the precise categories of documents in respect of which discovery is sought[192] and will generally simply repeat the categories as set out in the letter seeking voluntary discovery. That notice of motion must be grounded on the affidavit of the party seeking discovery and that affidavit should contain the following:

(i) A means of knowledge clause.

(ii) A reference to the proceedings had in the matter.

(iii) An enumeration of the documents sought and a recitation of the reasons why each category of document is sought. It is important that a specific and sufficient reason should be given for each individual category. If the letter requesting voluntary discovery has been properly drafted, then it will suffice to transpose the relevant portions of it into the affidavit.

(iv) An averment that voluntary discovery was requested and that the party from which it was requested has failed, refused or neglected to make such discovery and/or has ignored the request. The request for voluntary discovery and any subsequent correspondence should be exhibited.

(v) An averment that discovery of the documents sought is necessary for fairly disposing of the cause or matter or for saving costs.

---

[190] Order 31, rule 12(4)(3).
[191] Order 63, rule 1(6).
[192] Order 31, rule 12(1).

(vi) A prayer for relief.

Proofs

7.050 The party moving the application for discovery should have the following in court:

(i)   the notice of motion;

(ii)   the grounding affidavit;

(iii)   the pleadings;

(iv)   an affidavit of service of the notice of motion and grounding affidavit on the party from whom discovery is sought; and

(v)   the name (and, if necessary, the position) of the deponent plus a time period within which discovery is to be made.

Hearing of the Motion

7.051 The Master has a broad discretion on such an application and may make an order for discovery in terms of the notice of motion or in amended terms. He may also refuse or adjourn the application if he is satisfied that discovery is not necessary or not necessary at that stage of the case, or where voluntary discovery has not been requested. The principal issue to be decided on the motion is whether the documents sought are relevant and this will be tested in accordance with the principles set out above. If there is a doubt about the relevance of a particular category of documents, the Master will often examine the pleadings to determine if they are relevant to an issue in the case and it is, therefore, important to have them in court.

On an application for discovery, the Master has jurisdiction to make an order on terms as to security for the costs of discovery or otherwise and either generally or limited to certain classes or documents as he may think fit.[193] Before the introduction of the new rules, it was common to seek a cross-order for discovery in general terms but because of the stipulation that an application for discovery must be grounded on an affidavit, it would seem that such an order can no longer be made.

Costs

7.052 Order 31, rule 25 provides that the costs of discovery are, unless otherwise ordered by the court, to be allowed as part of the costs of the party seeking discovery. However, rule 12(4)(5) provides that the costs of an application to

---

[193] Order 31, rule 12(2).

court for discovery in any case in which a request for voluntary discovery has not been made or within the time provided shall be in the discretion of the court. Generally, if the party seeking discovery is granted an order in terms of the notice of motion, then costs should follow the event unless the party failed to request voluntary discovery. If discovery is granted in terms of an amended notice of motion, then costs will generally be reserved but if discovery is refused, costs will generally be awarded against the applicant.

Order for Discovery

7.053 If the Master decides to make an order for discovery, the order will specify the categories of document of which discovery is to be made and the period of time within which discovery must be made. Generally, for straightforward discovery, a period of six weeks is allowed but if a large volume of documents is involved or if the deponent is out of the jurisdiction, a period of eight weeks or longer may be permitted.

The order will also specify who is to swear the affidavit and for this reason it is imperative to have the name of the deponent in court because an order will not be made without it. Sometimes, a doubt may arise as to the means of knowledge of the deponent and if so, it will be necessary to satisfy the Master that he or she has sufficient knowledge of the matters at issue and the documents to swear the affidavit. The deponent should be a person with adequate means of knowledge of the issues in the case and of the documents, generally the individual litigant or a person in an appropriate position within a company or organisation. The Master will not accept the solicitor of a party as the deponent.

Affidavit of Discovery

7.054 The affidavit of discovery, which must be in the form set out in Form 10 of Appendix C to the Rules, contains two schedules. The First Schedule is divided into two parts and Part I lists all documents relating to the matters in question (*i.e.* falling within the categories of documents ordered to be discovered) which are in the possession or power of the deponent and which he or she is discovering. Part II of the Schedule lists documents of that description in respect of which the deponent is claiming privilege. Although it was and, to some extent still is, common practice to list privileged documents by reference to generic categories rather than individually *e.g.* "correspondence between solicitor and counsel", this is not permissible. The correct approach to the drafting of Part II is to list individually each document for which privilege is claimed, indicate the general nature of the document and specify the type of privilege claimed.[194] The Second Schedule to the affidavit lists relevant documents which

---

[194] *Bula Ltd v Crowley* [1991] 1 IR 220, [1990] ILRM 756; *Bula Ltd v Tara Mines Ltd (No. 4)* [1991] 1 IR 217. These cases are discussed below in Chapter 8.

the deponent had but no longer has in his power or possession. In the body of the affidavit, the deponent should state when those documents were last in his possession or power and what has become of them and in whose possession they are now. Finally, the main body of the affidavit will contain an averment by the deponent that neither he nor his agents have or have had in their possession or control any document related to the matters in question other than those listed in the two schedules. Provided that the documents are included in the correct schedules, there do not appear to be any requirements with respect to the order in which documents are listed and it is open to a party to list them in any order.[195]

Appeal

7.055 A party has six days from the date of the perfecting of the Master's order to appeal to the High Court to discharge the order made or to make the order refused.[196]

Non Party Discovery

7.056 The procedure for non-party discovery is very similar to that for *inter partes* discovery but a number of points should be borne in mind.

Voluntary Discovery

7.057 Although Order 31, rule 29 does not contain any stipulation that voluntary discovery must be sought, the practice of the Master is to regard it as a prerequisite to bringing an application. Although a non-party may not object to making discovery once their costs of doing so are discharged, it will often refuse to make discovery in the absence of a court order because of confidentiality concerns.

Motion for Discovery

7.058 The application is brought in the Master's Court[197] by way of motion on notice to the non-party and all other parties to the proceedings. The notice of motion should specify with particularity the precise categories of documents sought and will be grounded upon an affidavit of the party seeking discovery which should contain the following:

(i)   A means of knowledge clause.

---

[195] McDonnell, "Discovery" (Continuing Legal Education lecture delivered at Blackhall Place on 9 October 1998), at 12.
[196] Order 63, rule 9.
[197] Order 63, rule 1(6).

(ii) A reference to the proceedings had in the matter.

(iii) An enumeration of the documents or categories of document sought with the reasons why it is likely that they exist and are or have been in the possession, custody or power of the non-party and why they are relevant to the proceedings. It is also important to establish that the documents cannot be obtained by an order for discovery against a party to the action or by any other means.

(iv) An averment that voluntary discovery was requested and that the party from which it was requested has failed, refused or neglected to make such discovery. The request for voluntary discovery and any subsequent correspondence should be exhibited.

(v) An undertaking (if necessary) that the confidentiality of the documents will be maintained.

(vi) An averment that the discovery of the documents sought is necessary for fairly disposing of the cause or matter or for saving costs.

(vii) A prayer for relief.

Proofs

7.059 The party moving the application for discovery should have the following in court:

(i)   the notice of motion.

(ii)   the grounding affidavit (which should exhibit the letter requesting voluntary discovery).

(iii) the pleadings.

(iv) an affidavit of service of the notice of motion and grounding affidavit on the non-party and on every other party. It is crucial to have an affidavit of service of the motion on the non-party because they will often not appear on the hearing of the motion.

(v)   the name of the deponent.

Hearing of the Motion

7.060 As noted above, the Master or court has an even broader discretion when adjudicating upon an application for non-party discovery. In order to obtain such an order, it is necessary to show that the non-party is likely to have or have had documents in his possession or power and that those documents are relevant. In addition, the court has a power to refuse to make an order where to do so would cause oppression or prejudice to the non-party which cannot be adequately compensated by the payment of costs.

Order for Discovery

7.061 If the Master or court decides to make an order for discovery, the order will specify the categories of document of which discovery is to be made, the period of time within which discovery must be made and the name of the deponent. In addition, if discovery of categories of documents is ordered, the pleadings should be annexed to the order to enable the non-party to determine which of the documents within that category are relevant.

Costs

7.062 An order for discovery against a non-party will only be made on the basis of an undertaking of the party seeking discovery to pay the costs of the non-party in making it and any costs incurred on the motion. As between the parties to the action, those costs will be reserved and so, will ultimately be borne by the unsuccessful party in the proceedings.

Further and Better Discovery

7.063 If it is believed that a party has failed to make full or adequate discovery, the first step is to write to that party pointing out the deficiencies in the discovery made and requesting that a new or supplemental affidavit be sworn making further and better discovery. If the party refuses to do this, then the next step is to issue a motion for further and better discovery returnable to the Master's Court.[198]

Notice of Motion

7.064 The motion is brought on notice to the defaulting party seeking an order pursuant to Order 31, rule 20(3) directing that party to state by affidavit whether any one or more specific documents, specified in the notice of motion, are or have at any time been in his possession or power, and if not then in his possession, when he parted with them and what has become of them. This motion will, at first instance, be heard in the Master's Court. This notice of motion must be grounded on the affidavit of the party seeking further and better discovery and that affidavit should contain the following:

(i)   A means of knowledge clause.

(ii) A reference to the proceedings had in the matter.

---

[198] Order 63, rule 1(6).

(iii) Details of the agreement for voluntary discovery or order for discovery on foot of which the affidavit of discovery was made together with details of how and why it is alleged that this affidavit is deficient. The affidavit must state that in the belief of the deponent the party against whom the application is made has, or at some time had, in his possession or power the document or documents specified in the application, and that they relate to the matters in question in the case. That statement will not be sufficient, in itself, to obtain an order and it is crucial that the affidavit set out reasonable grounds for suspecting that these documents exist and are or have been in the possession, power or procurement of the party alleged to be in default.

(iv) Details of writing to the party seeking further and better discovery on a voluntary basis and exhibit that letter and any reply thereto.

(v) A prayer for relief.

Proofs

7.065 The party moving the application for discovery should have the following in court:

(i) the notice of motion;

(ii) the grounding affidavit;

(iii) the pleadings;

(iv) an affidavit of service of the notice of motion and grounding affidavit on the party from whom further and better discovery is sought; and

(v) the affidavit of discovery already sworn in the matter.

Hearing of the Motion

7.066 If the Master is satisfied that there are reasonable grounds for suspecting that there are additional documents in existence, he will make an order for further and better discovery limited to certain documents or categories of documents.

Failure to Make Discovery

7.067 Where a party has failed to comply with an order for discovery, the most common remedy invoked is to make an application pursuant to Order 31, rule 21, to have the proceedings of the plaintiff dismissed for want of prosecution or the defence of the defendant struck out.

Notice of Motion

7.068 The application is brought in the Master's Court by way of motion to strike out the proceedings or the defence, as appropriate, on notice to the defaulting party. The motion is grounded on an affidavit of the moving party which should contain the following:

(i)   A means of knowledge clause.

(ii)   A reference to the proceedings had in the matter.

(iii)   Details of the making of the order for discovery.

(iv)   An averment that despite the elapsing of the time limited for discovery in the order, no discovery or inadequate discovery has been made. Although it is not required by the Rules, it is advisable to write to the defaulting party extending time to make discovery and warning them that a motion will issue if proper discovery is not made within that extended period. That letter, any reply thereto and any further correspondence should be exhibited.

(v)   An averment, if appropriate, that the failure to make proper discovery and comply with the order of the court is deliberate. Any evidence that the default is deliberate should be set out in the affidavit and/or exhibited.

(vi)   A prayer for relief.

Proofs

7.069 The party moving the application should have the following in court:

(i)   the notice of motion;

(ii)   the grounding affidavit;

(iii)   the pleadings;

(iv)   an affidavit of service of the notice of motion and grounding affidavit on the defaulting party; and

(v)   the order for discovery

Hearing of the Motion

7.070 In general, this motion is simply used as a tactic to force a party which has been dilatory to make discovery. It is common for the defaulting party to appear, make excuses why discovery could not be made within the time limited and request an extension of time. This will generally be given with the period of the extension varying depending on the reason proffered for not making discovery and the court's view of the *bona fides* of the defaulting party. Thus, the usual order on this motion is for the period for the making of discovery to be extended by a set period with costs awarded to the moving party. Where the default is alleged to have been deliberate and the grounding affidavit contains evidence to that effect, then the moving party may press the application to have the proceedings or pleading struck out. However, the courts are reluctant to take this course of action and convincing evidence will be required that the failure to make discovery was wilful.

INSPECTION

7.071 As Barron J stated in the course of his judgment in *Holloway v Belenos Publications Ltd (No. 2)*[199] "the essence of an order for discovery is that it requires the person to whom it is directed to list documents of which he is aware but of which the applicant for the order need not necessarily be aware. On the other hand, the essence of an order for inspection is knowledge of the existence of the particular documents to be inspected". Therefore what differentiates the two procedures is that in the case of inspection, the party making the application will always already be aware of the existence of the documents which he seeks to inspect. It has been stressed by Murphy J in *Gormley v Ireland*[200] that where inspection of documents is ordered by the court that these documents should only be made available for "the proper processing of the present litigation and not for any other purpose".

Order 31, rule 15 of the Rules of the Superior Courts 1986 provides that where reference is made to a document in the pleadings, affidavit or list of documents of his opponent, a litigant is entitled to give notice to this other party to produce such documents for the inspection of the party giving such notice or of his solicitor, and to allow copies to be made. The rule goes on to provide that any party not complying with such a notice will not be entitled to put any such documents in evidence on his behalf unless the document relates only to his title as a defendant, or he has an excuse which the court deems sufficient for not complying with such notice. Rule 16 provides that a notice to any party to produce documents referred to in his pleadings, affidavit or list of documents shall be in the form of a "Notice to Produce Documents" set out in From No. 11 of Appendix C to the Rules which requires an applicant to describe the documents he wishes to inspect. The recipient of such a notice is required to reply by way of a "Notice to Inspect Documents" set out in Form No. 12 Appendix C informing the applicant that he can inspect some or all of documents requested or that objection is made to permitting such inspection and if so, the grounds of objection shall be set out in the notice. According to the provisions of rule 17, the party to whom a notice to produce is given shall reply within two days from the

---

[199] [1988] IR 494, [1988] ILRM 685.
[200] [1993] 2 IR 75, 80.

receipt of such notice if all the documents therein referred to have been set out by him in his affidavit of discovery, or within four days from such receipt if any of the documents referred to in the notice have been set out in the affidavit. Rule 17 goes on to provide that the "Notice to Inspect Documents" shall state a time within three days of its delivery at which the documents which a party is prepared to produce may be inspected at his solicitor's office, or in the case of banker's books, other books of account or books in constant use for the purposes of any trade or business, at their usual place of custody.

7.072 An application to court may become necessary if the party served with a "Notice to Produce Documents" fails to give notice of a time for inspection or objects to giving inspection, or offers it at a location other than at his solicitor's office. Rule 18 provides that the court may make an order for inspection in such place and in such manner as it may think fit and that the application should be grounded on an affidavit, unless the documents are ones referred to in the pleadings or affidavits of the party against whom the application is made or disclosed in his affidavit or list of documents, which must set out what documents are sought, that the applicant is entitled to inspect them, and that they are in the possession or power of the other party. The provisions of rule 18 have recently been considered by Kelly J in *Cooper Flynn v Radio Telefís Éireann*[201] in which the defendants sought an order against the plaintiff's employer, a bank, requiring it to make available in an unredacted form the documents disclosed in the non-party discovery affidavit. Kelly J pointed out that rule 18 provides a mechanism whereby inspection of documents which have been included in a discovery affidavit may be ordered and that rule 18(2) makes it clear that the court ought not to make an order if it is not necessary for disposing fairly of the action of for saving costs. He commented that there appears to be little authority in this jurisdiction as to what is meant by the phrase "necessary for disposing fairly of the cause or matter" but that he derived considerable assistance from the English authorities to which he had been referred. Kelly J referred to the *dicta* of Simon Brown LJ in *Wallace Smith Trust Co. Ltd v Deloitte Haskins & Sells*[202] in which he stated that the burden lies on the party seeking inspection to show that it is necessary for the fair disposal of the action. In the view of Simon Brown LJ disclosure would be necessary if it would give "litigious advantage" to the party seeking inspection, the information sought was not otherwise available to that party and such an order would not be oppressive. If a *prima facie* case was made out for disclosure, the court should examine the documents involved to ensure that inspection was indeed necessary and to see if the loss of confidentiality involved could be mitigated. Kelly J expressed the view that these principles governed the application of rule 18 in this jurisdiction and that it fell upon the defendants to show that the disclosure of the names of

---

[201] [2000] 3 IR 344, [2001] 1 ILRM 208.
[202] [1997] 1 WLR 257, [1996] 4 All ER 403.

the bank's customers was necessary for the fair disposal of the action, bearing in mind the principle of banker confidentiality. He then referred to the *dicta* of Bingham MR in *Taylor v Anderton*[203] as follows:

> The crucial consideration is, in my judgment, the meaning of the expression "disposing fairly of the cause or matter". Those words direct attention to the question whether inspection is necessary for the fair determination of the matter, whether by trial or otherwise. The purpose of the rule is to ensure that one party does not enjoy an unfair advantage or suffer an unfair disadvantage in the litigation as a result of a document not being produced for inspection. It is, I think, of no importance that a party is curious about the contents of a document or would like to know the contents of it if he suffers no litigious disadvantage by not seeing it and would gain no litigious advantage by seeing it. That, in my judgment, is the test.

Kelly J concluded that allowing inspection of the customer files in an unredacted form which would disclose their identity to the defendants' representatives would confer a litigious advantage upon them and that to deny them this entitlement would not be conducive to the fair disposition of the action. However, he stated that he had borne in mind the undoubted duty of confidentiality which existed and he made the order on the basis that the inspection could only be carried out by solicitors and counsel acting for the first and second named defendants and named persons in the legal department of the first named defendant.

7.073 It should be noted that in *Barry v Director of Public Prosecutions*,[204] O'Neill J held that where an application for inspection has been heard and determined and there was no basis in the fresh affidavits served for contending that the case had been materially altered, an order for further inspection would not be made.

7.074 In relation to business books, rule 20(1) provides that the court may order a copy of entries to be furnished but this must be verified by the affidavit of a person who has examined the copy with the original entry and it must be stated therein whether there are any erasures, interlineations or alterations in the original book. Notwithstanding that a copy of a document has been supplied, the court may still order inspection of the original from which the copy was made. Where privilege is claimed on an application for an order for inspection, rule 20(2) provides that the court may inspect the documents for the purpose of determining the validity of the claim. Finally rule 21 provides that if any

---

[203] [1995] 1 WLR 447, 462, [1995] 2 All ER 420, 434.
[204] High Court (O'Neill J) 2 April 2001.

party fails to comply with an order for inspection, he shall be liable to attachment and if a plaintiff, to have his action dismissed for want of prosecution or if
a defendant, to have his defence struck out.[205]

---

[205] See *supra* paragraphs 7.024–7.025 in relation to the operation of rule 21 with regard
to failure to comply with an order for discovery.

CHAPTER EIGHT

PRIVILEGE

INTRODUCTION

8.001 As we have seen in the previous chapter, a party will generally be obliged to produce for inspection all relevant documents discovered by him and this process is considered crucial to the administration of justice and disposition of the issues before a court. As Bingham LJ observed in *Ventouris v Mountain*:[1]

> Our system of civil procedure is founded on the rule that the interests of justice are best served if parties to litigation are obliged to disclose and produce for the other party's inspection all documents in their possession, custody or power relating to the issues in the action.

Indeed, in *Murphy v Dublin Corporation*,[2] Walsh J emphasised that the "[p]ower to compel the attendance of witnesses and the production of evidence is an inherent part of the judicial power of government of the State and is the ultimate safeguard of justice in the State."

However, there are a number of instances examined in this chapter where a party or person may enjoy a privilege from being compelled to produce a document. The recognition of such a privilege or immunity inevitably cuts down the amount of relevant evidence before the courts and, hence, impairs the administration of justice. However, there are certain situations in which it is considered that this harm is outweighed by the damage to some other objective which it is the policy of the courts to promote.[3] To paraphrase Finlay CJ in *Smurfit Paribas Bank Ltd v AAB Export Finance Ltd*,[4] a privilege may be "granted by the courts in instances which have been identified as securing an objective which in the public interest in the proper conduct of the administration of justice can be said to outweigh the disadvantage arising from the restriction of disclosure of all the facts."

---

[1] [1991] 3 All ER 472, 476.

[2] [1972] IR 215, 233.

[3] See *Skeffington v Rooney* [1997] 1 IR 22, 32, [1997] 2 ILRM 56, 66. *Cf. Re Barings plc* [1998] Ch 356, 362, [1998] 1 All ER 673, 678, *per* Scott VC: "The rules of discovery, which require relevant documents available to one litigant to be made available also to the other litigants, are intended to assist and make more likely the achieving of a just result in litigation. However, it is recognised, and established by authority, that in some circumstances a greater public interest will override the right of a litigant to obtain relevant documents from his opponent."

[4] [1990] 1 IR 469, 477, [1990] ILRM 588, 594.

Before going on to examine the various privileges, something should be said of the relationship between a "private" privilege and "public interest" privilege. Although the two have traditionally been treated as quite distinct, it is evident from the discussion below, that each is ultimately grounded on a determination that the balance of public interest favours the recognition and upholding of the privilege.[5] Instead, the main difference between the two rests on the fact that there is no overt balancing involved in the application of a "private" privilege. Thus, a document is either privileged from production in accordance with the definition of the particular privilege or it is not and the courts do not balance the conflicting policy interests involved on a case by case basis. Instead, the balancing of conflicting policy objectives occurs *ab initio* in determining the parameters of the particular privilege.[6] Therefore, as in the case of public interest privilege, the courts are the ultimate arbiters of both the parameters and application of a "private" privilege. Indeed, it could not, consistent with the constitutional position, be otherwise. As Finlay CJ emphasised in *Smurfit Paribas Bank Ltd v AAB Export Finance Ltd*,[7] "the question as to whether or not a party to litigation will be privileged to refuse to produce particular evidence is a matter within the sole competence of the courts".[8]

LEGAL PROFESSIONAL PRIVILEGE

INTRODUCTION

8.002 The origins of legal professional privilege can be traced back to the later part of the sixteenth century but its policy and broad parameters were only settled in the nineteenth century when the various decisions of the common law and chancery courts were reconciled and the relationship of the privilege with the principles of discovery settled.

Initial development of the privilege focused on communications between the client and lawyer for the purpose of giving or receiving legal advice. The privilege which originally applied only to communications made to a barrister or

---

[5] See *Skeffington v Rooney* [1997] 1 IR 22, 32, [1997] 2 ILRM 56, 66, where Keane J did not draw any distinction between "private" and "public interest" privilege but seemed to regard all privileges as resting ultimately on a judgment as to where the balance of public interest lies.

[6] See *Skeffington v Rooney* [1997] 1 IR 22, 32, [1997] 2 ILRM 56, 66. *Cf.* the comments of Lord Taylor CJ in *R v Derby Magistrates' Court, ex p. B.* [1996] AC 487, 508, [1995] 4 All ER 526, 541 ("Legal professional privilege and public interest immunity are as different in their origin as they are in their scope. Putting it another way, if a balancing exercise was ever required in the case of legal professional privilege, it was performed once and for all in the sixteenth century, and since then has applied across the board in every case, irrespective of the client's individual merits.").

[7] [1990] 1 IR 469, 475, [1990] ILRM 588, 592.

[8] See also *Skeffington v Rooney* [1997] 1 IR 22, 32, [1997] 2 ILRM 56, 66.

solicitor after the commencement of litigation was, over time, extended to communications made in contemplation of litigation,[9] then to disputes where litigation was not yet contemplated[10] and, finally, to legal advice irrespective of whether litigation was contemplated or a dispute existed.[11]

Another strand of development related to communications with third parties in preparation for litigation and again, the process was of gradual extension.[12] First, protection was afforded to information obtained by a solicitor from third parties for the purpose of litigation and then to evidence gathered by agents employed by a solicitor for this purpose.[13] Next, privilege was extended to information gathered by the client at the request of the solicitor and then to information volunteered by the client.[14] Finally, it was held that documents prepared by a client for the purpose of litigation, whether at the request of the solicitor or not, were privileged if prepared with the *bona fide* intention of being laid before him to obtain his advice and whether actually laid before him or not.[15]

By the last quarter of the nineteenth century, it was recognised that the effect of these two lines of authority had been to create two distinct privileges identified by Mellish LJ in *Anderson v Bank of British Columbia*,[16] as "first, the privilege which protects a man from producing confidential communications made between him and his solicitor ... [and], secondly, the privilege which entitles him to refuse to communicate evidence which he has obtained for the purpose of litigation." The distinction between the two was copper-fastened by the decision in *Wheeler v Le Marchant*,[17] that privilege did not apply to communications between a solicitor and third parties for the purpose of enabling him or her to give legal advice and that third party communications were only protected from disclosure where they came into existence for the purposes of litigation which had commenced or was contemplated.

The existence of these two sub-categories of legal professional privilege, commonly termed "legal advice privilege" and "litigation privilege" respectively,[18] is now generally recognised though some uncertainty about their pre-

---

[9] *Gainsford v Grammar* (1809) 2 Camp 9; *Williams v Mudie* (1824) 1 C & P 158.

[10] *Clark v Clark* (1830) 1 Mo & Rob 3.

[11] *Foster v Hall* (1831) 12 Pick 89; *Greenough v Gaskell* (1833) 1 My & K 98, 101.

[12] See the account of the development of the law given by Jessel MR in *Anderson v Bank of British Columbia* (1876) 2 Ch D 644, 649-50.

[13] See *Greenough v Gaskell* (1833) 1 My & K 98, 103-4 and *Curling v Perring* (1835) 2 My & K 380, 381.

[14] See *Steele v Stewart* (1844) 1 Ph 471 and *Lafone v Falkland Islands Co.* (1857) 4 K & J 36.

[15] *Southwark and Vauxhall Water Co. v Quick* (1878) 3 QBD 315. This decision was followed in *Worthington v Dublin, Wicklow and Wexford Railway Co.* (1888) 22 LR Ir 310, 313.

[16] (1876) 2 Ch D 644.

[17] (1881) 18 Ch D 675, 681.

[18] See *Formica Ltd v Secretary of State acting by Export Credit Guarantee Department*

cise parameters and degree of overlap remains. In particular, it is uncertain whether communications between a client and his legal adviser regarding litigation in being or anticipated are protected only by legal advice privilege or by both.[19] For the reasons articulated below, the better view is that such communications are more properly protected by legal advice privilege alone and that litigation privilege should be regarded as applied to third party communications and work product only.

LEGAL ADVICE PRIVILEGE

8.003 Legal advice privilege entitles a client to refuse to disclose any communications with his lawyer made for the purpose of giving or receiving legal advice. Although that legal advice will often be sought in connection with litigation, the proximity or otherwise of litigation is irrelevant provided that the communications pass in the course of a professional legal relationship.[20]

Policy of the Privilege

8.004 Legal professional privilege began life as a privilege enjoyed by the lawyer based on consideration for his oath and honour.[21] However, the idea that the confidentiality of communications could be maintained on the basis of honour was subsequently rejected by the courts[22] and from the early eighteenth century onwards, a new theory began to emerge based on the desirability of protecting the inviolability of the lawyer/client relationship. One of the earliest expositions of this new theory is to be found in the old Irish case of *Annesley v Earl of Anglesea*[23] where Mounteney B explained that:

> [A]n increase of legal business, and the inabilities of parties to transact

---

[1995] 1 Lloyd's Rep 692, 696 and *Highgrade Traders Ltd* [1984] BCLC 151, 162 where this terminology was used. *Cf. Porter v Scott* [1979] NI 6, where Kelly J drew a distinction between legal professional privilege properly so called and lawyer's 'work product' privilege.

[19] As O'Hanlon J in *Silver Hill Duckling Ltd v Minister for Agriculture* [1987] IR 289, [1987] ILRM 516 seemed to contemplate.

[20] *Wheeler v Le Marchant* (1881) 17 Ch D 675, 682; *Minter v Priest* [1929] 1 KB 655, 675.

[21] See *Berd v Lovelace* (1577) Cary 62; *Dennis v Codrington* (1579) Cary 100 and, generally, Wigmore (3rd ed., 1940), VIII, § 2290. It might be noted that under § 3.4 of the Code of Conduct for the Bar of Ireland a "barrister is under a duty not to communicate to any third person information entrusted to him by or on behalf of his lay client".

[22] See *Duchess of Kingston's Case* (1776) 20 How St Tr 355, 586 and *Wilson v Rastall* (1792) 4 TR 753, 758-9.

[23] (1743) 17 How St Tr 1139, 1225.

that business themselves, made it necessary for them to employ ... other persons who might transact that business for them; that this necessity introduced with it the necessity of what hath very justly established, an inviolable secrecy to be observed by attornies, in order to render it safe for clients to communicate to their attornies all proper instructions for the carrying on those causes which they found themselves under a necessity of intrusting to their care.

This rationale, thus, proceeds on the basis, articulated by Jessel MR in *Anderson v Bank of British Columbia*:[24]

[T]hat as, by reason of the complexity and difficulty of our law, litigation can only be properly conducted by professional men, it is absolutely necessary that a man, in order to prosecute his rights or to defend himself from an improper claim, should have recourse to the assistance of professional lawyers, and it being so absolutely necessary, it is equally necessary, to use a vulgar phrase, that he should be able to make a clean breast of it to the gentleman with whom he consults with a view to the prosecution of his claim, or the substantiating his defence against the claims of others; that he should be able to place unrestricted and unbounded confidence in the professional agent, and that the communications he so makes to him should be kept secret, unless with his consent (for it is his privilege, and not the privilege of the confidential agent), that he should be enabled properly to conduct his litigation.[25]

However, this rationale is not complete because it fails to explain why the private interests of the client in having effective legal representation should be allowed to trump the administration of justice and the truth-finding function of the courts. As Finlay CJ pointed out in *Smurfit Paribas Bank Ltd v AAB Export Finance Ltd*:[26]

The existence of a privilege or exemption from disclosure for communications made between a person and his lawyer clearly constitutes a potential restriction and diminution of the full disclosure both prior to and during

---

[24] (1876) 2 Ch D 644, 649.

[25] In *Smurfit Paribas Bank Ltd v AAB Export Finance Ltd* [1990] 1 IR 469, 476, [1990] ILRM 588, 593, Finlay CJ quoted this passage with approval which, he said, identified the "superior interest of the common good in the proper conduct of litigation which justified the immunity of communications from discovery in so far as they were made for the purpose of litigation as being the desirability in that good of the correct and efficient trial of actions by the courts". See also *Buckley v Incorporated Law Society* [1994] 2 IR 44, 47 and *Murphy v Kirwan* [1993] 3 IR 501, 514, [1994] 1 ILRM 293, 302.

[26] [1990] 1 IR 469, 477, [1990] ILRM 588, 594.

the course of legal proceedings which in the interests of the common good is desirable for the purpose of ascertaining the truth and rendering justice. Such privilege should, therefore ... only be granted by the courts in instances which have been identified as securing an objective which in the public interest in the proper conduct of the administration of justice can be said to outweigh the disadvantage arising from the restriction of disclosure of all the facts.

The protection conferred by the privilege is, therefore, more directly attributable to the view of the courts that it ultimately aids the administration of justice. In *Greenough v Gaskell*,[27] Brougham LC opined that:

The foundation of this rule is not difficult to discover ... it is out of regard to the interests of justice, which cannot be upholden, and to the administration of justice, which cannot go on without the aid of men skilled in jurisprudence, in the practice of the courts, and in those matters affecting rights and obligations which form the subject of all judicial proceedings. If the privilege did not exist at all, every one would be thrown upon his own legal resources; deprived of all professional assistance, a man would not venture to consult any skilful person, or would only dare to tell his counsellor half his case.[28]

8.005 The precise manner in which privilege is thought to promote the administration of justice is not specified in these decisions but the following may be suggested. First, it can be argued that privilege is crucial to the effective functioning of our adversarial model of justice.[29] This relies heavily on the parties to seek out both the facts and the law that support their case and undermine that of their opponent. The likelihood that the court will reach the right result and justice will be done is intimately tied to the quality of those efforts which are, obviously, likely to be much better if the party is represented by a trained lawyer. For example, although cross-examination has been described by Wigmore[30] as the "greatest legal engine ever invented for the discovery of truth", its effectiveness is crucially dependent upon the forensic skills of the cross-examiner. Furthermore, many cases require legal argument and the citation of legal authorities and it is simply unrealistic to expect lay persons to have the requisite skill and knowledge in that regard. Second, the representation of the parties by

---

[27] (1833) 1 My & K 98, 103.

[28] See also *Holmes v Baddeley* (1844) 1 Ph 476, 480-1, 41 ER 713, 715; *Lyell v Kennedy* (1884) 27 Ch D 1, 18; *Kennedy v Lyell* (1883) 23 Ch D 387, 404.

[29] Cf. *ESSO Australian Resources Ltd v Dawson* [1999] FCA 363, paragraph 14, where the Federal Court of Australia opined that the absence of the privilege "would significantly undermine the proper functioning of the adversarial system of justice".

[30] Wigmore, *Evidence* (3rd ed., 1940), Vol. V, §1367.

persons with legal training and knowledge is likely to result in more efficient presentation and, hence, disposal of cases.[31] Third, the involvement of a lawyer who is emotionally and financially detached from the underlying dispute aids a realistic appraisal of its prospects of success and its settlement or proper conduct if the matter comes to trial.[32] The foregoing considerations are underpinned and reinforced by the ethical obligations which barristers[33] and solicitors[34] owe to the court, ethical obligations which are not owed by lay clients and which clearly promote the administration of justice.[35]

Once it is accepted that it is desirable, in the interests of justice, that a client should be legally represented, then it necessarily follows that he should be enabled to make full and frank disclosure to the lawyer so that the foregoing benefits may be realised. In the absence of privilege, a client would be discouraged by the possibility of future disclosure from consulting a lawyer and, even if he did, the natural temptation would be to hold back facts which he considered to be harmful to his or her case. This might well lead a lawyer to advise that the client had a good case when, armed with all the relevant facts, he might have advised not to institute or to settle proceedings rather than fight a weak case.

8.006 The foregoing justifications all relate to the conduct of litigation and do not explain why privilege was extended to legal advice unconnected with litigation but in *Greenough v Gaskell*[36] Brougham LC justified this extension on the basis that:

---

[31] See *Smurfit Paribas Bank Ltd v AAB Export Finance Ltd* [1990] 1 IR 469, 476, [1990] ILRM 588, 592-3.

[32] *Cf.* the comments of Bingham LJ in *Ventouris v Mountain* [1991] 3 All ER 472, 475: "The doctrine of legal professional privilege is rooted in the public interest, which requires that hopeless and exaggerated claims and unsound and spurious defences be so far as possible discouraged, and civil disputes so far as possible settled without resort to judicial decision."

[33] Pursuant to § 5 of the Code of Conduct for the Bar of Ireland, a barrister is, *inter alia*, obliged to act at all times with courtesy to the court before which he is appearing and to use his endeavours in every case to avoid unnecessary expense and waste of the court's time. In addition, he must not knowingly deceive or mislead the court, must not coach a witness and must, in civil cases, ensure that the court is informed of any relevant decision on a point of law or any legislative provision of which he is aware immediately in point whether it is for or against his contention. See further *R v O'Connell* (1845) 7 ILR 261.

[34] In *IPLG v Fry* High Court (Lardner J) 19 March 1992, it was held that a solicitor is an officer of the court and the court, thus, has an inherent jurisdiction to supervise a solicitor's conduct and to discipline him for misconduct. See further, O'Callaghan, *The Law on Solicitors in Ireland* (2000), § 1.06 ff.

[35] *Cf. New Victoria Hospital v Ryan* [1993] ICR 201, 203, where Tucker J stated that the application of legal professional privilege "should be strictly confined to legal advisers such as solicitors and counsel, who are professionally qualified, who are members of professional bodies, who are subject to the rules and etiquette of their professions, and who owe a duty to the court".

[36] (1833) 1 My & K 98.

[T]he protection would be insufficient, if it only included communications more or less connected with judicial proceedings; for a person oftentimes requires the aid of professional advice upon the subject of his rights and his liabilities, with no reference to any particular litigation, and without any other reference to litigation generally, than all human affairs have, in so far as every transaction may, by possibility, become the subject of judicial inquiry.[37]

In addition, Lord Brougham pointed out that conferring privilege on legal advice helps to avoid litigation: "If the privilege were confined to communications connected with suits begun, or intended, or expected, or apprehended, no one could safely adopt such precautions as might eventually render any proceedings successful, or all proceedings superfluous."[38] This argument was taken up by Wigmore[39] who opined:

Now it cannot be denied that professional legal advice is as often needed for avoiding litigation as for carrying it on; still less can it be denied that the avowed ideal of the law, and the prudent custom of the profession, is to diminish litigation by so ordering the affairs of clients that litigation is not needed to correct their plight. It is a truism that much of litigation is due to the very failure of clients to seek legal advice until a resort to the courts can be avoided. Thus the relation of client and legal adviser, and the freedom of entering into it, are of at least equal importance for matters that are still in the non-litigious stage; and the promotion of the relation in that stage tends to prevent its necessity in the further and less desirable stage.

In *Smurfit Paribas Bank Ltd v AAB Export Finance Ltd*,[40] Finlay CJ did not regard the case law as providing a satisfactory explanation for the expansion of privilege to legal advice but accepted that it was justified on the basis that:[41]

Where a person seeks or obtains legal advice there are good reasons to believe that he necessarily enters the area of potential litigation. The necessity to obtain legal advice would in broad terms appear to envisage the possibility of a legal challenge or query as to the correctness or effectiveness of some step which a person is contemplating. Whether such query

---

[37] *Ibid.* at 102. *Cf. Lawrence v Campbell* (1859) 4 Drew 485, 489; *Wilson v Northampton and Banbury Junction Railway Co.* (1872) LR 14 Eq 477; *Minter v Priest* [1929] 1 KB 655, 675.
[38] (1833) 1 My & K 98, 103.
[39] Wigmore, *Evidence* (3rd ed., 1940), VIII, § 2295.
[40] [1990] 1 IR 469, [1990] ILRM 588.
[41] *Ibid.* at 478, 594-5.

or challenge develops or not, it is clear that a person is then entering the area of possible litigation.

Thus, the obtaining of legal advice was sufficiently linked to the conduct of litigation and the function of administering justice in the courts that the "public interest in the proper conduct of the administration of justice can be said to outweigh the disadvantage arising from the restriction of disclosure of all the facts".[42]

Conditions Required to Establish Privilege

8.007 In order to succeed in a claim of legal advice privilege, it is necessary to show that the document or information sought to be disclosed consists of a confidential communication made in the course of a professional legal relationship for the purpose of giving or receiving legal advice. Taking each of these elements in turn.

(i) Communication

8.008 The concept of 'communication' is given a broad and somewhat artificial interpretation so as to bring within the scope of privilege all information which passes between the lawyer and client for the purpose of giving, receiving or formulating legal advice.[43] Thus, privilege will apply not only to written communications between a lawyer and client but also to notes or memoranda of oral conversations,[44] documents generated by the lawyer in the course of formulating legal advice,[45] a solicitor's bill of costs,[46] copies of documents containing legal advice[47] and documents which reproduce or incorporate legal advice.[48]

---

[42] *Ibid.* at 477, 594.

[43] *Stevens v Canada (Privy Council)* (1998) 161 DLR (4th) 85, 100. *Cf. Descôteaux v Mierzwinski* [1982] 1 SCR 860, 893, (1982) 141 DLR (3d) 590, 618, where the Canadian Supreme Court held that privilege attaches "to all communications made within the framework of the solicitor-client relationship".

[44] *Hurstridge Finance Ltd v Lismore Homes Ltd* High Court (Costello J) 15 February 1991 at 4.

[45] *Pearce v Foster* (1885) 15 QBD 114, 118; *Hurstridge Finance Ltd v Lismore Homes Ltd* High Court (Costello J) 15 February 1991 at 5 (notes made by solicitor for purpose of preparing draft letter held to be privileged).

[46] *Chant v Brown* (1852) 9 Hare 790; *Stevens v Canada (Privy Council)* (1998) 161 DLR (4th) 85.

[47] *Butler v Board of Trade* [1971] Ch 680, 686, [1970] 3 All ER 593, 596.

[48] *Bula Ltd v Crowley* High Court (Murphy J) 8 March 1991. Murphy J rejected a distinction made in Syle & Hollander, *Documentary Evidence* (2nd ed.) at 103, between a document which merely passes on legal advice within a firm or company which is privileged and a document which goes further in which case privilege is lost. He was unable to see how this precise boundary could be maintained and held that privilege

There are, however, a number of limitations on the concept of a "communication". First, privilege only applies to communications between the lawyer and client and does not extend to communications between either the lawyer or client and third parties even though these relate to matters upon which the client has sought legal advice.[49] However, it is not necessary that the communication pass directly between the lawyer and client. Law firms could not function without the use of agents such as secretaries and apprentices and a communication which is made to or by such an agent will be privileged on the same basis as if made to or by the lawyer.[50] The position in relation to clients is slightly more complicated and privilege will not extend to communications with every agent of the client but only those who are employed or engaged for the purpose of obtaining or receiving legal advice on behalf on the client.[51]

Second, the communication must owe its genesis to the professional legal relationship. It is, therefore, important to distinguish between documents created by the client for the purpose of submission to his lawyer in order to obtain legal advice which are privileged[52] and pre-existing documents created for a different purpose and submitted to a lawyer for his advice which are not privileged.[53] Indeed, pre-existing documents enjoy no greater protection from dis-

---

applied to documents which "would of necessity disclose to a material extent confidential legal advice".

[49] *Kerry County Council v Liverpool Salvage Association* (1903) 38 ILTR 7, 8; *Hurstridge Finance Ltd v Lismore Homes Ltd* High Court (Costello J) 15 February 1991 (privilege did not apply to notes of meetings with third parties which solicitors but not the client had attended); *Wheeler v Le Marchant* (1881) 17 Ch D 675, 680-82; *Guardian Royal Exchange Assurance v Stuart* [1985] 1 NZLR 596, 602. Privilege will, however, attach to a communication between a solicitor and client in which the solicitor relates information received by him from third parties (*Re Sarah C. Getty Trust* [1985] QB 956, [1985] 2 All ER 809).

[50] In *Wheeler v Le Marchant* (1881) 17 Ch D 675, 682, Jessel MR said that a communication "is equally protected whether it is made by the client in person or is made by an agent on behalf of the client, and whether it is made to the solicitor in person or to a clerk or subordinate of the solicitor who acts in his place and under his direction." See also *Lyell v Kennedy* (1884) 27 Ch D 1, 19; *Anderson v Bank of British Columbia* (1876) 2 Ch D 644, 649; *Hooper v Gumm* (1862) 2 J & H 602, 606; *Reid v Langlois* (1849) 1 Mac & G 627, 638-9; *Walker v Wildman* (1821) 6 Madd 47, 47-8; *Steele v Stewart* (1844) 1 Phil 471, 475; *Bunbury v Bunbury* (1839) 2 Beav 173, 176.

[51] *Wheeler v Le Marchant* (1881) 17 Ch D 675, 684; *General Accident Assurance Co. v Chrusz* (1988) 37 OR (3d) 790; *Goodman & Carr v Minister of National Revenue* [1968] 2 OR 814, (1968) 70 DLR (2d) 670; *Mudgway v New Zealand Insurance Co. Ltd* [1988] 2 NZLR 283; *C-C Bottlers Ltd v Lion Nathan Ltd* [1993] 2 NZLR 445.

[52] *Horgan v Murray* [1999] 1 ILRM 257; *Dunnes Stores Ltd v Smyth* High Court (Costello P) 24 July 1995; *M'Mahon v Great Northern Railway Co.* (1906) 40 ILTR 172, 173.

[53] *Graham v Bogle* [1924] 1 IR 68, 70; *Pearce v Foster* (1885) 15 QBD 114, 118. *Cf. R v Hayward* (1846) 2 C & K 234 (privilege did not apply to a forged will which had been sent to solicitor amongst a number of title for the ostensible purpose of seeking his advice but in reality so that he could find it and act upon it). But *cf. Sheehan v McMahon* Supreme Court, 29 July 1993.

closure in the hands of the solicitor than they would in the hands of the client.[54] *A fortiori*, privilege will not attach to copies of pre-existing documents which are made for the purpose of obtaining legal advice.[55]

Third, privilege only applies to facts communicated and not to every fact which a lawyer may learn in the course of his professional relationship with a client.[56] A distinction is, thus, drawn between facts communicated to a lawyer by the client and those which are patent to the senses.[57] In *Brown v Foster*,[58] Baron Martin stated that "what passes between counsel and client ought not to be communicated, and is not admissible in evidence, but with respect to matters which the counsel sees with his own eyes, he cannot refuse to answer." In that case, it was held that counsel could give evidence as to whether a particular entry had been made in a book because this was not information communicated to him by the client but, rather, knowledge acquired by his own observation. Similarly, a lawyer may be required to give evidence as to whether a particular document was given to him by the client,[59] whether he saw the client execute a deed,[60] and whether handwriting is that of his client.[61]

(ii) Confidence

8.009 In order for a claim of privilege to succeed, it is a fundamental prerequisite that the communication passed was intended to pass in confidence.[62] Thus, in *Bord na gCon v Murphy*,[63] where a client made a statement to his solicitor of his version of events for the express purpose of corresponding with the com-

---

[54] *R v Justice of the Peace for Peterborough, ex p. Hicks* [1978] 1 All ER 225, 228, [1977] 1 WLR 1371, 1374; *R v King* [1983] 1 All ER 929, 931, [1983] 1 WLR 411, 414.

[55] *Tromso Sparebank v Beirne* [1989] ILRM 257.

[56] *Dwyer v Collins* (1852) LR 7 Exch 639, 645-6; *Bursill v Tanner* (1885) 16 QBD 1, 5; *Commissioner of Taxation v Coombes* [1999] FCA 842, (1999) 164 ALR 131; *Coveney v Tannahill* (1841) 1 Hill 33, 35 (NY).

[57] *Sandford v Remington* (1793) 2 Ves Jun 189; *Greenough v Gaskell* (1833) 1 My & K 98, 104; *Brown v Foster* (1857) 1 H & N 736; *Sawyer v Birchmore* (1837) 3 My & K 572; *Kennedy v Lyell* (1883) 23 Ch D 387, 407; *Stevens v Canada (Privy Council)* (1998) 161 DLR (4th) 85.

[58] (1857) 1 H & N 736, 740.

[59] *Dwyer v Collins* (1852) 7 Exch 639. But see *Madge v Thunder Bay (City)* (1990) 44 CPC (2d) 186.

[60] *Duchess of Kingston's Trial* (1776) 20 St Tr 355, 613; *Sanford v Remington* (1793) 2 Ves Jr 189.

[61] *Hurd v Moring* (1824) 1 C & P 372.

[62] *Smurfit Paribas Bank Ltd v AAB Export Finance Ltd* [1990] 1 IR 469, 473, [1990] ILRM 588, 590 (*per* Costello J); *Webster v James Chapman & Co.* [1989] 3 All ER 939, 944; *Ventouris v Mountain* [1991] 3 All ER 472, 475; *Bursill v Tanner* (1885) 16 QBD 1, 5; *R v Dunbar* (1982) 138 DLR (3d) 221, 244; *Zielinski v Gordon* (1982) 40 BCLR 165; *Federal Commissioner of Taxation v Coombes* [1999] FCA 842, (1999) 164 ALR 131.

[63] [1970] IR 301.

plainant board, it was held that the letter was not privileged and the solicitor could be required to disclose whether he had been instructed to write it and to make the statements contained therein because its contents were not intended to be confidential.[64]

The determination of whether a communication was intended to pass in confidence will depend on the circumstances in which the communication was made including a consideration of any precautions taken to preserve the confidentiality of the communication. One factor which will militate strongly against an inference of confidentiality is the presence of a third party.[65] However, if the presence of the third party is reasonably necessary for the protection of the client's interests as where a relative or friend of the client is present, and it is clear from the circumstances that the communication was intended to pass in confidence, then privilege is likely to apply.[66]

(iii) Professional Legal Relationship

8.010 In order to ground privilege, the communication must be made to or by a lawyer during the course of a professional legal relationship[67] or with the intention of establishing one.[68] The definition of lawyer for this purpose includes, obviously, solicitors and barristers but also salaried in-house legal advisers,[69]

---

[64] See also *Buckley v Incorporated Law Society* [1994] 2 IR 44, 48; *Murphy v Kirwan* [1993] 3 IR 501, 514, [1994] 1 ILRM 293, 302; *Conlon v Conlons Ltd* [1952] 2 All ER 462 (instructions given by client to his solicitor for the purpose of presenting an offer of settlement to the other side held not to be privileged); *Fraser v Sutherland* (1851) 2 Gr 442 (Can) (communications made to a solicitor which were intended to be and were put before the client's creditors as compromise proposal held not to be privileged).

[65] *R v Braham* [1976] VR 547; *Vanhorn v Commonwealth* (1931) 40 SW 2d 372; *People v Castiel* (1957) 315 P 2d 779.

[66] Cf. *R v Dunbar* (1982) 138 DLR (3d) 221, 244.

[67] *Greenough v Gaskell* (1833) 1 My & K 98, 101. It is immaterial whether the lawyer is remunerated for his advice (*Matters v State* (1930) 232 NW 781).

[68] *Minter v Priest* [1930] AC 558, [1930] All ER 431. It does not matter whether a professional legal relationship is actually established (*Shedd v Boland* [1942] OWN 316) but a communication to a lawyer who has declined or ceased to act is not privileged (*R v Farley* (1846) 2 Cox CC 82; *R v Schmidt* (1893) 11 NZLR 703).

[69] *Geraghty v Minister for Local Government* [1975] IR 300, 312 endorsing the decision of the Court of Appeal to this effect in *Alfred Crompton Amusement Machines Ltd v Customs and Excise Commissioners (No. 2)* [1972] 2 QB 102, 109, [1972] 2 All ER 353, 376. See also *New Victoria Hospital v Ryan* [1993] ICR 201, 202; *R v Campbell* [1999] 1 SCR 565, 601, (1999) 171 DLR (4th) 193, 224-5; *IBM Canada Ltd v Xerox of Canada Ltd* [1978] 1 FC 513, 516; *Attorney General for the Northern Territory v Kearney* (1985) 158 CLR 500, 510. In European Community law, privilege is confined to communications from independent lawyers *i.e.* lawyers who are not bound to the client by a relationship of employment: *AM & S Europe v Commission* [1982] ECR 1575, [1982] CMLR 264, [1983] QB 878, [1983] 1 All ER 705.

foreign lawyers,[70] and the Attorney General.[71] However, it does not include persons without a professional legal qualification who give legal advice[72] or persons who have ceased to practice as a lawyer[73] on the basis that "privilege should be strictly confined to legal advisers such as solicitors and counsel, who are professionally qualified, who are members of professional bodies, who are subject to the rules and etiquette of their professions, and who owe a duty to the court".[74] Nevertheless, because legal professional privilege exists for the benefit of the client, it will apply where the client does not know of the disability and reasonably believes the person to be a practising lawyer.[75]

8.011 The mere fact that the person making or receiving the communication is a lawyer is not sufficient to establish privilege, the communication must be made to or by the lawyer in his professional capacity.[76] As Lamer J said in *Descôteaux v Mierzwinski*,[77] "the relationship must be a professional one at

---

[70] *Lawrence v Campbell* (1859) 4 Drew 485; *Macfarlan v Rolt* (1872) LR 14 Eq 580; *Re Duncan* [1968] P 306, [1968] 2 All ER 395; *Great Atlantic Insurance Co. v Home Insurance Co.* [1981] 2 All ER 485, 490; *Mutual Life Assurance Co. of Canada v Canada (Deputy Attorney General)* (1989) 28 CPC (2d) 101, 104.

[71] *Duncan v Governor of Portlaoise Prison (No. 2)* [1998] 1 IR 433, 442; *Quinlivan v Governor of Portlaoise Prision* Supreme Court 5 March 1997. Under Article 30 of the Constitution, the Attorney General is the legal advisor to the government "in matters of law and legal opinion".

[72] See *Re Dormeuil Trade Mark* [1983] RPC 131 (trade mark agent); *R v Umoh* (1986) 84 Cr App R 138 (prison officer acting as legal aid officer); *Lumonics Research Ltd v Gould* [1983] 2 FC 360, 366 (patent agent); *Naujokat v Bratushesky* [1942] WWR 97, [1942] 2 DLR 721 (newspaper); *Schubkagel v Dierstein* (1890) 131 P 46 (law student).

[73] *Calley v Richards* (1854) 19 Beav 401.

[74] *New Victoria Hospital v Ryan* [1993] ICR 201, 203 (*per* Tucker J). See also the *obiter* comment to the same effect by Gibbs CJ in *Attorney General for the Northern Territory v Kearney* (1985) 158 CLR 500, 510.

[75] *Calley v Richards* (1854) 19 Beav 401; *Global Funds Management (NSW) Ltd v Rooney* (1994) 36 NSWLR 122; *R v Choney* (1908) 17 Man R 467; *People v Barker* (1886) 60 Mich 277, 27 NW 539; *State v Russell* (1892) 83 Wis 330, 53 NW 441. But *cf. Feuerheerd v London General Omnibus Co.* [1918] 2 KB 565.

[76] *Per* Abbott CJ in *Bramwell v Lucas* (1824) 2 B & C 745, 749: "Whether the privilege extends to all confidential communications between attorney and client or not, there is no doubt that it is confined to communications … to the attorney in his character of attorney … but … where the communication might have been made by any other person as well as an attorney, and where the character or office of attorney has not been called into action, has never been held within the protection, and is not within the principle upon which the privilege is founded." See also *Dunnes Stores Ltd v Smyth* High Court (Costello P) 24 July 1995; *Greenlaw v R* (1838) 1 Beav 137, 145; *Desborough v Rawlins* (1838) 3 My & Cr 515, 521; *Minter v Priest* [1930] AC 558, 568, [1930] All ER 431, 434; *R v Campbell* [1999] 1 SCR 565, 601-2, (1999) 171 DLR (4th) 193, 225; *Descôteaux v Mierzwinski* [1982] 1 SCR 860, 872, (1982) 141 DLR (3d) 590, 803; *Police v Mills* [1993] 2 NZLR 592, 595.

[77] [1982] 1 SCR 860, 872, (1982) 141 DLR (3d) 590, 603.

the exact moment of the communication". Thus, in *Smith v Daniell*,[78] it was held that a legal opinion obtained by the plaintiff from an eminent former Chancellor, Lord Westbury, was not privileged from disclosure because it was clear that he had given it as a friend rather than in discharge of any professional duty.[79] Similarly, in *Buckley v Incorporated Law Society*[80] correspondence between the complainants and the respondent society regarding the alleged misconduct of a solicitor was held not to be privileged because the complainants were not consulting the Law Society as a legal adviser.

Problems can arise where a lawyer acts in a dual capacity as can be seen from the recent case of *Somatra Ltd v Sinclair Roche & Temperley*.[81] An action for professional negligence had been taken by the plaintiff company against the defendant firm of solicitors. It was argued that privilege attached to communications between the managing partner of the firm and other partners of the firm concerning settlement discussions which the managing partner had held with the plaintiffs. However, the plaintiff argued that privilege did not attach because these communications had been made in his capacity as managing partner not as a lawyer. The Court of Appeal held that privilege attached because, although the managing partner was in important respects acting in his capacity as such in trying to settle the plaintiff's claim, he was a lawyer and, thus, in position to give legal advice to the partnership. On balance, the court was prepared to accept the assertion made on affidavit that the managing partner in creating those documents had been exercising professional skill and judgment as a solicitor on behalf of the defendants.

(iv) Legal Advice

8.012 Not all communications that pass between a lawyer and client are privileged, only those made for the purpose of giving or receiving legal advice.[82] So, for example, no privilege attaches to advice on business matters even where it is provided by a lawyer.[83] This point was central to the seminal decision of the Supreme Court in *Smurfit Paribas Bank Ltd v AAB Export Finance Ltd*,[84] in which a distinction was drawn between communications seeking legal advice

---

[78] (1874) LR 18 Eq 649, 654.

[79] See also *Rudd v Frank* (1889) 17 OR 758.

[80] [1994] 2 IR 44.

[81] [2000] 2 Lloyd's Rep 673.

[82] *Miley v Flood* [2001] 1 ILRM 489; *Smurfit Paribas Bank Ltd v AAB Export Finance Ltd* [1990] 1 IR 469, [1990] ILRM 588; *Caldbeck v Boon* (1872) IR 7 CL 32, 36-7; *Gillard v Bates* (1840) 6 M & W 548; *Re Cathcart, ex p. Campbell* (1870) 5 Ch App 703, 705; *O'Rourke v Darbishire* [1920] AC 581, 629, [1920] All ER 1, 48; *Minter v Priest* [1930] AC 558, 580-1, [1930] All ER 431, 440; *Smith-Bird v Blower* [1939] 2 All ER 406; *R v Bencardino* (1973) 2 OR (2d) 351. *Cf. Federal Commissioner of Taxation v Coombes* [1999] FCA 842, (1999) 164 ALR 131.

[83] *R v Campbell* [1999] 1 SCR 565, 602, (1999) 171 DLR (4th) 193, 225.

[84] [1990] 1 IR 469, [1990] ILRM 588.

which are privileged and those seeking legal assistance which are not exempt from disclosure. In *Smurfit*, the plaintiff sought disclosure of correspondence and instructions passing between the defendant and the solicitors then acting for it in relation to a charge taken by the defendant over the assets of a third party. The trial judge found that the documents in question did not request or contain any legal advice and were not, therefore, privileged and this conclusion was upheld on appeal by the Supreme Court. Finlay CJ identified the basic principle to be applied in dealing with claims of legal advice privilege as follows:

> The existence of a privilege or exemption from disclosure for communications made between a person and his lawyer clearly constitutes a potential restriction and diminution of the full disclosure both prior to and during the course of legal proceedings which in the interests of the common good is desirable for the purpose of ascertaining the truth and rendering justice. Such privilege should, therefore, in my view only be granted in instances which have been identified as securing an objective which in the public interest in the proper conduct of the administration of justice can be said to outweigh the disadvantage arising from the restriction of disclosure of all the facts.[85]

Having regard to the rationale for legal professional privilege, he was satisfied that legal advice satisfied this test but legal assistance did not because it was not "closely and proximately linked to the conduct of litigation and the function of administering justice in the courts":[86]

> There are many tasks carried out by a lawyer for his client and properly within the legal sphere, other than the giving of advice, which could not be said to contain any real relationship with the area of potential litigation. For such communications there does not appear to me to be any sufficient public interest or feature of the common good to be secured or protected which could justify an exemption from disclosure.[87]

Of course, even if a client merely seeks legal assistance, this may entail the provision of legal advice because a solicitor's duty of care extends beyond the scope of the instructions given by the client and he is required "to consider not only what the client wishes him to do, but also the legal implications of the facts

---

[85] *Ibid.* at 477, 594.
[86] *Ibid.* at 478, 594.
[87] *Ibid.* at 478, 595. *Cf.* the Australian decision of *Federal Commissioner of Taxation v Coombes* [1999] FCA 842, (1999) 164 ALR 131, where it was stated that instructions to a lawyer to do a particular thing such as, for example, to draft a legal document such as a will, would generally not be privileged because instructions to do something do not necessarily amount to a request for advice.

which the client brings to his attention."[88] However, McCarthy J was explicit
that it is only if such advice is in fact given that privilege will apply. He reasoned that public policy did not require that privilege extend to such communications unless they had, in fact, given rise to legal advice. An example where
this occurred can be seen in *Hurstridge Finance Ltd v Lismore Homes Ltd.*[89]
Privilege was claimed in respect of certain communications between the controller of a company and the company's solicitors regarding the drafting of certain agreements. Costello J, upholding the claim of privilege, was satisfied from
the surrounding circumstances and from the documents themselves, that the
controller had consulted the solicitors not merely for the purpose of drafting
certain documents but also to obtain legal advice.[90]

8.013 The decision in *Smurfit* was followed by Kelly J in *Miley v Flood*[91] who
extracted from it the principle that a communication only attracts privilege if it
seeks or contains legal advice and that the communication of any other information is not privileged. He, therefore, rejected the contention that privilege could
be claimed in respect of the identity of a client on the basis that this was a "mere
collateral fact"[92] unconnected with the receipt or provision of legal advice.[93] A
similar characterisation can be applied to facts such as the address of a client[94]
and details of when the lawyer met the client.[95] Although these matters may
well constitute important information for the purpose of establishing and maintaining a professional relationship between a solicitor and client, it is only in
exceptional circumstances that they will be required by the solicitor in order to
give legal advice. However, a lawyer will not be required to disclose information of this type if it is so intertwined with the legal advice given that the effect
of revealing it would be to disclose the advice.[96]

---

[88] *Per* Barron J in *McMullen v Farrell* [1993] 1 IR 123, 143, [1992] ILRM 776, 792.
[89] High Court (Costello J) 15 February 1991.
[90] See also *R v Crown Court, ex p. Baines* [1987] 3 All ER 1025 where it was held that
communications between a solicitor and client giving legal advice in respect of a conveyancing transaction were privileged but records of a conveyancing transaction were
not because they did not contain advice.
[91] [2001] 1 ILRM 489. See also *Buckley v Bough* High Court (Morris P) 2 July 2001.
[92] A phrase used by James LJ in *Re Cathcart, ex p. Campbell* (1870) 5 Ch App 703, 705,
referring to the address of a client.
[93] See also *Bursill v Tanner* (1885) 16 QBD 1; *A. & D. Logging Co. v Convair Logging
Ltd* (1967) 63 DLR (2d) 618; *Cook v Leonard* [1954] VLR 591; *Southern Cross
Commodities Pty Ltd v Crinis* [1984] VR 697. Cf. *United States v Mammoth Oil Co.*
(1925) 56 OLR 635, [1925] 2 DLR 966; *Lavallee, Rackel and Heintz v Canada (AG)*
(1998) 160 DLR (4th) 508, 525; *Police v Mills* [1993] 2 NZLR 592. See, *contra*, Morrick,
"Professional Privilege: the Client's Identity" (1980) 124 SJ 303.
[94] *Re Cathcart, ex p. Campbell* (1870) 5 Ch App 703, 705; *R v Bell* (1980) 146 CLR 141.
[95] *R v Manchester Crown Court, ex p. Rogers* [1999] 4 All ER 35 (solicitors ordered to
produce any record or log which recorded the time of arrival of client at the solicitors'
premises on a particular date).
[96] Cf. *Miley v Flood* [2001] 1 ILRM 489; *Federal Commissioner of Taxation v Coombes*
[1999] FCA 842, (1999) 164 ALR 131 and *Police v Mills* [1993] 2 NZLR 592.

LITIGATION PRIVILEGE

8.014 Litigation privilege enables parties to prepare for litigation without having to disclose those preparations in advance of the trial.[97] Traditionally, the privilege has been discussed in terms of the protection which it gives to communications with third parties but, as will become evident below, it also operates to confer a measure of protection on what may best be described as a lawyer's "work product"[98] *i.e.* documents and materials generated or compiled in preparation for litigation even though no element of communication can really be said to be involved.

Policy of the Privilege

8.015 The extension of protection to communications with third parties was initially justified on the basis that they could not be disclosed without revealing the instructions of the client and the nature of the advice given by the legal adviser.[99] However, with the limitation of the ambit of protection to communications with third parties in contemplation of litigation,[100] the focus shifted to the role that the privilege plays in the adversarial system. In *Anderson v Bank of British Columbia*,[101] James LJ explained the cases on the basis "that as you have no right to see your adversary's brief, you have no right to see that which comes into existence merely as the materials for the brief".

Under the adversarial model, the quality of fact-finding is inextricably linked to the efforts of the parties to seek out evidence that supports their case. If both parties use their best endeavours, then the truth should out. The cloak of privilege is required to protect these efforts.[102] As O'Leary J explained in the Canadian decision of *Ottawa-Carleton (Regional Municipality) v Consumers' Gas Co.*:[103]

---

[97] It should be noted that privilege will apply not only to preparations to litigate a case but also to those for the purpose of compromising it because it is the policy of the courts to encourage settlement: *Horgan v Murray* [1999] 1 ILRM 257.

[98] To use the phrase adopted in the US: see *Hickman v Taylor* (1946) 329 US 495.

[99] *Anderson v Bank of British Columbia* (1876) 2 Ch D 644, 649 (*per* Jessel MR). *Cf. Re Barings plc* [1998] Ch 356, 366, [1998] 1 All ER 673, 681, where Scott VC reviewed the authorities and concluded that the only reason that privilege attached to documents brought into existence for the purposes of litigation is to keep inviolate communications between the client and his or her legal adviser.

[100] *Wheeler v Le Marchant* (1881) 17 Ch D 675.

[101] (1876) 2 Ch D 644, 656.

[102] In *Kennedy v Lyell* (1883) 23 Ch D 387, 404, Cotton LJ cautioned "that no one is to be fettered in obtaining materials for his defence and, if for the purpose of his defence obtains evidence, the adverse party cannot ask to see it before the trial". See also *Lyell v Kennedy* (1887) 27 Ch D 1, 18.

[103] (1990) 74 DLR (4th) 742, 748.

Civil Procedure

The adversarial system is based on the assumption that if each side presents its case in the strongest light the court will be best able to determine the truth. Counsel must be free to make the fullest investigation and research without risking disclosure of his opinions, strategies and conclusions to opposing counsel. The invasion of privacy of counsel's trial preparation might well lead to counsel postponing research and other preparation until the eve of or during the trial, so as to avoid early disclosure of harmful information. The result would be counter-productive to the present goal that the early and thorough investigation by counsel will encourage an early settlement of the case. Indeed, if counsel knows he must turn over to the other side the fruits of his work, he may be tempted to forgo conscientiously investigating his own case in the hope he will obtain disclosure of the research, investigations and thought processes compiled in the trial brief of opposing counsel...

It is, thus, feared that the net effect of such a disincentive to the evidence-gathering efforts of the parties would be a diminution in the accuracy of fact-finding and ultimately of the quality of justice.

8.016 Another idea running through the case law is that the privacy of a lawyer in preparing for trial should be respected and if protection for pre-trial preparations was not given, inefficiencies would result. In *Hickman v Taylor*,[104] Murphy J opined that:

In performing his various duties ... it is essential that a lawyer work with a certain degree of privacy, free from unnecessary intrusion by opposing parties and their counsel. Proper preparation of a client's case demands that he assemble information, sift what he considers to be the relevant from the irrelevant facts, prepare his legal theories and plan his strategy without undue and needless interference ... This work is reflected, of course, in interviews, statements, memoranda, correspondence, briefs, mental impressions, personal beliefs, and countless other tangible and intangible ways – aptly though roughly termed by the Circuit Court of Appeals in this case as the "work product of the lawyer". Were such materials open to opposing counsel on mere demand, much of what is now put down in writing would remain unwritten. An attorney's thoughts, heretofore inviolate, would not be his own. Inefficiency, unfairness and sharp practices would invariably develop in the giving of legal advice and in the preparation of cases for trial. The effect on the legal profession would be demoralizing. And the interests of the clients and the cause of justice would be poorly served.

---

[104] (1947) 329 US 495, 510-11.

This idea fitted in with the traditional notion of "trial by ambush" whereby a litigant was, within certain limits entitled to refuse to disclose the nature of his case until trial. As Lord Wilberforce put it in *Waugh v British Railways Board*,[105] "one side may not ask to see the proofs of the other side's witnesses or the opponent's brief or even know what witnesses will be called: he must wait until the card is played and cannot try to see it in the hand".

8.017 However, in recent times, the courts have begun to question whether the application of litigation privilege actually advances the administration of justice. In *Gallagher v Stanley*,[106] the Supreme Court was very critical of the "oak-like" attitude of the defendant hospital and its attempts to withhold innocuous documents. O'Flaherty J stated that the purpose of legal professional privilege is "to aid the administration of justice; not to impede it" and "[i]n general, justice will be best served where there is the greatest candour and where all relevant documentary evidence is available."[107] Evident in this decision is dissatisfaction on the part of the court with the imperialist tendencies of litigation privilege in the hands of parties who wish to withhold probative material from disclosure. That coupled with the policy consideration that as much relevant evidence as possible should be before the trial court, may signal that claims of litigation privilege will be subjected to more rigorous examination in the future.

Communications with Third Parties

8.018 Communications between either a client or his lawyer and third parties such as potential witnesses or experts are privileged where they are made in preparation for litigation which is, at the time of the communication, pending or reasonably apprehended.

In determining whether a communication has come into being in preparation for litigation, the courts have generally focussed on the proximity of litigation as the litmus test. Sufficient proximity obviously exists where litigation has commenced but beyond that the courts have struggled to find and apply a formulation which allows parties to make adequate preparations under cover of privilege for litigation which they reasonably anticipate may ensue but which

---

[105] [1980] AC 521, 531, [1979] 2 All ER 1169, 1172.
[106] [1998] 2 IR 267.
[107] *Ibid.* at 271. *Cf.* the comments of Lord Edmund-Davies in *Waugh v British Railways Board* [1980] AC 521, 543, [1979] 2 All ER 1169, 1182 that a court "should start from the basis that the public interest is, on balance, best served by rigidly confining within narrow limits the cases where material relevant to litigation may be lawfully withheld. Justice is better served by candour than suppression" and *Grant v Downs* (1976) 135 CLR 674, 686, where a plurality of the High Court of Australia criticised litigation privilege on the basis that it "detracts from the fairness of the trial by denying a party access to relevant documents or at least subjecting him to surprise".

does not result in the suppression of too much probative evidence.[108] Various formulations such as that litigation should be "apprehended", "contemplated" or "anticipated" have been put forward but none of them has an irreducible content. The question is, at the end of the day, one of policy and the approach of the courts has been to try and reconcile the competing policy objectives by requiring that litigation be reasonably proximate. As a synthesis of the law in this area, it is difficult to improve upon the following statement by Barwick CJ in the Australian case of *Grant v Downs*:[109]

> [A] document which was produced or brought into existence either with the dominant purpose of its author, or of the person or authority under whose direction, whether particular or general, it was produced or brought into existence, of using it or its contents in order to obtain legal advice or to conduct or aid in the conduct of litigation, at the time of its production in reasonable prospect, should be privileged and excluded from inspection.

This passage identifies the ingredients required for a successful claim of privilege which will be examined in turn.

Reasonable Prospect of Litigation

8.019 The starting point of the modern case law[110] on this issue is the decision of O'Hanlon J in *Silver Hill Duckling Ltd v Minister for Agriculture*.[111] The plaintiff sought damages and compensation arising out of the slaughter of its flock of ducks following an outbreak of avian influenza. The defendants claimed privilege in respect of a number of documents on the ground, *inter alia*, that

---

[108] Reference can be made once more to the admonition of Finlay CJ in *Smurfit Paribas Bank Ltd v AAB Export Finance Ltd* [1990] 1 IR 469, 477, [1990] ILRM 588, 594 that privilege "should only be granted by the courts in instances which have been identified as securing an objective which in the public interest in the proper conduct of the administration of justice can be said to outweigh the disadvantage arising from the restriction of disclosure of all the facts."

[109] (1976) 135 CLR 674, 677.

[110] The early Irish cases include: *Kerry County Council v Liverpool Salvage Association* (1903) 38 ILTR 7 (claim of litigation privilege failed because no litigation was then in contemplation); *M'Mahon v Great Northern Railway Co.* (1906) 40 ILTR 172 (third party communications only protected where procured after litigation has commenced or in view of anticipated litigation); *Rushbrooke v O'Sullivan* [1926] IR 500, 503 (*per* FitzGibbon J) ("documents prepared, not with a view to actual or threatened litigation, but with a view of ascertaining whether litigation should be initiated at some future time, are not entitled to the privilege given by the practice of the court"); *Moroney v Great Southern Railway Ltd* [1933] LJ Ir 93 (routine report about the condition of a train engine which it was claimed had been prepared because the defendant apprehended litigation and in case it occurred held to be privileged).

[111] [1987] IR 289, [1987] ILRM 516.

they had come into being in contemplation of and for the purpose of advising the minister and his officers in relation to the plaintiff's claim. O'Hanlon J was satisfied that:

> [A] sustainable claim [of legal professional privilege] may be made in respect of a wider category of documents than the conventional communications passing between a client and his legal adviser in contemplation of litigation ... once litigation is apprehended or threatened, a party to such litigation is entitled to prepare his case, whether by means of communications passing between him and his legal advisers, or by means of communications passing between him and third parties, and to do so under the cloak of privilege.[112]

Applying these principles to the facts of the case, he was of the view that litigation between the parties could fairly be regarded as apprehended or threatened, and privilege thus applied, from the point at which it became clear that there was such a large disparity between what the department was offering in compensation and what the plaintiff was seeking that it was apparent to both parties that the claim would ultimately have to be resolved by litigation.[113]

8.020 O'Hanlon J took a similar approach in *PJ Carrigan Ltd v Norwich Union Fire Society Ltd*.[114] The defendant insurers had been notified by the plaintiffs of a claim in respect of their premises which had been destroyed by fire. They immediately commissioned a report from a firm of loss adjusters because they viewed the claim with some suspicion and wished to know whether any evidence available at the scene of the fire suggested that their suspicions were well-founded. O'Hanlon J accepted that the possibility of repudiating liability was a very real factor in the defendant's thinking from the time the claim was made by the plaintiffs and that, when commissioning the report, they were concerned to obtain not merely an evaluation of the claim in terms of financial loss, but also expert advice as to the circumstances in which the fire broke out. He was, therefore, satisfied that the report had been obtained in apprehension of litigation because, even at that early stage, the defendant was contemplating the possibility of a showdown with the plaintiffs in which they might decide to repudiate liability under the policy and the plaintiffs in turn would then have to decide whether they were prepared to embark on litigation to enforce their claims under the policy.[115]

---

[112] *Ibid.* at 291, 518-519.
[113] In reaching that conclusion, he followed the view of the Court of Appeal in *Alfred Crompton Amusement Machines Ltd v Customs and Excise Commissioners (No.2)* [1972] 2 QB 102, [1972] 2 All ER 353.
[114] [1987] IR 618.
[115] See also *Re Highgrade Traders* [1984] BCLC 151.

In *Gallagher v Stanley*,[116] this test was only considered in passing but O'Flaherty J emphasised that "it is essential that litigation should be reasonably apprehended at the least before a claim of privilege can be upheld".

Dominant Purpose Test

8.021 Perhaps the most acute difficulties in this area have arisen with regard to situations where it is possible to identify more than one purpose or motive for a communication as, for example, where a company requires employees to complete an accident report form in the aftermath of an accident. If litigation subsequently ensues, the defendant will almost inevitably argue that the purpose of requiring the document to be completed was to brief the company's legal advisers in relation to the accident and to help the company to defend the claim. However, it may be possible to identify another purpose for the completion of the document such as accident prevention which would bring it outside the protection of the privilege. The question as to whether the document should be privileged in those circumstances is crucial because it will frequently contain the most contemporaneous account of events and, again, policy considerations loom large.

One solution to the problem of multiple purposes, adopted in a series of English cases in the first half of the twentieth century, was to hold that a document need not be disclosed if one of the purposes for its creation (even if merely a subsidiary one) was that it be given to a solicitor for the purpose of advising on apprehended litigation.[117] Another approach which found favour with the High Court of Australia in *Grant v Downs*[118] was that a document should be disclosed unless the sole purpose for its genesis was apprehended litigation. However, in *Waugh v British Railways Board*,[119] the House of Lords rejected both of these extremes in favour of the intermediate approach adopted by Barwick CJ in his dissenting judgment in *Grant v Downs*[120] whereby a document will be protected by privilege if the dominant purpose for its creation is apprehended litigation.[121]

8.022 In *Waugh*, the plaintiff's husband, an employee of the defendant was killed while working on the railways. She sought discovery of a standard accident report prepared two days after the accident. The House of Lords held that,

---

[116] [1998] 2 IR 267, 272.
[117] *Birmingham and Midland Motor Omnibus Co. Ltd v London and North Western Railway Co.* [1913] 3 KB 850; *Ankin v London and North Eastern Railway Co.* [1930] 1 KB 527, [1929] All ER 65; *Ogden v London Electric Railway Co.* [1933] All ER 896.
[118] (1976) 135 CLR 674.
[119] [1980] AC 521, [1979] 2 All ER 1169.
[120] (1976) 135 CLR 674.
[121] See also *Neilson v Laugharne* [1981] QB 736; *Re Highgrade Traders Ltd* [1984] BCLC 151.

in order to attract privilege, the dominant purpose for preparation of the reports must have been that of submission to a legal adviser for use in relation to anticipated or pending litigation. While this was undoubtedly one of the purposes of the reports, it was not the dominant one, another equally important purpose being to inform the board about the cause of the accident in order that steps could be taken to avoid recurrence. Thus, privilege could not be claimed and discovery was ordered. Lord Wilberforce emphasised the policy background when he stated:

> It is clear that the due administration of justice strongly requires disclosure and production of this report: it was contemporary; it contained statements by witnesses on the spot; it would be not merely relevant evidence, but almost certainly the best evidence as to the cause of the accident. If one accepts that this important public interest can be overridden in order that the defendant may properly prepare his case, how close must the connection be between the preparation of the document and the anticipation of litigation? ... It appears to me that unless the purpose of submission to the legal adviser in view of litigation is at least the dominant purpose for which the relevant document was prepared, the reasons which require privilege to be extended to it cannot apply. On the other hand to hold that the purpose ... must be the sole purpose would, apart from difficulties of proof ... be too strict a requirement, and would confine the privilege too narrowly.[122]

8.023 The dominant purpose test was endorsed in this jurisdiction[123] by O'Hanlon J in *Silver Hill Duckling Ltd v Minister for Agriculture*,[124] and subsequently applied by Lynch J in *Davis v St Michael's House*.[125] The plaintiff, who was mentally handicapped, was injured in a fall in the defendant's school. The defendant claimed privilege in respect of an accident report form and a number of witness statements on the basis that these documents came into being in contemplation of possible proceedings. The defendant pointed out that it was obliged to notify its insurer of all accidents and, in addition to completing an accident report form, the defendant frequently obtained witness statements with a view to assessing the defendant's position in relation to any claim that might arise as a result of the accident. Lynch J identified the purpose of obtaining such

---

[122] [1980] AC 521, 531-532, [1979] 2 All ER 1169, 1173-1174.
[123] The dominant purpose test has also been approved in Canada (*Supercom of California v Sovereign General Insurance Co.* (1998) 37 OR (3d) 597, 605; *New West Construction Co. v R* [1980] 2 FC 44, (1980) 106 DLR (3d) 272), New Zealand (*Guardian Royal Exchange Asssurance v Stuart* [1985] 1 NZLR 596) and is now applied in Australia under s.119 of the Evidence Act 1995 which has reversed the decision in *Grant v Downs* (1976) 135 CLR 674.
[124] [1987] IR 289, [1987] ILRM 516.
[125] High Court (Lynch J) 25 November 1993.

documents as being to ensure that there was an accurate record of what happened from as many persons who may know something about it as possible so
that in the event of a claim, the insurers would be forewarned and forearmed
therewith for submission to their legal advisers and witnesses would have a
contemporary record of the events by which they would be able to refresh their
memories at the trial of the action which could be many years later. He was,
therefore, satisfied that the dominant purpose for which the documents came
into being was in apprehension and/or anticipation of litigation and that the
claim of privilege was valid.[126]

The dominant purpose test has recently been endorsed by the Supreme Court
in *Gallagher v Stanley*.[127] The infant plaintiff had a very difficult birth in the
National Maternity Hospital, as a result of which he was severely disabled.
Discovery was granted and the defendants claimed privilege in respect of certain documents on the basis that they were created in contemplation of litigation. The documents in question were statements made by nurses on duty the
night of the birth. They had been requested to make these the following morning
by the matron of the hospital. In her affidavit, the matron stated that she had
requested the statements because she anticipated litigation and for the sole purpose of being furnished to the legal secretary of the hospital.

O'Flaherty J accepted that, in view of the increasingly litigious nature of
society, apprehension of litigation was a consideration on the part of the
matron in requesting the statements but it was not the sole purpose. Instead, he
was satisfied that the main concern of the matron was that she should be in a
position to account for the events of the night in question and how the staff
under her control had conducted themselves which information was required
for the proper management and running of the hospital. He read the documents
and this confirmed his belief that they were essentially straightforward accounts
of events and conversations, and did not contain any element that should attract
an entitlement to legal professional privilege. He observed that:

> Both principles, full disclosure on the one hand and legal professional
> privilege on the other, are there to advance the cause of justice. Some-
> times they may be on a collision course, but not, I think, here. This is not
> like a case where a client is expected to deal with his lawyer with the
> utmost disclosure so that the case will be properly presented. It is rather a
> case where both sides are entitled to know what exactly happened before
> and at the birth of the infant. After all the nurses are the mother and child's

---

[126] See also *Andrews v Northern Ireland Railways Co. Ltd* [1992] NI 1. *Cf. Power City
Ltd v Monahan* High Court (Kinlen J) 14 October 1996 (fax message from the solicitor of the defendants to their insurer's representatives made with a view to the insurer
dealing with any response to made to letters from the plaintiff held to be privileged).
[127] [1998] 2 IR 267 (SC).

nurses as well as being hospital employees. I believe it is likely to help the course of the trial if these documents are made available to the plaintiff's advisers now and I do not see that the principle of legal professional privilege suffers in any way.[128]

In their concurring judgments, Lynch J and Barron J also endorsed the dominant motive test. Lynch J pointed out that people often act for mixed motives and therefore the sole purpose test set too high a threshold for the application of privilege. The true test is that anticipation and/or contemplation of litigation should have been the dominant motive or reason. Barron J stressed that it was the court's view as to the purpose of the statements, not that of the hospital which was important. Bare assertion on the part of the hospital was not enough without anything to back it up. If there were good reasons why there was no need to take statements from the nurses in relation to hospital administration, this could have been put on affidavit.

8.024 It can be seen from the foregoing discussion of the cases that the conception and application of the dominant purpose test is strongly influenced by policy and lends itself to manipulation by the courts to achieve a desired result. A very obvious example of this can be seen in *Mark v Flexibox Ltd.*[129] While employed by the defendant, the plaintiff sought medical advice from a factory doctor about a rash and was referred to a consultant dermatologist who carried out tests. The plaintiff subsequently brought proceedings and sought discovery of the report of the results of these tests. The defendant argued that this was covered by litigation privilege because at the top of the report, there was the legend: "For the use of legal advisers in anticipation of litigation and for solicitors and counsel to advise." MacDermott LJ said that "the judicial determination of 'dominant purpose' is not concluded by protective headings or expressions of intent made by the maker of the document" and rejected the defendant's claim of privilege based on its awareness of the level of claims:

> It may be ... that this employer, like others, realises that employees in Northern Ireland tend to be litigious and thus an employer must always anticipate litigation and be vigilant in dealing with any situations which may be of relevance in subsequent litigation. If that is the point it is of such a sweepingly general nature as to be of little probative value when a judge is seeking to ascertain the "dominant purpose" for which a particular document came into being.[130]

The learned judge went on to say that these matters are always questions of fact

---

[128] *Ibid.* at 273.
[129] [1988] NI 58.
[130] *Ibid.* at 61.

and degree and that:

> the claims of humanity must surely make the dominant purpose of any
> report upon the health of an employee who attends his factory doctor for
> advice (particularly where injuries have been sustained or are suspected)
> that of discovering what his state of health is and why he is ill or injured,
> if he is, so that he may be advised and measures to prevent recurrence
> may be discussed and, if possible, devised. For my part I think it will
> always be difficult for a defendant to satisfy the dominance test in this
> type of case.[131]

Purpose is Determined Objectively

8.025 When assessing the dominant purpose of a communication, it "must be
borne in mind that the important matter is the purpose, which is not necessarily
the same as the intention of the person who composed it".[132] Thus, it is the
motive of the person who procured the making of the communication rather
than the person who made it which is determinative.[133] This can be seen in
Guinness Peat Properties Ltd v Fitzroy Robinson Partnership.[134] The defendants wrote to their insurers, in accordance with the terms of their professional
indemnity policy, enclosing the notification of a claim by the first named plaintiffs and other relevant memoranda and expressed their views on the merits of
the claim. The plaintiffs argued that the defendants were not entitled to claim
privilege for the letter because the dominant purpose for which it was written
was to comply with the requirements of their indemnity policy not for the purpose of obtaining legal advice or to assist in the conduct of litigation. However,
it was held by the Court of Appeal that the dominant purpose for which a document was written does not necessarily fall to be determined by reference to the
intention of the person who actually composed it. The dominant purpose of the
communication had to be viewed objectively, particularly by reference to the
intentions of the insurers who procured its genesis. Here the dominant purpose
was to produce a letter of notification which would be used in order to obtain
legal advice or to conduct or aid in the conduct of litigation which was at the
time of its production in reasonable prospect.[135]

---

[131] *Ibid.* at 61.

[132] *Downey v Murray* [1988] NI 600, 602-3 (*per* Carswell J).

[133] *M'Mahon v Great Northern Railway Co.* (1906) 40 ILTR 172, 173; *Feuerheerd v London General Omnibus Co. Ltd* [1918] 2 KB 565.

[134] [1987] 2 All ER 716.

[135] See also *Andrews v Northern Ireland Railways Co. Ltd* [1992] NI 1.

Work Product

8.026 The precise extent to which litigation privilege can be invoked so as to protect the "work product" of a lawyer preparing for litigation is unclear. However, it seems as if some protection is afforded to the preparations of a lawyer for trial which do not fall under the umbrella of communications with third parties so as to enable him to prepare for litigation in privacy. Thus, privilege will attach to documents such as draft pleadings,[136] draft expert reports,[137] draft written legal submissions, internal memoranda and notes *etc.* prepared by the lawyer.

However, it is important to note that privilege will not attach to documents which came into existence before litigation was contemplated[138] or copies of such documents[139] even if obtained by a party to litigation or his legal adviser for the purposes of the litigation.[140] In *Tromso Sparebank v Beirne,*[141] Costello J pointed out that the purpose of legal professional privilege was to enable a person to have recourse to his legal advisers in confidence and he did not agree that "the protection of the interests of the litigant requires the privilege to be extended to copies of documents which came into existence prior to the contemplation of litigation, documents which are themselves not privileged and which the other side could probably inspect as a result of third party discovery order and which they could have produced at the trial pursuant to a *subpoena duces tecum.*" He went on to say that the rules of court should be construed so as to further the rules of justice and should not be interpreted so as to prevent a party inspecting documents which might assist its case in circumstances where this could not conceivably injure the interests of the other party.

Communications with an Adverse Party

8.027 Litigation privilege operates to protect a party's case from disclosure to an adverse party and, therefore, by definition, communications with the other

---

[136] *Argyle Brewery Pty Ltd v Darling Harbourside (Sydney) Pty Ltd* (1993) 120 ALR 537.
[137] *Highland Fisheries Ltd v Lynk Electric Ltd* (1989) 63 DLR (4th) 493.
[138] *Ventouris v Mountain* [1991] 3 All ER 472.
[139] *Tromso Sparebank v Beirne* [1989] ILRM 257; *Lubrizol Corp v Esso Petroleum Co. Ltd* [1992] 1 WLR 957.
[140] A possible exception may exist where documents or materials have been assembled by the application of professional skill and judgment by a lawyer and disclosure would betray the trend of his legal advice to the client (*Lyell v Kennedy (No. 3)* (1884) 27 Ch D 1; *Ventouris v Mountain* [1991] 3 All ER 472; *Dubai Bank Ltd v Galadari (No. 7)* [1992] 1 All ER 658; *Ottawa-Carleton (Regional Municipality) v Consumers' Gas Co.* (1990) 74 DLR (4th) 742; *Nickmar Pty Ltd v Preservatrice Skandia Insurance Ltd* (1985) 3 NSWLR 44). However, in *Bond v JN Taylor Holdings Ltd* (1991) 57 SASR 21, 46, Debelle J argued with some force that this line of authority requires re-examination in the light of the modern law of discovery and the trend towards greater disclosure.
[141] [1989] ILRM 257.

side will not attract privilege even where they are made in contemplation of litigation.[142] In *McKay v McKay*, Hutton LCJ explained that:[143]

> [A]s the basis of the privilege is that the communications which a party makes to his professional lawyer should be kept secret from the adverse party and that the adverse party cannot ask to see them before the trial it follows that the privilege cannot apply where the adverse party has himself supplied the information and is therefore aware of it. In such a case there is no need to keep the information secret from the opposing party because he already knows of it.

Thus, in *Tobakin v Dublin Southern District Tramways Co.*,[144] a statement obtained from the plaintiff by an inspector of the defendant company three days after the accident the subject matter of the proceedings was held not to be privileged.[145] Similarly, in *Grant v Southwestern and County Properties*,[146] a claim of privilege in respect of a tape recording of a conversation between the plaintiffs and the second defendants made by the second plaintiff because he contemplated that litigation between the parties might ensue and wished to be able to instruct his solicitors was rejected.

8.028 It is often the case that a document such as an affidavit or written legal submissions will be prepared with the intention of being sent to or handed over to the other side either before or during proceedings. However, privilege will apply until such time as the document is actually handed over. In *Horgan v Murray*,[147] an issue was raised as to a memorandum which was prepared by the petitioner in the context of settlement negotiations and for the purpose of furnishing it to the respondents. However, relations between the parties deteriorated drastically and the petitioner decided not to hand over the document. O'Sullivan J rejected the contention of the respondents that because the dominant intention for the document coming into being was for the purpose of being handed over to the respondents, it was not privileged:

---

[142] *Tobakin v Dublin Southern District Tramways Co.* [1905] 2 IR 58; *McKay v McKay* [1988] NI 611; *Grant v Southwestern and County Properties* [1975] 1 Ch 185; *Kennedy v Lyell* (1883) 23 Ch D 387, 405; *Baker v London and South Western Railway Co.* (1867) LR 3 QB 91; *Flack v Pacific Press Ltd* (1970) 14 DLR (3d) 334.

[143] [1988] NI 611, 617.

[144] [1905] 2 IR 58.

[145] In *Feuerheerd v London General Omnibus Co. Ltd* [1918] 2 KB 565, the English Court of Appeal refused to follow *Tobakin* but the Irish decision was followed in preference to that in *Feuerheerd* in *McKay v McKay* [1988] NI 611 and *Flack v Pacific Press Ltd* (1970) 14 DLR (3d) 334.

[146] [1975] 1 Ch 185.

[147] [1999] 1 ILRM 257.

In the context of the 'to and fro conflicting elements' of negotiation, a document or memorandum may well be drafted by one of the parties who at the time of drafting intends to be handed over to the other but who subsequently changes his or her mind. I think it is unrealistic to require the production of such a document if the negotiations 'go sour' because I still think that this document came into being for the purposes of litigation, albeit for the specific purpose of being presented to the other side as part of an effort to avoid litigation by compromise.[148]

CRIMINAL PROSECUTIONS

8.029 The application of the principles of legal professional privilege to criminal prosecutions caused some difficulties in *Breathnach v Ireland (No. 3)*.[149] The plaintiff had instituted civil proceedings against the state for various torts and breaches of his constitutional rights arising out of his unsuccessful prosecution for the Sallins train robbery. Discovery of communications between the gardaí and members of the DPP's office was ordered and the plaintiff brought a motion seeking inspection of various documents in respect of which privilege was claimed.

Keane J rejected the claim of litigation privilege. He pointed out that in every case where the commission of a crime is suspected, documentary material will be assembled by the gardaí irrespective of whether a prosecution is ever initiated. The fact that the documents in question might be submitted to the DPP in order to obtain his decision as to whether a prosecution should be instituted could not possibly give that material the same status as a medical report obtained by a plaintiff in a personal injuries action solely for the purpose of his claim. Therefore, privilege did not attach. With regard to the claim of legal advice privilege, Keane J pointed out that the DPP does not stand in the relationship of client to any other lawyer. He is in a sense both lawyer and client because he decides whether or not to prosecute and then becomes one of the parties to the litigation. Despite this, Keane J held that the public policy underlying the legal advice category of privilege "applies equally to communications between the Director of Public Prosecutions and professional officers in his department, solicitors and counsel as to prosecutions by him which are in being or contemplated."[150] In saying this, it is unclear whether Keane J accepted or rejected the proposition that the DPP could claim legal professional privilege in respect of communications with those three categories of person. It is submitted that the better view is that he held that the DPP is entitled to claim legal advice

---

[148] *Ibid.* at 260.
[149] [1993] 2 IR 458, [1992] ILRM 755. See also *Logue v Redmond* [1999] 2 ILRM 498.
[150] *Ibid.* at 471, 765. *Cf. Evans v Chief Constable of Surrey* [1988] QB 588, [1989] 2 All ER 594.

privilege in respect of those communications but in *Corbett v DPP*,[151] O'Sullivan J reached the opposite conclusion.

EXCEPTIONS TO PRIVILEGE

Introduction

8.030 Having regard to the importance of legal professional privilege to the administration of justice, the common law courts have, traditionally, set their face against any exceptions to it even where the information sought to be disclosed was of strong probative value. In *Williams v Quebrada Railway, Land and Copper Co.*,[152] Kekewich J stressed that:

> It is of the highest importance, in the first place, that the rule as to privilege of protection from production to an opponent of those communications which pass between a litigant, or an expectant or possible litigant, and his solicitor should not be in any way departed from. However hardly the rule may operate in some cases, long experience has shewn that it is essential to the due administration of justice that the privilege should be upheld.[153]

The argument against exceptions proceeds on the basis of the "chilling effect" of disclosure.[154] It is argued that the effective functioning of the lawyer/client relationship is crucially dependent upon the client being able to place unbounded confidence in his lawyer secure in the knowledge that whatever he says can never be disclosed without his consent. Thus, if disclosure were to be made even in limited circumstances this would fatally undermine the relationship because the absolute guarantee of confidentiality would now be hedged about with caveats.

8.031 However, in recent times there has been a greater recognition that the privilege is rooted in public policy and should, therefore, only be granted where

---

[151] [1999] 2 IR 179, 186-87.

[152] [1895] 2 Ch 751, 754.

[153] See also *per* Cockburn CJ in *Southwark and Vauxhall Water Co. v Quick* (1878) 3 QBD 315, 317-18: "The relation between the client and his professional legal adviser is a confidential relation of such a nature that to my mind the maintenance of the privilege with regard to it is essential to the interests of justice and the well-being of society. Though it might occasionally happen that the removal of the privilege would assist in the elucidation of matters in dispute, I do not think that this occasional benefit justifies us in incurring the attendant risk." In *S. v Safatsa* 1988 (1) SA 868, 886, Botha JA stated that any claim to relaxation of the privilege must be approached with the greatest caution.

[154] See *R v Derby Magistrates' Court, ex p. B.* [1996] AC 487, [1995] 4 All ER 526.

the balance of advantage favours protection of confidentiality rather than disclosure. In the Canadian decision of *Smith v Jones*,[155] Cory J stated that:

> Just as no right is absolute so too the privilege, even that between solicitor and client, is subject to clearly defined exceptions. The decision to exclude evidence that would be both relevant and of substantial probative value because it is protected by the solicitor–client privilege represents a policy decision. It is based upon the importance to our legal system in general of the solicitor-client privilege. In certain circumstances, however, other societal values must prevail.

It is submitted that the Irish courts should take a similar approach. To repeat again the salient passage from the judgment of Finlay CJ in *Smurfit Paribas Bank Ltd v AAB Export Finance Ltd*:[156]

> The existence of a privilege or exemption from disclosure for communications made between a person and his lawyer clearly constitutes a potential restriction and diminution of the full disclosure both prior to and during the course of legal proceedings which in the interests of the common good is desirable for the purpose of ascertaining the truth and rendering justice. Such privilege should, therefore, in my view, only be granted by the courts in instances which have been identified as securing an objective which in the public interest in the proper conduct of the administration of justice can be said to outweigh the disadvantage arising from the restriction of disclosure of all the facts.

In *Smurfit*, the Supreme Court was concerned to align the parameters of the privilege with the balance of public interest but it can be contended that, notwithstanding the "chilling effect" referred to, exceptions can, and indeed have been made to legal professional privilege where this balance is tilted in favour of disclosure. Thus, it is argued that other exceptions have been and should be created where the public interest in disclosure clearly outweighs that in the maintenance of privilege. As O'Flaherty J said in *Gallagher v Stanley*,[157] the purpose of legal professional privilege "is to aid the administration of justice, not to impede it".

It is possible to identify from the case law, four categories of case where courts are or may be prepared to pierce privilege and each of these is examined in turn: (i) communications in furtherance of conduct which is criminal, fraudulent or injurious to the interests of justice; (ii) proceedings involving the welfare of children; (iii) testamentary dispositions; and (iv) where the innocence of a criminal defendant is at stake.

---

[155] [1999] 1 SCR 455, 477.
[156] [1990] 1 IR 469, 477, [1990] ILRM 588, 594.
[157] [1998] 2 IR 267, 271.

(i) Communications in Furtherance of Conduct which is Criminal, Fraudulent or Injurious to the Interests of Justice

8.032 It has long been established that legal privilege cannot be invoked to protect from disclosure communications in furtherance of a criminal or fraudulent purpose.[158] Subsequent decisions have broadened the exception to include fraudulent conduct and conduct injurious to the interests of justice but the courts have refused to extend it to conduct which is merely tortious and does not include any element of moral turpitude.

Initially, the courts adopted a definitional approach to hold that privilege could not attach to a communication in furtherance of criminal conduct on the basis that such a communication could not be said to pass in the course of a professional legal relationship because it is no part of a lawyer's professional occupation to facilitate the commission of a crime or fraud.[159] In addition, it was argued that the necessary ingredient of confidentiality was lacking because there could not be a confidence as to the disclosure of iniquity.[160] However, the impetus for the development of this exception in the last century has been a recognition that the rationale for privilege cannot be extended to such communications. As Stephen J explained in *R v Cox and Railton*,[161] "[t]he reason on which the rule is said to rest cannot include the case of communications criminal in themselves or intended to further any criminal purpose, for the protection of such communications, cannot possibly be otherwise than injurious to the interests of justice and to those of the administration of justice". It is this test, whether applying privilege would be injurious to the administration of justice which justifies the exception and establishes its parameters.

---

[158] *Annesley v Earl of Anglesea* (1743) 17 How St Tr 1229; *Kelly v Jackson* (1849) 1 Ir Jur 233; *R v Cox and Railton* (1884) 14 QBD 153; *Bullivant v AG for Victoria* [1901] AC 196, 201 (*per* Earl of Halsbury LC).

[159] See *Follett v Jefferyes* (1850) 1 Sim NS 3, 17, where Lord Cranworth VC stated that it was "not accurate to speak of cases of fraud contrived by the client and solicitor in concert together, as cases of *exception* to the general rule. They are cases not coming within the rule itself; for the rule does not apply to all which passes between a client and his solicitor, but only to what passes between them in professional confidence; and no court can permit it to be said that the contriving of a fraud can form part of the professional occupation of an attorney or solicitor". See also *Russell v Jackson* (1851) 9 Hare 387, 392; *R v Cox and Railton* (1884) 14 QBD 153, 165-6. *Cf. AG for the Northern Territory v Kearney* (1985) 158 CLR 500, 514.

[160] In *Gartside v Outram* (1856) 26 LJ Ch 113, 114, Page Wood VC stated: "The true doctrine is that there is no confidence as to the disclosure of iniquity. You cannot make me the confidant of a crime or a fraud, and be entitled to close up my lips upon any secret which you have the audacity to disclose to me relating to any fraudulent intention on your part. Such a confidence cannot exist." *Cf. Annesley v Earl of Anglesea* (1743) 17 How St Tr 1139, 1242.

[161] (1884) 14 QBD 153, 167.

Communications in Furtherance of Crime or Fraud

8.033 One of the earliest cases in which the court declined to apply the privilege to criminal conduct was *Annesley v Earl of Anglesea.*[162] The plaintiff brought ejectment proceedings in respect of land in County Meath against his uncle, the defendant, who he alleged had contrived to have him kidnapped and sold into slavery in America so that he could inherit the family estates when the plaintiff's father died. After returning to England from America, the plaintiff accidentally shot and killed a gamekeeper and was acquitted of his murder. However, the defendant then engaged a solicitor to start a private prosecution for murder saying that he would be willing to give £10,000 if he could get the plaintiff hanged. Mounteney B in the Irish Court of Exchequer said that this declaration was not privileged because it was:

> [of] that nature, and so highly criminal, that, in my opinion, mankind is interested in the discovery; and whoever it was made to, attorney or not attorney, lies under an obligation to society in general, prior and superior to any obligation he can lie under to a particular individual, to make it known.[163]

Later cases extended the exception to fraudulent conduct. In *Williams v Quebrada Railway, Land and Copper Co.,*[164] the exception was applied in circumstances where a claim was made that a charge had been entered into by a company with the intention of defeating the holders of floating debentures. Kekewich J held that the exception was applicable to civil as well as criminal cases and said that "where there is anything of an underhand nature or approaching to fraud, especially in commercial matters where there should be the veriest good faith, the whole transaction should be ripped up and disclosed in all its nakedness to the light of the court". Subsequently, in *Crescent Farm Sports v Sterling Offices,*[165] Goff J clarified that "fraud in this connection is not limited to the tort of deceit, and includes all forms of fraud and dishonesty, such as fraudulent breach of trust, fraudulent conspiracy, trickery and sham contrivances."[166]

Privilege will not automatically be pierced merely because a client consults

---

[162] (1743) 17 How St Tr 1139.

[163] *Ibid.* at 1243. A more recent example can be seen in *People (AG) v Coleman* [1945] IR 237, where the Court of Criminal Appeal upheld the view of the trial judge that privilege did not apply to a note written by the accused which sought to procure the subornation of witnesses because it contemplated and suggested the commission of a crime.

[164] [1895] 2 Ch 751, 754-5.

[165] [1972] Ch 553, 565.

[166] See *Gamlen Chemical Co. (UK) Ltd v Rochem Ltd* [1983] RPC 1, where the exception was applied to allegations of conspiracy by former employees to breach their duty and confidence to a company.

a lawyer before committing a crime or fraud.[167] In order for this to occur, it must be shown that the communication in question was made in preparation for or in furtherance of a criminal or fraudulent purpose.[168] However, complicity or knowledge on the part of the lawyer is not required and privilege will be set aside if a client seeks legal advice intended to facilitate him in the commission of a crime or a fraud even though the legal adviser is entirely ignorant of that purpose.[169]

Conduct Injurious to the Interests of Justice

8.034 The courts have drawn on the policy foundation of the privilege to broaden the scope of the exception beyond criminal and fraudulent conduct to include conduct injurious to the interests of justice.[170] The leading case in this jurisdiction is the decision of the Supreme Court in *Murphy v Kirwan*.[171] The plaintiff sought specific performance of an agreement but his claim was dismissed. The defendant had counterclaimed that the proceedings were vexatious, frivolous and an abuse of the process of the court and sought discovery of legal advice obtained by the plaintiff relating to the specific performance claim up to the date of the trial.

A majority of the Supreme Court was satisfied that privilege could be pierced. Taking a purposive approach, Finlay CJ stated that:

> the essence of the matter is that professional privilege cannot and must not be applied so as to be injurious to the interests of justice and to those in the administration of justice where persons have been guilty of conduct of moral turpitude or of dishonest conduct, even though it may not be fraud.[172]

---

[167] *R v Campbell* [1999] 1 SCR 565, (1999) 171 DLR (4th) 193.

[168] Thus, if the communication does not actually further that purpose, as where a lawyer issues an unsolicited warning of the consequences of persisting in a certain course of conduct, privilege will not be lost: *Butler v Board of Trade* [1971] Ch 680, [1970] 3 All ER 593. *Cf. R v Snaresbrook Crown Court, ex p. DPP* [1988] QB 532, [1988] 1 All ER 315.

[169] *R v Cox and Railton* (1884) 14 QBD 153, 165-6; *R v Orton* (1873) 18 Digest (Rep) 4116. In *Tichborne v Lushington* (1872) 22 Digest (Rep) 409, Bovill CJ justified this approach on the basis that "if any such privilege should be contended for or existed, it would work most grievous hardship on an attorney who, after he had been consulted upon what subsequently appeared a most manifest crime and fraud, would have his lips closed, and might place himself in the very serious position of being suspected to be a party to the fraud, and without his having an opportunity of exculpating himself".

[170] *Murphy v Kirwan* [1993] 3 IR 501, [1994] 1 ILRM 293; *Attorney General for the Northern Territory v Kearney* (1985) 158 CLR 500; *Police v Mills* [1993] 2 NZLR 592.

[171] [1993] 3 IR 501, [1994] 1 ILRM 293.

[172] *Ibid.* at 511, 300.

With regard to the allegation at hand, that the plaintiff had abused the processes of the court, he was satisfied that:

> Nothing could be more injurious to the administration of justice nor to the interests of justice than that a person should falsely and maliciously bring an action, and should abuse for an ulterior or improper purpose the processes of the court.[173]

8.035 The scope of this exception arose again for consideration in *Bula Ltd v Crowley (No. 2)*.[174] The plaintiffs brought proceedings claiming, *inter alia*, that the first named defendant had been negligent in failing to follow certain legal advice obtained by him in the course of carrying out his duties as receiver of the first named plaintiff. The plaintiffs sought discovery of documents containing this legal advice arguing that privilege did not protect from disclosure documents containing or seeking legal advice where the question whether, and in what terms, such advice was sought or received was in issue. Alternatively, it was argued that the court has a discretion to view the legal advices and, in the light of those advices and of the allegations made, it should, if it is satisfied that that is the essential ground on which that part of the plaintiff's claim rested, exercise a discretion exempting the documents from privilege.

This contention was rejected by the Supreme Court which held, following *Murphy v Kirwan*[175] that the exemption under this head was restricted to conduct which contained an element of fraud, dishonesty or moral turpitude and did not extend to allegations of tortious conduct. Finlay CJ said that the extension of the exception to "any case where it was proved that the nature of the legal advice obtained by a party was clearly relevant to an issue as to the commission of a tort would be inconsistent with the principles" he had set out in *Murphy v Kirwan* and was of the view that acceptance of the plaintiff's argument would involve "a massive undermining ... of the important confidence in relation to communications between lawyers and their clients which is a fundamental part of our system of justice".[176] For this reason, the court also rejected the further submission made by the plaintiffs that a court should inspect documents and order their disclosure if it finds them to be highly relevant to the issues in an action. While relevance was a necessary precondition to the application of the exception, it was not sufficient.

It is clear from this decision that the exception will only be applied where the conduct complained of is injurious to the interests of justice and this will be

---

[173] *Ibid.* at 511, 300. *Cf. Police v Mills* [1993] 2 NZLR 592, 600 (privilege would be pierced if it could be shown that client had consulted lawyer for the improper purpose of seeking to cloak with privilege information regarding a criminal offence which the lawyer had obtained outside of the professional relationship).
[174] [1994] 2 IR 54, [1994] 1 ILRM 495.
[175] [1993] 3 IR 501, [1994] 1 ILRM 293.
[176] [1994] 2 IR 54, 59, [1994] 1 ILRM 495, 498.

the case only if it involves some degree of moral turpitude. Sufficient moral turpitude will generally not be found where allegations of tortious conduct or breach of contract are made. However, sufficient moral turpitude will exist where legal advice is sought with the intention of defeating the legal rights and entitlements of a person.[177] The dividing line between the two can be hard to draw. Thus, in *Crescent Farm (Sidcup) Sports Ltd v Sterling Offices Ltd*,[178] it was held that the tort of inducing a breach of contract was not within the ambit of the exception. Goff J said that "parties must be at liberty to take advice as to the ambit of their contractual obligations and liabilities in tort and what liability they will incur whether in contract or tort by a proposed course of action without thereby in every case losing professional privilege".[179] However, *Crescent Farm* was distinguished by the High Court of Australia in *AG for the Northern Territory v Kearney*.[180] At issue were communications made for the purpose of giving and receiving legal advice which came into existence in connection with a scheme by the Administrator of the Northern Territory to make regulations with the object of defeating potential aboriginal land claims. It was held that these communications were not privileged because it "would be contrary to the public interest which the privilege is designed to secure – the better administration of justice – to allow it to be used to protect communications made to further a deliberate abuse of statutory power and by that abuse to prevent others from exercising their rights under the law".[181]

8.036 As regards the standard of proof which must be met by a party in order to bring himself within the scope of this exception, it was held in *Murphy v Kirwan*[182] that it suffices that a person's allegations are supported to an extent that they are, in the view of the court, viable and plausible.[183] Finlay CJ said that where the claim was one for malicious prosecution or abuse of the processes of the court, to require a person to prove an allegation as a matter of probability would make it impossible to obtain an order of discovery necessary for the fair trial of the action.[184] Although the comments of the Chief Justice

---

[177] *Crawford v Treacy* [1999] 2 IR 171, 177; *Barclays Bank plc v Eustice* [1995] 4 All ER 511.

[178] [1972] Ch 553.

[179] *Ibid.* at 565.

[180] (1985) 158 CLR 500.

[181] *Ibid.* at 515 (*per* Gibbs CJ).

[182] [1993] 3 IR 501, [1994] 1 ILRM 293.

[183] *Ibid.* at 512. *Cf. Quinlivan v Governor of Mountjoy Prison* High Court (Kelly J) 23 January 1997 (appeal dismissed by Supreme Court, 5 March 1997) where Kelly J dismissed as "extravagant speculation" with no evidence to support it, the submission of the applicant that the claim of legal professional privilege made by the notice parties was vitiated because of an alleged conspiracy between the Director of Public Prosecutions, the Minister for Justice and the Attorney General.

[184] He also specified that it would be necessary for the party making the claim of an abuse of process to establish either that the claim has failed in its entirety or that it is bound

were directed solely to instances where allegations of malicious prosecution or abuse of process are made, there is no reason in principle why a different standard of proof should apply to allegations made within this category of exception. Therefore, it would seem that unlike the position in England, a *prima facie* case will not be required.[185]

One instance where a higher standard of proof may be required is where the allegation of fraud relates to the actual conduct of the proceedings themselves. In *Chandler v Church*[186] the plaintiffs sought discovery of communications between the defendant and his solicitors on the basis that he had obtained their assistance to mount an allegedly bogus defence. The plaintiffs submitted *prima facie* evidence to support their allegation. However, Hoffman J held that disclosure at an interlocutory stage based on evidence of fraud in the very proceedings in which disclosure is sought carries a far greater risk of injury to the party against whom discovery is sought, should he turn out to have been innocent, than disclosure of advice concerning an earlier transaction. On the facts, the risk of injustice to the defendant in being required to reveal communications with his lawyers for the purpose of his defence, together with the damage to the public interest which the violation of such confidences would cause, outweighed the risk of injustice to the plaintiffs.[187] That is not to say that such an application would never succeed but the courts will have to be completely satisfied of the merits of the allegations made before doing so. Otherwise, a party would only have to make an allegation of fraud in order to gain access to his opponent's brief.

(ii) Proceedings Involving the Welfare of Children

8.037 There is a strong vein of authority to the effect that the rules of evidence should not be applied with the same vigour in inquisitorial proceedings involving the welfare of children because these rules of evidence, which were laid down in an adversarial context, are not appropriate where there is no *lis inter partes*.[188] Thus, in *L. (T.) v L. (V.)*,[189] McGuinness J held that legal profes-

---

to do so and that the failure of the claim was not derived from the resolution by the trial court of a conflict of evidence with regard to the primary facts or from a special legal defence raised by the defendant such as the Statute of Frauds (Ireland) 1695.

[185] See *O'Rourke v Darbishire* [1920] AC 581, [1920] All ER 1 (which was cited with approval by Egan J in his dissent in *Murphy v Kirwan* [1993] 3 IR 501, [1994] 1 ILRM 293 on this point); *Butler v Board of Trade* [1973] 3 All ER 593, 598 (*per* Goff J) ("what has to be shown *prima facie* is not merely that there is a *bona fide* and reasonably tenable charge of crime or fraud but a *prima facie* case that the communications in question were made in preparation for or in furtherance or as part of it.")

[186] [1987] NLJR 451.

[187] See also *R v Crown Court at Snarsebrook, ex p. DPP* [1988] 1 All ER 315; *Francis & Francis (a firm) v Central Criminal Court* [1988] 3 All ER 775.

[188] See, in relation to the rule against hearsay, *Eastern Health Board v M.K.* [1999] 2 IR 99 (also reported *sub nom In the Matter of M.K., S.K. and W.K.* [1999] 2 ILRM 321).

sional privilege could be pierced in proceedings concerning the welfare of children. She surveyed the English decisions and followed that of the Court of Appeal in *Oxfordshire County Council v M.*[190] where it held that proceedings under the English Children Act 1989 are not adversarial and that the court's duty is to investigate and to seek to achieve a result which is in the interests of the welfare of the child or children the subject of the proceedings. Such proceedings are not similar to ordinary adversarial litigation in which the doctrine of professional privilege applies but fall into a special category where the court is bound to undertake all necessary steps to arrive at an appropriate result in the paramount interests of the welfare of the child. Accordingly, the court has power to override legal professional privilege and order disclosure of a privileged communication. She was of the opinion that these principles could be applied equally to proceedings in this jurisdiction governed by s.3 of the Guardianship of Infants Act 1964 which requires a court to have regard to the welfare of the child as the paramount consideration. Indeed, the statutory duty of the court in this regard was strengthened by the well established constitutional right of the child to have its welfare promoted and protected by the court. Although it was not necessary for the purposes of her decision, the learned judge cited with approval a number of English decisions to the effect that not only were legal representatives in possession of material relevant to the determination but contrary to the interests of their client unable to resist disclosure by reliance on legal professional privilege, they have a positive duty to disclose it to the other parties and to the court.[191]

She did, however, emphasise a number of limitations. Firstly, the English decisions referred solely to medical and expert reports and clearly such reports are the type of material which would normally require to be disclosed in this context. She said that the same considerations do not necessarily apply to other matters normally covered by legal professional privilege and in each case "the desirability of disclosure must on the facts of the case be weighed against the desirability of maintaining the privilege and a decision taken in the light of the interests of the child concerned."[192] She went on to accept that the power to override privilege in such cases should "be exercised only rarely and only when the court is satisfied that it is necessary".[193] She ultimately decided not to order discovery of the document at issue because she did not think that the material was of such a nature that the interests of the child required that it be disclosed by way of discovery.

---

[189] [1996] 1 FLR 126.

[190] [1994] 2 All ER 269.

[191] See *Re R. (A Minor) (Disclosure of Privileged Material)* [1993] 4 All ER 702; *Essex County Council v R.* [1993] 2 FLR 826; *Re H. (D.) (A Minor) (Child Abuse)* [1994] 1 FLR 679.

[192] [1996] 1 FLR 126, 137.

[193] *Ibid.* at 137.

(iii) Testamentary Dispositions

8.038 In general, the fact that a client is dead does not affect the existence of legal professional privilege[194] which will enure for the benefit of his successors in title.[195] However, a possible exception may exist, the parameters of which are far from clear, in respect of testamentary dispositions.

The starting point in this area is the decision in *Russell v Jackson*[196] where it was contended that a gift of the residue of the testator's estate to the executors was made upon a secret trust for the founding of a socialist school in Birmingham. In order to establish this fact, it was sought to examine on interrogatory the solicitor who had drawn up the will as to the circumstances surrounding this alleged secret trust. He refused to answer the interrogatories on the ground of privilege. On the facts, Turner VC held that privilege could not be set up by the executor against the next of kin claiming against the estate because both were claiming under the testator. However, he also advanced the view that in the case of testamentary dispositions, the rationale for the privilege did not apply:

> The disclosure in such cases can affect no right or interest of the client. The apprehension of it can present no impediment to the full statement of his case to his solicitor ... In the cases of testamentary dispositions the very foundation on which the rule proceeds seem to be wanting; and in the absence, therefore, of any illegal purpose entertained by the testator there does not appear to be any ground for applying it ... Another view of the case is that the protection which the rule gives is the protection of the client; and it cannot, I think, be said to be for the protection of the client that evidence should be rejected, the effect of which would be to prove a trust created by him, and to destroy a claim to take beneficially by parties who have accepted that trust.[197]

This passage was cited with approval by the Ontario Court of Appeal in *Stewart v Walker*,[198] where Moss CJO explained that:

> The nature of the case precludes the question of privilege from arising. The reason on which the rule is founded is the safeguarding of the interests of the client, or those claiming under him when they are in conflict with the claims of third persons not claiming, or assuming to claim under

---

[194] *Bullivant v AG for Victoria* [1901] AC 196.
[195] In *Swidler & Berlin v United States* (1998) 524 US 399, Rehnquist CJ justified this on the basis that posthumous disclosure might be feared by a client as much as disclosure during his lifetime and, thus, maintaining the confidentiality of communications after death would help to foster full and frank communication between client and counsel.
[196] (1851) 9 Hare 387.
[197] *Ibid.* at 392.
[198] (1903) 6 OLR 495, 497.

him. And that is not this case, where the question is as to what testamentary dispositions, if any, were made by the client.[199]

It can be seen that this line of authority is predicated on the recognition that where a dispute arises about a testamentary disposition, the client has no recognisable interest in the maintenance of privilege. On the contrary, the concern of the deceased client is that his instructions and intentions would be carried into effect and there would have been no "chilling effect" on the solicitor/client relationship if the client had been aware that privileged communications could be disclosed after his death.

8.039 Another vein of authority has focussed on the partially inquisitorial role of the courts in probate matters. In *Re Fuld's Estate (No. 2)*,[200] Scarman J drew a distinction with regard to the application of legal privilege between the inquisitorial function of a court in relation to the execution of a will and its role in an adversarial dispute:

> [T]here can be in a probate case an apparent clash or conflict between the right of the court to know everything that its witness knows or has said about execution, and the right of a party to claim privilege for communications passing between that witness and himself or his solicitor for the purpose of collecting evidence for the hearing. If there be such a conflict, I have no doubt that it must be resolved in favour of the court. Strictly, however, there is no conflict because the court in its inquisitorial capacity is seeking the truth as to execution. The parties upon the issue of execution are assisting the court in its search for the truth.[201]

8.040 These strands of authority were considered by O'Sullivan J in *Crawford v Treacy*.[202] The case concerned a probate dispute. The first defendant sought to establish that she was the lawful wife of the deceased and was thus, entitled to a share of his estate in accordance with the provisions of Part IX of the Succession Act 1965. The plaintiffs who were the executors of the deceased's estate brought an application seeking directions of the court. In the course of discovery, an affidavit was sworn by the first named plaintiff claiming legal professional privilege in respect of a number of documents relating to the preparation of the will and a separation agreement.

---

[199] In *Re Ott* (1972) 2 OR 5, 24 DLR (3d) 517 it was emphasised that it was in the interests of justice that privilege not be invoked as otherwise it would be impossible to ascertain the true intention of the testator. *Cf. Gartside v Sheffield, Young & Ellis* [1983] NZLR 37.

[200] [1965] P 405, [1965] 2 All ER 657.

[201] *Ibid.* at 410, 659.

[202] [1999] 2 IR 171.

Having been requested to do so, O'Sullivan J examined the documents in dispute and concluded that some of them were privileged. He then went on to consider the submissions of the first named defendant that even if privilege attached to the documents, discovery should be ordered by reason of the application of two exceptions to the general rule. The first was stated to arise out of the consideration that the proceedings were not truly *inter partes* but rather proceedings brought by the executors of the will for directions. It was submitted that the court's primary concern was the ascertainment of the truth rather than the protection of the interests of one of the parties and that this concern was paramount over such interests of the deceased as might be protected by the claim to privilege. It was further submitted that it would be anomalous if privilege were to apply such that the plaintiffs would be in possession of more information than the court itself. Reliance was placed in this regard on the decisions in *Russell v Jackson* and *Re Fuld's Estate (No.2)*.

O'Sullivan J distinguished these cases on the basis that in both, justice clearly required production of the documents or evidence. In *Russell*, there was a question not only of a secret trust but a breach of the law. In *Fuld*, the court was concerned with establishing a central fact in relation to the execution of a will. With regard to the instant case, he pointed out that the document sought related to advice and that the facts upon which that advice was given would be known to the court independently from incidental recitals in the documents passing between solicitor, counsel and the deceased. Having considered the documents, he did not think that the truth could only be discovered by ordering disclosure of the documents. The outcome of the application for directions would not, in his view, be dependent upon or influenced by production of those documents to the court. He concluded that the interests of justice did not necessitate disclosure of the privileged documents.

(iv) Innocence of a Defendant

8.041 The question has not yet arisen in this jurisdiction as to whether privilege may be pierced where disclosure of a privileged communication is sought in order to prove the innocence of a defendant. It is clear that public interest immunity will yield to the interest of a defendant in proving his innocence[203] and it would seem as if private privilege, which ultimately rests on public policy, should also yield. This was indeed the view taken by Caulfield J who approached the matter free from the constraints of authority in *R v Barton*:[204]

> If there are documents in the possession or control of a solicitor which, on production, help to further the defence of an accused man, then in my

---

[203] *Director of Consumer Affairs v Sugar Distributors Ltd* [1991] 1 IR 225, 229; *Goodman International v Hamilton (No. 3)* [1993] 3 IR 320, 327.
[204] [1972] 2 All ER 1192, 1194.

judgment no privilege attaches. I cannot conceive that our law would permit a solicitor or other person to screen from a jury information which, if disclosed to the jury, would perhaps enable a man either to establish his innocence or to resist an allegation made by the Crown.

This decision was approved in *R v Ataou*,[205] where the Court of Appeal held that where a defendant sought to pierce privilege claimed by a client or solicitor, he bore the burden of showing on the balance of probabilities that the claim for privilege could not be sustained because there was no ground on which the client could any longer reasonably be regarded as having a recognisable interest in asserting the privilege and the legitimate interest of the defendant in seeking to breach the privilege outweighed that of the client in seeking to maintain it. French J stated that "the resolution of the problem in each individual case involves balancing the competing interests of the public in the due and orderly administration of justice, on the one hand, and of the public and the accused, in ensuring that all evidence supportive of his case is before the court, on the other hand".

8.042 However, this line of authority was overturned by the House of Lords in *R v Derby Magistrates' Court, ex p. B*.[206] The appellant had been arrested on suspicion of having murdered a girl. He admitted being solely responsible for the murder but later changed his story and stated that his stepfather had killed the girl and that he had taken part under duress. He was tried and acquitted of the girl's murder and was subsequently called as a witness by the prosecution at the committal proceedings of his stepfather on a charge of murdering the girl. Counsel for the stepfather sought to cross-examine him on the instructions which he had given to his solicitors during the period between his first account and his second account. The appellant refused to waive privilege and an application was made for a witness summons directing the solicitor to produce certain privileged documents.

The House of Lords took the view that *Ataou* had been incorrectly decided and that it was impermissible to engage in such a balancing exercise which cut across the fundamental principle of "once privileged, always privileged" unless the client chooses to waive privilege. Lord Taylor CJ took the view that legal professional privilege is much more than an ordinary rule of evidence but is a fundamental condition on which the administration of justice as a whole rests, and rejected the proposition that there could be exceptions to it:

[T]he drawback to that approach is that once any exception to the general rule is allowed, the client's confidence is necessarily lost. The solicitor,

---

[205] [1988] 2 All ER 321.
[206] [1996] AC 487, [1995] 4 All ER 526. See also *Carter v Managing Partner of Northmore Hale Davey & Leake* (1995) 183 CLR 121.

instead of being able to tell his client that anything which the client might say would never in any circumstances be revealed without his consent, would have to qualify his assurance. He would have to tell the client that his confidence might be broken if in some future case the court were to hold that he no longer had "any recognisable interest" in asserting his privilege. One can see at once that the purpose of the privilege would thereby be undermined.[207]

Lord Lloyd said that there could not be a balancing exercise because "the courts have for many years regarded legal professional privilege as the predominant public interest. A balancing exercise is not required in individual cases, because the balance must always come down in favour of upholding the privilege, unless, of course, the privilege is waived." He also rejected the idea that privilege could be set aside where the client could be shown to have no recognisable interest in maintaining it.

If the client had to be told that his communications were only confidential so long as he had "a recognisable interest" in preserving the confidentiality, and that some court on some future occasion might decide that he no longer had any such recognisable interest, the basis of the confidence would be destroyed or at least undermined. There may be cases where the principle will work hardship on a third party seeking to assert his innocence. But in the overall interests of the administration of justice it is better that the principle should be preserved intact.[208]

Lord Nicholls pointed to the practical difficulties of any balancing test and the impossibility of setting satisfactory parameters to it. He characterised the prospect of a balancing exercise as "a veritable will-o'-the wisp". He was attracted to the argument that the client could not assert privilege where he had no recognisable interest in maintaining it *i.e.* where no rational person would regard himself as having any continuing interest in protecting the privilege. However, the point did not arise for decision as this test was not satisfied in the instant case where he was likely to be accused in the upcoming murder trial of having committed the murder.

8.043 The Canadian courts have taken a different and, it is submitted, preferable approach. In *R v Dunbar,*[209] Martin JA took the view that:

No rule of policy requires the continued existence of the privilege in criminal cases when the person claiming the privilege no longer has any inter-

---

[207] *Ibid.* at 508, 541.
[208] *Ibid.* at 509-510, 543.
[209] (1983) 138 DLR (3d) 221.

est to protect, and when maintaining the privilege might screen from the jury information which would assist an accused.[210]

This decision has been approved by the Supreme Court of Canada in a number of decisions where it has been held that legal professional privilege may have to give way to the constitutional right of an accused to make full answer and defence to a criminal charge.[211] In *Smith v Jones*,[212] the Supreme Court disavowed the approach in *Derby Magistrates'* pointing out that the privilege in Canada is subject to certain well defined and limited exceptions which are not closed and could be expanded in the future.

DURATION OF PRIVILEGE

8.044 In keeping with the policy behind legal advice privilege, "the law has considered it the wisest policy to encourage and sanction this confidence, by requiring that on such facts the mouth of the attorney shall be forever sealed".[213] Therefore, the general rule as stated by Lindley MR in *Calcraft v Guest*[214] is "once privileged always privileged"[215] and legal advice privilege will continue after the lawyer/client relationship has ended[216] and even after the death of the client.[217] This is justified on the basis that disclosure at any point in the future could potentially harm the interests of the client and would have a chilling effect on communications with his lawyer.[218]

In addition, the clear balance of authority is that the maxim of "once privileged always privileged" applies equally to communications protected by litigation privilege. In *Bullock v Corry*,[219] the plaintiffs brought proceedings against

---

[210] *Ibid.* at 252.

[211] *R v Seaboyer* [1991] 2 SCR 577, 607; *A. (L.L.) v B. (A.)* [1995] 4 SCR 536, 577; *Smith v Jones* [1999] 1 SCR 455, 477-8, (1999) 169 DLR (4th) 385, 391; *R v Campbell* [1999] 1 SCR 565, 610-11, (1999) 171 DLR (4th) 193, 231-2.

[212] [1999] 1 SCR 455, (1999) 169 DLR (4th) 385.

[213] *Per* Shaw CJ in *Hatton v Robinson* (1833) 14 Pick 416, 422. See also *Wilson v Rastall* (1792) 4 Term Rep 753, 759 (*per* Buller J) ("the privilege ... never ceased at any period of time ... it is not sufficient to say that the cause is at an end; the mouth of such person is closed forever").

[214] [1898] 1 QB 759.

[215] *Ibid.* at 761. See also *Bullock v Corry* (1878) 3 QBD 356; *Pearce v Foster* (1885) 15 QBD 114, 118; *Mann v American Automobile Insurance Co.* (1938) 52 BCR 460, [1938] 2 DLR 261.

[216] *Cholmondeley v Clinton* (1815) 19 Ves Jun 261, 268; *Bell v Smith* [1968] SCR 664, (1968) 68 DLR (2d) 751.

[217] *Russell v Jackson* (1851) 9 Hare 387; *Gartside v Sheffield, Young & Ellis* [1983] NZLR 37.

[218] *Porter v Scott* [1979] NI 6, 16-17.

[219] (1878) 3 QBD 356.

the defendants for failing to unload cargo at a certain port. It was held that the defendants were not entitled to inspection of the papers in the plaintiffs' possession relating to a previous action brought against them by the shipowner including correspondence between them and their solicitor and between their solicitor and other persons because those papers would have been privileged from discovery in the former action and the fact that such action had terminated did not deprive them of their privilege. Cockburn CJ said:

> The privilege which attaches by the invariable practice of our courts to communications between solicitor and client ought to be carefully preserved. In my opinion, the rule is, once privileged, always privileged. This will apply, *a fortiori*, where the succeeding action is substantially the same as that in which the documents were used.[220]

That decision was followed in *Pearce v Foster*,[221] where Brett MR said that "if a document is once so privileged, the fact that it is another action in which it is being inquired about will not destroy the privilege".

8.045 The leading case in this jurisdiction is *Quinlivan v Tuohy*.[222] The plaintiff instituted proceedings claiming damages for personal injuries arising out of a car accident. She had been involved in a previous accident in which she had suffered similar injuries and the defendants sought disclosure of two medical reports prepared in connection with proceedings arising out of that accident. The plaintiff argued that privilege continued to subsist in these reports and Barron J agreed. He regarded the issue as settled by authority and followed *Bord na Móna v Sisk*[223] in which Costello J had approved the holding in *The Aegis Blaze*.[224] In that case, the English Court of Appeal held that privilege could be claimed in respect of a surveyor's report prepared for the purpose of earlier proceedings and refused to impose a requirement that the subject matter of the two actions be identical or substantially the same or that the parties to the two actions should be the same. Barron J, therefore, held that the reports were privileged and "that it would be to the plaintiff's detriment and contrary to the principles from which the privilege was granted in the first place to allow this report now to be seen by the defendants".[225]

In *Quinlivan*, Barron J declared that, even in the absence of authority, he would still have regarded the public interest as requiring the maintenance of privilege. However, a strong argument can be made that the balance of public

---

[220] *Ibid.* at 358.
[221] (1885) 15 QBD 114, 118.
[222] High Court (Barron J) 29 July 1992. The issue was also raised but not decided in *Breathnach v Ireland (No. 3)* [1993] 2 IR 458.
[223] [1990] 1 IR 85.
[224] [1986] 1 Lloyd's Rep 203.
[225] High Court (Barron J) 29 July 1992 at 3.

interest is against maintaining litigation privilege in subsequent proceedings and that the correct approach is to be found in the judgment of Kelly J in *Porter v Scott*.[226] He distinguished between legal advice privilege and litigation privilege and held that the maxim "once privileged always privileged" applied to the former but not to the latter unless the subject-matter of the proceedings was the same:

> There is sound public policy in applying this rule "once privileged always privileged" to strict legal privilege *i.e.* lawyer/client communications. What a client reveals to his lawyer for professional purposes should not only be secret but is intended to remain permanently so or at least until the client decides otherwise. To reduce or qualify the permanency of this secret would be to inhibit free and unreserved communication and this is essential to our system of law. The element of permanency does not seem to pervade communications made in contemplation of litigation. Such communications are not generally intended to remain unrevealed – indeed more often than not it is intended that they should be revealed at the appropriate time in one form or another during the course of legal proceedings. They come into existence for the precise and limited purpose of use in contemplated litigation and I do not see on any grounds of public policy or otherwise why they should remain clothed with privilege when the proceedings for which they were made have been disposed and abandoned.[227]

Having regard to the admonition of Finlay CJ in *Smurfit Paribas Bank Ltd v AAB Export Finance Ltd*,[228] that the parameters of privilege should only be drawn as broad as necessary to advance the advantages secured by it, it is submitted that this reasoning is convincing and that litigation privilege should only apply to communications in the proceedings for which they came into being unless the identity of the parties and the subject matter of the proceedings are the same.

Indeed, such an approach was taken in a decision which does not seem to have been drawn to the attention of Barron J in *Quinlivan*. In *Kerry County Council v Liverpool Salvage Association*[229] the plaintiffs sued the defendants for having caused an obstruction of Valentia harbour by depositing a wreck there. The defendants, who had been employed by an insurance company to salvage the vessel, resisted disclosure of certain correspondence on the ground

---

[226] [1979] NI 6.

[227] *Ibid.* at 16. The Canadian courts have also distinguished between those communications protected by legal advice privilege and those protected by litigation privilege and held that litigation privilege ends with the litigation for which the communications were prepared (*Meaney v Busby* (1977) 15 OR (2d) 71; *Boulianne v Flynn* [1970] 3 OR 84).

[228] [1990] 1 IR 469, 477, [1990] ILRM 588, 594.

[229] (1904) 38 ILTR 7.

that it was privileged. It was argued that this correspondence had come into being in connection with an anticipated claim by the shipowner against the insurance company and was therefore privileged and that this privilege subsisted in these subsequent proceedings. The claim of privilege was rejected by the Court of Appeal on the ground that the correspondence would not have been privileged in the first action. However, two members of the Court did go on to deal, *obiter,* with the plaintiff's invocation of the maxim "once privileged, always privileged". Fitzgibbon LJ distinguished between legal advice privilege and litigation privilege. In relation to the latter, he said that the person claiming privilege must "show some connection between the parties, or the subject-matter, or both".[230] Holmes LJ was also of the opinion that privilege would not extend "to all cases, whatever might be the change of subject-matter or of parties".[231]

ASSERTION AND LOSS OF PRIVILEGE

Assertion of Privilege

8.046 Privilege belongs to the client[232] not the lawyer.[233] Therefore, the decision as to whether to assert privilege is one for the client to make, although the lawyer is under a duty to tell the client that he or she can claim privilege[234] and to assert it on his or her behalf unless otherwise instructed.[235] In *McMullen v Carty,*[236] Lynch J stressed that "[a] lawyer, whether solicitor or barrister, is under a duty not to communicate to any third party information entrusted to him by or on behalf of his client" and, there is authority to the effect that, if a lawyer attempts to give evidence in breach of this duty, a court can of its own motion, intervene to protect the interests of the client.[237]

---

[230] *Ibid.* at 8.

[231] *Ibid.* at 8.

[232] Or to the client's successors in title: *Chant v Brown* (1849) 7 Hare 79; *Re Konigsberg* [1989] 3 All ER 289 (trustee in bankruptcy); *Geffen v Goodman Estate* [1991] 2 SCR 353, (1991) 81 DLR (4th) 211.

[233] *Gallagher v Stanley* [1998] 2 IR 267, 271; *McMullen v Carty* Supreme Court, 27 January 1998 at 9; *Breathnach v Ireland (No. 3)* [1993] 2 IR 458, 471; *Wilson v Rastall* (1792) 4 Term Rep 753, 759; *Wright v Mayer* (1801) 6 Ves Jr 281; *Minter v Priest* [1930] AC 558, 579, [1930] All ER 431, 439; *Schneider v Leigh* [1955] 2 All ER 173; *Geffen v Goodman Estate* [1991] 2 SCR 353, (1991) 81 DLR (4th) 211; *R v Craig* [1975] 1 NZLR 597, 598. In *Ventouris v Mountain* [1991] 3 All ER 472, 475, Bingham LJ criticised the term "legal professional privilege" as "unhappy" because it falsely suggested a privilege enjoyed by the legal profession rather than the client.

[234] *R v Barton* [1972] 2 All ER 1192, 1194; *Re Cross* [1981] 2 NZLR 673, 677.

[235] *Bell v Smith* [1968] SCR 664, (1968) 68 DLR (2d) 751; *R v Craig* [1975] 1 NZLR 597, 598. *Cf. McMullen v Carty* Supreme Court, 27 January 1998.

[236] Supreme Court, 27 January 1998.

[237] *Beer v Ward* (1821) Jacob 77; *Stevens v Canada (Privy Council)* [1998] 4 FC 89,

Where clients jointly retain a lawyer, privilege cannot be claimed *inter se* in respect of communications passing between either of them and the lawyer but will be maintained against third parties unless waived jointly.[238] In addition, the courts have recognised a species of legal professional privilege, termed "common interest privilege" where a joint retainer does not exist but nevertheless a person has a common interest with the client in the subject matter of the privileged communication.[239] This privilege cannot be claimed as between the client and the person with the common interest in respect of communications which came into being during the currency of the common interest but can be asserted against any person who does not share the common interest.[240] Examples of persons with a common interest can, depending on the circumstances, include partners, a company and its shareholders, a trustee and *cestui que trust*, a lessor and lessee, a principal and agent and a husband and wife.

Privilege cannot, however, be invoked by persons who are strangers to the lawyer/client relationship. Thus, in *Schneider v Leigh*,[241] it was held that a doctor who had carried out an examination and written a medical report at the request of a defendant company could not assert litigation privilege in respect of that report in subsequent proceedings for libel taken against him. Similarly, in *R v Jack*[242] it was held that the accused, who was charged with the murder of his wife, could not assert privilege on her behalf in respect of a conversation which she had had with her lawyer shortly before her death.

Waiver of Privilege

8.047 Privilege may be waived expressly or impliedly[243] and, again, the decision as to whether privilege is waived is that of the client.[244] In general, a law-

---

[238] (1998) 161 DLR (4th) 85; *Geffen v Goodman Estate* [1991] 2 SCR 353, 383-4, (1991) 81 DLR (4th) 211, 232; *Bell v Smith* [1968] SCR 664, (1968) 68 DLR (2d) 751.

[238] *The Sagheera* [1997] 1 Lloyd's Rep 160; *Re Konigsberg* [1989] 3 All ER 289; *R v Dunbar* (1982) 138 DLR (3d) 221.

[239] *Bula Ltd v Crowley* High Court (Murphy J) 8 March 1991; *Buttes Gas and Oil Co. v Hammer (No. 3)* [1981] QB 223, [1980] 3 All ER 475; *CIA Barca de Panama SA v George Wimpey & Co. Ltd* [1980] 1 Lloyd's Rep 598; *Leif Hoegh & Co. A/S v Petrolsea Inc (No. 2)* [1993] 1 Lloyd's Rep 363; *Supercom of California Ltd v Sovereign General Insurance Co.* (1998) 37 OR (3d) 597. Cf. *Lee v South West Thames Regional Health Authority* [1985] 1 WLR 845.

[240] *CIA Barca de Panama SA v George Wimpey & Co. Ltd* [1980] 1 Lloyd's Rep 598; *Talbot v Marshfield* (1865) 2 Dr & Sm 549; *Ontario (AG) v Ballard Estate* (1994) 119 DLR (4th) 750; *Platt v Buck* (1902) 41 DLR 421.

[241] [1955] 2 All ER 173.

[242] (1992) 70 CCC (3d) 67.

[243] *McMullen v Carty* Supreme Court, 27 January 1998 at 9.

[244] *Gallagher v Stanley* [1998] 2 IR 267, 271; *McMullen v Carty* Supreme Court, 27 January 1998 at 9; *Breathnach v Ireland (No. 3)* [1993] 2 IR 458, 471; *Century Insurance Office Ltd v Falloon* [1971] NI 234, 235; *Minter v Priest* [1930] AC 558, 579, [1930] All ER 431, 439.

yer does not have authority to waive privilege and cannot do so without the express consent of his client.[245] However, he may be regarded as having implied authority to waive privilege in the course of proceedings in accordance with the general principle that a lawyer has ostensible authority to conduct proceedings on behalf of the client as he thinks fit.[246] Privilege will be taken to have been waived where a privileged document or its contents are disclosed by a lawyer to an adverse party unless it is expressly reserved.[247] Thus, reference to the contents of a privileged communication in a pleading or affidavit will waive privilege.[248] However, a mere reference to its existence will not do so.[249]

Although privilege may be waived in whole or in part, a person intending to make a partial waiver only may, nonetheless, be taken to have impliedly waived privilege in the whole of a document where unfairness might result from partial disclosure.[250] As a practical matter, this means that "if a document is privileged then privilege must be asserted, if at all, to the whole document unless the document deals with separate subject matters so that the document can in effect be divided into two separate and distinct documents each of which is complete."[251] Similarly, although waiver of privilege in one of a series of communications will not, generally, be construed as waiver of privilege in all,[252] a party will not be permitted to waive privilege in such a partial and selective manner that unfairness or misunderstanding may result.[253]

---

[245] *McMullen v Carty* Supreme Court, 27 January 1998 at 9; *Porter v Scott* [1979] NI 6, 17.

[246] *Great Atlantic Insurance Co. v Home Insurance Co.* [1981] 2 All ER 485; *Causton v Mann Egerton* [1974] 1 WLR 162, 167; *Porter v Scott* [1979] NI 6, 17.

[247] *Porter v Scott* [1979] NI 6; *Caldbeck v Boon* (1877) IR 7 CL 32. Privilege will be lost at the point when the document is handed over and it is not necessary that the document actually be opened in court (*Porter v Scott*).

[248] Cf. *Hannigan v Director of Public Prosecutions* [2002] 1 ILRM 48 (public interest privilege in document waived in circumstances where it was summarised in an affidavit).

[249] *Tromso Sparebank v Beirne* [1989] ILRM 257; *Buttes Gas & Oil Co. v Hammer (No. 3)* [1981] QB 223, [1980] 3 All ER 475; *Tate & Lyle International Ltd v Government Trading Corp.* [1984] LS Gaz R 3341; *Lac La Ronge Indian Board v Canada* (1996) 6 CPC (4th) 110. Cf. *R v Campbell* [1999] 1 SCR 565, (1999) 171 DLR (4th) 193. This accords with the position as set out in the Rules. Order 31, rule 15 makes provision for a party to be required to produce for inspection a document referred to in its pleadings but that party is entitled to object to its production (Order 31, rule 17).

[250] *AG for the Northern Territory v Maurice* (1986) 161 CLR 475; *Argyle Brewery Pty Ltd v Darling Harbourside (Sydney) Pty Ltd* (1993) 120 ALR 537; *Equiticorp Industries Group Ltd v Hawkins* [1990] 2 NZLR 175.

[251] *Great Atlantic Insurance Co. v Home Insurance Co.* [1981] 2 All ER 485.

[252] See, *contra*, *Smith v Smith* [1958] OWN 135.

[253] *Paragon Finance plc v Freshfields* [1999] 1 WLR 1183, 1188; *R v Secretary of State for Transport, ex p. Factortame* (1997) 9 Admin LR 591, 598. In *Nea Karteria Maritime Co. Ltd v Atlantic and Great Lakes Steamship Corp. (No. 2)* [1981] Com LR 138, 139, Mustill J said that "where a party is deploying in court material which would otherwise be privileged, the opposite party and the court must have an opportunity of

Civil Procedure

8.048 As seen above, the protection afforded by privilege is predicated on confidentiality and, therefore, if a client discloses a privileged communication to the public or a significant part of it, confidentiality and the consequent entitlement to claim privilege will be lost and a party will be taken to have waived privilege.[254] However, more limited disclosure to persons not including the adverse party may not be taken as waiver. It has, thus, been held that privilege will not be lost where the communication is disseminated to third parties who share a common interest in the subject matter of the communication with the client,[255] or even where a copy is sent to or shown to a third party for a specific purpose unconnected to the prosecution of the proceedings.[256] *A fortiori*, privilege will continue to subsist where the communication is disclosed on the condition that confidentiality be maintained.[257] Thus, in *Downey v Murray*,[258] a copy of a statement made by the plaintiff had been sent to the police subject to the condition that it would not form part of any police report or be communicated to any other person. It was held that the plaintiff was entitled to claim privilege for the document because the effect of sending a copy of the document to the police was not a general waiver. The plaintiff's solicitors were entitled to impose a condition on the use of the copy statement and the waiver of the privilege was limited to the purposes specified by them.

Communications put in issue by the client

8.049 Considerations of fairness dictate that if a client puts the contents of privileged communications in issue, then he will be taken to have impliedly waived privilege to the extent necessary for a fair disposition of the issue. Thus, implied waiver will occur where a client pleads that he acted in good faith in reliance on particular legal advice,[259] where he disputes the authority of his

---

satisfying themselves that what the party has chosen to release from privilege represents the whole of the material relevant to the issue in question. To allow an individual item to be plucked out of context would be to risk injustice through its real weight or meaning being misunderstood."

254 *Bula Ltd v Crowley* High Court (Murphy J) 8 March 1991; *Chandris Lines Ltd v Wilson & Horton Ltd* [1981] 2 NZLR 600.

255 *Bula Ltd v Crowley* High Court (Murphy J) 8 March 1991; *Buttes Gas and Oil Co. v Hammer (No. 3)* [1981] QB 223, [1980] 3 All ER 475; *Gotha City v Sotheby's* [1998] 1 WLR 114.

256 *Wilson v Liquid Packaging Ltd* [1979] NI 165, 169 (copy of a witness statement which had come into being in anticipation of litigation had been sent to the plaintiffs' MP to see whether the plaintiffs could obtain redress by political means rather than by litigation); *British Coal Corp. v Dennis Rye Ltd (No. 2)* [1988] 3 All ER 816 (documents disclosed in accordance with party's duty to assist in the prosecution of criminal proceedings); *Harbour Inn Seafood Ltd v Switzerland General Insurance Co. Ltd* [1990] 2 NZLR 381, 384; *C-C Bottlers Ltd v Lion Nathan Ltd* [1993] 2 NZLR 445.

257 *Goldberg v Ng* (1994) 33 NSWLR 639, 651.

258 [1988] NI 600.

259 *R v Campbell* [1999] 1 SCR 565, (1999) 171 DLR (4th) 193.

legal advisers to enter into a settlement agreement on his behalf,[260] or where he sues his legal advisers. [261]

The principles applicable where solicitors and/or barristers are being sued have recently been reviewed in *McMullen v Carty*.[262] The appellant instituted proceedings against the respondent firm of solicitors for negligence arising out of the conduct and disposal of previous proceedings brought by him. At the trial in the High Court, evidence was given by the senior counsel briefed by the respondents in the previous proceedings and on appeal it was contended by the appellant that this evidence had been given in breach of legal professional privilege. Lynch J, delivering the judgment of the Supreme Court, explained the basis of the waiver as follows:

> When a client sues his solicitor for damages for alleged negligence arising out of the conduct of previous litigation against third parties and especially as in this case arising out of the settlement of such previous litigation the client thereby puts in issue all the communications as between the solicitor and the client and the barrister and the client and also as between the barrister and the solicitor relevant to the settlement of the case and thereby impliedly waives the privilege of confidentiality ... It would be manifestly unjust and wrong if the solicitor was precluded by the rule of confidentiality from making his case before the court.[263]

He went on to say that the same principles applied where the barrister was sued and where the solicitor alone was sued. Thus, the senior counsel in question had not breached legal professional privilege (which had been impliedly waived) by giving evidence against the client.[264] It can be seen, therefore, that it is the fact that advices are put in issue rather than the identity of the party sued that is determinative. If a solicitor being sued could not put in evidence communica-

---

[260] *Century Insurance Office Ltd v Falloon* [1971] NI 234; *Conlon v Conlons Ltd* [1952] 2 All ER 462; *Newman v Nemes* (1979) 8 CPC 229.

[261] *McMullen v Carty* Supreme Court, 27 January 1998; *Lillicrap v Nalder & Son* [1993] 1 All ER 724. Implied waiver will not occur in circumstances where the client puts together a team to advise on a transaction which includes lawyers and other professionals such as accountants and subsequently sues the accountants but not the lawyers: *Nederlandse Reassurantie Groep Holding NV v Bacon & Woodrow* [1995] 1 All ER 976. As to the extent of the waiver, see *Paragon Finance plc v Freshfields* [1999] 1 WLR 1183.

[262] Supreme Court, 27 January 1998.

[263] *Ibid.* at 9-10.

[264] Note that § 3.4(c) of the Code of Conduct for the Bar of Ireland which deals with the obligation of confidentiality owed by a barrister to a client provides that: "When an accusation is made by the lay client against his solicitor a barrister is still bound to maintain secrecy as to matters coming to his knowledge as counsel and may not give a statement or give evidence concerning such matters without the consent of the lay client."

tions with the barrister briefed by him, his ability to defend himself would be severely impaired and injustice could result.[265]

Privileged Communications Disclosed by Inadvertence or Misconduct

8.050 The traditional common law approach was that disclosure of privileged communications, whether by inadvertence or misconduct, resulted in the loss of the privilege and evidence of the privileged communications whether original or secondary was admissible. This approach was closely linked to that adopted in respect of illegally obtained evidence and in *Calcraft v Guest*,[266] Lindley MR endorsed a passage from the judgment of Parke B in *Lloyd v Mostyn*[267] to the effect that:

> Where an attorney instructed confidentially with a document communicates the contents of it, or suffers another to take a copy, surely the secondary evidence so obtained may be produced. Suppose the instrument were even stolen, and a correct copy taken, would it not be reasonable to admit it?

However, some measure of protection was restored by the decision in *Lord Ashburton v Pape*[268] that the admissibility in evidence of copies of privileged communications did not affect the jurisdiction of the court to protect the underlying confidence where those copies had been obtained surreptitiously. Thus, in that case an injunction was granted to restrain the defendant from using copies of privileged correspondence between the plaintiff and his solicitors that he had obtained by trick.

A number of attempts to reconcile those two decisions have been made[269] and in *Guinness Peat Properties Ltd. v Fitzroy Robinson Partnership*,[270] Slade LJ synthesised the English position as follows. The general rule is that once the other party has inspected a document protected by privilege, it is too late for the first party to correct the mistake by applying for injunctive relief. However, if the other party has either (a) procured inspection of the relevant document by fraud, or (b) on inspection realised that he has been permitted to see the docu-

---

[265] *Cf. Nederlandse Reassurantie Groep Holding NV v Bacon & Woodrow* [1995] 1 All ER 976.
[266] [1898] 1 QB 759.
[267] (1842) 10 M & W 478, 481-2.
[268] [1913] 2 Ch 469.
[269] See *Goddard v Nationwide Building Society* [1986] 3 All ER 264, [1986] 3 WLR 734; *Re Briamore Manufacturing Ltd* [1986] 3 All ER 132; *Guinness Peat Properties Ltd v Fitzroy Robinson Partnership* [1987] 2 All ER 716; *Webster v James Chapman & Co.* [1989] 3 All ER 939.
[270] [1987] 2 All ER 716.

ment only by reason of an obvious mistake,[271] the court has power to grant an injunction.[272] In such cases, the court should ordinarily grant the injunction unless it can properly be refused having regard to the general principles governing the grant of a discretionary remedy.[273]

8.051 It is submitted that the English approach is unduly complicated[274] and suffers from the problem that the availability of relief will turn to a large degree on when the party found out about the error or impropriety rather than on any matter of principle.[275] It also fails to distinguish between legal advice privilege and litigation privilege and thereby emasculates the policy considerations in this area.

Taking first legal advice privilege, it is submitted that the English approach confers insufficient protection and that the Irish courts should follow instead the approach of the New Zealand Court of Appeal in *R v Uljee*.[276] In that case, a conversation between the accused and his solicitor had been overheard by a police officer and the issue arose of the admissibility of the evidence of the officer as to what he had heard. The court declined to follow *Calcraft v Guest*,[277] preferring to approach the question on the basis of principle. Richardson J drew attention to the chilling effect which the possible disclosure would have on the relationship between client and lawyer. If confidentiality was not assured because of the possibility that an eavesdropper could give evidence of what has passed between them, this would have an inhibiting effect on the freedom of communication which is essential to the relationship between them. Therefore, it was held that privilege applied and the evidence of the officer was inadmissible.

This decision points the way forward for the Irish courts. As noted above, legal advice privilege is predicated on the advantages to the administration of justice which accrue when free communication between a client and lawyer is

---

[271] As to whether disclosure has occurred as the result of an obvious mistake, see *IBM Corp. v Phoenix International* [1995] 1 All ER 413.

[272] See *Goddard v Nationwide Building Society* [1986] 3 All ER 264; *English and American Insurance Co. Ltd v Herbert Smith & Co.* [1987] NLJR 148.

[273] *Cf. Webster v James Chapman & Co.* [1989] 3 All ER 939 where Scott J placed a gloss on these principles. He said that the court was required to exercise its discretion by balancing the legitimate interests of the plaintiff in seeking to keep the confidential information suppressed and the legitimate interests of the defendant in seeking to make use of it and, in carrying out this exercise, the manner in which the privileged document came into the possession of the other side, the issues in the action, the relevance of the document and all the other circumstances will have to be taken into account.

[274] See the exceptions laid down in *ITC Film Distributors v Video Exchange Ltd* [1982] Ch 431; *Butler v Board of Trade* [1971] Ch 680.

[275] A point noted by Tapper, "Legal Professional Privilege and Third Parties" (1972) 35 MLR 601.

[276] [1982] 1 NZLR 561.

[277] [1898] 1 QB 759.

secured. The possibility that such communications could be intercepted and used in evidence could have a chilling effect on that relationship. It is important that the client can be assured that what he communicates to his legal adviser cannot be disclosed or used against him in any circumstances even where the disclosure results from mere inadvertence. Applying the test enunciated by Finlay CJ in *Smurfit Paribas Bank Ltd v AAB Export Finance Ltd*,[278] the availability of privilege in such circumstances is necessary to advance the advantages secured by it.

This argument may seem inconsistent with that made above that privilege should be pierced where the communication will help an accused person to establish his innocence but that proposed exception is predicated upon, and subject to, the important caveat that the client has no further recognisable interest in maintaining the privilege. However, the interest of the client in the privilege will not be spent simply by the disclosure of the communication whether deliberately or inadvertently. This takes too narrow a view of privilege and betrays its origin in the law relating to discovery. What animates a client who avails of the privilege to tell all to his lawyer is not the mere fact of disclosure though that is, of course, a concern. His principal worry is that what he relates to his adviser may be used *against* him.[279] Thus, he still has a recognisable interest to assert which should be protected.

8.052 Turning to litigation privilege, as has been argued above, it essentially erects a screen around trial preparation and serves to protect third party communications or work product until a party is ready to reveal it before or during litigation. Disclosure of communications covered by litigation privilege would not have an inhibiting effect on these preparations but would, rather, give a greater incentive to maintain their confidentiality and ensure that this is not compromised by mistake or otherwise. However, the courts should not permit themselves to become a party to wrongdoing or fraud and, therefore, if it can be shown that a party has come into possession of an original or secondary evidence of a privileged communication in those circumstances, the courts should not allow such evidence to be given.

STATUS OF THE PRIVILEGE

8.053 The traditional common law view of legal professional privilege was that it was merely a rule of evidence, the application of which was tied to the

---

[278] [1990] 1 IR 469, [1990] ILRM 588.
[279] See *Holmes v Baddeley* (1844) 1 Ph 476, 480-1, 41 ER 713, 715.

curial context. However, recent decisions in England,[280] Canada,[281] Australia[282] and New Zealand,[283] have taken the view that the privilege is more than a rule of evidence and have ascribed to it a substantive content which is capable of application in pre-trial and non-curial contexts. The Canadian courts have, perhaps, gone the furthest in that regard. Dickson J, delivering the judgment of the Supreme Court of Canada in *Solosky v Canada*,[284] described the right to communicate in confidence with one's legal adviser as "a fundamental civil and legal right, founded upon the unique relationship of solicitor and client". More recently, in *Smith v Jones*,[285] Cory J stated that legal professional privilege was "an element that is both integral and extremely important to the functioning of the legal system" and "the highest privilege recognized by the courts".

In *Miley v Flood*,[286] Kelly J referred with approval to those developments and reiterated the view previously taken by him in *Duncan v Governor of Portlaoise Prison*[287] that:

> Legal professional privilege is more than a mere rule of evidence. It is a fundamental condition on which the administration of justice as a whole rests.

These comments echo those of Hamilton CJ in *Quinlivan v Governor of Portlaoise Prison*,[288] that the privilege has "always been regarded by the courts as absolutely essential and of paramount importance in the administration of justice" and Finlay CJ in *Bula Ltd v Crowley (No. 2)*,[289] who referred to "the important confidence in relation to communications between lawyers and their clients which is a fundamental part of our system of justice and is considered in all the authorities to be a major contributor to the proper administration of justice."

---

[280] See *R v Derby Magistrates' Court, ex p. B.* [1996] AC 487, 507, [1995] 4 All ER 526, 540-41; *General Mediterranean Holdings SA v Patel* [1999] 3 All ER 673.

[281] See *Smith v Jones* [1999] 1 SCR 455; *Stevens v Canada (Privy Council)* (1998) 161 DLR (4th) 85; *Descôteaux v Mierzwinski* [1982] 1 SCR 860, (1982) 141 DLR (3d) 590; *Solosky v Canada* [1980] 1 SCR 821, (1980) 105 DLR (3d) 745; *Re Director of Investigation and Research and Canada Safeway Ltd* (1972) 26 DLR (3d) 745.

[282] See *ESSO Australia Resources Ltd v Dawson* [1999] FCA 363, (1999) 162 ALR 79; *Carter v Northmore Hale Davy & Leake* (1995) 183 CLR 121; *Baker v Campbell* (1983) 153 CLR 52.

[283] *Rosenberg v Jaine* [1983] NZLR 1.

[284] (1980) 105 DLR (3d) 745, 760.

[285] [1999] 1 SCR 455, 474-5.

[286] [2001] 1 ILRM 489, 504.

[287] [1997] 1 IR 558, 575, [1997] 2 ILRM 296, 311 (quoting in both cases the statement to that effect of Lord Taylor CJ in *R v Derby Magistrates' Court, ex p. B.* [1996] AC 487, 507, [1995] 4 All ER 526, 540-41). See also *Irish Haemophilia Society Ltd v Lindsay* High Court (Kelly J) 16 May 2001 at 11.

[288] Supreme Court, 5 March 1997.

[289] [1994] 2 IR 54, 59.

8.054 These *dicta* raise the possibility that the privilege, or at least some aspects of it, may be found to have a constitutional foundation.[290] It could, for example, be argued that the right to communicate in confidence with a legal adviser is protected in the civil context by Article 40.3 as a facet of the right of access to the courts[291] and in the criminal context by the right to legal representation.[292] Alternatively, supra-legal protection may be provided by Article 6 of the European Convention on Human Rights which guarantees the right to fair trial. In *Niemietz v Germany*,[293] the European Court of Human Rights stated that "where a lawyer is involved, an encroachment on professional secrecy may have repercussions on the proper administration of justice and hence on the rights guaranteed by Article 6".[294] In addition, confidential communications passing between a lawyer and client are protected under Article 8 which guarantees the privacy of correspondence. In *Campbell v United Kingdom*,[295] the court held that it is in the public interest "that any person who wishes to consult a lawyer should be free to do so under conditions which favour the full and uninhibited discussion"[296] and, therefore, correspondence with a solicitor is privileged under Article 8. European decisions in this area will assume additional significance with the incorporation of the convention into Irish law.

WITHOUT PREJUDICE PRIVILEGE

BASIS OF THE PRIVILEGE

8.055 The privilege granted in respect of communications in furtherance of settlement, commonly referred to as without prejudice privilege, rests on two

---

[290] But see the view of Advocate-General Warner in *AM & S Europe Ltd v Commission* [1983] 1 All ER 705, 721, who pointed out that legal professional privilege was not expressly protected in the convention or in the constitution of any member state and that while it was a right that was generally recognised, he did not think that it was a fundamental human right.

[291] See *Macauley v Minister for Posts and Telegraphs* [1966] IR 345. *Cf. R v Campbell* [1999] 1 SCR 565, 601, (1999) 171 DLR (4th) 193, 224, where Binnie J declared that: "Access to justice is compromised where legal advice is unavailable".

[292] See *State (Healy) v Donoghue* [1976] IR 325.

[293] (1992) 16 EHRR 97.

[294] Previously, in *S. v Switzerland* (1992) 14 EHRR 670, it had been held that the ability to communicate in confidence with a lawyer of one's choice without those communications being intercepted was one of the basic requirements of a fair trial in a democratic society and was protected by Article 6(3)(c) of the convention which guarantees the right of a defendant to obtain legal assistance in criminal trials.

[295] (1993) 15 EHRR 137.

[296] *Ibid.* at 160.

bases, public policy and convention.[297] The primary justification for the rule is the public policy "of encouraging litigants to settle their differences rather than litigate them to a finish".[298] As Keane J explained in *Greencore Group plc v Murphy*,[299] it is in the public interest that:

> parties should be encouraged as far as possible to settle their disputes without recourse to litigation and should not be discouraged by the knowledge that anything that is said in the course of negotiations may be used in the course of proceedings.[300]

The privilege, thus, promotes the settlement of disputes by enabling parties to discuss their dispute and the relative strengths and weaknesses of their cases with complete candour, secure in the knowledge that anything said in the course of the negotiations cannot be used to their prejudice in the course of the proceedings. In the absence of such a privilege any concession made in the course of settlement negotiations or even the fact that an offer of compromise was made, would be admissible as an admission and "[i]f this were permitted, the effect would be that no attempt to compromise a dispute could ever be made".[301] Therefore, although the privilege results in the exclusion of relevant evidence, any disadvantage to the administration of justice occasioned thereby is far outweighed by the advantages flowing from the settlements that are thereby facilitated. For this reason, the courts have generally given it an expansive application[302] and in *Dixons Stores Group Ltd v Thames Television plc*,[303] Drake J noted that "the modern tendency has been to enlarge the cloak under which negotiations may be conducted without prejudice".

This public policy justification is reinforced by the convention or implied agreement that when parties embark on settlement negotiations on a without

---

[297] *Cutts v Head* [1984] Ch 290, 313-14, [1984] 1 All ER 597, 611; *Forster v Friedland* Court of Appeal, 10 November 1992 (*per* O'Neill LJ); *Unilever plc v Proctor & Gamble Co.* [2000] 1 FSR 344, 351.

[298] *Rush & Tompkins v Greater London Council* [1989] AC 1280, 1299, [1988] 3 All ER 737, 739 (*per* Lord Griffiths). See also *Ryan v Connolly* [2001] 2 ILRM 174, 181; *Greencore Group plc v Murphy* [1995] 3 IR 520, 525, [1996] 1 ILRM 210, 216; *Quinlivan v Tuohy* High Court (Barron J) 29 July 1992 at 4; *Cutts v Head* [1984] Ch 290, 306, [1984] 1 All ER 597, 605-6; *Tomlin v Standard Telephones and Cables Ltd* [1969] 3 All ER 201, 205; *I. Waxman and Sons Ltd v Texaco Canada Ltd* [1968] 1 OR 642, 656, (1968) 67 DLR (2d) 295, 309; *Field v Commissioner for Railways for New South Wales* (1957) 99 CLR 285, 291; *Cedenco Foods v State Insurance* [1996] 3 NZLR 205, 210.

[299] [1995] 3 IR 520, 525, [1996] 1 IR 210, 216.

[300] See, to the same effect, *per* Keane CJ in *Ryan v Connolly* [2001] 2 ILRM 174, 181.

[301] *Per* Romilly MR in *Jones v Foxall* (1852) 15 Beav 388, 396.

[302] In *I Waxman and Sons Ltd v Texaco Canada Ltd* [1968] OR 642, 656, (1968) 67 DLR (2d) 295, 309, Fraser J said that it was "in the public interest that it not be given a restrictive application".

[303] [1993] 1 All ER 349, 351.

prejudice basis they do so on the understanding that the contents of those discussions will not be used to the prejudice of either party.[304] The English courts have taken the view that the convention justification is separate from the public policy justification and may operate to modify or even expand its application.[305] However, it would seem that in this jurisdiction due to constitutional considerations, the contractual justification must be considered to be subsidiary to the public policy justification and could not be invoked to justify the application or extension of the privilege beyond the parameters supported by public policy.

CONDITIONS REQUIRED TO ESTABLISH PRIVILEGE

8.056 In order for a claim of privilege to succeed, the party claiming it must establish that the communication in question was made (i) in a *bona fide* attempt to settle a dispute between the parties; and (ii) with the intention that, if negotiations failed, it could not be disclosed without the consent of the parties. These two tests can be seen to be closely related to the twin rationales identified above which also influence how they are applied.[306]

(i) Bona Fide Attempt to Settle Dispute

8.057 The party seeking to assert privilege must show that at the time the communication was made, a dispute existed between the parties in respect of which legal proceedings had commenced or were contemplated[307] and the communication was made in a genuine attempt to further negotiations to settle that dispute.

The fact that a communication concerns a dispute between parties is not sufficient to confer privilege – it must be made in furtherance of the settlement of the dispute. This is clear from the decision of Costello J in *O'Flanagan v Ray-Ger Ltd.*[308] The defendant objected to the admission of a letter written by its solicitor and headed "without prejudice" which contained an admission that the defendant held disputed property in trust for the plaintiff. The learned judge heard evidence from both the plaintiff and defendant about the circumstances

---

[304] *Cutts v Head* [1984] Ch 290, 313-14, [1984] 1 All ER 597, 611; *South Shropshire District Council v Amos* [1987] 1 All ER 340, 343; *Muller v Linsley* (1994) 139 SJ LB 43.

[305] See *Hodgkinson & Corby Ltd v Wards Mobility Services Ltd* (1997) 24 FSR 178, 190. *Cf. Muller v Linsley* (1994) 139 SJ LB 43.

[306] In *Muller v Linsley* (1994) 139 SJ LB 43, Hoffmann LJ noted a trend towards a more rationale based analysis of the privilege.

[307] It is not necessary that proceedings have commenced: *Rush & Tompkins Ltd v Greater London Council* [1988] 1 All ER 549, 554 (*per* Balcombe LJ); *Warren v Gray Goose Stage Ltd* [1937] 1 WWR 465, 472.

[308] High Court (Costello J) 28 April 1983 at 14.

surrounding the genesis of the letter. He noted that the plaintiff had not threatened legal proceedings and that her main concern was to ascertain from the defendant's solicitor what the true position was about her property. He concluded that the letter was admissible because it was not an offer to settle a dispute but a statement as to the rights of the plaintiff and her husband in relation to certain property.[309]

In *O'Flanagan*, Costello J approved the statement in *Re Daintrey, ex p. Holt,*[310] that the privilege "has no application unless some person is in dispute or negotiation with another, and terms are offered for the settlement of the dispute or negotiation" and there is Commonwealth authority to the effect that privilege only applies to communications which contain terms for settlement.[311] The balance of authority, however indicates that it is not necessary for a communication to contain terms[312] and privilege extends to all communications that are part of the negotiation process including a document which merely seeks to initiate settlement discussions[313] provided that it indicates a clear willingness to negotiate.[314] Privilege will not, however, apply to a communication made not as part of but after negotiations have concluded unsuccessfully[315] unless reference is made to the contents of the previous "without prejudice" letter.[316]

8.058 Although the designation of a communication by a party as "without prejudice" is a *prima facie* indication that the communication is in furtherance of settlement negotiations,[317] those words "possess no magic properties"[318] and

---

[309] Cf. *Buckinghamshire County Council v Moran* [1990] Ch 623, [1989] 2 All ER 225; *William Allan Real Estate Co. v Robichaud* (1987) 37 BLR 286.

[310] [1893] 2 QB 116, 119 (*per* Vaughan Williams J).

[311] *Drabinsky v Maclean-Hunter Ltd* (1980) 28 OR (2d) 23, 108 DLR (3d) 391; *Lamoureux v Smit* (1982) 40 BCLR 151; *Cedenco Foods v State Insurance* [1996] 3 NZLR 205, 211.

[312] *South Shropshire District Council v Amos* [1987] 1 All ER 340, 344; *Pirie v Wyld* (1886) 11 OR 422 (privilege applies to all communications fairly made for the purpose of expressing the writer's views on the matter of litigation or dispute as well as overtures for settlement or compromise).

[313] *South Shropshire District Council v Amos* [1987] 1 All ER 340, 344; *Phillips v Rodgers* (1988) 62 Atla LR (2d) 146.

[314] In *Buckinghamshire County Council v Moran* [1990] Ch 623, 634, [1989] 2 All ER 225, 231, Slade LJ said that the public policy on which the privilege rests does not "justify giving protection to a letter which does not unequivocally indicate the writer's willingness to negotiate". In that case privilege was held not to apply to a letter marked "without prejudice" which contained an assertion of the defendant's rights rather than an indication of any willingness to negotiate.

[315] *Holland v McGill* High Court (Murphy J) 16 March 1990; *Dixons Stores Group Ltd v Thames Television plc* [1993] 1 All ER 349, 351.

[316] *Somatra Ltd v Sinclair Roche & Temperley* [2000] 2 Lloyd's Rep 673, 681.

[317] *South Shropshire District Council v Amos* [1987] 1 All ER 340, 344.

[318] *O'Flanagan v Ray-Ger Ltd* High Court (Costello J) 28 April 1983 at 13.

will not be regarded as conclusive.[319] As Hoffman LJ emphasised in *Forster v Friedland*,[320] "whatever the parties may stipulate, the rule covers only those communications which are genuinely aimed at a settlement to avoid litigation". The propensity of parties, and particularly their solicitors, to mis-characterise their communications as being without prejudice has been the subject of adverse judicial comment.[321] A court will not, therefore, hesitate to go behind that phrase and examine a communication in order to ascertain whether a communication actually owes its genesis to an attempt to compromise a dispute.[322]

Indeed, the "without prejudice" tag is sometimes used by parties or their solicitors in an attempt to cloak from disclosure and absolve of legal consequence communications which have little or nothing to do with the settlement of disputes. This has prompted the courts to emphasise that privilege will only apply to communications made in a genuine[323] or *bona fide*[324] attempt to negotiate a settlement. As Walker LJ cautioned in *Unilever plc v Proctor and Gamble Co.*,[325] "without prejudice" is not a label which can be used indiscriminately so as to immunise an act from its normal consequences where there is no genuine dispute or negotiation. A good example of the attempted misuse of the privilege can be seen in *Kooltrade Ltd v XTS Ltd*.[326] The claimants sought to restrain threats of proceedings for patent infringement made by the defendants in connection with the importation of buggies for children by the claimants into the UK. One of these threats was allegedly contained in a letter marked "without prejudice" which had been sent to Tesco Home Shopping Ltd (the claimant's principal customer) and copied to the claimants. Pumfrey J held that letter was not privileged and could be admitted as an actionable threat because there were not, at the material time, any relevant negotiations taking place between the

---

[319] *Ryan v Connolly* [2001] 2 ILRM 174, 181; *South Shropshire District Council v Amos* [1987] 1 All ER 340, 344; *Dixons Stores Group Ltd v Thames Television plc* [1993] 1 All ER 349, 351; *Forster v Friedland* Court of Appeal, 10 November 1992; *Cote v Rooney* (1982) 137 DLR (3d) 371, 374.

[320] Court of Appeal, 10 November 1992.

[321] In *Christie v Odeon (Ireland) Ltd* (1958) 92 ILTR 106, 109, Kingsmill Moore J remarked that the use of the phrase "without prejudice" had "become quite indiscriminate in legal correspondence" and that "it would be to close one's eyes to all experience of the way correspondence is conducted between solicitors to suggest that all or even the majority of letters so headed have to do with attempts at settlement of the case". Cf. *Tomlin v Standard Telephones and Cables Ltd* [1969] 3 All ER 201, 205, where Ormrod J referred to instances of letters being headed "without prejudice" "in the most absurd circumstances".

[322] *Ryan v Connolly* [2001] 2 ILRM 174, 181.

[323] *Rush & Tompkins Ltd v Greater London Council* [1989] AC 1280, 1299, [1988] 3 All ER 737, 740.

[324] *Dixons Stores Group Ltd v Thames Television plc* [1993] 1 All ER 349, 351; *I Waxman and Sons Ltd v Texaco Canada Ltd* [1968] 1 OR 642, 644, (1968) 67 DLR (2d) 295, 297.

[325] [2000] FSR 344, 356, [2001] 1 All ER 783, 795.

[326] [2001] FSR 158.

parties. Moreover, the letter had not been sent to the claimant but to Tesco and he inferred that it had nothing whatever to do with negotiation and everything to do with making the claimant's position with Tesco as difficult as possible.[327]

8.059 It is important to note, however, that this stipulation of *bona fides* is directed towards ensuring that communications actually involve an attempt to resolve the parties' differences and does not import any general requirement of good faith.[328] This is evident from *WH Smith Ltd v Colman*[329] in which the plaintiff sought a variety of reliefs against the defendant arising from his opportunistic registration and subsequent offer for sale of the domain name WHSmith.com. After proceedings had been issued, the defendant wrote a letter to the chairman of the plaintiff headed "without prejudice" which contained a plea to settle amicably. The trial judge concluded that the letter was not privileged because he was not satisfied of the *bona fides* of the defendant and did not regard the letter as a genuine offer to negotiate a settlement. However, Walker LJ in the Court of Appeal said that whatever doubts there were about the merits of the defendant's case and his *bona fides*, his letter indicated that he was negotiating for a settlement in order to avoid litigation and, therefore, the letter was privileged.

Furthermore, the courts are unconcerned with the substance of the settlement proposals or the nature of the compromise sought to be brokered. This is clear from the decision in *Forster v Friedland*,[330] where it was held that the trial judge had erred in holding that privilege did not apply because there was no real dispute as to the legal issues and the purpose of the negotiations was simply to gain time. Hoffman LJ stated that there was no basis in authority or principle for limiting the rule to negotiations aimed at resolving the legal issues between the parties. Provided that the negotiations are genuinely aimed at settlement and the avoidance of litigation, "the nature of the proposals put forward or the character of the arguments used to support them, are irrelevant".

(ii) Intention that the Communication Would not be Disclosed

8.060 Settlement negotiations are not always conducted with the intention that any offers made should not subsequently be disclosed. Sometimes, a party will for tactical or other reasons, make an offer to compromise proceedings in "open" correspondence or negotiations. If that is the case, then the contents of those negotiations will be liable to production and admission in evidence in accord-

---

[327] See also *Re Daintrey, ex p. Holt* [1893] 2 QB 116, where it was held that a written notice sent by a debtor to one of his creditors that he has suspended or was about to suspend payment of his debts was admissible to prove an act of bankruptcy upon the hearing of a bankruptcy petition even though expressed to be 'without prejudice'.

[328] *Alizadeh v Nikbin* Court of Appeal, 25 February 1993; (1993) *Times*, March 19.

[329] [2001] FSR 91.

[330] Court of Appeal, 10 November 1992.

ance with general principles.[331] Therefore, it is essential to establish whether the communication at issue was made with the express or implied intention that it would not be disclosed if negotiations failed.

The universal means of evincing such an intention is to preface or head the communication "without prejudice" and the use of this phrase will constitute *prima facie* evidence of the author's intention that privilege apply.[332] However, it is not necessary that a communication be so described if the court is satisfied from an examination of the contents of the communication and the surrounding circumstances that the parties intended that the contents of their settlement negotiations would not be disclosed.[333] A court will generally be willing to infer the existence of such an intention where it finds that a communication was in furtherance of settlement negotiations[334] but will not do so if it finds evidence that it was intended to be open.[335]

If a communication is made to the other side which is expressed to be "without prejudice", then, in general, any answer to it will also be privileged even if not expressed to be "without prejudice".[336] However, one party cannot force another to negotiate under the cloak of privilege if the other party does not wish to do so and, therefore, an answer to a "without prejudice" letter will not be privileged if it is clearly written on an "open" basis (as where it is so headed).[337] Where negotiations have commenced on a "without prejudice" basis, the courts

---

[331] *Dixons Stores Group Ltd v Thames Television plc* [1993] 1 All ER 349, 351-2.

[332] *South Shropshire District Council v Amos* [1987] 1 All ER 340, 344; *Kirk v Tompkins* (1992) 86 DLR (4th) 759, 766-67. It is not necessary that the words be used to head the document, it will suffice if they appear in the main body: *Cory v Bretton* (1830) 4 C & P 462.

[333] *Greencore Group plc v Murphy* [1995] 3 IR 520, 525, [1996] 1 ILRM 201, 216; *Rush & Tompkins Ltd v Greater London Council* [1989] AC 1280, 1299, [1988] 3 All ER 737, 740; *Rodgers v Rodgers* (1964) 114 CLR 608, 614; *R v Secord* [1992] 3 NZLR 570, 572.

[334] See *Cheddar Valley Engineering Ltd v Chaddlewood Homes Ltd* [1992] 4 All ER 942 (communications in furtherance of settlement negotiations are *prima facie* privileged even if not headed "without prejudice"); *Forster v Friedland* Court of Appeal, 10 November 1992 (fact that a communication is aimed at settlement may be strong indication of an intention that it should be "without prejudice"). *Cf. William Allan Real Estate Co. v Robichaud* (1987) 37 BLR 286 (privilege arises if the communication is made for the purpose of effecting a settlement without any need for proof of intention).

[335] *Forster v Friedland* Court of Appeal, 10 November 1992. See, for example, *Podovinikoff v Montgomery* (1984) 58 BCLR 204, 14 DLR (4th) 716, where the British Columbia Court of Appeal reached the conclusion that privilege did not apply to letters which were not marked "without prejudice" because the author was an experienced loss-adjuster and the court, therefore, inferred that the decision not to mark them "without prejudice" was conscious.

[336] *Christie v Odeon (Ireland) Ltd* (1958) 92 ILTR 106, 109; *Paddock v Forrester* (1842) 3 Man & G 903; *Dixons Stores Group Ltd v Thames Television plc* [1993] 1 All ER 349, 351.

[337] *Marron v Louth County Council* (1938) 72 ILTR 101, 103.

will generally find that any subsequent communications were intended to be privileged[338] unless they find very clear evidence of an intention to change the character of the negotiations to "open".[339] Conversely, negotiations which commenced on an "open" basis may be found to have changed to "without prejudice" basis at a later point and any communications from that point onwards will be protected.[340]

AMBIT OF THE PRIVILEGE

8.061 A fundamental question which has yet to be definitively resolved by the Irish courts is the precise ambit of the privilege and, in particular, whether it applies only to admissions as to liability made in the course of settlement negotiations or whether it applies more broadly to prevent evidence being given of anything said in the course of settlement negotiations. Support for both approaches can be found in the case law of other common law countries and the authorities on this issue are not easy to reconcile.

8.062 The narrow view can be justified by reference to the genesis of the privilege which evolved to protect parties from being prejudiced by any admission made in the course of settlement negotiations.[341] It follows from this that the application of the privilege is confined to circumstances where it is sought to admit a without prejudice communication as an admission of liability at the trial of the action.[342] This viewpoint has, perhaps, been best articulated by Hoffmann LJ in *Muller v Linsley*:[343]

> If one analyses the relationship between the without prejudice rule and the other rules of evidence, it seems to me that the privilege operates as an exception to the general rule on admissions (which can itself be regarded

---

[338] *Bord na Móna v John Sisk and Son Ltd* [1990] 1 IR 85, 88; *Denovan v Lee* (1990) 40 CPC (2d) 54.

[339] *Cheddar Valley Engineering Ltd v Chaddlewood Homes Ltd* [1992] 4 All ER 942, 945 (the test is whether the change was made in circumstances as would have brought it home to the mind of a reasonable man in the position of the recipient).

[340] *Marron v Louth County Council* (1938) 72 ILTR 101; *South Shropshire District Council v Amos* [1987] 1 All ER 340.

[341] See *Waldridge v Kennison* (1794) 1 Esp 143 and *Jones v Foxall* (1852) 15 Beav 388, 397.

[342] *Marron v Louth County Council* (1938) 72 ILTR 101, 103; *Christie v Odeon (Ireland) Ltd* (1958) 92 ILTR 106, 109; *Rush & Tompkins Ltd v Greater London Council* [1989] AC 1280, 1299-1300, [1988] 3 All ER 737, 740; *Muller v Linsley* (1994) 139 SJ LB 43; *Dora v Simper* Court of Appeal, 15 March 1999; *Field v Commissioner for Railways for New South Wales* (1957) 99 CLR 285, 291; *Cedenco Foods Ltd v State Insurance Ltd* [1996] 3 NZLR 205, 210-11.

[343] (1994) 139 SJ LB 43.

as an exception to the rule against hearsay) that the statement or conduct of a party is always admissible against him to prove any fact which is thereby expressly or impliedly asserted or admitted. The public policy aspect of the rule is not in my judgment concerned with the admissibility of statements which are relevant otherwise than as admissions, *i.e.* independently of the truth of the facts alleged to have been admitted.

According to this theory, the privilege does not, therefore, prevent the admission of without prejudice communications where the relevance of the communication lies in the fact that it was made rather than in the truth of any fact asserted therein as, for example, where it is admitted to explain delay[344] or laches[345] or to ascertain whether a party in settling a claim acted reasonably to mitigate his loss.[346] Applying similar reasoning, it has been held that the privilege does not apply to objective facts ascertained in the course of settlement negotiations,[347] communications which are relevant as facts independently of the merits of the case[348] and statements made which do not relate to the negotiations such as statements as to future conduct.[349]

8.063 Other cases have taken a broader view based on the public policy and convention rationales outlined above and have applied the privilege so as to protect a party from being prejudiced in any way by anything said in the course of settlement negotiations.[350] An early example of this approach can be seen in

---

[344] *Marron v Louth County Council* (1938) 72 ILTR 101, 103; *Family Housing Association (Manchester) Ltd v Michael Hyde and Partners* [1993] 1 WLR 354, 363; *Jones v Foxall* (1852) 15 Beav 388, 397; *Schetky v Cochrane* (1917) 24 BCR 496; *Cedenco Foods v State Insurance* [1996] 3 NZLR 205, 210-11.
[345] *Walker v Wilsher* (1889) 23 QBD 335, 338.
[346] *Muller v Linsley* (1994) 139 SJ LB 43.
[347] *Field v Commissioner for Railways for New South Wales* (1957) 99 CLR 285, 291.
[348] In *Rush & Tompkins Ltd v Greater London Council* [1989] AC 1280, 1300, [1988] 3 All ER 737, 740, Lord Griffiths explained the "exceptional" case of *Waldridge v Kennison* (1794) 1 Esp 143 (in which without prejudice communications were admitted as proof of handwriting) as authority for the proposition that the admission of an "independent fact" in no way connected with the merits of the case is admissible even if made in the course of negotiations for a settlement. This holding was applied in *McDowell v Hirschfield Lipson & Rumney* [1992] 2 FLR 126, 132 where without prejudice correspondence was admitted on the issue of whether severance of a joint tenancy had taken place. See also *Tenstat Pty Ltd v Permanent Trustee Australia Ltd* (1992) 28 NSWLR 625 (without prejudice communications admitted to show notice of the exercise of an option).
[349] *Greencore Group plc v Murphy* [1995] 3 IR 520, 526, [1996] 1 ILRM 210, 217; *Holland v McGill*, High Court (Murphy J) 16 March 1990 at 8.
[350] See *Walker v Wilsher* (1889) 23 QBD 335, 337; *Simaan General Contracting Co. v Pilkington Glass Ltd* [1987] 1 All ER 345, 348; *Unilver plc v Proctor & Gamble* [2000] FSR 344, [2001] 1 All ER 783. But *cf. Cutts v Head* [1984] Ch 290, 306, [1984] 1 All ER 597, 605-6 where Oliver LJ took the view that the public policy

Walker v Wilsher[351] where Lindley LJ said that the words "without prejudice" meant "without prejudice to the position of the writer of the letter if the terms he proposes are not accepted". It was held that without prejudice communications could not be taken into consideration on the issue of costs and Bowen LJ justified this conclusion by reference to the justifications for the rule:

> In my opinion it would be a bad thing and lead to serious consequences if the courts allowed the action of litigants, on letters written to them without prejudice, to be given in evidence against them or to be used as material for depriving them of costs. It is most important that the door should not be shut against compromises, as would certainly be the case if letters written without prejudice and suggesting methods of compromise were liable to be read when a question of costs arose. The agreement that the letter is without prejudice ought, I think, to be carried out in its full integrity.[352]

The broader view has recently been endorsed by the English Court of Appeal in *Unilever plc v Proctor & Gamble*.[353] The claimant instituted proceedings seeking a declaration of non-infringement of the defendant's patent and sought to admit evidence of a claim of right and threat to bring enforcement proceedings made by the defendant during a without prejudice meeting between the parties. The defendant applied to strike out the proceedings as an abuse of process on the basis that the statement in question was privileged but the claimant, relying on the old decision of *Kurtz & Co. v Spence and Sons*,[354] argued that without prejudice privilege was confined in its application to admissions and did not extend to statements of the type at issue. Walker LJ, who delivered the leading

---

justification "essentially rests on the desirability of preventing statements or offers made in the course of negotiations for settlement being brought before the court of trial as admissions on the question of liability".

[351] (1889) 23 QBD 335.

[352] *Ibid.* at 339. But see *Cutts v Head* [1984] Ch 290, 306, [1984] 1 All ER 597, 605, where Oliver LJ propounded the narrower view that the privilege is confined to admissions of liability only and acknowledged that the decision in *Walker v Wilsher* could not be explained by this theory because at the point where the issue of costs came to be determined, there were no further issues of fact to be determined on which admissions could be relevant. He went on to say that the decision could not be said to rest on public policy because, contrary to the view of Bowen LJ, it would not encourage settlements: "As a practical matter, a consciousness of a risk as to costs if reasonable offers are refused can only encourage settlement, whilst, on the other hand, it is hard to imagine anything more calculated to encourage obstinacy and unreasonableness than the comfortable knowledge that a litigant can refuse with impunity whatever may be offered to him even if it is as much as or more than everything to which he is entitled in the action". Therefore, he held that the decision was grounded on the conventional rationale for the privilege.

[353] [2000] FSR 344, [2001] 1 All ER 783.

[354] (1888) 5 RPC 161.

judgment in the Court of Appeal, stated that the privilege "has a wide and compelling effect"[355] and took the view that:

> One party's advocate should not be able to subject the other party to speculative cross-examination on matters disclosed or discussed in without prejudice negotiations simply because those matters do not amount to admissions.[356]

Turning to the issue before the court, he refused to follow the decision in *Kurtz* and, instead, advocated a broader approach in line with the more modern authorities:

> Whatever difficulties there are in a complete reconciliation of [the modern] cases, they make clear that the without prejudice rule is founded partly in public policy and partly in the agreement of the parties. They show that the protection of admissions against interest is the most important practical effect of the rule. But to dissect out identifiable admissions and withhold protection from the rest of without prejudice communications (except for special reason) would not only create huge practical difficulties but would be contrary to the underlying objection of giving protection to the parties, in the words of Lord Griffiths in *Rush & Tompkins Ltd v Greater London Council*:[357] "to speak freely about all issues in the litigation both factual and legal when seeking compromise and, for the purpose of establishing a basis of compromise, admitting certain facts." Parties cannot speak freely at a without prejudice meeting if they must constantly monitor every sentence, with lawyers or patent agents sitting at their shoulders as minders.[358]

He, therefore, concluded that the trial judge had been right to conclude that it was an abuse of process for the plaintiff to be allowed to plead anything that was said at the meeting either as a threat or as a claim of right.

8.064 It is submitted that, ultimately, the question is one of policy and the parameters of the privilege should be dictated by the balance of public interest. In general, it is submitted that the balance of public interest will favour giving an expansive interpretation to the privilege. The privilege achieves its objective of promoting settlements by guaranteeing non-disclosure of the contents of the negotiations. This guarantee fosters the candour which is critical to the settlement process and which is undermined by disclosure. Thus, the privilege should

---

[355] [2000] FSR 344, 352, [2001] 1 All ER 783, 791.
[356] *Ibid.* at 354, 793.
[357] [1989] AC 1280, 1300, [1988] 3 All ER 737, 740.
[358] [2000] FSR 344, 357, [2001] 1 All ER 783, 796.

be applied to exclude evidence of without prejudice negotiations except where it can be clearly shown that greater damage to the interests of justice would be effected by non-admission than by disclosure.

It would seem as if the recent decision of the Supreme Court in *Ryan v Connolly*[359] is explicable on this basis. The plaintiff instituted proceedings seeking damages for personal injury against the defendant more than three years after the date of the accident in question but argued that the defendant was estopped from relying on the provisions of the Statute of Limitations 1957 as amended. In order to establish this plea, the plaintiff sought to rely on statements made by the defendant in "without prejudice" correspondence exchanged between the parties which, it was argued, induced him to refrain from issuing proceedings within time. Keane CJ, delivering the judgment of the Supreme Court, emphasised the importance of without prejudice privilege and the public interest underpinning it but went on to say that:

> The rule, however, although firmly based on considerations of public policy, should not be applied in so inflexible a manner as to produce injustice. Thus, where a party invites the court to look at "without prejudice" correspondence, not for the purpose of holding his opponent to admissions made in the course of negotiations, but simply in order to demonstrate why a particular course had been taken, the public policy considerations may not be relevant. It would be unthinkable that the attachment of the "without prejudice" label to a letter which expressly and unequivocally stated that no point under the Statute of Limitations would be taken if the initiation of proceedings was deferred pending negotiations, would oblige a court to decide, if the issue arose, that no action of the defendant had induced the plaintiff to refrain from issuing proceedings.[360]

The Chief Justice, therefore, concluded that the court was entitled to look at the "without prejudice" correspondence for the purpose of determining whether the defendants were estopped from maintaining their plea that the proceedings were statute barred and, having done so, he was satisfied that they were not so precluded.[361]

---

[359] [2001] 2 ILRM 174.

[360] *Ibid* at 181.

[361] See also *Family Housing Association (Manchester) Ltd v Michael Hyde and Partners* [1993] 1 WLR 354, 362-63 where it was held that without prejudice correspondence may be opened on an application to dismiss proceedings for want of prosecution.

                                                      Civil Procedure

EFFECT OF THE PRIVILEGE

8.065 The privilege is the joint privilege of the parties to the settlement negotiations[362] and, if negotiations fail, a privileged communication may only be disclosed to the court with the consent of each of the parties.[363] However, if negotiations succeed the reason for non-disclosure ceases and the fact of the compromise is admissible.[364] Further, "without prejudice" communications are admissible if a question arises as to whether they have resulted in agreement,[365] whether a settlement document reflects what was actually agreed between the parties,[366] or whether they give rise to an estoppel.[367]

The privilege may, of course, be expressly waived by the parties but, in addition, a party may, by his conduct, impliedly waive privilege. Thus, if a party deploys privileged material in support of its case on the merits of the action whether at the trial or on any interlocutory application, the other party will also be entitled to refer to the contents of those without prejudice communications to advance its case.[368]

In general, without prejudice communications will remain inadmissible in any subsequent litigation connected with the same subject matter, whether between the same or different parties.[369] This is because it would discourage settlements if a party believed that admissions made in settlement negotiations in other proceedings could be used against him in other, perhaps, more important

---

[362] *Cutts v Head* [1984] Ch 290, 314, [1984] 1 All ER 597, 611 (*per* Fox LJ) (the expression "without prejudice" "must be read as creating a situation of mutuality which enables both sides to take advantage of the 'without prejudice' protection"). Protection also extends to the parties' solicitors (*La Roche v Armstrong* [1922] 1 KB 485, 489 (*per* Lush J).

[363] *Marron v Louth County Council* (1938) 72 ILTR 101, 103; *Dixons Stores Group Ltd v Thames Televisions plc* [1993] 1 All ER 349, 351; *Walker v Wilsher* (1889) 23 QBD 335, 339.

[364] *Quinlivan v Tuohy* High Court (Barron J) 29 July 1992.

[365] *Tomlin v Standard Telephones and Cables Ltd* [1969] 3 All ER 201, 203; *Walker v Wilsher* (1889) 23 QBD 335, 337; *Pearlman v National Life Assurance Co. of Canada* (1917) 39 OLR 141, 142; *Butler v Countrywide Finance Ltd* (1992) 5 PRNZ 447. *Cf. Hunnisett v Owens* High Court (Denham J) 15 May 1992, where without prejudice correspondence was opened where a dispute arose as to whether the plaintiff's claim had been settled as a result of negotiations between the parties.

[366] *Allison v KPMG* (1994) 8 PRNZ 128. *Cf. Mespil Ltd v Capaldi* [1986] ILRM 373 where evidence of without prejudice communications was given where there was a disagreement as to what had actually been agreed.

[367] *Hodgkinson & Corby Ltd v Wards Mobility Services Ltd* [1997] FSR 178, 190-1.

[368] *Somatra Ltd v Sinclair Roche & Temperley* [2000] 2 Lloyd's Rep 673.

[369] *Greencore Group plc v Murphy* [1995] 3 IR 520, 525, [1996] 1 ILRM 210, 216; *Bord na Móna v John Sisk and Son Ltd* [1990] 1 IR 85, 88-89; *Rush & Tompkins Ltd v Greater London Council* [1989] AC 1280, 1301, [1988] 3 All ER 737, 741; *David J Instance Ltd v Denny Bros Printing Ltd* [2000] FSR 869, 879-80; *I Waxman & Sons Ltd v Texaco Canada Ltd* (1968) 67 DLR (2d) 295, 309.

proceedings.[370] In *Rush & Tompkins Ltd v Greater London Council*,[371] it was held that public policy also required that without prejudice communications should be privileged from production as against persons not involved in the settlement negotiations including other parties to the litigation. Lord Griffiths adverted to the possibility of one party taking up an unreasonably intransigent attitude and opined that it would "place a serious fetter on negotiations between other parties if they knew that everything that passed between them would ultimately have to be revealed to one obdurate litigant".[372] This decision was distinguished in *Gnitrow Ltd v Cape plc*[373] where the defendant in an action for indemnity or contribution brought against it by the plaintiff sought disclosure of the terms of a without prejudice agreement reached with another potential defendant. It was held by Court of Appeal that privilege did not attach to the agreement because the mischief identified by Lord Griffiths did not exist. However, Pill LJ confined his conclusion to the situation where a claimant has settled for a fixed sum a specific claim against him and seeks only an indemnity or contribution with respect to the sum paid by him. He acknowledged that the circumstances would be different, for example, if a claimant in an action for damages for personal injuries were to settle with one of two defendants. It could be a severe disincentive to negotiations generally if, by declining to negotiate, a party could routinely claim the advantage of knowing what other parties have agreed before condescending to negotiate for himself.

PIERCING PRIVILEGE

8.066 Apart from the instances, discussed in the foregoing section, where the courts have found the privilege not to apply, there are other exceptional circumstances where the courts will pierce the veil of privilege in the interests of justice.[374] As we have seen, the privilege is founded on public policy and, therefore, cannot be used in a way or to further ends which are contrary to public policy. Thus, parties will not be permitted to use privilege as a cloak for illegality or impropriety as where threats are made in the course of settlement negotiations. For example, in *Greenwood v Fitts*,[375] it was held that privilege did not apply in circumstances where the defendant told the plaintiffs in the course of without prejudice negotiations that unless they withdrew their claim for fraudulent misrepresentation he would give perjured evidence and bribe other witnesses to

---

[370] *Rush & Tompkins Ltd v Greater London Council* [1989] AC 1280, 1301, [1988] 3 All ER 737, 741.
[371] [1989] AC 1280, [1988] 3 All ER 737.
[372] *Ibid.* at 1305, 744
[373] [2000] 3 All ER 763.
[374] *Rush & Tompkins Ltd v Greater London Council* [1989] AC 1280, 1300, [1988] 3 All ER 737, 740.
[375] (1961) 29 DLR (2d) 260.

perjure themselves, and further, that if they nevertheless succeeded, he would leave the jurisdiction rather than pay damages. Shepherd JA said that the privilege "was never intended to give protection to this sort of thing".[376] Neither will parties be permitted to assert privilege where to do so would result in the court being deceived or misled.[377]

8.067 The scope of this exception has been considered in a series of cases involving the surreptitious recording of settlement meetings by one of the participants, the transcripts of which were later sought to be admitted on the basis that they disclosed impropriety on the part of the other party. In the first of these, *Hawick Jersey Ltd v Caplan*,[378] an analogy was drawn with the crime/fraud exception to legal professional privilege and the transcripts were admitted because they contained *prima facie* evidence that the transaction the subject matter of the proceedings had not taken place as alleged and that the plaintiffs were bringing the proceedings in order to put pressure on the defendants to settle other proceedings. Subsequently, in *Forster v Friedland*,[379] Hoffmann LJ in the Court of Appeal rejected as dangerous the analogies sought to be drawn with the crime/fraud exception to legal professional privilege. He said that: "If there is any analogy between the without prejudice rule and legal professional privilege, it is with advice as to the conduct of the litigation rather than advice as to a transaction which becomes the subject matter of litigation." He stressed the high threshold to be met before privilege could be pierced:

> I accept that a party, whether plaintiff or defendant, cannot use the without prejudice rule as a cloak for blackmail ... but the value of the without prejudice rule would be seriously impaired if its protection could be removed by anything less than unambiguous impropriety. The rule is designed to encourage parties to express themselves freely and without inhibition. I think it is quite wrong for tape recorded words of a layman, who has used colourful or even exaggerated language, to be picked over in order to support an argument that he intends to raise defences which he does not really believe to be true.

On the facts, he was satisfied that there had not been any blackmail. The plain-

---

[376] *Ibid.* at 269. See also *Underwood v Cox* (1912) 26 OLR 303, [1912] 4 DLR 66 and *Dora v Simper* Court of Appeal, 15 March 1999 (statements of defendants that they would transfer their assets so as to avoid the effect of any judgment obtained held to be capable of establishing the unambiguous impropriety required to set aside privilege).

[377] *McFadden v Snow* (1951) 69 WN (NSW) 8, 10; *Pitts v Adney* [1961] NSWR 535, 539; *JA McBeath Nominees Pty Ltd v Jenkins Development Corporation Pty Ltd* [1992] 2 Qd R 121.

[378] Queen's Bench Division, 26 February 1988, (1988) *Times*, March 11.

[379] Court of Appeal, 10 November 1992.

tiff argued that the tapes disclosed that the first defendant was threatening to advance what he knew to be a sham defence, namely, that there had been no agreement. However, the learned judge took the view that the tapes merely amounted to a restatement by the first defendant of his position that there had been no legally binding agreement.

8.068 In *Alizadeh v Nikbin*,[380] the test of "unambiguous impropriety" was applied and the claim of privilege was upheld because although the transcripts disclosed evidence of impropriety, that evidence was not unambiguous. Brown LJ explained why a high threshold was desirable in cases of this kind:

> There are in my judgment powerful policy reasons for admitting in evidence as exceptions to the without prejudice rule only the very clearest of cases. Unless this highly beneficial rule is most scrupulously and jealously protected, it will all too readily become eroded. Not least requiring of rigorous scrutiny will be claims for admissibility of evidence advanced by those (such as the first defendant here) who have procured their evidence by clandestine methods and who are likely to have participated in discussions with half a mind at least to their litigious rather than their settlement advantages. That distorted approach to negotiation to my mind is itself to be discouraged, militating, as inevitably it must, against the prospects of successful settlement.

The unambiguous impropriety test has been considered in a number of recent decisions which demonstrate its stringency. In *WH Smith Ltd v Colman*,[381] the Court of Appeal held that it did not apply on the facts with Walker LJ emphasising that the privilege "is not to be set aside simply because a party making a without prejudice communications appears to be putting forward an implausible or inconsistent case or to be facing an uphill struggle if the litigation continues." Neither was the test satisfied in *Kooltrade Ltd v XTS Ltd*,[382] where Pumfrey J took the view that a threat of infringement proceedings in circumstances where the person did not have a patent or design right was not "so grave and unambiguous an impropriety as would justify invasion of the without prejudice privilege if otherwise the privilege were available."

CALDERBANK LETTER

8.069 As noted above, without prejudice communications are inadmissible on

---

[380] Court of Appeal, 25 February 1993, (1993) *Times,* March 19.
[381] Court of Appeal, 20 March 2000.
[382] [2001] FSR 158, 164.

the issue of costs[383] but in *Calderbank v Calderbank*,[384] Scarman LJ suggested that a letter could be written on a without prejudice basis but with a reservation on the part of the writer of the right to refer to it on the issue of costs. This suggestion was made in the context of and confined to matrimonial proceedings relating to finances in order to overcome the disadvantages accruing from the lack of a lodgment procedure but was quickly taken up by practitioners who started to employ and rely on "Calderbank" letters in other contexts. In *Cutts v Head*,[385] the Court of Appeal endorsed the use of such letters in all cases where the subject matter is something more than a simple money claim in respect of which a payment into court would be the appropriate way of proceeding. The court took the view that a "Calderbank" letter would promote the settlement of actions because of the parties' consciousness of a potential costs penalty if a reasonable offer was refused.[386] So far as the conventional rationale for the privilege was concerned, this had been modified by the widespread practice of the courts to give effect to the reservation contained in the letter.

PUBLIC INTEREST PRIVILEGE

INTRODUCTION

8.070 While, as explained above, all privileges are ultimately founded on the public interest, this grounding is much more evident in the case of public interest privilege because, as will be seen below, a claim of public interest privilege will only be upheld after an individualised adjudication and finding that the balance of public interest favours the claim.

Before proceeding to examine the cases in this area, some explanation should be given of the nomenclature used. The expression "public interest privilege" has gained judicial currency[387] at the expense of the older phrase, "executive privilege"[388] reflecting the fact that the privilege is not confined in its application to the executive functions of the State but is available whenever the balance of public interest favours non-disclosure. In England, the term "public

---

[383] *Walker v Wilsher* (1889) 23 QBD 335, 339.
[384] [1976] Fam 93, [1975] 3 All ER 333.
[385] [1984] Ch 290, [1984] 1 All ER 597.
[386] Oliver LJ said that (*ibid.* at 306, 605): "As a practical matter, a consciousness of a risk as to costs if reasonable offers are refused can only encourage settlement, whilst, on the other hand, it is hard to imagine anything more calculated to encourage obstinacy and unreasonableness than the comfortable knowledge that a litigant can refuse with impunity whatever may be offered to him even if it is as much as or more than everything to which he is entitled in the action."
[387] See, for example, *McDonald v RTÉ* [2001] 2 ILRM 1; *Hughes v Commissioner of An Garda Síochána* High Court (Laffoy J), *ex tempore*, 20 January 1998.
[388] In *Murphy v Dublin Corporation* [1972] IR 215, 239, Walsh J said that he used it "for want of a better term".

interest immunity" is now favoured,[389] principally on the basis that the term "privilege" is only applicable to a claim which can be waived and public interest immunity, where it is found to apply, cannot be waived by the executive or any person.[390] However, as discussed below, the Irish courts have rejected the proposition that a claim of non-disclosure based on the public interest cannot be waived.[391] Thus, it is submitted that the term "public interest privilege" more accurately reflects the nature of the claim in this jurisdiction.[392]

DEVELOPMENT OF THE PRIVILEGE

8.071 At common law, the Crown enjoyed a prerogative, known as "Crown privilege" to refuse to produce documents or even to disclose their existence. If a minister, or a senior civil servant on his behalf certified, or swore an affidavit to the effect that disclosure of the documents sought would be prejudicial to the public interest, that was conclusive of the matter and a court could not examine the documents or otherwise go behind that certificate.[393]

That privilege was carried over into the law of the Irish Free State in *Leen v President of the Executive Council*,[394] where it was placed on the more republican footing of the public interest. Meredith J rejected the contention that the privilege could only be claimed by the Crown stating:

> I can see nothing ... in the authorities on this privilege in respect of discovery to suggest that the rule of law which has always been in force, and which has to be administered as heretofore under the Constitution of the Irish Free State, is dependent upon the magic of any particular nomencla-

---

[389] See, for example, *R v Whittle* [1997] 1 Cr App R 166; *Lonrho Plc v Fayed (No. 4)* [1994] QB 775, [1994] 1 All ER 870; *Makanjuola v Commissioner of Police of the Metropolis* [1992] 3 All ER 617. In *Rogers v Secretary of State for the Homes Department* [1973] AC 388, 400, [1972] 2 All ER 1057, 1060, Lord Reid criticised the older term "Crown privilege": "I think that the expression is wrong and may be misleading. There is no question of any privilege in the ordinary sense of the word. The real question is whether the public interest requires that the letter shall not be produced and whether that public interest is so strong as to override the ordinary right and interest of a litigant that he shall be able to lay before a court of justice all relevant evidence."

[390] *Rogers v Secretary of State for the Home Department* [1973] AC 388, 407, [1972] 2 All ER 1057, 1066 (*per* Lord Simon); *Air Canada v Secretary of State for Trade* [1983] 2 AC 394, 436, [1983] 1 All ER 910, 917.

[391] *McDonald v RTÉ* [2001] 2 ILRM 1; *Hannigan v Director of Public Prosecutions* [2002] 1 ILRM 48.

[392] But *cf. Murphy v Dublin Corporation* [1972] IR 215, 224, where Kenny J said that the word "privilege" was inaccurate to describe the claim being made.

[393] See *Duncan v Cammell Laird & Co. Ltd* [1942] AC 624, [1942] 1 All ER 587.

[394] [1926] IR 456.

ture. On the contrary, it appears to me to be broadbased upon the public interest ... The principle has roots in the general conception of State interests and the functions of Courts of Justice, which make it independent of the particular type of constitution under which the body of law which recognises that principle is administered.[395]

This privilege retained the incidents of the old and, therefore, once a claim of privilege was made in the appropriate form, it had to be accepted by the courts without any further inquiry.[396] However, it became evident over the course of the next half-century that the cloak of privilege was being abused to the extent that some of the claims made were judicially criticised as "grotesque" and "evidence not of any care for the public interest but of a remarkable elasticity of conscience".[397] It was not surprising, therefore, that in the landmark decision of *Murphy v Dublin Corporation*[398] the Supreme Court undertook a radical overhaul of this area.

8.072 In *Murphy* the plaintiff sought production of the report of an inspector relating to a compulsory purchase order which was resisted by the Minister for Local Government on the grounds that its production would be contrary to public policy and the public interest. Walsh J, with whom the other members of the court concurred, rejected the proposition that it was for the executive to decide whether documents were to be produced. He pointed out that:

> Under the Constitution the administration of justice is committed solely to the judiciary in the exercise of their powers in the courts set up under the Constitution. Power to compel the attendance of witnesses and the production of evidence is an inherent part of the judicial power of government of the State and is the ultimate safeguard of justice in the State. The proper exercise of the functions of the three powers of government set up under the Constitution, namely, the legislative, the executive and the judicial is in the public interest. There may be occasions when the different aspects of the public interest "pull in contrary directions".... If the conflict arises during the exercise of the judicial power then, in my view, it is the judicial power which will decide which public interest shall prevail.[399]

---

[395] *Ibid.* at 463.
[396] *Leen v President of the Executive Council* [1926] IR 456; *Smith v Commissioners of Public Works* [1936] Ir Jur Rep 67; *Malone v O'Hanlon* [1938] Ir Jur Rep 8; *Kenny v Minister for Defence* [1942] Ir Jur Rep 81; *O'Leary v Minister for Industry and Commerce* [1966] IR 676.
[397] *Per* Kenny J in *Murphy v Dublin Corporation* [1972] IR 215, 226.
[398] [1972] IR 215.
[399] *Ibid.* at 233.

Applying those principles to the claim of "executive privilege" made by the minister, he said:

> Where documents come into existence in the course of carrying out of the executive powers of the State, their production may be adverse to the public interest in one sphere of government in particular circumstances. On the other hand, their non-production may be adverse to the public interest in the administration of justice. As such documents may be any-where in the range from the trivial to the vitally important, somebody or some authority must decide which course is calculated to do the least in-jury to the public interest, namely, the production of the document or the possibility of the denial of right in the administration of justice. It is self evident that this is a matter which falls into the sphere of the judicial power for determination. In a particular case the court may be able to determine this matter having regard to the evidence available on the sub-ject and without examining the document in question, but in other cases it may be necessary as the court may think, to produce the document to the court itself for the purpose of inspecting it and making the decision having regard to the conflicting claims made with reference to the document.[400]

He made it clear that the court would not always decide that the interest of the litigant should prevail. However, once the court was satisfied that the document is relevant, the burden of satisfying the court that it should not be produced lies upon the party making the claim and a particularised objection would have to be made in respect of each document. Thus, he rejected the idea that there were any documents which could be withheld from production on the grounds that they belonged to a certain class of documents:

> Having regard to the nature of the powers of the courts in these matters, it seems clear to me that there can be no documents which may be withheld from production simply because they belong to a particular class of docu-ments. Each document must be decided upon having regard to the consid-erations which apply to that particular document and its contents. To grant or withhold the production of a document simply by reason of the class to which it belongs would be to regard all documents as being of equal im-portance notwithstanding that they may not be.[401]

---

[400] *Ibid.* at 234-35.

[401] *Ibid.* at 235. A striking example of this can be seen in *Ambiorix v Minister for the Environment (No. 1)* [1992] 1 IR 277, [1992] ILRM 209 where a class claim in respect of a certain category of documents was rejected by the trial judge who proceeded to examine the documents and concluded that the public interest involved in their pro-duction clearly outweighed any harm to the executive that might arise from disclosing them. On appeal, Finlay CJ noted (at 285, 214) that it had not been suggested "that

8.073 An attempt to partially overrule *Murphy* was rejected by the Supreme Court in *Ambiorix Ltd v Minister for the Environment (No. 1)*.[402] The defendants argued that documents emanating from a senior level of the Civil Service relating to the formulation of policy or proposals for legislation and intended for the ultimate consideration of ministers should be absolutely immune from production and inspection.[403] However, the Supreme Court was unanimous in rejecting this contention which Finlay CJ said suffered from the fundamental flaw of ignoring the constitutional origin of the decision in *Murphy*.[404] McCarthy J took a similar view, describing discovery as a constitutionally guaranteed fair procedure, and said that to depart from the decision in *Murphy* would "lessen or impair judicial sovereignty in the administration of justice".[405] The Chief Justice also pointed out the practical difficulties for plaintiffs which would flow from accepting the submission of the defendants. It would, for example, prevent plaintiffs from challenging a decision made by the government or a minister on the grounds that it was made without taking relevant material into account or in reliance on irrelevant material.[406]

In the course of his judgment, Finlay CJ codified the principles that had been laid down in *Murphy* as follows:[407]

1. Under the Constitution the administration of justice is committed solely to the judiciary by the exercise of their powers in the courts set up under the Constitution.

2. Power to compel the production of evidence (which, of course, includes a power to compel the production of documents) is an inherent part of the judicial power and is part of the ultimate safeguard of justice in the State.

3. Where a conflict arises during the exercise of the judicial power between the aspect of public interest involved in the confidentiality or exemption from documents pertaining to the exercise of the executive powers of the State, it is the judicial power which will decide which public interest shall prevail.

---

consideration of the individual documents as distinct from a consideration of the nature and character of the documents involved could lead to any other conclusion".

[402] [1992] 1 IR 277, [1992] ILRM 209.

[403] In *Geraghty v Minister for Local Government* [1975] IR 300, a class claim in respect of communications between the minister or his parliamentary secretary and civil servants had been rejected on the basis of the decision in *Murphy*.

[404] [1972] IR 215.

[405] [1992] 1 IR 277, 289, [1992] ILRM 209, 217.

[406] Citing the judgment of McCarthy J in *O'Keeffe v An Bord Pleanála* [1993] 1 IR 39, [1992] ILRM 237, who pointed out that capacity of an individual to challenge the decision of an administrative body depended on his right to avail of the procedures of interrogatories and discovery.

[407] [1992] 1 IR 277, 283, [1992] ILRM 209, 213. He stressed that these principles were re-stated "by way of summary, but not by way of expansion or qualification".

4.   The duty of the judicial power to make that decision does not mean that there is any priority or preference for the production of evidence over other public interests, such as the security of the State or the efficient discharge of the functions of the executive organ of the government.

5.   It is for the judicial power to choose the evidence upon which it might act in any individual case in order to reach that decision.

He went on to say that these principles led to a number of practical conclusions where a claim of public interest privilege was made:

(a)   The executive cannot prevent the judicial power from examining documents which are relevant to an issue in a civil trial for the purpose of deciding whether they must be produced.

(b)   There is no obligation on the judicial power to examine any particular document before deciding that it is exempt from production, and it can and will in many instances uphold a claim of privilege in respect of a document merely on the basis of a description of its nature and contents which it (the judicial power) accepts.

(c)   There cannot, accordingly, be a generally applicable class or category of documents exempted from production by reason of the rank in the public service of the person creating them, or of the position of the individual or body intended to use them.

THE BALANCING TEST

8.074 The effect of the decisions in *Murphy* and *Ambiorix* has been to establish a balancing test. In each case where a claim of public interest privilege is made, the court is required to balance the public interest in the proper administration of justice against the public interest put forward for non-disclosure in order to decide which is the superior public interest in the circumstances of the case.[408] It was emphasised in both decisions that the courts would not approach the application of this test with any preconceived notion of where the balance should lie and would not automatically favour the administration of justice over the competing public interest. However, as will be evident from the decisions examined below, the rejection of class claims and the requirement that a particularised reason be advanced for the non-disclosure of each individual document has, in practical terms, weighted the test in favour of disclosure.

---

[408] *Skeffington v Rooney* [1997] 1 IR 22, 32, [1997] 2 ILRM 56, 66; *Burke v Central Independent Television plc* [1994] 2 IR 61, 79, [1994] 2 ILRM 161, 176; *Breathnach v Ireland (No. 3)* [1993] 2 IR 458, 469, [1992] ILRM 755, 763; *Incorporated Law Society v Minister for Justice* [1987] ILRM 42, 44; *Hunt v Roscommon VEC* High Court (McWilliam J) 1 March 1981 at 3.

The Public Interest in the Proper Administration of Justice

8.075 The public interest in the proper administration of justice requires that a court should have all relevant evidence before it because this will help to ensure that justice is done and that the risk of adjudicative error is minimised. This public interest is closely allied to the interests of an individual litigant who avails of his constitutionally protected right of access to the courts[409] in order to vindicate his constitutional and legal rights.[410] In order for this right of access to be effective, a litigant must be afforded access to any documentation that helps to support his case or undermine that of his opponent. The withholding of any relevant material inevitably impairs his ability to make out a case.[411]

It follows from the foregoing that the most important indicator of the weight of the public interest in the proper administration of justice is the relevance of the information sought to the issues in the case and this has been used as a proxy in many cases for an assessment of this public interest. For example, in *Breathnach v Ireland (No. 3)*,[412] Keane J, having referred to the principles laid down in *Compagnie Financière et Commerciale du Pacifique v Peruvian Guano Co.*,[413] stated that in considering the public interest in the administration of justice, "it is necessary to determine to what extent, if any, the relevant documents may advance the plaintiff's case or damage the defendant's case or fairly lead to an enquiry which may have either of those consequences".[414] Thus, a court is likely to hold that the public interest in the administration of justice will trump the competing public interest where the documents sought are crucial or very relevant to the litigant's case.[415] Conversely, if the documents sought would be of some relevance but are not of vital importance, the balance may well lie in favour of non-disclosure.[416] So, for example, in *Hughes v Commissioner of An*

---

[409] See *Macauley v Minister for Posts and Telegraphs* [1966] IR 345.

[410] In *Gormley v Ireland* [1993] 2 IR 75, 78, Murphy J said that there had to be weighed against the grounds put forward for non-disclosure, "the conflicting interest of the litigant to have access to such documents as may be necessary to enable him to prosecute fairly and properly his actions in the courts set up under the Constitution".

[411] *Cf.* the comments of Finlay CJ in *Ambiorix Ltd v Minister for the Environment (No. 1)* [1992] 1 IR 277, 285, [1992] ILRM 209, 214.

[412] [1993] 2 IR 458, [1992] ILRM 755.

[413] (1882) 11 QBD 55, 63.

[414] [1993] 2 IR 458, 469, [1992] ILRM 755, 763. See to the same effect *Hughes v Commissioner of An Garda Síochána* High Court (Laffoy J) *ex tempore*, 20 January 1998; *Logue v Redmond* [1999] 2 ILRM 498, 507; *Corbett v DPP* [1999] 2 IR 179, 189.

[415] See *Hughes v Commissioner of An Garda Síochána* High Court (Laffoy J) *ex tempore*, 20 January 1998; *Logue v Redmond* [1999] 2 ILRM 498, 508. *Cf. Ahern v Minister for Industry and Commerce* High Court (Lardner J) 11 March 1988, where Lardner J refused to uphold a claim of privilege in circumstances where he was satisfied that the documents in question would be important evidence in the case.

[416] See *Hughes v Commissioner of An Garda Síochána* High Court (Laffoy J) *ex tempore*, 20 January 1998 and *Gormley v Ireland* [1993] 2 IR 75, 80, where Murphy J refused to order the disclosure of "highly confidential material, the disclosure of which might be

Garda Síochána,[417] Laffoy J ordered disclosure of documents which she considered to be centrally germane to the issues in the proceedings but refused to order disclosure of others which only had a marginal relevance.

Another factor to be considered is the nature of the litigant's case and the interests sought to be protected. In *Cahalane v Revenue Commissioners*,[418] McCracken J laid considerable stress on the fact that the plaintiff was seeking to vindicate a basic constitutional right, the right to earn a livelihood. For this reason, the public interest in the administration of justice in the case was of great importance and he ordered discovery of most of the documents sought.

These principles are attenuated when the innocence of a person is at stake because there is an overriding public interest in ensuring that an innocent person is not convicted. Therefore, if an accused can establish that certain documentation is, or may be, relevant to the question of his innocence, then this facet of the public interest will trump that in favour of non-disclosure.[419]

The Public Interest in Non-Disclosure

8.076 The categories of public interest in favour of non-disclosure are not closed[420] and hence, are not capable of exhaustive or comprehensive categorisation. However, a consideration of the decided cases discloses four main categories which have been identified to date: (i) national security, (ii) international relations, (iii) the proper functioning of the public service, and (iv) the prevention and detection of crime. Before examining these categories, two general observations can be made. First, in order for a claim of privilege to succeed, it is essential to show that the communication in question was brought into being in circumstances of confidentiality and, where this factor is lacking, a claim of privilege will fail *ab initio*.[421] Second, in keeping with the decision in *Murphy*, the Irish courts have taken a resolute stand against any attempts to establish class claims whether directly or by recourse to generic arguments which would

---

significantly detrimental to the public interest" because although the documents "might be of some value to the plaintiff in the conduct of his case", they were "in no sense fundamental to it".

[417] High Court (Laffoy J) *ex tempore*, 20 January 1998.

[418] High Court (McCracken J) 14 May 1999.

[419] In *Wong v Minister for Justice* High Court (Denham J) 16 March 1993, Denham J declined to order production of two confidential documents but she stated that if the documents aided the applicant and there was a prosecution pending, then the court might consider the balance differently. *Cf. Director of Consumer Affairs v Sugar Distributors Ltd* [1991] 1 IR 225, [1991] ILRM 395; *Goodman International v Hamilton (No. 3)* [1993] 3 IR 320 dealing with informer privilege.

[420] *Per* Keane J in *Skeffington v Rooney* [1997] 1 IR 22, 32, [1997] 2 ILRM 56, 66 (citing *D. v NSPCC* [1978] AC 171, 230, [1977] 1 All ER 589, 605 (*per* Lord Hailsham)).

[421] See *Skeffington v Rooney* [1997] 1 IR 22, [1997] 2 ILRM 56; *PMPS Ltd v PMPA Insurance plc* [1990] 1 IR 284.

apply equally to all documents within a certain class.[422] Thus, in order for a claim of privilege to succeed, it must be particularised and identify the damage to the public interest in question which will accrue from disclosure of each individual document.[423]

(i) National Security

8.077 In *Murphy*,[424] Walsh J identified national security as one of the vital interests of the State, and it is axiomatic that the public has an interest in the security of the State. Indeed, there may be cases involving the security of the State where even the disclosure of the existence of a document should not be allowed.[425] This does not mean, however, that a claim based on national security will automatically succeed and the courts, consistent with the principles established in *Murphy*, will scrutinise such a claim to ascertain if it is properly made out. This is evident from *Gormley v Ireland*[426] where the plaintiff civil servant sought discovery of documents concerning his internment pursuant to the Offences Against the State Act 1939 and the treatment by the government of civil servants who had been interned. Production of these documents was resisted on the basis that their disclosure would be injurious to the interests of national security. Adjudicating on this claim, Murphy J stated that, notwithstanding the involvement of the Offences Against the State Act 1939, he was not satisfied that all of the documents in respect of which privilege was claimed involved national security. On balance, he decided that production of some of the documents should be ordered even though they were "unquestionably confidential, sensitive documents" recording for the greater part submissions and advices by senior civil servants to ministers and the government.[427]

(ii) International Relations

8.078 There is an obvious public interest in fostering good international relations and in protecting the confidentiality of any document, the disclosure of which might endanger relations with other countries or international organisa-

---

[422] See *Breathnach v Ireland (No. 3)* [1993] 2 IR 458, [1992] ILRM 755; *W. v Ireland (No. 1)* [1997] 2 IR 132 *(sub nom Walker v Ireland* [1997] 1 ILRM 363); *Incorporated Law Society v Minister for Justice* [1987] ILRM 42, 44.

[423] See, for example, *W. v Ireland (No. 1)* [1997] 2 IR 132 *(sub nom Walker v Ireland* [1997] 1 ILRM 363).

[424] [1972] IR 215, 234.

[425] *Murphy v Dublin Corporation* [1972] IR 215, 234; *Breathnach v Ireland (No. 3)* [1993] 2 IR 458, 469, [1992] ILRM 755, 763.

[426] [1993] 2 IR 75.

[427] *Ibid.* at 78.

tions.[428] Thus, in *O'Mahony v Minister for Defence*,[429] Barrington J had little difficulty in accepting that privilege could be claimed in respect of the report of a UNIFIL inquiry into an incident in which an Irish soldier had been killed. This report had been given to the Irish government in circumstances of confidentiality and he accepted, as quite reasonable, the view of the government that it was obliged to maintain confidentiality in the report.[430]

The public interest in maintaining the confidentiality of inter-state communications was discussed in *W. v Ireland (No. 1)*.[431] The case arose out of the delay in extraditing a Catholic priest to Northern Ireland to face charges of sexual offences against minors. The plaintiff, who was one of the alleged victims, claimed that she had suffered personal injury, including psychiatric injury and mental distress, by reason of a negligent delay on the part of the Attorney General's office in processing the extradition request. Discovery was granted but the defendants claimed privilege in respect of a number of documents on the basis that they were supplied to the Irish Attorney General by the Attorney General for the United Kingdom and Northern Ireland on a confidential basis for the limited purpose of allowing the Irish Attorney General to decide whether to back the warrants for extradition. It was contended that disclosure of such documents would be prejudicial to the proper and effective operation of the extradition arrangements between the two states and that if the claim of privilege was not upheld, the free flow of information and consequently the effective operation of the extradition procedure would be seriously inhibited.

This was the first case in which the principles applicable to communications between sovereign states had arisen and in the absence of direct Irish authority on the point, Geoghegan J had recourse to the English decision of *Buttes Gas and Oil Co v Hammer (No. 3)*.[432] In that case, the Court of Appeal had refused to subscribe to the proposition that an absolute public interest privilege attached to confidential communications between states. Having regard to the provisions of the Irish Constitution, Geoghegan J said that there was an even stronger case in this jurisdiction for not countenancing any form of absolute privilege in relation to communications passing between sovereign states. He accepted that, as a general rule, documents in connection with an extradition request would be assumed by both states to be confidential and that there was a public interest in the State maintaining that confidentiality as far as possible.

However, having read the documents, he came to the conclusion that the

---

[428] *Cf. AG v Simpson* [1959] IR 105, 112, where Davitt P thought it clear that privilege must apply to documents containing state secrets, the disclosure of which might endanger diplomatic relations or international peace.

[429] High Court (Barrington J) *ex tempore*, 27 June 1989.

[430] Followed on this point by O'Hanlon J in *O'Brien v Ireland* [1995] 1 IR 568, [1995] 1 ILRM 22 who also relied on the provisions of s.9 of the Diplomatic Relations and Immunities Act 1967.

[431] [1997] 2 IR 132 (*sub nom Walker v Ireland* [1997] 1 ILRM 363).

[432] [1981] QB 223, [1980] 3 All ER 475.

balance of public interest lay in favour of disclosure. In arriving at this view, he attached importance to four factors: (i) the criminal proceeding to which the action related had long been disposed of; (ii) the State had failed to discharge the onus on it of establishing that there was a greater public interest in non-disclosure; (iii) there was no evidence before the court of any objection by the office of the Attorney General of Northern Ireland to the production of the documents; and (iv) while it would be understandable that both this State and the United Kingdom would want, as a matter of principle, to maintain the role of confidentiality in relation to such documentation, it was difficult to see any particular reason why the government of the United Kingdom would be concerned about the production of the particular documents sought to be produced in the case.

(iii) Proper Functioning of the Public Service

8.079 In *Murphy*,[433] it was held that a claim of "executive privilege" could only be made where the exercise of the executive functions of the State was at issue. However, this limitation was an undesirable accretion to the principles laid down therein and has been quietly dropped from the jurisprudence in this area.[434] It is now clear that a claim of privilege may be maintained on the broader ground that disclosure of the information sought would be detrimental to the public interest in the proper functioning of the public service.[435]

There is no precise definition as to what constitutes the public service but it extends beyond central government,[436] to include local authorities[437] and persons or bodies which perform important statutory functions in the public interest.[438] For example, in *Skeffington v Rooney*,[439] it was held that public interest

---

[433] [1972] IR 215, 237-38. See also *Geraghty v Minister for Local Government* [1975] IR 300, 312 (*per* Griffin J).

[434] The first indication that immunity would extend beyond the narrow confines of executive functions came in *Geraghty v Minister for Local Government* [1975] IR 300. In the High Court, Kenny J excluded from disclosure a document which was written by one civil servant to another and was, he said, clearly intended to be confidential. His conclusion in this regard was upheld without comment by the Supreme Court even though it purported to faithfully apply the decision in *Murphy*.

[435] *Skeffington v Rooney* [1997] 1 IR 22, 32, [1997] 2 ILRM 56, 66; *Director of Consumer Affairs v Sugar Distributors Ltd* [1991] 1 IR 225, 227; *Incorporated Law Society v Minister for Justice* [1987] ILRM 42, 44.

[436] *Per* Lord Edmund-Davies in *D. v NSPCC* [1978] AC 171, 245, [1977] 1 All ER 589, 618, quoted with approval by Geoghegan J in *Goodman International v Hamilton (No. 3)* [1993] 3 IR 320, 328.

[437] *Conway v Rimmer* [1968] AC 910, [1968] 1 All ER 874; *Campbell v Thameside Metropolitan Borough Council* [1982] QB 1065, [1982] 2 All ER 791.

[438] *Skeffington v Rooney* [1997] 1 IR 22, [1997] 2 ILRM 56 (Garda Síochána Complaints Board); *Haughey v Moriarty* High Court (Geoghegan J) 20 January 1998 (tribunal of inquiry); *Fitzpatrick v Independent Newspapers* [1988] IR 132 [1988] ILRM 707 (Bord na gCon); *PMPS Ltd v PMPA Insurance plc* [1990] 1 IR 284 (Registrar of Friendly

privilege could be claimed by the Garda Síochána Complaints Board in an appropriate case. Keane J stressed the policy considerations underpinning the Garda Síochána (Complaints) Act 1986 which had established the board[440] and said that, in determining the claim of privilege made by the board, "there must be weighed against the public interest in the disclosure of the documents relating to the complaint to the board, the public interest in ensuring that the statutory functions of the board are not frustrated."[441] Again, in *Haughey v Moriarty*,[442] Geoghegan J took the view that "the efficient discharge of the functions of a tribunal established by the resolution of each House of the Oireachtas would normally ... over-ride the conflicting public interest in the right to adduce evidence".

One decision which seems to be at variance with this line of authority is *Buckley v Incorporated Law Society*,[443] where Costello J held that the Law Society could not claim public interest privilege because it was not part of the public service even though he acknowledged that it carries out important statutory duties in the public interest. This decision may have been prompted by a desire to limit the potential ambit of the privilege but if so, such a desire seems misplaced. Such a limitation may have made sense at a time when a ministerial certificate was accepted without question, but does not do so now when claims of privilege are subject to scrutiny by the courts. Rather than adopting an *a priori* limitation on the bodies that can claim privilege, it is submitted that it would be better for the courts to adopt a broad approach to the question of whether a body is part of the public service and then decide the claim of privilege on its merits.

8.080 Claims that disclosure of documentation would undermine the proper functioning of the public service are based on the "candour argument". This proceeds on the basis that free and candid communication between persons in the public service is essential and the possibility that such communications could be disclosed will have a "chilling effect".[444] It is further argued that the efficiency of the public service will be adversely affected because officials will

---

Societies); *State (Williams) v Army Pensions Board* [1983] IR 308, 313 (Army Pensions Board).

[439] [1997] 1 IR 22, [1997] 2 ILRM 56.

[440] He pointed out (*ibid.* at 30, 64) that: "The establishment of procedures designed to ensure that complaints of misconduct against members of the garda may be the subject of an investigation under the supervision of an independent body is not only of value in protecting the rights of individual citizens who complain of misconduct. It can also play an important part in maintaining and enhancing the confidence of the public in the Garda Síochána."

[441] [1999] 1 IR 22, 35-36, [1997] 2 ILRM 56, 69.

[442] High Court (Geoghegan J) 20 January 1998.

[443] [1994] 2 IR 44.

[444] See the grounds for privilege put forward in *Incorporated Law Society v Minister for Justice* [1987] ILRM 42, 43.

tend, where possible, to communicate orally instead of in writing in order to obviate the possibility of disclosure.[445] Apart from the lack of any empirical evidence to support these assertions, the major difficulty with this argument is that it requires the recognition of a class claim because it is only where a blanket immunity from disclosure is conferred that the desired candour will be fostered. However, as we have seen, the concept of class claims was roundly rejected by the Supreme Court in *Murphy*.

It was for this reason that the candour argument was rejected by Murphy J in *Bula Ltd v Tara Mines Ltd*.[446] The Minister for Energy sought to resist the production of a number of documents, virtually all of which related to advice given by senior civil servants to ministers and submissions by ministers to the government based on such advice. It was argued on behalf of the minister that it was undesirable in the public interest that these documents should be disclosed because such disclosure would tend to inhibit civil servants in providing proper and candid advice to the executive. However, Murphy J pointed out that it was the possibility rather than the reality of disclosure which would tend to cause a deterioration in the scope and quality of advice available to a minister. As a result of the decision in *Geraghty v Minister for Local Government*,[447] all administrators had to be conscious of the fact that no absolute privilege attaches to documents containing advice to ministers and therefore, these hypothesised ill-effects must have occurred already.[448]

Of course, some weight must be given to the candour argument because the "chilling effect" on communication within the public service will bear a correlation to the perceived risk of disclosure; the more often disclosure is ordered, the greater the likelihood that candour will be undermined. However, this risk is of its nature small and unquantifiable in respect of an individual case. It is, therefore, likely to cede to the interests of the plaintiff in prosecuting his litigation, at least where some injustice to the plaintiff might accrue by refusing discovery. Thus, claims of privilege based on the proper functioning of the public service have generally been unsuccessful.[449]

---

[445] See the grounds for privilege put forward in *Hunt v Roscommon VEC* High Court (McWilliam J) 1 May 1981 at 6; *Incorporated Law Society v Minister for Justice* [1987] ILRM 42, 43 and *Ambiorix v Minister for Environment (No. 1)* [1992] 1 IR 277, 281, [1992] ILRM 209, 211.

[446] High Court (Murphy J) 25 July 1991.

[447] [1975] IR 300.

[448] See also *Hunt v Roscommon VEC* High Court (McWilliam J) 1 May 1981, where the candour argument was given short shrift by McWilliam J relying on *Conway v Rimmer* [1968] AC 910, [1968] 1 All ER 874 and *Burmah Oil Co. v Bank of England* [1980] AC 1090, [1979] 3 All ER 700 and *cf.* the comment of McCarthy J in *Ambiorix Ltd v Minister for the Environment (No. 1)* [1992] 1 IR 277, 287, [1992] ILRM 209, 216, that the progeny of *Murphy* gave an empirical answer to the candour argument.

[449] See *Geraghty v Minister for Local Government* [1975] IR 300; *Hunt v Roscommon VEC* High Court (McWilliam J) 1 May 1981; *Folens v Minister for Education* [1981] ILRM 121; *Incorporated Law Society of Ireland v Minister for Justice* [1987] ILRM

This bias in favour of disclosure is illustrated by the decision in *Incorporated Law Society v Minister for Justice*[450] where a claim of privilege was made on the ground that production of the documents sought would be detrimental to the proper functioning of the public service. Murphy J identified the function of the court as being to determine, first, whether the production of the documents at issue would be detrimental to the efficiency of the public service and, second, whether such prejudice outweighed the interest of the plaintiffs in their claim to have justice administered by the court. Applying this balancing test, he acknowledged that the possibility of future discovery of documentation could have an inhibiting effect on the manner in which advice would be transmitted and recorded within the public service. The danger attendant upon this possibility was accentuated in the instant case because the documentation in question included correspondence passing between ministers. However, he was satisfied that there was nothing in the documentation that had any *special* potential for damage to the proper administration of the public service.[451] On the other hand, although he found it difficult to evaluate the benefits which would flow to the plaintiffs from the disclosure of the documents, he was of the opinion that to deny the plaintiffs access to the documentation would be to impose some measure of injustice on them and "that injustice is almost necessarily greater than the potential damage to the public service".[452]

8.081 Special mention should be made of the principles which govern disclosure of cabinet discussions.[453] In *Attorney General v Hamilton (No. 1)*,[454] the chairman of a tribunal of inquiry set up to investigate allegations of fraud and malpractice in the beef processing industry (commonly known as the "Beef Tribunal") sought to question a former government minister about whether a particular decision had been taken by the government at a cabinet meeting. A majority of the Supreme Court acceded to the contention that absolute confidentiality attached to cabinet discussions pursuant to the collective responsibility

---

42; *Ahern v Minister for Industry and Commerce* High Court (Lardner J) 4 March 1988; *Ambiorix Ltd v Minister for the Environment (No. 1)* [1992] 1 IR 277, [1992] ILRM 209; *Gormley v Ireland* [1993] 2 IR 75; *Skeffington v Rooney* [1994] 1 IR 480 (High Court).

[450] [1987] ILRM 42.

[451] An important factor in reaching this conclusion was the fact that the documentation showed "a degree of expertise and involvement by the ministers concerned ... which is more likely to advance the interests of the public service than to damage it" (*ibid.* at 44). However, if the converse was the case *i.e.* the documentation showed a lack of expertise, then because of the great relevance which the documents would have to the plaintiff's case, the test would also be weighted in favour of disclosure.

[452] [1987] ILRM 42, 44.

[453] For a more comprehensive discussion, see Hogan & Morgan, *Administrative Law in Ireland* (3rd ed., 1998) at 939-942 and Hogan, "The Cabinet Confidentiality Case of 1992" (1993) 8 Irish Political Studies 131.

[454] [1993] 2 IR 250, [1993] ILRM 81.

provisions of Article 28.4.2°. In reaching this decision, the majority distinguished *Murphy* and *Ambiorix* on the basis that they were concerned with the exercise of the judicial power, whereas the tribunal was set up pursuant to the legislative power.

The decision in *Hamilton* expressly left open the question as to whether a similar constitutional immunity would apply if the issue arose in the context of the administration of justice.[455] However, the view was subsequently taken by O'Hanlon J in *O'Brien v Ireland*[456] that, given its constitutional foundation, the effect of the decision was to create an absolute prohibition on the disclosure of the contents and details of cabinet discussions with no scope for a balancing by the courts of the competing public interests involved.[457]

The issue is now governed by the provisions of Article 28.4.3° which was inserted by an amendment of the Constitution in 1997. This article provides, *inter alia*, that the confidentiality of cabinet discussions must be respected except where the High Court determines that disclosure should be made in respect of a particular matter in the interests of the administration of justice. The effect would appear to be that the principles laid down in *Murphy* and *Ambiorix* will apply, *mutatis mutandis*, to cabinet discussions.

(iv) Prevention and Detection of Crime

8.082 The public clearly has an interest in the prevention and detection of crime and it may therefore, be in the public interest to protect the confidentiality of certain communications in order to facilitate this aim. The leading decision on the application of this head of public interest is *Breathnach v Ireland (No. 3)*.[458] The plaintiff had been convicted of the Sallins train robbery and subsequently brought civil proceedings against the State and named gardaí seeking damages for various torts and breach of his constitutional rights. In order to prosecute these proceedings, the plaintiff sought discovery from the DPP of all communications between the investigating gardaí concerning the arrest, detention and interrogation of the plaintiff. Privilege was claimed in respect of these

---

[455] [1993] 2 IR 250, 271, [1993] ILRM 81, 99.
[456] [1995] 1 ILRM 22.
[457] See also *Lang v Government of Ireland* High Court (O'Hanlon J) 7 July 1993 but compare the view of Keane J in *Skeffington v Rooney* [1997] 1 IR 22, 32, [1997] 2 ILRM 56, 66, that the decision in *Hamilton* offered an apparent rather than a real exception to the principles established by *Murphy* and *Ambiorix* because the evidence was not sought in the course of any proceedings in the courts and, in any event, the immunity against disclosure rested on the particular constitutional position of the government.
[458] [1993] 2 IR 458, [1992] ILRM 755. See also *Logue v Redmond* [1992] 2 ILRM 498; *Corbett v DPP* [1999] 2 IR 179; *Cahalane v Revenue Commissioners* High Court (McCracken J) 14 May 1999 where the principles laid down in *Breathnach* are approved and applied.

documents on a number of grounds including the following: (i) that the documents were brought into existence for the purpose of communicating with the DPP in relation to matters relevant to the exercise of his functions; (ii) that the communications were made by members of the gardaí in circumstances where they held a reasonable belief that the communications were, and would remain, confidential; (iii) that it was necessary to maintain the confidentiality of such communications in order to ensure full disclosure by the gardaí of any fact considered to be of relevance to the DPP in the discharge of his office; and (iv) that the documents might make reference to the opinion of gardaí as to the involvement in the offence of the accused or others who were not charged and their opinion as to whether these persons are members of particular organisations.

In dealing with these contentions, Keane J began by reiterating his conclusion in *State (Hanley) v Holly*,[459] that a class claim in respect of communications between one member of the gardaí and another in the course of their duties was unsustainable having regard to the principles laid down in *Murphy*.[460] As regards the specific grounds put forward by the defendants, he pointed out that virtually all of the grounds stated would apply equally to any other criminal prosecution. Therefore, if the court were to accept these contentions without considering any countervailing considerations or inspecting the documents, it would follow that a similar course would have to be adopted in every case where those objections were raised and this was not in accordance with the constitutional position as laid down in the case law. He went on to elaborate on the proper approach to apply:

> [T]he court, as I understand the law, is required to balance the public interest in the proper administration of justice against the public interest reflected in the grounds put forward for non-disclosure in the present case. The public interest in the prevention and prosecution of crime must be put in the scales on the one side. It is only where the first public interest outweighs the second public interest that an inspection should be undertaken or disclosure should be ordered.[461]

In considering the first public interest, it was necessary to determine to what extent, if any, the relevant documents might advance the plaintiff's case or damage the defendant's case. In considering the second public interest, the factors identified by the defendant had to be given due weight.[462] Of these, the most

---

[459] [1984] ILRM 149. In *Hanley*, he had overruled an earlier decision of a divisional High Court in *Attorney General v Simpson* [1959] IR 105, which had held that a class privilege attached to communications between gardaí in the course of their duties.

[460] [1972] IR 215.

[461] [1993] 2 IR 458, 469, [1992] ILRM 755, 763.

[462] See also *Logue v Redmond* [1999] 2 ILRM 498, 507.

important was the desirability of free communication between the gardaí and
the DPP. The extent to which that freedom of communication might be inhibited
by the knowledge that the documents furnished to the DPP might subsequently
be disclosed in court proceedings was clearly a matter which had to be taken
into consideration in determining whether the public interest in the particular
case required their production. Drawing a distinction between civil and criminal cases, he said:

> In civil proceedings, the desirability of preserving confidentiality in the
> case of communications between members of the executive has been sig-
> nificantly eroded as a factor proper to be taken into account by the courts
> ... However, different considerations would appear to apply to communi-
> cations between gardaí and the Director of Public Prosecutions, where the
> public interest in the prevention and prosecution of crime must be given
> due weight. It would be clearly unacceptable if in every case where a
> person was acquitted of a criminal charge, he could, by instituting pro-
> ceedings for wrongful arrest or malicious prosecution, embark on a fish-
> ing expedition though all the files of the gardaí relating to the case. The
> circumstances of the particular case must determine, in the light of the
> constitutional principles to which I have referred, whether an inspection
> should be undertaken by the court and whether, as a result of that inspec-
> tion, production of any of the documents should be ordered.[463]

Weighing up these factors in the circumstances of the case, he pointed out that
the plaintiff's claim included one for damages for malicious prosecution. He
was of opinion that the disputed documentation might well furnish evidence
which would be of significance in establishing a want of reasonable cause for
the prosecution. Therefore, he was satisfied that the public interest in the administration of justice outweighed the general desirability of preserving the confidentiality of such documents and he examined them in order to decide whether
they should be produced.

DETERMINATION OF CLAIM OF PRIVILEGE

8.083 In *Murphy v Dublin Corporation*,[464] it was held that once a particular
document is established to be relevant, the burden of satisfying the court that it
should be privileged from production lies upon the party making the claim of
privilege. In this regard, it is essential that the affidavit of discovery be sworn in
the proper form such that the documents in respect of which privilege are claimed
are listed individually and the grounds on which privilege is claimed particular-

---

[463] [1993] 2 IR 458, 472-73, [1992] ILRM 755, 766.
[464] [1972] IR 215, 235.

ised.[465] In *O'Brien v Minister for Defence*,[466] where this had not been done and a general claim of privilege had been made in respect of bundles of documents and files, the Supreme Court stated that it was unable to assess whether a claim of public interest privilege could be maintained.[467]

In any case where a claim of privilege is made, the court has the power to examine the documents[468] and will generally do so before upholding the claim.[469] However, there is no requirement to examine the documents and the court may uphold a claim merely on the basis of a description of the nature and contents of the document.[470] Conversely, if the court is satisfied that a *prima facie* claim of privilege has not been made out, it is not required to inspect the documents to vouchsafe that conclusion.[471] Recently, in *McDonald v RTÉ*,[472] Murphy J has sounded a cautionary note in relation to the examination of documents, stating that although this procedure will generally be the best method for adjudicating on a claim of privilege, there are circumstances where it will not be. In particular, there were cases where the examination of documents by a judge without any information as to the significance of particular documents or any explanation as to how they might benefit one party or embarrass the other could lead to an injustice.

8.084 In some cases where the public interest is finely balanced or even weighted

---

[465] In accordance with the principles laid down by the Supreme Court in *Bula Ltd v Tara Mines Ltd* [1991] 1 IR 217, *Bula Ltd v Crowley* [1991] 1 IR 220, [1990] ILRM 756 and *O'Brien v Minister for Defence* [1998] 2 ILRM 156. See *Corbett v DPP* [1999] 2 IR 179, 188-89, where a dispute arose as to whether a claim of public interest privilege had been competently raised.

[466] [1998] 2 ILRM 156.

[467] See also *Hunt v Roscommon VEC* High Court (McWilliam J) 1 May 1981, where McWilliam J refused to remedy the deficiencies in the affidavit claiming privilege by examining the disputed documents. The learned judge criticised the failure to particularise the grounds on which privilege was claimed in respect of each document and said that "to ask the court to examine all these documents under the circumstances of this case seems to me to be getting very close to asking the court to prepare the parts of the affidavit of discovery."

[468] *Murphy v Dublin Corporation* [1972] IR 215, 235; *Ambiorix Ltd v Minister for the Environment (No. 1)* [1992] 1 IR 277, 283, [1992] ILRM 209, 213.

[469] In *Corbett v DPP* [1999] 2 IR 179, 189, O'Sullivan J took the view that once a *prima facie* claim of privilege has been established, then the courts should proceed to examine the documents to ascertain whether the claim is properly founded.

[470] *Murphy v Dublin Corporation* [1972] IR 215, 235; *Ambiorix Ltd v Minister for the Environment (No. 1)* [1992] 1 IR 277, 283, [1992] ILRM 209, 213; *Skeffington v Rooney* [1997] 1 IR 22, 35, [1997] 2 ILRM 56, 69. In *Breathnach v Ireland (No. 3)* [1993] 2 IR 458, 469, [1992] ILRM 755, 764, Keane J held that the burden of satisfying the court that it should not proceed to examine the documents lies upon the person seeking to withhold the documents.

[471] See *Hunt v Roscommon VEC* High Court (McWilliam J) 1 May 1981 and *Skeffington v Rooney* [1997] 1 IR 22, [1997] 2 ILRM 56.

[472] [2001] 2 ILRM 1.

in favour of non-disclosure, the courts have edited the documents and ordered partial disclosure. [473] This enables the courts to place the maximum amount of information possible before the party seeking disclosure while at the same time paying due attention to the countervailing public interest. Thus, in *Bula Ltd v Tara Mines Ltd*[474] where the Minister for Energy was anxious that the form in which certain cabinet documents are cast should not be disclosed, disclosure of the documents was ordered but the minister's concerns were addressed by the pasting over of parts of the documents.[475]

Another technique which had been used in some cases was to restrict inspection of documents to the lawyers of the party seeking disclosure upon their undertaking not to reveal the contents to anyone without the leave of the court.[476] However, the Supreme Court in *Burke v Central Independent Television plc*[477] cast doubt on the propriety of this practice. Finlay CJ said that this would result in the lawyers for the plaintiffs having access to a number of documents which might well be significant and weighty tools to be used in cross-examination of witnesses adduced on behalf of the defendant and be unable to use such documents or explain to their clients their failure to use them. He opined that this would constitute an unprecedented and wholly undesirable breach of the duty which counsel owe to their client and an interference in the trust which should exist between a client and his lawyers.[478]

ASSERTION AND WAIVER OF PRIVILEGE

8.085 Because of its nature, public interest privilege does not fit easily within the conceptual framework of a privilege which requires that a privilege exist for the benefit of an identified person or persons who can choose to assert it or waive it as they see fit. Public interest privilege exists to further the public interest and, therefore, in so far as a holder of the privilege can be identified, it is the public as a whole. For this reason, the view has been taken that it can be invoked by any party to litigation or, if no objection is otherwise taken, the issue can and should be raised by the court of its own motion in an appropriate case.[479]

---

[473] See, for example, *Gormley v Ireland* [1993] 2 IR 75, 79; *Wong v Minister for Justice* High Court (Denham J) 16 March 1993 and *Bula Ltd v Tara Mines Ltd* High Court (Murphy J) 25 July 1991.

[474] High Court (Murphy J) 25 July 1991.

[475] See also *Wong v Minister for Justice* High Court (Denham J) 16 March 1993.

[476] *Ambiorix Ltd v Minister for the Environment (No. 1)* [1992] 1 IR 277, 286, [1992] ILRM 209, 215; *Gormley v Ireland* [1993] 2 IR 75, 80.

[477] [1994] 2 IR 61, [1994] 2 ILRM 161.

[478] See also *DPP v Special Criminal Court* [1999] 1 IR 60, 84-88 and *R v Davis* [1993] 1 IR 613, 616.

[479] *AG v Simpson* [1959] IR 105, 133; *Duncan v Cammell Laird & Co. Ltd* [1942] AC 624, [1942] 1 All ER 587.

A controversial question is whether the privilege may be waived. In England, the view has been taken that because it involves an adjudication of where the balance of public interest lies, the doctrine of waiver has no application.[480] However, the Irish courts have taken a different approach and in two recent Supreme Court decisions, *Hannigan v Director of Public Prosecutions*,[481] and *McDonald v RTÉ*,[482] it was held that privilege may be waived. Thus, in *Hannigan*, it was held that privilege had been waived in respect of a document which had been summarised in an affidavit. Hardiman J said that the deployment of the document for litigious purposes was inconsistent with an assertion of the harmful effects following from its disclosure and it was just and equitable that the appellant should have access to it.[483]

MISCELLANEOUS PRIVILEGES

INFORMER PRIVILEGE

8.086 It has long been recognised[484] that privilege can be claimed in respect of the identities of informers and documents from which their identities can be established.[485] It is founded on the two interlinking justifications that, first, disclosure of the identities of informants might well place them in physical danger[486] and, second, if privilege is not granted, the flow of information from

---

[480] *Rogers v Secretary of State for the Home Department* [1973] AC 388, 407, [1972] 2 All ER 1057, 1066; *Air Canada v Secretary of State for Trade* [1983] 2 AC 394, 436, [1983] 1 All ER 910, 917.

[481] [2002] 1 ILRM 48.

[482] [2001] 2 ILRM 1.

[483] *Cf. Hughes v Commissioner of An Garda Síochána* High Court (Laffoy J), *ex tempore*, 20 January 1998 where Laffoy J rejected as unsustainable a claim of public interest privilege in respect of documents relating to matters which had been aired in court in earlier proceedings.

[484] *R v Hardy* (1794) 24 St Tr 199; *Attorney General v Briant* (1846) 15 M & W 169, 185. One of the earliest examples of its successful invocation in Ireland is to be found in *R v Smith O'Brien* (1848) 7 St Tr NS 123, 126, where, at the trial of William Smith O'Brien for treason arising out of the Young Irelander's rebellion, the court refused to compel a witness to disclose the identity of a person who had given him certain information.

[485] *Buckley v Incorporated Law Society of Ireland* [1994] 2 IR 44; *Director of Consumer Affairs v Sugar Distributors Ltd* [1991] 1 IR 225, [1991] ILRM 395; *Ward v Special Criminal Court* [1998] 2 ILRM 493; *Marks v Beyfus* (1890) 25 QBD 494; *D. v NSPCC* [1978] AC 171, [1977] 1 All ER 589. In addition, in *People (DPP) v Eccles* (1986) 3 Frewen 36, 63, and *People (DPP) v Reddan* [1995] 3 IR 560, 571-72, it was held that a garda witness could refuse to identify an informant as garda or civilian on the basis that it would be dangerous to do so.

[486] *R v Smith O'Brien* (1848) 7 St Tr NS 123; *R v Hennessy* (1978) 68 Cr App Rep 419; *Cf. Burke v Central Independent Television plc* [1994] 2 IR 61, [1994] 2 ILRM 161.

them would dry up.[487] Although this privilege is sometimes regarded as a discrete example of public interest privilege,[488] it is better regarded as a distinct category of privilege because, except where the "innocence at stake" exception is at issue, its application does not involve any case by case balancing exercise.[489]

Informers Protected by the Privilege

8.087 The traditional view of the privilege was that it was grounded on the public interest in the prevention and detection of crime[490] and, therefore, only applied to police or prison[491] informants. However, the range of informants protected by the privilege has been greatly expanded and it now appears as if privilege will extend to all communications between informers and bodies with law enforcement functions and powers. The landmark case in this regard is the decision of the House of Lords in *D. v NSPCC*[492] where privilege was conferred on communications by informers to the defendant society concerning alleged abuse of children. Lord Diplock justified the extension of privilege from police informers to NSPCC informers on the basis that the public interest served by preserving the anonymity of both classes of informers is analogous. The NSPCC was an organisation authorised by statute to bring legal proceedings for the welfare of children and the public interest in the effective exercise of its functions in this regard was as weighty as that in respect of police informers.

This decision was followed in *Director of Consumer Affairs v Sugar Distributors Ltd*[493] where Costello J held that privilege applied to the contents of a complaint made by a company to the Director that the defendant had breached restrictive practices legislation:

[T]he Oireachtas has conferred on the Director important law enforce-

---

[487] *Attorney General v Simpson* [1959] IR 105, 125; *D. v NSPCC* [1978] AC 171, 218, [1977] 1 All ER 589, 595 (*per* Lord Diplock).

[488] *Cf. Director of Consumer Affairs v Sugar Distributors Ltd* [1991] 1 IR 225, 227, [1991] ILRM 395, 397; *Buckley v Incorporated Law Society of Ireland* [1994] 2 IR 44, 49; *Breathnach v Ireland (No. 3)* [1993] 2 IR 458, 469, [1992] ILRM 755, 763.

[489] As far back as *Marks v Beyfus* (1890) 25 QBD 494, 498, Esher MR declared that "this rule of public policy is not a matter of discretion; it is a rule of law, and as such should be applied by the judge at the trial, who should not treat it as a matter of discretion whether he should tell the witness to answer or not". See also *Ward v Special Criminal Court* [1998] 2 ILRM 493, 504; *D. v NSPCC* [1978] AC 171, 218, [1977] 1 All ER 589, 595 (*per* Lord Diplock).

[490] See *Ward v Special Criminal Court* [1998] 2 ILRM 493, 504; *Buckley v Incorporated Law Society of Ireland* [1994] 2 IR 44, 49; *Director of Consumer Affairs v Sugar Distributors Ltd* [1991] 1 IR 225, 227, [1991] ILRM 395, 397.

[491] *State (Comerford) v Governor of Mountjoy Prison* [1981] ILRM 86.

[492] [1978] AC 171, [1977] 1 All ER 589.

[493] [1991] 1 IR 225, [1991] ILRM 395.

ment functions. I am satisfied that it is in the public interest that the court should protect the effective functioning by the Director of his statutory powers. I am further satisfied that to enable him to exercise his powers effectively he must be able to assure complainants that information given to him (and, indeed, in certain circumstances the names of the complainants) will be treated in confidence and not disclosed as otherwise complaints may not be forthcoming and breaches of ministerial orders are likely to go undetected.[494]

He subsequently distinguished this decision in *Buckley v Incorporated Law Society of Ireland*,[495] where privilege was claimed by the Law Society in respect of complaints of misconduct made to it. He pointed to what he regarded as a crucial distinction between the duties of the Law Society and those of the Director of Consumer Affairs in that the Director was concerned to investigate possible breaches of the criminal law whereas the defendant was concerned with allegations of professional misconduct. The fact that in some cases, the misconduct might involve breaches of the criminal law did not alter the fundamental nature of the defendant's statutory duties. He, therefore, had to consider whether informer privilege should be extended to complaints made to the Law Society and he did so by balancing the competing public interests.[496] The exemption from disclosure of documents would clearly constitute a potential restriction and diminution of the full disclosure which was desirable for the purpose of ascertaining the truth and rendering justice in civil proceedings. However, it was argued by the defendant that if it is known that documents relating to complaints to the defendant might be disclosed at some future time, persons with legitimate complaints might be discouraged by the fear of public disclosure of their private affairs from coming forward, thus reducing the effectiveness of the defendant's supervisory role.

He was in no doubt as to where the balance lay. It was a demonstrable probability that if inspection was refused this would result in the frustration of the court's duty to ascertain the truth and do justice between the parties. This probability outweighed what he considered to be a small risk that complainants would be deterred from approaching the defendant.

8.088 The decision in *D. v NSPCC*[497] was also relied upon by Geoghegan J in *Goodman International v Hamilton (No. 3)*.[498] This case arose out of the decision by the respondent, who was chairman of the Tribunal of Inquiry into the Beef Industry, that a number of TDs could rely on privilege to protect the iden-

---

[494] *Ibid.* at 228, 399.
[495] [1994] 2 IR 44.
[496] Applying the test laid down by Finlay CJ in *Smurfit Paribas Bank Ltd v AAB Export Finance Ltd* [1990] 1 IR 469, 477, [1990] ILRM 588, 594.
[497] [1978] AC 171, [1977] 1 All ER 589.
[498] [1993] 3 IR 320.

tity of their sources. Geoghegan J relied on the principle enunciated by Lord Edmund-Davies in *D. v NSPCC*[499] that where a confidential relationship exists and disclosure would be in breach of some ethical or social value involving the public interest, the court has a discretion to uphold a refusal to disclose relevant evidence provided it considers that, on balance, the public interest would be better served by excluding such evidence. He opined that most Irish people would regard it as important that matters of actual or potential public concern may be confidentially brought to the attention of elected national public representatives without fear of the confidence being broken. Therefore, having regard to all the circumstances of the case,[500] the balance lay in favour of non-disclosure.

The decision of the Supreme Court in *Skeffington v Rooney*,[501] may indicate that the courts will take an even broader approach in the future and recognise informer privilege where it is essential to the proper functioning of a statutory body. In that case, Keane J seemed to take the view that informer privilege could apply to the identity of informants and the substance of complaints made to the Garda Síochána Complaints Board. It might be noted though that, in that case, the court stressed the importance of the functions of the board and, even though that board has no law enforcement powers as such, if a complaint is made which the board is of opinion may constitute an offence committed by the garda concerned, it must refer the matter to the DPP.

The 'Innocence at Stake' Exception

8.089 Almost as old as informer privilege itself is the recognition that it is subject to what O'Flaherty J in *Ward v Special Criminal Court*[502] termed the "innocence at stake" exception which was described as follows by Esher MR in *Marks v Beyfus*:[503]

> [I]f upon the trial of a prisoner the judge should be of opinion that the disclosure of the name of the informant is necessary or right in order to show the prisoner's innocence, then one public policy is in conflict with another public policy, and that which says that an innocent man is not to

---

[499] [1978] AC 171, 245, [1977] 1 All ER 589, 618.

[500] These circumstances included the fact that informants reasonably believed that their identity would be protected by constitutional privilege pursuant to Article 15 and the fact that the respondent had at all times made it clear that hearsay evidence would not be admitted to undermine the good names of the applicants.

[501] [1997] 1 IR 22, 36, [1997] 2 ILRM 56, 69.

[502] [1998] 2 ILRM 493, 501. See, further, O'Connor, "The Privilege of Non-Disclosure and Informers" (1980) 15 Ir Jur 111.

[503] (1890) 25 QBD 494, 498. *Cf.* the opinion of Dixon J in *Attorney General v Simpson* [1959] IR 105, 141, that this proposition is based on a *non sequitur*.

be condemned when his innocence can be proved is the policy that must prevail.

A similar view was taken by Costello J in *Director of Consumer Affairs v Sugar Distributors Ltd*.[504] He said that where a claim of informer privilege is made, the court should examine the documents and permit inspection where it "concludes that the documents might tend to show that the defendant had not committed the wrongful acts alleged against him".[505]

Journalist's Sources

8.090 In *Re Kevin O'Kelly*,[506] the Court of Criminal Appeal rejected a claim of privilege in respect of the identity of a journalist's source. However, such a claim may succeed as a variation of informer privilege where disclosure of the identity of the source would put that person's life and/or bodily integrity at risk. In *Burke v Central Independent Television plc*,[507] the plaintiffs had instituted proceedings against the defendant for libel arising out of a television programme broadcast by the defendant in which it was alleged that certain premises were being used as the financial nerve centre of the IRA. The defendant objected to the disclosure of documents which would, or would be likely to, lead to the identification of its sources of information on the ground, *inter alia*, that the life and safety of those sources would be put at risk if their identities became known.

In the Supreme Court, Finlay CJ identified the two conflicting public interests in the case. On the one hand, there is the public interest in protecting Irish citizens from the risk of death or bodily injury at the hands of terrorists. On the other, there is the public interest in the administration of justice which requires that the plaintiffs should be entitled to the discovery which they are seeking if that is necessary for the protection and vindication of their constitutional right to their good names. Implicitly applying the theory of a hierarchy of constitutional rights, he was satisfied that the constitutional right of individual citizens to the protection of their life and bodily integrity must of necessity take precedence over the right of citizens to the protection and vindication of their good name and, therefore, upheld the claim of privilege.

---

[504] [1991] 1 IR 225, [1991] ILRM 395. See also *Goodman International v Hamilton (No. 3)* [1993] 3 IR 320, 327.

[505] *Ibid.* at 229. *Cf. Ward v Special Criminal Court* [1998] 2 ILRM 493, where the application of informer privilege and the "innocence at stake" exception was considered by the Supreme Court in the criminal context. The court stressed that prosecution counsel, who have an overall responsibility to ensure that a trial is fair and just, play a crucial role in the application of the privilege and owe a duty to disclose any possible source of evidence that may help the defence. If a doubt arises as to whether a particular document should be disclosed, then it is a matter for the trial judge to decide having, if necessary, examined the documents.

[506] (1974) 109 ILTR 97.

[507] [1994] 2 IR 61, [1994] 2 ILRM 161.

STATUTORY PRIVILEGE

8.091 The decisions in *Murphy*[508] and *Ambiorix*,[509] which emphasised that the question of whether documents were privileged from production was a matter solely for the judicial power, might seem to cast some doubt as to the competence of the Oireachtas to create statutory privileges. However, in *O'Brien v Ireland*[510] O'Hanlon J stated that, notwithstanding the absoluteness of the language used, neither decision:

> was intended to convey that the power of the legislature to intervene and confer the privilege of exemption from production on specified categories of documentary or other evidence was curtailed or restricted in any way, save insofar as any legislation enacted must not conflict with the overriding provisions of the Constitution.

That conclusion was endorsed by the Supreme Court in *Skeffington v Rooney*[511] and it would appear, therefore, that it is open to the Oireachtas to create a statutory privilege in respect of a specified category of documentation within the parameters set by the Constitution. Furthermore, such a statutory privilege will supersede any common law privilege which might otherwise have been applicable.[512]

Where a claim of statutory privilege is made, it is a question of statutory interpretation as to whether a privilege had been created and what communications and persons/bodies are protected by it.[513] Among the legislative provisions that have been held to create statutory privileges are s.8 of the Adoption Act 1976,[514] s.16 of the Central Bank Act 1989,[515] s.9 of the Diplomatic Relations and Immunities Act 1967[516] and article 11(2) of the Defence Forces Regulations 1982.[517] However, a claim that s.12 of the Garda Síochána (Complaints)

---

[508] [1972] IR 215.

[509] [1992] 1 IR 277, [1992] ILRM 209.

[510] [1995] 1 ILRM 22, 29.

[511] [1997] 1 IR 22, 36-37, [1997] 2 ILRM 56, 70-71.

[512] *B. (P.) v L. (A.)* [1996] 1 ILRM 154, 158; *M. (S.) v M. (G.)* [1985] ILRM 186, 187.

[513] See, for example, *M. (S.) v M. (G.)* [1985] ILRM 186, 188 and *O'Brien v Minister for Defence* [1998] 2 ILRM 156, 159.

[514] See *M. (S.) v M. (G.)* [1985] ILRM 186; *B. (P.) v L. (A.)* [1996] 1 ILRM 154; *C. (D.) v M. (D.)* [1999] 2 IR 150.

[515] *Cf. Cully v Northern Bank Finance Corp Ltd* [1984] ILRM 683 where O'Hanlon J held that the predecessor to s.16 of the Act of 1989, s.31 of the Central Bank Act 1942, created a statutory privilege in favour of information and documents coming into the possession or control of officers of the Central Bank.

[516] *O'Brien v Ireland* [1995] 1 IR 568, [1995] 1 ILRM 22.

[517] *O'Brien v Minister for Defence* [1998] 2 ILRM 156 (decision of O'Hanlon J in the High Court reported *sub nom O'Brien v Ireland* [1995] 1 IR 568, [1995] 1 ILRM 22); *O'Mahony v Minister for Defence* High Court (Barrington J) 27 June 1989.

Act 1986 had created a privilege from disclosure failed in *Skeffington v Rooney*[518] and it would appear from that decision that clear evidence of a legislative intention to create a privilege is required.

COMMUNICATIONS WITH SPIRITUAL ADVISORS

8.092 The generally accepted view is that prior to the Reformation, the common law recognised a sacerdotal privilege whereby a priest could not be compelled to reveal what had been communicated to him by a penitent in confession.[519] The position in the aftermath of the Reformation in England was unclear but in *Wheeler v Le Marchant*,[520] Jessel MR declared that communications "made to a priest in the confessional on matters perhaps considered by the penitent to be more important even than his life or his fortune are not protected". In Ireland, there was some authority which went the other way with *obiter dicta* in *Re Keller*[521] and *Tannian v Synott*[522] recognising the existence of a sacerdotal privilege but refusing to extend it further to confidential communications between a priest and parishioner.

It was against that background that Gavan Duffy J delivered his judgment in *Cook v Carroll*.[523] The issue in the case was whether a priest who refused to testify in an action for seduction as to the contents of a conversation he had had with the defendant and the plaintiff's daughter at his house was guilty of contempt. Gavan Duffy J availed of the opportunity to repudiate the common law position as stated in *Wheeler v Le Marchant*.[524] He referred to Article 44.1.2° of the then recently adopted Constitution wherein the State recognised the special position of the Catholic Church as the guardian of the faith professed by the great majority of the citizens and stated:

> In a State where nine out of every ten citizens to-day are Catholics and on a matter closely touching the religious outlook of the people, it would be intolerable that the common law, as expounded after the Reformation in a Protestant land, should be taken to bind a nation which persistently repudiated the Reformation as heresy. When, as a measure of necessary convenience, we allowed the common law generally to continue in force, we meant to include all the common law in harmony with the national spirit.

---

[518] [1997] 1 IR 22, 37, [1997] 2 ILRM 56, 71.

[519] See Callahan, "Historical Inquiry into the Priest-Penitent Privilege" (1976) 36 Jurist 328.

[520] (1881) 17 Ch D 675, 681. See also *Anderson v Bank of British Columbia* (1876) 2 Ch D 644, 651.

[521] (1887) 22 LR Ir 158.

[522] (1903) 37 ILTSJ 275.

[523] [1945] IR 515.

[524] (1881) 17 Ch D 675, 681.

> We never contemplated the maintenance of any construction of the common law affected by sectarian background.[525]

In the absence of binding authority, he approached the issue as a matter of first principles by reference to the conditions laid down by Wigmore[526] for the recognition of privileges:

(1) the communications must originate in a confidence that they will not be disclosed;

(2) this element of confidentiality must be essential to the full and satisfactory maintenance of the relation;

(3) the relation must be one which in the opinion of the community ought to be sedulously fostered; and

(4) the injury which would enure to the relation by the disclosure of the communications must be greater than the benefit thereby gained for the correct disposal of litigation.

He found those conditions to be satisfied and held that communications made in confidence to a priest, in private consultation between him and his parishioners, were privileged and that such privilege could not be waived by a party thereto without the consent of the priest.

8.093 The nature and application of this privilege has recently been clarified by Geoghegan J in *Johnston v Church of Scientology*.[527] The plaintiff alleged, *inter alia*, that she had been "brainwashed" by the defendants. An order for discovery was granted and the defendants sought to resist the disclosure of certain "counselling notes" on the basis of sacerdotal privilege. These counselling notes were generated during "spiritual practices" of scientology called "auditing" and "training". The defendant explained that auditing and training were conducted on a one to one confidential basis and it was claimed that for an auditor to disclose any of the communications he had with the other person, even if that person was to waive any privilege in respect of them, would be so fundamentally contrary to the beliefs and tenets of the Church of Scientology as to render him liable to eternal damnation.

Although Geoghegan J criticised the decision of Gavan Duffy J in *Cook v Carroll* on the basis that it proceeded on the erroneous view that there were constitutional and legal effects arising from the then "so-called" special position of the Catholic Church, he took the view that "as matter of common sense and justice, it was reasonable for the courts to revive what Gavan Duffy says

---

[525] [1945] IR 515, 519.
[526] Evidence (3rd ed., 1940), VIII, § 2285.
[527] High Court (Geoghegan J) 30 April 1999.

was the pre-reformation common law protecting the seal of the confessional even against waiver by the penitent". However, this absolute and unwaivable sacerdotal privilege which attached to the "priest penitent relationship in the confessional" was *sui iuris* and could not be successfully invoked by the defendants in the circumstances of the instant case. He rejected the analogy which they sought to make between the teachings of Scientology and the seal of confessional. He pointed out that no evidence had been adduced that it was part of the doctrines of Scientology that any disclosure of what transpired in auditing or training sessions led to some kind of eternal punishment. Moreover, the question as to whether the Church of Scientology even constituted a religion remained controversial.

Geoghegan J also accepted that there could be a broader counselling privilege which would apply to counselling by a parish priest of a parishioner. However, this could be waived by the person being counselled and here the plaintiff had waived any privilege which was alleged to exist.

The decision of Geoghegan J sets the law in this area on a course of more rational development. As recognised by the learned judge, there are two separate privileges which may apply to communications between a spiritual adviser and a parishioner: (i) sacerdotal privilege, and (ii) a privilege in respect of communications between a spiritual advisor and parishioner made for the purpose of giving or receiving spiritual guidance. It is important to distinguish between the two because their nature and incidents are quite distinct. In particular, the identity of the holders of the privilege is different in respect of each privilege.

Amongst the arguments in favour of sacerdotal privilege is that there are very strong ethical obligations with serious consequences imposed on ministers of a wide variety of religions not to reveal confessional communications. For example, the Canon Law of the Catholic Church states that the sacramental seal of confession is inviolable. Because of this, priests and ministers will face civil or penal sanctions rather than submit to any attempt to compel disclosure of such communications. There is, therefore, a strong argument to be made that the priest or minister is the ultimate holder or at least a co-holder of sacerdotal privilege because waiver by the penitent will still not relieve the priest or minister of his ethical and religious obligations to protect the secrecy of the confessional.

Quite different considerations attach, however, to any sort of counselling privilege which is recognised in respect of communications between a priest or minister and a parishioner. Such privilege exists primarily to protect the interests of the parishioner and to promote his ability to make frank disclosure in order to obtain spiritual guidance. Therefore, such privilege should be capable of being waived by the parishioner.

MARITAL PRIVILEGE

Marriage Counsellors

8.094 In Article 41.3.1° of the Constitution, the state pledges itself "to guard with special care the institution of marriage, on which the family is founded, and to protect it against attack" and this article may be invoked to justify the recognition of privilege in circumstances where it advances this objective.

In *R. (E.) v R. (J.)*,[528] Carroll J considered a claim of privilege made in respect of communications made to a priest who acted as a marriage counsellor in his capacity as such. She applied the four conditions for the recognition of a privilege articulated by Wigmore (which are set out above), to determine whether privilege should be granted. Taking the first two conditions, she was satisfied that:

> The nature of the relationship is such that a priest acting as marriage coun-
> sellor will be consulted by a spouse or spouses in order to get advice in
> connection with difficulties in their marriage. I consider that confidential-
> ity is an essential element in that relationship. I can imagine nothing less
> conducive to frank and open discussion between priest and spouses, pos-
> sibly leading to admissions to faults and failings on both sides, than the
> possibility that total confidentiality will not be observed.[529]

Turning to the third requirement that "the relation must be one which in the opinion of the community ought to be sedulously fostered", she adverted to Article 41 and opined that "[t]he provision of confidential marriage counselling which may help a married couple over a difficulty in their marriage is protection of the most practical kind for the family and should be fostered."[530] Finally, she was also satisfied that the fourth requirement was met on the basis that "any benefit which could be gained in litigation by having the evidence available does not outweigh the possible injury to the relationship if disclosure can be compelled".[531] She further specified that the privilege belonged to the spouses and could only be waived by both.[532]

An important factor in *R. (E.) v R. (J.)* was that the counsellor was also a priest and Carroll J reserved the question as to whether privilege could arise where the counsellor was not a minister of religion. However, given the ground-ing of the privilege in Article 41 rather than Article 44 and the strong public policy in protecting and promoting the institution of marriage, it is difficult to

---

[528] [1981] ILRM 125.

[529] *Ibid.* at 126.

[530] *Ibid.* at 126.

[531] *Ibid.* at 126.

[532] Following the decision of *Pais v Pais* [1970] P 119, [1970] 2 All ER 491 in this regard.

see why this factor should be determinative and in *Johnston v Church of Scientology*,[533] Geoghegan J took the view that the privilege in respect of marriage counselling should be available on a secular basis.

Marital Privacy

8.095 A privilege may also exist in respect of communications, the disclosure of which would injure marital privacy. Spouses formerly enjoyed a privilege not to disclose any communications made by the other spouse during the subsistence of the marriage both in civil[534] and criminal[535] proceedings. This privilege was abolished by s.3 of the Criminal Evidence Act 1992[536] but s.26 of that Act contains a saver in respect of marital privacy. Therefore, it would seem that privilege can be claimed where necessary to protect marital privacy.

CONFIDENTIALITY

8.096 It will be evident from the discussion of the various privileges above that a fundamental prerequisite for a privilege from disclosure to arise is that the communication be confidential in nature. However, the corollary does not follow and the mere fact that a communication came into being in the course of a confidential relationship and/or was intended to pass in confidence will not clothe it with privilege.[537] In *Re Kevin O'Kelly*,[538] Walsh J emphasised that:

> The fact that a communication was made under terms of expressed confidence or implied confidence does not create a privilege against disclosure. So far as the administration of justice is concerned the public has a right to every man's evidence except for those persons protected by a constitutional or other established and recognised privilege.

Thus, the courts have rejected claims of privilege in respect of communications

---

[533] High Court (Geoghegan J) 30 April 1999.

[534] S.3 of the Evidence (Amendment) Act 1853.

[535] S.1(d) of the Criminal Justice (Evidence) Act 1924.

[536] Implementing the recommendation of the Law Reform Commission in its *Report on the Competence and Compellability of Spouses as Prosecution Witnesses* (LRC 13-1985) at 27.

[537] *Miley v Flood* [2001] 1 ILRM 489; *Cooper Flynn v RTÉ* [2000] 3 IR 344, 351, [2001] 1 ILRM 208, 217; *Johnston v Church of Scientology* High Court (Geoghegan J) 30 April 1999; *Skeffington v Rooney* [1997] 1 IR 22, 35, [1997] 2 ILRM 56, 69; *In re Kevin O'Kelly* (1974) 108 ILTR 97, 101; *Duchess of Kingston's Case* (1776) 20 How St Tr 355, 586; *Greenlaw v R* (1838) 1 Beav 137, 145; *Wheeler v Le Marchant* (1881) 17 Ch D 675, 681.

[538] (1974) 108 ILTR 97, 101.

passing between a doctor and patient,[539] a banker and customer,[540] an account-ant and client,[541] an agent and principal,[542] and a probation officer and proba-tioner.[543] Neither can a privilege from disclosure be created by a contractual stipulation that information is not to be disclosed.[544]

However, as is clear from the decision in *Cooper Flynn v RTÉ*,[545] the courts recognise that there is a public interest in maintaining the confidentiality of certain communications. Thus, although this will not be a sufficient basis, of itself, to resist the disclosure of information, it is a factor which will be taken into account and will influence the court in deciding whether to order the dis-covery, production or inspection of documents.[546] In addition, if an order for the disclosure of confidential information is made, the courts will, where possible, take steps to ameliorate the effects of disclosure by, for example, ordering dis-closure in redacted form only or limit it to a party's legal advisers.[547]

PROCEDURAL MATTERS

MAKING A CLAIM TO PRIVILEGE

8.097 The fact that a claim of privilege can properly be made in respect of a document does not exempt it from the discovery process and all relevant docu-

---

[539] *Miley v Flood* [2001] 1 ILRM 489; *Duchess of Kingston's Case* (1776) 20 How St Tr 355; *Wheeler v Le Marchant* (1881) 17 Ch D 675, 681; *Anderson v Bank of British Columbia* (1876) 2 Ch D 644, 651; *Campbell v Thameside Metropolitan Borough Council* [1982] QB 1065, [1982] 2 All ER 791. Cf. *W. (W.) v B. (P.)* High Court (Barr J) 18 March 1999 where a claim of privilege in respect of the plaintiff's medical, psychiatric and counselling records and reports was rejected in circumstances where the plaintiff instituted proceedings alleging that the defendant had sexually assaulted him.

[540] *Cooper Flynn v RTÉ* [2000] 3 IR 344, 351, [2001] 1 ILRM 208, 217; *Loyd v Freshfield* (1826) 2 C & P 325.

[541] *Chantrey Martin & Co. v Martin* [1953] 2 QB 286, [1953] 2 All ER 691.

[542] *Kerry County Council v Liverpool Salvage Association* [1905] 2 IR 38, 44; *Anderson v Bank of British Columbia* (1876) 2 Ch D 644, 648; *Slade v Tucker* (1880) 14 Ch D 824, 827.

[543] *R v Umoh* (1986) 84 Cr App R 138; *R v Walker* (1992) 74 CCC (3d) 97.

[544] *Johnston v Church of Scientology* High Court (Geoghegan J) 30 April 1999; *Federal Commissioner of Taxation v Coombes* [1999] FCA 842, (1999) 164 ALR 131; *South-ern Cross Commodities Pty Ltd v Crinis* [1984] VR 697.

[545] [2001] 1 ILRM 208, 217.

[546] *Cooper Flynn v RTÉ* [2000] 3 IR 344, 351, [2001] 1 ILRM 208, 217-18; *Wallace Smith Trust Co. Ltd v Deloitte Haskins & Sells* [1996] 4 All ER 403, 417; *Science Research Council v Nassé* [1980] AC 1028, 1089, [1979] 3 All ER 673, 699.

[547] *Ibid.*

ments over which privilege is claimed must be listed in Part II of the First Schedule to an affidavit of discovery.[548]

Where a claim to privilege is made, the proper format is to list each document individually with a description of the general nature of the document[549] and an indication of the type of privilege claimed[550] and, if this is not done, further and better discovery may be ordered.[551] It is essential that the claim of privilege be particularised so that the party seeking discovery can evaluate the claim of privilege made and decide whether to challenge it[552] or, if a challenge is made, to enable the court to adjudicate upon it.[553] However, there is a marked tendency for parties to make generic claims of privilege in respect of bundles of documents and it has been necessary for the Supreme Court, on more than one occasion, to remind parties of their obligations in that regard.[554] For example, in *O'Brien v Minister for Defence*,[555] Hamilton CJ stressed that it was not sufficient to claim general privilege in respect of bundles of documents or files and that:

> The onus is on the defendants to specify in detail by number each of the documents in their possession relating to matters the subject matter of the proceedings and to specify in detail the nature of the privilege claimed in respect of each document and the basis for such privilege.

Where a claim of privilege is made in respect of an individual document, it is also important that it is made in the proper form and the claim may be unsuc-

---

[548] See *Bula Ltd v Tara Mines (No. 5)* [1994] 1 IR 487 and *Spring Grove Services (Ireland) Ltd v O'Callaghan* High Court (Herbert J) 31 July 2000.

[549] In *Irish Haemophilia Society Ltd v Lindsay* High Court (Kelly J) 16 May 2001, the notice party, the BTSB, had sworn a supplemental affidavit of discovery which described the documents over which privilege was claimed in general terms. Kelly J rejected the argument of the applicant that description of the documents in greater detail was required. He cautioned that "care must be taken to ensure that privilege is not abused on the one hand and on the other that the requirements for its assertion are not such as to in effect dilute or destroy it".

[550] See Appendix C, Form 10.

[551] See, for example, *Bula Ltd v Crowley* [1991] 1 IR 220, [1990] ILRM 756 and *Flynn v Northern Banking Co.* (1898) 32 ILTR 67.

[552] *Flynn v Northern Banking Co.* (1898) 32 ILTR 67; *Rushbrooke v O'Sullivan* [1926] IR 500.

[553] See, for example, *O'Brien v Minister for Defence* [1998] 2 ILRM 156, 159, where the Supreme Court said that it was unable to rule on the claim of privilege made "in the absence of having available to it particulars of the documentation in the possession of the defendants relating to the matter and without having particulars with regard to the nature of the privilege claimed in respect of each document."

[554] *Rushbrooke v O'Sullivan* [1926] IR 500; *Bula Ltd v Tara Mines Ltd* [1991] 1 IR 217; *Bula Ltd v Crowley* [1991] 1 IR 220, [1990] ILRM 756; *O'Brien v Minister for Defence* [1998] 2 ILRM 156.

[555] [1998] 2 ILRM 156, 160.

cessful if the affidavit of discovery is improperly drafted. For example, in *Worthington v Dublin, Wicklow & Wexford Railway Co.*,[556] it was held that the defendants were bound to produce an engineer's report regarding the subject matter of the plaintiff's claim because there was no statement in the affidavit to the effect that it had been prepared in contemplation of litigation.[557] However, an undue level of specificity is not required and in *Bula Ltd v Crowley*,[558] it was held that, where it is sought to claim litigation privilege, it is not necessary to assert in the affidavit of discovery that the dominant purpose for the genesis of the document was for the purpose of litigation unless a duality of reasons for the creation of the document, one of which would attract privilege and one of which would not, is evident.

PROCEDURE FOR CHALLENGING A CLAIM OF PRIVILEGE

8.098 If a party wishes to challenge a claim of privilege made by another party, the proper procedure is to bring an application seeking to have that issue decided, most properly by means of a motion seeking to inspect the documents. Although the issue of privilege is frequently raised by means of a motion for further and better discovery, this type of motion is more properly reserved for situations where a party believes that there are other documents in existence which have not been discovered or where documents are improperly or generically listed in the affidavit of discovery.

The onus is on the person claiming privilege to establish that the documents are privileged.[559] However, once the party claiming privilege has discharged this onus, it then falls on the party impugning the claim of privilege to do so by evidence.[560]

Although a court may be satisfied simply from a description of the document that it is privileged, it has an inherent jurisdiction, irrespective of the way in which the issue is raised before the court,[561] to adjudicate on a claim of privilege. In *Smurfit Paribas Bank Ltd v AAB Export Finance Ltd*,[562] McCarthy J said that:

---

[556] (1888) 22 LR Ir 310.

[557] See also *Smith v Daniell* (1874) LR 18 Eq 649.

[558] High Court (Murphy J) 8 March 1991.

[559] *Quinlivan v Governor of Portlaoise Prison* Supreme Court 5 March 1997 (*per* Hamilton CJ); *Irish Haemophilia Society Ltd v Lindsay* High Court (Kelly J) 16 May 2001; *Waugh v British Railways Board* [1980] AC 521, 541, [1979] 2 All ER 1169, 1181.

[560] *Irish Haemophilia Society Ltd v Lindsay* High Court (Kelly J) 16 May 2001.

[561] Where the issue is raised by way of an application for an order of inspection, Order 31, rule 20(2) expressly provides that the court may inspect the document for the purpose of deciding as to the validity of the claim of privilege.

[562] [1990] 1 IR 469, 480, [1990] ILRM 588, 597.

[T]he question as to whether or not a party to litigation will be privileged to refuse to produce particular evidence is a matter within the sole competence of the courts. It follows that the courts have whatever power is necessary to examine any relevant documents, irrespective of the wishes of the parties and to determine whether any communication, written or otherwise, between a party to litigation and any other person or body is privileged from disclosure.[563]

8.099 In *Duncan v Governor of Portlaoise Prison*,[564] the issue arose as to whether it is possible to cross-examine the deponent of an affidavit of discovery. Kelly J accepted that an affidavit of discovery was not conclusive and could be the subject of cross-examination:

It appears to me that the administration of justice, which is vested by the Constitution in the courts, requires that the courts have the ability to adjudicate fully upon the adequacy and accuracy of an affidavit of discovery. In exceptional cases this may involve the cross-examination of the deponent of such an affidavit. To hold otherwise would mean that the court would be deprived from investigating the accuracy or adequacy of an affidavit of discovery and would have to accept at face value what is averred therein.[565]

However, the circumstances in which this would be permitted were extremely rare. This was because there were a variety of other remedies available to test matters contained in an affidavit of discovery including orders for further and better discovery, the delivery of interrogatories and the inspection by the court itself of documents referred to in an affidavit of discovery. In addition, it was "wholly undesirable that the court should, save in the most exceptional cases, be called upon to deal with questions such as the existence or non-existence of a document in circumstances where such a question might impinge to a serious extent on the issues in the action".[566] He declined to specify the circumstances in which a court might permit cross-examination on an affidavit of discovery but emphasised that it could only arise where the alternative remedies had proven inadequate.[567]

Another submission was made to the effect that the court should direct the production of the documents with a view to the court reading them and extracting from them the factual content, in respect of which legal professional privi-

---

[563] *Cf. Murphy v Dublin Corporation* [1972] IR 215, 235; *Kerry County Council v Liverpool Salvage Association* [1905] 2 IR 38, 43.
[564] [1997] 1 IR 558, [1997] 2 ILRM 296.
[565] *Ibid.* at 573, 309.
[566] *Ibid.* at 573, 309.
[567] See also *Irish Haemophilia Society Ltd v Lindsay* High Court (Kelly J) 16 May 2001.

lege would not apply. However, Kelly J rejected this "unprecedented" proposition which, he said, would "dilute in very considerable measure the whole notion and effect of legal professional privilege". He took the view that to allow this would "be an unwarranted and dangerous course to embark upon" and would seriously interfere with legal professional privilege which had been described as "a fundamental condition on which the administration of justice as a whole rests".[568] He went on to point out the practical difficulties attendant upon the proposition:

> If [counsel] is correct in his submission, any case in which legal professional privilege is claimed may, on the simple request of the opponent, result in the court being called upon to go through the entire of the documents with a view to ascertaining, not the validity of the claim to legal professional privilege, but rather to engage in the work of editing the documents with a view to extracting from them factual material to be disclosed to the other side. This exercise would have to be conducted at a time in advance of the trial when no judge can be fully apprised of the entire factual matrix against which the action is brought. The conduct of such an exercise would, in my view, be much more likely to work against the administration of justice than in its favour.[569]

This proposition was also rejected by the Supreme Court on appeal.[570] Keane J said that this proposition was "unsupported by authority, [was] clearly incorrect in principle and, if admitted, would undermine the whole basis of legal professional privilege."

---

[568] *R v Derby Magistrates' Courts, ex p. B.* [1996] AC 487, 507, [1995] 4 All ER 526, 540 (*per* Taylor LCJ).
[569] [1997] 1 IR 558, 576, [1997] 2 ILRM 296, 311-312.
[570] *Sub nom Quinlivan v Governor of Portlaoise Prison* Supreme Court, 5 March 1997.

CHAPTER NINE

INTERROGATORIES

INTRODUCTION

9.001 The term "interrogatories" describes the procedure whereby a litigant seeks discovery of facts within the knowledge of the opposing party by posing a series of questions which the latter must answer on affidavit. As Lynch J stated in *Bula Ltd v Tara Mines Ltd*:[1] "the basic purpose of interrogatories is to avoid injustice where only one party has knowledge and the ability conveniently to prove facts which are important to be established in aid of the opposing party's case, such opposing party not having such knowledge nor the ability to prove the facts either at all or without undue difficulty". The purpose of employing this procedure is to ascertain information about the issues which arise in the action or to obtain admissions from the opposing party,[2] with a view to narrowing the issues in dispute between the parties and thus saving time and expense at the trial. Doyle J summarised the purpose of interrogatories in the course of his judgment in *Long v Conway*[3] as follows:

> [T]o facilitate and to expedite the trial of actions by enabling a party to obtain from his opponent information as to facts material to the questions in dispute between them and to obtain admissions of any facts which he has to prove on any issue which is raised between them.

Interrogatories therefore provide a useful means of preventing a party denying facts which he knows to be true and of establishing the veracity of facts which might otherwise be difficult to prove. As Cotton LJ stated in *Attorney General v Gaskill*:[4] "the object of interrogatories is not to learn what the issues are, but to see whether the party who interrogates cannot obtain an admission from his opponent which will make the burden of proof easier than it would otherwise have been".

---

[1] [1995] 1 ILRM 401, 405.
[2] *Mercantile Credit Co. of Ireland Ltd v Heelan* [1994] 2 IR 105, 110, [1994] 1 ILRM 406, 411. See also *Attorney General v Gaskill* (1882) 20 Ch D 519.
[3] High Court (Doyle J) 25 July 1977 at 5.
[4] (1882) 20 Ch D 519, 528-529.

THE PROCEDURE FOR SEEKING INTERROGATORIES

9.002 Order 31, rule 1 of the Rules of the Superior Courts 1986 provides that in any matter where relief by way of damages or otherwise is sought on the ground of fraud or breach of trust, the plaintiff may at any time after delivering his statement of claim, or if a defendant, at or after delivery of his defence, deliver interrogatories in writing to the opposite party, provided that no party shall deliver more than one set of interrogatories to the same party without an order for that purpose. In every other cause or matter a party may only deliver interrogatories by leave of the court and while no specific provision is made in relation to the time of their delivery, the suggestion has been made that generally the parties must have filed the appropriate pleadings before such leave will be granted[5] and it has been stated that "the service of interrogatories before witness statements have been exchanged will almost always be premature".[6] The rule also requires that interrogatories when delivered shall have a note at their foot stating which interrogatories each person is required to answer.[7]

9.003 A copy of the interrogatories which a party proposes to deliver shall be delivered with the notice of application for leave to deliver them unless the court orders otherwise and the court shall consider whether particular interrogatories shall be permitted.[8] Application for leave to deliver interrogatories shall be brought by way of motion on notice and may be heard by the Master.[9] The Rules set out a number of principles about the types of interrogatories which may be allowed. Interrogatories which do not relate to any matters in question in the cause or matter shall be deemed irrelevant.[10] In addition, leave

---

[5] Ó'Floinn and Gannon *Practice and Procedure in the Superior Courts* (1996) at 236.

[6] *Per* Colman J in *Det Danske Hedeselskabet v KDM International plc* [1994] 2 Lloyd's Rep 534. See also *Hall v Sevalco Ltd* [1996] TLR 183 where interrogatories served before exchange of witness statements or receipt of answers to requests for further and better particulars were held to be premature. Note also that in the decision of the English Court of Appeal in *UCB Bank plc v Halifax* 10 June 1997, Butler-Sloss J commented that "a suitable time if at all for interrogatories to be administered is after discovery and exchange of witness statements and to do so at an earlier stage will almost always be premature". Quoted by Shanley J in *Woodfab Ltd v Coillte Teoranta* [2000] 1 IR 20, 29, [1998] 1 ILRM 381, 389.

[7] In *McClatchey v Reilly* [1960] NI 118 Black LJ stressed that the plaintiff who had delivered interrogatories to two defendants was at fault in not stating which of them was to answer particular interrogatories.

[8] Order 31, rule 2. The rule provides that in deciding upon such an application, the court shall take into account any offer which may be made by the party sought to be interrogated, to deliver particulars or to make admissions, or to produce documents, relating to any matter in question.

[9] Order 63, rule 1(6). Cahill suggests in *Discovery* (1996) at 65 that "an affidavit in support is not usually necessary but in more complex cases it may greatly facilitate the application".

[10] Order 31, rule 1. As Costello J stated in *Mercantile Credit Co. of Ireland Ltd v Heelan*

will only be given in relation to interrogatories which shall be "considered necessary either for disposing fairly of the cause or matter or for saving costs".[11] The interrogatories are required to be in the form set out in Form 8 of Appendix C of the Rules and should be in the form of leading questions which can be answered 'yes' or 'no'. Order 31, rule 7 goes on to provide that any interrogatories "may be set aside on the ground that they have been exhibited unreasonably or vexatiously, or struck out on the ground that they are prolix, oppressive,[12] unnecessary, or scandalous" and states that any application for this purpose shall be made within seven days after service of the interrogatories. In *Bula Ltd v Tara Mines Ltd*[13] Lynch J stated that in his view a large number of the interrogatories asked were "quite unnecessary" and that others were impermissible for vagueness or for asking for opinions or evidence as distinct from facts. In these circumstances he stated that the principles set out by Myers J in the Australian decision of *American Flange Manufacturing Co. Inc. v Rheem (Australia) Pty (No. 2)*[14] could be applied, namely that "interrogatories which were prolix and oppressive or unnecessary could be disallowed as a whole, even though some of them were proper, and that the court was not required to go through interrogatories of that kind and ascertain which were admissible and which were not". However, Lynch J stated that having regard to the costs involved in an application for leave to deliver interrogatories and in order to ensure that the case should continue without any further interruptions due to interlocutory applications, he decided to go through the interrogatories with a view to deciding whether any and if so, which of them, ought to be allowed.

9.004 Interrogatories must be answered by affidavit within ten days of their delivery or within such time as the court may allow,[15] and the affidavit shall be in the form set out in Form No. 9 in Appendix C. An objection to answering one or more of the interrogatories may be set out in the affidavit in answer on the ground that it is "scandalous or irrelevant, or not *bona fide* for the purpose of the cause or matter, or that the matters inquired into are not suffi-

---

[1994] 2 IR 105, 110, [1994] 1 ILRM 406, 410 interrogatories must relate to "any matter in question" in the action. He went on to say that while at first sight this might seem to permit a party to interrogate an opponent on every issue which might arise in the action and so permit evidence on oath on every issue to be used at the trial as the interrogator may consider useful to the case, this is not so.

[11] Order 31, rule 2. See also *Conlon v Times Newspapers Ltd* Supreme Court, 28 July 1997.

[12] In *Det Danske Hedeselskabet v. KDM International plc* [1994] 2 Lloyd's Rep 534 Colman J held that an interrogatory was oppressive on the basis that it was inappropriate that a party should be asked to prepare statistical information which might require a substantial investigatory exercise giving rise to the answer requested.

[13] [1995] 1 ILRM 401.

[14] [1965] NSWLR 193.

[15] Order 31, rule 8.

ciently material at that stage".[16] The Rules go on to provide that the sufficiency
or otherwise of any affidavit objected to as insufficient shall be determined by
the court on motion[17] and that if the person interrogated omits to answer or
answers insufficiently, the party interrogating may apply to the court for an
order requiring him to answer or to answer further as the case may be.[18] Finally, it should be noted that Order 31, rule 3 provides that if the Taxing Master
or the court considers that the interrogatories have been exhibited "unreasonably, vexatiously, or at improper length" the costs occasioned by them shall be
paid by the party at fault.

    Order 31, rule 21 provides that if any party fails to comply with an order to
answer interrogatories, he shall be liable to attachment, or to have his action
dismissed for want of prosecution or to have his defence, if any, struck out and
the party interrogating may apply to the court for an order to that effect.[19] In
addition, Order 31, rule 29 now provides that a non-party may by leave of the
court, be directed to answer interrogatories if he is likely to be in a position to
give evidence relevant to an issue arising or likely to arise out of the cause or
matter and that the provisions of Order 31 shall apply *mutatis mutandis* to such
orders.

WHEN WILL INTERROGATORIES BE CONSIDERED NECESSARY?

9.005 These provisions of Order 31, rule 2 have been considered on a number
of occasions by the courts in this jurisdiction and overall, it is possible to
discern a movement towards a less flexible interpretation of what will be considered "necessary for disposing fairly of the action or for saving costs". In *J.
& L.S. Goodbody Ltd v Clyde Shipping Company Ltd*[20] Walsh J stated as
follows:

> While Order 31 rule 2 of the Rules of the Superior Courts provides that
> leave to deliver interrogatories shall be given only when it is considered
> necessary either for disposing fairly of the action or for saving costs, it is
> well established that one of the purposes of interrogatories is to sustain
> the plaintiff's case as well as to destroy the defendant's (see the judg-
> ment of this Court in *Keating v Healy*) and that interrogatories need not
> be confined to the facts directly in issue but may extend to any facts, the

---

[16] Order 31, rule 6.
[17] Order 31, rule 10.
[18] In *Lloyd v Morley* (1879) 5 LR Ir 74, 75 Chatterton VC stated that while the rules make
no specific provision in relation to the time within which an application for an order
requiring a further answer to interrogatories should be made, it should be made within a
reasonable time.
[19] See further paragraphs 7.024–7.025.
[20] Supreme Court, 9 May 1967 at 3.

existence or non-existence of which is relevant to the existence or non-existence of facts directly in issue. Furthermore the interrogatories sought need not be shown to be conclusive on the questions in issue but it is sufficient if the interrogatories sought should have some bearing on the question and that the interrogatory might form a step in establishing the liability. It is not necessary for the person seeking leave to deliver the interrogatory to show that it is in respect of something he does not already know.

This statement was quoted by Hamilton J in the course of his judgment in *Quilligan v Sugrue*[21] although the conclusion reached by the court would suggest that a more restrictive approach than that set out by Walsh J was being followed. Hamilton J had to consider whether to allow a number of interrogatories relating to an accident in respect of which the plaintiff said that he had no recollection. He pointed out that the accident had been witnessed by a number of people who had given statements to the gardaí and a statement in relation to it had also been made by the defendant. Hamilton J concluded that having regard to the fact that these witnesses and the defendant's statement would be available to the plaintiff at the trial[22] he would vary the Master's order and refuse leave to allow the interrogatories which asked specific questions about the trial to be delivered.

9.006 More recently in *Mercantile Credit Co. of Ireland Ltd v Heelan*[23] Costello J stated that in considering the fair disposal of an action commenced by plenary summons the court must bear in mind that such actions are in principle to be heard on oral evidence and that the use of evidence on affidavit given in reply to interrogatories is an exception which must be justified by some special exigency in the case which, in the interests of doing justice, requires the exception to be allowed. Commenting on the aim of saving costs Costello J further stated in *Mercantile*,[24] that although the rule allows interrogatories to be served for the purpose of saving costs, the interest of doing justice between the parties is the paramount consideration and so an order will be refused if a fair hearing of the issues between the parties might be prejudiced, even if the cost of proceedings could be reduced by making the order. In addition, it should be noted that in *Det Danske Hedeselskabet v KDM International plc*[25] Colman

---

[21] High Court (Hamilton J) 13 February 1984.
[22] In *Griebart v Morris* [1920] 1 KB 659, 663 Bankes LJ had stated that in many running down cases it may be correct not to allow interrogatories as they will not be necessary because *e.g.* the plaintiff can call witnesses who saw the accident.
[23] [1994] 2 IR 105, 110, [1994] 1 ILRM 406, 410. See also *McCole v Blood Transfusion Service Board* High Court (Laffoy J) 11 June 1996 at 2. Quoted with approval by Shanley J in *Woodfab Ltd v Coillte Teoranta* [2000] 1 IR 20, 28, [1998] 1 ILRM 381, 389.
[24] *Ibid.* at 116, 415.
[25] [1994] 2 Lloyd's Rep 534.

J commented that requests for information which, although it may be relevant to matters in issue, can only be provided by means of detailed research or investigation which the party interrogated would not otherwise carry out for the purpose of preparing for trial will hardly ever qualify as being necessary either for disposing fairly of the action or for saving costs.

9.007 Apart from cases where damages are sought on the grounds of fraud or breach of trust,[26] the view that interrogatories will only be deemed necessary in special circumstances would certainly seem to be borne out by the subsequent judgment of Shanley J in *Woodfab Ltd v Coillte Teoranta*.[27] Counsel for the defendant had relied strongly on the *dicta* of Bingham MR in *Hall v Sevalco Ltd*[28] where he had stated as follows: "Interrogatories should not be regarded as a source of ammunition to be routinely discharged as part of an interlocutory bombardment preceding the main battle. The interrogator had to be able to show that his interrogatories, if answered when served, would serve a clear litigious purpose by saving costs or promoting the fair and efficient conduct of the action". Shanley J stressed that "no party has a right to have interrogatories delivered and answered" and said that the authorities suggested that "a plaintiff will not be permitted as of right to deliver interrogatories but will have to satisfy the court either that a special exigency and some necessity exists which warrants the delivery and answering of interrogatories".[29] In his view the case law identified the delivery and answering of interrogatories as an "unusual step" in an action commenced by plenary summons and he quoted from the judgment of Butler-Sloss J in *UCB Bank plc v Halifax*[30] to the effect that the administering of interrogatories is not "a normal step" and that they must serve a "clear litigious purpose". He continued as follows:

> The various decisions to which I have been referred have gone to some length to emphasise that giving leave to deliver interrogatories must be regarded as an exception in any case to be heard on oral evidence and must be justified by the party seeking to deliver interrogatories.... However, it does appear that once the party seeking to deliver interrogatories satisfies that court that such delivery would serve a clear litigious purpose by saving costs or promoting the fair and efficient conduct of the action in question then the court should be prepared to allow the delivery of interrogatories unless it is satisfied that the delivery and answering of the interrogatories would work an injustice on the party interrogated.[31]

---

[26] See Order 31, rule 1 and paragraph 9.002 *supra*.
[27] [2000] 1 IR 20, [1998] 1 ILRM 381.
[28] [1996] TLR 183. Bingham MR had commented that "necessity [is] a stringent test".
[29] [2000] 1 IR 20, 28, [1998] 1 ILRM 381, 389.
[30] Court of Appeal, 10 June 1997.
[31] [2000] 1 IR 20, 29, [1998] 1 ILRM 381, 389.

Shanley J concluded that while he did not accept that the fact the case before him related to the Competition Act 1991 constituted a "special exigency", he was satisfied that the answers to the interrogatories which he proposed to allow to be delivered would save costs and time during the course of the trial and that by permitting them he would ensure that no injustice to the plaintiff would result from having to call the deponent and being deprived of the right to cross-examine him.

9.008 These views were considered in detail by O'Sullivan J in *Money Markets International Stock Brokers Ltd v Fanning*.[32] He concluded that the necessity referred to in the rules can be satisfied if the party exhibiting interrogatories can establish that answers to them would save costs or promote the fair and efficient conduct of the action in question. However, he added that the directing of replies must at all times be subject to the overriding principle that compelling such replies would not work an injustice upon the party interrogated.

It should also be noted that O'Sullivan J subsequently pointed out that in recent decisions the Supreme Court appeared to place less emphasis than the High Court on the fact that interrogatories are the exception rather than a normal step in pre-trial case preparation which should be encouraged. He referred to the fact that in the *J. & L.S. Goodbody* case, Walsh J appeared largely to subordinate the necessity to establish an exigency to the principle that one of the purpose of interrogatories is to sustain the plaintiff's case as well as to destroy the defendant's. O'Sullivan J also said that the judgment of Walsh J suggested that once it is established that the purpose of an interrogatory is either to sustain the plaintiff's case or to destroy the defendant's, then it may be regarded as necessary for fairly disposing of the cause or matter or for saving costs. Certainly the approach adopted by O'Sullivan J in *Money Markets* is more in line with that of the Supreme Court in *J. & L.S. Goodbody* and shows a movement away from the "special exigency" test suggested by Shanley J in *Woodfab*.

THE TYPE OF INFORMATION WHICH MAY BE OBTAINED BY INTERROGATORIES

9.009 Interrogatories may be delivered either to obtain information from the interrogated party about the issues that arise in the action or to obtain admissions from him.[33] Where information is sought it must relate to the issues raised

---

[32] [2000] 3 IR 215, [2001] 1 ILRM 1. See further Dodd [2001] 3(2) P & P 12.
[33] *Mercantile Credit Co. of Ireland Ltd v Heelan* [1994] 2 IR 105, 110, [1994] 1 ILRM 406, 411. See also *McCole v Blood Transfusion Service Board* High Court (Laffoy J) 11 June 1996 at 2. As Cotton LJ stated in *Attorney General v Gaskill* (1882) 20 Ch D

in the pleadings and not to the evidence which a party wishes to adduce in order to establish his case.[34] So a distinction must be drawn between interrogatories which relate to the facts in dispute and those which relate to the evidence of the facts in dispute. As Lord Esher MR commented in *Marriott v Chamberlain*:[35] "it is not permissible to ask what is mere evidence of the facts in dispute, but forms no part of the facts themselves" although he pointed out that "the right to interrogate is not confined to the facts directly in issue, but extends to any facts the existence or non-existence of which is relevant to the existence or non-existence of the facts directly in issue".[36] O'Sullivan J pointed out in *Money Markets International Stock Brokers Ltd v Fanning*[37] that the distinction between "... what is mere evidence of the facts in dispute ..." and "... the facts themselves ..." is a difficult one because the facts themselves become evidence once replies are furnished to interrogatories. He expressed the view that the line between what is and is not permissible is even more difficult to lay down in the light of the right to interrogate not only in relation to the facts directly at issue but in relation to any facts "the existence or non-existence of which is relevant to the existence or non-existence of the facts directly at issue". O'Sullivan J suggested that the formulation of Buckley LJ in *Hooton v Dalby*[38] to the effect that one may interrogate as to facts which tend to support ones case or to impeach that of ones opponent but not as to facts which support ones opponent's case provides a useful gloss on what he described as the "somewhat delphic" formulation of Lord Esher MR in *Marriott*.

A slightly different formulation was put forward by Lynch J in *Bula Ltd v Tara Mines Ltd*[39] in the following terms:

> Interrogatories to be allowable must be as to facts in issue or facts reasonably relevant to establish facts in issue. Interrogatories as to mere evi-

---

519, 529 "the object is to get from the defendant ... an admission of that which no doubt he denied by his defence, but not on oath, *viz.* a fact supposed to be within his knowledge ... and an admission of it by him must obviously save an enormous amount of expense at the trial".

[34] *Mercantile Credit Co. of Ireland Ltd v Heelan* [1994] 2 IR 105, 111, [1994] 1 ILRM 406, 411. See also *McCole v Blood Transfusion Service Board* High Court (Laffoy J) 11 June 1996 at 2.

[35] (1886) 17 QBD 154, 163.

[36] *Ibid.* at 163. See also *Nash v Layton* [1911] 2 Ch 71, 76 & 80. Quoted with approval by Costello J in *Mercantile Credit Co. of Ireland Ltd v Heelan* [1994] 2 IR 105, 111-112, [1994] 1 ILRM 406, 411-412. See also *McCole v Blood Transfusion Service Board* High Court (Laffoy J) 11 June 1996 at 2.

[37] [2000] 3 IR 125, [2001] 1 ILRM 1.

[38] [1907] 2 KB 18.

[39] [1995] 1 ILRM 401, 405. This view that questions as to opinions, the meaning or effect of documents or as to statements or conduct should not be permitted was adopted by Shanley J in *Woodfab Ltd v Coillte Teoranta* [2000] 1 IR 20, 30, [1998] 1 ILRM 381, 390.

dence as distinct from facts or as to opinions or matters of law such as the meaning or effect of documents or statements or conduct are not permissible. Nor is it appropriate that unnecessary interrogatories should be put such as to facts within the knowledge of and readily capable of proof by the interrogating parties.

9.010 In relation to admissions, Costello J stated in *Mercantile Credit Co. of Ireland Ltd v Heelan*,[40] that interrogatories which seek admissions as to the existence of documents and signatures to documents identified in discovery documents will normally be allowed, unless there are special reasons why in the interests of justice an order should not be made. He said that in such cases the court will allow such interrogatories because to refuse them would only add unnecessary costs and might also bring about a possible injustice as the interrogating party might be required to call the deponent at the trial to prove the relevant documents orally and thus deprive himself of the right to cross-examine the witness. In addition, Costello J stated that interrogatories which seek admissions about the facts surrounding documents identified in discovery affidavits must relate to the issues raised in the pleadings and cannot be used as a means of proving an interrogating party's case.[41]

As Bankes LJ stressed in *Griebart v Morris*[42] "it is not permissible to deliver interrogatories which are of a "fishing" character, or which seek to obtain the names of the opponent's witnesses". This reluctance to allow such "fishing" interrogatories can also be seen in a number of decisions in this jurisdiction, such as in the judgment of Doyle J in *Long v Conway*.[43] It is also evident in the judgments of both Hanna J and of the members of the Supreme Court in *Edgill v Cullen*[44] although the plaintiff's appeal in relation to one interrogatory in that case was allowed on the basis that it was fair and reasonable and asked for specific information necessarily within the defendant's knowledge and was not merely an attempt at "fishing".

9.011 The distinction between eliciting information through interrogatories at an interlocutory stage and through cross-examination at trial was considered by

---

[40] [1994] 2 IR 105, [1994] 1 ILRM 406.
[41] However, note that O'Sullivan J stated in *Money Markets International Stock Brokers Ltd v Fanning* [2000] 3 IR 215, [2001] 1 ILRM 1 that the purpose of exhibiting interrogatories is to seek admissions which will become evidence to be relied upon by the interrogating party, which while they will not prove the entire of that party's case, will lighten the burden of doing so to the extent that certain elements required to be proved will be established in the replies. He concluded "I am unable to see, therefore, how admissions about facts 'cannot be used as a means to prove the interrogating party's case'".
[42] [1920] 1 KB 659, 664.
[43] High Court (Doyle J) 25 July 1977 at 6. See also *Money Markets International Stock Brokers Ltd v Fanning* [2000] 3 IR 215, [2001] 1 ILRM 1.
[44] [1932] IR 734.

Laffoy J in her judgment in *McCole v Blood Transfusion Service Board*.[45]
Having summarised the principles set out by Costello J in *Mercantile,* she quoted
the following passage from the judgment of Colman J in *Det Danske
Hedeselskabet v KDM International plc*[46] which, it was submitted, was consistent with the fundamental rubric identified by Costello J, namely the existence of some special exigency:

> ... requests for information ascertainable by cross-examination at the trial
> are inappropriate unless the party questioning can establish that it is es-
> sential for the proper preparation of his case that such information is
> made available to him before trial, in the sense that if the matter is left
> until cross-examination at the trial that party will, or probably will be
> irremediably prejudiced in his conduct of the trial or the trial may be un-
> duly interrupted or otherwise disorganised by the late emergence of the
> information.

Applying this test, Laffoy J concluded that in her view the plaintiff had not
established that it was essential for the proper preparation of her case that
some of the interrogatories under consideration be furnished at that juncture
and said that the matters raised were matters for oral evidence at the trial.

Finally it should be noted that Lynch J in *Bula Ltd v Tara Mines Ltd*[47]
reiterated the point made by Murphy J in an earlier application in that case[48]
that "the making of an order of this nature does not lend credence, respect or
support of any description to the plaintiffs' claim" and that he regarded this
procedural relief as no more than ancillary to the institution of proceedings
themselves.

WHO MAY BE COMPELLED TO MAKE ENQUIRIES?

9.012 A final issue which arises is whether a party can be compelled to make
enquiries for the purpose of answering interrogatories where they have deposed to a lack of personal knowledge. In *J. & L.S. Goodbody Ltd v Clyde
Shipping Co. Ltd*[49] interrogatories were delivered to the secretary of the defendant company. Walsh J pointed out that in answering them he was not answering for himself but for the company and in doing so he must obtain such
information as he could from other servants of the company who had personally

---

[45] High Court (Laffoy J) 11 June 1996.
[46] [1994] 2 Lloyd's Rep 534, 537. This statement was approved of by the Court of Appeal
in *Hall v Sevalco Ltd* [1996] TLR 183.
[47] [1995] 1 ILRM 401.
[48] [1987] IR 85, 94 .
[49] Supreme Court, 9 May 1967.

conducted the transaction in question and had personal knowledge of the facts sought. He continued as follows: "On behalf of the company he is bound to answer according to information and belief acquired or formed from personal knowledge or from information obtained from others who are servants or agents of the company and have acquired information in that capacity." A slightly different situation arose in *Money Markets International Stock Brokers Ltd v Fanning*[50] in which the defendants sought to distinguish *Clyde Shipping* on the basis that they were individual directors rather than a company and were only giving their own answers and submitted that they should not be compelled to give answers which were not within their personal knowledge. However, O'Sullivan J referred to further *dicta* of Walsh J in *Clyde Shipping* which he said made it clear that the latter drew no distinction between an individual and a body corporate and condemned both if they answered in such a way as to leave the other party in doubt as to whether or not such individual or body had availed himself of the information properly at his disposal. O'Sullivan J therefore concluded that if information could be said to be properly at the disposal of the defendants, then notwithstanding that they are being interrogated as individuals rather then as officers of a company, they may not avoid giving answers to interrogatories merely on the grounds that the subject matter thereof is not within their personal knowledge.

A further issue which arose in *Money Markets* was whether the information sought could be said to be "properly at the disposal" of the defendants. The correct position had been set out by Colman J in *Det Danske Hedeselskabet v KDM International plc*[51] and referred to by Laffoy J in *McCole* to the effect that "the person other than the party interrogated whose knowledge may, for the purpose of interrogatories, be treated as the knowledge of the party interrogated must be a person for whose knowledge that party is responsible". O'Sullivan J expressed the view that it was artificial for the defendants to say that they had no personal knowledge of information in documents in respect of which (at the time they were brought into existence) they were, as directors of the company, in a position of responsibility. He considered that the defendants had available to them information "properly at [their] disposal" and as such might not, on the sole ground of lack of personal knowledge, decline to respond.

---

[50] [2000] 3 IR 215, [2001] 1 ILRM 1.
[51] [1994] 2 Lloyd's Rep 534.

CHAPTER TEN

SECURITY FOR COSTS

INTRODUCTION

10.001 The primary purpose of Order 29 of the Rules of the Superior Courts 1986 is arguably to protect defendants from spurious claims which may be brought against them by plaintiffs who reside out of the jurisdiction of the court and who for this reason may be able to evade any subsequent order as to costs made against them.[1] However, as Matthews[2] has pointed out in the context of the then equivalent English provision,[3] a defendant may seek to rely on the order even where a plaintiff has a good claim and may attempt to use it as a "tactical weapon" in the context of the proceedings as a whole. As Murphy J pointed out in the course of his judgment in *Proetta v Neil*[4] the order does not state a requirement in positive terms that a person resident outside the jurisdiction may be required to provide security for costs but "rather ... proceeds on the footing that such is the case". So, it is now accepted that an order for security for costs may be granted against a plaintiff who is ordinarily resident outside the jurisdiction where a defendant establishes on affidavit that he has a *prima facie* defence on the merits and there are no other special circumstances which might influence the exercise of the court's discretion.

Order 29, rule 1 provides that when a party requires security for costs, he should apply to the other party for such security and if within 48 hours of service of this notice the other party fails to provide it, the former party shall be at liberty to apply to the court for an order that the latter should furnish such security.[5] Rule 6 provides that where the court has made an order that a party

---

[1] As Finlay P commented in *Collins v Doyle* [1982] ILRM 495, 496: "In general it would appear to me that the principles underlying the defendant's right to security for costs must be that he should not suffer from an inability to recover the cost of successfully defending the claim arising from the fact that the unsuccessful plaintiff resides and has his assets outside the jurisdiction of the court".

[2] "Security for Costs and European Law" [1994] LMCLQ 454, 455.

[3] Order 23, rule 1(1)(a) of the Rules of the Supreme Court.

[4] [1996] 1 IR 100, 102, [1996] ILRM 457, 459.

[5] Note that in *Lancefort Ltd v An Bord Pleanála* [1998] 2 IR 511 Morris J stated that while undoubtedly the party seeking security is required to make the appropriate demand, failure to do so would only be relevant in his view if it transpired that the applicant were prepared to give security and never had the opportunity to do so by reason of the failure of the moving party to make the demand. In these circumstances Morris J suggested that the appropriate relief would be to make such order as to costs

should furnish security, the amount, time at which, and manner and form in which it shall be given shall be determined by the Master.

SECURITY FOR COSTS IN RELATION TO INDIVIDUAL PLAINTIFFS

The Circumstances in Which an Order for Security Will be Granted

10.002 At the outset it should be stated that security for costs of proceedings in the High Court[6] will only be granted in the case of individual as opposed to corporate plaintiffs in circumstances where that person is resident outside the jurisidction. In addition, such security will only be ordered by the court where it is necessary, so in *Hogan v Hogan*[7] where the plaintiff had admitted the defendant's entitlement to part of the sum claimed and proposed to lodge this sum (which exceeded any sum which might have been ordered by way of security) in court, the court refused to make an order for security on the grounds that it was now unnecessary.

The provisions of Order 29 provide some guidance about the circumstances in which an order for security will be granted although as Keane J has recently noted[8] the language of the order "assumes the existence of an existing practice rather than defining it in precise terms". Order 29, rule 3 provides that "No defendant shall be entitled to an order for security for costs by reason of any plaintiff being resident out of the jurisdiction of the court, unless upon a satisfactory affidavit that such defendant has a defence upon the merits". The phrase "satisfactory affidavit" was considered by the Irish Court of Appeal in *Walker v Atkinson*[9] in which Fitzgibbon LJ stated that it must mean "an affidavit that satisfies the court of something" and went on to say that a defendant must give some evidence to satisfy the court that there is a reasonable prospect of his establishing some more or less specific or ascertainable defence. Similarly in *Denman v O'Callaghan*[10] Ashbourne LC spoke of the need for a satisfactory affidavit "showing grounds on which we can arrive at the conclusion that [the defendant] has merits" and Fitzgibbon LJ stated that "the defendant must make a satisfactory affidavit that he has a specific and definite defence".[11] In addi-

---

as was required including the costs of the party attending court and in his view the failure to make the demand did not invalidate the application.
[6] The provisions governing security for the costs of an appeal are dealt with by Order 58, rule 17 and will be considered *infra*.
[7] [1924] 2 IR 14.
[8] *Pitt v Bolger* [1996] 1 IR 108, 114, [1996] 2 ILRM 68, 74. Referring to comments made by Murphy J in *Proetta v Neil* [1996] 1 IR 100, [1996] 1 ILRM 457.
[9] [1895] 1 IR 246, 249. See also the *dicta* of Walker LC (at 249) that as the defendant is bound to lay a satisfactory affidavit before the court "he must at least, state facts which suggest a defence".
[10] (1897) 31 ILTR 141, 142.
[11] *Ibid.* at 142. See also the *dicta* of Fitzgibbon LJ in *Dennis v Leinster Paper Co. Ltd* [1901] 2 IR 337, 346 that a "defendant must indicate a definite defence, and show a

tion, the comment of Budd J in *Cohane v Cohane*[12] on the interpretation of the relevant requirements in Order 29, rule 3 is worth noting:

> What the rule says is that an order for security shall not be made in the case of a plaintiff resident out of the jurisdiction unless the defendant files a satisfactory affidavit of merits; it does not say that, if a satisfactory affidavit of merits is filed, security must be given in the case of a plaintiff outside the jurisdiction.

10.003 As Walsh J stated in *Power v Irish Civil Service (Permanent) Building Society*:[13] "What will amount to a satisfactory affidavit that a defendant has a defence on the merits in any particular action must necessarily depend upon the circumstances of the case and upon the nature and details of the claim and the allegations made". In this case the plaintiff had, in the opinion of the court, not pleaded any stateable cause of action and the defendant's affidavit contained the averment that it had a good defence on the merits. The majority of the Supreme Court concluded that the affidavit was "satisfactory" within the meaning of rule 3 "having regard to the complete absence of the grounds of the plaintiff's alleged claim".[14]

10.004 It was established in *Gardiner v Harris*[15] that *prima facie* the affidavit to satisfy the provisions of Order 29, rule 3 should be sworn by the defendant himself. This was confirmed by Murphy J in *Banco Ambrosiano SPA v Ansbacher & Co. Ltd,*[16] in which the affidavit had been sworn by a solicitor on behalf of the defendant, who commented that "the failure to have the affidavit sworn by the defendant himself would have been sufficient grounds for refusing the order".[17] This question was also considered by Murphy J in *Proetta v Neil*[18] where he stated, referring to the *Banco* case, that he would have expected the defendant to have sworn an affidavit himself and to have dealt more precisely with the basis of his defence. However, he recognised that any justification for

---

reasonable prospect of sustaining it" and the *dicta* of Ashbourne LC (at 345) that "we have only to be satisfied on the facts disclosed in the affidavits that there is a reasonable prospect of a defence being established".

[12] [1968] IR 176, 181. Budd J held that the High Court judge had erred in so far as he considered that he had no discretion but to make the order once a reasonable prospect of establishing a defence had been shown.

[13] [1968] IR 158, 163. See also the *dicta* of Fitzgerald J (at 164) that "the assessment of whether an affidavit is satisfactory or not must be made with due regard to the nature of the action, the facts pleaded in the statement of claim and the cause of action, or causes of action, therein pleaded".

[14] *Per* Walsh J at 163.

[15] (1881) 8 LR Ir 352.

[16] High Court (Murphy J) 19 July 1985.

[17] *Ibid.* at 3.

[18] [1996] 1 IR 100.

the alleged libel was not likely to be within his direct knowledge and that at this stage in the proceedings he had to rely on information obtained from other sources. Although Murphy J held that he felt obliged to dismiss the defendant's claim for security having regard to the provisions of the EC Treaty,[19] he did conclude that the circumstances disclosed in the affidavits were not such as would normally have justified him in exercising his discretion against the defendant's claim for security.

The effect of other rules in Order 29 should also be noted. Rule 2 provides that a defendant shall not be entitled to an order for security "solely on the ground that the plaintiff resides in Northern Ireland". The effect of an earlier version of rule 2 which provided that a defendant should not be entitled to an order for security "solely on the ground that the plaintiff resides in England or Scotland" was considered by the Irish Court of Appeal in *Watson v Porter.*[20] Sir Samuel Walker C stated that some effect must be given to the word "solely" in the rule and that it clearly pointed to the existence of circumstances which taken in conjunction with a plaintiff's residence in England or Scotland would entitle a defendant to require him to provide security for costs. Order 29, rule 4 provides that a plaintiff ordinarily resident out of the jurisdiction may be ordered to give security for costs though he may be temporarily resident within the jurisdiction.

10.005 It is fair to say that while consideration has been given by the courts on a number of occasions to establishing a set of principles for determining the circumstances in which security for costs should be granted, it remains a discretionary jurisdiction to be exercised on the basis of the facts in a given case. Nevertheless it is possible to identify the factors which will influence the court and to deduce certain principles which will govern the exercise of its discretion in such cases.

In *Heaney v Malocca*[21] Maguire CJ stated that *prima facie* a defendant is entitled to an order for security for costs when the plaintiff resides outside the jurisdiction and that in order to deprive him of this right, some special circumstance must be shown, *e.g.* that there is no defence to the action,[22] or where it is

---

[19] Article 12EC, originally Article 7 of the Treaty of Rome, renumbered as Article 6 by the Treaty on European Union 1993.

[20] [1907] 2 IR 341.

[21] [1958] IR 111.

[22] In *Perpetual Trustee Co. Ltd v Bolger* (1933) 67 ILTR 259 O'Byrne J stated that the court requires to have before it such evidence as will enable it to decide on the facts whether the defendant has a defence or not and that it not sufficient for the defendant merely to state that he has a good defence. Similarly in *Birch v Purtill* [1936] IR 122 O'Byrne J concluded that there were facts "which go to show that the cause of action as against [the plaintiff] is well founded, and no ground for defence is suggested". In both these cases the applications for security were refused on the basis of a lack of evidence that the defendant had a good defence. However, note that in *Cohane v Cohane* [1968] IR 176 Budd J stated that if what the plaintiff had said about her means was true, the

established that the plaintiff has ample assets within the jurisdiction. Maguire CJ concluded that in view of the fact that it had been suggested by the defendant on the basis of an engineer's report that she had a good defence and as there were no other circumstances to justify refusing the application, he would grant an order for security.

10.006 Perhaps the most important decision to consider in this context is that of Finlay P in *Collins v Doyle*[23] in which he stated that *"prima facie* a defendant establishing a *prima facie* defence to a claim made by a plaintiff residing outside the jurisdiction has got a right to an order for security for costs."[24] However, he stressed that such a right is not an absolute one and that the court must exercise its discretion based on the facts of each individual case.[25] He also stated that poverty on the part of the plaintiff making it impossible for him to comply with an order for security for costs is not, even when *prima facie* established, of itself automatically a reason for refusing the order. Nevertheless, he accepted that amongst the matters which the court should have regard to in exercising its discretion is whether a *prima facie* case has been made by the plaintiff that his inability to provide security flows from the defendant's wrong,[26] and he added that he was impressed by the apparent injustice of requiring a person who cannot give security to do so when this inability *may* flow from the wrong of the defendant.

10.007 It is useful at this point to consider the court's attitude towards poverty on the part of the plaintiff in more detail. In *Graham v Wray*[27] O'Brien LCJ stated that he was of the opinion that the case before him was governed by the decision in *Jones v Evans*[28] in which it was decided that poverty, in addition to foreign residence, is not a sufficient ground to compel the plaintiff to provide security. This is similar to the view expressed by Hamilton CJ in *Malone v*

---

effect of making an order for security for costs would be to effectually shut her out from endeavouring to assert her legal rights against the defendant and "to leave her to live on charity" and he decided to exercise his discretion against ordering security.

[23] [1982] ILRM 495. The principles set out by Finlay P were quoted with approval by O'Flaherty J in *Fares v Wiley* [1994] 2 IR 379, [1994] 1 ILRM 465 and by Hamilton CJ in *Malone v Brown Thomas & Co. Ltd* [1995] 1 ILRM 369. See also *Jahwar v Owners of the MV Betta Livestock 17* High Court (Barr J) 29 May 2001 in which the High Court refused to grant security for costs in respect of a claim by a ship's master for wages and disbursements.
[24] *Ibid.* at 496.
[25] See also *Malone v Brown Thomas & Co. Ltd* [1995] 1 ILRM 369, 372.
[26] See also in relation to corporate plaintiffs *Peppard & Co. Ltd v Bogoff* [1962] IR 180; *Jack O'Toole v MacEoin Kelly Associates* [1986] IR 277; *Irish Commercial Society Ltd v Plunkett* [1986] IR 258, [1987] ILRM 504; *Beauross v Kennedy* High Court (Morris J) 18 October 1995.
[27] (1901) 35 ILTR 237.
[28] (1901) 35 ILTR 237n.

Brown Thomas & Co. Ltd[29] in which he said that poverty should not be a sufficient justification for compelling an appellant to lodge security.[30] The effect of
poverty was also considered in *Flynn v Rivers*[31] in which Casey J concluded
that having regard to the plaintiff's lack of financial resources, to make an order
for security would be tantamount to a judicial determination of the action, and
that it should therefore be refused. This approach was followed by Murnaghan
J in the High Court in *Heaney v Malocca*[32] who expressed the view that he
should exercise his discretion to refuse an order for security. However, this
decision was reversed by the Supreme Court; Maguire CJ said that in his opinion the decision in *Flynn* went too far[33] and he restated that a defendant has a
prima facie entitlement to an order for security where a plaintiff resides outside
the jurisdiction in the absence of special circumstances which would deprive
him of that right and made no suggestion that poverty should be considered in
this regard. The most accurate summary of the effect of the plaintiff's poverty is
perhaps contained in the judgment of Maguire J in *Heaney*; in his view "mere
poverty is not in itself a sufficient ground either for refusing or granting an
order for security for costs".[34]

10.008 A related issue is the question of how poverty has been considered in
the light of the constitutional guarantee of access to the courts and again a marked
lack of consistency in approach is evident. In *Salih v General Accident Fire
and Life Assurance Corporation Ltd*[35] O'Hanlon J stated that "any right of
access to the courts to prosecute civil claims cannot be an unfettered one" and
that the right to apply for security was intended to do justice between parties
and was not in breach of any constitutional right which the plaintiff might be
able to assert in the case before him. However, in *Malone v Brown Thomas &
Co. Ltd*[36] Hamilton CJ stated that "access to the courts is the constitutional
right of every citizen" and that "no unnecessary monetary obstacle should be
placed in the path of those who seek access to the courts".[37] It is interesting to
note that in *Salih* the court concluded that it should exercise its discretion to
order that the plaintiff furnish security whereas in *Malone* the opposite conclu-

---

[29] [1995] 1 ILRM 369, 372.
[30] Bankruptcy as such is not a ground for ordering a plaintiff to give security for costs, see
Tormey v ESRI [1986] IR 615.
[31] (1951) 86 ILTR 85.
[32] [1958] IR 111.
[33] Note that in *Collins v Doyle* [1982] ILRM 495 Finlay P stated that he accepted the
disapproval expressed by the Supreme Court in *Heaney* of the decision in *Flynn v
Rivers* (1951) 86 ILTR 85.
[34] [1958] IR 111, 115.
[35] [1987] IR 628.
[36] [1995] 1 ILRM 369, 373.
[37] It is arguable that on the facts of *Malone*, where the plaintiff had bank accounts in the
jurisdiction and intended to resume residence here, that security would probably have
been refused in any event without recourse to constitutional principles.

sion was reached and it might be argued that the constitutional guarantee of access to the courts seems to be an issue which may be accorded significance or not depending on the surrounding circumstances in the case.

10.009 The fact that it is necessary for the plaintiff to establish a *prima facie* case that his inability to provide security flows from the defendant's wrong if it is to be a factor which will influence the exercise of the court's discretion was restated by the High Court in *Salih v General Accident Fire and Life Assurance Corporation Ltd.*[38] The plaintiff sought a declaration that the defendant was liable under an insurance policy for loss and damage caused when the plaintiff's premises was damaged by fire. The defendant brought an action for security for costs as the plaintiff was resident outside the jurisdiction. O'Hanlon J held that as the plaintiff was a person resident outside the jurisdiction and the defendant had shown that it had a defence on the merits, the defendant had a *prima facie* right to an order. Nevertheless, he stressed that the jurisdiction to make the order was a discretionary one and said that it might be refused if there were special circumstances justifying the exercise of the court's discretion in the plaintiff's favour. O'Hanlon J said that while the plaintiff's current financial problems might well be attributable to the losses incurred as a result of the fire, he was not prepared to say that the plaintiff had been impoverished by the defendant when it was fighting on the merits the plaintiff's entitlement to recover anything under the terms of the policy and concluded that the plaintiff should be required to furnish security.

10.010 A good example of how difficult it may be to predict the result which the application of the *Collins v Doyle* principles will lead to is the decision in *Fares v Wiley.*[39] The plaintiff, who resided outside the jurisdiction in Libya, brought a claim against the defendant in respect of injuries sustained by him in a road traffic accident in the State. The defendant applied to the High Court for an order for security for costs on the grounds that he had a good defence and that the plaintiff had no assets within the jurisdiction, although it was conceded that he had such assets elsewhere. MacKenzie J refused the application but the Supreme Court allowed the defendant's appeal. O'Flaherty J said that he would accept the principles laid down by Finlay P in *Collins v Doyle* as being correct and found that the defendant had put forward evidence that he had a good defence. He concluded that in all the circumstances of the case and having regard in particular to the fact that the plaintiff was a "man of some means", the court should exercise its discretion in the defendant's favour.[40]

---

[38] [1987] IR 628.

[39] [1994] 2 IR 379. This can be contrasted with the conclusion reached by the Supreme Court in *Malone v Brown Thomas & Co. Ltd* [1995] 1 ILRM 369 in which Hamilton CJ laid emphasis on the fact that the plaintiff had expressed her intention to return permanently to reside in the jurisdiction.

[40] See also *Guion v Heffernan* [1929] IR 487 where O'Byrne J stated that the case before

10.011 As a general principle a defendant cannot be called upon to provide security for costs; as Johnston J stated in *Leonard v Scofield*:[41] "It would be almost a mockery of justice if a plaintiff, having brought a defendant before a court, could demand that he should be obliged to give security for the costs of being allowed to defend himself against the proceedings".[42] However, as is made clear below, where security is sought for the costs of an appeal, the fact that the party moving for security is the plaintiff will not prevent the court from exercising its discretion in his favour.[43] In addition, it should be noted that in admiralty proceedings bail for the release of a ship under arrest can include a sum for security for costs.

10.012 The principles which apply where there are a number of plaintiffs in an action,[44] some of whom reside outside the jurisdiction, were considered by Hanna J in *Re Bonis Mooney*,[45] which concerned an action to have a grant of probate recalled. One of three plaintiffs resided outside the jurisdiction but there was a suggestion made that the other two plaintiffs, who had already been paid legacies under the impugned will, had been added in order to prevent an order for security for costs being made. Hanna J summarised the relevant principles as follows:

> [T]he ordinary and normal rule is that security for costs will not be ordered against a plaintiff out of the jurisdiction when there is joined with such a plaintiff another *bona fide* plaintiff, or plaintiffs, residing within the jurisdiction; but that the court can, within its jurisdiction, deal with the plaintiff, or plaintiffs, within the jurisdiction if of opinion that such plaintiff, or plaintiffs, are not real and substantial plaintiffs in the action, or are not entitled to the relief claimed therein, or that they have been

---

him was not one in which an order to provide security would amount to a denial of justice, as the plaintiff had ample means, and the court made the orders sought.

[41] [1936] IR 715, 719. Johnston J stated that this "universal rule" extends to protect a defendant who has filed a counterclaim, at any rate one which arises out of the same transaction as the plaintiff's claim. He relies on the decision of Palles CB in *Compania Naviera Vascongada v Hall Ltd* (1906) 40 ILTR 114 to support this proposition, although it is far from clear that this point was decided in that case. Note also the decision of the English Court of Appeal in *The Silver Fir* [1980] 1 Lloyd's Rep 371 to the effect that where two opposing parties applied for security for costs against a claim and counterclaim, they were both entitled to security.

[42] However, see *Ward v Skeehan* [1907] 2 IR 1 where it was held that a defendant caveator resident out of the jurisdiction may in a proper case be ordered to provide security. See also *O'Leary v Stack* (1900) 34 ILTR 54.

[43] *Midland Bank Ltd v Crossley-Cooke* [1969] IR 56.

[44] The situation where co-plaintiffs include both individuals and companies is considered *infra*. See *Bula Ltd v Tara Mines Ltd* [1987] IR 494.

[45] [1938] IR 354.

joined merely to oust the jurisdiction to order security for costs against the foreign plaintiff.[46]

In the circumstances, Hanna J held that the justice of the case would be met by requiring the legacies already given to the two plaintiffs resident within the jurisdiction to be paid into court and that in default of such lodgment that the other plaintiff be required to provide security for costs.

It should also be noted that a plaintiff may be ordered to provide security notwithstanding the fact that he sues in a representative capacity. This was established by the statement made by Meredith MR in *Wheelan v Irwin*[47] to the effect that when the plaintiff resides out of the jurisdiction and there is a real question to be tried and the defendant is not entering a sham defence, the court may order that security be provided whether the plaintiff is "peer or pauper, suing for himself or in a representative capacity".

Finally, it was confirmed by the High Court in *Dockery v Croghan*[48] that security for costs may be granted in relation to an appeal from the Circuit Court to the High Court. As Hanna J stated once the notice of appeal has been served and lodged, the appeal becomes a matter in the High Court, to which the Rules of the Superior Courts apply.

Security for the Costs of an Appeal to the Supreme Court

10.013 Order 58, rule 17 of the Rules of the Superior Courts 1986 provides that "such deposit or other security for the costs to be occasioned by any appeal shall be made or given as may be directed under special circumstances by the Supreme Court". One aspect of rule 17 which should be noted is that no reference is made to the relevance of any specific factor, *e.g.* residence outside the jurisdiction or insufficiency of assets and for this reason, some of the authorities dealing with the interpretation of Order 29 should be treated with a degree of caution.[49] As Walsh J commented in *Midland Bank Ltd v Crossley-Cooke*[50] the court will "consider the special circumstances of each case and the effect of the combination of various grounds which might arise in each case, and [will] consider whether ... the justice of the case require[s] that the court should exercise its discretion in favour of ordering security to be given".

---

[46] *Ibid.* at 358.
[47] [1909] 1 IR 294, 296. Quoted with approval by Johnston J in *Re Julian* [1936] IR 126, 130.
[48] [1931] IR 466.
[49] *E.g.* in a number of cases, security has been ordered against an appellant who resides within the jurisdiction, see *Somers v Erskine (No. 3)* [1945] IR 308; *Oakes v Lynch* Supreme Court, 27 November 1953 (referred to in *Midland Bank Ltd v Crossley-Cooke* [1969] IR 56, 60); *Fallon v An Bord Pleanála* [1992] 2 IR 380, [1991] ILRM 799.
[50] [1969] IR 56.

In *Perry v Stratham*,[51] in which the former Supreme Court considered an application made pursuant to the equivalent provision in the 1905 Rules,[52] Fitzgibbon J commented that "the rules and practice which govern such applications in the High Court do not apply here". He stated that he was not deciding that mere residence outside the jurisdiction, or poverty alone, was a sufficient justification for compelling an appellant to lodge security for costs and that all the circumstances of the case must be taken into account.[53] Amongst the circumstances which he considered relevant in the case before him were the fact that the appellant was not resident in the jurisdiction, that there was an outstanding judgment of the High Court against him and in favour of the respondent, that there was no satisfactory evidence of any tangible assets in or outside the jurisdiction and that a judgment obtained in the jurisdiction could not be enforced outside it. While Fitzgibbon J stressed that the Supreme Court could not enter into a discussion of the merits of the appeal on such a preliminary application,[54] he was satisfied having regard to the circumstances set out above that the appellant should be ordered to provide security for costs.

10.014 The meaning of the words "special circumstances" were considered by the Supreme Court in *Somers v Erskine (No. 3)*.[55] Murnaghan J stated that in practice it has generally been held that the fact that the appellant resides out of the jurisdiction[56] or the fact that he is an undischarged bankrupt amounts to special circumstances. Although neither of these factors applied in the case before him, Murnaghan J concluded that having regard to such issues as the lengthy delay in bringing the proceedings and the complexity and number of the questions to be resolved in the action, special circumstances did exist to justify the making of an order for security.

10.015 Perhaps the most important judgment dealing with an application to the Supreme Court for security for the costs of an appeal, is that of Walsh J in *Midland Bank Ltd v Crossley-Cooke*.[57] Having reviewed a number of previous decisions, he stated that four points emerge clearly from them; that the courts

---

[51] [1928] IR 580.

[52] Order LVIII, rule 15 of the Rules of the Supreme Court (Ireland) 1905 was identical in its terms except that it read "the Court of Appeal" rather than "the Supreme Court".

[53] See also *Malone v Brown Thomas & Co. Ltd* [1995] 1 ILRM 369, 372 *per* Hamilton CJ.

[54] See also *Somers v Erskine (No. 3)* [1945] IR 308, 313-314; *Malone v Brown Thomas & Co. Ltd* [1995] 1 ILRM 369, 373.

[55] [1945] IR 308.

[56] Although this statement is somewhat at odds with that of Fitzgibbon J in *Perry v Stratham* [1928] IR 580, 582 approved of by Hamilton CJ in *Malone v Brown Thomas & Co. Ltd* [1995] 1 ILRM 369, 372 that he was not deciding that mere residence outside the jurisdiction was a sufficient justification for compelling an appellant to lodge security for costs.

[57] [1969] IR 56.

are free to order security in any type of case, that poverty alone is not sufficient to warrant the making of an order,[58] that poverty or insufficiency of assets on the part of the appellant was an essential prerequisite for the making of an order and that if a point of law of public importance was at issue, the court would not order security to be provided.[59] He continued as follows:

> It would appear that in the circumstances of any particular case the court could have felt itself justified in making such an order when there was a combination of poverty of the appellant and any one or more of the several factors mentioned in those cases, such as a party being resident outside of the jurisdiction, or there being no apparent *prima facie* grounds for the appeal, or the complexity of the issues,[60] or long delays on the part of the appellant in the conduct of the litigation,[61] or where the appellant is simply a nominal appellant;[62] or, where there are several appellants and poverty is common to each of them, a combination of that and one or more of the other factors even if the other factors affect only one of the appellants.[63]

A further important point clarified by Walsh J in *Midland* is that in his view "the fact that the party moving for security on the appeal is the plaintiff is not a matter to be taken into consideration in ease of the appellant or defendant".[64] He stated that the fact that the party who had succeeded in the High Court was the plaintiff did not make the case analogous to *Leonard v Scofield*[65] and noted

---

[58] See also the *dicta* of Fitzgerald J at 63.

[59] See also *Moore v Attorney General (No. 2)* [1929] IR 544 and *Irish Press plc v Ingersoll Irish Publications Ltd* [1995] 2 IR 175, [1995] 1 ILRM 117. See also *Lancefort Ltd v An Bord Pleanála* [1998] 2 IR 511 in the context of an application for security against a company.

[60] Note that in *Bula Ltd v Tara Mines Ltd* Supreme Court, 26 March 1998 at 17, Keane J stated that the reference to the "complexity of the issues" must be seen in the context of the remainder of the passage and said the presumably Walsh J was indicating that the court might look less favourably on an application for security where, although the appellant was impoverished, the appeal was unlikely to prove lengthy and expensive and there appeared to be an arguable case.

[61] See also the comment of O'Byrne J in *Guion v Heffernan* [1929] IR 487, 488 to the effect that there had been unreasonable delay on the plaintiff's part in bringing the proceedings. In the circumstances he decided to exercise his discretion in favour of ordering security to be granted. Equally, it would appear that delay on the defendant's part may be a relevant factor, see *e.g. Duffy v Joyce* (1890) 25 LR Ir 42 in which Porter MR stated that he was of the opinion that the defendant had lost his right to security by delay in applying for it.

[62] See *Fallon v An Bord Pleanála* [1992] 2 IR 380.

[63] [1969] IR 56, 61. Quoted with approval by Keane J in *Bula Ltd v Tara Mines Ltd* Supreme Court, 26 March 1998 at 17.

[64] *Ibid.* at 62.

[65] [1936] IR 715. Johnston J held that the defendant cannot be called upon to provide security for costs, see *supra*.

that in a number of earlier unreported decisions,[66] the party who had successfully moved for security on the appeal was the plaintiff.

10.016 The principles set out by Walsh J in *Midland* were applied in a slightly
different way by Finlay CJ in *Fallon v An Bord Pleanála* who treated poverty
on the part of the appellant and the fact that the question at issue was not a
question of law of public importance as "mandatory" conditions. Provided these
conditions were satisfied the court could proceed to consider whether there were
"special circumstances" which would justify the making of an order. In the case
before him, Finlay CJ was satisfied that these circumstances existed and referred to the fact that there was a probability that the appellant had been chosen
as a man of straw, that no explanation had been given about why he was imper-
illing his financial future by taking the action and that the allegation that the
proceedings had been taken to try to prevent completion of a development had
not been contradicted.

10.017 A further recent example of an application for an order for security for
the costs of an appeal is the decision of the Supreme Court in *Malone v Brown
Thomas & Co. Ltd.*[67] The appellant, who lived in Australia, claimed damages
against the respondents for wrongful arrest, false imprisonment and defamation. Security for costs was furnished before the High Court heard the case; it
dismissed the claim and the appellant appealed to the Supreme Court. The first
named respondent then brought an application to the Supreme Court for an order for security for the costs of the appeal. Hamilton CJ quoted with approval
from *Midland Bank* and stated that having considered all the circumstances of
the case, including the fact that the appellant intended to return permanently to
reside in the jurisdiction within the year, the fact that the sum lodged before the
High Court hearing was still on deposit and having regard to the appellant's
constitutional right of access to the courts, he must exercise his discretion in her
favour. Finally, it should be noted that Hamilton CJ commented that while the
court could not enter into any consideration of the merits of the appeal, he observed that the notice of appeal disclosed at least arguable grounds of appeal.
This approach is very much in line with that adopted in relation to corporate
plaintiffs, as will be seen below.[68]

---

[66] *Oakes v Lynch* Supreme Court, 27 November 1953; *Greham v Muldarrig* Supreme
Court, 29 October 1958.
[67] See *e.g. SEE Co. Ltd v Public Lighting Services Ltd* [1987] ILRM 255, 259.
[68] [1995] 1 ILRM 369.

SECURITY FOR COSTS IN RELATION TO CORPORATE PLAINTIFFS

Introduction – s. 390 of the Companies Act 1963

10.018 S.390 provides that where a limited company is a plaintiff in any action, a judge may "if it appears by credible testimony that there is reason to believe that the company will be unable to pay the costs of the defendant if successful in his defence", require sufficient security to be given for the costs and may stay the proceedings until this is given.[69] This jurisdiction has been accepted as being discretionary in nature but as Megarry VC stated in *Pearson v Naydler*:[70] "The court must not show such a reluctance to order security for costs that this becomes a weapon whereby an impecunious company can use its inability to pay costs as a means of putting unfair pressure on a more prosperous company". While McGuinness J has recently stated in the course of her judgment in *Irish Press plc v E.M. Warburg Pincus & Co. International Ltd*[71] that, on considering the relevant authorities in this area, she had gained the impression that on balance the courts have tended to lean against the making of orders for security for costs against companies, other decisions such as that of the Supreme Court in *Lismore Homes Ltd v Bank of Ireland Finance Ltd*[72] suggest that a more stringent attitude may be taken.

Provisions in Relation to Corporate and Individual Plaintiffs

10.019 Before considering the manner in which the provisions of s.390 have been interpreted in more detail it should be noted that the courts have not always been clear about the distinctions which should be drawn between the principles which apply to seeking an order for security for costs against an individual on the one hand and a company on the other hand. In *Bula Ltd v Tara Mines Ltd (No. 3)*[73] Murphy J referred to the "clear distinction" which had been drawn by Megarry VC in *Pearson v Naydler*[74] "in both the nature and origin of the rule with regard to security as it affected natural persons and limited companies".

---

[69] This provision also applies to judicial review proceedings. See *Lancefort Ltd v An Bord Pleanála* [1998] 2 IR 511. See also Order 84, rule 20(6).

[70] [1977] 1 WLR 899, 906, [1977] 3 All ER 531, 537.

[71] [1997] 2 ILRM 263, 274. In delivering the judgment of the Supreme Court, 29 July 1998, Lynch J stated that he did not think that there was any substance in the argument that this statement was incorrect.

[72] [1999] 1 IR 501.

[73] [1987] IR 494, 499.

[74] [1977] 1 WLR 899, [1977] 3 All ER 531. Megarry VC had stated that while insolvency is not a ground for requiring security from natural persons, in the case of corporations, the basic rule is reversed. See also *Philip Harrington Daly & Co. v JVC (UK) Ltd* High Court (O'Hanlon J) 16 March 1995 at 17-18.

However, it was suggested by Budd J in *Cohane v Cohane*[75] that the same considerations and principles established in relation to the Companies Act provisions are equally applicable to litigation between individuals.[76] Nevertheless, a detailed consideration of the manner in which s.390 has been interpreted reveals a number of clear principles which differ in several material respects from those considered above in relation to individual litigants. In summary, with regard to corporate plaintiffs, likely inability to pay the costs of a successful defendant is the essential prerequisite for obtaining an order for security,[77] and place of residence is not a factor. However, in the case of individual plaintiffs, residence out of the jurisdiction is the essential issue and while lack of assets within the jurisdiction is also an important consideration, poverty on the plaintiff's part may be interpreted by the court in different ways.[78] As Murphy J stated in *Bula Ltd v Tara Mines Ltd*:[79] "It is clear beyond debate that section 390 ... may impose a serious handicap on an impecunious limited liability company where a lack of funds would not create the same problem for an individual litigant".

10.020 The reason for drawing such a distinction is adverted to by Barrington J in his judgment in *Lismore Homes Ltd v Bank of Ireland Finance Ltd*[80] in the following terms: "Insolvent limited liability companies are in a different category simply because the liability of their shareholders is limited" and the threat of bankruptcy will not hang over them as it would in the case of individual plaintiffs.[81] It is also clear from both the judgment of Keane J in the High Court[82] and of Lynch J in the Supreme Court in *Lismore* that the courts take a

---

[75] [1968] IR 176, 191. See also *Banco Ambrosiano SPA v Ansbacher & Co. Ltd* High Court (Murphy J) 19 July 1985 at 2.

[76] See also *Lough Neagh Exploration Ltd v Morrice* [1998] 1 ILRM 205 in which Laffoy J stated that "in broad terms, the same principles govern the determination whether a plaintiff should be ordered to furnish security for a defendant's costs under s.390 and under Order 29 of the RSC 1986" and *Bula Ltd v Tara Mines Ltd* Supreme Court, 26 March 1998 in which the Supreme Court suggested that similar principles applied in relation to seeking security for the costs of an appeal pursuant to Order 58, rule 17 and s.390.

[77] Although as Barrington J commented in *Lismore Homes Ltd v Bank of Ireland Finance Ltd* [1999] 1 IR 501, 507 "the mere fact that a plaintiff is impecunious has never, on its own been a reason for awarding security for costs against him" and the crucial factor is likely inability to pay.

[78] Contrast, *e.g. Flynn v Rivers* (1951) 86 ILTR 85 and *Cohane v Cohane* [1968] IR 176 with *Heaney v Malocca* [1958] IR 111 and *Collins v Doyle* [1982] ILRM 495.

[79] [1987] IR 494, 496.

[80] [1999] 1 IR 501, 507.

[81] See Buttimore *Security for Costs* (1999) at 3 where he points out that an individual plaintiff is faced with the threat of bankruptcy if a successful defendant's order for costs cannot be satisfied out of his assets, whereas there is no such deterrent in relation to a limited liability company.

[82] [1992] 2 IR 57.

stricter attitude towards impoverished companies than they would towards individual plaintiffs. Keane J stated that to refrain from granting an order for security in the case of a impecunious company simply because it might have the effect of stifling the plaintiff company's action would be to render the section nugatory, a conclusion with which Lynch J agreed.

The Discretionary Nature of the Section and the Onus of Proof

10.021 The equivalent pre-1963 provision, s.278 of the Companies Consolidation Act 1908, was considered by the Supreme Court in *Peppard & Co. Ltd v Bogoff*[83] in which Kingsmill Moore J laid down the important principle, repeated in almost every decision since, that the power conferred by the section is discretionary in nature. He stated as follows:

> I am of the opinion that the section does not make it mandatory to order security for costs in every case where the plaintiff company appears to be unable to pay the costs of a successful defendant, but that there still remains a discretion in the court which may be exercised in special circumstances.[84]

One of these special circumstances was the fact that the poor financial position of the plaintiff company may be due to the very actions of the defendant for which he is being sued and on the facts of the case, he decided to reverse the decision to order security.

10.022 Another important matter is where the onus of proof lies, first, in relation to establishing inability to pay the costs of a successful defendant and secondly, in relation to establishing "special circumstances" which may justify refusing an order for security. This issue was considered by Finlay CJ in *Jack O'Toole Ltd v MacEoin Kelly Associates*[85] where he stated that "where it is established or conceded, as arises in this case, that a limited liability company which is a plaintiff would be unable to meet the costs of a successful defendant ... if a plaintiff company seeks to avoid an order for security for costs, it must, as a matter of onus of proof, establish to the satisfaction of the judge the special circumstances which would justify the refusal of an order". With regard to the initial onus which lies on the defendant, Murphy J stated in *Bula Ltd v Tara Mines Ltd (No. 3)*[86] that "all that the section requires is that it should appear by

---

[83] [1962] IR 180.

[84] *Ibid.* at 188.

[85] [1986] IR 277, 283. See also *Bula Ltd v Tara Mines Ltd (No. 3)* [1987] IR 494, 500; *Lismore Homes Ltd v Bank of Ireland Finance Ltd* [1992] 2 IR 57, 62; [1992] ILRM 798, 802 (HC). *Philip Harrington Daly & Co. v JVC (UK) Ltd* Supreme Court, 21 February 1997 at 9.

[86] [1987] IR 494, 499. This *dicta* was accepted by McGuinness J in *Irish Press plc v E.M. Warburg Pincus & Co. International Ltd* [1997] 2 ILRM 263, 271.

credible testimony 'that there is *reason to believe* that the company would be unable to pay the costs of the defendant if successful in his defence'" and he said that he did not think it necessary to enter into a detailed analysis of the assets and liabilities of the company for this purpose. A useful restatement of the shifting onus of proof is contained in the judgment of Morris P in *Inter Finance Group Ltd v KPMG Peat Marwick*[87] in the following terms:

> [T]here is an onus on the moving party the defendant to establish (a) that he has a *prima facie* defence to the plaintiff's claim and (b) that the defendant will not be able to pay the defendant's costs if successful in his defence.
>
> On establishing these two facts then the order sought should be made unless it can be shown that there are specific circumstances in the case which would cause the court to exercise its discretion not to make the order sought. Such special circumstances might be;
> (I) that the plaintiff's inability to discharge the defendant's costs of successfully defending the action flow from the wrong allegedly committed by the parties seeking the security or
> (II) there has been delay by the moving party in seeking the relief now claimed
> (III) some other circumstance which might arise in the case.

10.023 A recent case in this area which illustrates well how the shifting onus of proof operates in practice is *Irish Press plc v E.M. Warburg Pincus & Co. International Ltd*[88] in which the defendants sought an order requiring the plaintiff in an action for negligent misrepresentation to provide security for costs. McGuinness J stated that it was "for the defendants ... to establish that the plaintiff company would be unable to meet the costs, and for the plaintiff ... to establish the existence of the necessary special circumstances". The defendants accepted that the plaintiff company had an arguable case but contended that they had reason to believe that the plaintiff company would be unable to meet the defendants' costs if they were successful as the plaintiff was no longer trading and had substantial continuing costs. The plaintiff asserted that it would be in a position to meet the costs in the event of the defendants succeeding or alternatively, that any impecuniosity suffered by it had been caused by the wrongful acts of the defendants. McGuinness J stated that in determining the plaintiff's ability to pay, the costs of the High Court action alone should be considered

---

[87] High Court (Morris P) 29 June 1998 at 4. See also the *dicta* of Morris J in *Beauross v Kennedy* High Court, 18 October 1995 at 3: "On the defendant establishing a *prima facie* defence and establishing that there is 'reason to believe' that the plaintiff would not be able to pay the defendant's costs if successful ... the onus shifts to the plaintiff to establish the special circumstances upon which he chooses to rely".

[88] [1997] 2 ILRM 263 (HC), Supreme Court, 29 July 1998. See also *Wexford Rope and Twine Co. Ltd v Gaynor* High Court (Barr J) 6 March 2000.

and not the costs of a possible appeal to the Supreme Court which she said would have to be the subject of a further application to that court. In the circumstances, she decided to refuse the application for security and concluded that on balance the plaintiff had sufficient resources to meet any order for costs. She stated that while the company's assets appeared to be diminishing, it was not insolvent and also had regard to the fact that it continued to have some investment income and that its future costs would not be large. On appeal, Lynch J reiterated that the onus of proving inability to pay lies on the defendants and if they establish such inability to pay, the onus of proving special circumstances to justify not making the order lies on the plaintiff. Having assessed the plaintiff's financial circumstances, Lynch J stated that he was satisfied that it would be able to pay the defendants' costs if these were awarded at the present time or within the next two years or so. While this would not be the position if the case were to drag on for another three or four years, he concluded that in the ultimate analysis, the defendants had not established that there was reason to believe that the plaintiff would be unable to pay their costs if they were successful in their defence and Lynch J therefore decided to dismiss the defendants' appeal.

Special Circumstances which may Justify Refusal of the Order

10.024 It is now necessary to consider in more detail what will constitute "special circumstances" which may justify refusing an order for security even where the plaintiff's inability to pay the costs of a successful defendant has been established. Clearly the onus lies on the party attempting to resist the order for security to establish that special circumstances exist.[89] As noted above, Kingsmill Moore J referred in *Peppard & Co. Ltd v Bogoff*[90] to the poor financial position of the plaintiff company being due to the very actions of the defendant for which he is being sued and this issue was formulated in the following terms by McCarthy J in *SEE Co. Ltd v Public Lighting Services Ltd*,[91] namely, "has a *prima facie* case been made to the effect that the inability identified by the section flows from the wrong allegedly committed by the party seeking security?". However, as Finlay CJ stressed in *Jack O'Toole Ltd v MacEoin Kelly Associates*[92] it is not a sufficient discharge of the onus of proof which lies on a

---

[89] *Jack O'Toole Ltd v MacEoin Kelly Associates* [1986] IR 277, 283 and *Village Residents Association Ltd v An Bord Pleanála* [2000] 4 IR 321, 331, [2001] 2 ILRM 22, 32.

[90] [1962] IR 180.

[91] [1987] ILRM 255, 259. See also *Jack O'Toole Ltd v MacEoin Kelly Associates* [1986] IR 277; *Bula Ltd v. Tara Mines Ltd (No. 3)* [1987] IR 494; *Lismore Homes Ltd v Bank of Ireland Finance Ltd* [1992] 2 IR 57; [1992] ILRM 798 (HC); *Lough Neagh Exploration Ltd v Morrice* [1998] 1 ILRM 205.

[92] [1986] IR 277, 284. See also *Bula Ltd v Tara Mines Ltd (No. 3)* [1987] IR 494, 500; *Lismore Homes Ltd v Bank of Ireland Finance Ltd* [1992] ILRM 798, 801-802 (HC) and [1999] 1 IR 501, 512, 529 (SC); *Philip Harrington Daly & Co. v JVC (UK) Ltd* High Court (O'Hanlon J) 16 March 1995 at 16-18 and Supreme Court, 21 February 1997 at 9.

plaintiff company "to make a mere bald statement of the fact that the insolvency of the company has been caused by the wrong the subject-matter of the claim".

10.025 A further "special circumstance" which may justify refusing an order for security is the question of whether there has been "undue delay on the part of the moving party".[93] Delay was treated by Finlay CJ in *SEE Co. Ltd v Public Lighting Services Ltd*,[94] as being of "considerable significance" and he noted that between the service of the notice of appeal and the bringing of the motion seeking security, the plaintiff must have incurred significant costs. Similarly in *Beauross v Kennedy*[95] Morris J, as he then was, stated that if the party seeking security for costs has delayed to such an extent as to cause the plaintiff to act to its detriment by incurring a level of costs it would not have incurred had it known it would be required to provide security, the court would not make the order and he decided to refuse relief on this basis and because he was satisfied that the plaintiff's inability to pay flowed from the wrong allegedly committed by the defendant. Barr J has recently reiterated in *Wexford Rope and Twine Co. Ltd v Gaynor*[96] that delay on the part of a defendant in bringing an application for security may amount to a "special circumstance" but he concluded that in the case before him it was reasonable for the defendants to await the statement of claim before bringing an application for security.

10.026 Arguably, the fact that the plaintiff has raised a point of law of exceptional public importance may also constitute a special circumstance justifying refusal of an order for security which might otherwise be warranted. While this point was considered by Morris P in *Lancefort Ltd v An Bord Pleanála*[97] he held that he was unable to conclude that the point of law raised was "of such gravity and importance that it transcends the interests and consideration of the parties actually before the court" and he granted the application for security. Similarly, in *Village Residents Association Ltd v An Bord Pleanála*,[98] Laffoy J found that the point at issue did not raise a question of law of public importance

---

[93] *Per* Finlay CJ in *SEE Co. Ltd v Public Lighting Services Ltd* [1987] ILRM 255, 259. See also *Lismore Homes Ltd v Bank of Ireland Finance Ltd* [1992] 2 IR 57, 63; [1992] ILRM 798, 803 (HC), although Keane J stated that he did not think that there had been such undue delay as to justify a refusal on that ground alone.

[94] [1987] ILRM 255, 259. See also *Oakes v Lynch* Supreme Court, 27 November 1953.

[95] High Court (Morris J) 18 October 1995. Morris J made it clear that it will be the level of legal costs incurred as a result of the delay rather than the period of the delay itself which will be the significant feature in this regard. See also *Village Residents Association Ltd v An Bord Pleanála* [2000] 4 IR 321, [2001] 2 ILRM 22 where Laffoy J concluded that there was no evidence that the applicant had altered its position to its detriment by reason of the application not having been made at the leave stage.

[96] High Court (Barr J) 6 March 2000.

[97] [1998] 2 IR 511, 516.

[98] [2000] 4 IR 321, [2001] 2 ILRM 22.

and she held that no special circumstances had been established by the applicant and that the second named respondent was entitled to an order for security.

Not the Function of the Court to Assess Likelihood of Success

10.027 While the strength of the defendant's case will clearly be a factor in considering an application for security for costs, it is accepted as a general principle that in most cases the strength of the plaintiff's case will be irrelevant. Although the issue has not been entirely unproblematic it now appears to be reasonably well accepted that the court should not attempt to predict the outcome of the case in determining whether security should be ordered. As O'Hanlon J stated in *Philip Harrington Daly & Co. v JVC (UK) Ltd*[99] the court cannot be expected to embark on a full and final assessment of the issue of liability for the purpose of deciding whether it is appropriate to make an order for the giving of security for costs. In *Bula Ltd v Tara Mines Ltd (No. 3)*[100] Murphy J stated as follows:

> [I]t is no part of my function as I see it to forecast the outcome of the litigation or to prejudge the facts or express an interim view on the questions of law involved. On behalf of the defendants it was argued that the weakness of the plaintiffs' case is a factor to which regard should be had. Whilst it must be established that the plaintiffs do have an arguable case it does not seem to me that it is either necessary or proper to evaluate the prospects of success.

10.028 As Barron J stated in *Lismore Homes Ltd v Bank of Ireland Finance Ltd*[101] what may or may not be an arguable case has not been precisely defined but he said that it seemed to him that since the application is heard on affidavit, there must "at least be a case which would be sufficiently strong as that which would entitle a defendant in a motion for liberty to enter final judgment to be permitted to defend". The statement of Murphy J in *Bula* set out above was endorsed by McCarthy J in *Comhlucht Paipear Riomhaireachta Teo v Údarás na Gaeltachta*[102] where he also made it clear that the fact that the plaintiff had

---

[99] High Court (O'Hanlon J) 16 March 1995 at 17.

[100] [1987] IR 494, 501. Murphy J noted that in *Jack O'Toole Ltd v MacEoin Kelly Associates* [1986] IR 277 McCarthy J had recognised that on the facts before the court it was not possible to assess the prospects of success and in *SEE Co. Ltd v Public Lighting Services Ltd* [1987] ILRM 255 he had been content to find that the appellants could make out an arguable case based on inferences drawn by the court of first instance.

[101] [1999] 1 IR 501, 529.

[102] [1990] 1 IR 320, 331-332, [1990] ILRM 266, 275. These principles were also endorsed by Keane J in *Lismore Homes Ltd v Bank of Ireland Finance Ltd* [1992] 2 IR 57, 62; [1992] ILRM 798, 802 (HC) and [1999] 1 IR 501 (SC) by Lynch J (at 513) and Barron J (at 530). See also *Lough Neagh Exploration Ltd v Morrice* [1998] 1 ILRM

a very strong case was not an appropriate consideration unless it could be shown that its strength was such that there was no real defence in which case the application should be refused. This approach is slightly difficult to reconcile with the view expressed by Costello J in *Irish Commercial Society Ltd v Plunkett*[103] that he could take "all the circumstances of the case into consideration" and these would include, in his opinion, "the strength of the plaintiff's claim and the conduct of the applicant for security". However, it would appear that the view expressed by Murphy J in *Bula* is the better one and it has certainly met with a greater degree of approval in recent decisions.[104]

Relevance of Individual Co-Plaintiff

10.029 Another issue which has been considered is the significance of there being an individual co-plaintiff within the jurisdiction to whom the defendant may look for payment of his costs. In *Peppard & Co. Ltd v Bogoff*[105] the fact that there was a co-plaintiff within the jurisdiction was characterised as one of two special circumstances which influenced the court to exercise its discretion to refuse to order security. However, it is more difficult to assess the significance of such a factor on the basis of the *dicta* of Murphy J in *Bula Ltd v Tara Mines Ltd*.[106] Having pointed out that there is a clear distinction between the nature of the rules with regard to security as they affect natural persons and companies, he said that it would seem therefore that the addition of individual plaintiffs "should have no direct bearing on the question of whether a corporate co-plaintiff would be required to give security".[107] He went on to say that while the presence of individual co-plaintiffs is a factor to be considered in all cases it was not in the case before him of particular significance "still less of decisive importance". Murphy J then concluded his judgment by referring to the *dicta* of Kingsmill Moore J in *Peppard* and said that while he himself would attach little significance to the presence of individual co-plaintiffs in the circumstances, it was nonetheless a factor to be taken into account and that the conclusion reached by Kingsmill Moore J was, by coincidence, equally applicable to the case before him. It should

---

205, 210 and *Village Residents Association Ltd v An Bord Pleanála* [2000] 4 IR 321, [2001] 2 ILRM 22.

[103] [1988] IR 1, 5, [1989] ILRM 461, 465.

[104] *E.g. Wexford Rope and Twine Co. Ltd v Gaynor High Court* (Barr J) 6 March 2000; *Village Residents Association Ltd v An Bord Pleanála* [2000] 4 IR 321, [2001] 2 ILRM 22.

[105] [1962] IR 180. Kingsmill Moore J stated that he had no doubt that where an application for security is made on the grounds that an individual plaintiff is outside the jurisdiction it will be refused if there is another plaintiff within the jurisdiction who would be answerable for costs and that he was of the view that in principle, the same arguments would seem to apply where the ground for seeking security was based on the Companies Act provisions.

[106] [1987] IR 494.

[107] *Ibid.* at 499.

certainly be recognised that where there is an individual co-plaintiff, he will have more to lose if an order for costs is made against him, and for this reason some significance should probably be attached to the fact, although as we have seen uncertainty surrounds the question of its relative importance.

Security for the Costs of an Appeal

10.030 It is also necessary to consider whether any different principles apply when an application is brought for security for the costs of an appeal by an appellant company. In *Personal Service Laundry Ltd v National Bank Ltd*[108] Kingsmill Moore J applied the provisions of s.390 as interpreted by the Supreme Court in *Peppard & Co. Ltd v Bogoff* and made no attempt to suggest that any different principles should apply in relation to seeking security for the costs of an appeal. Similarly in *SEE Co. Ltd v Public Lighting Services Ltd*[109] Finlay CJ applied the principles established in *Peppard,* although he did refer to the power conferred by Order 58, rule 17 of the RSC in relation to security for the costs of an appeal.[110] While he stated that he would not attempt to make an exhaustive list of the circumstances which might justify the court in refusing to order security, he did refer to the question of whether there was an arguable case stated in the notice of appeal,[111] a factor which would be in line with that suggested by Murphy J in *Bula Ltd v Tara Mines Ltd (No. 3)* in relation to applications brought before the High Court, namely that it must be established that the plaintiff has an arguable case. One further point which McCarthy J stressed in *SEE Co. Ltd* was that an order for security for the costs of the appeal should be confined to the costs incurred in relation to the appeal. He stated as follows:

> In my judgment, on the true construction of the section, it is not to be read as enabling an order for security for costs of an appeal to encompass the costs of trial in the High Court or, indeed, any costs other than those incurred after the demand for security has first been made. It would, in my opinion, be intolerable if a limited company, having embarked on the relatively uncharted seas of litigation, having failed in an action, and possibly

---

[108] [1964] IR 49.

[109] [1987] ILRM 255, 259. See also the *dicta* of Hamilton CJ in *Malone v Brown Thomas & Co. Ltd* [1995] 1 ILRM 369, 373 in relation to individual plaintiffs.

[110] Note that in *Bula Ltd v Tara Mines Ltd* Supreme Court, 26 March 1998 the Supreme Court suggested that similar principles applied in relation to seeking security for the costs of an appeal in relation to individual plaintiffs pursuant to Order 58, rule 17 and corporate plaintiffs pursuant to s.390. However, much of the judgment of Keane J is devoted to the principles which applied to an application made pursuant to Order 58, rule 17 and he simply stated that he was also satisfied that in the case of corporate plaintiffs it would be reasonable to make an order under s.390.

[111] See further *Lismore Homes Ltd v Bank of Ireland Finance Ltd* [1999] 1 IR 501, 529.

as a direct result of either the failure or of the facts that gave rise to the action, be shown to be unable to pay future costs, should, then, as a condition of being entitled to proceed with an appeal, be made liable to give security for what could be very large costs already incurred.[112]

One further matter made clear by Finlay CJ in *Jack O'Toole Ltd v MacEoin Kelly Associates*[113] and endorsed by Barron J in *Lismore Homes Ltd v Bank of Ireland Finance Ltd*[114] was that a court on appeal must exercise its discretion in relation to granting security independently of the manner in which it was exercised in the court below and that the Supreme Court has a right and obligation to substitute its discretion for that of the High Court, if it is satisfied that it should do so.

Conclusions

10.031 While the above consideration of the case law in this area shows certain differences of opinion in relation to some of the issues discussed, it is possible to identify a number of well established principles. First, it is clearly accepted that the jurisdiction conferred upon the court by the section is discretionary in nature. In addition, the onus lies on the defendant to establish a *prima facie* defence and that there is reason to believe that the plaintiff would be unable to pay the defendant's costs if successful, and if he succeeds in doing this, the onus lies on the plaintiff to establish "special circumstances" which may justify the court in refusing to order security. Such special circumstances will include the fact that a plaintiff's inability to provide security flows from a wrong allegedly committed by the defendant – although it will not suffice to make a "vague general assertion"[115] to this effect – or that there has been undue delay by the moving party in bringing the application which has resulted in the plaintiff incurring additional unnecessary costs.[116]

In assessing whether these respective onuses of proof have been met the court must seek to balance the need to allow an impoverished company access to the courts[117] with the need to protect more prosperous companies from litiga-

---

[112] [1987] ILRM 255,258.

[113] [1986] IR 277, 283.

[114] [1999] 1 IR 501, 529.

[115] *Per* O'Hanlon J *Philip Harrington Daly & Co. v JVC (UK) Ltd* High Court (O'Hanlon J) 16 March 1995 at 16. See also *Jack O'Toole Ltd v MacEoin Kelly Associates* [1986] IR 277, 284.

[116] *SEE Co. Ltd v Public Lighting Services Ltd* [1987] ILRM 255, 259; *Beauross v Kennedy* High Court (Morris J) 18 October 1995.

[117] See the comments of McCarthy J in *SEE Co. Ltd v Public Lighting Services Ltd* [1987] ILRM 255, 258 and of McGuinness J in *Irish Press plc v E.M. Warburg Pincus & Co. International Ltd* [1997] 2 ILRM 263, 274 although she stated that she accepted the submission of counsel for the defendants that "the constitutional right of access to the courts is primarily available to natural persons".

tion where no effective sanction exists against an unsuccessful plaintiff who cannot reimburse a defendant its costs in defending the action. It remains to be seen whether the comment of McGuinness J in *Irish Press plc v E.M. Warburg Pincus & Co. International Ltd*[118] to the effect that "the courts have tended to lean against the making of an order for security for costs" will reflect future practice in this area although the tenor of the judgments of the Supreme Court in *Lismore Homes Ltd v Bank of Ireland Finance Ltd*[119] would suggest otherwise.

MISCELLANEOUS ISSUES

The Amount of Security

10.032 The question of the amount of security which should be furnished has been considered by the Supreme Court on a number of occasions. In *Gibson v Coleman*[120] Dixon J held that where security is ordered, the amount fixed should not be less than the amount of the costs to which the defendant would, on a fair and reasonable computation, probably be put in defending the action. However, it was suggested by Kingsmill Moore J giving judgment in *Thalle v Soares*[121] that the authorities did not seem to support such a test.[122] The plaintiff commenced proceedings seeking the sum of £25,000 which was half the value of a sweepstake ticket which had won a first prize of £50,000. The High Court ordered the plaintiff to provide security for costs and when the Master fixed the security at the sum of £2,500, the plaintiff appealed on the grounds that the sum was excessive. It was upheld by the High Court but varied by the Supreme Court to the sum of £1,000. Kingsmill Moore J stated as follows:

> Security for costs must be so fixed as to advance the ends of justice and not to hinder them. If the amount is too small a plaintiff with a speculative or even dishonest case may be able to force a defendant into an unfavourable settlement by the threat of expensive litigation whose costs may be irrecoverable; if too large a defendant may be able to defeat an honest and substantial claim because the plaintiff cannot find the necessary security.

---

[118] [1997] 2 ILRM 263, 274.
[119] [1999] 1 IR 501.
[120] [1950] IR 50.
[121] [1957] IR 182.
[122] It should be noted that Kingsmill Moore J drew a distinction between the phrase "sufficient security" used in s.278 of the Companies Act 1908 which he stated would seem to mean security which would be equal to the probable costs of the action and the provisions contained in the rules which he said seemed "studiously to have avoided any approach to definiteness, leaving each case to be decided by an uncontrolled discretion" (at 188).

Somewhere between Scylla and Charybdis a way has to be found but there can be no Admiralty chart, no succinct sailing directions.[123]

Kingsmill Moore J continued by quoting with approval the remarks of Fitzgibbon J in *Perry v Stratham*[124] to the effect that "security is not intended either as an indemnity against all costs which may be incurred or as an encouragement to luxurious litigation". He also referred to the fact that in his own experience it had been customary to require as security an amount of not more than about one third of the costs which would probably be incurred by the defendant and the figure of £1,000 was approximately one third of the defendant's estimate of his probable costs.

10.033 It was subsequently accepted by the Supreme Court in *Fallon v An Bord Pleanála*[125] that there is a rule of practice that the amount of security to be fixed should be approximately one third of the estimated costs likely to be incurred by the party against whom the security has been granted. Hederman J accepted that the court has a discretion as to the amount of security to be fixed having regard to the individual facts of each case based on the balance of justice but concluded that to depart from the well established practice "the court would have to be satisfied on evidence that the interest of justice could only be served by increasing the amount for security for costs to a sum substantially in excess of one third of the costs to be incurred".[126] McCarthy J stressed the importance of the constitutional right of access to the courts and said that in assessing the amount of security which should be provided, the fact that the plaintiff was a man of straw acting as a front for people with means was not a consideration. He also said that if the amount fixed was such as to be an indemnity to the defendant, the rules would be being used as "a weapon not of deterrence but of defeat",[127] something which he would not permit. It should be noted that Finlay CJ dissented and held that there were additional factors which prompted him to depart from the usual practice, namely the fact that it was likely that the plaintiff had been specifically chosen as an individual without means and the probability that one of the major reasons behind the institution of proceedings was to delay the completion of the development being challenged.

10.034 It remains to consider whether different principles should apply in relation to corporate plaintiffs. In *Gibson v Coleman*[128] Dixon J said that he did not believe that the use of the word "sufficient" imported a different norm in rela-

---

[123] [1957] IR 182, 193.
[124] [1928] IR 580.
[125] [1992] 2 IR 380.
[126] *Ibid.* at 392.
[127] *Ibid.* at 397.
[128] [1950] IR 50.

tion to the amount of security to that implicit in the simple criterion of "security for costs" and he expressed the view that the fact that an application might be brought pursuant to the Companies Act should not affect the amount of security fixed. In *Thalle v Soares*[129] Kingsmill Moore J made reference to the fact that Dixon J had rejected the idea that there was any difference between the measure of security to be given under the Companies Act and where a plaintiff is resident out of the jurisdiction and said that he was unable to take that view. He stated that "[t]he statute lays down reasonably precise instructions as to the measure of security while the rule makers and the judges seem studiously to have avoided any approach to definiteness, leaving each case to be decided by an uncontrolled discretion".[130] This issue was considered by McCracken J in *Lismore Homes Ltd v Bank of Ireland Finance Ltd.*[131] McCracken J referred to the *dicta* of Kingsmill Moore J and also to the decision of the English Court of Appeal in *Innovare Displays plc v Corporate Broking Services Ltd*[132] where Legatt LJ had expressed the view that the equivalent section "does not mean ... complete security. It can only mean security of a sufficiency in all the circumstances of the case to be just". However, McCracken J pointed out that the English authorities did not seem to be compatible with the decision in *Thalle*. He said that while it is arguable that the use of the word "may" in s.390 gives a general discretion to the court, on the whole he thought it more likely that the word referred to the making of the order for security rather than the amount thereof. McCracken J expressed the view that if the discretion was intended to be in relation to the amount, the word "sufficient" would not have been used. However, it was used in the section and he stated its only logical construction was that it meant sufficient for the costs of the defendant if he were successful in his defence. While it was customary to require security of approximately one third of the probable costs where the plaintiff was out of the jurisdiction, McCracken J stated that he did not see how under any circumstances this could be called "sufficient security" and he concluded that "the section can only mean that the security required must approximate to the probable costs of the defendant should he succeed".[133] These principles were subsequently applied by McCracken J in *Windmaster Developments Ltd v Airogen Ltd*[134] in which the defendants sought an order pursuant to s.390 of the Companies Act that the plaintiff should provide security for the defendants' costs. McCracken J referred to his judgment in Lismore and to the fact that he had held that the words "sufficient security" in s.390 meant that the security required was to approximate to the probable costs of the defendant should it succeed and assessed the security on that basis.

---

[129] [1957] IR 182.

[130] *Ibid.* at 192.

[131] High Court (McCracken J) 24 March 2000.

[132] [1991] BCC 174, 179.

[133] High Court (McCracken J) 24 March 2000 at 5.

[134] High Court (McCracken J) 10 July 2000.

10.035 A similar conclusion was reached by the Supreme Court in *Hot Radio Co. Ltd v IRTC*[135] although it should be pointed out that Keane CJ merely concluded that it was just in the case before him to order the full measure of security because there was no suggestion that the action would be stifled by such an award. Keane CJ referred to the *dicta* of Kingsmill Moore J in *Thalle v Soares* but pointed out that it might be regarded as *obiter* since the learned judge was dealing with a case brought pursuant to the Rules of Court and not the companies legislation. The Chief Justice then referred to the decision of the English Court of Appeal in *Innovare Displays* and said that it was clear that in that case a matter which weighed significantly with the court was the fact that there was a danger the claim would be stifled if security for costs at the full measure was ordered; the opinion of the court was that sufficient security meant security sufficient in all the circumstances to be just. Keane CJ then stated that even applying those criteria and assuming that this view of the law was to be preferred to the view expressed by McCracken J, it was just in the case before him to order the full measure of security because there was no suggestion that the action would be stifled by the award of this amount. Therefore it was not possible to draw any firm conclusions from the decision of Keane CJ in *Hot Radio* as to whether the approach of McCracken J or the English courts would be followed in the future. On the facts of the case before him both tests led to the same conclusion but on balance it appeared that Keane CJ, although he avoided expressing a preference for either option, favoured the "sufficient in all the circumstances to be just" approach.

Any residual doubts about the position of the Supreme Court on this issue have been laid to rest by the recent decision of the court in *Lismore Homes Ltd v Bank of Ireland Finance Ltd.*[136] Murphy J stated that he found himself disagreeing with the conclusions reached by the Court of Appeal in England on this point, although he added that he did so with hesitation. However, in upholding the conclusion reached by McCracken J in relation to the measure of security which should be ordered, he stated that he was greatly comforted to find himself in full agreement with the views expressed by Kingsmill Moore J in *Thalle v Soares.*[137] Murphy J expressed the view that the plain meaning of the words "sufficient security" in s.390 of the Companies Act 1963 is clear. He stated as follows:

> The word "sufficient" in its plain meaning signifies adequate or enough and it is directly related in the section to the defendant's costs. The section does not provide – as it might have – a sufficient sum "to meet the justice of the case" or some such phrase as would give a general discretion to the

---

[135] Supreme Court, 14 April 2000. See Lowe and Dowling [2000] 2(2) P & P 6.
[136] Supreme Court, 5 October 2001.
[137] [1957] IR 182.

court. Harsh though it may be, I am convinced that sufficient security involves making a reasonable estimate or assessment of the actual costs which it is anticipated that the defendant will have to meet.[138]

The Consequences of Failure to Comply with an Order for Security

10.036 The issue of the circumstances in which a claim may be struck out for failure to comply with an order for security for costs was considered briefly by O'Byrne J in *Mitchell v Mitchell*[139] in which he stated that if he had the jurisdiction to take such a step, he would not exercise it unless it were shown that the defendant was "wilfully in default". More recently the question has received more detailed consideration by both O'Sullivan J in the High Court and by the Supreme Court in *Lough Neagh Exploration Ltd v Morrice (No. 2).*[140] O'Sullivan J accepted that the jurisdiction which he was being asked to exercise was discretionary and stated that the jurisdiction must be exercised only sparingly and in clear cases and not for the purpose of punishing a defaulter but for the purpose of ensuring that court orders are complied with. O'Sullivan J referred to the following principles from the *White Book* dealing with the court's inherent jurisdiction to dismiss in default of giving security, namely that it has power to dismiss where it is satisfied that (i) the action is not being pursued with due diligence (ii) that there is no reasonable prospect that the security will be paid and (iii) that the time limit prescribed by the court for the giving of security has been disregarded. He added that it was clear from the English decision in *Speed Up Holdings Ltd v Gough & Co.*[141] that these tests were not cumulative but alternates. O'Sullivan J concluded that in the circumstances the plaintiff was in breach of the order of the court and had not advanced a sufficient or any justification for such breach. Accordingly he decided to accede to the application made on behalf of the defendants and made an order striking out the proceedings by reason of the plaintiff's failure to provide security for costs. The Supreme Court affirmed the decision of O'Sullivan J and Hamilton CJ referred to the decision in *Giddings v Giddings*[142] as authority for the proposition that where time is limited for the provision of security, the proceedings may be dismissed for failure to comply with that time limit and to the decision in *Speed Up Holding Ltd v Gough & Co.* as identifying a number of circumstances in which it would be appropriate to dismiss proceedings for this reason. Hamilton CJ stated that the learned High Court judge had a discretion as to whether to dismiss the claim and that he was satisfied that the order made by him represented a proper exercise by him of that discretion.

---

[138] Supreme Court, 5 October 2001 at 15.
[139] (1932) 66 ILTR 55.
[140] [1999] 4 IR 515; [1999] 1 ILRM 62 (HC).
[141] [1986] FSR 330.
[142] (1847) 10 Beav 29.

THE EFFECT OF EC LAW ON SECURITY FOR COSTS

10.037 As we have seen above, traditionally an order for security for costs will be granted against a plaintiff who is ordinarily resident outside the jurisdiction where a defendant establishes on affidavit that he has a *prima facie* defence on the merits. However, this practice has had to be re-assessed in the wake of a judgment delivered by the European Court of Justice[143] on the interpretation of Article 12EC[144] of the EC Treaty, which prohibits overt or covert discrimination on grounds of nationality, and in the light of the "radical change"[145] effected by the Brussels Convention to the practice of enforcing judgments in States which are party to it.

Article 12EC provides: "Within the scope of the application of this Treaty, and without prejudice to any special provisions contained therein, any discrimination on grounds of nationality shall be prohibited". In addition the fourth indent of Article 293EC[146] provides, in the words employed by the European Court of Justice in its decision in *Mund & Fester v Hatrex International Transport*[147] that "the member states shall, so far as is necessary, enter into negotiations with each other with a view to securing for the benefit of their nationals the simplification of formalities governing the reciprocal recognition and enforcement of judgments of courts or tribunals". It was on the basis of this article, and within the framework defined by it, that the member states concluded the Brussels Convention on Jurisdiction and Enforcement of Judgments in Civil and Commercial Matters in 1968, which was passed into Irish law by the Jurisdiction of Courts and Enforcement of Judgments (European Communities) Act 1998. Order 29, rule 8 now provides that "no defendant shall be entitled to an order for security for costs in proceedings for the enforcement of a judgment under the 1988 Act solely on the ground that the plaintiff is a foreign national or that he is domiciled or resident in the State".

10.038 The terms of Article 12EC were interpreted by the European Court of Justice in *Boussac Saint-Freres SA v Gerstenmeier*[148] as meaning that "[it] forbids not only overt discrimination by reason of nationality but also all covert forms of discrimination which, by the application of other criteria of differentiation, lead in fact to the same result." One interpretation of this article put forward by Staughton LJ in his judgment in *Berkeley Administration Inc. v McClelland*[149] was that "provisions which are 'tantamount as regards their

---

[143] *Mund & Fester v Hatrex International Transport* (Case C–398/92) [1994] ECR I–467.
[144] This article was originally Article 7 and was renumbered as Article 6 by the Treaty on European Union 1993.
[145] *Per* Keane J in *Pitt v Bolger* [1996] 1 IR 108, 115, [1996] 2 ILRM 68, 75.
[146] Formerly Article 220.
[147] (Case C–398/92) [1994] ECR I–467, 478.
[148] (Case 22/80) [1980] ECR 3427, 3436.
[149] [1990] 2 QB 407, 427-428, [1990] 2 WLR 1021, 1036, [1990] 1 All ER 958, 971.

practical effect' to discrimination on grounds of nationality qualify as indirect, or as community law would say covert, discrimination[150] or provisions which 'principally affect' nationals of other member states".[151] It is in the light of such an interpretation that questions arose about the domestic laws of member states which might appear to indirectly discriminate on grounds of nationality *e.g.* provisions relating to security for costs.

As Murphy J noted in *Proetta v Neil*[152] the equivalent rule in England which deals with security for costs contains a difference in emphasis if not in principle from its counterpart here. Order 23, rule 1(1)(a) of the Rules of the Supreme Court provides that where it appears that a plaintiff is "ordinarily resident[153] out of the jurisdiction" then if, having regard to all the circumstances of the case, the court thinks it just to do so, it may order the plaintiff to give security for costs. While this provision gives the court considerable discretion, its authority under this rule is undoubtedly premised on the fact that a plaintiff resides out of the jurisdiction and questions began to be asked about whether it could be interpreted as indirectly discriminating against an EU national.

10.039 This point was canvassed before Browne-Wilkinson VC in *Porzelack KG v Porzelack (UK) Ltd*[154] and examined more fully by Lord Donaldson MR in *De Bry v Fitzgerald*,[155] although in the circumstances the Master of the Rolls found that it was unnecessary for him to express any view on the argument based on Article 12EC. Lord Donaldson anticipated that this discrimination argument would need to be addressed, particularly in view of the fact that trade between member states was becoming freer and litigation of this nature more frequent.[156] This issue was directly examined by the Court of Appeal in *Berkeley Administration Inc. v McClelland*[157] and it is interesting to compare the conclusions reached. While all the members of the court agreed that the defendant's appeal against the finding that no order for security for costs be made should be dismissed, only Parker and Russell LJJ based their decision on the finding that Order 23, rule 1(1)(a) did not discriminate overtly or covertly on grounds of nationality contrary to Article 12EC. As Russell LJ stated: "Order 23 is concerned with residence irrespective of nationality; Article [12EC] is concerned with nationality irrespective of residence".[158] In other words as resi-

---

[150] *Sotgiu v Deutsche Bundespost* (Case 152/73) [1974] ECR 153, 164.
[151] *Boussac Saint-Freres SA v Gerstenmeier* (Case 22/80) [1980] ECR 3427, 3436.
[152] [1996] 1 IR 102, 103, [1996] 1 ILRM 457, 460.
[153] See *Re Little Olympian Each Ways Ltd* [1995] 1 WLR 560, [1994] 4 All ER 561.
[154] [1987] 1 WLR 420, [1987] 1 All ER 1074.
[155] [1990] 1 WLR 552, [1990] 1 All ER 560. See also *Thune v London Properties Ltd* [1990] 1 WLR 562, [1990] 1 All ER 972.
[156] *Ibid.* at 558, 565.
[157] [1990] 2 QB 407, [1990] 2 WLR 1021, [1990] 1 All ER 958. See further Matthews [1994] LMCLQ 454.
[158] *Ibid.* at 424, 1033, 968. See also the comments of Parker LJ that under the terms of the

dence, not nationality, determined the applicability of the order it could not be impugned on the ground that it infringed Article 12EC. Staughton LJ took a more enlightened approach and found that provisions directed at those not ordinarily resident in the jurisdiction were tantamount in their practical effect to provisions directed at non-nationals. However, he concluded that it was objectively justifiable to provide a discretion to order security for costs in cases where a plaintiff was ordinarily resident outside the jurisdiction since it was in those cases that a successful defendant was more likely to have difficulty in enforcing an order for costs.

10.040 It remained to re-assess this latter conclusion in the light of developments in the recognition and enforcement of judgments within EU member states which are party to the Brussels Convention, an issue addressed by the European Court of Justice in the landmark decision of *Mund & Fester v Hatrex International Transport*[159] which forced a re-assessment of the position both in England[160] and in this jurisdiction. In its judgment, the court re-appraised the question of whether such forms of indirect discrimination based on grounds of nationality could be justified in the light of current practice in relation to enforcement of judgments. The plaintiff, a German company which had brought a claim against an international carrier with a registered office in the Netherlands, sought a seizure order against a lorry belonging to the defendant which remained in Germany. The relevant order provided that: "The fact that a judgment is to be enforced abroad shall be considered sufficient grounds for a seizure order".[161] In his opinion, which was upheld by the court, Advocate General Tesauro stated that while it might have been presumed that there would be a greater degree of difficulty in enforcing judgments obtained in other states prior to the entry into force of the Brussels Convention, this argument could no longer be relied on with regard to countries which are signatories to the convention. As he stated:

> The reduction in the number of obstacles to the recognition and enforcement of decisions given in another Contracting State and also the simplification of the procedures for obtaining an order for enforcement ensure, within the scope of the Convention, enforcement of judgments which is not in practice less rapid or less certain than when the judgment is en-

---

order "all persons who select residence within the jurisdiction are, irrespective of nationality, treated alike, and all persons who select residence outside the jurisdiction are equally, irrespective of nationality treated alike." (at 421, 1030, 965).

[159] (Case C–398/92) [1994] ECR I–467.

[160] As Matthews points out (1994) LMCLQ 454, 460, the decision of the European Court of Justice in *Mund & Fester* destroyed the reasoning underpinning the views expressed by both the majority and minority in *Berkeley Administration Ltd v McClelland* [1990] 2 QB 407, [1990] 2 WLR 1021, [1990] 1 All ER 958.

[161] Paragraph 917 of the Zivilprocessordnung (German Code of Civil Procedure).

forced within the country in which it is delivered but within the territorial
jurisdiction of another court.[162]

These comments would seem to deal with the arguments put forward by Staughton
LJ in *Berkeley* on the issue of whether it was objectively justifiable to discriminate and the Court of Justice agreed with the conclusion of the Advocate General. The court was satisfied that the national provision which it was considering
involved a covert form of discrimination and that it was not justified by objective circumstances, at any rate where the subsequent judgment was to be enforced in a member state of the Community, which were all parties to the Brussels
Convention.

10.041 An opportunity for the High Court to re-assess the effect of Order 29 on
persons not resident within the jurisdiction in the light of the judgment of the
European Court of Justice in *Mund & Fester* arose in *Maher v Phelan*.[163] The
plaintiff, who was resident in England, argued that the defendant should not
succeed in obtaining an order for security for costs, on the basis that the law in
this area had "radically changed" since the enactment of the Jurisdiction of
Courts and Enforcement of Judgments (European Communities) Act 1988.
Carroll J considered the findings and conclusions of the European Court of
Justice in *Mund & Fester* which she said "put the matter beyond doubt" and
held that as an individual litigant who is resident in Ireland cannot be ordered to
provide security for costs, a plaintiff resident outside Ireland but within the EU
should not be so ordered. Carroll J said even if she were wrong in that view, she
would not in any event grant an order as the rationale for granting one no longer
exists as far as EU member states in which judgments are enforceable with
comparative ease under the Brussels Convention and the Jurisdiction of Courts
and Enforcement of Judgments (European Communities) Act 1988 are concerned. She concluded that even without reference to the question of discrimination on grounds of nationality, the plaintiff was not impecunious and had
assets within as well as outside the jurisdiction.

10.042 The interpretation of the European Court of Justice in *Mund & Fester*
was also relied on by Murphy J in refusing an order for security for costs against
a plaintiff, resident outside the jurisdiction but within the EU, in *Proetta v Neil*.[164]
The proceedings between the parties arose out of a statement made by the defendant on a television programme broadcast by RTÉ which the plaintiff, who
is a Spanish national residing in Gibraltar, claimed was defamatory of her. The
plaintiff sought damages for libel and the defendant brought an application for
security for costs on a full indemnity basis. Murphy J made reference to the

---

[162] Paragraph 12 of his opinion.
[163] [1996] 1 IR 95, [1996] 1 ILRM 359.
[164] [1996] 1 IR 100, [1996] 1 ILRM 457.

decision of the Court of Appeal in *Berkeley Administration Inc. v McClelland*[165] but also referred to the judgment of the European Court of Justice in *Mund & Fester* which had been delivered subsequently, and held that the conclusion reached in the latter case was equally applicable to the facts before him. However, he added that were it not for the provisions of the Treaty of Rome, he would, in the exercise of his discretion on the basis of the information before him, have ordered the plaintiff to provide security for costs.

10.043 An attempt was made to distinguish these decisions in a recent case on the basis that the plaintiff, while a national of an EU country, was not ordinarily resident there. In *Pitt v Bolger*,[166] the plaintiff, who was a UK national resident in the Isle of Man, brought proceedings against the defendants claiming that they had acted fraudulently and in breach of their duty to her or, in the alternative, had been negligent in advising her in relation to an agreement to sell a horse in which she had an interest. The second named defendant sought an order for security for costs on the basis that the plaintiff resided out of the jurisdiction, namely in the Isle of Man, and claimed that affidavits had been sworn which should satisfy the court that he had a defence on the merits within the meaning of Order 29, rule 3 of the RSC 1986. The plaintiff averred that while she had resided in the Isle of Man, she had recently acquired a property in England, that she was currently living in both places and intended to reside in England permanently as soon as she had sold her home in the Isle of Man. Counsel for the second named defendant sought to distinguish the decisions in *Maher v Phelan* and *Proetta v Neil* on the basis that at the time the proceedings were initiated, the plaintiff was ordinarily resident in the Isle of Man which is neither a member state of the European Union or one of the contracting parties to the Brussels Convention. Counsel for the plaintiff submitted that as a citizen of the United Kingdom she was entitled to the benefit of the principle laid down in *Mund & Fester.*

Keane J embarked upon a comprehensive review of the relevant authorities in the area and said that the nature of the jurisdiction of the court had been explained in *Collins,* namely that *prima facie* a defendant establishing a *prima facie* defence to a claim made by a plaintiff residing outside the jurisdiction is entitled to an order for security for costs but this was not an absolute right and, amongst the matters to which a court might have regard in exercising its discretion against ordering security, was a *prima facie* case that the plaintiff's inability to give security flowed from the wrong committed by the defendant. Keane J said that the Brussels Convention had effected a "radical change" in the enforcement of judgments throughout the member states of the EU and the rules of private international law in this context had been entirely altered.

---

[165] [1990] 2 QB 407, [1990] 2 WLR 1021, [1990] 1 All ER 958.
[166] [1996] 1 IR 108, [1996] 2 ILRM 68.

Keane J referred to the *Maher* and *Proetta* decisions and to a decision of the English Court of Appeal in *Fitzgerald v Williams*,[167] in which Bingham MR had concluded that the equivalent English provision, which empowered the court to make orders against plaintiffs ordinarily resident out of the jurisdiction which it could not make against plaintiffs ordinarily resident within it, involved discrimination in the sense used by the European Court of Justice in *Mund & Fester.* On this basis Keane J concluded that "the undoubted discretion under the rule should never be exercised by an Irish court to order security to be given by an individual plaintiff who is a national of and resident in another member state which is a party to the convention" subject to the possible qualification referred to by Bingham MR in *Fitzgerald v Williams,* namely, where there is "very cogent evidence of substantial difficulty in enforcing a judgment in another member state".

Finally, Keane J had to consider whether the fact that the plaintiff was ordinarily resident in the Isle of Man at the time proceedings were instituted should alter the position. He concluded that where, as in the case before him, the plaintiff was a national of a member state of the EU and the evidence was that while resident in the past in a non-member state she had significant assets in the member state and intended to reside there permanently in the future, it seemed to him that the principles in *Mund* were clearly applicable. Accordingly he refused to grant the order for security for costs.[168]

10.044 As a result of these three recent decisions of the High Court, in particular the comprehensive judgment of Keane J (as he then was), it would appear that the courts should not exercise their discretion under Order 29 to order security for costs to be given by an individual plaintiff who is a national of and resident in another member state of the EU which is a party to the Brussels Convention in the absence of very cogent evidence of substantial difficulty in enforcing a judgment in another member state. Equally, on the authority of *Pitt v Bolger* this would seem to be the case even in the context of a EU national whose place of residence is not altogether unproblematic, provided the court is satisfied that any judgment will be enforced within the framework of the Brussels Convention.

However, the position is not so clear cut in certain other situations. In order for the principles discussed above to apply, the plaintiff must be a national of and resident in another member state of the EU which is a party to the Brussels Convention. At the time of the judgment of the European Court of Justice in

---

[167] [1996] QB 657, [1996] 2 WLR 447, [1996] 2 All ER 171.

[168] One further point which Keane J made reference to was the fact that under the Foreign Judgments (Reciprocal Enforcement) Act 1933 which had been applied to the Isle of Man, judgments obtained in that jurisdiction might be enforced in the United Kingdom and he said that it seemed clear that an order for costs given by the Irish courts could have been enforced against the plaintiff in the Isle of Man.

Hayes v Kronenberger GmbH[169] some member states of the EU were not yet parties to the Brussels Convention[170] or Lugano Convention[171] and as a result as between some member states there was a real risk that enforcement would be impossible or at least considerably more difficult. While the court did not find it necessary to express a view as to whether that situation might warrant the imposition of security for costs on non-residents where such a risk existed, it would in all likelihood constitute objectively justifiable grounds for discrimination. This should be borne in mind in the context of the proposed enlargement of the European Union if additional states become members but are not parties to the Brussels or Lugano Conventions.

10.045 Similarly, the European Court of Justice made clear in its judgment in *Mund & Fester*,[172] that difficulties in enforcing a judgment may arise where enforcement is to take place in a non-member country of the EU, and any discrimination on grounds of nationality might be objectively justified where these difficulties remain. So, if proceedings were brought against a national of a member state who was resident outside the EU and enforcement was to take place outside the countries of the Union, discrimination might be objectively justified on the grounds of potential difficulties in enforcement and security for costs might be ordered. Equally in litigation to which the provisions of the Brussels Convention do not apply, *i.e.* outside the scope of civil and commercial cases, discrimination may also be objectively justified for this reason. While Carroll J seemed to conclude in *Maher v Phelan* that she could support her decision merely on the basis of discrimination on grounds of nationality, it is submitted that the second ground on which she relied, namely, the ease with which judgments may now be enforced in convention countries, is an integral part of any conclusion that security for costs should not be ordered on the grounds of discrimination if one is to avoid the "objectively justifiable" clause relied on by Staughton LJ in *Berkeley Administration*.

10.046 Another related issue is whether the protection of Article 12EC can extend to non-EU nationals resident within the Union. If it is interpreted to apply to such persons,[173] then it is likely that they would be entitled to the benefit of the reasoning employed in *Mund & Fester* and applied in the decisions of the Irish High Court as there would in theory be no difficulties in enforcing any judgment obtained within the framework of the Brussels Convention. Further clarification will be required before these questions can be answered with any degree of certainty. What is evident, however, is that the decision of

---

[169] (Case C–323/95) [1997] ECR I–1711.
[170] Austria, Finland and Sweden.
[171] Belgium and Greece.
[172] (Case C–398/92) [1994] ECR I–467.
[173] See *Diatta v Land Berlin* (Case 267/83) [1985] ECR 567, [1986] 2 CMLR 164.

the European Court of Justice in *Mund & Fester* and the advancements in the enforcement of judgments achieved by the Brussels Convention have brought about a radical change in the manner in which the courts in this jurisdiction may exercise their discretion to make an order for security for costs under Order 29 of the Rules of the Superior Courts 1986.

10.047 Finally it is important to recall that different considerations apply to applications for security for costs against corporate plaintiffs and that it is the impoverished state of the company rather than its place of residence which is significant. So where security for costs is granted against a plaintiff company resident in the EU because of its impecunious state, this will not constitute discrimination contrary to Article 12EC as an order would be made against a company resident in the jurisdiction on the same basis, *i.e.* its likely inability to pay the costs of a successful defendant. This is illustrated by *Chequepoint Sarl v McClelland*[174] in which the Court of Appeal held that where a court exercises its discretion under Order 23, r.1(1)(a) to order an impecunious foreign company ordinarily resident in a member state of the EC to give security for costs, it does not thereby discriminate against that company contrary to community law since an English company in a similar position will be treated in the same manner and may also be required to provide security.[175] The plaintiff, a company incorporated under French law and ordinarily resident there, appealed against an order made ordering it to give security for costs in its action for defamation against the defendants. In addressing the question of whether the exercise of discretion in this case offended against principles of community law, Lord Bingham CJ stated as follows: "The object of community law in this area is to ensure that member states do not treat nationals and enterprises of other member states prejudicially as compared with the way in which they treat their own nationals and enterprises".[176] He concluded that if the exercise of the court's discretion involved no prejudicial treatment of a foreign company as compared with an English one, and the interests of justice called for an order to be made, it could not be struck down as unlawful.

---

[174] [1997] QB 51, [1996] 3 WLR 341, [1997] 2 All ER 384.
[175] Pursuant to s.726 of the Companies Act 1985.
[176] [1997] QB 51, 59; [1996] 3 WLR 341, 347; [1997] 2 All ER 384, 389.

CHAPTER ELEVEN

DISMISSAL FOR WANT OF PROSECUTION ON GROUNDS OF INORDINATE AND INEXCUSABLE DELAY

INTRODUCTION

11.001 As Finlay CJ commented in *Sweeney v Horan's (Tralee) Ltd*[1] "the courts have a consistent duty to try and convey both to litigants and lawyers the necessity for the bringing of cases to trial with due expedition" and an action may be dismissed on the basis that the plaintiff's delay in proceeding with his claim is such that the defendant could not reasonably be expected to defend it. Order 63, rule 1(8) of the Rules of the Superior Courts 1986 provides that the Master of the High Court may make an order, *inter alia*, "to dismiss an action with costs for want of prosecution ..." and the circumstances in which an action may be dismissed pursuant to the Rules of the Superior Courts for want of prosecution include default of pleading,[2] a failure to give notice of trial,[3] or "in any cause or matter in which there has been no proceeding for two years from the last proceeding had".[4] In addition, as Hamilton CJ stated in *Primor plc v Stokes Kennedy Crowley*:[5] "the courts have an inherent jurisdiction to control their own procedure and to dismiss a claim when the interests of justice require them to do so."[6] Such inherent jurisdiction may be exercised where there has been inordinate and inexcusable delay on the part of the plaintiff and where the balance of justice is against allowing the case to proceed.[7] However, in making

---

[1] [1987] ILRM 240, 243.

[2] Order 27, rule 1.

[3] Order 36, rules 12 and 13.

[4] Order 122, rule 11.

[5] [1996] 2 IR 459, 475. See also the comments of Nicholson J in *NIHE v Wimpey Construction (UK) Ltd* [1989] NI 395, 402.

[6] As was made clear in the context of similar guidelines which apply in England by Balcombe LJ in *Halls v O'Dell* [1992] QB 393, 404 [1992] 2 WLR 308, 316 the same principles apply whether the court is asked to dismiss a claim under its inherent jurisdiction or under an express rule of court. See also *Barratt Manchester Ltd v Bolton MBC* [1998] 1 WLR 1003, 1009, [1998] 1 All ER 1, 7.

[7] Note that there is a useful list of some of the relevant factors which may influence a court in deciding whether to dismiss an action for want of prosecution set out in the judgment of McPherson JA in the decision of the Queensland Court of Appeal in *Cooper v Hopgood* [1999] 2 Qd R 113, 124 which include "matters such as the duration of the time lapse involved; the cogency of any explanation for delay; the probable impact of

any such decision the court is required to strike a balance between the rights of both parties and the conduct of both plaintiff and defendant may be relevant. In practice, cases may come before the court in a number of different ways. A plaintiff may be granted[8] or refused[9] an extension of the period allowed for delivering a statement of claim by the Master[10] and the unsuccessful party may appeal to the High Court. Often where a defendant contests the granting of such an extension, he will also seek to have the claim dismissed for want of prosecution.[11] Similarly, a defendant may apply to have a claim dismissed for want of prosecution or pursuant to the court's inherent jurisdiction on grounds of inordinate and inexcusable delay.[12]

THE RATIONALE BEHIND THIS JURISDICTION

11.002 The need for such a jurisdiction is clear particularly where disputed facts have to be ascertained from the evidence of witnesses whose recollection of events will inevitably become less certain and therefore less reliable with the passage of time. As Diplock LJ stated in *Allen v Sir Alfred McAlpine & Sons Ltd*:[13] "The chances of the court's being able to find out what really happened

---

procrastination on fading recollection; the death or disappearance of critical witnesses or records; costs already or likely in the future to be expended or thrown away; the apparent prospects of success or otherwise at a trial of the action; and the progressively growing problem of effectively hearing and determining questions of fact arising out of events that have taken place many years before."

[8] *Rainsford v Limerick Corporation* [1995] 2 ILRM 561.

[9] *Dowd v Kerry County Council* [1970] IR 27.

[10] See Order 63, rule 1(5).

[11] *O'Reilly v Coras Iompair Éireann* [1973] IR 278. See also *Ó Domhnaill v Merrick* [1984] IR 151, [1985] ILRM 40 where an appeal was taken by the defendant from a decision of the Master to grant an extension and a motion was brought by the defendant to have the claim dismissed.

[12] Note that in *Collins v Dublin Bus* Supreme Court, 22 October 1999 the distinction between an application to dismiss for want of prosecution pursuant to Order 122, rule 11 and to dismiss on grounds of inordinate and inexcusable delay pursuant to the court's inherent jurisdiction was clarified by the Supreme Court. Counsel for the plaintiff had argued that the learned trial judge had not been entitled to dismiss the plaintiff's claim "for want of prosecution" as in accordance with Order 122, rule 11 an action cannot be dismissed for want of prosecution where proceedings have been taken in the two years prior to the application. Murphy J stated that counsel was correct in that submission but that it related more to the form of order as drawn up than to the substance of the ruling made by Flood J in the High Court. He concluded that the learned High Court judge had been correct in striking out the plaintiff's claim but stated that he believed that the form in which the order was expressed was incorrect and said that he would rectify the terms in which it had been made by ordering that the action be dismissed for inordinate and inexcusable delay on the part of the plaintiff to the prejudice of the defendant.

[13] [1968] 2 QB 229, 255, [1968] 2 WLR 366, 379, [1968] 1 All ER 543, 553.

are progressively reduced as time goes on. This puts justice to the hazard." However, such an order can also inflict considerable hardship on a plaintiff who may have suffered serious injury and have no other means of compensation and, as Diplock LJ also commented in *Allen*, an order to dismiss "will not lightly be made".[14]

One point which the courts both in this jurisdiction and in England have been careful to stress traditionally is that an action will not be struck out in order to punish a plaintiff for his delay but rather with a view to ensuring that justice is done. This was made clear by Murphy J in the course of his judgment in *Hogan v Jones*[15] in the following terms:

> The draconian penalty of dismissing proceedings as against a particular defendant in circumstances which will wholly defeat that claim of the plaintiff is not an order which is made with a view to punishing a party for his dilatoriness in proceeding with the action or for his failure to meet some artificial regime. The order is made only where it is necessary to protect the legitimate interests of the party sued and in particular his constitutional right to a trial in accordance with fair procedures.

11.003 The possibility of extending the jurisdiction to dismiss for want of prosecution to achieve a deterrent effect was canvassed before the House of Lords in *Department of Transport v Chris Smaller (Transport) Ltd*,[16] although the idea was firmly rejected by Lord Griffiths who said that "[t]o extend the principle purely to punish the plaintiff in the illusory hope of transforming the habits of other plaintiffs' solicitors would, in my view, be an unjustified way of attacking a very intractable problem." Clearly as Finlay CJ stated in *Sweeney v Horan's (Tralee) Ltd*[17] while the courts must encourage the bringing of proceedings to trial with all due speed, the balance of justice between the parties cannot be disturbed by a desire on the part of the court to deter others from lengthy delay. Similar sentiments were expressed by O'Flaherty J in *Primor plc v Stokes Kennedy Crowley*[18] where he stated that "Courts do not exist for the sake of discipline but rather to deal with the essential justice of the case before them."

---

[14] *Ibid.* at 259, 383, 556. See further the comment of Millett LJ in *Barratt Manchester Ltd v Bolton MBC* [1998] 1 WLR 1003, 1011, [1998] 1 All ER 1, 9 that "the dismissal of an action is a draconian measure".

[15] [1994] 1 ILRM 512, 518.

[16] [1989] AC 1197, 1207, [1989] 2 WLR 578, 585, [1989] 1 All ER 897, 903. However, note the recent comments of Lord Woolf in *Arbuthnot Latham Bank Ltd v Trafalgar Holdings Ltd* [1998] 1 WLR 1426, [1998] 2 All ER 181, see further *infra*.

[17] [1987] ILRM 240, 243.

[18] [1996] 2 IR 459, 516. Referring to his comment in *Murphy v Minister for Defence* [1991] 2 IR 161.

THE GUIDELINES ADOPTED

11.004 Where a court is required to decide whether to dismiss an action for
want of prosecution or pursuant to its inherent jurisdiction on grounds of inordinate and inexcusable delay, it would appear that essentially the same principles
apply.[19] The court will be influenced by the concepts of fairness and justice and
must balance the interests of both plaintiff and defendant *i.e.* "whether it is fair
to the defendant to allow the action to proceed and whether it is just to the
plaintiff to strike out the action".[20] The importance of this balancing process
was stressed by Ó Dálaigh CJ in *Dowd v Kerry County Council*[21] where he
stated that "in weighing the extent of one party's delay, the court should not
leave out of account the inactivity of the other party.... [l]itigation is a two-party
operation and the conduct of both parties should be looked at." The importance
of achieving a balance between the rights of both parties was stressed again by
Henchy J in *Ó Domhnaill v Merrick*[22] where he said that whether delay should
be treated as barring the prosecution of a claim must inevitably depend on the
circumstances of a case. However, where, as in the case before him, the delay
had been inordinate and inexcusable, it was not likely to be overlooked unless
there were countervailing circumstances, such as acquiescence on the defendant's part or the plaintiff's inability to control the delay of his agents. As he
stated: "In all cases the problem of the court would seem to be to strike a balance between a plaintiff's need to carry on his or her delayed claim against a
defendant and the defendant's basic right not to be subjected to a claim which
he or she could not reasonably be expected to defend".[23]

11.005 A number of general guidelines were laid down by Finlay P in *Rainsford
v Limerick Corporation*[24] which have been quoted with approval in numerous
subsequent cases.[25] First, he stated that it should be established whether the

---

[19] *Per* Salmon LJ in *Allen v Sir Alfred McAlpine and Sons Ltd* [1968] 2 QB 229, 268,
[1968] 2 WLR 366, 390, [1968] 1 All ER 543, 561. See also *Department of Health and
Social Services v Derry Construction Co. Ltd* [1980] NI 187, 189; *Bannon v Craigavon
Development Commission* [1984] NI 387, 390.

[20] *Per* Hamilton CJ in *Primor plc v Stokes Kennedy Crowley* [1996] 2 IR 459, 466. See
also *Whearty v ACC* High Court (McCracken J) 31 October 1997 at 7.

[21] [1970] IR 27, 41-42.

[22] [1984] IR 151.

[23] *Ibid.* at 157. Quoted with approval by O'Hanlon J in *Celtic Ceramics Ltd v IDA* [1993]
ILRM 248, 254, by Finlay CJ in *Toal v Duignan (No. 2)* [1991] ILRM 140, 143 and by
Murphy J in *Southern Mineral Oil Ltd v Cooney* High Court (Murphy J) 10 February
1995. See also the *dicta* of Barron J in the Supreme Court decision of *Kelly v Cullen*
Supreme Court, 27 July 1998 to the effect that the ultimate test in determining whether
to dismiss proceedings is whether or not justice could be done as between the parties.

[24] [1995] 2 ILRM 561 (31 July 1979).

[25] *Ó Domhnaill v Merrick* [1984] IR 151, [1985] ILRM 40; *Guerin v Guerin* [1992] 2 IR
287, [1993] ILRM 243; *Celtic Ceramics Ltd v IDA* [1993] ILRM 248; *Hogan v Jones*
[1994] 1 ILRM 512; *Primor plc v Stokes Kennedy Crowley* [1996] 2 IR 459; *Whearty v*

delay has been inordinate and inexcusable and that the onus of establishing this would appear to lie on the party seeking a dismissal. Even where the delay has been inordinate and inexcusable, the court must exercise its discretion to decide whether the balance of justice is in favour of or against the case proceeding. Finlay P added that delay on the part of the defendant in seeking a dismissal may be an ingredient in the exercise by the court of its discretion and that while a party must to an extent be vicariously liable for the inactivity of his solicitor, the litigant's own personal blameworthiness is material to the exercise of the court's discretion. Similar guidelines were laid down by Hamilton CJ in *Primor plc v Stokes Kennedy Crowley*[26] having conducted an extensive review of the relevant authorities, and it is useful to set out these principles in full:

(a) the courts have an inherent jurisdiction to control their own procedure and to dismiss a claim when the interests of justice require them to do so;

(b) it must, in the first instance, be established by the party seeking a dismissal of proceedings for want of prosecution on the ground of delay in the prosecution thereof, that the delay was inordinate and inexcusable;

(c) even where the delay has been both inordinate and inexcusable the court must exercise a judgment on whether, in its discretion, on the facts the balance of justice is in favour of or against the proceeding of the case;

(d) in considering this latter obligation the court is entitled to take into consideration and have regard to:
   (i) the implied constitutional principles of basic fairness of procedures,
   (ii) whether the delay and consequent prejudice in the special facts of the case are such as to make it unfair to the defendant to allow the action to proceed and to make it just to strike out the plaintiff's action,
   (iii) any delay on the part of the defendant because litigation is a two party operation the conduct of both parties should be looked at,

---

ACC High Court (McCracken J) 31 October 1997; *Daly v Limerick Corporation* (Morris P) 11 July 2001.

[26] [1996] 2 IR 459, 475-476. These principles have been approved in numerous decisions, *e.g. Carroll Shipping Ltd v Mathews Mulcahy & Sutherland Ltd* High Court (McGuinness J) 18 December 1996; *PMPA Ltd v PMPS Ltd* High Court (Costello P) 20 February 1997; *Robert McGregor and Sons (Ireland) Ltd v Mining Board* High Court (Carroll J) 5 October 1998; *Dunne v ESB* High Court (Laffoy J) 19 October 1999; *Truck and Machinery Sales Ltd v General Accident Fire and Life Assurance Corporation plc* High Court (Geoghegan J) 12 November 1999; *Glynn v Rotunda Hospital* High Court (O'Sullivan J) 6 April 2000; *Kelly v O'Leary* High Court (Kelly J) 22 June 2001.

(iv) whether any delay or conduct of the defendant amounts to acquiescence on the part of the defendant in the plaintiff's delay,
(v) the fact that conduct by the defendant which induces the plaintiff to incur further expense in pursuing the action does not, in law, constitute an absolute bar preventing the defendant from obtaining a striking out order but is a relevant factor to be taken into account by the judge in exercising his discretion whether or not to strike out the claim, the weight to be attached to such conduct depending upon all the circumstances of the particular case,
(vi) whether the delay gives rise to a substantial risk that it is not possible to have a fair trial or is likely to cause or have caused serious prejudice to the defendant,
(vii) the fact that the prejudice to the defendant referred to in (vi) may arise in many ways and be other than that merely caused by the delay, including damage to a defendant's reputation and business.

On the facts before him, Hamilton CJ was satisfied that there had been inordinate and inexcusable delay on the plaintiff's part and went on to consider whether the balance of justice was in favour of or against the case proceeding. He found that the defendants' conduct was not such as would amount to a countervailing circumstance as would negative or provide an answer to the inordinate and inexcusable delay on the part of the plaintiff. He concluded that the prejudice caused to the defendants by the plaintiff's delay was such as to place an inexcusable and unfair burden on the defendants in defending the proceedings and was such as to make it impossible that a fair trial between the parties could now proceed. O'Flaherty J agreed that there had been inordinate and inexcusable delay on the part of the plaintiff and that the prejudice chronicled by the defendants was "total and insurmountable".

11.006 While the guidelines outlined above are now well established principles, it is not possible to state with certainty what period of inactivity will suffice to constitute "inordinate delay".[27] While in *Carroll Shipping Ltd v Mathews Mulcahy and Sutherland Ltd*[28] a delay of over 15 years since the issue of the plenary summons was described as "undoubtedly inordinate", much shorter periods of time have been found to meet this criteria.[29] A further issue which has proved problematic over the years is the extent to which delay prior to the commencement of proceedings within the relevant limitation period can be con-

---

[27] Note that a plaintiff may sometimes concede that a delay has been inordinate but argue that it is excusable, *e.g. Dunne v ESB* High Court (Laffoy J) 19 October 1999.
[28] High Court (McGuinness J) 18 December 1996.
[29] *E.g.* in *Byrne v ITGWU* High Court (Morris J) 30 November 1995 a period of four years was held to be inordinate.

sidered in assessing whether a claim should be dismissed. The following principles set out by Lord Diplock in *Birkett v James*[30] have been approved in this jurisdiction[31] and would seem to reflect the correct position:

> [T]ime elapsed before the issue of a writ within the limitation period cannot of itself constitute inordinate delay however much the defendant may already have been prejudiced by the consequent lack of early notice of the claim against him, the fading recollections of potential witnesses, their death or their untraceability. To justify dismissal of an action for want of prosecution the delay relied on must relate to time which the plaintiff allows to lapse unnecessarily after the writ has been issued. A late start makes it the more incumbent on the plaintiff to proceed with all due speed and a pace which might have been excusable if the action had been started sooner may be inexcusable in the light of the time that has already passed before the writ was issued.

11.007 A similar approach was adopted by Henchy J in *Sheehan v Amond*[32] where he stated that when the period of limitation for instituting proceedings has been all but allowed to expire, "a plaintiff's solicitor should be astute to ensure that he is not dilatory in regard to any of the further procedural steps that are necessary to avoid the taint of prejudicial delay". These principles were applied by Murphy J recently in *Collins v Dublin Bus*[33] where he held that a delay of eight years between the issue of the plenary summons and the delivery of the statement of claim was inordinate, particularly having regard to the fact that the plaintiff had only instituted proceedings just prior to the expiration of the statutory period of limitation. It should also be noted that in some instances delay prior to the institution of proceedings has itself been characterised as

---

[30] [1978] AC 297, 322, [1977] 3 WLR 38, 50, [1977] 2 All ER 801, 808. See also the *dicta* of Lord Griffiths in *Department of Transport v Chris Smaller Ltd* [1989] AC 1197, 1208, [1989] 2 WLR 578, 586, [1989] 1 All ER 897, 903 where he stated that "long delay before issue of the writ will have the effect of any post writ delay being looked at critically by the court and more readily being regarded as inordinate and inexcusable than would be the case if the action had been commenced soon after the accrual of the cause of action" and the comments of Lord Denning MR in *Biss v Lambeth, Southwark and Lewisham Health Authority* [1978] 1 WLR 382, 390, [1978] 2 All ER 125, 132 to the effect that "if the plaintiff is guilty of inordinate and inexcusable delay before issuing the writ, then it is his duty to proceed with it with expedition after the issue of the writ". See also *Re Noble Trees Ltd* [1993] BCLC 1185, 1190 and *Re Manlon Trading Ltd* [1995] 3 WLR 839, 846, 851, [1996] Ch 136, 162, 168, [1995] 4 All ER 14, 23, 28.

[31] *Hogan v Jones* [1994] 1 ILRM 512, 516.

[32] [1982] IR 235, 237. Quoted with approval by McCarthy J in *Ó Domhnaill v Merrick* [1984] IR 151, [1985] ILRM 40, by Hamilton CJ in *Primor plc v Stokes Kennedy Crowley* [1996] 2 IR 459 and by Murphy J in *Collins v Dublin Bus* Supreme Court, 22 October 1999.

[33] Supreme Court, 22 October 1999.

"inordinate"[34] and in other cases delay in processing a claim both before and after the institution of proceedings appears to have been taken into account.[35]

11.008 A further issue related to what will constitute unacceptable delay which was considered by Macken J in *Brennan v Western Health Board*[36] is the extent to which delay caused by a servant or agent of the plaintiff can be taken into account for the purpose of deciding whether the latter's delay has been inordinate and inexcusable. Macken J stated as follows:

> What appears from the authorities, so far as they go, on this matter is that delay caused by the servant or agent of a party may not be taken into account unless such servant or agent was under the control of the party against whom delay is pleaded. Here, as in almost all cases involving infants there could be no control by the plaintiff over her parents while she was a minor, and no suggestion is made that such was the case.[37]

However, it should be noted that in cases such as this which involve claims brought by plaintiffs who sustained injuries while minors, the court may find that it would be unjust to a defendant that it should have to defend the case after such lapse of time irrespective of how the delay arose. Therefore the fact that a plaintiff may not be held responsible for delay on a parent's part may not alter the outcome of the case, as in *Brennan* where Macken J concluded that the case could not be defended properly by the defendant having regard to the decisions of the Supreme Court in *Ó Domhnaill v Merrick*[38] and *Toal v Duignan (No. 1)*.[39]

11.009 What may be considered "excusable" in this context may vary depending on the circumstances of the case and in *Guerin v Guerin*[40] Costello J held that an inordinate delay was excusable as the plaintiff and his family came from what he described as "an economically and socially deprived world from which the world so familiar to lawyers in which people sue and are sued was remote and arcane".[41] The circumstances which may be taken into account in assessing whether delay is excusable have been given more detailed consideration recently by Geoghegan J in *Truck and Machinery Sales Ltd v General Accident Fire and Life Assurance Corporation plc.*[42] The action was one for damages

---

[34] See *Guerin v Guerin* [1992] 2 IR 287, 293, [1993] ILRM 243, 247.
[35] *Celtic Ceramics Ltd v IDA* [1993] ILRM 248, 259 (HC).
[36] High Court (Macken J) 18 May 1999.
[37] At 8-9.
[38] [1984] IR 151.
[39] [1991] ILRM 135.
[40] [1992] 2 IR 287, [1993] ILRM 243.
[41] *Ibid.* at 293, 247.
[42] High Court (Geoghegan J) 12 November 1999.

on foot of a contract of insurance for failure to indemnify the plaintiff on the basis of a policy in respect of fire damage to the plaintiff's business premises and its contents which occurred in December 1982. Geoghegan J stated that he had no doubt that the delay in the case before him had been inordinate but that the question of whether it was inexcusable was more difficult. He stated that a director of the plaintiff company had sought to use the fact that it was involved in other litigation which threatened its continued existence and said that he doubted whether those were the kind of excuses, however genuine, which the Supreme Court had in mind when it used the expression "inexcusable". Geoghegan J continued as follows:

> Strictly speaking it would seem to me that the excuses relied on should relate in some way to the actual proceedings in hand because an opposing party can hardly be expected to stand aside and wait while the other party resolves its problems which have nothing to do with the litigation. Nevertheless I am satisfied that all the surrounding circumstances including so called excuses based on extraneous activities must to some extent be taken into account and weighed in the balance in finally considering whether justice requires that the action be struck out or allowed to proceed.[43]

Geoghegan J concluded that even if the delay was to be regarded as inexcusable, a point which he did not find it necessary finally to decide, he was of the view that it would not be just to strike out the action. The issue between the parties would largely be determined on documentary evidence and there was no real suggestion, still less had it been established as a matter of probability, that the defendant could not properly defend the case.

11.010 A further point initially highlighted by Finlay P in *Rainsford v Limerick Corporation*[44] which has resurfaced recently is that the extent of a litigant's personal blameworthiness for delay may be material to the exercise of the court's discretion. In *Silverdale and Hewetts Travel Agencies Ltd v Italiatour Ltd*[45] Finnegan J stressed that in considering a party's personal blameworthiness the court must look at the circumstances of the party. Whereas in the case of an infant plaintiff, this circumstance will most likely justify delay during minority, a plaintiff such as the one before the court, which was a commercial enterprise of considerable size, must be expected to pursue litigation with reasonable expedition and to that end to take steps to ensure that its legal advisors act in an appropriately expeditious manner.

Clearly where a plaintiff seeks an extension of time in circumstances where there has been excessive delay, it is in his interests to provide some excuse for

---

[43] At 4-5.
[44] [1995] 2 ILRM 561.
[45] [2001] 1 ILRM 464.

this delay. This issue was considered by Carswell J in *Hughes v Hughes*[46] where he stated that where an applicant for an extension makes no attempt to explain the delay or states that he can provide no excuse for it, the court starts from the position that the application should *prima facie* be refused. However, he conceded that in some cases, although not in the case before him, the presumption which the lack of explanation creates may be rebutted by showing that there are other factors strongly in the applicant's favour or that the balance of prejudice is such as to make it necessary in the interests of justice that he should be granted an extension of time.

11.011 It must be stressed that even where delay is shown to be inordinate and inexcusable, as Finlay P pointed out in *Rainsford,* and reiterated by Hamilton CJ in *Primor*, the court must exercise a judgment on whether in its discretion on the facts the balance of justice is in favour of or against the proceeding of the case. A good example of how this discretion may be exercised is the decision of Laffoy J in *Dunne v ESB*.[47] Laffoy J held that the plaintiff's delay had been inordinate and inexcusable and then proceeded to consider whether, in the exercise of the court's discretion, on the facts the balance of justice was in favour of or against proceeding with the case. She stated that two questions arose, namely whether the defendant was prejudiced by the delay and whether there was anything in the defendant's conduct which militated against granting the relief sought. Having considered the facts put before her, Laffoy J was satisfied that the dealings between the parties over the years had been well documented and she concluded that she did not believe that the defendant had established a serious prejudice or a substantial risk that it was not possible to have a fair trial. She distinguished the facts of the case before her from those in *Toal v Duignan (No. 1)*[48] on the basis that while the claim there came as it were "out of the blue", in the instant case the rights asserted by the plaintiff had been a source of controversy since the early 1960s which inevitably was going to have to be resolved at some stage. In addition, Laffoy J was satisfied that the defendant's conduct both before and after the initiation of the proceedings militated against granting the relief sought. It had not at any time prior to the initiation of proceedings sought to restrain the plaintiff from exercising the rights he asserted, and despite a period of inactivity of four and a half years the defendant had taken no steps to have the proceedings brought to trial or dismissed during that time. Laffoy J concluded that this inaction by the defendant during the four and a half years tilted the balance of justice against acceding to the defendant's application and she held that the defendant's application must be refused. A similar conclusion was reached in *Rainsford v Limerick Corporation,*[49] where despite

---

[46] [1990] NI 295.
[47] High Court (Laffoy J) 19 October 1999.
[48] [1991] ILRM 135.
[49] [1995] 2 ILRM 561 (31 July 1979).

a delay of almost a decade since the cause of action had accrued, Finlay P found that the chances of major injustice to the plaintiff if the action was dismissed were significantly greater than the chance of such injustice being inflicted on the defendants if it were allowed to proceed. This can be contrasted with the case of *Celtic Ceramics Ltd v IDA*,[50] in which the plaintiff alleged negligence and breach of contract in relation to the construction of a factory premises. While the delay was of a similar length to that in *Rainsford*, both the High Court and the Supreme Court concluded that the balance of justice was in favour of dismissing the claim for want of prosecution. However, clearly in cases where there has been an excessive delay since the accrual of a cause of action, the balance of justice is almost invariably likely to favour the dismissal of a claim.[51]

As Hamilton CJ made clear in *Primor* the court must exercise its discretion in assessing whether the balance of justice is in favour of or against the case proceeding and he went on to list a number of relevant factors set out above. It is proposed now to consider these factors in turn.

IMPLIED CONSTITUTIONAL PRINCIPLES OF BASIC FAIRNESS OF PROCEDURES

11.012 In *Ó Domhnaill v Merrick*,[52] which concerned a claim instituted by a plaintiff 16 years after she had suffered injuries as a three year old child, Henchy J referred to "implied constitutional principles of basic fairness of procedures"[53] as supporting a claim to have an action dismissed where it places "an inexcusable and unfair burden" on a defendant. In the view of Henchy J: "While justice delayed may not always be justice denied, it usually means justice diminished, and in a case such as this, it puts justice to the hazard to such an extent that to allow the case to proceed to trial would be an abrogation of basic fairness".[54] These views also underlie the decisions of the Supreme Court in *Toal v Duignan (No. 1)*[55] and *Toal v Duignan (No. 2)*,[56] in which a delay of 23 years had ensued before proceedings were commenced. In the latter decision, Finlay CJ stated that the court has inherent jurisdiction in the interests of justice to dismiss a claim where the length of time which has elapsed between the events out of which it arises and the time when it comes on for hearing is in all the circum-

---

[50] [1993] ILRM 258; Supreme Court, 4 February 1993.
[51] *E.g. Ó Domhnaill v Merrick* [1984] IR 151, [1985] ILRM 40; *Toal v Duignan (No. 1)* [1991] ILRM 135 and *Toal v Duignan (No. 2)* [1991] ILRM 140.
[52] [1984] IR 151.
[53] *Ibid.* at 159.
[54] *Ibid.* at 159. See also the comments of O'Flaherty J in *Primor plc v Stokes Kennedy Crowley* [1996] 2 IR 459, 521.
[55] [1991] ILRM 135.
[56] [1991] ILRM 140.

stances so great that it would be unjust to call upon the defendant to defend himself against the claim made. In his view to conclude otherwise would be to give the Oireachtas a supremacy over the courts which would be inconsistent with the Constitution.

THE TYPE OF PREJUDICE WHICH MAY OCCUR

11.013 As Hamilton CJ has stated in *Primor plc v Stokes Kennedy Crowley*[57] "if prejudice to a defendant's capacity to defend a case brought against [him] is caused by inordinate and inexcusable delay on the part of a plaintiff and as a result thereof a fair trial cannot now be held, a defendant should not be further prejudiced by the further delay which would inevitably be caused by a long and difficult hearing of the action". He went on to say that the nature, extent and effect of any prejudice should be considered at the time the application is brought to dismiss the proceedings for want of prosecution. In assessing the issue of prejudice it should be noted that different considerations apply to cases which will largely involve documentary evidence and those in which greater reliance will be placed on the evidence of witnesses. As McGuinness J stated in *Carroll Shipping Ltd v Mathews Mulcahy & Sutherland Ltd*[58] "where matters are at issue which are not, or are not fully, covered by documentary evidence, there is a greater likelihood of prejudice resulting from delay". So, in cases like *Truck and Machinery Sales Ltd v General Accident Fire and Life Assurance Corporation plc*[59] where the issue was one which would be largely determined on the basis of documentary evidence, it will be considerably more difficult to establish that the defendant could not properly defend the case.[60] However, the issue of the type of evidence which will be relied upon is only a guide and a defendant may fail to establish sufficient prejudice even where the case is clearly not a "documents only" one.[61] Equally, it must be acknowledged that there is a greater likelihood of the destruction of records where there has been a considerable lapse of time. However, this will not automatically lead to greater prejudice being suffered by the defendant and it has been pointed out that such destruction

---

[57] [1996] 2 IR 459, 497. It is well established that delay alone will not provide sufficient grounds on which to dismiss an action and that "the delay must have occasioned prejudice to the defendant" (*per* Millett LJ in *Barratt Manchester Ltd v Bolton MBC* [1998] 1 WLR 1003, 1011, [1998] 1 All ER 1, 9.

[58] High Court (McGuinness J) 18 December 1996 at 11.

[59] High Court (Geoghegan J) 12 November 1999.

[60] See also *Dunne v ESB* High Court (Laffoy J) 19 October 1999 where the dealings between the parties were documented over the years, the court similarly concluded that the defendant had not established serious prejudice or a substantial risk that it was not possible to have a fair trial.

[61] *Superwood Holdings plc v Scully* Supreme Court, 4 November 1998. See also *Glynn v Rotunda Hospital* High Court (O'Sullivan J) 6 April 2000.

may also cause problems for a plaintiff bearing in mind the onus of proof which will lie upon him.[62]

11.014 A number of difficulties may arise due to lapse of time in relation to witnesses whose evidence is required at a trial. The most obvious of these is that where an essential witness has died[63] the defendant may be gravely prejudiced by this fact. In addition, undue delay in proceeding with a claim may lead to considerable difficulty in finding witnesses,[64] particularly where they have left their previous employment[65] or are living outside the jurisdiction.[66] A further problem is that as a general proposition "memories fade and become less reliable with the passage of time"[67] and lapse of time may have dimmed the recollection of witnesses whom the defendant may wish to call in his defence[68] and will make it difficult for witnesses to give an accurate account of events.[69] This latter proposition can equally cause detriment to a plaintiff but its overall effect is to make it likely that there is "a substantial risk that it is not possible to have a fair trial"[70] which may lead to a claim being struck out.

11.015 It has also been established that the type of prejudice which the court may consider is not confined to that which will affect the actual conduct of the trial. In *Biss v Lambeth, Southwark and Lewisham Health Authority*[71] the Court of Appeal accepted that the difficulty experienced by nurses faced by the threat of litigation questioning their professional competence amounted to prejudice. As Lord Denning MR stated: "There is much prejudice to a defendant in having

---

[62] *Sterling v G. Cohen and Sons & Co. Ltd* [1987] NI 409, 414 *per* Murray J.

[63] *Hogan v Jones* [1994] 1 ILRM 512; *Byrne v ITGWU* High Court (Morris J) 30 November 1995; *Carroll Shipping Ltd v Mathews Mulcahy & Sutherland Ltd* High Court (McGuinness J) 18 December 1996; *Brennan v Western Health Board* High Court (Macken J) 18 May 1999; *Hughes v Moy Contractors Ltd* High Court (Carroll J) 29 July 1999.

[64] *Robert McGregor and Sons (Ireland) Ltd v Mining Board* High Court (Carroll J) 5 October 1998.

[65] *Carroll Shipping Ltd v Mathews Mulcahy & Sutherland Ltd* High Court (McGuinness J) 18 December 1996.

[66] *Hogan v Jones* [1994] 1 ILRM 512.

[67] *Superwood Holdings plc v Scully* Supreme Court, 4 November 1998 *per* Murphy J. However, Murphy J expressed the view that there were special features in the case before him which would provide considerable reassurance for those who might be called to give evidence on the defendants' behalf (reports and notes which might assist in refreshing the witnesses' memories) and concluded that he did not believe that the evidence had established that any prejudice to the defendants was such that a fair trial between the parties could not be held.

[68] *Hogan v Jones* [1994] 1 ILRM 512, 518.

[69] *Bannon v Craigavon Development Commission* [1984] NI 387.

[70] *Per* Hamilton CJ in *Primor plc v Stokes Kennedy Crowley* [1996] 2 IR 459, 476.

[71] [1978] 1 WLR 382, 389. See also *Department of Transport v Chris Smaller Ltd* [1989] AC 1197, 1208-1209, [1989] 2 WLR 578, 586-587, [1989] 1 All ER 897, 904 *per* Lord Griffiths.

an action hanging over his head indefinitely, not knowing when it is going to be
brought to trial; like the prejudice to Damocles when the sword was suspended
over his head at the banquet". This view was confirmed by O'Hanlon J in *Celtic
Ceramics Ltd v IDA*[72] where he stated that "[i]t seems very unfair and unjust
that persons whose professional standing and competence are under attack should
be left with litigation hanging over their heads for years by reason of inordinate
and inexcusable delay on the part of a plaintiff." Indeed, it has recently been
acknowledged by O'Flaherty J at the conclusion of his judgment in *Primor* that
there was much in counsel's suggestion that once it has been established that
there has been inordinate and inexcusable delay, "prejudice would seem to follow almost inexorably".[73] Certainly in cases involving claims brought by minors who may often have a substantial period of time within which to bring
proceedings,[74] this statement is particularly apposite.

THE RELEVANCE OF THE DEFENDANT'S CONDUCT

11.016 As has already been made clear the conduct of both parties must be
assessed by the court in deciding whether to dismiss a claim for want of prosecution; as Ó Dálaigh CJ commented in *Dowd v Kerry County Council*[75] "litigation is a two party operation". It is clearly established that delay on the
defendant's part is a factor to be taken into account[76] and that it may defeat an
otherwise valid claim to have a case dismissed.[77] However, it is clear from the
decision of Murphy J in *Hogan v Jones*[78] that delay on the defendant's part *e.g.*
in delivering a defence[79] will be considered in conjunction with what may be

---

[72] [1993] ILRM 248, 258-259.
[73] [1996] 2 IR 459, 521. See also the comments of McGonigal J in *Department of Health and Social Services v Derry Construction Co. Ltd* [1980] NI 187, 200 quoted with approval by Carswell J in *Bannon v Craigavon Development Commission* [1984] NI 387, 395.
[74] E.g. *Ó Domhnaill v Merrick* [1984] IR 151, [1985] ILRM 40; *Toal v Duignan (No. 1)* [1991] ILRM 135 and *Toal v Duignan (No. 2)* [1991] ILRM 140.
[75] [1970] IR 27, 42.
[76] *Primor plc v Stokes Kennedy Crowley* [1996] 2 IR 459, 490. See also *Hughes v Moy Contractors Ltd* High Court (Carroll J) 29 July 1999 at 9. However, it should be stressed that while the court accepted this point in principle, on the facts of the case Carroll J concluded that the delay of the defendants in filing their defences was "absolutely negligible" in relation to the overall delay and she made an order dismissing the plain-tiff's claim.
[77] *Hogan v Jones* [1994] 1 ILRM 512.
[78] [1994] 1 ILRM 512.
[79] In this case a delay of four years in delivering a defence. See also the comments of Hamilton CJ in *Primor plc v Stokes Kennedy Crowley* [1996] 2 IR 459, 490 that "[d]elay on the part of a defendant seeking a dismiss of the action and to some extent a failure on his part to exercise his right to apply at any given time for the dismiss of an action for want of prosecution are ingredients in the exercise by the court of its discretion".

perceived as a defendant's failure to exercise his right to apply to the court to dismiss the claim at an earlier stage in the proceedings.[80] As Murphy J stated "when the defendants assert that their professional and financial reputation was damaged or tarnished as a result of the proceedings being outstanding, it might have been inferred that these would be factors ... which would influence the defendants in pressing the plaintiffs to proceed with the action".[81] Yet the extent of the obligation which lies on the defendant in this respect is far from clear. In *Celtic Ceramics Ltd v IDA*[82] Finlay CJ stated that "it is the plaintiff who must bring forward his litigation" whereas in *Dunne v ESB*[83] Laffoy J pointed to the fact that the defendant had taken no steps despite a period of inactivity of four and a half years to have the proceedings brought to trial or dismissed for want of prosecution and held that this inaction tilted the balance of justice against acceding to the defendant's application. Effectively the court must assess whether the defendant's conduct amounts to acquiescence;[84] as Henchy J stated in *Ó Domhnaill v Merrick*[85] "where delay has been inordinate and inexcusable, such delay is not likely to be overlooked unless there are counterveiling circumstances, such as conduct akin to acquiescence on the part of the defendant ...". However what will amount to acquiescence is difficult to define and in *Byrne v ITGWU*[86] Morris J made it clear that delivery of a notice for particulars did not amount to such conduct.

11.017 One issue which has only been resolved relatively recently is the degree to which the defendant's conduct in taking positive action to participate in the proceedings may influence the court. This principle was considered by both Diplock and Salmon LJJ in *Allen v Sir Alfred McAlpine & Sons Ltd*[87] and Diplock LJ commented that "if ... the defendant so conducts himself as to induce the plaintiff to incur further costs in the reasonable belief that the defendant intends to exercise his right to proceed to trial notwithstanding the plaintiff's

---

[80] As Ó Dálaigh CJ commented in *Dowd v Kerry County Council* [1970] IR 27, 41: "The adage about sleeping dogs may be wise, but it is not specifically conceived to advance the cause of justice". See also the *dicta* of McCracken J in *Whearty v ACC* High Court (McCracken J) 31 October 1997 that proceedings exist for a defendant who feels prejudiced by delay to apply to have a case struck out and if a defendant chooses not to use such proceedings it must "very much weaken" any case of prejudice due to delay which he makes.

[81] *Ibid.* at 520. Quoted by Carroll J in *Hughes v Moy Contractors Ltd* High Court (Carroll J) 29 July 1999 at 9.

[82] Supreme Court, 4 February 1993 at 7.

[83] High Court (Laffoy J) 19 October 1999.

[84] *Primor plc v Stokes Kennedy Crowley* [1996] 2 IR 459, 476.

[85] [1984] IR 151, 157. Quoted by O'Hanlon J in *Celtic Ceramics Ltd v IDA* [1993] ILRM 248, 254.

[86] High Court (Morris J) 30 November 1995. See also *Carroll Shipping Ltd v Mathews Mulcahy & Sutherland Ltd* High Court (McGuinness J) 18 December 1996 at 11.

[87] [1968] 2 QB 229, [1968] 2 WLR 366, [1968] 1 All ER 543.

delay, he cannot obtain dismissal of the action ..."[88] The Court of Appeal in *County and District Properties Ltd v Lyell* [89] took an even more forceful approach on this issue. Roskill LJ drew a distinction between positive action taken by or on behalf of the defendant and passive inaction on his part and said that if any positive action taken has led the plaintiff or his advisers to believe that the defendant was consenting to the action proceeding and in this belief, the plaintiff has *e.g.*, incurred further costs, the court does not have the power to insist on the plaintiff's action being dismissed.[90] More recently, in *Roebuck v Mungovin*,[91] the House of Lords firmly rejected such an approach and held that *Lyell's* case should be overruled. In the opinion of Lord Browne-Wilkinson, the defendant's conduct would give rise to an equitable estoppel which would not impose an automatic legal bar to obtaining a striking out order but rather would give the court power to do what is equitable in the circumstances. He stated as follows:

> Where a plaintiff has been guilty of inordinate and inexcusable delay which has prejudiced the defendant, subsequent conduct by the defendant which induces the plaintiff to incur further expense in pursuing the action does not, in law, constitute an absolute bar preventing the defendant from obtaining a striking out order. Such conduct of the defendant is, of course, a relevant factor to be taken into account by the judge in exercising his discretion whether or not to strike out the claim, the weight to be attached to such conduct depending upon all the circumstances of the particular case.[92]

11.018 The question of whether conduct on the part of the defendant which might induce a plaintiff to incur further expense in pursuing the action should constitute an absolute bar to relief or merely amount to a relevant factor which might influence the manner in which the court's discretion is exercised has recently been examined in this jurisdiction in *Primor plc v Stokes Kennedy Crowley*.[93] The actions concerned claims brought by the plaintiff company which was under administration alleging negligence, breach of duty and breach of statutory duty against two firms of accountants which had acted as auditors for

---

[88] *Ibid.* at 260, 383, 556. See also the *dicta* of Salmon LJ at 272, 394, 563-564.

[89] [1991] 1 WLR 683.

[90] These principles appeared to be accepted by the Court of Appeal in *Reynolds v British Leyland Ltd* [1991] 1 WLR 675, [1991] 2 All ER 243 although Russell LJ admitted that he found the idea that such conduct might remove the court's discretion "a little surprising". See also the decision of the Court of Appeal in *Trill v Sacher* [1993] 1 WLR 1379, 1390-1392, [1993] 1 All ER 961, 971-973 although on the facts of the case, no estoppel arose.

[91] [1994] 2 AC 224, [1994] 2 WLR 290, [1994] 1 All ER 568.

[92] *Ibid.* at 236, 298, 576.

[93] *Primor plc v Stokes Kennedy Crowley* (O'Hanlon J) 11 February 1994 and *Primor plc v Oliver Freaney & Co.* (Johnson J) 9 February 1995. The appeals were heard together by the Supreme Court.

it. The Master of the High Court had granted applications brought pursuant to Order 63, rule 1(8) of the Rules of the Superior Courts 1986 to dismiss the plaintiff's claims against both defendants for want of prosecution and in both cases the Master's order was set aside on appeal to the High Court. In delivering his judgment in the action against Stokes Kennedy Crowley, O'Hanlon J laid emphasis on the fact that the defendant had participated in the discovery process and had induced the plaintiff to embark on the "mammoth task" of discovering countless thousands of documents. O'Hanlon J referred to the judgment of Roskill LJ in *Lyell's* case and said that he believed it gave "at least a very good guideline as to the manner in which the judicial discretion should be exercised" and that in such cases the balance of justice would in most, if not all, cases be seen to be tilted in favour of allowing the action to proceed. He concluded that this feature of the case was fatal to the defendant's claim to have the matter dismissed and said that his decision was reinforced by the defendant's lengthy delay in delivering its defence. Johnson J reached the same conclusion in the claim against the defendant Oliver Freaney & Co. He said that many of the factors which had governed the decision of O'Hanlon J also governed the case before him and referred in particular to the defendant's participation in the process of discovery.

The Supreme Court heard both appeals together and were unanimous in overturning the decisions of the High Court. Hamilton CJ undertook a detailed review of the relevant decisions both in this jurisdiction and in England and in particular referred to the decision of the House of Lords in *Roebuck v Mungovin* which had been handed down after O'Hanlon J had heard the *Stokes Kennedy Crowley* case but just before he had delivered judgment. Hamilton CJ[94] concluded that the learned trial judge would have been entitled to regard the defendant's conduct as relevant in exercising his discretion but instead he had treated it as being fatal to its claim and in so holding, in his view, had erred in law. As a result of applying such an approach, neither trial judge had properly considered the effect of the prejudice which the defendants had undoubtedly suffered by reason of the plaintiff's delay. This discretionary approach was also adopted by McGuinness J in her judgment in *Carroll Shipping Ltd v Mathews Mulcahy & Sutherland Ltd*[95] in which she concluded that she did not accept that the conduct of the defendant, while at times encouraging the plaintiff to incur further expenditure in the proceedings, could operate as a bar to the obtaining of an order striking out the action.

This approach is undoubtedly preferable and allows a judge an element of flexibility when exercising his discretion to decide where the 'balance of justice' lies in such cases. Obviously the extent of the defendant's participation or

---

[94] Denham J concurring. O'Flaherty J delivered a separate judgment and also allowed the defendants' appeals.
[95] High Court (McGuinness J) 18 December 1996 at 11.

acquiescence will vary from case to case as will the effect which this conduct may have on the plaintiff and it would seem to be important to maintain an element of discretion.

POSSIBLE FUTURE DEVELOPMENTS

11.019 There have been signs of increasing impatience being expressed by the judiciary in England over the past decade over excessive and often inexplicable delays in bringing cases to trial. In *Department of Transport v Chris Smaller (Transport) Ltd*[96] Lord Griffiths commented as follows:

> I believe that a far more radical approach is required to tackle the prob-lems of delay in the litigation process than driving an individual plaintiff away from the courts when his culpable delay has caused no injustice to his opponent. I, for my part, recommend a radical overhaul of the whole civil procedure process and the introduction of court controlled case man-agement techniques designed to ensure that once a litigant has entered the litigation process his case proceeds in accordance with a timetable as pre-scribed by the Rules of Court as modified by a judge: see the Civil Justice Review, Report of the Review Body on Civil Justice (1988) (Cmnd 394).

However, nearly a decade later, Lord Woolf commented that "[t]he period which has elapsed since Lord Griffiths's speech has not seen any improvement in the problems caused by delay in the conduct of civil proceedings".[97] This growing exasperation manifested itself in a fairly radical change in approach being put forward by Lord Woolf MR in *Arbuthnot Latham Bank Ltd v Trafalgar Hold-ings Ltd.*[98] Lord Woolf stated that in *Birkett v James* the consequence to other litigants and to the courts of inordinate delay was not a consideration which was in issue but said that it is going to be a consideration of increasing signifi-cance and that "delay which occurs from now on will be assessed not only from the point of view of the prejudice caused to particular litigants whose case it is, but also in relation to the effect it can have on other litigants who are wishing to have their cases heard, and the prejudice which is caused to the due administra-tion of justice."[99] He continued "the more ready recognition that wholesale failure as such to comply with the rules justifies an action being struck out as long as it is just to do so will avoid much time and expense being incurred in investigating questions of prejudice and allow the striking out of actions whether or not the limitation period has expired."

---

[96] [1989] AC 1197, 1207, [1989] 2 WLR 578, 585-586, [1989] 1 All ER 897, 903.
[97] *Grovit v Doctor* [1997] 1 WLR 640, 644.
[98] [1998] 1 WLR 1426.
[99] *Ibid.* at 1436.

11.020 Key[100] in a recent article commenting on the position in England states that the pendulum in England is swinging markedly towards much greater court control in this area than hitherto and quite rightly points out that the Court of Appeal in *Arbuthnot* has announced its intention to exercise henceforth a rigorous control over plaintiffs who flout court procedures. He states while this change in approach is dramatic, the precise manner in which courts will apply this doctrine remains as yet unclear. In addition, it should be noted that Rule 1.1.2 of the Civil Procedure Rules 1998 provides that dealing with a case justly includes, so far as practicable, "(d) ensuring that it is dealt with expeditiously and fairly; and (e) allotting to it an appropriate share of the court's resources, while taking into account the need to allot resources to other cases". Given the nature of these provisions and the tenor of Lord Woolf's comments in *Arbuthnot*, litigants who fail to progress an action with sufficient expedition or observe the rules of court are likely to suffer the consequences. Certainly the *dictum* of Lord Woolf has been referred to on a frequent basis[101] and particularly since the coming into force of the Civil Procedure Rules 1998, adherence to time limits has been regarded as increasingly important.[102]

To date there have been no signs of a similar "change of culture"[103] being adopted in this jurisdiction and the courts have repeatedly stressed that the jurisdiction to dismiss a claim should only be exercised where the essential justice of the case requires it[104] and not in order to further the demands of the administration of justice generally. However, given the steady increase in the number of the applications to dismiss on grounds of delay and the growing demands on the courts, a move towards a more rigorous approach, provided that it respects the constitutional rights of parties involved in litigation, cannot be ruled out.

CONCLUSIONS

11.021 It would appear that the law in this area is now fairly well settled in this jurisdiction, namely that it must be established that a plaintiff's delay has been inordinate and inexcusable and that if this is so, the court must proceed to

---

[100] (1999) 115 LQR 208.

[101] See *e.g. Braustein v Mostafazan Janbazan Foundation* Court of Appeal, 18 March 1999, *Johnson v. Coburn* Court of Appeal, 24 November 1999, *Securum Finance Ltd v Ashton* [2000] 3 Ch 291, [2000] 3 WLR 1400, *Circuit Systems Ltd v Zuken-Radac (UK) Ltd* [2001] Build LR 253 and *Austin v Newcastle Chronicle* [2001] EWCA Civ 834.

[102] *Biguzzi v Rank Leisure plc* [1999] 1 WLR 1926, 1932, [1999] 4 All ER 934, 939. See also *Annodeus Entertainment v Gibson* Chancery Division (Neuberger J) 2 February 2000.

[103] *Omgate Ltd v Gordon* Chancery Division, 9 April 2001 *per* Anthony Mann QC.

[104] *Per* O'Flaherty J in *Primor plc v Stokes Kennedy Crowley* [1996] 2 IR 459, 516.

determine whether on the facts the balance of justice is in favour of or against the case proceeding. The relevance of the rights and conduct of both parties in this balancing process has now been clarified, as has the type of prejudice which must be suffered. While the conduct of both parties is clearly relevant, whatever its nature it should not constitute an absolute bar to that party's success in the hearing of an application to dismiss a claim but should be regarded as a factor which may influence a court in the exercise of its discretion. In this regard, the reasoning of Lord Browne-Wilkinson in *Roebuck v Mungovin* and the approach followed by Hamilton CJ in *Primor plc v Stokes Kennedy Crowley* are to be welcomed. If the balancing exercise which the court is required to perform is to achieve a fair and just result having regard to the interests of both parties, it must be permitted to exercise its discretion in each case in a relatively unfettered manner, provided it does so within the general perameters accepted as applying to cases of this nature.

CHAPTER TWELVE

STRIKING OUT WHERE NO REASONABLE CAUSE OF ACTION OR WHERE CLAIM FRIVOLOUS OR VEXATIOUS

JURISDICTION PURSUANT TO ORDER 19, RULE 28

12.001 Order 19, rule 28 of the Rules of the Superior Courts 1986 provides that a court may order a pleading to be struck out on the grounds that "it discloses no reasonable cause of action or answer" and that in any case where the action or defence is shown by the pleadings to be "frivolous or vexatious", the court may order that the action be stayed or dismissed or that judgment may be entered accordingly. It was stressed by O'Higgins CJ in *McCabe v Harding*[1] that in order for this rule to apply "vexation or frivolity must appear from the pleadings alone" or as Costello J commented in *Barry v Buckley*[2] "the court can only make an order under this rule when a pleading discloses no reasonable cause of action on its face". These principles were affirmed by Costello J in the course of his judgment in *D.K. v King*[3] where he stated that rule 28 only applies where it can be shown that the text of the plaintiff's summons or statement of claim discloses no reasonable cause of action or that the action is frivolous or vexatious. So, for the purposes of considering whether to accede to an application based on rule 28 the court should consider the pleadings alone, ignoring any affidavit evidence filed.[4] The scope of what constitutes "pleadings" for this purpose was considered by Macken J in *Leinster Leader Ltd v Williams Group (Tullamore) Ltd*[5] in which she stated that while strictly speaking a notice for particulars and its reply were not necessarily "pleadings", in case they should be considered as such, she was prepared to look at them to ascertain whether their contents made it certain that the plaintiff could not succeed in its claim. However, she concluded that even taking the request for particulars and the reply into account, it seemed to her that a court could not say with certainty that the plaintiff could not succeed or was bound to fail. Clearly, given the rather restrictive wording of rule 28 it will often prove difficult in practice to establish

---

[1] [1984] ILRM 105, 108.
[2] [1981] IR 306, 308.
[3] [1994] 1 IR 166, 170.
[4] *Supermac's Ireland Ltd v Katesan (Naas) Ltd* High Court (Macken J) 15 March 1999 at 5, *Ratcliffe v Wilson* High Court (Macken J) 23 March 1999 at 3 and *Leinster Leader Ltd v Williams Group (Tullamore) Ltd* High Court (Macken J) 9 July 1999 at 5.
[5] High Court (Macken J) 9 July 1999.

that a pleading discloses no reasonable cause of action on its face. One recent example of a decision in which it was felt that these criteria had been met is *Moffitt v Bank of Ireland*[6] in which the Supreme Court was satisfied that even reading the statement of claim in as expansive a manner as possible, it seemed to disclose no cause of action whatever against the second named defendant.

INHERENT JURISDICTION OF THE COURT

12.002 While the power to dismiss pursuant to rule 28 has been interpreted restrictively, the courts also possess an inherent power to strike out claims on similar grounds. In exercising this jurisdiction "the court is not limited to considering the pleadings of the parties, but is free to hear evidence on affidavit relating to the issues in the case".[7] This inherent jurisdiction may be used to dismiss an action on the basis that "on admitted facts, it cannot succeed"[8] or as O'Higgins CJ commented in *McCabe v Harding*[9] where vexation is established by undisputed facts which explain the nature of the claim made or pleading. The rationale behind this jurisdiction was explained in the following terms by Costello J in *Barry v Buckley*:[10]

> Basically its jurisdiction exists to ensure that an abuse of the process of the courts does not take place. So, if the proceedings are frivolous or vexatious they will be stayed. They will also be stayed if it is clear that the plaintiff's claim must fail *per* Buckley LJ in *Goodson v Grierson* [1908] 1 KB 761, 765.

[6] Supreme Court, 19 February 1999. See also *McCabe v Dolan Cosgrove & Co.* High Court (Lynch J) 14 October 1991.

[7] *Per* Costello J in *Barry v Buckley* [1981] IR 306, 308. See also *Tassan Din v Banco Ambrosiano SPA* [1991] 1 IR 569, 572, *Landers v Garda Síochána Complaints Board* [1997] 3 IR 347, 360.

[8] *Per* McCarthy J in *Sun Fat Chan v Osseous Ltd* [1992] 1 IR 425, 428. See also *McManus v Cable Management (Ireland) Ltd* High Court (Morris J) 8 July 1994 and the *dicta* of Herbert J in *O'Connell v Environmental Protection Agency* [2002] 1 ILRM 1, 13 to the effect that the court should only act "where confident that the claim must inevitably fail".

[9] [1984] ILRM 105, 108.

[10] [1981] IR 306, 308. Quoted with approval in *Stud Managers Ltd v Marshall* [1985] IR 83, 86, *Ennis v Butterly* [1996] 1 IR 426, 430, [1997] 1 ILRM 28, 31, *Landers v Garda Síochána Complaints Board* [1997] 3 IR 347, 359, *Supermac's Ireland Ltd v Katesan (Naas) Ltd* High Court (Macken J) 15 March 1999 at 2, *Leinster Leader Ltd v Williams Group (Tullamore) Ltd* High Court (Macken J) 9 July 1999 at 12 and *Ruby Property Co. Ltd v Kilty* High Court (McCracken J) 1 December 1999. See also the *dicta* of Costello J in *D.K. v King* [1994] 1 IR 166, 170 : "Basically, the jurisdiction exists to ensure that an abuse of the court's process does not take place. It is established by satisfactory evidence that the proceedings are frivolous or vexatious or if it is clear that the plaintiff's claim must fail then the court may stay the action". Quoted with approval by Blayney J in *O'Neill v Ryan* [1993] ILRM 557, 561.

12.003 It should be noted that it has been stated that this inherent jurisdiction "should be exercised sparingly and only in clear cases"[11] and as McCarthy J said in *Sun Fat Chan v Osseous Ltd*[12] "generally the High Court should be slow to entertain an application of this kind". However, McCarthy J stated that he inclined to the view that if the statement of claim admitted of an amendment which might save it and the action founded upon it, the claim should not be dismissed.[13] The reason for the caution which McCarthy J urged the courts to show was set out by him in the following terms:

> Experience has shown that the trial of an action will identify a variety of circumstances perhaps not entirely contemplated at earlier stages in the proceedings; often times it may appear that the facts are clear and established but the trial itself will disclose a different picture.[14]

12.004 As Macken J commented in *Supermac's Ireland Ltd v Katesan (Naas) Ltd*:[15] "I bear in mind in particular that the Supreme Court has stated that while the facility to strike out a case *in limine* on the grounds that it cannot possibly succeed is one from which the court should not shirk, it is equally the case that the Supreme Court has stated that it is a remedy which ought to be applied sparingly, and in general ought to be applied only to circumstances where there

---

[11] *Per* Costello J in *Barry v Buckley* [1981] IR 306, 308. See also *D.K. v King* [1994] 1 IR 166, 170, *Olympia Productions Ltd v Mackintosh* [1992] ILRM 204, 207, *Weldon v Mooney* High Court (O Caoimh J) 25 January 2001 at 2 and *Jestdale Ltd v Millennium Theatre Co. Ltd* High Court (Lavan J) 31 July 2001 at 7.

[12] [1992] 1 IR 425, 428. Quoted with approval in *Philip Harrington Daly & Co. v JVC (UK) Ltd* Supreme Court, 20 February 1997, *Flanagan v Kelly* High Court (O'Sullivan J) 26 February 1999, *Supermac's Ireland Ltd v Katesan (Naas) Ltd* High Court (Macken J) 15 March 1999, *Leinster Leader Ltd v Williams Group (Tullamore) Ltd* High Court (Macken J) 9 July 1999, *Jodifern Ltd v Fitzgerald* High Court (McCracken J) 28 July 1999 and *Ruby Property Co. Ltd v Kilty* High Court (McCracken J) 1 December 1999.

[13] *Ibid.* at 428. See also *D.K. v King* [1994] 1 IR 166, 174, *Landers v Garda Síochána Complaints Board* [1997] 3 IR 347, 360, *Flanagan v Kelly* High Court (O'Sullivan J) 26 February 1999 at 1 and *Ewing v Kelly* High Court (O'Sullivan J) 16 May 2000 at 3; *Riordan v Hamilton* High Court (Smyth J) 26 June 2000.

[14] *Ibid.* Quoted with approval in *Ennis v Butterly* [1996] 1 IR 426, 430, [1997] 1 ILRM 28, 31, *Doe v Armour Pharmaceutical Inc.* High Court (Morris J) 31 July 1997 at 6, *Philip Harrington Daly & Co. v JVC (UK) Ltd* Supreme Court, 20 February 1997 at 7, *Supermac's Ireland Ltd v Katesan (Naas) Ltd* High Court (Macken J) 15 March 1999 at 3, *Leinster Leader Ltd v Williams Group (Tullamore) Ltd* High Court (Macken J) 9 July 1999 at 12 and *Jodifern Ltd v Fitzgerald* High Court (McCracken J) 28 July 1999. This approach is also borne out by the conclusion reached by O'Flaherty J in *Philip Harrington Daly & Co. v JVC (UK) Ltd* Supreme Court, 20 February 1997 that while he could see the force in the argument that the plaintiff's case against the third named defendant was very tentative at that time, he held that it would be preferable that this defendant should remain in the proceedings until its role was clarified.

[15] High Court (Macken J) 15 March 1999 at 20-21. See also the *dicta* of O'Donovan J in *Moran v Oakley Park Developments Ltd* High Court (O'Donovan J) 31 March 2000.

are undisputed facts." Clearly a balance must be struck by the courts in exercising its inherent jurisdiction in this regard and it will be more suited to some types of dispute than others. As Costello J pointed out in *Barry v Buckley*[16] the jurisdiction is one which enables the court to avoid injustice particularly in cases where the outcome depends on "the interpretation of a contract or agreed correspondence". In this case the plaintiff offered to buy the defendant's land and the defendant stipulated that no binding contract would be created until a written agreement had been executed by each party and a deposit paid by the plaintiff. The defendant decided to treat the transaction as at an end and did not sign the contract nor did the plaintiff pay any deposit. The plaintiff then brought an action seeking an order directing the defendant to perform his obligations under the alleged contract of sale and registered a *lis pendens* affecting the defendant's land. The defendant successfully brought an application for an order striking out the plaintiff's action and vacating the *lis pendens*. Costello J concluded "as the case is a clear one and as considerable injustice could result if the matter is not disposed of now, it seems that to allow the case to proceed to trial would be to permit an abuse of the court's processes". Similarly in *Sun Fat Chan v Osseous Ltd*[17] McCarthy J commented that "the procedure is peculiarly appropriate to actions for the enforcement of contracts", a point reiterated by Keane J delivering the judgment of the Supreme Court in *Jodifern Ltd v Fitzgerald*[18] where he pointed out that in such cases it may well be that the action will inhibit or preclude the party sued from entering into a new contract in respect of the same subject matter.

12.005 If the court is to exercise its inherent jurisdiction to dismiss a claim, it is important that there is no dispute between the parties on issues of fact. In *Doe v Armour Pharmaceutical Inc.*[19] Morris J referred to the fact that McCarthy J had made it clear in his judgment in *Sun Fat Chan v Osseous Ltd* that the court will only exercise this jurisdiction where it is clear beyond doubt that the plaintiff could not succeed and said that "such circumstances would clearly envisage that no dispute could arise on issues of fact". If such a dispute did arise, Morris J stated that in his view it could only be determined by the trial judge at the hearing of the action. In the case before him Morris J pointed out that neither the plaintiff nor the remaining defendants accepted as matters of fact the facts relied upon by the third named defendant and held that until such time as the facts were established, in his view it was not open to the court to make the order sought. Similar views were expressed by Costello J in *Olympia Productions Ltd v Mackintosh*[20] where he said that when, as in the case before him, contro-

---

[16] [1981] IR 306, 308. See also *Stud Managers Ltd v Marshall* [1985] IR 83.
[17] [1992] 1 IR 425, 429.
[18] [2000] 3 IR 321.
[19] High Court (Morris J) 31 July 1997 at 6.
[20] [1992] ILRM 204, 207. See also the *dicta* of Carroll J in *Mehta v Marshs* High Court

versial issues of fact exist which can only be resolved by oral testimony, it seemed to him that the court could not conclude that the proceedings are vexatious.

12.006 These principles have been reiterated in a number of recent cases and in *Ruby Property Co. Ltd v Kilty*[21] McCracken J commented that if there is a dispute on facts on affidavit which is not resolved by admitted documents, then it will be virtually impossible for a defendant to have proceedings struck out as being unsustainable. So, in refusing the relief sought by the defendant in *Supermac's Ireland Ltd v Katesan (Naas) Ltd*[22] Macken J commented that "the very last thing that can be said about these proceedings is that there is any area in which there are undisputed facts". It is also instructive to compare the opposite conclusions reached by the High Court and the Supreme Court in *Jodifern Ltd v Fitzgerald*[23] which concerned a claim for specific performance in relation to an alleged contract for the sale of land. In granting the defendants' application to have the claim struck out in the High Court, McCracken J stated that there was "very little dispute on the facts between the parties, as virtually the entire negotiation was carried out in correspondence, all of which has been exhibited". However, in reversing his decision Keane J commented that the correspondence entered into between the parties "could undoubtedly be regarded as somewhat inconclusive in some respects". He concluded that while the case might or might not succeed if the action were allowed to proceed to trial, it was an unsustainable proposition to say that this was a case which could not possibly succeed.

12.007 A related issue is that it has been accepted that in so far as there may be a conflict between matters averred to by the plaintiff and the defendant, such conflict must be resolved in favour of the plaintiff. It was conceded by counsel for the defendant in *Ennis v Butterly*[24] that the court must assume that every fact pleaded by the plaintiff is correct and can be proved at trial[25] and that every fact asserted by the plaintiff on affidavit is likewise correct and can be proved at trial.[26] This was interpreted by O'Sullivan J in *O'Keeffe v Kilcullen*[27] to mean that the court must accept fully all averments and assertions deposed to on the plaintiff's behalf even where these are traversed in opposing pleadings or are

---

(Carroll J) 5 March 1996 that as there were no agreed facts, the inherent jurisdiction of the court to dismiss the action could not be invoked.

[21] High Court (McCracken J) 1 December 1999, [1994] 3 IR 321 (SC).

[22] High Court (Macken J) 15 March 1999.

[23] High Court (McCracken J) 28 July 1999.

[24] [1996] 1 IR 426, [1997] 1 ILRM 28.

[25] *Ewing v Kelly* High Court (O'Sullivan J) 16 May 2000 at 3.

[26] See also *Sunreed Investment Ltd v Gill* High Court (Finnegan J) 3 June 2000.

[27] High Court (O'Sullivan J) 24 June 1998.

contested on affidavit.[28] This approach has been accepted as the correct one in a number of subsequent cases,[29] and while McCracken J commented in *Ruby Property Co. Ltd v Kilty*[30] that he thought the concession made in *Ennis* had been "somewhat rash", he was satisfied that the court can only exercise its inherent jurisdiction where there was no possibility of success.

12.008 Finally some useful comments about the nature of the evidence which a court should consider where an application is made to dismiss a claim on grounds of abuse of process were made by Barron J in the Supreme Court decision in *Jodifern Ltd v Fitzgerald*:[31]

> One thing is clear, disputed oral evidence of fact cannot be relied upon by a defendant to succeed in such an application. Again, while documentary evidence may well be sufficient for a defendant's purpose, it may well not be if the proper construction of the documentary evidence is disputed. If the plaintiff's claim is based upon allegations of fact which will have to be established at an oral hearing, it is hard to see how such a claim can be treated as being an abuse of the process of the court. It can only be contested by oral evidence to show that the facts cannot possibly be true. This however would involve trial of that particular factual issue.
>
> Where the plaintiff's claim is based upon a document as in the present case then clearly the document should be before the court upon an application of this nature. If that document clearly does not establish the case being made by the plaintiff then a defendant may well succeed. On the other hand, if it does, it is hard to see how a defendant can dispute this *prima facie* construction of the document without calling evidence and having a trial of that question.

GROUNDS FOR EXERCISE OF THE COURT'S INHERENT JURISDICTION

12.009 Consideration was given by Murphy J in *Tassan Din v Banco*

---

[28] Although as O'Higgins J pointed out in *Fagan v McQuaid* High Court (O'Higgins J) 12 May 1998 at 20 "even if the entire contents of the statement of claim were proven" there may not be a reasonable chance of the plaintiff succeeding.

[29] *Supermac's Ireland Ltd v Katesan (Naas) Ltd* High Court (Macken J) 15 March 1999 at 6, *Leinster Leader Ltd v Williams Group (Tullamore) Ltd* High Court (Macken J) 9 July 1999 at 8 and *Moran v Oakley Park Developments Ltd* High Court (O'Donovan J) 31 March 2000 at 4.

[30] High Court (McCracken J) 1 December 1999 at 26.

[31] [2000] 3 IR 321, 332. Referred to by Geoghegan J in *Supermac's Ireland Ltd v Katesan (Naas) Ltd* [2000] 4 IR 273, [2001] 1 ILRM 401 and by Lavan J in *Jestdale Ltd v Millennium Theatre Co. Ltd* High Court, 31 July 2001.

Ambrosiano SPA[32] to what will be vexatious and an abuse of the process of the court and this will include seeking to litigate any matter which has already been concluded by a final and binding order of the court. In *McSorley v O'Mahony*[33] Costello P also ordered that the action should be stayed on the grounds that it was vexatious and an abuse of the court's process. In his view the first cause of action between the parties no longer existed and in the second, the plaintiff could obtain no benefit from maintaining the proceedings. Costello P gave the following explanation of what will amount to an abuse of process:

> It is an abuse of the process of the courts to permit the court's time to be taken up with litigation which can confer no benefit on a plaintiff. It is also an abuse to permit litigation to proceed which will undoubtedly cause detriment to a defendant and which can confer no gain on a plaintiff.[34]

It will often prove difficult to establish that a claim is vexatious. In *Olympia Productions Ltd v Mackintosh*[35] Costello J stated that where, as in the case before him, controversial issues of fact existed which could only be resolved by oral testimony, it seemed to him that the court could not conclude that the proceedings were vexatious. He said that while it might well be that the plaintiff's claim against one or more of the defendants would ultimately fail, that was not the same thing as saying that any of the claims were vexatious.

12.010 Even if it cannot be established that a claim is frivolous or vexatious, the court may strike out a claim where there is satisfactory evidence that it is clearly unsustainable.[36] So, in *Ennis v Butterly*[37] where the cohabitation contract contended for by the plaintiff was unenforceable as a matter of public policy the court struck out the plaintiff's claim for breach of contract.[38] However, it would appear that provided the court reaches the conclusion that the plaintiff's case is one which he should be permitted to make and that it is not so devoid of merit as to justify the conclusion that by making it the court's processes have been abused, a claim to have the action struck out will not succeed.[39]

---

[32] [1991] 1 IR 569, 574.

[33] High Court (Costello P) 6 November 1996.

[34] *Ibid.* at 21.

[35] [1992] ILRM 204, 207. (The defendants' appeal was dismissed by the Supreme Court on 15 March 1996).

[36] *D.K. v King* [1994] 1 IR 166, 171; *O'Neill v Ryan* [1993] ILRM 557, 561; *Ennis v Butterly* [1996] 1 IR 426, 430, [1997] 1 ILRM 28, 32; *Flanagan v Kelly* High Court (O'Sullivan J) 26 February 1999 at 11; *Supermac's Ireland Ltd v Katesan (Naas) Ltd* High Court (Macken J) 15 March 1999 at 3 and *Leinster Leader Ltd v Williams Group (Tullamore) Ltd* High Court (Macken J) 9 July 1999 at 13.

[37] [1996] 1 IR 426, [1997] 1 ILRM 28.

[38] Although Kelly J held that the plaintiff's claim for damages for misrepresentation should not be struck out as he could not say that it had to fail.

[39] *D.K. v King* [1994] 1 IR 166, 174.

So, in *Leinster Leader Ltd v Williams Group Tullamore Ltd*[40] Macken J concluded that there was no question of the court being able to come to the view at that time that the claims of the plaintiff were unsustainable. In her view the kernel of the plaintiff's claim would be dependent on the establishment of the representations made and the effect of those representations and none of this was dependent on written contracts or documents but rather on statements allegedly made orally which would have to be considered in the light of the overall evidence tendered. This may be contrasted with the conclusion reached by O'Sullivan J in *Flanagan v Kelly*[41] where he held that there was satisfactory evidence that the proceedings were unsustainable in the sense that they were bound to fail. In his view the statement of claim failed to show a reasonable cause of action and even if it were amended along the lines indicated by counsel for the plaintiff, this position would not change.

Finally it should be noted that McCarthy J stated in *Sun Fat Chan v Osseous Ltd*[42] that a defendant may be denied the right to defend an action in plenary hearing if the facts are clear and it is shown that the defence is unsustainable. However, it should be pointed out that as Murphy J stated in *Phonographic Performance (Ireland) Ltd v Chariot Inns Ltd*[43] the potential for abuse by pleading in a defence (otherwise than by counterclaim) must be limited.

CONCLUSIONS

12.011 Clearly in exercising its power to strike out a claim both pursuant to the Rules of the Superior Courts and on the basis of its inherent jurisdiction, the court must seek to balance the rights of plaintiff and defendant. The implied constitutional right of access to the courts[44] has been interpreted as encompassing the right "to litigate claims which are justiciable"[45] and "to initiate litigation in the courts"[46] but clearly the courts also have a duty to uphold the integrity of the judicial system by declining to adjudicate on matters which constitute an abuse of the court's process. While the circumstances in which the pleadings themselves disclose no reasonable cause of action on their face will be relatively limited, the inherent jurisdiction of the court to look beyond the pleadings

---

[40] High Court (Macken J) 9 July 1999.
[41] High Court (O'Sullivan J) 26 February 1999.
[42] [1992] 1 IR 425, 428. See also *Ruby Property Co. Ltd v Kilty* High Court (McCracken J) 1 December 1999.
[43] Supreme Court, 16 February 1998.
[44] *Macauley v Minister for Post and Telegraphs* [1966] IR 345. Although note that this right of access to the courts is not an unqualified one, see generally Kelly, *The Irish Constitution* eds. Hogan and Whyte (3rd ed., 1994) at 770-773 and Casey, *Constitutional Law in Ireland* (3rd ed., 2000) at 413-420.
[45] *O'Brien v Manufacturing Engineering Ltd* [1973] IR 334, 364.
[46] *State (McCormack) v Curran* [1987] ILRM 225, 237.

has meant that it can act at a relatively early stage to strike out proceedings where a claim is clearly unsustainable and on the admitted facts cannot suc-ceed. As a consideration of the case law has shown, a crucial precondition to the exercise of this inherent jurisdiction is that there is no dispute between the parties on issues of fact[47] and for this reason it has tended to be invoked suc-cessfully in cases involving the interpretation of an alleged contract[48] or where the dealings between the parties have been well documented. However, the very existence of the jurisdiction acts as a deterrent to litigants who seek to pursue vexatious or unsustainable claims and it represents an important weapon in the armoury of the courts to prevent abuse of process.

---

[47] *Doe v Armour Pharmaceutical Inc.* High Court (Morris J) 31 July 1997.
[48] *Barry v Buckley* [1981] IR 306 and *Stud Managers Ltd v Marshall* [1985] IR 83.

CHAPTER THIRTEEN

THIRD PARTY PROCEDURE

INTRODUCTION

13.001 Order 16 of the Rules of the Superior Courts 1986 provides a procedure whereby a third party may be joined in an action involving plaintiff and defendant. The defendant may have a claim against another party arising out of the same set of circumstances and rather than having two separate actions it may be desirable to dispose of both issues in the same case. As Lavery J stated in *Gilmore v Windle*:[1]

> The procedure allowing a party to an action to bring in a third party is not new, though it has been greatly extended. The object of the old procedure, and of its extension, is to avoid multiplicity of actions and to enable, so far as can be done with just regard to the interests of the several parties involved, all issues arising out of the particular incident or transaction to be determined by the one court at one time; thus avoiding repetition of evidence and argument before different tribunals. The procedure is most useful but it must be availed of with caution as, if unduly extended, it might lead to confusion rather than simplification and might cause injustice to one of the parties involved.

13.002 Order 16, rule 1(1) provides that where a defendant claims against any person not already party to an action[2] that he is entitled to a contribution or indemnity or to any relief or remedy relating to the original subject matter of the action and substantially the same as some relief claimed by the plaintiff, the

---

[1] [1967] IR 323, 329. See also the *dicta* of Finlay CJ in *International Commercial Bank plc v Insurance Corporation of Ireland plc* [1989] IR 453, 468, [1989] ILRM 788, 799-800: "The modern development of procedures against third parties in respect of claims for contribution or indemnity, in my view, indicates a clear recognition by the courts of the requirement of justice which so frequently involves the necessity as far as possible to ensure that a party against whom a claim has been made and who has legal rights against some other party which may relieve him from some or even all of the consequences of that claim should be entitled to have the issue of his liability and of his consequential rights determined in a single set of proceedings and as far as possible at the same time".

[2] Where contribution is sought from an existing party, such as a co-plaintiff, service of a third party notice will be inappropriate, see *Cullen v Clein* [1970] IR 146 in which the Supreme Court held that the defendant was correct in seeking to advance his claim by way of counterclaim.

court may give leave to issue and serve a third party notice.[3] Rule 1(2) provides that the application for leave shall be made on notice to the plaintiff, although unless the plaintiff wishes to add the third party as a defendant, his attendance at the hearing of the motion shall not be necessary. In practice, the plaintiff may wish to join the third party as if the plaintiff loses his case against the defendant, even if the defendant wins his case against the third party (*i.e.* the third party is found totally to blame and the defendant absolved), the plaintiff cannot recover against the third party. The motion must be grounded on an affidavit which should set out why the third party may be responsible and must convince the court that the issue between the defendant and the third party arises out of substantially the same facts and circumstances as that arising between the plaintiff and defendant. It should be noted that Hederman J has stated in *Darcy v Roscommon County Council*[4] that where an affidavit is put in a third party application it is undesirable that the solicitor appearing for the relevant party should be the person making the affidavit and the individual who has first hand knowledge of the facts intended to be offered in support of the application is the one who should swear it. Rule 2(2) provides that the third party notice shall, unless otherwise ordered by the court, be served within 28 days from the making of the order and that a copy of the originating summons and any pleading delivered in the action shall be served with it.[5]

DISCRETIONARY CONSIDERATIONS

13.003 It has been stressed that where a person claims as against any person not already a party to the action that he is entitled to a contribution or indemnity, the court may give leave to issue and serve a third party notice in accordance with Order 16 but that such jurisdiction is discretionary in nature. In bringing such an application the defendant must have given the court "sufficient information to indicate with clarity the grounds on which the defendant would seek to rely".[6] As Egan J stated in *Johnston v Fitzpatrick*[7] "the order says 'may give leave' and this must mean that facts must be alleged by the defendant which would support a claim by him that the proposed third party or third parties contributed to the accident". While it is not necessary for the defendant to prove his case fully against the third party at this stage in the proceedings, "at

---

[3] The third party notice shall be in the form set out in Appendix C Form 1 or 2.

[4] Supreme Court, 11 January 1991.

[5] See *International Commercial Bank plc v Insurance Corporation of Ireland plc* [1989] IR 453, [1989] ILRM 788 in relation to service of third party notices out of the jurisdiction.

[6] *Per* Hederman J in *Darcy v Roscommon County Council* Supreme Court, 11 January 1991.

[7] [1992] ILRM 269.

least a *prima facie* case is required to be made out".[8] It should also be noted that in *Quirke v O'Shea*[9] counsel for the defendant conceded for the purpose of the appeal that it was necessary that he should establish to the satisfaction of the court a *prima facie* case of negligence against the proposed third party and the Supreme Court accepted that this was correct. However as Finlay CJ went on to point out, the discretion which the court must exercise in such case is a wide one and extends beyond the question of whether the issues arising between the parties are similar or appropriately tried together to such considerations as whether the purpose of seeking to join the third party is *bona fide* and the relevance of whether the proposed third party is the next friend of the plaintiff.[10]

13.004 The question of whether leave to issue and serve third party proceedings should be granted where the proposed third party is the next friend of the plaintiff has been considered by the Supreme Court on a number of occasions and it seems clear that the likely disruption which this might cause may lead to a reassessment of the principle that where possible all issues should be resolved in the same set of proceedings. In *Darcy v Roscommon County Council*[11] Hederman J pointed out that in exercising his discretion in the matter the trial judge was correct in taking into account the fact that making the order sought might well affect the ability of the parent and next friend to maintain parental independence in considering the running of the case and any settlement which might be offered. In *Johnston v Fitzpatrick*[12] the Supreme Court concluded that the defendant had failed to establish sufficient grounds for the issue of a third party notice and Finlay CJ stated that he would prefer to leave a decided view on the relevance of the proposed third party being a next friend to a case in which it arose as an issue necessary for the determination of the rights between the parties. The issue was considered in some detail in *Quirke v O'Shea*,[13] in which the Supreme Court accepted that the defendants had made out a *prima facie* case of negligence against the plaintiff's mother and next friend. Finlay CJ stated that where an application is made to join a next friend as a third party the court is entitled to balance the disruption to the existing proceedings which could arise against the convenience of trying all the issues in the one action. He continued as follows:

The result of balancing those two factors will depend very greatly on the

---

[8] *Fox v Armagh Education Authority* [1956] NI 171 *per* Lord MacDermott LCJ. See also *Dowsett Engineering Construction Ltd v Sloan* [1955-56] Ir Jur Rep 31; *Andrews v Dunn & Co. Ltd* [1960] NI 181.
[9] [1992] ILRM 286.
[10] Considered further *infra*.
[11] Supreme Court, 11 January 1991.
[12] [1992] ILRM 269.
[13] [1992] ILRM 286.

individual facts of each case. It is possible to conceive a situation in which a next friend has such a high potential responsibility as a concurrent wrong-doer for the wrong in respect of which the infant is claiming, that it would be in the actual interests of the infant, and therefore, in the interests of the just procedures in the case, that he or she should be removed as a next friend so as to avoid any conflict of interest which would arise. On the other hand, there may be cases where a potential liability of the next friend is, even if established, very small, proportionately, and where the reality of the next friend's assets being made available to satisfy any claim, if established, is small. In such a case it would appear probable that the disruption involved from the appointment of another or different next friend and the removal of one parent from the control of the infant plaintiff's action is not justified by the convenience of trying both issues together.[14]

Finlay CJ stated that the case before him fell into the latter category and concluded that in the interests of justice the defendant's appeal from the decision to refuse leave to join the third party should be dismissed. These principles were subsequently applied by O'Hanlon J in the High Court decision of *Hallahan v Keane*[15] in which he pointed to the "very limited means" of the next friend to defray the costs of the proceedings. However, he stressed that he was refusing the defendant's application without prejudice to his entitlement to bring separate proceedings against the father and next friend of the plaintiff seeking contribution should he elect to do so.

TIME LIMITS LAID DOWN BY THE RULES OF THE SUPERIOR COURTS

13.005 Order 16, rule 1(3) of the RSC provides that application for leave to issue a third party notice shall, "unless otherwise ordered by the court, be made within 28 days from the time limited for delivering the defence or, where the application is made by the defendant to a counterclaim, the reply". The provisions of Order 16, rule 1(3) have been considered on a number of occasions[16] and as Kelly J noted in *S.F.L. Engineering v Smyth Cladding Systems Ltd*[17] the rule requires the application for leave to issue a third party notice to be made "within 28 days from the time limited for delivering the defence" and not within

---

[14] *Ibid.* at 291.

[15] [1992] ILRM 595.

[16] Although where the case concerns concurrent wrongdoers and the provisions of s.27 (1)(b) of the Civil Liability Act 1961 are applicable, submissions have tended to be confined to the interpretation of the subsection, see *e.g. Dillon v MacGabhann* High Court (Morris J) 24 July 1995 at 2-3.

[17] High Court (Kelly J) 9 May 1997.

28 days from the delivery of the defence.[18] Kelly J went on to say that "[i]t is clear therefore that the Rules of Court contemplate an application for the joinder of a third party being made at quite an early stage in the proceedings". However, in his judgment in the High Court in *Connolly v Casey*[19] while Kelly J pointed out that the third party was placing reliance on the defendants' failure to comply with the provisions of Order 16, rule 1(3), he commented that "experience indicates that only a tiny percentage of applications to join a third party are made within the time prescribed by this rule". He said that it would in his view "require very exceptional circumstances for the court to accede to an application of this sort if the only complaint related to a failure to observe strict compliance with the provisions of this rule".[20] Similarly in *Golden Vale plc v Food Industries plc*,[21] McCracken J referred to the 28 day limit as one which is "frequently breached". In the case before him the court had made an order on foot of an application for leave to issue a third party notice well over a year after the 28 day period had expired and so had by implication extended the time provided for in the rule.

The same type of attitude towards the question of technical non-compliance with the rules is evident in *Ward v O'Callaghan*[22] in which the third party brought an application under Order 16, rule 8(3) to set aside a third party notice on the grounds that there had been unnecessary and unreasonable delay in serving the notice and that the third party had suffered prejudice as a result of the delay. The third party notice was not served until approximately one year and five months after delivery of the statement of claim despite the fact that the rules provided that the application is to be made within 28 days from the time limited for the delivery of the defence to the plaintiff's statement of claim. Morris P stated that in his view, while clearly the first named defendant had failed to comply with the time limit provided in the rules, this delay alone would not be of such significance as to constitute a ground for setting aside the third party procedure. In order to do so, it would be necessary for delay of this length to be

---

[18] At 3. As Kelly J noted in a case where a defendant does not by notice require a statement of claim, the defence must be delivered within 28 days from the entry of appearance and in any other case it must be delivered within 28 days of the date of delivery of the statement of claim or from the time limited for appearance, whichever shall be the later.

[19] High Court (Kelly J) 12 June 1998.

[20] Kelly J observed that in the case before him, the third party could *prima facie* complain of matters which went "far beyond a technical non-compliance with the provisions of this rule" and he decided the case on the basis of the requirement in s.27(1)(b), see further *infra*. The defence ought to have been delivered within 28 days of the date of delivery of the statement of claim and it followed that in order to comply with the Rules of Court, the application to join the third party ought to have been made within 56 days of 3 March 1995. In fact the application was not set down for hearing until 25 July 1997.

[21] [1996] 2 IR 221.

[22] High Court (Morris P) 2 February 1998.

coupled with circumstances which amounted to prejudice[23] which the third party had suffered based on this delay and as in his view no prejudice arose in the case before him, he accordingly refused to set aside the third party notice.

As we have seen in *Connolly v Casey*, Kelly J pointed out that the third party could, *prima facie*, complain about matters which went far beyond "a technical non-compliance" with the rule and he based his conclusions on the interpretation of the provisions of s.27(1)(b) of the Civil Liability Act 1961. Essentially then in the case of concurrent wrongdoers it is the "temporal imperative"[24] contained in s.27(1)(b) which requires that a third party notice shall be served as soon as reasonably possible which has prompted most judicial consideration and it is to this subsection that our attention must now turn.

CONCURRENT WRONGDOERS – S.27 OF THE CIVIL LIABILITY ACT 1961

Introduction

13.006 S.27(1) of the Civil Liability Act 1961 provides as follows:

> A concurrent wrongdoer who is sued for damages or for contribution and who wishes to make a claim for contribution under this part –
>
> (a) shall not if the person from whom he proposes to claim contribution is already a party to action, be entitled to claim contribution except by a claim made in the said action, whether before or after judgment in the action; and
>
> (b) shall, if the said person is not already a party to the action, serve a third party notice upon such person as soon as is reasonably possible and, having served such notice, he shall not be entitled to claim contribution except under the third party procedure. If such third party notice is not served as aforesaid, the court may in its discretion refuse to make an order for contribution against the person from whom the contribution is claimed.

In *Board of Governors of St Laurence's Hospital v Staunton*[25] Finlay CJ referred to Order 16, rule 1(3) and stated that "[t]his provision of the Rules and the discretion vested in the court by it must, of course, be exercised subject to the statutory provisions which give rise to that jurisdiction" and so, in the case of concurrent wrongdoers, the discretion must be exercised subject to the provi-

---

[23] On the issue of prejudice, see further *infra*.
[24] *Per* Kelly J in *S.F.L. Engineering v Smyth Cladding Systems Ltd* High Court (Kelly J) 9 May 1997 at 3.
[25] [1990] 2 IR 31, 36.

sions of s.27(1)(b) of the Act of 1961 which require service of the third party notice "as soon as is reasonably possible". The purpose of requiring such a notice to be served within such time constraints was stated by McMahon J in *A. & P. (Ireland) Ltd v Golden Vale Products Ltd*[26] as being "to put the contributor in as good a position as is possible in relation to knowledge of the claim and opportunity of investigating it".

13.007 O'Keeffe J stated in *Gilmore v Windle*[27] that s.27 of the Act of 1961 is clearly intended to ensure that, as far as possible, all questions relating to the liability of concurrent wrongdoers, or persons who may be concurrent wrong-doers, should be tried in a single proceeding. Its purpose is also to prevent a multiplicity of actions; as Denham J stated in *Connolly v Casey*[28] "a multiplicity of actions is detrimental to the administration of justice, to the third party and to the issue of costs". In addition, as Finlay CJ stated in *Board of Governors of St Laurence's Hospital v Staunton*: [29]

> I am quite satisfied upon the true construction of that sub-section that the only service of a third-party notice contemplated by it and, therefore, the only right of a person to obtain from the High Court liberty to serve a third-party notice claiming contribution against a person who is not already a party to the action, is a right to serve a third-party notice as soon as is reasonably possible.

The question of whether there is any alternative to serving a third party notice in order to claim contribution in the case of concurrent wrongdoers was also addressed by Finlay CJ. He said that he was driven to the conclusion that the express vesting in the court of a discretion to refuse to make an order for contri-

---

[26] High Court (McMahon J) 7 November 1978 at 7. See also *Dowling v Armour Pharmaceutical Co. Inc.* High Court (Morris J) 18 April 1996 at 7.

[27] [1967] IR 323, 334. Quoted with approval by Barron J in *McElwaine v Hughes* High Court, 30 April 1997 at 3. See also the *dicta* of Finlay CJ in *Board of Governors of St Laurence's Hospital v Staunton* [1990] 2 IR 31, 35 that the general policy of that part of the Civil Liability Act 1961 was to make "claims for contribution and indemnity as well as claims for damages all preferably heard together in the one proceedings and at approximately the same time".

[28] [2000] 1 IR 345, 351, [2000] 2 ILRM 226, 231. See also *Molloy v Dublin Corporation* Supreme Court, 28 June 2001, *per* Murphy J at 5.

[29] [1990] 2 IR 31, 36. Quoted with approval by Kelly J in *S.F.L. Engineering v Smyth Cladding Systems Ltd* High Court, 9 May 1997 at 4 and in *Connolly v Casey* High Court, 12 June 1998 at 10-11. As Kelly J commented in *S.F.L.* the view expressed by Finlay CJ was clearly authority for the proposition that the obligation to serve the third party notice as soon as reasonably possible was mandatory in nature and a failure to comply with the temporal obligation might lead to the application for liberty to issue and serve the third party notice being refused, or if granted, being set aside on the application of the newly joined third party.

bution upon the failure of the claimant for such contribution to serve a third party notice "as aforesaid" made it necessary to construe the subsection as leaving open the bringing of a substantive claim for contribution.[30] However, as Finlay CJ made clear, having regard to the terms of the subsection, any substantive claim for contribution which the defendant may make becomes subject to the proviso that "the defendants having failed to serve a third party notice in the action, there is vested in the court a new and separate discretion by this subsection to refuse to make an order for contribution in their favour, even if it were satisfied that they could establish a right to contribution on the facts presented to it".[31] In the view of Barron J in *McElwaine v Hughes*[32] a similar result will arise where a third party notice is set aside and he suggested that failure to serve a third party notice on a person not already a party to the proceedings as soon as reasonably possible does not bar a defendant completely from recovering contribution but makes him subject to a separate discretion on the part of the court. Similarly in *Connolly v Casey*[33] Kelly J commented that failure to serve a third party notice will not automatically prevent a defendant from recovering an indemnity or contribution but that any claim which the latter may make will be subject to the discretion of the court as to whether to allow it to proceed. These views appear to be somewhat at odds with the *dicta* of O'Keeffe J in *Gilmore v Windle*[34] who suggested that a defendant who serves a third party notice "shall not be entitled to claim contribution except under the third party procedure". However, Barron J in *McElwaine*, correctly it is submitted suggests, that this provision in s.27(1)(b) is intended to apply "only where the procedure laid down by that subsection has been followed by a valid third party notice".[35] In any event, where a third party notice has been set aside the defendant's chances of recovery will be slim. As Barron J pointed out in *McElwaine* it will have two serious consequences, first, "the defendant would be at risk of circumstances arising which would justify the court refusing him relief in fresh proceedings" and secondly assuming that no such adverse circumstances arose,

---

[30] *Ibid.* at 35. Quoted with approval by Barron J in *McElwaine v Hughes* High Court (Barron J) 30 April 1997. See also the *dicta* of O'Keeffe J in *Gilmore v Windle* [1967] IR 323, 336, of McMahon J in *A. & P. (Ireland) Ltd v Golden Vale Products Ltd* High Court, 7 December 1978 at 7-8 and of Kelly J in *Connolly v Casey* High Court, 12 June 1998 at 11 to the effect that "a failure to serve a third party notice on a person not already a party to the proceedings as soon as is reasonably possible does not of course bar a defendant completely from recovering an indemnity or contribution".

[31] *Ibid.* at 36-37. However, as Dignam comments (1997) (4) P&P 2, 3 "the discretion vested in the courts by the second sentence of s.27(1)(b) is of little comfort as consideration of the case law in this area illustrates that the courts will seldom exercise their discretion in favour of a defaulting defendant particularly in light of the repeated acknowledgement by the courts of the general policy of the 1961 Act".

[32] High Court (Barron J), 30 April 1997.

[33] High Court (Kelly J), 12 June 1998.

[34] [1967] IR 323, 336.

[35] At 5.

the overall policy of the Act to have all claims heard together in the one proceeding would be defeated.

Onus of Proof and Date at which Assessment of Delay should be Made

13.008 It has been made clear that in analysing the delay to determine whether
the third party notice has been served as soon as reasonably possible "the whole
circumstances of the case and its general progress must be considered".[36] As
Barron J stated in *McElwaine v Hughes*[37] since the obligation is on the defendant to serve the third party notice within a reasonable time, it seemed to him that
the onus of proof of showing that the delay, if there was one, was not unreasonable lies on the defendant. In *Connolly v Casey* Kelly J expressed agreement
with this view and reiterated that in view of the obligation which lies on the
defendant to serve the notice as soon as reasonably possible, the onus should
also lie on him to show that any delay was not unreasonable. Clearly where the
delay is significant, some explanation should be offered for it if it is to be excused and in the absence of such explanation it is likely to be held to be significant. So, in *Neville v Margan*[38] the defendant alleged that the plaintiff's injuries
had been caused by the third party in its defence delivered in May 1980 but no
application to join the third party was made until nine months later. Blayney J
characterised such delay as "clearly unreasonable" and pointed out that no explanation had been offered which might excuse it.[39]

13.009 A further issue of interpretation which has been considered is whether
in assessing the question of whether the "as soon as is reasonably possible"
requirement has been complied with, the relevant date is the date of service of
the third party notice or the date of the application to the court for leave to issue
such a notice. In *Dillon v MacGabhann*[40] Morris J stated that the submission
that the court should look at the date upon which the third party notice was

---

[36] *Per* Denham J in *Connolly v Casey* [2000] 1 IR 345, 351, [2000] 2 ILRM 226, 231. See
also *Molloy v Dublin Corporation* Supreme Court, 28 June 2001, *per* Murphy J at 7.

[37] High Court (Barron J) 30 April 1997.

[38] [1988] IR 734. See also *O'Brien v Ulster Bank Ltd* High Court (Carney J) 21 December
1993 where similarly there had been a significant delay and no explanation had been
offered to excuse it. These decisions can be compared with *Gilmore v Windle* [1967] IR
323 where the explanation furnished by the defendant for the delay (of 17 months
between the delivery of the statement of claim and the application for leave to issue
and serve the third party notice) was accepted.

[39] Blayney J also made reference to the fact that as the third party notice had not been
served until after the plaintiff's claim against the defendant had been settled, the claim
for contribution was no different from what it would have been if it had been made in
a separate action.

[40] High Court (Morris J) 24 July 1995.

served appeared to be correct but said that in determining whether the service had been as soon as reasonably possible, the court would have to consider all the elements which contributed to any possible delay in effecting such service.[41] However, in *McElwaine v Hughes*[42] Barron J expressed the view that "[a]lthough the wording of the section refers to the service of the notice, nevertheless, it seems to me that unless there are circumstances arising between the issue of the application to issue and serve a third party notice and its ultimate service following an order to that effect, that the time to be considered should end at the date of issue of the application to the court". Subsequently in *Connolly v Casey*[43] Kelly J stated that in so far as there was a conflict between these two views, he preferred that of Morris J in *Dillon* since it accorded precisely with the wording of the section and it was the date of service of the third party notice which he took into account in the case before him.

13.010 Another point worth noting is the statement made by Kelly J in *S.F.L. Engineering v Smyth Cladding Systems Ltd*[44] to the effect that "in considering applications of this sort, the court is not concerned with any question of prejudice arising as a result of the delay in applying for liberty to join the third party", which he said seemed to follow from the interpretation placed on the relevant provision by Finlay CJ in the *Board of Governors of St Laurence's Hospital v Staunton*.[45] It should be noted that in the latter case, the question of whether the third party was seriously prejudiced was not fully argued before the Supreme Court and Finlay CJ did not express a concluded view on the issue. However, Finlay CJ did not suggest that absence of prejudice could afford a defendant an argument sufficient to counter an unreasonable delay and the conclusion reached by Kelly J on the issue of prejudice would appear to be in accordance with the general tenor of the former's judgment.

13.011 It is also interesting to note the comments of Morris P in his decision in *Ward v O'Callaghan*[46] referred to above which appeared to countenance consideration of prejudice. Morris P stated that to constitute a ground for setting aside third party proceedings, it would be necessary for delay – in this case of about one year and five months since the delivery of the statement of claim – to

---

[41] This included in the case before him, the fact that the notice was missed in the court list when originally listed and was struck out.

[42] High Court (Barron J) 30 April 1997 at 6.

[43] High Court (Kelly J) 12 June 1998 at 12.

[44] High Court (Kelly J) 9 May 1997 at 6. Note that in *McElwaine v Hughes* High Court, 30 April 1997 Barron J commented that although the effect of allowing the third party procedure to go ahead might have a prejudicial effect on either the plaintiff or the third party, this was something which, if it existed, would in most cases be capable of remedy by other procedural means.

[45] [1990] 2 IR 31.

[46] High Court (Morris P) 2 February 1998.

be coupled with circumstances which amounted to prejudice which the third party had suffered based on this delay. He reiterated that it has been the view of the courts that, save in exceptional circumstances, it is desirable that all issues about indemnity or contribution as between third parties and defendants should be disposed of at the same time as the issues relating to the defendant's liability towards the plaintiff, and stated that such a view should only be departed from where serious prejudice would arise as a result of following this course. In his opinion, no such prejudice arose in the case before him and he accordingly refused to set aside the third party proceedings. Most recently, in *Connolly v Casey* Kelly J commented that it was accepted that he should not be concerned with any question of prejudice arising as a result of the delay in applying for liberty to join the third party and stated that this seemed to follow from the judgment of Finlay CJ in the *St Laurence's Hospital* case.

What Does "as Soon as is Reasonably Possible" Mean?

13.012 As stated above, Denham J made it clear in the course of her judgment in *Connolly v Casey*[47] that "in analysing the delay – in considering whether the third party notice was served as soon as reasonably possible – the whole circumstances of the case and its general progress must be considered". The meaning of the words "as soon as is reasonably possible" have recently been examined in some detail by Murphy J, delivering the judgment of the Supreme Court in *Molloy v Dublin Corporation*.[48] The court concluded that it had been possible for the second named defendant on the information available to it to make a "prudent and responsible decision" to apply to join the third party several months before it had done so and on that basis, the court agreed that the third party order should be set aside. Murphy J stated as follows:

> The terms in which the time limit was expressed do appear severe. The use of the word "possible" rather than the words "practicable" as is invoked elsewhere, suggests a brief and inflexible time limit. It might suggest that if it is physically possible to serve the appropriate notice within an identified period that any further delay would be impermissible. However, such a draconian approach would be inconsistent with the nature of the problems to be confronted by a defendant and of the decisions to be made by him or his advisors. The statute is not concerned with physical possibilities but legal and perhaps commercial judgments. Proceedings cannot and should not be instituted or contributions sought against any party without assembling and examining the relevant evidence and obtaining appropriate advice thereon. It is in that context that the word "possible" must be understood. Furthermore the qualification of the word

---

[47] [2000] 1 IR 345, 351, [2000] 2 ILRM 226, 231.
[48] Supreme Court, 28 June 2001.

"possible" by the word "reasonable" gives a further measure of flexibility.[49]

Clearly, in order to assess whether a defendant acted "as soon as is reasonably possible" it will be necessary for the court to establish at what point the defendant possessed sufficient knowledge to appreciate that a third party might bear responsibility in relation to the plaintiff's claim. In *Board of Governors of St Laurence's Hospital v Staunton*[50] the plaintiff was admitted to the defendant's hospital under the care of the proposed third party, a consultant neurologist, and sustained injuries when he fell from a window. Finlay CJ stated that probably from the time that particulars were filed in July 1984, the defendants were aware of the nature of the plaintiff's claim[51] and it followed that they were also aware at that time of any potential claim for contribution which they might have against the third party. In the circumstances, Finlay CJ concluded that in serving a third party notice in November 1987, after the conclusion of the plaintiff's claim, the defendant had not met the requirement of serving it as "soon as is reasonably possible".

13.013 In *Dillon v MacGabhann*[52] Morris J was satisfied that since the delivery of the plaintiff's statement of claim on 11 November 1991, the defendant had been aware of all the details of the claim which must have made it clear to them that she was blaming her injury on a defect in the working of a lift which the third party was responsible for maintaining. In his view it was clear that "at that stage [the defendant] appreciated and realized" that a maintenance contract existed which would enable them to look to the third party for an explanation of how the defect in the lift could have arisen. Morris J stated that since late 1991 or certainly by a date in August 1992 when the defendant's solicitors had written to the proposed third party reminding them of their obligations under the maintenance agreement, the way was clear for the defendant to seek to join the third party. No attempt was made to do this until July 1994 and Morris J concluded that "under no circumstances could this timescale be described as moving 'as soon as is reasonably possible'".

13.014 In the view of Barron J in *McElwaine v Hughes*[53] the real question

---

[49] *Ibid*. at 6. See also the *dicta* of Barron J in *McElwaine v Hughes* High Court (Barron J) 3 April 1997 referred to by Murphy J to the effect that: "Clearly the words 'as soon as reasonably possible' [sic] denote that there should be as little delay as possible, nevertheless use of the word 'reasonable' indicates that circumstances may exist which justify some delay in the bringing of proceedings."

[50] [1990] 2 IR 31.

[51] Although Finlay CJ accepted that they might have been unaware as to whether the claim would succeed or not.

[52] High Court (Morris J) 24 July 1995.

[53] High Court (Barron J) 30 April 1997.

hinges on what is reasonable in a particular case and that in turn may depend on the behaviour of the defendant or rather that of his legal advisers. In his opinion the first question to be determined is at what point in time would a reasonably prudent solicitor acting for the defendant be in a position to advise the institution of third party proceedings and if these proceedings are not instituted at that time, it must be asked whether the delay was reasonable. He added that such time should be allowed as is reasonably necessary to reach a decision whether to institute third party proceedings and to obtain such evidence as may be required on which to base them. Once there is sufficient evidence upon which to base such a decision, the defendant's solicitor should be in a position to give the appropriate advice. Delays to get further evidence for some purpose other than that of reaching such decision would be unreasonable, although time may be taken to obtain counsel's advice where they have been instructed. In *McElwaine* it appeared from an early stage in the proceedings that oysters consumed by the plaintiff at the defendant's hotel premises had been the cause of the personal injuries allegedly suffered by the plaintiff in November 1991. However, it was not confirmed until replies to the notices for particulars were furnished in April 1994 that the plaintiff was relying on the oysters as the cause of his injuries and an expert's opinion, which the defendant's solicitors had sought on the advice of counsel, was not furnished until January 1995. A defence was filed later that month and notices of motion for liberty to serve third party notices were issued in February 1995 and the orders made in May 1995. Barron J accepted that it had been reasonable for the defendant's solicitor to wait until the replies to the notices for particulars were received as until then he could not have been sure that this was the case being relied upon by the plaintiff and while further time elapsed awaiting the expert's report, this was the latter's fault and not that of the solicitor. In the circumstances, Barron J was satisfied that the third party proceedings had been brought as soon as was reasonably possible and the application by the third parties to have the third party notices set aside was refused.

13.015 This approach of assessing whether it was reasonable to await the replies to particulars is in line with that adopted by Denham J in delivering the judgment of the Supreme Court in *Connolly v Casey*,[54] although it is at odds with the attitude towards this issue taken by Kelly J in the High Court in that decision. The plaintiff's claim against the defendant solicitors was for professional negligence and the third party, a barrister, brought an application for an order that a third party notice be struck out on the basis of the defendants' alleged failure to comply with the requirement to serve the notice as soon as reasonably possible. The delay which was particularly contentious was between the delivery of the defence in April 1996 and the application to seek liberty to serve the third party proceedings in July 1997. The defendants argued that they

---

[54] [2001] 1 IR 345, [2000] 2 ILRM 226.

were awaiting the delivery of the replies to particulars before they could move to join the third party. In addition, it was asserted on their behalf that a solicitor who was no longer employed by them had been given full instructions in the case and that it was essential for them to obtain a detailed statement from him – which was not supplied until March 1997 – before bringing any application in relation to the third party. In relation to this first explanation, Kelly J expressed the view that the insertion of pleas alleging negligence and breach of duty on the part of the third party in the defence suggested that at the time of its delivery, the defendants possessed sufficient information to justify such a plea. The defendants argued that they were awaiting the delivery of replies to particulars before they could move to join the third party but Kelly J was not satisfied that such replies would have materially altered the defendants' state of knowledge. Kelly J concluded that he was not prepared to hold that the explanations furnished for the delay in commencing the third party proceedings were justified. He was satisfied that when the defence was delivered, the defendants had sufficient information to warrant the application being brought at that time. He therefore concluded that the third party notice was not served as soon as reasonably possible and ordered that the third party proceedings be set aside.

The crucial question in his view was whether the replies to particulars materially altered the defendants' state of knowledge in relation to any matter of relevance concerning the joinder of a third party and Kelly J was satisfied that they did not. However, on appeal, Denham J stated that this was the wrong test and that instead it should be "whether it was reasonable to await the replies to particulars". In her view the queries raised in the notice for particulars were relevant to the claim against the third party and thus it had been reasonable to await the replies.[55]

In relation to the second explanation given for the delay, Denham J was satisfied that Kelly J had been in error in considering that the defendants were not justified in waiting for the instructing solicitor to give a statement. She stated that even though there were pleas in the defence relevant to the third party, there was a difference between a general plea in a defence and swearing an affidavit setting out the basis on which it was alleged that the third party was negligent. In her opinion a statement from the instructing solicitor was relevant to this and it had not been unreasonable to have awaited the arrival of this statement. Denham J concluded that she was satisfied that the proceedings had been served within the time frame permitted under s.27(1)(b) of the 1961 Act and she stated that she would allow the appeal.

13.016 It is submitted that this difference in approach as between the High Court and the Supreme Court may be significant and should be considered further. Commenting on the position following the High Court decision in *Connolly,*

---

[55] See also *Dowling v Armour Pharmaceutical Co. Inc.* High Court (Morris J) 18 April 1996.

Breen stated as follows:[56] "The court will therefore concern itself with evidence which tends to show the exact point in time that the defendant acquired knowledge, or realised that the third party might share the responsibility for the circumstances which gave rise to the proceedings being issued against the defendant". However, this view must be re-evaluated in the light of the judgment of Denham J in *Connolly*. Arguably the defendant must have realised when it delivered its defence in April 1996 that it had grounds to make a claim for contribution against the proposed third party. As Kelly J commented:

> The insertion of these pleas in the defence suggests to me that at the time of its delivery the defendants were possessed of sufficient information to justify the inclusion of such a plea. An allegation of professional negligence is a serious matter and ought not be made unless there are reasonable grounds for so doing. I do not believe that either counsel who signed the defence would have done so unless they were satisfied that such grounds did exist.[57]

The test adopted by Denham J, namely whether it was reasonable to await the replies to particulars, therefore requires a re-evaluation of the "realisation that the third party might share the responsibility approach" suggested by Breen. Given the conclusion which Denham J reached, it should be easier to justify delay provided that it is reasonable, a yardstick which will be based, in the case of particulars, on the likely relevance of additional material which may come to light. However, it should be pointed out that Denham J stressed that her determination that the defendants' delay was not unreasonable in the circumstances should not be read as an endorsement of "a culture of delay". She explained her decision in the following terms, namely that it is important in cases of professional negligence to act reasonably and to ensure that proceedings have an appropriate basis. Reference had already been made to the need to develop modern case management where professional negligence was at issue[58] and in the view of Denham J, the facts before her illustrated the need to consider the introduction of such case management in this type of case.

Failure to Apply to Have Third Party Notice Set Aside in Time

13.017 While a court may refuse to give liberty to join a third party on the grounds that the requirement laid down in s.27(1)(b) of the Civil Liability Act 1961 has not been complied with, the question of whether a third party notice has been served as soon as reasonably possible usually arises when an application is made for an order setting aside the third party proceedings pursuant to

---

[56] [1999] 1 P & P 2, 3.
[57] *Ibid.* at 15-16.
[58] *Cooke v Cronin* Supreme Court, 14 July 1999.

Order 16, rule 8(3).[59] In such cases the question also arises whether the third party has acted sufficiently promptly in order to succeed in having the proceedings against him set aside and this issue was considered in some detail by Morris J in a trilogy of cases decided a number of years ago. In *Carroll v Fulflex Ltd*[60] the plaintiff claimed to have suffered injuries driving a forklift truck while employed by the defendant when the floor of a container on which he was driving collapsed. The statement of claim was delivered in March 1992 and the order giving leave to issue the third party notice was not made until March 1994. Morris J stated that given that the defendants were aware from March 1992 that a claim was being made against them arising out of a defect in a container, he found it impossible to accept that it had taken almost two years to establish the identity of the person responsible for its condition or any possible defects in it. He concluded that were it not for "other features" in the case, it would have been an appropriate one in which to make the order sought by the third party. However, Morris J referred to the fact that the defendants, having been served with the third party statement of claim, had delivered a full defence and said that the third party proceedings had been set down and were listed for hearing in the immediate future. He continued as follows:

> In the circumstances it appears to me to be entirely inappropriate that now, when the action is ready to be heard, the third party should come to court seeking to set aside a procedure in which they have taken an active part and effectively urge the court to set at nought the costs and expenses incurred in this procedure and then require an existing party come before the court by way of a separate action, as they are entitled to do under the provisions of the Civil Liability Act 1961 in order to seek to enforce the rights they claim to have in the present proceedings. A motion to set aside a third party notice should only be brought before that defendant has taken an active part in the third party proceedings and I believe that an application of this nature must itself be brought within the time-scale identified in s.27(1) of the Civil Liability Act 1961, that is to say, "as soon as is reasonably possible". While that limitation is not spelt out in the Act, I believe that a fair interpretation of the Act must envisage that a person seeking relief under s.27 would himself move with reasonable speed and certainly before significant costs and expenses have been incurred in the third party procedures.[61]

---

[59] *O'Brien v Ulster Bank Ltd* High Court (Carney J) 21 December 1993; *Dillon v MacGabhann* High Court (Morris J) 24 July 1995; *McElwaine v Hughes* High Court (Barron J) 30 April 1997; *S.F.L. Engineering v Smyth Cladding Systems Ltd* High Court (Kelly J) 9 May 1997; *Connolly v Casey* High Court (Kelly J) 12 June 1998.
[60] High Court (Morris J) 18 October 1995.
[61] *Ibid.* at 3-4.

In the circumstances, Morris J concluded that it would be improper to grant the relief sought and said that in his view the correct procedure would be that the issues arising between the defendants and the third party should be tried in the existing proceedings.

13.018 Similarly, in *Tierney v Fintan Sweeney Ltd*[62] where there was a delay of two and a half years between delivery of the statement of claim – in which the plaintiff pleaded that the lawnmower which had allegedly caused her injuries had been manufactured by the third parties – and the order giving liberty to serve the third party notice, Morris J accepted that in the ordinary course of events this would have been a case for setting aside the third party proceedings. However, he pointed out that the third parties had entered a defence to the third party statement of claim and had allowed the action between the plaintiff and defendant to proceed to its conclusion before bringing the motion to set aside the third party proceedings. Morris J, in refusing the relief sought, reiterated that an application of this nature should be brought with reasonable expedition and in accordance with the time-scale in s.27(1)(b), namely "as soon as is reasonably possible" and save in exceptional circumstances should not extend beyond the point where a defence has been delivered to the third party statement of claim.

13.019 These principles were again endorsed by Morris J in *Grogan v Ferrum Trading Co. Ltd.*[63] He stated that "if there is to be an orderly conduct of litigation" the parties are entitled to assume that once a statement of claim and defence have been delivered in the third party proceedings, that this procedure meets with the approval of the third parties and that they will not attempt to retreat from it. Morris J said that he believed that an argument could be made to support the proposition that it would be open to a third party to enter an appearance to a third party notice without prejudicing his position in order to allow him time to consider the situation and make an application to the court if so advised. However, having entered a defence, he must be assumed to have received all appropriate advice including in relation to the desirability of setting aside the third party notice and Morris J concluded that "the delivery of the defence is, in my view, an election by the third party which precludes him from thereafter moving the court to set aside the notice".[64] While he accepted that there was no statutory provision nor rule limiting the time for making an application of this nature, Morris J was of the view that a "cut-off point" must be established and it seemed to him that it should be not later than the entry of the defence by the third party.

---

[62] High Court (Morris J) 18 October 1995.
[63] [1996] 2 ILRM 216.
[64] *Ibid.* at 221.

These cases clearly illustrate that a third party must act promptly in seeking to have a third party notice set aside and that the "as soon as is reasonably possible" requirement is applied by analogy to such applications. It would also appear that the crucial factor is not so much the length of the delay, although this is obviously relevant, but rather whether the proposed third party has taken an active role in the proceedings, specifically whether he has delivered a defence to the third party proceedings.

Conclusion

13.020 Clearly, whatever the context in which the plaintiff's claim against the defendant is made, a balancing exercise must be carried out by the courts when a defendant seeks to join a third party. As Barron J commented in *McElwaine v Hughes*[65] "while a court should not construe 'as soon as is reasonably possible' too liberally, it should not at the same time be too astute to set aside a third party notice on such grounds". It has been acknowledged that "it is desirable that all issues as to indemnity or contribution as between third parties and defendants should be disposed of at the same time as the issues relating to the defendant's liability towards the plaintiff",[66] and that there is a clear policy argument in favour of avoiding a multiplicity of actions.[67] However, as against this there are equally clear arguments in favour of achieving speedy resolution of legal disputes between parties and not condoning conduct which might be perceived as encouraging the "culture of delay". Clearly this creates a dilemma for the courts in seeking to reconcile these two principles where there are plainly issues relating to contribution or indemnity to be resolved but in circumstances where a defendant has delayed unduly in seeking to join a third party.

PROCEDURE FOR JOINING A THIRD PARTY

Motion

13.021 An application for leave to issue and serve a third party notice is made by motion on notice to the plaintiff (and not to the proposed third party). If the application is on consent, then the motion may be made returnable to the Master's Court.[68] Otherwise, it will be returnable to the common law motion list or Court 5 or 6 if it is a chancery matter. The notice of motion should be grounded on the affidavit of the defendant seeking leave (not his or her solicitor[69]) and

---

[65] High Court (Barron J) 30 April 1997 at 5.
[66] *Per* Morris J in *Dillon v MacGabhann* High Court, 24 July 1995.
[67] See *Gilmore v Windle* [1967] IR 323 at 329 *per* Lavery J and at 334 *per* O'Keeffe J and *per* Denham J in *Connolly v Casey* [2000] 1 IR 345, 351, [2000] 2 ILRM 226, 231.
[68] Order 63, rule 1(34).
[69] *Darcy v Roscommon County Council* Supreme Court, 11 January 1991.

that affidavit should contain the following:
- (i) A means of knowledge clause.
- (ii) A summary of the plaintiff's case and a reference to the proceedings had in the matter.
- (iii) The reason why the third party should be joined in the proceedings. Three grounds for joining a third party are set forth in Order 16, rule 1 and, whichever is applicable, the affidavit must set forth sufficient facts and reasons why it is appropriate to join the third party. The ground usually put forward is that the defendant is entitled to contribution or indemnity from the third party. In this instance, the affidavit must detail facts sufficient to establish a *prima facie* case against the third party and it is common in this regard to make reference to a paragraph in the defence alleging that the third party is wholly or partly answerable for the plaintiff's claim. The draft third party notice should also be exhibited and this will state the nature and grounds of the claim or the nature of the question or issue sought to be determined and the nature and extent of any relief or remedy claimed.[70]
- (iv) If the application is being made outside the time limits laid down in Order 16, rule 1(3), then an explanation for the delay should be given.
- (v) A prayer for relief.

Proofs

- (i) A notice of motion seeking leave to issue and serve a third party notice and, if necessary, an order extending the time for bringing the application.
- (ii) A grounding affidavit in the form prescribed above.
- (iii) The pleadings.
- (iii) An affidavit of service of the notice of motion and grounding affidavit on the plaintiff (and not on the third party).

Hearing of the Motion

13.022 Order 16, rule 2 specifies that, unless the plaintiff wishes to join the third party as a defendant, his attendance at the hearing of the motion is not necessary and that, if he does attend, he shall not be entitled to the costs of doing so except by special direction of the court. It can be seen from rule 2 that the primary reason for giving notice to the plaintiff is to allow him to join the proposed third party as a defendant and he will generally not appear unless he wishes to do this. Therefore, the application is generally uncontested, though, if there has been serious delay in the matter, the defendant will have to satisfy the judge that he should exercise his discretion to make the order sought. In addi-

---

[70] Order 16, rule 2(1).

tion, the application may sometimes be opposed by the plaintiff on the basis that it will delay the hearing of the substantive matter. The costs of the application will generally be reserved.

Issue and Service of Third Party Notice

13.023 If the court makes the order giving leave to issue and serve the third party notice, the notice must be served within 28 days unless the court orders otherwise.[71] An appearance must be entered to the notice within eight days of service or within such other period as may be directed by the court and specified in the notice.[72]

---

[71] Order 16, rule 2(2).
[72] Order 16, rule 4(1).

CHAPTER FOURTEEN

REMITTAL OR TRANSFER OF ACTIONS

REMITTAL OR TRANSFER OF ACTIONS TO A LOWER COURT

From the High Court to the Circuit Court or the District Court

14.001 S.25 of the Courts of Justice Act 1924 as amended provides that when any action shall be pending in the High Court which might have been commenced in the Circuit Court, any party to such action may, at any time before the commencement of the trial[1], apply to the High Court to have the action remitted or transferred to the Circuit Court. The High Court may retain such action if it considers that it is fit to be prosecuted in that court or it may remit or transfer it to the Circuit Court or, where the action might have been commenced in the District Court, to the District Court. Such cases shall be remitted to be tried before the judge assigned to the Circuit or District, "as may appear to the High Court suitable and convenient", upon such terms and subject to such conditions, as to costs or otherwise as may appear to be just. S.25 also contains a proviso that the High Court shall have jurisdiction to remit or transfer any action, "whatever may be the amount of the claim formally made", if the court is of the opinion that the action should not have been commenced in the High Court but in the Circuit Court or in the District Court if at all.[2]

14.002 S.25 was amended by s.11 of the Courts of Justice Act 1936. S.11(2)(a)

---

[1] As originally enacted s.25 provided that such an application had to be made before service of the notice of trial. S.11(1) of the Courts of Justice Act 1936 clarified this to provide that an application might be made at any time after an appearance had been entered and before service of the notice of trial and provided further that where the summons in an action was required by the rules of court to be set down for hearing before the Master of the High Court, an application might be made notwithstanding the fact that the summons had not been set down. This position was changed again by s.2 of the Courts Act 1988 which provided for remittals at any time before the commencement of trial in the case of actions to which s.1(1) of Act of 1988 – which made provision for the abolition of juries in certain civil actions before the High Court – applied. This principle was further extended by s.15(3) of the Courts Act 1991 which provided that the jurisdiction of the High Court under s.25 might be exercised "at any time before the commencement of the trial".
[2] This proviso was considered by Gavan Duffy J in the course of his judgment in *Royal Bank of Ireland v Daly* [1938] IR 192. The learned judge stated *obiter* that he had no doubt that the words in the proviso "whatever may be the amount of the claim formally made" were inserted in the section to defeat the expedient of retaining a case in the High Court by exaggerating a plaintiff's financial claim.

provides that notwithstanding the provisions of s.25, an action shall not be remitted if the High Court is satisfied that, having regard to all the circumstances, notwithstanding the fact that such an action could have been commenced in the Circuit Court, it is reasonable that it should have been commenced in the High Court.[3] The question of the correct interpretation and construction of s.11(2)(a) was considered by Morris J in *O'Shea v Mallow UDC*.[4] The plaintiff brought an application seeking an order that his personal injuries action be remitted to the Circuit Court when it became apparent that the injuries which he had sustained were not as serious as had initially been thought at the time proceedings against the defendant were instituted in the High Court. Counsel for the defendants opposed the application on the basis that the correct interpretation of the provisions of s.11(2)(a) was that the court might only transfer and remit an action where it was not reasonable that the action should have been commenced in the High Court. It was submitted that it would follow that any order remitting the action to the Circuit Court must therefore contain an express finding that it was not reasonable to have commenced the action in the High Court, the corollary of this proposition being that in these circumstances no award in excess of Circuit Court jurisdiction could be made. However, Morris J was satisfied that this construction of the subsection was incorrect. He stated:

> The provisions of s.11(2)(a) of the Courts of Justice Act 1936 were enacted so as to provide for the circumstance where an action involves issues which were capable of being resolved in the Circuit Court and fell within the jurisdiction of that court but, for valid reason, should properly be dealt with in the High Court. The subsection removes from the High Court the obligation to transfer an action simply because the subject matter of the action fell within the Circuit Court jurisdiction. The subsection provided for a circumstance where, notwithstanding the fact that the subject matter of the action fell within the jurisdiction of the Circuit Court, it was nevertheless reasonable and proper to retain the action in the High Court. If such circumstance existed then the High Court had the power to retain the action and not transmit it to the Circuit Court.[5]

---

[3] In *Stokes v Milford Co-operative Creamery Ltd* (1956) 90 ILTR 67, Dixon J stated that he was of the view that the subsection meant that where there were some specific circumstances by reason of which the action should have been brought in the High Court, it should not be remitted. However, he did not see any circumstances in the case before him which made it reasonable to have commenced the action in the High Court and he accordingly made an order that the matter be remitted. See also *Neary v McDonnell* (1971) 105 ILTR 121 where it was held by O'Keeffe P that in view of the amount of the poor law valuation of the premises in relation to the sale of which a dispute had arisen, the matter should be remitted to the Circuit Court.

[4] [1994] 2 IR 117, [1993] ILRM 884.

[5] *Ibid.* at 119-120, 886.

On the basis of this reasoning, Morris J concluded that it did not necessarily follow that, simply because the court might make an order remitting the action to the Circuit Court for hearing, it was unreasonable to have commenced the proceedings in the High Court. He stated that he found support for this interpretation of the subsection in the provisions of s.20 of the Act of 1936, which provided that in actions remitted to the Circuit Court, there might be an award in excess of the normal Circuit Court jurisdiction. In these circumstances, Morris J concluded that he should make an order remitting the action to the Circuit Court for hearing.

14.003 S.11(2)(b) of the Act of 1936 provides that an action for the recovery of a liquidated sum should not be remitted or transferred unless the plaintiff consents or the defendant either satisfies the High Court that he has a good defence to the action or discloses facts which in the opinion of the court are sufficient to entitle him to defend the action.[6] As mentioned above, it should also be noted that s.20 of the Courts of Justice Act 1936, as amended,[7] provides that where an action claiming unliquidated damages is remitted or transferred by the High Court to the Circuit Court, the Circuit Court shall have jurisdiction to award damages in excess of £30,000, to be increased to €100,000 from 1 January 2002.[8]

S.25 was also amended by s.13 of the Courts of Justice Act 1953 which provides that the power to remit or transfer an action conferred by s.25 may, with the consent of the parties to the action, be exercised by the Master of the High Court.

14.004 The "suitable and convenient" Circuit Court referred to in s.25 is to be determined with reference to the maxim *actor sequitur forum rei*.[9] As Kennedy CJ pointed out in *O'Connor v O'Brien*:[10] "[T]he policy of the [1924] Act is unmistakable. It is that the great bulk of the ordinary litigation not involving very heavy financial consequences ... shall be dealt with and disposed of in the local venue" and s.25 provides a means whereby this policy may be carried out. Kennedy CJ reiterated this view in *Hosie v Lawless*[11] by stating that ordinary

---

[6] See *United Drug and Chemical Co. Ltd v McSweeney* [1959] IR 149, where Murnaghan J refused to make an order remitting the case to the Circuit Court holding that the defendant had not succeeded in satisfying the court that she had a good defence to the action and stating that in his opinion, the affidavits filed on the defendant's behalf did not disclose facts sufficient to entitle her to defend the action. See also *Winters v Elizabeth James Models (Manufacturing) Ltd* [1955] IR 348.

[7] S.20 was amended by s.19(2) of the Courts of Justice Act 1953, by s.2(4)(a), s.25(4) of the Courts Act 1971, by s.2(3)(a), s.33(3) of the Courts Act 1981 and by s.2(3)(a), s.23(3) of the Courts Act 1991.

[8] See s.12 of the Courts and Court Officers Bill 2001.

[9] *Meagher v Shanahan* (1932) 66 ILTR 94.

[10] [1925] 2 IR 24, 28.

[11] [1927] IR 464.

everyday actions, *i.e.* those which do not involve very large sums of money or raise exceptional questions for determination, should in the ordinary course be tried in the local venue by the Circuit Court. Referring to the general policy of the 1924 Act, he stated as follows:

> The policy was decentralization of jurisdiction, though no doubt the High Court has, under the Constitution, and still keeps, original jurisdiction, which may be exercised in any case; but as we have stated in this Court on many occasions, if an action is *prima facie* within the jurisdiction of the Circuit Court, and there are no special circumstances indicating that it ought to be withdrawn from that court, then it ought to be tried in the Circuit Court.[12]

14.005 Where a claim is within the procedural and jurisdictional limits of the Circuit Court an application may be brought, by means of a motion on notice, to remit the matter.[13] So, in *Sligo Corporation v Gilbride*,[14] the Supreme Court ordered that actions commenced in the High Court, *inter alia*, seeking injunctions, should be transferred to the Circuit Court on the grounds that the actions could have been commenced in that court and were within its jurisdiction. For such an application to succeed, the action must be one which might have been commenced in the Circuit Court. In *Byrne v Hughes*[15] it was held that the question of whether an action might or might not have been commenced in the Circuit Court depends on that court's jurisdiction to entertain a claim and that where the court has jurisdiction to entertain a case it cannot be deprived of that jurisdiction by the non-existence of the necessary procedural rules or forms. Reversing Meredith J, the Supreme Court held that the action in question should be remitted to the Circuit Court as being within the jurisdiction of that court despite the fact that at the time the action was commenced it could not have been initiated in the Circuit Court owing to the fact that no rules had as yet been made regulating procedure in that court.[16] This can be contrasted with the approach taken by the court in *McCormack v Hardwith*[17] where a procedural inadequacy was held to be sufficient to sustain the argument that the case was not one "which might have been commenced in the Circuit Court" within the

---

[12] *Ibid.* at 471.
[13] See *e.g. Stokes v Milford Co-operative Creamery Ltd* (1956) 90 ILTR 67 where the action in question was an equity matter within the jurisdiction of the Circuit Court.
[14] [1929] IR 351.
[15] [1925] 1 IR 126.
[16] Note that a similar finding was made by the Supreme Court in *O. v M.* [1977] IR 33 in relation to a claim under the provisions of the Illegitimate Children (Affiliation Orders) Act 1930 to the effect that the High Court could exercise its jurisdiction for the purposes of the Act, notwithstanding the absence of the appropriate rules of court.
[17] (1931) 65 ILTR 54.

meaning of s.25. It has also been established that where the affidavit grounding the application to remit does not disclose facts sufficient to entitle the defendant to defend the action, the matter cannot be transferred or remitted.[18]

14.006 The meaning of the last words of the first paragraph of s.25, "subject to such conditions as to costs or otherwise as may appear to be just" was considered by the High Court in *McEvoy v Fitzpatrick*.[19] Meredith and Johnston JJ agreed that the phrase meant that the question of costs was to be dealt with at the time the action was transferred by the High Court judge, and that he is given full power by the section to deal with this question in whatever manner he deems just. Meredith J was of the opinion that even if the High Court judge had made no order as to costs, the Circuit Court judge would have no jurisdiction to subsequently take the matter up and the effect of the High Court order was to conclude the issue of costs. In the instant case, the plaintiff had not been allowed any costs in the High Court, and it was held that the Circuit Court judge had no power to allow such costs.[20]

14.007 The primary test to be applied by the High Court on a motion to remit was laid down by Fitzgibbon J in *O'Connor v O'Brien*[21] as follows:

> ... if the amount of damages recoverable is the only question involved in the decision, the court must consider whether the plaintiff could reasonably contemplate the recovery of a sum of damages beyond the jurisdiction of the Circuit Court.

In *Ronayne v Ronayne*,[22] in which this test was cited with approval by Ó Dálaigh CJ, the Supreme Court had to consider an appeal from the decision of the High Court that the case before the court should be remitted. Ó Dálaigh CJ stated that, in his opinion, s.20 of the Courts of Justice Act 1936, which provided that in a remitted case the Circuit Court should have jurisdiction to award damages in excess of its normal jurisdictional limit, did not alter the test laid down in *O'Connor v O'Brien*. Ó Dálaigh CJ added that the policy of decentralization, which as Kennedy CJ had pointed out in *Hosie v Lawless*[23] lay behind the

---

[18] See *United Drug and Chemical Co. Ltd v McSweeney* [1959] IR 149.
[19] [1931] IR 212.
[20] Note that Order 49, rule 7 of the Rules of the Superior Courts 1986 provides that "the High Court ... may remit or transfer an action on such terms and subject to such conditions as to costs as may appear just".
[21] [1925] 2 IR 24, 31. Similarly, in *Mitofsky v Tolkin* (1930) 64 ILTR 40, it was held that the action was a proper matter to be retained in the High Court on the basis that a jury might reasonably have come to the conclusion that the plaintiff was entitled to recover a sum in excess of the jurisdictional limit of the Circuit Court and if such a sum were awarded it could not be set aside by a court as being excessive in the circumstances.
[22] [1970] IR 15.
[23] [1927] IR 464.

establishment of the Circuit Court, did not in his opinion require that actions within the lower range of the High Court's jurisdiction should be remitted for trial before the Circuit Court. In the circumstances he was satisfied that the High Court order remitting the matter should be set aside on the basis that an award of damages in excess of the then jurisdictional limit of the Circuit Court would not be set aside as an excessive amount on appeal.

14.008 The constitutional validity of s.25 was challenged in *Ward v Kinahan Electrical Ltd.*[24] The plaintiff, resisting an application by the defendant to have the action remitted, contended that the section was invalid on the grounds that Article 34.3.1° of the Constitution gives every citizen the right to have his case, however trivial, determined in the High Court, and he relied on the judgment of Kenny J in *Macauley v Minister for Posts and Telegraphs*[25] in support of his claim. McMahon J rejected his argument in the following terms:

> In my opinion, Article 34.3 cannot be construed as conferring a universal right of recourse to the High Court from the determination of all justiciable disputes. . . . It cannot be construed as creating a right of access to the High Court for the determination of all matters and questions because Article 36 enables laws to be made for the distribution of jurisdiction and business among all the courts which may be established under the Constitution, including courts of first instance other than the High Court. It follows, therefore, that business which falls within the full original jurisdiction of the High Court may be assigned within the limits express and implied in the Constitution, to some other court.[26]

McMahon J therefore concluded that s.25, as amended by s.11 of the Courts of Justice Act 1936, was not inconsistent with the Constitution.

From the Circuit Court to the District Court

14.009 S.15 of the Courts Act 1991 makes similar, although not identical provision in relation to remittals from the Circuit Court to the District Court. It provides that when any action is pending in the Circuit Court which might have been commenced in the District Court, any party to the action may, at any time before the commencement of the trial, apply to the Circuit Court to have the action remitted or transferred to the District Court. If the court does not consider the action fit to be prosecuted in the Circuit Court, it may remit or transfer the action to the District Court to be prosecuted before the judge assigned to such district court district as may appear to the Circuit Court suitable and convenient

---

[24] [1984] IR 292.
[25] [1966] IR 345.
[26] [1984] IR 292, 295.

upon such terms and subject to such conditions as to costs or otherwise as may appear to it to be just. S.15 also contains the following proviso that "the Circuit Court may remit or transfer any action, whatever may be the amount of the claim formally made therein, if the court is of opinion that the action should not have been commenced in the Circuit Court but in the District Court if at all".

This procedure differs from that in relation to remittals from the High Court to the Circuit Court, where the Circuit Court has unlimited jurisdiction. In such cases, the District Court may award damages in excess of its jurisdictional limit of £5,000 to be increased to €20,000 on 1 January 2002,[27] but it may not award damages in excess of £10,000, to be increased to €40,000 from that date.[28] It should also be noted that Regulation 7(1) of the District Court (Costs) Rules 1992 (SI No. 225 of 1992) provides as follows:

> Where an action is remitted or transferred to the District Court by the High Court under s.25 of the Act of 1924 or by the Circuit Court under s.15 of the Act of 1991 the plaintiff shall, within 14 days from the date of the order for remittal or transfer, lodge with the clerk a certified copy of such order together with the summons or other originating document (or a copy thereof) and copies of all documents already delivered and orders made in the action. Where the plaintiff omits or refuses to lodge those documents within the time prescribed, the defendant may do so at any time after the expiration of the said 14 days. The party lodging these documents shall, within 14 days of such lodgment, serve notice on the other party that the said documents have been so lodged. Upon receipt of the documents lodged the clerk shall enter and list the action for hearing and notify the parties of the place, date and time fixed therefor. The action shall then be heard and determined by the court as if it had originally been commenced therein. A note of the remittal or transfer shall be entered on the court record and on any court order issued in the action.

TRANSFER OF ACTIONS TO A HIGHER COURT

14.010 S.22(8)(a) of the Courts (Supplemental Provisions) Act 1961 as amended[29] provides that any interested party may at any time apply to the judge

---

[27] See s.13 of the Courts and Court Officers Bill 2001.

[28] S.15(2) of the Courts Act 1991 as amended by s.17 of the Courts and Court Officers Bill 2001.

[29] S.21 of the Courts Act 1971 substituted a new subsection (8) in s.22 of the Courts (Supplemental Provisions) Act 1961 as a result of which civil proceedings may be transferred from either the District or the Circuit Court to the High Court. The need for extending this power to the District Court arose primarily as a result of the necessity to determine the liability of all the parties in a case in one action in accordance with the objectives of the Civil Liability Act 1961 where *e.g.* a claim which fell within the

of the Circuit Court before whom an action commenced in that court or an appeal from the District Court is pending to have the action or appeal forwarded to the High Court. In cases where the action or appeal is one fit to be tried in the High Court and the High Court appears to be the more appropriate tribunal in the circumstances, the Circuit Court judge may send forward the action or appeal to the High Court upon such terms and subject to such conditions as to costs or otherwise as may appear to him to be just. An appeal shall lie under s.38 of the Courts of Justice Act 1936, as applied by s.48 of the Act of 1961, from the decision of the judge granting or refusing any such application.

S.22(8)(b) makes equivalent provision in relation to actions pending before the District Court to enable the action to be transferred to the Circuit Court or the High Court and provides that an appeal shall lie under s.84 of the Courts of Justice Act 1924, as applied, from the decision of the district judge granting or refusing any such application.

S.21(1) of the Courts of Justice Act 1936 provides that the Circuit Court shall have power to strike out with costs actions which that court has no jurisdiction to hear and determine. However, s.21(2) goes on to provide that whenever a judge of the Circuit Court is required by the foregoing sub-section to order an action to be struck out, such judge may, if he so thinks proper having regard to all the circumstances of the case, in lieu of making such order, transfer the action to the High Court and make such order as to the costs of the proceedings had in the Circuit Court as shall appear to him to be proper.

TRANSFER OF ACTIONS IN THE CIRCUIT COURT

14.011 S.22(9) of the Courts (Supplemental Provisions) Act 1961 provides that a judge of the Circuit Court may, on the application of any party or on his own motion, by order change the venue for the trial of any action pending before him from one place of hearing to any other within his circuit, and that an appeal shall lie under s.38 of the Courts of Justice Act 1936, as applied by s.48 of the Act of 1961, from the decision of the judge of the Circuit Court. S.22(10) provides that a judge of the Circuit Court may, on the application of any party to an action which has been partly heard, transfer the remainder or any portion of the hearing to another venue within his circuit or within the Dublin Circuit and makes the same provision in relation to an appeal from the making or refusing of such an order.

S.22(12) provides that where an action is pending before a judge of the Circuit Court for the time being assigned to a particular circuit, and an application is made by any party to such action for the transfer of such action to another

---

jurisdiction of the Circuit Court might involve a counterclaim which fell outside the jurisdictional limit of that court.

circuit for hearing by the judge of the Circuit Court for the time being assigned to such other circuit, the first-mentioned judge may, with the consent of the other judge, transfer such action accordingly and provision is made for an appeal under s.38 of the Courts of Justice Act 1936 from the making or refusing of such an order.

Note that provision is made for the transfer of trials in criminal cases by judges of the Circuit Court under s.32 of the Courts and Court Officers Act 1995.

CHAPTER FIFTEEN

LODGMENTS

INTRODUCTION

15.001 Order 22 of the Rules of the Superior Courts 1986 makes provision in relation to the payment of money into and out of court, known as the lodgment procedure. Rule 1(1) applies to any action for a debt or damages, other than an action to which s.1(1) of the Courts Act 1988 applies, and provides that a defendant may, at any time after he has entered an appearance and before the action is set down for trial, or at any later time by leave of the court, on notice to the plaintiff pay into court a sum of money in satisfaction of the plaintiff's claim. Rule 1(2) goes on to provide that a defendant may once, without leave and upon notice to the plaintiff, pay an additional sum into court. Such notice must be given and payment made at least three months before the date on which the action is first listed for hearing. This increased lodgment will then become the sum paid into court and the date of the increased payment the date of the payment into court. In general a lodgment may be made with or without an admission of liability but it should be noted that in actions for libel or slander, or where the defence raises questions of title to land or incorporeal hereditaments, money may not be paid into court unless liability is admitted in the defence.[1] In addition, rule 1(5) provides that where money is paid into court in satisfaction of one or more of several causes of action, the notice of lodgment shall specify the cause or causes of action in respect of which payment is made, and the sum paid in respect of each, unless the court orders otherwise. The provisions of rules 1(3) and (5) have recently been considered by Kelly J in *Norbrook Laboratories Ltd v Smithkline Beecham (Ireland) Ltd*[2] in which the plaintiffs sought damages against the defendant for slander of goods and libel. The defendant sought an order giving directions as to whether a payment into court by it pursuant to Order 22 in respect of the plaintiffs' allegation of slander of goods and in respect of some but not all of their allegations of defamation would be a valid payment into court. Kelly J stated that rule 1(3) has long been a source of controversy and that he did not believe that there was any convincing reason to justify a differentiation between defamation and other tort actions when it came to the issue of payments into court. Notwithstanding this, as Kelly J pointed out, the rules in this jurisdiction have not been amended to reflect this point of view and he had to give effect to rule 1(3) which requires an admission of liability in

---

[1] Order 22, rule 1(3).
[2] [1999] 2 IR 192, [1999] 2 ILRM 391.

defamation cases. Kelly J further held that each of the innuendoes pleaded constituted a separate cause of action for the purposes of rule 1(5) and he stated
that the practical effect of this is that in defamation proceedings it is possible to
make a lodgment with an admission of liability to part of a plaintiff's claim
provided that the defendant makes the necessary admissions in the defence and
identifies in the notice of lodgment the particular allegations in respect of which
payment is made.

LODGMENTS IN CASES TO WHICH S. 1(1) OF THE COURTS ACT 1988 APPLIES

15.002 Rules 1(7) & (8)[3] and (9) & (10)[4] make provision in relation to
lodgments in cases to which s.1(1) of the Courts Act 1988 applies, namely
personal injuries actions, fatal injuries actions taken pursuant to s.48 of the
Civil Liability Act 1961 and actions taken pursuant to s.18 of the Air Navigation and Transport Act 1936.[5] In such actions a defendant may once, without
leave and upon notice to the plaintiff, pay into court a sum of money in satisfaction of a claim either at the time of the delivery of the defence or within a period
of four months from the date of the notice of trial. A defendant who has not
made such payment within the time permitted or who wishes to increase the sum
lodged may only do so with the leave of the court and upon such terms and
conditions as the court may impose. Rule 1(8) provides that in such actions, the
pleadings shall not disclose either the fact that a lodgment has been made or the
amount thereof. These facts shall not be communicated to the judge although he
may, before or at the trial of the action, enquire "for good and sufficient reason"
whether and in what amount a lodgment has been made. Notwithstanding the
provisions of rule 1(7), in any case in which the plaintiff has served a notice of
replies to particulars or additional particulars, without a request for these, after
the time within which a defendant could make a payment into court without
leave has expired, the defendant may without leave make a payment or increase
any payment into court within 21 days from the date thereof on notice to the
plaintiff.[6] In addition, in any case in which a period in excess of 18 months has
elapsed since the date of the notice for trial, a defendant may without leave
make a payment into court within 21 days on notice to the plaintiff, provided
that the payment, if not accepted by the plaintiff shall not take effect for two
months from the date on which it was made or increased.[7]

---

[3] Inserted by Rules of the Superior Courts (No. 3) 1990 (SI No. 229 of 1990).
[4] Inserted by Rules of the Superior Courts (No. 2) 1993 (SI No. 265 of 1993).
[5] Inserted by s.4 of the Air Navigation and Transport Act 1965.
[6] Order 22, rule 1(9) inserted by Rules of the Superior Courts (No. 2) 1993 (SI No. 265 of 1993).
[7] Order 22, rule 1(10) inserted by Rules of the Superior Courts (No. 2) 1993 (SI No. 265 of 1993).

LATE LODGMENTS

15.003 As noted above, Order 22, rule 1(1) allows a defendant, upon notice to the plaintiff, to pay into court a sum of money in satisfaction of the plaintiff's claim before the action is set down for trial, or at a later time by leave of the court. As Ó Dálaigh CJ stated in *Ely v Dargan*:[8]

> The rule is in the widest terms, and it clearly allows of an application being made to the court before a retrial as well as before a trial. The only question, in the former case, is what conditions the court may properly impose in granting leave.

An example of a successful application for a late lodgment being made in the case of a retrial is *Hanley v Randles*[9] in which the Supreme Court had found for the infant plaintiff on the issue of liability but had directed a new trial on the issue of damages. After the service of the notice of trial the defendant sought to increase the lodgment and offered to pay all the costs incurred by the plaintiff to the date of the motion. Counsel for the defendant submitted that the plaintiff would be in no way prejudiced if the order sought were made but counsel for the plaintiff submitted that the court should not be used as a sounding board for the defendant to test the plaintiff by raising the lodgment to see what the plaintiff would take in settlement of the claim. Murnaghan J stated that the application had been undoubtedly brought at the eleventh hour but concluded that if the plaintiff was not prejudiced by being under a risk for costs already incurred, the application was unanswerable.

15.004 A similar result was arrived at by the Supreme Court in *Ely v Dargan*[10] in which leave was granted to increase a lodgment in circumstances where the Supreme Court had directed a retrial on the question of damages. Ó Dálaigh CJ stated that "the defendant was right to urge that the public interest was served by allowing a defendant, even at the eleventh hour, to proffer to the plaintiff under the lodgment machinery of the courts a sum that the defendant considers adequately meets the plaintiff's claim". However, he stressed that the public interest does not require that a defendant, who is allowed to avail of the lodgment machinery by leave of the court, should do so on any more favourable conditions than he would have done if he had used that machinery in the ordinary way without the court's leave. He said that while cases may arise in which there are circumstances requiring special consideration,

> [I]n the ordinary way where a defendant wishes to increase the amount of

---

[8] [1967] IR 89, 94.
[9] [1960] Ir Jur Rep 67.
[10] [1967] IR 89.

his original lodgment he may properly be required as a condition of obtaining liberty, to restore the plaintiff to the position in which he would have been if the increased lodgment had been an original lodgment made under the Rules without leave; that is to say, that the defendant should undertake to recoup the plaintiff in respect of all costs already incurred, or ordered to be paid by him, subsequent to the date of the original lodgment.[11]

15.005 The circumstances in which a court may refuse leave to make a late lodgment outside the time limits laid down by Order 22, rule 1(7), were considered by Barr J in *Brennan v Iarnród Éireann*[12] in which the plaintiff sought damages for personal injuries, although the general principles which determine whether a late lodgment should be allowed are the same. No lodgments had been made during the time permitted and in the course of settlement negotiations the plaintiff disclosed all medical reports relating to her injuries. The defendants then sought liberty to make a late lodgment. Barr J refused the application and held that in the absence of special circumstances, a defendant should not be allowed to use information obtained in unsuccessful settlement negotiations as a means of calculating the amount of a lodgment. He commented that there are circumstances where in fairness to the defendant, the court should exercise its discretion to allow a late lodgment, notwithstanding a full disclosure of the plaintiff's case in the course of unsuccessful settlement negotiations *e.g.* where it emerged for the first time during such negotiations that the plaintiff's injuries were more serious than those pleaded. However, in the case before him it was not suggested that the plaintiff's injuries had transpired to be different or more serious than indicated in the particulars pleaded. The decision of Barr J was clearly based on the reasoning that "*bona fide* settlement negotiations in personal injury actions are often in the best interest of the parties and are to be encouraged". He stated as follows:

> It seems to me that if such negotiations are unfruitful, the defendant ought not to be allowed to capitalise on the plaintiff's full disclosure of his or her case as to personal injuries and/or on liability, and to use the information obtained in such negotiations as a measure for calculating what is intended to be a tight lodgment.[13]

15.006 This statement was quoted with approval by O'Sullivan J in *Rhatigan v Gill*[14] in which the defendant applied unsuccessfully to increase his lodgment on the day on which the hearing of the trial was due to begin. O'Sullivan J

---

[11] *Ibid.* at 95.
[12] [1992] 2 IR 167, [1993] ILRM 134.
[13] *Ibid.* at 169, 135.
[14] High Court (O'Sullivan J) 16 December 1998.

stressed that like Barr J in *Brennan*, he was anxious to protect the integrity of settlement negotiations in exercising his discretion on an application of this nature. The defendant had made a nominal lodgment because, his counsel asserted, he was not in possession of sufficient information to assess what a realistic amount should be. However, O'Sullivan J stated that he considered that the responsibility for the lack of information available to the defendant's legal advisers at the time of making this lodgment must rest with the defendant rather than the plaintiffs. He also made reference to the fact that the defendant sought following negotiations to increase his lodgment and said that the close proximity of the application and negotiations to the commencement of the hearing involved a risk or a perception of risk that something may have been said in the course of negotiations which enabled the defendant to make a better assessment from a tactical point of view thereby resulting in an unfair advantage to him. O'Sullivan J therefore concluded that in all the circumstances it would not be just to the plaintiffs to allow the defendant to make an increased lodgment.

15.007 However, it should be noted that some doubt has now been cast on the validity of the approach adopted by Barr J in *Brennan* and it was distinguished in *Dawson & Dawson v Irish Brokers Association*[15] in which Moriarty J acceded to an application for a late lodgment in circumstances where the Supreme Court had directed a retrial on the question of damages alone. Moriarty J commented that "there is no question here of a background of settlement discussions or other negotiations having enabled the defendants to know the plaintiffs' hand to a level of potential unfairness with regard to a lodgment, such as influenced the court to refuse leave for a late lodgment in *Brennan*".

15.008 Similarly, in the recent decision of *Noble v Gleeson McGrath and Baldwin*,[16] Quirke J seemed to rely on the reasoning underlying the Supreme Court decision in *Ely v Dargan* in granting an application for a late lodgment and in distinguishing *Brennan*. Quirke J observed that the proceedings in the case before him had been listed for hearing in ten days time and noted that leave granted pursuant to rule 1(1) even at this late stage would not affect or interfere with the plaintiff's right to have all the costs he had incurred to date taxed and paid for by the defendant. He went on to say that while there were factual similarities between *Brennan* and the case before him it was clear that they were distinguishable from one another. While in *Brennan* Barr J had refused the application on the grounds, *inter alia*, that to grant relief might encourage defendants or their indemnifiers to enter into spurious settlement negotiations, there was no such suggestion in the case before him, a fact acknowledged by the plaintiff. However, it should be noted that while the cases were distinguishable on one level, in both sets of circumstances the defendants were fully aware at

---

[15] High Court (Moriarty J) 23 June 1997.
[16] High Court (Quirke J) 19 February 2000.

the time the applications were brought of the details of the plaintiff's case, albeit for different reasons. This in turn casts doubt on the continuing validity of the rationale employed by Barr J in *Brennan* as providing a ground for refusing the application for a late lodgment.

Furthermore, as Sheridan comments,[17] the view expressed by Barr J in *Brennan* must now fall to be considered in the light of the fact that Order 39, rule 46[18] now provides for the exchange of reports prior to the hearing, giving the defendant comprehensive information about the plaintiff's case in any event. He submits that it would appear that the findings of Barr J have been overtaken by these new provisions and suggests that there is a resonance of the judgment of Ó Dálaigh CJ in *Ely v Dargan* in these new rules. Therefore the approach adopted in *Brennan* and followed in *Rhatigan v Gill* may need to be reassessed, both in view of the re-emergence of the reasoning of the Supreme Court in *Ely* and in the light of the new rules on disclosure of expert reports.

ACCEPTANCE OF LODGMENT

15.009 Where a lodgment has been made, the plaintiff may within 14 days of receipt of the notice of payment or within such further period as may be agreed between the parties, accept it by giving notice to the defendant.[19] Where the plaintiff refuses to accept the lodgment and is not awarded more than the amount paid into court, then unless the trial judge directs otherwise the following principles apply. The excess shall be repaid to the defendant and the plaintiff shall be entitled to the costs of the action up to the time when the lodgment was made and the defendant shall be entitled to the costs from this point on.[20]

It should also be noted that in a case where damages are claimed by or on behalf of an infant or a person of unsound mind, no settlement or lodgment shall be valid without the approval of the court.[21]

LODGMENT BY ONE OF SEVERAL DEFENDANTS

15.010 Order 22, rule 12 provides that a lodgment may be made by one or more of several defendants on notice to the other defendant(s). If the plaintiff chooses to accept the lodgment within the time limited he is required to give notice to each defendant and all further proceedings in the action shall be stayed

---

[17] (2001) 6 BR 389, 391.
[18] Inserted by Rules of the Superior Courts (No. 6) (Disclosure of Reports and Statements) 1998 (SI No. 391 of 1998). See further Chapter 17.
[19] Order 22, rule 4(1). See Form 6 in Appendix C.
[20] Order 22, rule 6.
[21] Order 22, rule 10(1).

and the money shall not be paid out except in pursuance of a court order dealing with the whole costs of the action. An issue as to the application of rule 12 arose in *Superwood Holdings plc v Sun Alliance and London Insurance plc*[22] which concerned an application by the plaintiff seeking to extend the time in which to accept a lodgment made by the fourth named defendant. Smyth J refused this application concluding that there was no evidence on which he could grant the relief sought and stating that he was "not in a position to deal with the whole costs of the action" within the meaning of Order 22, rule 12. However the plaintiff's application was allowed on appeal to the Supreme Court. Hamilton CJ stated that it was clear from the judgment of the learned trial judge that he considered that the provisions of Order 22, rule 12 applied to the circumstances of the application and the Chief Justice said that the respondents had relied on the provisions of rule 12 to support their submission that the monies lodged by the fourth named respondent could not be paid to the appellant unless and until the costs of the action had been dealt with by the trial judge. However, in his opinion it could only apply in the circumstances set out in the rule, namely:

1.   The money is paid into court by one or more several defendants sued jointly or in the alternative,

2.   is accepted on the basis that all further proceedings in the action or in respect of the specified cause or causes of action (as the case may be) shall be stayed, and

3.   the court is in a position to deal with the whole costs of the action, there being no question of the action continuing against the remaining defendants.

Hamilton CJ concluded that these conditions had not been satisfied in the case before him and said that while the appellant had settled its claim against the fourth named respondent, no settlement had been reached in relation to the claims of the other respondents. In his opinion the application did not fall under rule 12 or the terms of any other provision of Order 22 and he concluded that there was no rule of law, nor did the interests of justice require, that there should be any impediment to the implementation of a settlement of even a part of what he described as "these long protracted proceedings".

OFFER OF PAYMENT IN LIEU OF LODGMENT

15.011 By virtue of the Rules of the Superior Courts (No. 5) (Offer of Payment in Lieu of Lodgment) 2000,[23] a new Order 22, rule 14 was inserted to provide

---

[22] High Court (Smyth J) 15 May 1998, [1999] 4 IR 531 (SC).
[23] SI No. 328 of 2000.

for the making of an offer of tender of payment in lieu of lodging money in court. Rule 14(2) provides that where a qualified party[24] is entitled to make or increase a lodgment on his own behalf or on behalf of any other party, then he may in lieu of lodging any money in court, make an offer of tender of payment to the other party. Any tender offer of payment shall be deemed to be a lodgment and to have the same effect as a lodgment and the provisions of Order 22 shall apply *mutatis mutandis* to such tender offers as regards the time for making and accepting same.[25]

A tender offer is to be made in accordance with Form No.4A or 5A in Appendix C and shall state whether liability is admitted or denied and notice of acceptance of the tender shall be in the Form 6A in Appendix C.[26] Where a tender offer has been accepted, the party having made the offer shall pay it within four weeks of the date of receipt of notice of acceptance of it[27] and where it has not been paid within the time required, that party shall continue to be liable to pay the sum together with interest.

---

[24] Defined in rule 14(1) as a minister of government, the Attorney General, the government, the State, any party in respect of whom the State is providing an indemnity, an indemnifier of any party and authorized to carry on business in the State as an insurance undertaking pursuant to the law for the time being in force, the Motor Insurers Bureau or the Visiting Motor Insurers Bureau.

[25] Order 22, rule 14(3).

[26] Order 22, rule 14(4).

[27] Order 22, rule 14(5).

CHAPTER SIXTEEN

SUMMARY AND SPECIAL SUMMONS PROCEDURE

SUMMARY SUMMONS PROCEDURE

INTRODUCTION

16.001 Procedure by summary summons is intended for use in cases which are capable of summary disposition, without pleadings,[1] and upon affidavit without the necessity for oral evidence.[2] Its aim is, thus, to enable a plaintiff to obtain judgment against a defendant expeditiously in circumstances where the plaintiff's claim is easily quantifiable and the defendant does not have any valid defence. As Lavery J stated in *Prendergast v Biddle*:[3]

> The procedure by summary summons is provided in order to enable speedy justice to be done in particular cases where there is either no issue to be tried or the issues involved are simple and capable of being easily determined.[4]

To that end, the procedure has a number of stages each of which is designed to filter out those cases where a defendant may have a *bona fide* defence from those where judgment should be entered summarily.

The virtue of the summary summons procedure from the plaintiff's point of view, namely its expedition, is precisely its vice from the defendant's point of view in that judgment may be granted without him being afforded an adequate opportunity to contest the plaintiff's claim. For this reason, the provisions of Order 13 and Order 37 which govern the summary summons procedure have been construed quite strictly. As Lord O'Hagan C explained in *Kiely v Massey*[5] "the exercise of summary jurisdiction...ought to be strictly guarded, and...there should not be any looseness of practice in a matter in which...the court is required summarily to make final adjudication".

---

[1] Order 20, rule 1 provides that when procedure by summary or special summons is used, no statement of claim or other pleading can be delivered except by order of the Court.

[2] Order 1, rule 3.

[3] Supreme Court, 31 July 1957. See also *Criminal Assets Bureau v Kelly* [2000] 1 ILRM 271, 275.

[4] *Ibid.* at 5.

[5] (1880) 6 LR Ir 445, 447.

WHERE SUMMARY SUMMONS PROCEDURE MAY BE USED

16.002   The classes of claim which may be commenced by summary summons have already been discussed in detail in chapter 2 and it suffices to say that there are four categories of case where it can be used: (1) actions where the plaintiff seeks to recover a debt or liquidated demand in money (with or without interest) on foot of a contract, other instrument or statute; (2) ejectment actions against a tenant whose term has expired or been duly determined by a notice to quit or for non-payment of rent; (3) claims in which the plaintiff in the first instance desires to have an account taken; and (4) where all the parties consent.[6] The first category, that of claims for liquidated amounts is by far the most common class of claim commenced by summary summons and it is with the procedure adopted in respect of such claims that this chapter is concerned.

JUDGMENT IN DEFAULT OF APPEARANCE IN THE CENTRAL OFFICE

16.003   The first opportunity for a plaintiff to enter judgment will arise if the defendant or any of the defendants fails to enter an appearance within the eight days limited for doing so.[7] If this occurs, and it is not uncommon in debt collection cases, then the plaintiff will be able "to obtain a judgment in the office expeditiously and cheaply without involving himself in the substantial costs which are incidental to an action in court."[8]

Procedure for Entering Judgment

16.004   The procedure is governed by Order 13 which provides that where a summary summons is indorsed with a claim for a liquidated demand, and the defendant or all of the defendants fail to appear thereto, the plaintiff, after filing an affidavit of service of the summons or notice in lieu of the summons,[9] may enter final judgment in the Central Office.[10] That judgment will be for the sum specified in an affidavit of debt as the sum then actually due[11] (which cannot exceed the sum indorsed on the summons) together with interest (if any) to the date of the judgment and costs.[12] If there are several defendants, of whom one

---

[6]   Order 2.

[7]   Order 12, rule 2.

[8]   *Per* Shiel J in *Joseph Morton (Banbridge) Ltd v Boyle* [1959] NI 141, 143.

[9]   Order 13, rule 2. The affidavit must establish that service was properly effected and if an order for substituted service was obtained that the terms of the order were strictly complied with.

[10]   Order 13, rule 3.

[11]   This is required by Order 13, rule 18.

[12]   Order 13, rule 3. Those costs can include the taxed costs of a motion for substituted

or more appear to the summons and another or others fail to appear, the plaintiff may enter final judgment against those that have not appeared (and issue execution upon such judgment), without prejudice to his right to proceed against such of the defendants as have appeared.[13]

Claims in Foreign Currencies

16.005 It is no impediment to the entry of judgment that the sum claimed is expressed in a foreign currency. In *Damen v O'Shea*,[14] the plaintiffs applied in the Central Office for judgment against the defendant in default of appearance to a summary summons in which the claim was for a sum in Dutch guilders. The application was refused on the ground that the practice was to give judgment in Irish currency only. However, upon application being made to the High Court, McMahon J granted the application stating that "the requirements of international commerce are clearly better met by a rule which enables the court to give judgment in whatever currency the plaintiff is entitled to under the terms of the contract and there is nothing to prevent this Court from adopting the rule which permits justice to be done more effectively".[15]

Interest

16.006 Although it would appear that the Registrar of the Central Office has the power to award interest pursuant to s.22 of the Courts Act 1981[16] in an appropriate case,[17] the practice of the Registrar is not to award such interest.

---

service of the summons: *Eager v Buckley* (1881) 8 LR Ir 99. It should also be noted that in *Gilsenan v M'Govern* (1891) 30 LR Ir 300, it was held that where judgment is marked in the office for the amount claimed on a solicitor's bill of costs, there should not be any reference for taxation *i.e.* it should be treated as an ordinary action for a liquidated claim.

[13] Order 13, rule 8. See further paragraph 4.010.

[14] [1976-77] ILRM 275.

[15] *Ibid.* at 276.

[16] S.22 provides that: "Where in any proceedings a court orders the payment by any person of a sum of money (which expression includes in this section, damages) the judge concerned may, if he thinks fit, also order the payment by the person of interest at the rate *per annum* standing specified for the time being in s.26 of the Debtors (Ireland) Act 1840, on the whole or any part of the sum in respect of the whole or any part of the period between the date when the cause of action accrued and the date of judgment." This is subject to qualification in relation to compound interest, interest payable pursuant to contract, bills of exchange and personal injuries contained in subs (2) and (3).

[17] S.50(2) of the Courts and Court Officers Act 1995 provides that: "Where, in the case of a claim in the High Court for a debt or a liquidated sum, an application is made for judgment in default of appearance, the Registrar of the Central Office may exercise the discretion to award interest conferred by s.22 of the Courts Act 1981." The interaction between this section and Order 13, rule 19 which provides that a plaintiff who is entitled to enter final judgment in the Central Office may apply to the court *ex parte* for an

Therefore, if a party wishes to seek interest, it will be necessary to make an application to the court *ex parte* for an order for judgment inclusive of interest.[18] Such applications are, however, uncommon because a plaintiff is usually more concerned with obtaining judgment expeditiously rather than pursuing what may be a relatively small sum of interest.

Cases Where Judgment will not be Entered in the Central Office

16.007 Judgment cannot be entered in the office in the normal way pursuant to Order 13 in two categories of case: (i) proceedings by moneylenders; and (ii) proceedings on foot of a hire-purchase agreement. In either case, judgment cannot be entered in the Central Office without the leave of the Master or the court having first been obtained.[19] In addition, the Registrar may refuse to enter judgment if he is not satisfied that the plaintiff's papers are in order or where there is some doubt as to the amount claimed. In those circumstances, the plaintiff must apply to the Master in accordance with the procedure discussed below for liberty to enter final judgment.

JUDGMENT IN THE MASTER'S COURT

16.008 If the defendant does enter an appearance, then the plaintiff is required by Order 37, rule 1, to set the summons down before the Master by issuing a motion seeking liberty to enter final judgment for the amount claimed together with interest (if any).

Grounding Affidavit

16.009 Order 37, rule 1 requires the notice of motion to be grounded on an affidavit, served therewith,[20] and sworn either by the plaintiff or by another person who can swear positively to the facts, showing that the plaintiff is entitled to the relief claimed and stating that, in the belief of the deponent, there is no defence to the action.[21] This is a crucial proof and in *Masterson v Scallan*,[22]

---

order for judgment inclusive of interest pursuant to s.22 is unclear. *Cf. Mellowhide Products Ltd v Barry Agencies Ltd* [1983] ILRM 152.

[18] *Cf. Mellowhide Products Ltd v Barry Agencies Ltd* [1983] ILRM 152.
[19] Order 13, rules 14 & 15. See further paragraphs 4.013-4.014.
[20] But note that in *Masterson v Scallan* [1927] IR 453, 461, it was held by Kennedy CJ that the requirement to serve the grounding affidavit with the summons was purely directory and did not go to jurisdiction except that such affidavit must be on the record of the court before summary judgment can be granted. Therefore, an omission to serve it at the time provided for in the Rules can be relieved against on terms.
[21] Order 37, rule 1. It is essential that the affidavit (and any supplemental affidavit) is filed as otherwise it is not on the record and cannot ground an order granting liberty to enter final judgment: *Masterson v Scallan* [1927] IR 453.

FitzGibbon J emphasised that "no party ought to get summary judgment until there is before the court an affidavit completely verifying the cause of action and the amount of the debt claimed".[23]

Entitlement to Relief

16.010 The affidavit[24] is required to show that the plaintiff is entitled to the relief claimed by satisfying the court "that on the facts stated in the affidavit [the plaintiff] is entitled in law to judgment for his cause of action".[25] In many cases, this is done simply by verifying the particulars set out in the special indorsement of claim in the summons and, provided that those particulars establish a good cause of action,[26] this will suffice.[27] However, it is important that the deponent actually "unequivocally depose to the necessary facts" as opposed to simply repeating the wording used in the summons.[28]

No Defence to the Action

16.011 In addition to establishing that the plaintiff is entitled to the relief claimed, the deponent is also required to state his belief that there is no defence to the action and failure to do so will result in the application for liberty to enter final judgment being refused.[29] A statement that the plaintiff was "advised and believed that the defendant had no defence on the merits to the action" will suffice in this regard.[30] Although not required by the Rules, it is also common to aver that the appearance has been entered solely for the purposes of delay.

---

[22] [1927] IR 453.

[23] *Ibid.* at 461.

[24] Verification of the action must be contained in the affidavit.

[25] *Caulfied v Bolger* [1927] IR 117, 126 *per* Hanna J.

[26] See *Bond v Holton* [1959] IR 302 where the special indorsement of claim was defective in failing to establish a cause of action and an affidavit which merely repeated the wording of the summons was, therefore, held to be insufficient.

[27] *Murphy v Nolan* (1886) 18 LR Ir 468. However, FitzGibbon LJ (at 471) stated that the court's conclusion in that case was "not to be taken as implying any approval of the looseness with which the plaintiff's case had been brought forward".

[28] *O'Gorman v Long* (1958) 93 ILTR 3, 4. It follows that it is not sufficient to merely refer to the summons without deposing to the particulars contained therein: *M'Conville v Nolan* (1883) 17 ILTR 24. Cf. *Hayward Brothers and Eckstein Ltd v Callen* (1901) 36 ILTR 56 which concerned an application for judgment in respect of goods sold and delivered. There, an affidavit which stated that the goods were "sold" but did not say they were "delivered" was held to constitute sufficient verification of the cause of action.

[29] *Kiely v Massey* (1880) 6 LR Ir 445; *Lord Bellew v Markey* (1878) 12 ILTR 52.

[30] *Manning v Moriarty* (1883) 12 LR Ir 372. Although note that in *Henzell v Martin* (1881) 15 ILTR 233 an averment that "the defendant had no legal defence on the merits" was held to be defective and the motion was refused.

Deponent

16.012 The affidavit will usually be sworn by the plaintiff because he is generally the person with the best means of knowledge but, as rule 1 makes clear, it
can be sworn by any person who is in a position to swear positively to the facts.
So, in *Roche v Sullivan*,[31] where a defendant made admissions of liability to the
plaintiff's solicitor and there was plainly no defence to the action, the solicitor's
affidavit verifying those admissions and deposing that in his belief the defendant had no defence sufficed. However, in *Imperial Tobacco Co. Ltd v
McAllister*,[32] the affidavit was held to be defective in circumstances where it
was sworn by a bookkeeper in the employment of the plaintiff company who did
not show or allege that the facts deposed to were within his own knowledge and
who did not allege that he had the authority of the plaintiff to make the affidavit.

Defects in the Affidavit

16.013 As noted at the outset, the courts take a strict approach to compliance
with the summary summons procedure[33] and thus, even where the foregoing
requirements are complied with, any other irregularity in the affidavit may lead
to the application being refused. So, for example, in *M'Alpine v Craig*[34] the
court refused to grant final judgment where the copy of the affidavit served did
not contain a jurat or the defendant's signature. A similar conclusion was reached
in *Best v Woods*[35] where the copy of the affidavit omitted the signature of the
deponent and the name of the place where the affidavit was sworn. It should be
noted in this regard that, if the grounding affidavit is insufficient or irregular in
some respect, then the Master may give the plaintiff an opportunity to mend his
hand by giving him liberty to file a supplemental affidavit which remedies the
lacuna or defect in the original.[36]

Hearing of the Motion

16.014 The motion will be returned for a date fixed by the Master which must
be not less than four clear days from the service thereof.[37] What occurs at the

---

[31] (1878) 12 ILTR 93.
[32] (1916) 50 ILTR 156. See also *Lagos v Grunwaldt* [1910] 1 KB 41 in which the deponent swore the affidavit on information and belief, the information having been obtained principally from correspondence with the plaintiff. The Court of Appeal held
that the affidavit was defective and that the court had no jurisdiction to make any order.
[33] *Per* Lord O'Hagan C in *Kiely v Massey* (1880) 6 LR Ir 445, 447.
[34] (1881) 15 ILTR 51.
[35] (1904) 39 ILTR 44.
[36] See *Caulfield v Bolger* [1927] IR 117, 127. See also *Masterson v Scallan* [1927] IR
453.
[37] Order 37, rule 1.

hearing of the motion will depend on whether the case is contested or uncontested.

(i) Uncontested Cases

16.015 In uncontested cases, the Master is empowered to deal with the matter summarily and to make such order for the determination of the action as may seem just.[38] He may, thus, give liberty to enter judgment for the relief to which the plaintiff may appear to be entitled or, alternatively, he may dismiss the action.[39] Before granting liberty to enter judgment, the Master will examine the plaintiff's papers carefully to ensure that they are in order.[40] If the Master has any difficulty or doubt about the case, he can transfer it to the Judges' List in the High Court for hearing notwithstanding that he would have jurisdiction to deal with it.[41]

16.016 If the Master does decide to grant liberty to enter judgment, that judgment may include an award of interest on the whole or part of the sum claimed in respect of the period between the date when the cause of action accrued and the date of the judgment pursuant to s.22 of the Courts Act 1981.[42] In *Mellowhide Products Ltd v Barry Agencies Ltd*,[43] Finlay P considered the wording of s.22 and held that it could not be construed as giving the Master jurisdiction to make an order under the section. He went on to say that he reached this conclusion with reluctance because it created an anomaly:

> If in order to recover interest before judgment a creditor suing in default of appearance or in default of a defence has to seek to have the matter put in the judge's list then such creditor will be put to additional cost and expense and if the amount is recoverable in full the debtor will be put to additional cost and expense even if he does not appear or defend.[44]

Finlay P took the view that there was no logical reason why the Master should not exercise the discretion contained in s.22 and s.50(1) of the Courts and Courts Officers Act 1995 now provides that in the case of a claim in the High Court for

---

[38] Order 37, rule 4. The Master must, however, act within jurisdiction because the power to deal with the matter summarily relates to procedure and not to jurisdiction: *Roe v McMullan* [1927] IR 9.

[39] Order 37, rule 4.

[40] Order 37, rule 2 provides that the Master can hear oral evidence but this is very rare.

[41] Order 37, rule 12.

[42] Interest under s.22 can be awarded even though it is not claimed in the summons though the inclusion of a claim for such interest in the summons is the wiser course of action: *Mellowhide Products Ltd v Barry Agencies Ltd* [1983] ILRM 152.

[43] [1983] ILRM 152.

[44] *Ibid.* at 155.

a debt or liquidated sum, the Master may exercise the discretion to award interest conferred on a judge by s.22 in the case of applications for judgment in default of defence.[45]

(ii) Contested Cases

16.017 If the case is contested, the defendant will usually appear on the return date and seek an adjournment to enable him to file a replying affidavit setting out his full or partial defence to the claim.[46] This may well precipitate a further affidavit from the plaintiff and a reply thereto and it is only when the exchange of affidavits is completed that the matter will be ready for hearing.

It is clear from the judgment of O'Byrne J in *Grace v Molloy*[47] that the Master has no jurisdiction to make an order giving liberty to enter final judgment where a claim is contested. Therefore, when he is satisfied that the papers are in order and the case is ready for hearing, he must transfer it to the Judge's List for hearing at the first opportunity.[48] For this purpose, he may extend the time for filing affidavits and may give such directions as he thinks fit.[49] Alternatively, where the parties consent, he may adjourn the case to plenary hearing and make such directions as to pleadings, discovery or settlement of issues as may be appropriate.[50]

JUDGMENT IN COURT

16.018 The motion for liberty to enter judgment is heard on affidavit unless the court otherwise orders[51] and it is rare for the motion to be heard on oral evidence because if that course is appropriate, the case is one which should be adjourned to plenary hearing. However, that is not to say that oral evidence may not be heard and issues of fact resolved in appropriate circumstances. In *Criminal Assets Bureau v Kelly*,[52] O'Higgins J rejected the submission of counsel for the defendant that the very presence of a factual dispute precludes summary

---

[45] That section overtakes the provisions of Order 37, rule 5 which provides that, if the plaintiff claims interest under s.22, the Master must transfer the application to the Judges' List for hearing.
[46] Order 37, rule 3 provides that the defendant may show cause against a motion for liberty to enter final judgment by affidavit and such affidavit shall state whether the defence alleged goes to the whole or to part only, and if so to what part, of the plaintiff's claim. Rule 3 further provides that a defendant may show cause by offering to bring into court the sum indorsed on the summons.
[47] [1927] IR 405.
[48] Order 37, rule 6.
[49] Order 37, rule 6.
[50] Order 37, rule 6.
[51] Order 37, rule 2.
[52] [2000] 1 ILRM 271.

disposal of a matter. The learned judge said that the provision for notice to cross-examine[53] indicates that a court may resolve issues of fact in summary proceedings. In addition, the court may order the defendant, or in the case of a corporation, any officer thereof, to attend and be examined on oath, or to produce any documents or copies or extracts from any of them.[54]

Order 37, rule 7 provides that, upon the hearing of the motion, the court may make such order for determination of the question in issue in the action as may seem just. It may, thus: (i) dismiss the action; (ii) grant judgment to the plaintiff for such relief as to which he appears to be entitled;[55] or (iii) grant leave to defend with or without an order adjourning the proceedings to plenary hearing.

Dismissal of the Action

16.019 The plaintiff's claim may be dismissed where the court is satisfied that it discloses no cause of action or the plaintiff is otherwise not entitled to relief. In *Bond v Holton*,[56] the plaintiff claimed a sum allegedly due under a conacre agreement and, in his affidavit grounding the motion for summary judgment, he merely repeated the wording in the summons. It was held by the Supreme Court that the summons failed to disclose a cause of action because no contract, express or implied, was pleaded in the special indorsement of claim. Further, any cause of action which could possibly be spelled out of the pleading was not supported by evidence in the affidavit. The court, therefore, refused the application for summary judgment and dismissed the action.

Grant of Judgment

16.020 The motion for liberty to enter judgment is in the nature of an interlocutory motion[57] and it has been emphasised that summary judgment should only be granted in clear cases and not "where any serious conflict as to matter of fact or any real difficulty as to matter of law arises".[58] In *Bank of Ireland v Educational Building Society*,[59] Murphy J referred to the detailed written submissions made by both parties, the arguments of counsel and the analysis of those

---

[53] Order 37, rule 2 provides that any party desiring to cross-examine a deponent who has sworn an affidavit on behalf of his opponent may serve upon that party a notice in writing requiring the production of the deponent for cross-examination and, unless such deponent is produced accordingly, his affidavit cannot be used as evidence unless by special leave of the court.

[54] Order 37, rule 3.

[55] Note that the court *gives* judgment whereas the Master is only entitled to give *liberty* to enter judgment which is then entered in the Central Office.

[56] [1959] IR 302.

[57] *Crawford v Gillmor* (1891) 30 LR Ir 238, 243.

[58] *Per* Sir Peter O'Brien CJ in *Crawford v Gillmor* (1891) 30 LR Ir 238, 245. See also *Goodchild v Duncan* [1895] 2 IR 393 and *Dolan v Henry* (1905) 39 ILTR 70.

[59] [1999] 1 IR 220, 231, [1998] 2 ILRM 451, 461.

arguments which was required and endorsed the comments of Barry LJ in *Crawford v Gillmor*,[60] that:

> [T]he mere length of time which has been occupied by the argument of this case – and I do not think one moment of our time was occupied unnecessarily – shows that it does not come within the rule which allows final judgment to be marked on motion.[61]

The complexity of a case may therefore, of itself, be a reason for refusal to deal with it in a summary manner.

Tests for Granting Judgment/Leave to Defend

16.021 The tests for deciding whether liberty to enter judgment or leave to defend should be granted are essentially the same because if judgment is not granted upon the motion, leave to defend is impliedly given to the defendant.[62]

The leading case is *First Commercial Bank plc v Anglin*.[63] The plaintiff issued a summary summons seeking judgment on foot of a personal guarantee allegedly given by the defendant and the Master directed that the case should be placed in the Judge's List. Costello J refused to give the defendant leave to defend the action on the basis that there was no credible evidence of a real *bona fide* defence to the plaintiff's claim and granted summary judgment to the plaintiff. On appeal by the defendant, the Supreme Court, in a judgment delivered by Murphy J, held that for the court to grant summary judgment and refuse leave to defend it is not sufficient that the court should have reason to doubt the *bona fides* of the defendant or to doubt whether the defendant has a genuine defence.

Murphy J adopted the test laid down in *Banque de Paris v de Naray*[64] and reaffirmed in *National Westminster Bank plc v Daniel*,[65] namely that, in deciding whether to grant summary judgment to a plaintiff and to refuse leave to defend, the court has to look at the whole situation to see whether the defendant has satisfied the court that there is a fair and reasonable probability of the defendant having a real or *bona fide* defence or whether what the defendant had said in his defence was credible. In this regard, the mere assertion in an affidavit of a given situation which was to form the basis of the defence did not, of itself, constitute a ground for granting leave to defend. Murphy J concluded, in dismissing the defendant's appeal, that there was no credible evidence for the defence which he sought to assert and that he had failed to establish either on the law or on the facts, a probable defence to the plaintiff's claim.

---

[60] (1891) 30 LR Ir 238.
[61] *Ibid.* at 245.
[62] *Rae v Langford* (1881) 15 ILTR 105; *Ogilby v O'Donnell* (1882) 16 ILTR 53.
[63] [1996] 1 IR 75.
[64] [1984] 1 Lloyd's Rep 21.
[65] [1993] 1 WLR 1453, [1994] 1 All ER 156.

16.022 These principles have been applied in a number of recent decisions[66] including *ACC Bank plc v Malocco*[67] which concerned an action to recover a debt secured by a mortgage. Laffoy J reiterated that in deciding whether to grant summary judgment, the court should look at the whole situation, including the cogency of the evidence adduced by the parties, to see whether there was a fair or reasonable probability of a real or *bona fide* defence.[68] She concluded that in the case before her, this probability could not be excluded and she refused to grant summary judgment and made an order adjourning the case for plenary hearing.

Judgment for Part of Claim

16.023 There are a number of circumstances where judgment may be entered in favour of a plaintiff for part of the amount claimed. The most common situation is where the defence put forward by the defendant applies to part only of the plaintiff's claim or where he admits part of the plaintiff's claim. If this is the case, then the court will give the plaintiff judgment forthwith for the undefended portion of the claim, subject to such terms as to suspending execution as the court may order[69] and the defendant will be permitted to defend the balance of the plaintiff's claim provided that he satisfies the court that he may have a *bona fide* defence.[70] So, in *Quinn v Donoghue*[71] a writ was endorsed for a liquidated sum which the defendant in part admitted and in part disputed. The High Court gave judgment for the sum admitted to be due and made it clear that the amount claimed in the writ should be amended accordingly. In addition, it would appear from the judgment of Palles CB in *Scott v M'Mullen*[72] that a plaintiff may obtain judgment for a sum less than that claimed where the defendant has paid

---

[66] See *Tedcastle McCormack & Co. Ltd v McCrystal* High Court (Morris P) 15 March 1999 (summary judgment refused and matter adjourned to plenary hearing) and *Criminal Assets Bureau v Hutch* High Court (Morris P) 14 May 1999 (summary judgment granted because the defendant had not established that he had any real or *bona fide* defence to be tried by the court); *ACC Bank plc v Malocco* [2000] 3 IR 191; *Criminal Assets Bureau v Kelly* [2000] 1 ILRM 271 (matter remitted for plenary hearing where defendant had raised factual and legal issue); *Aer Rianta Cpt v Ryanair Ltd* High Court (Kelly J) 5 December 2000 (summary judgment granted because defendant had failed to establish by credible evidence that there was a fair or reasonable possibility of it having a real or *bona fide* defence).

[67] [2000] 3 IR 191.

[68] See also *Aer Rianta Cpt v Ryanair Ltd* High Court (Kelly J) 5 December 2000 at 14, where Kelly J stated that "a mere assertion in an affidavit of a given situation which is said to be the basis of a defence does not of itself constitute a ground for granting leave to defend".

[69] See further *Newton v Byrne* (1887) 21 ILTR 82.

[70] Order 37, rule 8.

[71] (1892) 26 ILTR 10.

[72] (1880) 14 ILTR 26.

part of the debt since the proceedings were instituted on the basis that such a case comes within the spirit of the summary summons procedure.[73]

Terms on Which Leave may be Granted

16.024 Order 37, rule 10 provides that leave to defend may be given unconditionally or subject to such terms as to give security, or time and mode of trial, or otherwise as the court may think fit. So, in *Sketchley v Corrigan*[74] the defendant was given leave to defend on condition that he lodged a sum of money into court. This practice was, however, disapproved by the Supreme Court in *Calor Teoranta v Colgan*.[75] It was held that, in circumstances where a defendant has been given leave to defend, it could not be a condition precedent to the exercise of that right that he lodge a sum of money in court because this would obstruct his constitutional right of access to the courts.[76] However, terms may be imposed where there has been default on the part of the defendant. In *Decospan NV v Benhouse Ltd*,[77] the Master had ordered the defence and counterclaim of the defendants in proceedings commenced by summary summons to be struck out for failure to make discovery. Subsequently, Morris J reinstated the defence and counterclaim on terms that the sum of £30,000 should be lodged in court as an earnest of *bona fides* or security in respect of the matter. The defendants' appeal against this order was dismissed by the Supreme Court. O'Flaherty J referred to the provisions of rule 10 and said that it seemed to him that the High Court was giving the defendants a further opportunity to defend the matter and clearly had jurisdiction to impose a condition such as to require the lodgment of a sum of money.

Delivery of Defence

16.025 Where a defendant has been granted leave to defend, he must deliver his defence within such time as is limited in the order granting leave or, if no time is thereby limited, within fourteen days from the order.[78] If the defendant

---

[73] See also *Rye v Hawkes* (1885) 16 LR Ir 12 where the court held that a plaintiff was entitled to judgment in respect of part of a claim initially made where the balance had been included by mistake.

[74] (1878) 12 ILTR 50.

[75] Supreme Court, 22 June 1990. For a detailed analysis of this decision, see Doyle, "Summary Procedure: Leave to Defend and Lodgments" (1990) 8 ILT 255.

[76] See also *Laundry and Clothing Engineers Ltd v Keatings* (1953) 87 ILTR 113 where the Supreme Court held that where a matter commenced by summary summons is sent for plenary hearing, the court has no power to order the defendant to pay a sum of money to the plaintiff in part discharge of the plaintiff's claim before the plenary hearing.

[77] [1995] 2 ILRM 620.

[78] Order 21, rule 2.

thereupon fails to deliver a defence, the plaintiff can proceed to apply for judgment in default of defence even though he has not delivered a statement of claim.[79]

Adjournment to Plenary Hearing

16.026 Once a defendant has established to the satisfaction of the court that he should be granted leave to defend, it will generally follow, as a matter of course, that the matter will be adjourned to plenary hearing. However, the questions of whether leave to defend should be given and whether the proceedings should be adjourned to plenary hearing are distinct and, thus, if there is no dispute as to the facts and/or the court is satisfied that it may hear the matter on the basis of affidavit evidence, it may direct trial on affidavit.

Plenary trial will be appropriate where serious issues of fact arise between the parties that can best be resolved by oral evidence. This may be the case where the defendant alleges certain facts in affidavits filed on his behalf which, if proved, would provide him with a defence to the claim and the plaintiff disputes the existence of those facts.[80] Thus, in *Irish Dunlop Co. Ltd v Ralph*[81] where the defendant had disclosed facts which might constitute a *prima facie* defence to the plaintiff's claim, the Supreme Court held that the matter should go forward for plenary hearing.[82] A similar conclusion was reached by Costello J in *Munster Base Metals Ltd v Bula Ltd*[83] where the proceedings revolved around the issue of whether the defendant had breached a warranty that it had disclosed all material matters. In deciding whether to grant summary judgment, the learned judge asked:

> Can I determine the issue that thus arises between the parties on this motion? Can I decide that the plaintiffs' legal rights are so clear that the defence raised by Bula Limited is not a *bona fide* one? I do not think so. This does not seem to me to be an issue which can be determined without the benefit of an oral hearing of expert testimony on the matter.[84]

---

[79] *Rae v Langford* (1881) 15 ILTR 105.

[80] It is not necessary that the defendant have personal knowledge of the facts alleged in his affidavit in order to have a case sent for plenary hearing, statements as to his belief with the grounds thereof may be sufficient to entitle him to such an order: *William P. Lucas Ltd v Sunvalley Preserves Ltd* (1955) 95 ILTR 8.

[81] (1958) 95 ILTR 70.

[82] See also *MacNiece v Madden* (1949) 84 ILTR 34. *Cf. Munster & Leinster Bank Ltd v Coffey* (1940) 74 ILTR 84 where it was held that the defendant's affidavit had not disclosed any facts which might give rise to a defence and, therefore, the case should not have been sent for plenary hearing.

[83] High Court (Costello J) 29 July 1983.

[84] *Ibid.* at 5.

He thus concluded that the case was not appropriate for determination in a summary manner and he adjourned it to plenary hearing with oral evidence.

16.027 In addition, as is clear from the decision of the Supreme Court in *Bank of Ireland v Educational Building Society*,[85] a plenary trial may be appropriate even where the defence of the defendant is based on legal grounds. In that case, the plaintiff sought summary judgment against the defendant and the Master put the matter into the Judges' List. Morris J ordered that the case be sent for plenary hearing on the basis that there was a fair and reasonable probability of the defendant having a real and *bona fide* defence to the proceedings and the plaintiff appealed on the grounds that the affidavits filed by the defendant did not disclose any issue of fact which justified the case being remitted for plenary hearing.

In the Supreme Court, Murphy J took the view that it could hardly be disputed that there was a fair and reasonable probability of the defendant having a real and *bona fide* defence to the proceedings. The issue, therefore, was the appropriateness of sending the matter for plenary hearing. He believed that the defendant had identified issues of fact which needed to be explored and clarified before the issues of law could be properly dealt with. He added that even if the position were otherwise, once the trial judge had been satisfied that the defendant had a real and *bona fide* defence, whether based on fact or law, he was bound to afford it an opportunity of having the issue tried in the appropriate manner. Murphy J therefore concluded that the sending of the motion for trial by plenary hearing represented a proper exercise by Morris J of his discretion to select the mode of trial.

Barron J pointed out that liberty to defend is usually sought on the ground that there is an issue of fact to be determined and when the issue is solely one of law, the court can determine that issue and give final judgment. However, he added that where, as in the instant case, the court would be in a better position to determine the issue of law after a closer examination of the facts, then the defendant should be given liberty to defend. He concluded as follows:

> The issues of law require to be determined in the light of facts which will ultimately be found following a full oral hearing. Since it cannot be said that whatever picture develops, the plaintiff must succeed, it is clear that the defendant should be given liberty to defend.[86]

Delivery of Pleadings

16.028 Order 20, rule 1 stipulates that where the summary summons procedure is adopted, no statement of claim or other pleading can be delivered except

[85] [1999] 1 IR 220, [1998] 2 ILRM 451.
[86] *Ibid.* at 233, 463.

by order of the court.[87] Therefore, if the court decides to adjourn the case for plenary hearing, it must further decide what directions as to pleadings are required in order the settle the issues between the parties.[88] Although the exchange of a statement of claim and defence or points of claim and defence will generally be ordered, it may be unnecessary where the affidavits filed by the parties identify the issues between them with sufficient particularity.[89] The court may also make an order for discovery and any other ancillary orders it deems appropriate.[90] Thereafter, the action will be treated as if it had been commenced by way of plenary summons.[91]

Counterclaim and Set-off

16.029 The difficulties which arise where a defendant raises a counterclaim or set-off in defence to a motion for summary judgment were considered by the Supreme Court in *Prendergast v Biddle*.[92] The plaintiff sought leave to enter summary judgment for a liquidated sum but the defendant filed a defence in which she sought to set up a counterclaim for a greater sum. Kingsmill Moore J acknowledged that where a defendant admits a claim but raises a counterclaim, it is difficult to reconcile the competing interests of the parties and do justice between them:

> On the one hand it may be asked, why a plaintiff with a proved and perhaps uncontested claim should wait for judgment or execution of judgment on his claim because the defendant asserts a plausible but unproved and contested counterclaim. On the other hand it may equally be asked why a defendant should be required to pay the plaintiff's demand when he asserts and may be able to prove that the plaintiff owes him a larger amount.[93]

---

[87] It is immaterial that the defendant, by his appearance, required a statement of claim to be delivered: *Salters Co. v McCleary* (1891) 28 LR Ir 283. See also *Forrester v Exham* (1898) 32 ILTR 141.

[88] Order 37, rule 7.

[89] See, for example, *Church & General Insurance plc v Moore* [1996] 1 ILRM 202, where the requirement for a statement of claim was dispensed with.

[90] Order 37, rule 7.

[91] Order 37, rule 7. It should be noted that the power to adjourn the proceedings to plenary hearing and treat the action as if it had been commenced by plenary summons can only be exercised if the proceedings are properly before the court and cannot be used to treat as a plenary summons, a summary summons which has been used to commence proceedings in contravention of the Rules: *Meares v Connolly* [1930] IR 333.

[92] Supreme Court, 31 July 1957. See Doyle, "Set-Off and Counterclaim – Deciphering the Irish Rules" (1989) GILSI 367 for a detailed analysis of this decision which casts doubt on whether the judgment of Kingsmill Moore J represents the majority view in the case.

[93] *Ibid.* at 7.

He thus concluded that there could be no hard and fast answer as to whether the court should enter judgment and suggested a number of relevant factors which should be considered by the court:

> It seems to me that a judge in exercising his discretion may take into account the apparent strength of the counterclaim and the answer suggested to it, the conduct of the parties and the promptitude with which they have asserted their claims, the nature of their claims and also the financial position of the parties. If, for instance, the defendant could show that the plaintiff was in embarrassed circumstances it might be considered a reason why the plaintiff should not be allowed to get judgment or execute judgment, on his claim till after the counterclaim had been heard, for the plaintiff having received payment might use the money to pay his debts or otherwise dissipate it so that judgment on the counterclaim would be fruitless. I mention only some of the facts which a judge before whom the application comes may have to take into consideration in the exercise of his discretion.[94]

16.030 These criteria were subsequently applied by Barrington J in *Agra Trading Ltd v Minister for Agriculture*.[95] The plaintiff sought to enter final judgment against the defendant for a large sum in respect of export refunds allegedly due by the defendant in respect of the export by the plaintiff of beef to Russia. A counterclaim was made by the defendant on the basis of non-compliance with the relevant Regulations. The plaintiff, relying on Order 19, rule 2, argued that the defendant should not be allowed to plead his claim in the proceedings by way of counterclaim but, rather, should be left to bring his claim in independent proceedings. Barrington J weighed up the plaintiff's claim which he regarded as proved and the defendant's claim which he characterised as 'problematical' and one which, even if proved, did not appear to involve any loss quantifiable in money. He pointed out that there would be considerable delay if the defendant's counterclaim, which involved a reference to the European Court of Justice, was to be litigated and that there had been no suggestion that the plaintiff company was not solvent or that it would not be able to pay any sum of money which might, at the end of the day, be found to be due from it to the minister. In the circumstances, he concluded that it would be "wrong" to deprive the plaintiff, which was a trading company, of such a large sum of money while the counterclaim was being litigated and he granted the plaintiff leave to enter final judgment.[96]

---

[94] *Ibid.* at 8.
[95] High Court (Barrington J) 19 May 1983.
[96] See also *Hibernia Meats Ltd v Minister for Agriculture* High Court (Barron J) 29 July 1983 where the decision of Barrington J in *Agra Trading* was applied by Barron J on similar facts.

16.031 A similar approach was taken by Geoghegan J in *Soanes v Leisure Corporation International Ltd.*[97] The plaintiff brought an application for leave to enter judgment against the defendant for a liquidated sum on foot of an employment agreement between the parties and the defendant sought to have the action adjourned for plenary hearing on the basis that it had a valid counterclaim for rescission of the agreement or alternatively that it had a counterclaim for damages. Geoghegan J was satisfied that the defendant had no valid counterclaim for rescission and that although there might conceivably be a counterclaim for damages, this was highly unlikely. He, therefore, decided not to adjourn the matter for plenary hearing to enable the defendant to pursue a counterclaim explaining that:

> In exercising my discretion I have balanced against the slim chance of the defendants succeeding in a claim for damages the obvious hardship which would be caused to the plaintiff by being delayed in the payment of monies due to him in consideration of terminating a valuable employment agreement.[98]

In those circumstances, he concluded that justice required that he give leave to the plaintiff to enter judgment.

Miscellaneous

Amending the Indorsement of Claim

16.032 Order 37, rule 11 provides that if, on the hearing of any motion under the order, it appears that any claim which could not have been specially indorsed under Order 2 has been included in the indorsement on the summons, the Master or the court may forthwith amend the indorsement by striking out such claim, or may deal with the claim specially indorsed as if no other claim had been included in the indorsement, and allow the action to proceed in relation to the balance of the claim.[99] So, in *Stokes v Kerwick*,[100] a claim for interest which fell outside the then equivalent to Order 2 was disallowed because there was no agreement to pay it but the court struck out the claim for interest and gave final judgment for the amount claimed. Furthermore, it has been held that where there are two or more distinct claims indorsed on the summons, judgment

---

[97] High Court (Geoghegan J) 18 December 1992.
[98] *Ibid.* at 6.
[99] This rule was included in Order 37 to overcome the difficulty identified by Dixon J in *Starkey v Purfield* [1946] IR 358 (on the authority of *Caulfied v Bolger* [1927] IR 117 and *Seales v McSweeney* [1944] IR 25) that the master did not have the power to order the amendment of a summons except in conjunction with adjourning it for plenary hearing.
[100] (1921) 56 ILTR 24.

may be granted in respect of any one of them if the requirements for leave to enter judgment are met.[101]

More than one defendant

16.033 Order 37, rule 9 provides that if it appears to the court that any defendant has a good defence or ought to be permitted to defend an action and that another defendant does not and should not be permitted to defend, the former may be permitted to defend and the plaintiff shall be entitled to enter final judgment against the latter. The plaintiff may issue execution against the latter defendant without prejudice to his right to proceed with his action against the former defendant.

SPECIAL SUMMONS PROCEDURE

INTRODUCTION

16.034 As outlined in chapter 2, a special summons is intended for use in proceedings which are capable of summary disposition without pleadings on affidavit without the need for oral evidence.[102] A consideration of the miscellany of claims that may be brought by special summons[103] indicates that their suitability for summary disposition arises from the common factor that they raise issues of law with, at most, discrete issues of fact. The special summons procedure bears a strong resemblance to that employed in respect of summary summonses and will, therefore, be considered here in outline only.

ISSUE AND SERVICE OF THE SUMMONS

16.035 At the time of issue, the summons will be given a return date which must be not less than seven days from the date of issue except in cases where the parties consent to an earlier date or where no service is required (as in the case of certain probate matters).[104] Where service is necessary, it must be effected on the parties concerned at least four days before the return date[105] and if this is not done, it will be necessary to apply to the Master for a new return date.

---

[101] *M'Allister v Allen* (1878) 12 ILTR 49. However, note that the decision in *M'Allister* was distinguished in *Borland v Curry* (1878) 12 ILTR 149 on the grounds that there were separate endorsements in the former case.
[102] Order 1, rule 4.
[103] See paragraph 2.018.
[104] Order 38, rule 1.
[105] Order 38, rule 1.

After the summons has been issued, an affidavit verifying the issue and indorsement of claim on the summons must be sworn and filed[106] and notice of the filing given to the parties concerned. Although this is not required, it is common for the summons and the affidavit to be served together.

PROCEDURE BEFORE THE MASTER

16.036 The procedure adopted before the Master will depend on whether the Master has jurisdiction to determine the matter.[107] If the Master has jurisdiction, then he has the same powers to hear and determine the matter as the court.[108] Alternatively, he can put the matter into the Judges' List for hearing.[109]

If the Master does not have jurisdiction to deal with the matter or if he decides not to deal with it, his function will be essentially administrative in nature *i.e.* to ensure that the matter is ready for hearing before transferring it to the Judges' List.[110] If the defendant fails to appear and the matter is uncontested, the Master will have to be satisfied as to service before sending the matter forward.[111] If the defendant does enter an appearance,[112] then the Master will grant him an opportunity to file such replying affidavits as he may wish.

When the exchange of affidavits between the parties is complete, the Master will transfer the matter, on the application of the plaintiff, if he is satisfied that the papers are in order *i.e.* if the plaintiff has in court: (i) the original special summons and a certified copy of the verifying affidavit (sworn after the issue of the summons) with the original exhibits; (ii) the appearance filed by the defendant or, if no appearance has been filed, satisfactory proof of service; (iii) certified copies of any other affidavits filed in the matter.

---

[106] Order 38, rule 1.

[107] See the interaction of Order 2 and Order 63.

[108] Order 38, rules 4, 5, 7, 9.

[109] Order 38, rule 5.

[110] Order 38, rule 6 provides that, in all cases in which the Master does not have jurisdiction, and in all other such cases which he shall decide to put in the Judges' List for hearing, the Master must transfer the summons, when in order for hearing, at the first opportunity. Rule 7 further provides that, for the purposes of rule 6, the Master may extend the time for filing affidavits and give such directions and adjourn the case before himself as he thinks fit.

[111] Note that, if the defendant fails to appear, the court will have to be satisfied that the proceedings were properly served and that it has jurisdiction before making the reliefs sought: *R. v R.* [1984] IR 296.

[112] Order 12, rule 2(2) provides that a defendant to proceedings commenced by special summons may enter an appearance thereto at any time, but shall not, without the leave of the court, be entitled to be heard in such proceedings unless he has entered an appearance.

PROCEDURE BEFORE THE COURT

Hearing of the Summons

16.037 As noted above, special summonses usually raise issues of law rather than issues of fact and, therefore, unless the court otherwise orders, the hearing of the proceedings will take place on affidavit[113] subject to the entitlement of a party to serve a notice to cross-examine.[114] In addition, Order 38, rule 8 allows for the determination of discrete issues of fact in order to obviate the expense of a plenary trial.[115] It provides that, if the determination of questions of fact is necessary for the proper decision or ruling as to the relief to be granted in such proceedings or as to any matter arising therein, the court may determine such questions either by directing the trial of issues in regard thereto or in such other manner (whether summary or otherwise) as may seem convenient for doing justice between the parties. Evidence as to the said questions of fact may be given either orally or by affidavit or partly orally and partly by affidavit as the court may in the circumstances think proper.[116]

Determination of the Court

16.038 On the hearing of the special summons, the court is given a broad discretion and may make such order for determination of the questions in issue as may be just.[117] In that regard, the court has three options open to it: (i) it may give the plaintiff judgment for such relief as he may appear to be entitled; (ii) it may dismiss the action; or (iii) it may adjourn the proceedings for plenary hearing with such directions as to pleadings, discovery etc. as may be appropriate.[118]

---

[113] Order 38, rule 3.

[114] Order 38, rule 3 provides that "any party desiring to cross-examine a deponent who has made an affidavit filed on behalf of the opposite party may serve upon the party by whom such affidavit has been filed a notice in writing requiring the production of the deponent for cross-examination, and unless such deponent is produced accordingly, his affidavit shall not be used as evidence unless by the special leave of the court".

[115] *Cf. Meegan v Harvey* (1939) 73 ILTR 167, 171

[116] Order 38, rule 8.

[117] Order 38, rule 8.

[118] Order 38, rule 8. The provisions of Order 20, rule 1 should be noted. It provides that, when the procedure is by special summons, no statement of claim or other pleading can be delivered except by order of the court, which order may be made in any case in which the delivery of such statement of claim or other pleading appears to be requisite. Such an order is necessary even where the defendant has, by his appearance, required such a pleading: *Salters Co. v McCleary* (1891) 28 LR Ir 283; *Forrester v Exham* (1898) 32 ILTR 141.

Adjournment to Plenary Hearing

16.039 The provision for adjournment to plenary hearing is in virtually identical terms to that contained in Order 37, rule 7 in relation to summary summons and the principles discussed in relation thereto are equally applicable.[119] The question, therefore, is whether issues of fact arise, the resolution of which are necessary for the determination of the proceedings, and which can only or best be resolved by plenary hearing. In addition, adjournment to plenary hearing may be ordered where the complexity of the issues raised is such that the action cannot be disposed of in a summary manner and plenary trial preceded by an exchange of pleadings is the more appropriate mode of trial.[120]

One case where the question of adjournment to plenary hearing was considered is *National Irish Bank Ltd v Graham*.[121] The plaintiff sought an order of possession under a mortgage agreement which was resisted on the basis that the mortgage was void under s.3 of the Family Home Protection Act 1976. The affidavits filed initially on behalf of the plaintiff in support of the application contained a number of material inaccuracies which were corrected in later affidavits and in oral testimony. The fourth named defendant argued the case was not an appropriate one for summary judgment because of inconsistencies contained in the affidavits but this contention was rejected by the Supreme Court. Finlay CJ took the view that the purpose of a plenary hearing instead of a summary judgment in this type of case was in order to resolve a dispute of fact between the parties, the resolution of which was necessary for the decision in the case. However, there was no longer any dispute or uncertainty in relation to the material facts and, in the circumstances, he was satisfied that there was "no general principle nor any requirement of justice which would make necessary a plenary hearing and the refusal of a summary judgment".[122]

---

[119] See paragraphs 16.026-16.028.
[120] See, for example, *In re Killcullen Parochial Hall* [1947] IR 458.
[121] [1995] 2 IR 244, [1994] 2 ILRM 109.
[122] *Ibid.* at 249, 112.

CHAPTER SEVENTEEN

DISCLOSURE IN PERSONAL INJURY ACTIONS

INTRODUCTION

17.001 The traditional approach of the common law courts, justified by reference to the adversarial model of justice, was that a party was entitled to prepare for trial secure in the knowledge that those preparations would not be disclosed to the other side in advance of the trial. A party was entitled to claim litigation privilege (a branch of legal professional privilege) in respect of any communications with third parties including witnesses and expert witnesses[1] and could even refuse to disclose the identity of the witnesses whom he intended to call.[2]

This approach, which fostered surprise and "trial by ambush", became the subject of increasing criticism on the basis that it militated against the possibility of settlement and thereby prolonged litigation and increased costs. In *O'Sullivan v Herdmans Ltd*,[3] Lord Mackay pointed to the benefits of production before the trial of medical reports and said that:

> The interests of justice are, in my opinion, served by the promotion of settlements rather than the prolongation of litigation and by the possibility of early, complete preparation for both parties to a trial rather than by obliging one party to delay its full preparation until after the trial has actually started.[4]

These considerations led to calls for some form of pre-trial disclosure[5] and provision in that regard was finally made in s.45 of the Courts and Court Officers Act 1995 which empowered the Superior Courts Rules Committee to make rules abridging legal professional privilege by requiring parties to personal injury actions to disclose certain specified categories of information including expert reports and the names of witnesses which it was intended to call.

---

[1] See the discussion of litigation privilege at paragraphs 8.014–8.028.
[2] *Eade v Jacobs* (1877) 3 Ex D 335, 337; *Marriott v Chamberlain* (1886) 17 QBD 154, 163. *Cf. McAvoy v Goodyear Tyre and Rubber Co.* [1971] NI 185.
[3] [1987] 1 WLR 1047, [1987] 3 All ER 129.
[4] *Ibid.* at 1056, 136.
[5] As far back as 1967, Walsh J in *P.W. v CIE* [1967] IR 137, 140, stated that: "In all matters of evidence of a scientific or technical nature it would ... be highly desirable to institute the practice of exchanging between the parties the reports of the experts whose evidence is relied upon by the parties."

Rules to that effect were promulgated in the Rules of the Superior Courts (No. 7) 1997[6] which added a new Part VI to Order 39 providing for disclosure and admission of reports and statements.[7] Concerns about the application of the rules to pre-existing actions led to a Practice Direction[8] and amending rules in the Rules of the Superior Court (No. 8) (Disclosure and Admission of Reports and Statements) (Amendment) 1997.[9] Further consideration of the difficulties created by the rules[10] ultimately led to their replacement by the Rules of the Superior Courts (No. 6) (Disclosure of Reports and Statements) 1998.[11] Those rules are referred to in this chapter as the "disclosure rules".[12]

DISCLOSURE RULES

General

17.002 In *Galvin v Murray*,[13] Murphy J commented that the disclosure rules "represent a radical change in the manner in which personal injury litigation will be processed in this jurisdiction". The nature of that change was elaborated upon by Lord Donaldson MR in *Naylor v Preston Health Authority*[14] where he explained that, under the new disclosure regime, "whilst a party is entitled to

---

[6] SI No. 348 of 1997.

[7] For a detailed analysis of the 1997 rules and the policy considerations raised thereby, see O'Neill, "Disclosure in Personal Injuries Actions" (1997) 4 BR 77. See also Pierse, "New Superior Court Rules on Disclosure and Admission of Reports and Statements" (1997) 15 ILT 190.

[8] Practice Direction of 15 September 1997.

[9] SI No. 471 of 1997.

[10] For a discussion of those problems, see Brady, "The Disclosure and Exchange of Experts' Reports in Personal Injuries Litigation" (1999) 5 BR 181 and an editorial in (1997) 4 BR 49.

[11] SI No. 391 of 1998. It is provided in the rules that they are deemed to have come into operation on 1 September 1997 and that the Rules of the Superior Courts (No. 7) 1997 (SI No. 348 of 1997) and the Rules of the Superior Courts (No. 8) (Disclosure and Admission of Reports and Statements) (Amendment) 1997 (SI No. 471 of 1997) were revoked as and from 14 October 1998. It is further provided that they do not apply to proceedings instituted before 1 September 1997 or to any report or statement coming into existence before that date for the purposes of any proceedings (whether instituted before or after that date). However, it is important to note that the old rules may continue to operate in a small number of cases.

[12] For an analysis of the rules, see Brady, "The Disclosure and Exchange of Experts' Reports in Personal Injuries Litigation" (1999) 4 BR 181; Barr, "Expert Evidence – A Few Personal Observations and the Implications of Recent Statutory Developments" (1999) 4 BR 185; Marray, "New Disclosure Rules in Personal and Fatal Injuries Actions" (1998) (6) P & P 4; Carolan, "New Superior Court Rules on Disclosure of Expert Reports in Personal Injury Actions – a Sea Change in Irish Law" (1999) 3 IILR 3.

[13] [2001] 2 ILRM 234, 240.

[14] [1987] 1 WLR 958, 967, [1987] 2 All ER 353, 360.

privacy in seeking out the "cards" for his hand, once he has put his hand together, the litigation is to be conducted with all the cards face up on the table".[15]

Given the novelty of the disclosure rules, it is unsurprising that a number of
uncertainties in relation to their precise scope and application arise which remain to be resolved[16] and this area is likely to see significant judicial contour-
ing in the next few years.

Actions to Which the Rules Apply

17.003 Rule 45(1) provides that the disclosure rules apply only to personal
injury actions. A personal injury action is defined as including any claim for
damages in respect of any personal injuries[17] to a person howsoever caused.
Further clarification of the definition of "personal injury action" is given by the
express inclusion within it of claims for fatal injuries brought pursuant to s.48
of the Civil Liability Act 1961[18] and the exclusion of actions in respect of
which a party is entitled, by virtue of s.1(3) of the Courts Act 1988, to trial by
jury, *viz.* an action where the damages claimed consist of damages for false
imprisonment or intentional trespass to the person.[19]

An interesting issue arising out of the definition of a personal injury action
is whether the application of the disclosure rules is confined to a claim for dam-

---

[15] *Cf.* Lord Wilberforce's synopsis of the traditional position in *Waugh v British Railways
Board* [1980] AC 521, 531, [1979] 2 All ER 1169, 1172, that "one side may not ask to
see the proofs of the other side's witnesses or the opponent's brief or even know what
witnesses will be called: he must wait until the card is played and cannot try to see it in
the hand".

[16] *Cf. Galvin v Murray* [2001] 2 ILRM 234, 239, where Murphy J stated that "the problems to which the disclosure rules give rise and which were identified in argument
before this Court are serious and may not admit of a simple or immediate solution".

[17] Personal injuries are defined as including any disease and any impairment of a person's physical or mental condition.

[18] S.48(1) provides that: "Where the death of a person is caused by the wrongful act of
another such as would have entitled the party injured, but for his death, to maintain an
action and recover damages in respect thereof, the person who would have been so
liable shall be liable to an action for damages for the benefit of the dependants of the
deceased."

[19] S.1(1) of the Courts Act 1988 abolished the right to trial by jury in respect of three
categories of actions: (a) claiming damages in respect of personal injuries to a person
caused by negligence, nuisance or breach of duty (whether the duty exists by virtue of
a contract or a provision made by or under a statute or independently of any such
contract or any such provision), (b) under s.48 of the Civil Liability Act 1961 and (c)
under s.18 of the Air Navigation and Transport Act 1936 (as inserted by the Air Navigation and Transport Act 1965). Subs.(3) provides that the section does not apply in
relation to an action where the damages claimed consist only of damages for false
imprisonment or intentional trespass to the person or both.

ages arising *directly* from personal injuries suffered by a person or whether they would extend to claims for damages arising *indirectly* as, for example, where a plaintiff sues a solicitor who failed to institute proceedings within the limitation period. Rule 45(1) uses the phrase "in respect of" and these words were interpreted by Mann CJ in *Trustees Executors & Agency Co. Ltd v Reilly*[20] as having "the widest possible meaning of any expression intended to convey some connection or relation between ... two subject matters".

17.004 The foregoing explanation was quoted with approval by Boreham J in *Paterson v Chadwick*[21] who interpreted the wording "a claim in respect of personal injuries to a person or in respect of a person's death" as used in s.32(1) of the English Administration of Justice Act 1970 as extending to a claim made against a solicitor for negligence in failing to institute proceedings within the limitation period. He took the view that the nature and extent of the plaintiff's personal injuries would form an essential ingredient in the proof of her claim and, whatever the nature of her cause of action, there was a clear and firm connection or relation between her claim and her personal injuries.[22] It remains to be seen whether this reasoning would recommend itself to an Irish court.

Information Which Must be Disclosed

17.005 The categories of information which must be disclosed are specified by a combination of s.45(1)(a) of the Courts and Courts Officers Act 1995 and Order 39, rule 46 as follows:

(1)   All reports from expert witnesses intended to be called;

(2)   The names and addresses of all witnesses intended to be called to give evidence as to facts in the case;

(3)   A full statement of all items of special damage together with appropriate vouchers, or statements from witnesses by whose evidence such loss would be proved in the action;

(4)   A written statement from the Department of Social Welfare showing all payments made to a plaintiff subsequent to an accident or an authorisation from the plaintiff to the defendant to apply for such information.

A number of issues arise out of these categories of information which are examined below.

---

[20] [1941] VLR 110, 111.
[21] [1974] 1 WLR 890, [1974] 2 All ER 772.
[22] See also *Burns v Shuttlehurst Ltd* [1999] 1 WLR 1449, [1999] 2 All ER 27; *Howe v David Brown Tractors (Retail) Ltd* [1991] 4 All ER 30.

Restriction of Disclosure Obligation to Witnesses Intended to be Called

17.006 It is important to note that the obligation of disclosure only arises in respect of witnesses and experts whom it is *intended to call to give evidence*. Thus, if an expert has been consulted by a party who does not intend to call him, litigation privilege continues to apply with full force to any report provided by him and no obligation of disclosure arises. In *Galvin v Murray*,[23] Murphy J emphasised the limited abridgement of legal professional privilege effected by the disclosure rules:

> It is only if and when [a party] determines to call the authors of the reports to give evidence that the requirement of disclosure arises.... It is still open to any litigant to obtain reports from a variety of experts and decide to call as witnesses some but not others of them. It is only in respect of those whom he determines to call as witnesses that he must provide the required report.[24]

Thus, if a party does not wish to disclose a particular expert report, it is possible to circumvent the rules simply by not calling that person as a witness.

Definition of an Expert

17.007 No actual definition of an "expert" is given in the disclosure rules although a non-exhaustive list is provided in rule 45(1) which specifies accountants, actuaries, architects, dentists, doctors, engineers, occupational therapists, psychologists, psychiatrists and scientists. Apart from these specific categories of person, it appears from s.45(3) of the 1995 Act that an expert is a person "qualified to give expert evidence" and that, therefore, a person will be expert when he is qualified by his experience, training or knowledge to provide evidence in relation to a subject calling for expertise.[25]

17.008 It is evident from the foregoing that the classification of a person as a witness is related to his skill or knowledge and not his relationship to a party in the proceedings and this was the basis of the decision of the Supreme Court in *Galvin v Murray*.[26] The plaintiff instituted proceedings seeking damages for personal injury arising out of a road traffic accident. His claim against the second named defendant, Cork County Council, was advanced on the basis that it had been negligent in constructing or alternatively taking in charge a bridge which was unsound and not sufficiently durable to withstand the volume and weight of traffic which travelled over it. The second named defendant sought to

---

[23] [2001] 2 ILRM 234.
[24] *Ibid.* at 239-40. See also *Derby & Co. Ltd v Weldon* (1990) *Times*, November 9.
[25] *AG (Ruddy) v Kenny* (1960) 94 ILTR 185, 190.
[26] [2001] 2 ILRM 234.

resist the disclosure of reports generated for the purpose of the proceedings by engineers employed by it on the basis that they had furnished reports, not as experts, but as employees. This contention was accepted by Johnson J in the High Court and the plaintiff appealed.

Murphy J, delivering the judgment of the Supreme Court, evinced little difficulty in concluding that the engineers were experts for the purpose of the disclosure rules:

> Whatever the consequences, it seems to me that the two engineers are beyond doubt experts and accordingly if the council are determined to call them as witnesses to give evidence of the technical matters included in the reports that those documents would fall squarely within the disclosure rules. In general terms an expert may be defined as a person whose qualifications or expertise give an added authority to opinions or statements given or made by him within the area of his expertise. Here experts are expressly identified in the disclosure rules as including "engineers". The fact that an engineer is employed by one or other of the parties may affect his independence with a consequent reduction in the weight to be attached to his evidence but could not deprive him of his status as an expert.[27]

He went on to point out the consequences of accepting the contention advanced on behalf of the county council:

> In the present case the county council feel that they are placed in an invidious position because the engineers in question being their employees have reported more fully and widely than might be expected by an independent expert. On the other hand if that or any other factor of itself were to permit an employee/expert to escape the requirements of the disclosure rules it would mean that substantial corporations with a wide variety of in-house experts would have the advantage of knowing the expert evidence to be adduced by their opponents without having themselves to provide a comparable facility. That would be a manifest injustice.[28]

Murphy J reinforced his conclusion by reference to the English decision of *Shell & Pensions Trust Ltd v Pell Frischmann & Partners*.[29] In that case, it was pointed out that the equivalent English Rules applied to "expert evidence" and not "evidence given by independent experts" and that they, therefore, applied to

---

[27] *Ibid.* at 239. *Cf. Field v Leeds City Council* [2000] 17 EGLR 54, 55, where Lord Woolf MR in the Court of Appeal stressed that if the defendant city council wished to use an employee as an expert, it was important that they show that he had full knowledge of the requirements for an expert to give evidence before the court and that he was fully familiar with the need for objectivity.

[28] *Ibid.* at 240.

[29] [1986] 2 All ER 911.

evidence given by any expert including "in-house" experts and the parties themselves.

Definition of Expert Report

17.009 Rule 45(1) defines "report" for the purpose of the disclosure rules as meaning a report or statement from an expert intended to be called to give evidence in relation to an issue in a personal injury action containing "the substance of the evidence to be adduced and shall also include any maps, drawings, photographs, graphs, charts, calculations or other like matter referred to in any such report".[30] Further elucidation of the concept is provided by s.45(3) of the 1995 Act which provides that references to an expert report or to a report of statements from an expert are to be construed as references to evidence in whatever form or a written report by a person dealing wholly or mainly with matters on which that person is qualified to give expert evidence.

17.010 The concept of the "substance" of an expert's evidence requires some elaboration and reference may be made to the observations of Ackner J in *Ollett v Bristol Aerojet Ltd*,[31] where he stated that the obligation to disclose the substance of an expert's report:

> [W]as not satisfied by the experts merely setting out factual descriptions of the machine and the alleged circumstances in which the accident happened and leaving out any conclusions as to the defects in the machine, the system of work or other relevant opinion evidence. This seems to me to be a total misconception of the ordinary meaning of the word "substance". It is also a misconception of the function of an expert. An expert, unlike other witnesses, is allowed, because of his special qualifications and/or experience to give *opinion* evidence. It is for his opinion evidence that he is called, not for a factual description of the machine or the circumstances of the accident, although that is often necessary in order to explain and/or justify his conclusions. When the substance of the expert's report is to be provided, that means precisely what it says, both the substance of the factual description of the machine and/or the circumstances of the accident and his expert opinion in relation to that accident, which is the very justification for calling him.[32]

---

[30] The definition also extends to: "Any copy report (including a copy report in the form of a letter), copy statement or copy letter however made, recorded or retained from any such expert mentioned above intended to be called to give evidence in relation to an issue or action and containing the substance of the evidence to be adduced, the original of which has been concealed, destroyed, lost, mislaid or is not otherwise readily available".

[31] [1979] 1 WLR 1197, [1979] 3 All ER 544.

[32] *Ibid.* at 1197, 544.

Thus, it would appear that a party must disclose both: (i) all information upon which the opinion of the expert is based; and (ii) any conclusions reached by the expert including the nature of any inferences drawn by him from the information before him. However, the obligation of disclosure is not unlimited and is restricted to the "substance" of the expert's evidence. It would not, for example, be necessary to disclose any letter or other document which deals with matters peripheral to or unrelated to the substance of the expert's evidence such as, for example, the terms of his appointment.

17.011 The next and, perhaps, the most important issue arising in relation to the disclosure rules is whether the disclosure obligation extends to information that is unfavourable to the case of the party calling the expert. The answer to this question depends, to a considerable extent, on the purpose of the disclosure rules. A plausible argument can be advanced that their purpose is simply to remove the element of surprise in litigation and to put other parties on notice of the expert evidence which a party intends to call. This seems to have been the purpose ascribed to them by Murphy J in *Galvin v Murray*[33] who said that:

> Clearly the disclosure rules are designed to forewarn other parties of expert evidence with which they may be confronted. The rules have no role to play in investigating the strengths or weaknesses of an opponent's case.[34]

It would seem to follow that all that is required to comply with the disclosure obligation is a précis of the expert's evidence containing "the substance of the evidence" which the expert intended to give on behalf of the party calling him. Thus, if an expert did not intend to give evidence in relation to a matter unfavourable to the case of the party calling him, then, arguably, there is no obligation to disclose that matter. That, indeed, was the opinion of Staughton LJ in *Derby & Co. Ltd v Weldon*[35] who took the view that what had to be disclosed was the substance of the evidence which it was intended that the expert should give and not all the evidence which the expert could conceivably give.[36]

17.012 However, an alternative interpretation of the rules is that they are directed not just towards removing the element of surprise but towards disclosure *per se*. This was the view taken by Wright QC in *Kenning v Eve Construction Ltd*,[37] who stated that a solicitor in deciding whether to call an expert was presented with a simple choice:

---

[33] [2001] 2 ILRM 234.
[34] *Ibid.* at 239-40.
[35] (1990) *Times*, November 9.
[36] He, therefore, disapproved of the decision in *Kenning v Eve Construction Ltd* [1989] 1 WLR 1189 which is discussed below.
[37] [1989] 1 WLR 1189.

He must make up his mind whether he wishes to rely upon that expert, having balanced the good parts of the report against the bad parts. If he decides that on balance the expert is worth calling, then he must call him on the basis of all the evidence that he can give, not merely the evidence that he can give under examination-in-chief, taking the good with the bad together. If, on the other hand, the view that the solicitor forms is that it is too dangerous to call that expert, and he does not wish to disclose that part of his report, then the proper course is that that expert cannot be called at all.[38]

This interpretation of the disclosure obligation can be bolstered by consideration of rule 50(1) which provides a mechanism whereby a party can apply for an order that, in the interests of justice, the disclosure obligations should not apply to any particular report or statement (or portion thereof). This provision would not seem to be necessary if a party could discharge his obligations by disclosing a "sanitised" expert report which merely set out the substance of the evidence which he intended to give on examination-in-chief. Indeed, if this was the case, then the application of the County Council in *Galvin* was unnecessary and its concerns misplaced.

17.013 Interpreted in this way, the disclosure rules serve to reinforce the duties and responsibilities owed by an expert to the court[39] and can be viewed as, at least in part, an attempt to restore in some small measure the impartiality and independence of experts which was originally the hallmark and, indeed, to some extent, the justification for their evidence[40] but which has become very much eroded in recent years.[41] The knowledge that any report or statement by him has been disclosed should discourage attempts by an expert to tailor his evidence in court for the benefit of the party calling him, as he could well find himself being cross-examined on an inconsistent statement made by him in a previous report. However, any apparent benefits in terms of ensuring greater

---

[38] *Ibid.* at 1195. *Cf. Derby & Co. Ltd v Weldon* (1990) *Times*, November 9, where the majority cast doubt on the ambit of the decision in *Kenning* in so far as the damaging material did not relate to the case as pleaded against the defendant and Staughton LJ in his concurring judgment took the view that the decision stated the obligation of disclosure too broadly and, to that extent, had been wrongly decided.

[39] See the list of duties enumerated by Cresswell J in *National Justice Cia Naviera SA v Prudential Assurance Co. Ltd* [1993] 2 Lloyd's Rep 68, 81 and discussed in Chapter 19 at paragraph 19.036.

[40] In *Davie v Edinburgh Magistrates* 1953 SC 34, 40, Lord President Cooper said that the function of expert evidence "is to furnish the judge or jury with the necessary scientific criteria for testing the accuracy of their conclusions, so as to enable the judge or jury to form their own independent judgment by the application of these criteria to the facts proved in evidence".

[41] See, for example, *News Datacom Ltd v Lyons* [1994] 1 ILRM 450, 456 where Flood J referred to "the opinion of a partisan expert" in the case before him.

impartiality on the part of experts are likely to prove illusory. The practical effect is more likely to be that experts will simply become more careful in drafting their reports to omit anything that could be construed as damaging to the case of the party retaining them, reserving such comments for oral communication. Indeed, it might be questioned whether the rules might not be counterproductive in this regard because a party will be unlikely to call as a witness an expert who has furnished an impartial and balanced report for fear of having to disclose it.

Another important ambiguity which arises is whether the disclosure obligation can be met by the compilation of a report specifically for the purpose of disclosure or whether, it is necessary, once a decision has been taken to call a particular expert, to disclose all reports and statements from that witness which touch upon the substance of the evidence which he intends to give. Again, the resolution of this issue depends on the purpose attributed to the disclosure rules.

17.014 A final point which might be made is in relation to the enhanced role which it can be anticipated that solicitors and, perhaps, counsel, will play in the formulation of expert reports. It is interesting to note that in *Galvin v Murray*[42] Murphy J contemplated the involvement of lawyers in the process of producing expert reports:

> [I]t may be anticipated that expert witnesses – with the assistance of the lawyers concerned – will produce reports in such a manner as will enable the parties to comply with the disclosure rules as effectively, expeditiously and as inexpensively as the draftsman intended.[43]

However, lawyers would be well advised to remember the cautionary words of Lord Wilberforce in *Whitehouse v Jordan*[44] that:

> While some degree of consultation between experts and legal advisers is entirely proper, it is necessary that expert evidence presented to the court should be, and should be seen to be, the independent product of the expert, uninfluenced as to form or content by the exigencies of litigation. To the extent that it is not, the evidence is likely to be not only incorrect but self-defeating.[45]

---

[42] [2001] 2 ILRM 234.
[43] *Ibid.* at 240.
[44] [1981] 1 WLR 246, [1981] 1 All ER 267.
[45] *Ibid.* at 256-57, 276.

Exchange of Reports and Statements

Timetable for Exchange

17.015 Rule 46 makes provision for the staggered exchange[46] of reports and statements in accordance with the following timetable:

(i)   Within one month of the service of the notice of trial or within such further time as may be agreed by the parties or permitted by the court, the plaintiff must furnish to the other parties a schedule listing all reports from expert witnesses intended to be called.

(ii)   Within seven days of receipt of the plaintiff's schedule, the defendant or any other parties must furnish to the plaintiff or any other party or parties a schedule listing all reports from expert witnesses intended to be called.

(iii) Within seven days of the receipt of the schedule of the defendant or other party or parties, the parties shall exchange copies of the reports listed in the relevant schedule.

(iv)   Also within one month of the service of the notice of trial or within such further time as may be agreed by the parties or permitted by the court, the parties must exchange:

    (a) the names and addresses of all witnesses intended to be called to give evidence as to facts in the case;

    (b) a full statement of all items of special damage together with appropriate vouchers or statements from witnesses by whose evidence such loss would be proved in the action;

    (c) a written statement from the Department of Social, Community and Family Affairs showing all payments made to the plaintiff subsequent to the accident or authorisation from the plaintiff to the defendant to apply for such information.

If a party certifies in writing that no expert report exists which requires to be exchanged, then any other party must, on the expiry of the time fixed, agreed or permitted, deliver any report within the meaning of the section to all other parties to the proceedings.[47]

---

[46] The staggered exchange provides for some element of mutuality and improves on simple sequential exchange but still falls short of the simultaneous exchange recommended by the Report of the Committee on Personal Injuries Litigation (1968) (Cmnd 3691), para. 279.

[47] Order 39, rule 46(3).

17.016 According to Marray[48] the staggered disclosure procedure with the exchange of reports was introduced in order to ensure mutuality and fairness. It also guards against the possibility of selective disclosure by the defendant or other parties, who if they were to receive copies of the plaintiff's reports before disclosing the names of their experts might be tempted to rely on those reports where the reports from their own experts were less favourable.

Parties who Must Make Disclosure

17.017 The concept of a "party" for the purpose of the disclosure rules is given a broad definition as including a plaintiff or co-plaintiff, defendant or co-defendant or any third party, counterclaimant or notice party to the action save where the context otherwise requires.[49]

Continuing Obligation of Disclosure

17.018 A party is under a continuing obligation of disclosure in accordance with the disclosure rules. Thus, if a party, subsequent to the exchange of expert reports, obtains any expert report or the name and address of any further witness, he must forthwith deliver a copy of any such report or details of the name and address of any such witness to the other parties.[50]

Service of Reports and Information

17.019 Rule 46(5) provides that service of any report, statement or information requiring to be exchanged or delivered may be effected by letter in writing enclosing the report, statement or information and may be sent by ordinary prepaid post. That letter must specifically state that the service is for the purpose of complying with the requirements of s.45 of the Act and the disclosure rules. It is further provided that the court may, on application to it by any party to an action, or of its own motion, require an affidavit to be filed by any party in relation to proof of disclosure and service in any case in which it appears to the court necessary so to do.

Withdrawal of Information

17.020 Rule 46(6) provides that a party who has previously delivered any report or statement or details of a witness may withdraw reliance on such by confirming by letter in writing that he does not now intend to call the author of such report or statement or such witness to give evidence in the action.[51] Al-

---

[48] "New Disclosure Rules in Personal and Fatal Injuries Actions" (1998) (6) P & P 4, 6. It should be noted that the author is a member of the Superior Courts Rules Committee.

[49] Order 39, rule 45(1).

[50] Order 39, rule 46(4). *Cf. Vernon v Bosley (No. 2)* [1999] QB 18, [1997] 3 WLR 683, [1997] 1 All ER 614.

[51] Order 39, rule 46(6).

though, normally, the disclosure of a privileged document to an adverse party in the course of litigation would constitute a waiver of privilege,[52] it is expressly provided that if a party withdraws reliance on a report or details of a witness, the privilege (if any) which existed in relation thereto is deemed to have always applied to it notwithstanding any exchange or delivery which may have taken place.[53]

Application for Exemption from Disclosure

17.021 Rule 50(1) provides that, in any case, application may be made to the court by motion on notice by any party for an order that in the interests of justice the provisions of rule 46 shall not apply in relation to any particular report or statement (or portion thereof), which is in the possession of such party and which he maintains should not be disclosed and served as required. The court may, upon such application, make such order as to it seems just.

The decision in *Galvin v Murray*[54] discussed above arose on foot of an application pursuant to rule 50(1) and, after deciding that engineers employed by the County Council were experts for the purpose of the disclosure rules, the Supreme Court remitted the matter back to the High Court to afford it the opportunity of arguing that certain parts of the reports of the engineers should be deleted before being disclosed to the plaintiff.

Non-Compliance with the Disclosure Rules

17.022 The problem of non-compliance is dealt with in two separate rules, one intended to deal with problems that arise pre-trial and the other with the situation which arises where a problem becomes manifest in the course of the trial.

Motion for Directions

17.023 Rule 47 makes provision for a motion for directions when any party alleges that any other party to an action has failed to comply with the requirements of rule 46 or any provision thereof. Application may be made to the court by motion on notice seeking the directions of the court in relation to any such alleged default, grounded upon the affidavit of the party concerned. On the hearing of the motion the court may, if satisfied that the party alleged to be in default has failed to comply with all or any of the requirements of s.45 or the disclosure rules, direct compliance with such requirements forthwith or within such period as the court may fix. Alternatively, the court may make such other order as the justice of the case may require including an order providing that in default of

---

[52] *Porter v Scott* [1979] NI 6; *Caldbeck v Boon* (1877) IR 7 CL 32.
[53] Order 39, rule 46(6).
[54] [2001] 2 ILRM 234.

such compliance the party in default be prohibited from adducing such evidence or that in default of such compliance the claim or defence (as the case may be) be struck out and may make such further order in relation to costs as seems meet.

Non-Compliance Uncovered During the Trial of the Action

17.024 Rule 48 deals with the situation where non-compliance with the disclosure rules comes to light during the trial of the action. It provides that, if at any stage of the hearing of an action it appears to the court that there has been non-compliance with any provision of the section or these rules, the court may, having heard any such evidence as may be adduced by the parties in relation to such non-compliance, make such order as it deems fit including an order prohibiting the adducing of evidence in relation to which such non-compliance relates. Alternatively, the court may adjourn the action to permit compliance with the provisions of s.45 or the disclosure rules on such terms and conditions as seem appropriate and may make such order as to costs as appears just in the circumstances.

Admission of Evidence Which Has Not Been Disclosed

17.025 Rule 50(2) provides that, in any case in which there has been non-compliance by any party with any relevant requirement of the section or these rules, such party, in the absence of the consent of the other party or parties may apply by motion on notice to the court for an order seeking the leave of the court permitting the adducing of such evidence as has not been disclosed and the court may make such order on such application as appears just in the circumstances. The English courts have taken a strict approach towards non-adherence to the disclosure rules and the failure to disclose adequate expert reports within the required timetable.[55] It remains to be seen if the Irish courts will adopt a more indulgent attitude.

---

[55] See *Baron v Lovell* [2000] PIQR 20.

CHAPTER EIGHTEEN

TRIAL OF PRELIMINARY ISSUES OF LAW

INTRODUCTION

Provisions of the Rules

18.001 Issues of law may arise in pleadings which lend themselves to being determined by means of the trial of a point of law as a preliminary issue. Two different orders make provision for the determination of a point of law as a preliminary issue. Order 25, rule 1 of the Rules of the Superior Courts 1986 provides that by the consent of the parties,[1] or by order of the court on the application of either party, any point of law may be set down for hearing and disposed of at any time before the trial. Order 25, rule 2 goes on to provide that if in the opinion of the court, the decision on this point substantially disposes of the action, or any distinct cause of action, ground of defence, counterclaim or reply, the court may dismiss the claim or make such other order as may be just. In addition, Order 34, rule 2 provides that if it appears to the court that any question of law arises which it would be convenient to have decided before any evidence is given or any question or issue of fact is tried, it may direct such question of law to be raised for the opinion of the court. As Lavery J stated in *McDonald v Bord na gCon*[2] these two rules "cover the same ground". In his view the only relevant difference between them is that Order 34, rule 2 expressly provides that it should appear to the judge to be convenient to have the particular issue decided before any evidence is given or any question of fact tried, whereas Order 25, rule 2 is more general in its terms.

Purpose of the Procedure

18.002 The purpose behind the procedure for setting down a preliminary point of law for trial is to save time and costs.[3] Certainly in some cases, considerable savings in both time and expense can be achieved where a question of law is determined as a preliminary issue where it results in the dismissal of the plain-

---

[1] *E.g. Garvey v Ireland* [1981] IR 75; *Moyne v Londonderry Port and Harbour Commissioners* [1986] IR 299; *Thomas v Leitrim County Council* [1998] 2 ILRM 74 (HC) [2001] 2 ILRM 385 (SC).

[2] [1964] IR 350, 357.

[3] *Duffy v News Group Newspapers Ltd (No. 2)* [1994] 3 IR 63, 77, [1994] 1 ILRM 364, 372 *per* O'Flaherty J. See also the judgment of Kenny J in *McDonald v Bord na g Con* [1964] IR 350 in which he held that considerations of time and expense indicated that an order directing trial of a preliminary issue of law should be made.

tiff's claim.[4] The difficulty for a judge in deciding whether to accede to an application of this nature is to weigh up the likelihood of achieving such savings as when the determination of the preliminary issue results in the necessity for a full trial of the substantive questions raised, costs will inevitably be increased.[5]

APPLICATIONS FOR TRIAL OF A PRELIMINARY ISSUE

18.003 An application for an order that a point of law be tried as a preliminary issue may be made by either party although in practice such applications tend to be made more frequently by defendants[6] than by plaintiffs.[7] More than one preliminary issue may be tried together[8] or an order may be subsequently varied to include a provision that a further question be tried as a preliminary issue.[9] Preliminary issues may be ordered to be tried on more than one occasion in the course of proceedings,[10] although this will rarely happen in practice. Where the trial of the preliminary point of law results in a finding in the defendant's favour, the claim will be dismissed, otherwise the action will proceed on the basis of the pleadings delivered in the case.[11]

Appeals to the Supreme Court

18.004 Decisions made by the High Court on the trial of a preliminary issue of law may be appealed to the Supreme Court,[12] although where the application

---

[4] *E.g. W. v Ireland (No.2)* [1997] 2 IR 141.

[5] Note the *dicta* of Lavery J in *McDonald v. Bord na gCon* [1964] IR 350, 359 to the effect that "the question of costs which may be involved, if proper to be considered at all, cannot override the real considerations".

[6] *E.g. Reamsbottom v Raftery* [1991] 1 IR 531; *McKinley v Minister for Defence* [1992] 2 IR 333; *Guerin v Guerin* [1992] 2 IR 287, [1993] ILRM 243; *Reidy v McGreevy* High Court (Barron J) 19 March 1993; *Walsh v Butler* [1997] 2 ILRM 81; *Irish Equine Foundation Ltd v Robinson* [1999] 2 IR 442, [1999] 2 ILRM 289; *Kelly v Minister for Agriculture, Food and Forestry* High Court (Butler J) 1 May 2001.

[7] *E.g. Allen and Hanburys Ltd v Controller of Patents, Designs and Trademarks* [1996] 3 IR 401, [1997] 1 ILRM 416.

[8] *Guerin v Guerin* [1992] 2 IR 287, [1993] ILRM 243.

[9] *Walsh v Butler* [1997] 2 ILRM 81.

[10] *E.g.* in *Breathnach v Ireland* High Court 1982 No. 4021P a preliminary issue was tried by Lardner J (see [1989] IR 491) and a separate issue subsequently tried by Blayney J (High Court, 4 March 1990).

[11] *Per* O'Flaherty J in *Duffy v News Group Newspapers (No. 2)* [1994] 3 IR 63, 75, [1994] 1 ILRM 364, 370.

[12] *E.g. Hegarty v O'Loughran* [1990] 1 IR 148, [1990] ILRM 403; *J.P.D. v M.G.* [1991] 1 IR 47, [1991 ILRM 217; *McKinley v Minister for Defence* [1992] 2 IR 333; *Chambers v An Bord Pleanala* [1992] 1 IR 134, [1992] ILRM 296; *Scanlon v McCabe* [1997] 1 IR 63, [1997] 2 ILRM 337; *Bowes v MIBI* Supreme Court, 30 July 1999; *Ryan v Connolly* [2001] 2 ILRM 174.

has been brought by the defendant, this will inevitably lead to further delay and the incurring of additional costs if the matter is not resolved in his favour. In many cases, the Supreme Court decision will not dispose of the matter as between the parties and O'Flaherty J made an interesting comment on this point in *Lawless v Bus Eireann,*[13] in which the plaintiff had instituted proceedings against the defendant arising out of the death of her husband. In dismissing the point of law raised by the defendant as a preliminary issue, O'Flaherty J commented that, in view of the length of time which had elapsed, it would seem fitting that the case should now have the same priority as it would have had if the preliminary issue leading to a hearing in the High Court as well as an appeal had not been set down.

CIRCUMSTANCES IN WHICH TRIAL OF PRELIMINARY ISSUE MAY BE ORDERED

Issue Must be Tried in the Context of Agreed Facts

18.005 As O'Flaherty J stated in *Duffy v News Group Newspapers Ltd (No. 2)*[14] "the Order 25 procedure is only appropriate where words can be placed before the judge, without the necessity of calling evidence." Equally, as Lynch J made clear in *McCabe v Ireland*[15] a preliminary issue of law cannot be tried *in vacuo*, it must be tried in the context of agreed or established facts. So, in *Tara Exploration and Development Co. Ltd v Minister for Industry and Commerce*[16] Kenny J held, in dismissing the defendant's application pursuant to Order 34, rule 2 for an order that certain questions of law be determined as a preliminary issue, that the proposed questions could not be answered without reference to the relevant facts and these were still undetermined. The Supreme Court agreed with his conclusion, O'Higgins CJ stating that "Order 34, rule 2 can only apply to questions of pure law where no evidence is needed and no further information is required".[17] Where, as in the case before the court, the answers to the suggested questions of law were dependent on facts that had not yet been ascertained, the procedure could not be utilised.[18]

---

[13] [1994] 1 IR 474.

[14] [1994] 1 ILRM 364, 371, [1994] 3 IR 63, 76.

[15] [1999] 4 IR 151, 157, [2000] 1 ILRM 410, 415. See also *Ryan v Minister for Justice* Supreme Court, 21 December 2000 at 9.

[16] [1975] IR 242.

[17] *Ibid.* at 257.

[18] Note the *dicta* of Humphreys J in *S.C. Taverner & Co. Ltd v Glamorgan County Council* (1940) 57 TLR 243 to the effect that "[i]t is very rarely that the facts are so clearly and definitely stated in pleadings… that the court can say it has all necessary facts before it".

18.006 These issues were considered by Ó Dálaigh CJ in *Kilty v Hayden*[19] in the context of an application brought pursuant to Order 25, rule 1 where the Chief Justice stated that:

> When Order 25 is contrasted with Order 36 it becomes clear that Order 25 is not providing for the separate trial of issues which are partly of fact and partly of law, but for the separate trial of a net point of law dissociated from issues of fact, that is to say, the point of law must arise on the basis of the facts being as the opposing party on his pleadings alleges them to be.

This passage was quoted recently by Lynch J in the Supreme Court decision of *McCabe v Ireland*[20] where he said that facts must be agreed or the moving party must accept, for the purposes of the trial of the preliminary issue which he raises, the facts alleged by the opposing party. However, he also stated that while the facts relevant to the preliminary issue must not be in dispute,[21] "they may be agreed for the purposes of the preliminary issue of law only without prejudice to the right to contest the facts if the actual determination of the preliminary issue should not dispose of the matter". The Supreme Court upheld the decision of Kinlen J directing the trial of preliminary issues of law on the basis that for the purposes thereof, but no further, the averments in the plaintiff's statement of claim were true.

18.007 The fact that a defendant may accept the facts alleged in the statement of claim and replies to particulars for the purposes of the trial of a preliminary issue of law only, was confirmed by the Supreme Court in its recent decision in *Ryan v Minister for Justice*.[22] The defendants sought an order pursuant to Order 25, rule 1 and/or Order 34, rule 2 directing the trial of preliminary issues of law concerning whether they owed the plaintiff, who alleged that she had been abducted and raped by an individual on temporary release from prison, a duty of care in relation to whether to release offenders in this manner or to provide sufficient prison places to accommodate sentenced persons. In the High Court, Kinlen J concluded that the issue as to whether a duty of care arose depended to a great extent on the knowledge of the prison authorities and in his view it was not possible to segregate the factual issues from the legal ones which he was being asked to direct should be tried as preliminary questions. In their written submissions to the Supreme Court, the defendants stated that the trial of preliminary issues of law, if directed by the court, could proceed on the basis that the facts alleged by the plaintiff in the statement of claim and replies to particu-

---

[19] [1969] IR 261, 265.
[20] [1999] 4 IR 151, 157, [2000] 1 ILRM 410, 415.
[21] See also *O'Reilly v Granville* [1971] IR 90, 109 *per* Budd J.
[22] Supreme Court, 21 December 2000.

lars were not in issue. The defendants relied on the fact that an order had been made by the Supreme Court in *McCabe v Ireland* that a preliminary issue be tried in a very similar situation, although counsel for the plaintiff pointed out that the decision to direct the trial of a preliminary issue was a discretionary one. While Murphy J accepted that the latter argument was technically correct, he stated that it would be highly undesirable for the Supreme Court to endorse two conflicting orders made on substantially the same facts. In addition, he did not accept that there was a dispute of fact given the concession made by the defendants about accepting the facts alleged by the plaintiff for the purposes of the trial of the preliminary issues of law. In these circumstances, Murphy J allowed the defendants' appeal against the order of Kinlen J and directed the trial of the preliminary issues of law sought.

18.008 In determining what issues of law can be tried in a preliminary manner, it is important to identify matters "which could have no further light thrown upon them by a trial".[23] In addition, if a judge finds that there is any evidence which a party could call which would assist in the determination of the question of law, he should refuse to make an order that it be tried as a preliminary issue.[24]

Finally, it should be noted that where an order is made that a preliminary issue be tried, "care should be taken that a real point of law is being raised and ... there should be a clear definition of what the point of law raised is".[25]

Limited Application of the Principle

18.009 The limited circumstances in which trial of preliminary issues of law should be ordered was considered in the context of an application brought pursuant to Order 34, rule 2 in *Tara Exploration and Development Co. Ltd v Minister for Industry and Commerce*.[26] In dismissing the defendant's application for an order that questions of law should be determined as preliminary issues, O'Higgins CJ described it as a procedure which is rarely availed of by the courts and continued as follows:

> The infrequent use of this procedure may be explained by the restricted field in which it can operate. First of all, there must be a question of law which can be identified amongst the issues in the action. Further, this question of law must be such that it can be decided before any evidence is given. If special facts have to be proved or if facts are in dispute, the rule

---

[23] *Per* Roche J in *M. Issacs and Sons Ltd v Cook* [1925] 2 KB 391, 401.

[24] *S.C. Taverner & Co. Ltd v. Glamorgan County Council* (1940) 57 TLR 243, 244 *per* Humphreys J.

[25] *Per* MacKinnon LJ in *National Real Estate and Finance Co. v Hassan* [1939] 2 KB 61, 77.

[26] [1975] IR 242. See also *McDonald v Bord na gCon* [1964] IR 350.

does not apply. In addition, it must appear to the court to be convenient to try such question of law before any evidence is given. This will involve a consideration of the effect on other issues in the case and whether its resolution will reduce these significantly, or shorten the hearing. Convenience in this respect must also be considered in the light of what appears fair, proper and just in the circumstances.[27]

A more recent example of an application being made pursuant to Order 34, rule 2 is *James McMahon Ltd v Bedford Row Investment Ltd,*[28] which concerned a claim for damages, in which Flood J dismissed the defendant's application. Flood J concluded that "the very nature of this case is such as to render it unsuitable for preliminary issues" and said that he took on board the caveats expressed by Kenny J in the *Tara* case in which he had quoted with approval from the decisions of Lord Evershed MR and Harman LJ in *Windsor Refrigerator Co. Ltd v Branch Nominees Ltd.*[29] Lord Evershed MR had stated that:

> [T]he course which this matter has taken emphasises as clearly as any case in my experience has emphasised, the extreme unwisdom – save in very exceptional cases – of adopting this procedure of preliminary issues. My experience has taught me (and this case emphasises the teaching) that the shortest cut so attempted inevitably turns out to be the longest way round.[30]

Clearly, this will not always be the case and this *dicta* must be treated with a degree of caution. Subsequently in *Carl Zeiss Stiftung v Herbert Smith & Co.*[31] Lord Denning MR dismissed as incorrect the principle that a preliminary issue should only be ordered to be tried "when, *whichever way it is decided*, it is conclusive of the whole matter." In his opinion, the better view was as set out by Romer LJ in *Everett v Ribbands*[32] in the following terms:

> Where you have a point of law which, *if decided in one way*, is going to be decisive of litigation, then advantage ought to be taken of the facilities afforded by the Rules of Court to have it disposed of at the close of pleadings, or very shortly after the close of pleadings.

---

[27] *Ibid.* at 256.
[28] High Court (Flood J) 20 November 1996.
[29] [1961] Ch 375, [1961] 2 WLR 196, [1961] 1 All ER 277.
[30] *Ibid.* at 396, 210, 283. See also the *dicta* of Harman LJ at 396, 210, 283 to the effect that "the number of conditions [Lord Evershed MR] has found it necessary to use to fence in the expression of this court's opinion shows at once the undesirability of this kind of procedure."
[31] [1969] 1 Ch 93, [1968] 3 WLR 281, [1968] 2 All ER 1002.
[32] [1952] 2 QB 198, 206-207, [1952] 1 All ER 823, 827.

Issues Not Suitable for Determination in this Manner

18.010 By their nature, some issues will not be suitable for determination in this manner as they are essentially matters of fact which must be resolved in the course of the trial by a judge, or where relevant, by a jury. So, in *Murphy v Dow Jones Publishing Co. (Europe) Inc.*[33] Flood J refused the defendant's application brought pursuant to Order 25, rule 1 that an issue raised, namely that the words of which the plaintiff complained were published on an occasion of qualified privilege, be determined as a preliminary issue by a judge of the High Court sitting without a jury. In his view, the essence of the protection of privilege was that a report was a "fair and accurate" one and he concluded that "in principle the fairness and accuracy of anything concerned with defamation are factual matters and have been held to be eminently suitable for decision by a jury". In addition, in *Duffy v News Group Newspapers Ltd (No. 2)*[34] the Supreme Court reversed the order of the High Court directing that a preliminary point of law be tried as to whether the words complained of were capable of bearing any meaning defamatory of the plaintiff. In the view of the Supreme Court the issue of whether the words used were capable of such meaning was one which might be supported by oral testimony and the court concluded that it was impossible to dispose of the issue as a preliminary point of law.

CONSIDERATIONS WHERE PRELIMINARY ISSUE OF CONSTITUTIONAL LAW RAISED

18.011 It is a well-established principle that where the relief which a plaintiff seeks rests on two distinct grounds, as a general rule the court should consider first whether it can be granted on the ground which does not raise a question of constitutional validity. If so, the court ought not to rule on the issue of the constitutional validity of the law in question.[35] So, in *Cooke v Walsh*[36] O'Higgins CJ stated that: "It is well settled that the consideration of any question involving the validity of a statute or a section thereof, should, in appropriate circumstances, be postponed to the consideration of any other question, the resolution of which will determine the issue between the parties."

The Supreme Court confirmed that this was the approach which it favoured in *Murphy v Roche*[37] in holding that where matters in dispute between the parties can be disposed of by the resolution of an issue of law other than constitutional law, the court should consider that issue first and if it determines the

[33] High Court (Flood J) 11 January 1995.
[34] [1994] 3 IR 63, [1994] 1 ILRM 364.
[35] *Per* O'Higgins CJ in *M v An Bord Uchtala* [1977] IR 287, 293.
[36] [1984] IR 710, 728, [1984] ILRM 208, 213.
[37] [1987] IR 106.

case, should decline to express any view of the constitutional issue which may have been raised. The plaintiff brought a claim for personal injuries against an unincorporated club of which he was a member and the defendants pleaded that as a member of the club, he was estopped from maintaining proceedings against it. The plaintiff denied that he was so estopped and contended that any estoppel alleged by the defendants was repugnant to the Constitution. The plaintiff applied to have the points of law raised determined as preliminary issues and the defendants were prepared to consent to this. However, the Attorney General, on whom notice had been served, objected on the grounds that the trial of any question involving constitutional law as a preliminary issue was inappropriate and might ultimately prove to have been the determination of an issue of constitutional law in the form of a moot. The Supreme Court agreed and Finlay CJ stated that it must decline to decide any question which is in the form of a moot and the decision of which is not necessary for the determination of the rights of the parties before it. Finlay CJ continued as follows:

> [I]t has also been clearly established that where the issues between parties can be determined and finally disposed of by the resolution of an issue of law other than constitutional law, the court should proceed to consider that issue first and, if it determines the case, should refrain from expressing any view on the constitutional issue that may have been raised.[38]

The Supreme Court concluded that the issue of whether the plaintiff might sue the club should be tried as a preliminary issue and adjourned the constitutional question until this point had been determined.

18.012 The view expressed by the Supreme Court in *Murphy* is in line with the approach subsequently adopted by that court in *McDaid v Sheehy*[39] in which it declined to follow the view of the majority in *McDonald v Bord na gCon*,[40] which had held that the constitutionality of legislation should be tried as a preliminary issue on the grounds that it would be quite inappropriate to try the other issues until the constitutional question had been decided.[41] In *McDaid*,

---

[38] *Ibid.* at 110.
[39] [1991] 1 IR 1, [1991] ILRM 250.
[40] [1964] IR 350.
[41] In a strong dissenting judgment, Ó Dálaigh CJ pointed to the fact that with respect to considerations of time and expense, the course proposed by Kenny J looked only at the possibility of the legislation being held to be repugnant to the Constitution. If the decision were to go the other way, then the plaintiff would have to back to the High Court to litigate the rest of his claim and the time and costs involved for the parties would be greater than in an unsevered trial. While this was not the course which he advocated in the case before him, Ó Dálaigh made some interesting observations about the considerations which arise where a constitutional question is being tried as a preliminary issue. He stated that it is usually considered an advantage to a court to examine a question of law in relation to specific facts and in deciding constitutional ques-

the applicant sought to quash his conviction of an offence under legislation which had been amended by statutory instrument and subsequently confirmed by further legislation. The Supreme Court held that the subsequent legislation gave validity to the order, that at all material times the latter had been of full force and effect and that it had not been necessary for the High Court to pronounce on the validity of the legislation which allowed for the making of the order. Finlay CJ referred to the decision of the majority in *McDonald* which he said appeared to be entirely directed towards questions of convenience in the procedures adopted and in which no question of inappropriateness of trying the constitutional validity of the statute as a moot arose. He added that in so far as *McDonald* constituted a break with what appeared to be a relatively consistent attitude by the Supreme Court, he would feel obliged to refuse to follow it. Finlay CJ stated that having regard to the view which he had taken of the legal effect of the provisions of the subsequent legislation, the applicant had not been prejudiced or damaged by the operation of the Act or of any statutory order made pursuant to it. He concluded that the courts should not pronounce on the constitutional validity of legislation unless it was necessary for its decision to do so, and here it clearly was not.[42]

As a result of the decision in *McDaid v Sheehy*, it is clear that the reasoning of the majority in *McDonald v Bord na gCon* will no longer be followed. While the constitutionality of legislation may still be determined as a preliminary issue in appropriate circumstances,[43] the principle of addressing constitutional issues last seems to be well established.

---

tions, it may be beneficial to a court to see a problem set in the framework of a defined case or controversy. Ó Dálaigh CJ added that he doubted whether it would be proper to pronounce a statute repugnant to the Constitution except in a situation where the specific facts of the case themselves exemplified the repugnancy complained of.

[42] McCarthy J delivered a dissenting judgment in which he stated that the executive was entitled to clarification of the law not merely when an issue had been raised but when it has been determined adversely to the executive at a level below that of the Supreme Court. Notwithstanding the view expressed by the Chief Justice, in his opinion, the resolution by the Supreme Court of the constitutional challenge to the legislation could not be avoided.

[43] See *e.g. Carway v Attorney General* [1996] 3 IR 300, [1997] 1 ILRM 110; *Molyneux v Ireland* [1997] 2 ILRM 241.

CHAPTER NINETEEN

PLENARY TRIAL

INTRODUCTION

19.001 The centrepiece of our adversarial system of justice is the plenary trial. It is in the course of such a trial, which involves the examination and cross-examination of witnesses, that the strengths of the adversarial model come to the fore. The purpose of this chapter is to outline the procedural and evidential rules which govern the conduct of a plenary trial.

BURDEN OF PROOF

Where the Burden Lies

19.002 The general principle applied in civil cases is encapsulated in the Latin maxim: *Ei incumbit probatio qui dicit, non qui negat i.e.* he who asserts must prove. Thus, whichever party contends for the existence of a particular fact must bear the burden of proving its existence on the balance of probabilities and a party cannot circumvent this rule by pleading his case by way of negative allegation.[1] In addition, a party may have to prove a negative where it is an essential part of his claim. Thus, in *Abrath v North Eastern Railway*,[2] the Court of Appeal held that in an action for malicious prosecution, the plaintiff bore the burden of proving not only that the defendant instituted proceedings against him, but also that he did so without reasonable and probable cause.

Application of the foregoing principles means that, in general, proof of the facts necessary to establish a cause of action will rest on the party bringing the case whilst proof of a defence to the action, which is more than a mere denial of the claim, will lie on the party raising the defence. Thus, in a negligence action, the burden of proving duty, breach and damages will rest on the plaintiff while the burden of establishing contributory negligence lies on the defendant.[3] Fur-

---

[1] *Soward v Leggatt* (1836) 7 C & P 613.
[2] (1883) 11 QBD 440.
[3] *Clancy v Commissioners of Public Works* [1992] 2 IR 449, 467, [1991] ILRM 567, 574-575. It was held in *Clancy* that because the onus was on the defendants to establish contributory negligence, the trial judge had been wrong in adopting the view of the facts most favourable to the defendants for the purpose of assessing the issue of contributory negligence.

ther, where a defence raises a counterclaim, then the defendant will bear the burden of proof in respect of that counterclaim.[4]

Standard of Proof

19.003 The standard of proof to be met in civil cases is proof on a balance of probabilities[5] and whether a party has met this standard and discharged the burden of proof upon him is decided at the conclusion of the case by the judge (where he is sitting alone) or the jury as appropriate. In reference to this standard, Denning J in *Miller v Minister of Pensions*[6] said that "[i]f the evidence is such that the tribunal can say: 'we think it more probable than not', the burden is discharged, but if the probabilities are equal it is not."

19.004 If a particularly serious allegation is made, then this general standard will be applied in a more rigorous fashion. However, the Irish courts have consistently rejected the contention that there are any categories to which a higher standard than that of proof on the balance of probabilities applies.[7] The seminal case is *Banco Ambrosiano SPA v Ansbacher & Co. Ltd*[8] which involved an allegation of fraud. Henchy J in the Supreme Court rejected the contention that some sort of intermediate standard applied to such an allegation. He adverted to the difficulties of expressing such a standard and of the risk of confusing juries and took the view that it would introduce an element of uncertainty into the law.[9] In response to the argument that a higher standard should be required because of the moral condemnation and serious consequences which accompanied a finding of fraud, he pointed out that similar condemnation and consequences could follow a finding against a defendant in other civil proceedings, which only required proof on a balance of probabilities. He therefore, concluded that there was no rational reason why fraud in civil cases should require a higher degree of proof than that required for other issues in civil claims.[10] However, the learned judge did accept that the consequences of a finding of

---

[4] *Rhatigan v Gill* [1999] 2 ILRM 427, 442.
[5] *Best v Wellcome Foundation Ltd* [1993] 2 IR 421, [1992] ILRM 609.
[6] [1947] 2 All ER 372, 374.
[7] *Banco Ambrosiano SPA v Ansbacher & Co. Ltd* [1987] ILRM 669; *Masterfoods Ltd v HB Ice Cream Ltd* [1993] ILRM 145; *Superwood Holdings plc v Sun Alliance & London Insurance plc* [1995] 3 IR 303; *Hanafin v Minister for the Environment* [1996] 2 IR 321, [1996] 2 ILRM 161; *S.C. v P.D.* High Court (McCracken J) 14 March 1996; *Mehigan v Duignan* [1997] 1 IR 340, [1997] 1 ILRM 171; *O'Keeffe v Ferris* [1997] 3 IR 463, [1997] 2 ILRM 161; *Georgopoulus v Beaumont Hospital Board* [1998] 3 IR 132. *Cf. O'Laoire v Medical Council* Supreme Court, 25 July 1997; *Hearn v Collins* High Court (O'Sullivan J) 3 February 1998.
[8] [1987] ILRM 669.
[9] [1987] ILRM 669, 701.
[10] *Ibid.* at 701.

fraud should be taken into account in deciding whether it had been established.[11] The position is, perhaps, best summarised by O'Flaherty in *O'Laoire v Medical Council*[12] who surveyed the authorities and stated:

> The common law panorama at this time gives the impression that there is but one standard of proof in civil cases though, of necessity, it is a flexible one. This flexibility will ensure that the graver the allegation the higher will be the degree of probability that is required to bring home the case against the person whose conduct is impugned.

It is, thus, clear that while there is not any formal raising of the standard of proof from that of proof on a balance of probabilities, the courts will be careful to apply the standard of proof with sufficient stringency to ensure that justice is done and that an adverse finding is not made without satisfactory proof.

Application for a Non-Suit

19.005 As stated, the question of whether a party has discharged the burden of proof upon him by proving his case on a balance of probabilities is decided, once, at the conclusion of the case by the tribunal of fact. However, an issue will not even reach the tribunal of fact for this adjudication if a party fails to satisfy the evidential burden placed upon him to make out a *prima facie* case.[13] Whether a party has done this can be tested by a defendant by means of an application for a non-suit after the conclusion of the plaintiff's case.

19.006 The principles to be applied by a trial judge in dealing with such an application in a contract or tort action were laid down by the Supreme Court in *Hetherington v Ultra Tyre Service Ltd*[14] and *O'Toole v Heavey*.[15] In the latter case, Finlay CJ differentiated between actions that were tried with a jury and those that were tried by a judge sitting alone. In the case of the former, the judge is required to consider whether the plaintiff had made out a *prima facie* case *i.e.*

---

[11] *Ibid.* at 702. See also *Masterfoods Ltd v HB Ice Cream Ltd* [1993] ILRM 145, 183; *S.C. v P.D.* High Court (McCracken J) 14 March 1996; *O'Keeffe v Ferris* [1997] 3 IR 463, [1997] 2 ILRM 161; *Georgopoulus v Beaumont Hospital Board* [1998] 3 IR 132; *Hearn v Collins* High Court (O'Sullivan J) 3 February 1998; *Hornal v Neuberger Products Ltd* [1957] 1 QB 247, 266, [1956] 3 WLR 1034, 1048, [1956] 3 All ER 970, 978.
[12] Supreme Court, 25 July 1997.
[13] *O'Toole v Heavey* [1993] 2 IR 544, [1993] ILRM 343.
[14] [1993] 2 IR 535, [1993] ILRM 353.
[15] [1993] 2 IR 544, [1993] ILRM 343. The principles laid down in these decisions have been applied in a number of cases including *Bank of Ireland v McCabe* High Court (Flood J) 25 March 1993; *Hanafin v Minister for the Environment* [1996] 2 IR 321, [1996] 2 ILRM 161; *Chanelle Veterinary Ltd v Pfizer (Ireland) Ltd* [1999] 1 IR 365, [1998] 1 ILRM 161 (HC); *Cranny v Kelly* [1998] 1 IR 54; *Gill v Egan* High Court (O'Sullivan J) 16 October 1998.

whether, on the evidence adduced by the plaintiff, it would be open to a jury, if no other evidence was given, or if they accepted that evidence, even though contradicted in its material facts, to enter a verdict for the plaintiff.

The situation in relation to an action tried without a jury is somewhat more complex. If an action is brought against one defendant and an application to dismiss the proceedings is brought, the trial judge should, first, inquire from the defendant as to whether in the event of a refusal of that application, he intends to go into evidence. If the defendant indicates that he does intend to go into evidence if the application is refused, then the trial judge has to decide whether the plaintiff has made out a *prima facie* case. If, on the other hand, the defendant indicates that he does not intend to go into evidence on the issue of liability if the application is refused, then the trial judge is required to determine whether, having regard to his view of the evidence of the plaintiff, the plaintiff has established as a matter of probability the facts necessary to support a verdict in his favour.[16] If he is not so satisfied, then the trial judge must dismiss the action. However, if he is so satisfied, he must give judgment for the plaintiff.

The Chief Justice went on to consider the situation where more than one defendant is sued. He stated that, where claims or cross-claims for contribution have been made between the defendants on the basis that they are joint tortfeasors, the trial judge should not decide on an application for a non-suit at the conclusion of the plaintiff's evidence unless he is completely satisfied that the eventual outcome of the case could not result in the patently unjust anomaly that a plaintiff having sued more than one defendant and one of the defendants having been dismissed out of the action at the conclusion of the plaintiff's evidence, the other defendant or defendants could also escape liability by affixing the blame through their evidence on the defendant already dismissed. He took the view that, the only way in most cases that a trial judge would be in a position to satisfy himself that such a risk did not exist would be by ascertaining what the intention of all the defendants was in relation to the calling of evidence and the precise nature of the case which each of them would be making in the event of giving such evidence. However, he did enter the caveat that, where a plaintiff did not make out any form of plausible or arguable case against any of the defendants, the trial judge had a discretion to dismiss the action in its entirety.

19.007 In *Cranny v Kelly*,[17] an appeal was allowed by the Supreme Court because of a departure from those principles. The plaintiff's claim arose out of the death of her husband in a road traffic accident involving a car in which he and the first named defendant were travelling. The plaintiff contended that the accident had been caused by the negligence of the first named defendant driving the car. However, while she was able to adduce evidence to show that the car

---

[16] Note that if the defendant indicates that he intends to go into evidence on the issue of damages but not of liability, the same position obtains (at 547, 345).
[17] [1998] 1 IR 54.

had been driven negligently, none of the witnesses could say who was driving it.

At the conclusion of the evidence for the plaintiff, the first named defendant applied for a non-suit on the basis that the evidence had not established the identity of the driver. The trial judge put the first named defendant to his election as to whether he intended to call evidence and he was informed by counsel that the first named defendant would not be calling evidence. Notwithstanding this, the trial judge refused the application on the basis that the first named defendant had a case to answer and invited him to change his mind and give evidence. The first named defendant then gave evidence to the effect that the plaintiff's husband had been driving the car. Although the trial judge rejected much of the evidence given by the first named defendant, he ultimately held that he was not satisfied that the first named defendant had been driving the car on the day in question.

Murphy J, delivering the judgment of the Supreme Court, was satisfied that, in ruling on the application for a non-suit, the trial judge had departed from the principles laid down in *Hetherington* and *O'Toole* in that, having been informed that the first named defendant did not intend to go into evidence, he did not dismiss the action or give judgment for the plaintiff. While he acknowledged that it would be desirable to avoid the expense and delay of a further trial, he concluded that this was unavoidable and the case was remitted to the High Court for a re-trial.

RELEVANCE AND ADMISSIBILITY OF EVIDENCE

Relevance

19.008 An essential pre-condition for the admission of any evidence is that it is relevant to the issues in the case. Evidence will be relevant "if it is logically probative or disprobative of some matters which requires proof…[if it] makes the matters which requires proof more or less probable".[18] A straightforward example of the application of this definition can be seen in *Holcombe v Hewson*.[19] The plaintiff brewer brought an action against the defendant publican for breach of covenant to buy his beer from the plaintiff. The defendant's defence was that the plaintiff had supplied sub-standard beer and in order to rebut this allegation, the plaintiff wished to call other publicans to give evidence that he had supplied them with good beer. However, this evidence was excluded on the basis that it merely proved the good quality of beer supplied by the plaintiff to other publicans. Given that a brewer might supply good beer to one publican and not another, this evidence was irrelevant to the issues at hand.

---

[18] *Per* Lord Simon in *R v Kilbourne* [1973] AC 729, 756, [1973] 2 WLR 254, 276-277, [1973] 1 All ER 440, 461.
[19] (1810) 2 Camp 391.

19.009 It is important to emphasise, however, that the concept of relevance is not purely one of logic. Policy considerations may also be taken into account in assessing relevance and may dictate that a given piece of evidence should be deemed to be irrelevant. This can be seen in *Browne v Tribune Newspapers plc*[20] where it was held by the Supreme Court that evidence that the plaintiff had recovered damages for libel in other unrelated actions was not admissible in mitigation of damages in libel proceedings. A very important factor in reaching that conclusion was that permitting the introduction of evidence of this nature would involve the court in trying collateral issues. Keane CJ pointed to the nature of the inquiry which admission of such evidence would require and commented that it would be "remarkable that a court would be obliged to try collateral issues of this nature simply in order to determine whether ... the plaintiff's damages should be reduced because of his readiness to bring defamation proceedings in the past".[21]

Admissibility

19.010 All relevant evidence is admissible unless excluded by one of the exclusionary rules. There are a number of exclusionary rules that are potentially applicable in civil proceedings but, by far, the two most important are the rules against hearsay and opinion evidence.

Rule Against Hearsay[22]

19.011 The rule against hearsay stipulates that a statement other than one made by a person testifying in the proceedings in which it is sought to be admitted, is inadmissible as evidence of the truth of any fact asserted.[23] The scope of application of the rule is very broad and extends to all statements, whether oral,[24] written[25] or by conduct.[26] However, it is important to note that it does not apply to all out of court statements. As emphasised by Kingsmill Moore J in *Cullen v Clarke*:[27]

---

[20] [2001] 2 ILRM 424.

[21] *Ibid.* at 435.

[22] For a comprehensive statement and analysis of the Irish law with regard to the rule against hearsay, see the Law Reform Commission, *The Rule Against Hearsay* (Working Paper No. 9 – 1980).

[23] This definition is based on that advanced by Kingsmill Moore J in *Cullen v Clarke* [1963] IR 368, 378 and Tapper (ed.), *Cross & Tapper on Evidence* (9th ed.), at 530.

[24] See *Stobart v Dryden* (1836) 1 M & W 615; *R v Gibson* (1887) 18 QBD 537; *Teper v R* [1952] AC 480, [1952] 2 All ER 447.

[25] See *Patel v Comptroller of Customs* [1966] AC 356, [1965] 3 WLR 1221, [1965] 3 All ER 593; *Myers v Director of Public Prosecutions* [1965] AC 1001, [1964] 3 WLR 145, [1964] 2 All ER 881.

[26] *Chandrasekera v R* [1937] AC 220.

[27] [1963] IR 368.

[T]here is *no* general rule of evidence to the effect that a witness may not testify as to the words spoken by a person who is not produced as a witness. There is a general rule subject to many exceptions that evidence of the speaking of such words is inadmissible to prove the truth of the facts which they assert. ... This is known as the rule against hearsay. If the fact that the words were spoken rather than their truth is what it is sought to prove, a statement is admissible.[28]

The hearsay rule is also subject to a large number of exceptions which are examined below. However, it should be acknowledged that recourse to these exceptions may not be necessary because hearsay is often admitted in civil cases in the discretion of the trial judge at least where it does not go to the crucial facts at issue between the parties.[29]

(i) Admissions

19.012 An admission is a statement made by a party which is adverse to his case and it may be adduced to prove the truth of its contents. A statement made in the presence of a party may constitute an admission if, having regard to the circumstances, he can be considered to have accepted or admitted the truth of what was stated.[30] Admissions made by persons in privity with a party such as a predecessor in title[31] or an agent[32] may also be addduced.

(ii) Statements Forming Part of the Res Gestae

19.013 Under the inclusionary doctrine of *res gestae*, a statement of fact or opinion which is so closely associated in time, place and circumstances with some act or event which is in issue that it can be said to form part of the same

---

[28] *Ibid.* at 378. Examples of out of court statements which are admissible as non-hearsay or original evidence include: (i) statements which demonstrate the ability to speak; (ii) operative words (*Director of Public Prosecutions v O'Kelly* High Court (McCracken J) 10 February 1998); (iii) where the falsity of the statement is relevant (*Attorney General v Good* (1825) M'Cle & Yo 286); (iv) where the statement reveals esoteric knowledge (*R v Olisa* [1990] Crim LR 721); (v) to show impact upon the person hearing or reading it (*Hoare v Allen* (1801) 3 Esp 276); and (vi) where it constitutes circumstantial proof (*R v Lydon* [1987] Crim LR 407).

[29] The Law Reform Commission (*op. cit.* at 11) noted that the disadvantages of the hearsay rule were, in practice, alleviated by the fact that judges often discouraged counsel from pressing points on hearsay or by insisting on hearing an item of hearsay evidence *de bene esse.*

[30] *People (AG) v Finkel* (1951) 1 Frewen 123; *R v Christie* [1914] AC 545, [1914-15] All ER 63.

[31] *McKenna v Earl of Howth* (1893) 27 ILTR 48; *Woolway v Rowe* (1834) 1 Ad & El 114.

[32] *Dwyer v Larkin* (1905) 39 ILTR 40; *Bord na gCon v Murphy* [1970] IR 301.

transaction as the act or event in issue, is itself admissible in evidence.[33] The doctrine can be subdivided into four classes of statement: (i) statements by participants in or observers of events;[34] (ii) statements concerning the maker's performance of an act;[35] (iii) statements concerning the maker's state of mind or emotion;[36] (iv) statements of physical sensation.[37]

(iii) Declarations in the Course of Duty

19.014 An oral or written statement of a deceased person, made by a person in pursuance of a duty owed to another to report or record an act, is admissible as evidence of the truth of its contents provided that the record or report was made more or less contemporaneously with his doing of the act and he had no motive to misrepresent or mislead.[38] The conditions of admissibility are that: (i) the declarant must have performed an act which he was under a duty to record or report;[39] (ii) the statement must have been made roughly contemporaneously with it;[40] and (iii) the declarant must have had no motive to misrepresent or mislead.[41]

(iv) Declarations Against Interest

19.015 A statement by a deceased person as to a fact which he knew to be against his pecuniary or proprietary interest when he made the declaration is admissible as evidence of that fact and of collateral matters mentioned in the declaration. The conditions of admissibility are that the statement (i) must be against the proprietary or pecuniary interest of the maker;[42] (ii) must have been

---

[33] See *People (AG) v Crosbie* [1966] IR 490; *Teper v R* [1952] AC 480, 486, [1952] 2 All ER 447, 449.

[34] See *R v Lunny* (1854) 6 Cox CC 477; *People (AG) v Crosbie* [1966] IR 490; *Ratten v R* [1972] AC 378, [1971] 3 WLR 930, [1971] 3 All ER 801; *R v Andrews* [1987] AC 281, [1987] 2 WLR 413, [1987] 1 All ER 513.

[35] See *Gresham Hotel v Manning* (1867) IR 1 CL 125; *Wright v Doe d Tatham* (1838) 4 Bing (NC) 489; *Peacock v Harris* (1836) 5 Ad & El 449; *Howe v Malkin* (1878) 40 LT 196.

[36] See *Davis v Adair* [1895] 1 IR 379; *Moffet v Moffet* [1920] 1 IR 57; *Cullen v Clarke* [1963] IR 368; *Thomas v Connell* (1838) 4 M & W 267; *R v Vincent* (1840) 9 C & P 275; *Sudgen v Lord St Leonards* (1876) 1 PD 154.

[37] *Donaghy v Ulster Spinning Co. Ltd* (1912) 46 ILTR 33; *Gilbey v Great Western Railway Co.* (1910) 102 LT 202; *Aveson v Lord Kinnaird* (1805) 6 East 188.

[38] See *Malone v L'Estrange* (1839) 2 Ir Eq R 16; *Dillon v Tobin* (1879) 12 ILTR 32; *Mulhern v Clery* [1930] IR 649; *Price v Earl of Torrington* (1703) 1 Salk 285.

[39] *Ryan v Ring* (1890) 25 LR Ir 184; *Harris v Lambert* [1932] IR 504; *Somers v Erskine (No. 2)* [1944] IR 368; *Smith v Blakey* (1867) LR 2 QB 326.

[40] *Price v Earl of Torrington* (1703) 1 Salk 285; *The Henry Coxon* (1878) 3 PD 156.

[41] *The Henry Coxon* (1878) 3 PD 156.

[42] *Richards v Gogarty* (1870) 4 ICLR 300; *Conner v Fitzgerald* (1883) 4 LR Ir 106; *Flood v Russell* (1891) 29 LR Ir 91; *Domvile v Calwell* [1907] 2 IR 617; *Power v United Dublin Tramways Co.* [1926] IR 302.

against the interest of the maker at the time it was made;[43] (iii) the declarant must have known that it was against his interest;[44] and (iv) the declarant must have had personal knowledge of the facts stated.[45]

(v) Declarations as to Pedigree

19.016 Oral or written declarations of a deceased person as to pedigree may be admissible as evidence of the facts asserted.[46] The conditions of admissibility are that (i) the declaration should relate to a question of pedigree, *viz.* demonstrate a genealogical purpose;[47] (ii) the declarant must have been a blood relation, or the spouse of a blood relation, of the person whose pedigree is in issue;[48] and (iii) the declaration must have been made before the dispute in which it is tendered had arisen.[49]

(vi) Declarations as to Public and General Rights

19.017 The oral or written declaration of a deceased person concerning the reputed existence of a public or general right is admissible as evidence of the existence of such a right provided that it was made prior to the commencement of the dispute to which it relates.[50] An additional requirement in the case of the reputed existence of a general right, is that the declarant have competent knowledge.[51]

(vii) Testamentary Declarations

19.018 Declarations made by a testator, both before and after the execution of his will, are, in the event of its loss, admissible as secondary evidence of its contents.[52]

---

[43] *Lalor v Lalor* (1879) 4 LR Ir 678; *Re Tollemache, ex p. Edwards* (1884) 14 QBD 415.

[44] *Ward v HS Pitt & Co.* [1913] 2 KB 130; *Tucker v Oldbury UDC* [1912] 2 KB 317.

[45] *Sussex Peerage Case* (1844) 11 Cl & Fin 85; *Sturla v Freccia* (1880) 5 App Cas 623.

[46] See *Goodright d Stevens v Moss* (1777) 2 Cowp 591; *Whitelocke v Baker* (1807) 13 Ves 510.

[47] *Duke of Devonshire v Neill* (1877) 2 LR Ir 132; *Palmer v Palmer* (1885) 18 LR Ir 192; *Smith v Smith* (1876) 1 LR Ir 206; *Haines v Guthrie* (1884) 13 QBD 818.

[48] *Beamish v Smeltzer* [1934] IR 693; *Johnson v Lawson* (1824) 2 Bing 86; *Shrewsbury Peerage Case* (1858) 7 HL 1.

[49] *Berkeley Peerage Case* (1811) 4 Camp 401.

[50] *Duke of Devonshire v Neill* (1877) 2 LR Ir 132; *Giant's Causeway Co. Ltd v Attorney General* (1905) 5 NIJR 381; *Berkeley Peerage Case* (1811) 4 Camp 401; *Moseley v Davies* (1822) 11 Price 162; *Mercer v Denne* [1905] 2 Ch 538.

[51] *Thomas v Jenkins* (1837) 6 Ad & El 788.

[52] *R v Ball* (1890) 25 LR Ir 556; *Sugden v Lord St Leonards* (1876) 1 PD 154.

(viii) Statements in Public Documents

19.019 A diverse range of documents classified as public documents are admissible of the facts stated therein including entries in the public books of a corporation relating to matters of public interest,[53] the statutory returns of a company[54] and census returns.[55] Because of the variety in the classes of documents to which this exception applies, the conditions of admissibility vary somewhat but as a general rule, it would seem as if a public document is only admissible if (i) it concerns a public matter;[56] (ii) it was made by a public officer acting under a duty to inquire and records the results of such inquiry;[57] and (iii) it was intended to be retained for public reference or inspection.[58]

(ix) Testimony in Former Proceedings

19.020 A statement made by a witness concerning a particular issue while testifying is admissible in relation to the same issue in subsequent proceedings between the same parties (or those in privity with them) if the witness in question was subject to cross-examination and is dead or otherwise unable to attend the subsequent proceedings.[59]

(x) Works of Reference

19.021 Authoritative published works of reference such as dictionaries,[60] historical works[61] and medical texts[62] are admissible to prove facts of a public nature[63] stated therein.

(xi) Statements of Children in Welfare Proceedings

19.022 S. 23 of the Children Act 1997, which applies in proceedings concerning the welfare of a child or a person with a mental disability, provides that a

---

[53] *Shrewsbury v Hart* (1823) 1 C & P 113.

[54] *R v Halpin* [1975] QB 907, [1975] 3 WLR 260, [1975] 2 All ER 1124.

[55] *Dublin Corporation v Bray Townships* [1900] 2 IR 88.

[56] *Cf. Heath v Deane* [1905] 2 Ch 86.

[57] *Irish Society v Bishop of Derry* (1846) 12 Cl & Fin 641; *Doe d France v Andrews* (1850) 15 QB 756; *R v Halpin* [1975] QB 907, [1975] 3 WLR 260, [1975] 2 All ER 1124.

[58] *Mercer v Denne* [1905] 2 Ch 538; *R v Sealby* [1965] 1 All ER 701.

[59] *Doncaster Corporation v Day* (1810) 3 Taunt 262; *Llanover v Homfray* (1881) 19 Ch D 224. *Cf. R v Hall* [1973] QB 496, [1972] 3 WLR 974, [1973] 1 All ER 1.

[60] *Marchioness of Blandford v Dowager Duchess of Marlborough* (1743) 2 Atk 542; *R v Agricultural Land Tribunal, ex p. Benney* [1955] 2 QB 140.

[61] *Read v Bishop of Lincoln* [1892] AC 644.

[62] *McCarthy v Owners of the Melita* (1923) 16 BWCC 222.

[63] The exception does not extend to facts of a private or local nature: *Evans v Getting* (1834) 6 C & P 586; *Fowke v Berington* [1914] 2 Ch 308.

statement made by a child can be admitted as evidence of any fact therein of which direct oral evidence would be admissible, notwithstanding the rule against hearsay, where the court considers that the child is unable to give evidence by reason of age, or the giving of oral evidence by the child would not be in the interests of the welfare of the child.[64] Certain safeguards are built into the section with subs.(2) stipulating that a statement cannot be admitted if the court is of the opinion that, in the interests of justice, the statement or that part of the statement ought not to be so admitted. In considering this issue, the court must have regard to all the circumstances, including any risk that the admission will result in unfairness to any of the parties to the proceedings. Provision is also made for advance notification of the intention to adduce hearsay evidence under the section.[65]

Opinion Evidence

19.023 The general rule is that a witness may only give evidence of facts perceived by him and may not express an opinion as to any fact in issue which is a function reserved to the tribunal of fact.[66] However, a witness may be permitted to give opinion evidence where it is necessary to do so because: (i) fact and inference therefrom are indivisible as where a witness gives evidence as to the age of a person[67] or the sanity of a testator[68]; (ii) the tribunal of fact is not in as good a position as to the witness to make the inference as, for example, where a witness gives identification evidence[69]; or (iii) where it is simply expedient to admit such evidence. In addition, an expert can give opinion evidence as to matters within his expertise and this exception is examined below.

THE COURSE OF EVIDENCE

Calling of Witnesses

19.024 Under our adversarial model of justice, strategic decisions relating to what witnesses to call and the order in which to call them is primarily a matter for the parties themselves. A party is free to call as many witnesses as he wishes subject to a potential costs penalty if the witnesses he calls are either unneces-

---

[64] *Cf. Eastern Health Board v M.K.* [1999] 2 IR 99 (*sub nom In the Matter of M.K., S.K. and W.K.* [1999] 2 ILRM 321); *Southern Health Board v C.H.* [1996] 1 IR 219, [1996] 2 ILRM 142.

[65] Subs. (3). See also s.24 which deals with the weight to be attached to a statement admitted pursuant to s.23 and s.25 which deals with evidence as to the credibility of the child.

[66] *Attorney General (Ruddy) v Kenny* (1960) 94 ILTR 185, 190.

[67] *R v Cox* [1898] 1 QB 179.

[68] *Wright v Doe d Tatham* (1838) 4 Bing NC 489.

[69] *Attorney General (Ruddy) v Kenny* (1960) 94 ILTR 185, 190.

sary or superfluous. Further, there are no witnesses which he is obliged to call and there are no restrictions on the order in which he may call his witnesses.[70]

The power of a judge to intervene in the calling of witnesses is very limited. A judge has no right to call witnesses without the consent of the parties,[71] except in cases of civil contempt[72] or child care proceedings.[73] A judge does, however, have the power to recall a witness previously called by a party.[74]

Course of Evidence

19.025 At common law, the plaintiff has the right to begin, subject to the judge's discretion to the contrary, unless the defendant bears the evidential burden in respect of every issue.[75] Assuming that he has the right to begin, the plaintiff opens the case to the court, calls his witnesses and sums up if the defendant does not go into evidence. The defendant then replies. If the defendant does go into evidence, then the plaintiff will not sum up at the conclusion of his case. Instead, the defendant opens his case, calls his witnesses and sums up, leaving the plaintiff with the right of reply. This procedure is reversed if the defendant has the right to begin calling evidence.

The course of evidence in the case of a trial by jury is expressly regulated by Order 36, rule 35[76] which provides that the party who begins, or his counsel, is permitted at the close of his case, if his opponent does not announce any intention to adduce evidence, to address the jury a second time for the purpose of summing up the evidence. If, on the other hand, the opposite party, or his counsel, decides to go into evidence, then he is permitted to open his case and to sum up the evidence with the plaintiff granted a right to reply.

Non-appearance by a Party

19.026 Order 36, rule 28 provides that if, when the trial is called on, the plaintiff appears, and the defendant does not appear, the plaintiff may prove his claim, so far as the burden of proof lies upon him.[77] Similarly, if the defendant appears but not the plaintiff, the defendant is entitled to judgment dismissing the action subject to the caveat that, if he has a counterclaim, then he prove it so far as the

---

[70] *Briscoe v Briscoe* [1968] P 501, [1966] 2 WLR 205, [1966] 1 All ER 465.
[71] *Re Enoch and Zaretzky, Bock & Co.'s Arbitration* [1910] 1 KB 327, cited with approval by Molony LJ in *Shea v Wilson & Co.* (1916) 50 ILTR 73.
[72] *Yianni v Yianni* [1966] 1 WLR 120, [1966] 1 All ER 231.
[73] *Eastern Health Board v Mooney* High Court (Carney J) 20 March 1998.
[74] *Fallon v Calvert* [1960] 2 QB 201, [1960] 2 WLR 346, [1960] 1 All ER 281.
[75] *Mercer v Whall* (1845) 5 QB 447.
[76] See also Order 36, rule 36 which makes special provision for defamation actions.
[77] Special provision is made with regard to actions for the recovery of land: Order 36, rules 29–31.

burden of proof lies upon him.[78] However, Order 36, rule 33 provides that any verdict or judgment obtained where a party does not appear at the trial may be set aside by the court upon such terms as may seem fit, upon an application made within six days after trial.[79]

Adjournment

19.027 Order 36, rule 34 provides that a judge may, if he thinks it expedient for the interests of justice, postpone or adjourn a trial for such time, and upon such terms, if any, as he shall think fit.[80] It is clear from the decision in *A. and B. v Eastern Health Board*,[81] that the discretion to grant an adjournment is not untrammelled but is, rather, governed by the requirements of fair procedures.[82] The third respondent, who was the child of the applicants, had been 13 years of age when she was raped and became pregnant as a result. The Eastern Health Board applied to the District Court for an interim care order and directions permitting the termination of the third respondent's pregnancy and, at the hearing, counsel for the applicants requested a short adjournment so that he could consult a psychiatrist with a view to cross-examining a paediatric psychiatrist who had given evidence. The district judge refused to grant the adjournment because of the urgency of the matter and Geoghegan J concluded that "she wrongly and unreasonably refused the application as, although the matter was urgent, there had to be a balance between the urgency and the adoption of fair procedures".[83]

WITNESSES

Competence and Compellability of Witnesses

19.028 The general rule at common law, is that, in civil proceedings, all persons capable of understanding the nature of the oath, and capable of giving rational testimony, are competent and compellable witnesses.[84] The most important exception to this rule relates to children and persons with a mental disability which is examined below.[85] The burden of proving competence is on the

---

[78] Order 36, rule 32.

[79] Time for bringing such an application may be enlarged pursuant to Order 122, rule 7.

[80] *Cf. Ward v Walsh* Supreme Court, 31 July 1991.

[81] [1998] 1 IR 464.

[82] *Cf. Carey v Hussey* High Court (Kearns J) 21 December 1999; *Carroll v Mangan* High Court (Laffoy J) 10 November 1998; *Byrne v McDonnell* High Court (Keane J) 19 December 1995.

[83] [1998] 1 IR 464, 475.

[84] *Cf. Eastern Health Board v Mooney* High Court (Carney J) 20 March 1998.

[85] It should also be noted that diplomats cannot be compelled to give evidence: s.5 of the Diplomatic Relations Immunities Act 1967.

party tendering the witness and if an issue is raised as to competence, the witness can be examined and cross-examined in order to reach a determination.[86] The question as to whether a particular witness is competent to testify is determined by the trial judge but if the witness is found to be competent, the question of the weight to be attached to his testimony is a matter for the tribunal of fact.

Sworn Evidence

19.029 The general rule is that the evidence of any witness should be sworn and, once a witness is deemed to be competent, the witness must be sworn.[87] The oath may take any form that the witness wishes[88] and it is immaterial that the person taking the oath has no religious belief.[89] Should a person object to being sworn and states as the ground of his objection either that he has no religious belief or that the taking of an oath is against his religious belief, he will be permitted to make a solemn affirmation instead.[90]

In *Mapp v Gilhooley*,[91] one of the points raised on appeal was that the trial judge had erred in admitting the unsworn evidence of a young boy. It was held by the Supreme Court that *viva voce* evidence must be given on oath or affirmation. Finlay CJ stated that the broad purpose of this rule is to ensure, as far as possible, that such *viva voce* evidence is true by the provision of a moral or religious and legal sanction against deliberate untruth. Such a rule could not, therefore, be inconsistent with the Constitution, either on the basis of being discriminatory or on the basis of being an impermissible restriction of the right of access to the courts.[92] It followed that the trial judge did not have any jurisdiction to accept the unsworn evidence of the child even if both parties expressly agreed and even if he concluded that the child was a competent witness in the sense that he understood what he was saying and was able to give a coherent and truthful account of what had occurred.

19.030 The situation with regard to children and persons with a mental disability is now governed by s.28(1) of the Children Act 1997, which provides that in any civil proceedings, "the evidence of a child who has not attained the age of 14 years may be received otherwise than on oath or affirmation if the court is satisfied that the child is capable of giving an intelligible account of events which are relevant to the proceedings." Subs.(3) extends the application of the

---

[86] *Cf. People (AG) v Kehoe* [1951] IR 70.
[87] *Cf.* Order 39, rule 18 which provides that any officer of the court or other persons, directed to take the examination of any witness or person, may administer oaths.
[88] S.2 of the Oaths Act 1909.
[89] S.3 of the Oaths Act 1888.
[90] S.1 of the Oaths Act 1888.
[91] [1991] 2 IR 253, [1991] ILRM 695.
[92] *Ibid.* at 262, 700.

section to persons with a mental disability who are aged 14 or over.[93] Where it is sought to rely on s.28(3) to permit the introduction of unsworn evidence, the trial judge must hold an inquiry and be satisfied that: (i) the person has a mental handicap, and (ii) that he is capable of giving an intelligible account of events which are relevant to the proceedings.[94]

Language and Interpreters

19.031 Evidence in this jurisdiction may, as a matter of course, be given in either English or Irish.[95] However, if a witness does not have a sufficient grasp of either English or Irish, he may give evidence in any language and an interpreter will be provided to facilitate this.[96] The parties to litigation are also entitled to have the proceedings conducted in a language that they understand and to have interpreters provided if necessary.[97] In *O Monacháin v An Taoiseach*,[98] Henchy J took the view that it would not be permissible to hear a case in any language (even Irish) without giving those who do not speak it a full opportunity to understand the case.

Expert Witnesses

19.032 As an exception to the general prohibition against opinion evidence, an expert is entitled to give evidence expressing his expert opinion in respect of matters which call for expertise.[99]

Definition of Expert

19.033 An expert is a person who is qualified to provide evidence in relation to a subject calling for expertise.[100] The categories of expert are not closed but

---

[93] A person with a mental disability is defined by s.20 as a person who has a mental disability to such an extent that it is not reasonably possible for the person to live independently.

[94] *Cf. O'Sullivan v Hamill* [1999] 2 IR 9.

[95] *Cf.* Article 8 of the Constitution and *Attorney General v Joyce* [1929] IR 526.

[96] *Attorney General v Joyce* [1929] IR 526, 531. Order 120, rule 1 provides that there must be such number of interpreters as the Chief Justice and the President of the High Court respectively may, from time to time, by requisition in writing addressed to the Minister for Justice, request. Such interpreters must attend the courts and the offices of the superior courts and be available to attend those courts as required for the hearing of any cause or matter.

[97] *R (O Coiléan) v Crotty* (1927) 61 ILTR 81; *State (Buckan) v Coyne* (1936) 70 ILTR 185; *O Monacháin v An Taoiseach* [1986] ILRM 660; *People (AG) v Saunders* (1963) 1 Frewen 283.

[98] [1986] ILRM 660.

[99] *Attorney General (Ruddy) v Kenny* (1960) 94 ILTR 185, 190. See generally Hardiman, "The Role of the Expert Witness" in Daly (ed.), *The Role of the Expert Witness* (1999).

[100] *Attorney General (Ruddy) v Kenny* (1960) 94 ILTR 185, 190. *Cf. McFadden v Murdock* (1867) 1 ICLR 211, 218.

include accountants, actuaries, architects, dentists, doctors, engineers, occupational therapists, psychologists, psychiatrists and scientists.[101] Expert evidence may be given in relation to matters of foreign law[102] but not in relation to domestic law.[103]

Persons may be considered to be experts by reason of their experience, training or knowledge.[104] Although some expertise in the area is necessary,[105] formal qualifications are not necessary provided the judge is satisfied as to the witness's expertise.[106] For example, in *McFadden v Murdock*,[107] it was held that a witness was qualified by virtue of his experience to give expert testimony. In an action for wages due, the defendant pleaded set off in respect of monies which he said had come into the hands of the plaintiff in the course of his employment as a shop assistant and for which he had not accounted. The plaintiff put the discrepancies down to wastage and was permitted to call a witness who had run a business similar to that of the defendant for many years in order to testify that according to his experience in such business, the amount of wastage alleged was not unreasonable.

Facts on Which Expert Opinion may be Based

19.034 An expert may give his opinion upon facts which are either admitted or proved by admissible evidence.[108] These facts may be proved either by the expert himself or by other witnesses[109] but where the expert has no first-hand knowledge of the facts upon which his opinion is based he can state a hypothesis upon assumed facts.[110] These assumed facts must be proved by admissible

---

[101] *Cf.* the definition of expert given in Order 39, rule 45(1) (inserted by the Rules of the Superior Courts (No. 6) (Disclosure of Reports and Statements) 1998 (SI No. 391 of 1998).

[102] *O'Callaghan v O'Sullivan* [1925] 1 IR 90; *Sussex Peerage Case* (1844) 11 Cl & Fin 85.

[103] *Society for the Protection of Unborn Children (Ireland) Ltd v Grogan (No. 3)* [1992] 2 IR 471; *F. v Ireland* [1995] 1 IR 321, [1994] 2 ILRM 401 (HC), [1995] 2 ILRM 321 (SC).

[104] *Attorney General (Ruddy) v Kenny* (1960) 94 ILTR 185, 190.

[105] *R v Wilbain* (1863) 9 Cox CC 448.

[106] *McFadden v Murdock* (1867) 1 ICLR 211; *R v Silverlock* [1894] 2 QB 766. The lack of formal qualifications does, however, go to the weight to be attached to the testimony.

[107] (1867) 1 ICLR 211.

[108] *T. v P. (Orse T.)* [1990] 1 IR 545, 551. See also *Attorney General (Ruddy) v Kenny* (1960) 94 ILTR 185, 190.

[109] *Ibid.* at 551.

[110] *Ibid.* at 551. *Cf. Rotheram v Midland Great Western Railway Co.* (1903) 37 ILTR 23; *McFadden v Murdock* (1867) 1 ICLR 211. If an expert does not have first-hand knowledge of the facts upon which he bases his opinion, this will affect the weight to be attached to his testimony: *K.(D.) v H.(.T) (Orse K.(T.))* High Court (O'Higgins J) 25 February 1998.

evidence or else the expert's opinion will be of little or no weight. The nature of expertise is such that it will usually be based at least in part on matters of which the expert does not have personal knowledge. Therefore, in derogation of the general rule, an expert witness may give evidence as to matters which he, himself, did not perceive. Thus, an expert is entitled to draw on the work of others as part of the process of arriving at his conclusion.[111] Such material may include learned treatises, reference works, particular studies (whether published or unpublished[112]) and other information acquired in the course of his profession.[113]

Functions and Duties of Expert Witness

19.035 In *Davie v Edinburgh Magistrates*,[114] Lord President Cooper explained that the function of experts "is to furnish the judge or jury with the necessary scientific criteria for testing the accuracy of their conclusions, so as to enable the judge or jury to form their own independent judgment by the application of these criteria to the facts proved in evidence." It follows from this that the evidence of an expert should be independent and impartial and not coloured by the requirements of the party calling him. However, this level of independence is rarely achieved in practice leading Taylor to comment that "it is often quite surprising to see with what facility and to what extent their views can be made to correspond with the wishes or the interests of the parties who call them."[115] Indeed, it is difficult to escape the conclusion that in many cases, especially personal injury cases, experts are merely "hired guns" with little conception of their proper function and responsibility to the court.[116]

19.036 It is not surprising, therefore, that in recent times, the courts have felt the need to articulate the duties and responsibilities of experts. The most notable example in this regard is *National Justice Cia Naviera S.A. v Prudential Assurance Co. Ltd*[117] where Cresswell J enumerated a list which included the following:

1. Expert evidence presented to the court should be, and should be seen to be, the independent product of the expert uninfluenced as to form or content by the exigencies of litigation.

---

[111] *R v Abadom* [1983] 1 WLR 126, [1983] 1 All ER 364 (CA).
[112] *R v Abadom* [1983] 1 WLR 126, [1983] 1 All ER 364 (CA).
[113] *English Exporters (London) Ltd v Eldonwall Ltd* [1973] Ch 415, [1973] 2 WLR 435, [1973] 1 All ER 726.
[114] 1953 SC 34, 40.
[115] *Treatise on the Law of Evidence* (12th ed.), p.59. *Cf. News Datacom Ltd v Lyons* [1994] 1 ILRM 450, 456, where Flood J referred to "the opinion of a partisan expert".
[116] *Cf.* Barr, "Expert Evidence – A Few Personal Observations and the Implications of Recent Statutory Developments" (1999) 4 BR 185.
[117] [1993] 2 Lloyd's Rep 68.

2.　　An expert witness should provide independent assistance to the court by way of objective unbiased opinion in relation to matters within his expertise. An expert witness should never assume the role of advocate.

3.　　An expert witness should state the facts or assumptions upon which his opinion is based. He should not omit to consider material facts which could detract from his concluded opinion.

4.　　An expert witness should make it clear when a particular question or issue falls outside his expertise.

5.　　If an expert's opinion is not properly researched because he considers that insufficient data is available, then this must be stated with an indication that the opinion is no more than a provisional one.[118]

19.037 This list has not yet been expressly endorsed by the Irish courts but a similar approach is evident in *Fitzpatrick v Director of Public Prosecutions*.[119] The complainants were two sisters who alleged that they had been sexually abused over a long period by members of their family and a neighbour, the applicant. The applicant brought judicial review proceedings seeking an order of prohibition preventing his trial on a number of counts of sexual abuse offences on the ground of delay. One of the affidavits filed by the respondent was sworn by a senior clinical psychologist. The purpose of this affidavit was to give expert evidence to explain why such a long period had elapsed between the alleged offences and the complaints eventually made by the complainants. In the affidavit, he failed to mention the abuse of the complainants by members of their family or the psychological effect which this might have had on them. Under cross-examination, he sought to explain this omission on the basis that did not know of the allegations against the members of the family and he did not think that the fact that the complainants had been abused by someone else should form part of his report. Speaking of this failure, which he characterised as 'astonishing', McCracken J said that:

> It is my strongly held view that where a witness purports to give evidence in a professional capacity as an expert witness, he owes a duty to ascertain all the surrounding facts and to give that evidence in the context of those facts, whether they support the proposition which he is being asked to put forward or not.[120]

He did not accept that the background of abuse of the complainants was not relevant and as a consequence, he gave little weight to the evidence of the psychologist.

---

[118] *Ibid.* at 81.
[119] High Court (McCracken J) 5 December 1997.
[120] *Ibid.* at 3.

Evidence of Medical Practitioners in Personal Injuries Cases

19.038 A practice direction dated 8 September 1993 provides that, in actions in which damages for personal injuries are claimed, counsel should consider whether the attendance at the trial of medical witnesses who have provided medical reports is necessary to supplement or explain such reports. If attendance is not necessary for this purpose then a request should be made to admit in evidence the contents of such reports without the necessity to adduce oral testimony. The practice direction also stipulates that copies of all medical reports provided by medical witnesses who are called to give oral testimony should be made available to the court unless reasonable grounds exist for their exclusion. In addition, when medical witnesses are called to give evidence they should be asked, first, to confirm the correctness of the facts and opinions contained in any medical reports they had provided unless they have been excluded. If so confirmed, the reports may be admitted in evidence and the witness should then be asked to explain or supplement the report.

19.039 Although the savings in time and costs generated by adherence to the practice direction are obvious, these benefits may potentially come at a price as can be seen from the decision in *Curran v Finn*.[121] The case revolved around the question of whether accident trauma could aggravate the condition of multiple sclerosis. Murphy J in the Supreme Court commented that the task of the trial judge in this regard had been made more difficult by the decision of the parties not to call expert medical witnesses who had examined the plaintiff. A crucial issue in the case was the pre-accident condition of the plaintiff and the most important doctor to have treated the plaintiff during that period was Dr Callaghan. He did not give evidence but notes made by him on the occasion of the plaintiff's admission to hospital prior to the accident were admitted by consent of the parties. In considering those notes the trial judge misunderstood the notation used and, as a result, attributed symptoms to the plaintiff which she was not, in fact, suffering from. On appeal to the Supreme Court, the plaintiff sought and was granted leave to introduce by way of further evidence an affidavit of Dr Callaghan to explain the notation used and diagnosis made. All of this led Murphy J to comment that: "The facts of this case underscore the dangers and difficulties of examining or analysing documents provided on discovery or put in evidence by agreement without the sworn testimony of the author and his explanation of the records made by him."

---

[121] Supreme Court, 20 May 1999.

EXAMINATION OF WITNESSES

Necessity for Oral Evidence

19.040 One of the cardinal principles of our system of justice is that of orality, whereby the primary form of proof is the oral testimony of witnesses given before the tribunal of fact. That principle is enshrined in Order 39, rule 1 which provides that:

> In the absence of any agreement in writing between the solicitors of all parties ... the witnesses at the trial of any action, or at any assessment of damages shall be examined *viva voce* and in open Court, but the Court may, at any time for sufficient reason, order that any particular fact or facts may be proved by affidavit, or that the affidavit of any witness may be read at the hearing or trial, on such conditions as the Court may think reasonable, or that any witness whose attendance in Court ought for some sufficient cause to be dispensed with be examined by interrogatories or otherwise before a commissioner or examiner; provided that, where it appears to the Court that the other party, *bona fide*, desires the production of a witness for cross-examination, and that such witness can be produced, an order shall not be made authorising the evidence of such witness to be given by affidavit.

19.041 The interpretation of the predecessor of this rule was considered by Palles CB in *Cronin v Paul*.[122] He distinguished between evidence going to the gist of the issues in the action which could not be proved by affidavit and evidence in relation to formal matters which could be so proved:

> It is the ordinary practice that everything going to the gist of the action should be proved by oral evidence in cases of trial by jury. If proof of mere formal matter were required I would grant this application; but here the evidence required goes to the issues in the action; and the plaintiff's evidence as to these matters would also, I think, be confined to evidence by affidavit.[123]

19.042 These principles were endorsed and refined in what is now the leading authority, *Phonographic Performance (Ireland) Ltd v Cody*.[124] The case concerned a dispute about the payment of royalties in respect of recordings played in the defendants' hotel. In their defence, the defendants put in issue the plaintiff's claim that copyright subsisted in the recordings and that the plaintiff was

---

[122] (1881) 15 ILTR 121. Followed by Maguire P in *Northridge v O'Grady* [1940] Ir Jur Rep 19.
[123] *Ibid.* at 122.
[124] [1998] 4 IR 504, [1994] 2 ILRM 241 (HC), [1998] 2 ILRM 21 (SC).

the owner or exclusive licensee of such copyrights. In the alternative, they pleaded that they were willing to pay such equitable remuneration as the plaintiff might be entitled to, under the provisions of the Copyright Act 1963. The plaintiff brought a motion seeking, *inter alia*, leave to prove these matters on affidavit rather than by oral evidence. The plaintiff argued that, having regard to the multiplicity of witnesses who would be required and the difficulty in obtaining their attendance, it would be wholly impractical for the plaintiff to prove these matters by oral evidence.

In the High Court, Keane J took the view that the court had a discretion as to whether to make an order under Order 39, rule 1 permitting any particular fact to be proved by affidavit. However, given that "the rule that witnesses at the trial of any action must be examined *viva voce* and in open court is of central importance in our system of justice and is not to be lightly departed from",[125] he held that such an order could only be made where four requirements were met: (i) the facts sought to be proved did not relate to issues significantly in dispute between the parties;[126] (ii) the court was not satisfied that the other party *bona fide* required the production of the deponent for cross-examination; (iii) the difficulty or expense of producing the deponent in court was such that there was a serious risk of injustice to the party seeking to adduce the evidence on affidavit; and (iv) the application was made as a preliminary application before the trial of the action.[127]

Applying those criteria to the facts before him, he was satisfied that the case was an appropriate one in which to make such an order. Important factors in reaching this conclusion were his view that the pleas denying the copyright in the recordings and the plaintiff's legal interest in the copyright did not go to the gist of the action and that the defendants had failed to indicate that they had any serious doubts about the correctness of the averments sought to be made on affidavit or that they were in possession of material on the basis of which they wished to cross-examine the proposed deponents.

An appeal against the determination of Keane J on this point was allowed by the Supreme Court. Delivering the judgment of the court, Murphy J agreed with the emphasis placed by Keane J on the importance of examination of witnesses *viva voce* but took the view that he had overstated the degree of discretion enjoyed by a court under Order 39, rule 1 and had misapplied it on the facts. Murphy J endorsed the analysis of Palles CB in *Cronin v Paul*[128] that an order dispensing with oral evidence could only be made in relation to formal or

---

[125] [1998] 4 IR 504, 515.
[126] *Cronin v Paul* (1881) 15 ILTR 121; *Northridge v O'Grady* [1940] Ir Jur Rep 19; *McGlinchey v Ireland (No. 2)* [1990] 2 IR 220.
[127] *Cf. Shannon v Ireland* [1984] IR 548, [1985] ILRM 449 where Finlay P allowed evidence to be given on affidavit by a person who was in custody in Northern Ireland on foot of an application made in the course of the trial but emphasised that the application should be made as a preliminary application before the trial.
[128] (1881) 15 ILTR 121.

collateral matters and not in respect of issues that went to the gist of the action. He disagreed, in that regard, with the conclusion of Keane J that the gist of the action was the reasonableness of the remuneration sought by the plaintiff. He accepted that this was part of the gist of the action but another part of it was the right of the plaintiff to receive such remuneration. The defendants were entitled to put the plaintiff on proof of its title and the strength or weaknesses of the case to be made by either side did not alter the importance of the issue.

That conclusion was sufficient for the disposition of the appeal but the learned judge went on to make some comments as to the proviso of whether the defendants *bona fide* desired the production of the deponents for cross-examination. He accepted that the onus was on them to establish the *bona fide* desire for the production of a witness but he did not accept that it necessarily followed that the defendants would have to show the existence of evidence casting doubt upon that to be offered by the deponent. It might be sufficient simply to point to the complexities of the matters in respect of which it was sought to tender proof by affidavit and assert the right to explore with the witnesses their competence and credibility in giving evidence in relation to them. He also stated that, where a *bona fide* desire is shown and the proviso is satisfied, the matter ceases to be one of discretion and the order for dispensation with oral evidence must be refused.

Examination-in-Chief

19.043 Examination-in-chief is the questioning of a witness by the party calling him. Its object is to elicit testimony which supports the version of the facts in issue which is contended for by that party. A number of rules regulate the manner in which examination-in-chief may be conducted and what questions may be asked and each of these is considered in outline.

Leading Questions

19.044 The general rule is that on examination-in-chief, a party may not be asked leading questions.[129] A leading question is one which suggests the answer desired, or assumes the existence of disputed facts as to which the witness is to testify. The difference between leading and other questions is not a clear one and there is no ready test available to distinguish the two.[130] Strict adherence to the rule would make examination-in-chief unduly cumbersome and slow and, therefore, a degree of latitude is often afforded by counsel on the other side

---

[129] Evidence elicited by leading questions is not inadmissible but the weight to be attached thereto may be reduced accordingly: *Moor v Moor* [1954] 1 WLR 927, [1954] 2 All ER 459.

[130] Best, *Law of Evidence* (12th ed.), at 562, emphasised that "leading" is a relative, not an absolute term.

and the judge. In addition, there are also a number of recognised exceptions to the rule and a witness may be asked leading questions: (i) in respect of introductory matters and facts which are not in dispute; (ii) to help him identify objects or people or if required to aid his recollection;[131] and (iii) if he has been classified as hostile.

Refreshing Testimony

19.045 A witness will not be permitted to read from a prepared statement[132] but can refresh his memory from any written statement made by him or other document prior to giving evidence.[133] A witness will also be permitted to refresh his memory from a document while giving evidence provided that the document in question was either made or verified contemporaneously with the matters to which it relates. In *Lord Talbot de Malahide v Cusack*,[134] O'Brien J elaborated on what is required in this regard. If the document was complied by the witness himself, it suffices that it was made "at the time of the transaction to which it refers, or shortly afterwards when the facts were fresh in his recollection".[135] Alternatively, if the document was prepared by another person, then it must have been either "made in his presence, and read by him at the time of the transactions, or read and examined by him shortly afterwards when the facts were fresh in his recollection, and when he was enabled to ascertain that the facts stated in the entries were true".[136]

19.046 It should be noted that it is not necessary that sight of the document used to refresh testimony actually awaken an independent recollection on the part of the witness. In *Northern Banking Co. v Carpenter*,[137] Kennedy CJ explained that "[i]f the witness can say that, from seeing his own writing, he is sure of the fact stated therein, such statement by him is admissible in evidence of the fact." The only difference is that in this situation of "past recollection recorded", the witness can only use the original document[138] or an exact copy[139] whereas in the case of "present recollection revived", it is permissible to use a

---

[131] *Acerro v Petroni* (1815) 1 Stark 100.
[132] *Dineen v Delap* [1994] 2 IR 228.
[133] *Cf. People (DPP) v Donnelly* Court of Criminal Appeal, 22 February 1999; *R v Richardson* [1971] 2 QB 484, [1971] 2 WLR 889, [1971] 2 All ER 773.
[134] (1864) 17 ICLR 213.
[135] *Ibid.* at 217. The requirement of contemporaneity is a matter of fact and degree (*R v Simmonds* (1967) 51 Cr App R 316) and should not be confined to an over-short period (*R v Richardson* [1971] 2 QB 484, [1971] 2 WLR 889, [1971] 2 All ER 773).
[136] *Ibid.* at 217. Aural as well as visual verification will suffice (*R v Kelsey* (1981) 74 Cr App R 213).
[137] [1931] IR 268, 276.
[138] *Doe d Church v Perkins* (1790) 3 Term Rep 749.
[139] *Lord Talbot de Malahide v Cusack* (1864) 17 ICLR 213.

copy of the original document which substantially reproduces the original.[140] In
either case, the document must be available for inspection by the other side and
the court if required.

It is important to emphasise that where a witness refreshes his memory, it is
the oral testimony of the witness and not the document from which he refreshes
his memory that constitutes evidence in the case.[141] The document is hearsay
and as such is inadmissible. This point is well illustrated by *Northern Banking
Co. v Carpenter.*[142] In that case a memorandum which was used to refresh the
memory of a witness contained two express statements of fact. When giving
evidence, the witness only testified as to the second statement of fact. Kennedy
CJ pointed out that because of the failure of the witness to use the memorandum
to enable him to depose to the first statement of fact, neither the memorandum
nor his testimony provided any evidence upon that issue.

Previous Consistent Statements

19.047 A witness who wished to give false or exaggerated testimony could
confer artificial and unjustified credibility on himself by repeating his version
of events to a number of persons and then having them called to support his
evidence. Therefore, the general rule is that previous statements by a witness to
the same effect as his evidence are not admissible in confirmation thereof.[143]
This is the case even if the evidence of the witness is impeached on cross-
examination.[144]

The principal exception to this rule which is applicable in civil cases relates
to allegations of recent fabrication. Thus, if, on cross-examination, a witness's
testimony is impugned as a fabrication, statements made by him to the same
effect prior to the date when the evidence was allegedly fabricated may be adduced in order to show his consistency.[145] Thus, in *Flanagan v Fahy*,[146] which
concerned a suit to establish a will, one of the witnesses for the defendants
stated that the will had been written after the death of the deceased, that he had
been invited to sign as a witness and that he was given a bribe to keep silent.
The cross-examination of this witness was directed towards showing that he
had fabricated the story because of hostility between him and the plaintiff's

---

[140] *Topham v McGregor* (1844) 1 Car & Kir 320. *Cf. R v Chisnell* [1992] Crim LR 507; *R
v Cheng* (1976) 63 Cr App R 20.
[141] *Young v Denton* [1927] 1 DLR 426.
[142] [1931] IR 268.
[143] *R. v Coll* (1889) 24 LR Ir 522; *Flanagan v Fahy* [1918] 2 IR 361; *Fox v General
Medical Council* [1960] 1 WLR 1017, [1960] 3 All ER 225; *Corke v Corke* [1958] P
93, [1958] 2 WLR 110, [1958] 1 All ER 224.
[144] *R v Coll* (1889) 24 LR Ir 522, 541.
[145] *R v Coll* (1889) 24 LR Ir 522; *Flanagan v Fahy* [1918] 2 IR 361; *Nominal Defendant
v Clements* (1960) 104 CLR 476.
[146] [1918] 2 IR 361.

family. It was held by the Court of Appeal that the trial judge had properly allowed the witness's employer to be called in order to prove that the witness had told him the same story before the cause of the hostility had arisen.

Hostile Witnesses

19.048 The general rule is that a party may not impeach the credit of a witness he calls, even if the witness fails to come up to proof on the matters in respect of which he was called. His only option is to call other witnesses to give evidence of the matters in respect of which the unfavourable witness has failed to come up to proof.[147] The situation is, however, different with respect to a hostile witness, namely a witness who shows no desire to tell the truth at the instance of the party calling him. Leading questions may be put to such a witness[148] who may be cross-examined by the party calling him as to any previous inconsistent statement made by him.[149]

The decision as to whether to treat a witness as hostile is a matter for the discretion of the judge, upon application by the party who called the witness. The judge has a wide discretion in this regard[150] and among the matters which he may take into account are the witness's refusal (if any) to answer questions, the existence of an obvious disregard on the part of the witness of his duty to the proper administration of justice[151] and the extent to which any prior statement made by him is inconsistent with his testimony.[152]

Cross-Examination

19.049 Cross-examination takes place after examination-in-chief of a witness has concluded and may be carried out by any other party to the proceedings. It is central to our adversarial model of justice and has been described by Wigmore,[153] with some justification, as the "greatest legal engine ever invented for the discovery of truth". The right to cross-examine is, therefore, regarded as a crucial element of natural and constitutional justice, particularly the principle of *audi alterem partem*, and a judgment will be set aside if an adequate oppor-

---

[147] See *Ewer v Ambrose* (1825) 3 B & C 746.

[148] *O'Flynn v Smithwick* [1993] 3 IR 589, [1993] ILRM 627.

[149] S.3 of the Criminal Procedure Act 1865 (which despite the title also applies in civil cases).

[150] *O'Flynn v Smithwick* [1993] 3 IR 589, [1993] ILRM 627 ; *People (AG) v Hannigan* [1941] IR 252.

[151] *O'Flynn v Smithwick* [1993] 3 IR 589, [1993] ILRM 627.

[152] *O'Flynn v Smithwick* [1993] 3 IR 589, [1993] ILRM 627; *People (AG) v Hannigan* [1941] IR 252. *Cf. Attorney General v K.* (1948) 82 ILTR 67. The procedure to be adopted where it is sought to have a witness classified as hostile on the basis of a prior inconsistent statement is laid down in *People (AG) v Taylor* [1974] IR 97.

[153] Wigmore, *Evidence* (3rd ed.), Vol. V, §1367.

tunity is not afforded to each party to test the evidence of the other by cross-examination.[154]

Supervisory Role of the Judge

19.050 Notwithstanding the importance of cross-examination, Order 36, rule 37, vests in a judge a supervisory jurisdiction and he may, in any case, disallow any questions put in cross-examination of any party or other witness which appear to him to be vexatious and not relevant to any matter proper to be inquired into in the cause or matter. He may also disallow questions which he considers to be improper[155] or oppressive and may curtail cross-examination which is excessive in length.[156] However, a judge must be careful not to intervene excessively in a way which is unfairly disruptive or which gives the impression that he is leaning in favour of one party.[157] Furthermore, the judge must not prevent a party from adequately testing the case against him.[158]

Liability to Cross-Examination

19.051 All witnesses are liable to cross-examination with three exceptions: (i) a witness who is not sworn, being called merely to produce a document;[159] (ii) a witness called by mistake, because he is unable to testify as to the matters supposed to be within his knowledge, where the mistake is discovered before the examination-in-chief has begun but after the witness has been sworn; and (iii) a witness called by the judge, in which case neither party is entitled to cross-examine him without the leave of the judge although such leave should be given if the evidence is adverse to either party.[160]

Objects of Cross-Examination

19.052 There are two principal objects of cross-examination: (i) to elicit evidence which supports the version of events for which the cross-examiner is contending; and (ii) to undermine the credibility of the witness.

(i) Cross-Examination as to Matters in Issue

19.053 Any question may be put to the witness which relates to any fact in issue or relevant to a fact in issue and the cross-examining party is not re-

---

[154] *Cf. Kiely v Minister for Social Welfare (No. 2)* [1977] IR 267.
[155] *R v Baldwin* (1925) 18 Cr App Rep 175.
[156] *R v Kalia* [1975] Crim L R 181.
[157] See *Browne v Tribune Newspapers plc* [2001] 2 ILRM 424.
[158] *Cf. O'Broin v Ruane* [1989] IR 214.
[159] *Summers v Moseley* (1834) 2 Cr & M 477.
[160] *Coulson v Disborough* [1894] 2 QB 316; *R v Cliburn* (1898) 62 JP 232.

stricted to matters proved in examination-in-chief. However, it should be noted that the ordinary rules controlling the admissibility of evidence apply equally to cross-examination. Therefore, no evidence is admissible on cross-examination which would not be admissible in examination-in-chief.[161]

(ii) Cross-Examination as to Credit

19.054 The objective of cross-examination as to credit is to undermine the credibility of the witness[162] by attacking the evidence given or the witness himself. A witness may be asked to explain any mistakes, omissions or inconsistencies in his evidence. He can be questioned about his means of knowledge of the facts of which he has testified and can be challenged as to the quality of his memory and powers of perception. The witness may also be cross-examined about previous inconsistent statements, previous convictions, previous misconduct, his general reputation for untruthfulness, and matters tending to show bias on his part. However, the entitlement of a party to ask questions as to credit is not untrammelled and is subject to the supervisory jurisdiction of the court. In *Hobbs v Tinling*[163] Sankey LJ laid down a number of considerations to be taken into account in deciding whether a question as to credit should be disallowed:

(1) Such questions are proper if they are of such a nature that the truth of the imputation conveyed by them would seriously affect the opinion of the court as to the credibility of the witness on the matter to which he testifies.

(2) Such questions are improper if the imputation which they convey relates to matters too remote in time, or of such a character, that the truth of the imputation would not affect, or would affect in a slight degree, the opinion of the court as to the credibility of the witness on the matter to which he testifies.

(3) Such questions are improper if there is a great disproportion between the importance of the imputation made against the witness's character and the importance of his evidence.[164]

Finality of Answers to Collateral Questions

19.055 As a general rule, the answers given by a witness under cross-examination to questions concerning collateral matters must be treated as final.[165] Thus, even if a party on cross-examination fails to elicit the desired answer,

---

[161] *R v Treacy* [1944] 2 All ER 229; *R v Gillespie* (1967) 51 Cr App Rep 172.

[162] *Browne v Tribune Newspapers plc* [2001] 2 ILRM 424, 439.

[163] [1929] 2 KB 1.

[164] *Ibid.* at 51.

[165] *R v Burke* (1858) 8 Cox CC 44; *People (DPP) v Barr* Court of Criminal Appeal, *ex tempore*, 2 March 1992; *Attorney General v Hitchcock* (1847) 1 Exch 91.

they are generally confined to the terms of that answer and may not call further evidence in rebuttal if the matter is collateral. The test of whether a matter is collateral laid down in *R v Burke*[166] is whether it is one in respect of which the cross-examining party would be allowed to introduce evidence in chief because of its connection with the issues in the case. The facts of *Burke* furnish a very good example of a collateral matter. In that case, a witness was called to give evidence on behalf of the defendant. He pleaded a lack of competence in English, and no objection being taken by the Crown, he was sworn and gave evidence in Irish. On cross-examination he was asked whether he had, on a recent occasion, spoken in English to two persons who were present in court and were shown to the witness. He denied this, and the two persons were called to contradict him. On appeal, it was held by a majority of the Court of Criminal Appeal that the evidence had been improperly admitted. Christian J was of the view that the question whether the witness could speak English was "wholly beside and collateral to the issue which the jury had to try, which was the guilt or innocence of the prisoner."[167]

To the general rule as to the finality of answers to collateral matters, there are three recognised exceptions which apply in respect of: (i) previous inconsistent statements; (ii) previous convictions; and (iii) bias.

(i) Previous Inconsistent Statements

19.056 If a witness denies a previous oral or written statement made by him which is relevant to an issue in the case and inconsistent with his testimony, that statement may be proved against him.[168] If the cross-examiner wishes to contradict the witness using a prior inconsistent statement, he should hand it to the witness, direct his attention to the relevant part of its contents, ask him to read that part of the document to himself and then inquire whether he still wishes to stand by the evidence which he has given.[169] If the witness adopts the previous statement, it becomes part of his evidence, which has therefore changed, and to that extent his credibility will have been impeached. If the witness adheres to his original evidence, the cross-examiner may accept the answer given and move on, there being no obligation on him to put the document in evidence. However, if he does wish to contradict the witness, he must then prove the document and put it in evidence.[170] It is important to note that, if this occurs, the previous statement merely goes to credibility and is not admissible of the facts stated in it.[171]

---

[166] (1858) 8 Cox CC 44 (adopting the test laid down in *Attorney General v Hitchcock* (1847) 1 Exch 91).

[167] *Ibid.* at 54.

[168] Ss. 4 and 5 of the Criminal Procedure Act 1865 (which despite the title also governs the situation in civil cases).

[169] *People (AG) v Cradden* [1955] IR 130, 138.

[170] *Cf. Attorney General v Murray* [1926] IR 266.

[171] *People (AG) v Cradden* [1955] IR 130, 138. *Cf. People (AG) v Flynn* [1963] IR 255.

(ii) Previous Convictions

19.057 A witness may be questioned as to whether he has been convicted of a criminal offence and if he denies or does not admit the fact of his conviction, the cross-examiner can prove conviction.[172]

(iii) Bias

19.058 Where the line of cross-examination goes further than merely attacking the credibility of a witness and seeks to establish partiality, bias or improper motive, a cross-examiner is not bound by the answers received.[173] Bias or improper motive may relate to either the parties to an action or the issues in the action and as such, encompasses any matter which might provide an incentive for a party to give false testimony.[174] A good example is furnished by *People (DPP) v McGinley*[175] where the appellant was charged with larceny of cattle. At his trial, the principal evidence against him was that of an alleged accomplice. Counsel for the appellant cross-examined the accomplice as to matters pertaining to his earlier trial with the object of showing that he had received a suspended sentence by reason of an undertaking on his part to co-operate in the prosecution of the appellant. Not being satisfied with the answers given by the accomplice, he wished to adduce evidence in rebuttal. However, the trial judge ruled that the questions went merely to the credit of the witness and thus, the appellant was bound by his answers. On appeal, it was held that the trial judge had erred because the line of questioning fell "within the general category of questioning seeking to lead to the establishing of partiality, bias or improper motive on the part of the witness, as distinct from a general assertion of lack of credit."[176]

Re-Examination

19.059 A party who has been cross-examined may be re-examined by the party who called him. The object of re-examination is to repair such damage as has been done by the cross-examining party in so far as he has elicited evidence from the witness supporting his version of the facts in issue or has impugned the witness's credibility. The cardinal rule of re-examination is that it must be confined to such matters as arose out of the cross-examination.[177] Thus, although the witness may be asked to clarify or explain any matters, including evidence of new facts, which arose in cross-examination, questions on other matters may only be asked with the leave of the judge.

---

[172] S.6 of the Criminal Procedure Act 1865.
[173] *People (DPP) v McGinley* [1987] IR 340.
[174] *Cf. R v Burke* (1858) 8 Cox CC 44.
[175] [1987] IR 340.
[176] *Ibid.* at 345.
[177] *Prince v Samo* (1838) 7 Ad & El 627.

Special Procedures in Cases Concerning the Welfare of Children

19.060 A number of recent cases have recognised that the rules of procedure and evidence which evolved in the adversarial context are unsuitable to the inquisitorial jurisdiction exercised by a court in cases concerning the welfare of a child or a person with a mental disability.[178] Such proceedings are now governed by Part III of the Children Act 1997[179] which makes special provision for the examination of such persons.

S.21 provides that evidence by a child may be given by live television link with the leave of the court. No guidelines are given as to when such leave should be granted and it seems as if a trial judge will enjoy considerable discretion in this regard. However, it would appear that, at a minimum, some evidence that a child would suffer trauma if required to testify, will have to be adduced. S.22 further provides that where the evidence of a child is being given through live television link, the court may, of its own motion or on the application of a party to the proceedings, if satisfied that, having regard to the age or mental condition of the child, any questions to be put to the child should be put through an intermediary, direct that any such question be so put.

JUDGMENT

Entry of Judgment

19.061 Order 36, rule 38 provides that the judge may, at or after a trial, direct that judgment be entered for any or either party, or adjourn the case for further consideration before him.[180] If the judge directs judgment to be entered, then the Registrar is obliged to enter judgment accordingly.[181] Order 41, rule 6 further provides that particulars of every judgment or order must be entered in proper books to be kept for that purpose and filed in the Central Office.[182] Every judgment or order pronounced or made when so filed is deemed to have

---

[178] *Cf. Eastern Health Board v M.K.* [1999] 2 IR 99 (*sub nom In the Matter of M.K., S.K. and W.K.* [1999] 2 ILRM 321); *Southern Health Board v C.H.* [1996] 1 IR 219, [1996] 2 ILRM 142.

[179] Part III applied to civil proceedings before any court concerning the welfare of a child or the welfare of a person who is of full age but has a mental disability to such an extent that it is not reasonably possible for the person to live independently (s.20).

[180] No judgment can be entered without the order of the judge: Order 36, rule 38.

[181] Order 36, rule 40. Order 36, rule 39 further provides that, upon every trial, the Registrar or other proper officer must record all findings of fact as the judge may direct and the directions, if any, of the judge as to judgment, and the certificates, if any, granted by the judge in a book kept for the purpose.

[182] A copy of every judgment and order of the Supreme Court must also be filed in the Office of the Registrar of the Supreme Court.

been duly entered. The judgment will be dated as of the day on which it was pronounced unless the court otherwise directs.[183]

Amending/Setting Aside Judgments

19.062 As a general principle "in the absence of a clear provision to the contrary in a statute or a rule of court, once a final order has been made and perfected in the High Court, the jurisdiction of the High Court as to the matters determined by that order is exhausted, save possibly to the extent that a subsidiary or supplementary order may be made subsequently by consent".[184] However, the Rules of the Superior Courts[185] confer the power to correct mistakes or errors on the courts, which, in addition, possess an inherent jurisdiction to amend or vary orders made by them, even where they are of a final nature.

Jurisdiction to Correct Mistakes under the Rules of the Superior Courts

19.063 Order 28, rule 11 provides that "clerical mistakes in judgments or orders, or errors arising therein from any accidental slip or omission,[186] may at any time be corrected by the court on motion without an appeal". In addition, Order 28, rule 12 provides that the court may at any time and on such terms as to costs or otherwise as it may think fit, amend any defect or error in any proceedings and requires that all necessary amendments shall be made for the purpose of determining the real question or issue raised by or depending on the proceedings.

An example of an accidental slip within the meaning of Order 28, rule 11 is provided by the decision in *McCaughey v Stringer*[187] in which the original order made followed the terms of the plaintiff's notice of motion which had mistakenly set out the incorrect amount sought. O'Connor MR stated that while there was no mistake in the sense that the order made did not carry out the intention of the court, there was still a mistake induced by the form of the notice of motion and he held that he had the jurisdiction to correct it.

19.064 More detailed consideration was given to the provisions of rule 11 by McCracken J in *Concorde Engineering Co. Ltd v Bus Átha Cliath*[188] in which the plaintiff sought to have an order amended, either under Order 28 or pursuant

---

[183] Order 41, rule 6.

[184] *Per* Henchy J in *Hughes v O'Rourke* [1986] ILRM 538, 540.

[185] Order 28, rule 11.

[186] This wording in the equivalent rule in Northern Ireland (Order 20, rule 11 of the Rules of the Supreme Court (Northern Ireland), was interpreted by Lowry LCJ in *McNicholl v Neely* [1983] NI 43, 48 as "including a slip or omission made by counsel or the court".

[187] [1914] 1 IR 73.

[188] [1995] 3 IR 212, [1996] 1 ILRM 533.

to the inherent jurisdiction of the court, to include a decree for interest on the principal sum awarded. McCracken J pointed out that the plaintiff must satisfy the court that it is a proper case in which to intervene as the rule seems to make it quite clear that the power to amend is discretionary. He stated that the wording of the rule, referring as it does to any "accidental slip or omission" must be construed as encompassing only matters which were omitted from the judgment or order by reason of a slip or omission and suggested that were it not for such an error, the amendment requested would of necessity have been in the original order. McCracken J said that he doubted whether the rule envisaged an application being made after a final order and added that even if the rule could be read as permitting such a claim to be made at that stage, the court would have to have regard to the rights of a defendant to know the exact extent of liability at the time of the perfection of an order. He pointed out that in the case before him the application had been made almost nine months after the perfection of the order and if granted, would allow the plaintiff to plead a head of damages which had not been referred to at all at the hearing of the action. In the circumstances, McCracken J concluded that he would refuse the application.

Inherent Jurisdiction of the Court to Amend or Vary an Order

19.065 In addition to the power conferred by Order 28, the courts have recognised that there is a "wider and more fundamental jurisdiction" to amend an order previously made even though it is a final order which has been perfected.[189] However, as O'Higgins J stated in *Limerick VEC v Carr*,[190] this power should be "exercised sparingly and only when the court finds that a judgment as drawn up does not correctly state what the court actually decided or intended".

This power was considered in some detail by the Supreme Court in *Belville Holdings Ltd v Revenue Commissioners*[191] in which Finlay CJ referred with approval to the following principles set out by Romer J in *Ainsworth v Wilding*:[192]

> So far as I am aware, the only cases in which the court can interfere after the passing and entering of the judgment are these:
>
> (1) Where there has been an accidental slip in the judgment as drawn up, in which case the court has power to rectify it under Order 28, rule 11;
>
> (2) When the court itself finds that the judgment as drawn up does not correctly state what the court actually decided and intended.

---

[189] See *Cregan v Rafter* [1940] Ir Jur Rep 80; *McClean v McClean* (1947) 81 ILTR 91; *O'Sullivan v Dwyer (No. 2)* [1973] IR 81.

[190] High Court (O'Higgins J) 25 July 2001 at 11.

[191] [1994] 1 ILRM 29. See also *Re Creeney's Estate* [1988] NI 167.

[192] [1896] 1 Ch 673, 677.

19.066 Finlay CJ also referred to the views expressed by the members of the Court of Appeal in *Re Swire,*[193] also quoted by Romer J in *Ainsworth v Wilding*. Cotton LJ had stated that it is only in special circumstances that the court will interfere with an order which has been passed and entered except in the case of a mere slip or verbal inaccuracy. In addition, Lindley LJ made it clear that where an order does not express the order actually made the court has jurisdiction to intervene, whether or not the order has been passed and entered and whether or not it arises from a clerical slip. Bowen LJ spoke in similar terms and said that in such circumstances the amendment should be made provided this can be achieved without injustice or on terms which preclude injustice. In his judgment in *Belville*, Finlay CJ continued as follows:

> I am satisfied that these expressions of opinion validly represent what the true common law principle is concerning this question. I would emphasise, however, that it is only in special or unusual circumstances that an amendment of an order passed and perfected, where the order is of a final nature, should be made by the court. The finality of proceedings both at the level of trial and, possibly more particularly, at the level of the ultimate appeal is of fundamental importance to the certainty of the administration of law and should not lightly be breached.[194]

These principles have been approved in subsequent decisions[195] and were summarised in the following terms by Hamilton CJ in *Re Greendale Developments Ltd (No. 3)*:[196]

> Where a final order has been made and perfected it can only be interfered with
>
> (1) in special or unusual circumstances, or
>
> (2) where there has been an accidental slip in the judgment as drawn up, or

---

[193] (1885) 30 Ch D 239.

[194] [1994] 1 ILRM 29, 37. See also *Silverstone Designs Ltd v Ryan* High Court (Smyth J) 28 February 2000 at 4 and *Bula Ltd v Tara Mines Ltd* Supreme Court, 3 July 2000 *per* McGuinness J at 20.

[195] *Attorney General (SPUC (Ireland) Ltd) v Open Door Counselling Ltd* [1994] 2 IR 333, 339-340, [1994] 1 ILRM 256, 260; *McMullen v Clancy* High Court (McGuinness J) 3 November 1999 at 5-6; *McG. v W. (No.2)* [2000] 1 ILRM 121, 135 (HC); *Re Greendale Developments Ltd (No. 3)* [2000] 2 IR 514, 527, [2001] 1 ILRM 161, 185; *Bula Ltd v Tara Mines Ltd* Supreme Court, 3 July 2000 *per* McGuinness J at 20; *Limerick VEC v Carr* High Court (O'Higgins J) 25 July 2001 at 8.

[196] [2000] 2 IR 514, 527-528, [2001] 1 ILRM 161, 174. See also *Bula Ltd v Tara Mines Ltd* Supreme Court, 3 July 2000 *per* McGuinness J at 19 and *Rooney v Minister for Agriculture and Food* [2001] 2 ILRM 37, 50.

(3) where the court itself finds that the judgment as drawn up does not correctly state what the court actually decided and intended.

In addition, Hamilton CJ added that the restriction on the power of a court to amend or vary an order which has been made and perfected set out above must apply to an application to set aside an order.

Setting Aside a Final Order of the Supreme Court

19.067 Additional factors may also come into play where it is sought to vary or set aside an order made by the Supreme Court. As Finlay CJ pointed out in *Belville Holdings Ltd v Revenue Commissioners*[197] the finality of proceedings, particularly at the level of the ultimate appeal is of fundamental importance to the certainty of the administration of the law.[198] However, it was stressed by Denham J in *McG. v W. (No. 2)*[199] that the inherent jurisdiction of the court as expressed by Finlay CJ in *Belville* does not trench on the principle of the finality of litigation but rather ensures that the intent of the court in making an order is met. In addition, as Murray J stated in his judgment in *McG.*, the power to amend a final order is limited to correcting the final judgment so as to ensure that it accurately reflects the adjudication made and gives "true and final effect to what the court had actually decided".[200]

19.068 It should also be noted that Article 34.4.6° of the Constitution provides that "the decision of the Supreme Court shall in all cases be final and conclusive".[201] So, as Hamilton CJ commented in *Re Greendale Developments Ltd (No. 3)*[202] the common law and public policy recognised the desire for finality in proceedings *inter partes* and Article 34.4.6° incorporated this desire into the Constitution and expressed it in clear and unambiguous terms. In *Greendale* the applicants sought to have the judgment and order of the Supreme Court set aside on the basis that the central issue had been decided by the court without affording them any proper opportunity to argue the point. In refusing the appli-

---

[197] [1994] 1 ILRM 29, 37.

[198] Similarly, in *Re Greendale Developments Ltd (No. 3)* [2000] 2 IR 514, 529, [2001] 1 ILRM 161, 175 Hamilton CJ emphasised that public policy requires a definite and decisive end to litigation.

[199] [2000] 4 IR 1, 14 , [2000] 2 ILRM 451, 464.

[200] *Ibid.* at 30, 479. Note that it was held by McGuinness J (see [2000] 1 ILRM 121) in a decision upheld by the Supreme Court that even where there had been a highly unusual change in circumstances subsequent to the final order being entered, the court had no jurisdiction on that basis to alter the order it had previously made.

[201] As Barron J commented in *Re Greendale Developments Ltd (No. 3)* [2000] 2 IR 514, 546, [2001] 1 ILRM 161, 192 the Constitution requires the decisions of the Supreme Court to be final and conclusive for good reason as there must be certainty in the administration of justice and "uncertainty can lead to injustice".

[202] [2000] 2 IR 514, 536, [2001] 1 ILRM 161, 183.

cation, the Supreme Court held that all the issues raised by the appellants had been dealt with in the judgment of the court and that regard had been had to both the oral and written submissions of their counsel. Hamilton CJ concluded that Article 34.4.6° was intended to apply to all cases and that there was nothing in the circumstances of the appeal which would justify disregarding it.

Similarly, in *Bula Ltd v Tara Mines Ltd*[203] McGuinness J stessed that "very great weight" must be given to the principle of finality and to the provisions of Article 34.4.6°, although she acknowledged that the court has the jurisdiction to set aside a final order in circumstances where its duty to protect constitutional rights or natural justice arises. However, McGuinness J emphasised that this power will only be exercised in exceptional circumstances and that a very heavy onus lies on the applicant to establish that these exist.[204] Denham J reiterated this latter point in her judgment in *Bula*[205] and said that this inherent jurisdiction while it may apply in relation to an order of the Supreme Court will only arise in "rare and exceptional cases".

19.069 Another important decision which addresses the issue of the circumstances in which the Supreme Court has jurisdiction to set aside or vary an order previously made by it is *Attorney General (SPUC (Ireland) Ltd) v Open Door Counselling Ltd*[206] in which the question arose whether the Supreme Court could discharge or vary part of an order made by it in the light of a constitutional amendment enacted subsequent to the decision being handed down. Having referred to the principles set out in *Belville*, Finlay CJ, speaking for the majority, concluded that the Supreme Court, having delivered a judgment and made an order in accordance with the law as it was at that time, which was perfectly correct and carried into effect the full meaning and intent of the court, could not subsequently discharge or vary that order by virtue of an amendment in the law which had occurred since the decision had been made.[207]

19.070 It should also be noted that it was stated by Finlay CJ in *Attorney General (SPUC (Ireland) Ltd) v Open Door Counselling Ltd*[208] that an exception to the principles set out in *Belville* may occur in cases where it is established that a judgment has been obtained by fraud, although as he pointed out no such

---

[203] Supreme Court, 3 July 2000.

[204] See also *Kearney v Ireland* Supreme Court, 10 November 2000 at 3.

[205] Supreme Court, 3 July 2000 at 22-23. See also *Re Greendale Developments Ltd (No. 3)* [2000] 2 IR 514, 539, [2001] 1 ILRM 161, 186

[206] [1994] 2 IR 333, [1994] 1 ILRM 256.

[207] It should also be noted that Denham J, delivering a dissenting judgment, held that there were unique and specific factors, including the fact that the order granted was no longer consistent with the Constitution, which required the court to exercise its inherent jurisdiction to discharge the order previously made by it.

[208] [1994] 2 IR 333, 340, [1994] 1 ILRM 256, 261. See also *Re Greendale Developments Ltd (No. 3)* [2000] 2 IR 514, 528-529, [2001] 1 ILRM 161, 175.

considerations arose in the case before him. This issue had been considered in more detail by the High Court in *Tassan Din v Banco Ambrosiano SPA*,[209] in which the plaintiffs brought proceedings seeking to have the order of the Supreme Court made in the original proceedings set aside alleging that evidence had been deliberately concealed by the defendants. The defendants' application to strike out the plaintiffs' proceedings was granted by Murphy J who stated that there was no authority for the proposition that a decision of a final court of appeal can be challenged in subsequent proceedings on the basis of new evidence. As he said " in the very nature of a court of final appeal such an action would involve a contradiction in terms".[210] Murphy J added that it had been accepted that a decision of the Supreme Court can be set aside for fraud[211] and that this does not truly represent an exception to the provisions of Article 34.4.6° as an order obtained by fraud is a mere nullity. However, referring to the decision of the House of Lords in *The Ampthill Peerage*[212] he made it clear that nothing short of fraud pleaded with sufficient particularity and ultimately established on the balance of probabilities would be sufficient grounds in the case before the court for upsetting the decision given by the Supreme Court.

---

[209] [1991] 1 IR 569.

[210] *Ibid.* at 580.

[211] *Waite v House of Spring Gardens Ltd* High Court (Barrington J) 6 June 1985; *St Albans Investment Co. v London Insurance and Provincial Insurance Co. Ltd* High Court (Murphy J) 27 June 1990.

[212] [1977] AC 547.

CHAPTER TWENTY

APPEALS

INTRODUCTION

20.001 While Order 58, rule 1 of the Rules of the Superior Courts 1986 provides that appeals to the Supreme Court shall be "by way of re-hearing", as Henchy J commented in *Northern Bank Finance Corporation Ltd v Charlton*[1] "the expression 're-hearing' in this context is necessarily a term of art in its application to cases such as this" and the Supreme Court will normally be precluded from hearing or seeing witnesses whose oral testimony formed the basis of the proceedings before the High Court. As he stated:

> So, the appeal will be "by way of re-hearing" only to the extent that that will be possible by examining documentary material, particularly a written version or report of the evidence, save for those exceptional cases when fresh or re-presented evidence is received, usually in the form of oral testimony or by way of visual consideration of a person or object.[2]

The Supreme Court may exercise appellate jurisdiction in relation to questions of law and of fact, although its jurisdiction in relation to the latter is necessarily restricted to the extent that it cannot put itself in the position of the trial judge. While Order 58, rule 8 provides that the Supreme Court shall have power to draw inferences of fact, this power "must be read subject to the necessarily implied limitation that conflicts of oral testimony are usually more likely to be correctly resolved in the forensic atmosphere of the trial than on appeal in this Court, where subtleties, inflexions and countless matters of direct personal impression tend to be distorted or blurred or even totally lost in the transmutation of the live trial into a written record."[3]

PREPARATIONS FOR AN APPEAL

The Notice of Appeal

20.002 All appeals, save from the refusal of an *ex parte* application, must be

---

[1]   [1979] IR 149, 188.
[2]   *Ibid.* at 188.
[3]   *Northern Bank Finance Corporation Ltd v Charlton* [1979] IR 149, 193.

brought by way of a notice of motion called a notice of appeal.[4] The notice of appeal must give at least 10 days notice of the return date and subject to the provisions of Order 58, must be served not later than 21 days from the perfecting of the judgment or order appealed against.[5]

Time for Appealing

20.003 The Supreme Court is empowered to abridge the time appointed by the Rules for notice of an appeal[6] or to enlarge the time fixed for the service of such a notice.[7] The circumstances in which the Supreme Court will grant an order enlarging time for service of a notice of appeal have been considered in a number of decisions and are now well established. A power to extend time also existed pursuant to Order 38 of the Rules of the High Court and Supreme Court 1926 which conferred a discretion to be exercised upon such terms, if any, as the justice of the case might require.[8] These provisions were considered by the Supreme Court in *Éire Continental Trading Co. Ltd v Clonmel Foods Ltd*[9] in which Lavery J accepted the submission of counsel that the following conditions were "proper matters for the consideration of the court in determining whether time should be extended":

1.   The applicant must show that he had a *bona fide* intention to appeal formed within the permitted time.

2.   He must show the existence of something like mistake and that mistake as to procedure and in particular the mistake of counsel or solicitor as to the meaning of the relevant rule was not sufficient.

3.   He must establish that an arguable ground of appeal exists.

However, Lavery J stressed that these conditions must be considered in relation to all the circumstances of the particular case and he quoted the words of Sir Wilfred Greene MR in *Gatti v Shoesmith*[10] that "the discretion of the court being, as I conceive it, a perfectly free one, the only question is whether, upon the facts of this particular case, that discretion should be exercised". On the facts of the case before him, Lavery J was satisfied that the defendants had the intention to appeal or at least the intention to consider whether an appeal would be justified and should be taken. In addition, he stated that the court had mate-

---

[4]   Order 58, rule 1.
[5]   Order 58, rule 3(1).
[6]   Order 58, rule 3(3).
[7]   Order 58, rule 3(4).
[8]   See *Moore v Attorney General* [1930] IR 560 and *McGonagle v McGonagle* [1951] Ir Jur Rep 13.
[9]   [1955] IR 170.
[10] [1939] 1 Ch 841, [1939] 3 All ER 916.

rial before it which justified it in coming to the conclusion that there were or might be substantial matters in issue and he also pointed to the fact that the President of the High Court had made an order staying execution. In these circumstances, Lavery J held that the order extending the time for appealing against the judgment and order of the High Court should be granted.

20.004 The principles in *Éire Continental* have been consistently applied and while the courts have tended to consider whether there has been compliance with the three conditions set out above,[11] they have also stressed the importance of the "free discretion" referred to.[12] The manner in which these principles should be applied was considered by the Supreme Court in *Hughes v O'Rourke*[13] in which an application for leave to extend the time for service of an appeal was granted. Henchy J referred to the *dicta* of Lavery J in *Éire Continental* and stated that as was emphasised by the Supreme Court in *Carroll v McManus*[14] the three matters set out must be considered in the light of all the circumstances of the case and the court still has a "free discretion". Henchy J stated that in his experience, the court's discretion is "liberally exercised" so that a would be appellant who has allowed time for an appeal to slip by through a mistake will not be prevented from appealing unless an extension of time would not be warranted in the circumstances. Hederman J spoke in similar terms and said that it was clear from the judgment of Lavery J in *Éire Continental* that the court is not confined to considering the three conditions and its discretion should be exercised in each case in the light of its particular facts.

20.005 There is also evidence in the judgment of Finlay CJ in *Dalton v Minister for Finance*[15] of a fairly flexible approach to the application of the three conditions set out in *Éire Continental* although on the facts of the case none of these were satisfied. The Supreme Court concluded that in these circumstances, there could be no question of the court exercising its discretion in the plaintiff's favour "which might conceivably arise were some but not all of these preconditions satisfied", a statement which clearly suggests that a court might be free to extend time in circumstances where not all three conditions had been met. This is borne out by the approach adopted by Murphy J in *Blascaod Mór Teoranta v Commissioners of Public Works in Ireland*,[16] albeit in the context of an application under Order 63, rule 9 of the Rules to extend time for appealing an order

---

[11] See *e.g. Outdoor Billposting Ltd v Newspaper Security Services Ltd* Supreme Court, 11 March 1994 where an extension of time was refused on the ground that there was no arguable ground of appeal even though the conditions relating to an intention to appeal gave rise to no difficulty.
[12] *Dowdall v O'Brien* (1955) 90 ILTR 145.
[13] [1986] ILRM 538.
[14] Supreme Court, 15 April 1964.
[15] [1989] IR 209, [1989] ILRM 519.
[16] [1994] 2 IR 372.

of the Master of the High Court. Murphy J pointed out that neither affidavit filed in support of the application identified "the existence of something like mistake". However, he went on to quote the *dicta* of Sir Wilfred Greene MR in *Gatti v Shoesmith* quoted above about the court's discretion being a free one and concluded that in the circumstances it was an appropriate case in which to grant the extension of time sought.

Therefore, it appears that while the three conditions set out in *Éire Continental* are a useful guide to the manner in which the jurisdiction of the court will be exercised in such cases, the overriding consideration is that the court has a discretion which must be properly exercised in all the circumstances of the case.[17] So, it will not necessarily be fatal if one, or possibly more, of the conditions is not satisfied provided the court is disposed to granting an application to extend time based on all the circumstances of the case. Equally, as McCarthy J made clear in *Bank of Ireland v Breen,*[18] although this did not arise in the matter before him, there may be cases in which an applicant might have fulfilled the three criteria and still fail in his application because of the prejudice which granting it would cause to the prospective respondent.

Grounds of Appeal

20.006 Order 58, rule 5 provides that a notice of appeal shall in every case state "the grounds of appeal and the relief sought or the order (if any) in lieu of the judgment or order appealed sought by the appellant". It is clear from the judgment of O'Brien LCJ in *Hughes v Dublin United Tramways Co.*[19] that a statement of the grounds of appeal should be specific and sufficiently stated. The notice of appeal must be served on all the parties directly affected by the appeal and the Supreme Court may direct that it shall also be served on any parties to the action or other proceedings or on any person not a party and in the meantime may adjourn the hearing of the appeal on such terms as may be just.[20]

Amending of Notice of Appeal

20.007 Order 58, rule 6 provides that a "notice of appeal may be amended at any time on such terms as the Supreme Court may think fit" and the Supreme Court may give an appellant leave to amend a notice of appeal.[21] The *dicta* of Finlay CJ in *Mapp v Gilhooley*[22] suggests that it is inappropriate to wait until the commencement of the hearing of the appeal before applying to add a further

---

[17] *Bank of Ireland v Breen* Supreme Court, 17 June 1987 *per* McCarthy J at 5.

[18] Supreme Court, 17 June 1987.

[19] [1911] 2 IR 114. See also the *dicta* of McCarthy J in *State (Gallagher Shatter & Co.) v. de Valera* Supreme Court, 8 February 1990.

[20] Order 58, rule 5.

[21] *E.g. Goulding Chemicals Ltd v Bolger* [1977] IR 211.

[22] [1991] 2 IR 253, [1991] ILRM 695.

ground. In his view any party seeking to extend the grounds of an appeal should ordinarily obtain an order, whether by consent or otherwise, amending the notice of appeal in sufficient time to enable the members of the court, when considering the documents which are read before the hearing, to be aware of the issues which are to be raised.[23]

20.008 The circumstances in which amendment of a notice of appeal may be permitted was considered by the Supreme Court in *Balkanbank v Taher*,[24] in which the defendants sought to amend a notice of appeal which had been delivered by adding certain parties and expanding the existing grounds. While the notice of appeal had been served in time, counsel for the defendants approached the matter – rightly in the view of the court – as if it were an application for an extension of time *simpliciter*. In granting the application, O'Flaherty J pointed to the fact that this was not a case of a litigant who had not appealed at all within the required time, but rather one in which an extension of the grounds of appeal and the addition of parties was sought, and he stated that he believed that the requirement of justice in this case was that the amendments to the notice of appeal should be allowed.

20.009 It should be noted that as a general principle, leave to argue an appeal on the basis of a new ground will not be granted as this would allow an issue which had not been considered by the High Court to be raised for the first time before the Supreme Court.[25] As Henchy J stated in *Movie News Ltd v Galway County Council*:[26] "It should not – except for exceptional reasons which do not exist in this case – under the guise of an appeal, enter on the trial of a matter as of first instance and thereby deprive the party aggrieved with its decision of the constitutional right of appeal which he would have if that matter had been decided in the High Court." A similar point was made by Denham J in *Attorney General (SPUC (Ireland) Ltd) v Open Door Counselling Ltd* [27] where she stated that in general the Supreme Court should not hear and determine an issue which has not been tried and decided by the High Court. However, she acknowledged that there may be rare exceptional cases other than those explicitly set out by the Constitution in which the Supreme Court may exercise a non-appellate jurisdiction when a constitutional right or justice lies to be protected. Finlay CJ spoke in similar terms in that case, commenting that the Supreme Court "has consistently declined, otherwise than in the most exceptional cir-

---

[23] Although it should be noted that in this case the Supreme Court allowed an additional ground to be added and at the commencement of the hearing of the appeal counsel on behalf of the defendant abandoned all other grounds and successfully based his case on this additional ground.

[24] Supreme Court, 19 May 1994.

[25] *Movie News Ltd v Galway County Council* Supreme Court, 25 July 1973.

[26] Supreme Court, 25 July 1973 at 4.

[27] [1994] 2 IR 333, [1994] 1 ILRM 256.

cumstances, dictated by the necessity of justice, to consider an issue of constitutional law which, though arising in a case not yet determined by it, has not been fully argued and decided in the High Court".[28] This *dicta* has recently been quoted with approval by Denham J in *Blehein v Murphy*[29] in which she agreed that in exceptional cases the Supreme Court will consider issues of constitutional law which have not been argued in the High Court.

20.010 It is also clear from the recent judgment of Geoghegan J in *Carlton v Director of Public Prosecutions*[30] that leave to amend a notice of appeal will not be granted where it would be unfair to the applicant or where the proposed amendments are very substantial and would change the nature of the appeal. Macken J had granted an order of prohibition to prevent the District Court having seisin of certain summonses brought against the applicant and had quashed the appointment of an inspector to investigate a complaint of alleged misconduct by gardaí essentially on the basis that the latter was based in the same division, and in some cases in the same district, as the gardaí being investigated.[31] The respondents initially filed a notice of appeal which did not seek in express terms to set aside the order of prohibition or the order quashing the appointment. They then brought a motion to amend the notice of appeal to set aside the orders made by the High Court although counsel for the respondents conceded that an inspector from the same district as some of the gardaí complained about ought not to have been appointed. In refusing leave to amend the notice of appeal, Geoghegan J stated that the amendments sought were very substantial and changed the nature of the appeal. He also said that they were sought "far too late" and were basically unfair to the applicant who was led to believe that the prosecutions would not be going ahead.

20.011 It should be noted that Order 58, rule 10 provides that it shall not be necessary for a person served with a notice of appeal to give notice by way of cross appeal, but if such person intends to contend that the judgment or order appealed from should be varied, he shall within four days of such service upon him or within such extended time as may be allowed by the Supreme Court, give notice of such intention to any parties who may be affected by this conten-

---

[28] *Ibid.* at 341-342, 262.
[29] [2000] 2 IR 231, 239, [2000] 2 ILRM 481, 489. However, note the *dicta* of Keane CJ in *Dunnes Stores Ireland Co. v Ryan* Supreme Court, 8 February 2000 that it was not open to the Supreme Court to determine an issue of constitutional law which had not been the subject of adjudication in the High Court.
[30] [2000] 3 IR 269.
[31] The original summonses against the applicant were struck out and new ones issued based on the same information. The applicant then filed a cross appeal seeking a complete prohibition on the prosecution of these summonses which was ultimately allowed by the Supreme Court.

tion.[32] So, it is clear that if either party seeks to contend that any aspect of the order of the High Court should be varied, he must give notice of this.[33]

The rule goes on to provide that the omission to give such notice shall not diminish the powers conferred by statute or by the Rules of the Supreme Court, but may in the discretion of that court, be grounds for an adjournment of the appeal or a special order as to costs.

Lodging an Appeal

20.012 Order 58, rule 11 provides that all appeals to the Supreme Court shall be entered in the Office of the Registrar of the Supreme Court within seven days of service of the notice of appeal, or of the last service if there has been more than one. In *Dowdall v O'Brien*[34] the defendant had served a notice of appeal on the plaintiff but failed to lodge one in the Supreme Court office within the time limited by the Rules owing to a mistake made by an assistant in the office. Maguire CJ commented that the principles which apply in cases of this kind had been settled in *Éire Continental Trading Co. v Clonmel Foods Ltd*[35] although he acknowledged that the circumstances in the matter before him were different to those in that decision. Maguire CJ stated that service of a notice of appeal was the best evidence of the appellant's intention to proceed with the appeal. While he said that it might have been better to have stated the ground on which the judgment was to be challenged in the affidavit, the court accepted the appellant's assertion that there was an arguable ground of appeal and also pointed to the fact that the granting of a stay by the trial judge was a *prima facie* indication that the latter shared this view. Maguire CJ concluded by saying that in matters of this nature, the court has a free discretion and held that it would be exercised in favour of granting the extension of time conditional on the lodging of the amount of the decree in court and the payment of costs to the respondent.

The appellant must lodge with the Registrar an attested copy of the judgment or order appealed from and leave a copy of the notice of appeal, indorsed with sufficient particulars of service, to be filed.[36] The appellant is also required to lodge "without delay" in the Office of the Registrar five books of appeal[37] each containing copies of the pleadings and all other documents required for the hearing with a sufficient index and a true copy of this index must have been previously furnished to every other party affected by the appeal.[38]

---

[32] *E.g. Garvey v Ireland* [1981] IR 75.

[33] *Hanratty v Drogheda Web Offset Printers Ltd* Supreme Court, 2 June 1994.

[34] (1955) 90 ILTR 145.

[35] [1955] IR 170.

[36] Order 58, rule 11.

[37] Order 58, rule 12 provides that in an appeal within rule 2, which relates to appeals of jury trials, three books of appeal shall be lodged initially unless the court shall order otherwise.

[38] Order 58, rule 12.

Listing of an Appeal

20.013 As soon as the necessary papers are in order, the Registrar shall set down the appeal by entering it in the list of appeals and it will come on to be heard according to its order in the list, unless the Supreme Court shall direct otherwise.[39] In practice, appeals which are ready for hearing will be listed for mention for the purpose of ascertaining whether they are proceeding, the realistic time required for the hearing of the appeal, whether written submissions by the parties will be required and finally, for the purpose of fixing a date for the hearing of the appeal. When a date has been allocated, unless alternative directions are given by the court on foot of a specific application in this regard, written submissions must be lodged by the appellant in the Supreme Court office not later than three weeks before the date of the hearing and the respondent's submissions are to be lodged in the office within one week thereafter.[40]

Stay on Order of the High Court

20.014 Order 58, rule 18 provides that an appeal to the Supreme Court shall not operate as a stay of execution or of proceedings under the decision appealed from unless the High Court or the Supreme Court orders otherwise. A party who is unsuccessful in the High Court may apply to that court for a stay pending an appeal to the Supreme Court[41] or may apply directly to the Supreme Court for such a stay.[42] In addition, where the High Court has granted a stay on an order, an application may be made to the Supreme Court to have this stay removed.[43]

It has been stated that the overriding consideration in deciding whether to grant a stay is to maintain a balance so that justice will not be denied to either party.[44] In *O'Toole v Radio Telefís Éireann (No. 1)*[45] O'Hanlon J had directed the defendants to issue a directive to their staff in order to comply with the findings he had previously made in relation to the interpretation of s.31 of the Broadcasting (Authority) Act 1960. The Supreme Court granted a stay pending the appeal, Finlay CJ stating that it was necessary to balance a number of factors including the right to freedom of expression on the one hand, with the fact that the Act provides protection for the authority of the State on the other hand. Balancing these factors and having regard to the fact that there would be a relatively early appeal, he concluded that a stay should be ordered.

---

[39] Order 58, rule 11.
[40] Practice Direction, 3 November 2000.
[41] *E.g. O'Toole v Radio Telefís Éireann (No. 1)* [1993] ILRM 454.
[42] *E.g. Redmond v Ireland* [1992] 2 IR 362, [1992] ILRM 291.
[43] *E.g. Emerald Meats Ltd v Minister for Agriculture* [1993] 2 IR 443.
[44] *Per* McCarthy J in *Redmond v Ireland* [1992] 2 IR 362, 366, [1992] ILRM 291, 294 and in *Emerald Meats Ltd v Minister for Agriculture* [1993] 2 IR 443, 446.
[45] [1993] ILRM 454.

20.015 The difficult balancing exercise which must be carried out by the Supreme Court in deciding whether to grant or refuse a stay in the context of a monetary award is well summarised by Egan J in *Redmond v Ireland*[46] in the following terms. On the one hand, if a stay is granted and the plaintiff later succeeds in upholding the award he will inevitably have suffered delay in receiving his money for which interest payments will not always compensate. On the other hand, if a stay is refused and the defendant subsequently wins the appeal, the award may no longer be recoverable. It is generally accepted that the court must do its best to balance the conflicting considerations which must arise in such cases although it has been acknowledged that "there may be no perfect solution".[47]

A useful summary of the factors which may be taken into account by the Supreme Court in considering an application for a stay is set out by McCarthy J in *Redmond v Ireland*[48] as follows:

(1) liability is genuinely in issue;

(2) a heavy responsibility lies upon the legal advisers of those seeking a stay of execution to assist the court on the reality of the appeal on liability;

(3) the court should not be trying the appeal;

(4) the issue is raised upon an argument that findings of fact are unsupported by any credible evidence;

(5) there may be cases in which monies paid on foot of a decree might not be recoverable;

(6) the bringing of an appeal can be, of itself, damaging to an injured person;

(7) appeals have been brought and may be brought again, not as *bona fide* appeals with any legitimate chance of success, but as a bargaining weapon;

(8) the length of time between accident and trial and the prospective length of time between trial and the hearing of the appeal;

(9) the absence of any application for a stay at the trial.

The relevance of this final factor, namely the absence of any application for a stay in the High Court is an interesting issue and as Finlay CJ commented in his dissenting judgment in *Redmond* "the failure of a party to apply to the High Court for a stay, whilst not fatal to an application for a stay in this Court, must be a significant factor in the various matters which must be taken into consid-

---

[46] [1992] 2 IR 362, 367, [1992] ILRM 291, 295.
[47] *Redmond v Ireland* [1992] 2 IR 362, 367, [1992] ILRM 291, 295 *per* Egan J.
[48] [1992] 2 IR 362, 366, [1992] ILRM 291, 294.

eration".[49] A further opinion expressed by McCarthy J in *Redmond* is that where a trial judge has delivered a reasoned judgment on liability, then unless it is demonstrably wrong, the fact that an appeal has been taken on liability should not be taken into account.

20.016 A more contentious factor is that suggested by Egan J in *Redmond* and in *Emerald Meats Ltd v Minister for Agriculture*,[50] namely, that "the court must form some view (even though not a final view) on the reality of the likely outcome of the appeal", although he acknowledged in the latter decision that any such assessment cannot lead to a concluded view on the final outcome of the case. Some support for this approach can be found in the dissenting judgment of Finlay CJ in *Redmond*, – although it is interesting to note that these judges reached different conclusions on the question of whether a stay should be granted[51] – where he stated that he would approach the issue by taking a *prima facie* view of the appeal on the issue of liability.

20.017 Additional consideration was given to this issue by Finlay CJ in *Irish Press plc v Ingersoll Irish Publications*[52] in which the respondent sought a further stay on orders made by the High Court in proceedings brought by the petitioner under s.205 of the Companies Act 1963 alleging oppression. Finlay CJ said that the application must be dealt with on the basis of the views expressed by the court in *Redmond* and *Emerald Meats*. He said that in so far as an earlier decision of the court in *Corish v Hogan*[53] appeared to state that for a defendant to be entitled to a stay where liability is an issue raised by him on appeal it is necessary for him to prove a probability that his appeal on liability would succeed, it must not be followed. Finlay CJ said that to raise that standard would be to impose on the court an obligation practically to hear the whole appeal in a *prima facie* fashion and the court could not and should not do this. Instead the court should look at the extent to which the appeal is arguable and then assess the balance of convenience. Therefore, it would appear that in order

---

[49] *Ibid.* at 364, 293.

[50] [1993] 2 IR 443.

[51] The plaintiff was awarded damages of £49,969 for personal injuries. The defendants did not apply to the High Court for a stay on the order but appealed against the order on the issue of liability and damages. Subsequently, by notice of motion, the defendants applied to the Supreme Court for a stay of execution on the award of damages pending the hearing of the appeal. The Supreme Court ordered that £15,000 should be paid to the plaintiff immediately and ordered a stay on the balance pending the delivery of its reserved judgment. When this was delivered the majority (McCarthy and Egan JJ) refused to order a stay on the balance of the award pending the appeal. Finlay CJ dissented and held that the stay should continue, expressing the view that the immediate hardship on the plaintiff appeared to have been relieved by the payment of the £15,000.

[52] [1995] 1 ILRM 117.

[53] Supreme Court, 1 December 1990.

to be entitled to a stay, a defendant does not have to prove that there is a probability the appeal on liability will succeed.

THE CONDUCT OF THE APPEAL

Review of Evidence on Appeal

20.018 For the purpose of appellate jurisdiction, questions of fact may be divided into two categories: questions of primary fact which are "determinations of fact depending on the assessment of the trial judge of the credibility and quality of the witnesses"[54] and questions of secondary or inferred facts which do not follow directly from an assessment of the credibility of witnesses or the weight to be attached to their evidence but derive from the inferences which a judge draws from the facts found or admitted. Because the findings of primary fact depend on the oral evidence given and accepted by the court of trial, an appellate court will not interfere with such findings if there is credible evidence to support them.[55] This will normally be the case even if the Supreme Court deems other findings to be more appropriate or even if the findings made appear to it to be incorrect.[56] As Finlay CJ stated in *Pernod Ricard & Comrie plc v FFI Fyffes plc*:[57] "findings by a trial judge of primary or basic facts which depend upon the assessment by him of the credibility and quality of a witness[58] will only be interfered with by this court on appeal when such findings of primary fact cannot in all reason be held to be supported by the evidence."

---

[54] *Per* Henchy J in *J.M. v An Bord Uchtála* [1987] IR 510, 522-523, [1988] ILRM 203, 205.

[55] *Hay v O'Grady* [1992] 1 IR 210, 217, [1992] ILRM 689, 694 and *Duffy v Rooney* Supreme Court, 23 April 1998.

[56] *J.M. v An Bord Uchtála* [1987] IR 510, 522-523, [1988] ILRM 203, 205. Quoted with approval by Henchy J in *Hanrahan v Merck, Sharp and Dohme (Ireland) Ltd* [1988] ILRM 629, 637 and by O'Flaherty J in *Best v Wellcome Foundation Ltd* [1993] 3 IR 421, 482, [1992] ILRM 609, 642. However, note also the *dicta* of O'Higgins CJ in *Northern Bank Finance Corporation Ltd v Charlton* [1979] IR 149, 181 who went as far as to say that "insofar as the judge's findings of fact are based directly on evidence which he heard and believed, it being open to him to accept such evidence or reject it, such findings cannot be interfered with by this Court in my view".

[57] Supreme Court, 11 November 1988 at 7. See also the *dicta* of Holmes LJ stated in *Re SS Gairloch* [1899] 2 IR 1, 18 "when a judge after trying a case upon *viva voce* evidence comes to a conclusion regarding a specific and definite matter of fact, his finding ought not to be reversed by a court that has not the same opportunity of seeing and hearing the witnesses unless it is so clearly against the weight of the testimony as to amount to a manifest defeat of justice". See also *Northern Bank Finance Corporation Ltd v Charlton* [1979] IR 149, 178 and *Maguire v Keane* [1986] ILRM 235, 237.

[58] Note that Finlay CJ stated (at 8) that the reference to the question of the assessment by the judge of trial of the credibility of a witness is a reference to "credibility of its legal sense, namely reliability of memory and testimony, and is in no way confined to credibility in its narrow sense of truthfulness".

20.019 However, in respect of inferred facts the advantage gained by the trial judge is of less importance and an appeal court is free to draw its own inferences from the facts proved or admitted if it considers that those drawn by the court of trial were incorrect.[59] For this reason it will be important for a trial judge to make a clear statement of his findings of primary facts, the inferences to be drawn and his conclusions.[60] A useful distinction was drawn by Henchy J in *Northern Bank Finance Corporation Ltd v Charlton*[61] in the following terms. He said that in a civil case where a court has decided a question of specific fact and the resolution of the question depended wholly or in substantial measure on the choice of one version of controverted oral testimony as against another, a court of appeal, which is dependent on a written record of the oral evidence given at the trial, will not normally reject that finding merely because an alternative version of the oral testimony seems more acceptable. In his opinion "the court of appeal will only set aside findings of fact based on one version of the evidence when, on taking a conspectus of the evidence as a whole, oral and otherwise, it appears to the court that, notwithstanding the advantages which the tribunal of fact had in seeing and hearing the witnesses, the version of the evidence which was acted on could not reasonably be correct."[62] On the other hand, Henchy J expressed the view that if the question of fact answered in the court of trial does not depend on a choice of alternatives arising out of divergent oral testimony, but amounts to a conclusion in the nature of an evaluation of proved or admitted facts, the court of appeal will consider itself free to rely on its own judgment as to whether the evaluation made by the tribunal was correct or not, on the grounds that its competence to evaluate the fact in question is no less than that of the tribunal of fact.[63]

20.020 A comprehensive summary of the principles which apply to the review of evidence on appeal is contained in the judgment of McCarthy J in *Hay v O'Grady*[64] which included the following points:

---

[59] *Northern Bank Finance Corporation Ltd v Charlton* [1979] IR 149, 192 *per* Henchy J. See also *Cullen v Clein* [1970] IR 146, 152, *J.M. v An Bord Uchtála* [1987] IR 510, 522-523, [1988] ILRM 203, 205, *Pernod Ricard & Comrie plc v FFI Fyffes plc* Supreme Court, 11 November 1988 at 8, *Mullen v Quinnsworth Ltd (No. 2)* [1991] ILRM 439, 445 and *Coleman v Clarke* [1991] ILRM 841, 845-846.

[60] *Hay v O'Grady* [1992] 1 IR 210, 218, [1992] ILRM 689, 694.

[61] [1979] IR 149, 188.

[62] *Ibid.* at 191. See also *Dunne v National Maternity Hospital* [1989] IR 91, 107, [1989] ILRM 735, 743 and *Nolan Transport (Oaklands) v Halligan* [1999] 1 IR 128.

[63] *Ibid.* at 192. See also *Maguire v Keane* [1986] ILRM 235, 238 and *Banco Ambrosiano SPA v Ansbacher & Co. Ltd* [1987] ILRM 669, 698.

[64] [1992] 1 IR 210, 217. Quoted with approval by O'Flaherty J in *Best v Wellcome Foundation Ltd* [1993] 3 IR 421, 483, [1992] ILRM 609, 643. See also *Tuohy v Courtney* [1994] 3 IR 1, 50, [1994] 2 ILRM 503, 517, *Superwood Holdings plc v Sun Alliance and London Insurance plc* [1995] 3 IR 303, 325-326, *Southern Health Board v An*

1. An appellate court does not enjoy the opportunity of seeing and hearing the witnesses as does the trial judge who hears the substance of the evidence but, also, observes the manner in which it is given and the demeanour of those giving it. The arid pages of a transcript seldom reflect the atmosphere of a trial.

2. If the findings of fact made by the trial judge are supported by credible evidence, this Court is bound by those findings, however voluminous and apparently weighty the testimony against them. The truth is not the monopoly of any majority.

3. Inferences of fact are drawn in most trials; it is said that an appellate court is in as good a position as the trial judge to draw inferences of fact. I do not accept that this is always necessarily so. It may be that the demeanour of a witness in giving evidence will, itself, lead to an appropriate inference which an appellate court would not draw. In my judgment, an appellate court should be slow to substitute its own inference of fact where such depends upon oral evidence or recollection of fact and a different inference has been drawn by the trial judge. In the drawing of inferences from circumstantial evidence, an appellate court is in as good a position as the trial judge.

Admission of Further Evidence on Appeal

20.021 Order 58, rule 8 provides that the Supreme Court shall have full discretionary power to receive further evidence on questions of fact to be taken either by oral examination in court, by affidavit or by deposition. This power to receive further evidence on questions of fact was considered by the Supreme Court in *B. v B.*[65] and the majority concluded that leave should be granted for additional oral evidence to be given by both parties. Walsh J stated that the power of the court to accept such evidence for the purpose of determining the appeal was inherent in the court by virtue of its establishment and by virtue of the appellate jurisdiction conferred on it by the Constitution. In his view Order 58, rule 8 recognises the existence of this jurisdiction and seeks to regulate the hearing of further evidence to a limited extent by distinguishing between matters which have occurred after the date of the decision from which the appeal was brought and other matters.[66] If, on the hearing of any appeal the examination of the further evidence is necessary or desirable, then in the opinion of Walsh J, the court has ample jurisdiction within its appellate jurisdiction to allow the appeal to be conducted on that basis. This broad approach can be contrasted with the views expressed by McLoughlin J who dissented on the question of whether

---

Bord Uchtála [2000] 1 IR 165, 175-176 and *Kelly v Dublin Bus* Supreme Court, 16 March 2000 at 3.

[65] [1975] IR 54.
[66] See further *infra*.

leave should be granted to adduce additional evidence. In his opinion such further evidence should only be directed to an issue upon which the order of the High Court was based and not upon an entirely different and substantial issue of fact originating for the first time during the hearing of the appeal. Rule 8 continues as follows:

> Such further evidence may be given without special leave upon any appeal from an interlocutory judgment or order or in any case as to matters which have occurred after the date of the decision from which the appeal is brought. Upon any appeal from a final judgment or order such further evidence (save as to matters subsequent as aforesaid) shall be admitted on special grounds only, and not without special leave of the Supreme Court (obtained upon application therefor by motion on notice setting forth such special grounds).

20.022 It is clear from the terms of rule 8 that the court has a discretionary power to receive further evidence on questions of fact and that this may be permitted without special leave in relation to matters which have occurred after the date of the decision appealed against. However, it is also clear that where the evidence relates to matters which occurred before the date of the decision, it should be admitted on special grounds only and not without special leave of the court.[67] The special grounds upon which the court will exercise its power to permit further evidence of this nature were considered by Walsh J in the course of his judgment in *Lynagh v Mackin*[68] and set out by Finlay CJ in *Murphy v Minister for Defence*[69] in the following terms:

1. The evidence sought to be adduced must have been in existence at the time of the trial and must have been such that it could not have been obtained with reasonable diligence for use at the trial;

2. The evidence must be such that if given it would probably have an important influence on the result of the case, though it need not be decisive.

3. The evidence must be such as is presumably to be believed or, in other words, it must be apparently credible, though it need not be incontrovertible.

20.023 These principles are now well established and have been applied on numerous occasions.[70] In *Re Greendale Developments Ltd (No. 2)*[71] Keane J

---

[67] *Per* Walsh J in *Lynagh v Mackin* [1970] IR 180, 189.
[68] [1970] IR 180.
[69] [1991] 2 IR 161, 164.
[70] *Smyth v Tunney* [1996] 1 ILRM 219, 229; *Pat O'Donnell & Co. Ltd v Truck and Machinery Sales Ltd* Supreme Court, 18 February 1997; *Re Greendale Developments (No. 2)* [1998] 1 IR 8, 15; *Allied Irish Coal Supplies Ltd v Powell Duffryn International Fuels Ltd* [1998] 2 IR 519, 538, [1998] 2 ILRM 61, 73.
[71] [1998] 1 IR 8.

stated that "evidence" in this context connotes evidence of facts relevant to the issues in the action, which would have had an important influence on the result and which was not available to the court of trial. In his opinion, the documents which the first named respondent sought to introduce in that case did not constitute "new evidence" and could at best have been used in cross-examination to test the credibility of witnesses. As such, its admissibility fell to be determined by reference to the stricter test set out in the following terms by Holroyd Pearce LJ in *Meek v Fleming*:[72]

> Where, however, the new evidence does not relate directly to the issue, but is merely evidence as to the credibility of an important witness, this court applies a stricter test. It will only allow its admission (if ever) where, ... *per* Tucker LJ in *Braddock v Tillotson's Newspapers Ltd* [1950] 1 KB 47:
>
>> 'the evidence is of such a nature and the circumstances of the case are such that no reasonable jury could be expected to act on the evidence of the witness whose character has been called in question'
>
> or, *per* Cohen LJ:
>
>> '...where the court is satisfied that the additional evidence *must* have led a reasonable jury to a different conclusion from that actually arrived at in that case'.

Keane J stated that it could not be said with any plausibility that the production of the additional evidence in the case before him must have led the trial judge to a different conclusion on the facts and he concluded that he was satisfied that the application to adduce new evidence must be refused in these circumstances.

20.024 Where the further evidence which a party seeks to adduce relates to "matters which have occurred after the date of the decision from which the appeal is brought", while no special leave is required, "the position remains nonetheless that the power of the court to receive the evidence is discretionary".[73] The manner in which this discretion should be exercised was considered by the Supreme Court in *O'Connor v O'Shea*[74] in which Finlay CJ, in rejecting the application to adduce further evidence, said that there is a very strong presumption against permitting the re-opening of a case on the assessment of damages for personal injuries by reason of the progress, or apparent progress, of those injuries after the conclusion of the trial.[75] On the other hand, he accepted

---

[72] [1961] 2 QB 366, 378, [1961] 3 WLR 532, 537-538, [1961] 3 All ER 148, 153.
[73] *Per* Blayney J in *Fitzgerald v Kenny* [1994] 2 IR 383, 396, [1994] 2 ILRM 8, 18.
[74] Supreme Court, 24 July 1989.
[75] See also the *dicta* of Finlay CJ in *Dalton v Minister for Finance* [1989] IR 269, 273,

that in principle where there has been "what could fairly and accurately be described as a dramatic alteration in the circumstances upon which the verdict in the court below was based", it may be proper having regard to the requirements of justice that the Supreme Court should consider that alteration in circumstances in relation to the question as to whether an appeal with regard to the amount of damages should be allowed. However, this "dramatic alteration" test was subsequently rejected by the Supreme Court in *Fitzgerald v Kenny*[76] in favour of what it considered to be more appropriate guidelines for the court to follow in exercising its discretion as to whether to admit further evidence. Both O'Flaherty and Blayney JJ quoted with approval the following "non-exhaustive indications" from the speech of Lord Wilberforce in *Mulholland v Mitchell*:[77]

> I do not think that, in the end, much more can usefully be said than, in the words of my noble and learned friend, Lord Pearson, that the matter is one of discretion and degree (*Murphy v Stone-Wallwork (Charlton) Ltd* [1969] 1 WLR 1023, 1036). Negatively, fresh evidence ought not to be admitted when it bears upon matters falling within the field or area of uncertainty, in which the trial judge's estimate has previously been made. Positively, it may be admitted if some basic assumptions, common to both sides, have clearly been falsified by subsequent events, particularly if this has happened by the act of the defendant. Positively, too, it may be expected that the courts will allow fresh evidence when to refuse it would affront common sense, or a sense of justice.

Blayney J went on to say that these guidelines were in fact consistent with the statement of Finlay CJ in *O'Connor v O'Shea* referred to above that there is a strong presumption against permitting the re-opening of an assessment of damages for personal injuries by reason of the progress or apparent progress of those injuries after the trial is over. In the view of Blayney J evidence of this nature would come within what Lord Wilberforce described as "the field of uncertainty in which the trial judge's estimate has previously been made" and should not be admitted for that reason. Applying the guidelines set out above to

---

[1989] ILRM 519, 522: "With particular regard to the assessment of damages for personal injuries, it is clear that very many plaintiffs indeed feel after the conclusion of their case and with the passage of years and reflecting upon the matter that they have been inadequately compensated. Many defendants may equally be of the impression, seeing the plaintiff, if they happen to do so, moving around and apparently being able to cope with life that the plaintiff has been exorbitantly compensated. To allow either of these two categories of persons subsequently to seek a variation of the assessment of damages based on after events would be to cut across the entire finality of litigation in this context."

[76] [1994] 2 IR 383, [1994] 2 ILRM 8.
[77] [1971] AC 666, 679, [1971] 2 WLR 93, 102, [1971] 1 All ER 307, 313.

the facts of the case, the Supreme Court concluded that the court's discretion should be exercised to admit evidence of the plaintiff's subsequent loss of his job as a garda four years after the trial on medical grounds and further evidence of his injuries connected to this.[78] O'Flaherty J said that the matter of the plaintiff's loss of career was a completely new fact arising after the trial and therefore was to be approached as not requiring any form of special leave under the Rules. Nevertheless the court had to apply a discretion which had to be exercised in a fair and just manner and in the circumstances of the case he held that the possibility that a serious injustice would be suffered by the plaintiff must prevail over the desirability of having finality in litigation. Blayney J agreed and said that it was quite clear from the transcript, and was conceded by counsel for the defendants, that none of the witnesses had suggested that the plaintiff's injuries were such that they could cause him to lose his job. So, it was on this basis that damages had been assessed, a premise which had been falsified by subsequent events. In addition, Blayney J stated that he would also favour the court exercising its discretion to admit further evidence because to refuse to do so would be an affront to justice.

20.025 Order 58, rule 8 also provides that "further evidence may be given without special leave upon any appeal from an interlocutory judgment or order" and another issue of interpretation which must be considered is what will constitute an interlocutory order in this context. Rule 8 goes on to provide that upon any appeal from a final judgment or order, further evidence save as to matters subsequent, may only be admitted on special grounds and not without special leave of the court.[79] This question was recently considered in some detail by the Supreme Court in *Minister for Agriculture, Food and Forestry v Alte Leipziger Versicherung Aktiengesellchaft*[80] in which Laffoy J had concluded that the plaintiff was entitled to sue the defendants for indemnity pursuant to Article 8 of the Brussels Convention and the defendant had appealed to the Supreme Court. Prior to the hearing of the appeal, a supplemental written submission on behalf of the defendants was lodged in which the conflicts of evidence disclosed by the affidavits filed subsequent to the lodging of the notice of appeal were set out in detail. Counsel on behalf of the plaintiff submitted that as this was not an ap-

---

[78] O'Flaherty J stated that if the evidence of the exacerbation of the plaintiff's injuries had stood alone, he would not have allowed it to be admitted but it seemed to him that it was inextricably linked with the evidence concerning the loss of his job and so should be allowed. Blayney J stated that if this further medical evidence had been the only matter to be considered, it was possible that leave to introduce it would not have been given as it probably fell within the area of uncertainty in which the trial judge's estimate had been made, but as it in all likelihood had a connection with the plaintiff's loss of his job, he considered that the court's discretion should be exercised in favour of receiving it.

[79] *Kennan & Sons Ltd v Housing Corporation of Great Britain Ltd* [1932] IR 192.

[80] [2000] 4 IR 32, [2001] 1 ILRM 582.

peal from an "interlocutory judgment or order" within the meaning of Order 58, rule 8, the evidence contained in the affidavits sworn and filed after the hearing in the High Court could be admitted only on special grounds and with the special leave of the Supreme Court obtained on application by a motion on notice. Counsel on behalf of the defendants accepted that the evidence contained in the affidavits did not relate to matters which occurred after the date of the High Court decision but submitted that as this was an appeal from an interlocutory judgment or order, special leave of the Supreme Court was not required for the admission of the further affidavits. The majority of the Supreme Court agreed with the submission of counsel on behalf of the plaintiff that the order in the case before it was, for the purposes of Order 58, rule 8 a final order. Barron J concluded that the order in question, while it did not readily fall into the category of "interlocutory" or "final", was one which was much more in the nature of a final order. The application before the court dealt with the issue as to whether a particular cause of action was justiciable in this jurisdiction and in his view the determination of such a question should be final, subject to an appeal, as to treat it otherwise would in effect be to allow the issue to be tried twice. However, the conclusion reached by Keane CJ in his dissenting judgment following an extensive review of the English authorities should also be noted. In his view, an order such as the one in the case before the court, which did no more than reject a preliminary objection as to jurisdiction, could not be said to be final in its nature and he expressed the opinion that the policy considerations which had led the courts to impose specific limitations on the admission of additional evidence were wholly absent.

20.026 Finally, it should be noted that Order 58, rule 14 provides that when any question of fact is involved in an appeal, the evidence taken in the High Court bearing on such question shall, subject to any special order, be brought before the Supreme Court in the following manner. Where the evidence has been taken by affidavit, copies of the affidavits shall be produced and where evidence has been given orally, copies of the judge's notes or such other materials as the Supreme Court shall deem expedient, shall be introduced. Considering this provision, O'Higgins CJ stated in *Northern Bank Finance Corporation Ltd v Charlton*[81] that it follows that in a normal case, while the evidence given at trial may be heard subsequently on the appeal in the form of the judge's notes or the transcript, the witness who gave the evidence will not be heard again.

Miscellaneous Provisions Relating to Appeals

20.027 Order 58, rule 8 provides that the Supreme Court shall have all the powers and duties as to amendment or otherwise as the High Court. However,

---

[81] [1979] IR 149, 178.

as was pointed out by Henchy J in *Hughes v O'Rourke*,[82] this provision refers only to appeals pending before the Supreme Court and it has no reference to an intermediate matter arising between hearing and appeal.

Order 58, rule 13 provides that where an *ex parte* application has been refused in whole or in part by the High Court, an application for a similar purpose may be made to the Supreme Court on an *ex parte* basis within four days from the date of such refusal or within such enlarged time as the Supreme Court may allow.[83] Rule 16 provides that no interlocutory order or rule from which there has been no appeal shall operate so as to bar or prejudice the Supreme Court from giving such decision on the appeal as may be just. Rule 9 provides that if, on the hearing of an appeal, it appears to the Supreme Court that there ought to be a new trial, it may order that the judgment or order appealed against be set aside and that a new trial take place.

Order 58, rule 20 provides that on an appeal from the High Court, "interest for such time as execution has been delayed by the appeal shall be allowed" unless the Supreme Court orders otherwise and the Taxing Master or other proper officer may compute such interest without any order for that purpose. It is clear from the decision in *O'Sullivan v Dwyer (No. 2)*[84] that by virtue of this rule, the defendant is bound to pay interest on a sum of damages awarded from the date of the High Court order to the date of the payment of that sum to the plaintiff. It should also be noted that where an order for costs is made,[85] interest accrues thereon from the date of the order and not from the date of taxation.

Appeals in Cases where there has been a Trial with a Jury

20.028 Order 58, rule 2 provides that in any matter where there has been a trial with a jury, or where an issue in a matter has been tried by a jury, every notice of appeal shall include an application for a new trial and such other relief as may be sought *e.g.* to set aside the verdict and finding of the jury or to enter judgment for the appellant. Rule 7 goes on to provide that in any appeal falling within rule 2 the following provisions shall apply. First, the Registrar of the Supreme Court shall apply to the trial judge for a report of the trial for the information of the Supreme Court, so far as he may deem it necessary. Secondly, a new trial shall not be granted on the ground of mis-direction or because of the improper admission or rejection of evidence, or because the jury's verdict was not taken on a question which the judge at the trial was not asked to leave

---

[82] [1986] ILRM 538, 540-541.

[83] As Hederman J commented in *Hughes v O'Rourke* [1986] ILRM 538, 543 it is clear from this rule (and from rule 10) that only the Supreme Court may deal with applications for extension of time for appealing from the High Court to the Supreme Court.

[84] [1973] IR 81.

[85] *Hickey v Norwich Union Fire Insurance Ltd* High Court (Murphy J) 23 October 1987
Best v Wellcome Foundation Ltd (No. 2) [1995] 2 IR 393, [1995] 1 ILRM 554.

with them unless in the opinion of the Supreme Court some substantial wrong or miscarriage has been thereby occasioned at the trial. Thirdly, a new trial may be ordered on any question without interfering with the finding or decision on any other question. Rule 15 provides that if, on the hearing of any appeal, a question arises as to the ruling or direction of a judge to a jury or assessors, the Supreme Court shall have regard to verified notes or other evidence and to such other materials as the Supreme Court may deem expedient.

CHAPTER TWENTY ONE

JUDICIAL REVIEW

INTRODUCTION

21.001 The purpose of judicial review is to provide a form of supervision in relation to decisions made by lower courts and administrative bodies to ensure that the functions conferred on these authorities are carried out correctly and legally. Perhaps the most frequently quoted statement of the perceived role of the judicial review mechanism is that of Lord Brightman in *Chief Constable of the North Wales Police v Evans*[1] in which he commented that "judicial review is concerned not with the decision, but with the decision making process". Essentially judicial review involves an assessment of the manner in which a decision has been made; it is not an appeal and the jurisdiction exercised is supervisory in nature.[2] While traditionally the attention of the courts in judicial review proceedings was directed towards the issue of whether a decision maker had acted beyond the limits of his powers, whether statutory or common law, the scope of this review process is now much more comprehensive. It has been said[3] that the purpose of the courts' supervisory jurisdiction in judicial review proceedings is not to vindicate rights as such, but to ensure that public powers are exercised in accordance with basic standards of legality, fairness and rationality.[4]

Prior to the introduction of Order 84 of the Rules of the Superior Courts

---

[1] [1982] 1 WLR 1155, 1173, [1982] 3 All ER 141, 154. This statement has been approved in this jurisdiction on numerous occasions. See *State (Keegan) v Stardust Victims' Compensation Tribunal* [1986] IR 642, [1987] ILRM 202, *ACT Shipping (PTE) Ltd v Minister for the Marine* [1995] 3 IR 406, [1995] 2 ILRM 30, *National Association of Regional Game Councils v Minister for Justice* High Court (Quirke J) 12 June 1998, *Ní Eilí v Environmental Protection Agency* Supreme Court, 30 July 1999 and *Ryanair Ltd v Flynn* [2000] 3 IR 240, [2001] 1 ILRM 283.

[2] See *Murphy v Director of Public Prosecutions* Supreme Court, 24 February 1999. As Lawton LJ commented in *Laker Airways Ltd v Department of Trade* [1977] QB 643, 724, [1977] 2 WLR 234, 267, [1977] 2 All ER 182, 208: "I regard myself as a referee. I can blow my judicial whistle when the ball goes out of play; but when the game restarts I must neither take part in it nor tell the players how to play".

[3] Alder, "Obsolescence and renewal: Judicial review in the private sector" in *Administrative Law Facing the Future* Leyland and Woods eds. (1997) at 163.

[4] These three touchstones have in one form or other become well established as the grounds upon which administrative action is subject to control by judicial review and Lord Diplock in the significant decision of *Council of Civil Service Unions v Minister for the Civil Service* [1985] AC 374, [1984] 1 WLR 1174, [1984] 3 All ER 935 referred to these grounds as "illegality", "irrationality" and "procedural impropriety".

1986 public law remedies were not interchangeable with remedies which operated in private law and a litigant who had a good case on the merits might be deprived of relief because he chose the wrong form of remedy. Order 84 introduced a comprehensive new judicial review procedure which brought about greater flexibility and allowed the courts to grant whichever form of relief was considered appropriate.[5]

While a number of important issues arise in relation to the nature and scope of judicial review[6] these have already been extensively considered elsewhere[7] and it will suffice to state briefly a number of fundamental principles relating to seeking relief by way of judicial review. Traditionally judicial review will only lie to review decisions of public bodies which concern issues of public law.[8] In addition, it must be borne in mind that public law remedies are discretionary in nature and that relief will not automatically be granted once a substantive ground for review is made out.[9]

RELIEF WHICH MAY BE CLAIMED IN JUDICIAL REVIEW PROCEEDINGS

21.002 Order 84, rule 18 sets out some of the remedies which may be sought by way of judicial review and it is useful to explain them briefly.

Certiorari

21.003 *Certiorari* lies to quash a decision of a public body made in excess of or in abuse of its jurisdiction or where an error appears on the face of the record.

---

[5] As Hederman J commented in *O'Neill v Iarnród Éireann* [1991] ILRM 129, 133 "Order 84 of the 1986 Rules eliminates procedural technicalities relating to the machinery of administrative law, mainly by removing procedural differences between the remedies which an applicant was formerly required to select as the most appropriate to his case".

[6] *E.g.* the question of whether the Superior Courts Rules Committee had authority to make the changes effected by Order 84 (see Hogan and Morgan, *Administrative Law in Ireland* (3rd ed., 1998) at 693-695 and Collins and O'Reilly, *Civil Proceedings and the State in Ireland: A Practitioner's Guide* (1990) at 75-78 and the relationship between judicial review and plenary proceedings (see Hogan and Morgan, *Administrative Law in Ireland* (3rd ed., 1998) at 788-798 and Collins and O'Reilly, *Civil Proceedings and the State in Ireland: A Practitioner's Guide* (1990) at 73-75).

[7] See generally Hogan and Morgan, *Administrative Law in Ireland* (3rd ed., 1998), Collins and O'Reilly, *Civil Proceedings and the State in Ireland: A Practitioner's Guide* (1990) and Bradley, *Judicial Review* (2000).

[8] See further Hogan and Morgan, *Administrative Law in Ireland* (3rd ed., 1998) Chapter 14. A further traditional limitation was that judicial review would lie only to review decisions which affected rights or imposed liabilities, although as Hogan and Morgan explain (at 696-698) there has been a movement away from such orthodox principles.

[9] See further *infra* in relation to discretionary factors.

As O'Higgins CJ stated in *State (Abenglen Properties Ltd) v Dublin Corporation*[10] its purpose is to supervise the exercise of jurisdiction by bodies or tribunals having legal authority to affect rights and having a duty to act judicially and "to control any usurpation or action in excess of jurisdiction".

Prohibition

21.004 Prohibition lies to restrain a public body from acting in a manner which would be in excess of jurisdiction. It issues "for the purpose of preventing the inferior court from usurping a jurisdiction with which it was not legally vested, or in other words, to compel courts entrusted with judicial powers to keep within the limits of their jurisdiction".[11] The function of prohibition is therefore in some respects similar to that of *certiorari* except that it is sought before a public body has acted whereas *certiorari* is the appropriate remedy where a determination has already been made.

Quo Warranto

21.005 Proceedings by way of *quo warranto* may be brought against a person claiming any office, franchise, liberty or privilege of a public nature requiring him to establish by what authority he claims it. While the remedy still exists[12] it is rarely used and proceedings for a declaration and an injunction would achieve the same result.

Mandamus

21.006 An order of *mandamus* lies to compel the performance of a legal duty[13] of a public nature. Performance of this duty must have been demanded and refused,[14] although such refusal may be inferred from the circumstances.[15]

---

[10] [1984] IR 381, 392, [1982] ILRM 590, 597.
[11] Short and Mellor, *Practice of the Crown Office* (2nd ed.) Quoted with approval by Samuels J in *R. (Kelly) v Maguire* [1923] 2 IR 58, 68-69.
[12] The Law Reform Commission recommended that this procedure be abolished in Working Paper No. 8 - 1979 paragraph 5-2.
[13] It would appear that the obligation in question must impose a duty and *mandamus* will not lie to compel performance of a power or discretion, see *Minister for Labour v Grace* [1993] 2 IR 53, 55.
[14] *R.(Butler) v Navan UDC* [1926] IR 466, 470-471. See also *State (Modern Homes (Ireland) Ltd) v Dublin Corporation* [1953] IR 202.
[15] *Point Exhibition Co. Ltd v Revenue Commissioners* [1993] 2 IR 551, 555, [1993] ILRM 621, 623.

Other remedies

21.007 In addition to public law remedies which must be sought by way of an application for judicial review, Order 84, rule 18(2) provides that an application for a declaration or an injunction may be made by way of an application for judicial review[16] if the court considers that it would be just and convenient to do so having regard to:

(a) the nature of the matters in respect of which relief may be granted by way of an order of *mandamus*, prohibition, *certiorari*, or *quo warranto*;

(b) the nature of the persons and bodies against whom relief may be granted by way of such order, and

(c) all the circumstances of the case

The origins of the declaratory order can be traced to s.155 of the Chancery (Ireland) Act 1867[17] and of the injunction to s.28(8) of the Supreme Court of Judicature (Ireland) Act 1877. A declaration can apply to situations which might also be dealt with by the use of *certiorari*, prohibition or *mandamus*, but its effect will, theoretically at least, be limited to declaring the rights of the parties.[18] An injunction, which can be either prohibitory or mandatory in nature, may be granted in all cases where it is "just and convenient to do so"[19] and prior to the introduction of the new Rules of the Superior Courts in 1986 both remedies could only be sought in proceedings commenced by way of plenary summons.

21.008 As noted above, prior to the coming into effect of Order 84 of the Rules of the Superior Courts 1986, if an applicant sought the incorrect remedy the court could not grant relief. However, since the introduction of Order 84, traditional public law remedies together with remedies such as the declaration, in-

---

[16] Note that in *McBride v Galway Corporation* [1998] 1 IR 485 the respondent submitted that the applicant should have proceeded by way of plenary summons rather than by way of judicial review as he was seeking declaratory and injunctive relief on foot of oral evidence. In the light of his findings, Quirke J found that it was not necessary for him to deal with the argument relating to the nature of the relief sought although he remarked that *"prima facie* the court would appear the have jurisdiction under Order 84 ... to grant, in appropriate cases, the relief which is being sought herein".

[17] Now see Order 19, rule 29 of the Rules of the Superior Courts 1986.

[18] However, note the *dicta* of Costello J in *O'Donnell v Dun Laoghaire Corporation* [1991] ILRM 301, to the effect that "a declaratory judgment is one which declares the rights of parties and because defendants, and in particular public bodies, respect and obey such judgments they have the same legal consequences as if the court were to make orders quashing the impugned orders and decisions".

[19] It was held by the Supreme Court in *Garda Representative Association v Ireland*, 18 December 1987 that the same considerations were relevant to the jurisdiction of the court to grant an injunction sought under Order 84 as would ordinarily apply.

junction and damages are effectively interchangeable and the court is free to grant a remedy even though it has not been specifically sought. Order 84, rule 19 now provides that any relief referred to in rule 18 may be claimed in an application for judicial review "as an alternative or in addition to any other relief" and that the court may grant any relief mentioned in rule 18 which it considers appropriate notwithstanding that it has not been specifically claimed, provided that it arises out of or is connected to the same matter.

LEAVE TO APPLY FOR JUDICIAL REVIEW

Introduction

21.009 Pursuant to Order 84 of the Rules of the Superior Courts 1962 an applicant for judicial review was required to obtain a conditional order and if the respondent could not show cause why it should not be granted, it was made absolute. The equivalent of obtaining a conditional order under Order 84 of the Rules of the Superior Courts 1986 is the granting of leave to bring an application for judicial review and it provides a mechanism for weeding out unmeritorious claims at this *ex parte* stage. In *G. v Director of Public Prosecutions*[20] Denham J spoke about the aim of requiring an applicant to seek leave as being to effect a screening process and to prevent trivial and unstateable cases proceeding and thus impeding public authorities unnecessarily.[21] A similar point was made by Kelly J in *O'Leary v Minister for Transport, Energy and Communications*[22] where he stated that "the judicial review procedure is designed so as to ensure that cases which are frivolous, vexatious or of no substance cannot be begun, hence the necessity for judicial screening at the stage when leave is sought". As Lord Diplock commented in *Inland Revenue Commissioners v National Federation of Self Employed and Small Businesses Ltd*:[23]

> Its purpose is to prevent the time of the court being wasted by busybodies with misguided or trivial complaints of administrative error, and to remove the uncertainty in which public officers and authorities might be left as to whether they could safely proceed with administrative action while proceedings for judicial review of it were actually pending even though misconceived.

---

[20] [1994] 1 IR 374, 382. See also the comments of McCracken J in *O'Ceallaigh v An Bord Altranais* High Court 26 May 1998 (at 13) that "[i]t is frequently necessary to have procedures of this kind to filter out unstateable cases".

[21] See also *O'Donnell v Dun Laoghaire Corporation* [1991] ILRM 301, 314 *per* Costello J.

[22] [2000] 1 ILRM 391, 397.

[23] [1982] AC 617, 642-643, [1981] 2 WLR 722, 739, [1981] 2 All ER 93, 105.

Making an Application for Leave

21.010 Order 84, rule 20(2) provides that an application for leave shall be made by motion *ex parte* grounded on a notice in Form 13 in Appendix T and on an affidavit which verifies the facts relied on. The statement of grounds and the affidavit verifying the facts must be filed in the Central Office of the High Court. The meaning of the requirement in rule 20(2)(b) that the affidavit should verify the facts relied on has recently been considered by McGuinness J in *Director of Public Prosecutions v Hamill*.[24] While the second named respondent had complained that affidavits did not "verify" the facts relied on in the applicant's statement, McGuinness J stated that she believed this submission was based on a misunderstanding of the phraseology of the rule. In her view "[t]he rule requires that the facts relied on should be set out in an affidavit; it does not require that the actual word 'verify' must be used in the affidavit". The first paragraph of the affidavit in question which was in the standard form, averred the truth of what was set out in the body of the affidavit and this was confirmed in the jurat. The body of the affidavit set out the same facts as were relied upon in the statement of grounds and so stated that they were true or "verified" them. This conclusion was upheld on appeal to the Supreme Court,[25] Keane CJ stating that the word "verify" does not require an applicant to state that he is verifying the petition or the application for judicial review or to use any phrase of that nature and that it is sufficient if he sets out the facts in the affidavit grounding the application.

Factors for the Consideration of the Court

21.011 Order 84, rule 20(3) provides that a court hearing an application for leave may allow the applicant's statement to be amended by specifying different or additional grounds of relief on such terms if any as it thinks fit. A useful summary of the factors which an applicant must establish in a *prima facie* manner in his affidavit and submissions before he will be granted leave is set out by Finlay CJ in *G. v Director of Public Prosecutions*,[26] although he stressed that these conditions were not intended to be exclusive:

(a) That he has a sufficient interest in the matter to which the application relates to comply with rule 20(4).

(b) That the facts averred in the affidavit would be sufficient, if proved, to support a stateable ground for the form of relief sought by way of judicial review.

---

[24] [2000] 1 ILRM 150.
[25] Supreme Court, 11 May 2000.
[26] [1994] 1 IR 374, 377-378.

(c) That on those facts an arguable case in law can be made that the applicant is entitled to the relief which he seeks.

(d) That the application has been made promptly and in any event within the three months or six months time limit provided for in Order 84, rule 21(1), or that the court is satisfied that there is a good reason for extending the time limit ...

(e) That the only effective remedy, on the facts established by the applicant, which the applicant could obtain would be an order by way of judicial review or, if there be an alternative remedy, that the application by way of judicial review is, on all the facts of the case, a more appropriate method of procedure.

As stated above, the purpose of the leave stage in judicial review proceedings has been described as "to effect a screening process of litigation against public authorities"[27] and to weed out trivial or unstateable cases at the *ex parte* stage. Thus public authorities need not be involved at all in proceedings which the High Court considers are unwarranted at the leave stage.[28] The function of the court at this stage is simply to satisfy itself that the applicant's case is arguable and as Finlay CJ stated in *O'Reilly v Cassidy*[29] it is not appropriate or proper for it to express any view on whether the grounds put forward are strong or weak, nor is it concerned with trying to ascertain what the eventual result will be.

21.012 However, it should be noted that the Oireachtas has imposed the requirement in certain types of cases[30] that leave to bring judicial review proceedings should not be granted unless the High Court is satisfied that there are

---

[27] *Per* Denham J in *G. v Director of Public Prosecutions* [1994] 1 IR 374, 382.

[28] However, it should be noted that some types of applications for judicial review are required to be on notice to other parties, see s.82(3B)(a)(ii) of the Local Government (Planning and Development) Act 1963, as amended, s.50(4)(b) of the Planning and Development Act 2000, s.55A(2)(b) of the Roads Act 1993 as amended, s.12(2)(b) of the Transport (Dublin Light Rail) Act 1996, s.43(5)(b) of the Waste (Management) Act 1996, s.13(3)(b) of the Irish Takeover Panel Act 1997, s.73(2)(b) of the Fisheries (Amendment) Act 1997 and s.5(2)(b) of the Illegal Immigrants (Trafficking) Act 2000, considered *infra*.

[29] [1995] 1 ILRM 306, 309.

[30] Amongst the most commonly invoked provisions are s.82(3B)(a)(ii)of the Local Government (Planning and Development) Act 1963, as amended, s.50(4)(b) of the Planning and Development Act 2000, s.43(5)(b)(ii) of the Waste (Management) Act 1996 and s.5(2)(b) of the Illegal Immigrants (Trafficking) Act 2000 (see (2000) 6 Bar Review 170). See also s.55A(2)(b) of the Roads Act 1993 (as amended by the Roads (Amendment) Act 1998), s.12(2)(b) of the Transport (Dublin Light Rail) Act 1996, s.13(3)(b) of the Irish Takeover Panel Act 1997 and s.73(2)(b) of the Fisheries (Amendment) Act 1997.

"substantial grounds"[31] for contending that the impugned decision is invalid or ought to be quashed. This was interpreted by Carroll J in *McNamara v An Bord Pleanála*[32] in the context of an application for judicial review of a planning decision as meaning reasonable, arguable and weighty and "not trivial or tenuous". More recently, the Supreme Court commenting on this test in *In re Article 26 and ss. 5 and 10 of the Illegal Immigrants (Trafficking) Bill 1999*[33] stated that the interpretation put forward by Carroll J was appropriate. The court concluded that the imposition of a requirement of "substantial grounds" in an application for leave to apply for judicial review was one which fell within the discretion of the legislature and was not so onerous, either in itself or in conjunction with a fourteen day limitation period,[34] as to infringe the constitutional right of access to the courts or the right to fair procedures.

Circumstances in Which There May be an *Inter Partes* Hearing at Leave Stage

21.013 It should be noted that while Order 84, rule 20(2) provides that an application for leave shall be made *ex parte*, it may be decided not to determine the application without giving the respondents an opportunity to be heard and to conduct an *inter partes* hearing at this stage, a procedure which according to Kelly J in *Gorman v Minister for the Environment*[35] is used in a small number of cases, but it may also be said, with increasing frequency. In this case counsel on both sides had agreed initially that notwithstanding the fact that the hearing was *inter partes*, the burden of proof to be satisfied was that set out by the Supreme Court in *G. v Director of Public Prosecutions*,[36] namely that the applicant had made out an arguable case. Kelly J concluded that he must proceed to decide the case on the basis of that standard given the fact that counsel had proceeded to open the case in reliance on it, but he expressed the view that he was "by no means convinced that this low standard is appropriate on an *inter partes* hearing." He then stated that there was much to be said in favour of the standard put forward by Glidewell LJ in *Mass Energy Ltd v Birmingham City Council*[37] that the applicant's case should be not merely arguable but "strong,

---

[31] Interpreted by Carroll J in *McNamara v An Bord Pleanála* as meaning reasonable, arguable and weighty and "not trivial or tenuous".

[32] [1995] 2 ILRM 125, 130. See also *Scott v An Bord Pleanála* [1995] 1 ILRM 424, 428-429 and *Lancefort Ltd v An Bord Pleanála* [1997] 2 ILRM 508, 516.

[33] [2000] 2 IR 360, 395. See also *Zgnat'ev v Minister for Justice, Equality and Law Reform* High Court (Finnegan J) 29 March 2001 and *P. v Minister for Justice, Equality and Law Reform* [2002] 1 ILRM 16.

[34] Imposed by s.5(2) of the Illegal Immigrants (Trafficking) Act 2000.

[35] High Court (Kelly J) 7 December 2000.

[36] [1994] 1 IR 374.

[37] [1994] Env LR 298, 308. Applied by Keene J in *R. v Cotswold District Council, ex p. Barrington Parish Council* (1998) 75 P & CR 515, 530.

that is to say, likely to succeed". In the view of Kelly J this approach appeared to make for a more economic use of court time than the application of the substantially lower standard of an arguable case, although he stressed that the question must be decided in another case in which the issue could be fully debated.

21.014 It should be noted that subsequently in *Irish Haemophilia Society Ltd v Lindsay*[38] Kelly J applied the ordinary onus of proof as set out in *G v Director of Public Prosecutions* to an *inter partes* leave application, although he reiterated that there might well be grounds for believing that a higher threshold was appropriate in cases of this nature. In *Halpin v Wicklow County Council*[39] in which the applicant sought leave to extend the grounds on which leave to bring judicial review proceedings had been granted, O'Sullivan J stated that in his view the standard laid down by the Supreme Court in *G v Director of Public Prosecutions* should apply, notwithstanding the observations of Kelly J in *Gorman*, although he went on to say that he agreed that he could not shut his mind to the case being made by the respondent which was a notice party to the application. Similarly, in *Gilligan v Governor of Portlaoise Prison*[40] McKechnie J, having commented that a state of uncertainty exists in relation to this issue which is evidently unsatisfactory, proceeded to apply the threshold of arguability but suggested that he would in the evaluation process "take into account those parts of the respondent's evidence which [he could] confidently accept as being accurate and also the submissions made thereon."[41]

21.015 It should also be noted that certain types of judicial review applications governed by statute are required to be on notice to other parties, such as applications brought pursuant to s.5(2) of the Illegal Immigrants (Trafficking) Act 2000 which are required to be brought on notice to the Minister for Justice and any other person specified by order of the High Court.[42] In *P. v Minister for Justice, Equality and Law Reform*[43] in considering an application for judicial review brought pursuant to s.5 of the Act of 2000, which provides that leave shall not be granted unless there are "substantial grounds" for contending that

---

[38] High Court (Kelly J) 16 May 2001.
[39] High Court (O'Sullivan J) 15 March 2001.
[40] High Court (McKechnie J) 12 April 2001.
[41] *Ibid.* at 9.
[42] See also s.82(3B)(a)(ii) of the Local Government (Planning and Development) Act 1963 (inserted by s.19 of the Local Government (Planning and Development) Act 1992), s.50(4)(b) of the Planning and Development Act 2000 which requires applications for leave to be made on notice to An Bord Pleanála and each other party to the appeal or reference (see *McCarthy v An Bord Pleanála* [2000] 1 IR 42 and *Murray v An Bord Pleanála* [2000] 1 IR 58). In addition, see the provisions of s.43(5)(b)(ii) of the Waste Management Act 1996, s.55A(2)(b) of the Roads Act 1993 as amended, s.12(2)(b) of the Transport (Dublin Light Rail) Act 1996, s.13(3)(b) of the Irish Takeover Panel Act 1997 and s.73(2)(b) of the Fisheries (Amendment) Act 1997.
[43] [2002] 1 ILRM 16.

the decision ought to be quashed, Smyth J stated that he was not satisfied that imposing the ordinary standard of establishing a stateable case was suitable at an *inter partes* hearing and that it was appropriate to apply the views expressed by Kelly J in *Gorman v Minister for the Environment* to cases decided pursuant to the legislation. In dismissing the applicants' appeal, Hardiman J, speaking for the Supreme Court, focused on the "substantial grounds" standard imposed in order to obtain leave pursuant to s.5. He said that for the purpose of the case before him, he had not found it necessary to consider whether any more onerous standard was required by that phrase and he decided not to express any view on the findings made by the trial judge in relation to this question.

Therefore, considerable doubt remains about whether the views expressed by Kelly J in *Gorman v Minister for the Environment* will gain approval in the context of "ordinary" leave applications heard *inter partes* which are not governed by legislative schemes imposing a requirement to establish "substantial grounds". Given the increasing frequency with which such hearings now appear to be taking place, it would be most useful if this issue were clarified.

Appeal Against Refusal to Grant Leave

21.016 Where leave to apply for judicial review is refused by the High Court an applicant may appeal on an *ex parte* basis within four days from the date of such refusal or within the enlarged time as the Supreme Court may allow.[44] It would appear that the Supreme Court will be reluctant to rule out an applicant's claim at this *ex parte* stage if he has an arguable case.[45] In *O'Neill v Iarnrod*

---

[44] Order 58, rule 13. Note that Order 84, rule 23(2) provides that the court may allow the applicant to amend his statement of grounds at the hearing of the motion or summons, so even if leave is refused is respect of certain grounds, application may subsequently be made to add them.

[45] However, note that no appeal shall lie to the Supreme Court in respect of a determination of the High Court on an application for leave or an application for review in planning matters save with the leave of the High Court which shall only be granted where the High Court certifies that its decision involves a point of law of exceptional public importance and that it is desirable in the public interest that an appeal shall be taken, see s.82(3B)(b)(i) of the Local Government (Planning and Development) Act 1963 and s.50(4)(f) of the Planning and Development Act 2000. It has been held that the High Court alone has power to issue such a certificate and that accordingly the Supreme Court has no jurisdiction to hear an appeal from a refusal to grant one, see *Irish Asphalt Ltd v An Bord Pleanála* [1996] 2 IR 179, [1987] 1 ILRM 81 and *Irish Hardware Ltd v South Dublin County Council* [2001] 2 ILRM 291. By virtue of s.5(3)(a) of the Illegal Immigrants (Trafficking) Act 2000 similar provisions apply to applications for judicial review in respect of orders made regarding non-nationals pursuant to, *inter alia*, the Refugee Act 1996 and the Immigration Act 1999. See also s.55A(4)(a) of the Roads Act 1993, s.43(5)(c)(i) of the Waste Management Act 1996, s.12(4)(a) of the Transport (Dublin Light Rail) Act 1996, s.13(6) of the Irish Takeover Panel Act 1997 and s.73(3) of the Fisheries (Amendment) Act 1997.

Eireann[46] the Supreme Court allowed an appeal against the decision of the High Court refusing leave to apply for judicial review on the basis that "it would not appear to be correct to cut out the applicant from his opportunity to pursue a relief by way of judicial review and at least to argue at the hearing of such application his right to proceed in this manner",[47] although all the members of the Supreme Court clearly had misgivings about whether judicial review properly lay in this case, given the ostensibly contractual nature of the relationship between the parties. However, as against this, the purely supervisory role of judicial review must be also borne in mind and as Murphy J has recently commented in *Devlin v Minister for Arts, Culture and the Gaeltacht*[48] "it would be regrettable if this procedure, which achieved so much good, was to be invoked unnecessarily or in such a way as to delay or defeat the proper exercise of administrative powers".[49]

Application to Set Aside Order Granting Leave

21.017 It would now appear that the High Court has jurisdiction to set aside an order granting leave to bring judicial review proceedings made on an *ex parte* basis, although it has been suggested that this jurisdiction should "only be exercised sparingly and in a very plain case".[50] In *Adams v Director of Public Prosecutions*[51] the third named respondent, the British Home Secretary, successfully applied to have the order granting leave to issue proceedings[52] against him set aside. In a decision upheld by the Supreme Court, Kelly J referred to the *dicta* of McCracken J in *Voluntary Purchasing Groups Inc. v Insurco Ltd*[53] to the effect that the courts possess an inherent jurisdiction, in the absence of an express statutory provision to the contrary, to set aside an order made *ex parte* on the application of any party affected by that order. Kelly J stated that he had no hesitation in following this line of reasoning and that it would be most unjust to deny a party against whom an *ex parte* order has been made the opportunity of applying to have it set aside and instead to insist that the only remedy was an appeal to the Supreme Court. Kelly J concluded that it is the established practice of the High Court to hear applications to set aside orders made *ex parte* and in his view such applications could be entertained by any judge of the High

---

[46] [1991] ILRM 129. See also *Arnold v Windle* Supreme Court, 4 March 1999.

[47] *Ibid.* at 131 *per* Finlay CJ.

[48] [1999] 1 IR 47, 58, [1999] 1 ILRM 462, 474.

[49] Note that Bradley has commented in *Judicial Review* (2000) at 222 that "[t]o date there is no evidence of either an express or implicit judicial policy to manage the judicial review case-load by adopting a restrictive approach at the leave stage".

[50] *Per* McGuinness J in *Adam v Minister for Justice* [2001] 2 ILRM 452, 469.

[51] [2001] 2 ILRM 401.

[52] The applicant sought, *inter alia*, an order of *certiorari* to quash the Home Secretary's certificate purporting to waive the rule of specialty in relation to the applicant's extradition.

[53] [1995] 2 ILRM 145, 147.

Court, not merely by the judge who had made the *ex parte* order in the first instance.

21.018 These principles were subsequently applied by the High Court to an application to set aside leave to take judicial review proceedings in *Adam v Minister for Justice*.[54] The applicants had been granted leave by Kinlen J to bring judicial review proceedings in respect of the respondents' decision to make deportation orders against them and the respondents sought to have the order granting leave discharged. O'Donovan J acknowledged that while Kinlen J had filtered and evaluated the applicants' applications for leave to apply for judicial review, nevertheless he had only heard one party to the proceedings and certainly had not had the full facts before him. O'Donovan J stated that like McCracken J in *Voluntary Purchasing* he thought it would be quite unjust if an order could be made against a party in his absence and without notice to it which could not be reviewed on the application of the party affected. O'Donovan J concluded that the applications of the applicants in respect of whom deportation orders had been made or threatened were without substance and that the order of the court in so far as it affected those applicants ought to be discharged.

21.019 A similar issue arose before Morris P in *Iordache v Minister for Justice*[55] and given that the decision in *Adam* was under appeal, he decided to review the relevant authorities and consider the question afresh. He concluded that for the reasons stated in the decisions considered above he was in no doubt that the fact that a case had been considered on an *ex parte* basis by a judge of the High Court and that he had formed a view on it should not be a bar to an application by a respondent seeking to have the original order set aside. In the circumstances, Morris P held that the order granting leave to apply for judicial review should be set aside. Similarly in *Byrne v Wicklow County Council*[56] Morris P stated that it is within the capacity of the High Court to review an order made *ex parte* in judicial review proceedings in an appropriate case. However, he stressed that the correct practice is to apply to the court on notice to the applicant for an order setting aside the original order well in advance of the hearing of the substantive application and he said that in this way the costs of the substantive hearing will be avoided if the original *ex parte* order is set aside.

21.020 The appeals in *Adam* and *Iordache* were heard together by the Supreme Court which concluded that the decisions made by O'Donovan J and Morris P should be upheld.[57] McGuinness J rejected the contention of the applicants that the decision in *Adams v Director of Public Prosecutions* should

[54] High Court (O'Donovan J) 16 November 2000.
[55] High Court (Morris P) 30 January 2001.
[56] High Court (Morris P) 7 February 2001.
[57] [2001] 2 ILRM 452.

be distinguished as a case dealing with material non-disclosure or other conduct akin to lack of *bona fides*. In her view the conclusions reached in the High Court that the grant of leave should be set aside were correct although she accepted the submission of counsel for the applicant, with which counsel for the respondent agreed, that this jurisdiction should only be exercised very sparingly and in a very plain case. In this regard, McGuinness J referred to the comments of Bingham LJ in *R v Secretary of State for the Home Department ex p. Chinoy*[58] to the effect that it would be an unfortunate development if the granting of leave were to be followed by applications to set aside the grant of leave which would then be followed, if leave were not set aside, by a full hearing. McGuinness J continued as follows:

> One could envisage the growth of a new list of applications to discharge leave to be added to the already lengthy list of applications for leave. Each application would probably require considerable argument – perhaps with further affidavits and/or discovery. Where leave was discharged, an appeal would lie to this Court. If the appeal succeeded, the matter would return to the High Court for full hearing followed, in all probability, by a further appeal to this Court. Such a procedure would result in a wasteful expenditure of court time and an unnecessary expenditure in legal costs; it could be hardly said to serve the interests of justice. The exercise of the court's inherent jurisdiction to discharge orders giving leave should, therefore, be used only in exceptional cases.[59]

Hardiman J reached the same conclusion that the High Court had jurisdiction to set aside an order giving leave to seek judicial review. He expressed the view that any order made *ex parte* must be regarded as an order of a provisional nature only and that the fact that a party may be affected by it without notice and without having had the opportunity of being heard may, depending on the facts of the case, constitute a grave injustice to him. He referred to the case of *Adams v Director of Public Prosecutions* and stated that it appeared to have been accepted here and in neighbouring jurisdictions that there is an inherent jurisdiction to strike out an order giving leave to seek judicial review. In his view "once it is accepted that the jurisdiction invoked here by the respondents exists, it is difficult to justify any hard and fast restrictions on it".[60] He concluded that the grant of leave, especially when coupled with a stay, was quite sufficient to constitute the respondents as parties affected by an order and that they must in a suitable case be entitled to attack the grant of leave. The tenor of the judgment delivered by McGuinness J is undoubtedly more restrictive, and it could be argued, more pragmatic, and it remains to be seen whether the rather

---

[58] [1991] COD 381.
[59] *Ibid.* at 469.
[60] *Ibid.* at 475.

stringent test she suggested will be followed.

Sufficient Interest

21.021 In order to obtain leave to issue judicial review proceedings, the applicant must establish that he has a "sufficient interest" in the matter to which the application relates.[61] Even before the introduction of the 1986 Rules of the Superior Courts, it was accepted that the test of interest should be broadly speaking the same both in relation to public law remedies and those which also operated in the realm of private law.[62] As Hogan and Morgan observe,[63] the policy of the new rules is to achieve uniformity and given that Order 84, rule 20(4) applies to all remedies, they suggest that "this must mean that the *locus standi* requirements do not vary from remedy to remedy". In *State (Lynch) v Cooney*[64] Walsh J commented that such rules as do exist regarding what is "sufficient interest" are judge made rules and as such can be altered by the judiciary; more importantly he said "they must be flexible so as to be individually applicable to the particular facts of any given case".

21.022 One question which has provoked discussion both in this jurisdiction and in England is the extent to which the issue of standing should be determined at the leave stage or whether it should largely be left for consideration at the hearing of the substantive application.[65] Collins and O'Reilly[66] have commented that the issue of whether an applicant has a sufficient interest to maintain an application for judicial review is "by and large too complex and controversial to be resolved at the hearing of the application for leave" and this tends to reflect judicial thinking on this question. In *R v Inland Revenue Commissioners, ex p. National Federation of Self-Employed and Small Businesses Ltd*[67] Lord Diplock stated that "the discretion that the court is exercising at this stage is not the same as that which it is called upon to exercise when all the evidence

---

[61] Order 84, rule 20(4). However, note that s.50(4)(b) of the Planning and Development Act 2000 imposes a requirement that an applicant establish that he has a "substantial interest" before leave to bring judicial review proceedings will be granted in respect of certain types of planning decisions. S.50(4)(d) goes on to provide that a "substantial interest" in this context is not limited to an interest in land or other financial interest. For a discussion of this requirement, see Simons "The Implications of the New Act for Judicial Review Proceedings" in *The Planning and Development Act 2000: Implications for Practitioners* (2001) at 4-6.
[62] *State (Lynch) v Cooney* [1982] IR 337, 369, [1983] ILRM 89, 100 *per* Walsh J.
[63] *Administrative Law in Ireland* (3rd ed., 1998) at 741.
[64] [1982] IR 337, 369, [1983] ILRM 89, 101.
[65] Note that the question of *locus standi* should be raised by the respondent or notice party in the statement of opposition if it is intended to challenge the applicant's standing, see *O'Connor v Dublin Corporation* High Court (O'Neill J) 3 October 2000 at 45.
[66] *Civil Proceedings and the State in Ireland: A Practitioner's Guide* (1990) at 88.
[67] [1982] AC 617, 643-644, [1981] 2 WLR 722, 740, [1981] 2 All ER 93, 106.

is in and the matter has been fully argued at the hearing of the application". This statement was quoted with approval by Denham J in *G. v Director of Public Prosecutions*[68] who commented that on the actual application for judicial review, the applicant has "an altogether heavier burden of proof to discharge". Linked to this is the point made by Walsh J in *State (Lynch) v Cooney*[69] that the question of whether a person has a sufficient interest must depend on the circumstances of each particular case. In his view, while the question of sufficient interest is a mixed one of fact and law, greater importance should be attached to the facts, and it is clear that a detailed examination of the facts of the case may only take place at the hearing of the substantive application for judicial review.

These principles were drawn together by Keane J in his judgment in *Lancefort Ltd v An Bord Pleanála*[70] in considering whether *locus standi* should be determined as a threshold issue on an application for leave or whether, assuming that leave is granted, it should be determined at the substantive hearing. In the view of Keane J the approach adopted by Walsh J in *State (Lynch) v Cooney* was consistent with determining standing as a threshold issue on an application for leave only where it was obvious that a person did not have a sufficient interest.

Discretion to Adjourn Application for Leave

21.023 Order 84, rule 20(5) provides that where leave is sought to apply for an order of *certiorari* to quash any order which is subject to an appeal and a time is limited for the bringing of an appeal, the court may adjourn the application for leave until the appeal is determined or the time for appealing has expired. In *State (Roche) v Delap*[71] after the prosecutor's appeal to the Circuit Court had come on for hearing, the district judge adjourned the matter so as to enable him to bring proceedings for *certiorari*. In refusing the order sought, Henchy J held that while the appeal was pending it was not open to him to apply for *certiorari* and that he should have elected either to bring an appeal or to seek *certiorari*. However, in *State (Glover) v McCarthy*[72] Gannon J, although he refused to grant an order of *certiorari*, held that the fact that the prosecutrix had appealed to the Circuit Court was not of itself a reason for refusing such an order in an appropriate case. In his view "the principal factor which would guide the court in the exercise of its discretion in a case where the alternatives of *certiorari* and appeal lie is the objective of achieving a just resolution of the matters at issue with minimal inconvenience consistent with regularity of judicial procedures".[73] Whether the *Roche* decision could be distinguished on the basis that the appeal

---

[68] [1994] 1 IR 374, 382.
[69] [1982] IR 337, 369, [1983] ILRM 89, 101. See also *Lancefort Ltd v An Bord Pleanála* [1999] 2 IR 270, 310-311, [1998] 2 ILRM 401, 435 *per* Keane J.
[70] [1999] 2 IR 270, 310-311, [1998] 2 ILRM 401, 435.
[71] [1980] IR 170.
[72] [1981] ILRM 47.
[73] *Ibid.* at 51. Quoted with approval by Hamilton P in *Byrne v Grey* [1988] IR 31, 41.

before the Circuit Court was actually in the process of being heard is unclear but it is likely that the approach of Gannon J in *Glover* is the better one irrespective of the progress of the appeal.

The manner in which the availability of an alternative remedy and specifically, a right to appeal a decision on the merits, will affect the exercise of a judge's discretion to grant or withhold relief in judicial review proceedings will be fully considered below. However, it is fair to say that the predominant, and it is submitted, the correct view, appears to be that where the legal validity of a decision is called into question, the taking of proceedings by way of judicial review is the appropriate remedy and the availability of an appeal on the merits should not be a factor.[74] In any event Order 84, rule 20(5) merely confers a discretion on the court to adjourn an application for judicial review and given recent trends it is likely that it will not often be exercised.

Awarding of Costs, Stays and Interim Relief

21.024 While the question of the awarding of costs will not generally be determined at the leave stage of proceedings,[75] Order 84, rule 20(6) provides that where a court grants leave "it may impose such terms as to costs as it thinks fit" and may require that an undertaking as to damages be given.[76] Order 84, rule 20(7)(a) provides that where leave to apply for judicial review is granted and the relief sought is prohibition or *certiorari* and the court so directs, the grant of leave shall operate as a stay of the proceedings to which the application relates until the determination of the application or until the court otherwise orders. Rule 20(7)(b) provides that if any other relief is sought, the court may at any time grant such interim relief as could be granted in an action begun by plenary summons.

21.025 The operation of the provisions of rule 20(6) in particular was considered in some detail by Laffoy J in *Broadnet Ireland Ltd v Office of the Director of Telecommunications Regulation*[77] in which the applicant company, which had been granted leave to apply for judicial review was required to provide an

---

[74] *P. & F. Sharpe Ltd v Dublin City and County Manager* [1989] IR 701, [1989] ILRM 565; *Mythen v Employment Appeals Tribunal* [1990] 1 IR 98, [1989] ILRM 844 and *Tennyson v Dun Laoghaire Corporation* [1991] 2 IR 527.

[75] Although note that Laffoy J accepted *obiter* in *Village Residents Association Ltd v An Bord Pleanála* [2000] 4 IR 321, [2001] 2 ILRM 22 that the High Court does have jurisdiction to make a pre-emptive order for costs. See also *R v Lord Chancellor, ex p. CPAG* [1991] 1 WLR 347, [1998] 2 All ER 755 and Costello (2000) 35 Ir Jur 121, 134-136.

[76] As Collins and O'Reilly point out in *Civil Proceedings and the State in Ireland: A Practitioner's Guide* (1990) at 92, this latter requirement is necessitated by the fact that Order 84, rule 20(7)(b) allows the court to grant interim injunctive relief.

[77] [2000] 3 IR 281, [2000] 2 ILRM 241. See further Costello (2000) 35 Ir Jur 121, 131-134.

undertaking as to damages. Laffoy J stated that she was satisfied that the court's jurisdiction to require an undertaking as to damages provided for in subrule (6) was not limited to situations in which a stay is granted under subrule (7)(a) or an interim injunction under subrule (7)(b). In her view subrule (6) by implication recognises that granting leave to impugn the decision of a public body may have the potential to cause damage not only to the public body but also to third parties affected by that body's decision. Laffoy J said that in her view subrule (6) was open to the construction that the court might, at the leave stage, on its own motion condition the grant of leave by requiring an undertaking as to damages. She had no doubt that this course was open under subrule (6) because the application for leave being an *ex parte* one, a respondent or notice party would have no opportunity to seek an undertaking until after leave had been granted. In addition, the High Court may also entertain an application after leave is granted from a respondent or notice party that it be a term of the continuance of the leave and the proceedings that an undertaking as to damages be given by the applicant. In relation to the manner in which the court's jurisdiction pursuant to subrule (6) should be exercised, Laffoy J stated as follows:

> In considering whether to exercise the discretion under subrule (6) to require an undertaking as to damages as a condition to the grant or the continuance of leave to apply for judicial review, the essential test is whether such requirement is necessary in the interests of justice or, put another way, whether it is necessary to mitigate injustice to parties directly affected by the existence of the pending application. If, in substance, the existence of the application has an effect similar to the effect of an interlocutory injunction in private litigation – that activity which would otherwise be engaged in is put 'on hold' pending final determination of the controversy, with resulting loss and damage – in my view, it is appropriate for the court to adopt the approach traditionally adopted in private law litigation in determining whether an interlocutory injunction should be granted and to require that the applicant should give an undertaking to make good that loss and damage if it is ultimately found that the applicant's case is unsustainable, provided there is no countervailing factor arising from the public nature of the jurisdiction it exercised under O.84 which precludes it from adopting that approach.[78]

Laffoy J concluded that it would be patently unfair and unjust to allow the proceedings to continue without the applicant carrying the risk occasioned by them if the proceedings were ultimately found to be unsustainable.

---

[78] *Ibid.* at 300, 258-259. Quoted with approval in *Seery v An Bord Pleanála* [2001] 2 ILRM 151.

21.026 The effect of rule 20(7)(a) seems to be that the High Court is empowered to grant the equivalent of an interlocutory injunction where *certiorari* or prohibition is sought after a purely *ex tempore* hearing,[79] although normally an applicant for interlocutory relief would have to apply on notice to the respondent for such an order. As Kelly J pointed out in *Fitzpatrick v Garda Commissioner*[80] this may give rise to difficulties as normally where injunctive relief is granted on an *ex parte* basis, it is purely of an interim nature and imposes on a successful applicant the obligation to apply for an interlocutory injunction on notice to the respondent. However, in the case before the court, the order made was to continue until the determination of the judicial review proceedings and no proviso was inserted entitling the respondent to apply to discharge the order on giving notice to the applicant.

Time Limits in Judicial Review Proceedings Generally

21.027 As Denham J stated in *de Roiste v Minister for Defence*[81] "time is more of the essence, more urgent, in judicial review proceedings" and the period in which a claim may be brought is a shorter time span than that required in other proceedings. Prior to the introduction of the Rules of the Superior Courts 1986, the particular period of inactivity which might debar a person from obtaining relief would depend on the circumstances of the case.[82] The court would consider both the nature of the decision which it was sought to quash and the effect of the delay on the parties and on any third parties who might have been prejudiced by the decision. It was suggested by McCarthy J in *State (Furey) v Minister for Defence*[83] that where the order which it was sought to challenge involved a form of public wrong, delay should not "of itself" disentitle an applicant to relief.[84] However in respect of other types of decision, the fact that delay might have prejudicially affected third parties was often considered fatal to an application.[85]

---

[79] See Hogan and Morgan, *Administrative Law in Ireland* (3rd ed., 1998) at 711.

[80] High Court (Kelly J) 16 October 1996.

[81] [2001] 2 ILRM 241, 261.

[82] *Per* Henchy J in *State (Cussen) v Brennan* [1981] IR 181.

[83] [1988] ILRM 89,100.

[84] However, note the comments of Keane CJ and Denham J in *de Roiste* in relation to this *dicta*. Keane CJ stated at 11 that in the light of the explanation of the relevant law provided by Denham and Fennelly JJ, with which he agreed, that passage could no longer be regarded as a correct statement of the law. Denham J commented that the words of McCarthy J were not an absolute statement that delay cannot disentitle an applicant to relief but rather that it should not "of itself" disentitle.

[85] So in *State (Cussen) v Brennan* [1981] IR 181 a delay of four months in bringing proceedings was considered fatal in circumstances where a rival candidate had accepted the position which the applicant sought. However, this should be contrasted with the decision in *M. v An Bord Uchtála* [1977] IR 287 where a delay of three years in chal-

21.028 Order 84, rule 21(1) now lays down requirements in relation to time limits and as Denham J commented in *de Roiste v Minister for Defence*[86] it sets out a scheme "which indicates a specific, short, time span within which to bring an application". Rule 21(1) provides that an application for leave to apply for judicial review shall be made[87] "promptly, and in any event within three months from the date when grounds for the application first arose, or six months where the relief sought is *certiorari*, unless the court considers that there is good reason for extending the period within which the application shall be made".[88] One important preliminary point made by Fennelly J in *de Roiste v Minister for Defence*[89] is that Order 84, rule 21 does not operate in the same way as a period of limitation, although it does "impose a preliminary obligation to proceed with despatch". It should also be noted at the outset that even where leave is granted on the basis that any delay is not such as to disentitle the applicant from seeking judicial review, the issue of delay may still debar an applicant from obtaining relief at the substantive hearing.[90] As Hederman J stated in *O'Flynn v Mid-Western Health Board*[91] "[e]ven if leave is granted at the *ex parte* stage, nonetheless, when the trial judge comes to hear the matter he must adjudicate upon whether the delay was reasonable and such as may be excused or not".

21.029 Rule 21(1) requires that an application for leave to apply for judicial review should be made "promptly", a precondition described by Ackner LJ in the Court of Appeal in relation to the same wording in the then equivalent Eng-

---

lenging an adoption order was overlooked even though the consequences for the adoptive parents and the child were extremely serious.

[86] [2001] ILRM 241, 257.
[87] It is clear from the judgment of Barr J in *Tennyson v Dun Laoghaire Corporation* [1991] 2 IR 527 that the provisions relating to time limits apply to the date on which the initial application for leave is made. So, the adjournment of an application for leave to a date outside the two month time limit laid down in relation to planning decisions did not affect compliance with this requirement in circumstances where the initial application was made within the relevant time limits.
[88] Certain shorter time limits have been created by statute: see s.82(3B) of the Local Government (Planning and Development) Act 1963 (inserted by s.19 of the Local Government (Planning and Development) Act 1992) as modified by s.50(4) of the Planning and Development Act 2000, s.78(2) of the Housing Act 1966, s.85(8) of the Environmental Protection Agency Act 1992, s.55A(1) of the Roads Act 1993 (inserted by s.6 of the Roads (Amendment) Act 1998), s.12(2) of the Transport (Dublin Light Rail) Act 1996, 43(5)(a) of the Waste Management Act 1996, s.13(3) of the Irish Takeover Panel Act 1997, s.73(1) of the Fisheries (Amendment) Act 1997 and s.5(2)(a) of the Illegal Immigrants (Trafficking) Act 2000.
[89] [2001] 2 ILRM 241, 266. See also Collins and O'Reilly *Civil Proceedings and the State in Ireland: A Practitioner's Guide* (1990) at 94 to the effect that the provisions of rule 21(1) should be regarded as guidelines and "ought not to be regarded as akin to limitation periods".
[90] *Solan v Director of Public Prosecutions* [1989] ILRM 491, 494 *per* Barr J.
[91] [1991] 2 IR 223, 236.

lish provision[92] as the "essential requirement" and it was acknowledged by him in his decision in *R v Stratford-on-Avon DC, ex p. Jackson*[93] that the fact that an application has been made within the time period laid down in the rules does not necessarily mean that it has been made "promptly". A similar view was expressed by McCracken J in *de Roiste v Minister for Defence*[94] where he said that the primary provision is that an application for judicial review must be made promptly, and it is only a secondary requirement that, in any event, the application must be made within the stated time depending on the nature of the application.[95] So, as McCracken J pointed out, an application for judicial review may fail even if it is made within the stated time unless it is also made promptly.[96] On appeal, Denham J also stated that the first condition as to time is that the application be brought promptly and that whether this requirement is met will depend on the circumstances.[97]

21.030 While there have been few examples of cases in this jurisdiction in which judicial review has been refused on grounds of lack of promptness within the three and six month time periods specified in the rules, it should be noted that in limited circumstances this may happen. In *Director of Public Prosecutions v Macklin*[98] the Director sought orders of *certiorari* and *mandamus* directed towards the respondent district judge in respect of orders which the latter had made in a criminal case. A delay of five and a half months had ensued before the proceedings were instituted and Lardner J said that although he was satisfied that the judge had erred in law, he would not grant the relief sought. In relation to the order of *mandamus*, he said that the application had not been brought within the three month period prescribed and there was no good reason for extending this. He then referred to the *dicta* of Henchy J in *State (Cussen) v Brennan*[99] where the latter had stated that "if anything wrong had taken place the party aggrieved should move at once" and in relation to the application for *certiorari*, he said that in all the circumstances it should fail because it had not been made promptly. A similar conclusion was reached by Laffoy J in *Director*

---

[92] Order 53, rule 4.
[93] [1985] 1 WLR 1319, 1322-1323, [1985] 3 All ER 769, 772.
[94] High Court (McCracken J) 28 June 1999 at 2.
[95] This view is in line with that expressed by Herbert J in *O'Connell v Environmental Protection Agency* [2002] 1 ILRM 1 to the effect that s.85(8) of the Environmental Protection Agency Act 1992, while imposing a non-expandable upper time limit within which an application for leave must be brought, does not in any way suspend or lessen the requirement that every application for leave to apply for judicial review must be made promptly within that stipulated period.
[96] See also *Grimes v Censorship of Publications Board* High Court (Smyth J) 22 February 2001 at 1.
[97] [2001] 2 ILRM 241, 255.
[98] [1989] ILRM 113.
[99] [1981] IR 181, 196.

of Public Prosecutions v Kelly[100] in which the applicant sought *certiorari* to quash the order of the respondent directing the jury to acquit the notice party. The application for leave was made four days before the expiration of the six month time limit and Laffoy J concluded that the application should fail, *inter alia,* because of this delay. While it should be borne in mind that in both these cases judicial review was being sought by the Director of Public Prosecutions and not by an accused person, the decisions nevertheless show that a failure to act promptly even within the time periods laid down in the rules may be fatal to an application for judicial review. However, the usual position would appear to be that if an applicant acts within the three or six month time periods, albeit only just within them, it is unlikely that a court will find that the application has not been made promptly provided no prejudice has been suffered by the respondent or third parties as a result of this delay. In *Eurocontainer Shipping plc v Minister for the Marine*[101] the question arose whether the applicant's application for judicial review of the validity of a gross tonnage certificate for a container ship, which was made one day short of six months from the date of issue of the certificate, was made promptly. Barr J concluded that in all the circumstances it was fair and reasonable to regard the application as having been made within time and he pointed to the fact that the respondent had suffered no loss as a result of the alleged delay and that there was no evidence that any third party had been prejudiced by it.

Where the applicant feels that he has failed to act promptly, he should explain the circumstances of the delay[102] and seek to provide an explanation for it in the affidavit verifying the facts in the statement of grounds. Similarly, as Hederman J commented in *O'Flynn v Mid-Western Health Board*[103] "where the time limit prescribed by the rules of court has passed ... the judge should be furnished with the reasons for the delay in the grounding affidavit and he should decide whether there are grounds for excusing the delay". Equally if the respondent wishes to contest the application on grounds of delay, he should raise it in his notice of opposition.[104]

---

[100] [1997] 1 IR 405, [1997] 1 ILRM 497.

[101] High Court (Barr J) 11 December 1992. See also *McEniry v Flynn* High Court (McCracken J) 6 May 1998 where McCracken J stated that while the applicant had almost allowed the six month period to expire, there had been no prejudice caused to the respondent and he concluded that the application had been brought within time and *Director of Public Prosecutions v Windle* [1999] 4 IR 280 where McCracken J reached a similar conclusion in circumstances where the application had been made only one day short of the six month period, although this included the long vacation.

[102] See the *dicta* of Barr J in *Director of Public Prosecutions v McDonnell* High Court, 1 October 1990 at 4 to the effect that "the obligation to apply promptly for ... relief is a primary requirement which ought not be ignored and where, patently, prompt application has not been made, then an explanation for the delay should be put before the court".

[103] [1991] 2 IR 223, 236.

[104] *Director of Public Prosecutions v McMenamin* High Court (Barron J) 23 March 1996.

21.031 A further aspect of rule 21(1) which should be examined is the power of the court to exercise its discretion to extend the three and six month time limits provided that there is "good reason" for doing so.[105] As Denham J made clear in *de Roiste v Minister for Defence*[106] the onus is on the applicant to show good reason why time should be extended. This power may be exercised in an applicant's favour provided the delay can be satisfactorily explained and there is no evidence of prejudice being caused to the respondent[107] or to third parties as a result of it.[108] In her judgment in *de Roiste*, Denham J stated that in analysing the facts of a case to determine whether there is good reason to extend time, the following factors may be taken into account, although she stressed that this list was not exclusive.

(i)   the nature of the order or actions the subject of the application;

(ii) the conduct of the applicant;

(iii) the conduct of the respondents;

(iv) the effect of the order under review on the parties subsequent to the order being made and any steps taken by the parties subsequent to the order to be reviewed;

(v) any effect which may have taken place on third parties by the order to be reviewed;

(vi) public policy that proceedings relating to the public law domain take place promptly except when good reason is furnished.[109]

As Barr J commented in *Solan v Director of Public Prosecutions*[110] "[i]n the

---

[105] See *e.g. Director of Public Prosecutions v Hamill* [2000] 1 ILRM 150.

[106] [2001] 2 ILRM 241, 254. McCracken J also stated in *de Roiste* that "[w]hile this may not be an absolute rule, I have no doubt that in the vast majority of cases the onus is on the applicant to produce the evidence to show such a good reason". See also the *dicta* of Barr J in *Solan v Director of Public Prosecutions* [1989] ILRM 491, 493 to the effect that where the application, as in the case before him, was made out of time "the applicant is obliged to satisfy the court that in all the circumstances it is in the interest of justice that time for the making of the application should be extended".

[107] *Director of Public Prosecutions v Hamill* [2000] 1 ILRM 150, 159.

[108] See the *dicta* of McCarthy J in *Flynn v Mid-Western Health Board* [1991] 2 IR 223, 239 to the effect that "[i]n principle it is right to relieve against delay in challenging an administrative decision where the delay has not prejudiced third parties".

[109] [2001] 2 ILRM 241, 259.

[110] [1989] ILRM 491, 493. It should be noted that in this decision, as in *Connors v Delap* [1989] ILRM 93 and *White v Hussey* [1989] ILRM 109, the court appeared to place importance on the fact that there was no evidence that the criminal convictions in each case were not properly made on the merits in refusing to extend to the time for bringing applications for judicial review. This approach can be open to criticism given that the purpose of judicial review proceedings is to examine the legality of a decision rather than its merits.

absence of evidence explaining delay, there is no basis on which the court can exercise its discretion to grant an extension of time for making the applications". So in *Flynn v Mid-Western Health Board*[111] the Supreme Court refused to grant judicial review quashing a decision establishing a committee to investigate complaints against the applicant doctors eight months after it was made in circumstances where no explanation was offered for this delay. A similar delay had ensued in *O'Connor v Minister for the Marine*[112] where Geoghegan J concluded that the delay point was well made in the circumstances and that there was no good reason for extending the time. He commented that while strictly speaking under Order 84, rule 21 it is the application for leave which has to be brought promptly it has always been accepted that a respondent may raise a time issue as otherwise it would effectively mean that this question would be dealt with finally at the *ex parte* stage at which the respondent would have no hearing which would not be a fair procedure.

21.032 Where the delay can be satisfactorily explained and there is no evidence that the respondent has been prejudiced by it, it may be overlooked. However, as Fennelly J stated in *de Roiste v Minister for Defence*,[113] a longer delay will require a more cogent explanation and "explicable delays have usually been a matter of months and very rarely years". In *Murphy v Minister for Social Welfare*[114] the applicant delayed for 15 months in bringing judicial review proceedings seeking to quash a finding that his employment was not insurable employment. Blayney J found that the respondent was not prejudiced by this delay and referred to the fact that there was on-going communication between the parties and that the applicant had not been inactive following the decision of the appeals officer. In the circumstances he concluded that it was perfectly reasonable for the applicant not to take steps to quash the decisions made in his case while he was in correspondence with the Department of Social Welfare in relation to his claim and Blayney J extended the time and granted *certiorari* to quash the decisions. A similar result ensued in *Eastern Health Board v Farrell*[115] in which the applicant sought judicial review in relation to an inquest originally convened 16 months before the application had been made and then adjourned. The respondent contended that the application had not been made promptly and that there was no justification for extending the time and Geoghegan J accepted that this issue was a serious one which he would have to consider carefully. While he agreed that the application had not been made promptly, Geoghegan J expressed the view that the issues in the case were far too important to allow the judicial review application to be determined on a time point alone unless some

---

[111] [1991] 2 IR 223.
[112] High Court (Geoghegan J) 6 October 1999.
[113] [2001] 2 ILRM 241, 271.
[114] [1987] IR 295.
[115] [2000] 1 ILRM 446.

serious prejudice was going to be caused. He concluded that no serious injury would follow and stated that in all the circumstances he thought that he should deal with the application on its merits.[116]

21.033 A useful explanation of what will constitute "good reason" for this purpose is provided by Costello J in his judgment in *O'Donnell v Dun Laoghaire Corporation*.[117] Although the case concerned plenary proceedings brought to challenge the validity of water charges imposed by the corporation, Costello J decided to apply by analogy the rules and principles contained in Order 84, rule 21. He stated as follows:

> The phrase "good reasons" is one of wide import which it would be futile to attempt to define precisely. However, in considering whether or not there are good reasons for extending the time I think it is clear that the test must be an objective one and the court should not extend the time merely because an aggrieved plaintiff believed that he or she was justified in delaying the institution of proceedings. What the plaintiff has to show (and I think the onus under Order 84, rule 21 is on the plaintiff) is that there are reasons which both explain the delay and afford a justifiable excuse for the delay.[118]

Costello J concluded that the evidence established to his satisfaction that the plaintiff's conduct in seeking the assistance of his public representatives from the time his water supply was cut off did constitute good reason for extending the time within which proceedings could be brought. He was satisfied that this was a "reasonable explanation" as to why for a period of 13 months he had not instituted proceedings and in the circumstances he held that the plaintiff's delay did not disentitle him to the declaratory order sought.

21.034 The requirements of explanation and justification also formed the basis for the conclusions reached by Fennelly J in *de Roiste v Minister for Defence*.[119] In his opinion the applicant had neither explained nor justified his failure to commence proceedings over a period of more than 29 years and he expressed the view that an extremely long delay without cogent explanation and justification may in itself constitute a ground for refusing relief. Fennelly J referred to the fact the applicant had sought to explain away the delay by reference to the

---

[116] This can be contrasted with the approach of the Supreme Court in *Gilligan v Ireland* [2001] 1 ILRM 473 in which leave to apply for judicial review was refused on the basis that the application had been brought "far too late."

[117] [1991] ILRM 301.

[118] *Ibid.* at 315. This passage was quoted by Fennelly J in *de Roiste* who said that the view that delay in making an application for judicial review requires both explanation and justification is fully consistent with the provisions of Order 84, rule 21.

[119] [2001] 1 ILRM 241.

general severe disruption of his life, but without attempting to explain why he was prevented from instructing a solicitor or otherwise taking action. He concluded that the applicant had come nowhere near establishing "good reason" for his delay and he stated that he would dismiss the applicant's appeal. Denham J agreed that the applicant had not shown good reason why time should be extended and that his appeal should be dismissed. She expressed the view that while the actions which the applicant sought to have reviewed were serious and did affect his life, his subsequent conduct, the considerable delay in seeking relief and the prejudice caused to the respondents were circumstances which justified the court in refusing to extend the period in which the application could be made.

Time Limits in Relation to Judicial Review of Certain Types of Decisions

21.035 Over the past decade the Oireachtas has prescribed an exclusive procedure and specific time limits for judicial review applications in particular areas on a number of occasions.[120] The most frequently invoked of these provisions relate to decisions in planning matters and s.82(3B)(a)(i) of the Local Government (Planning and Development) Act 1963 laid down a two month time limit for bringing an application for judicial review of a decision of a planning authority or An Bord Pleanála commencing on the date the decision is given.[121] This provision is now modified by s.50(4) of the Planning and Development Act 2000 which applies to a decision of a planning authority on an application for permission or to proceed with a proposed local authority development or to a decision of An Bord Pleanála in a range of areas.[122] S.50(4)(a) lays down an eight week time period, commencing on the date of the decision in the case of an application for permission. An important innovation is contained in s.50(4)(a)(iii)of the Planning and Development Act 2000 which empowers the High Court to extend the eight week period prescribed for the bringing of judicial review proceedings, although it provides that the High Court shall not do so "unless it considers that there is good and sufficient reason for doing so". Given the difference in phraseology from Order 84, rule 21, the fact that the jurisdiction to extend time is phrased in a negative as opposed to a positive manner, and

---

[120] See *e.g.* s.85(8) of the Environmental Protection Agency Act 1992 (two months), s.55A(2)(b) of the Roads Act 1993 as amended (two months), s.43(5)(b) of the Waste Management Act 1996 (two months), s.12(2)(a) of the Transport (Dublin Light Rail) Act 1996 (two months), s.13(3)(a) of the Irish Takeover Panel Act 1997 (seven days), s.73(2)(a) of the Fisheries (Amendment) Act 1997 (three months) and s.5(2)(a) of the Illegal Immigrants (Trafficking) Act 2000 (14 days).

[121] See *Brady v Donegal County Council* [1989] ILRM 282.

[122] See Simons "The Implications of the New Act for Judicial Review Proceedings" in *The Planning and Development Act 2000: Implications for Practitioners* (2001) at 1-2.

the general reluctance of the courts to countenance delay in planning matters, it is unlikely that the case law considered above in a general context will prove of use in considering how this provision will be interpreted.[123] It remains to be seen how this new provision will be construed by the courts, although it should be noted that Simons[124] suggests that it is probable that the court will focus on the conduct of the applicant and on whether any delay on his part has been contributed to by the developer.

Provision has also been made in s.5(2)(a) of the Illegal Immigrants (Trafficking) Act 2000[125] for a time limit which should not be extended unless there is "good and sufficient reason" for doing so, although the period specified is only 14 days as opposed to eight weeks. The constitutionality of this provision was upheld by the Supreme Court in *Re Article 26 and the Illegal Immigrants (Trafficking) Bill 1999.*[126]

PROCEDURE FOR BRINGING APPLICATIONS FOR JUDICIAL REVIEW

Introduction

21.036 Order 84, rule 22(1) provides that an application for judicial review shall be made by originating notice of motion unless the court directs that it should be made by plenary summons.[127] The notice of motion is required to be filed in the Central Office of the High Court before it is served[128] and a return date will be allocated by the office. The notice of motion or summons, a copy of the order giving leave to apply for judicial review, a copy of the statement of grounds and a copy of the verifying affidavit must be served personally on all persons directly affected by the application, except where the applicant is in custody, in which case all the necessary documents may be served by registered prepaid post.[129] Where the notice of motion or summons relates to any proceedings in or before a court and the object of the application is either to compel the court or an officer of the court to do any act in relation to the proceedings or to quash them or any order made in them, the notice or summons must also be served on the clerk or registrar of the court.[130]

---

[123] See further Simons *op. cit.* at 3.

[124] *Ibid.* at 3.

[125] S.5 applies to applications brought to challenge the validity of certain order and decisions made in respect of non-nationals pursuant to, *inter alia*, the Refugee Act 1996 and the Immigration Act 1999.

[126] [2000] 2 IR 360, 388-391.

[127] In the vast majority of cases applications are made by way of notice of motion.

[128] Order 52, rule 2.

[129] Order 84, rule 23(1) and Practice Direction [1987] ILRM 127.

[130] Order 84, rule 22(3).

Service of Notice or Summons

21.037 The notice of motion or summons must be served within 14 days of the grant of leave or within such other period as the court may direct.[131] In default of service within such period the stay of proceedings referred to in rule 20(7) will lapse.[132] If the notice of motion is not served within 14 days from the grant of leave, an application for an order extending the time for service may be made on an *ex parte* basis.[133] The power of the court to grant such an extension of time for the service of the notice of motion was considered in *Director of Public Prosecutions v Hamill*.[134] The second named respondent opposed the application for judicial review on the grounds that he had not been served with the notice of motion within an initial period of 21 days allowed by Geoghegan J in his order granting leave. It was contended that once this 21 day period had expired the court had no power to further extend the time for service for an additional period of seven days and that an order made extending the time for service for a further seven days was a nullity. However, McGuinness J was satisfied that Order 122, rule 7, which allows the court to enlarge the time fixed by the rules for the doing of any act, applied to permit it to extend the time for service of the notice of motion in the case before her and she concluded that the second named respondent had been correctly served with the judicial review proceedings in the circumstances. On appeal to the Supreme Court, in view of his finding that the order extending time had not in fact been appealed, Keane CJ stated that it was not necessary to express any view on the distinctions drawn by McGuinness J, although he commented that "she may very well [have] been correct in distinguishing the two earlier cases and indeed there are good grounds for supposing that she was correct in so doing".[135]

Affidavit of Service

21.038 Before the hearing of the motion or summons, an affidavit of service, giving the names and addresses of and the places and dates of service on all persons who have been served with the notice of motion or summons, must be filed and the affidavit must be before the court on the hearing of the motion or summons.[136] If any person who ought to have been served has not been, the affidavit must state that fact and the reason for it.[137] Where an applicant has

---

[131] Order 84, rule 22(3).

[132] *Ibid.*

[133] Practice Direction [1987] ILRM 127. The new provisions in Order 84 of the Rules of the Superior Courts 1986 effectively overruled *State (Fitzsimons) v Kearney* [1981] IR 406 in which it was held that if service was not effected within the time limit prescribed, the conditional order would lapse.

[134] [2000] 1 ILRM 150.

[135] Supreme Court, 11 May 2000 at 4.

[136] Order 84, rule 22(5).

[137] *Ibid.*

failed to comply with the requirements as to service, an order may be made by
the court pursuant to Order 9, rule 15 to declare the service actually effected
sufficient.[138]

Statement of Opposition

21.039 A respondent who intends to oppose an application for judicial review
by way of motion on notice is required to file a statement of opposition which
shall include the name and registered place of business of the respondent's solicitor if any.[139] If any facts are relied on in the statement of opposition, an
affidavit verifying such facts must be filed with it.[140] It was pointed out by
Denham J in *H. v Director of Public Prosecutions*[141] that it was correct for the
respondent to file a statement of opposition directed solely to the grounds upon
which the High Court granted relief to apply for judicial review ignoring those
grounds upon which leave had not been granted. It has been stated that where
the respondent is a person exercising a judicial function it is undesirable that he
swear an affidavit himself and that it would be more appropriate in such circumstances for the affidavit to be sworn by the court clerk or registrar.[142]

21.040 The respondent is required to serve a copy of the statement of opposition and any verifying affidavit on all parties to the proceedings not later than
seven days from the date of service of the notice of motion. It is generally accepted that it is difficult in practice to comply with this time requirement and an
application may be made on an *ex parte* basis to extend the time. While the
Supreme Court accepted in *Butler v Ruane*[143] that such an application may
properly be made *ex parte* it should be noted that McCarthy J suggested in his
judgment that "it may well be that a judge hearing such an application would, if
the circumstances so require, refuse to grant the order sought *ex parte* and direct that the motion be brought on notice".[144]

Listing and Hearing of Motion

21.041 New provisions relating to the listing and hearing of a notice of motion
in judicial review applications are contained in a Practice Direction of 12 February 2001. Where the court grants leave to apply for judicial review by notice

---

[138] See *Lancefort Ltd v An Bord Pleanála* High Court (Morris J) 13 May 1997.
[139] Order 84, rule 22(4).
[140] *Ibid.*
[141] [1994] 2 IR 589, 607, [1994] 2 ILRM 285, 294.
[142] *State (Freeman) v Connellan* [1986] IR 433, 441, [1987] ILRM 470, 476 *per* Barr J
referring to the *dicta* of Henchy J in *State (Sharkey) v McArdle* Supreme Court, 4 June
1981 at 8.
[143] [1989] ILRM 159.
[144] *Ibid.* at 161.

of motion it will, at the time of granting such order, fix the date for which the notice of motion seeking substantive relief is to be made returnable. Such notices of motion will be made returnable for every day of the week and not exclusively for a Monday which had previously been the case. Upon the first listing of the notice of motion, a short *inter partes* hearing will be conducted and directions will be given for the exchange of pre-trial documents. At this hearing the parties should be in a position to apprise the judge of the main issues in the case and suggest realistic time limits for the exchange of pre-trial documents. Appropriate directions will be given and the motion will then be adjourned to a date subsequent to the final date for the exchange of such documents. It is expected that the court order as to directions will be complied with within the permitted time and only in exceptional cases will further extensions of time be granted.

Once the court is satisfied that all pre-trial matters have been disposed of the motion will be adjourned to the next available list to fix dates with a view to having a trial date assigned.[145] In addition, it should be noted that a Practice Direction of 26 February 1993 provides as follows:

> Practitioners are requested to lodge with the registrar seven days in advance of the hearing of the notice of motion for judicial review a bound book containing the following documents
>
> (i)   copy notice of motion;
> (ii)   copy order granting leave to make application for judicial review;
> (iii) copy grounding statement (notice of application);
> (iv)   copy verifying affidavit;
> (v)   copy exhibits;
> (vi)   copy affidavits verifying statement of opposition (if any);
> (vii) affidavit of personal service of motion, statement, affidavit and order giving leave on all parties to be served (Order 84, rule 22(5));
> (viii) in applications for order of *certiorari* copy of order/decision subject of application verified by affidavit (if not already exhibited above)(see Order 84, rule 26(2)).

If, on the hearing of the motion or summons, the court is of opinion that any person who ought to have been served has not been served, the court may adjourn the hearing on such terms as it may direct.[146] In addition, an application may be made when the matter appears in the motion list to join a notice party or such a party may be joined at the direction of the court.

---

[145] Practice Direction 12 February 2001.
[146] Order 84, rule 22(6).

NOTICE PARTIES

Introduction

21.042 An application for judicial review will often affect the rights and interests of persons other than those against whom relief is sought. Natural justice requires that such persons should be notified of the proceedings because they may wish to intervene in support of the impugned decision and, to this end, Order 84, rule 22(2) requires an applicant to serve judicial review proceedings "on all persons directly affected".[147] No further elaboration of the meaning of a person directly affected is given but it has been held to include a person "vitally interested in the outcome of the proceedings"[148] and where an order for *certiorari* is sought, "any person whose rights would be affected by the avoidance of the decision impugned".[149] It should be noted that in the recent decision of *Miley v Flood*[150] Kelly J held that the Law Society should be joined as a notice party to the applicant's application for judicial review which concerned the issue of whether legal professional privilege applied to the identity of his client "because the issue of legal professional privilege may have implications for the profession as a whole".

Service of the proceedings will, of itself, make the person served a party to the proceedings entitling him to appear and be heard even though he is not named on the record[151] and there is, therefore, no need for such persons to be joined as parties in the proceedings. However, the practice has arisen of formally recognising the status of such persons served with the proceedings but against whom no relief is sought[152] by joining them as notice parties even though the concept of a "notice party" is not mentioned in Order 84.[153]

---

[147] The rule further provides that where the application relates to any proceedings in or before a court and the object of the application is either to compel the court or an officer of the court to do any act in relation to the proceedings or to quash them or any order made therein, the proceedings must also be served on the clerk or registrar of the court and, where any objection to the conduct of the judge is to be made, on the clerk or registrar on behalf of the judge. Although it is common to join the judge as a party in circumstances where an order of *certiorari* is sought to quash an order made by the judge, the Supreme Court in *O'Connor v Carroll* [1999] 2 IR 160 questioned the propriety of doing so.

[148] *Spin Communications v IRTC* Supreme Court, 14 April 2000 (*ex tempore*).

[149] *O'Keeffe v An Bord Pleanála* [1993] 1 IR 39, 78, [1992] ILRM 237, 268.

[150] [2001] 2 ILRM 459.

[151] See the definition of "party" in Order 125.

[152] Where relief is sought against a person, then he should be joined as a party to the proceedings (see *Village Residents Association Ltd v An Bord Pleanála* [2000] 4 IR 321, [2001] 2 ILRM 22.

[153] Some degree of statutory recognition of the concept of notice parties is to be found in s.50 of the Planning and Development Act 2000 which prescribes certain persons who must be put on notice of the motion for leave to apply for judicial review. See further *McCarthy v An Bord Pleanála* [2000] 1 IR 42, *Murray v An Bord Pleanála* [2000] 1

A person who has not been served by the applicant with judicial review proceedings may still be entitled to be heard in the matter. If the court is of the opinion that a person who ought to have been served has not been served, it will direct that the person be served with the proceedings[154] and may adjourn the proceedings to enable this to be done.[155] Again, although it is not necessary, it is common for the person on whom service is directed to be joined as a notice party. Alternatively, a person who has not been served with the proceedings but who opposes the application may appear at the hearing and apply to be heard and that application will be granted if the court is satisfied that he is a proper person to be heard.[156]

The Role of Notice Parties

21.043 The role of notice parties in judicial review proceedings has been clarified somewhat by the decision of the Supreme Court in *Spin Communications v IRTC*.[157] The case concerned a challenge by the applicant to a decision of the respondent to award a radio licence to the notice party. The trial judge granted security for costs to the IRTC but refused to grant it to the notice party on the basis that, although it was vitally interested in the outcome, the only live issue in the case was bias which was an issue which only arose between the applicant and the respondent and in the resolution of which the notice party would have no role. The Supreme Court allowed an appeal from that decision on the basis that the trial judge had erred in his approach and had misconceived the role of the notice party. Keane CJ distinguished the situation where there are a multiplicity of notice parties, not all of whose presence is necessary, and where the court could exercise its discretion by declining to order costs except in favour of one representative notice party. He pointed out that the notice party had a vital interest in the outcome of the matter and was a necessary party to the proceedings:

> In those circumstances, it seems to me that once the notice party is there, once he is in the proceedings protecting his interests, he may find himself

---

IR 58 and *Village Residents Association Ltd v An Bord Pleanála* [2000] 4 IR 321, [2001] 2 ILRM 22.
[154] *O'Keeffe v An Bord Pleanála* [1993] 1 IR 39, 78, [1992] ILRM 237, 268; *Spin Communications v IRTC* Supreme Court, 14 April 2000 (*ex tempore*).
[155] Order 84, rule 22(6). The question of joining a person as a notice party will generally be considered by the court at the leave stage but the court may direct that a person be joined at any stage of the proceedings: See *Smith v Minister for Marine* High Court (Geoghegan J) 18 June 1998, where Geoghegan J considered joining a person affected by his decision as a notice party for the purpose of making submissions before making a final order.
[156] Order 84, rule 26(1). *Cf. O'Keeffe v An Bord Pleanála* [1993] 1 IR 39, [1992] ILRM 237 where the developer was joined as a respondent by the Supreme Court on appeal.
[157] Supreme Court, 14 April 2000 (*ex tempore*).

in precisely the same position as the respondent. He may find himself in
the position that he has been there, of necessity, to protect his interest, to
advance arguments that may not have been advanced by the IRTC and to
have had the benefit of his own counsel and solicitor to protect his interest. It would be quite unjust that he should have to pay his costs because
the applicant company has no assets, where he has been brought there as
a necessary party.[158]

On the basis of this *dicta* it would seem, therefore, that a person joined as a
notice party who decides to participate in judicial review proceedings is in the
same position as if he had been joined as a respondent. It would appear that he
will, thus, have *locus standi* to raise any argument of law or fact in defence of
the proceedings and will be entitled to an order for costs or security for costs as
appropriate.[159]

AMENDMENTS TO THE GRANT OF LEAVE/ADDITIONAL AFFIDAVITS

21.044 Order 84, rule 23(1) provides that subject to rule 23(2) no grounds
shall be relied on or any relief sought at the hearing except the grounds and
relief set out in the statement in support of the application for judicial review.
Rule 23(2) then goes on to provide that the court on the hearing of the motion or
summons may allow the applicant or respondent to amend his statement whether
by specifying different or additional grounds of relief or opposition or otherwise on such terms, if any, as it thinks fit. In addition the court may allow
further affidavits to be used if they deal with new matters arising out of an
affidavit of any other party to the application. Rule 23(3) provides that where
the applicant or respondent intends to apply for leave to amend his statement or
to use further affidavits, he shall give notice of his intention and of any proposed amendment to every other party.[160]

21.045 A fairly strict interpretation was placed on the words "on the hearing of
the motion or summons" by Blayney J in *Ahern v Minister for Industry and*

---

[158] *Ibid.* at 5.
[159] However, it should be noted that in the recent decision of *O'Connell v Environmental
Protection Agency* [2002] 1 ILRM 1, in which Herbert J held that a notice party could
bring an application to strike out judicial review proceedings, he also stated that he
had "very considerable reservations" as to the power of the court to make any form of
order either against or in favour of a notice party, including an order as to costs.
[160] Even where no notice of intention to apply for leave to amend is given in compliance
with rule 23(3), the court has power to deal with such an application by virtue of
Order 124, see *Dooner v Garda Síochána Complaints Board* High Court (Finnegan J)
2 June 2000.

Commerce[161] in which he stated that the court had no jurisdiction to amend at an earlier stage in the proceedings. In addition, he expressed the view that the definition of "pleading" in Order 125 did not include a statement grounding an application for judicial review so that the jurisdiction given to the court under Order 28 to amend pleadings did not extend to such a statement. However, a more liberal interpretation was placed on Order 84, rule 23(2) by Finlay CJ in *Molloy v Governor of Limerick Prison*[162] who stated as follows:

> I take the view that the proper interpretation of Order 84, rule 23(2) is that the court may after the time that either a notice of motion with a return date has passed the date of the return date, or in the case of applications for judicial review, where liberty has been granted to issue them by summons after the summons has been issued, that the court may, on the basis that either the summons or the motion concerned is then properly to be described as "a hearing", "pending hearing" or "at hearing" in the High Court, that the court may on the application of an applicant amend the documents concerned as provided for in that sub-rule.

Finlay CJ dealt with the argument that the applicant might greatly extend the nature and character of the application by stating that the application seeking the amendment was liable to the same onus of proof as in the original application for leave.[163]

21.046 As Kelly J commented in *O'Leary v Minister for Transport, Energy and Communications*[164] the test for an application to amend the grounds for seeking judicial review is "much more stringent" than that applicable to amending pleadings generally pursuant to Order 28, rule 1.[165] The circumstances in which the High Court would allow a grounding statement to be amended were considered by Costello P in *McCormack v Garda Síochána Complaints Board*[166] in which the applicant sought judicial review of the decision of the respondent that no action was to be taken on foot of a complaint by him. He also sought an order amending the statement grounding his application for judicial

---

[161] [1990] 1 IR 55.

[162] Supreme Court, 12 July 1991 at 5-6.

[163] However, Bradley in *Judicial Review* (2000) at 409 raises the question of whether it is appropriate to re-impose the burden of proof applicable at the leave stage when the action may be at the substantive stage at which a correspondingly higher burden might be more appropriate, see *G. v Director of Public Prosecutions* [1994] 1 IR 374.

[164] [2000] 1 ILRM 391, 398.

[165] Kelly J held that notwithstanding the delivery of a statement of claim the proceedings before him retained the character of judicial review proceedings. However, on appeal the Supreme Court held that the application to amend fell to be considered pursuant to Order 28, rule 1 and granted the relief sought by the applicant (see [2001] 1 ILRM 132).

[166] [1997] 2 IR 489, [1997] 2 ILRM 321.

review by adding additional grounds of relief in the form of claims that the respondents had failed to properly investigate the complaints made and had failed to properly instruct the investigating officer. Costello P decided to allow the amendment sought in the circumstances, but laid down the following general principle:

> It seems to me that only in exceptional circumstances would liberty to amend a grounding statement be made because the court's jurisdiction to entertain the application is based on and limited by the order granting leave. But when facts come to light which could not be known at the time leave was obtained and when the amendment would not prejudice the respondents, then it seems a proper exercise of the court's power of amendment to permit the amendment rather than require that the new "grounds" be litigated in fresh proceedings.[167]

21.047 It was accepted in *Twomey v Minister for Tourism and Transport*[168] that due to the "very special circumstances" of the case the applicant should be permitted to amend his motion before the Supreme Court pursuant to rule 23(2) by specifying an additional ground of relief. Egan J stated that the matter should then be dealt with by the High Court within the framework of the existing proceedings with full particulars of the claim being delivered by the appellant and grounds of defence being delivered by the respondent.

Delay in Seeking to Amend Statement of Grounds

21.048 A further issue which arises in the context of an application to amend a statement of grounds is what, if any, time constraints should apply. The courts do not appear to tolerate unacceptable delay in bringing an application to amend a statement of grounds and there are *dicta* to suggest that similar time constraints to those which apply in respect of an application seeking leave may be imposed. In *Toner v Ireland*[169] Kinlen J made it clear that amendments under

---

[167] *Ibid.* at 503-504. Applied by Kelly J in *O'Leary v Minister for Transport, Energy and Communications* [2000] 1 ILRM 391. In *Dooner v Garda Síochána Complaints Board* High Court (Finnegan J) 2 June 2000 Finnegan J also accepted that the approach to be adopted on an application for leave to amend grounds is that set out by Costello P in *McCormack*. He granted leave on the basis that the applicant had no knowledge of certain relevant material until the date of the hearing and he was satisfied that no injustice would be worked on the respondent by allowing an amendment "even at this late stage". Note that the test set out by Costello P in *McCormack* has been criticised by Hogan and Morgan in *Administrative Law in Ireland* (3rd ed., 1998) at 705 on the basis that it seems to be too strict and they correctly point out that the Rules themselves "expressly envisage that the grounding statement can be amended".

[168] Supreme Court, 12 February 1993.

[169] High Court (Kinlen J) 11 February 2000.

rule 23(2) should not be allowed unless the applicant can justify the delay in seeking to introduce new material. He referred to the decision of the Supreme Court in *Molloy v Governor of Limerick Prison*[170] where he said "it was held that a statement of grounds could be amended subject to the applicant discharging the same onus as an applicant for leave under Order 84 – *i.e.* the time limit of six months referred to above applies unless the applicant can justify a departure from it." Kinlen J then made reference to the decision of O'Hanlon J in *Rajah v RCSI*[171] where the latter had decided with some reluctance to allow the applicant to extend her grounds, although Kinlen J said that it should be noted that the application to amend was determined by O'Hanlon J within six months from the date of the events giving rise to the application for judicial review.

21.049 Subsequently in *Aquatechnologie Ltd v National Standards Authority of Ireland*[172] Murray J held, in deciding to grant the application for leave to amend the statement of grounds, that the proposed amendments did not extend the ambit of the proceedings in a significant manner and that the delay was excusable. The respondents had opposed the application submitting that the plaintiff had failed to bring his action promptly, was out of time and had failed to explain or excuse the delay. Murray J stated that if the appellant knew or ought to have known of the alleged decision which prompted it to seek to amend its grounds on service of an affidavit, it was out of time for the making of its application by a short period. However, he stated that having regard to all the circumstances of the case, the delay was excusable and he granted the application for leave to amend the statement of grounds.

It is certainly arguable that Murray J was not advocating that the requirements as to time limits laid down in Order 84, rule 21 should be strictly adhered to by analogy in bringing an application to amend a statement of grounds. However, he merely stated that the delay was excusable in the circumstances; he clearly took this issue seriously and was not suggesting that undue delay should be overlooked. It should also be noted that the time limits laid down in Order 84, rule 21 may be extended for "good reason" and so it could equally be argued that Murray J was in favour of applying similar requirements to those contained in rule 21 when considering applications to amend a statement of grounds. Irrespective of which view is correct, it would seem that excessive delay in making applications of this nature will not be tolerated.

Time Constraints in Specific Forms of Judicial Review

21.050 Different considerations apply in the context of judicial review appli-

---

[170] Supreme Court, 12 July 1991.
[171] [1994] 1 IR 384, [1994] 1 ILRM 233.
[172] Supreme Court, 10 July 2000.

cations to which statutory time limits apply[173] and the most commonly encountered of these are the eight week time limit for judicial review laid down by s.82(3B) of the Local Government (Planning and Development) Act 1963 as modified by s.50(4) of the Planning and Development Act 2000 in relation to planning matters and the two month time limit laid down by s.85(8) of the Environmental Protection Agency Act 1992. As Finlay CJ stated in *K.S.K. Enterprises Ltd v An Bord Pleanála*[174] in relation to s.82(3B) before its recent amendment:[175] "The general scheme of the subsection ... is very firmly and strictly to confine the possibility of judicial review in challenging or impugning a planning decision". The question of whether an applicant can expand the grounds of challenge beyond the statutory time limit was subsequently answered in the negative by Murphy J in *Keane v An Bord Pleanála*[176] in which he stated that the time limit was an extraordinarily brief one within which to bring proceedings "but to permit an amendment at a later stage, however well founded the new ground might appear to be, [seemed] to be impermissible". In *McNamara v An Bord Pleanála*[177] Barr J rejected the submission put forward on behalf of the applicant that additional grounds of challenge not previously notified might be introduced after the statutory time limit had expired. Instead he interpreted the legislation to mean that "not only must [the applicant] initiate proceedings and specify the relief claimed within the two month time limit, but when so doing, he must also specify the grounds on which the relief is sought".[178] However, it should be noted that Barr J accepted that the applicant was not precluded from introducing evidence after the expiration of the two month time limit to support or amplify the grounds he was relying on provided these were specified in the original documentation which had been served on all relevant parties within time.

21.051 A further example of this approach is the decision in *Ní Eilí v Environmental Protection Authority*[179] in which leave to amend the grounds on which an application for judicial review was sought outside the statutory time limit[180] and was refused albeit in circumstances where the amendment sought amounted to "an additional and entirely new case". Kelly J concluded that the applicant could not expand her challenge by seeking new reliefs on new grounds outside

---

[173] See *supra*.

[174] [1994] 2 IR 128, 135, [1994] 2 ILRM 1, 5. See also *McNamara v An Bord Pleanála* [1996] 2 ILRM 339, 349, *Ní Eilí v Environmental Protection Authority* [1997] 2 ILRM 458, 465, *McCann v An Bord Pleanála* [1997] 1 IR 264, 271, [1997] 1 ILRM 314, 319-320 and *Henry v Cavan County Council* [2001] 2 ILRM 161.

[175] Although this reasoning could be applied to any of the short time limits provisions set out *supra*.

[176] High Court (Murphy J) 23 May 1995.

[177] [1996] 2 ILRM 339.

[178] *Ibid.* at 351.

[179] [1997] 2 ILRM 458.

[180] Two months pursuant to s.85(8) of the Environmental Protection Agency Act 1992.

the statutory time limit. In his view "[t]o allow such a thing to occur would run counter to the statute, negative its intent, and in effect permit of no time bar at all in respect of the additional reliefs sought".[181]

It should be noted that s.50(4)(a)(iii) of the Planning and Development Act 2000 empowers the High Court to extend the eight week period prescribed for the bringing of judicial review proceedings in relation to specified types of planning decisions, although it provides that the High Court shall not do this "unless it considers that there is good and sufficient reason for doing so".[182] Given this new element of flexibility to extend time for the bringing of judicial review proceedings in such cases, the *dicta* set out above in cases decided prior to the introduction of this new provision must now be considered in the light of this change. However, given the fact that the jurisdiction to extend time is phrased in a negative as opposed to a positive manner and the general reluctance of the courts to countenance delay in planning matters, applications to amend a grant of leave brought outside the eight week time period are unlikely to meet with much success.

MISCELLANEOUS ISSUES

Damages in Judicial Review Proceedings

21.052 Prior to the introduction of the Rules of the Superior Courts 1986, it was not possible to claim a public law remedy and damages in the same proceedings. This position was changed by Order 84, rule 24 of the 1986 Rules which provides that on an application for judicial review the court may award damages to the applicant if certain conditions are met. First, the court must be satisfied that if the claim had been made in a civil action, the applicant would have been awarded damages. In addition, the provisions of Order 19, rules 5 and 7 shall apply to a statement relating to a claim for damages. The effect of this provision is that an applicant must set out the particulars of the wrongdoing alleged and any items of special damages in the same way as would be necessary in an ordinary action. Should further particulars be required, the court has jurisdiction to direct their delivery.

One question which arises in relation to rule 24 is whether it is possible to utilize the Order 84 procedure where a claim is being made solely for damages. The better view is that Order 84 does not create an independent cause of action for damages and that damages can only be claimed pursuant to rule 24 where they are sought as an ancillary remedy to one of the established public law remedies. This raises the issue of how the courts should deal with an application

---

[181] [1997] 2 ILRM 458, 466.

[182] See also s.5(2)(a) of the Illegal Immigrants (Trafficking) Act 2000 which provides that the 14-day time limit shall not be extended unless there is "good and sufficient reason" for doing so.

for judicial review in which a public law remedy is claimed which appears to have been brought solely for the purpose of enabling an applicant to seek damages by means of this speedier and more cost effective procedure. Hogan and Morgan[183] suggest that provided the claim for damages by way of judicial review is *bona fide*, the courts should entertain it.

Interlocutory Applications

21.053 Order 84, rule 25 provides that any interlocutory application may be made to the court in judicial review proceedings[184] and this expressly includes an application for an order under Order 31 or Order 39, rule 1 or for an order dismissing the proceedings by consent of the parties. Order 31 makes provision for the granting of orders for the delivery of interrogatories or for discovery[185] or inspection and Order 39, rule 1 deals with the giving of evidence and allows, *inter alia*, for the proof of particular facts by affidavit. An application may be made pursuant to Order 40, rule 1 for an interlocutory order permitting cross-examination of a deponent on the contents of an affidavit. Such an order may be made where there is a serious conflict of fact evident from the affidavits filed by both sides. At this point it should be noted that Order 84, rule 26(5) provides that proceedings commenced by way of judicial review seeking a declaration, an injunction or damages may be ordered to continue as if they had been begun by way of plenary summons.

Other Miscellaneous Provisions

21.054 Order 84, rule 25(2) provides that where the relief sought includes an order of *mandamus*, the practice and procedure provided for in Order 57, which relates to interpleader actions, will apply in so far as the nature of the case will admit.

Order 84, rule 26 makes further provision in relation to miscellaneous issues associated with the hearing of judicial review applications. Rule 26(1) allows any party who has not been served with the notice of motion or summons to be heard in opposition to it provided that it appears to the court that he is a "proper person" to be heard.[186] In *TDI Metro Ltd v Delap (No. 1)*[187] the Supreme Court allowed the Attorney General's application to intervene in the hear-

---

[183] *Administrative Law in Ireland* (3rd ed., 1998) at 800.
[184] *E.g.* for an interlocutory injunction, see *Birr v Birmingham UDC* [1998] 2 ILRM 136.
[185] See further *supra* paragraphs 7.035–7.036 in relation to discovery and judicial review proceedings.
[186] Collins and O'Reilly point out in *Civil Proceedings and the State in Ireland: A Practitioner's Guide* (1990) at 108 that in practice the application for judicial review will be adjourned to enable this person to file a statement of opposition and verifying affidavit.
[187] [2000] 4 IR 337, [2001] 1 ILRM 321.

ing of an appeal on the basis that he was a proper person to be heard. The Supreme Court was satisfied that there was no bar to the joinder of a party at the appeal stage[188] but stressed that the intervention of the Attorney General did not mean that additional grounds might be added.

21.055 Rule 26(2), (3) and (4) relate only to cases where an order of *certiorari* is sought; rule 26(2) provides that where it is sought to have an order quashed, a copy of this order the subject of the application verified by affidavit must be lodged with the registrar prior to the hearing of the motion,[189] or the applicant must account for his failure to do so to the satisfaction of the court. Rule 26(4) makes provision for the remittal of any matter to the relevant court, tribunal or authority where an order is made quashing a decision.[190] The reason for the need for such a power of remittal was adverted to by Lynch J in the course of his judgment in *Dawson v Hamill*[191] when he commented that "[g]enerally speaking judicial review is more concerned with the methods whereby the court of limited jurisdiction arrived at its decision rather than with the merits of the case ..." This power to remit has been exercised in numerous cases[192] and commenting on the provision in *Sheehan v Reilly*,[193] Finlay CJ stated as follows:

> Neither this provision nor any rule similar to it was contained in the Rules of the Superior Courts 1962. It must first clearly be stated that this rule, which on the face of it, gives to the court a discretion as to whether or not to remit a matter in which an order has been quashed for further consideration, cannot, having regard to the limitation of the powers vested in the rule-making authority pursuant to the Courts of Justice Acts be the grant of any new or different power that is not already vested in the courts by virtue of statute or by virtue of inherent jurisdiction.

Having regard to the fact that no similar provision existed in earlier Rules, it should be noted that some doubts have been raised about the power of the Rules Committee to make provision for remittal on the grounds that it may be a matter of substantive law.[194]

---

[188] Denham J referred to *O'Keeffe v An Bord Pleanála* [1993] 1 IR 39, [1992] ILRM 237 and *Canada v EAT* [1992] 2 IR 484, [1992] ILRM 325.

[189] See Practice Direction of 26 February 1993 referred to *supra*.

[190] See further Hogan and Morgan, *Administrative Law in Ireland* (3rd ed., 1998) at 712-715 and Bradley *Judicial Review* (2000) at 384-392. See also Costello (1993) 2 ICLJ 145.

[191] [1989] IR 275, 284, [1990] ILRM 257, 265. (This decision was reversed by the Supreme Court, see [1991] 1 IR 213).

[192] *E.g. Comerford v O'Malley* [1987] ILRM 595, *Coughlan v Pattwell* [1993] 1 IR 31, [1992] ILRM 808, *Hurley v MIBI* [1993] ILRM 886 and *Sweeney v Brophy* [1993] 2 IR 202, [1993] ILRM 449.

[193] [1993] 2 IR 81, 92, [1993] ILRM 427, 434.

[194] See Hogan and Morgan, *Administrative Law in Ireland* (3rd ed., 1998) at 694-695 and

21.056 Order 84, rule 26(5), as noted above, provides that proceedings commenced by way of judicial review seeking a declaration, an injunction or damages may be ordered to continue as if they had been begun by way of plenary summons rather than refusing the application. There is no converse power to convert an action begun by plenary summons into an action for judicial review probably, as Hogan and Morgan suggest,[195] as it might encourage litigants to circumvent the procedural requirements as to leave and in relation to time limits which are designed to protect public authorities. It should also be noted that rule 26(7) provides that the court may direct a plenary hearing with directions as to pleadings, discovery *etc.* at any stage in proceedings in which an order of prohibition or *quo warranto* is sought.

Finally, rule 26(6) provides the court with the power to order that proceedings for *mandamus* may be continued where the respondent has died, resigned or been removed from office.

THE DISCRETIONARY NATURE OF REMEDIES

21.057 The public law remedies[196] discussed above are all discretionary in nature and although a plaintiff may succeed in proving his case, he may nevertheless be refused relief on discretionary grounds. So in addition to establishing a ground for judicial review the applicant must satisfy the court that "it would be just and proper in all the circumstances" to grant the relief sought.[197] It would appear that such discretion should be exercised on the basis of established principles irrespective of the nature of the proceedings.

Traditionally it was assumed that relief should issue *ex debito justitiae* to a person aggrieved except in limited circumstances *e.g.* where to grant relief would prejudice the rights of third parties.[198] Where a criminal conviction was involved, as Maguire CJ stated *obiter* in *State (Vozza) v O'Floinn*,[199] he would find it "difficult ... to imagine conduct on the part of the applicant for *certiorari* which would disentitle him to an order of *certiorari* in regard to a conviction of any sort, where it is established that it was made without jurisdiction".

The Level at Which Discretion Should Operate

21.058 However, in recent years a certain amount of controversy has grown up around the question of the level at which this discretion should operate and

---

Bradley *Judicial Review* (2000) at 49-50. However, see the view expressed by Costello (1993) 2 ICLJ 145.
[195] *Administrative Law in Ireland* (3rd ed., 1998) at 790.
[196] The remedies of declaration and injunction are also discretionary in nature.
[197] *Per* Henchy J in *State (Cussen) v Brennan* [1981] IR 181, 195.
[198] *State (Cussen) v Brennan* [1981] IR 181.
[199] [1957] IR 227, 244.

essentially two views have emerged on the subject. One approach, advocated by Henchy J in *State (Abenglen Properties Ltd) v Dublin Corporation*,[200] is that in civil cases a person aggrieved is entitled to a remedy purely on a discretionary basis. This view seems to be line with that expressed more recently by Finlay CJ in *G. v Director of Public Prosecutions*[201] that "judicial review in many instances is an entirely discretionary remedy". However, the more traditional view has continued to be upheld in a number of decisions, including *State (Furey) v Minister for Defence*[202] in which McCarthy J made it clear that where the applicant has suffered some form of public wrong, he should be entitled to a remedy *ex debito justitiae*. While it might have been possible to reconcile these conflicting authorities on the basis of distinguishing between a "public wrong" such as a wrongful criminal conviction and an *ultra vires* administrative act , this has now become more difficult in the light of a number of decisions involving criminal convictions where relief was refused on the basis of delay.[203] However, it is also fair to say that the result in these cases was clearly influenced by the fact that the court concluded that there were no merits on the substance of the case, a factor which arguably should have had no bearing on the issue of the manner in which the court's discretion should be exercised. A useful summary of a middle ground approach which generally reflects current practice is provided by O'Higgins CJ in *State (Abenglen Properties Ltd) v Dublin Corporation*[204] in the following terms:

> Where ... [an] applicant has been affected or penalised and is an aggrieved person, it is commonly said that *certiorari* issues *ex debito justitiae*. This should not be taken as meaning that a discretion does not remain in the High Court as to whether to give the relief or to refuse it. There may be exceptional and rare cases where a criminal conviction has been recorded otherwise than in due course of law and the matter cannot be set right except by *certiorari*. In such circumstances the discretion may be exercisable only in favour of quashing.... In the vast majority of cases, however, a person whose legal rights have been infringed may be awarded *certiorari ex debito justitiae* if he can establish any of the recognised grounds for quashing; but the court retains a discretion to refuse his application if his conduct has been such as to disentitle him to relief or, I may add, if the relief is not necessary for the protection of those rights.

[200] [1984] IR 381, 403.
[201] [1994] 1 IR 374, 378. See also *Buckley v Kirby* [2000] 3 IR 431, [2001] 2 ILRM 395.
[202] [1988] ILRM 89.
[203] *Connors v Delap* [1989] ILRM 93, *White v Hussey* [1989] ILRM 109 and *Solan v Director of Public Prosecutions* [1989] ILRM 491.
[204] [1984] IR 381, 393. This *dicta*, while it relates specifically to the remedy of *certiorari*, can be of general application.

21.059 In her judgment in *de Roiste v Minister for Defence*,[205] Denham J quoted this passage and said that the discretion of the court is not absolute; it must be exercised in accordance with established principles and in reaching a decision the court may weigh conflicting rights to achieve a balance which is just. She continued by saying that where there is a conviction on record made without jurisdiction it is probable that the court will only exercise its discretion one way *i.e.* by granting relief, but even in such cases other factors may have to be considered such as the conduct of the applicant and the availability of alternative remedies. In her view while an applicant will be in a stronger position if he has been particularly aggrieved, the court retains its discretion in all applications. In the case before her, Denham J was satisfied that the actions which the applicant sought to have reviewed were serious and did affect his life but she said his subsequent conduct, the considerable delay in seeking relief and the prejudice caused to the respondents were circumstances which justified the court in refusing to extend the period in which the application could be made.[206]

21.060 The recent approach of Geoghegan J in *Carr v Minister for Education and Science*[207] which suggests that discretionary principles should not always be applied should also be borne in mind. In his view there are cases, such as the one before him, where a court should not exercise its discretion to withhold a remedy where the decision, in this case to suspend the applicant, has no statutory basis. He stated that to refuse *certiorari* would be to condone an open illegality by the minister in the face of the wording of the relevant statute and that if he were to refuse a remedy, the unreasonable behaviour of the applicant would have effectively conferred on the minister a statutory power which he did not possess. However, despite this finding, it is likely that the view of Denham J in *de Roiste* is to be preferred and it would seem to better reflect current practice.

Factors Which May Influence the Exercise of Discretion

1. Conduct

21.061 The conduct of the applicant may have an important influence on the manner in which a court exercises it discretion to grant or withhold relief in judicial review proceedings and an applicant must show good faith in making an application.[208] Full and accurate disclosure will be necessary in the applicant's affidavit and in cases where there has been "not merely an omission to

---

[205] [2001] 2 ILRM 241.
[206] *Ibid.* at 260. See also the judgment of Fennelly J at 271.
[207] [2001] 2 ILRM 272.
[208] *Per* Finlay CJ in *G. v Director of Public Prosecutions* [1994] 1 IR 374, 378.

disclose but concealment of material facts"[209] an applicant cannot expect to obtain an order for judicial review.

The issue of lack of good faith has been considered on a number of occasions. In *State (Vozza) v O'Floinn*[210] it was held in the High Court that the applicant had disentitled himself to relief because of the gross exaggeration contained in his affidavits. However, on appeal the Supreme Court concluded that the applicant was entitled to an order of *certiorari ex debito justitiae* to quash his conviction despite the element of lack of candour. In *State (Furey) v Minister for Defence*[211] the State contested the prosecutor's right to seek judicial review, *inter alia*, because of the lack of honesty in his grounding affidavit in which he stated that he had never been in any trouble with his superiors or been disciplined in any way. McCarthy J accepted that there might have been some lack of candour in failing to reveal some minor disciplinary offences, but he pointed out that the authorities themselves had been less than fair in saying that his rating as "unsatisfactory" was justified. He took a similar approach to the Supreme Court in *Vozza* and said that the applicant had not in the circumstances disentitled himself to relief by reason of his conduct.

21.062 The net effect of *Vozza* and *Furey* would appear to be that at least where a criminal conviction or a public wrong which continues to mar the life of the applicant is concerned, he will be entitled to relief *ex debito justitiae* unless there is some very good reason for refusing it. In the case of *ultra vires* administrative action, it is likely that the applicant's conduct in bringing the application will be of more importance in weighing up how the court will exercise its discretion. In *Ahern v Minister for Industry and Commerce (No. 2)*[212] disciplinary procedures were brought against the applicant who was employed in a senior position in the Patents Office. It was decided to refer the matter to the Chief Medical Officer of the Civil Service for consideration and he advised that a psychiatrist's opinion was required. The applicant refused to attend a psychiatrist as there was a dispute about whether the department would pay if he attended a doctor of his choice. The applicant was then placed on compulsory sick leave although subsequently he saw a psychiatrist and was certified fit to return to work which he did. His application for judicial review of the decision to have him placed on compulsory sick leave was refused on the grounds, *inter alia,* that in view of his own unreasonable attitude and the fact that *certiorari* would not confer any benefit on him the court would refuse to exercise its discretion in his favour. Blayney J characterised his refusal to attend a psychiatrist as unrea-

---

[209] *Per* Griffin J in *Cork Corporation v O'Connell* [1982] ILRM 505, 511. See further the judgment of Henchy J where he commented that there had been "duplicitous use of the processes of the courts".

[210] [1957] IR 227.

[211] [1988] ILRM 89.

[212] [1991] 1 IR 462. See also the comments of Blayney J in *Connolly v Collector of Customs and Excise* High Court, 5 October 1992.

sonable and said that he had sought to allege *mala fides* against his superiors when there was no grounds whatsoever for such an allegation. However, it should be borne in mind, as Geoghegan J pointed out in *Carr v Minister for Education and Science*,[213] that the actual basis of the refusal of relief was the fact that the order sought was not necessary for the protection of the applicant's legal rights and the comments of Blayney J on the relevance of the applicant's conduct were strictly *obiter*. It is also clear from the *Carr* decision that there are limits on the effect which conduct may have on the manner in which discretion to withhold relief may be exercised. Counsel for the respondent argued that the court ought to exercise its discretion to refuse a remedy notwithstanding the illegality committed by the minister in view of what he characterised as the "wholly unreasonable behaviour" of the applicant. While Geoghegan J stated that there could be circumstances in which the unreasonable behaviour of the applicant would justify the court in refusing relief as a matter of discretion, this was not such a case and the decision made by the minister to suspend the applicant had in his view "no conceivable statutory basis".

21.063 An applicant's motives for seeking an order for judicial review may also be relevant to the court in exercising its discretion. In *State (Abenglen Properties Ltd) v Dublin Corporation*[214] the applicant sought judicial review of the respondent's decision to grant planning permission for a development subject to restrictive conditions. However, it emerged that if the applicant succeeded in obtaining the order of *certiorari* sought, it intended to claim that as no valid decision had been made within the two month period required by statute, it was entitled to permission by default. The Supreme Court was clearly influenced by the applicant's questionable motives in reaching the decision to refuse the order sought. As O'Higgins CJ stated: "[t]he purpose of their application for *certiorari* was not, primarily, to correct a grievance which they had suffered, as a result of a process alleged to have been without legal authority, but to avail of the alleged irregularity to obtain a benefit not contemplated by the planning code".[215]

Finally it should be noted that the conduct of the respondent may also influence the court in deciding how to exercise its discretion. So, in *Flynn and O'Flaherty Properties Ltd v Dublin Corporation*[216] Kelly J made reference to the behaviour of the respondents in delaying in communicating its decision about the grant of planning permission to the applicant in holding that the latter should be entitled to a default permission.

---

[213] [2001] 2 ILRM 272.
[214] [1984] IR 381.
[215] *Ibid.* at 394.
[216] [1997] 2 IR 558.

2. Delay

21.064 This issue is dealt with *supra* in considering the provisions of Order 84, rule 21(1).

3. Whether Any Useful Purpose Would be Served by Granting Judicial Review

21.065 It has been clearly established that no relief will issue in judicial review proceedings where it would be a "meaningless exercise" to grant the order sought.[217] So, where granting judicial review would confer no practical benefit on the applicant, the court may decline to act.[218] This point is well illustrated by the decision of Costello P in *Ryan v Compensation Tribunal*[219] in which the applicant sought to challenge a decision made by the respondent tribunal, set up to compensate persons who had contracted hepatitis C from blood products. In refusing the application for judicial review, Costello P stated that even if the tribunal had erred in law in determining the compensation payable in relation to assistance in the home, he would not have granted the order sought as the health board was now effectively obliged by statute to provide this service. To this extent he agreed with the submission of counsel for the respondent that "it is well established that if an order will confer no practical benefit on an applicant relief would be refused".

21.066 This issue was also considered by Keane J in the High Court and by Denham J in the Supreme Court in *Barry v Fitzpatrick*[220] in which the applicants sought judicial review of orders made by district judges remanding them on bail on the grounds that there was no jurisdiction to remand them for a period exceeding eight days unless they gave their consent to this. Keane J pointed out that the remand orders were purely temporary in effect and were of no further significance once spent. In his view "[i]t ceases to affect anyone's rights, and the grant of an order of *certiorari* once it ceases to have any effect is a pointless exercise and one which no court should undertake". The Supreme Court held that the trial judge had been correct in exercising his jurisdiction to refuse the relief sought on the grounds that the orders were spent, although the court accepted that the district judges had exceeded their jurisdiction.[221]

---

[217] *Per* O'Hanlon J in *Minister for Labour v Grace* [1993] 2 IR 53, 56.

[218] *Ahern v Minister for Industry and Commerce (No. 2)* [1991] 1 IR 462.

[219] [1997] 1 ILRM 194.

[220] [1996] 1 ILRM 512.

[221] This approach can be contrasted with that adopted in *State (Furey) v Minister for Defence* [1988] ILRM 89 and *Bane v Garda Representative Association* [1997] 2 IR 449 in which orders of judicial review were granted in order to vindicate the applicants' reputation.

4. Acquiescence and Waiver

21.067 The principle that waiver or acquiescence may constitute a ground on which the court may, in its discretion, refuse relief is firmly established in this jurisdiction.[222] In *State (Byrne) v Frawley*[223] it emerged during the course of the prosecutor's trial[224] that the jury panel selected to try him could be challenged as unconstitutional. Although fully aware of the significance of the decision, he did not apply to have the jury discharged and he even appealed unsuccessfully without making reference to this invalidity. The majority of the Supreme Court held that although the prosecutor's mode of trial was unconstitutional, his acquiescence in the alleged invalidity precluded him from obtaining relief. This decision is surprising in some respects particularly as the liberty and good name of the prosecutor had been threatened and no prejudice had been suffered by any third parties.

5. The Availability of Alternative Remedies

21.068 While this is undoubtedly a discretionary factor in itself, often it may be not so much the failure of an applicant to pursue an alternative remedy which will prejudice the court's decision but rather his motive for doing so. Where an appeal can deal only with the merits of a case and not with its legality or jurisdictional aspects, judicial review will be the appropriate means of redress open to a person and the existence of a right of appeal should not *per se* be a ground for refusing relief. Conversely, where judicial review would seem to be a "singularly inappropriate" remedy as compared to an appeal, leave to seek review should be refused.[225] An analysis of the case law in this area over the last two decades reveals remarkably diverse attitudes towards the question of the exhaustion of alternative remedies and while it is now possible to identify a middle ground approach, it is nevertheless necessary to be aware of these differences in judicial opinion.[226] Much of the case law relates to planning matters and before examining it in some detail, it should be noted that s.50(3) of the Planning and Development Act 2000 now provides that the High Court is empowered to stay judicial review proceedings pending the making of a decision by An Bord Pleanála in relation to a parallel statutory appeal.

21.069 The most hard line approach is illustrated by the judgment of Henchy J in *State (Abenglen Properties Ltd) v Dublin Corporation*[227] in which the applicant, which sought to challenge the imposition of restrictive conditions at-

---

[222] See *R (Kildare County Council) v Commissioner for Valuation* [1901] 2 IR 215.
[223] [1978] IR 326.
[224] As a result of the decision of the Supreme Court in *de Burca v Attorney General* [1976] IR 38.
[225] *Buckley v Kirby* [2000] 3 IR 431, [2001] 2 ILRM 395.
[226] See generally Steen (2000) 2 Hibernian Law Journal 294.
[227] [1984] IR 381, [1982] ILRM 590.

tached to a grant of planning permission by way of judicial review, also had the option of pursuing an appeal to An Bord Pleanála. Henchy J stated that the Planning Acts envisaged "a self-contained administrative code, with resort to the courts only in exceptional circumstances"[228] and concluded that even if he found grounds for review, he would in the exercise of his discretion have refused to grant *certiorari* on the ground that the applicant should have pursued the appellate procedure open to it under the Acts. O'Higgins CJ adopted a more flexible approach towards this question, which, it is submitted, achieves a better balance. He stated as follows:

> The question immediately arises of the existence of a right of appeal or an alternative remedy as to the effect on the exercise of the court's discretion. It is well established that the existence of such right or remedy ought not to prevent the court from acting. It seems to me to be a question of justice. The court ought to take into account all the circumstances of the case, including the purpose for which *certiorari* has been sought, the adequacy of the alternative remedy and, of course, the conduct of the applicant. If the decision impugned is made without jurisdiction or in breach of natural justice then, normally, the existence of a right of appeal or of a failure to avail of such, should be immaterial. Again, if an appeal can only deal with the merits and not with the question of the jurisdiction involved, the existence of such ought not to be a ground of refusing relief. Other than these, there may be cases where the decision exhibits an error of law and a perfectly simple appeal can rectify the complaint, or where administrative legislation provides adequate appeal machinery which is particularly suitable for dealing with errors in the application of the code in question. In such cases, while retaining always the power to quash, the court should be slow to do so, unless satisfied that, for some particular reason, the appeal or alternative remedy is not adequate.[229]

21.070 The approach of Henchy J in *Abenglen* was followed in a number of subsequent decisions[230] including *Memorex World Trade Corporation v Employment Appeals Tribunal*[231] in which Carroll J declined to grant an order of *certiorari* quashing the decision of the respondent on the grounds that the appeal procedure open to the applicant, namely an appeal to the Circuit Court, was adequate. However, this reasoning can be criticised on the basis that it deprives the applicant of the opportunity to have his case considered properly at first instance and ignores the fact that there may be a difficulty with the legality of the decision making process which should be rectified.

---

[228] *Ibid.* at 404, 607.
[229] *Ibid.* at 393, 597.
[230] *Nova Colour Graphic Supplies v Employment Appeals Tribunal* [1987] IR 426 and *O'Connor v Kerry County Council* [1988] ILRM 660.
[231] [1990] 2 IR 184.

Civil Procedure

21.071   An alternative approach, which can be contrasted with that adopted by
Henchy J in *Abenglen* is that put forward by Finlay CJ in *P. & F. Sharpe v
Dublin City and County Manager.*[232] This case also concerned a challenge to
the validity of a decision made in a planning context, in this case by the respondent county manager, although it should be noted that, in addition to the
judicial review proceedings, an appeal to An Bord Pleanála had also been lodged.
Finlay CJ pointed out that "[t]he powers of an Bord Pleanála on the making of
an appeal to it would be entirely confined to the consideration of the matters
before it on the basis of the proper planning and development of the area and
would have no jurisdiction to consider the question of the validity, from a legal
point of view, of the purported decision of the county manager".[233] He held that
it would not be just for the applicant to be deprived of its right to have the
decision quashed for want of validity and concluded that proceedings by way of
judicial review had been properly brought in the circumstances. Similarly, in
Mythen v Employment Appeals Tribunal[234] Barrington J granted an order of
certiorari in relation to a refusal by the respondent to entertain the applicant's
claim on the grounds that it had erred as to its jurisdiction. He stated that he did
not think the applicant should be denied relief in the form of judicial review
because he could have appealed to the Circuit Court and that he was entitled to
have the facts investigated by a court of first instance. The rationale behind this
approach is that a person is entitled to a proper decision at an initial stage in
proceedings without the expense and delay often involved in an appeal and it
certainly better reflects the true purpose of judicial review.

21.072   The most recent pronouncements in this area seem to fall somewhere in
between the two approaches outlined above and tend to reflect the attitude adopted
by O'Higgins CJ in *Abenglen*. In *McGoldrick v An Bord Pleanála*[235] Barron J
stated as follows:

> The real question to be determined where an appeal lies is the relative
> merits of an appeal as against the granting of relief by way of judicial
> review. It is not just a question whether an alternative remedy exists or
> whether the applicant has taken steps to pursue such remedy. The true
> question is which is the more appropriate remedy considered in the con-
> text of common sense, the ability to deal with the questions raised and
> principles of fairness; provided, of course, that the applicant has not gone
> too far down one road to be estopped from changing his or her mind.

---

[232] [1989] IR 701, 721, [1989] ILRM 565, 581. This approach was applied by Barr J in
Tennyson v Dun Laoghaire Corporation [1991] 2 IR 527.
[233] *Ibid.* at 721, 581.
[234] [1990] 1 IR 98, [1989] ILRM 844.
[235] [1997] 1 IR 497. Quoted with approval by Kelly J in *Cremin v Smithwick* High Court
(Kelly J) 27 June 2001 at 4.

On the facts, Barron J concluded that the applicant was entitled to have the particular issues of fact on which his application had been refused determined before the respondent and he granted judicial review. This approach has recently been approved *obiter* by Geoghegan J in the Supreme Court decision of *Buckley v Kirby*[236] where he considered the appropriate course of action for the court to take where an applicant has brought an appeal which is pending and has moved for judicial review in circumstances where either remedy would be equally appropriate. Geoghegan J stated that he would adopt the view of Barron J in *McGoldrick* and that the High Court on an application for leave is not bound to refuse it merely because an appeal is pending.

21.073 In *Duff v Mangan*[237] Denham J expressed the view that *certiorari* is a discretionary remedy which will be granted "cautiously where there is an adequate alternative remedy which has been inadequately prosecuted"[238] although she decided in the circumstances that the court's jurisdiction should be exercised in the appellant's favour. One point in her judgment which should be treated with caution is her statement that "*certiorari* will not lie regarding a matter which is pending before an appellate court".[239] In the case before her the appellant's appeal to the Circuit Court had been concluded and thus it was, she said, not an absolute bar to judicial review but rather a factor for consideration by the court. It is difficult to reconcile this approach with that of Finlay CJ in *P. & F. Sharpe* and Barr J in *Tennyson v Dun Laoghaire Corporation*[240] where the court placed no significance on the fact that appeals to An Bord Pleanála were also pending. The correct view is probably that expressed by O'Sullivan J in *Nevin v Crowley*[241] to the effect that the principle that *certiorari* will not lie where a matter is pending before an appellate court is not an absolute rule. He stated "what I have to consider is whether justice can be done by refusing the appellant relief and allowing him to prosecute his appeal or whether it is more appropriate in the interests of justice to quash the impugned decision". In the circumstances O'Sullivan J decided to grant *certiorari* to quash the decision made by the District Court, a finding upheld on appeal by the Supreme Court.[242] A further relevant factor may be an applicant's motive in deciding whether to pursue an appeal or proceed by way of judicial review. In *Bridgeman v Limerick Corporation*[243] Finnegan J commented that in the case before him "there was not ... a deliberate choice not to avail of the remedy of appeal" and he

---

[236] [2000] 3 IR 431, [2001] 2 ILRM 395.
[237] [1994] 1 ILRM 91.
[238] *Ibid.* at 101. See also *Arnold v Windle* Supreme Court, 4 March 1999 at 5.
[239] *Ibid.* at 96.
[240] [1991] 2 IR 527.
[241] [1999] 1 ILRM 376, 381.
[242] Supreme Court, 17 February 2000.
[243] High Court (Finnegan J) 2 June 2000.

concluded that if he had found for the applicant on substantive grounds, it would have been appropriate for him to exercise his discretion in the latter's favour.

21.074 One further general consideration which may be relevant is the nature of the error or illegality which an applicant seeks to correct. In *Sweeney v Brophy*[244] Hederman J suggested that *certiorari* was not the appropriate remedy for a "routine mishap" which might occur in the course of a trial and that an appeal would be the correct remedy in such circumstances. However, this approach is open to criticism on the grounds that it overlooks the distinction between appeal and review and should be viewed with some caution. At the other end of the spectrum, there is some authority for the proposition that if the error made amounts to a breach of the principles of natural and constitutional justice, the availability of an alternative remedy should not be a consideration. This was suggested by O'Higgins CJ in *State (Abenglen Properties Ltd) v Dublin Corporation*[245] where he stated that if the decision impugned is made without jurisdiction or in breach of natural justice then, normally the existence of a right of appeal or a failure to avail of it should be immaterial. The tenor of the judgment of O'Sullivan J in *Nevin v Crowley*[246] also supports this view and he stated that in his opinion "it would be an inadequate response from the High Court, faced with [a] failure of natural and constitutional justice ... simply to allow the appeal to proceed as if nothing untoward had happened". This approach was also favoured by Murray J in the Supreme Court in the same case[247] where he quoted with approval the statement of O'Higgins CJ in *Abenglen* and said that where a trial has been conducted in a manner which is in breach of a fundamental principle of constitutional justice "the mere existence of a right of appeal cannot be an obstacle to the granting of an order of *certiorari*".[248]

Finally it is important not to overlook the fact that any hard line approach to the exhaustion of alternative remedies requirement will have the effect of blurring the distinction between an appeal on the merits and a review of the legality of a decision. In view of the fact that judicial review is the appropriate mechanism for controlling the legality of decisions made by administrative bodies and lower courts, it may be important to allow review to take place even where an alternative appeal procedure is open in order to ensure that confidence in the decision making process is maintained.

---

[244] [1993] 2 IR 202, 211, [1993] ILRM 449, 453. See also *Moore v Martin* High Court (Finnegan J) 29 May 2000 where Finnegan J held that in circumstances where the error in question did not appear on the face of the record, there had been no breach of natural justice and the applicant had an appeal pending before the Circuit Court, it was not appropriate that an order of *certiorari* should be made. See also *Maher v O'Donnell* [1995] 3 IR 530, 539-540.

[245] [1984] IR 381, [1982] ILRM 590.

[246] [1999] 1 ILRM 376.

[247] Supreme Court, 17 February 2000.

[248] *Ibid*. at 7.

CHAPTER TWENTY TWO

CASE STATED PROCEDURE

APPEAL BY WAY OF CASE STATED

Introduction

22.001 S.51 of the Courts (Supplemental Provisions) Act 1961 extends the provisions of s.2 of the Summary Jurisdiction Act 1857 to allow any party to summary proceedings before the District Court (other than proceedings relating to an indictable offence which was dealt with summarily by that court) to request a district judge,[1] after he has heard and determined a matter, to state a case to the High Court on a point of law.

The scope of the jurisdiction conferred by s.51 was considered by Barrington J in the course of his judgment in *McMahon v McDonald*.[2] He said that it appeared to him to be a general grant of jurisdiction which could be invoked to challenge any determination of law made by a district judge in the course of the exercise of any statutory powers from time to time conferred upon him and it was not in his view necessary "that each statute conferring jurisdiction on the District Court in relation to any matter should incorporate a power authorising him to state a case in relation to any matter of law arising under that statute". This was subject to the exemption set out in the section itself relating to "proceedings relating to an indictable offence which was not dealt with summarily by the court", presumably, as Barrington J suggested, because any question of law arising in such proceedings could be dealt with by the court of trial.

22.002 It is clear from the wording of s.2 of the 1857 Act as amended that the proceedings in the District Court must be "heard and determined" before the appeal by way of case stated procedure can be utilized.[3] Initially there was some doubt about whether questions as to the jurisdiction of a district judge could be raised by way of appeal by case stated. In *Attorney General (McNamara) v Beirne*[4] the High Court held that rulings of a district judge on

---

[1] In this chapter all references will be to "district judge". The effect of s.21(2) of the Courts Act 1991 is that all references to "justice" of the District Court should be construed as references to "judge" of the District Court and for the sake of consistency this change has been effected throughout the text.
[2] High Court (Barrington J), 3 May 1988. See also the decision of the Supreme Court, 27 July 1988.
[3] *Director of Public Prosecutions v Early* High Court (McGuinness J) 2 December 1997 at 17-18.
[4] [1943] IR 480.

objections which went to jurisdiction could not be tested by means of the case stated procedure and that the defendant should instead have sought *certiorari*. The rationale behind this approach was summarised in *Attorney General v Burke*[5] to the effect that the defendant was in a dilemma: if he succeeded in establishing that the judge had no jurisdiction, he also succeeded in showing that he had no power to state a case. If he failed to show that the judge had no jurisdiction, then he had jurisdiction to state the case but the defendant must inevitably lose. However, it seems that the principle laid down in *Beirne* should be regarded "as applying only to the facts of that case and not as establishing any wider proposition"[6] and this interpretation is borne out by the decision of Blayney J in *Sports Arena Ltd v O'Reilly*.[7] The applicant had applied to the District Court for the renewal of licensing certificates and the respondent district judge had concluded that the applications were not properly before him and had struck them out. The applicant's request for a case stated was refused by the respondent district judge and he sought judicial review of this decision. Blayney J referred to *Beirne* and stated that it seemed to him that it was a decision on special facts which did not lay down any general principle. In so far as it decided anything it was that "a district [judge] is entitled to refuse to state a case at the request of the party who is contending that the district [judge] had no jurisdiction to hear the case." But, as he pointed out, this was not the position in the case before him; the applicant was contending that the district judge had jurisdiction and it was the judge himself who refused jurisdiction and struck out the applications. It was held by Blayney J in granting an order of *mandamus*, that where a district judge strikes out a case before him on the grounds that he has no jurisdiction to hear it, he may not refuse to state a case on this issue. In the opinion of Blayney J the only ground on which the district judge could have refused to state the case in the matter before the court was on the basis that it was "frivolous" within the meaning of s.4 of the Summary Jurisdiction Act 1857, and being satisfied that this was not the case, he held that the applicant was entitled to the relief which he sought. The fact that a case may be stated on a point going to the jurisdiction of a district judge was also confirmed by Hamilton P in *Director of Public Prosecutions v Nolan*[8] in which he rejected the argument that a judge may not state a case on a jurisdictional question.

22.003 S.4 of the Summary Jurisdiction Act 1857 provides that if a district judge is of opinion that an application is frivolous, but not otherwise, he may refuse to state a case and shall, on the request of the appellant, sign and deliver

---

[5] [1955] IR 30, 38.
[6] See Collins and O'Reilly, *Civil Proceedings and the State in Ireland: A Practitioner's Guide* (1990) at 3.
[7] [1987] IR 185.
[8] [1990] 2 IR 526, 531.

to him a certificate of such refusal.[9] However, he may not refuse to state a case where the application is made by or under the direction of a Minister, the Attorney General, the Director of Public Prosecutions or the Revenue Commissioners.[10] In *Eastern Health Board v Ballagh*[11] the respondent district judge refused to accede to an application to have a case stated for the opinion of the High Court on the basis that it was frivolous. The notice party had been prosecuted in relation to a contaminated carton of yoghurt and a preliminary issue had arisen as to whether the writing on the carton amounted to a warranty such as would entitle it to be discharged from the prosecution under the terms of the Health Act 1947. Morris J stated that given that most of the writing on the carton was required by EU legislation the determination of whether this information amounted to a warranty would be of importance in future District Court prosecutions under the Health Act and he concluded that the application was not merely frivolous.

22.004 Where a district judge refuses to state a case, the appellant may apply to the High Court for a ruling calling upon the judge to show cause why the case should not be stated.[12] In *State (Turley) v O'Floinn*[13] an application for a case stated was made and a certificate of refusal was issued by the district judge on the grounds that he was of the opinion that the request was frivolous. Ó Dálaigh CJ referred to the fact that the ground of the district judge's refusal to state a case was that there was no question of law involved but said that the question of whether there was sufficient evidence in law to support a conviction was not a question of fact but of law. Given that there was a stateable question of law to be decided he was satisfied that the application for a case stated could not be regarded as merely frivolous and he held that the prosecutor was entitled to have the issue determined by the High Court by way of a case stated. Similarly in *Sports Arena Ltd v O'Reilly*[14] the applicant successfully sought an order of *mandamus* directing the respondent district judge to state and sign a case for

---

[9] See also Order 102, rule 15 of the District Court Rules 1997 which provides that the certificate shall be in the form set out in Form 102.6 Schedule D.

[10] Rule 202 of the District Court Rules 1948 (now see Order 102, rule 15 of the District Court Rules 1997) extended the original provisions of s.4 of the Summary Jurisdiction Act 1857 which referred only to the Attorney General. Note that Collins and O'Reilly in *Civil Proceedings and the State in Ireland: A Practitioner's Guide* (1990) at 6, footnote 38 have queried whether such an extension is within the competence of the District Court Rules Committee.

[11] [1999] 1 ILRM 544.

[12] S.5 of the Summary Jurisdiction Act 1857.

[13] [1968] IR 245.

[14] [1987] IR 185. Note that the applicant was granted leave to apply by way of judicial review for a rule pursuant to s.5 of the Summary Jurisdiction Act 1857 calling upon the respondent district judge to show cause why he should not state and sign a case for the opinion of the High Court and for an order of *mandamus* directing the respondent to state and sign such a case.

the opinion of the High Court. Blayney J quoted with approval the statement made by O'Keeffe P in *Turley* to the effect that s.5 of the 1857 Act appears "to enable the High Court to form its own opinion on whether the facts warrant consideration by the High Court".

22.005 S.2 of the Summary Jurisdiction Act 1857 as amended makes it clear that the case stated procedure may only be utilized to determine questions of law. It would appear that on a case stated, "jurisdiction is confined to questions of law and that findings of fact are conclusive, unless it appears that there was no evidence to support them".[15] However, there is also authority for the proposition that mixed findings of fact and law may be considered in a case stated.[16] In *Rahill v Brady*[17] the Supreme Court held that a decision by a district judge as to whether a particular occasion constituted a "special event" within the meaning of s.11 of the Intoxicating Liquor Act 1961 was open to review in an appeal by way of case stated. In the view of Budd J a decision on such a matter was not a decision on a question of fact only, but "a decision on a mixed question of law and fact" which involved the construction of a statute.

22.006 The question of whether the High Court can entertain an appeal by way of case stated from a judge who, on the date he signed the case stated, had been appointed a judge of the Circuit Court was considered by Geoghegan J in *Director of Public Prosecutions v Galvin*.[18] A preliminary objection as to the jurisdiction of the High Court to hear the case stated, which concerned an appeal from an acquittal by direction at the end of the prosecution case, was raised on behalf of the respondent. Geoghegan J stated that it is well established that the observance of the preliminary requirements under the Summary Jurisdiction Act 1857 is a condition precedent to the jurisdiction of the High Court to hear a case stated and he said that the expression "the said justice" used in s.51(1) suggests that it is clearly intended that the judge of the District Court who hears the case signs the case stated. However, he stated that in his view it was also implicit in the wording of s.51 that at the time of signing the case stated the particular judge was still a judge of the District Court. Geoghegan J concluded that for two distinct reasons he did not think that a district judge who has been appointed a judge of the Circuit Court can sign a case stated. He pointed to the fact that the case stated procedure, whether it be an appeal by way of case stated or a consultative case stated, normally contemplates that the case will return to the same district judge because the case stated itself arises from a

---

[15] *Per* Gibson J in *Donaghy v Walsh* [1914] 2 IR 261, 273. So, "the question of whether there is any evidence to support a finding of fact is in itself a matter of law" *per* Andrews LCJ in *Luke v Bracewell* (1948) 82 ILTR 123, 125.
[16] *Murphy v Bayliss* Supreme Court, 22 July 1976.
[17] [1971] IR 69.
[18] [1999] 4 IR 18, [1999] 2 ILRM 277.

particular view which that judge took of the law. However, in the case before him the matter could not go back to the district judge who had heard the case and if the High Court were to take the view that his decision had been wrong, a completely new hearing would have to take place in the District Court which would mean that the hearing of the case stated would be to some extent a moot. Geoghegan J added that even if it was thought sensible that a judge of the District Court who had been promoted to the Circuit Court should be allowed to sign a case stated after the date of his promotion, he was unable to interpret s.2 and s.51 as permitting this and it would in his view require a statutory amendment to allow it to be done.

Procedure

Application for Case Stated

22.007 The jurisdiction of the High Court to hear a case stated under s.2 of the Summary Jurisdiction Act 1857 as amended by s.51 of the Courts (Supplemental Provisions) Act 1961 is a statutory one and in order to invoke it, an applicant must comply with the procedure laid down in the legislation. S.51(1) of the Act of 1961 provides that a party wishing to appeal by case stated must apply within 14 days of the determination of the district judge to the said judge to state and sign a case for the opinion of the High Court. It would appear that this 14 day time limit must be complied with and that it cannot be extended by the District Court. Where such an application for a case stated is made, the determination of the matter is suspended, where the district judge grants the application, until the case stated has been heard and determined[19] and where he refuses to grant the application, until he so refuses.[20]

Order 102, rule 8(1) and (2) of the District Court Rules 1997 provides that an application pursuant to s.2 of the Act of 1857 as extended shall be by notice in the Form 102.3 Schedule D and that such notice shall be lodged with the clerk for the court area in which the proceedings were heard and determined within 14 days after the determination. Order 102, rule 8(3) requires that a copy of such notice shall be served by registered post on every other party to the proceedings, also within 14 days.

Entry into Recognizance

22.008 The applicant must also enter into a recognizance with sureties in such sum as the district judge may determine, conditioned to prosecute such case stated without delay and to submit to the judgment of the High Court and pay

---

[19] S.51(2)(a) of the Courts (Supplemental Provisions) Act 1961 and Order 102, rule 10(a) of the District Court Rules 1997.

[20] S.51(2)(b) of the Courts (Supplemental Provisions) Act 1961 and Order 102, rule 10(b) of the District Court Rules 1997.

such costs as may be awarded by that court.[21] Order 102, rule 9 of the District
Court Rules 1997 now provides that the appellant shall within 14 days after the
determination of the proccedings, enter into a recognisance with or without a
surety or sureties in such sum(s) as the judge may determine.[22] The recognizance when completed, should be lodged with the District Court clerk of the
area in which the decision has been given.

Preparing and Signing a Case Stated

22.009 The district judge is required to prepare and sign a case stated within
six months from the date of the application.[23] It was held by Davitt P in
Prendergast v Porter[24] that after such a period has elapsed, either party may
institute proceedings for an order of *mandamus* to compel a judge to prepare
and sign the case stated. Davitt P stated that the purpose of rule 17 of the District Court Rules 1955[25] which lays down this requirement was "to provide a
period after which the [judge] could clearly be said to have neglected or refused
to perform his duty; and to enable *mandamus* proceedings then to be instituted". Davitt P added that it could never have been intended to deprive a party
of his right of appeal by way of case stated by interpreting the wording in the
District Court Rules as mandatory in nature. This statement was approved of by
Egan J in *Irish Refining plc v Commissioner of Valuation*[26] who stressed that
there is a distinction between this type of provision and provisions which pre-
scribe time limits for parties to proceedings. In upholding this interpretation,
Finlay CJ pointed out that if the opposite view were taken "the position of a
person seeking a case stated would be that he would be entirely at the mercy of
the judge concerned" and he concluded that "such a manifestly unfair or unjust
procedure should not be assumed to have been the real intention of the legislature".[27] This view was confirmed by Costello J in *McMahon v McClafferty*[28]
in which he held that the fact that a case stated is signed after the six month

---

[21] S.3 of the Summary Jurisdiction Act 1857. See also Order 102, rule 9 of the District
Court Rules 1997. Note that a Minister of State, a member of the Garda Siochána, the
Attorney General (and since 1974 the Director of Public Prosecutions) are exempt
from the requirement to enter into recognizances for the purpose of taking an appeal
(see s.18 of the Criminal Justice Act 1951).

[22] In the Form 102.4 Schedule D. Rule 199 of the District Court Rules 1948 originally
provided that the lodging of the notice and the entering into a recognizance should be
carried out within seven days from the date upon which the decision was given. The
time limit in respect of lodging notice was extended to 14 days by s.51(1) of the Courts
(Supplemental Provisions) Act 1961.

[23] Order 102, rule 12 of the District Court Rules 1997.

[24] [1961] IR 440.

[25] Now see Order 102, rule 12 of the District Court Rules 1997.

[26] [1990] 1 IR 568, 574.

[27] *Ibid.* at 577.

[28] [1989] IR 68, [1990] ILRM 32.

period has elapsed does not deprive the court of jurisdiction to entertain it. However, it is clear from the recent decision of Kelly J in *Director of Public Prosecutions v Rice*[29] that excessive delay in preparing and signing a case stated
will not be overlooked. The case against the respondent was heard by the District Court in November 1998 and was dismissed on the merits. The appellant
served a notice requiring a case to be stated and in May 1996 the draft case
stated was sent to the respondent's solicitors. In September 1997 the draft was
forwarded to the district judge, who requested that it be amended in January
1998. The case stated was finally signed by the district judge in April 1999 and
then was served on the respondent's solicitors and filed in the Central Office.
As Kelly J pointed out the delay from the time when the complaint had been
before the District Court was almost four years and it had been nearly five
years since the incident giving rise to the complaint had occurred. In the circumstances, Kelly J, relying on the decision of the Supreme Court in *Director of
Public Prosecutions v Flahive*,[30] concluded that there had undoubtedly been a
delay for which no adequate justification had been provided and he concluded
that the case stated in the proceedings should be stayed.

22.010 To secure agreement between the parties as to the facts, at any time
within two months from the date of the lodgment of the notice, the district judge
may submit a draft of the case to or receive a draft from the parties, but in the
event of a dispute between the parties as to the facts, such facts shall be found
by the judge.[31] It has been made clear that in order to deal with a question of
law sought to be raised by a case stated, the court must have before it the precise facts found by the judge who stated the case and any inferences or conclusions of fact which he drew from the facts found by him. Murphy J so held in the
decision of the Northern Ireland Court of Appeal in *Emerson v Hearty*[32] in
which he set out the following useful summary of the principles which ought to
be observed in drafting a case stated.

> The case stated should be stated in consecutively numbered paragraphs,
> each paragraph being confined, as far as possible to a separate portion of
> the subject matter. After the paragraphs setting out the facts of the case
> there should follow separate paragraphs setting out the contentions of the
> parties and the findings of the judge.
>   The case stated should set out clearly the judge's findings of fact, and
> should also set out any inferences or conclusions of fact which he drew
> from those findings. The task of finding the facts and of drawing the proper
> inferences and conclusions of fact from the facts so found is the task of the

---

[29] [2000] 2 ILRM 393.
[30] [1988] ILRM 133.
[31] Order 102, rule 12 of the District Court Rules 1997.
[32] [1946] NI 35.

judge. It does not fall within the province of this Court. Accordingly, it is not legitimate by setting out the evidence in the case stated and omitting any findings of fact to attempt to pass the task of finding the facts on to the Court of Appeal. What is required in the case stated is a finding by the judge of the facts, and not a recital of the evidence. Except for the purpose of elucidating the findings of fact it will rarely be necessary to set out any evidence in the case stated save in the one type of case where the question of law intended to be submitted is whether there was evidence before the judge which would justify him in deciding as he did.

The point of law upon which this Court's decision is sought should of course be set out clearly in the case. But we think the judge is certainly entitled to expect the party applying for the case stated to indicate the precise point of law upon which he wishes to have the decision of the appellate court. It would be convenient practice that this should ordinarily be done in the written application for the case stated.[33]

22.011 In his judgment in *Mitchelstown Co-Operative Society Ltd v Commissioner for Valuation,*[34] Blayney J stated that he was in complete agreement with and adopted this statement of the principles to be followed in drafting a case stated. He added that the facts must be found and stated that the court should not be required to go outside the case stated to some other document in order to discover them. In the matter before him, which concerned a case stated pursuant to s.5 of the Valuation Act 1988, Blayney J was satisfied that the case stated did not contain any clear statement of the facts found by the tribunal, although the entire transcript of the evidence was annexed, and he concluded that it must be returned to the tribunal for amendment and if necessary re-statement.[35]

Service of Copy of Case Stated

22.012 When the case has been stated and signed, the appellant shall receive the case stated from the District Court clerk.[36] Then, the appellant must first give notice in writing of the appeal and serve a copy of the case stated on the other party to the proceedings.[37] This notice must be served before the case

---

[33] *Ibid.* at 36-37.
[34] [1989] IR 210.
[35] Note that the principles set out in *Emerson v Hearty* [1946] NI 35, 36-37 and *Mitchelstown Co-Operative Society Ltd v Commissioner for Valuation* [1989] IR 210, 212-213 were quoted with approval by Denham J in *McGinley v Criminal Assets Bureau* Supreme Court, 30 May 2001 where she stated that these were the correct principles to apply to the stating of cases pursuant to s.16 of the Courts of Justice Act 1947.
[36] Order 102, rule 13 of the District Court Rules 1997.
[37] S.2 of the Summary Jurisdiction Act 1857.

stated is transmitted to the Central Office of the High Court.[38] In *Director of Public Prosecutions v Nangle*[39] it was held by Finlay P that a copy of the case stated accompanied by a letter informing the respondents that it was the intention of the solicitor for the appellant to transmit the case stated to the High Court was sufficient notice to comply with the statutory requirement. However, subsequently in *Director of Public Prosecutions v O'Connor*[40] Finlay P held that a letter which enclosed a copy of the case stated and sought an endorsement of acceptance of service did not constitute sufficient compliance with the provisions of s.2 of the Act of 1857. Finlay P stated that if he had had any discretion in relation to compliance by the applicant with the terms of the section, he would have exercised it in his favour, but in his view he did not have any such discretion and he concluded that it would do violence to the meaning of the phrase "notice in writing on such appeal" to hold that the statutory requirement had been complied with in the circumstances. In addition, it was held by Blayney J in *Crowley v McVeigh*[41] that where it has not been possible to serve the respondent, but every possible effort has been made to serve him, service on the solicitor who acted for him in the District Court will be sufficient.

Transmission of Case Stated to Central Office

22.013 The appellant is also required, within three days of receiving the case stated to transmit it to the Central Office of the High Court.[42] It was held by the Supreme Court in *Attorney General v Shivnan*[43] that this three day period may be extended under the power conferred by what is now Order 122, rule 7 to enlarge the time appointed by the Rules for doing any act or taking any proceeding. Lavery J said that the rules had adopted the three day period of the statute but subject to the power contained in the rules to enlarge it.[44]

Time Limit and Notice Requirements

22.014 The time limit and notice requirements laid down in s.2 of the Sum-

---

[38] Order 62, rule 5 of the Rules of the Superior Courts 1986 which provides that "immediately before transmitting the case to the Central Office" the appellant shall give notice to every other party to the proceedings. See also *Thompson v Curry* [1970] IR 61.

[39] [1984] ILRM 171 and on this point see *Director of Public Prosecutions v O'Connor* High Court (Finlay P) 9 May 1983 at 6-8.

[40] High Court (Finlay P) 9 May 1983.

[41] [1989] IR 73, 79, [1990] ILRM 220, 226.

[42] S.2 of the Summary Jurisdiction Act 1857 and Order 62, rule 1.

[43] [1970] IR 66.

[44] However, note that Collins and O'Reilly in *Civil Proceedings and the State in Ireland: A Practitioner's Guide* (1990) at 13 query whether the rule making committee had power to amend the professions of a statute, see *State (Gallagher Shatter & Co.) v de Valera* [1986] ILRM 3, 7 *per* McCarthy J.

mary Jurisdiction Act 1857 were considered by the High Court in *Director of Public Prosecutions (Murphy) v Regan*,[45] namely whether a case stated to that court could no longer be entertained by reason of the appellant's alleged failure to comply with the time limits laid down for the serving of a case stated after it had been completed by the District Court judge and for transmitting it to the Central Office of the High Court. O'Hanlon J reviewed a number of authorities dealing with the question of the time limits specified in s.2 of the 1857 Act and noted that this matter is now also dealt with by Order 62, rule 1 and comes within the ambit of Order 122, rule 7 which gives the court jurisdiction to enlarge the time for doing any act or taking any proceedings where it is appropriate to do so. He concluded that he would have no hesitation in enlarging the time for transmission of the case stated by one day in order to remedy what he termed the "slight oversight" which had occurred. However, in relation to the apparent failure on the part of the appellant to give notice in writing of the appeal with a copy of the case stated signed by the district judge to the other party to the proceedings within three days of receiving the case, O'Hanlon J pointed out that no power to extend the time limit for this purpose arose by virtue of the Rules of Court. He referred to the fact that no effort had been made to effect personal service on the respondent and he concluded that it would "extend the scope of previous decisions considerably" were he to hold that the service effected in the case before him was sufficient, where a copy of the case stated and the notice of appeal had merely been served on the solicitors who had represented the respondent at the initial prosecution in the District Court. Accordingly, O'Hanlon J dismissed the appeal by way of case stated.

Function of the High Court

22.015 The High Court is required to hear and determine the question or questions of law raised in the case stated and shall "reverse, affirm or amend" the determination of the District Court or may remit the matter to the District Court with its opinion or may make such other order as to the court may seem fit.[46] In *Revenue Commissioners v Bradley*[47] it was confirmed by the Supreme Court that the High Court is bound to hear and consider arguments on points of law which were raised in the District Court but as to which no specific questions were put by the district judge.

The High Court also has the power to cause the case to be sent back to the District Court for amendment[48] as happened in *O'Friel v Director of Public Prosecutions*[49] where a case was sent back to enable the district judge to set out the facts and inferences from facts on the basis of which he had made his find-

---

[45] [1993] ILRM 335.
[46] S.6 of the Summary Jurisdiction Act 1857.
[47] (1942) 76 ILTR 87, 90.
[48] S.7 of the Summary Jurisdiction Act 1857.
[49] Supreme Court, 30 July 1999.

ings. However, it would appear that where a case is sent back to the District Court that court may not hear further evidence in relation to the matter. It was held by the Supreme Court in *T. v T.* [50] that once a district judge has heard and determined such proceedings and has stated a case for the opinion of the High Court, he is *functus officio* and has no jurisdiction to hear further evidence in the matter. A case was stated pursuant to s.2 of the 1857 Act as amended and the High Court judge referred the matter back to the district judge, who heard additional evidence and made certain findings. Henchy J concluded that this was "an unpermitted expedient in view of the fact that the matter was an appeal by case stated and the district judge was then *functus officio*". [51]

22.016 While s.6 of the Summary Jurisdiction Act 1857 provides that the order of the High Court in a case stated is to be "final and conclusive", it would appear that a decision by a district judge made after and in consequence of an order of the High Court may be appealed to the Circuit Court. [52] In addition it would seem that despite the wording of s.6, an appeal lies to the Supreme Court from any decision of the High Court in relation to an appeal by way of case stated under the Act of 1857. In *Attorney General (Fahy) v Bruen* [53] Murnaghan J suggested that such an appeal would lie as a result of the constitutional guarantee of an appeal from all decisions of the High Court "with such exceptions as may be prescribed by law". He pointed out that it had been determined that such exceptions must be found in a law made subsequently to the adoption of the 1922 Constitution. Given the similar wording contained in Article 34.4.3° of the 1937 Constitution, the fact that an appeal will lie to the High Court in this respect seems clearly established.

Costs

22.017 The awarding of the costs of case stated proceedings lies in the discretion of the High Court subject to the provisions of s.6 of the Act of 1857 which lays down that a district judge shall not be liable for any costs in relation to such an appeal. The issue of costs was considered by the Supreme Court in *Brennan v O'Brien* [54] in which the High Court in a case stated concluded that convictions against the defendant could not be sustained but it made no order as to costs. In considering whether the High Court had exercised its discretion in this regard on a proper ground, Maguire CJ stated that "there would appear to have been

---

[50] [1983] IR 29, [1982] ILRM 217.
[51] *Ibid.* at 33, 220. It should be noted that a different view was taken in the earlier decision of *Veterinary Council v Good* [1935] IR 884. See also *Forte v McAlister* [1917] 2 IR 387.
[52] Collins and O'Reilly, *Civil Proceedings and the State in Ireland: A Practitioner's Guide* (1990) at 14.
[53] [1936] IR 750, 764.
[54] (1960) 103 ILTR 36.

no ground on which the court was entitled to deprive the defendant of his costs" and the order of the High Court on the issue of costs was reversed. Finally it should be noted that it has been stated that "those charged with the carriage of a case stated or conducting appeals in this Court should bear in mind that their duty to the court and to their client is to move with reasonable expedition and that, if they fail to do so, they may be liable in costs or be made answerable in some other way".[55]

CONSULTATIVE CASE STATED

By the District Court

Nature of Case Stated Jurisdiction

22.018 Unlike the procedure provided for by s.2 of the 1857 Act as amended, which allows for an appeal by way of case stated after a district judge has heard and determined proceedings, s.52 provides a mechanism for a "consultative case stated", which allows for the stating of a case in the course of the proceedings before the District Court. The latter section states that a district judge shall, if requested to do so by any party who has been heard in proceedings before him (other than the preliminary examination of an indictable offence) unless he considers the request frivolous, state a case to the High Court on a point of law. In addition, a district judge himself may without request refer such a question of law to the High Court for determination where it arises in the course of the proceedings before him. This has been interpreted to mean that a district judge "if requested must state a case for the opinion of the High Court unless the district judge considers the request to be frivolous and also may of his own motion and without any request from any of the parties state such a case for the opinion of the High Court".[56] It had been accepted in the context of the original consultative case stated procedure provided for in s.83 of the Courts of Justice Act 1924 that the section seemed "to make the district [judge] the sole judge of whether an application for a case stated is frivolous".[57]

22.019 As Murnaghan J commented in *Attorney General (Fahy) v Bruen*[58] in relation to s.83 of the Courts of Justice Act 1924 it was "a new consultative case stated before determination" and it was accepted by Barron J in *Fernandes*

---

[55] *Per* Kenny J in *Southern Health Board v Reeves-Smith* [1980] IR 26, 31. See also *Brown v Donegal County Council* [1980] IR 132, 145-146.

[56] *Per* Lynch J in *McKenna v Deery* [1998] 1 IR 62, 74.

[57] *Per* Murnaghan J in *Attorney General (Fahy) v Bruen* [1936] IR 750, 763. Note also that Walsh J commented in *Campus Oil Ltd v Minister for Industry and Energy* [1983] IR 82, 86 that "it may be noted that in Irish law no appeal lies against the decision of any judge to state a consultative case".

[58] [1936] IR 750, 764.

v Bermingham[59] that *"prima facie* [s.52] gives the District Court power to state a case at any stage in the proceedings".[60] So it would appear that a district judge may state a case at any stage up until he makes his final determination in the matter; as Ó Dálaigh J commented in *Attorney General v Simpson*[61] "every question of law may be said to be 'arising' in the case while the [judge] is still not *functus officio"*. However, it will clearly be necessary for the district judge to hear the evidence relating to the point of law arising before stating the case. The correct procedure in this regard is set out in the following terms by Lynch J in *DPP (Travers) v Brennan*:[62]

> The proper procedure leading to the stating of a consultative case for the opinion of the Superior Courts is for the district judge to hear all the evidence relevant to the point of law arising, to find the facts relevant to such point of law in the light of such evidence, then to state the case posing the questions appropriate to elucidate the point of law and finally, on receiving the answers to those questions to decide the matter before him on the basis of those answers.

22.020 Ryan and Magee in *The Irish Criminal Process*[63] point out that the majority of cases in which the case stated procedure is utilized involve the procedure laid down by s.2 of the Summary Jurisdiction Act 1857 as amended, probably because of the reluctance of a party to incur the expense of further proceedings before a decision against him has actually been given and because the appeal mechanism under s.52 is restricted. Under s.52(2) an appeal will only lie to the Supreme Court where the leave of the High Court has been obtained. However, under the procedure provided for by s.2 of the 1857 Act as amended, an appeal lies to the Supreme Court without the necessity of first obtaining leave to appeal.[64] The issue of whether an appeal lay from the decision of a judge of the High Court refusing leave to appeal against his determination of a question of law raised on a consultative case stated from the District Court pursuant to s.52 was considered by the Supreme Court in *Minister for Justice v Wang Zhu Jie*.[65] Counsel for the appellant submitted, *inter alia*, that the decision of the High Court judge to refuse leave to appeal was a "decision of the High Court" within the meaning of Article 34.4.3° of the Constitution and that therefore there was a constitutional right of appeal to the Supreme Court from such a decision. It was further contended that even if the provisions of s.52(2) were to be construed as a form of regulation or exception applicable to

---

[59] High Court (Barron J) 22 May 1985.
[60] See also *Doyle v Hearne* [1987] IR 601, 610-611, [1988] ILRM 318, 327.
[61] [1959] IR 335, 346.
[62] [1998] 4 IR 67, 70, [1998] 2 ILRM 128, 131-132.
[63] (1983) at 417.
[64] *Attorney General (Fahy) v Bruen* [1936] IR 750, 764.
[65] [1993] 1 IR 426, [1991] ILRM 823.

the decision of the High Court in such a case, they did not unambiguously except the decision of the High Court on a case stated from the provisions of Article 34.4.3° and that, accordingly a right of appeal existed. In refusing to entertain the appeal, Finlay CJ stated that the provisions of Article 34.4.3° clearly envisaged and provided for exceptions to and regulation of the general right of appeal from decisions of the High Court to the Supreme Court to be prescribed by law, namely by Act of the Oireachtas. The Chief Justice concluded that the provisions of s.52 should be construed as effecting an exception from the absolute right of appeal provided for in Article 34.4.3° of the Constitution from decisions of the High Court to the Supreme Court and substituting therefor a regulated right of appeal which is subject to the final discretion of the judge of the High Court answering the consultative case stated.

22.021 The interpretation of the phrase "other than proceedings relating to an indictable offence which is not being dealt with summarily by the court" in s.52 was considered by Lavan J in *People (DPP) v Delaney*.[66] The accused had appeared before the District Court charged with certain offences and the district judge had formed the view that they were not minor offences fit to be tried summarily. The Director of Public Prosecutions declined to give an explanation of his decision not to prosecute these offences on indictment and contended that upon electing to have the offences tried in the District Court, rather than upon indictment, the Director had discharged his statutory function in the matter. It was further contended on his behalf that in electing not to seek trial on indictment, the Director was not deciding whether or not the offence was a minor one which was a question for the district judge. The district judge formed the view that these submissions were not correct in law and stated a case for the opinion of the High Court on the matter. It was submitted on behalf of the Director that as the district judge had formed the opinion that the offences in question were not minor offences fit to be tried summarily, they fell into the category of indictable offences not being dealt with summarily by the court and as such could not properly be the subject matter of a consultative case stated. In addition, in support of his submission that the questions raised in the case stated were moot, counsel for the Director referred to the *dicta* of Sullivan P in *Attorney General v McLoughlin*[67] in relation to the earlier procedure provided for by s.83 of the Courts of Justice Act 1924 to the effect that "the only question of law which a district justice can refer to this Court is a question of law arising in any case before him, and that he has no right to ask this Court to answer questions 'extraneous to the issues affecting the defendant's case'". Lavan J concluded that "the inclusion of 'other than proceedings relating to an indictable offence which is not being dealt with summarily by the court' is in the opinion of this Court

---

[66] [1995] 2 IR 511. Reported in [1996] 1 ILRM 70 *sub nom Director of Public Prosecutions (Whelan) v Delaney*.
[67] [1931] IR 430, 440-441.

sufficient to expressly exclude from the case stated procedure a question of law arising from an offence which the district judge has decided to send forward for trial on indictment". In addition, he stated that the district judge had formed the view that the offences were not minor offences fit to be tried summarily and the questions of law which formed the subject matter of the case stated were therefore moot and the court could not entertain the case stated under s.52 of the Act of 1961. Further consideration was given to the meaning of the words "other than proceedings relating to an indictable offence which is not being dealt with summarily by the court" by Kearns J in *Attorney General v Oldridge*[68] where he held that it would be a "perverse and distorted interpretation" of the section to hold that extradition proceedings are caught by those words. In his view the process of extradition was altogether different from the process to which those bracketed words referred.

It is clear that the case stated procedure can only be used where a question of law arises in the particular context of the proceedings before the court. In *O'Neill v Butler*[69] McMahon J stressed that the where a district judge refers to the High Court a question of law arising in proceedings before him under s.52 of the Act of 1961, this question must relate to the facts of the case as found by him. As McMahon J stated, a district judge "cannot ask the High Court to define generally and without reference to particular facts the meaning of expressions used in a statute".[70]

22.022 Another issue which might have been open to question was whether a district judge may refer questions of law to the High Court concerning his jurisdiction to hear and decide a case, but it is clear from the decision of Finlay P in *Minister for Agriculture v Norgro Ltd*[71] that this is permissible. The question of law submitted by the district judge in that case was whether he was correct in holding that he had no jurisdiction to embark on the hearing of a complaint where the summons did not disclose on its face the fact that the complaint was made within a period of six months as required by statute.[72] Finlay P answered this question in the negative and concluded that the complainant should have been permitted to prove the date of the issue of the summons.

22.023 The question of whether a case may be stated pursuant to s.52 where an

---

[68] [2000] 4 IR 593, [2000] 2 ILRM 233.
[69] [1979] ILRM 243.
[70] *Ibid.* at 244. See also the comments of Hanna J in *Attorney General v McLoughlin* [1931] IR 430, 442 to the effect that "this Court is not a moot for the decision of any questions which may occur to the district [judge] under an Act of parliament".
[71] [1980] IR 155. See also *Director of Public Prosecutions v O'Donnell* [1995] 2 IR 294 where Geoghegan J held that where an issue as to jurisdiction is put forward in the course of a hearing, there is no reason why the district judge should not raise it in a consultative case stated.
[72] S.10 of the Petty Sessions (Ireland) Act 1851.

issue of the interpretation of domestic legislation having regard to the provisions of an EU directive arose was answered in the affirmative by Morris P in *Director of Public Prosecutions v O'Connor*.[73] Article 234 EC (formerly Article 177) of the EC Treaty provides, *inter alia,* that where a question of interpretation of the Treaty or of the validity and interpretation of the acts of the community institutions is raised in a case pending before a court or tribunal of a member state against whose decision there is no judicial remedy under national law, that court or tribunal shall bring the matter before the European Court of Justice. A question arose as to whether a garda is entitled to make a demand for the production of a certificate of insurance in respect of a vehicle which is deemed to be based in another member state and the district judge stated a case to the High Court pursuant to s.52. Morris P rejected the submission made by counsel for the accused that by virtue of the provisions of Article 234 EC the issues raised in the case must be brought before the Court of Justice. He stated that it appeared to him that his determination of the consultative case stated would result in the matter returning to the District Court and the accused, if convicted, had a right of appeal *de novo* to the Circuit Court. In these circumstances, he was of the view that the decision of the High Court could not be regarded as one against which there was no judicial remedy under national law. In any event, Morris P stated that it would be his intention to grant leave to either party to appeal his determination to the Supreme Court under s.52 and accordingly he held that Article 177 did not preclude the High Court from determining the issues before it.[74]

22.024 Finally, it is clear that a district judge is not entitled to state a case to the High Court on a question concerning the validity of a statutory provision having regard to the Constitution. This was made clear by O'Hanlon J in *Minister for Labour v Costello*[75] who stated that "the district [judge] must proceed on the assumption that powers conferred on him by Act of the Oireachtas, enacted subsequent to the enactment of the Constitution of 1937, may be lawfully exercised by him unless and until the statute has been successfully impugned in proceedings appropriate for that purpose".[76] This issue has recently been considered in some detail by Geoghegan J in *Director of Public Prosecutions v Dougan*.[77] The defendant had pleaded guilty to two road traffic offences and the district judge hearing the matter was of the opinion that due to the penalty and disqualification attaching to one of them, it might be that the offence could not be regarded as a minor one, and that as such he would be exceeding his

---

[73] High Court (Morris P) 22 July 1998.
[74] Note that the respondent's appeal to the Supreme Court was dismissed on 17 November 1999 [2000] 1 IR 300, [2000] 2 ILRM 137.
[75] [1988] IR 235, [1989] ILRM 485.
[76] *Ibid.* at 241, 490. Relying on the decision of the former Supreme Court in *Foyle Fisheries Commission v Gallen* [1960] Ir Jur Rep 35.
[77] [1997] 1 ILRM 550.

jurisdiction under the Constitution if he were to proceed with the matter. The district judge therefore decided to state a case to the High Court asking, *inter alia,* whether the offence in question was a minor one and in the proceedings before the High Court counsel for the Director of Public Prosecutions submitted that the district judge had no jurisdiction to state the case as he was effectively challenging the constitutionality of the provisions of the Road Traffic Acts which he was precluded from doing by the provisions of Article 34.3.2° of the Constitution. Geoghegan J concluded that:

> There is absolutely no doubt that a District Court judge is not entitled to state a case to the High Court on a question of the validity of a statutory provision having regard to the Constitution. The direct effect of [Article 34.3.2°] prevents him deciding the question himself and he can obviously only state a case on questions which he himself would be entitled to decide independently of the case stated. The mere fact, therefore, that the High Court is given jurisdiction under the Constitution to determine a question of the constitutionality of a statutory provision does not mean that this can be done by way of case stated and the former Supreme Court of Justice has made this absolutely clear in *Foyle Fisheries Commission v Gallen* ...[78]

While Geoghegan J accepted that the district judge did have jurisdiction under s.52 to send forward the consultative case stated, he stressed that the mere fact that the judge had jurisdiction to do this did not mean that he was *per se* entitled to specific answers to the questions posed.

Procedure

22.025 Where a district judge refers a question of law to the High Court for determination pursuant to s.52, he is required to adjourn the case to the sitting of the District Court for the court area to be held next after the expiration of 14 days from the day on which the decision of the High Court is given.[79] Before adjourning the proceedings, the judge may require the party requesting the case stated to enter into a recognizance with or without a surety or sureties in such sum(s) as he may determine,[80] which when completed shall be lodged with the District Court clerk. Order 102, rule 11(2) of the District Court Rules 1997 also provides that in civil cases or in cases of summary jurisdiction of a civil nature a party may in lieu of entering into a recognizance lodge with the District

---

[78] *Ibid.* at 555.
[79] Order 102, rule 11(1) of the District Court Rules 1997.
[80] Order 102, rule 11(2) of the District Court Rules 1997. See Form 102.4 Schedule D. Note that Collins and O'Reilly state in *Civil Proceedings and the State in Ireland: A Practitioner's Guide* (1990) at 21 that "in practice the requirement that a recognizance be enforced is largely ignored or waived".

Court clerk a sum determined by the judge which shall be retained until the judge finally adjudicates on the proceedings.

The district judge is required to prepare and sign the case stated within six months from the date of the request or decision to state the case.[81] He may within two months of this date submit to or receive from the parties a draft of the case stated but in the event of a dispute the facts shall be as found by the judge.[82]

22.026 S.91 of the Courts of Justice Act 1924 as re-enacted by s.48 of the Courts (Supplemental Provisions) Act 1961 expressly excludes from the competence of the District Court rule making authority the power to make rules in relation to the hearing by the High Court of cases stated. In the view of Walsh J in *Thompson v Curry*[83] "s.91 of the Act of 1924 also excludes from the competence of this authority the making of rules for the transmission of the case stated to the High Court or other matters subsequent in time to the receipt by the appellant of the case stated" which are matters reserved to the High Court rule-making authority by s.36 of the Courts of Justice Act 1924 as matters pertaining to "the hearing ... of cases stated by the District Court". Therefore the relevant procedural requirements relating to the transmission of the case stated are those contained in Order 62 of the Rules of the Superior Courts 1986 and rule 3 provides that the case may be transmitted to the Central Office of the High Court by the person or tribunal stating the same or by any party to the proceedings. Where a judge refers a question of law for determination without a request being made by one of the parties, the District Court clerk is required to give notice in writing to the parties informing them that the case stated has been prepared and signed and giving notice that it will be transmitted to the Central Office of the High Court immediately.[84]

By the Circuit Court

22.027 S.16 of the Courts of Justice Act 1947 provides that a Circuit Court judge may, if an application is made to him by any party to a matter[85] pending before him, refer any question of law arising in such matter by way of case stated to the Supreme Court and may adjourn the pronouncement of his judgment or order in the matter pending the determination of the case stated.

Finlay CJ commented in *Doyle v Hearne*[86] that this provision is "of fundamental importance to the relationship between [the Supreme Court] and the Circuit Court and to the nature of the assistance which [the Supreme Court] can

---

[81] Order 102, rule 12 of the District Court Rules 1997.
[82] Order 102, rule 12 of the District Court Rules 1997.
[83] [1970] IR 61, 65.
[84] Order 102, rule 14 of the District Court Rules 1997 and Form 102.5 Schedule D.
[85] Other than a re-hearing under s.196 of the Income Tax Act 1918.
[86] [1987] IR 601, 609, [1988] ILRM 318, 325.

give to judges of the Circuit Court on questions of law". The procedure provided for by s.16 differs in one important respect from that set out in s.52 of the Act of 1961 in relation to consultative cases stated from the District Court. A request for a case stated must be made by a party to the matter before the court and the Circuit Court judge has no power to decide to state a case on his own initiative.[87]

It would appear that the Supreme Court may consider any issue which may assist the Circuit Court judge in arriving at the correct legal decision, even if this point has not been argued and decided before the High Court. This point emerges from the decision of Finlay CJ in *Dublin Corporation v Ashley*[88] where he stated as follows:

> The purpose and effect of a consultative case stated by a Circuit Court judge to the Supreme Court is to enable him to obtain the advice and opinion of the Supreme Court so as to assist him in reaching a correct legal decision. Having regard to that purpose and the relationship which exists between the two courts, it would, in my view, be quite inappropriate for the Supreme Court, for any reason of procedure, to abstain from expressing a view on an issue of law which may determine the result of the case before the learned Circuit Court judge.[89]

Stage at Which Case May be Stated

22.028 The question of whether a judge may refer a question of law to the Supreme Court at a stage in the proceedings before all the evidence which might fall to be considered by him has been concluded is one which has been answered in the affirmative by the majority of the Supreme Court in *Doyle v Hearne*[90] but was for some time the subject matter of divergent judicial opinion. In *Corley v Gill*[91] the Supreme Court unanimously concluded that until a Circuit Court judge has heard or received all the evidence to be tendered in the matter before him, he has no jurisdiction to state a case to the Supreme Court pursuant to s.16. O'Higgins CJ considered the wording of s.16 which enabled a judge to "adjourn the pronouncement of his judgment or order" pending the determination of the case stated and said that in his view this form of wording was an intentional adoption of that used in s.38(3) of the Courts of Justice Act 1936 which made provision for the stating of a case by a High Court judge hearing circuit appeals to the Supreme Court. O'Higgins CJ was of the opinion that the express power to adjourn the pronouncement of the judgment conferred

---

[87] See *McKenna v Deery* [1998] 1 IR 62, 73.
[88] [1986] IR 781.
[89] *Ibid.* at 875. Quoted with approval by Denham J in *Director of Public Proseuctions v Best* [2000] 2 IR 17, [2000] 2 ILRM 1.
[90] [1987] IR 601, [1988] ILRM 318.
[91] [1975] IR 313.

by s.16 clearly indicated that it was only at the conclusion of the evidence brought before the Circuit Court judge that he had jurisdiction to refer a question of law pursuant to the section.[92]

22.029 In *Director of Public Prosecutions v Gannon*[93] in which the Supreme Court refused to entertain a case stated under s.16 by a Circuit Court judge on the hearing of an appeal from a conviction in the District Court, Finlay CJ relied, *inter alia,* on the fact that it had not been shown that all the evidence had been given by the time the case was stated. It is interesting to note that Finlay CJ in finding that the case stated had been incorrectly applied for, also placed reliance on the fact that the prosecution had applied for and been granted a case stated at a stage in the proceedings when a ruling in its favour was about to be made by the Circuit Court judge. He said that while s.16 did not define which party should seek a case stated, he was satisfied that "it was quite clear that it is intended to provide a shield to a party who has reason to anticipate or fear that a decision which is caused by an error in law is going to be made against him". The Chief Justice stated that the proper interpretation of s.16 of the 1947 Act is that all in effect that must be left in a case before a Circuit Court judge may state a case under that section is his judgment or order, and that it cannot be stated before all the evidence is concluded.

22.030 However, a change in attitude had occurred by the time the case of *Doyle v Hearne*[94] came before the Supreme Court the following year. A preliminary issue had arisen in *Doyle* as to the jurisdiction of a Circuit judge to state a case to the Supreme Court pursuant to s.16 where all the evidence which might fall to be considered by the judge had not been concluded at the stage when the case was stated. While Finlay CJ accepted that as a general proposition it was desirable that all the material facts should be found and the evidence concerning them heard before a question of law was raised for determination

---

[92] See also the comments of Henchy J in *State (Harkin) v O'Malley* [1978] IR 269, 285-286. In considering a similar question in relation to the interpretation of s.38(3) of the Courts of Justice Act 1936, the majority of the Supreme Court held in *Dolan v Corn Exchange* [1975] IR 315 that as a general principle a case should not be stated pursuant to that section before the moment at which all the evidence to be tendered at the hearing of the appeal has been heard or received by the High Court judge so that the latter's only remaining function is to pronounce judgment in the light of the answers to the questions posed in the case stated, although it was acknowledged that a judge retains an inherent jurisdiction to take such steps as he considers necessary to ensure that justice is done. This can be contrasted with the approach taken by Barron J in *Fernandes v Bermingham* High Court, 22 May 1985 where he stated that s.52(1) of the Courts (Supplemental Provisions) Act 1961, which enabled a district judge to state a case for the opinion of the High Court, "*prima facie* [gave] the District Court power to state a case at any stage of the proceedings".

[93] Supreme Court, 3 June 1986.

[94] [1987] IR 601, [1988] ILRM 318.

before the Supreme Court, he concluded that in the circumstances the court did have jurisdiction to hear the case stated. He said:

> It is clear that every court has an inherent jurisdiction in order to secure the due administration of justice to adjourn any part of the hearing of a case before it. For s.16 of the Act of 1947 to be interpreted as removing that jurisdiction once a case had been stated under the section would, in my view, require very clear and unambiguous terms. I do not so read s.16 as to contain those terms and I therefore conclude that I should approach the construction of it bearing in mind the purpose of the section and the procedure which by it the legislature clearly intended to create.[95]

McCarthy J agreed with the conclusion reached by the Chief Justice and said that he was content to leave it to the individual Circuit or High Court judge to determine the time, having heard evidence, at which he would state a case to the Supreme Court. However, Henchy and Griffin JJ in dissenting judgments, put forward the view that it was the intention of the legislature to make provision for the stating of a case pursuant to s.16 only when all the evidence had been heard. Henchy J was of the opinion that the wording of s.16 necessarily implied that it was only when that point of the decision had been reached that the case might be stated and that the only adjournment allowed by s.16 was one pending the pronouncement of the judgment or order. Griffin J agreed with this reasoning and stated that there were no compelling reasons in the instant case for departing from the previous decisions of the Supreme Court in relation to this issue.

22.031 A related question which had earlier been considered by the Supreme Court in *Tralee UDC v McSweeney*[96] is whether a case stated must be one which will allow a final determination of the matter before the court at the time the case is stated. Murnaghan J stated that the wording of s.16 seemed to him to allow a case to be stated on a point of law which did not necessarily determine the entire matter before the Circuit Court. He commented quite rightly that a point might arise for example in relation to the interpretation of a statute which if answered in one way might determine the matter before the court but if answered differently would still leave questions to be determined.

22.032 It was established in *People (Attorney General) v McGlynn*[97] that a Circuit Court judge has no jurisdiction to state a case pursuant to s.16 in the course of a criminal trial after the accused has been given in charge of the

---

[95] *Ibid.* at 607-608, 324.
[96] [1954] IR 233.
[97] [1967] IR 232.

jury.[98] The accused had been charged in the Circuit Court with criminal offences to which he had pleaded not guilty and had been given in charge of the jury. At the conclusion of the evidence, but before the jury's verdict had been given, the Circuit Court judge stated a case to the Supreme Court pursuant to s.16 and directed that the prosecution should bear the costs of the case stated. The Supreme Court rejected the argument that the provisions of s.16 were repugnant to the Constitution, Ó Dálaigh CJ placing reliance on the *dicta* of Walsh J in *State (Browne) v Feran*.[99] The Supreme Court also had to consider the question of the jurisdiction of the Circuit Court judge to state a case, or to make a costs order, in the matter before him. Ó Dálaigh CJ made reference to the inconvenience and "virtual impracticability" of adjourning a criminal trial *in media re* but stressed that the true question for determination by the court must be whether s.16 could be construed so as to permit such a course of action. In his opinion it could not, and he concluded that the power conferred by s.16 was not exercisable in respect of questions of law arising after an accused had been given in charge to the jury and before the verdict had been reached. Budd J stressed that the words of s.16 in their ordinary literal meaning conferred jurisdiction on a Circuit Court judge "to state a case on any question of law arising in a matter pending before him and him alone; and not in a matter pending before him and a jury". Fitzgerald J also agreed with the conclusion reached by the Chief Justice and said that it appeared to him that a criminal trial proceeding before a Circuit Court judge is not a matter pending before a Circuit Court judge within the meaning of s.16. In his opinion, s.16 was never intended to permit a Circuit Court judge to interrupt a criminal trial before a judge and jury as had been done in the case before him. In addition, Fitzgerald J expressed the view that the judge had no jurisdiction to make an order that the prosecution should pay the costs of the case stated; even if the latter had such jurisdiction, Fitzgerald J questioned the validity of such an order on the basis that the issue before the court had been raised by the accused and was one which the prosecution had rightly contended was ill-founded and not capable of being put forward by way of case stated.

22.033 In *People (Attorney General) v Doyle*[100] it was held by Ó Dálaigh CJ that a Circuit Court judge had no jurisdiction to enter on the trial of a count in an indictment that was undisposed of and that there was no matter pending before the court within the meaning of s.6 of the Criminal Justice Act 1951. Accordingly, it was held that the Circuit Court judge had no jurisdiction to state a case

---

[98]   See also *People (Director of Public Prosecutions) v McCormack* [1984] IR 177. However, where the accused has not been arraigned and put in charge of a jury the court may still state a case pursuant to s.16, see *Director of Public Prosecutions v E.F.* Supreme Court, 24 February 1994.

[99]   [1967] IR 147, 157.

[100]   (1966) 101 ILTR 136.

to the Supreme Court in relation to issues raised in the matter before the court. The basis for this decision was questioned subsequently by Henchy J in *State (Harkin) v O'Malley*,[101] in which he said that he was unable to accept the court's conclusion in *Doyle* that there was not "any matter pending" as is required for the operation of s.16 as being a good ground for holding that the case stated was not properly before the court. Therefore the reason given by the court for rejecting jurisdiction in *Doyle* was one which Henchy J found "unacceptable".[102]

Case Cannot be Stated Regarding Validity of Statute

22.034 It was held by the former Supreme Court in *Foyle Fisheries v Gallen*[103] that a Circuit Court judge may not state a case regarding the validity of a statute having regard to the provisions of the Constitution. It was held that the constitutional validity of legislation cannot be challenged in a consultative case stated in view of the provisions of Article 34.3.2° of the Constitution. In *Greany v Scully*[104] the Supreme Court held that a Circuit Court judge had jurisdiction to rule on the question of whether a statutory instrument was *ultra vires* and to refer that question to the Supreme Court by way of case stated. The Supreme Court applied its previous decision in *Listowel UDC v McDonagh* in reaching this conclusion although Henchy J expressed some doubts about whether he would have proceeded on the basis of this reasoning if the matter was *res integra*.

Circumstances in Which Case Should be Stated

22.035 The circumstances in which a Circuit Court judge should state a case have recently been considered by the Supreme Court in some detail in *McKenna v Deery*[105] in which it allowed an appeal by the notice party, the Director of Public Prosecutions, against a decision to grant, *inter alia*, an order of *mandamus* compelling the respondent to state a case for the opinion of the Supreme Court pursuant to s.16. Counsel for both sides referred to the test set out by Lardner J in his judgment in *McHale v Devally*[106] to the effect that there must be (a) an arguable case of some substance placed before the Circuit Court judge by the applicant for the case stated and (b) whether the interests of justice between the parties concerned require the stating of a case. Counsel for the Director of Public Prosecutions submitted that the test laid down by Lardner J in paragraph (a)

---

[101] [1978] IR 269.
[102] Although it should be noted that Henchy J stated that he nevertheless considered that the court in *Doyle* had had no jurisdiction to entertain the case stated on the basis on the principle laid down in *Corley v Gill*.
[103] [1960] Ir Jur Rep 35.
[104] [1981] ILRM 340.
[105] [1998] 1 IR 62. See Dignam [1999] 1 P & P 30.
[106] High Court (Lardner J) 29 May 1993.

did not set a sufficiently high threshold and argued that an applicant for a case stated must show not merely an arguable case but substantial grounds which mean more than probable or *prima facie* grounds and should be interpreted as amounting to real, weighty and solid grounds. Counsel for the applicant on the other hand submitted that the test laid down by Lardner J in *McHale v Devally* was the correct one and argued that in the instant case the Circuit Court judge had not addressed either of these criteria in declining the applicant's request for a case stated. In considering the effect of s.16, Lynch J stated that it provides for a consultative case stated and that the terms of the section do not qualify the discretion possessed by the Circuit Court judge to accede to or refuse an application. In addition, he said that it should be noted that a Circuit Court judge cannot state a case of his own motion pursuant to s. 16 and that an application must be made by at least one of the parties to the matter pending before him in order for him to state a case. He continued as follows:

> The discretion conferred on the Circuit Court judge by s.16 of the 1947 Act is in terms unlimited but all discretions conferred on courts must be exercised judicially. Nevertheless, consultative cases stated are primarily for the guidance and assistance of the judge who is asked to state such a case and if the judge is quite clear in his own mind as to the proper decision in the case, *prima facie* he is entitled to refuse the application and to go ahead and decide the case in accordance with his firm and positive views. The Superior Courts should be slow to interfere in such a case and should only do so if there is not merely an arguable case, but substantial, weighty and solid grounds calling for a decision by the Supreme Court on the question or questions of law the subject matter of the application by one of the parties to the proceedings.[107]

Lynch J concluded that the standard laid down by Lardner J in *McHale v Devally* at paragraph (a) of his test was "on the low side" and stated that a higher threshold was preferable. He said that as far as paragraph (b) of the test was concerned, it was conceded that if paragraph (a) was satisfied, then so would paragraph (b) and he said that for this reason he did not have to consider the latter paragraph. Lynch J was satisfied that in the case before him if the Circuit Court judge were to accede to the application for a case stated and were to set out the facts as decided by him as the facts of the case then the questions of law which were requested by the applicant would simply not arise and the whole case stated would be moot. In the circumstances the Supreme Court decided to reverse the order of the High Court and dismiss the application for judicial review.[108]

---

[107] [1998] 1 IR 62, 75.
[108] See also *Sports Arena Ltd v Devally* High Court (Kinlen J) 30 July 1998.

Form of Case Stated

22.036 In her judgment in *McGinley v Criminal Assets Bureau*[109] Denham J quoted with approval the principles relating to the form of a case stated to the High Court set out in *Emerson v Hearty*[110] and *Mitchelstown Co-Operative Society Ltd v Commissioner for Valuation*.[111] These include the point that the case stated should set out clearly the judge's findings of fact and any inferences or conclusions of fact which he drew from those findings and that what is required is a finding of facts and not a recital of the evidence. She commented that it was most unusual to append a transcript of the evidence as had been done in the case before her but she concluded that in all the circumstances it would not be appropriate to return the matter to the Circuit Court judge for restatement. Fennelly J stated that he agreed with Denham J on the form of the case stated and said that in the ordinary way the Circuit Court should make any findings of fact which are necessary to enable the Supreme Court to provide answers to the questions posed. He stressed that the Supreme Court cannot express any view on the facts and that in so far as the case stated left open some of the issues of fact or mixed issues of fact and law, he would refer to the material furnished with the case stated.

By the High Court

Nature of Case Stated Jurisdiction

22.037 S.38(3) of the Courts of Justice Act 1936 provides that a judge hearing an appeal under s.38 may refer any question of law arising in the appeal to the Supreme Court by way of case stated and "may adjourn the pronouncement of his judgment or order on such appeal pending the determination of such case stated". A number of relevant points about the nature of this case stated jurisdiction were made by Walsh J in the course of his dissenting judgment in *Dolan v Corn Exchange*.[112] First, it is a consultative case stated and therefore the judgment or order of the High Court may not be pronounced until after the determination by the Supreme Court of the case stated. Secondly, the case may be stated only on a question of law which actually arises in the appeal and may not be stated in respect of a hypothetical point of law or one which has not yet arisen. Thirdly, the judge must also be actually hearing the appeal when he states the case; if he has declined to hear an appeal because of lack of jurisdiction, he has no power to state a case to the Supreme Court.

---

[109] Supreme Court, 30 May 2001.
[110] [1946] NI 35, 36-37.
[111] [1989] IR 210, 212-213.
[112] [1975] IR 315, 320.

22.038 As Budd J pointed out in *Hanley v Martin*,[113] "an appeal from the Circuit Court does not lie to the High Court by reason of any inherent jurisdiction but exists only by reason of statute". The existence of a right of appeal is provided for in ss.37 and 38 of the Courts of Justice Act 1936 and as Budd J pointed out, to distinguish between the rights conferred by the sections it is necessary to refer to their wording. S.38 deals with appeals from the Circuit Court in cases not otherwise provided for and the case stated procedure in s.38(3) cannot be utilised if the appeal does not come within the scope of the section. S.37 of the Act of 1936 provides for an appeal to the High Court sitting in Dublin subject to the exceptions laid down by the legislation,[114] from a matter "at the hearing or for the determination of which no oral evidence was given". S.38 deals with appeals in cases not otherwise provided for and makes provision for an appeal from the Dublin Circuit Court to the High Court sitting in Dublin and in every other case to the High Court on Circuit. So, as the decision in *Hanley v Martin*[115] illustrates, the jurisdiction of the High Court to state a case under s.38(3) only arises where the appeal has been properly brought under s.38. The plaintiff had brought proceedings in the Circuit Court sitting in Galway and when the case came on for hearing the plaintiff did not call any evidence. The claim was dismissed and the plaintiff appealed to the High Court on Circuit sitting in Galway. Budd J, in holding that he had no jurisdiction to hear the appeal, pointed out that there had been no oral evidence given before the Circuit Court, and that the case therefore fell within the terms of s.37. Accordingly, any appeal to the High Court in the case had to be heard and determined by a judge of the High Court sitting in Dublin. Budd J therefore concluded that he had no jurisdiction to state a case since the appeal before him should have been taken and lay under s.37.

22.039 It is difficult to reconcile this decision with that of the Supreme Court in *H. Wigoder & Co. Ltd v Moran*[116] which concerned an appeal from a decision of the Circuit Court which was based on affidavit evidence only. Finlay P stated a case pursuant to s.38(3) which was considered by the Supreme Court despite the fact that both Henchy and Kenny JJ accepted that the case before the High Court was an appeal from the Circuit Court under s.37. Clearly on the wording of s.37, the High Court has no jurisdiction to state a case in this way and the decision in *Wigoder* must be of doubtful authority.

It was held by O'Sullivan CJ in *Cork County Council v Commissioners for Public Works*[117] that the subsection contemplates that the same judge who states a case to the Supreme Court should pronounce judgment after determination of

---

[113] [1961] Ir Jur Rep 34.
[114] See s.31 of the Courts of Justice Act 1936.
[115] [1961] Ir Jur Rep 34.
[116] [1977] IR 112.
[117] (1943) 77 ILTR 195.

the case stated. He said that s.38(3) "emphasized the individuality rather than the office of the judge" and the Supreme Court declined to entertain a case stated where the Circuit Court judge who had referred the questions of law to that court had died in the interim.

Stage in Proceedings at Which a Case May be Stated

22.040 The wording employed in s.38(3) that a judge "may adjourn the pronouncement of his judgment or order on such appeal pending the determination of such case stated" is identical to that used in s.16 of the Courts of Justice Act 1947 considered above and this raises the question of at what stage in the proceedings a judge may state a case for determination by the Supreme Court. This issue was considered in detail by the Supreme Court in *Dolan v Corn Exchange*,[118] where a High Court judge hearing a Circuit Appeal stated a case to the Supreme Court concerning an application for a new tenancy pursuant to the Landlord and Tenant Act 1931. When the matter was referred back to the High Court, the landlord sought leave to adduce additional evidence and a further case was stated for the opinion of the Supreme Court on the question of the jurisdiction of the High Court to permit such evidence to be heard. A majority of the Supreme Court held that it could not entertain a second case stated in the same appeal. However, the opportunity was taken by a number of the members of the court to examine the manner in which s.38(3) should operate. Henchy J was of the opinion that a judge has jurisdiction to state a case only at the stage of the hearing when the adjournment of the appeal is for the pronouncement of the judgment or order. He stated:

> The mandatory adjournment, once the case has been stated, means that the appeal passes out of the hands of the judge while the question of law is being decided in the Supreme Court; when the question has been answered there, the appeal returns to the judge for "the pronouncement of his judgment or order" – not, be it noted, for the hearing or the further hearing of the appeal. The word "pronouncement", by which is meant the oral delivery of the judicial determination of the appeal, was obviously chosen by the legislature to denote the stage of the hearing when the case may be stated, namely, when it appears to the judge that nothing remains to complete the hearing before him except the pronouncement of his decision.[119]

However Henchy J acknowledged that while a judge may only state a case under s.38(3) when the adjournment of the appeal is for the pronouncement of the judgment or order, it does not follow that his jurisdiction thereafter is necessarily limited to pronouncing the judgment or order. He continued that "[w]ithin

---

[118] [1975] IR 315.
[119] *Ibid.* at 325-326.

the confines of the rules of evidence and the principles of elementary fairness to both sides, the judge is entitled, where events render it necessary in the interests of justice, to hear further evidence or legal argument so as to ensure that his judgment or order will be soundly based in law and in fact".[120] In a dissenting judgment, Walsh J concluded that s.38(3) conferred jurisdiction on the High Court to state a case at any stage of the proceedings on appeal prior to the determination of the appeal. He stated as follows:

> Many important questions of law may arise in the course of an appeal – some at a very early stage.... I do not think it would be desirable that a judge on appeal should be compelled to hear the evidence before he has had a ruling upon the admissibility of it.... Likewise, a preliminary point taken at the commencement of the hearing of an appeal, if decided in a particular way may render unnecessary any further hearing of what could well be a long and protracted hearing.[121]

22.041 It is interesting to note that the approach adopted by the majority of the Supreme Court in *Doyle v Hearne*[122] in relation to the similar power contained in s.16 of the Courts of Justice Act 1947 for the stating of a case from the Circuit Court to the Supreme Court is in line with the view taken by Walsh J in *Dolan v Corn Exchange*. For this reason it is likely that the view of the majority in *Dolan* would not now be followed and that a case may be stated for determination by the Supreme Court at any stage in the proceedings before the High Court. This question has been considered more recently by O'Flaherty J in *O'Rourke v Revenue Commissioners*[123] where he stated as follows:

> While the case will be returned to the trial judge "for the pronouncement of his judgment or order" under s.38 of the Courts of Justice Act 1936, he is not required to act as perfunctorily as that phrase suggests but retains an inherent jurisdiction, within the rules of evidence and without unfairly affecting the rights of any party, to take such steps as he considers necessary to ensure that the issues outstanding will be decided according to the true facts and a correct version of the law. In that regard he has jurisdiction to hear further evidence or to make further findings of fact (*Dolan v Corn Exchange* [1975] IR 315) or, in my view, to amend the pleadings.

While this statement does not resolve the question fully, it would appear that O'Flaherty J is at least advocating a more flexible approach which involves a

---

[120]   *Ibid.* at 330.
[121]   *Ibid.* at 321.
[122]   [1987] IR 601, [1988] ILRM 318.
[123]   Supreme Court, 15 May 1996 at 2-3.

High Court judge possessing the inherent jurisdiction to hear further evidence should he deem this necessary.

22.042 The fundamental question which was considered by the Supreme Court in *Dolan v Corn Exchange*[124] is whether a High Court judge can entertain more than one case stated in the same appeal. This question had been considered by the Supreme Court in *Gavin Low v Field (No. 2)*[125] in which O'Sullivan CJ, for the majority, concluded that when the question determined by the Supreme Court is such that the answer to it decides the only question between the parties on the facts stated, that determination should be accepted by the judge stating the case. However, Black J dissented and held that no authority had been cited to show that the Circuit Court judge was precluded from allowing the case to be reopened in this manner. In his view the judge had seisin of the case right up to the time he gave his final decision and while "the result of having two successive cases stated may be inconvenient and undesirable" if that were so, the problem was one for the legislature to resolve. In *Dolan* Walsh J in his dissenting judgment distinguished *Gavin Low* and described it as at best only authority for the proposition that "if a case is stated upon the basis that it deals with all the points to be raised, a second case cannot be stated in the same proceeding". On the other hand, Henchy J, with whom Griffin J agreed, was satisfied that in confining a case stated under s.38(3) to the stage when the hearing has come to the point of adjudication, the legislature cannot have intended that there could be more than one case stated in any appeal. However, as noted above, Henchy J did not rule out the possibility that the interests of justice might require a judge stating a case to hear further evidence or argument to ensure that his judgment or order would be soundly based in fact and in law. This point, coupled with the decision of the majority of the Supreme Court in *Doyle v Hearne*[126] in relation to the same wording in s.16 of the Courts of Justice Act 1947 that a consultative case stated could be stated at any stage in the proceedings, certainly throws some doubt on the principle that a judge hearing an appeal under s.38 may never state a second case stated. While, as Collins and O'Reilly[127] point out, the decision in *Doyle*, although of persuasive authority, is not binding on the Supreme Court in construing s.38, it is likely that there are at least sufficient grounds to require a re-evaluation of the principles which the majority judgments in *Dolan* purport to lay down.

---

[124] [1975] IR 315.
[125] [1942] IR 610. The case was stated pursuant to s.22 of the Courts of Justice Act 1936 which was replaced by s.16 of the Courts of Justice Act 1947.
[126] [1987] IR 601, [1998] ILRM 318.
[127] Collins and O'Reilly, *Civil Proceedings and the State in Ireland: A Practitioner's Guide* (1990) at 30-31.

Procedure in Relation to Consultative Cases Stated from the Circuit Court and High Court

22.043 No specific provision is made in the Circuit Court Rules in relation to the stating of cases to the Supreme Court and the provisions set out in Order 59 of the Rules of the Superior Courts 1986 apply. Order 59, rule 2 sets out the procedure which shall apply to cases stated to the Supreme Court both by the Circuit Court and by the High Court. As soon as the case stated is signed and lodged with the County Registrar, the latter shall endorse on it the date of lodgment, the name of the party or parties who applied for the case stated, the name of the party who is to have carriage of it and the names and addresses of the parties' solicitors.[128] Within seven days of the lodgment, the county registrar is required to serve notice of it by registered post on every party who appeared in the matter and to transmit the original case stated to the Registrar of the Supreme Court.[129] The Registrar of the Supreme Court is then required to set the matter down for hearing. Order 59, rule 2(3) provides that any interested party shall be entitled to obtain one or more copies of the case stated from the Registrar of the Supreme Court upon payment of the prescribed fee. Order 59, rule 2(4) also provides that the party having carriage of the case stated shall within 21 days after the service of the notice of the signing and lodgment lodge five copies of the case stated and any documents referred to therein with the Registrar of the Supreme Court.

The procedure in relation to a case stated under s.38(3) is essentially the same at that set out above with the functions of the County Registrar being performed by the Registrar of the High Court.

OTHER FORMS OF CASE STATED

22.044 In addition to the general case stated procedure from the District Court to the High Court and from the Circuit Court and the High Court to the Supreme Court, various legislation makes provision for the stating of a case in particular contexts. These are considered in detail by Collins and O'Reilly in *Civil Proceedings and the State in Ireland*[130] and the most commonly used are merely referred to here. S.428 of the Income Tax Act 1967 provides for the stating of a case by Appeal Commissioners to the High Court and s.430 of the Act of 1967 provides that a case may be stated by a Circuit Court judge to the High Court where he has heard an appeal by way of a full rehearing. S.5 of the Valuation Act 1988 provides for the stating of a case by the Valuation Tribunal to the

---

[128] Order 59, rule 2(2).
[129] *Ibid.*
[130] Collins and O'Reilly, *Civil Proceedings and the State in Ireland: A Practitioner's Guide* (1990).

High Court and s.35 of the Arbitration Act 1954 provides that an arbitrator may state a case to the High Court. S.18 of the Malicious Injuries Act 1981 provides for a form of consultative case stated to the Supreme Court and by virtue of s.20 of the Adoption Act 1952 the Adoption Board may state a case to the High Court.

CHAPTER TWENTY THREE

THE RECOGNITION AND ENFORCEMENT
OF FOREIGN JUDGMENTS

INTRODUCTION

23.001 The Brussels Convention on Jurisdiction of Courts and Enforcement of Judgments in Civil and Commercial Matters and subsequent Accession Conventions introduced a new and simplified procedure for enforcing judgments obtained in contracting states which was given the force of law in this State by the Jurisdiction of Courts and Enforcement of Judgments (European Communities) Act 1988.[1] By virtue of the Convention on Jurisdiction and the Enforcement of Judgments in Civil and Commercial Matters 1988 (the Lugano Convention) the European Union and certain contracting states of the European Free Trade Association[2] entered into similar arrangements and this was ratified in the State by the Jurisdiction of Courts and Enforcement of Judgments Act 1993.[3] The provisions of Irish law relating to jurisdiction of courts and enforcement of judgments under these conventions were consolidated by the Jurisdiction of Courts and Enforcement of Judgments Act 1998[4] which also gave force of law to the Accession Convention on new EU member states to the Brussels Convention.[5]

The substantive principles relating to the interpretation of the Conventions are beyond the scope of this work and are well documented elsewhere,[6] so it will suffice to set out a brief outline of the main features of its operation. Article

---

[1] Note that from 1 March 2002, Council Regulation (EC) No. 44/2001 on Jurisdiction and the Recognition and Enforcement of Judgments in Civil and Commercial Matters will come into effect in the Member States of the EU excluding Denmark.

[2] Austria, Finland, Iceland, Norway, Sweden and Switzerland.

[3] This Act also gave force of the law of the Accession Convention of Spain and Portugal to the Brussels Convention.

[4] Brought into force by the Jurisdiction of Court and Enforcement of Judgments Act 1998 (Commencement) Order 1999 (SI No. 353 of 1999).

[5] Austria, Finland and Sweden.

[6] See Byrne, *The European Union and Lugano Conventions on Jurisdiction and the Enforcement of Judgments* (2nd ed., 1994); Moloney and Robinson eds., *The Brussels Convention on Jurisdiction and the Enforcement of Foreign Judgments* (ICEL, 1989); Stone, *Civil Jurisdiction and Judgments in Europe* (1998); Kennett, *The Enforcement of Judgments in Europe* (2000). See also the reports listed in s.6(2) of the Jurisdiction of Courts and Enforcement of Judgments Act 1998 which provides that judicial notice shall be taken of, in particular the Jenard Report.

1 of the Brussels Convention provides that the convention shall apply in civil and commercial matters[7] whatever the nature of the court or tribunal[8] but states that it shall not extend in particular to revenue, customs or administrative matters and shall not apply to the status or legal capacity of natural persons, rights in property arising out of a matrimonial relationship, wills and succession; bankruptcy, proceedings relating to the winding up of insolvent companies or other legal persons, judicial arrangements, compositions and analogous proceedings; social security or arbitration.[9] The *lis alibi pendens* rule set out in Article 21 of the Brussels Convention provides that where proceedings involving the same cause of action[10] and between the same parties are brought in the courts of different contracting states, any court other than the court first seised of the action shall, of its own motion, decline jurisdiction.

23.002 The fundamental jurisdictional principle upon which the Brussels Convention is founded is contained in Article 2 which provides that subject to the exceptions provided for elsewhere in the convention, "persons domiciled in a contracting state shall whatever their nationality, be sued in the courts of that state". It is also well established that articles constituting a derogation of this principle must be restrictively interpreted.[11] Therefore, the onus lies on a plaintiff who seeks to have his claim tried in the jurisdiction of a contracting state other than the one in which the defendant is domiciled to establish that such a claim unequivocally comes within the relevant exception.[12]

Article 52 paragraph 1 of the Convention provides that in order to determine whether a party is domiciled in the contracting state whose courts are seised of a matter, the court shall apply its own internal law. However, it was agreed that Ireland and the UK would include a definition of domicile in their enabling legislation which would be closer to its meaning in civil law. The Ninth Schedule, Part I of the Jurisdiction of Courts and Enforcement of Judgments Act 1998 therefore provides that an individual is domiciled in a state if, but only if, he is ordinarily resident there. In addition, Part III of the Schedule provides that a corporation or association has its seat in the State if, but only if, it was incorpo-

---

[7] In *Gourdian v Nadler* (Case 133/78) [1979] ECR 733, [1979] 3 CMLR 180 the Court of Justice stated that the concept of "civil and commercial matters" must be interpreted according to the general legal principles common to the law of the contracting states.

[8] See *Lufttransportunternehmen GmbH & Co. KG v Eurocontrol* (Case 29/76) [1976] ECR 1541, 1551.

[9] On the scope of the convention, see Byrne, *The European Union and Lugano Conventions on Jurisdiction and the Enforcement of Judgments* (2nd ed., 1994) at 14-35.

[10] See *The Nordglimt* [1988] QB 183, [1988] 2 WLR 338, [1988] 2 All ER 531.

[11] *Gannon v B. & I. Steampacket Co. Ltd* [1993] 2 IR 359, 368 *per* Denham J.

[12] *Handbridge Ltd v British Aerospace Communications Ltd* [1993] 3 IR 342, 358, [1994] 1 ILRM 39, 45 *per* Finlay CJ. See also *Hanley v Someport-Walon* [1995] 2 IR 132, 140, *Ewins v Carlton UK TV Ltd* [1997] 2 ILRM 223, 227; *Hunter v Gerald Duckworth & Co. Ltd* [2000] 1 IR 510, 516; *Bio-Medical Research Ltd v Delatex SA* [2000] 4 IR 307, 315, [2001] 2 ILRM 51, 60.

rated or formed under the law of the State or its central management and control is exercised in the State.[13] As Costello J commented in *Deutsche Bank AG v Murtagh*[14] in relation to the equivalent Schedule in the 1988 Act "this means that the traditional common law principles relating to the concept of domicile are not to be applied; instead the court will consider whether the defendant is 'ordinarily resident' in the State".

RECOGNITION AND ENFORCEMENT

Introduction

23.003 As Griffin J stated in *Rhatigan v Textiles y Confecciones Europeas SA*:[15] "The 1968 Convention is clearly designed to provide an expeditious and comparatively simple and uncomplicated method of enforcing a judgment of one contracting state against the judgment debtor in the contracting state in which he is domiciled, and in which his assets are, therefore, likely to be." The wording of Article 25 of the Convention illustrates that for the purposes of the Convention a judgment refers solely to judicial decisions actually given by a court or tribunal of a contracting state and "the decision must emanate from a judicial body of a contracting state deciding on its own authority on the issues between the parties".[16]

23.004 Article 31 of the Brussels Convention provides that a judgment given in a contracting state and enforceable in that state shall be enforced in another contracting state when, on the application of any interested party, the order for its enforcement has been issued there. The provisions of the Convention were interpreted by the European Court of Justice in *De Wolf v Cox BV*[17] as prescribing a mandatory procedure as regards enforcement. In other words, as the court ruled, a party who has obtained a judgment in his favour in a contracting state, being a judgment for which an enforcement order under Article 31 may issue in another contracting state, is prevented by the Convention from applying to a court in the latter state for a judgment against the other party in the same terms as the judgment delivered in the former state.[18] Finally, the comments of

---

[13] See further Gill, "Jurisdiction of Courts and the Brussels Convention" in *The Brussels Convention on Jurisdiction and the Enforcement of Foreign Judgments* (ICEL, 1989) at 12-19.

[14] [1995] 2 IR 122, 128, [1995] 1 ILRM 381, 385.

[15] [1990] 1 IR 126, 133, [1990] ILRM 825, 831.

[16] *Solo Kleinmotoren GmbH v Boch* (Case 414/92) [1994] ECR I-2237, 2255.

[17] (Case 42/76) [1976] ECR 1759.

[18] *Ibid.* at 1768.

the European Court of Justice in *Debaecker v Bouwman*[19] should be borne in mind; namely that although the Judgments Convention is intended to simplify the formalities governing the reciprocal recognition and enforcement of foreign judgments, that aim cannot be attained by undermining in any way the right to a fair hearing.

Recognition

23.005 In practice, in most cases recognition of a judgment is merely a precondition to enforcement, although in limited circumstances *e.g.* where a judgment is of a purely declaratory nature and incapable of enforcement,[20] the provisions of the Convention relating to recognition alone may be relevant. Order 42A,[21] rule 15 provides that the rules of procedure considered below shall apply to an application for recognition of a judgment as they shall apply to an application for enforcement, with the exception that an applicant will not be required to produce the documents referred to in Order 42A, rules 5(3) and (4).[22]

Article 26 of the Convention provides that a judgment given in a contracting state shall be recognised in the other contracting states without any special procedure being required. An interested party who raises the recognition of a judgment as the principal issue in a dispute may apply for a decision that the judgment be recognised and if the outcome of the proceedings in a court of a contracting state depends on the determination of an incidental question of recognition, that court shall have jurisdiction over that question. In addition, Article 29 provides that under no circumstances may a foreign judgment be reviewed as to its substance. However, it is the provisions of Articles 27 and 28 which set out the circumstances in which a judgment shall not be recognised, which have received the most judicial attention, as they are also grounds for resisting enforcement and these will be considered below.[23]

Enforcement

23.006 The procedure governing enforcement of such judgments provided for in s.7 of the Jurisdiction of Courts and Enforcement of Judgments Act 1998 is set out in general terms in Title III Section 2 of the Brussels Convention and more specifically in Order 42A of the Rules of the Superior Courts.[24]

---

[19] (Case 49/84) [1985] ECR 1779. See also *Isabelle Lancray SA v Peters and Sickert KG* (Case C-305/88) [1990] ECR I-2725, 2748.

[20] See Gill in *Legal Implications of 1992* (ICEL, 1988) at 86.

[21] Inserted by the Rules of the Superior Courts (No. 1) 1989 (SI No. 14 of 1989).

[22] Documents which establish that, according to the law of the state in which it has been given, the judgment is enforceable and has been served and where appropriate, a document showing that the applicant was in receipt of legal aid in the state in which the judgment was given.

[23] See paragraphs 23.015–23.018.

[24] Inserted by the Rules of the Superior Courts (No. 1) 1989 (SI No. 14 of 1989).

Applications for the Enforcement of Judgments

23.007 Applications for the enforcement of a foreign judgment in cases governed by the Brussels Convention and the Accession Conventions are made *ex parte* to the Master of the High Court.[25] The application is made by motion grounded upon affidavit specifying the protective measures (if any) requested by the applicant and the contents of the affidavit are specified in Order 42A, rules 5 and 6. The affidavit shall exhibit:[26]

(1) The judgment which is sought to be enforced;

(2) In the case of a default judgment, the original or a certified copy of the document which establishes that the party in default was served with the document(s) instituting the proceedings in sufficient time to enable him to arrange for his defence;

(3) Documents which establish that, according to the law of the state in which it has been given, the judgment is enforceable and has been served;

(4) Where appropriate, a document showing that the applicant was in receipt of legal aid in the state in which the judgment was given.[27]

The affidavit grounding the application for enforcement must also state:[28]

(1) Whether the judgment provides for the payment of a sum(s) of money;

(2) Whether interest is recoverable on the judgment in accordance with the law in the state in which the judgment was given and if so, the rate of interest, the date from which interest is recoverable and the date on which interest ceases to accrue.

(3) An address within the State for service of proceedings on the party making the application, and to the best of the deponent's knowledge and belief, the name and usual or last known address or place of business of the person against who judgment was given;

(4) The grounds on which the right to enforce the judgment is vested in the party making the application;

---

[25] S.7 of the Jurisdiction of Courts and Enforcement of Judgments Act 1998; Order 42A, rule 4 of the Rules of the Superior Courts and Article 32 of the Brussels Convention.

[26] Order 42A, rule 5.

[27] These requirements are based on the provisions of Articles 46 and 47 of the Convention. Note the revised requirements imposed by Articles 53 and 54 of Council Regulations (EC) No. 44/2001 which will come into force on 1 March 2002. A party seeking a declaration of enforceability will be required to produce a copy of the judgment which satisfies the conditions necessary to establish its authenticity and a certificate in the form set out in Annex V to the regulations.

[28] Order 42A, rule 6.

(5) As the case may require, that at the date of the application the judgment has not been satisfied, or not been fully satisfied, and the part in respect of which it remains unsatisfied.

23.008 If the party making the application for enforcement does not produce the documents referred to in rules 5 and 6, the Master of the High Court has a discretion to adjourn the application or to accept equivalent documents or to dispense with production of the said documents.[29] However, it should be noted that Article 33 of the Convention requires that the applicant "must give an address for service of process within the area of jurisdiction of the court applied to". While the article contains no provision stipulating the time at which an address for service should be given, it was held by the European Court of Justice in *Carron v Germany*[30] that this requirement must be observed "no later than the date on which the decision authorising enforcement is served". This finding was considered by the Supreme Court in *Rhatigan v Textiles y Confecciones Europeas SA*[31] in which the court held that it was not a requirement of Article 33 that the applicant's address for service within the jurisdiction be stated in the order of the Master authorising enforcement. In the view of the court the evidence established that the address had been given at the time the application was made to the Master and this satisfied the requirements of Article 33.

Decision on the Application

23.009 Article 34 of the Convention provides that the decision on an application for enforcement shall be given "without delay" and expressly states that the party against whom enforcement is sought shall not be entitled to make any submissions at this stage of the proceedings.[32] It also provides that an application may be refused only for one of the reasons specified in Articles 27 and 28 of the Convention, so if the requirements of Order 42A, rules 5 and 6 have been complied with, the Master may only refuse the application for the enforcement order on these grounds.[33] It should also be noted that both Articles 29 and 34 provide that under no circumstances may a foreign judgment be reviewed as to its substance. Article 35 also requires that the decision on the enforcement application shall "without delay" be brought to the notice of the applicant.[34] The order granting leave to enforce a judgment shall state the period within which

---

[29] Order 42A, rule 7.
[30] (Case 198/85) [1986] ECR 2437, [1987] 1 CMLR 838.
[31] [1990] 1 IR 126, [1990] ILRM 825.
[32] *Firma P. v Firma K.* (Case 178/83) [1984] ECR 3033, 3045-3046, [1985] 2 CMLR 271, 276-277 *per* Advocate General Darmon.
[33] These are considered in detail under the heading "Recognition", see *infra*.
[34] This need for expedition is referred to by Griffin J in *Rhatigan v Textiles y Confecciones Europeas SA* [1990] 1 IR 126, 134, [1990] ILRM 825, 832.

an appeal may be made against the order for enforcement,[35] which is within one month of service of the order, or if the party is domiciled in another contracting state, within two months.[36] The order granting leave shall also contain a notification that execution of the judgment will not issue until after the expiration of the period within which an appeal may be brought and shall specify the protective measures, if any granted by the Master pending execution.[37]

Service of the Order

23.010 Notice of an order granting leave to enforce a judgment shall be served together with the order on the defendant by delivering it to him personally or in such other manner as the Master may direct.[38] In *Barnaby (London) Ltd v Mullen,*[39] the Master's order and the enforcement notice were served on the defendant by handing two copies and showing the originals of each document to the defendant's wife at the family home. In refusing the defendant's application for a declaration that he had not been validly served with the Master's order, Kinlen J held that he was satisfied that the court has a discretion to deem service good under its own rules and concluded that in the circumstances, the service effected was sufficient. However, the Supreme Court allowed the defendant's appeal against the decision of the High Court that the Master's order was valid and effective and complied with the requirements of Title III of the Brussels Convention. Murphy J stated that the procedure "envisages and requires the service of the order personally or in any other manner prescribed by the Master so as to fix the defendant with knowledge of the order and also the date on which he is deemed to have that knowledge". This purpose could not be effected by an inference, however strong it might be, that the party in question did become aware after a short but undefined interval of documents inadequately or improperly served. Furthermore, it seemed to him that it would not be feasible for the court to "deem good" a form of service which did not comply with that prescribed by the Master. Hamilton CJ agreed and added that where personal service became impracticable, the correct solution was to apply to the Master for a variation of his order to permit substituted service.

---

[35] Order 42A, rule 8.

[36] Order 42A, rule 11 and Article 36.

[37] Order 42A, rule 8.

[38] Order 42A, rule 9. In *Paper Properties Ltd v Power Corporation* [1996] 1 ILRM 475 Carroll J held that service of an enforcement notice was sufficient where the party was served in circumstances which did not comply precisely with the Master's order. As to service by fax, the first named defendant was served at its Dublin office (which according to the fax directory was the only fax number shown) rather than at its registered office.

[39] [1996] 2 ILRM 24 (HC), [1997] 2 ILRM 341 (SC).

Service of the Order out of the Jurisdiction

23.011 The notice and order may be served out of the jurisdiction without leave and the provisions of Order 11A of the Rules of the Superior Courts 1986 apply as if the notice were an originating summons. Order 42A, rule 10 provides that the notice of enforcement shall state:

(a) full particulars of the judgment declared to be enforceable and the order for enforcement;

(b) the name of the party making the application and his address for service within the State;

(c) the protective measures, if any, granted in respect of the property of the person against whom judgment was given;

(d) the right of the person against whom judgment was given to appeal to the High Court against the order for enforcement, and

(e) the period within which an appeal against the order for enforcement may be made.

The provisions of rule 10 were considered by Carroll J in *Paper Properties Ltd v Power Corporation*[40] in which the plaintiff sought to enforce a judgment of the English Court of Appeal against the first named defendant in this jurisdiction. This defendant argued that the notice did not contain full particulars of the order of the Court of Appeal, whereas the plaintiff contended that those parts of the judgment relevant for enforcement were cited. Carroll J found for the plaintiff on this point, stating that "it seems to me that full particulars of the part of the judgment sought to be enforced is what is required, not a lot of detail which has no relevance".[41] In addition, Carroll J held that a letter sent for the purpose of notifying a party of protective measures did not constitute a formal enforcement notice for the purposes of Order 42A, rules 9 and 10.

Appeal to the High Court

23.012 If enforcement is authorised by the Master, the party against whom enforcement is sought may appeal to the High Court[42] against the order within one month of service thereof or within two months if that party is domiciled in another contracting state.[43] Article 36, which makes provision for such appeals has been interpreted by the European Court of Justice as excluding an appeal by an interested third party, even where such a procedure is available to third par-

---

[40] [1996] 1 ILRM 475.
[41] *Ibid.* at 480.
[42] Article 37 of the Convention.
[43] Order 42A, rule 11 and Article 36 of the Convention.

ties under the domestic law of the state in which the enforcement order is granted.[44] In addition, the Court of Justice has held that Article 36 must be interpreted as meaning that a party who has not appealed against an enforcement order in accordance with the timeframe laid down by the article, is precluded, at the stage of execution of the judgment, from relying on a valid ground which he could have pleaded in an appeal if it had been brought initially.[45]

Appeals to the High Court shall be brought by notice of motion which shall be served on the party in whose favour the enforcement notice was granted.[46] Order 42A, rule 13 provides that execution shall not issue on a judgment declared enforceable until after the period specified in accordance with rule 11 or such extended period as may have been granted by the court.[47] If an appeal is brought to the High Court under rule 11, execution shall not issue until after such appeal is determined and this extends to any further appeal to the Supreme Court on a point of law. An affidavit of service of the order granting leave to enforce the judgment and of any order made by the Master, the High Court or the Supreme Court in relation to the judgment must be produced to the appropriate officer if execution is sought.

23.013 If the application for enforcement of the judgment is refused, the applicant may appeal to the High Court within five weeks of the perfection of the Master's order.[48] The appeal must be brought by way of notice of motion grounded on an affidavit establishing that the party against whom enforcement is sought has been notified of the appeal and the date set for it in sufficient time to enable him to arrange for his defence. Article 40 of the Convention provides that "the party against whom enforcement is sought shall be summoned to appear before the appropriate court" in such cases and as the decision of the European Court of Justice in *Firma P. v Firma K.* [49] illustrates, this provision is strictly applied. It was held that the court hearing an appeal by the party seeking enforcement is required to hear the party against whom enforcement is sought even though the application for enforcement was dismissed simply on the basis of a technicality. In addition, Article 40 goes on to provide that if the party against whom enforcement is sought fails to appear at the hearing, the service provisions of Article 20, paragraphs 2 and 3 must be complied with even where the judgment debtor is not domiciled in any of the contracting states.

---

[44] *Deutsche Genossenschaftsbank v SA Brasserie du Pecheur* (Case 148/84) [1985] ECR 1981, [1986] 2 CMLR 496.

[45] *Hoffman v Krieg* (Case 145/86) [1988] ECR 645.

[46] Order 42A, rule 11 and Articles 37(2) and Article 41 of the Convention.

[47] Article 39 of the Convention provides that "during the time specified for an appeal pursuant to Article 36 and until any such appeal has been determined, no measures of enforcement may be taken other than protective measures taken against the property of the party against whom enforcement is sought."

[48] Order 42A, rule. 12.

[49] (Case 278/83) [1984] ECR 3033, [1985] 2 CMLR 271.

Appeal to the Supreme Court

23.014 Where the High Court makes a finding on an appeal against a decision either to authorise or refuse enforcement, either the applicant or the respondent may appeal this to the Supreme Court on a point of law.[50] However, an appeal by an interested third party is precluded by the interpretation placed on Article 37(2) by the European Court of Justice,[51] even where the domestic law of the State in which enforcement is sought confers such a right.

Such an appeal is brought by notice of appeal in accordance with the provisions of Order 58, rule 1 and must be served within five weeks of the perfection of the order of the High Court. It is the duty of the Registrar of the Supreme Court to apply to the appropriate Registrar of the High Court for a signed copy of the note made by the High Court judge of any question of law raised before him and of the facts and evidence relating to it and of his decision. The Supreme Court Registrar must also apply to the appropriate High Court Registrar for transmission to him of a file of all the documents and papers relating to the case.[52] Finally rule 14(3) provides that subject to the above provisions, Order 58 shall, so far as practicable, apply to an appeal on a point of law under the Convention.

Defences to Enforcement and Recognition

23.015 Article 27(1) provides for a situation where recognition is "contrary to public policy in the state in which recognition is sought".[53] It has been suggested that the public policy clause "ought to operate only in exceptional circumstances"[54] and in the view of the convention requirement that under no circumstances may a foreign judgment be reviewed as to its substance,[55] this provision cannot be invoked to facilitate a review of the merits of a judgment.

Article 27(2) deals with cases where judgment has been obtained in default of appearance[56] and provides that such judgments shall not be recognised if a

---

[50] Order 42A, rule 14.

[51] *Sonntag v Waidmann* (Case C-172/91) [1993] ECR 1-1963.

[52] Order 42, rule 14(2).

[53] See *Westpac Banking Corporation v Dempsey* [1993] 3 IR 331, 340 where the argument based on public policy was raised but rejected.

[54] Jenard Report at 44. See also *Hoffmann v Krieg* (Case 145/86) [1988] ECR 645, 668. Note that Article 34(1) of Council Regulation (EC) No. 44/2001, which comes into force on 1 March 2002, provides that a judgment shall not be recognised "if such recognition is *manifestly* contrary to public policy in the state in which recognition is sought" (emphasis added).

[55] See Articles 29 and 34.

[56] Article 27(2) cannot be relied upon where the defendant is deemed to have appeared. It was held by the European Court of Justice in *Sonntag v Waidmann* (Case C-172/91) [1993] ECR I-1963, 2001-2002 that a defendant is deemed to have appeared for the purposes of Article 27(2) of the Convention where, in connection with a claim for compensation joined to criminal proceedings, he answered at the trial, through counsel

defendant was not duly served with the documents which instituted the proceedings or with an equivalent document in sufficient time to arrange for his defence.[57] According to the European Court of Justice in its judgment in *Klomps v Michel*,[58] the purpose of Article 27(2) is to ensure that a judgment is not recognised or enforced under the Convention if the defendant has not had an opportunity of defending himself before the court first seised of the action. It was held by the European Court of Justice in *Hendrikman v Magenta Druck v Verlag GmbH*[59] that Article 27(2) applies where the defendant was not properly represented during the initial proceedings, even though the judgment was not formally given in default of appearance, in circumstances where someone purported to represent the defendant but in fact acted without his authority.

23.016 As the court observed in *Klomps v Michel*, Article 27(2) lays down two conditions; the first of which, that service be duly effected,[60] entails a decision based on the legislation of the state in which the judgment was given and on the conventions binding that state in relation to service and the second, which concerns the time necessary to enable the defendant to arrange for his defence, involves appraisals of a factual nature.[61] This point was reiterated by the European Court of Justice in *Isabelle Lancray SA v Peters and Sickert KG*,[62] where it was stated that the requirements of due service and service in sufficient time constitute two separate and concurrent safeguards for a defendant who fails to appear. In terms of what will constitute adequate time to arrange for a defence, it was held by O'Sullivan J in *Societe Lacoste SA v Keely Group Ltd*[63] that service of the relevant documents had been established and that nine weeks was sufficient time to enable the defendant to arrange for his defence.

23.017 A further point clarified by the European Court of Justice in *Klomps*, is

---

of his own choice, to the criminal charges but did not express a view on the civil claim, on which oral argument was also submitted in the presence of his counsel.

[57] Note that Article 34(2) of Council Regulation (EC) No. 44/2001 adds the words "unless the defendant failed to commence proceedings to challenge the judgment when it was possible to do so".

[58] (Case 166/80) [1981] ECR 1593. See also *Minalmet GmbH v Brandeis Ltd* (Case C-123/91) [1992] ECR I-5661, 5678; *Sonntag v Waidmann* (Case C-172/91) [1993] ECR 1963.

[59] (Case C-78/95) [1996] ECR I-4943.

[60] Note that it was held by the European Court of Justice in *Minalmet GmbH v Brandeis Ltd* (Case C-123/91) [1992] ECR I-5661, 5679 that Article 27(2) must be interpreted as precluding a judgment given in default of appearance in one contracting state from being recognised in another contracting state where the defendant was not duly served with the document which instituted the proceedings, even if he subsequently became aware of the judgment which was given and did not avail himself of the legal remedies provided for in the State where the judgment was delivered.

[61] *Ibid.* at 1607.

[62] (Case C-305/88) [1991] ECR I-2725.

[63] [1999] 3 IR 534, [1999] 1 ILRM 510.

that even if the court in which the judgment was given has held, in subsequent adversary proceedings, that service was duly effected, Article 27(2) still requires the court in which enforcement was sought to examine whether service was effected in sufficient time to enable the defendant to arrange for his defence. Subsequently in *Pendy Plastic Products BV v Pluspunkt Handelgesellschaft mbH*,[64] the court ruled that the court of the state in which enforcement is sought may, if it considers that the conditions laid down in Article 27(2) are fulfilled, refuse to grant recognition and enforcement of a judgment even though the court of the state in which the judgment was given regarded it as proven that the defendant had an opportunity to receive service of the document instituting the proceedings in sufficient time to enable him to make arrangements for his defence. Further consideration was given to the concept of service in sufficient time by the Court of Justice in *Debaecker v Bouwman*,[65] in which the court held that regard must be had to facts which, although occurring after service was effected, may nonetheless have had the consequence that service did not in fact enable the defendant to arrange for his defence. The court concluded that the fact the plaintiff was apprised of the defendant's new address after service was effected and the fact that the defendant was responsible for the failure of the duly served document to reach him are matters which the court in which enforcement was sought might take into account in assessing whether service was effected in sufficient time.

23.018 Article 27(3) provides that a judgment shall not be recognised if it is irreconcilable with a judgment given in a dispute between the same parties in the state in which recognition is sought. "Irreconcilable" in this context has been interpreted to mean having legal consequences which are mutually exclusive.[66] So, in *Hoffman v Krieg*[67] the European Court of Justice held that a foreign judgment ordering a person to make maintenance payments to his spouse was irreconcilable within the meaning of Article 27(3) with a subsequent national judgment granting a divorce. In addition, it was held by Murphy J in *Tassan Din v Banco Ambrosiano SPA*[68] that a decision of the Appeal Court of Milan should not be recognised, *inter alia*, as it was irreconcilable with the judgment given by the Supreme Court in this jurisdiction.

Article 27(5) provides that a judgment shall not be recognised if it is irreconcilable with an earlier judgment given in a non-contracting state involving the same cause of action and between the same parties provided that this latter judgment fulfils the conditions necessary for its recognition in the State addressed.

---

[64] (Case 228/81) [1982] ECR 2723.
[65] (Case 49/84) [1985] ECR 1779.
[66] *Hoffman v Krieg* (Case 145/86) [1988] ECR 645, 668.
[67] (Case 145/86) [1988] ECR 645.
[68] [1991] 1 IR 569.

Article 28 paragraph (1) sets out the only circumstances in which review of jurisdiction of the court in which the judgment was given may be carried out. A judgment may not be recognised on jurisdictional grounds if it conflicts with the provisions of ss. 3, 4 or 5 of Title II which deal with rules on insurance, consumer contracts and exclusive jurisdiction under Article 16 respectively or in a case provided for in Article 59. Article 28 goes on to provide that in any examination of the grounds of jurisdiction, the court shall be bound by the findings of fact on which the court of the state in which the judgment was given based its jurisdiction. In addition, Article 28 paragraph (3) prevents a court invoking public policy as a basis for applying different jurisdictional rules.

Miscellaneous Provisions Relating to Enforcement

23.019 Order 42A, rule 16 provides that the rules set out above in relation to enforcement shall apply as appropriate to applications for the enforcement of authentic instruments and court settlements[69] except that the application for enforcement shall be made in the first instance to the High Court and not to the Master.[70]

Where any judgment, order or document which is required for the purposes of Order 42A is not in one of the official languages of the State, a translation certified by a person competent and qualified for this purpose in one of the contracting states shall be admissible and the competence and qualifications of the translator shall be verified by affidavit.[71]

S.14 of the Jurisdiction of Courts and Enforcement of Judgments Act 1998 and Order 42A, rules 18 and 19 relate to the provision of documents by the courts in the State to an interested party seeking recognition and enforcement of a judgment given in this jurisdiction in another contracting state. Rule 18 provides that the Registrar of the High Court or the Supreme Court, as appropriate, shall at the request of an interested party give to him a copy of the order and the written judgment of the court duly authenticated.[72] In addition, rule 19 provides that an application for a certificate signed by the appropriate registrar shall be made on affidavit which shall:

---

[69] See Article 50 and 51 of the Convention.

[70] Hogan notes in "Rules of the Superior Courts (No. 1) 1989" in *The Brussels Convention on Jurisdiction and the Enforcement of Foreign Judgments* Moloney and Robinson eds. (ICEL, 1989) at 75 that the court settlements referred to in rule 16 have no exact equivalent in this jurisdiction; they are a form of arrangement designed to put an end to litigation and are enforceable without a court order. He further points out that a consent order made in a common law jurisdiction would be regarded as a judgment for the purposes of Article 25 of the Convention and that therefore an application to enforce such an order must be made in the first instance to the Master and not to the High Court.

[71] Order 42A, rule 17. See also s.12(3) of the Jurisdiction of Courts and Enforcement of Judgments Act 1998.

[72] See also s.14(a) of the Act of 1998.

(a) state the nature of the proceedings,

(b) state the particular provision(s) of the 1968 Convention by which the court assumed jurisdiction,

(c) state the date on which time for the lodging of an appeal against the judgment will expire or if it has expired, the date on which it expired,

(d) state whether notice of appeal against, or in any case where the defendant does not appear, a notice to set aside, the judgment has been entered,

(e) state whether the judgment is for the payment of a sum of money, the rate of interest, if any, payable on the sum and the date from which interest is payable,

(f) include annexed thereto two certified copies of the originating summons or other process by which the proceedings were commenced together with one copy of all the proceedings.

PROVISIONAL AND PROTECTIVE MEASURES

Introduction

23.020 Article 24 of the Brussels Convention provides that application may be made to the courts of a contracting state for such provisional, including protective measures "as may be available under the law of that State" even if the courts of another contracting state have jurisdiction as to the substance of the matter.[73] The expression "provisional, including protective measures" must be understood in this context as referring to "measures which, in matters within the scope of the Convention, are intended to preserve a factual or legal situation so as to safeguard rights the recognition of which is sought elsewhere from the court having jurisdiction as to the substance of the matter".[74]

23.021 As the European Court of Justice commented in *Denilauler v Couchet Frères*,[75] the courts of the place where the assets subject to the measures sought are located are those best able to assess the circumstances which may lead to the grant or refusal of the measures sought or to the laying down of procedures and conditions which the plaintiff must observe in order to guarantee the "provisional and protective character" of the measures ordered. However, Article 24 only applies where the substantive dispute falls within the scope of the Convention and it cannot be relied upon "to bring within the scope of the Conven-

---

[73] A similar provision is contained in Article 31 of Council Regulation (EC) No. 44/2001, which comes into force on 1 March 2002.
[74] *Reichert v Dresdner Bank AG (No. 2)* (Case C-261/90) [1992] ECR I-2149, 2184.
[75] (Case 125/79) [1980] ECR 1553.

tion provisional or protective measures relating to matters which are excluded therefrom".[76] So, the inclusion of provisional or protective measures in the scope of the Convention is determined not by their own nature but by the nature of the rights which they serve to protect.[77] In addition, as the European Court of Justice pointed out in *Van Uden Maritime BV v Kommanditgesellschaft in Firma Deco-Line*[78] the grant of provisional measures is conditional on the existence of "a real connecting link between the subject matter of the measures sought and the territorial jurisdiction of the contracting state of the court before which those measures are sought".

In this jurisdiction, by virtue of s.13 of the Jurisdiction of Courts and Enforcement of Judgments Act 1998, power to grant provisional, including protective measures[79] is given to the High Court in proceedings that, apart from the 1998 Act, are within its jurisdiction, if they have been or are to be commenced in another contracting state and the subject matter of the proceedings is within the scope of Article 1 of the 1968 Convention, whether or not the Convention has effect in relation to the proceedings.

Provisional, Including Protective Measures in Cases where a Cause of Action is Pending or About to be Commenced

23.022 By virtue of s.13(1) of the Act of 1998, the courts in this jurisdiction have power to grant provisional, including protective measures where the courts of another contracting state have jurisdiction to hear a claim which has been commenced or is about to be commenced under the Convention, even where the plaintiff has no independent cause of action within the jurisdiction.[80] S.13(2) provides that the High Court may refuse to grant the measures sought on an application brought pursuant to subs.(1) if in its opinion, the fact that, apart from that section, the courts does not have jurisdiction in relation to the subject matter of the proceedings makes it inexpedient for it to grant the measures.

23.023 A similar provision in s.25(2) of the English Civil Jurisdiction and Judgments Act 1982 has recently been fairly broadly interpreted in *Credit Suisse*

---

[76] *De Cavel v De Cavel* (Case 143/78) [1979] ECR 1055, 1067.

[77] *De Cavel v De Cavel* (Case 143/78) [1979] ECR 1055, 1066. See also *Reichert v Dresdner Bank AG (No. 2)* (Case C-261/90) [1992] ECR I-2149.

[78] (Case C-391/95) [1998] ECR I-7091, 7138.

[79] As Hogan and O'Reilly point out in *Guide to Changes in the Rules of the Superior Courts 1986 as a Consequence of the Coming into Operation of the Jurisdiction of Courts and Enforcement of Judgments (European Communities) Act 1988* (1989) at 16, a provisional measure implies any judicial order which by its nature is not final whereas a protective measure is one which seeks to conserve or freeze the defendant's assets. A protective measure will generally be provisional in nature but this is not necessarily so.

[80] This effectively reversed the finding of the Supreme Court in *Caudron v Air Zaire* [1985] IR 716, [1986] ILRM 10.

Fides Trust SA v Cuoghi.[81] Millett LJ accepted that an ancillary jurisdiction ought to be exercised with caution and that care should be taken not to make orders which conflict with those of the court seised of the substantive proceedings. However, he did not accept that interim relief should be limited to that which would be available in the court trying the substantive dispute. Although the worldwide Mareva injunction sought would not have been available in Switzerland, where the substantive action had been initiated, Millett LJ was satisfied that there was no danger of conflicting jurisdiction and concluded that it was not inexpedient to grant the protective measures sought. Bingham LJ reached the same conclusion and made the following useful comments about the relationship between the substantive proceedings and applications for protective measures:

> It would be unwise to attempt to list all of the considerations which might be held to make the grant of relief under s.25 inexpedient or expedient, whether on a municipal or a worldwide basis. But it would obviously weigh heavily, probably conclusively, against the grant of interim relief if such grant would obstruct or hamper the management of the case by the court seized of the substantive proceedings ("the primary court") or give rise to a risk of conflicting, inconsistent or overlapping orders in other courts. It may weigh against the grant of relief by this court that the primary court could have granted such relief and has not done so, particularly if the primary court has been asked to grant such relief and declined. On the other hand, it may be thought to weigh in favour of granting such relief that a defendant is present in this country and so liable to effective enforcement of an order made *in personam*, always provided that by granting such relief this court does not tread on the toes of the primary court or any other court involved in the case. On any application under s.25 this court must recognise that its role is subordinate to and must be supportive of that of the primary court.[82]

23.024 This reasoning was considered by the Court of Appeal in *Refco Inc. v Eastern Trading Co.*[83] where protective measures were refused in circumstances where the court was satisfied that no Mareva relief would have been granted even if the substantive proceedings had been brought in England. Morritt LJ advocated first considering whether the facts would warrant the interim relief sought being granted if the substantive proceedings had been brought within the jurisdiction and if the answer to that question was in the affirmative, then considering whether the fact that the court had no jurisdiction apart from the section made it inexpedient to grant the relief sought.

---

[81] [1998] QB 818, [1997] 3 WLR 871, [1997] 3 All ER 724.
[82] *Ibid.* at 831-832, 882, 734.
[83] [1999] 1 Lloyd's Rep 159.

The procedure relating to applications for provisional, including protective measures brought pursuant to s.13(1), in other words in cases where an action is either pending or about to be instituted in another contracting state,[84] is set out in Order 42A, rule 1 of which provides that such an application must be made *ex parte* to the High Court. Order 42A, rule 2 provides that the application must be grounded on an affidavit specifying the measures sought pursuant to s.13(1), which in addition to setting out the information and exhibiting the documents necessary to ground the application, must:

(a) state the nature of the proceedings or intended proceedings and exhibit a certified true copy of the document(s) used or proposed to be used to institute the proceedings;

(b) specify the contracting state in which the proceedings have been commenced or are to be commenced;

(c) state the particular provision(s) of the Convention by which the court of the contracting state has assumed jurisdiction, or in the case of intended proceedings, would be entitled to assume jurisdiction.

In addition, Order 42A, rule 3 provides that the High Court may make an interim order on an *ex parte* basis and that every application for an interlocutory order pursuant to s.13(1) shall be brought by notice of motion.

On the basis that s.13(1) creates a separate and distinct cause of action enabling the High Court to grant protective measures in aid of proceedings pending or about to the commenced in the courts of other contracting states, Order 1, rule 6 seems to require that such proceedings be commenced by plenary summons.[85]

Provisional, Including Protective Measures in Cases where an Applicant is Seeking to Enforce a Final Judgment Already Obtained

23.025 Article 39 of the Convention contemplates the granting of protective measures where an appeal has been taken against enforcement and provided that "the decision authorizing enforcement shall carry with it the power to proceed to any such protective measures". In so doing, it seeks to balance the inter-

---

[84] As distinct from where protective measures are sought as part of an application for enforcement of a judgment already obtained in a contracting state which will be considered below.

[85] As Hogan notes in "Protective Measures and the Judgments Convention - A Practical Guide" in *The Brussels Convention on Jurisdiction and the Enforcement of Foreign Judgments* (ICEL, 1989) at 81, there is no difficulty in serving the proceedings out of the jurisdiction under Order 11A, rule 1; there is no breach of the *lis alibi pendens* rule as the cause of action in this jurisdiction is different from the substantive cause of action in the other contracting states.

ests of both parties by giving a plaintiff the right to protective measures while at the same time ensuring that no measures of enforcement, other than such protective measures, may be taken until the appeal has been determined. S.13(3) of the Act of 1998 provides that subject to Article 39, an application to the Master of the High Court for an enforcement order may include an application for protective measures which "the High Court has power to grant in proceedings that, apart from this Act, are within its jurisdiction". S.13(4) goes on to provide that where an enforcement order is made, the Master *shall* grant any protective measures that are sought in the application for the enforcement order (emphasis added).[86] This wording illustrates the crucial distinction between an application for protective measures where an action is either pending or about to be instituted in another contracting state, which will be dealt with by the High Court on a purely discretionary basis, and an application for such measures on foot of an enforcement order where the Master is obliged to grant the relief sought.[87] The mandatory nature of the jurisdiction to grant protective measures when the application is made in the context of an enforcement application can be seen from the judgment of the European Court of Justice in *Cappelloni v Pelkmans*[88] where it was held that by virtue of Article 39, a party who has applied for and obtained authorisation for enforcement may[89] proceed directly with protective measures against the property of the party against whom enforcement is sought and is under no obligation to obtain specific authorisation. In addition, the court made it clear that a party who has proceeded with protective measures is under no obligation to obtain any confimatory judgment required by the national law of the court in question. The principle laid down in *Cappelloni* was applied by Carroll J in *Elwyn (Cottons) Ltd v Pearle Designs Ltd*[90] in which the plaintiff in its application for enforcement, sought protective measures to prevent the defendant reducing its assets below a certain level pending enforcement of a judgment. The Master granted the order for enforcement but refused to grant the protective measures sought. Carroll J held that the Master was not entitled to refuse the protective measures; if he was satisfied that this was relief which the High Court had power to grant in proceedings within its jurisdiction, then once the enforcement order was made, it should have included a provision including the protective measures applied for. As regards the appropriate procedure in such cases, Carroll J noted that there was no provision for an appeal to the High Court against a refusal to grant protective measures.

---

[86] As the Jenard Report states at 52, this is seen as a counterbalance to the *ex parte* nature of the enforcement procedure.

[87] See also *Elwyn (Cottons) Ltd v Pearle Designs Ltd* [1989] IR 9, 11, [1989] ILRM 162, 163 *per* Carroll J.

[88] (Case 119/84) [1985] ECR 3147.

[89] Within one month of service of the enforcement decision or if the party is domiciled in a state other than that in which the decision authorising enforcement is given, within two months, see Article 36.

[90] [1989] IR 9, [1989] ILRM 162.

In the circumstances she was satisfied that the correct course of action was to bring an application for leave to apply for judicial review seeking an order of *mandamus* directed to the Master and then interim relief in the form of a Mareva injunction could be applied for under Order 84, rule 7.

23.026 As mentioned above, where an application is made for enforcement, Order 42A, rule 5 requires it to be grounded on affidavit specifying the protective measures, if any, that are being sought and rule 8 provides that where an order granting leave to enforce a judgment is granted, it shall contain a notification that execution of the judgment shall not issue until after the period within which an appeal may be brought and shall specify the protective measures, if any, granted pending execution. In addition, rule 10 provides that the notice of enforcement shall set out any protective measures granted in respect of the property of the person against whom judgment was given.

CHAPTER TWENTY FOUR

RES JUDICATA

INTRODUCTION

24.001 The doctrine of estoppel *per rem judicatam*,[1] better known by the short-hand term *res judicata*,[2] provides that the final judgment of a judicial tribunal of competent jurisdiction is conclusive and, therefore, a party is precluded from re-litigating the matters decided in the judgment or giving evidence to contradict it in subsequent proceedings.

The doctrine is firmly rooted in the public policy considerations of ensuring the finality of litigation[3] and preventing vexatious litigation.[4] These concerns are commonly encapsulated in the twin Latin maxims of *"interest rei publicae ut sit finis litium"*[5] (it is in the public interest that there should be an end to litigation) and *"nemo debet bis vexari pro eadem causa"* (no one should be sued twice in respect of the same cause). In *Dublin Corporation v Building and Allied Trade Union*,[6] Keane J said that the public interest referred to in the former maxim reflected:

> [T]he interest of all citizens who resort to litigation in obtaining a final and conclusive determination of their disputes. However severe the stresses

---

[1] The benchmark text on the area is the excellent book by McDermott, *Res Judicata and Double Jeopardy* (1999). Recourse should also be had to Spencer Bower, Turner & Handley, *Res Judicata* (3rd ed., 1996).

[2] The term "res judicata" derives from the Latin phrase *"Res judicata pro veritate accipitur"* which translates as "the decided issue is to be taken as correct" (see *per* Hardiman J in *People (DPP) v O'Callaghan* Court of Criminal Appeal, 18 December 2000 at 19). The doctrine was also known historically as estoppel by record but this expression which derives from Coke, *The First Part of the Institutes of the Laws of England; or a Commentary Upon Littleton*, Vol II (1832), at 352a, is misleading because it is the *judicium* not the record which creates the estoppel and it is not essential for the application of the doctrine that the judicial tribunal be required to keep a record of its decisions (*Carl Zeiss Stiftung v Rayner & Keeler Ltd (No. 2)* [1967] 1 AC 853, 933, [1966] 3 WLR 125, 160, [1966] 2 All ER 536, 564 (*per* Lord Guest)). It should be noted that all courts in this jurisdiction are courts of record with the District Court having been made a court of record by s.13 of the Courts Act 1971.

[3] *Irish Land Commission v Ryan* [1900] 2 IR 565, 584 *per* Holmes LJ.

[4] *Kildare County Council v Keogh* [1971] IR 330, 344 *per* McLoughlin J.

[5] Cited by Keane J in *Dublin Corporation v Building and Allied Trade Union* [1996] 1 IR 468, [1996] 2 ILRM 547 and in *Belton v Carlow County Council* [1997] 1 IR 172, [1997] 2 ILRM 405.

[6] [1996] 1 IR 468, [1996] 2 ILRM 547.

of litigation may be for the parties involved – the anxiety, the delays, the costs, the public and painful nature of the process – there is at least the comfort that at some stage finality is reached. Save in those exceptional cases where his opponent can prove that the judgment was procured by fraud, the successful litigant can sleep easily in the knowledge that he need never return to court again.[7]

Another, and not insignificant, policy factor is that of underpinning the legitimacy of the judicial system and the administration of justice by ensuring consistency of decision making. Finally, there is the theoretical idea, promoted mainly in older cases and commentary, that a final and conclusive judgment has the character of an admission by the party against whom it is invoked.[8]

24.002 *Res judicata* is a branch of the law of estoppels and it has been said of estoppels that they "are odious as compelling a person to admit that to be true which is not true".[9] This generalised criticism would not seem to apply with the same force to *res judicata*. In *New Brunswick Railway Co. v British and French Trust Corp. Ltd*[10] Lord Maugham LC said that:

> [T]he doctrine of estoppel (*per res judicatam*) is one founded on considerations of justice and good sense. If an issue has been distinctly raised and decided in an action, in which the parties are represented, it is unjust and unreasonable to permit the same issue to be litigated afresh between the same parties or persons claiming under him.

Indeed, in *Cox v Dublin City Distillery Co. Ltd (No. 3)*[11] O'Brien LC lauded *res judicata* as affording "a convenient means, and sometimes the only means, of defending a position which may be just and fair as between man and man".

However, despite the lack of a truth impairment effect *per se*, the applica-

---

7   *Ibid.* at 481, 556. *Cf.* the comments of Lord Simon in *The Ampthill Peerage* [1977] AC 547, 575, [1976] 2 WLR 777, 792-793, [1976] 2 All ER 411, 423, which were quoted by Murphy J in *Tassan Din v Banco Ambrosiano SPA* [1991] 1 IR 569 and again in *Pringle v Ireland* [1994] 1 ILRM 467.

8   See, for example, the notes to the *Duchess of Kingston's Case* (1776) 20 How St Tr 355, (1776) 1 East PC 468, [1775-1802] All ER 623, in Smith, *Leading Cases* (12th ed.), Vol II, at 767; *Ord v Ord* [1923] 2 KB 432, 440, [1923] All ER 206, 211 *per* Lush J. For a more recent invocation of this idea, see *Donohoe v Browne* [1986] IR 90, 99 *per* Gannon J.

9   *Per* FitzGibbon LJ in *Irish Land Commission v Ryan* [1900] 2 IR 565. See also, *Lampon v Corke* (1822) 5 B & Ald 606, 611 *per* Holroyd J; *Baxendale v Bennett* (1878) 3 QBD 525, 529 (*per* Bramwell LJ).

10 [1939] AC 1, 19-20, [1938] 4 All ER 747, 754-755.

11 [1917] 1 IR 203, 220. *Cf. New Brunswick Rail Co. v British and French Trust Corporation Ltd* [1939] AC 1, at 19-20, [1938] 4 All ER 747, 754-755 (*per* Lord Maugham LC).

tion of the doctrine may sometimes have that result.[12] This cost was acknowledged by Keane J in *Dublin Corporation v Building and Allied Trade Union*,[13] but he took the view that the interest of the public in the finality of litigation should be "given precedence by the law over the injustices which inevitably sometimes result."[14] It might be noted in that regard that a party who is dissatisfied with a decision generally has the option of an appeal and a number of recent decisions have emphasised that where an appeal is open, this should be prosecuted rather than attempting to relitigate the matters in new proceedings.[15]

ELEMENTS REQUIRED TO PLEAD RES JUDICATA

24.003 In order to successfully plead *res judicata*,[16] it must be shown that the same matter has been determined in previous proceedings[17] involving the same parties or their privies by the final decision of a judicial tribunal of competent jurisdiction. These elements will be examined under the following headings: (1) judicial tribunal of competent jurisdiction; (2) final and conclusive judgment; (3) identity of parties; and (4) identity of subject matter.

---

[12] In *Murphy v AG* [1982] IR 241, 314, Henchy J identified *res judicata* as a rule which may operate to debar a person from obtaining redress in the courts for injury which would otherwise be justiciable and redressable.

[13] [1996] 1 IR 468, [1996] 2 ILRM 547.

[14] *Ibid.* at 481, 556.

[15] See *O'Reilly v Daly* Supreme Court, 11 February 1999; *Cooney v Ireland* Supreme Court, *ex tempore*, 11 October 1999.

[16] The traditional position was that it was essential to plead *res judicata* (*Nowlan v Gibson* (1847) 12 LR Ir 5) and if a party failed to do so, then the prior judgment was only an item of evidence in favour of the party which the tribunal of fact could choose whether or not to follow (*Vooght v Winch* (1819) 2 B & Ald 662). While it is still necessary to plead an estoppel (*McMahon v Jackson's Garage Ltd* (1968) 102 ILTR 197; Casson, *Odgers on High Court Practice and Pleading* (23rd ed., 1991), at 227) it appears that the courts will freely allow pleadings to be amended so as to allow the plea to be raised (see, for example, *Lawless v Bus Éireann* [1994] 1 IR 474, *Gilroy v McLoughlin* [1988] IR 44, [1989] ILRM 133; *McMahon v Jackson's Garage Ltd* (1968) 102 ILTR 197).

[17] The availability of the plea of *res judicata* is dictated by the date on which proceedings were determined, not when they were instituted. Thus, a party may be bound by a judgment in an action which was commenced later in time but came on for hearing first. Where more than one set of proceedings is instituted, a party may gain a procedural or tactical advantage from having their case heard first (see, for example, *Donohoe v Browne* [1986] IR 90, where the damages claimed by the plaintiff would have exceeded the jurisdiction of the District Court in which the defendant had instituted proceedings) and the courts are generally reluctant to interfere with the priority of hearing (see *Troy v CIÉ* [1971] IR 320; *Murphy v Hennessy* [1984] IR 378, [1985] ILRM 100).

JUDICIAL TRIBUNAL OF COMPETENT JURISDICTION

24.004 In order to ground an estoppel, the judgment must be that of a court[18] or other judicial tribunal with jurisdiction to enter upon the adjudication and make the order or declaration sought. If this authority is lacking, then the judgment is made without jurisdiction.[19] The concept of jurisdictional competence extends to the doing of an act required before a judgment can become effective. If that act is not done, then no estoppel may be raised on the judgment.[20] Provided that the court had authority to enter upon the adjudication, it will not be deprived of jurisdictional competence merely by reason of an error made during the course of adjudication.[21]

Judicial Tribunals

24.005 The doctrine of *res judicata* applies not only to the decisions of courts but also to those of judicial tribunals. In order to found an estoppel, the decision of the tribunal must involve "the exercise of limited powers of a judicial nature, so that the decision is properly described as a judicial decision pronounced by a judicial tribunal".[22] Examples of such decisions include the awards of arbitrators[23] and the decision of planning authorities.[24] If a body merely exercises fact-finding as opposed to adjudicative functions, then *res judicata* will not apply.[25]

---

[18] It is immaterial that the court is not one of record (*Martin v Keilty* (1902) NIJR 250; *Williams v Jones* (1845) 13 M & W 628; *Re May* (1885) 28 ChD 516) though, as noted above, at paragraph 24.001, all Irish courts are courts of record. It should also be noted that, provided the court has jurisdictional competence, it is immaterial that the decision is that of a subordinate court: *Cassidy v O'Rourke* High Court (Carroll J) 18 May 1983; *Clare County Council v Mahon* [1995] 3 IR 193, [1996] 1 ILRM 521; *Re Irwin Estate* (1933) 67 ILTR 218; *McMahon v Jackson's Garage Ltd* (1968) 102 ILTR 197.

[19] *Butler Lloyd v Trinity College* (1901) 35 ILTR 232; *Re Estate of Lynham* [1928] IR 127.

[20] *Hanrahan v Stapleton* (1927) 62 ILTR 11.

[21] See *Belton v Carlow County Council* [1997] 1 IR 172, [1997] 2 ILRM 405 in which it was held that even if the judge had made an error of law in reaching his conclusion in the previous proceedings, his judgment remained conclusive as to all matters of law and fact on which it was founded.

[22] *Per* Gavan Duffy J in *Athlone Woollen Mills Co. Ltd v Athlone Urban District Council* [1950] IR 1, 9.

[23] *Dublin Corporation v Building and Allied Trade Union* [1996] 1 IR 468, [1996] 2 ILRM 547.

[24] *Athlone Woollen Mills Co. Ltd v Athlone Urban District Council* [1950] IR 1; *State (Kenny and Hussey) v An Bord Pleanála* High Court (Carroll J) 23 February 1984.

[25] *Re National Irish Bank (No. 2)* [1999] 3 IR 190, [1999] 2 ILRM 443.

Foreign Judgments

24.006 The decision of a foreign court or judicial tribunal[26] can also found a plea of *res judicata* provided it is made within jurisdiction.[27] In *Gaffney v Gaffney*[28] it was held that the plaintiff, in order to defeat a plea of estoppel, was entitled to adduce evidence in order to show that the decree of an English court granting the divorce was made without jurisdiction because a judgment made without jurisdiction could not ground an estoppel. It would also appear that an estoppel cannot be grounded on a foreign judgment which was reached in proceedings that departed from the requirements of natural and constitutional justice.[29]

If two inconsistent foreign judgments exist, both of which have been handed down by judicial tribunals of competent jurisdiction, then it is the earlier one in time which is the operative judgment for the purposes of estoppel.[30]

FINAL AND CONCLUSIVE JUDGMENT

24.007 In order for a plea of *res judicata* to succeed, the judgment on which it is sought to ground the estoppel must be a final and conclusive judgment on the merits.

Final Judgment

24.008 The requirement of finality excludes from the application of *res judicata*, judgments which are provisional in character[31] or subject to review.[32] An interlocutory judgment will generally not possess the requisite quality of finality[33] but may do so if "it was clearly intended finally to determine rights between the parties".[34]

---

[26] For example, the Industrial Tribunal of England and Wales (see *Amstrad plc v Walker* High Court (Carney J) 19 July 1993).

[27] *Gaffney v Gaffney* [1975] IR 133; *Deighan v Sunday Newspapers Ltd* [1987] NI 105; *Carl Zeiss Stiftung v Rayner & Keeler Ltd (No. 2)* [1967] 1 AC 853, [1966] 3 WLR 125, [1966] 2 All ER 536; *The Sennar* [1985] 1 WLR 490, [1985] 2 All ER 104, [1985] 1 Lloyd's Rep 521.

[28] [1975] IR 133.

[29] See *Gaffney v Gaffney* [1975] IR 133 where Kenny J approved *dicta* from the judgment of Lindley MR in *Pemberton v Hughes* [1899] 1 Ch 781, 790 that a court will examine the foreign proceedings in order to establish whether they "offended against English views of substantial justice".

[30] *Showlag v Mansour* [1995] 1 AC 431, [1994] 2 WLR 615, [1994] 2 All ER 129.

[31] See *McDonnell v Alcorn* [1894] 1 IR 274; *Re Estate of Lynham* [1928] IR 127.

[32] *Tracy v Great Southern Railways (No. 2)* [1943] IR 41.

[33] *Sweeney v Horan's (Tralee) Ltd* [1987] ILRM 240; *Schlieske v Minister for Immigration and Ethnic Affairs* (1987) 79 ALR 554; *Kinex Exploration Pty Ltd v Tasco Pty Ltd* [1995] 2 VR 318 (bail application). It is for this reason that no estoppel can arise where

Judgment on the Merits

24.009 The necessity for an adjudication on the issues raised by the parties, sometimes expressed as the requirement that there must have been a decision on the merits,[35] means that an order of the court dismissing an action without proceeding to the merits will not constitute a final judgment.[36] Thus, no bar to fresh proceedings is created by the dismissal of an action for want of prosecution[37] or because it is premature.[38] Similarly, where a plaintiff discontinues an action in accordance with Order 26, such discontinuance is not a defence to any subsequent action.[39]

Default and Consent Judgments

24.010 An estoppel *per rem judicatam* may also be raised on foot of a default[40] or consent judgment.[41] In *Re South American and Mexican Co., ex p. Bank of England,* [42] Vaughan Williams J explained that:

> It has always been the law that a judgment by consent or default raises an estoppel, just as in the same way as a judgment after the court has exercised a judicial discretion in the matter. The basis of the estoppel is that, when parties have once litigated a matter, it is in the interest of the estate that litigation should come to an end; and if they agree upon a result, or upon a verdict, or upon a judgment, or upon verdict and judgment, as the case may be, an estoppel is raised as to all the matters in respect of which an estoppel would have been raised by judgment if the case had been fought to the bitter end.

---

the welfare of children is at issue because any order relating to the welfare of infants is necessarily interlocutory in character (*D. v D.* High Court (Doyle J) 21 July 1977).

[34] *Per* Judge Davitt in *Kinsella v Byrne* (1940) 74 ILTR 157. See also *McDaid v O'Connor and Bailey Ltd* [1954] IR 25, *Midland Bank Trust Co. Ltd v Green* [1981] AC 513, [1981] 2 WLR 28, [1981] 1 All ER 153; *Schlieske v Minister for Immigration and Ethnic Affairs* (1987) 79 ALR 554.

[35] *Bradshaw v M'Mullan* [1920] 2 IR 412, 424 (*per* Lord Shaw).

[36] *Cf. White v Spendlove* [1942] IR 224 (order of trial judge in previous proceedings that the defendant's counterclaim be dismissed, same not having been proceeded with, held to be sufficient to ground an estoppel).

[37] *Byrne v Frere* (1828) 2 Mol 157; *Pople v Evans* [1969] 2 Ch 255, [1968] 3 WLR 97, [1968] 2 All ER 743.

[38] *Barber v McQuaig* (1900) 31 OR 593.

[39] Order 26, rule 1. See *Owens v Minoprio* [1942] 1 KB 193, [1942] 1 All ER 30. *Cf. White v Spendlove* [1942] IR 224.

[40] *Irish Land Commission v Ryan* [1900] 2 IR 565.

[41] *Thomson v Moore* (1889) 23 LR Ir 599; *Doyle v Clancy* (1926) 61 ILTR 150; *Kinsella v Byrne* (1940) 74 ILTR 157.

[42] [1895] 1 Ch 37, 45.

However, it is important to note that, as emphasised by Davitt J in *Kinsella v Byrne*,[43] a consent can only give rise to an estoppel where it has resulted in a judgment by the court. This is because it is not the agreement of the parties which creates an estoppel but the judgment given on the basis of that agreement.[44] Thus, in *Kinsella*, where the order of the court merely made the consent a rule of court and stayed all further proceedings, the consent did not operate as an estoppel because there was no adjudication on any of the issues raised by the parties.[45]

Appeals

24.011 The requirement of finality will be satisfied if the judgment "is one that cannot be varied, reopened or set aside by the court that delivered it or any other court of co-ordinate jurisdiction although it may be subject to appeal to a court of higher jurisdiction".[46] Thus, a judgment will be sufficiently final and conclusive not only where the time limit for an appeal has elapsed[47] but even where a right of appeal to a superior court remains open.[48] Furthermore, it appears from the decision of Carswell J in *Deighan v Sunday Newspapers Ltd*[49] that a judgment will still be final even if there remains the possibility that the decision of the appeal court may be set aside. This merely means that the judgment is still subject to appeal.

Where an appeal is taken, the judgment of the appeal court will generally be the operative one for the purposes of *res judicata* but an estoppel may still be raised on an issue decided at first instance if the decision on that point is not appealed[50] or the appeal is unsuccessful.[51]

---

[43] (1940) 74 ILTR 157.

[44] *Cf.* the comments of Lord Shaw in *Bradshaw v M'Mullan* [1920] IR 412, 424-5, who expressed the view, *obiter*, that the estoppel arising from a consent judgment was more properly characterised as an estoppel *in pais* (by conduct). This comment may well have been based on the view that the estoppel arose from the fact of consent. It is, of course, possible that a consent which does not give rise to an estoppel *per res judicatam* may give rise to an estoppel by conduct.

[45] See also *Kinsella v Connor* (1942) 76 ILTR 141.

[46] *Per* Lord Diplock in *The Sennar* [1985] 1 WLR 490, 494, [1985] 2 All ER 104, 106, [1985] 1 Lloyd's Rep 521, 523.

[47] *O'Reilly v Daly* Supreme Court, 11 February 1999.

[48] *Deighan v Sunday Newspapers Ltd* [1987] NI 105; *Cooney v Ireland* Supreme Court, *ex tempore*, 11 October 1999.

[49] [1987] NI 105, 117.

[50] *Re National Irish Bank (No. 2)* [1999] 3 IR 190, [1999] 2 ILRM 443.

[51] *People (DPP) v Quilligan and O'Reilly (No. 3)* [1993] 2 IR 305; *Breathnach v Ireland* [1989] IR 489.

IDENTITY OF PARTIES

24.012 Perhaps the best statement of what is contemplated by the requirement of identity of parties is to be found in the judgment of Barwick CJ in *Ramsay v Pigram*[52] who explained that the previous judgment must have been "between the same parties in the same respective interests or capacities, or between a privy of each, or between one of them and a privy of the other in each instance in the same interest or capacity."[53] This passage contains a number of elements which require elaboration.

(a) Same Parties

24.013 Apart from persons actually joined in previous proceedings and named on the record, a person will be considered to have been a party to those proceedings if he has been served with notice or attended those proceedings.[54] In addition, a person may be bound by the result of proceedings where they are taken in the form of a test case on behalf of that person and others or where he consents to be bound by the result thereof and such consent is embodied in an order of the court.[55]

While the concept of identity of interest is crucial in determining whether privity exists between parties, it would seem as if it is irrelevant to the question of whether a party has participated in prior proceedings. In *McGuinness v Motor Distributors Ltd*,[56] the plaintiff instituted proceedings for breach of contract arising out of a road traffic accident which had been the subject of previous proceedings involving the plaintiff and the defendant. The defendant pleaded estoppel based on the earlier proceedings which the plaintiff sought to resist on the basis that, although he had been named as a party to those proceedings, he had not been a "real" party because, in reality, it was his insurance company and not he who had been in control of the proceedings. In the High Court, Barron J accepted that the earlier proceedings had been controlled by the insurance company but refused to hold that this relieved the plaintiff from his status as a party. His conclusion on this point was upheld on appeal by the Supreme Court on the basis that there had been a clear privity of interest between the parties.

---

[52] (1968) 118 CLR 271.

[53] *Ibid.* at 276. This passage was quoted with approval by Gannon J in *Donohoe v Browne* [1986] IR 90, 98.

[54] See Order 125, rule 1. A person cited to probate proceedings is considered to be a party to those proceedings and is bound by the decision reached therein unless the proceedings are compromised without this knowledge: *Ritchie v Malcolm* [1902] 2 IR 403.

[55] *Cf. Cox v Dublin City Distillery Co. Ltd (No. 2)* [1915] 1 IR 345 and *Cox v Dublin City Distillery Co. Ltd (No. 3)* [1917] 1 IR 203.

[56] [1997] 2 IR 171 (HC); Supreme Court, 17 July 1997.

24.014 The decision in *McGuinness* was subsequently followed in *O'Grady v Laois County Council.*[57] The principal contention advanced by the plaintiff in that case was that the requirements for issue estoppel were not met because there was not sufficient identity between the parties to the two sets of proceedings. He argued that because the conduct of the case in the District and Circuit Courts had been in the hands of his insurance company which instructed their own solicitors, he had not had sufficient input into how the case was run. In particular, he averred that certain witnesses might have been called to advance the case more strongly against the county council if he had been in charge of the proceedings with his own legal team. This contention was, however, rejected by the Supreme Court. Lynch J took the view that there was a clear identity of parties between the third party issue tried in the earlier District and Circuit Court proceedings and the instant proceedings pointing out that there was an identity of interest between the plaintiff and his insurers.[58] O'Flaherty J concurred but, interestingly, opined that because of the operation of the doctrine of *res judicata*, an insurance company taking over the conduct of proceedings owes a duty to the insured to conduct them properly.

24.015 Although unfairness may sometimes result, it is submitted that there are strong policy reasons in favour of the approach adopted by the Supreme Court. First, it would lead to complexity and uncertainty if, in each case that involved an insurance company, the courts were to go behind the parties on the record in order to ascertain the "real" parties. Secondly, because so much litigation is effectively fought out between insurance companies, the policy goal of finality of litigation would be significantly undermined if a party could escape the binding force of a previous decision on that basis.

(b) Same Capacity

24.016 The parties must sue and be sued in the same capacity.[59] Thus, in *Blake v O'Kelly*[60] no estoppel was held to arise where the defendant, who was being sued as a fraudulent donee, had previously been sued in his capacity as an executor *de son tort*. Similarly, in *Manton v Cantwell*,[61] it was held by the House of Lords that an employer was not estopped from denying liability in proceedings taken by dependants under the Workmen's Compensation Act 1906 by virtue of an admission of liability made by him in proceedings previously taken

---

[57] Supreme Court, *ex tempore*, 18 May 1998.
[58] *Cf. Shaw v Sloan* [1982] NI 393, 397, where Lowry LCJ opined that "there is, so far as policy can be relevant, an argument against allowing a party to be prejudiced in later proceedings by the way in which his insurers have in their own interest conducted the earlier proceedings".
[59] *McMahon v Jackson's Garage Ltd* (1968) 102 ILTR 197, 199 (*per* Walsh J).
[60] (1874) IR 9 Eq 54.
[61] (1920) 54 ILTR 93.

by the workman while he was alive because the plaintiffs sued under an independent cause of action as dependants, not as representatives of the deceased.

(c) Privies

24.017 A person is a privy of a party "by blood, title or interest when he stands in his shoes and claims through or under him".[62] There is little authority on when privity may be established by blood. Indeed, a Canadian case has doubted the continued existence of this concept.[63] Privity by title or estate is based on the idea that it is reasonable that the privy should be estopped because his estate was represented at the time of the recovery of the judgment.[64] Where it is relied upon, it must be shown that the privy derived title from the party by act or operation of law subsequent to the recovery of the previous judgment.[65] Privies by title or estate include the relationships of vendor and purchaser,[66] principal and agent,[67] executor and deceased,[68] and lessor and lessee provided of course that the privy claims title or estate through or under the party.[69] There is also authority in England to the effect that it suffices if title is derived after the commencement of the proceedings in the course of which the judgment was given.[70]

Privity of Interest

24.018 Most of the recent case law has centred on the third category of privity, that of privity by interest. This is a rather amorphous category, the parameters of which are not clearly established, but its essence would seem to have been identified by Megarry VC in *Gleeson v J. Wippell & Co. Ltd*[71] when he stated that "there must be a sufficient degree of identification between the two to make it just to hold that the decision to which one was party should be binding in proceedings to which the other is party." This criterion of justice was also em-

---

[62] *Per* Lowry LCJ in *Shaw v Sloan* [1982] NI 393, 396. This formulation was quoted with approval by the Supreme Court in *Belton v Carlow County Council* [1997] 1 IR 172, [1997] 2 ILRM 405 and *McCauley v McDermot* [1997] 2 ILRM 486. See also, *per* Lord Reid in *Carl Zeiss Stiftung v Rayner & Keeler Ltd (No. 2)* [1967] 1 AC 853, 910, [1966] 3 WLR 125, 140, [1966] 2 All ER 536, 550.

[63] *Cassidy v Ingoldsby* (1875) 36 UCQB 339, 341.

[64] *Re De Burgho's Estate* [1896] 1 IR 274, 280.

[65] *Re De Burgho's Estate* [1896] 1 IR 274; *McConnell v Lombard and Ulster Banking Ltd* [1982] NI 203.

[66] *Board v Board* (1873) LR 9 QB 48.

[67] *McConnell v Lombard and Ulster Banking Ltd* [1982] NI 203.

[68] *Ennis v Rochford* (1884) 14 LR Ir 285. See also, *Douglas v Forrest* (1828) 4 Bing 686; *Reimers v Druce* (1857) 26 LJ Ch 196.

[69] *McConnell v Lombard and Ulster Banking Ltd* [1982] NI 203; *Cassidy v Ingoldsby* (1875) 36 UCQB 339.

[70] *Pople v Evans* [1969] 2 Ch 255, [1968] 3 WLR 97, [1968] 2 All ER 743.

[71] [1977] 1 WLR 510, 515, [1977] 3 All ER 54, 60.

phasised by O'Donnell LJ in *Shaw v Sloan*[72] in cautioning against an overbroad concept of privity:

> Privity means something more than being interested in the outcome. It must involve such interest as would enable the privy to have a voice or say in how the proceedings are, or will be conducted or concluded. Any other meaning could operate to cause grave injustice to servants or agents, who while not parties to the proceedings, and having no voice in their conduct, could be held to be bound by them.[73]

24.019 A straightforward example of where sufficient identification of interest was missing can be seen in *Belton v Carlow County Council*[74] where the Supreme Court, applying settled law as to the separate legal personality of a company and its shareholders, held that there was not sufficient privity between them. While the interests of the company and its shareholders might often coincide, they would not always do so and did not do so on the facts of the case.

Road Traffic Accidents

24.020 Most of the recent case law on privity by interest has concerned road traffic accidents. In *Donohoe v Browne*[75] the plaintiff claimed damages for personal injuries sustained in a collision between a motorcycle driven by him and a car owned by the first defendant and driven by the second defendant. In previous proceedings taken by the first defendant for damage to her car, it had been held by the Circuit Court (on appeal), that the plaintiff had been solely to blame for the collision. In the instant proceedings, the defendants pleaded that, by virtue of the determination in the Circuit Court, the plaintiff was estopped from proceeding with his claim. The second defendant had not been a party to the previous proceedings and, hence, the question arose as to whether he could claim estoppel on the basis of privity of interest. Gannon J pointed out that the second named defendant made no claim on his own behalf and that his position as defendant derived solely from his position as the driver of the car with the consent of the owner. The learned judge pointed out that, by virtue of s.118 of the Road Traffic Act 1961, the first defendant was vicariously liable for the negligence of the second defendant and he, therefore, concluded that their interests were identical with respect to the plaintiff's claim.

24.021 However, the interests of the owner and driver of a vehicle may not necessarily coincide and are much less likely to do so where it is sought to rely

---

[72] [1982] NI 393.
[73] *Ibid.* at 410.
[74] [1997] 1 IR 172, [1997] 2 ILRM 405.
[75] [1986] IR 90.

on a previous decision *against* a putative privy. In *Reamsbottom v Raftery*[76] the plaintiff was the driver of a car, owned by her husband, which had been involved in an accident with a car owned and driven by the defendant. The defendant had previously brought an action in the Circuit Court against the plaintiff's husband who was found to be solely responsible for the accident. The plaintiff had not been a party to those proceedings, had not been represented at the trial and had not even given evidence because of the injuries sustained by her in the accident. It was in those circumstances that the question arose as to whether privity of interest existed between the plaintiff as driver and her husband as owner of the car such that she was estopped from the earlier determination from maintaining the instant proceedings.

Johnson J distinguished the decision in *Donohoe v Browne*[77] on the basis that it was open to both the defendant and the plaintiff's husband to have joined the plaintiff as a party to the Circuit Court proceedings and this had not been done. He took the view that an injustice could be done to the plaintiff by holding that she was precluded from bringing her action as a result of an action to which she was not a party, over which she had no control and in which she had not offered evidence. He bolstered this conclusion by reference to a passage from the judgment of Megarry VC in *Gleeson v J. Wippel & Co. Ltd*[78] where the learned judge stated that:

> Any contention which leads to the conclusion that a person is liable to be condemned unheard is plainly open to the gravest of suspicions. A defendant ought to be able to put his own defence in his own way, and to call his own evidence. He ought not to be concluded by the failure of the defence and evidence adduced by another defendant in other proceedings unless his standing in those other proceedings justifies the conclusion that a decision against the defendant in them ought fairly and truly to be said to be in substance a decision against him.

24.022 The reasoning in *Reamsbottom v Raftery*[79] was endorsed by the Supreme Court in *Lawless v Bus Éireann*.[80] The plaintiff brought fatal injury proceedings on behalf of herself and the statutory dependants of the deceased who had been killed in a collision between the van that he was driving and a bus owned by the first named defendant. In a previous action brought by a passenger in the bus against Bus Éireann and a representative of the deceased who had been nominated by the deceased's insurance company, it was held that the de-

---

[76] [1991] 1 IR 531.
[77] [1986] IR 90.
[78] [1977] 1 WLR 510, 516, [1977] 3 All ER 54, 60. This passage was also quoted by O'Donnell LJ in *Shaw v Sloan* [1982] NI 393.
[79] [1991] 1 IR 531.
[80] [1994] 1 IR 474.

ceased had been solely to blame. The defendants in the instant proceedings sought to raise a plea of *res judicata* on the basis of that determination, but it was held by the Supreme Court that the plea failed because of the lack of sufficient identity between the parties. The plaintiff and dependants had not been represented at the first trial and the court concluded that there was no identity of interest between them and the nominee of the insurance company. O'Flaherty J, with whom the other members of the court agreed, based this conclusion on "the entitlement of a person to have an opportunity to present his or her case in court; to decide the tempo of the case; decide what witnesses should be called or not called, and so forth."[81] He also adverted to the importance of the case to the plaintiff and the distress which she would suffer should she be prevented from prosecuting her claim.

24.023 This line of case law was examined by the Supreme Court in *McCauley v McDermott*[82] where a strict approach to the question of identity of parties was taken. This case also arose out of a collision between motor vehicles, this time between a car and a tractor. Earlier proceedings taken by the car owner against the tractor owner in respect of the damage to his car had resulted in a finding that the collision was due to the negligence of the tractor driver and that there had been no contributory negligence on the part of the car driver. The instant proceedings were brought by a passenger in the car against the tractor owner who sought to join the car driver as a third party. The question therefore arose as to whether the issues arising between the car driver, who had not been a party to the earlier proceedings, and the tractor driver were *res judicata*. Keane J, delivering the judgment of the Supreme Court, held that despite the provisions of s.118 of the Road Traffic Act 1961, which renders the owner of a vehicle vicariously liable for the negligence of a person driving that vehicle with his permission, it did not follow that there was a sufficient identity of interest to make one the privy of the other.[83] Although this case was distinguishable from earlier decisions in that it was sought to raise an estoppel *against* the tractor driver who had been a party to the earlier proceedings, Keane J nevertheless concluded that the car driver could not be considered to be a privy of the car owner.

24.024 The foregoing decisions evince a great reluctance to find a person bound by a decision in proceedings in which they were not directly involved and this strict approach to identity of parties can be justified on constitutional grounds. A person has a constitutional right to access to the courts[84] and, hence, it is only

---

[81] *Ibid.* at 478.

[82] [1997] 2 ILRM 486.

[83] Following in this regard the decisions in *Ramsay v Pigram* (1967) 118 CLR 271 and *Shaw v Sloan* [1982] NI 393.

[84] See *Macauley v Minister for Posts and Telegraphs* [1966] IR 345 and *Murphy v Greene* [1990] 2 IR 566, [1991] ILRM 404.

where he has been a party to a previous decision or was *effectively represented* by a party to that decision that it is fair to deprive him of that right of access. In order that a person be effectively represented in the earlier proceedings, it is imperative that there is some connection between the parties such that their interests are identical in both type and degree. This point was tellingly made by O'Flaherty J in *Lawless v Bus Éireann*[85] when he drew attention to the fact that "for the insurance company the case was surely just another case to be disposed of – naturally on the best basis possible; but for the widow and her children and other dependants the case is likely to be one of the most important things to be decided in their lifetimes".[86]

Proceedings Involving the State

24.025 The issue of privity requires special consideration in relation to proceedings involving the State. In particular, the question arises as to the extent to which privity can be said to exist between different organs of State. This question was considered by O'Hanlon J in *Kelly v Ireland*.[87] The plaintiff, who had been convicted of the Sallins train robbery, sued the defendants, Ireland and the Attorney General, for, *inter alia*, damages for assault allegedly committed upon him while he was in custody. The defendants argued that the plaintiff was estopped from making the allegations of assault on the basis that they had previously been made and rejected before the Special Criminal Court in a challenge to the voluntariness of his confession. However, the plaintiff sought to argue that no privity existed between the Director of Public Prosecutions and the defendants in the instant case and that, therefore, *res judicata* did not arise. This contention was rejected by O'Hanlon J. He pointed out that in criminal proceedings on indictment, the Director acts in a representative capacity on behalf of the People of Ireland[88] and that in defending a civil claim against the State the Attorney General acts in the same capacity.[89] He was, therefore, satisfied that the requisite privity existed.[90]

---

[85] [1994] 1 IR 474.

[86] *Ibid.* at 479.

[87] [1986] ILRM 318 (approved by Blayney J in *Breathnach v Ireland (No. 2)* [1993] 2 IR 448).

[88] Article 30.3 of the Constitution also provides that: "All crimes and offences prosecuted in any court constituted under Article 34 of this Constitution other than a court of summary jurisdiction shall be prosecuted in the name of the People and at the suit of the Attorney General or some other person authorised in accordance with law to act for that purpose." The Director of Public Prosecutions is authorised by s.3 of the Prosecution of Offences Act 1974 to exercise all functions capable of being performed in relation to criminal matters by the Attorney General. However, this Article was held to be inapplicable in *Kelly* because the Special Criminal Court is not a court constituted under Article 34 of the Constitution.

[89] Relying on *Byrne v Ireland* [1972] IR 241.

[90] The same conclusion was reached by Blayney J in *Breathnach v Ireland (No. 2)* [1993] 2 IR 448.

24.026 In *McGrath v Commissioner of An Garda Síochána*,[91] McCarthy J
went further and advanced the broad proposition that "[w]here one organ of
State has been a contestant in the first trial of the issue, then … another organ of
State has the necessary privity" for the purpose of issue estoppel. As to what
constituted an organ of the State, he opined that the Attorney General, the Director of Public Prosecutions and the Commissioner of An Garda Síochána would
certainly came within that category.

It would seem as if both O'Hanlon J and McCarthy J considered that representation of a common principal, namely the State, is sufficient *per se*, to confer
the requisite privity. However, this ignores the point that there must be an identity of interest on the facts of the individual case. Generally, there will be a
coincidence of interest between various organs of the State but not necessarily
and, therefore, future decisions may seek to apply a gloss in terms of identity of
interest to these *dicta*.

24.027 A related question which arose for consideration in *Breathnach v Ireland (No. 2)*[92] is whether privity exists between individual members of the
gardaí and the Director of Public Prosecutions. The plaintiff had been a co-
defendant of Kelly in the Sallins train robbery case and like Kelly, he brought a
civil claim seeking damages for various alleged breaches of his rights. However, in addition to suing Ireland and the Attorney General, he also joined as
defendants several members of the gardaí whom he alleged had assaulted him.
Blayney J thought it unlikely that the gardaí could be held to have been parties
or privies to the criminal trial but did not need to decide the issue because of his
invocation of the doctrine of abuse of process. However, if this question were to
arise again for resolution, it seems unlikely that privity would be found to exist.
Though both are employed by the State, there is no direct relationship between
an individual garda and the Director of Public Prosecutions. To hold that they
are in privity would be to stretch the concept beyond its natural meaning. It can
hardly be contended that two employees are in privity of interest simply by
virtue of their employment by a common employer.

(d) Mutuality

24.028 It has frequently been emphasised that *both* parties to the later proceedings must have been party or privy to the earlier proceedings: "It is essential to an estoppel that it be mutual, so that the same parties and privies may
both be bound and take advantage of it."[93] This requirement of mutuality is

---

[91] [1991] 1 IR 69, 75, [1990] ILRM 817, 822.
[92] [1993] 2 IR 448.
[93] *Per* Alderson B in *Petrie v Nuttall* (1886) 11 Ex Ch 569, 575-76 (cited with approval
by Keane J in *McCauley v McDermot* [1997] 2 ILRM 486, 495). See also *Shaw v Sloan*
[1982] NI 393, 410.

central to the policy basis of *res judicata*[94] and a person will not be allowed to take advantage of an earlier determination unless he would have been bound by it. For example, in *Clare County Council v Mahon*[95] Carroll J held that the defendant could not plead *res judicata* based on a decision in earlier proceedings between the plaintiff and another defendant because "[i]f the case had gone the other way, they would have been properly entitled to say they were not bound by the decision".[96]

24.029 As is evident from the decision in *McCarthy Construction Ltd v Waterford County Council*,[97] adherence to the principle of mutuality has contributed significantly to the narrow approach to the identity of parties taken by the Irish courts. In *McCarthy*, the owners of a hotel which had been destroyed by fire had successfully applied in the Circuit Court for compensation under the Malicious Injuries Act 1981 and compromised their claim before an appeal to the High Court came on for hearing. The applicants, who owned property destroyed in the fire, argued that the issue of liability for the fire was *res judicata*. However, Lynch J held that the applicants were not in privity with the owners of the hotel and therefore, *res judicata* did not apply. A very important factor in reaching this conclusion was that if the county council were to be estopped where the first claim for compensation succeeded, then an applicant would similarly have been estopped if the first claim failed. If the first claim had been incompetently pursued, this could result in a person being estopped from claiming compensation to which he would otherwise be legally entitled. He took the view that, to deprive a person of his right of access to the courts in such circumstances, "would be a grave injustice".[98]

Similar reasoning was employed by the Supreme Court in *McCauley v McDermot*.[99] Although the facts of *McCauley* were distinguishable from those in *Reamsbottom v Raftery*[100] and *Lawless v Bus Éireann*,[101] in that it was sought to raise an estoppel against the tractor driver who had been a party to and participated in the earlier proceedings, an equally narrow approach to the question of privity was justified by Keane J on the basis of mutuality. If the Circuit Court had decided the issue in the previous proceedings against the car owner and in favour of the tractor owner, the car driver would not have been estopped because he was not party or privy to the earlier proceedings. That being so, he could not take advantage of the decision against the tractor owner.

[94] *Donohoe v Browne* [1986] IR 90, 99.
[95] [1995] 3 IR 193, [1996] 1 ILRM 521.
[96] *Ibid.* at 206, 532. See also *McCarthy Construction Ltd v Waterford County Council* High Court (Lynch J) 6 July 1987.
[97] High Court (Lynch J) 6 July 1987.
[98] *Ibid.* at 6.
[99] [1997] 2 ILRM 486.
[100] [1991] 1 IR 531.
[101] [1994] 1 IR 474.

Non-Mutual Preclusion

24.030 The strong commitment of the Irish courts to the principle of mutuality has stymied any attempts to create a doctrine of non-mutual preclusion along the lines developed by the US courts.[102] However, there is a strong argument to be made that the principle of mutuality should be abandoned on the basis that the reasons, rooted in fairness, which lie behind the non-preclusion of a person who was not a party or privy to the earlier proceedings do not apply where it is sought to raise estoppel against a person who was actually a party or privy to the earlier proceedings. Furthermore, it undermines the policy goal of finality of litigation to allow an issue which has been determined against a party to be re-opened merely by changing defendants.[103] As Keane J acknowledged in *McCauley v McDermot*,[104] although issue estoppel was not available on the facts, it remained the case that the tractor owner was "seeking to relitigate an issue which was conclusively and finally determined against him in the Circuit Court proceedings, the very mischief which the doctrine of issue estoppel was intended to prevent." However, as will be seen below, this reluctance to abandon mutuality and thereby create a doctrine of non-mutual preclusion has been tempered to some degree by the willingness of the courts in *McCauley* and in other cases to employ the doctrine of abuse of process in order to achieve substantially the same result.

IDENTITY OF SUBJECT MATTER

24.031 In its modern incarnation, the term estoppel *per rem judicatam* is an umbrella term which encompasses two distinct branches: "cause of action estoppel" and "issue estoppel". The hiving off of issue estoppel into a separate category is of relatively recent origin[105] and the conferment of the term "cause

---

[102] The landmark cases are *Bernhard v Bank of American National Trust and Savings Association* 122 P 2d 892, 19 Cal 2d 807 (1942), *Blonder-Tongue Laboratories Inc. v University of Illinois Foundation* 402 US 313 (1971) and *Parkland Hosiery Co. v Shore* 439 US 322 (1979).

[103] As Bentham argued in a passage quoted in *McCauley v McDermot* [1997] 2 ILRM 486: "There is reason for saying that a man shall not lose his cause in consequence of the verdict given in a formal proceeding to which he was not a party; but there is no reason whatever for saying he shall not lose his cause in consequence of the verdict in a proceeding to which he was a party, merely because his adversary was not. It is right enough that a verdict obtained by A against B should not bar the claim of a third party C: but that it should not be evidence in favour of C against B, seems the very height of absurdity."

[104] [1997] 2 ILRM 486.

[105] In *Countess of Mountcashell's Estate* [1920] 1 IR 1, 5-6, Ross J referred to the proposition, which he did not regard as well established, that "whenever an allegation of fact is made on the record and issue taken upon it, and that issue has been found one way or other and followed by judgment, neither of the parties can afterwards reopen that question of fact."

of action" estoppel upon the rump of *res judicata* more recent still.[106] However, the distinction between the two is now well understood[107] and is important in terms of the degree of identity of subject matter which must be shown between the two actions. In summary, cause of action estoppel will arise where the causes of action in the two cases are the same whereas issue estoppel can be successfully pleaded where an issue has previously been decided.

(a) Cause of Action Estoppel

24.032 As Diplock LJ explained in *Thoday v Thoday*,[108] cause of action estoppel is that branch of estoppel *per res judicatam* which:

> prevents a party to an action from asserting or denying, as against the other party, the existence of a particular cause of action, the non-existence or existence of which has been determined by a court of competent jurisdiction in previous litigation between the same parties.[109]

It thus precludes a party from contradicting the previous determination of a court on a cause of action.

The constituent elements of cause of action estoppel are that in previous proceedings between the parties or their privies, the existence or non-existence of an identical cause of action has been determined by the final and conclusive judgment of a court of competent jurisdiction. These elements have already been considered with the exception of the requirement of identity of cause of action which will be considered further here.

24.033 The leading authority is the decision of the Supreme Court in *White v Spendlove*.[110] The defendant had previously brought an action against the plaintiff claiming specific performance of an agreement dated 9 February 1935 for the sale of a premises. In her defence to that action, the plaintiff had pleaded that she had entered into a different contract dated 12 February 1934 for the purchase of the said premises subject to certain conditions precedent. She alleged that these conditions had not been fulfilled and counterclaimed for rescission of the alleged agreement and repayment of money which she alleged had been paid on foot of the agreement. The defendant's action was dismissed on the ground that a valid agreement did not exist and the plaintiff not having proceeded with her counterclaim, it was also dismissed by the court. In the instant proceedings,

---

[106] It would appear that the phrase was first coined by Diplock LJ in *Thoday v Thoday* [1964] P 181, [1964] 2 WLR 371, [1964] 1 All ER 341.
[107] See the explanation given by Lord Diplock LJ in *Thoday v Thoday* [1964] P 181, 197-198, [1964] 2 WLR 371, 384, [1964] 1 All ER 341, 352.
[108] [1964] P 181, [1964] 2 WLR 371, [1964] 1 All ER 341.
[109] *Ibid.* at 197, 384, 352.
[110] [1942] IR 224.

the plaintiff claimed the return of the money allegedly paid on foot of the contract of 12 February 1934. She repeated the contention that this agreement had been subject to conditions precedent which had not been complied with by the defendant and that there had, therefore, been a total failure of consideration.

There was a division of opinion in the Supreme Court as to whether identity of cause of action existed. A majority of the Supreme Court held that the plaintiff's claim was based on substantially the same cause of action as her counterclaim which had been dismissed in the former action and that she was, therefore, estopped from seeking to recover the same sum. Meredith J, dissenting, reached a different conclusion based on the proposition put forward by Lord Cranworth in *Moss v Anglo-Egyptian Navigation Co.*[111] that there is no estoppel unless "everything that was in controversy in the second suit as the foundation for the relief sought was also in controversy in the first." He was not satisfied that this condition was satisfied on the facts because, in his opinion, the counterclaim in the previous proceedings was based on the allegation of an agreement whereas the claim in the instant case was based on the non-existence of any agreement and the allegation of total failure of consideration. The latter issue had not been determined in the earlier proceedings and, therefore, the matters in controversy were not the same.

It can be seen from this case that the identification and comparison of causes of action required for the application of cause of action estoppel can give rise to considerable difficulties and, as will be seen below, may require a very detailed and technical analysis of the relevant cause of actions. This, perhaps, explains the relative under-utilisation of cause of action estoppel as compared to issue estoppel which does not pose the same problems.

Merger of Judgments

24.034 Cause of action estoppel is primarily directed towards the non-contradiction of a previous determination as to the existence or non-existence of a cause of action. However, it also has a further effect which flows from the doctrine of merger or *transit in rem judicatam.*[112] According to this theory, when a judgment as to the existence or non-existence of a cause of action is given, the cause of action is extinguished by that decision such that "the very right or cause of action claimed ... has in the formal proceedings passed into judgment, so that it is merged and has no longer an independent existence".[113]

One consequence of this theory is that where proceedings are brought in respect of a cause of action, the plaintiff must make all claims open to him and

---

[111] (1865) 1 Ch App 108, 114.

[112] See, *per* Diplock LJ in *Thoday v Thoday* [1964] P 181, 197, [1964] 2 WLR 371, 384, [1964] 1 All ER 341, 352.

[113] *Per* Dixon J in *Blair v Curran* (1939) 62 CLR 464, 531-2 (quoted with approval by the Supreme Court in *Belton v Carlow County Council* [1997] 1 IR 172, [1997] 2 ILRM 405).

the defendant must raise all defences available to him because the judgment operates as a comprehensive declaration of all the rights and duties of the parties arising out of the cause of action.[114] Fragmentation of litigation is thereby prevented because parties and their privies will not be allowed to reopen a case at a later date by making claims which could have been made during the earlier proceedings.

24.035 Perhaps the best known statement of this principle is that of Wigram VC in *Henderson v Henderson*:[115]

> [W]here a given matter becomes the subject of litigation in, and of adjudication by, a court of competent jurisdiction, the court requires the parties to that litigation to bring forward their whole case, and will not (except under special circumstances) permit the same parties to open the same subject of litigation in respect of matter which might have been brought forward as part of the subject in contest, but which was not brought forward, only because they have, from negligence, inadvertence, or even accident, omitted part of their case. The plea of *res judicata* applies, except in special cases, not only to points upon which the court was actually required by the parties to form an opinion and pronounce a judgment, but to every point which properly belonged to the subject of litigation, and which the parties exercising reasonable diligence, might have brought forward at the time.

24.036 A similar principle was propounded by Palles CB in *Cox v Dublin City Distillery Co. Ltd (No. 2)*[116] where he expressed the view that the defendants were estopped by the decision in an earlier case "from raising as against the plaintiff in that suit, not only any defences which they did raise in that suit, but also any defence which they might have raised, but did not raise therein."[117] This proposition was subsequently approved and applied by the Court of Appeal in *Cox v Dublin City Distillery Co. Ltd (No. 3)*[118] where the defendants argued that certain debentures were invalid because the meeting which purported to authorise their issue had not been properly constituted. However, it was held that they were estopped from raising this defence by their failure to do so in earlier proceedings in which a declaration had been made that the plaintiff was entitled to a lien on certain debentures.

---

[114] Sopinka, Lederman and Byrant, *The Law of Evidence in Canada* (2nd ed., 1999), at §19.67.
[115] (1843) 3 Hare 100, 114.
[116] [1915] 1 IR 345.
[117] *Ibid.* at 372 (emphasis omitted).
[118] [1917] 1 IR 203.

24.037 A conflation of these two facets of cause of action estoppel *i.e.* non-contradiction and non-fragmentation seems to have led to a rather extreme application of *res judicata* in *Dublin Corporation v Building and Allied Trade Union*.[119] The case arose out of a road-widening scheme that necessitated the demolition of part of the defendant's premises. A compulsory purchase order was made and at the arbitration to determine the amount of compensation payable, the defendant was awarded an increased amount of compensation on the basis that it *bona fide* intended to reinstate the premises. It subsequently failed to do so and in fact demolished the premises in question. The plaintiffs then instituted proceedings arguing that the defendants had been unjustly enriched but were met by a plea that the arbitrator's award was *res judicata*.

The Supreme Court, stressing the public interest in the finality of litigation, agreed that the award was *res judicata* and that the plaintiffs could not reopen it by bringing forward additional evidence or matters which were not before the arbitrator. However, it is arguable that the court misapplied the *Henderson* principle. In that case, Wigram VC stated that the decision on a cause of action is conclusive as to every point "which the parties exercising reasonable diligence, might have brought forward *at the time*."[120] However, the claim for unjust enrichment did not arise until the defendants failed to reinstate the hall. It could not have been raised before the arbitrator and, therefore, did not come within the ambit of the principle.

24.038 An example of a case where a party could not with reasonable diligence have brought forward a point during earlier proceedings is *Iarnród Éireann v Ireland*.[121] The proceedings arose out of a collision between a train and a herd of cattle in which a large number of people were injured. One of those injured, Gaspari, sued for personal injuries and recovered judgment against Iarnród Éireann and Diskin, the owner of the cattle. In the instant proceedings, Iarnród Éireann challenged the constitutionality of ss. 12 and 14 of the Civil Liability Act 1961 which dealt with contribution between concurrent wrongdoers. They were facing a total of 230 claims and the effect of the provisions was that it would have to pay the full amount of all claims arising out of the collision because of the limited circumstances of Diskin.

Gaspari, who had been named as a defendant in the instant proceedings, argued that the issues between him and Iarnród Éireann were *res judicata* and could not be reopened even if the impugned provisions were found to be unconstitutional. However, Keane J noted that in the earlier proceedings, Iarnród Éireann had attempted to challenge the validity of the legislation but was unable to do so because of a ruling by the Supreme Court, on appeal, that such a

---

[119] [1996] 1 IR 468, [1996] 2 ILRM 547. See O'Dell, "Restitution and *res judicata* in the Irish Supreme Court" (1997) 113 LQR 245.
[120] (1843) 3 Hare 100, 114.
[121] [1996] 3 IR 321, [1995] 2 ILRM 161(HC), [1996] 2 ILRM 500 (SC).

claim would have to be made in a separate proceeding. Thus, it was "neither undesirable nor impractical nor, least of all, impossible"[122] to treat Gaspari as being in the same position as any of the other plaintiffs if the challenge of Iarnród Éireann was upheld.

Negligence Actions

24.039 Particular difficulties in applying cause of action estoppel arise in circumstances where an act of negligence results in both damage to property and personal injuries. The question arises as to whether that act of negligence gives rise to one or two causes of action. The leading English decision is *Brunsden v Humphery*[123] where it was held that material damage and personal injuries arising out of the same incident give rise to two distinct causes of action. This decision was followed in Northern Ireland in *Davidson v North Down Quarries Ltd*[124] where Nicholson J pointed out that the existence of a duty of care or the standard of care may vary from case to case as between personal injury and damage to property:

> [While] on a given set of facts, there may be no duty in respect of one type of damage such as damage to privacy or economic loss, the standard of care required may have been met in respect of other damage such as damage to personal property so that the plaintiff's claim for damage to personal property may be defeated and there may have been duty, breach and personal injury damage, entitling the plaintiff to succeed in respect of the personal injury claim.[125]

However, this reasoning was rejected in this jurisdiction by Gannon J in *Donohoe v Browne*:[126]

> In my opinion the fact that a person sustains personal injury and damage to property in the same event does not constitute one or more causes of action for compensation. These harmful consequences of an incident involving another party may be the cause, in the sense only of the motivation, for instituting proceedings. ... if the cause of action is negligence on the part of the defendant a claim will not be entertained unless it be established that injury or damage attributable to the negligence has in fact been

---

[122] *Ibid.* at 365, 201.
[123] (1884) 14 QBD 141.
[124] [1988] NI 214. The decision in *Brunsden* was also endorsed by the High Court of Australia in *Port of Melbourne Authority v Anshun* (1981) 147 CLR 589 but was rejected by the Supreme Court of Canada in *Cahoon v Franks* (1963) 63 DLR (2d) 274.
[125] *Ibid.* at 220.
[126] [1986] IR 90.

sustained and is quantifiable in damages. . . . It follows therefore that although the issue of the fact that personal injury loss or expenses has been sustained is a pre-requisite to a successful claim for damages for negligence, the claim for compensation is not the cause of action. The cause of action is the breach of the duty of care which the law imposes in the relevant circumstances. In an action of that nature there are issues which can be distinguished and separated, but the issue of liability for breach of the duty of care is so fundamental that the issue of compensation and its value does not arise for determination unless and until the breach of the duty of care and its connection as a causative factor with the damage for which compensation is claimed has been established.[127]

24.040 The question was considered again recently in *Hayes v Callanan*.[128] The plaintiff in that case had collided with the defendant's tractor while trying to overtake it and then with a wall. Soon afterwards, the plaintiff's solicitors commenced proceedings in the District Court to recover damages in respect of the damage to her car. The district judge found against the defendant and made no finding of contributory negligence against the plaintiff. She subsequently issued separate proceedings claiming damages for personal injury and was met with the defence that her claim was barred by cause of action estoppel and/or that it was an abuse of process. On the trial of a preliminary issue as to whether the plaintiff was estopped from maintaining the proceedings, Smith J defined the questions before him as follows:

> It seems to me that what I have to decide in this case is whether all issues that could have been dealt with at the same time, should in fact have been dealt with at the same time *i.e.* in the one set of proceedings. I must also consider whether the second set of proceedings before me is contrary to public policy and could be regarded as an abuse of the process of the courts.[129]

In deciding these questions, he sought to balance the competing policy considerations. On the one hand, it was desirable, if possible, that the legal liability of parties to an accident should be litigated upon as soon as possible after the occurrence of the accident. On the other, it was also desirable that plaintiffs who suffer material damage, in addition to personal injuries, should not have to wait many years before they are compensated for such losses. On the facts before him, Smith J took the view that the plaintiff had adopted an acceptable course in claiming first for material damage to her car and, subsequently, for personal injuries. The defendant's insurers made the case that had they realised

---

[127] *Ibid.* at 100.
[128] [2000] 1 IR 321.
[129] *Ibid.* at 327.

that a substantial claim for personal injuries was pending, they would almost
certainly have appealed the findings of the district judge and that on appeal,
there might well have been a finding of contributory negligence against the
plaintiff. However, the learned judge considered it unlikely that such a finding
would have been made. He observed that personal injury actions should not be
rushed and concluded that:

> If I were to rule that the plaintiff is estopped from bringing these proceed-
> ings I consider that a great injustice could be done to the plaintiff and in so
> doing I am bearing in mind that of necessity there must be some injustice
> done to the defendant's insurers.[130]

24.041 The approach of Smith J presents an interesting contrast to that of Gannon
J in *Donohoe v Browne*.[131] It can be seen that in order to decide whether cause
of action estoppel arose, Gannon J engaged in a technical analysis of a claim in
negligence whereas Smith J sought to assess the applicability of the doctrine on
the basis of policy and justice. Although it is difficult to take issue with the
technical correctness of Gannon J's approach, it may be that the policy based
approach adopted by Smith J is preferable.[132]

(b) Issue Estoppel

24.042 The concept of issue estoppel derives from the fact that an adjudication
upon a cause of action may involve the determination of many different issues.
As Diplock LJ explained in *Thoday v Thoday*:[133]

> [T]here may be cases where the fulfilment of an identical condition is a
> requirement common to two or more different causes of action. If in liti-
> gation upon one such cause of action any of such separate issues as to
> whether a particular condition has been fulfilled is determined by a court
> of competent jurisdiction, either upon evidence or upon admission by a
> party to the litigation, neither party can, in subsequent litigation between
> one another upon any cause of action which depends upon the fulfilment
> of the identical condition, assert that the condition was fulfilled if the
> court has in the first litigation determined that it was not, or deny it was
> fulfilled if the court in the first litigation determined that it was.[134]

---

[130] *Ibid.* at 328.
[131] [1986] IR 90, 100.
[132] McDermott, *Res Judicata and Double Jeopardy*, (1999), at 62, argues that: "the problem should not be resolved solely on technical arguments as to whether one defines a
cause of action exclusively in terms of the defendant's negligence or in terms of the
different consequences of that negligence. Ultimately it should be a question of policy
based on the purposes of the *res judicata* doctrine."
[133] [1964] P 181, [1964] 2 WLR 371, [1964] 1 All ER 341.
[134] *Ibid.* at 198, 385, 352.

Thus, issue estoppel greatly expands the parameters of *res judicata* because there is no requirement of exact identity of causes of action; identity of issue will suffice.

24.043 There is, however, one crucial difference between cause of action estoppel and issue estoppel which prevents the latter from being viewed merely as a subset of the former. The doctrine of merger does not apply to issue estoppel because it is the cause of action not the individual issues that merge in the former judgment. Therefore, despite *dicta* to the contrary,[135] the principle of *Henderson v Henderson*[136] does not apply to issue estoppel.[137] Indeed, it is difficult to see how it could sensibly be said to apply. As will be seen, one of the prerequisites of issue estoppel is that the issue was determined in previous proceedings. How, then, can it be said that a party is to be estopped from raising an issue which could not have been determined in the earlier proceedings because it was not even raised. In addition, there may be good reasons why a litigant failed to raise or abandoned an issue in earlier proceedings and it would be unjust to preclude him from raising that issue in subsequent proceedings.[138] Indeed, if such preclusion were a possibility, then this would create an incentive for parties to dispute every possible issue for fear of being estopped from doing so at a later date with the effect of prolonging trials.

24.044 The enumeration of the elements of issue estoppel which has most often been endorsed by the Irish courts[139] is that of Gibson LJ in *Shaw v Sloan*:[140]

> It would seem that before estoppel of an issue can arise there must have been a final determination of the same issue in previous proceedings by a court of competent jurisdiction and the parties bound by this earlier deci-

---

[135] *Deighan v Sunday Newspapers Ltd* [1987] NI 105, 115-6 (*per* Carswell J), *Fidelitas Shipping Co. Ltd v V/O Exportchleb* [1966] 1 QB 630, 640, [1965] 2 All ER 4, 9 (*per* Lord Denning MR) and *Arnold v National Westminster Bank plc* [1991] 2 AC 93, 105-109, [1991] 2 WLR 1177, 1184-1187, [1991] 3 All ER 41, 47-50 (*per* Lord Keith).

[136] (1843) 3 Hare 100.

[137] *Cf. Application of Woods* [1970] IR 154, where the Supreme Court held that a previous decision on a *habeas corpus* application would not preclude an applicant from raising a new ground at a later date even though that ground might have been, but was not, put forward on the first application. Although this conclusion was reached on the basis that the principles which apply in litigation *inter partes* are not applicable in *habeas corpus* applications, it is submitted that the same principles apply.

[138] *Carl Zeiss Stiftung v Rayner & Keeler Ltd (No. 2)* [1967] 1 AC 853, 917, 947, [1966] 3 WLR 125, 146, 171, [1966] 2 All ER 536, 554, 573 (*per* Lords Reid and Upjohn).

[139] By the High Court in *Gilroy v McLoughlin* [1988] IR 44, [1989] ILRM 133, *Breathnach v Ireland (No. 2)* [1993] 2 IR 448, 452, and by the Supreme Court in *Lawless v Bus Éireann* [1994] 1 IR 474, 478.

[140] [1982] NI 393, 398.

sion must have been either the same parties as are sought in the later proceedings to be estopped or their privies.[141]

The questions of (i) final and conclusive judgment; (ii) court of competent jurisdiction and (iii) identity of parties, have already been examined so it just remains to elaborate upon the requirement of identity of issues.

In order to establish the requisite identity of issues, the issue in question must be identical with an issue decided in previous proceedings.[142] In addition, it must also be shown that in the previous proceedings, the issue actually arose for decision, and that it was necessarily determined by the court as a matter fundamental to its decision. The ascertainment of whether these requirements have been met involves a careful exposition of the law and an examination of the judgment and/or order in the first action,[143] the pleadings in both,[144] and any other relevant and admissible evidence.[145]

(i) Identical Issues

24.045 The issue determined in the previous action and that upon which it is sought to raise an estoppel must be identical[146] and where the previous determi-

---

[141] *Cf.* the formulations of Diplock LJ in *Mills v Cooper* [1967] 2 QB 459, 468, [1967] 2 WLR 1343, 1350, [1967] 2 All ER 100, 104, and of Lord Brandon in *The Sennar* [1985] 1 WLR 490, 499, [1985] 2 All ER 104, 110, [1985] 1 Lloyd's Rep 521, 526.

[142] *Cf.* the comments of Murnaghan J in *Royal Bank of Ireland Ltd v O'Rourke* [1962] IR 159, 160 that it had to be shown that the issue raised in the later proceedings was "substantially the same" as that determined in the earlier proceedings.

[143] See, for example, *Rhatigan v Gill* [1999] 2 ILRM 427, where O'Sullivan J engaged in a detailed and careful examination of the court orders made in the earlier proceedings. Where no written judgment or order exists, reference may be had to an entry in the Registrar's Book (*White v Spendlove* [1942] IR 224), the court file (see *Rhatigan v Gill* [1999] 2 ILRM 427) or a contemporaneous note taken by counsel or a solicitor for one of the parties (*Cooney v Ireland* Supreme Court, *ex tempore*, 11 October 1999; *Dublin County Council v Taylor* High Court (Blayney J) 18 November 1988; *Gilroy v McLoughlin* [1988] IR 44, [1989] ILRM 133; *Waite v House of Spring Gardens Ltd* High Court (Barrington J) 26 June 1985).

[144] See, for example, the examination undertaken by Carswell J in *Deighan v Sunday Newspapers Ltd* [1987] NI 105.

[145] See *Rhatigan v Gill* [1999] 2 ILRM 427, where the evidence of a Land Registry official was considered by O'Sullivan J in considering the interpretation of the High Court order in earlier proceedings relating to a boundary dispute. See also, *Trainor v McKee* [1988] NI 556; *Cloutte v Storey* [1911] 1 Ch 18.

[146] It is important to note that it is the issues, not the method of proof, which must be the same. Although a coincidence in the *facta probantia* between the two actions is a factor indicating that the issues are the same, differences in evidence do not render otherwise identical issues different (*Deighan v Sunday Newspapers Ltd* [1987] NI 105, 115 (*per* Carswell J).

nation involved a finding of fact, no estoppel will arise if there has been any change in circumstances.[147]

A straightforward example where there was identity of issue can be seen in *Nolan v Listowel UDC*.[148] The plaintiff had been the passenger in a car which collided with a mound of rubble on the road. In a previous action, another passenger in the car had successfully sued both the council and the owner of the car (who was vicariously liable for any negligence on the part of the driver) and on the issue of contribution and indemnity, it had been held that the council was solely liable. In the instant case, the council sought to join the owner of the car as a third party and it was held that they were estopped by the previous decision from raising again the issue of the fault of the driver of the car.[149]

Three areas which have given rise to particular difficulty in determining identity of issues and which merit separate consideration are (i) collisions involving motor vehicles, (ii) taxation matters, and (iii) planning decisions.

Collisions Involving Motor Vehicles

24.046 The difficulties in this area flow from the different duties imposed on road users to other road users and themselves. In *Donohoe v Browne*,[150] the plaintiff, Donohoe, claimed damages for personal injuries sustained in a collision between a motorcycle driven by him and a car owned by the first defendant, Browne and driven by the second defendant, McCabe. In previous proceedings taken by Browne for damage to her car, it was held by the Circuit Court that Donohoe had been solely to blame for the collision and the defendants pleaded that he was estopped from proceeding with his claim by virtue of this determination. Gannon J advocated a broad approach based on the substance of the issue rather than the technical definition thereof[151] and adopted

---

[147] *O'B. v O'B.* [1984] IR 182, [1984] ILRM 1; *DPP v Gray* Supreme Court, *ex tempore*, 10 November 1997.

[148] [1966] IR 56. See also *White v Spendlove* [1942] IR 224 (defendant not estopped from raising defence that two agreements combined constituted valid agreement because this issue had not been determined in previous proceedings between the parties).

[149] No point was taken as to any difference between the duties owed to the passengers. *Cf. Black v Mount and Hancock* [1965] SASR 167. Black was a passenger in a car driven by Hancock which collided with a car driven by Mount. In a previous action taken by another passenger in Hancock's car, Hunt, it was held that Hancock was 85% liable and Mount was 15% liable. It was held that Hancock was estopped from denying, as against Mount, that he was 85% to blame for the injuries sustained by Black. Although there was a distinction in law between the duties owed by the drivers to each of the passengers, Chamberlain J observed that the "duties of care of each driver owed to the two passengers, the breach of those duties and the extent of their responsibility for the damage depended on precisely identical facts in each case" (at 170).

[150] [1986] IR 90.

[151] Relying on *Ord v Ord* [1923] 2 KB 432, [1923] All ER 206, and the *dictum* of Bowen LJ in *Brunsden v Humphrey* (1884) 14 QBD 141, 148 that "the application of the rule

the criterion of "whether the same evidence considered in relation to an issue in the earlier proceedings will be required and relied upon to support a determination upon the same issue between the same parties in the later proceeding".[152]

The learned judge recognised that there is a distinction in law between the nature of the duty of care, the breach of which is imputed by a plea of contributory negligence, and the duty of care to all road users, imputed in a plea of ordinary negligence.[153] Where pleaded by a defendant, the gist of a plea of contributory negligence is that a plaintiff failed to take reasonable care for the safety of himself or for his property whilst a plea of ordinary negligence alleges the person failed to take reasonable care for the safety of all road users who might reasonably have been expected to be present. Because the pleadings from the lower court were not produced he did not know whether a plea of ordinary negligence had been made by Donohoe in those proceedings. However, he was of the opinion that it was clear from an examination of the Circuit Court order (which included the finding that "the defendant was negligent and the plaintiff was not negligent") that the judge had considered the question of whether Donohoe was the only party entirely liable in negligence for the collision. Thus, this matter having been necessarily and directly determined against him, the plaintiff was estopped from bringing his claim.

24.047 In *Gilroy v McLoughlin*[154] a collision had occurred between two cars. Earlier proceedings, taken by the defendant, McLoughlin and his brother against the plaintiff had been dismissed on appeal by the High Court on the ground that the McLoughlins had failed to discharge the onus of proof on them to show that Gilroy had been negligent. In the instant proceedings, the plea made by the defendant was that "the collision was caused entirely or alternatively contributed to by the negligence and breach of duty of the plaintiff" and the question for resolution was whether he was estopped from making this plea by reason of the dismissal of the earlier proceedings.

Blayney J examined the plea and concluded that it was simply a plea of contributory negligence. Although ordinary negligence was pleaded, this could not mean a breach of the duty of care owed by the plaintiff to the defendant as negligence in that sense would have no place in such a plea. Accordingly, the question was whether the defendant was estopped from pleading contributory negligence and he was in no doubt as to the answer. The only negligence on the part of Gilroy which had been considered in the earlier proceedings was ordi-

---

depends, not upon any technical consideration of the identity of forms of action, but upon matter of substance".
[152] [1986] IR 90, 99 (quoting Brett MR in *Brunsden v Humphrey* (1884) 14 QBD 141, 148: "it is whether the same sort of evidence would prove the plaintiff's case in the two actions").
[153] *Jackson v Goldsmith* (1950) 81 CLR 446.
[154] [1988] IR 44, [1989] ILRM 133.

nary negligence. The issue of his contributory negligence did not and could not have arisen because Gilroy made no counterclaim against McLoughlin in those proceedings and it is only if he had that it would have been appropriate for the issue of Gilroy's contributory negligence to be made. In addition, the question of contributory negligence only arises where there is already a finding of negligence against the other party and since McLoughlin had not been found to have been negligent, the question of Gilroy's contributory negligence could not have been considered in the previous proceedings.

One issue expressly left open by Blayney J was whether the dismissal of the earlier action on the ground that the McLoughlins had failed to discharge their onus of proof was equivalent to a holding that Gilroy had not been negligent. Arguably, it is not. To say that a party cannot prove that another is negligent is quite different from saying that that party is not negligent.[155] Such a finding is inherently equivocal on the question of the other party's negligence except where the issues in the case coupled with the terms of the judgment indicate otherwise.[156]

24.048 Although Blayney J was of the opinion that *Donohoe v Browne*[157] was clearly distinguishable on the facts because of the express finding by the Circuit Court judge that the plaintiff had been negligent, there is a basic contradiction between the two decisions. This is because of Blayney J's assertion that a plea of ordinary negligence cannot be made in defence. It is implicit in the judgment of Gannon J that he considered that a plea of ordinary negligence could properly be made in a defence and that if made, it could be adjudicated upon by the trial judge. Indeed, if a plea of ordinary negligence cannot properly be made, then the determination of this issue was not a necessary matter fundamental to the decision of the action and no estoppel could be based on it.

The better view would seem to be that ordinary negligence can be pleaded in defence. If, for example, a defendant manages to prove that a collision was caused entirely by the plaintiff's failure to take reasonable care for the safety of the defendant, then this would be a complete defence to the plaintiff's claim. In addition, as a matter of policy, it is clearly better if the issue of the plaintiff's negligence can be raised and determined because this increases the potential application of *res judicata* and, thus, promotes finality of litigation.

---

[155] See the comments made by Palles CB in a different context in *Lennon v Meegan* [1905] 2 IR 189, 196.

[156] See *Belton v Carlow County Council* [1997] 1 IR 172, [1997] 2 ILRM 405, where a finding that the plaintiff in previous proceedings had failed to satisfy the court on the balance of probabilities that a fire in its factory had been caused by the malicious act of a third party was held to constitute a finding that the fire had been started by the owners of the company where it was common case that the fire had been started deliberately and the issue between the parties to the previous proceedings was whether the owners of the company or a third party had started the fire.

[157] [1986] IR 90.

24.049 This still leaves to be resolved the basic question of the relationship between pleas of negligence and of contributory negligence. This issue arose in the Supreme Court decision in *McCauley v McDermott*.[158] The plaintiff was the passenger in a car which was involved in a collision with a tractor. The car owner instituted proceedings in the District Court against the tractor owner claiming damages for material damage to his car and, on appeal, it was held by the Circuit Court that the collision was due to the negligence of the tractor driver and that there was no contributory negligence on the part of the car driver. The instant proceedings were instituted by the plaintiff against the tractor owner claiming damages for personal injuries. The tractor owner was granted liberty to issue and serve a third party notice against the car driver and a motion was subsequently brought to strike out the third party notice on the grounds that the issues arising between the tractor owner and the car driver were *res judicata* or alternatively, an abuse of the process of the court. The first question to be decided by the Supreme Court was that of identity of issues and after examining the issues in both sets of proceedings, the court concluded that the same issue, namely whether the car driver was in breach of his duty to the tractor owner, was involved in both.

In view of the fact that the finding of the Circuit Court judge was limited to a finding that there had been no contributory negligence on the part of the car driver, not that there had been no negligence on his part, the decision of the Supreme Court seems to proceed on the basis that there is an equivalence between the two pleas for the purposes of issue estoppel. This case would thus seem to herald a shift towards what Gibson LJ has described as "the broad common sense approach"[159] from the more narrow technical approach exhibited in the earlier cases. According to the narrow approach, there is a bright line distinction between negligence and contributory negligence. Therefore, a finding of contributory negligence on the part of a plaintiff in one action does not create an estoppel on the issue of his negligence in a later action. The broad approach looks past the technicalities of the various duties of care and asks whether the issue in the later case was substantially determined in the earlier case.

24.050 The Northern Ireland Court of Appeal had to choose between these two approaches in *Shaw v Sloan*[160] and faced with the divergence of approach exhibited by the English courts, it plumped for the broader approach both on the basis that it represented the weight of authority in England[161] and on policy

---

[158] [1997] 2 ILRM 486.

[159] *Shaw v Sloan* [1982] NI 393, 399.

[160] [1982] NI 393.

[161] Though some cases have taken a narrow approach (*e.g. Randolph v Tuck* [1962] 1 QB 175, [1961] 2 WLR 855, [1961] 1 All ER 814), the weight of English authority favours the broad approach (*e.g. Marginson v Blackburn Borough Council* [1939] 2 KB 426; *Bell v Holmes* [1956] 1 WLR 1359, [1956] 3 All ER 449; *Wood v Luscombe* [1966] 1

grounds.[162] Gibson LJ pointed out that if the narrow view is taken, then the scope for the operation of issue estoppel is drastically reduced with respect to collisions between motor vehicles. He gave the simple example of a collision involving two cars driven by their respective owners, A and B. If A sues B for negligence and B pleads contributory negligence, the issues are: (i) was B in breach of his duty of care to A? and (ii) was A in breach of his duty of care to himself? If B later sues A, then the issues are reversed and because of this, according to the narrow view, there is no issue estoppel.

24.051 It would seem, therefore, that the broad approach is preferable in terms of promoting finality of litigation and consistency of decision making. Thus, in the fact scenario outlined by Gibson LJ, there may or may not be an estoppel in the second case. This is because, if as has been argued, it is open to B in the first action to allege negligence *simpliciter* on the part of A, that issue may well have been determined by the judge in the first action. Alternatively, even if ordinary negligence is not pleaded or is not considered by the judge, his determination of the existence or absence of contributory negligence may possibly equate with a determination of the question of negligence on the part of A. This is because there are certain facts which go to prove contributory negligence only such as failure to wear a seat belt whereas there are other facts such as failure to keep a proper lookout at a junction which may constitute both contributory and ordinary negligence.

Where the evidence is the same in both actions and there is no material difference in the evidence which goes to prove contributory negligence and that which goes to prove negligence, then it seems unduly technical to say that the determination of the issue of contributory negligence in the first action does not determine the issue of negligence in the second. As stated above, what is needed in each case is a careful examination of the judgment in the first action, the pleadings in both and the evidence in both cases in order to determine whether *substantially the same* issue has already been determined in earlier proceedings whatever the differences in legal nomenclature and effect.

QB 169, [1965] 3 WLR 998, [1964] 3 All ER 972; *Wall v Radford* [1991] 2 All ER 741). In contrast, the bulk of Australian authority favours the narrower, more technical approach *e.g. Jackson v Goldsmith* (1950) 81 CLR 446, *Ramsay v Pigram* (1967) 118 CLR 271 but there is some support for a broader approach *e.g. Black v Mount and Hancock* [1965] SASR 167.

[162] *Shaw v Sloan* was followed by Carswell J in *Trainor v McKee* [1988] NI 556, who summarised the holding in *Shaw* on this point as follows: "Where two parties to a road traffic accident sue each other in separate actions, the issues are the same for the purposes of estoppel, notwithstanding the technical difference between the duties owed in negligence and contributory negligence."

Taxation Matters

24.052 Divergent approaches have been taken on the question of whether a decision on a point of law in respect of the assessment for one tax year can ground a plea of issue estoppel if the same point arises in respect of a subsequent tax year. In *Hoystead v Taxation Commissioner*[163] the Privy Council answered this question in the affirmative. However, in a judgment delivered only a few months earlier in *Broken Hill Proprietary Co. v Broken Hill Municipal Council,*[164] a differently constituted board had held that a decision as to liability for taxes or rates for a particular period could not ground a plea of *res judicata* with regard to a claim by the taxing or rating authority in respect of a subsequent period on the basis that the claim relates to a different period and is therefore founded on different facts even if the question of law involved is the same. This view now predominates in England. *Hoystead* was effectively overruled by the Privy Council in *Caffoor v Income Tax Commissioner*[165] and the narrow approach has since been adopted by the House of Lords in *Society of Medical Officers of Health v Hope.*[166]

24.053 The choice between these conflicting authorities fell to be made by the Supreme Court in *Kildare County Council v Keogh.*[167] The plaintiffs sued the defendants for arrears of rates for the years 1955-61 and in their defence, the defendants contended that the matter was *res judicata* by reason of a decision of the High Court in 1953. In that case, the plaintiffs had sought to recover rates for the years 1951-52 but it was held that the defendants were not liable to pay rates by virtue of the operation of s.11(2) of the Electricity (Supply) (Amendment) Act 1930.

A majority of the Supreme Court preferred to follow the decisions in *Broken Hill* and *Caffoor* rather than that in *Hoystead*. Walsh J pointed out that the subject matter of the claim before the court was for a period subsequent to the previous determination and expressed the opinion that "the question of liability for rates for one year is always to be treated as inherently a different question to that of liability for another year, even though there might be an identity on the question of law involved".[168] An important factor in making this choice was his

---

[163] [1926] AC 155, [1925] All ER 56.
[164] [1926] AC 94, [1925] All ER 672.
[165] [1961] AC 584, [1961] 2 WLR 794, [1961] 2 All ER 436.
[166] [1960] AC 551, [1960] 2 WLR 404, [1960] 1 All ER 317.
[167] [1971] IR 330 (followed on this point by Carroll J in *Clare County Council v Mahon* [1995] 3 IR 193, [1996] 1 ILRM 521). *Cf. Aylmer v Mahaffey* [1925] NI 167, where the Northern Ireland Court of Appeal applied the ordinary principles of *res judicata* to hold that the Special Commissioners hearing an appeal from a tax assessment for the year 1922-23 were bound by the previous decision of the Recorder of Belfast that a deduction had been properly claimed for the year 1921-22.
[168] *Ibid.* at 342-3.

conclusion that there can be no estoppel as to the construction of an Act of the legislature: "It would be contrary to public policy that an erroneous construction of a statute should be perpetuated so as to decide successive claims between the same parties."[169]

McLoughlin J, dissenting, preferred the approach in *Hoystead* which he thought to be more in accordance with the policy behind the principle of *res judicata*, namely the achievement of finality in disputes between parties and the restraint of vexatious litigation. He pointed out that if estoppel did not apply, then the plaintiffs could have brought fresh proceedings every year after the initial decision until they found a judge willing to overrule the earlier decision. There is much force in this point though it might be speculated that repeated actions of this nature would be restrained as an abuse of the process of the court.

24.054 The approach of the majority has recently been endorsed and applied by the Supreme Court in *Gael Linn Teo. v Commissioner of Valuation*,[170] where Keane J summarised the principle laid down by Walsh J as follows:[171]

> [I]n a case of issues regarding rates and taxation liability in any event, the issue of liability for one year is not the same as liability for another year, although the issue of law may be exactly the same.

The learned judge also supported his conclusion that *res judicata* did not apply by reference to s.3(1) of the Valuation Act 1988 which allows the question of valuation to be reopened and the decision in *Mayor of Limerick v Commissioner of Valuation*[172] where it was held by the Queen's Bench that the fact that the legislature gave an opportunity for a review of one year's valuation the following year, meant that an estoppel could not arise.

Planning Decisions

24.055 As noted above, where the previous determination involved a finding of fact, no estoppel will arise if there has been any change in circumstances. This means that although the decisions of planning authorities on planning applications potentially come within the scope of *res judicata*, they will rarely do so in practice because, unless the applications submitted are identical or virtually identical, the planning issues involved in adjudicating on the application will be different.[173] So, in *State (Kenny and Hussey) v An Bord Pleanála*,[174] it

---

[169] *Ibid.* at 343.
[170] [1999] 3 IR 296.
[171] *Ibid.* at 304.
[172] (1872) IR 6 CL 420.
[173] See *Delgany Area Residents Association Ltd v Wicklow County Council* High Court

was held by Carroll J that an earlier decision of the board refusing planning permission for a single storey house was not a refusal covering all single storey houses.[175] She pointed out that the second application which had been considered by the board was for a house that was different in conception and design and therefore, *res judicata* did not apply. In addition, even if exactly the same application were to be submitted, the matter would not be *res judicata* if the planning considerations relevant to the area had changed.

(ii) At Issue Between the Parties

24.056 The point must have been distinctly put in issue by the parties.[176] Thus, it must actually have been in contention during the hearing as opposed to being merely raised in the pleadings.[177] This requirement rules out any idea of "estoppel by implication" unless the decision of the party not to contest an issue can be construed as an admission on that point.[178]

In *D. v C.*,[179] the petitioner had obtained an order in 1981 barring the respondent from the family home. An application for a barring order could only be made by a spouse and in support of her application the petitioner had filed an affidavit in which she averred that she had been married to the respondent. In the instant proceedings, she sought a decree of nullity and the respondent argued that she was precluded from claiming that the marriage was invalid by reason of the grant of the barring order. Rejecting this contention, Costello J held that "[b]efore an issue estoppel can arise it must ... be shown that a point arising in the second action was clearly put in issue in the first and was with certainty determined in the first action."[180] Although, the court had acted on the assumption that the petitioner was the spouse of the respondent in the earlier proceedings, the validity of the marriage was not put in issue nor was the court asked to determine it. Therefore, no estoppel arose on that point.

24.057 In *Rhatigan v Gill*,[181] a dispute arose between the plaintiff, who had

---

(Barr J) 28 May 1998. *Cf. Athlone Woollen Mills Co. Ltd v Athlone UDC* [1950] IR 1 and *O'Dea v Minister for Local Government* (1953) 91 ILTR 169.

[174] High Court (Carroll J) 23 February 1984.

[175] See also *Murray v Buckley* High Court (Barron J) 5 December 1990.

[176] *Robertson & Co. v Mulvenna* (1942) 76 ILTR 1, 4; *Green v Martin* (1986) 63 ALR 627.

[177] *Cf.* the comments of Holmes LJ in *Irish Land Commission v Ryan* [1900] 2 IR 565, 583, that "an unnecessary averment in a record that is neither pleaded to nor admitted cannot be used as an estoppel."

[178] See, for example, *Hennerty v Bank of Ireland* High Court (O'Hanlon J) 5 July 1988, where O'Hanlon J viewed the failure of the plaintiff to contest certain matters in earlier proceedings as concessions on his part which estopped him from raising those matters in later proceedings.

[179] [1984] ILRM 173.

[180] *Ibid.* at 193-194.

[181] [1999] 2 ILRM 427.

purchased a site from the defendant, as to the ownership of a 12 foot strip of land. In his counterclaim, the defendant contended that the plaintiffs were estopped from raising the issue of ownership of this strip because it had been decided in previous proceedings concerning a boundary dispute between the defendant and the purchasers of another site from the defendant. The plaintiffs argued that the previous litigation did not address the question of the ownership of the 12 foot strip. O'Sullivan J examined the decisions in *Kelly v Ireland*,[182] *Breathnach v Ireland*[183] and *Breathnach v Ireland (No. 2)*,[184] and stated:[185]

> From the foregoing it will be seen that the court's approach to the application of the doctrine of issue estoppel is precise and strict. The issue must be identical with the issue already determined in earlier litigation and the determination, when it is an issue of fact, must be a formal determination of that issue in the same manner as it would have arisen in the second set of proceedings and not by reason, only, of the application of a principle of law which would not apply in the second set of proceedings.

Having examined the pleadings and orders made by the Circuit Court and High Court in the earlier proceedings, O'Sullivan J concluded that the issue as to the ownership of the 12 foot strip had not been raised or determined in the earlier proceedings which were concerned with an entirely different question. In particular, he was satisfied that the order made by the High Court determined the only relevant issue established by the pleadings and that it was not necessary to the determination of that issue that there be a conclusion as to the ownership of the 12 foot strip.

(iii) Definitely and Necessarily Determined

24.058 It is essential to show that the issue was actually determined in the earlier proceedings.[186] This point was emphasised by Lord Shaw in *Bradshaw v M'Mullan*[187] when he stated that the question of *res judicata* cannot arise unless you have a *judicium i.e.* an adjudication on some issue of law or fact. Difficulties may arise in some cases in ascertaining whether and how an issue was determined. The general principle would seem to be that, where no grounds are given for the decision and there are a number of grounds upon which it could have been reached, then the judgment will not give rise to an estoppel on any issue raised because it is impossible to tell what issues were determined by the

---

[182] [1986] ILRM 318.
[183] [1989] IR 489.
[184] [1993] 2 IR 448.
[185] [1999] 2 ILRM 427, 438.
[186] *O'Grady v Synan* [1900] 2 IR 602; *Royal Bank of Ireland Ltd v O'Rourke* [1962] IR 159.
[187] [1920] 2 IR 412, 424.

court.[188] This is subject to the caveat that in some cases, it may be possible, by an examination of the pleadings or otherwise to determine the grounds of the decision despite their non-enumeration in the judgment.[189]

Necessarily Determined

24.059 Not every issue decided in previous proceedings can ground an estoppel. An estoppel may only be raised if determination of the issue was necessary for or fundamental to the decision in the earlier proceedings.[190] It is, thus, necessary:

> [T]o distinguish the matters fundamental or cardinal to the prior decision or judgment, or necessarily involved in it as its legal justification or foundation, from matters which, even though actually raised and decided as being in the circumstances of the case the determining considerations, yet are not in point of law the essential foundation or groundwork of that judgment.[191]

24.060 In *Dublin County Council v Taylor*[192] the applicant county council sought an order restraining the respondent from making an unauthorised use of his premises. In his defence, the respondent contended that he had been granted a default retention planning permission and that this issue was *res judicata* because of the decision of a district judge to dismiss a previous summons against the respondent on the ground that such a default permission had been granted. Applying the test laid down by Spencer-Bower and Turner of whether "the determination upon which it is sought to found an estoppel [is] so fundamental to the substantive decision that the latter *cannot stand* without the former",[193]

---

[188] *Irish Land Commission v Ryan* [1900] 2 IR 565; *O'Grady v Synan* [1900] 2 IR 602. But see, *contra, Blake v O'Kelly* (1874) IR 9 Eq 54.

[189] See, for example, *White v Spendlove* [1942] IR 224.

[190] See *Blair v Curran* (1939) 62 CLR 464, 531-2 (*per* Dixon J) (in a passage quoted with approval by the Supreme Court in *Belton v Carlow County Council* [1997] 1 IR 172, [1997] 2 ILRM 405). See also *Kildare County Council v Keogh* [1971] IR 330, 344 (*per* McLoughlin J), *O'Grady v Synan* [1900] 2 IR 602, 608 *per* Gibson J, *Countess of Mountcashell's Estate* [1920] 1 IR 1, 6 *per* Ross J, *In re Estate of Lynham* [1928] IR 127 and *Healy v Spillane* [1915] 2 IR 195.

[191] *Per* Dixon J in *Blair v Curran* (1939) 62 CLR 464, 533. *Cf.* the test proposed by Lord Wilberforce in *Carl Zeiss Stiftung v Rayner and Keeler Ltd (No. 2)* [1967] 1 AC 853, 965, [1966] 3 WLR 125, 187, [1966] 2 All ER 536, 584 (relying on the *dicta* of Coleridge J in *R v Township and Inhabitants of Hartington Middle Quarter* (1855) 4 E & B 780, 794) of whether the determination of an issue "is a 'necessary step' to the decision or a 'matter which it was necessary to decide and which was actually decided as the groundwork of the decision'". This test was endorsed by O'Hanlon J in *Kelly v Ireland* [1986] ILRM 318, 329.

[192] High Court (Blayney J) 18 November 1988.

[193] *The Doctrine of Res Judicata* (2nd ed., 1969), at 181-2.

Blayney J held that no issue estoppel arose. Although the district judge purported to found his decision on his conclusion that a default permission had been granted, determination of this issue was neither necessary nor even relevant for his decision. This was because the summons related to the failure of the respondent to comply with a warning notice during a period *prior* to the making of the application for retention planning permission and retention permission, even if granted, would not have retrospective effect.

Ultimately, no matter what the precise formula employed, there is a degree of discretion in deciding whether the determination of a particular issue was fundamental or necessary to a previous decision. It is to be expected that, in some cases at least, the resolution of this problem will be influenced by the later court's opinion as to the correctness of the prior decision.

Default Judgments

24.061 Special difficulties arise as to the identification of the issues definitely and necessarily determined by default judgments. In *McConnell v Lombard and Ulster Banking Ltd*,[194] Gibson LJ pointed out that where judgment is granted in default of appearance or defence, then as between the parties and for the purpose of the action, all allegations in the statement of claim are deemed to have been admitted by the defaulting party and to that extent he will generally be estopped from setting up in any subsequent proceeding any matter of defence which was "necessarily and with complete precision"[195] decided against him by the previous default judgment. However:

> the courts will scrutinise such judgments with extreme particularity in order to ascertain the bare essence of what must necessarily have been decided and to avoid implying as having been decided by a judgment in default any more than is necessarily involved by reason of the fact that judgment has been obtained.[196]

24.062 At one point, the view was taken that the grounds of the decision could only be ascertained from the terms of the judgment itself. In *Irish Land Commission v Ryan*,[197] Fitzgibbon J stated that "the ground and extent" of an estoppel raised upon a default judgment must be:

> [F]ound on the face of the judgment itself, and cannot be inferred or de-

---

[194] [1982] NI 203.

[195] *Per* Lord Maugham LC in *New Brunswick Railway Co. v British & French Trust Corporation Ltd* [1939] AC 1, 21, [1938] 4 All ER 747, 756.

[196] *Per* Gibson LJ in *McConnell v Lombard & Ulster Banking Ltd* [1982] NI 203, 207, adopting the comments of Lord Radcliffe in *Kok Hoong v Leong Cheong Kweng Mines Ltd* [1964] AC 993, 1012, [1964] 2 WLR 150, 158, [1964] 1 All ER 300, 306.

[197] [1900] 2 IR 565. See also *Collins v Stapleton* (1914) 48 ILTR 243.

duced from the pleading of the party who has obtained the judgment, when the defendant has said nothing, and done nothing, and has merely allowed the judgment to go by default.[198]

However, the better view would seem to be that reference may also be had to the pleadings of the plaintiff and the defendant (if any). In *Kinsella v Connor*,[199] the plaintiff brought an action seeking to recover sums allegedly paid by him in excess of the correct rent under the Rent Restrictions Acts. In his defence, the defendant landlord contended that the plaintiff was estopped from denying that the rent was due by virtue of a judgment in default of appearance that had been obtained by the landlord in an action for arrears of rent. The civil bill in that case expressly referred to a consent previously entered into between the parties in which the plaintiff admitted that he owed a certain amount in rent. Judge Shannon distinguished the decision in *Irish Land Commission v Ryan*[200] and held that the plaintiff could not re-litigate a matter which he had admitted on the record even though such admission was only by default of appearance or defence.

Criminal Judgments

24.063 The difficulties attendant upon discerning what issues had been determined in a criminal trial gave rise to doubts about whether issue estoppel could be raised in a civil case on foot of a previous decision in a criminal trial. The question was addressed for the first time in *Kelly v Ireland*,[201] the facts of which are set out above. O'Hanlon J referred to the decision of the House of Lords in *Director of Public Prosecutions v Humphrys*[202] where one of the arguments put forward by Lord Salmon against the importation of the concept of issue estoppel into criminal law was the difficulty of identifying the issues. There were no pleadings defining the issues and no judgments explaining how the issues were decided even if identifiable. However, in the case before him it was possible to identify the issue and there was a judgment of the Special Criminal Court defining the issue and explaining how it had been decided. He therefore held that:

> In the rare case where a clearly identifiable issue has been raised in the course of a criminal trial and has been decided against a party to those proceedings by means of a judgment explaining how the issue has been decided, I would be prepared to hold that such decision may give rise to issue estoppel in later civil proceedings in which that party is also in-

[198] *Ibid.* at 572.
[199] (1942) 76 ILTR 141.
[200] [1900] 2 IR 565.
[201] [1986] ILRM 318.
[202] [1977] AC 1, [1976] 2 WLR 857, [1976] 2 All ER 497.

volved. Such estoppel would arise, not only in relation to the specific issue determined (in this case, whether the statement was made freely and voluntarily) but also to findings which were fundamental to the court's decision on such issue.[203]

24.064 In *Breathnach v Ireland*,[204] this passage was approved and applied by Lardner J. Breathnach, who had been a co-accused of Kelly, brought a civil action claiming damages for *inter alia* assault and battery alleged to have occurred while he was in detention. He had challenged the admissibility of his confession on this basis at his trial but the Special Criminal Court held that he had not been assaulted and admitted his confession. His conviction was subsequently quashed by the Court of Criminal Appeal because it was not satisfied beyond a reasonable doubt that the inculpatory statements made by him were voluntary. However, the court expressly refused to interfere with the findings of fact by the Special Criminal Court on the issue of assault and battery.

Lardner J examined the trial before the Special Criminal Court and found that it had made a determination, following a lengthy *voir dire*, that the statements of the plaintiff had not been made as the result of any assaults by the gardaí and that the injuries of the plaintiff had not been inflicted or caused by any member of the gardaí. On appeal, the Court of Criminal Appeal had expressly left the findings of fact of the lower court in relation to the allegations of assault undisturbed and therefore, the decision of the Special Criminal Court was a subsisting decision on that issue. He, therefore, concluded that the plaintiff was estopped from litigating this issue again.

A further preliminary issue was directed to be tried as to whether the defendants were estopped from raising in their defence the issues as to the legality of the arrest and detention of the plaintiff, and whether his constitutional right of access to a solicitor had been denied. This was decided by Blayney J in *Breathnach v Ireland (No. 2)*[205] who endorsed the reasoning of O'Hanlon J in *Kelly v Ireland*.[206] He held that the determination by the Special Criminal Court that the plaintiff's arrest and subsequent detention had been unlawful constituted a clear finding against the People, as represented by the Director of Public Prosecutions and was of such a nature as to operate as an estoppel. However, in finding that the plaintiff's request for a solicitor had been denied, the court of trial had been acting upon the principle that in a criminal trial, the construction of the evidence most favourable to the accused must be preferred and had not made a positive finding of fact in relation to the issue. Therefore, the defendants were not estopped from raising an issue in their defence as to whether the plaintiff's request for a solicitor had been denied.

---

[203] [1986] ILRM 318, 328.
[204] [1989] IR 489.
[205] [1993] 2 IR 448.
[206] [1986] ILRM 318.

JUDGMENTS IN REM

24.065 The foregoing discussion has dealt with the requirements for *res judicata* in respect of judgments *in personam*.

As we have seen, one of the vital requirements for *res judicata* is that of identity of parties. However, even where this element is missing, the judgment of a judicial tribunal of competent jurisdiction may still found an estoppel where it constitutes a judgment *in rem*. This was defined by Costello J in *D. v C.*[207] as:

> [A] judgment of a court of competent jurisdiction determining the status of a person or thing or the disposition of a thing, as distinct from a particular interest in it, of a party to the litigation.[208]

It should, thus, be contrasted with a judgment *in personam* which was defined by Costello J in that case as:

> [A judgment] which determine[s] the rights of parties between one another to or in the matter in suit and [does] not affect the status of any person or thing or make any disposition of property.[209]

24.066 The difference between judgments *in rem* and *in personam* and the importance of the distinction is illustrated by the litigation concerning regulation 15 of the Law Society's regulations. This regulation made provision for the granting of exemptions to students from certain named universities which did not include Queen's University Belfast. This situation was challenged by students from Queen's in *Bloomer v Incorporated Law Society of Ireland*[210] and it was held by Laffoy J at first instance and by the Supreme Court that regulation 15 was invalid because it was in breach of Article 6 (now Article 12) of the EC Treaty.

Subsequently in *Abrahamson v Law Society of Ireland*,[211] proceedings were taken by a group of students seeking, *inter alia*, an order that notwithstanding the decision in *Bloomer*, regulation 15 was not invalid in so far as it affected them. These students had not been parties to *Bloomer* and therefore the question of whether they were bound by it turned on whether that judgment was *in rem* or *in personam*. McCracken J offered the following definition of a judgment *in rem*:

> A decision *in rem* is one which determines once and for all, the status of a

---

[207] [1984] ILRM 173.
[208] *Ibid.* at 192.
[209] *Ibid.* at 192.
[210] [1995] 3 IR 14.
[211] [1996] 1 IR 403, [1996] 2 ILRM 481.

particular *res* or thing. It is not a determination which depends upon the relationship between the parties to the action.[212]

Applying this definition to the facts, he stated that if Laffoy J had decided that the plaintiffs in *Bloomer* had been discriminated against because they were graduates of Queen's, that would have been a decision in *personam* as it affected the status of the plaintiffs. However, the decision in the case was that regulation 15 was invalid because it offended against Article 6 of the EC Treaty. Therefore, although the decision as to the validity of regulation 15 was given in the context of the particular circumstances of the Queen's students, if the regulation was invalid as against those students, it was invalid as against the world.[213]

24.067 Although it is not necessary to show identity of parties in order to ground an estoppel on a judgment *in rem*, it is important that the other requirements, namely a final judgment of a court of competent jurisdiction and identity of subject matter are met. So, in *Clare County Council v Mahon*[214] an estoppel based on a putative judgment *in rem* failed because of a lack of jurisdictional competence. The plaintiffs sought declaratory relief that the defendants were liable to pay water charges. The defendants contended that they were entitled to free water under an old lease which it was argued created a charitable trust. Previous proceedings taken by the plaintiffs against another recalcitrant water user had been dismissed by the District and Circuit Courts on the ground that the person was entitled to free water under the lease and the defendants argued that this was a judgment *in rem* such that the plaintiffs was estoped from maintaining the proceedings against them. However, it was held that the dismissal was not a judgment *in rem* because the District Court hearing the action, which was for recovery of the water charges as a simple contract debt, only had jurisdiction to consider that claim and did not have jurisdiction to make a finding as to the existence of a trust.

It should also be noted that a judgment *in rem* is conclusive against all persons only as to the legal result of the decision, not as to the grounds or facts upon which it is based. So, for example, if a defendant is acquitted of an offence and sues for malicious prosecution, the record of the court of trial is conclusive as to the acquittal but not as to his innocence.[215]

---

[212] *Ibid.* at 414, 490.

[213] *Abrahamson* is authority for the proposition that any finding of invalidity in relation to a statute or statutory instrument, whether on the grounds of *ultra vires*, unconstitutionality or breach of European law will constitute a judgment *in rem* and therefore will bind the whole world.

[214] [1995] 3 IR 193, [1996] 1 ILRM 521.

[215] *Purcell v Macnamara* (1807) 9 East 157.

DEFENCES TO RES JUDICATA

FRAUD

24.068 A judgment may be set aside on the ground of fraud[216] and if it is rescinded on this ground, no estoppel may be grounded on it. In order to succeed in such an application, the fraud alleged must be pleaded with particularity[217] and it must be proved that there was "conscious and deliberate dishonesty" and that the judgment was obtained by it.[218]

FRESH EVIDENCE

24.069 The availability of fresh evidence will not defeat a plea of cause of action estoppel,[219] nor can a judgment be set aside on this ground.[220] However, a plea of issue estoppel will not succeed where "further material which is relevant to the correctness or incorrectness of the assertion by that party in the previous proceedings has since become available to him."[221]

In *Kelly v Ireland*,[222] the plaintiff sought to defeat the pleas of issue estoppel and abuse of process by adducing fresh medical evidence which supported his allegations that he had, *inter alia*, received severe blows to his ears while in custody. This consisted of first, the evidence of John Fitzpatrick, who had been arrested and detained at around the same time as the plaintiff, that he had been assaulted in a similar manner; and secondly, the evidence of a specialist, to whom the plaintiff had been referred after his trial, that both he and John Fitzpatrick had suffered trauma to the ear. It was argued that this evidence strongly supported the plaintiff's allegations of severe blows to the ears while in custody.

---

[216] *Waite v House of Spring Gardens Ltd* High Court (Barrington J) 6 June 1985; *St Alban's Investment Co. v London Insurance and Provincial Insurance Co. Ltd* High Court (Murphy J) 27 June 1990; *Tassan Din v Banco Ambrosiano SPA* [1991] 1 IR 569.

[217] *Waite v House of Spring Gardens Ltd* High Court (Barrington J) 6 June 1985; *Tassan Din v Banco Ambrosiano SPA* [1991] 1 IR 569.

[218] *The Ampthill Peerage* [1977] AC 547, 571, [1976] 2 WLR 777, 788, [1976] 2 All ER 411, 419 (*per* Lord Wilberforce).

[219] *McDaid v O'Connor and Bailey Ltd* [1954] IR 25; *Workington Harbour Board v Trade Indemnity Co. (No. 2)* [1938] 2 All ER 101. See also *Tassan Din v Banco Ambrosiano SPA* [1991] 1 IR 569.

[220] *Tassan Din v Banco Ambrosiano SPA* [1991] 1 IR 569; *Re Barrell Enterprises* [1973] 1 WLR 19, 24. In *Tassan Din*, the judgment in question was one of the Supreme Court and therefore Article 34.4.6° which provides that the decision of the Supreme Court shall in all cases be final and conclusive was relied upon by Murphy J but the decision would seem to be of more general import.

[221] *Per* Diplock LJ in *Mills v Cooper* [1967] 2 QB 459, 468-469, [1967] 2 WLR 1343, 1350, [1967] 2 All ER 100, 104.

[222] [1986] ILRM 318.

In assessing the significance of this evidence, O'Hanlon J adopted the test articulated by Goff LJ in the Court of Appeal in *Hunter v Chief Constable of the West Midlands*:[223]

> First, it must be evidence of such a character as "changes the whole aspect of the case"; secondly, it must be evidence which could not, by the exercise of reasonable diligence, have been made available at the previous hearing, and thirdly, it must be evidence which is "well capable of belief in the context of the circumstances as a whole".

Applying this test to the facts of the case, he was of opinion that the evidence of John Fitzpatrick could have been available at the trial of the plaintiff had reasonable diligence been exercised. As regards the medical evidence, this merely reinforced that given at the trial and O'Hanlon J was not satisfied that it was of such a character that, "if presented in the course of the criminal trial, it would have changed the whole aspect of the case in relation to the court's decision to reject the plaintiff's allegations about the circumstances under which he came to make the inculpatory statement."[224]

24.070 The approach of O'Hanlon J was endorsed by Murphy J in *Pringle v Ireland*[225] but subject to the caveat that such an approach could not be applied where the purpose of the civil proceedings was to reverse the judgment of a criminal court. The difference between the two cases turns on the fact that in *Kelly*, the plaintiff sought to reopen an issue which had been determined at his trial whilst in *Pringle* the plaintiff sought to reopen the correctness of his conviction. However, he was precluded from doing so by the criminal analogue of cause of action estoppel and as has already been stated, cause of action estoppel cannot be defeated by fresh evidence.[226]

---

[223] Reported *sub. nom. McIlkenny v Chief Constable of the West Midlands* [1980] QB 283, 334-335, [1980] 2 WLR 689, 717, [1980] 2 All ER 227, 248-9. Goff LJ had himself adopted the test of Earl Cairns LC in *Phosphate Sewage Co. v Molleson* (1879) 4 App Cas 801, 814 that "the new evidence must be such as entirely changes the aspect of the case". The test laid down by Goff LJ was endorsed by the House of Lords on appeal (see, *per* Lord Diplock [1982] AC 529, 545, [1981] 3 WLR 906, 917, [1981] 3 All ER 727, 736).

[224] [1986] ILRM 318, 333.

[225] [1994] ILRM 467.

[226] See now, s.2 of the Criminal Procedure Act 1993, which provides for the review by the Court of Criminal Appeal of a conviction or sentence where a convicted person alleges that a new or newly-discovered fact shows that there has been a miscarriage of justice in relation to the conviction or that the sentence imposed is excessive.

CHANGE IN THE LAW

24.071 Although, in general, it is irrelevant to the question of raising an estoppel that the decision in the previous proceedings was wrong or given on an incorrect legal basis, there may be situations where a matter will not be held to be *res judicata* because of a change in the law. Again, a distinction has to be made between cause of action and issue estoppel. It is now relatively well settled that a plea of issue estoppel will not succeed where the issue determined was a point of law and there has been a change of law in the interim.[227] However, it appears as if a plea of cause of action estoppel will not be defeated by a change in the law between the two sets of proceedings.[228]

It is less clear whether it is possible to invoke cause of action estoppel in respect of a decision which was given on an unconstitutional basis. *Dicta* of Henchy J in *Murphy v Attorney General*[229] suggest that *res judicata* may apply in such circumstances but in *Iarnród Éireann v Ireland*[230] Keane J expressly left open the question of whether these *dicta* were "intended to convey that the principle of *res judicata* would in all circumstances prevent the reopening of accounts between parties where those accounts had been settled on a basis subsequently found to be unconstitutional."

CONTRARY TO STATUTE

24.072 It is clear that a plea of estoppel, including a plea of *res judicata* cannot be raised in defiance of a statute[231] and in *Lipschitz v Tierney*[232] Murnaghan J regarded it as:

> [A] well established principle that a statutory injunction, by which I mean a provision that something "shall" be done, cannot be set at naught or defeated by a previous judgment or agreement between the parties, upon which a plea of *res judicata* or of estoppel might in other circumstances properly be based.[233]

---

[227] *Convoy Reformed Presbyterian Church v Boyton* (1902) 36 ILTR 118; *Arnold v National Westminster Bank plc* [1991] 2 AC 93, [1991] 2 WLR 1177, [1991] 3 All ER 41.
[228] *Arnold v National Westminster Bank plc* [1991] 2 AC 93, [1991] 2 WLR 1177, [1991] 3 All ER 41.
[229] [1982] IR 241, 314.
[230] [1996] 3 IR 321, 364, [1995] 2 ILRM 161, 200.
[231] *Bradshaw v M'Mullan* [1920] IR 412, 425-6 (*per* Lord Shaw); *Dempsey v O'Reilly* [1958] Ir Jur Rep 75 (plaintiff not estopped from setting up the illegality of a contract prohibited by statute).
[232] [1959] IR 144.
[233] *Ibid.* at 147.

In *Nolan v Dublin Board of Assistance*,[234] a previous application by the applicant under the Workmen's Compensation Act 1934 had been dismissed both by
the Circuit Court and by the Supreme Court on appeal. He brought another
application pursuant to s.7(1) of the Workmen's Compensation (Amendment)
Act 1948 and it was argued that he was estopped from doing so by reason of the
earlier dismissal. S.7(1) provided that an action could be maintained, notwithstanding any rule or anything contained in the 1934 Act provided certain conditions were fulfilled and it was held by Judge Shannon that because the terms of
the section were mandatory, no estoppel could be raised.

24.073 It has also been held that an estoppel cannot be raised as to the construction of a statute. In *Kildare County Council v Keogh*,[235] Walsh J stated
that any litigant is entitled to submit what he believes to be the true construction
of a statutory provision and cannot be estopped from doing so.[236] The basis of
this exception is not articulated in the judgment and no explanation is given as
to why the question of the construction of a statute should be differentiated from
a decision on any other point of law. It may well be that the Supreme Court in
that case was influenced by its opinion that the earlier decision had clearly
proceeded on the basis of an erroneous statutory construction.

However, it is difficult to see why statutory construction should be singled
out as a special exception to issue estoppel. It may well be invidious to hold a
party bound by an erroneous interpretation of a statute in subsequent proceedings but no more invidious than to hold that party bound by an erroneous interpretation of the common law. Thus, it is submitted that no special rule should
apply to statutory interpretation. Instead, questions of statutory interpretation
should be subject to the general exception, set out above, in respect of changes
in the law. The important difference is that the parties to a judgment which
involves a point of statutory construction will be bound by the determination
thereof until such time as the construction is shown to be erroneous by a decision in a case involving other parties. This satisfies the requirements of justice
in that the parties will not be bound by an erroneous interpretation once it is
shown to be wrong but also advances the goal of finality of litigation because
that determination cannot come about as the result of further litigation between
the parties.

---

[234] (1950) 85 ILTR 88.
[235] [1971] IR 330 (followed on this point by Carroll J in *Clare County Council v Mahon*
[1995] 3 IR 193, [1996] 1 ILRM 521).
[236] *Ibid.* at 342.

ESTOPPEL

24.074 A party may be estopped from relying on a plea of *res judicata* if he has by his words or conduct made a representation to the other party with the intention, whether actual or presumed, and with the result, of inducing the other party to alter his position to his detriment.[237] In *Limerick VEC v Carr*,[238] O'Higgins J quoted with approval a passage from McDermott where he summarised the doctrine of counter-estoppel as follows:

> However where an estoppel by *res judicata* meets an estoppel by conduct or representation, there is a genuine cross-estoppel. In such a case the party against whom the plea of *res judicata* is made does not deny that he is estopped, but insists that the other party is estopped from saying so.[239]

An early decision which is explicable on this basis is *Eckfort v Shortt*[240] where it was held that, if an appeal against a judgment is abandoned on foot of a settlement between the parties which differs from the judgment, either party will be thereafter estopped from raising a plea of *res judicata* on foot of that judgment.

24.075 In *Cassidy v O'Rourke*[241] two sets of proceedings were issued as a result of a collision between the motor cycle of the plaintiff and the car of the defendant. In 1979, proceedings were instituted by O'Rourke in the Circuit Court claiming damages for damage to his car. Then, in 1980, Cassidy issued a plenary summons in the High Court claiming damages for personal injuries sustained in the accident. At the trial of the Circuit Court action, Cassidy was found to be 100% negligent and an appeal against this finding was dismissed by the High Court. Payment on foot of the Circuit Court decree was made by the insurers for Cassidy but was stated in the accompanying letter to be "without admission of liability". Subsequently, a preliminary issue was raised as to whether O'Rourke was estopped from raising a plea of *res judicata* in the High Court action by reason of the acceptance by his solicitor of the cheque on this basis. Carroll J held that he was so estopped because in the circumstances, it would be unconscionable for him to rely on a plea of *res judicata*.

24.076 Another case where a party was estopped by his conduct from pleading *res judicata* is *Littondale Ltd v Wicklow County Council*.[242] The applicant had

---

[237] This definition of estoppel by representation is adapted from Spencer-Bower and Turner, *The Law Relating to Estoppel by Representation* (3rd ed., 1996), at 4.

[238] High Court (O'Higgins J) 25 July 2001.

[239] McDermott, *Res Judicata and Double Jeopardy* (1999) § 17.10.

[240] (1903) 37 ILTR 219.

[241] High Court (Carroll J) 18 May 1983.

[242] [1996] 2 ILRM 519.

applied to the respondent to extend the duration of a planning permission and when that application was refused brought judicial review proceedings. The respondent contended that the matter was *res judicata* by virtue of a previous decision it had made refusing to extend the duration of the permission coupled with the fact that there had been no change of circumstances in the meantime. However, Laffoy J held that the respondent was estopped by its conduct from raising the plea of *res judicata*: it had accepted the application of the applicant, requested and accepted the prescribed fee, adjudicated on the application, and notified the applicant of its decision.

24.077 A defence of estoppel by representation or conduct can only succeed where the requisite elements of estoppel are made out *i.e.* an unambiguous representation is made which is relied on by the other party to its detriment. So, for example, in *Kelly v Ireland*[243] the contention that the respondents were estopped from pleading *res judicata* by virtue of their conduct failed on the basis that no representation had been held out and, further, because there was no evidence that the plaintiff had been induced to act to his detriment. The same conclusion was reached in *Limerick VEC v Carr*,[244] where an argument that the first named defendant was estopped from relying on the doctrine of *res judicata* because of the representations made on her behalf was also rejected on the facts. O'Higgins J was satisfied that no representation of the nature contended for had been given and, in any event, there was no evidence that the plaintiff had acted to its detriment by reason of the alleged representation.

ABUSE OF PROCESS

INTRODUCTION

24.078 A doctrine which has been invoked in some cases in order to deal with the inevitable interstices created by the technicality of *res judicata* is the inherent power of the courts to stay proceedings which are an abuse of the process of the court. Indeed, in *Donohoe v Browne*,[245] Gannon J described the entire doctrine of *res judicata* "as a matter of pleading to prevent as a matter of justice an abuse of the process of the administration of justice". This abuse of process being the "apparent disclaimer of a binding court order by the party bound by it."[246]

The doctrine of abuse of process has been deployed by the courts as something of a residuary weapon with which to advance the policy interest of the

---

[243] [1986] ILRM 318.
[244] High Court (O'Higgins J) 25 July 2001.
[245] [1986] IR 90, 99.
[246] *Ibid.* at 99.

finality of litigation and is of increasing importance because of the willingness of the courts to employ it to uphold the decision of a court of competent jurisdiction when a plea of estoppel *per rem judicatam* would not be successful. In particular, there has been a tendency for the courts to channel the pressures for the abandonment of the strictures of issues estoppel, notably those of privity and mutuality, into the development and application of this doctrine. Thus, it has been invoked in a number of cases where it has been shown that an identical question has already been decided by a court of competent jurisdiction.

24.079 It is, however, important to keep the doctrine of abuse of process within reasonable bounds because as Lowry LCJ pointed out in *Shaw v Sloan*[247] with regard to issue estoppel, the "entire corpus of authority on issue estoppel is based on the theory that it is *not* an abuse of process to relitigate a point where any of the three requirements of the doctrine is missing". Thus, it is submitted that the utilisation of the doctrine should be confined to egregious cases where one party seeks to obtain an unfair advantage or to in some way manipulate the requirements of *res judicata* to his own ends. As has already been stated, it is not desirable that it should be pressed into service in a broader spectrum of cases in order to alleviate the constraints of estoppel *per rem judicatam*.

EVOLUTION OF THE DOCTRINE

24.080 The jurisdiction to strike out a claim as an abuse of the process of the court on the ground that it seeks to relitigate a matter which has already been decided by a court of competent jurisdiction can be traced back to two English decisions at the end of the last century, namely, *Reichel v Magrath*[248] and *Stephenson v Garnett.*[249] In the former, Lord Halsbury LC stated that "it would be a scandal to the administration of justice if, the same question having been disposed of by one case, the litigant were to be permitted by changing the form of the proceedings to set up the same case again"[250] and in the latter, A.L. Smith LJ confirmed that the court had a jurisdiction to strike out a claim when it was shown that "the identical question sought to be raised has been already decided by a competent court".[251]

24.081 However, the potential impact of this jurisdiction had lain practically unnoticed until the decision in *Hunter v Chief Constable of West Midlands.*[252]

---

[247] [1982] NI 393, 337 (emphasis in the original).
[248] (1889) 14 App Cas 665.
[249] [1898] 1 QB 677.
[250] (1889) 14 App Cas 665, 668.
[251] [1898] 1 QB 677, 680-1.
[252] [1982] AC 529, [1981] 3 WLR 906, [1981] 3 All ER 727.

In this case, the "Birmingham Six" instituted a civil action claiming damages for assaults allegedly suffered by them when they were in custody being questioned about the bombing of two Birmingham pubs which had resulted in the deaths of twenty-one people. At their trial for murder, the plaintiffs had challenged the admissibility of confessions made by them on the basis that they had been beaten in custody but after a lengthy *voir dire* the statements were admitted and the plaintiffs were convicted. The defendant applied to have the action struck out on the ground that it raised an issue identical to that which had been finally determined at the accuseds' murder trial.

In the Court of Appeal[253] Goff LJ preferred to rest his judgment on the basis that the action of the plaintiffs was an abuse of process and this approach was endorsed on appeal by the House of Lords who were unanimously of the opinion that the proceedings constituted an abuse of process. Lord Diplock, with whom the other members of the House concurred, stated that:

> The abuse of process which the instant case exemplifies is the initiation of proceedings in a court of justice for the purpose of mounting a collateral attack on a final decision against the intending plaintiff which has been made by another court of competent jurisdiction in previous proceedings in which the intending plaintiff had a full opportunity of contesting the decision in the court by which it was made.[254]

An important factor in reaching the conclusion that the proceedings were an abuse of process was that the dominant purpose for bringing them was not to recover damages but to put pressure on the Home Secretary to release the men.[255]

24.082 The decision in *Hunter* was first followed in this jurisdiction in *Kelly v Ireland*,[256] where O'Hanlon J advanced as an alternative basis for his judgment, the proposition that:

> [I]n the absence of special circumstances, an effort to challenge the correctness of a decision made by a court of competent jurisdiction against a party in the course of a criminal trial, by means of civil proceedings insti-

---

[253] Reported *sub. nom. McIlkenny v Chief Constable of West Midlands* [1980] QB 283, [1980] 2 WLR 689, [1980] 2 All ER 227.

[254] *Ibid.* at 541, 913, 733.

[255] In *Brady v Chief Constable, RUC* [1988] NI 32, Murray J identified this factor as the essence of the decision in *Hunter* and he distinguished it from the case before him on the basis that this factor was missing. He also held that the doctrine of abuse of process could only be invoked against a party to the earlier criminal proceedings. Thus, preclusion did not apply where the plaintiff had made the same allegations in a criminal trial in which he appeared as a witness and the trial judge stated that he did not believe his evidence.

[256] [1986] ILRM 318.

tuted by such person after that decision has been made, should normally be restrained as an abuse of the process of the court.[257]

This line of authority was endorsed by Blayney J in *Breathnach v Ireland (No. 2)*[258] where he had to decide whether estoppel arose with respect to a number of points decided during the plaintiff's criminal trial. Dealing first with the allegation that the plaintiff had signed an alleged confession and verbally repeated it in fear of assault and that the confession was extracted by oppression, he held that this issue had been finally determined against the plaintiff by the Special Criminal Court (which determination had not been disturbed by the Court of Criminal Appeal) and it would be an abuse of process to raise it again.

Secondly, he held that it would be an abuse of process for the defendants to deny that the plaintiff had been unlawfully detained during his second period of detention by reason of the finding of the Special Criminal Court to this effect. In coming to this conclusion, he rejected the contention of counsel for the defendants that an estoppel could only arise where an issue had been determined against an accused and not where an issue had been determined in his favour. No reason is given by Blayney J for rejecting the contention of the defendants that abuse of process operates in a non-mutual fashion with regard to criminal trials and this is unfortunate because there is a strong argument in favour of that contention.

24.083 By virtue of the burden and standard of proof in a criminal trial, the determination of an issue *against* an accused means that the prosecution have proved the point beyond a reasonable doubt. There are therefore, strong grounds for saying that it is an abuse of process to reopen the issue in civil proceedings where proof is to the lower standard of on the balance of probabilities. The same conclusion does not follow when an issue in a criminal trial is decided *in favour of* an accused. Although the prosecution failed to prove the point beyond a reasonable doubt, it may be possible to do so on the balance of probabilities in subsequent civil proceedings. Hence, it is arguable that it is not an abuse of process to relitigate the issue because a different conclusion in the civil proceedings would not necessarily imply that the decision in the criminal case was wrong. However logical this argument would be, the net result would be unfairness to an accused because of the complete lack of mutuality and this may be why Blayney J opted for mutual preclusion.

24.084 The question of launching a collateral attack in civil proceedings upon the verdict in a criminal case was also considered by Murphy J in *Pringle v Ireland*.[259] The plaintiff had been convicted of robbery and murder and his

---

[257] *Ibid.* at 330.
[258] [1993] 2 IR 448.
[259] [1994] 1 ILRM 467.

conviction had been upheld on appeal by the Court of Criminal Appeal. He issued civil proceedings in which he claimed that his prosecution, trial, conviction and sentence were conducted, carried out and imposed in violation of his constitutional rights. The defendants claimed that the matters raised in the plaintiff's statement of claim had already been adjudicated upon by the Special Criminal Court and the Court of Criminal Appeal and were thus *res judicata*. They further relied on s.29 of the Courts of Justice Act 1924 which provides that the determination by the Court of Criminal Appeal of any appeal or other matter which it has power to determine shall be final.

Murphy J took the view that the proceedings instituted by the plaintiff were an attempt to appeal from and overturn the decision of the Court of Criminal Appeal. He held that the terms of s.29 making the decision of the Court of Criminal Appeal final were "clear and inescapable" and accepted "the basic proposition that a conviction secured in a criminal court of competent jurisdiction cannot be set aside or reviewed in civil proceedings least of all in civil proceedings conducted in a court of subordinate jurisdiction".[260]

24.085 Although the decision of the House of Lords in *Hunter* turned on the ulterior motive of the plaintiffs, it would seem as if a broader proposition emerges from *Kelly* and *Breathnach (No. 2)*[261] to the effect that any attempt in civil proceedings to contradict the final determination of an issue in earlier criminal proceedings, whether made in favour of or against the accused, will constitute an abuse of process unless there are special circumstances. These special circumstances were not enumerated by O'Hanlon J in *Kelly* but some guide as to what they might be emerges from *Breathnach v Ireland*.[262] In deciding that the plaintiff was precluded from litigating the issue of assault, Lardner J expressed his satisfaction that "the plaintiff had a full and fair opportunity of presenting his case on this issue to the Special Criminal Court and that he fully availed of this opportunity" and that "neither justice nor fairness requires that the plaintiff ... should be allowed to re-open this issue in civil proceedings".[263] Thus, it would seem that preclusion will not apply if a different conclusion is reached as to these matters.

---

[260] *Ibid.* at 479.
[261] See also *Breathnach v Ireland* [1989] IR 489, 495. Although Lardner J did not actually use the term "abuse of process", he described the action as an example "of civil proceedings being instituted for the purpose of mounting a collateral attack on the decision made".
[262] [1989] IR 489.
[263] *Ibid.* at 495.

APPLICATION IN CIVIL CASES

24.086 In recent times, the doctrine of abuse of process has been employed in a number of purely civil cases. In *McCauley v McDermot*,[264] the facts of which are set out above, the Supreme Court decided that issue estoppel did not apply to the determination of liability by the Circuit Court because of the lack of privity between the car owner in those proceedings and the car driver in the later proceedings. It was conceded on behalf of the tractor owner that the only reason for not joining the car owner in the later proceedings was that he would have been met with an unanswerable plea of *res judicata* and Keane J concluded that "[t]o allow that party to bring about the same result by the stratagem of suing the motorist rather than the car owner would be to ignore the maxim *interest rei publicae ut sit finis litium* and facilitate an abuse of process."[265] Although satisfied that the case before the court was a blatant one which clearly called for intervention, he did enter the caveat that the inherent jurisdiction to strike out proceedings as being an abuse of process should be exercised only with great caution.[266]

24.087 A case where such caution was exercised is *Belton v Carlow County Council*.[267] A factory was destroyed by fire and the company which owned it had brought a claim for compensation under the Malicious Injuries Act 1981. It was common case that the fire had been started deliberately, the only question was by whom. The county council contended that it had been started by the owners of the company and on appeal to the High Court, the claim was dismissed on the basis that the company had failed to satisfy the onus of proof that the fire was started by the malicious act of a third party.

The fire had also caused damage to adjoining premises owned by the applicant and the instant proceedings had been instituted by him seeking compensation. Liability was not disputed by the county council but they claimed an indemnity from the owners of the company, arguing that they were estopped by the decision of the High Court from denying that they had deliberately started the fire or alternatively that the proceedings should be struck out as an abuse of process.

Regarding the latter contention, Keane J pointed out that the owners of the company had not initiated the proceedings for the purpose of mounting any

---

[264] [1997] 2 ILRM 486.

[265] *Ibid.* at 496. He thereby departed from the decision of the Northern Ireland Court of Appeal in *Shaw v Sloan* [1982] NI 393, and his own previous decision in *McGinn v McShane* High Court (Keane J) 18 May 1995.

[266] For other decisions which emphasise the caution to be adopted in striking out proceedings as an abuse of the process of the court but which do not deal with attempts to evade the rules of *res judicata*, see *Barry v Buckley* [1981] IR 306, 308 *per* Costello J and *Mulgrew v O'Brien* [1953] NI 10, 14 *per* Black LJ.

[267] [1997] 1 IR 172, [1997] 2 ILRM 405.

form of attack upon the High Court decision. Rather, the proceedings had been initiated by the local authority and "their invocation of the abuse of process principle is intended to deprive the defendants of a defence, which they might otherwise have upon the merits, to the present claim."[268] This decision thus confirms what had been apparent in the earlier cases dealing with abuse of process in the criminal context that the doctrine of abuse of process is directed at parties who attack previous determinations *against* them.

24.088 In *Bula Ltd v Crowley*,[269] Barr J effectively conflated issue estoppel and abuse of process to create a doctrine of non-mutual preclusion. The plaintiffs in this case wished to controvert findings that had been made against them in separate proceedings in which they were also the plaintiffs. Barr J acknowledged that issue estoppel did not apply because there was no identity between the defendants in the instant case and any of the parties in the other proceedings. Thus, the question of whether the plaintiffs were bound by the findings in the other proceedings depended on whether "it would be unjust in all the circumstances and an abuse of the process of the court" to allow such findings to be revisited in the instant action. Relying on the decisions in *Breathnach (No. 2)* and *Hunter*, he held that when "an issue has been finally determined by a court of competent jurisdiction it is an abuse of the process of the court to seek to have it relitigated in new proceedings".

Thus far his judgment was in chartered waters, but he then went on to quote with approval an enumeration of the elements of issue estoppel by Dixon J in *Blair v Curran*,[270] and stated that it applied where the plaintiffs but not the defendants were the same in both actions. He concluded that there were three questions to be addressed by a court in determining whether a party was bound by findings of fact or law by a court of competent jurisdiction in earlier proceedings: (i) is the party seeking to re-open an issue of fact or law which was decided against them in the earlier proceedings? (ii) was the finding in question necessary to the determination, in the earlier proceedings, of the issue to which it relates? (iii) is the finding relevant to an issue raised by that party in the instant proceedings? Applying these tests to the facts of the case, he held that they were satisfied and that the plaintiffs were precluded from controverting the findings against them in the earlier proceedings.

24.089 In *McCauley* and *Bula*, we can see a willingness on the part of the courts to use the doctrine of abuse of the process of the courts to achieve a partial doctrine of non-mutual preclusion. However, it would be preferable if this were achieved by a dilution or abandonment of mutuality accompanied by the development of a principled approach within the parameters of *res judicata*

---

[268] *Ibid*. at 183, 416.
[269] High Court (Barr J) 29 April 1997.
[270] (1939) 62 CLR 464, 531-2.

rather than through invocation of the amorphous doctrine of abuse of process. Instead, that doctrine should be confined to egregious cases where one party seeks to obtain an unfair advantage or to in some way manipulate the requirements of *res judicata* to his own ends.

Indeed, *Bula* indicates the practical desirability of developing such a doctrine. The earlier proceedings, *Bula Ltd v Tara Mines*, had run for 277 days and the findings which the plaintiffs sought to challenge had been reached by Lynch J after assessment of a huge volume of evidence. If reopened, they would have added greatly to the duration and expense of the instant proceedings. It is easy to sympathise with the opinion of Barr J that there "was no acceptable reason in justice to revisit such findings and to permit the plaintiffs to challenge them".

INDEX